Alan Greenwood launched *Vintage Guitar* magazine in 1986 and in '90 started *The Official Vintage Guitar Price Guide*. The company has expanded to include the massive daily-updated Vintage Guitar Online at www.Vintage-Guitar.com, the free *Overdrive* email newsletter, large followings on Facebook, Instagram, YouTube, and Twitter, and co-sponsorship of guitars shows across the country. His collection includes several vintage instruments from the '20s to the '80s, as well as newer production and custom-made guitars, amps, effects, lap steels, and ukuleles. He lives in Bismarck, North Dakota.

Gil Hembree began collecting guitars in 1966 while working at Kitt's Music, in Washington, D.C. Familiarity with the professional musicians playing on Georgetown's M-Street allowed him to dabble in early buy-sell, but his academic interest in finance led to a corporate job in Michigan. Throughout his financial career, he played in bands and searched for original-owner vintage guitars in Flint, Saginaw, Bay City, Port Huron, Pontiac, Battle Creek, and Kalamazoo. In 2000, freshly retired from corporate finance, he became the co-author of *The Official Vintage Guitar Price Guide*. In 2007, Hal Leonard released his biography of Ted McCarty: *Gibson Guitars: Ted McCarty's Golden Era: 1948-1966*. After residing in Michigan for 35 years, Hembree and his wife, Jane, relocated to Austin, Texas.

The Official Vintage Guitar® magazine Price Guide
By Alan Greenwood and Gil Hembree

Vintage Guitar magazine, PO Box 7301, Bismarck, ND 58507, (701) 255-1197, Fax (701) 255-0250, publishers of *Vintage Guitar*® magazine and Vintage Guitar® Online at www.VintageGuitar.com. Vintage Guitar is a registered trademark of Vintage Guitar, Inc.

ISBN: 978-1-884883-43-9

Cover: 1958 Gretsch White Falcon (left) courtesy of Dave's Guitar Shop. 1956 Gretsch White Penguin (right) courtesy of Scott Chinery. Photos property of *VG* Archive.
Back: 1968 Fender Telecaster Thinline: *VG* Archive. 1958 Gibson Les Standard courtesy of Gary's Classic Guitars/*VG* Archive. Elliot Easton: Rob Shanahan. Buzzy Levine: Lark Street Music. Myles Goodwyn: Darren Lulka. Drew Berlin: Drew Berlin's Vintage Guitars. Steve Wariner: David McClister.

Cover Design: Doug Yellow Bird/Vintage Guitar, Inc.

Printed in the United States of America

— VINTAGE —
TAKEN HIGHER

GuitarPlayer EDITORS' PICK

PG PREMIERGuitar PREMIER GEAR

For our 50th we wanted to do something fun and take a look back to our Roots and all the wonderful sounds we grew up on **in the 60s ...and maybe even one-up them.** That led to a revolution here at MESA® that birthed two new Tweed-blooded, Vintage-voiced Models; The **California Tweed™** 6V6 4:40, and the Fillmore™ ...a Line of 2 Channel amps comprised of 25, 50 and 100-Watt models.

These born-classic amplifiers take Traditional to new heights of Tone and expression and invite you in while giving back in ways we find most vintage gems rarely can. From Single Channel simplicity and patented Power possibilities in the California Tweed,™ to the Dual Cloned Channel's 3-Mode versatility in the Fillmore™, experience our mission to reinvent Vintage Tone and take Traditional higher than you've ever experienced.

1317 Ross Street · Petaluma, CA 94954 (707) 778-6565 · www.mesaboogie.com

TABLE OF CONTENTS

Fender Stratocasters from 1965 and '63 in Lake Placid Blue along with a '66 in Ice Blue, all backed by a '64 Bandmaster.

ORIGINAL COLLECTION

EXPLORE THE ORIGINAL COLLECTION AT **GIBSON.COM**

USING THE GUIDE

UNDERSTANDING THE VALUES

The values presented in T*he Of-ficial Vintage Guitarw Price Guide* are for excellent-condition, all-original instruments. Our definition of excellent condition allows for some wear, but the instrument should be well-maintained, with no significant blemishes, wear, repairs, or damage. All-original means the instrument has the parts and finish it had when it left the factory. Replacement parts and refinishes can greatly affect value, as can the appropriate case (or cover) in excellent condition. In many instances, a "wrong" case will not greatly affect value, but with the top-dollar collectibles, it can.

We use a range of excellent-condition values, as there is seldom agreement on a single price point for vintage and used instruments. A tighter range suggests there is a general consensus, while a wide range means the market isn't in strict agreement. A mint-condition instrument can be worth more than the values listed here, and anything in less-than-excellent condition will have a reduced value.

Repairs affect value differently. Some repair is necessary to keep an instrument in playable condition. The primary concern is the level of expertise displayed in the work and an amateurish repair will lower the value more than one that is obviously professional. A refinished guitar, regardless of the quality of the work, is generally worth 50% or less of the values shown in *The Guide*. A poorly executed neck repair or significant body repair can mean a 50% reduction in a guitar's value. A professional re-fret or minor, nearly invisible body repair will reduce a guitar's value by only 5%.

The values in the The *Guide* are for unfaded finishes. Slight color fade reduces the value by only 5%, but heavily faded examples can reduce the value by 25% to 50%.

FINDING THE INFORMATION

The table of contents shows the major sections and each is organized in alphabetical order by brand, then by model. In a few instances, there are separate sections for a company's most popular models, especially when there is a large variety of similar instruments. Examples include Fender's Stratocasters, Telecasters, Precision and Jazz basses, and Gibson's Les Pauls. The outer top corner of each page uses a dictionary-type header that tells the models or brands on that page. This provides a quick way to navigate each section.

The Guide has excellent brand histories and in most cases the guitar section has the most detailed information for each brand. When possible, The Guide lists each model's years of availability and any design changes that affect values.

More information on many of the brands covered in *The Guide* is available in the pages of *Vintage Guitar* magazine and on the "Features" section of our website, www.VintageGuitar.com.

The authors of *The Guide* appreciate your help, so if you find any errors or have additional information on certain brands or models, we'd like to hear from you. Feel free to drop us a line at Alan@Vintage-Guitar.com.

NEW RETAIL PRICING INFORMATION

The Guide continues to add information on individual luthiers and smaller shops. It's difficult to develop values on used instruments produced by these builders because much of their output is custom work, production is low, and/or they haven't been producing for a period of time sufficient to see their instruments enter the used/resale market. To give you an idea about their instruments, we've developed five grades of retail values for new instruments. These convey only the prices charged by the builder, and are not indicative of the quality of construction. *The Guide* applies this scale to all builders and manufacturers of new instruments.

The five retail-price grades are:
Budget - up to $250,
Intermediate - $251 to $1,000,
Professional - $1,001 to $3,000,
Premium - $3,001 to $10,000,
Presentation - more than $10,000.

The Guide uses the terms "production" and "custom" to differentiate between builders who do true custom work versus those who offer standard production models. "Production" means the company offers specific models, with no variations. "Custom" means they do only custom orders, and "production/custom" indicates they do both. Here's an example:

JayMan Guitars
2010-present. Premium grade, custom solidbody guitars built by luthier Jayden Flanagin in Mandan, North Dakota. He also builds effects.

This tells who the builder is, the type of instruments they build, where they build them, how long they've been operating under that brand, that they do only custom work, and that they ask between $3,000 and $10,000 for their guitars (premium-grade).We've applied the retail price grades and production and/or custom labels to most new-instrument manufacturers.

INTRODUCTION

Welcome to the 2021 edition of *The Official Vintage Guitar Price Guide*. We, of course, were working on this book throughout 2020, and what a hell of a year it was! We'll get to that in a moment, but first a few notes.

Regular buyers of *The Guide* noticed the 2020 edition was missing the usual sections for banjos and mandolins. We did this primarily because we wanted to maintain *The Guide*'s physical size even as the Guitars section continues to expand. Given the relative stability/lack of change in values in the banjo, mandolin, ukulele, and steel-guitar market segments, we opted to rotate those sections on alternating years. So, the Banjos and Mandolins sections have returned this year while Ukuleles and Steel Guitars will sit out.

THE VIRUS

The coronavirus pandemic affected virtually everything in 2020, and the guitar industry was no exception. Early on, it had all the markings of a disaster for collectibles markets like guitars and related gear. We had never been down this road, at least not in the memory of most people, so we had no idea what to expect. Did business closures and the resulting job and income loss around the world affect values of the guitars and amps in your practice room?

To get a better feel, we surveyed 250 instrument dealers for a *Vintage Guitar* magazine feature titled "Dealing in Diligence: Covid 19 and the Market for Vintage Instruments." The piece asked how events were affecting their stores and the broader market for vintage instruments. You can read it in the September '20 issue, but I'll touch on the main takeaways, keeping in mind the information was gathered in July, 2020.

A 1970 Ampeg Dan Armstrong and '66 Epiphone Casino.

Among those who responded, 70 percent operate retail space and two-thirds of those reported at some point being closed to walk-in customers. And while overall sales held steady for those with an internet presence, mandated store closures greatly impacted the rest, leading to nearly half reporting an overall decline (one-third said sales actually increased).

Half of the dealers faced challenges finding quality inventory mostly because they saw no walk-ins at their stores and guitar shows were cancelled. While none mentioned the possibility of going out of business, some are not going back to retail business as usual, opting to permanently shift to appointment-only operation.

In a bit of good news for collectors, just over 75 percent of dealers said the pandemic had not affected asking prices for vintage or used gear. Also, many manufacturers and online retailers reported some of the best monthly sales in a long time – or ever – during the spring and summer of 2020. That could have been because people had more time on their hands and were looking for new challenges. Some anecdotal evidence shows that one of the attractions is that, since learning guitar is one of a few pastimes requiring one's total concentration, it's a great break from the crazy outside world (something you and I have known all along, right?). The consensus is that much of that was driven by people new to guitar playing. And much of them were younger and female. For some time, guitar playing has been dominated by an aging, male demographic, so it's great to hear that its appeal is reaching to a younger, more diverse group. Looks like our favorite instrument (and the music it makes) will be around for a *long* time!

WHAT'S HOT

Here are a few examples of instruments that increased in value by 20% or more in this year's *Guide*.

The Ampeg Dan Armstrong Lucite Guitar from 1969-'71,

43rd Annual
DALLAS INTERNATIONAL
digf
GUITAR FESTIVAL

APRIL 30–MAY 2   2021

DALLAS MARKET HALL ★ WWW.GUITARSHOW.COM

both "clear" and "smoke," increased 33% (Lucite basses increased also but only by 18%). The 1987-'98 BC Rich ST III (USA) guitar increased 21%. Burns Bisons from 1961-'65, both albino and black, are up by 32%. The early models with four pickups and flat headstock fetch more than the later three pickup and scroll headstock versions.

Earlier Charvels saw nice gains, with the 1986-'89 Models 1, 1A, 1C, 2, 3, 3A, 3DR, 3L, 4, 4A, 5, 5A, 6, and 7 and the 1989-'96 Charvel Fusion and Fusion Deluxe all up 30%.

The Epiphone 1966-1970 FT110 Frontier has increase over 20% two years in a row, while the '66 Casino with two pickups is up 22% and the 2001 Epi Ace Frehley Les Paul Custom 20%.

Custom color Fender Electric XII models are hot with those from 1966-'69 up 33%, while the 1966-'69 Coronado XII in custom colors, sunburst, Wildwood and Antiqua increased 24%. Several Strats increased over 20%, including the '91 Jeff Beck Signature 1st year collector grade (the '92

Authors Alan Greenwood and Gil Hembree

GUITAR DEALER PARTICIPANTS

The information refined on these pages comes from several sources, including the input of many knowledgeable guitar dealers. Without the help of these individuals, it would be very hard for us to provide the information here and in each issue of *Vintage Guitar* magazine. We deeply appreciate the time and effort they provide.

Brian Goff
Bizarre Guitars

Garrett Tung
Boingosaurus Music

Dave Belzer
Burst Brothers

Walter Carter
Carter Vintage

Daniel Escauriza
Chicago Music Exchange

John Majdalani
Cream City Music

Dave Rogers
Dave's Guitar Shop

Drew Berlin
Drew Berlin's Vintage Guitars

Stan Werbin & S.J. "Frog" Forgey
Elderly Instruments

Dewey Bowen
Freedom Guitar

Rick Hogue
Garrett Park Guitars

Gary Dick
Gary's Classic Guitars

Alex Gray
Goat Peak Strings

Eric Newell
Gruhn Guitars

Richard Johnston
Gryphon Strings

Kennard Macho & Leonard Coulson
Intermountain Guitar & Banjo

Jim Singleton
Jim's Guitars

Kevin Borden
Kebo's BassWorks

Dave Hinson
Killer Vintage

Timm Kummer
Kummer's Vintage Instruments

Buzzy Levine
Lark Street Music

Larry Wexer
Laurence Wexer, Ltd.

Artie Leider
McKenzie River Music

Neal Shelton
Neals Music (California)

Lowell Levinger
Players Vintage Instruments

Howie Statland
Rivington Guitars

Eliot Michael
Rumble Seat Music

Sammy Ash
Sam Ash Music Stores

Eric Schoenberg
Schoenberg Guitars

Richard Gellis
Union Grove Music

Fred Oster
Vintage Instruments

Richard Friedman
We Buy Guitars

Nate Westgor
Willie's American Guitars

and '93 versions did not increase), the 1995-'01 Bonnie Raitt, the 1985-'87 Contemporary Stratocaster 7/8 scale made in Japan (33%), and the 2000-'08 Custom Classic Custom Shop Stratocaster. The 1990-2013 Albert Collins Custom Shop Telecaster jumped 28%.

The 1976-'77 Gibson Marauder Custom with sunburst finish jumped 31%. Flying Vs seeing 30% gains are the 1981-'82 Heritage in natural finish increased 30% (other colors did not increase), and the 1983 Korina. The Explorer versions of those models also increased 30% and sell at the same price level.

The 2006-'07 Gibson ES-335 Alvin Lee with COA is up 33% and near the original retail selling price.

The 1975-'84 Guild M-80 and M-80CS are up 23% with the Brian May Pro for 1994-'95 up 28% and the George Gruhn designed F-46NT, made only in 1984, up 28%.

From Martin, the electric 1961-'65 F-55 and F-65 both increased 31%, and both

A 1981 Gibson Flying V Heritage and ES-335 Alvin Lee.

the 1992 HJ-28 Limited Edition Guitar of the Month, with 69 offered, and the similar 1994 HJ-28M, 72 offered, both up 26%.

The 1982-'93 Mosrite Ventures (Jonas Ridge/Boonville) increased 29% and they are selling at prices not seen since 2011. The 1975-'82 Ovation Viper III Model 1273 and Viper Model 1271 both increased 25% and the 1999-'04 Peavey EVH Wolfgang with standard top, 25%.

The 1976-'78 Yamaha SG-500 and SG-700 and the 1982-'85 SG-3000 SBG Custom Pro all increased 30%.

The 1964 English-made Vox Phantom VI and Phantom XII both increased significantly in value (the Italian-made 1965 models are worth much less).

42 INDEX

A perennial favorite, *Vintage Guitar*'s 42 Index tracks the cumulative value of a selection of models from the three biggest companies of the "classic era" – 14 each from Fender, Gibson, and Martin. The Index excludes the most-valuable instruments for each brand, such as pre-war D-45s, Les Paul 'Bursts, early Explorers, first-year Teles and Strats. The list at right shows the instruments in the Index. Since the Index only includes pre-1970 instruments from those three American manufacturers, it doesn't necessarily reflect the overall market, but it shows how values have changed over time.

The Index rose 1.5% from 2020, which was based on a slight decline in the Fender group, a 2.3% increase in the

THE 42 INDEX

FROM FENDER
1952 blond Precision Bass
1952 blond Esquire
1953 blond Telecaster
1956 sunburst Stratocaster
1958 sunburst Jazzmaster
1958 blond Telecaster
1960 sunburst Stratocaster
1961 sunburst, stack knob, Jazz Bass
1962 sunburst, 3-knob, Jazz Bass
1963 sunburst Telecaster Custom
1963 sunburst Esquire Custom
1964 Lake Placid Blue Jaguar
1964 sunburst Precision Bass
1966 Candy Apple Red Stratocaster

FROM GIBSON
1952 sunburst ES-5
1952 Les Paul Model
1954 Les Paul Jr.
1958 sunburst EB-2 Bass
1958 Les Paul Custom

1958 natural ES-335
1958 Super 400CES
1959 Les Paul Jr.
1959 J-160E
1961 ES-355
1961 Les Paul SG
1964 sunburst Thunderbird II Bass
1965 EB-3 Bass
1969 sunburst Citation

FROM MARTIN
1931 OM-28
1936 00-28
1935 D-18
1944 scalloped-brace 000-28
1944 D-28
1950 D-28
1958 000-18
1959 D-18
1959 D-28E
1962 D-28
1967 GT-75
1968 000-18
1969 N-20
1969 D-45

Build
Your
Tone

(((AmplifiedParts)))

Gibson group, and 2.4% increase in the Martin group. Only Martin saw an increase in all of its instruments in the Index. Vintage Gibson and Fender basses in the Index continue their recent trend of dropping in value. Guitar-wise, there were mixed results in the Fender and Gibson groups.

When we started tracking these 42 guitars in 1991, their average value (in excellent condition) was $3,660. Today that average value is $18,884, up from last year's $18,763.

The 42 Guitar Index 1991 - 2021

MODEL YEAR	FEATURES	EXC. COND. LOW	HIGH

'06 he licensed the names of his standard models to Fender (see Benedetto FMIC); during that period, Benedetto only made special order instruments. In '06, Howard Paul joined Benedetto as President of the company to begin manufacturing a broader line of more affordable professional instruments.

Benny
1990s-present. Electric chambered single-cut mahogany body, carved spruce top, 2 humbuckers.

1990s-2019	Signed or factory	$2,000	$2,700

Benny Deluxe
1990s-2011. Deluxe version of the Benny.

1990s-2011	Signed or factory	$3,500	$4,800

Bravo Deluxe
2004-present. Electric 1 pickup archtop, laminated back and top, deluxe binding.

2004-2019	Signed or factory	$2,500	$3,400

Cremona
1988-present. Acoustic/electric archtop, single-cut, 17" body, natural.

1988-2019	Signed or factory	$8,500	$11,500

Fratello
1980s-present. Electric archtop, single-cut, 17" body, blond or sunburst.

1988-2019	Signed or factory	$6,600	$8,900

La Venezia
1990s-present. Acoustic archtop, single-cut, 17" body, sunburst.

1990s-2019	Signed or factory	$7,200	$9,700

Limelite Custom
1990s. Single-cut, neck pickup, select aged wood, blond.

1990s	Signed or factory	$13,100	$17,700

Manhattan
1989-present. Archtop with 16" body, neck pickup, blond.

1989-2019	Signed or factory	$6,100	$8,200

Manhattan Custom
1990s. Carved 17" body, blond.

1990s	Signed or factory	$8,400	$11,200

Benedetto (FMIC)
1999-2006. Premium and presentation, production/custom, acoustic and electric archtops. From '99 to '06, Bob Benedetto had an agreement with Fender (FMIC) to build Benedetto guitars under his guidance and supervision. The guitars were originally built in the FMIC Guild Custom Shop in Nashville, and later in Fender's Corona, California, facility.

Artist/Artist Award
Full body, rounded cutaway, single neck pickup, natural or sunburst.

2000-2003		$5,400	$7,100

Benedict
1988-present. Founded by Roger Benedict. Professional and premium grade, production/custom, solid and semi-hollow body guitars and basses built by luthier Bill Hager in Cedar, Minnesota.

Beneteau
1974-present. Custom, premium grade, classical, baritone and steel string acoustic guitars built first in Ottawa, Ontario, and since 1986 in St. Thomas, Ontario by luthier Marc Beneteau. He also builds ukuleles.

Bennett Music Labs
1998-present. Custom guitars built by luthier Bruce Bennett, who helped design the first Warrior line of instruments with J.D. Lewis. He also built amps and Brown Sound effects and also guitars for J. Backlund Designs.

Bently
Ca.1985-1998. Student and intermediate grade copy style acoustic and electric guitars imported by St. Louis Music Supply. Includes the Series 10 electrics and the Songwriter acoustics (which have a double reversed B crown logo on the headstock). St. Louis Music replaced the Bently line with the Austin brand.

Berkowitz Guitars
1995-present. Luthier David D. Berkowitz builds his premium grade, custom/production, steel string and baritone guitars and basses in Washington, D.C.

Bernie Rico Jr. Guitars
Professional and premium grade, production/custom, solidbody electrics guitars and basses built by luther Bernie Rico, Jr., the son of B.C. Rich founder, in Hesperia, California.

Bertoncini Stringed Instruments
Luthier Dave Bertoncini began building in 1995, premium grade, custom, flat-top guitars, in Olympia, Washington. He has also built solidbody electrics, archtops, mandolins and ukuleles.

Beyond The Trees
1976-present. Luthier Fred Carlson offers a variety of innovative designs for his professional and presentation grade, production/custom 6- and 12-string flat-tops in Santa Cruz, California. He also produces the Sympitar (a 6-string with added sympathetic strings) and the Dreadnautilus (a unique shaped headless acoustic).

Big Lou Guitar
Mid-2010-present. Located in Perris, California, owner Louis Carroll imports his intermediate grade, production, electric guitars from China.

Big Tex Guitars
Production/custom, professional grade, vintage-style replica guitars, started in 2000, built for owner Eric Danheim, by luthiers James Love, Mike Simon and Eddie Dale in Houston and Dripping Springs, Texas and Seattle, Washington.

Benedetto Cremona

Bennett Music Labs JBD-800

1949 Bigsby
Imaged by Heritage Auctions, HA.com

Bill Foley BF-2

MODEL YEAR	FEATURES	EXC. COND. LOW	HIGH

Bigsby

Pedal steel guitars, hollow-chambered electric Spanish guitars, electric mandolins, doublenecks, replacement necks on acoustic guitars, hand vibratos, all handmade by Paul Arthur Bigsby, machinist and motorcycle enthusiast (designer of '30s Crocker motorcycles), in Downey, California. Initially built for special orders.

Bigsby was a pioneer in developing pedal steels. He designed a hand vibrato for Merle Travis. In '48, his neck-through hollow electrics (with Merle Travis) influenced Leo Fender, and Bigsby employed young Semie Moseley. In '56, he designed the Magnatone Mark series guitars and 1 Hawaiian lap steel. He built guitars up to '63.

He built less than 50 Spanish guitars, 6 mandolins, 70 to 150 pedal steels and 12 or so neck replacements. SN was stamped on the end of fingerboard: MMDDYY. In '65, the company was sold to Gibson president Ted McCarty who moved the tremolo/vibrato work to Kalamazoo. Bigsby died in '68. Fred Gretsch purchased the Bigsby company from Ted McCarty in '99 and sold it to Fender in 2019. A solidbody guitar and a pedal steel based upon the original Paul Bigsby designs were introduced January, 2002. These were modeled on the 1963 Bigsby catalog but look very similar to the typical Bigsby solidbodys made in the early '50s. Early Bigsby guitars command high value on the collectible market and values here assumes authentication by an industry expert.

Standard Solidbody (Spanish)

Late-1940s-1950s, 2002. Standard Guitar, solidbody, natural. Reissue offered in '02.

MODEL YEAR	FEATURES	EXC. COND. LOW	HIGH
1948		$185,000	$290,000
1949		$115,000	$280,000
1950-1956		$65,000	$250,000
2002	Reissue	$2,850	$3,700

Standard Models (Japan)

2007-2008. Various models made in Japan.

MODEL YEAR	FEATURES	EXC. COND. LOW	HIGH
2007	Model BY-48N	$1,000	$1,300
2007	Model BY-50	$1,000	$1,300
2007	Model BYS-48	$1,000	$1,300

Bil Mitchell Guitars

1979-present. Luthier Bil Mitchell builds his professional and premium grade, production/custom, flat-top and archtop guitars originally in Wall, New Jersey, and since '02 in Riegelsville, Pennsylvania.

Bill Foley Fine Instruments

2012-present. Luthiers Bill Foley, his son Sam, and Brad Lewis build professional and premium grade, custom electric guitars and basses in Columbus, Ohio.

Bilt Guitars

2010-present. Professional grade, production/custom, solidbody and semi-hollowbody electric guitars built in Des Moines, Iowa by luthiers Bill Henss and Tim Thelen.

MODEL YEAR	FEATURES	EXC. COND. LOW	HIGH

Birdsong Guitars

2001-present. Luthiers Scott Beckwith and Jamie Hornbuckle build their professional grade, production/custom, solidbody guitars and basses in Wimberley, Texas.

Bischoff Guitars

1975-present. Professional and premium-grade, custom-made flat-tops built by luthier Gordy Bischoff in Eau Claire, Wisconsin.

Bishline

1985-present. Luthier Robert Bishline, of Tulsa, Oklahoma, mainly builds banjos, but did build flat-tops and resonators in the past, and still does occasionally.

Black Jack

1960s. Violin-body hollowbody electric guitars and basses, possibly others. Imported from Japan by unidentified distributor. Manufacturers unknown, but some may be Arai.

Blackbird

2006-present. Luthier Joe Luttwak builds his professional grade, production/custom, carbon fiber acoustic guitars in San Francisco, California. He also offers a uke.

Blackshear, Tom

1958-present. Premium and presentation grade, production, classical and flamenco guitars made by luthier Tom Blackshear in San Antonio, Texas.

Blade

1987-present. Intermediate and professional grade, production, solidbody guitars and basses from luthier Gary Levinson and his Levinson Music Products Ltd. located in Switzerland.

California Custom

1994-2010. California Standard with maple top and high-end appointments.

MODEL YEAR	FEATURES	EXC. COND. LOW	HIGH
1994-2010		$625	$850

California Deluxe/Deluxe

1994-1995. Standard with mahogany body and maple top.

1994-1995		$475	$625

California Hybrid

1998-1999. Standard with piezo bridge pickup.

1998-1999		$400	$550

California Standard

1994-2007. Offset double-cut, swamp ash body, bolt neck, 5-way switch.

1994-2007		$300	$400

R 3

1988-1993. Offset double-cut maple solidbody, bolt maple neck, 3 single-coils or single/single/humbucker.

1988-1993		$475	$625

R 4

1988-1993. R 3 with ash body and see-thru color finishes.

1988-1992		$475	$625

MODEL YEAR	FEATURES	EXC. COND. LOW	HIGH

Texas Series
2003-present. Includes Standard (3 single-coils) and Deluxe (gold hardware, single/single/hum pickups).

2003-2010	Deluxe	$350	$475
2003-2010	Special	$325	$450
2003-2019	Standard	$325	$450

Blanchard Guitars
1994-present. Luthier Mark Blanchard builds premium grade, custom steel-string and classical guitars originally in Mammoth Lakes, California, and since May '03, in northwest Montana.

Blindworm Guitars
2008-present. Luthiers Andrew J. Scott and Steven Sells build premium and presentation grade, production/custom, acoustic, electric and electric-acoustic guitars, basses, mandolins, banjos and others in Colorado Springs, Colorado.

Blount
1985-present. Professional and premium grade, production/custom, acoustic flat-top guitars built by luthier Kenneth H. Blount Jr. in Sebring, Florida.

Blue Star
1984-present. Luthier Bruce Herron builds his production/custom guitars in Fennville, Michigan. He also builds mandolins, lap steels, dulcimers and ukes.

Bluebird
1920s-1930s. Private brand with Bluebird painted on headstock, built by the Oscar Schmidt Co. and possibly others. Most likely made for distributor.

13" Flat-Top

| 1930s | | $125 | $160 |

Bluebird Guitars
2011-present. Luthiers Rob Bluebird and Gian Maria Camponeschi build premium grade, custom, archtop and solidbody guitars in Rome, Italy. They build production resonator guitars in Bali, Indonesia. They also offer basses and ukuleles.

Blueridge
Early 1980s-present. Intermediate and professional grade, production, solid-top acoustic guitars distributed by Saga. In '00, the product line was redesigned with the input of luthier Greg Rich (Rich and Taylor guitars).

Bluesouth
1991-ca. 2006. Custom electric guitars built by luthier Ronnie Knight in Muscle Shoals, Alabama. He also built basses.

Boaz Elkayam Guitars
1985-present. Presentation grade, custom steel, nylon, and flamenco guitars made by luthier Boaz Elkayam in Chatsworth, California.

Boedigheimer Instruments
2000-present. Luthier Brian Boedigheimer builds his professional and premium grade, production/custom, semi-hollowbody electric guitars in Red Wing, Minnesota.

Bohmann
1878-ca. 1926. Acoustic flat-top guitars, harp guitars, mandolins, banjos, violins made in Chicago Illinois, by Joseph Bohmann (born 1848, in Czechoslovakia). Bohmann's American Musical Industry founded 1878. Guitar body widths are 12", 13", 14", 15". He had 13 grades of guitars by 1900 (Standard, Concert, Grand Concert sizes). Early American use of plywood. Some painted wood finishes. Special amber-oil varnishes. Tuner bushings. Early ovalled fingerboards. Patented tuner plates and bridge design. Steel engraved label inside. Probably succeeded by son Joseph Frederick Bohmann.

Ca. 1896 12" body faux rosewood, 13", 14" and 15" body faux rosewood birch, 12", 13", 14" and 15" body sunburst maple, 12", 13", 14" and 15" body rosewood. By 1900 Styles 0, 1, 2 and 3 Standard, Concert and Grand Concert maple, Styles 1, 2, 3, 4, 5, 6, 7, 8, 9, 10, 11 and 12 in Standard, Concert, and Grand Concert rosewood.

14 3/4" Flat-Top
Solid spruce top, veneered Brazilian rosewood back and sides, wood marquetry around top and soundhole, natural. Each Bohmann should be valued on a case-by-case basis.

| 1896-1900 | Brazilian | $900 | $1,200 |
| 1896-1900 | Other woods | $450 | $600 |

Harp Guitar

| 1896-1899 | All styles | $2,700 | $3,500 |

Bolin
1978-present. Professional and premium grade, production/custom, solidbody guitars and basses built by luthier John Bolin in Boise, Idaho. Bolin is well-known for his custom work. His Cobra guitars are promoted and distributed by Sanderson Sales and Marketing as part of the Icons of America Series.

NS
1996-2011. Slot-headstock, bolt-on neck, single-cut solidbody, Seymour Duncan passive pickups or EMG active, from '96 to the fall of 2001 custom-built serial numbers to 0050 then from the fall of '01 to the present production model build starting with SN 0051.

| 1996-2001 | Custom-built | $1,600 | $2,100 |
| 2001-2011 | Standard production | $700 | $900 |

Bolt
1988-1991. Founded by luthier Wayne Bolt and Jim Dala Pallu in Schnecksville, Pennsylvania, Bolt's first work was CNC machined OEM necks and bodies made for Kramer and BC Rich. In '90, they started building solidbody Bolt guitars, many with airbrushed graphics. Only about 100 to 125 were built, around 40 with graphics.

Blindworm The Mighty Kraken

Blueridge BG-1500E

Bourgeois Country Boy

2015 Bourgeois JOM
Imaged by Heritage Auctions, HA.com

MODEL YEAR	FEATURES	EXC. COND. LOW	HIGH

Bond

1984-1985. Andrew Bond made around 1,400 Electraglide guitars in Scotland. Logo says 'Bond Guitars, London'.

ElectraGlide

1984-1985. Black carbon graphite 1-piece body and neck, double-cut, 3 single-coils (2 humbuckers were also supposedly available), digital LED controls that required a separate transformer.

1984-1985	With attachments	$1,275	$1,650

Borges Guitars

2000-present. Luthier Julius Borges builds his premium grade, production/custom, acoustic guitars in Groton, Massachusetts.

Boucher

2005-present. Professional and premium grade, acoustic guitars built by luthier Robin Boucher in Quebec.

Boulder Creek Guitars

2007-present. Intermediate and professional grade, production, imported dreadnought, classical, and 12-string guitars, basses and ukes distributed by Morgan Hill Music of Morgan Hill, California.

Bourgeois

1993-1999, 2000-present. Luthier Dana Bourgeois builds his professional and premium grade, production/custom, acoustic and archtop guitars in Lewiston, Maine. Bourgeois co-founded Schoenberg guitars and built Schoenberg models from '86-'90. Bourgeois' 20th Anniversary model was issued in '97. Bourgeois Guitars, per se, went of business at the end of '99. Patrick Theimer created Pantheon Guitars, which included 7 luthiers (including Bourgeois) working in an old 1840s textile mill in Lewiston, Maine and Bourgeois models continue to be made as part of the Pantheon organization.

A-500

Top-of-the-line acoustic cutaway archtop, natural.

1997		$3,600	$4,700

Blues

1996. D-style, all koa.

1996		$2,300	$3,000

Country Boy

1998-present. Pre-war D-style designed for Ricky Skaggs, Sitka spruce top, mahogany back and sides, Ricky Skaggs label, natural.

1998-2019		$2,100	$2,750

Country Boy Custom

1999-2016. Adirondack spruce top, figured mahogany back and sides.

1999-2016		$2,300	$3,000

Country Boy Deluxe

2003-2015. Country Boy with Adirondack spruce top, rosewood binding.

2003-2015		$2,300	$3,000

D - 20th Anniversary

1997. 20 made, bearclaw spruce top, rosewood back and sides, mother-of-pearl 'board, ornate abalone floral pattern inlay, abalone rosette and border, natural.

1997		$2,300	$3,000

D-150/Style 150

2002-present. Brazilian rosewood, premium Adirondack, abalone rosette. Called Style 150 in '20.

2002-2019		$3,600	$4,700

DBJC

Jumbo cutaway, Indian rosewood back and sides, redwood top, gloss finish.

2007		$2,500	$3,300

Georgia Dreadnought

2003. Mahogany, Adirondack.

2003		$1,650	$2,200

JOM

1993-2015. Jumbo Orchestra Model flat-top, 15 5/8". Model includes one with cedar top, mahogany back and sides, and one with spruce top, Brazilian rosewood back and sides.

1993	Brazilian rosewood	$3,600	$4,700
1993	Mahogany	$1,650	$2,200
1993-2015	Indian rosewood	$1,650	$2,200

JOMC/OMC

1995-2015. JOM (jumbo) cutaway.

1995	OMC, figured mahogany	$2,700	$3,600
1995-2015	JOMC200, Indian rosewood	$2,300	$3,100

JR-A

1990s. Artisan Series, 15 5/8", spruce top, rosewood back and sides.

1990s		$950	$1,300

LC-4 Archtop Limited Edition

2002. Limited edition of 12, signed and numbered, premium sitka and carved curly maple.

2002		$8,400	$11,000

Martin Simpson

1997-2003. Grand auditorium with unusual cutaway that removes one-half of the upper treble bout, Englemann spruce top, Indian rosewood back and sides, natural.

1997-2003		$1,900	$2,500

OM

1993-1999. Standard size OM, spruce top, rosewood back and sides.

1993-1999		$2,500	$3,300

OM Deluxe Artisan

2002. Indian rosewood, sitka.

2002		$1,650	$2,200

OM Soloist

1990s-present. Full-sized, soft cutaway flat-top, Adirondack spruce top, figured Brick Red Brazilian rosewood back and sides, natural.

1990-2019		$3,500	$4,600

Ricky Skaggs Signature

1998. D-style, rosewood sides and back, spruce top.

1998		$2,300	$3,000

MODEL YEAR	FEATURES	EXC. COND. LOW	HIGH

Slope D
1993-present. D-size, 16", spruce top, mahogany back and sides.

1993-2019		$2,300	$3,000

Vintage D
2000-present. Adirondack spruce (Eastern red spruce) top, optional rosewood back and sides.

2000-2019	Indian rosewood	$1,850	$2,450
2000s	Brazilian rosewood	$3,500	$4,700

Vintage OM
2005. Madagascar rosewood and Italian spruce top.

2005		$2,600	$3,400

Bown Guitars
Luthier Ralph Bown builds custom steel-string, nylon-string, baritone, and harp guitars, starting 1981, in Walmgate, U.K.

Bozo
1964-present. Bozo (pronounced Bo-zho) Podunavac learned instrument building in his Yugoslavian homeland and arrived in the United States in '59. In '64 he opened his own shop and has built a variety of high-end, handmade, acoustic instruments, many being one-of-a-kind. He has built around 570 guitars over the years. There were several thousand Japanese-made (K. Yairi shop) Bell Western models bearing his name made from '79-'80; most of these were sold in Europe. He currently builds premium and presentation grade, custom guitars in Port Charlotte, Florida.

Acoustic
1970s-1980s. Indian rosewood.

1970s-80s	12-string	$1,400	$1,800
1970s-80s	6-string	$1,400	$1,800

Classical
1969. Limited production.

1969		$1,400	$1,800

Cutaway 12-String
1977-1998. Often old world Balkan ornamentation, generally Sitka spruce top, Indian rosewood back and sides, widow-style headstock, ornamentation can vary (standard or elaborate).

1977	Standard	$1,450	$1,900
1993	Elaborate	$2,400	$3,100
1998	Elaborate Custom	$2,800	$3,700

Bradford
Mid-1960s. Brand name used by the W.T. Grant Company, one of the old Five & Ten style retail stores similar to F.W. Woolworth and Kresge. Many of these guitars and basses were made in Japan by Guyatone.

Acoustic Flat-Top

1960s		$140	$185

Electric Solidbody

1960s	1 or 2 pickups	$150	$200
1960s	3 pickups	$200	$275
1960s	4 pickups	$260	$350

Bradley
1970s. Budget Japanese copy models imported by Veneman's Music Emporium.

MODEL YEAR	FEATURES	EXC. COND. LOW	HIGH

Brawley Basses
Headquartered in Temecula, California, and designed by Keith Brawley, offering solidbody guitars and basses made in Korea.

Brazen
Starting in 2005, owner Steve Tsai, along with luthier Eddie Estrada, offered professional and premium grade, production, electric guitars. Steve also imports a line of intermediate grade guitars from China which are set up in the U.S.

Breedlove
1990-present. Founded by Larry Breedlove and Steve Henderson. Intermediate, professional, premium, and presentation grade, production/custom, steel and nylon string flat-top built in Bend, Oregon and imported. They also build mandolins, basses, lapsteels and ukes. Several available customoptions may add to the values listed here. They offered chambered electric guitars starting in 2008 but in January 2010, Breedlove discontinued all electric guitar production. Also in '10, they became part of Two Old Hippies.

Brentwood
1970s. Student models built by Kay for store or jobber.

K-100
1970s. 13" student flat-top, K-100 label inside back, K logo on 'guard.

1970s		$40	$55

Brian May Guitar Company
2006-present. Guitarist Brian May teamed up with Barry Moorhouse and Pete Malandrone to offer versions of his Red Special Guitar. They also offered a bass.

Brian May Special
2006-present. Mahogany solidbody, 3 pickups, various colors

2006-2019		$350	$475

Brian Moore
1992-present. Founded by Patrick Cummings, Brian Moore and Kevin Kalagher in Brewster, New York; they introduced their first guitars in '94. Initially expensive custom shop guitars with carbon-resin bodies with highly figured wood tops; later went to all wood bodies cut on CNC machines. The intermediate and professional grade, production, iGuitar/i2000series was introduced in 2000 and made in Korea, but set up in the U.S. Currently the premium grade, production/custom, Custom Shop Series guitars are handcrafted in La Grange, New York. They also build basses and electric mandolins.

C/DC/MC Series
1994-2011. Various models.

1994-2011		$800	$1,400

Breedlove Pacific

Brian May BMG Special

1938 Bronson Honolulu Master
Blue Moon Music

R. E. Bruné 30-S

MODEL YEAR	FEATURES	EXC. COND. LOW	HIGH

iGuitar Series
2000-present. Various models.

2000-2019		$625	$825

Brian Stone Classical Guitars
Luthier Brian Stone builds his classical guitars in Corvallis, Oregon.

Briggs
1999-present. Luthier Jack Briggs builds his professional and premium grade, production/custom, chambered and solidbody guitars in Raleigh, North Carolina.

Broman
1930s. The Broman brand was most likely used by a music studio (or distributor) on instruments made by others, including Regal-built resonator instruments.

Bronson
Ca. 1934-early 1960s. George Bronson was a steel guitar instructor in the Detroit area and his instruments were made by other companies. They were mainly lap steels (usually sold with a matching amp), but some other types were also offered.

Honolulu Master Hawaiian
1938		$3,000	$3,900

Student Hawaiian
1930s	13" flat-top	$150	$200

Brook Guitars
1993-present. Simon Smidmore and Andy Petherick build their production/custom Brook steel-string, nylon-strings, and archtops in Dartmoor, U.K.

Brown's Guitar Factory
1982-present. Luthier John Brown builds professional and premium grade, production/custom, solidbody guitars, basses and lap steels in Inver Grove Heights, Minnesota.

Bruné, R. E.
1966-present. Luthier Richard Bruné builds his premium and presentation grade, custom, classical and flamenco guitars in Evanston, Illinois. He also offers his professional and premium grade Model 20 and Model 30, which are handmade in a leading guitar workshop in Japan. Bruné's "Guitars with Guts" features appear in *Vintage Guitar* magazine.

Bruno and Sons
Distributor Bruno and Sons marketed a variety of brands, including their own. Later became part of Kaman Music.

Harp Guitar
1924		$1,800	$2,300

MODEL YEAR	FEATURES	EXC. COND. LOW	HIGH

Hollowbody Electric
1960s-1970s. Various imported models.

1960s		$145	$200

Parlor Guitar
1880-1920. Various woods used on back and sides.

1880-1920	Birch	$400	$525
1880-1920	Brazilian rosewood	$825	$1,100
1880-1920	Mahogany	$450	$575

Buddy Blaze
1985-present. Professional and premium grade, custom/production, solidbody electric guitars built by luthier Buddy Blaze from '85 to '87 in Arlington, Texas, and presently in Kailua Kona, Hawaii. He also designs intermediate grade models which are imported.

Bunker
1961-present. Founder Dave Bunker built custom guitars and basses while performing in Las Vegas in the '60s and developed a number of innovations. Around '92 Bunker began PBC Guitar Technology with John Pearse and Paul Chernay in Coopersburg, Pennsylvania, building instruments under the PBC brand and, from '94-'96, for Ibanez' USA Custom Series. PBC closed in '97 and Bunker moved back to Washington State to start Bunker Guitar Technology and resumed production of several Bunker models. In early 2002, Bunker Guitars became part of Maple Valley Tone Woods of Port Angeles, Washington. Currently Bunker offers intermediate, professional, and premium grade, production/custom, guitars and basses built in Port Angeles. Most early Bunker guitars were pretty much custom-made in low quantities.

Burke
Ca. 1960-ca. 1966. 6- and 12- string electric guitars built by Glen Burke's Tuning Fork Guitar Company in Eugene and Grants Pass, Oregon and mostly sold in kit form. The guitars featured an aluminum neck-thru design with the body portion of the neck shaped being a rectangular box where the body wings are attached. Being kit guitars finishes, pickups, options and build quality will vary.

Burlesk Guitars
1994-present. Professional and premium grade, custom, solidbody electric guitars and basses, built by luthier James Burley in Alberta, Canada.

Burly Guitars
2007-present. Luthier Jeff Ayers builds his professional and premium grade, custom, solid and semi-hollowbody guitars in Land O' Lakes, Wisconsin. He plans on adding basses.

Burns
1960-1970, 1974-1983, 1992-present. Intermediate and professional grade, production, electric guitars built in the U.K. and Asia. They also build basses.

MODEL YEAR	FEATURES	EXC. COND. LOW	HIGH

Jim Burns began building guitars in the late-'50s and established Burns London Ltd in '60. Baldwin Organ (see Baldwin listing) purchased the company in '65 and offered the instruments until '70. The Burns name was revived in '91 by Barry Gibson as Burns London, with Jim Burns' involvement, offering reproductions of some of the classic Burns models of the '60s. Jim Burns passed away in August '98.

Baby Bison
1965. Double-cut solidbody, scroll headstock, 2 pickups, shorter scale, tremolo.

1965		$600	$800

Bison
1964-1965, 2003-present. Double-cut solidbody, 3 pickups, tremolo, black or white, scroll-headstock, replaced flat headstock Black Bison. Has been reissued with both types of headstocks.

1961-1962	Black, 4 pus, flat hs	$1,450	$1,950
1962-1965	Black, 3 pus, scroll hs	$1,350	$1,750
1962-1965	White, 3 pus, scroll hs	$1,350	$1,750
2003-2019	Reissue	$400	$525

Brian May Signature - Red Special
2001-2006. Replica of May's original 'Red Special' but with added whammy-bar, red finish. Korean-made.

2001-2006		$575	$750

Cobra
2004-present. Double-cut solid, 2 pickups.

2004-2019		$105	$135

Double Six
1964-1965, 2003-present. Solidbody 12-string, double-cut, 3 pickups, greenburst. Reissue made in Korea.

1964-1965		$1,250	$1,650
2003-2019		$200	$260

Flyte
1974-1977. Fighter jet-shaped solidbody, pointed headstock, 2 humbucking pickups, silver, has been reissued.

1974-1977		$600	$775

GB 66 Deluxe
1965. Like 66 Standard, but with bar pickups and add Density control.

1965		$700	$925

GB 66 Deluxe Standard
1965. Offset double-cut, f-holes, 2 Ultra-Sonic pickups.

1965		$650	$850

Jazz
1962-1965. Offset double-cut solid, shorter scale, 2 pickups.

1962-1965		$825	$1,075

Jazz Split Sound
1962-1965. Offset double-cut solid, 3 pickups, tremolo, red sunburst.

1962-1965		$1,000	$1,325

Marquee
2000-present. Offset double-cut solid, 3 pickups, scroll headstock

2000-2019		$200	$260

Marvin
1964-1965. Offset double-cut solidbody, scroll headstock, 3 pickups, tremolo, white.

1964-1965		$1,400	$1,800

Nu-Sonic
1964-1965. Solidbody, 2 pickups, tremolo, white or cherry, has been reissued.

1964-1965		$725	$925

Sonic
1960-1964. Double shallow cut solid, 2 pickups, cherry.

1960-1964		$600	$775

Split Sonic
1962-1964. Solidbody, 3 pickups, bound neck, tremolo, red sunburst.

1962-1964		$850	$1,100

Steer
2000-present. Semi-hollowbody, sound-hole, 2 pickups, non-cut and single-cut versions.

2000-2019		$300	$385

TR-2
1963-1964. Semi-hollow, 2 pickups, red sunburst.

1963-1964		$775	$1,000

Vibraslim
1964-1965. Double-cut, f-holes, 2 pickups, red sunburst.

1964-1965		$775	$1,000

Virginian
1964-1965. Burns of London model, later offered as Baldwin Virginian in '65.

1964-1965		$975	$1,275

Vista Sonic
1962-1964. Offset double-cut solid, 3 pickups, red sunburst.

1962-1964		$650	$850

Burnside
1987-1988. Budget solidbody guitars imported by Guild.

Solidbody Electric/Blade
1987-1988. Solidbody, fat pointy headstock.

1987-1988		$150	$195

Burns-Weill
1959. Jim Burns and Henry Weill teamed up to produce three solidbody electric and three solidbody bass models under this English brand. Models included the lower end Fenton, a small single-cutaway, 2 pickups and an elongated headstock and the bizarrely styled RP2G. Henry Weill continued to produce a slightly different RP line under the re-named Fenton-Weill brand.

Burny
1980s-1990s. Solidbody electric guitars from Fernandes and built in Japan, Korea or China.

Burrell
1984-2010. Luthier Leo Burrell built his professional grade, production/custom, acoustic, semi-hollow, and solidbody guitars and basses in Huntington, West Virginia. Leo retired in '10.

1963 Burns Sonic
Imaged by Heritage Auctions, HA.com

1990 Burny RSG-140
Craig Brody

GUITARS

Byrd Super Avianti

*2008 Carvin Allan
Holdsworth Signature*
Robbie Keene

MODEL YEAR	FEATURES	EXC. COND. LOW	HIGH

Burton Guitars

1980-present. Custom classical guitars built by luthier Cynthia Burton in Portland, Oregon.

Buscarino Guitars

1981-present. Luthier John Buscarino builds his premium and presentation grade, custom archtops and steel-string and nylon-string flat-tops in Franklin, North Carolina.

Byers, Gregory

1984-present. Premium grade, custom classical and Flamenco guitars built by luthier Gregory Byers in Willits, California.

Byrd

1998-present. Custom/production, professional and premium grade, V-shaped electric guitars, built by luthiers James Byrd and Joe Riggio, in Seattle and several other cities in the state of Washington.

C. Fox

1997-2002. Luthier Charles Fox built his premium grade, production/custom flat-tops in Healdsburg, California. In '02 he closed C. Fox Guitars and moved to Portland, Oregon to build Charles Fox Guitars.

C.F. Mountain

1970s-early 1980s. Japanese copy acoustics made by Hayashi Musical Instrument Ltd with headstock logo that looks very much like that of a certain classic American guitar company.

Acoustic

MODEL YEAR	FEATURES	LOW	HIGH
1970s-80s		$55	$75

CA (Composite Acoustics)

1999-2010, 2011-present. Professional grade, production, carbon fiber composite guitars that were built in Lafayette, Louisiana. The company ceased production in February, '10. At the end of '10 CA was acquired by Peavey, which launched the new Meridian, Mississippi-based line in January, '11.

Califone

1966. Six and 12-string guitars and basses made by Murphy Music Industries (maker of the Murph guitars) for Rheem Califone-Roberts which manufactured tape recorders and related gear. Very few made.

Callaham

1989-present. Professional, production/custom, solidbody electric guitars built by luthier Bill Callaham in Winchester, Virginia. They also make tube amp heads.

Camelli

1960s. Line of solidbody electric guitars imported from Italy.

Solidbody Electric

MODEL YEAR	FEATURES	LOW	HIGH
1960s		$500	$650

MODEL YEAR	FEATURES	EXC. COND. LOW	HIGH

Cameo

1960s-1970s. Japanese- and Korean-made electric and acoustic guitars. They also offered basses.

Electric

MODEL YEAR	FEATURES	LOW	HIGH
1960s-70s	Higher-end	$275	$360

Campbell American Guitars

2005-2015. Luthier Dean Campbell built his intermediate and professional grade, production/custom, solidbody guitars originally in Pawtucket, Rhode Island, then in Westwood, Massachusetts. From '02 to '05, he built guitars under the Greene & Campbell brand.

Campellone

1978-present. Luthier Mark Campellone builds his premium grade, custom archtops in Greenville, Rhode Island. He also made electrics and basses in the '70s and '80s, switching to archtops around '90.

Deluxe

1990-present. 16" to 18" archtop, middle of the company product line, blond or sunburst.

MODEL YEAR	FEATURES	LOW	HIGH
1990-2019		$3,200	$4,100

Special

1994-present. 16" to 18" archtop, top of the company product line, carved spruce top, carved flamed maple back, flamed maple sides, blond or sunburst.

MODEL YEAR	FEATURES	LOW	HIGH
1994-2019		$4,400	$5,700

Standard

2000-present. 16" to 18" archtop, lower of the 3 model lines offered.

MODEL YEAR	FEATURES	LOW	HIGH
2000-2019		$2,700	$3,500

Canvas

2004-2012. Budget and intermediate grade, production, acoustic and electric guitars and basses imported from China by America Sejung Corp. until '11, then in South Korea.

Carbonaro

Luthier Robert Carbonaro began building in 1975, premium grade, production/custom, archtop and flat-top guitars in Santa Fe, New Mexico. Relocated his shop to Mexico in 2016, then Vietnam in '19.

Carl Fischer

1920s. Most likely a brand made for a distributor. Instruments built by the Oscar Schmidt Co. and possibly others.

Carlos

Ca.1976-late 1980s. Imported copies of classic American acoustics distributed by Coast Wholesale Music.

Acoustic Flat-Top

MODEL YEAR	FEATURES	LOW	HIGH
1976-1980s	Various models	$50	$200

MODEL YEAR	FEATURES	EXC. COND. LOW	HIGH

Carson Robison

1933-1938. Wards sold guitars endorsed by popular country artist Carson Robison. Built by Gibson, the guitars were the same as models sold under the Kalamazoo brand.

Model K

1933-1938. Flat top, ladder, K #926 same as Kalamzoo KG-11, K #1281/#1115 same as Kalamzoo K-14. Becomes the Recording King (Ward's main brand) Model K in '38.

1933-1935	K#926	$1,000	$1,300
1936-1938	K#1281/1115	$1,575	$2,100

Carvin

1946-present. Intermediate and professional grade, production/custom, acoustic and electric guitars and basses built in San Diego, California. They also offer amps and mandolins. Founded in Los Angeles by Hawaiian guitarist and recording artist Lowell C. Kiesel as the L.C. Kiesel Co. making pickups for guitars. Bakelite Kiesel-brand electric Hawaiian lap steels are introduced in early-'47. Small tube amps introduced ca. '47. By late-'49, the Carvin brand is introduced, combining parts of names of sons Carson and Gavin. Carvin acoustic and electric Spanish archtops are introduced in '54. Instruments are sold by mail-order only. Kiesel brand name revived by Carvin in '15 for use on their guitars.

2,000-4,000 guitars made prior to '70 with no serial number. First serial number appeared in '70, stamped on end of fingerboard, beginning with #5000. All are consecutive. Later SN on neck plates.

Approximate SN ranges include:
1970: First serial number #5000 to 10019 ('79).
'80-'83: 10768 to 15919.
'84-'87: 13666 to 25332.
'88-'90: 22731 to 25683.
'91-'94: 25359 to 42547.
'95-'99: 45879 to 81427.
'00-present: 56162 upward.

Casa Montalvo

1987-present. Intermediate and professional grade, production/custom flamenco and classical guitars made in Mexico for George Katechis of Berkeley Musical Instrument Exchange.

Casio

In 1987 Casio introduced a line of digital MIDI guitars imported from Japan, sporting plastic bodies and synthesizer features. They offered them for just a few years.

DG1

1980s. Squared plastic body.

1980s		$55	$85

DG10

1987-1989. Self-contained digital guitar.

1987-1989		$125	$165

MODEL YEAR	FEATURES	EXC. COND. LOW	HIGH

DG20

1987-1989. Midi-capable digital guitar.

1987-1989		$165	$240

MG-500 Series MIDI Guitar

1987-1989. Cut-off teardrop (MG-500) or Strat-shaped (MG-510), basswood body, maple neck, rosewood 'board, 3 pickups.

1987-1989	500	$400	$575
1987-1989	510	$350	$475

PG-300

1988-1989. Similar to PG-380, but with less features.

1988-1989		$300	$400

PG-310

1988-1989. Similar to PG-380, but with less features.

1988-1989		$375	$500

PG-380

1988-1989. Guitar synth, double-cut, over 80 built-in sounds, midi controller capable.

1988-1989		$500	$700

Casper Guitar Technologies

2009-present. Professional grade, production/custom, solidbody electric guitars and basses built by luthier Stephen Casper in Leisure City, Florida.

Cat's Eyes

1980s. Made by Tokai, Cat's Eyes headstock logo, see Tokai guitar listings.

Champion

Ca. 1894-1897. Chicago's Robert Maurer built this brand of instruments before switching to the Maurer brand name around 1897.

Champlin Guitars

2006-present. Professional and premium grade, custom, flat-top and archtop guitars, and mandolinettos, built by Devin Champlin in Bellingham, Washington.

Chandler

Intermediate and professional grade, production/custom, solidbody electric guitars built by luthiers Paul and Adrian Chandler in Chico, California. They also build basses, lap steels and pickups. Chandler started making pickguards and accessories in the '70s, adding electric guitars, basses, and effects in '84.

555 Model

1992-2000s. Sharp double-cut, 3 mini-humbuckers, TV Yellow.

1992-2000s		$550	$725

Austin Special

1991-1999. Resembles futuristic Danelectro, lipstick pickups, available in 5-string version.

1991-1999		$475	$625

Austin Special Baritone

1994-1999. Nicknamed Elvis, gold metalflake finish, mother-of-toilet-seat binding, tremolo, baritone.

1994-1999		$475	$625

Casper CGT-20 Series Classic

1995 Chandler 555

Imaged by Heritage Auctions, HA.com

GUITARS

Char

1990 Charvel 750XL Soloist
Imaged by Heritage Auctions, HA.com

MODEL YEAR	FEATURES	EXC. COND. LOW	HIGH

LectraSlide
2000s. Single-cut, Rezo 'guard, 2 pickups.

2000s		$525	$675

Metro
1995-2000. Double-cut slab body, P-90 in neck position and humbucker in the bridge position.

1995-2000		$475	$625

Telepathic
1994-2000. Classic single-cut style, 3 models; Basic, Standard, Deluxe.

1994-2000	Basic	$400	$525
1994-2000	Deluxe 1122 Model	$475	$625
1994-2000	Standard	$450	$575

Chantus
Premium grade, production/custom, classical and flamenco guitars built in Austin, Texas, by luthier William King starting in '84. He also builds ukes.

Chapin
Professional and premium grade, production/custom, semi-hollow, solidbody, and acoustic electric guitars built by luthiers Bill Chapin and Fred Campbell in San Jose, California.

Chapman
1970-present. Made by Emmett Chapman, the Stick features 10 strings and is played by tapping both hands. The Grand Stick features 12 strings.

Stick
1970-present. Touch-tap hybrid electric instrument, 10 or 12 strings.

1970-2019	10- or 12-string	$1,400	$1,800

Char
1985-present. Premium grade, custom, classical and steel string acoustic guitars built in Portland, Oregon by luthier Kerry Char. He also builds harp-guitars and ukuleles.

Charis Acoustic
1996-present. Premium grade, custom/production, steel-string guitars built by luthier Bill Wise in Bay City, Michigan.

Charles Fox Guitars
1968-present. Luthier Charles Fox builds his premium and presentation grade, custom, steel and nylon string guitars in Portland, Oregon. He also produced GRD acoustic and electric guitars for '78-'82 and C. Fox acoustic guitars for '97-'02. He also operates The American School of Lutherie in Portland.

Charles Shifflett Acoustic Guitars
Premium grade, custom, classical, flamenco, resonator, and harp guitars, basses and banjos built by luthier Charles Shifflett, starting 1990, in High River, Alberta.

Charvel
1976 (1980)-present. Intermediate and professional grade, production, solidbody electric guitars. They also build basses. Founded by Wayne Charvel as Charvel Manufacturing in '76, making guitar parts in Asuza, California. Moved to San Dimas in '78. Also in '78 Grover Jackson bought out Charvel. In '79 or early '80 Charvel branded guitars are introduced. U.S.-made to '85, a combination of imports and U.S.-made post-'85. Charvel also manufactured the Jackson brand.

Charvel licensed its trademark to IMC (Hondo) in '85. IMC bought Charvel in '86 and moved the factory to Ontario, California. On October 25, 2002, Fender Musical Instruments Corp. (FMIC) took ownership of Jackson/Charvel Manufacturing Inc.

Pre-Pro (Pre-Production) Charvels began in November 1980 and ran until sometime in 1981. These are known as 'non-plated' indicating pre-production versus a production neck plate. Production serialized neck plates are considered to be San Dimas models which have a Charvel logo, serial number, and a PO Box San Dimas notation on the neck plate. These Serialized Plated Charvels came after Pre-Pros. Late '81 and '82 saw the early serialized guitars with 21-fret necks; these are more valuable. During '82 the 22-fret neck was introduced. The so-called Soft Strat-, Tele-, Flying V-, and Explorer-style headstocks are associated with the early San Dimas Charvel models. In late '82 the pointy headstock, called the Jackson style, was introduced. In '82 the Superstrat style with a neck plate was introduced. Superstrats with a Kahler tailpiece have a lower value than the Pre-Pro models (with Fender-style trem tailpiece).

Collectors of vintage Charvels look for the vintage Charvel 3-on-a-side logo. This is a defining feature and a cutoff point for valuations. Bogus builders are replicating early Charvels and attempting to sell them as originals so fakes can be a problem for Charvel collectors, so buyer beware.

Other electric guitar manufacturing info:
1986-1989 Japanese-made Models 1 through 8
1989-1991 Japanese-made 550 XL, 650 XL/ Custom, 750 XL (XL=neck-thru)
1989-1992 Japanese-made Models 275, 375, 475, 575
1990-1991 Korean-made Charvette models
1992-1994 Korean-made Models 325, 425

Early Charvel serial numbers (provided by former Jackson/Charvel associate Tim Wilson):
The first 500 to 750 guitars had no serial number, just marked "Made In U.S.A." on their neckplates. Five digit serial numbers were then used until November '81 when 4-digit number adopted, starting with #1001.
1981: 1001-1095
1982: 1096-1724
1983: 1725-2938
1984: 2939-4261
1985: 4262-5303
1986: 5304-5491

MODEL YEAR	FEATURES	EXC. COND. LOW	HIGH

Pre-Pro

November 1980-1981. Pre-Pros came in different configurations of body styles, pickups, and finishes. There are five basic Pre-Pro formats: the Standard Body, the Bound Body, the Graphic Body, the Flamed Top, and the Matching Headstock. It is possible to have a combination, such as a Bound Body and Matching Headstock. Line items are based on body style and can feature any one of four neck/headstock-styles used: the so-called Tele-headstock, Strat-headstock, Flying V headstock, and Explorer headstock. Finishes included white, black, red, metallic Lake Placid Blue, and special graphics. All original parts adds considerable value and it is often difficult to determine what is original on these models, so expertise is required. An original Fender brass trem tailpiece, for example, adds considerable value. The Pre-Pro models were prone to modification such as added Kahler and Floyd Rose trems. Price ranges are wide because this is a relatively new market without mature pricing.

1980-1981	Bound body	$2,300	$3,000
1980-1981	Flamed top, stained body	$3,100	$4,100
1980-1981	Graphic body	$2,700	$3,600
1980-1981	Matching headstock & body	$3,400	$4,500
1980-1981	Standard body	$1,900	$2,500

275 Deluxe Dinky

1989-1991. Made in Japan, offset double-cut solidbody, 1 single-coil and 1 humbucker in '89, 2 humbuckers after, tremolo.

1989-1991		$450	$575

325SL

1992-1994. Dot inlays.

1992-1994		$450	$575

325SLX

1992-1994. Surfcaster-like thinline acoustic/electric, dual cutaways, f-hole, on-board chorus, shark inlays, made in Korea.

1992-1994		$450	$575

375 Deluxe

1989-1991. Maple or rosewood 'board, dot inlays, single-single-humbucker.

1989-1991		$450	$575

475 Deluxe/Special

1989-1991. Introduced as Special, changed to Deluxe in '90, bound rosewood board, shark tooth inlays, 2 oval stacked humbuckers and 1 bridge humbucker. Was also offered as Deluxe Exotic with figured top and back.

1989-1991		$450	$575

525

1989-1994. Acoustic-electric, single-cut.

1989-1994		$450	$575

550XL

1987-1989. Neck-thru (XL), dot markers, 1 single-coil and 1 bridge humbucker.

1987-1989		$525	$675

625-C12

1993-2000. Acoustic-electric cutaway 12-string, spruce top.

1993-2000		$375	$490

625F/625ACEL

1993-1995. Acoustic-electric cutaway, figured maple top.

1993-1995		$375	$490

650XL/Custom

1989-1990. Introduced as neck-thru XL and discontinued as Custom, shark fin markers, 2 stacked oval humbuckers and 1 bridge humbucker, custom version of 550XL.

1989-1990		$900	$1,175

750XL Soloist

1989-1990. Shark fin markers, cutaway body, 2 humbuckers, large Charvel logo.

1989-1990		$1,000	$1,300

Avenger

1990-1991. Randy Rhoads-style batwing-shaped solidbody, 1 humbucker, 1 single-coil, tremolo, made in Japan.

1990-1991		$425	$550

Charvette

1989-1991. Charvette Series made in Korea, superstrat-style, model number series 100 through 300.

1990-1991		$325	$425

CX Series

1991-1994. Imported solidbodies, body-mounted or pickguard mounted pickups, standard or deluxe tremolo.

1991-1994		$250	$325

EVH Art Series

2004-2007. Offset double-cut solidbody, 1 humbucker, striped finish.

2004-2007	Black/white	$1,050	$1,400
2004-2007	White/black on red	$1,250	$1,600
2004-2007	Yellow/black	$1,050	$1,400

Fusion Deluxe

1989-1991. Double-cut solidbody, tremolo, 1 humbucker and 1 single-coil, made in Japan.

1989-1991		$525	$675

Fusion Standard/AS FX 1

1993-1996. Double-cut solidbody, tremolo, 1 regular and 2 mini humbuckers, made in Japan, also named AS FX1.

1993-1996		$475	$625

Model 1/1A/1C

1986-1988. Offset double-cut solidbody, bolt-on maple neck, dot inlays, 1 humbucker, tremolo, made in Japan. Model 1A has 3 single-coils. Model 1C has 1 humbucker and 2 single-coils.

1986-1988		$475	$625

Model 2

1986-1988. As Model 1, but with rosewood 'board.

1986-1988		$475	$625

Model 3/3A/3DR/3L

1986-1989. As Model 2, but with 1 humbucker, 2 single coils. Model 3A has 2 humbuckers. Model 3DR has 1 humbucker and 1 single-coil.

1986-1989		$475	$625

Model 4/4A

1986-1988. As Model 2, but with 1 regular humbucker and 2 stacked humbuckers (no pickguard), active electronics, dots in '86, shark-fin inlays after. Model 4A has 2 regular humbuckers and dot markers.

1986-1988		$600	$775

1987 Charvel Model 1
Imaged by Heritage Auctions, HA.com

1986 Charvel Model 3
Imaged by Heritage Auctions, HA.com

GUITARS

Charvel Model 5

Chris George

MODEL YEAR	FEATURES	EXC. COND. LOW	HIGH

Model 5/5A
1986-1988. As Model 4A, but neck-thru, with JE1000TG active elctronics. Model 5A is single humbucker and single knob version, limited production, made in Japan.

1986-1988		$600	$775

Model 6
1986-1988. As HSS Model 4, but with shark's tooth inlays, standard or various custom finishes.

1986-1988		$675	$875

Model 7
1988-1989. Single-cut solidbody, bound top, reversed headstock, 2 single-coils, made in Japan.

1988-1989		$675	$875

Model 88 LTD
1988. Double-cut solidbody, 1 slanted humbucker, shark fin inlay, 1000 built, made in Japan.

1988		$675	$875

Predator
1989-1991. Offset double-cut, bridge humbucker, single-coil neck, bolt-on.

1989-1991		$360	$465

San Dimas Serialized Plated
1981-1986, 1995-1997. U.S.-made with San Dimas neck plate, bolt neck, rounded headstock early production, pointy headstock later, reissued in mid-'90s.

1981-1982	Soft headstock	$1,750	$2,300
1982-1986	Pointy headstock	$1,150	$1,500
1995-1997	Soft headstock	$500	$650

San Dimas LTD 25th Anniversary
2006. About 100 made, 25th Anniversary logo on neck plate with production number, highly figured top, high-end appointments.

2006		$1,375	$1,775

San Dimas Reissue (FMIC)
2004-present. Alder body, bolt neck.

2004-2019		$525	$975

So-Cal Series
2008-2012. Offset double-cut solidbody.

2008-2012	Various options	$400	$850

ST Custom
1990-1991. Offset double-cut ash solidbody, 2 single-coils and 1 humbucker, rosewood 'board, tremolo, made in Japan.

1990-1991		$425	$550

ST Deluxe
1990-1991. Same as ST Custom but with maple 'board.

1990-1991		$400	$525

Standard
2002-2003. Typical offset double-cut Charvel body, 2 Seymour Duncan humbucker pickups, various opaque colors.

2002-2003		$300	$400

Star
1980-1981. The Star is considered by early-Charvel collectors to be Charvel's only original design with its unique four-point body.

1980-1981		$2,600	$3,400

Surfcaster
1991-1996. Offset double-cut, f-hole, various pickup options, bound body, tremolo, made in Japan.

1991-1996	1 single, 1 hum	$1,025	$1,325
1991-1996	2 singles, hardtail	$1,025	$1,325
1991-1996	2 singles, vibrato	$1,125	$1,450

Surfcaster 12
1991-1996. Made in Japan, 12-string version of Surfcaster, no tremolo.

1991-1996		$1,075	$1,400

Surfcaster Double Neck
1992. Very limited production, 6/12 double neck, Charvel logo on both necks, black.

1992		$1,750	$2,300

Surfcaster HT (Model SC1)
1996-2000. Made in Japan. Hard Tail (HT) non-tremolo version of Surfcaster, has single-coil and bridge humbucker.

1996-2000		$1,025	$1,325

Chiquita
1979-present. Intermediate grade, production guitars made by Erlewine Guitars in Austin, Texas (see that listing). There was also a mini amp available.

Travel Guitar
1979-present. Developed by Mark Erlewine and ZZ Top's Billy Gibbons, 27" overall length solidbody, 1 or 2 pickups, various colors.

1979-2019		$225	$475

Chris George
1966-present. Professional and premium grade, custom, archtop, acoustic, electric and resonator guitars built by luthier Chris George in Tattershall Lincolnshire, U.K.

Christopher Carrington
1988-present. Production/custom, premium grade, classical and flamenco acoustic guitars built by luthier Chris Carrington in Rockwall, Texas.

Chrysalis Guitars
1998-2015. Luthier Tim White built his premium grade, production/custom Chrysalis Guitar System, which included interchangeable components that can be quickly assembled into a full-size electric/acoustic guitar, in New Boston, New Hampshire. White introduced his new brand, Ridgewing, at January 2016 NAMM.

Cimar/Cimar by Ibanez
Early-1980s. Private brand of Hoshino Musical Instruments, Nagoya, Japan, who also branded Ibanez. Headstock with script Cimar logo or Cimar by Ibanez, copy models and Ibanez near-original models such as the star body.

Cimar
1982	Classical	$55	$75
1982	Double-cut solidbody	$165	$225
1982	Star body style	$165	$225

MODEL YEAR	FEATURES	EXC. COND. LOW	HIGH

Cimarron

1978-present. Luthiers John Walsh and Clayton Walsh build their professional grade, production/custom, flat-top acoustic guitars in Ridgway, Colorado. Between '94 and '98 they also produced electric guitars.

Cipher

1960s. Solidbody electric guitars and basses imported from Japan by Inter-Mark. Generally strange-shaped bodies.

Electric Solidbody

1960s. For any student-grade import, a guitar with any missing part, such as a missing control knob or trem arm, is worth much less.

1960s		$150	$250

Citron

1995-present. Luthier Harvey Citron builds his professional and premium grade, production/custom solidbody guitars and basses in Woodstock, New York. He also builds basses. In '75, Citron and Joe Veillette founded Veillette-Citron, which was known for handcrafted, neck-thru guitars and basses. That company closed in '83.

Clark

1985-present. Custom, professional grade, solidbody electric guitars and basses, built by luthier Ed Clark, first in Amityville, New York ('85-'90), then Medford ('91-'99) and presently Lake Ronkonkoma.

Clifford

Clifford was a brand manufactured by Kansas City, Missouri instrument wholesalers J.W. Jenkins & Sons. First introduced in 1895, the brand also offered mandolins.

Clovis

Mid-1960s. Private brand guitars, most likely made by Kay.

Electric Solidbody

Mid-1960s. Kay slab solidbody, 2 pickups.

1965		$285	$385

CMG Guitars

2012-present. Owner Chris Mitchell imports intermediate grade, acoustic and acoustic-electric guitars from China. He also offers professional grade, production/custom, electric guitars built by luthiers Russell Jones and James Horel in Statesboro, Georgia.

Cole

1890-1919. W.A. Cole, after leaving Fairbanks & Cole, started his own line in 1890. He died in 1909 but the company continued until 1919. He also made mandolins and banjos.

Parlor

1897. Small size, Brazilian rosewood sides and back, spruce top, ebony 'board, slotted headstock, dot markers.

1897		$675	$900

Coleman Guitars

1976-1983. Custom made presentation grade instruments made in Homosassa, Florida, by luthier Harry Coleman. No headstock logo, Coleman logo on inside center strip.

Collings

1986-present. Professional, premium, and presentation grade, production/custom, flat-top, archtop and electric guitars built in Austin, Texas. They also build mandolins and ukuleles. Bill Collings started with guitar repair and began custom building guitars around '73. In '80, he relocated his shop from Houston to Austin and started Collings Guitars in '86. In '06 they moved to a new plant in southwest Austin.

0-1

2005-present. Mother-of-pearl inlays, sitka spruce, mahogany neck, back & sides, ebony 'board and bridge, high gloss lacquer finish.

2005-2019		$2,200	$3,000

0-1A

2010-2017. As 0-1 with Adirondack spruce top.

2010-2017		$3,000	$4,000

0-1G

As 0-1 with German spruce top.

2009		$2,700	$3,500

0-1SB

Sitka spruce, mahogany.

2006-2015		$2,550	$3,300

0-2G

German spruce, sunburst.

1996		$3,200	$4,200

0-2H

Parlor, 12 frets.

2008		$2,400	$3,200

0-2SB

Parlor, 12 frets, 12-string.

2016		$3,200	$4,200

00-1G

German spruce.

2009		$2,900	$3,800

00-1MH

All mahogany body.

2010		$2,550	$3,300

00-2H

1999-present. Indian rosewood.

1999-2019		$2,550	$3,300

00-41

2001. Premium Brazilian rosewood back and sides, Adirondack spruce top, abalone top purfling.

2001		$6,200	$8,000

000-1

1990s-present. Mahogany body, spruce top.

1990s	000-1 Sitka	$2,900	$3,800
1990s-2019	000-1A		
	Adirondack	$3,100	$4,200

000-1 ICC

000-1 with Indian rosewood back and sides.

2000s		$2,100	$3,000

Cimarron Model P

Collings 000-1

Collings AT-17

Collings I-35

MODEL YEAR	FEATURES	EXC. COND. LOW	HIGH

000-1Mh
2006. All mahogany body, 000 size.

| 2006 | | $2,100 | $3,000 |

000-2H
1994-present. 15" 000-size, Indian rosewood back and sides, spruce top, slotted headstock, 12-fret neck, dot markers. AAA Koa back and sides in '96.

1994-1995	Indian rosewood	$2,400	$3,200
1996	AAA Koa	$2,700	$3,500
2007-2019	Indian rosewood	$2,400	$3,200

000-41
1999. Indian rosewood sides and back, Sitka spruce top, slotted headstock.

| 1999 | | $4,000 | $5,100 |

290 Series
2004-present. Solid Honduran mahogany body, East Indian rosewood 'board, 2 P-90 style pickups, '50s style wiring, high gloss lacquer finish.

| 2004-2019 | Deluxe | $1,650 | $2,200 |

360 LT
2015-present. Solidbody electric, level top (LT), mahogany, ash or alder body, rosewood 'board, high gloss nitro finish.

| 2015-2019 | | $2,200 | $2,900 |

AT-17
2008-present. Collings' archtops are built in limited numbers, AT-17 is a 17" single-cut, with f-holes, Adirondack or European spruce top, premium flamed maple back and sides, and premium appointments, sunburst or blonde. Options include scale length, pickup and bindings.

| 2008-2019 | | $10,000 | $13,000 |

Baby Series
1997-present. Various 3/4 size models, Englemann (E) or German (G) spruce top, rosewood back and sides, Ivoroid with herringbone trim, tortoise 'guard, gloss nitro lacquer finish.

| 1997-2019 | Various models | $2,200 | $2,800 |

C-10
1986-present. 000-size, mahogany back and sides, spruce top, sunburst or natural.

| 1986-2019 | | $2,350 | $3,050 |

C-10 Deluxe
1986-present. C-10 with Indian rosewood back and sides (mahogany, flamed maple or koa optional), sunburst or natural.

1986-2019	Indian rosewood	$2,800	$3,650
1994-2000s	Flamed maple	$2,800	$3,650
1994-2000s	Koa option	$2,800	$3,650
1994-2000s	Varnish	$2,800	$3,650
1994-2019	Mahogany	$2,800	$3,650

C-100
1986-1994. Quadruple 0-size, mahogany back and sides, spruce top, natural, replaced by CJ Jumbo.

| 1986-1994 | | $2,100 | $2,800 |

C-100 Deluxe
1986-1994. C-100 with rosewood back and sides.

| 1986-1994 | | $2,350 | $3,000 |

CJ Jumbo
1995-present. Quadruple 0-size, Indian rosewood back and sides, spruce top, natural.

| 1995-2019 | | $2,600 | $3,400 |

CJ Koa ASB
2007. Adirondack spruce top, scalloped bracing ASB, flamed koa sides and back.

| 2007 | | $3,100 | $4,000 |

CJ-35
2014-present. Sitka spruce top, Honduran mahogany back, sides and neck, tigerstripe 'guard.

| 2014-2019 | | $3,000 | $3,900 |

CL Series (City Limits)
2004-present. City Limits Jazz series, fully carved flame maple top, solid Honduran mahogany body, East Indian rosewood 'board, high gloss lacquer finish.

| 2004-2019 | | $2,900 | $3,800 |

Clarence White
1989-2000. Adirondack top, Brazilian rosewood back and sides (CW-28), or mahogany (CW-18), herringbone trim.

| 1989-2000 | Brazilian CW-28 | $6,200 | $8,000 |
| 1993-2000 | Mahogany CW-18 | $3,100 | $4,100 |

CW Indian A
2019-present. Collings Winfield (CW), named after the Walnut Valley Festival in Winfield, Kansas, modified version of standard dreadnought, Adirondack spruce top, East Indian rosewood back and sides, ivoroid binding with herringbone purfling.

| 2019 | | $3,400 | $4,400 |

D-1
1994-present. D-style, 15 5/8", spruce top, mahogany back and sides, natural.

| 1992-2019 | | $2,300 | $3,000 |

D-1 Gruhn
1989. Short run for Gruhn Guitars, Nashville, Gruhn script headstock logo, signed by Bill Collings, choice of Indian rosewood or curly maple back and sides, Engelman spruce top.

| 1989 | | $2,750 | $3,550 |

D-1A
1992-2018. Upgrade D-1 with Adirondack spruce top and higher appointments, natural.

| 1992-2018 | | $3,300 | $4,400 |

D-1H
1992-2018. Same as D-1 with herringbone purfling.

| 1992-2018 | | $2,100 | $2,800 |

D-2
1986-1995. D-1 with Indian rosewood back and sides, natural.

| 1986-1995 | | $2,300 | $3,000 |

D-2H
1986-present. Dreadnought, same as D-2 with herringbone purfling around top edge.

| 1986-2019 | | $2,450 | $3,150 |

D-2HA
2004-2010. Indian or Brazilian rosewood back and sides, Adirondack spruce top, top herringbone trim, gloss natural finish.

| 2004-2006 | | $3,250 | $4,300 |
| 2007-2010 | | $3,100 | $4,000 |

D-2HAV
2004-2010. Varnish finish option.

| 2004-2010 | | $3,100 | $4,000 |

MODEL YEAR	FEATURES	EXC. COND. LOW	HIGH

D-2HB

1994-2001. Grade AA Brazilian rosewood, Adirondack spruce top.

| 1994-2005 | | $6,200 | $8,000 |

D-2HG SB

German spruce, sunburst varnish.

| 2008 | | $4,200 | $5,500 |

D-2HV

1994. D-2H with V shaped neck.

| 1994 | | $2,150 | $2,800 |

D-3

1990-present. Similar to D-2H but with abalone purfling/rosette, Brazilian or Indian rosewood. A is Adirondack upgrade.

1990-1999	Brazilian	$5,500	$7,100
2000-2019	Indian	$2,550	$3,300
2004	D-3A, Adirondack	$3,700	$4,800

D-42

2000s. Brazilian rosewood back and sides, fancy.

| 2000s | | $6,200 | $8,100 |

DS-1/DS-1A

2004-present. D-size, slope shoulders, 12 fret neck, slotted headstock, mahogany back and sides, A is Adirondack upgrade.

| 2004-2019 | | $2,800 | $3,600 |

DS-2H/DS-2HA

1995-present. D size, slope shoulders, 12 fret neck, slotted headstock. A is Adirondack upgrade.

| 1995-2019 | | $3,000 | $3,800 |

DS-41

1995-2007. Indian rosewood, abalone top trim, snowflake markers.

| 1995-2007 | | $3,500 | $4,500 |

I-35 Deluxe

2007-present. Fully carved flame or quilted maple top, mahogany body, Brazilian or Madagascar rosewood 'board, high Gloss lacquer finish.

| 2007-2019 | | $3,200 | $4,200 |

OM-1 Series

1994-present. Grand concert, sitka spruce top, mahogany back and sides, natural. OM-1A/OM-1A Cutaway includes Adirondack spruce upgrade.

1994-2005	OM-1A	$2,800	$3,700
1994-2019	OM-1	$2,500	$3,200
2000-2016	OM-1 Koa	$2,650	$3,400
2000-2016	OM-1MH Mahogany	$2,800	$3,600
2007-2016	OM-1A Cutaway	$2,800	$3,800

OM-2

2008. Cutaway, Indian rosewood back and sides.

| 2008 | | $2,750 | $3,575 |

OM-2H

1990-present. Indian rosewood back and sides, herringbone binding.

| 1990-2019 | | $2,600 | $3,400 |

OM-2H GSS

2008. Indian rosewood sides and back, German spruce, herringbone trim top.

| 2008 | | $2,700 | $3,500 |

OM-2H SSB

Brazilian rosewood, herringbone binding.

| 2001 | | $6,200 | $8,000 |

OM-2HA/OM-2HA Custom

Adirondack spruce top, rosewood or mahogany back and sides.

| 2003-2018 | OM-2HA, rosewood | $3,500 | $4,500 |
| 2010 | OM-2HA Custom, mahogany | $3,500 | $4,500 |

OM-2HAV

1998. Adirondack spruce top, Brazilian rosewood back and sides, ivoroid-bound body.

| 1998 | | $6,200 | $8,000 |

OM-3

1998-present. Brazilian rosewood back and sides, Adirondack spruce top, fancy rosette, later Indian rosewood or figured maple or mahogany.

1998	B, Brazilian, fancy	$6,300	$8,100
2002-2019	Indian	$3,000	$3,900
2003	Figured maple	$2,900	$3,800
2008	Mahogany	$2,900	$3,800

OM-3A

2004-2007. Adirondack spruce, Indian rosewood.

| 2004-2007 | | $3,400 | $4,400 |

OM-3HBA

1994-2007. Brazilian rosewood, Adirondack spruce.

| 1994-2007 | | $6,300 | $8,100 |

OM-3HC

1986-1996. Single-cut, 15", Indian rosewood back and sides, spruce top, herringbone purfling.

| 1986-1996 | | $3,050 | $4,000 |

OM-41BrzGCut

2007. Brazilian rosewood sides and back, German spruce top, rounded cutaway.

| 2007 | | $6,200 | $8,000 |

OM-42B

Brazilian rosewood back and sides, Adirondack spruce top, fancy rosette and binding.

| 2000 | | $6,800 | $9,000 |

OM-42G

Indian rosewood.

| 1999 | | $3,400 | $4,500 |

OMC-2H

Adirondack top, Brazilian rosewood back and sides, herringbone trim.

| 2008 | | $6,200 | $8,000 |

SJ

1986-present. Spruce top, quilted maple back and sides or Indian rosewood (earlier option), later mahogany.

| 1986-2019 | Various options | $2,500 | $3,200 |

SJ-41

1996. Brazilian rosewood back and sides, cedar top.

| 1996 | | $6,200 | $8,000 |

SoCo Deluxe

2007-present. Premium figured maple top over semi-hollow mahogany body, rosewood 'board, f-holes, various finish options.

| 2007-2019 | | $2,900 | $3,750 |

Collings SJ

Collings SoCo DLX

Conrad Acoustical Slimline 12-String (40100)
Imaged by Heritage Auctions, HA.com

1968 Coral Hornet
Robbie Keene

MODEL YEAR	FEATURES	EXC. COND. LOW	HIGH

Winfield
2004-2006. D-style, Adirondack spruce top, Brazilian or Indian rosewood back and sides, later mahogany.

2004	Indian	$3,100	$4,000
2005-2006	Brazilian	$6,200	$8,000
2006	Mahogany	$3,100	$4,000

Columbia
Late 1800s-early 1900s. The Columbia brand name was used on acoustic guitars by New York's James H. Buckbee Co. until c.1987 and afterwards by Galveston's Thomas Goggan and Brothers.

Comins
1992-present. Premium and presentation grade, custom archtops built by luthier Bill Comins in Willow Grove, Pennsylvania. He also builds mandolins and offers a combo amp built in collaboration with George Alessandro.

Commander
Late 1950s-early 1960s. Archtop acoustic guitars made by Harmony for the Alden catalog company.

Concertone
Ca. 1914-1930s. Concertone was a brand made by Chicago's Slingerland and distributed by Montgomery Ward. The brand was also used on other instruments such as ukuleles.

Conklin
1984-present. Intermediate, professional and premium grade, production/custom, 6-, 7-, 8-, and 12-string solid and hollowbody electrics, by luthier Bill Conklin. He also builds basses. Originally located in Lebanon, Missouri, in '88 the company moved to Springfield, Missouri. Conklin instruments are made in the U.S. and overseas.

Conn Guitars
Ca.1968-ca.1978. Student to mid-quality classical and acoustic guitars, some with bolt-on necks, also some electrics. Imported from Japan by band instrument manufacturer and distributor Conn/Continental Music Company, Elkhart, Indiana.

Acoustic
1968-1978. Various models.

1968-1978		$105	$175

Classical
1968-1978. Various student-level models.

1968-1978		$80	$125

Electric Solidbody
1970s. Various models.

1970-1978		$150	$200

Connor, Stephan
1995-present. Luthier Stephan Connor builds his premium grade, custom nylon-string guitars in Waltham, Massachusetts.

MODEL YEAR	FEATURES	EXC. COND. LOW	HIGH

Conrad Guitars
Ca. 1968-1978. Mid- to better-quality copies of glued-neck Martin and Gibson acoustics and bolt-neck Gibson and Fender solidbodies. They also offered basses, mandolins and banjos. Imported from Japan by David Wexler and Company, Chicago, Illinois.

Acoustic 12-String
1970s. Dreadnought size.

1970s		$125	$175

Acoustical Slimline (40080/40085)
1970s. Rosewood 'board, 2 or 3 DeArmond-style pickups, block markers, sunburst.

1970s		$350	$450

Acoustical Slimline 12-String (40100)
1970s. Rosewood 'board, 2 DeArmond-style pickups, dot markers, sunburst.

1970s		$350	$450

Bison (40035/40030/40065/40005)
1970s. 1 thru 4 pickups available, rosewood 'board with dot markers, six-on-side headstock.

1970s		$350	$450

Bumper (40223)
1970s. Clear Lucite solidbody.

1970s		$425	$575

Classical Student (40150)

1970s		$100	$140

De Luxe Folk Guitar
1970s. Resonator acoustic, mahogany back, sides and neck, Japanese import.

1970s		$200	$300

Master Size (40178)
1972-1977. Electric archtop, 2 pickups.

1972-1977		$325	$425

Resonator Acoustic
1970s. Flat-top with wood, metal resonator and 8 ports, round neck.

1970s		$400	$525

Violin-Shaped 12-String Electric (40176)
1970s. Scroll headstock, 2 pickups, 500/1 control panel, bass side dot markers, sunburst.

1970s		$400	$525

Violin-Shaped Electric (40175)
1970s. Scroll headstock, 2 pickups, 500/1 control panel, bass side dot markers, vibrato, sunburst.

1970s		$400	$525

White Styrene 1280
1970s. Solid maple body covered with white styrene, 2 pickups, tremolo, bass side dot markers, white.

1970s		$350	$450

Contessa
1960s. Acoustic, semi-hollow archtop, solidbody and bass guitars made in Italy by Zero Sette and imported by Hohner. They also made banjos.

Acoustic

1960s		$75	$200

Electric Solidbody
1967. Various models.

1960s		$225	$350

MODEL YEAR	FEATURES	EXC. COND. LOW	HIGH

Contreras

See listing for Manuel Contreras and Manuel Contreras II.

Coral

1967-1969. In '66 MCA bought Danelectro and in '67 introduced the Coral brand of guitars, basses and amps.

Bellzouki 7021

1967. 12-string electric, modified teardrop shape with body points on treble and bass bouts, 2 pickups.

Year	Features	Low	High
1967		$1,050	$1,400

Combo/Vincent Bell Combo

1967-1969. Cutaway acoustic/electric,1 or 2 pickups.

1967-1969	V1N6, 1 pu	$2,075	$2,725
1967-1969	V2N6, 2 pu	$2,375	$3,100

Firefly

1967-1969. Double-cut, f-holes, 2 pickups, with or without vibrato.

1967-1969	2N, red	$650	$850
1967-1969	2N, sunburst	$650	$850
1967-1969	2V, vibrato, red	$950	$1,275
1967-1969	2V, vibrato, sunburst	$950	$1,275
1968-1969	F2N12, Electric XII, red	$950	$1,275
1968-1969	F2N12, Electric XII, sunburst	$950	$1,275

Hornet

1967-1969. Solidbody, 2 or 3 pickups, with or without vibrato, sunburst, black or red.

1967-1969	2N, 2 pu, black or red	$950	$1,250
1967-1969	2N, 2 pu, sunburst	$825	$1,075
1967-1969	2V, 2 pu, vibrato, black or red	$1,050	$1,400
1967-1969	2V, 2 pu, vibrato, sunburst	$850	$1,150
1967-1969	3N, 3 pu, black or red	$1,050	$1,400
1967-1969	3N, 3 pu, sunburst	$950	$1,250
1967-1969	3V, 3 pu, vibrato, black or red	$1,125	$1,500
1967-1969	3V, 3 pu, vibrato, sunburst	$950	$1,250

Long Horn

1967-1969. Deep double-cut hollowbody, 2 lipstick tube pickups, 6 or 12-string, sunburst.

1967-1969	L2N12, Electric XII	$1,150	$1,525
1967-1969	L2N6, 2 pu	$1,050	$1,400

Scorpion

1967-1969. Offset double-cut solidbody, 2 or 3 lipstick tube pickups, 12-string.

1967-1969	2N12, 2 pu, black or red	$950	$1,275
1967-1969	2N12, 2 pu, sunburst	$825	$1,075
1967-1969	2V12, 2 pu, vibrato, black or red	$950	$1,275
1967-1969	2V12, 2 pu, vibrato, sunburst	$950	$1,275
1967-1969	3N12, 3 pu, black or red	$1,100	$1,475
1967-1969	3N12, 3 pu, sunburst	$950	$1,275
1967-1969	3V12, 3 pu, vibrato, black or red	$1,150	$1,525
1967-1969	3V12, 3 pu, vibrato, sunburst	$950	$1,275

Sitar

1967-1969. Six-string guitar with drone strings and 3 pickups (2 under the 6 strings, 1 under the drones), kind of a USA-shaped body.

1967-1969	3S18, 18-string	$1,900	$2,500
1967-1969	3S19, 19-string	$2,000	$2,700
1967-1969	3S9, 9-string	$1,700	$2,250

Teardrop

1967-1969. Teardrop shaped hollowbody, 2 lipstick tube pickups.

1968	T2N6	$1,625	$2,100

Córdoba

Line of classical guitars handmade in Portugal and imported by Guitar Salon International. By '13, U.S. production was added.

Classical

2000s	Higher-end	$500	$1,800
2000s	Mid-level	$300	$500
2000s	Student-level	$175	$300

Cordova

1960s. Classical nylon string guitars imported by David Wexler of Chicago.

Grand Concert Model WC-026

1960s. Highest model offered by Cordova, 1-piece rosewood back, laminated rosewood sides, spruce top, natural.

1960s		$225	$300

Corey James Custom Guitars

2005-present. Luthier Corey James Moilanen builds his professional and premium grade, production/custom solidbody guitars and basses in Howell, Michigan.

Coriani, Paolo

1984-present. Production/custom nylon-string guitars and hurdy-gurdys built by luthier Paolo Coriani in Modeila, Italy.

Cort

1973-present. North Brook, Illinois-based Cort offers budget, intermediate and professional grade, production/custom, acoustic and solidbody, semi-hollow, hollow body electric guitars and basses built in Korea.

Cort was the second significant Korean private-label (Hondo brand was the first) to come out of Korea. Jack Westheimer entered into an agreement with Korea's Cort to do Cort-brand, private-label, and Epiphone-brand guitars.

1968 Coral Sitar
Craig Brody

Cort Classic TC

CP Thornton Improv

CSR Serenata

CP Thornton Guitars

1985-present. Luthier Chuck Thornton builds professional and premium grade, production/custom, semi-hollow and solidbody electric guitars in Sumner, Maine. Up to '96 he also built basses.

Crafter

1986-present. Crafter offers budget and intermediate grade, production, classical, acoustic, acoustic/electric, and electric guitars, basses and mandolins made in Korea. They also offer the Cruzer and Ashland brands of instruments. From '72 to '86 they made Sungeum classical guitars.

Cranium

Introduced 1996, professional grade, production/custom, hollow, semi-hollow, and solidbody electrics built by luthier Wayne O'Connor in Peterborough, Ontario.

Crescent Moon

Professional grade, production/custom, solidbody guitars and basses built by luthier Craig Muller in Baltimore, Maryland, starting 1999.

Creston

2004-present. Professional grade, custom, solidbody electric guitars and basses built by luthier Creston Lea in Burlington, Vermont.

Crestwood

1970s. Copies of the popular classical guitars, flat-tops, electric solidbodies and basses of the era, imported by La Playa Distributing Company of Detroit.

Acoustic 12-String

MODEL YEAR	FEATURES	LOW	HIGH
1970s		$175	$225

Electric

1970s. Various models include near copies of the 335 (Crestwood model 2043, 2045 and 2047), Les Paul Custom (2020), Strat (2073), Jazzmaster (2078), Tele (2082), and the SG Custom (2084).

1970s		$225	$475

Crimson Guitars

2005-present. Luthiers Benjamin Crowe and Aki Atrill build professional and premium grade, custom, solidbody guitars and basses in Somerset, U.K.

Cromwell

1935-1939. Budget model brand built by Gibson and distributed by mail-order businesses like Grossman, Continental, Richter & Phillips, and Gretsch & Brenner.

Acoustic Archtop

1935-1939. Archtop acoustic, f-holes, pressed mahogany back and sides, carved and bound top, bound back, 'guard and 'board, no truss rod.

MODEL YEAR	FEATURES	LOW	HIGH
1935-1939	Various models	$650	$1,075
1935-1939	With '30s era pickup	$1,100	$1,400

Acoustic Flat-Top

MODEL YEAR	FEATURES	LOW	HIGH
1935-1939	G-2 (L-00)	$1,500	$1,900

GT-2 Tenor

1935-1939	1474" flat-top	$650	$1,075

GT-4 Tenor

1935-1939	16" archtop	$650	$1,075

Cromwell (Guild)

1963-1964. Guild imported these 2- or 3-pickup offset double cut solidbodies from Hagstrom. These were basically part of Hagstrom's Kent line with laminated bodies and birch necks. About 500 were imported into the U.S.

Solidbody

MODEL YEAR	FEATURES	LOW	HIGH
1963-1964		$900	$1,125

Crook Custom Guitars

1997-present. Professional grade, custom, solidbody electric guitars and basses built in Moundsville, West Virginia by luthier Bill Crook.

Crossley

2005-present. Professional grade, production/custom, solidbody and chambered electric guitars built in Melbourne, Victoria, Australia by luthier Peter Crossley.

Crown

1960s. Violin-shaped hollowbody electrics, solidbody electric guitars and basses, possibly others. Imported from Japan.

Acoustic Flat-Top

1960s. 6-string and 12-string.

MODEL YEAR	FEATURES	LOW	HIGH
1960s		$110	$150

Electric Archtop

1960s. Double pointed cutaways, 2 humbucking pickups, laminated top, full-depth body.

1960s		$350	$450

Electric Solidbody/Semi-Hollow

1960s. Student-level Japanese import.

1960s	Copy models	$250	$350
1960s	Standard models	$150	$200
1960s	Violin-shaped body	$250	$350

Crucianelli

Early 1960s. Italian guitars imported into the U.S. by Bennett Brothers of New York and Chicago around '63 to '64. Accordion builder Crucianelli also made Imperial, Elite, PANaramic, and Elli-Sound brand guitars.

Cruzer

Intermediate grade, production, solidbody electric guitars, basses, amps and effects made by Korea's Crafter Guitars.

CSR

1996-present. Father and daughter luthiers Roger and Courtney Kitchens build their premium grade, production/custom, archtop guitars and basses in Byron, Georgia.

MODEL YEAR	FEATURES	EXC. COND. LOW	HIGH

Cumpiano

1974-present. Professional and premium grade, custom steel-string and nylon-string guitars, and acoustic basses built by luthier William Cumpiano in Northampton, Massachusetts.

Curbow String Instruments

1994-2007. Premium grade, production/custom, solidbody guitars and basses built by luthier Doug Somervell in Morganton, Georgia. Founded by Greg Curbow who passed away in '05.

Custom

1980s. Line of solidbody guitars and basses introduced in the early '80s by Charles Lawing and Chris Lovell, owners of Strings & Things in Memphis, Tennessee.

Custom Kraft

Late-1950s-1968. A house brand of St. Louis Music Supply, instruments built by Valco and Kay. They also offered basses and amps.

Electric Solidbody

1950s-1960s. U.S.-made or import, entry-level, 1 or 2 pickups.

1950s-60s	Import	$150	$225
1950s-60s	USA, Kay, 2 pickups	$425	$550

Sound Saturator

1960s	12-string	$350	$450

Super Zapp

1960s		$400	$500

Thin Twin Jimmy Reed (style)

Late-1950s-early-1960s. Single cut, 2 pickups, 4 knobs and toggle, dot markers.

1959	US-made	$575	$700

D.J. Hodson

1994-2007. Luthier David J. Hodson built his professional and premium grade, production/custom, acoustic guitars in Loughborough, Leicestershire, U.K. He also built ukes. He passed away in '07.

Daddy Mojo String Instruments Inc.

2005-present. Luthiers Lenny Piroth-Robert and Luca Tripaldi build their intermediate and professional grade, production/custom, solidbody electric, resonator and cigar box guitars in Montreal, Quebec.

Dagmar Custom Guitars

Luthier Pete Swanson builds custom, premium and presentation grade, acoustic and electric archtop guitars in Niagara, Ontario, starting in 2008.

D'Agostino

1976-early 1990s. Acoustic and electric solidbody guitars and basses imported by PMS Music, founded in New York City by former Maestro executive Pat D'Agostino, his brother Steven D'Agostino, and

Mike Confortti. First dreadnought acoustic guitars imported from Japan in '76. First solidbodies manufactured by the EKO custom shop beginning in '77. In '82 solidbody production moved to Japan. Beginning in '84, D'Agostinos were made in Korea. Overall, about 60% of guitars were Japanese, 40% Korean. They also had basses.

Acoustic Flat-Top

1976-1990. Early production in Japan, by mid-'80s, most production in Korea.

1976-1990		$150	$500

Electric Semi-Hollowbody

1981-early 1990s. Early production in Japan, later versions from Korea.

1981-1990		$150	$700

Electric Solidbody

1977-early 1990s. Early models made in Italy, later versions from Japan and Korea.

1981-1990		$150	$700

Daily Guitars

1976-present. Luthier David Daily builds his premium grade, production/custom classical guitars in Sparks, Nevada.

Daion

1978-1984. Mid- to higher-quality copies imported from Japan. Original designs introduced in the '80s. Only acoustics offered at first; in '81 they added acoustic/electric and solid and semi-hollow electrics. They also had basses.

Acoustic

1978-1985. Various flat-top models.

1978-1985	Higher-end	$400	$1,050
1978-1985	Lower-end	$150	$400

Electric

1978-1985. Various solid and semi-hollow body guitars.

1978-1985	Higher-end	$400	$1,050
1978-1985	Lower-end	$150	$400

Daisy Rock

2001-present. Budget and intermediate grade, production, full-scale and 3/4 scale, solidbody, semi-hollow, acoustic, and acoustic/electric guitars and basses. Founded by Tish Ciravolo as a Division of Schecter Guitars, the Daisy line is focused on female customers.

D'Ambrosio

2001-present. Luthier Otto D'Ambrosio builds his premium grade, custom/production, acoustic and electric archtop guitars in Providence, Rhode Island.

Dan Armstrong

Dan Armstrong started playing jazz in Cleveland in the late-'50s. He moved to New York and also started doing repairs, eventually opening his own store on 48th Street in '65. By the late-'60s he was designing his Lucite guitars for Ampeg (see

Dagmar Custom

Daily Classical

1960s Danelectro Convertible
Tom Pfeifer

1964 Danelectro
3923 Doubleneck
Izzy Miller

MODEL YEAR	FEATURES	EXC. COND. LOW	HIGH

Ampeg for those listings). He moved to England in '71, where he developed his line of colored stomp boxes. He returned to the States in '75. Armstrong died in '04.

Wood Body Guitar
1973-1975. Sliding pickup, wood body, brown.

1973-1975		$1,600	$2,100

Dan Armstrong Guitars
Introduced 2015, professional grade, production/custom, acrylic solidbody electrics based on the original Dan Armstrong models, built in Everett, Washington.

Dan Kellaway
1976-present. Production/custom, premium grade, classical and steel string guitars built by luthier Dan Kellaway in Singleton NSW, Australia. He also builds mandolins and lutes.

Danelectro
1946-1969, 1996-present. Founded in Red Bank, New Jersey, by Nathan I. (Nate or Nat) Daniel, an electronics enthusiast with amplifier experience. In 1933, Daniel built amps for Thor's Bargain Basement in New York. In '34 he was recruited by Epiphone's Herb Sunshine to build earliest Electar amps and pickup-making equipment. From '35 to '42, he operated Daniel Electric Laboratories in Manhattan, supplying Epiphone. He started Danelectro in '46 and made his first amps for Montgomery Ward in '47. Over the years, Danelectro made amplifiers, solidbody, semi-hollow and hollowbody electric guitars and basses, electric sitar, and the Bellzouki under the Danelectro, Silvertone, and Coral brands. In '48, began supplying Silvertone amps for Sears (various coverings), with his own brand (brown leatherette) distributed by Targ and Dinner as Danelectro and S.S. Maxwell. He developed an electronic vibrato in '48 on his Vibravox series amps. In '50 he developed a microphone with volume and tone controls and outboard Echo Box reverb unit. In the fall of '54, Danelectro replaced Harmony as provider of Silvertone solidbody guitars for Sears. Also in '54, the first Danelectro brand guitars appeared with tweed covering, bell headstock, and pickups under the pickguard. The Coke bottle headstock debuts as Silvertone Lightning Bolt in '54, and was used on Danelectros for '56 to '66. The company moved to Red Bank, New Jersey in '57, and in '58 relocated to Neptune, New Jersey. In '59, Harmony and Kay guitars replace all but 3 Danelectros in Sears catalog. In '66, MCA buys the company (Daniel remains with company), but by mid-'69, MCA halts production and closes the doors. Some leftover stock is sold to Dan Armstrong, who had a shop in New York at the time. Armstrong assembled several hundred Danelectro guitars as Dan Armstrong Modified with his own pickup design.

Rights to name acquired by Anthony Marc in late-'80s, who assembled a number of thinline hol-lowbody guitars, many with Longhorn shape, using Japanese-made bodies and original Danelectro necks and hardware. In '96, the Evets Corporation, of San Clemente, California, introduced a line of effects bearing the Danelectro brand. Amps and guitars, many of which were reissues of the earlier instruments, soon followed. In early 2003, Evets discontinued offering guitar and amps, but revived the guitar and bass line in '05.

MCA-Danelectro made guitars were called the Dane Series. Dane A model numbers start with an A (e.g. A2V), Dane B models start with a B (e.g. B3V), Dane C (e.g. C2N), and Dane D (e.g. D2N). The least expensive series was the A, going up to the most expensive D. All Dane Series instruments came with 1, 2 or 3 pickups and with hand vibrato options. The Dane Series were made from '67 to '69. MCA did carry over the Convertible, Guitarlin 4123, Long Horn Bass-4 and Bass-6 and Doubleneck 3923. MCA also offered the Bellzouki Double Pickup 7021. Each Dane Series includes an electric 12-string. Danelectro also built the Coral brand instruments (see Coral).

Baritone 6-String Reissue
1999-2003, 2008-present. Danelectro has offered several models with 6-string baritone tuning, often with various reissue-year designations, single- or double-cut, 2 or 3 pickups.

1999-2019	Various models	$375	$475

Bellzouki
1963-1969. 12-string electric. Teardrop-shaped body, 1 pickup, sunburst (7010) for '63-'66. Vincent Bell model (7020) with modified teardrop shape with 2 body points on both treble and bass bouts and 2 pickups for '63-'66. Same body as Coral Electric Sitar for '67-'69.

1963-1969	1 pu, teardrop body	$750	$975
1963-1969	2 pu, pointy body	$1,025	$1,325
1967-1969	2 pu, sitar body	$1,600	$2,100

Companion
1959-1960. Hollowbody double-cut, 2 pickups, concentric TV knobs.

1959-1960	Pickup installed, rare color	$1,325	$1,725

Convertible
1959-1969. Acoustic/electric, double-cut, guitar was sold with or without the removable single pickup.

1959-1969	Acoustic, no pu, natural	$300	$400
1959-1969	Pickup installed, natural	$475	$625
1967-1969	Red, white, blue	$750	$975

Convertible Reissue
1999, 2000-2003. The Convertible Pro was offered '00-'03 with upgraded Gotoh tuners and metalflake and pearl finishes.

1999-2003	Blond or green	$240	$315

Dane A Series
1967-1969. 1or 2 pickups, with or without vibrato (V), solid wood slab body, hard lacquer finish with 4 color options, 12-string also offered.

1967-1969	1N12, Electric XII	$1,125	$1,475
1967-1969	2N12, Electric XII	$1,250	$1,625

MODEL YEAR	FEATURES	EXC. COND. LOW	HIGH
1967-1969	N, 6-string, 1 pu	$825	$1,075
1967-1969	N, 6-string, 2 pu	$975	$1,275
1967-1969	V, 6-string, 1 pu	$975	$1,275
1967-1969	V, 6-string, 2 pu	$1,050	$1,375

Dane B Series
1967-1969. 2 or 3 pickups, with or without vibrato (V), semi-solid Durabody, 6 or 12 strings.

1967-1969	12-string	$1,025	$1,350
1967-1969	6-string, 2 pu	$825	$1,075
1967-1969	6-string, 3 pu	$950	$1,250

Dane C Series
1967-1969. 2 or 3 pickups, with or without vibrato (V), semi-solid Durabody with 2-tone Gator finish, 6 or 12 strings.

1967-1969	12-string	$1,475	$1,925
1967-1969	6-string	$1,250	$1,650

Dane D Series
1967-1969. 2 or 3 pickups, with or without vibrato (V), solid wood sculptured thinline body, 'floating adjustable pickguard-fingerguide', master volume with 4 switches, 6 or 12 strings.

1967-1969	12-string	$1,200	$1,575
1967-1969	6-string, 2 pu	$950	$1,250
1967-1969	6-string, 3 pu	$1,075	$1,425

Danoblaster Series
2000-2003. Offset double-cuts, 3 pickups, built-in effects – distortion on the Hearsay, distortion, chorus, trem and echo on Innuendo. Also in 12-string and baritone.

2000-2003		$115	$145

DC-3/DDC-3
1999-2003. Shorthorn double-cut, 3 pickups, seal-shaped pickguard, Coke bottle headstock, solid and sparkle finishes.

1999-2003		$275	$350

DC-12/Electric XII
1999-2003. 12-string version of 59-DC.

1999-2003		$325	$425

59-DC/'59 Dano (Standard Double Pickup Reissue)
1998-1999, 2007. Shorthorn double-cut, 2 pickups, seal-shaped pickguard, Coke bottle headstock, '07 version called '59 Dano.

1998-1999		$240	$310

Deluxe Single Pickup
1959-1966. Double-cut, Coke bottle headstock, 1 pickup, 2 knobs.

1959-1960	Walnut or white	$1,025	$1,350
1961-1966	Walnut, white, honey	$925	$1,200

Deluxe Double Pickup
1959-1966. As Single above, but with 2 pickups, and added master volume on later models.

1959-1960	Walnut or white	$1,050	$1,400
1961-1966	Walnut, white, honey	$1,025	$1,325

Deluxe Triple Pickup
1959-1966. As Single above, but with 3 pickups, 3 knobs, and added master volume on later models.

1959-1960	Walnut or white	$1,150	$1,500
1961-1966	Walnut, white, honey	$1,075	$1,400

Doubleneck (3923)
1958-1966. A shorthorn double-cut, bass and 6-string necks, 1 pickup on each neck, Coke bottle headstocks, white sunburst.

1958-1966		$1,425	$1,850

Doubleneck Reissue
1999-2003. Baritone 6-string and standard 6-string double neck, shorthorn body style, or the 6-12 model with a 6-string and 12-string neck. Price includes $75 for a guitar case, but many sales do not seem to include a guitar case because of unusual body size.

1999-2003		$460	$600

Electric Sitar
1968-1969. Traditional looking, oval-bodied sitar, no drone strings as on the Coral Sitar of the same period.

1968-1969		$1,925	$2,500

Guitarlin (4123)
1958-1966. The Longhorn guitar, 2 huge cutaways, 31-fret neck, 2 pickups.

1958-1960		$1,875	$2,450
1961-1966		$1,750	$2,300

Hand Vibrato Single Pickup (4011)
1958-1966. Short horn double-cut, 1 pickup, batwing headstock, simple design vibrato, black w/ white guard.

1958-1966		$800	$1,025

Hand Vibrato Double Pickup (4021)
1958-1960. Same as Single Pickup, but with 2 pickups and larger pickguard.

1958-1960		$900	$1,175

Hawk
1967-1969. Offered with 1 or 2 pickups, vibrato (V models) or non-vibrato (N models), 12-string model also offered.

1967-1969	1N, 1 pu	$925	$1,200
1967-1969	1N12, Electric XII	$1,150	$1,500
1967-1969	1V, 1 pu	$1,025	$1,325
1967-1969	2N, 2 pu	$1,025	$1,325
1967-1969	2N12, Electric XII	$1,300	$1,700
1967-1969	2V, 2 pu	$1,125	$1,450

Hodad/Hodad 12-String
1999-2003. Unique double-cut with sharp horns, 6 or 12 strings, sparkle finish.

1999-2003		$300	$400

Model C
1955. Single-cut, 1or 2 pickups, ginger colored vinyl cover.

1955		$500	$650

Pro 1
1963-1964. Odd-shaped double-cut electric with squared off corners, 1 pickup.

1963-1964		$700	$900

Pro Reissue
2007. Based on '60s Pro 1, but with 2 pickups.

2007		$230	$300

Slimline (SL) Series
1967-1969. Offset waist double-cut, 2 or 3 pickups, with or without vibrato, 6 or 12 string.

1967-1969	12-string	$1,100	$1,425
1967-1969	6-string, 2 pu	$850	$1,100
1967-1969	6-string, 3 pu	$1,025	$1,325

1965 Danelectro Guitaralin
Binky Philips

1964 Danelectro 4021
Craig Brody

GUITARS

1957 Danelectro U2

Imaged by Heritage Auctions, HA.com

1937 D'Angelico Excel

MODEL YEAR	FEATURES	EXC. COND. LOW	HIGH

Standard Single Pickup
1958-1966. Nicknamed the Shorthorn, double-cut, 1 pickup, 2 regular control knobs, kidney-shaped pickguard originally, seal-shaped 'guard by ca. 1960, Coke bottle headstock, in black or bronze.

1958-1959	Kidney guard	$750	$975
1960-1966	Seal guard	$750	$975

Standard Double Pickup
1958-1966. As Single Pickup above but with 2 pickups and 2 stacked, concentric volume/tone controls, in black, bronze and later blond. The black, seal-shaped pickguard version of this guitar is often referred to as the Jimmy Page model because he used one. Reissued in 1998 as 59-DC.

1958-1959	Kidney guard, black	$800	$1,050
1960-1966	Bronze	$775	$1,025
1960-1966	Jimmy Page, black	$1,150	$1,500
1961-1966	Blond	$925	$1,200

Standard Triple Pickup
1958. As Single Pickup above but with 3 pickups and 3 stacked, concentric pointer volume/tone controls, in white to bronze sunburst, very rare.

1958		$1,025	$1,325

Tweed Models
1954-1955. First production models, single-cut, bell-shape headstock, 1 or 2 pickups, tweed vinyl cover.

1954-1955	1 pu	$2,225	$2,925
1954-1955	2 pu	$2,425	$3,175

U-1
1955-1958. Single-cut, 1 pickup, 2 regular knobs, bell-shape headstock originally, switching to Coke bottle in late '55. The U Series featured Dano's new 'solid center' block construction.

1955	Enamel, bell hdsk	$1,750	$2,300
1956-1957	Enamel, Coke hdsk	$1,600	$2,075
1956-1957	Ivory, Coke hdsk	$1,650	$2,150
1958	Enamel, Coke hdsk	$1,375	$1,800
1958	Ivory, Coke hdsk	$1,600	$2,100

U-1 '56 Reissue
1998-1999. Reissue of '56 U-1, various colors.

1998-1999		$195	$250

U-2
1955-1958. As U-1, but with 2 pickups and 2 stacked concentric volume/tone controls.

1955	Enamel, bell hdsk	$1,900	$2,475
1956-1957	Enamel, Coke hdsk	$1,725	$2,250
1956-1957	Ivory, Coke hdsk	$1,875	$2,450
1958	Enamel, Coke hdsk	$1,600	$2,100
1958	Ivory, Coke hdsk	$1,725	$2,250

U-2 '56 Reissue
1998-2003. Reissue of '56 U-2, various colors.

1998-2003		$200	$260

U-3
1955-1958. As U-2, but with 3 pickups and 3 stacked concentric volume/tone controls.

1958	Enamel, Coke hdsk	$1,750	$2,300

U-3 '56 Reissue
1999-2003. Reissue of '56 U-3, various colors.

1999-2003		$250	$350

MODEL YEAR	FEATURES	EXC. COND. LOW	HIGH

D'Angelico
John D'Angelico built his own line of archtop guitars, mandolins and violins from 1932 until his death in 1964. His instruments are some of the most sought-after by collectors. The binding on some D'Angelico guitars can become deteriorated and requires replacing. Replaced binding, even if excellent work, reduces the values shown by 20% or more.

D'Angelico (L-5 Snakehead)
1932-1935. D'Angelico's L-5-style with snakehead headstock, his first model, sunburst.

1932-1935		$9,400	$12,200

Excel/Exel (Cutaway)
1947-1964. Cutaway, 17" width, 1- and 3-ply bound f-hole.

1947-1949	Natural, original binding	$30,000	$38,000
1947-1949	Sunburst, original binding	$26,000	$34,000
1950-1959	Natural, original binding	$29,000	$38,000
1950-1959	Sunburst, original binding	$26,000	$34,000
1960-1964	Natural	$30,000	$40,000
1960-1964	Sunburst	$27,000	$35,000

Excel/Exel (Non-Cutaway)
1936-1949. Non-cut, 17" width, 1- and 3-ply bound f-hole, natural finishes were typically not offered in the '30s, non-cut Excels were generally not offered after '49 in deference to the Excel cutaway.

1936-1939	Sunburst, straight f-hole	$15,000	$20,000
1938-1939	Sunburst, standard f-hole	$15,000	$20,000
1940-1949	Natural	$16,000	$21,000
1940-1949	Sunburst	$13,500	$17,500

New Yorker (Non-Cutaway)
1936-1949. Non-cut, 18" width, 5-ply-bound f-hole, New Yorker non-cut orders were overshadowed by the cut model orders starting in '47.

1936-1939	Sunburst	$21,000	$27,000
1940-1949	Natural	$22,000	$29,000
1940-1949	Sunburst	$20,000	$26,000

New Yorker Deluxe (Cutaway)
1947-1964. Cutaway, 18" width, 5-ply-bound f-hole, New Yorker non-cut orders were overshadowed by the cut model orders starting in '47.

1947-1949	Natural	$42,000	$54,000
1947-1949	Sunburst	$36,700	$47,000
1950-1959	Natural	$42,000	$54,000
1950-1959	Sunburst	$36,000	$46,000
1960-1964	Natural	$36,000	$46,000
1960-1964	Sunburst	$32,000	$42,000

New Yorker Special
1947-1964. Also called Excel New Yorker or Excel Cutaway New Yorker Cutaway, 17" width, New Yorker styling, not to be confused with D'Angelico Special (A and B style).

1947-1959	Natural	$28,000	$36,000
1947-1959	Sunburst	$25,000	$33,000
1960-1964	Natural	$25,000	$33,000
1960-1964	Sunburst	$22,000	$29,000

MODEL YEAR	FEATURES	EXC. COND. LOW	HIGH

Special (Cutaway)
1947-1964. Generally Style A and B-type instruments made for musicians on a budget, plain specs with little ornamentation, not to be confused with New Yorker Special.

| 1947-1959 | Sunburst | $9,500 | $12,300 |
| 1960-1964 | Sunburst | $8,500 | $11,000 |

Special (Non-Cutaway)
1947-1964. Non-cut Special, not to be confused with New Yorker Special.

| 1947-1959 | Sunburst | $5,800 | $7,500 |
| 1960-1964 | Sunburst | $5,000 | $6,500 |

Style A
1936-1945. Archtop, 17" width, unbound f-holes, block 'board inlays, multi-pointed headstock, nickel-plated metal parts.

| 1936-1939 | Sunburst | $10,000 | $13,000 |
| 1940-1945 | Sunburst | $9,000 | $11,700 |

Style A-1
1936-1945. Unbound f-holes, 17" width, arched headstock, nickel-plated metal parts.

| 1936-1939 | Sunburst | $10,000 | $13,000 |
| 1940-1945 | Sunburst | $9,000 | $11,700 |

Style B
1933-1948. Archtop 17" wide, unbound F-holes, block 'board inlays, gold-plated parts.

| 1936-1939 | Sunburst | $11,000 | $14,500 |
| 1940-1948 | Sunburst | $10,400 | $13,500 |

Style B Special
1933-1948. D'Angelico described variations from standard features with a 'Special' designation, Vintage dealers may also describe these instruments as 'Special'.

| 1936-1939 | Sunburst | $11,500 | $15,000 |
| 1940-1948 | Sunburst | $10,900 | $14,100 |

D'Angelico (D'Angelico Guitars of America)
1988-present. Intermediate and professional grade, production/custom, archtop, flat-top, and solidbody guitars made in South Korea and imported by D'Angelico Guitars of America, of Colts Neck, New Jersey. From 1988 to '04, they were premium and presentation grade instruments built in Japan by luthier Hidesato Shino and Vestax. In '12, GTR announced they bought the brand name and are offering premium grade D'Angelicos built in the U.S.

D'Angelico (Lewis)
1994-2011. Luthier Michael Lewis built presentation grade, custom/production, D'Angelico replica guitars in Grass Valley, California, under an agreement with the GHS String Company, which owned the name in the U.S. He also builds guitars and mandolins under the Lewis name.

D'Angelico II
Mid-1990s. Archtops built in the U.S. and distributed by Archtop Enterprises of Merrick, New York. Mainly presentation grade copies of Excel and New Yorker models, but also made lower cost similar models.

MODEL YEAR	FEATURES	EXC. COND. LOW	HIGH

Jazz Classic
1990s. Electric archtop, cutaway, carved spruce top, figured maple back and sides, single neck pickup, transparent cherry.

| 1990s | | $2,300 | $3,000 |

Daniel Friederich
1955-2015. Luthier Daniel Friederich built his custom/production, classical guitars in Paris, France.

D'Aquisto
1965-1995. James D'Aquisto apprenticed under D'Angelico until the latter's death, at age 59, in '64. He started making his own brand instruments in '65 and built archtop and flat-top acoustic guitars, solidbody and hollowbody electric guitars. He also designed guitars for Hagstrom and Fender. He died in '95, at age 59.

Avant Garde
1987-1994. 18" wide, non-traditional futuristic model, approximately 5 or 6 instruments were reportedly made, because of low production this pricing is for guidance only.

| 1990 | Blond | $70,000 | $90,000 |

Centura/Centura Deluxe
1993-1994. 17" wide, non-traditional art deco futuristic archtop, approximately 10 made, the last guitars made by this luthier, due to the low production this pricing is for guidance only.

| 1993-1994 | Centura, sunburst | $85,000 | $110,000 |
| 1993-1994 | Deluxe, sunburst | $90,000 | $120,000 |

Excel (Cutaway)
1965-1992. Archtop, 17" width, with modern thin-logo started in '81.

1965-1967	Blond or sunburst	$29,000	$38,000
1968-1980	Blond or sunburst	$29,000	$38,000
1981-1992	Blond or sunburst	$29,000	$38,000

Excel (Flat-Top)
1970s-1980s. Flat-top, 16", flamed maple back and sides, Sitka spruce top, about 15 made, narrow Excel-style headstock, oval soundhole, D'Aquisto script logo on headstock.

| 1970s-80s | | $16,000 | $21,000 |

Hollow Electric
Early model with bar pickup, D'Aquisto headstock, '70s model with humbuckers.

| 1960s-80s | Sunburst | $14,000 | $18,000 |

New Yorker Classic (Archtop)
1986. Single-cut acoustic archtop with new modern design features such as large S-shaped soundholes.

| 1986 | | $51,000 | $66,000 |

New Yorker Classic (Solidbody)
1980s. Only 2 were reported to be made, therefore this pricing is for guidance only.

| 1980s | | $16,000 | $21,000 |

New Yorker Deluxe (Cutaway)
1965-1992. Most are 18" wide.

| 1965-1979 | Blond or sunburst | $36,000 | $47,000 |
| 1980-1992 | Blond or sunburst | $35,000 | $45,000 |

New Yorker Special (7-String)
1980s. Limited production 7-string, single-cut.

| 1980s | | $29,000 | $38,000 |

1961 D'Angelico New Yorker
Cartwright Thompson

1967 D'Aquisto New Yorker
Imaged by Heritage Auctions, HA.com

GUITARS

Davis, J. Thomas

1980 Dean Golden E'Lite
Olivia's Vintage

MODEL YEAR	FEATURES	EXC. COND. LOW	HIGH

New Yorker Special (Cutaway)
1966-1992. Most are 17" wide.

| 1966-1992 | Blond or sunburst | $24,000 | $31,000 |

Solo/Solo Deluxe
1992-1993. 18" wide, non-traditional non-cut art deco model, only 2 reported made, because of low production this pricing is for guidance only.

| 1992-1993 | Blond | $90,000 | $115,000 |

D'Aquisto (Aria)
May 2002-2013. Premium grade, production, D'Aquisto designs licensed to Aria of Japan by D'Aquisto Strings, Inc., Deer Park, New York.
Various Models

| 2002-2013 | | $1,400 | $1,800 |

Dauphin
1970s-late 1990s. Classical and flamenco guitars imported from Spain and Japan by distributor George Dauphinais, located in Springfield, Illinois.

Dave King Acoustics
1980-present. Premium grade, custom/production, acoustic and resonator guitars built by luthier Dave King in Berkshire, U.K.

Dave Maize Acoustic Guitars
1991-present. Luthier Dave Maize builds his professional and premium grade, production/custom, flat-tops and basses in Cave Junction, Oregon.

David Rubio
1960s-2000. Luthier David Spink built his guitars, lutes, violins, violas, cellos and harpsichords first in New York, and after '67, in the U.K. While playing in Spain, he acquired the nickname Rubio, after his red beard. He died in '00.

David Thomas McNaught
1989-present. Professional, premium, and presentation grade, custom, solidbody guitars built by luthier David Thomas McNaught and finished by Dave Mansel in Locust, North Carolina. In '97, they added the production/custom DTM line of guitars.

Davis, J. Thomas
1975-present. Premium and presentation grade, custom, steel-string flat-tops, 12-strings, classicals, archtops, Irish citterns and flat-top Irish bouzoukis made by luthier J. Thomas Davis in Columbus, Ohio.

Davoli
See Wandre listing.

DBZ
2008-2012. Solidbody electric guitars from Dean B. Zelinsky, founder of Dean Guitars, and partners Jeff Diamant and Terry Martin. Dean left the partnership February, '12 and established Dean Zelinsky Private Label guitars.

MODEL YEAR	FEATURES	EXC. COND. LOW	HIGH

de Jonge, Sergei
1972-present. Premium grade, production/custom classical and steel-string guitars built by luthier Sergei de Jonge originally in Oshawa, Ontario, and since '04 in Chelsea, Quebec.

De Paule Stringed Instruments
1969-1980, 1993-present. Custom steel-string, nylon-string, archtop, resonator, and Hawaiian guitars built by luthier C. Andrew De Paule in Eugene, Oregon.

Dean
1976-present. Intermediate, professional and premium grade, production/custom, solidbody, hollowbody, acoustic, acoustic/electric, and resonator guitars made in the U.S., Korea, the Czech Republic and China. They also offer basses, banjos, mandolins, and amps. Founded in Evanston, Illinois, by Dean Zelinsky. Original models were upscale versions of Gibson designs with glued necks, fancy tops, DiMarzio pickups and distinctive winged headstocks (V, Z and ML), with production beginning in '77. In '80 the factory was relocated to Chicago. Dean's American manufacturing ends in '86 when all production shifts to Korea. In '91 Zelinsky sold the company to Tropical Music in Miami, Florida. For '93-'94 there was again limited U.S. (California) production of the E'Lite, Cadillac and ML models under the supervision of Zelinsky and Cory Wadley. Korean versions were also produced. In '95, Elliott Rubinson's Armadillo Enterprises, of Clearwater, Florida, bought the Dean brand. In '97 and '98, Dean offered higher-end USA Custom Shop models. In '98, they reintroduced acoustics. From 2000 to '08, Zelinsky was once again involved in the company.

Dating American models: First 2 digits are year of manufacture. Imports have no date codes.
Baby ML
1982-1986, 2000-2014. Downsized version of ML model.

| 1982-1986 | Import | $325 | $425 |
| 1982-1986 | US-made | $475 | $625 |

Baby V
1982-1986, 2000-2014. Downsized version of the V model.

| 1982-1986 | Import | $325 | $425 |
| 1982-1986 | US-made | $475 | $625 |

Baby Z
1982-1986, 2000-2014. Downsized version of the Z model.

| 1982-1986 | Import | $325 | $425 |
| 1982-1986 | US-made | $475 | $625 |

Bel Aire
1983-1984. Solidbody, possibly the first production guitar with humbucker/single/single pickup layout, U.S.-made, an import model was introduced in '87.

| 1980s | Import | $325 | $425 |
| 1983-1984 | US-made | $475 | $625 |

MODEL YEAR	FEATURES	EXC. COND. LOW	HIGH

Budweiser Guitar
Ca.1987. Shaped like Bud logo.

1987		$175	$250

Cadillac (U.S.A.)
1979-1985. Single long treble horn on slab body.

1979-1985		$1,425	$1,850

Cadillac 1980
2006-2018. Block inlays, 2 humbuckers, gold hardware.

2006-2018		$350	$450

Cadillac Deluxe (U.S.A.)
1993-1994, 1996-1997. Made in U.S., single longhorn shape, various colors.

1993-1997		$1,000	$1,300

Cadillac Reissue (Import)
1992-1994. Single longhorn shape, 2 humbuckers, various colors.

1992-1994		$275	$350

Cadillac Select
2009-2017. Made in Korea, figured maple top, mahogany, pearl block inlays.

2009-2017		$325	$425

Cadillac Standard
1996-1997. Slab body version.

1996-1997		$1,250	$1,600

Del Sol
2008. Import, small double-cut thinline semi-hollow, ES-335 style body, rising sun fretboard markers.

2008		$290	$375

Dime O Flame (ML)
2005-2018. ML-body, Dimebuckers, burning flames finish, Dime logo on headstock.

2005-2018		$325	$425

Eighty-Eight (Import)
1987-1990. Offset double-cut solidbody, import.

1987-1990		$175	$225

E'Lite
1978-1985, 1994-1996. Single-horn shape.

1978-1985		$950	$1,250
1994-1996		$875	$1,125

E'Lite Deluxe
1980s. Single-horn shape.

1980s		$1,150	$1,500

EVO XM
2004-present. Single-cut slab body, 2 humbuckers.

2004-2019		$100	$135

Golden E'Lite
1980. Single pointy treble cutaway, fork headstock, gold hardware, ebony 'board, sunburst.

1980		$1,150	$1,500

Hollywood Z (Import)
1985-1986. Bolt-neck Japanese copy of Baby Z, Explorer shape.

1985-1986		$125	$165

Jammer (Import)
1987-1989. Offset double-cut body, bolt-on neck, dot markers, six-on-a-side tuners, various colors offered.

1987-1989		$125	$165

Leslie West Standard
2008-2017. Flame maple top, mahogany body, rosewood 'board.

2008-2017		$350	$450

Mach I (Import)
1985-1986. Limited run from Korea, Mach V with six-on-a-side tunes, various colors.

1985-1986		$125	$165

Mach V (Import)
1985-1986. Pointed solidbody, 2 humbucking pickups, maple neck, ebony 'board, locking trem, various colors, limited run from Korea.

1985-1986		$125	$165

Mach VII (U.S.A.)
1985-1986. Mach I styling, made in America, offered in unusual finishes.

1985-1986		$1,000	$1,300

ML (ML Standard/U.S.A.)
1977-1986. There is a flame model and a standard model.

1977-1986	Burst flamed top	$1,950	$2,525
1977-1986	Burst plain top	$1,850	$2,425
1977-1986	Common opaque finish	$1,550	$2,000

ML (Import)
1983-1990. Korean-made.

1983-1990		$425	$550

Soltero SL
2007-2010. Made in Japan, single-cut solidbody, 2 pickups, flame maple top.

2007-2010		$1,250	$1,600

USA Time Capsule Exotic V
2005-2014. Flying V style, solid mahogany body with exotic spalted and flamed maple top, Dean V neck profile (split V headstock).

2005-2014		$1,900	$2,500

USA Time Capsule Z
2000-2014. Explorer style body, figured maple top.

2000-2014		$1,900	$2,500

V Standard (U.S.A.)
1977-1986. V body, there is a standard and a flame model offered.

1977-1981	Burst flamed top	$2,200	$2,900
1977-1981	Burst plain top	$1,900	$2,500
1977-1981	Common opaque finish	$1,600	$2,100
1982-1986	Burst flamed top	$1,850	$2,400
1982-1986	Burst plain top	$1,700	$2,200
1982-1986	Common opaque finish	$1,400	$1,800

Z Standard (U.S.A.)
1977-1986. Long treble cutaway solidbody, 2 humbuckers.

1977-1983	Common finish	$1,300	$1,700
1977-1983	Rare finish	$1,700	$2,200

Z Autograph (Import)
1985-1987. The first Dean import from Korea, offset double-cut, bolt neck, dot markers, offered in several standard colors.

1985-1987		$200	$260

Z Coupe/Z Deluxe (U.S.A. Custom Shop)
1997-1998. Mahogany body offered in several standard colors, Z Deluxe with Floyd Rose tremolo.

1997-1998		$825	$1,025

1981 Dean V Standard

1979 Dean Z Standard

Imaged by Heritage Auctions, HA.com

72

Dean Z Korina — **Delgado**

2000 DeArmond Starfire Special

2000 DeArmond X-155

MODEL YEAR	FEATURES	EXC. COND. LOW	HIGH

Z Korina (U.S.A. Custom Shop)
1997-1998. Z Coupe with korina body, various standard colors.
1997-1998 — $950 — $1,225

Z LTD (U.S.A. Custom Shop)
1997-1998. Z Coupe with bound neck and headstock, offered in several standard colors.
1997-1998 — $950 — $1,225

Dean Markley
The string and pickup manufacturer offered a limited line of guitars and basses for a time in the '80s. They were introduced in '84.

Dean Zelinsky Private Label
2012-present. Premium grade, production/custom, hollow, semi-hollow and solidbody electric guitars built in Chicago, Illinois by luthier Dean Zelinsky, founder of Dean Guitars. He also imports a line of intermediate grade guitars from South Korea and Indonesia.

DeArmond Guitars
1999-2004. Solid, semi-hollow and hollow body guitars based on Guild models and imported from Korea by Fender. They also offered basses. The DeArmond brand was originally used on pickups, effects and amps built by Rowe Industries.
Electric
1999-2004. Various import models, some with USA electronic components.
1999-2004 Jet Star (Polara style) — $350 — $450
1999-2004 Various models — $200 — $600

Dearstone
1993-2017. Luthier Ray Dearstone built his professional and premium grade, custom, archtop and acoustic/electric guitars in Blountville, Tennessee. He also built mandolin family instruments and violins.

Decar
1950s. A private brand sold by Decautur, Illinois music store, Decar headstock logo.
Stratotone H44 Model
1956. Private branded Stratotone with maple neck and fretboard instead of the standard neck/fretboard, 1 pickup and other Harmony H44 Stratotone attributes, bolt-on neck.
1956 — $600 — $750

DeCava Guitars
1983-present. Professional and premium grade, production/custom, archtop and classical guitars built by luthier Jim DeCava first in Stratford, then Ansonia, Connecticut. He also builds ukes, banjos, and mandolins.

Decca
Mid-1960s. Acoustic, solid and hollow body guitars, basses and amps made in Japan by Teisco and imported by Decca Records, Decca headstock logo, student-level instruments.
Acoustic Flat-Top
1960s. Decca label on the inside back.
1960s — $75 — $175
Electric Solidbody
1960s. Teisco-made in Japan, 3 pickups, sunburst.
1960s — $275 — $350

Defil
Based out of Lubin, Poland, Defil made solid and semi-hollowbdy electric guitars at least from the 1970s to the '90s.

DeGennaro
2003-present. Premium grade, custom/production, acoustic, archtop, semi-hollow and solidbody guitars, basses and mandolins built by luthier William DeGennaro in Grand Rapids, Michigan.

Del Oro
1930s-1940s. Flat-top (including cowboy stencil models) and resonator guitars, built by Kay. At least the cowboy stencils were sold by Spiegel.
Small Acoustic
1930s — 13" to 14" body — $150 — $225

Del Pilar Guitars
1956-1986. Luthier William Del Pilar made his classical guitars in Brooklyn, New York.
Classical (Rosewood)
1950s-1980s. Brazilian rosewood back and sides, cedar top, quilt rosette, 9-ply top binding.
1950s-80s — $3,000 — $4,000

Del Vecchio
1902-present. Casa Del Vecchio builds a variety of Spanish instruments including acoustic and resonator guitars in São Paulo, Brazil.

Delaney Guitars
2004-present. Luthier Mike Delaney builds his professional grade, production/custom, chambered, solidbody, and semi-hollowbody electric guitars and basses in Atlanta, Georgia. Prior to 2008 he built in Florence, Montana.

Delgado
1928-present. Delgado began in Torreon, Coahuila, Mexico, then moved to Juarez in the '30s with a second location in Tijuana. In '48 they moved to California and opened a shop in Los Angeles. Since 2005, Manuel A. Delgado, a third generation luthier, builds his premium and presentation grade, production/custom, classical, flamenco and steel string acoustic guitars in Nashville, Tennessee. He also builds basses, mandolins, ukuleles and banjos.

MODEL YEAR	FEATURES	EXC. COND. LOW	HIGH

Delirium Custom Guitars

Luthiers Patrick and Vincent Paul-Victor along with Gael Canonne build their professional and premium grade, production/custom, solidbody electric guitars in Paris and Toulouse, France.

Dell'Arte

1997-present. Production/custom Maccaferri-style guitars from John Kinnard and Alain Cola. In '96, luthier John Kinnard opened a small shop called Finegold Guitars and Mandolins. In '98 he met Alain Cola, a long time jazz guitarist who was selling Mexican-made copies of Selmer/Maccaferri guitars under the Dell'Arte brand. Cola wanted better workmanship for his guitars, and in October '98, Finegold and Dell'Arte merged. As of May '99 all production is in California.

Delta Guitars

2005-2010. Acoustic, acoustic/electric, and solidbody electric guitars from Musician's Wholesale America, Nashville, Tennessee.

Dennis Hill Guitars

Premium and presentation grade, production/custom, classical and flamenco guitars built by luthier Dennis Hill in Panama City, Florida. He has also built dulcimers, mandolins, and violins.

Desmond Guitars

1991-present. Luthier Robert B. Desmond builds his premium grade, production/custom classical guitars in Orlando, Florida.

DeTemple

1995-present. Premium grade, production/custom, solidbody electric guitars and basses built by luthier Michael DeTemple in Sherman Oaks, California.

DeVoe Guitars

1975-present. Luthier Lester DeVoe builds his premium grade, production/custom flamenco and classical guitars in Nipomo, California.

Diamond

Ca. 1963-1964. Line of sparkle finish solidbody guitars made in Italy for the Diamond Accordion company.

Ranger

Ca. 1963-1964. Rangers came with 1, 2, 3, or 4 pickups, sparkle finish.

1960s		$500	$675

Dick, Edward Victor

1975-present. Luthier Edward Dick currently builds his premium grade, custom, classical guitars in Denver, Colorado (he lived in Peterborough and Ottawa, Ontario until '95). He also operates the Colorado School of Lutherie.

Dickerson

1937-1947. Founded by the Dickerson brothers in '37, primarily for electric lap steels and small amps. Instruments were also private branded for Cleveland's Oahu company, and for the Gourley brand. By '47, the company changed ownership and was renamed Magna Electronics (Magnatone).

Dillion

1996-present. Dillion, of Cary, North Carolina, offers intermediate grade, production, acoustic, acoustic/electric, hollow-body and solidbody guitars, basses and mandolins made in Korea and Vietnam.

Dillon

1975-2006. Professional and premium grade, custom, flat-tops and basses built by luthier John Dillon in Taos, New Mexico, and in Bloomsburg, Pennsylvania ('81-'01).

Dino's Guitars

Custom, professional grade, electric solidbody guitars built by a social co-op company founded by Alessio Casati and Andy Bagnasco, in Albisola, Italy. They also build effects.

DiPinto

1995-present. Intermediate and professional grade, production retro-vibe guitars and basses from luthier Chris DiPinto of Philadelphia, Pennsylvania. Until late '99, all instruments built in the U.S., since then all built in Korea.

Ditson

1835-1937. Started in Boston by music publisher Oliver Ditson, by the end of the 1800s the company was one of the East Coast's largest music businesses, operating in several cities and was also involved in distribution and manufacturing of a variety of instruments, including guitars and ukes. From 1916-1930 Ditson guitars were made by Martin. The majority of Martin production was from '16 to '22 with over 500 units sold in '21. Ditson also established Lyon and Healy in Chicago and the John Church Company in Cincinnati.

Values for Ditson Models 111 and 1-45 would be equivalent to those for Martin models from that era with similar specs.

Concert Models

1916-1922. Similar in size to Martin size 0. Models include Style 1, Style 2 and Style 3.

1916-1922	Style 1	$4,200	$5,500
1916-1922	Style 2	$4,900	$6,500
1916-1922	Style 3	$5,400	$7,100

Standard Models

1916-1922. Small body similar to Martin size 3, plain styling. Models include Style 1, Style 2 and Style 3.

1916-1922	Style 1	$2,700	$3,600
1916-1922	Style 2	$3,200	$4,300
1916-1922	Style 3	$4,200	$5,600

Del Vecchio V01P01

DeTemple Spirit Series Stellacasta

MODEL YEAR	FEATURES	EXC. COND. LOW	HIGH

Dobro D-10
Bernunzio Uptown Music

1937 Dobro Model 62
Bernunzio Uptown Music

D'Leco Guitars

1991-2003. Guitarist Maurice Johnson and luthier James W. Dale built premium grade, production/custom archtops in Oklahoma City, Oklahoma.

DM Darling Guitars

Beginning 2006 luthier Denis Merrill builds professional and premium grade, custom, acoustic, classical, resonator and solidbody guitars in Tacoma, Washington. From 1978 to '06 he built under his own name and Merrill Custom Shop. He also builds mandolin family instruments.

Dobro

1929-1942, ca. 1954-2019. Currently, professional and premium grade, production, wood and metal body resophonic guitars offered by Gibson.

Founded 1929 in Los Angeles by John Dopyera, Rudy Dopyera, Ed Dopyera and Vic Smith (Dobro stands for Dopyera Brothers). Made instruments sold under the Dobro, Regal, Norwood Chimes, Angelus, Rex, Broman, Montgomery Ward, Penetro, Bruno, Alhambra, More Harmony, Orpheum, and Magn-o-tone brands.

Dobro instruments have a single cone facing outward with a spider bridge structure and competed with National products. Generally, model names are numbers referring to list price and therefore materials and workmanship (e.g., a No. 65 cost $65). Because of this, the same model number may apply to various different instruments. However, model numbers are never identified on instruments!

In '30, the company name was changed to Dobro Corporation, Ltd. In '32, Louis Dopyera buys Ted Kleinmeyer's share of National. Louis, Rudy and Ed now hold controlling interest in National, but in '32 John Dopyera left Dobro to pursue idea of metal resophonic violin. In December of '34 Ed Dopyera joins National's board of directors (he's also still on Dobro board), and by March of '35 Dobro and National have merged to become the National Dobro Corporation. Dobro moves into National's larger factory but continues to maintain separate production, sales and distribution until relocation to Chicago is complete. Beginning in early-'36 National Dobro starts relocating its offices to Chicago. L.A. production of Dobros continues until '37, after which some guitars continue to be assembled from parts until '39, when the L.A. operations were closed down.

All resonator production ended in '42. Victor Smith, Al Frost and Louis Dopyera buy the company and change the name to the Valco Manufacturing Company. The Dobro name does not appear when production resumes after World War II.

In mid-'50s - some sources say as early as '54 - Rudy and Ed Dopyera began assembling wood-bodied Dobros from old parts using the name DB Original. In about '59, some 12-fret DB Originals were made for Standel, carrying both DB Original and Standel logos. In around '61, production was

moved to Gardena, California, and Louis Dopyera and Valco transferred the Dobro name to Rudy and Ed, who produce the so-called Gardena Dobros. At this time, the modern Dobro logo appeared with a lyre that looks like 2 back-to-back '6s'. Dobro Original debuts ca. '62. In late-'64 the Dobro name was licensed to Ed's son Emil (Ed, Jr.) Dopyera. Ed, Jr. designs a more rounded Dobro (very similar to later Mosrites) and has falling out with Rudy over it.

In '66 Semi Moseley acquires the rights to the Dobro brand, building some in Gardena, and later moving to Bakersfield, California. Moseley introduced Ed, Jr's design plus a thinline double-cutaway Dobro. He also made MoBros during this time period. Moseley Dobros use either Dobro or National cones. In '67 Ed, Sr., Rudy and Gabriella Lazar start the Original Music Instrument Company (OMI) and produce Hound Dog brand Dobros. In '68 Moseley goes bankrupt and in '70 OMI obtains the rights to the Dobro brand and begins production of OMI Dobros. In '75 Gabriella's son and daughter, Ron Lazar and Dee Garland, take over OMI. Rudy Dupyera makes and sells Safari brand resonator mandolins. Ed, Sr. dies in '77 and Rudy in '78. In '84 OMI was sold to Chester and Betty Lizak. Both wood and metal-bodied Dobros produced in Huntington Beach, California. Chester Lizak died in '92. Gibson purchased Dobro in '93 and now makes Dobros in Nashville, Tennessee.

Dobros generally feature a serial number which, combined with historical information, provides a clue to dating. For prewar L.A. guitars, see approximation chart below adapted from "Gruhn's Guide to Vintage Guitars." No information exists on DB Originals.

Gardena Dobros had D prefix plus 3 digits beginning with 100 and going into the 500s (reportedly under 500 made). No information is available on Moseley Dobros.

OMI Dobros from '70-'79 have either D prefix for wood bodies or B prefix for metal bodies, plus 3 or 4 numbers for ranking, space, then a single digit for year (D XXXX Y or B XXX Y; e.g., D 172 8 would be wood body #172 from '78). For '80-'87 OMI Dobros, start with first number of year (decade) plus 3 or 4 ranking numbers, space, then year and either D for wood or B for metal bodies (8 XXXX YD or 8 XXX YB; e.g., 8 2006 5B would be metal body #2008 from '85). From '88-'92, at least, a letter and number indicate guitar style, plus 3 or 4 digits for ranking, letter for neck style, 2 digits for year, and letter for body style (AX XXXX NYYD or AX XXX NYYB).

L.A. Guitars (approx. number ranges, not actual production totals):
1929-30   900-2999
1930-31   3000-3999
1931-32   BXXX (Cyclops models only)
1932-33   5000-5599
1934-36   5700-7699
1937-42   8000-9999

MODEL YEAR	FEATURES	EXC. COND. LOW	HIGH

Angelus
1933-1937. Wood body, round or square neck, 2-tone walnut finish, continues as Model 19 in Regal-made guitars.

1933-1937	Round neck	$1,125	$1,450
1933-1937	Square neck	$1,200	$1,550

Artist M-16
1934-1935. German silver alloy body, engraved.

1934-1935	H square neck	$3,300	$4,300
1934-1935	M round neck	$5,300	$6,900

Columbia D-12
1967-1968. Acoustic 12-string, typical Dobro resonator with spider style bridge, made during Dobro-Moseley era.

1967-1968		$725	$950

Cyclops 45
1932-1933. Bound walnut body, 1 screen hole.

1932-1933	Round neck	$2,400	$3,200
1932-1933	Square neck	$2,900	$3,800

D-40 Texarkana
1965-1967. Mosrite-era (identified by C or D prefix), traditional Dobro style cone and coverplate, dot inlays, Dobro logo on headstock, sunburst wood body. Red and blue finishes available.

1965-1967	Sunburst, square neck	$925	$1,200

D-40E Texarkana
1965-1967. D-40 electric with single pickup and 2 knobs.

1965-1967		$1,000	$1,300

D-100 The Californian
1965-1969. Dobro's version of Mosrite (thus nicknamed the "Mobro") thinline double-cut, resonator, 2 small metal ports, 2 pickups, 2 knobs, sunburst.

1965-1969		$1,400	$1,800

DM-33 California Girl/DM-33H
1996-2006. Chrome-plated bell brass body, biscuit bridge, spider resonator, rosewood 'board. Girl or Hawaiian-scene (H) engraving.

1996-2006		$1,275	$1,650

Dobjo
Dobro body, banjo neck, 5-string.

1989		$1,000	$1,300

Dobro/Regal Model 19
Ca.1934-1938. In the 1930s Dobro licensed Chicago's Regal Company to build Dobro-style guitars. The headstocks on these models can have a Dobro logo, Regal logo, or no logo at all. The 19 is a lower-end model, round holes in coverplate, square neck.

1934-1938		$1,050	$1,400

Dobro/Regal Model 46/47
1935-1942. Dobro/Regal 46, renamed 47 in '39, aluminum body, round neck, 14 frets, slotted headstock, silver finish. Degraded finish was a common problem with the Dobro/Regal 47.

1935-1938	46	$1,400	$1,800
1939-1942	47, original finish	$1,900	$2,500

Dobro/Regal Model 62/65
1935-1942. Renamed Model 65 in '39, nickel-plated brass body, Spanish dancer etching, round or square neck. Note: Dobro/Regal 65 should not be confused with Dobro Model 65 which discontinued earlier.

1935-1938	62, round neck	$2,300	$3,000
1935-1938	62, square neck	$2,550	$3,300
1939-1942	65, round neck	$2,300	$3,000
1939-1942	65, square neck	$2,550	$3,300

Dobro/Regal Tenor Model 27-1/2
1930. Tenor version of Model 27.

1930		$525	$675

Dobrolektric
1996-2005. Resonator guitar with single-coil neck pickup, single-cut.

1996-2005		$1,075	$1,400

DS-33/Steel 33
1995-2000. Steel body with light amber sunburst finish, resonator with coverplate, biscuit bridge.

1995-2000		$850	$1,125

DW-90C
2001-2006. Single sharp cutaway, wood body, metal resonator, f-hole upper bass bout.

2001-2006		$825	$1,100

E3 (C, M, W, B)
Late 1970s-1986. Double-cut solidbodies with necks and bodies of laminated select hardwoods (Cinnamon, Maple, Walnut) or plain Black (B) finish, 2 pickups.

1979-1986	C, M, W	$1,125	$1,500

F-60/F-60 S
1986-2005. Round neck (60, discontinued '00) or square neck (60 S), f-holes, brown sunburst.

1986-2005		$1,075	$1,400

Gardena
1968. Electric Dobro body, 2 knobs, single-coil soap bar pickup.

1968		$700	$925

Hound Dog
2002-2019. Laminated wood, 10 1/2" spider-bridge resonator.

2002-2019		$375	$500

Hula Blues
1987-1999. Dark brown wood body (earlier models have much lighter finish), painted Hawaiian scenes, round neck.

1987-1999		$1,050	$1,375

Jerry Douglas
1995-2005. Mahogany body, square neck, limited run of 200 with signature, but also sold without signature.

1995-2005		$1,800	$2,400

Josh Graves
1995-2005. First 200 made were signed, single bound ample body, spider cone, nickel plated. Includes DW Josh Graves and Uncle Josh Limited models.

1995	Signed	$1,500	$2,000
1996-2005	Unsigned	$1,200	$1,600

Leader 14M/14H
1934-1935. Nickel plated brass body, segmented f-holes.

1934-1935	H square neck	$1,900	$2,500
1934-1935	M round neck	$1,600	$2,100

Model 25
1930-1935. Sunburst wood body, f-holes upper bout, large single metal cone, square neck.

1930-1935		$1,450	$1,900

Dobro Model 62
Bernunzio Uptown Music

1986 Dobro E3 C
Imaged by Heritage Auctions, HA.com

GUITARS

1973 Dobro Model 63
Imaged by Heritage Auctions, HA.com

1965 Domino Callifornian
Rivington Guitars

MODEL YEAR	FEATURES	EXC. COND. LOW	HIGH
Model 27 (OMI)			
1976-1994. Wood body, square neck.			
1976-1994		$1,175	$1,525
Model 27 Cyclops			
1932-1933.			
1932-1933	Round neck	$1,600	$2,100
1932-1933	Square neck	$1,700	$2,200
Model 27 Deluxe			
1995-2005. 27 with figured maple top, nicer appointments.			
1996-2005		$1,500	$2,000
Model 27/27G			
1933-1937. Regal-made, wooden body.			
1933-1937	Round neck	$1,275	$1,700
1933-1937	Square neck	$1,500	$2,000
Model 32			
1939-1941. Regal-made, wooden body.			
1939-1941		$1,750	$2,300
Model 33 (Duolian)			
1972. Only made in '72, becomes Model 90 in '73.			
1972		$900	$1,175
Model 33 H			
1973-1997 (OMI & Gibson). Same as 33 D, but with etched Hawaiian scenes, available as round or square neck.			
1980s-90s	Round neck	$1,300	$1,700
1980s-90s	Square neck	$1,300	$1,700
Model 35 (32)			
1935-1942. Metal body, called Model 32 (not to be confused with wood body 32) for '35-'38.			
1935-1942		$1,950	$2,550
Model 36			
1932-1937. Wood body with resonator, round or square neck.			
1932-1937	Round neck	$1,150	$1,500
1932-1937	Square neck	$1,500	$2,000
Model 36/36 S			
1970s-1997, 2002-2005. Chrome-plated brass body, round or square (S) neck, dot markers, engraved rose floral art.			
1970s-2005		$1,400	$1,800
Model 37			
1933-1937. Regal-made wood body, mahogany, bound body and 'board, round or square 12-fret neck.			
1933-1937	Round neck	$1,400	$1,800
1933-1937	Square neck	$1,700	$2,200
Model 37 Tenor			
1933-1937 (Regal). Tenor version of No. 37.			
1933-1937		$850	$1,100
Model 45			
1934-1939. Regal-made wood body, round or square neck.			
1934-1939	Round neck	$1,700	$2,200
1934-1939	Square neck	$2,000	$2,600
Model 55/56 Standard			
1929-1934. Model 55 Standard, renamed 56 Standard 1932-1934. Unbound wood body, metal resonator, bound neck, sunburst.			
1929-1934	Round neck	$1,500	$2,000
1929-1934	Square neck	$1,800	$2,400

MODEL YEAR	FEATURES	EXC. COND. LOW	HIGH
Model 60			
1933-1936. Similar to Model 66/66B.			
1933-1936	Round neck	$3,500	$4,600
1933-1936	Square neck	$4,400	$5,700
Model 60 Cyclops			
1932-1933. Round neck, 12-fret model, black walnut finish.			
1932-1933		$3,500	$4,600
Model 60/60 D (OMI)/60 DS			
1970-1993. Wood body (laminated maple) with Dobro resonator cone, model 60 until '73 when renamed 60 D, and various 60 model features offered, post-'93 was Gibson-owned production.			
1970-1993	Model 60 Series	$900	$1,300
Model 63			
1973-1996. Wood body, 8-string, square neck.			
1973-1996		$950	$1,250
Model 64			
1980s-1995. Walnut body, tree-of-life inlay.			
1982		$1,300	$1,700
Model 65/66/66 B			
1929-1933. Wood body with sandblasted ornamental design top and back, metal resonator, sunburst. Model 66 B has bound top.			
1929-1931	Model 65	$2,100	$2,700
1932-1933	Model 66	$2,100	$2,700
1932-1933	Model 66 B	$2,100	$2,700
Model 66/66 S			
1972-1995. Wood body with sandblasted ornamental design top and back, metal resonator, sunburst, round or square (S) neck.			
1972-1995		$825	$1,100
Model 75/Lily of the Valley			
1972-1997, 2002-2005. Chrome plated bell brass body resonator, round neck, Lily of the Valley engraving.			
1972-1997		$1,600	$2,100
Model 85/86			
1929-1934. Wood body, triple-bound, round or square neck, renamed 86 in '32.			
1929-1934		$2,150	$2,800
Model 90 (Duolian) (OMI)			
1972-1995. Chrome-plated, f-holes, etched Hawaiian scene.			
1972-1995	Various models	$750	$1,400
Model 90 (Woodbody)/WB90 G/WB90 S			
1980s-2005. Maple body with upper bout f-holes or sound holes, round neck, metal resonator with spider bridge, sunburst.			
1984-2005		$1,000	$1,300
Model 125 De Luxe			
1929-1934. Black walnut body, round or square neck, Dobro De Luxe engraved, triple-bound top, back and 'board, nickel-plated hardware, natural.			
1929-1934	Round neck	$4,900	$6,500
1929-1934	Square neck	$9,000	$12,000
Professional 15M/15H			
1934-1935. Engraved nickel body, round (M) or square (H) neck, solid peghead.			
1934-1935	H square neck	$2,400	$3,100
1934-1935	M round neck	$2,100	$2,700

MODEL		EXC. COND.	
YEAR	FEATURES	LOW	HIGH

Dodge

1996-present. Luthier Rick Dodge builds his intermediate and professional grade, production, solidbody guitars with changeable electronic modules in Tallahassee, Florida. He also builds basses.

Doitsch

1930s. Acoustic guitars made by Harmony most likely for a music store or studio.

Domino

Ca. 1967-1968. Solidbody and hollowbody electric guitars and basses imported from Japan by Maurice Lipsky Music Co. of New York, New York, previously responsible for marketing the Orpheum brand. Models are primarily near-copies of EKO, Vox, and Fender designs, plus some originals. Models were made by Arai or Kawai. Earlier models may have been imported, but this is not yet documented.

Electric

1967-1968. Various models include the Baron, Californian, Californian Rebel, Dawson, and the Spartan.

1967-1968		$250	$400

Dommenget

1978-1985, 1988-present. Luthier Boris Dommenget (pronounced dommen-jay) builds his premium grade, custom/production, solidbody, flat-top, and archtop guitars in Balje, Germany. From '78 to '85 he was located in Wiesbaden, and from '88-'01 in Hamburg. He and wife Fiona also make pickups.

Don Musser Guitars

Luthier Don Musser, in 1976, began building custom, classical and flat-top guitars in Silver City, New Mexico. He later moved his shop to Cotopaxi, Colorado.

Doolin Guitars

1997-present. Luthier Mike Doolin builds his premium grade, production/custom acoustics featuring his unique double-cut in Portland, Oregon.

Dorado

Ca. 1972-1973. Six- and 12-string acoustic guitars, solidbody electrics and basses. Brand used briefly by Baldwin/Gretsch on line of Japanese imports.

Acoustic Flat-Top/Acoustic Dobro

1972-1973. Includes folk D, jumbo Western, and grand concert styles (with laminated rosewood back and sides), and Dobro-style.

1972-1973	Higher-end models	$200	$325
1972-1973	Lower-end models	$125	$155
1972-1973	Mid-level models	$155	$200

Solidbody Electric

1972-1973. Includes Model 5985, a double-cut with 2 P-90-style pickups.

1972-1973		$200	$300

Douglas Ching

Luthier Douglas J. Ching builds his premium grade, production/custom, classical, acoustic, and harp guitars currently in Chester, Virginia, and previously in Hawaii ('76-'89) and Michigan ('90-'93). He also builds ukes, lutes and violins.

D'Pergo Custom Guitars

2002-present. Professional, premium, and presentation grade, production/custom, solidbody guitars built in Windham, New Hampshire. Every component of the guitars is built by D'Pergo.

Dragge Guitars

1982-2010. Luthier Peter Dragge builds his custom, steel-string and nylon-string guitars in Ojai, California.

Dragonfly Guitars

1994-present. Professional grade, production/custom, sloped cutaway flat-tops, semi-hollow body electrics, basses and dulcitars built by luthier Dan Richter in Roberts Creek, British Columbia.

Drive

Ca. 2001-ca. 2011. Budget grade, production, import solidbody electric guitars and basses. They also offered solidstate amps.

DTM

See David Thomas McNaught listing.

Dudley Custom Guitars

2005-present. Luthier Peter Dudley builds his custom, premium grade, chambered solidbody electric guitars in Easton, Maryland.

Duelin Guitars

Professional grade, production/custom, 6 ½ string guitars designed by Don Scheib of Simi Valley and built by luthier Mike Lipe in Sun Valley, California.

Duesenberg

1995-present. Professional and premium grade, production/custom, solid and hollow body electric guitars and basses built by luthier Dieter Goelsdorf in Hannover, Germany. Rockinger had a Duesenberg guitar in the 1980s.

Dunwell Guitars

Professional and premium grade, custom, flat-tops built by luthier Alan Dunwell in Nederland, Colorado.

Dupont

Luthier Maurice Dupont builds his classical, archtop, Weissenborn-style and Selmer-style guitars in Cognac, France.

Dwight

See info under Epiphone Dwight guitar.

D'Pergo Signature

Duesenberg Mike Campbell II

GUITARS

Eastman T146SM

EER Custom E-06 Classic

MODEL YEAR	FEATURES	EXC. COND. LOW	HIGH

Dyer

1902-1939. The massive W. J. Dyer & Bro. store in St. Paul, Minnesota, sold a complete line of music related merchandise though they actually built nothing but a few organs. The Larson Brothers of Chicago were commissioned to build harp guitar and harp mandolin pieces for them somewhat following the harp guitar design of Chris Knutsen, until 1912 when the Knutsen patent expired. Although the body design somewhat copied the Knutsen patent the resulting instrument was in a class by itself in comparison. These harp guitars have become the standard by which all others are judged because of their ease of play and the tremendous, beautiful sound they produce. Many modern builders are using the body design and the same structural ideas evidenced in the Larson originals. They were built in Styles 4 (the plainest), 5, 6, 7 and 8. The ornamentation went from the no binding, dot inlay Style 4 to the full treatment, abalone trimmed, tree-of-life fingerboard of the Style 8. All had mahogany back and sides with ebony fingerboard and bridge. There are also a very few Style 3 models found of late that are smaller than the standard and have a lower bout body point. Other Dyer instruments were built by Knutsen. Dyer also carried Stetson brand instruments made by the Larson Brothers.

Harp Guitar

1902-1920s	Style 3, smaller, short scale	$3,000	$3,900
1902-1920s	Style 4, no binding	$3,000	$3,900
1902-1920s	Style 5, bound top	$3,800	$4,900
1902-1920s	Style 6, bound top/bottom	$4,300	$5,600
1902-1920s	Style 7, fancy inlays	$5,000	$6,500
1902-1920s	Style 8, tree-of-life	$7,600	$9,800

Dynacord

1950-present. Dynacord is a German company that makes audio and pro sound amps, as well as other electronic equipment. In 1966-'67 they offered solidbody guitars and basses from the Welson Company of Italy. They also had the Cora guitar and bass which is the center part of a guitar body with a tube frame in a guitar outline. They also offered tape echo machines.

Dynelectron

1960s-late 1970s. This Italian builder offered a variety of guitars and basses, but is best known today for their almost exact copies of Danelectro Longhorns of the mid-'60s.

E L Welker

Luthier Eugene L. Welker began building in 1984, premium and presentation grade, production/custom, leather-wrapped archtop guitars in Claremont, New Hampshire.

E.L. Bashore Guitars

2011-present. Professional grade, custom, steel string and classical acoustic and solidbody electric guitars, basses and banjos built by luthier Eric L. Bashore in Danville, Pennsylvania.

Earthwood

1972-1985. Acoustic designs by Ernie Ball with input from George Fullerton and made in Newport Beach, California. One of the first to offer acoustic basses.

Eastman

1992-present. Intermediate and professional grade, production, archtop and flat-top guitars and basses, mainly built in China, with some from Germany and Romania. Beijing, China-based Eastman Strings started out building violins and cellos. They added guitars in '02 and mandolins in '04.

Eastwood

1997-present. Mike Robinson's company imports budget and intermediate grade, production, solid and semi-hollowbody guitars, many styled after 1960s models. They also offer basses and mandolins.

Eaton, William

1976-present. Luthier William Eaton builds custom specialty instruments such as vihuelas, harp guitars, and lyres in Phoenix, Arizona. He is also the Director of the Robetto-Venn School of Luthiery.

Echopark Guitars

2010-present. Premium and presentation grade, production/custom, solidbody electric guitars built by luthier Gabriel Currie in Detroit, Michigan, formerly in Los Angeles, California.

Ed Claxton Guitars

1972-present. Premium grade, custom flat-tops made by luthier Ed Claxton, first in Austin, Texas, and currently in Santa Cruz, California.

Eduardo Duran Ferrer

1987-present. Luthier Eduardo Duran Ferrer builds his premium grade, classical guitars in Granada, Spain.

Edward Klein

1998-present. Premium grade, custom, guitars built by luthier Edward Klein in Mississauga, Ontario.

EER Custom

2005-present. Professional and premium grade, custom, solidbody and semi-hollowbody electric guitars built by luthier Ernest E. Roesler in Forks, Washington.

Egmond

1935-1972. Founded by Ulke Egmond, building acoustic, archtop, semi-hollow and solidbody gui-

MODEL YEAR	FEATURES	EXC. COND. LOW	HIGH

tars originally in Eindhoven, later in Best Holland. They also made basses. Egmond also produced instruments under the Orpheum (imported into U.S.) Rosetti (England), Miller, Wilson and Lion brand names.

Electric
1960-1972. Solid or semi-hollow bodies.

1960-1972		$375	$500

Ehlers
1968-2011. Luthier Rob Ehlers built his premium grade, production/custom, flat-top acoustic guitars, originally in Oregon and from '06 to '11, in Veracruz, Mexico. Rob died in November, 2011.

15 CRC
Cutaway, Western red cedar top, Indian rosewood back and sides.

1996		$1,875	$2,450

15 SRC
Cutaway, European spruce top, Indian rosewood back and sides.

1998		$1,875	$2,450

16 BTM
European spruce top, mahogany back and sides, Troubadour peghead, black lacquer finish.

1998		$1,950	$2,525

16 C
16" lower bout, cutaway, flamed maple sides and back, European spruce top.

1990		$1,950	$2,525

16 SK Concert
16" lower bout, relatively small upper bout, small waist, European spruce top, flamed koa back and sides, diamond markers, natural.

1993		$1,775	$2,300

16 SM
European spruce top, mahogany back and sides.

1999		$1,675	$2,175

16 SSC
Cutaway, European spruce top, English sycamore back and sides.

1996		$1,775	$2,300

25 C
Limited Edition Anniversary Model, European spruce top, Indian rosewood back and sides, abalone top border.

2001		$2,600	$3,375

GJ (Gypsy Jazz)

2000s	D-style	$1,675	$2,175

Eichelbaum Guitars
Luthier David Eichelbaum builds his premium grade, custom, flat-tops in Santa Barbara, California.

EKO
1959-present. Originally acoustic, acoustic/electric, electric thinline and full-size archtop hollowbody, solidbody electric guitars and basses built by Oliviero Pigini and Company in Recanati, Italy, and imported by LoDuca Brothers, Milwaukee, Radio and Television Equipment Company in Santa

Ana, California and others. First acoustic guitars followed by sparkle plastic-covered electrics by '62. Sparkle finishes are gone ca. '66. Pigini dies ca. '67. LoDuca Bros. phases out in early-'70s. By '75 EKO offers some copy guitars and they purchased a custom shop to make other brands by '78. In '85 they ceased production in Italy, continuing the brand for a few years with Asian imports, and continued to distribute other brands. By 2004, the Eko line of guitar was revived with budget and intermediate grade, production, classical, acoustic, acoustic/electric, solidbody, solidbody, and hollowbody guitars made in Asia. They also make basses and amps.

Barracuda VI
1966-ca.1978. Double-cut semi-hollow, 2 pickups, 6-string.

1966-1978		$600	$800

Barracuda XII
1966-ca.1978. Double-cut semi-hollow, 2 pickups, 12-string.

1966-1978		$650	$850

Cobra I/II/III/XII
1966-1978. Double-cut solidbody, 2 knobs. Cobra I has 1 pickup, II 2 pickups and III 3 pickups. 12-string Cobra XII offered '67-'69, has 2 pickups.

1966-1978	Cobra I	$400	$550
1966-1978	Cobra II	$500	$650
1966-1978	Cobra III	$525	$725
1966-1978	Cobra XII	$525	$725

Commander
1965. Single-cut archtop electric, 1 pickup, 2 controls, EKO logo on upper bass bout, maple body in 'dura-glos' finish.

1965		$450	$600

Condor
1966-ca.1969. Double-cut solidbody with 3 or 4 pickups.

1966-1969		$600	$800

Dragon
1967-ca.1969. Single-cut archtop, 2 f-holes, 3 pickups, tremolo.

1967-1969		$700	$925

Flat-Top Acoustic
1960s. Various student-level flat-top acoustic models.

1960s		$250	$325

Florentine
1964-ca.1969. Double-cut archtop, 2 pickups.

1964-1969		$600	$800

Kadett/Kadett XII
1967-ca.1978. Double-cut solidbody with point on lower bass side of body, 3 pickups, tremolo. 12-string Kadett XII offered '68-'69.

1967-1978	Kadett	$600	$800
1968-1969	Kadett XII	$600	$800

Lancer Stereo
1967-1969. Lancer VI with stereo output (route output to 2 amplifiers requires EKO stereo cable for stereo application).

1967-1969		$475	$650

1998 Ehlers 16
Norton Graham

1960s EKO Model 995
Wayne Howland

1982 El Degas
Robbie Keene

*1976 Electra Elvin Bishop
Signature Model 2281*
Greg Perrine

MODEL YEAR	FEATURES	EXC. COND. LOW	HIGH
Lancer VI			
1967-ca.1969. Double-cut solidbody, 2 pickups.			
1967-1969		$350	$475
Lancer XII			
1967-1969. Double-cut solidbody electric, 12-string.			
1967-1969		$425	$575
Lark I/II			
1970. Thin hollow cutaway, sunburst. Lark I has 1 pickup and Lark II 2.			
1970	Lark I	$475	$650
1970	Lark II	$475	$650
Model 180			
1960s. Cutaway acoustic archtop.			
1960s		$350	$450
Model 285 Modello			
1960s. Thinline single-cut, 1 pickup.			
1962		$425	$575
Model 290/2V			
1963-1965. Maple body and neck, ebony 'board, dot markers, 2 pickups, tremolo, renamed Barracuda in '66.			
1963-1965		$600	$800
Model 300/375			
1962. Copy of Hofner Club-style electric, single-cut, 2 pickups, set-neck.			
1962		$850	$1,150
Model 400 Ekomaster			
1960-1962. Jazzmaster-style, 1, 2 or 4 (2+2) pickups, sparkle finish.			
1960-1962	4 pickups	$800	$1,075
Model 500/1 / 500/1V			
1961-1965. Plastic covered solidbody, 1 pickup. 500/1 no vibrato, 1V with vibrato.			
1961-1965	500/1	$675	$900
1961-1965	500/1V	$775	$1,025
Model 500/2 / 500/3V			
1961-1964. Plastic covered solidbody, plastic sparkle finish. 500/2 no vibrato, 2 pickups. 3V with vibrato, 3 pickups.			
1961-1965	500/2	$775	$1,025
1961-1965	500/3V	$825	$1,100
Model 500/4 / 500/4V			
1961-1964. Plastic covered solidbody, 4 pickups. 500/4 no vibrato, 4V with vibrato.			
1961-1965	500/4	$925	$1,250
1961-1965	500/4V	$1,000	$1,325
Model 540 (Classical)			
1960s. Nylon-string classical guitar.			
1960s		$200	$275
Model 700/3V			
1961-1964. Map-shape/tulip-shape body, 3 pickups, vibrato, woodgrain plastic finish.			
1961-1964		$1,175	$1,550
Model 700/4V			
1961-1967. Map-shape/tulip-shape body, 4 pickups, multiple switches, vibrato.			
1961-1967	Red, blue, silver sparkle	$1,350	$1,750
1961-1967	Standard finish	$1,175	$1,550

MODEL YEAR	FEATURES	EXC. COND. LOW	HIGH
Ranger 6/12			
1967-ca.1982. D-size flat-top acoustic, large 3-point 'guard, dot inlays, EKO Ranger label. Ranger 12 is 12-string.			
1967-1982	Ranger 12	$425	$575
1967-1982	Ranger 6	$425	$575
Ranger 6/12 Electra			
1967. Ranger 6/12 with on-board pickup and 2 controls, 6-string with dot markers, 12-string with block markers.			
1967	12 Electra	$450	$600
1967	6 Electra	$450	$600
Rocket VI/XII (Rokes)			
1967-ca.1969. Rocket-shape design, solidbody, 6-string, says Rokes on the headstock, Rokes were a popular English band that endorsed EKO guitars, marketed as the Rocket VI in the U.S.; and as the Rokes in Europe, often called the Rok. Rocket XII is 12-string.			
1967-1969	Rocket VI	$825	$1,100
1967-1969	Rocket XII	$825	$1,100

El Degas
Early-1970s. Japanese-made copies of classic America electrics and acoustics, imported by Buegeleisen & Jacobson of New York, New York.
Solidbody
Early-1970s. Copies of classic American models, including the Let's Play model.

1970s		$250	$325

El Maya
1970s-1980s. Also labeled Maya. Solidbody, archtop and semi-hollow guitars built by Japan's Chushin Gakki Co., which also built models for several other manufacturers.

Eleca
2004-present. Student/budget level, production, acoustic and electric guitars, imported by Eleca International. They also offer amps, effects and mandolins.

Electar
See Epiphone listing.

Electra
1970-1984, 2013-present. Imported from Japan by St. Louis Music. Most instruments made by Matsumoku in Japan. The Electra line replaced SLM's Japanese-made Apollo and U.S.-made Custom Kraft lines. First guitar, simply called The Electra, was a copy of the Ampeg Dan Armstrong lucite guitar and issued in '70, followed quickly by a variety of bolt-neck copies of other brands. In '75 the Tree-of-Life guitars debut and the line is expanded. Open-book headstocks changed to wave or fan shape by '78. Some Korean production begins in early-'80s. In the fall of '83, the Electra Brand becomes Electra Phoenix. By beginning of '84, the brand becomes Electra-Westone and by the end of '84 just Westone. In 2013, the brand was revived with guitars built by

MODEL YEAR	FEATURES	EXC. COND. LOW	HIGH

luthiers Ben Chafin and Mick Donner in Tampa, Florida. Matsumoku-made guitars have serial number in which first 1 or 2 digits represent the year of manufacture. Thus a guitar with a serial number beginning in 0 or 80 would be from 1980.

Concert Professional
Late 1970s. Howard Roberts style, single-cut electric flat-top with oval sound hole, single humbucking pickup, fancy markers.

1977		$750	$1,000

Custom
1970s. Double-cut solidbody, 2 pickups, Custom logo on truss rod, cherry finish.

1970s		$600	$775

Elvin Bishop
1976-ca.1980. Double-cut semi-hollow body, tree-of-life inlay.

1976-1980		$750	$1,000

Flying Wedge
1970s. V body, six-on-a-side tuners.

1970s		$500	$650

MPC Outlaw
1977-1980. Symmetric horn body, neck-thru, has separate modules (Modular Powered Circuits) that plug in for different effects. Includes X710 (peace sign burned into natural mahogany top), X720 (gray sunburst), X730 (tobacco sunburst) and X 740 (maple top).

1977-1980		$700	$925
1977-1980	MPC plug in module	$85	$115

MPC X310
1976-1980. MPC model, LP solidbody, 2 humbuckers (bridge w/ exposed zebra bobbins), 4 in-line control knobs plus 2 toggles, gold hardware, black finish.

1976-1980		$625	$825

MPC X320
1976-1980. Same as X310, but with transparent cherry red finish over mahogany top.

1976-1980		$625	$825

MPC X330
1976-1980. Same as X310, but with cherry sunburst finish on maple top.

1976-1980		$625	$825

MPC X340
1976-1980. Same as X310, but with Jacaranda rosewood top.

1976-1980		$625	$825

MPC X350
1977-1980. Same as X310, but with tobacco sunburst on a maple top.

1977-1980		$625	$825

Phoenix
1980-1984. Classic offset double-cut solidbody, Phoenix logo on headstock.

1980-1984		$300	$400

Rock
1971-1973. Single cut solidbody, becomes the Super Rock in '73.

1971-1973		$425	$550

Super Rock
1973-ca.1978. Renamed from Rock ('71-'73).

1973-1978		$500	$650

X135
1982. Offset double-cut solidbody, 2 humbucker pickups.

1982		$300	$400

X145 60th Anniversary
1982. Classic offset double-cut only made one year, Anniversary plate on back of headstock, single/single/hum pickups.

1982		$300	$400

X150
1975. Offset double-cut, 2 humbucker pickups.

1975		$425	$550

X220 Omega
1976-ca. 1980. Single-cut solidbody, block inlays, Omega logo on truss rod, black with rosewood neck, or natural with figured top and maple neck.

1976-1980		$525	$700

X280/X290 Working Man
1980-1984. Modified double-cut solidbody, 2 exposed-coil humbuckers, dot inlays, natural satin finish (X280) or jet black (X290).

1980-1984		$300	$400

X410
1975. Double-cut thinline acoustic archtop, 2 humbucker pickups, large split triangle markers, open-book style headstock shape.

1975		$750	$1,000

X420
1978. Double-cut thinline acoustic archtop, 2 humbucker pickups, dot markers, wave-shape style headstock.

1978		$525	$700

X935 Endorser
1983-1984. Double-cut solidbody, 2 humbucker pickups, tune-o-matic, dot markers.

1983-1984		$350	$475

X960 Ultima
1981. Hybrid single-cut with additional soft bass bout cutaway, slab solidbody, dot markers, 2 humbucker pickups, wave-shape style headstock.

1981		$400	$550

Electric Gypsy
See listing under Teye.

Electro
1964-1975. The Electro line was manufactured by Electro String Instruments and distributed by Radio-Tel. The Electro logo appeared on the headstock rather than Rickenbacker. Refer to the Rickenbacker section for models.

Electromuse
1940s-1950s. Mainly known for lap steels, Electromuse also offered acoustic and electric hollowbody guitars. They also had tube amps usually sold as a package with a lap steel.

Elferink
1993-present. Production/custom, premium grade, archtop guitars built in the Netherlands by luthier Frans Elferink.

Late-1970s Electra MPC X320

Elferink

GUITARS

Elliott Classical

1946 Epiphone Broadway
Bernunzio Uptown Music

MODEL YEAR	FEATURES	EXC. COND. LOW	HIGH

Elijah Jewel

2009-present. Luthier Michael Kerry builds his professional grade, production/custom, acoustic guitars in Mineola, Texas. He also builds mandolins.

Elite

1960s. Guitars made in Italy by the Crucianelli accordion company, which made several other brands.

Elk

Late-1960s. Japanese-made by Elk Gakki Co., Ltd. Many were copies of American designs. They also offered amps and effects.

Elliott Guitars

1966-present. Premium and presentation grade, custom, nylon-string classical and steel-string guitars built by luthier Jeffrey Elliott in Portland, Oregon.

Ellis

2000-present. Luthier Andrew Ellis builds his production/custom, premium grade, steel string acoustic and resophonic guitars in Perth, Western Australia. In 2008 he also added lap steels.

Elli-Sound

1960s. Guitars made in Italy by the Crucianelli accordion company, which made several other brands.

Ellsberry Archtop Guitars

2003-present. Premium and presentation grade, custom/production, acoustic and electric archtops built by luthier James Ellsberry previously in Torrance and Harbor City, California, and presently in Huntington Beach.

Emperador

1966-1992. Guitars and basses imported from Japan by Westheimer Musical Instruments. Early models appear to be made by either Teisco or Kawai; later models were made by Cort.

Acoustic

1960s	Archtop or flat-top	$125	$175

Electric Solidbody

1960s		$150	$200

Empire

1997-present. Professional and premium grade, production/custom, solidbody guitars from Lee Garver's GMW Guitarworks of Glendora, California.

Encore

Mid-1960s-present. Budget grade, production, classical, acoustic, and electric guitars imported from China and Vietnam by John Hornby Skewes & Co. in the U.K. They also offer basses.

MODEL YEAR	FEATURES	EXC. COND. LOW	HIGH

Engel Guitars

1990-present. Luthier Robert Engel builds his premium grade, production/custom, hollowbody and solidbody guitars in Stamford, Connecticut.

English Electronics

1960s. Lansing, Michigan, company named after owner, some private branded guitars and amps by Valco (Chicago), many models with large English Electronics vertical logo on headstock.

Tonemaster

1960s. National Val-Pro 84 with neck pickup and bridge mounted pickup, black.

1960s		$700	$875

Epcor

1967. Hollowbody electirc guitars and basses built by Joe Hall's Hallmark Guitars in Bakersfield, CA for manufacturer's rep Ed Preager (the EP in the name). Only about 35 were built.

Epi

1970s. Typical Japanese copy-import, Epi logo on headstock with capital letter split-E logo, inside label says "Norlin," probably for Japanese domestic market.

Acoustic Flat-Top

1970s. D-style, mahogany body.

1970s		$135	$175

Epiphone

Ca. 1873-present. Budget, intermediate, professional and premium grade, production, solidbody, archtop, acoustic, acoustic/electric, resonator, and classical guitars made in the U.S. and overseas. They also offer basses, amps, mandolins, ukes and banjos. Founded in Smyrna, Turkey, by Anastasios Stathopoulos and early instruments had his label. He emigrated to the U.S. in 1903 and changed the name to Stathoupoulo. Anastasios died in '15 and his son, Epaminondas ("Epi") took over. The name changed to House of Stathopoulo in '17 and the company incorporated in '23. In '24 the line of Epiphone Recording banjos debut and in '28 the company name was changed to the Epiphone Banjo Company. In '43 Epi Stathopoulo died and sons Orphie and Frixo took over. Labor trouble shut down the NYC factory in '51 and the company cut a deal with Conn/Continental and relocated to Philadelphia in '52. Frixo died in '57 and Gibson bought the company. Kalamazoo-made Gibson Epiphones debut in '58. In '69 American production ceased and Japanese imports began. Some Taiwanese guitars imported from '79-'81. Limited U.S. production resumed in '82 but sourcing shifted to Korea in '83. In '85 Norlin sold Gibson to Henry Juszkiewicz, Dave Barryman and Gary Zebrowski. In '92 Jim Rosenberg became president of the new Epiphone division.

AJ Masterbilt Series
2004-present. Sloped shoulder D size, solid spruce tops, solid rosewood or mahogany (M) back and sides.

MODEL YEAR	FEATURES	EXC. COND. LOW	HIGH
2004-2019 AJ-45ME		$475	$625

Alleykat
2000-2010. Single cut small body archtop, I humbucker and 1 mini-humbucker.

| 2000-2010 | | $250 | $325 |

B.B. King Lucille
1997-2019. Laminated double-cut maple body, 2 humbuckers, Lucille on headstock.

| 1997-2019 | | $400 | $525 |

Barcelona CE
1999-2000. Classical, solid spruce top, rosewood back and sides, EQ/preamp.

| 1999-2000 | | $250 | $325 |

Barcelone (Classical)
1963-1968. Highest model of Epiphone '60s classical guitars, maple back and sides, gold hardware.

1963-1964		$625	$825
1965		$525	$700
1966-1968		$500	$650

Bard 12-String
1962-1969. Flat-top, mahogany back and sides, natural or sunburst.

1962-1964		$1,100	$1,450
1965		$1,000	$1,300
1966-1969		$875	$1,125

Beverly
1931-1936. Flat-top, arched back, tenor or Hawaiian versions.

| 1931-1936 | Hawaiian | $675 | $875 |
| 1931-1936 | Tenor | $475 | $625 |

Biscuit
1997-2000, 2002-2010. Wood body resonator, biscuit bridge, round neck.

| 1997-2010 | | $250 | $325 |

Blackstone
1931-1950. Acoustic archtop, f-holes, sunburst.

1933-1934	Masterbilt	$850	$1,100
1935-1937		$725	$925
1938-1939		$625	$800
1940-1941		$575	$750
1948-1950		$475	$625

Broadway (Acoustic)
1931-1958. Non-cut acoustic archtop.

1931-1938	Sunburst, walnut body	$2,000	$2,600
1939-1942	Sunburst, maple body	$2,000	$2,600
1946-1958	Natural	$1,675	$2,200
1946-1958	Sunburst	$1,525	$2,000

Broadway Regent (Acoustic Cutaway)
1950-1958. Single-cut acoustic archtop, sunburst.

| 1950-1958 | | $1,675 | $2,200 |

Broadway (Electric)
1958-1969. Gibson-made electric archtop, single-cut, 2 New York pickups (mini-humbucking pickups by '61), Frequensator tailpiece, block inlays, sunburst or natural finish with cherry optional in '67 only.

1958-1959	Natural	$2,100	$2,700
1958-1959	Sunburst	$1,850	$2,400
1960-1964	Natural	$1,950	$2,550
1960-1964	Sunburst	$1,775	$2,300
1965	Natural	$1,600	$2,100
1965	Sunburst	$1,525	$1,975
1966-1967	Natural, cherry	$1,525	$1,975
1966-1967	Sunburst	$1,475	$1,926
1968-1969	Natural, cherry	$1,475	$1,926
1968-1969	Sunburst	$1,475	$1,926

Broadway Reissue
1997-2019. Full depth acoustic-electric single cut archtop, 2 humbuckers.

| 1997-2019 | | $425 | $550 |

Broadway Tenor
1937-1953. Acoustic archtop, sunburst.

| 1937-1953 | | $1,025 | $1,350 |

Byron
1949-ca.1955. Acoustic archtop, mahogany back and sides, sunburst.

| 1949-1955 | | $350 | $450 |

C Series Classical (Import)
1995-2006. Nylon-string classical guitars, including C-25 (mahogany back & sides), C-40 (cedar top, mahogany), C-70-CE (rosewood).

| 1998-2005 C-40 | | $125 | $165 |

Caiola Custom
1963-1970. Introduced as Caiola, renamed Caiola Custom in '66, electric thinbody archtop, 2 mini-humbuckers, multi-bound top and back, block inlays, walnut or sunburst finish (walnut only by '68).

1963-1964		$1,850	$2,400
1965		$1,675	$2,200
1966-1967		$1,525	$1,975
1968-1970		$1,475	$1,926

Caiola Standard
1966-1970. Electric thinbody archtop, 2 P-90s, single-bound top and back, dot inlays, sunburst or cherry.

| 1966-1967 | | $1,400 | $1,825 |
| 1968-1970 | | $1,250 | $1,650 |

Casino (1 Pickup)
1961-1969. Thinline hollowbody, double-cut, 1 P-90 pickup, various colors.

1961-1964		$3,700	$4,900
1965		$3,100	$4,000
1966-1969		$2,850	$3,700

Casino (2 Pickups)
1961-1970. Two pickup (P-90) version, various colors. '61-'63 known as Keith Richards model, '64-'65 known as Beatles model.

1961-1964		$4,900	$6,300
1965		$3,700	$4,800
1966-1970		$4,200	$5,500

Casino (Japan)
1982-1983. Epiphone built a few of its classic models, including the Casino, in Japan from mid-'82 to mid-'83.

| 1982-1983 | | $725 | $950 |

Casino J.L. U.S.A. 1965
2003-2006. 1,965 made.

| 2003-2006 | | $2,050 | $2,650 |

Epiphone AJ-500M Masterbilt
Rivington Guitars

1964 Epiphone Casino

To get the most from this book, be sure to read "Using *The Guide*" in the introduction.

GUITARS

2002 Epiphone Casino Reissue
Bernunzio Uptown Music

1964 Epiphone Coronet
Trey Rabinek <treyrabinek@google.com>

MODEL YEAR	FEATURES	EXC. COND. LOW	HIGH

Casino Reissue
1995-2019. Import, sunburst.
| 1995-2019 | | $450 | $575 |

Casino Revolution
1999-2005. Limited production 1965 reissue model, with certificate of authenticity, sanded natural.
| 1999-2005 | | $2,050 | $2,650 |

Casino 1961 50th Anniversary Limited Edition
2011. Trapeze (TD) or TremTone vibrato (TDV), total run of 1,961 built.
| 2011 | TDV | $625 | $800 |
| 2011 | Trapeze | $625 | $800 |

Century
1939-1970. Thinline archtop, non-cut, 1 pickup, trapeze tailpiece, walnut finish, sunburst finish available in '58, Royal Burgundy available '61 and only sunburst finish available by '68.
1939-1948	Oblong shape pu	$950	$1,225
1949-1957	Sunburst	$850	$1,100
1958-1962	Sunburst, P-90 pu, plate logo	$825	$1,075
1963-1964	Sunburst, P-90 pu, no plate logo	$825	$1,075
1965	Sunburst, cherry	$725	$950
1966-1970	Sunburst, cherry	$650	$850

Classic (Classical)
1963-1970.
1963-1964		$375	$500
1965		$325	$425
1966-1970		$325	$425

Collegiate
2004-2005. Les Paul-style body, 1 humbucker, various college graphic decals on body.
| 2004-2005 | | $150 | $200 |

Coronet (Electric Archtop)
1939-1949. Electric archtop, laminated mahogany body, 1 pickup, trapeze tailpiece, sunburst, name continued as an electric solidbody in '58.
| 1939-1949 | | $750 | $975 |

Coronet (Solidbody)
1958-1969. Solidbody electric, 1 New York pickup ('58-'59), 1 P-90 ('59-'69), cherry or black finish, Silver Fox finish available by '63, reintroduced as Coronet USA '90-'94, Korean-made '95-'98.
1958-1959	Cherry, NY pu	$2,900	$3,800
1959	Black (rare), NY pu	$5,000	$6,500
1960-1964	Various colors	$2,700	$3,500
1965	Standard color	$1,900	$2,450
1965-1966	Custom color	$3,800	$4,900
1966-1969	Standard color	$1,700	$2,200

Coronet U.S.A.
1990-1994. Made in Nashville, reverse banana headstock, typical Coronet styled body, single-coil and humbucker.
| 1990-1994 | | $650 | $825 |

Coronet (Import)
1995-1998. Import version.
| 1995-1998 | | $300 | $400 |

MODEL YEAR	FEATURES	EXC. COND. LOW	HIGH

Crestwood Custom
1958-1970. Solidbody, 2 New York pickups ('58-'60), 2 mini-humbuckers ('61-'70), symmetrical body and 3+3 tuners ('58-'62), asymmetrical and 1x6 tuners ('63-'70), slab body with no Gibson equivalent model.
1958-1960	Cherry, NY pus	$2,400	$3,150
1959-1960	Sunburst, NY pus	$2,400	$3,150
1961-1962	Cherry, mini-hums	$2,300	$3,000
1961-1962	White, mini-hums	$2,750	$3,600
1963-1964	Cherry, mini-hums, 1x6	$1,700	$2,250
1963-1964	Custom color	$3,100	$4,000
1965	Cherry	$1,600	$2,100
1965	Custom color	$3,000	$3,900
1966-1967	Cherry	$1,550	$2,000
1966-1967	Custom color	$1,950	$2,500
1968-1970	Cherry, white	$1,375	$1,800

Crestwood Deluxe
1963-1969. Solidbody with 3 mini-humbuckers, block inlay, cherry, white or Pacific Blue finish, 1x6 tuners.
1963-1964	Cherry, mini-hums	$1,950	$2,500
1963-1964	Custom color	$3,100	$4,000
1965	Cherry	$1,700	$2,250
1965	Custom color	$2,825	$3,700
1966-1967	Cherry	$1,550	$2,000
1966-1967	Custom color	$2,000	$2,600
1968-1969	Cherry, white	$1,550	$2,000

De Luxe
1931-1957. Non-cut acoustic archtop, maple back and sides, trapeze tailpiece ('31-'37), frequensator tailpiece ('37-'57), gold-plated hardware, sunburst or natural finish.
1931-1935	Sunburst, 17⅜"	$4,700	$6,100
1935-1944	Sunburst, 16⅜"	$4,100	$5,400
1939-1944	Natural	$4,100	$5,400
1945-1949	Natural	$3,500	$4,600
1945-1949	Sunburst	$3,300	$4,300
1950-1957	Natural	$3,400	$4,400
1950-1957	Sunburst	$3,000	$4,000

De Luxe Regent (Acoustic Archtop)
1948-1952. Acoustic cutaway archtop, high-end appointments, rounded cutaway, natural finish, renamed De Luxe Cutaway in '53.
| 1948-1952 | Natural | $5,600 | $7,300 |
| 1948-1952 | Sunburst | $4,700 | $6,100 |

De Luxe Cutaway/Deluxe Cutaway
1953-1970. Renamed from De Luxe Regent, cataloged Deluxe Cutaway by Gibson in '58, special order by '64 with limited production because acoustic archtops were pretty much replaced by electric archtops. There is also a FT Deluxe Cutaway flat-top (see FT listings).
1953-1957	Natural	$5,600	$7,300
1953-1957	Sunburst	$4,700	$6,100
1958-1959		$4,500	$5,900
1960-1964	Gibson Kalamazoo, rounded cutaway	$4,100	$5,400
1965-1970	Special order only	$3,500	$4,600

MODEL YEAR	FEATURES	EXC. COND. LOW	HIGH

De Luxe Electric (Archtop)
1954-1957. Single-cut electric archtop, 2 pickups, called the Zephyr De Luxe Regent from '48-'54. Produced with a variety of specs, maple or spruce tops, different inlays and pickup combinations.

1954-1957	Natural	$3,400	$4,400
1954-1957	Sunburst	$3,100	$4,100

Del Ray
1995-2000. Offset double-cut body, 2 blade humbuckers, dot markers, tune-o-matic, flamed maple top.

1995-2000		$300	$400

Devon
1949-1957. Acoustic archtop, non-cut, mahogany back and sides, sunburst finish, optional natural finish by '54.

1950-1957	Sunburst	$1,350	$1,750
1954-1957	Natural	$1,350	$1,750

Don Everly (SQ-180)
1997-2004. Jumbo acoustic reissue, large double 'guard, black gloss finish.

1997-2004		$500	$650

Dot (ES-335 Dot)/Dot Archtop
2000-present. Dot-neck ES-335.

2000-2019		$350	$450

Dot Studio
2004-2019. Simplified Dot, 2 control knobs, black hardware.

2004-2019		$275	$350

Dove Limited Edition
2008. Dove Limited Edition logo on label, Dove script logo on truss rod cover, classic dove logo art on 'guard and dove inlay on bridge, cherry or ebony.

2008		$225	$300

Dwight
1963, 1967. Coronet labeled as Dwight and made for Sonny Shields Music of St. Louis, 75 made in '63 and 36 in '67, cherry. National-Supro made Dwight brand lap steels in the '50s.

1963		$2,700	$3,500
1967		$1,700	$2,200

EA/ET/ES Series (Japan)
1970-1979. Production of the Epiphone brand was moved to Japan in '70. Models included the EA (electric thinline) and ET (electric solidbody).

1970-1975	EA-250 Riviera	$325	$425
1970-1975	ET-270	$425	$550
1970-1975	ET-275	$425	$550
1972	ES-255 Casino	$450	$575
1975-1979	ET-290 Crestwood	$425	$550

EJ-160E John Lennon
1997-2013. Based on John's Gibson acoustic/electric, sunburst, signature on body.

1997-2013		$325	$425

EJ-200 Series
1994-present. Solid spruce top, laminate maple body.

1994-2019	Various models	$200	$400

EJ-300
2004-2006. Solid spruce top, laminate rosewood body.

2004-2006		$350	$500

El Diablo
1994-1995. Offset double-cut acoustic/electric, on-board piezo and 3-band EQ, composite back and sides, spruce top, cherry sunburst.

1994-1995		$350	$450

Electar Model M
1935-1939. Epiphone's initial entry into the new electric guitar market of the mid-'30s, 14 3/4" laminate maple archtop, horseshoe pickup, trap door on back for electronics, Electar logo on headstock, oblong pickup replaces horseshoe in late-'37.

1935-1936	2 control knobs	$1,075	$1,400
1937-1939	3 control knobs	$1,075	$1,400

Electar Model M Tenor
1937-1939. Electric tenor 4-string with Electar specs.

1937-1939	3 knobs, natural	$1,000	$1,300

Elitist Series
2003-2019. Made in Japan, higher-grade series, using finer woods and inlays and U.S.-made Gibson pickups.

2003-2004	J-200	$1,250	$1,625
2003-2004	L-00/VS	$1,050	$1,350
2003-2005	'65 Texan	$1,250	$1,625
2003-2005	'61 SG Standard	$825	$1,075
2003-2005	Riviera	$1,425	$1,850
2003-2008	'63 ES-335 Dot	$1,300	$1,700
2003-2008	Byrdland/L5	$1,850	$2,400
2003-2009	Broadway	$1,250	$1,625
2003-2009	LP Custom	$825	$1,075
2003-2009	LP Standard	$825	$1,075
2003-2009	LP Standard '57 Goldtop	$825	$1,075
2003-2009	LP Studio	$675	$875
2003-2009	Sheraton	$1,425	$1,850
2003-2019	Casino	$1,250	$1,625
2004-2005	Jim Croce L-00	$825	$1,075
2005	Chet Atkins Country Gentleman	$1,250	$1,625
2007-2009	Les Paul Plus	$825	$1,075
2012	Dwight Yoakam Trash Casino	$1,250	$1,625

Emperor (Acoustic Archtop)
1935-1954. Acoustic archtop, non-cut, maple back and sides, multi-bound body, gold-plated hardware, sunburst, optional natural finish by '39.

1935-1939	Natural	$6,200	$8,100
1935-1939	Sunburst	$4,400	$5,700
1940-1949	Natural, Sunburst	$5,500	$7,200
1950-1954	Natural	$5,000	$6,500
1950-1954	Sunburst	$4,600	$6,000

Emperor Regent
1948-1953. Acoustic archtop with rounded cutaway, renamed Emperor Cutaway in '53.

1948-1953	Natural	$5,500	$7,200
1948-1953	Sunburst	$5,000	$6,600

Emperor Cutaway
1953-1957. Renamed from Emperor Regent, acoustic archtop, single-cut, maple back and sides, multi-bound body, gold-plated hardware, sunburst or natural.

1953-1957	Natural	$5,500	$7,200
1953-1957	Sunburst	$5,000	$6,600

Epiphone Dot

Epiphone Elitist 1965 Casino

GUITARS

*1959 Epiphone Emperor
(Thinline Electric)*

1958 Epiphone FT 79 Texan
Bernunzio Uptown Music

MODEL YEAR	FEATURES	EXC. COND. LOW	HIGH

Emperor Electric
1953-1957. Archtop, single-cut, 3 pickups, multi-bound body, sunburst, called the Zephyr Emperor Regent in '50-'53.

| 1953-1957 | | $3,000 | $3,900 |

Emperor (Thinline Electric)
1958-1969. Single-cut, thinline archtop, 3 New York pickups in '58-'60, 3 mini-humbuckers '61 on, multi-bound, gold-plated hardware, sunburst or natural finish until '65 when only sunburst was made.

1958-1959	Natural, 3 NY pus	$6,750	$8,800
1958-1959	Sunburst, 3 NY pus	$5,250	$6,800
1960-1962	Natural	$6,400	$8,300
1960-1962	Sunburst	$5,250	$6,800
1963-1969	Special order only	$4,500	$5,800

Emperor/Emperor II
1982-1994. Single-cut archtop jazz guitar, 2 humbuckers, blocks, gold hardware. II added to name in '93, became Joe Pass Emperor II (see that listing) in '95, although his name was on the guitar as early as '91.

| 1982-1989 | Matsumoku, Japan | $700 | $900 |
| 1990-1994 | | $700 | $900 |

Entrada (Classical)
1963-1968. Small classical, 13.25" bout, natural.

| 1963-1964 | | $375 | $500 |
| 1965-1968 | | $325 | $425 |

ES-175 Premium
2010-2019. Limited Edition, vintage "aged" lacquer finish, various colors.

| 2010-2019 | | $525 | $675 |

ES-295
1997-2001, 2003-2016. Epiphone's version of classic Gibson goldtop.

| 1997-2016 | | $575 | $750 |

ES-339 PRO
2012-present. Maple laminate body, 2 pickups.

| 2012-2019 | | $300 | $400 |

Espana (Classical)
1962-1968. Classical, U.S.-made, maple back and sides, natural, imported in '69 from Japan.

1962-1964		$550	$725
1965		$500	$650
1966-1968		$450	$600

Exellente
1963-1969, 1994-1995. Flat-top, Brazilian rosewood back and sides (Indian rosewood '68-'69), cloud inlays. Name revived on Gibson Montana insturment in '90s.

1963-1964	Brazilian	$5,700	$7,500
1965	Brazilian	$5,400	$7,000
1966-1967	Brazilian	$5,000	$6,500
1968-1969	Indian	$3,000	$4,000

1958 Korina Explorer
1998-2011. Explorer with typical appointments, korina body. This guitar was produced with a variety of specs, ranging from maple tops to spruce tops, different inlay markers were also used, different pickup combinations have been seen, natural or sunburst finish.

| 1998-2011 | | $385 | $500 |

1958 Gothic Explorer/Flying V
2002-2012. Flat black finish, V ends in 2010.

| 2002-2012 | | $375 | $475 |

Firebird
1995-2000. Two mini-humbuckers, Firebird Red, dot markers.

| 1995-2000 | | $375 | $475 |

Firebird 300
1986-1988. Korean import, Firebird Red.

| 1986-1988 | | $375 | $475 |

Firebird 500
1986-1988. Korean import, Firebird Red.

| 1986-1988 | | $375 | $475 |

1963 Firebird VII/Firebird VII
2000-2010. Three mini-humbuckers, gold hardware, Maestro-style vibrato, block markers, Firebird Red, reverse body. 1963 dropped from name in '03.

| 2000-2010 | | $450 | $600 |

Firebird Studio
2006-2011. Two humbuckers, with worn cherry finish.

| 2006-2011 | | $400 | $525 |

Flamekat
1999-2005. Archtop, flame finish, double dice position markers, 2 mini-humbuckers, Epiphone Bigsby.

| 1999-2005 | | $250 | $325 |

Flying V/'67 Flying V
1989-1998, 2003-2005. '67 or '58 specs, alder body, natural.

| 1989-1998 | '67 specs | $375 | $475 |
| 2003-2005 | '58 specs | $375 | $475 |

1958 Korina Flying V
1998-2011. Typical Flying V configuration, korina body.

| 1998-2011 | | $375 | $475 |

FT 30
1941-1949. Acoustic flat-top, brown stain, mahogany back and sides, reintroduced as Gibson-made FT 30 Caballero in '58.

| 1941-1943 | | $1,025 | $1,325 |
| 1944-1949 | | $875 | $1,150 |

FT 30 Caballero
1959-1970. Reintroduced from Epiphone-made FT 30, Gibson-made acoustic flat-top, natural, all mahogany body, dot inlay, tenor available '63-'68.

1959-1961		$850	$1,125
1962-1964		$625	$825
1965		$550	$725
1966-1970		$475	$625

FT 45
1941-1948. Acoustic flat-top, walnut back and sides, cherry neck, rosewood 'board, natural top, reintroduced as Gibson-made FT 45 Cortez in '58.

| 1941-1943 | | $1,500 | $1,925 |
| 1944-1948 | | $1,150 | $1,500 |

FT 45 Cortez
1958-1969. Reintroduced from Epiphone-made FT 45, Gibson-made acoustic flat-top, 16.5", mahogany back and sides, sunburst or natural top (sunburst only in '59-'62).

1958-1959	Sunburst	$1,250	$1,600
1960-1964	Sunburst, natural	$1,100	$1,450
1965-1966	Sunburst, natural	$1,000	$1,300
1967-1969	Sunburst, natural	$750	$1,000

MODEL YEAR	FEATURES	EXC. COND. LOW	HIGH

FT 79

1941-1958. Acoustic 16" flat-top, square shoulder dreadnought, walnut back and sides until '49 and laminated maple back and sides '49 on, natural, renamed FT 79 Texan by Gibson in '58.

1941-1943	Walnut	$2,200	$2,850
1944-1949	Walnut	$2,000	$2,600
1949-1958	Maple	$1,600	$2,075

FT 79 Texan

1958-1970, 1993-1995. Renamed from Epiphone FT 79, Gibson-made acoustic flat-top, mahogany back and sides, sunburst or natural top, Gibson Montana made 170 in '93-'95.

1958-1959		$2,400	$3,150
1960-1964		$2,350	$3,050
1965		$2,250	$2,950
1966-1967		$2,100	$2,750
1968-1969		$1,750	$2,300
1970		$1,525	$1,975

Paul McCartney 1964 Texan (U.S.A.)

2005-2006. Reproduction of McCartney's '64 Texan made in Gibson's Montana plant, two runs, one of 40 guitars ('05), second of 250 ('05-'06). First 40 were hand-aged and came with Sir Paul's autograph, display case and certificate; the 250 run were not-hand aged, but have signed labels.

2005-2006		$2,850	$3,700

Paul McCartney 1964 Texan (Japan)

2006-2010. Limited run of 1,964 guitars.

2006-2010		$1,100	$1,425

1964 Texan (Inspired By Series)

2010-2019. Imported production model, acoustic/electric, non-adjustable bridge.

2010-2019		$240	$310

FT 85 Serenader 12-String

1963-1969. 12 strings, mahogany back and sides, dot inlay, natural.

1963-1964		$850	$1,100
1965		$700	$900
1966-1969		$650	$850

FT 90 El Dorado

1963-1970. Dreadnought flat-top acoustic, mahogany back and sides, multi-bound front and back, natural.

1963-1964		$1,900	$2,450
1965		$1,450	$1,875
1966-1967		$1,350	$1,775
1968-1970		$1,275	$1,675

FT 95 Folkster

1966-1969. 14" small body, mahogany back and sides, natural, double white 'guards.

1966-1969		$550	$700

FT 98 Troubadour

1963-1969. 16" square shouldered drednought, maple back and sides, gold-plated hardware, classical width 'board.

1963-1964		$1,575	$2,050
1965		$1,450	$1,875
1966-1969		$1,350	$1,775

FT 110

1941-1958. Acoustic flat-top, natural, renamed the FT 110 Frontier by Gibson in '58.

1941-1943	Square shoulder	$3,500	$4,700
1944-1949	Square shoulder	$3,300	$4,300
1949-1954	Round shoulder	$3,100	$4,025
1954-1958	Mahogany neck	$3,100	$4,025

FT 110 Frontier

1958-1970, 1994. Renamed from FT 110, acoustic flat-top, natural or sunburst, Gibson Montana made 30 in '94.

1958-1959		$4,100	$5,400
1960-1964		$3,600	$4,800
1965		$3,377	$4,400
1966-1970		$3,200	$4,100

FT Deluxe

1939-1941. Acoustic flat-top, 16.5".

1939-1941		$5,000	$6,500

FT Deluxe Cutaway (FT 210)

1954-1957. Acoustic flat-top, cutaway, 16.5". Some labeled FT 210.

1954-1957		$4,900	$6,400

FT Series (Flat-Tops Japan)

1970s. In '70 Epiphone moved production to Japan. Various 6- to 12-string models were made, nearly all with bolt necks and small rectangular blue labels on the inside back, rangeing from the budget FT 120 to the top-of-the-line FT 570 Super Jumbo.

1970s	Various models	$150	$450

G 310

1989-2019. SG-style model with large 'guard and gig bag.

1989-2019		$200	$260

G 400

1989-2013. SG-style, 2 humbuckers, crown inlays.

1989-2013		$250	$325

G 400 Custom

1998-2000, 2003-2011. 3 humbucker version, gold harware, block inlays.

1998-2011		$350	$450

G 400 Deluxe

1999-2007. Flame maple top version of 2 humbucker 400.

1999-2007		$350	$450

G 400 Limited Edition

2001-2002. 400 with Deluxe Maestro lyra vibrola, cherry red.

2001-2002		$350	$450

G 400 Tony Iommi

2003-2011. SG-style model with cross 'board inlay markers, black finish.

2003-2011		$350	$450

G 1275 Custom Double Neck

1996-2011. SG-style alder body, 6- & 12-string, maple top, mahogany neck, cherry red, set neck. Also offered as bolt-neck Standard for '96-'98.

1996-2011		$550	$725

1955 Epiphone FT Deluxe Cutaway
Craig Brody

Epiphone G 400 Tony Iommi

GUITARS

*1967 Epiphone Howard
Roberts Standard*

Imaged by Heritage Auctions, HA.com

Epiphone Joe Pass Emperor II

MODEL YEAR	FEATURES	EXC. COND. LOW	HIGH

Genesis
1979-1980. Double-cut solidbody, 2 humbuckers with coil-taps, carved top, red or black, available as Custom, Deluxe, and Standard models, Taiwan import.

1979-1980		$625	$825

Granada (Non-cutaway Thinbody)
1962-1969. Non-cut thinline archtop, 1 f-hole, 1 pickup, trapeze tailpiece, sunburst finish.

1962-1964		$850	$1,100
1965-1969		$700	$900

Granada (Cutaway)
1965-1970. Single-cut version.

1965		$950	$1,225
1966-1970		$850	$1,100

Hollywood Masterbilt Tenor
1931-1936. Tenor version of the Triumph, acoustic archtop 15.4", 19-fret Brazilian rosewood 'board, diagonal diamond markers.

1931-1936		$1,400	$1,825

Howard Roberts Standard
1964-1970. Single-cut acoustic archtop, bound front and back, cherry or sunburst finish, listed in catalog as acoustic but built as electric.

1964		$1,800	$2,350
1965-1970		$1,475	$1,925

Howard Roberts Custom
1965-1970. Single-cut archtop, bound front and back, 1 pickup, walnut finish (natural offered '66 only).

1965-1970		$1,950	$2,550

Howard Roberts III
1987-1991. Two pickups, various colors.

1987-1991		$385	$500

Hummingbird/Hummingbird Pro
1994-present. Twin parallelogram inlays, hummingbird 'guard, replaced by Pro, with added electronics, in '13.

1994-2019		$200	$275

Inspiration Style A Tenor
1928-1929. Banjo resonator style body with round soundhole, A headstock logo, spruce top, walnut back, sides and neck.

1928-1929		$1,750	$2,250

Joe Pass/Joe Pass Emperor II
1995-2019. Single-cut archtop jazz guitar, 2 humbuckers, blocks, gold hardware, natural or sunbusrt, renamed from Emperor II (see that listing). Limited Edition all-gold finish or Wine Red were available early on.

1995-2019		$385	$500

Les Paul 100/LP-100
1993-2019. Affordable single-cut Les Paul, bolt-on neck.

1993-2019		$170	$220

Les Paul '56 Goldtop
1998-2013. Made in China, based on '56 Goldtop specs with 2 P-90s. Black finish was offered starting in '09.

1998-2013	Gold	$385	$500
2009-2013	Black	$385	$500

Les Paul Ace Frehley
2001. Les Paul Custom 3-pickups, Ace's signature on 22nd fret, lightning bolt markers.

2001		$700	$900

Les Paul Alabama Farewell Tour
2003. Limited production, 1 pickup single-cut Jr., American flag and Alabama logo graphics and band signatures on body, Certificate of Authenticity.

2003		$385	$500

Les Paul Black Beauty
1997-2019. Classic styling with three gold plated pickups, black finish, block markers.

1997-2019		$385	$500

Les Paul Classic
2003-2005. Classic Les Paul Standard specs, figured maple top, sunburst.

2003-2005		$385	$500

Les Paul Custom
1989-2011. Various colors.

1989-2011		$385	$500

Les Paul Custom Plus (Flame Top)
1998-2010. Flamed maple top version of 2 pickup Custom, gold hardware, sunburst.

1998-2010		$385	$500

Les Paul Custom Silverburst
2007-2008. 2 humbuckers, silverburst finish.

2007-2008		$385	$500

Les Paul Dale Earnhardt
2003. Dale Earnhardt graphics, 1 humbucker.

2003		$350	$450

Les Paul Deluxe
1998-2000. Typical mini-humbucker pickups.

1998-2000		$385	$500

Les Paul ES Limited Edition
1999-2000. Les Paul semi-hollow body with f-holes, carved maple top, gold hardware, cherry sunburst and other color options.

1999-2000	Custom	$525	$675
1999-2000	Standard	$525	$675

Les Paul Gold Top
1994-1998. Goldtop, 2 humbuckers. Listed as Les Paul Standard Goldtop in '94.

1994-1998		$385	$500

Les Paul Joe Perry Boneyard
2004-2006. Boneyard logo on headstock, figured Boneyard finish.

2004-2006		$450	$575

Les Paul Jr. '57 Reissue
2006. '57 Reissue on truss rod cover, logo and script Les Paul Junior stencil on headstock, lower back headstock states 'Epiphone Limited Edition Custom Shop'.

2006		$230	$300

Les Paul Music Rising
2006-2007. Music Rising (Katrina charity) graphic, 2 humbuckers.

2006-2007		$250	$325

Les Paul Sparkle L.E.
2001. Limited Edition LP Standard, silver, purple, red (and others) glitter finish, optional Bigsby.

2001		$350	$450

MODEL YEAR	FEATURES	EXC. COND. LOW	HIGH

Les Paul Special
1994-2000, 2020-present. Double-cut, bolt neck. Reintroduced in '20 with P-90 Pro pickups, CTS electronics, TV yellow finish.

1994-2000		$175	$225

Les Paul Special II
1996-2019. Economical Les Paul, 2 pickups, single-cut, various colors.

1996-2016	Player Pack with amp	$90	$120
1996-2019	Guitar only	$75	$100

Les Paul Special Limited Edition/TV Special
2006. Copy of single-cut late '50s Les Paul Special with TV finish.

2006		$210	$275

Les Paul Standard
1989-2019. Solid mahogany body, carved maple top, 2 humbuckers.

1989-2019	Various colors	$275	$350

Les Paul Standard Baritone
2004-2005. 27-3/4" long-scale baritone model.

2004-2005		$350	$450

Les Paul Standard Plus FMT
2003-2012. LP Standard figured curly maple sunburst top.

2003-2012		$310	$400

Les Paul Standard Ultra/Ultra II
2005-2012. LP Standard with chambered and contoured body, quilted maple top.

2005-2012	Ultra	$360	$465
2005-2012	Ultra II	$450	$575

Les Paul Studio
1995-present. Epiphone's version of Gibson LP Studio.

1995-2019		$210	$275

Les Paul XII
1998-2000. 12-string solidbody, trapeze tailpiece, flamed maple sunburst, standard configuration.

1998-2000		$390	$500

Slash Les Paul
1997-2000. Slash logo on body.

1997-2000		$600	$775

Slash Les Paul Goldtop
2008-2012. Limited Edition 2,000 made, goldtop finish, Seymour Duncan exposed humbuckers, Slash logo on truss rod cover, includes certificate of authenticity.

2008-2012	With COA	$650	$850

Slash Les Paul Standard Plus-Top
2008-2012. Figured top, exposed humbuckers, includes certificate of authenticity.

2008-2012	With COA	$725	$950

Zakk Wylde Les Paul Custom
2002-2019. Bull's-eye graphic, block markers, split diamond headstock inlay.

2002-2019		$390	$500

Madrid (Classical)
1962-1969. Classical, natural.

1962-1964		$325	$425
1965-1969		$225	$300

MD-30
1993. D-size, round metal resonator, spruce top with dual screens.

1993		$400	$525

Melody Tenor
1931-1937. 23" scale, bound body.

1931-1937	Masterbilt	$875	$1,150

Moderne
2000. Copy of '58 Gibson Moderne design, dot markers, Moderne script logo on 'guard, black.

2000		$525	$675

Navarre
1931-1940. Hawaiian flat-top, mahogany back and sides, bound top and back, dot inlay, brown finish.

1931-1937	Masterbilt label	$2,200	$2,850
1938-1940	Standard label	$2,000	$2,600

Nighthawk Standard
1995-2000. Epiphone's version of the Gibson Nighthawk, single-cut, bolt neck, figured top.

1995-2000		$250	$325

Noel Gallagher Union Jack/Super Nova
1997-2005. Limited edition, higher-end ES-335. Union Jack with British flag finish (introduced '99) or Supernova in solid blue.

1997-2005		$825	$1,075

Olympic (Acoustic Archtop)
1931-1949. Mahogany back and sides.

1931-1936	Smaller body	$750	$975
1937-1939	Larger body	$625	$800
1940-1949		$600	$775

Olympic Tenor (Acoustic Archtop)
1937-1949. 4-string version of the Olympic.

1937-1949		$550	$725

Olympic Single (Solidbody)
1960-1970. Slab body, the same as the mid-'60s Coronet, Wilshire and Crestwood Series, single-cut '60-'62, asymmetrical double-cut '63-'70, 2 Melody maker single-coil pickups, vibrato optional in '64 and standard by '65.

1960-1962	Sunburst, single-cut	$850	$1,100
1963-1964	Sunburst, double-cut	$750	$975
1965-1970	Sunburst	$650	$850

Olympic Double (Solidbody)
1960-1969. Slab body, the same as the mid-'60s Coronet, Wilshire and Crestwood Series, single-cut '60-'62, asymmetrical-cut '63-'70, 2 Melody Maker single-coils, vibrato optional in '64 and standard by '65.

1960-1963	Sunburst, single-cut	$1,450	$1,900
1963-1964	Sunburst, double-cut	$1,300	$1,700
1965-1969	Cherry, sunburst	$1,100	$1,400

Olympic (3/4 Scale Solidbody)
1960-1963. 22" scale, sunburst.

1960-1963		$800	$1,050

Olympic Special (Solidbody)
1962-1970. Short neck with neck body joint at the 16th fret (instead of the 22nd), single Melody Maker-style single-coil bridge pickup, small headstock, double-cut slab body, dot markers, Maestro or Epiphone vibrato optional '64-'65, slab body contour changes in '65 from symmetrical to asymmetrical with slightly longer bass horn, sunburst.

1962-1964	Symmetrical	$550	$700
1965-1970	Asymmetrical	$475	$625

Epiphone Les Paul Standard
Steve Alvito

1965 Epiphone Olympic Special
Carter Vintage Guitars

GUITARS

1964 Epiphone Professional
Rivington Guitars

1961 Epiphone Sheraton
Killer Vintage

MODEL YEAR	FEATURES	EXC. COND. LOW	HIGH
PR Series			
1980-2004. Budget acoustics, mainly D size but some smaller, cut and non-cut bodies.			
1980-2004	Various models	$175	$350
Pro 1			
1989-1996. Solidbody, double-cut, 1 single-coil and 1 humbucking pickup, bolt-on neck, various colors.			
1989-1996		$300	$390
Pro 2			
1995-1998. Higher-end Pro I with Steinberger DB bridge, set-neck, 2 humbuckers, various colors.			
1995-1998		$300	$390
Professional			
1962-1967. Double-cut, thinline archtop, 1 pickup, mahogany finish. Values include matching Professional amp.			
1962-1964	With matching amp	$2,150	$2,800
1965	With matching amp	$1,850	$2,400
1966-1967	With matching amp	$1,600	$2,100
Recording A			
1928-1931. Asymmetrical body flat-top with exaggerated treble bout cutaway, celluloid headstock veneer, dot inlays. All Recording models were offered in concert or auditorium body sizes.			
1928-1931	Standard 6-string	$1,400	$1,850
1928-1931	Tenor 4-string	$1,000	$1,300
Recording B			
1928-1931. As Recording A but with arched back, bound fingerboard, fancier body binding and zigzagging double slotted-diamond inlays.			
1928-1931		$1,950	$2,550
Recording C			
1928-1931. As Recording B but with arched top.			
1928-1931		$2,100	$2,700
Recording D			
1928-1931. As Recording C, but with large cross-hatched block inlays.			
1928-1931		$2,700	$3,500
Recording E			
1928-1931. As Recording D, but with large floral engraved block inlays.			
1928-1931		$3,500	$4,500
Ritz			
1940-1949. 15.5" acoustic archtop, large cello f-holes, dot inlays, no headstock ornamentation other than script Epiphone inlay, blond finish.			
1940-1949		$650	$850
Riviera			
1962-1970. Double-cut thinline archtop, 2 mini-humbuckers, Royal Tan standard finish changing to sunburst in '65, cherry optional by '66-'70, additional 250 were made in Nashville in '93-'94, a Riviera import was available in '82 and for '94-'06.			
1962-1964	Tan or custom cherry	$3,200	$4,200
1964	Sunburst	$3,100	$4,000
1965	Sunburst, cherry	$2,800	$3,600
1966-1967	Sparkling Burgundy	$2,700	$3,500
1966-1970	Sunburst, cherry	$2,600	$3,350
1967-1968	Walnut	$2,600	$3,350

MODEL YEAR	FEATURES	EXC. COND. LOW	HIGH
Riviera (U.S.A.)			
1993-1994. Made in U.S.A. on back of headstock.			
1993-1994		$975	$1,300
Riviera Reissue (Korea)			
1994-2006. Korean-made contemporary reissue, natural.			
1994-2006		$400	$525
Riviera 12-String			
1965-1970. Double-cut, 12 strings, thinline archtop, 2 mini-humbuckers, sunburst or cherry.			
1965-1970		$2,200	$2,850
Riviera 12-String Reissue (Korea)			
1997-2000. Korean-made reissue, natural.			
1997	Humbuckers	$700	$900
1998-2000	Mini-hums	$400	$525
Royal			
1931-1935. 15 1/2" acoustic archtop, mahogany back and sides, dot markers, sunburst, bound top, back and neck, Masterbilt headstock logo.			
1931-1935		$1,150	$1,500
S-900			
1986-1989. Neck-thru-body, locking Bender tremolo system, 2 pickups with individual switching and a coil-tap control.			
1986-1989		$300	$400
SC350			
1976-1979. Mahogany solidbody, scroll bass horn, rosewood 'board, dot inlays, bolt neck, 2 humbuckers, made in Japan.			
1976-1979	Mahogany	$525	$675
SC450			
1976-1979. Like SC350, but with maple body, glued neck, and coil tap.			
1976-1979	Maple	$525	$675
SC550			
1976-1979. Like SC450, but with gold hardware, block inlays, neck and body binding, and ebony 'board.			
1976-1979	Maple, gold hdwr	$525	$675
Seville EC-100 (Classical)			
1938-1941, 1961-1969 (Gibson-made). Classical guitar, mahogany back and sides, natural, the '61-'63 version also available with a pickup.			
1961-1964		$375	$500
1965-1969		$325	$425
SG Special			
2000-present. SG body, dot markers, 2 open-coil humbuckers.			
2000-2016	Player Pack with amp	$105	$135
2000-2019	Guitar only	$80	$105
Sheraton			
1958-1970, 1993-1994. Double-cut thinline archtop, 2 New York pickups '58-'60, 2 mini-humbuckers '61 on, frequensator tailpiece, multi-bound, gold-plated hardware, sunburst or natural finish with cherry optional by '65.			
1958-1960	Natural, NY pus	$7,500	$10,000
1959-1964	Sunburst, mini-hums	$6,700	$9,000
1961-1964	Natural, mini-hums	$7,500	$10,000

MODEL YEAR	FEATURES	EXC. COND. LOW	HIGH
1962	Cherry, few made	$6,700	$9,000
1965	Cherry, natural	$5,000	$6,700
1965	Sunburst	$4,000	$5,300
1966-1967	Natural	$4,800	$6,300
1966-1970	Cherry, sunburst	$3,700	$4,900

Sheraton (Japan)

1982-1983. Early reissue, not to be confused with Sheraton II issued later, natural or sunburst.

1982-1983		$1,300	$1,700

Sheraton (Reissue U.S.A.)

1993-1994, 2005. An additional 250 American-made Sheratons were built from '93-'94.

1993-1994		$1,750	$2,250
2005		$1,750	$2,250

Sheraton II (Reissue)

1986-present. Contemporary reissue, natural or sunburst.

1986-2019		$350	$460

Slasher

2001. Reverse offset double cut solidbody, bolt neck, six-on-a-side tuners, 2 pickups, dot markers.

2001		$325	$425

Sorrento (1 pickup)

1960-1970. Single-cut thinline archtop, 1 pickup in neck position, tune-o-matic bridge, nickel-plated hardware, sunburst, natural or Royal Olive finish, (cherry or sunburst by '68).

1960-1964		$1,575	$2,050
1965		$1,500	$1,950
1966-1970		$1,400	$1,800

Sorrento (2 pickups)

1960-1970. Single-cut thinline archtop, 2 pickups, tune-o-matic bridge, nickel-plated hardware, sunburst, natural or Royal Olive finish, (cherry or sunburst by '68).

1960-1964		$2,400	$3,100
1965		$2,000	$2,600
1966-1970		$1,900	$2,500

Sorrento (Reissue)

1994-2000. Reissue of 2 pickup model, import.

1994-2000		$450	$575

Spartan

1934-1949. Acoustic archtop, 16 3/8", laminated maple body, multi-bound, trapeze tailpiece, sunburst or natural.

1934-1939	Sunburst	$700	$925
1940-1949	Sunburst	$625	$825
1941-1947	Natural	$700	$925

Special/SG Special (U.S.A.)

1979-1983. SG Special body style, dot markers, 2 exposed humbuckers, Special logo on truss rod cover.

1979-1983		$625	$825

Spider/The Spider

1997-2000. Wood body resonator, spider bridge, square neck.

1997-2000		$375	$475

Spirit I/Spirit II

1982. U.S.-made electric solidbody, Spirit logo on truss rod cover, double-cut, flat-top with 1 (I) or 2 (II) humbuckers.

1982		$900	$1,175

SST

2007-2011. Acoustic/electric solidbody, either Classic (nylon) or Studio (steel). Chet Atkins model also available.

2007-2011		$250	$325

Tom Delonge Signature ES-333

2008-2019. One humbucker, dot inlays.

2008-2019		$325	$400

Trailer Park Troubadour Airscreamer

2003-2005. Airstream trailer-shaped body, identifying logo on headstock.

2003-2005		$375	$475

Triumph

1931-1957. 15 1/4" '31-'33, 16 3/8" '33-'36, 17 3/8" '36-'57, walnut back and sides until '33, laminated maple back and sides '33, solid maple back and sides '34, natural or sunburst.

1931-1932	Sunburst, laminated walnut	$1,200	$1,550
1933	Sunburst, laminated maple	$1,200	$1,550
1934-1935	Sunburst, solid maple	$1,250	$1,600
1936-1940	Sunburst 17 3/8" body	$1,250	$1,600
1941-1949	Natural	$1,250	$1,600
1941-1949	Sunburst	$1,250	$1,600
1950-1957	Natural	$1,250	$1,600
1950-1957	Sunburst	$1,150	$1,500

Triumph Regent (Cutaway)

1948-1969. Acoustic archtop, single-cut, F-holes, renamed Triumph Cutaway in '53, then Gibson listed this model as just the Triumph from '58-'69.

1948-1952	Regent, natural	$1,850	$2,400
1948-1952	Regent, sunburst	$1,600	$2,100
1953-1957	Cutaway, natural	$1,850	$2,400
1953-1957	Cutaway, sunburst	$1,600	$2,100
1958-1964	Sunburst	$1,600	$2,100
1965	Sunburst	$1,550	$2,000
1966-1969	Sunburst	$1,450	$1,900

USA Map Guitar

1982-1983. U.S.-made promotional model, solidbody electric, mahogany body shaped like U.S. map, 2 pickups, natural.

1982-1983		$2,100	$2,700

USA Map Guitar Limited Edition

2007	Import	$450	$575

Vee-Wee (Mini Flying V)

2003. Mini Flying V, single bridge pickup, gig bag.

2003		$75	$95

Wildkat

2001-2019. Thinline, single-cut, hollow-body, 2 P-90s, Bigsby tailpiece.

2001-2019		$250	$325

Wilshire

1959-1970. Double-cut solidbody, 2 pickups, tune-o-matic bridge, cherry.

1959	Symmetrical	$3,000	$3,900
1960-1962	Thinner-style, P-90s	$2,175	$2,800
1962-1963	Symmetrical, mini-hums	$2,250	$2,900

1962 Epiphone Sorrento
Bernunzio Uptown Music

Epiphone Wildkat

1964 Epiphone Wilshire
Imaged by Heritage Auctions, HA.com

Epiphone Zephyr De Luxe Regent

MODEL YEAR	FEATURES	EXC. COND. LOW	HIGH
1963-1964	Asymmetrical, mini-hums	$2,000	$2,600
1965-1966	Custom color	$2,200	$2,900
1965-1966	Standard color	$1,700	$2,200
1967-1970		$1,500	$1,950

Wilshire 12-String
1966-1968. Solidbody, 2 pickups, cherry.

1966-1968		$1,500	$1,950

Wilshire II
1984-1985. Solidbody, maple body, neck and 'board, 2 humbuckers, 3-way switch, coil-tap, 1 tone and 1 volume control, various colors.

1984-1985		$325	$425

Windsor (1 Pickup)
1959-1962. Archtop, 1 or 2 pickups, single-cut thinline, sunburst or natural finish.

1959-1960	Natural, NY pu	$1,850	$2,400
1959-1960	Sunburst, NY pu	$1,750	$2,300
1961-1962	Natural, mini-hum	$1,625	$2,100
1961-1962	Sunburst, mini-hum	$1,550	$2,000

Windsor (2 Pickups)
1959-1962. Archtop, 1 or 2 pickups, single-cut thinline, sunburst or natural finish.

1959-1960	Natural, NY pu	$2,200	$2,850
1959-1960	Sunburst NY pu	$2,100	$2,725
1961-1962	Natural, mini-hum	$1,900	$2,450
1961-1962	Sunburst, mini-hum	$1,800	$2,325

X-1000
1986-1989. Electric solidbody, Korean-made, various colors.

1986-1989		$250	$325

Zenith
1931-1969. Acoustic archtop, bound front and back, f-holes, sunburst.

1931-1933		$800	$1,050
1934-1935	14 3/4" body	$950	$1,250
1936-1949	16 3/8" body	$950	$1,250
1950-1957	Natural	$1,050	$1,375
1950-1957	Sunburst	$950	$1,250
1958-1969		$775	$1,000

Zephyr
1939-1957. Non-cut electric archtop, 1 pickup, bound front and back, blond or sunburst (first offered '53), called Zephyr Electric starting in '54.

1939-1940	Natural, 16 3/8", metal handrest pu	$1,050	$1,375
1941-1943	Natural, no metal handrest	$1,050	$1,375
1944-1946	Natural, top mounted pu	$1,050	$1,375
1947-1948	17 3/8", metal covered pu	$1,050	$1,375
1949-1957	Natural, NY pu	$950	$1,250
1953-1957	Sunburst, NY pu	$850	$1,125

Zephyr Regent
1950-1953. Single-cut electric archtop, 1 pickup, natural or sunburst, called Zephyr Cutaway for '54-'57.

1950-1953	Natural	$1,750	$2,300
1950-1953	Sunburst	$1,600	$2,100

MODEL YEAR	FEATURES	EXC. COND. LOW	HIGH

Zephyr Cutaway
1954-1957. Cutaway version of Zephyr Electric, called Zephyr Regent for 1950-'53.

1954-1957	Natural	$1,875	$2,450
1954-1957	Sunburst	$1,675	$2,200

Zephyr Electric (Cutaway)
1958-1964. Gibson-made version, thinline archtop, single-cut, 2 pickups, natural or sunburst.

1958-1959	Natural	$1,900	$2,450
1958-1959	Sunburst	$1,600	$2,075
1960-1964	Natural	$1,700	$2,200
1960-1964	Sunburst	$1,500	$1,950

Zephyr De Luxe (Non-cutaway)
1941-1954. Non-cut electric archtop, 1 or 2 pickups, multi-bound front and back, gold-plated hardware, natural or sunburst.

1941-1942	Natural	$1,600	$2,100
1945-1949	Natural, 1 pu	$1,875	$2,450
1945-1954	Natural, 2 pus	$2,025	$2,650
1950-1954	Sunburst, 2 pus	$1,875	$2,450

Zephyr De Luxe Regent (Cutaway)
1948-1954. Single-cut electric archtop, 1 or 2 pickups until '50, then only 2, gold-plated hardware, sunburst or natural finish. Renamed Deluxe Electric in '54.

1948-1949	Natural, 1 pu	$2,025	$2,650
1948-1949	Natural, 2 pus	$2,650	$3,400
1948-1949	Sunburst, 1 pu	$1,875	$2,450
1948-1949	Sunburst, 2 pus	$2,400	$3,100
1950-1954	Natural, 2 pus	$2,550	$3,300
1950-1954	Sunburst, 2 pus	$2,300	$3,000

Zephyr Emperor Regent
1950-1954. Archtop, single rounded cutaway, multi-bound body, 3 pickups, sunburst or natural finish, renamed Emperor Electric in '54.

1950-1954	Natural	$4,500	$6,000
1950-1954	Sunburst	$3,500	$4,700

Zephyr Tenor
1940-1950. Natural, figured top.

1940-1950		$700	$925

Zephyr Blues Deluxe
1999-2005. Based on early Gibson ES-5, 3 P-90 pickups.

1999-2005		$625	$800

Epoch
Economy level imports made by Gibson and sold through Target stores.

Equator Instruments
2006-present. Production/custom, professional and premium grade, solidbody, hollowbody, acoustic and classical guitars built in Chicago, Illinois by luthier David Coleman.

Erlewine
1979-present. Professional and premium grade, production/custom guitars built by luthier Mark Erlewine in Austin, Texas. Erlewine also produces the Chiquita brand travel guitar.

MODEL YEAR	FEATURES	EXC. COND. LOW	HIGH

Esoterik Guitars

Professional grade, production/custom, electric guitars built in San Luis Obispo, California by luthier Ryan Cook. He began with guitars in 2010 and plans to add basses.

ESP

1983-present. Intermediate, professional, and premium grade, production/custom, Japanese-made solidbody guitars and basses. Hisatake Shibuya founded Electronic Sound Products (ESP), a chain of retail stores, in '75. They began to produce replacement parts for electric guitars in '83 and in '85 started to make custom-made guitars. In '87 a factory was opened in Tokyo. In '86 ESP opened a sales office in New York, selling custom guitars and production models. From around '98 to ca. '02 they operated their California-based USA custom shop. In '96, they introduced the Korean-made LTD brand and in '03 introduced the Xtone brand, which was folded into LTD in '10. Hisatake Shibuya also operated 48th Street Custom Guitars during the '90s but he closed that shop in 2003.

20th Anniversary
1995. Solidbody, double-cut, ESP95 inlaid at 12th fret, gold.

1995		$950	$1,250

Eclipse Custom (U.S.A.)
1998-2002. U.S. Custom Shop-built, single-cut, mahogany body and maple top, various colors offered.

1998-2002		$625	$775

Eclipse Custom/Custom T (Import)
1986-1988, 2003-2010. Single-cut mahogany solidbody, earliest model with bolt dot marker neck, 2nd version with neck-thru and blocks, the Custom T adds locking trem. Current has quilt maple top.

1986-1987	Bolt, dots	$525	$650
1987-1988	Neck-thru, blocks	$625	$700
1987-1988	Neck-thru, Custom T	$550	$675

Eclipse Deluxe
1986-1988. Single-cut solidbody, 1 single-coil and 1 humbucker, vibrato, black.

1986-1988		$525	$650

Eclipse Series
1995-present. Recent Eclipse models.

1995-2000	Eclipse/Eclipse I	$450	$575
1996-2000	Eclipse Archtop	$450	$550

George Lynch M-1 Tiger/Sunburst Tiger
1996-present. Signature series, sunburst tiger finish.

1996-2019		$1,400	$1,800

Horizon (Import)
1986, 1996-2001. Double-cut neck-thru, bound ebony 'board, 1 single-coil and 1 humbucker, buffer preamp, various colors, reintroduced '96-'01with bolt neck, curved rounded point headstock.

1986		$550	$700
1996-2001		$550	$700

Horizon Classic (U.S.A.)
1993-1995. U.S.-made, carved mahogany body, set-neck, dot markers, various colors, optional mahogany body with figured maple top also offered.

1993-1995		$1,100	$1,350

Horizon Custom (U.S.A.)
1998-2001. U.S. Custom Shop-made, mahogany body, figured maple top, bolt-on neck, mostly translucent finish in various colors.

1998-2001		$1,100	$1,350

Horizon Deluxe (Import)
1989-1992. Horizon Custom with bolt-on neck, various colors.

1989-1992		$575	$725

Hybrid I (Import)
1986 only. Offset double-cut body, bolt maple neck, dots, six-on-a-side tuners, vibrato, various colors.

1986		$300	$375

Hybrid II (Import)
1980s. Offset double-cut, rosewood 'board on maple bolt neck, lipstick neck pickup, humbucker at bridge, Hybrid II headstock logo.

1980s		$325	$425

LTD EC-GTA Guitarsonist
2008. Flame graphic by Matt Touchard, 100 made.

2008		$1,000	$1,250

LTD EC-SIN Sin City
2008. Vegas graphic by Matt Touchard, 100 made.

2008		$1,550	$1,900

LTD Series
1998-present. Range of prices due to wide range of models.

1998-2018	Various models	$100	$550

Maverick/Maverick Deluxe
1989-1992. Offset double-cut, bolt maple or rosewood cap neck, dot markers, double locking vibrola, six-on-a-side tuners, various colors.

1989-1992		$325	$400

Metal I
1986 only. Offset double-cut, bolt maple neck, rosewood cap, dots, various colors.

1986		$325	$400

Metal II
1986 only. Single horn V body, bolt on maple neck with rosewood cap, dot markers, various colors.

1986		$350	$450

Metal III
1986 only. Reverse offset body, bolt maple neck with maple cap, dot markers, gold hardware, various colors.

1986		$375	$450

M-I Custom
1987-1994. Offset double-cut thru-neck body, offset block markers, various colors.

1987-1994		$450	$600

M-I Deluxe
1987-1989. Double-cut solidbody, rosewood 'board, 2 single-coils and 1 humbucker, various colors.

1987-1989		$450	$600

M-II
1989-1994, 1996-2000. Double-cut solidbody, reverse headstock, bolt-on maple or rosewood cap neck, dot markers, various colors.

1989-1994		$450	$600

ESP Eclipse E-II DB VB

ESP George Lynch M-1 Tiger

1996 ESP Vintage Plus S
Curtis Hill

Essex (SX) EH3D-CS

MODEL YEAR	FEATURES	EXC. COND. LOW	HIGH

M-II Custom
1990-1994. Double-cut solidbody, reverse headstock, neck-thru maple neck, rosewood cap, dot markers, various colors.

1990-1994		$450	$600

M-II Deluxe
1990-1994. Double-cut solidbody, reverse headstock, Custom with bolt-on neck, various colors.

1990-1994		$450	$600

Mirage Custom
1986-1990. Double-cut neck-thru solidbody, 2-octave ebony 'board, block markers, 1 humbucker and 2 single-coil pickups, locking trem, various colors.

1986-1990		$500	$700

Mirage Standard
1986 only. Single pickup version of Mirage Custom, various colors.

1986		$400	$525

Phoenix
1987 only. Offset, narrow waist solidbody, thru-neck mahogany body, black hardware, dots.

1987		$550	$650

Phoenix Contemporary
Late-1990s. 3 pickups vs. 2 on the earlier offering.

1998		$750	$875

S-454/S-456
1986-1987. Offset double-cut, bolt maple or rosewood cap neck, dot markers, various colors.

1986-1987		$425	$525

S-500
1991-1993. Double-cut figured ash body, bolt-on neck, six-on-a-side tuners, various colors.

1991-1993		$500	$600

SV-II
2009-2012. Neck-thru offset v-shaped solidbody, 2 pickups, dot inlays, part of Standard Series, made in Japan.

2009-2012		$1,400	$1,700

Traditional
1989-1990. Double-cut, 3 pickups, tremolo, various colors.

1989-1990		$525	$650

Vintage/Vintage Plus S
1995-1998. Offset double-cut, bolt maple or rosewood cap neck, dot markers, Floyd Rose or standard vibrato, various colors.

1995	20th Anniv Ed, gold	$750	$950
1995-1998		$700	$850

Viper Series
2004-present. Offset double-cut SG style, 2 humbuckers, various models

2010	300M	$275	$350

Espana
1963-ca. 1973. Primarily acoustic guitars distributed by catalog wholesalers Bugeleisen & Jacobson. Built by Watkins in England.

Classical
1963-1973. Guitars with white spruce fan-braced tops with walnut, mahogany, or rosewood back and sides.

1963-1973		$155	$200

EL (Electric) Series
1963-1973. Various double-cut models, 2 or 3 pickups, tremolo, '63-ca. '68 with nitro finish, ca. '69-'73 poly finish.

1963-1973	EL-30, 2 pickups	$225	$300
1963-1973	EL-31, 3 pickups	$275	$350
1963-1973	EL-32 (XII)	$225	$300
1963-1973	EL-36, 2 pickups	$275	$350

Jumbo Folk
1969-1973. Natural.

1969-1973		$175	$275

Essex (SX)
1985-present. Budget grade, production, electric and acoustic guitars imported by Rondo Music of Union, New Jersey. They also offer basses.

Solidbody Electric
1980s-1990s. Copies of classic designs like the Les Paul and Telecaster.

1980s		$105	$130

Este
1909-1939. Luthier Felix Staerke's Este factory built classical and archtop guitars in Hamburg, Germany. They also built high-end banjos. The plant ceased instrument production in '39 and was destroyed in WW II.

Esteban
2002-present. Budget grade, production, acoustic and classical import guitars sold as packages with classical guitarist Esteban's (Stephen Paul) guitar lesson program, other miscellany and sometimes a small amp.

Steel and Nylon Acoustics

2002-2019	Various models	$25	$155

EtaVonni
2008-2010. Luthier Ben Williams built premium grade, production/custom, carbon fiber and aluminum electric guitars in Kentwood, Michigan.

Euphonon
1930-1944. A Larson brothers brand, most Euphonons date from 1934-'44. Body sizes range from 13 ½" to the 19" and 21" super jumbos. The larger body 14-fret neck sizes have body woods of Brazilian rosewood, mahogany, or maple. Ornamentation and features are as important to value as rosewood vs. mahogany. Production also included mandolins, and most models were A-style, with teardrop body and flat backs.

Everett Guitars
1977-present. Luthier Kent Everett builds his premium and presentation grade, production/custom, steel-string and classical guitars in Atlanta, Georgia. From '01 to '03, his Laurel Series guitars were built in conjunction with Terada in Japan and set up in Atlanta. He has also built archtops, semi-hollow and solidbody electrics, resonators, and mandolins.

MODEL YEAR	FEATURES	EXC. COND. LOW	HIGH

Evergreen Mountain

1971-present. Professional grade, custom, flat-top and tenor guitars, basses and mandolins built by luthier Jerry Nolte in Cove, Oregon. He also built over 100 dulcimers in the '70s.

Everly Guitars

1982-2001. Luthier Robert Steinegger built these premium grade, production/custom flat-tops in Portland, Oregon (also see Steinegger Guitars).

EVH

2007-present. Eddie Van Halen works with FMIC to create a line of professional and premium grade, production, solidbody guitars built in the U.S. and imported from other countries. They also build amps.

Wolfgang Special

2010-present. Made in Japan, offset double-cut solidbody, figured maple top over basswood body, birdseye maple 'board, 2 pickups, tremolo.

2010-2019		$800	$1,050

Excelsior

The Excelsior Company started offering accordions in 1924 and had a large factory in Italy by the late '40s. They started building guitars around '62, which were originally plastic covered, switching to paint finishes in the mid '60s. They also offered classicals, acoustics, archtops and amps. By the early '70s they were out of the guitar business.

The Excelsior brand was also used ca.1885-ca.1890 on guitars and banjos by Boston's John C. Haynes & Co.

Dyno and Malibu

1960s. Offset, double cut, 2 or 3 pickups, vibrato.

1960s	Dyno I	$250	$350
1960s	Dyno II	$275	$375
1960s	Malibu I	$275	$375
1960s	Malibu II	$300	$400

Exlusive

2008-2013. Intermediate grade, production, electric guitars and basses, imported from Asia and finished in Italy by luthier Galeazzo Frudua.

Fairbuilt Guitar Co.

2000-present. Professional and premium grade, custom/production, archtop and flattop acoustic guitars built by luthiers Martin Fair and Stuart Orser in Loudoun County, Virginia. They also build mandolins and bouzoukis.

Falk

1989-present. Professional and premium grade, production/custom archtop guitars built by luthier Dave Falk, originally in Independence, Missouri, and currently in Amarillo, Texas. He also builds mandolins and dulcimers.

Fano

1995-present. Professional grade, production/custom, solidbody electric guitars and basses built by luthier Dennis Fano in Fleetwood, Pennsylvania.

Farnell

1989-present. Luthier Al Farnell builds his professional grade, production, solidbody guitars and basses in Ontario, California. He also offers his intermediate grade, production, C Series which is imported from China.

Fat Cat Custom Guitars

2004-present. Intermediate to premium grade, production/custom, solidbody and chambered electric guitars and basses built in Carpentersville, Illinois by luthier Scott Bond.

Favilla

1890-1973. Founded by the Favilla family in New York, the company began to import guitars in 1970, but folded in '73. American-made models have the Favilla family crest on the headstock. Import models used a script logo on the headstock.

Acoustic Classical

1960s-1973. Various nylon-string classical models.

1960s-1969		$155	$400
1970-1973	Import	$155	$400

Acoustic Flat-Top

1960s-1973. Various flat-top models, 000 to D sizes, mahogany to spruce.

1960s-1969	US-made, Crest logo	$155	$400
1970-1973	Import, Script logo	$155	$400

Fell

One of the many guitar brands built by Japan's Matsumoku company.

Fender

1946 (1945)-present. Budget, intermediate, professional and premium grade, production/custom, electric, acoustic, acoustic/electric, classical, and resonator guitars built in the U.S. and overseas. They also build amps, basses, mandolins, bouzoukis, banjos, lap steels, ukes, violins, and PA gear. Ca. 1939 Leo Fender opened a radio and record store called Fender Radio Service, where he met Clayton Orr 'Doc' Kauffman, and in '45 they started KF Company to build lap steels and amps. In '46 Kauffman left and Fender started the Fender Electric Instrument Company.

In January '65 CBS purchased the company and renamed it Fender Musical Instruments Corporation. The CBS takeover is synonymous with a perceived decline in quality among musicians and collectors, and Pre-CBS Fenders are more valuable. Fender experienced some quality problems in the late '60s. Small headstock is enlarged in '65 and the 4-bolt neck is replaced by the 3-bolt in '71. With high value and relative scarcity of Pre-CBS Fenders, even CBS-era instruments are now sought by collectors.

Fairbuilt Barnburner

Farnell Guitars

1960 Fender Stratocaster

1960 Fender Stratocaster
Folkway Music

Leo Fender was kept on as consultant until '70 and went on to design guitars for Music Man and G&L.

In '82 Fender Japan is established to produce licensed Fender copies for sale in Japan. Also in '82, the Fender Squier brand debuts on Japanese-made instruments for the European market and by '83 they were imported into U.S. In March '85, the company was purchased by an investor group headed by Bill Schultz but the purchase does not include the Fullerton factory. While a new factory was being established at Corona, California, all Fender Contemporary Stratocasters and Telecasters were made either by Fender Japan or in Seoul, Korea. U.S. production resumes in late '85. The Fender Custom Shop, run by Michael Stevens and John Page, opens in '87. The Mexican Fender factory is established in '90. In '95, Fender purchased the Guild guitar company. On January 3, 2002, Fender Musical Instruments Corporation (FMIC) recapitalized a minority portion of common stock, with partners including Roland Corporation U.S. and Weston Presidio, a private equity firm in San Francisco. In 2003, Fred Gretsch Enterprises, Ltd granted Fender the exclusive rights to develop, produce, market and distribute Gretsch guitars worldwide. Around the same time, Fender also acquired the Jackson/Charvel Guitar Company. In October, '04, Fender acquired Tacoma Guitars. On January 1, '08, Fender acquired Kaman Music Corporation and the Hamer, Ovation, and Genz Benz brands. The Groove Tubes brand was purchased by Fender in June, '08.

Dating older Fender guitars is an imprecise art form at best. While serial numbers were used, they were frequently not in sequence, although a lower number will frequently be older than a substantially higher number. Often necks were dated, but only with the date the neck was finished, not when the guitar was assembled. Generally, dating requires triangulating between serial numbers, neck dates, pot dates, construction details and model histories.

From '50 through roughly '65, guitars had more-or-less sequential numbers in either 4 or 5 digits, though some higher numbers may have an initial 0 or - prefix. These can range from 0001 to 99XXX.

From '63 into '65, some instruments had serial numbers beginning with an L prefix plus 5 digits (LXXXXX). Beginning in '65 with the CBS takeover into '76, 6-digit serial numbers were stamped on F neckplates roughly sequentially from 10XXXX to 71XXXX. In '76 the serial number was shifted to the headstock decal. From '76-'77, the serial number began with a bold-face 76 or S6 plus 5 digits (76XXXXX).

From '77 on, serial numbers consisted of a 2-place prefix plus 5 digits (sometimes 6 beginning in '91): '77 (S7, S8), '78 (S7, S8, S9), '79 (S9, E0), '80-'81 (S9, E0, E1), '82 (E1, E2, E3), '84-'85 (E4), '85-'86 (no U.S. production), '87 (E4), '88 (E4, E8), '89 (E8, E9), '90 (E9, N9, N0), '91 (N0), '92 (N2).

Serial numbers on guitars made by Fender Japan consist of either a 2-place prefix plus 5 digits or a single prefix letter plus 6 digits: '82-'84 (JV), '83-'84 (SQ), '84-'87, '85-'86+ (A, B, C), '86-'87 (F), '87-'88+

(G), '88-'89 (H), '89-'90 (I, J), '90-'91 (K), '91-'92 (L), '92-'93 (M).

Factors affecting Fender values: The sale to CBS in '65 is a major point in Fender instrument values as CBS made many changes collectors feel affected quality. The '70s introduced the 3-bolt neck and other design changes that aren't as popular with guitarists. Custom color instruments, especially Strats from the '50s and early-'60s, can be valued much more than the standard sunburst finishes. In '75 Fender dropped the optional custom colors and started issuing the guitars in a variety of standard colors.

Custom colors are worth more than standard colors. For a Stratocaster, Telecaster Custom and Esquire Custom the standard color is sunburst, while the Telecaster and Esquire standard color is blond. The first Precision Bass standard color was blond but changed to sunburst in the late 1950s. The Jazz Bass standard color is sunburst. The Telecaster Thinline standard color is natural. To understand a custom color, you need to know what the standard color is. Some custom colors are rarer than others. Below is a list of the custom colors offered in 1960. They are sorted in ascending order with the most valuable color, Shell Pink, listed last. For example, Fiesta Red is typically worth 12% more than a Black or Blond, though all are in the Common Color category. In the Rare Color group, Foam Green is normally worth 8% more than Shoreline Gold. The two Very Rare colors are often worth 30% more than Shoreline Gold. In our pricing information we will list the standard color, then the relative value of a common custom color, and then the value of a rare custom color. Remember that the amount of fade also affects the price. These prices are for custom colors with slight or no fade, which implies a lighter color, but with custom colors a faded example can also be much darker in color. Blue can fade to dark green. White can fade to deep yellow.

The various Telecaster and Stratocaster models are grouped under those general headings.

Common Color: Black, Blond, Candy Apple Red, Olympic White, Lake Placid Blue, Dakota Red, Daphne Blue, Fiesta Red

Rare Color: Shoreline Gold, Inca Silver, Burgundy Mist, Sherwood Green, Sonic Blue, Foam Green

Rare (Very Rare) Color: Surf Green, Shell Pink

1960 - 1962: Black, Blond, Burgundy Mist, Dakota Red, Daphne Blue, Fiesta Red, Foam Green, Inca Silver, Lake Placid Blue, Olympic White, Shell Pink, Sherwood Green, Shoreline Gold, Sonic Blue, Sunburst, Surf Green

1963 - 1964: Black, Blond, Burgundy Mist, Candy Apple Red, Dakota Red, Daphne Blue, Fiesta Red, Foam Green, Inca Silver, Lake Placid Blue, Olympic White, Sherwood Green, Shoreline Gold, Sonic Blue, Sunburst, Surf Green

1965 - 1969: Black, Blond, Blue Ice, Candy Apple Red, Charcoal Frost, Dakota Red, Fiesta Red, Firemist Gold, Firemist Silver,

MODEL YEAR	FEATURES	EXC. COND. LOW	HIGH

Foam Green, Lake Placid Blue, Ocean Turquoise, Olympic White, Sonic Blue, Sunburst, Teal Green

1970 - 1971: Black, Blond, Candy Apple Red, Firemist Gold, Firemist Silver, Lake Placid Blue, Ocean Turquoise, Olympic White, Sonic Blue, Sunburst

1972: Black, Blond, Candy Apple Red, Lake Placid Blue, Olympic White, Sonic Blue, Sunburst

1973: Black, Blond, Candy Apple Red, Lake Placid Blue, Natural, Olympic White, Sunburst, Walnut

1974 - 1977: Black, Blond, Natural, Olympic White, Sunburst, Walnut

1978 - 1979: Antigua, Black, Blond, Natural, Olympic White, Sunburst, Walnut, Wine

Arrow
1969-1972. See listing for Musiclander.

Avalon
1985-1995. California Series, acoustic import, 6-on-a-side tuners, mahogany neck, back and sides (nato after '93), spruce top, various colors.

1985-1995		$180	$235

Balboa
1983-1987. California Series, acoustic import.

1983-1987		$300	$400

Brawler Baritone (Custom Shop)
2019-2020. Journeyman Relic, masterbuilt by Carlos Lopez.

2019-2020		$5,500	$7,000

Broadcaster
Mid-1950-early-'51. For a short time in early-'51, before being renamed the Telecaster, models had no Broadcaster decal; these are called No-casters by collectors.

1950	Blond	$54,000	$70,000
1951	Clipped decal, "No Caster"	$43,000	$56,000

Broadcaster Leo Fender Custom Shop
1999 only. Leo Fender script logo signature replaces Fender logo on headstock, Custom Shop Certificate signed by Phyllis Fender, Fred Gretsch, and William Schultz, includes glass display case and poodle guitar case.

1999		$4,500	$5,900

'50s Relic/'51 NoCaster Custom Shop
1995-2014. Called the '50s Relic NoCaster for '96-'99, and '51 NoCaster in NOS, Relic, or Closet Classic versions 2000-'10, with the Relic Series being the highest offering. From June '95 to June '99 Relic work was done outside of Fender by Vince Cunetto and included a certificate noting model and year built, an instrument without the certificate is worth less than the value shown. Blonde or Honey Blonde finish. Also in '09, the Limited '51 NoCaster Relic was offered with Twisted Tele neck pickup, 50 each in 2-tone sunburst or Dakota Red.

1995-1997	Cunetto built Relic	$2,500	$3,200
1997-1999	Cunetto era Closet Classic	$1,750	$2,300

MODEL YEAR	FEATURES	EXC. COND. LOW	HIGH
1997-1999	Cunetto era NOS	$1,750	$2,300
1998-1999	Cunetto era Relic	$2,075	$2,700
2000-2009	Closet Classic	$1,750	$2,300
2000-2014	NOS	$1,750	$2,300
2000-2014	Relic	$1,900	$2,450

'51 NoCaster Limited Edition
2009. Custom Shop Limited Edition, as above but with Twisted Tele neck pickup, 50 each in 2-tone sunburst or Dakota Red.

2009	Relic	$1,900	$2,450

Bronco
1967-1980. Slab solidbody, 1 pickup, tremolo, red.

1967-1968	Nitro	$1,050	$1,400
1969-1980	Poly	$925	$1,200

Buddy Miller Signature
2007-2009. Flat-top, Fishman Ellipse Aura, 6-on-a-side tuner headstock.

2007-2009		$625	$800

Bullet/Bullet Deluxe
1981-1983. Solidbody, came in 2- and 3-pickup versions (single-coil and humbucker), and single- and double-cut models, various colors. Becomes Squire Bullet in '85.

1981-1983	Various models	$525	$700

Catalina
1983-1995. California Series, acoustic dreadnought, import.

1983-1995		$175	$225

CD (Classic Design) Series
2006-present. Imported, intermediate grade, various models, acoustic or acoustic-electric, steel or nylon string.

2006-2019	High-end models	$270	$475
2006-2019	Low-end models	$120	$275

CG (Classical Guitar) Series
1995-2005. Imported, various nylon-string classical acoustic and acoustic/electric models, label on the inside back clearly indicates the model number, back and sides of rosewood, mahogany or other woods.

1995-2005		$50	$300

Concert
1963-1970. Acoustic flat-top slightly shorter than King/Kingman, spruce body, mahogany back and sides (optional Brazilian or Indian rosewood, zebrawood or vermillion), natural, sunburst optional by '68.

1963-1970	Natural or sunburst	$800	$1,075

Concord
1986-1995. Dreadnought flat-top, 6-on-a-side headstock, natural.

1986-1995		$105	$140

Coronado I
1966-1969. Thinline semi-hollowbody, double-cut, tremolo, 1 pickup, single-bound, dot inlay.

1966-1969	Various colors	$1,250	$1,650

Coronado II
1966-1969 (Antigua finish offered until '70). Thinline semi-hollowbody, double-cut, tremolo optional, 2 pickups, single-bound, block inlay, available in standard finishes but special issues offered in Antigua and 6 different Wildwood finishes (labeled on the pickguard as Wildwood I through Wildwood VI

2003 Fender '51 Nocaster Custom Shop
Carter Vintage Guitars

1967 Fender Coronado II
Tom Pfeifer

GUITARS

1968 Fender Coronado XII
Tim Kummer

1964 Fender Duo-Sonic
Robbie Keene

MODEL YEAR	FEATURES	EXC. COND. LOW	HIGH

to designate different colors). Wildwood finishes were achieved by injecting dye into growing trees.

1966-1969	Various colors	$1,475	$1,900
1966-1969	Wildwood	$2,025	$2,625
1967-1970	Antigua	$1,475	$1,900

Coronado XII

1966-1969 (Antigua finish offered until '70). Thinline semi-hollowbody, double-cut, 12 strings, 2 pickups, block inlay, standard, Antigua and Wildwood finishes available.

1966-1969	Various colors	$1,400	$1,850
1966-1969	Wildwood	$2,450	$3,200
1967-1970	Antigua	$1,700	$2,200

Custom

1969-1971. Six-string solidbody that used up parts from discontinued Electric XII, asymmetrical-cut, long headstock, 2 split pickups, sunburst. Also marketed as the Maverick.

| 1969-1971 | | $2,500 | $3,300 |

Cyclone

1998-2006. Mexican import, solidbody, contoured offset waist, poplar body, various colors.

| 1998-2006 | Various options | $400 | $525 |

D'Aquisto Elite

1984, 1989-1994, 1994-2002. Part of Fender's Master Series, 16" laminated maple-side archtop, single-cut, glued neck, 1 pickup, gold hardware, made in Japan until '94, in '94 the Fender Custom Shop issued a version that retailed at $6,000, various colors.

| 1984-2002 | | $1,925 | $2,500 |

D'Aquisto Standard

1984 (Serial numbers could range from 1983-1985). Like D'Aquisto Elite, but with 2 pickups.

| 1984 | | $1,925 | $2,500 |

D'Aquisto Ultra

1984, 1994-2000. USA Custom Shop, made under the supervision of James D'Aquisto, solid flamed maple back and sides, spruce top, ebony tailpiece, bridge and 'guard, all hand carved.

| 1994-2000 | | $3,150 | $4,100 |

DG (Dreadnought Guitar) Series

1995-1999, 2002-2014. Made in China, various lower-end acoustic and acoustic/electric models.

| 1995-2014 | | $85 | $285 |

Duo-Sonic

1956-1969, 2016-present. Solidbody, 3/4-size, 2 pickups, Desert Sand ('56-'61), sunburst ('61-'63), blue, red or white after, short- and long-scale necks, short-scale necks listed here (see Duo-Sonic II for long-scale), reissued Mexican-made in '94.

1956-1958	Desert Sand	$2,200	$2,850
1959	Maple neck	$2,200	$2,850
1960	Rosewood 'board	$1,800	$2,300
1961-1963	Desert Sand	$1,800	$2,300
1963	Sunburst (rare)	$1,800	$2,300
1964	Blue, red or white	$1,800	$2,300
1965	Blue, red or white	$1,600	$2,050
1966-1969	Blue, red or white	$1,175	$1,525

Duo-Sonic II

1965-1969. Solidbody, 2 pickups, blue, red or white, long-scale neck, though the long-scale neck Duo-Sonic was

MODEL YEAR	FEATURES	EXC. COND. LOW	HIGH

not known as the Duo-Sonic II until '65, we have lumped all long-scales under the II for the purposes of this Guide.

| 1965-1969 | | $1,275 | $1,675 |

Duo-Sonic Reissue

1993-1997. Made in Mexico, black, red or white.

| 1994-1997 | | $250 | $325 |

Duo-Sonic HS

2017-present. Player Series, humbucker and single-coil pickups.

| 2017-2019 | | $250 | $325 |

Electric XII

1965-1969. Solidbody, 12 strings, long headstock, 2 split pickups. Custom colors can fade or become darker; for example Lake Placid Blue changes to green. The price ranges below are for instruments that are relatively unfaded. Many older guitars have some color fade and minor fade is factored into these values. Each custom color should be evaluated on a case-by-case basis.

Custom color Fenders can be forged and bogus finishes have been a problem. As the value of custom color Fenders has increased, so has the problem of bogus non-original finishes. The prices in the Guide are for factory original finishes in excellent condition. The prices noted do not take into account market factors such as fake instruments, which can have the effect of lowering a guitar's market value unless the guitar's provenance can be validated. Please refer to the Fender Guitar Intro Section for details on Fender color options.

1965-1969	Common color	$4,500	$6,000
1965-1969	Rare color	$5,800	$7,500
1965-1969	Sunburst	$3,025	$3,925

Electric XII Alternate Reality

2019. Modern updated reissue..

| 2019 | | $600 | $800 |

Ensenada Series

2005-2007. Made in Mexico acoustics, solid top, back and sides, A (grand auditorium), D (dreadnought), M (mini jumbo) and V (orchestra) sizes, E suffix denotes on-board electronics.

| 2005-2007 | Acoustic | $375 | $525 |
| 2005-2007 | Acoustic-electric | $425 | $600 |

Esprit Elite

1984. Master Series, made in Japan, double-cut, semi-hollow, carved maple top, 2 humbuckers, 4 controls, bound rosewood 'board, snowflake inlays.

| 1983-1985 | | $1,150 | $1,525 |

Esprit Standard

1984. Like Esprit Elite, but with dot inlays, 2 controls.

| 1983-1985 | | $1,100 | $1,450 |

Esprit Ultra

1984. Like Esprit Elite, but with bound ebony 'board, split-block inlays, gold hardware.

| 1984 | | $1,150 | $1,525 |

Esquire

1950-1970. Ash body, single-cut, 1 pickup, maple neck, black 'guard '50-'54, white 'guard '54 on. Please refer to the Fender Guitar Intro Section for details on Fender color options.

| 1950-1951 | Blond, black 'guard | $30,700 | $40,000 |

MODEL YEAR	FEATURES	EXC. COND. LOW	HIGH
1952-1953	Blond, black 'guard	$26,700	$35,100
1954	Blond, black 'guard	$23,500	$30,500
1954	Blond, white 'guard	$18,000	$24,000
1955	Blond, white 'guard	$17,700	$22,800
1956-1957	Blond	$18,000	$24,000
1958	Blond, backloader	$13,000	$17,000
1958	Blond, toploader	$13,000	$17,000
1959	Blond, maple 'board	$13,000	$17,000
1959	Blond, rosewood 'board	$13,000	$17,000
1960	Blond	$11,200	$14,600
1960	Sunburst	$12,100	$15,900
1961	Blond, slab 'board	$10,300	$13,500
1961	Custom color	$18,000	$30,000
1961	Sunburst, slab	$12,200	$16,000
1962	Blond, curved 'board	$9,300	$12,500
1962	Blond, slab	$10,300	$13,500
1962	Custom color	$18,000	$30,000
1962	Sunburst, curved	$11,200	$15,000
1962	Sunburst, slab	$12,200	$16,000
1963	Blond	$9,300	$12,500
1963	Common color	$17,000	$22,000
1963	Rare color	$22,000	$30,000
1963	Sunburst	$11,200	$15,000
1964	Blond	$9,500	$12,500
1964	Common color	$15,000	$20,000
1964	Rare color	$18,000	$26,000
1964	Sunburst	$12,000	$15,500
1965	Blond	$8,000	$10,500
1965	Common color	$12,000	$16,000
1965	Rare color	$16,000	$25,000
1965	Sunburst	$8,000	$10,500
1966	Blond	$6,800	$8,800
1966	Common color	$7,000	$10,000
1966	Rare color	$10,000	$14,000
1966	Sunburst	$7,500	$9,800
1967	Blond	$5,400	$7,200
1967	Blond, smuggler cavity	$7,700	$10,000
1967	Common color	$7,000	$10,000
1967	Rare color	$10,000	$14,000
1967	Sunburst	$7,500	$9,800
1968	Blond	$5,400	$7,200
1968	Common color	$7,000	$10,000
1968	Rare color	$10,000	$14,000
1968	Sunburst, nitro	$7,500	$9,800
1969	Blond	$4,800	$6,300
1969	Common color	$7,000	$10,000
1969	Rare color	$10,000	$14,000
1969	Sunburst, poly	$6,700	$8,800
1970	Blond	$4,100	$5,400
1970	Common color	$6,000	$8,500
1970	Rare color	$6,000	$12,000
1970	Sunburst	$4,100	$5,400

Esquire (Japan)
1985-1994. Made in Japan, '54 specs.

MODEL YEAR	FEATURES	EXC. COND. LOW	HIGH
1985-1986		$850	$1,100
1987-1989	'50s Esquire	$850	$1,100
1990-1994	'50s Esquire	$750	$975

'50s Esquire (Mexico)
2005-2010. Maple neck, ash body.

2005-2010		$425	$550

'52 Esquire
2012. Custom Shop model, price includes Certificate of Authenticity.

2012	NOS	$1,750	$2,300

'53 Esquire
2012. Custom Shop model, price includes Certificate of Authenticity.

2012	NOS	$1,750	$2,300

'59 Esquire
2003-2007, 2013-2016. Custom Shop model, Relic version lasted to '07, then came back in '13 for limited run.

2003-2013	Closet Classic	$1,750	$2,300
2003-2013	NOS	$1,750	$2,300
2003-2016	Relic	$1,900	$2,450

'60 Esquire
Custom Shop model, NOS.

2010		$1,750	$2,300

'70 Esquire
2008. Custom Shop model, only 20 made.

2008	Heavy Relic	$2,000	$2,600
2008	Relic	$1,900	$2,450

Custom Esquire '95
1995. Custom Shop limited edition of 12, stealth pickup under 'guard, bird's-eye maple neck.

1995		$1,750	$2,300

Esquire Custom
1959-1970. Same as Esquire, but with bound alder sunburst body and rosewood 'board.

1959	Sunburst	$23,000	$30,000
1960	Custom color	$23,000	$42,000
1960	Sunburst	$22,000	$28,000
1961	Custom color	$22,000	$41,000
1961	Sunburst	$21,000	$27,000
1962	Custom color	$19,000	$38,000
1962	Sunburst, curve	$18,000	$24,000
1962	Sunburst, slab	$20,000	$26,000
1963	Custom color	$17,000	$32,000
1963	Sunburst	$18,000	$24,000
1964	Custom color	$15,000	$27,000
1964	Sunburst	$18,000	$24,000
1965	Custom color	$14,000	$25,000
1965	Sunburst	$14,500	$19,000
1966	Custom color	$11,000	$20,000
1966	Sunburst	$10,000	$13,000
1967-1969	Sunburst	$10,000	$13,000
1970	Sunburst	$7,800	$10,200

Esquire Custom (Import)
1983-1994. Made in Japan with all the classic bound Esquire features, sunburst.

1983-1994		$650	$850

1965 Fender Electric XII
Richard F. Johnson

1961 Fender Esquire Custom
Carter Vintage Guitars

GUITARS

1997 Fender Jag-Stang
Imaged by Heritage Auctions, HA.com

1963 Fender Jaguar
David Hinds

MODEL YEAR	FEATURES	EXC. COND. LOW	HIGH
Esquire Custom GT/Celtic/Scorpion			
2003. Made in Korea, single-cut solidbody, 1 humbucker, 1 knob (volume), set-neck, solid colors.			
2003		$400	$525
Esquire Z			
2001. Custom Shop, black body and headstock, curly maple neck, ebony 'board, 25 made.			
2001		$4,200	$5,500
Jeff Beck Tribute Esquire (Custom Shop)			
2006. Also called Beck Artist Esquire or Tribute Series Jeff Beck Esquire, specs include an extremely lightweight 2-piece offset ash body with Beck's original contours, distressed for an appearance like Beck's original Esquire that was used on many Yardbird records.			
2006		$6,700	$8,700
F (Flat-Top) Series			
1969-1981. The F-Series were Japanese-made flat-top acoustics, included were Concert- and Dreadnought-size instruments with features running from plain to bound necks and headstocks and fancy inlays, there was also a line of F-Series classical, nylon-string guitars. A label on the inside indicates the model. FC-20 is a classical with Brazilian rosewood. There was also an Asian (probably Korean) import Standard Series for '82-'90 where the models start with a F.			
1969-1981	Dreadnought, laminated	$55	$135
1969-1981	Dreadnought, solid top	$130	$325
1972-1981	Classical (FC)	$130	$325
Flame Elite			
1984. Master Series, made in Japan, neck-thru, offset double-cut, solidbody, 2 humbuckers, rosewood 'board, snowflake inlays.			
1984-1988		$1,150	$1,525
Flame Standard			
1984-1988. Like Flame Elite, but with dot inlays.			
1984-1988		$1,100	$1,450
Flame Ultra			
1984. Like Flame Elite, but with split block inlays (some with snowflakes), gold hardware.			
1984-1988		$1,150	$1,525
FR-48 Resonator			
2003-2009. Made in Korea, steel body.			
2003-2009		$225	$300
FR-50 Resonator			
2000-2015. Spruce top, mahogany back and sides, sunburst, optional square-neck.			
2000-2015		$225	$300
FR-50CE Resonator			
2000-2015. Same as FR-50 with cutaway and pickups.			
2009-2015		$300	$400
FR-55 Hawaiian Resonator			
2012-2013. Bell brass nickel-plated body etched with scenes of South Seas.			
2012-2013		$350	$450
GA (Grand Auditorium) Series			
2001-2009. Various grand auditorium models made in Korea, an oval label on the inside back clearly indicates the model number.			
2001-2009		$110	$475

MODEL YEAR	FEATURES	EXC. COND. LOW	HIGH
GC (Grand Concert) Series			
1997-2009. Various grand concert models, an oval label on the inside back clearly indicates the model number.			
1997-2009		$110	$150
GDO (Global Design Orchestra) Series			
2004-2008. Various orchestra-sized acoustic models, an oval label on the inside back clearly indicates the model number.			
2004-2008		$310	$400
Gemini Series			
1983-1990. Korean-made flat-tops, label on inside indicates model. I is classical nylon-string, II, III and IV are dreadnought steel-strings, there is also a 12-string and an IIE acoustic/electric.			
1984-1987	Gemini II	$75	$175
1984-1988	Gemini I	$70	$140
1987-1988	Gemini III	$125	$200
1987-1990	Gemini IIE	$125	$200
1987-1990	Gemini IV	$125	$200
GN (Grand Nylon) Series			
2001-2007. Various grand nylon acoustic models, an oval label on the inside back clearly indicates the model number.			
2001-2007		$300	$390
Harmony-Made Series			
Late-1960s-1973. Various Harmony-made models, with white stencil Fender logo, mahogany, natural or sunburst.			
1960s	D-style model	$200	$850
1970-1973	Stella model	$75	$175
Jag-Stang			
1996-1999, 2003-2004. Made in Japan, designed by Curt Cobain, body similar to Jaguar, tremolo, 1 pickup, oversize Strat peghead, Fiesta Red or Sonic Blue. First year has 50th Anniversary label.			
1996-2004		$700	$900
Jaguar			
1962-1975. Reintroduced as Jaguar '62 in '95-'99. Custom colors can fade and often the faded color has very little similarity to the original color. The values below are for an instrument that is relatively unfaded. Each custom color should be evaluated on a case-by-case basis. As the value of custom color Fenders has increased, so has the problem of bogus non-original finishes. The prices in the Guide are for factory original finishes in excellent condition. Please refer to the Fender Guitar Intro Section for details on Fender color options.			
1962	Common color	$4,300	$5,700
1962	Rare color	$5,900	$8,200
1962	Sunburst	$3,800	$5,000
1963	Common color	$4,300	$5,700
1963	Rare color	$5,900	$8,200
1963	Sunburst	$3,600	$4,600
1964	Common color	$4,300	$5,700
1964	Rare color	$5,900	$8,200
1964	Sunburst	$3,600	$4,600
1965	Common color	$4,000	$5,500
1965	Rare color	$5,700	$8,000
1965	Sunburst	$3,200	$4,200

MODEL YEAR	FEATURES	EXC. COND. LOW	HIGH
1966	Common color	$3,500	$4,600
1966	Rare color	$4,700	$7,300
1966	Sunburst, block markers	$3,200	$4,200
1966	Sunburst, dot markers	$3,200	$4,200
1967-1969	Common color	$3,500	$4,600
1967-1969	Rare color	$5,000	$6,600
1967-1969	Sunburst	$3,200	$4,200
1970	Common color	$3,200	$4,200
1970	Rare color	$4,200	$6,000
1970-1975	Sunburst	$2,700	$3,500
1971-1975	Custom color	$2,650	$3,500

Jaguar '62
1986-2012. Reintroduction of Jaguar, Japanese-made until '99, then U.S.-made American Vintage series, basswood body, rosewood 'board, various colors.

1986-1999	Import	$850	$1,100
1999-2012	USA	$1,200	$1,575

Jaguar HH/Special Edition Jaguar HH
2005-2014. Japan, 2 Dragster humbuckers, matching headstock, chrome knobs and pickup covers.

2005-2014		$450	$600

50th Anniversary Jaguar
2012. USA, modeled after '62, classic 24" scale, new one-degree neck-angle pocket, repositioned tremolo plate, redesigned hot Jaguar single-coils, lacquer finish in Lake Placid Blue, Candy Apple Red, or burgundy.

2012		$1,075	$1,400

American Vintage '62 Jaguar
2000. Export version, Lake Placid Blue, Candy Apple Red, Shell Pink, Burgundy Mist Metallic and Ice Blue Metallic with matching headstocks, a special run for Yamano, Japan. Limited to 50 in each color.

2000		$1,175	$1,550

Blacktop Jaguar HH
2010-2014. Stripped-down electronics with 2 humbuckers, 1 volume, 1 tone, single 3-way switch, maple neck, rosewood 'board, black 'guard, black or silver.

2010-2014		$325	$425

Jaguar Baritone Special HH
2005-2010. Japan, limited edition, Baritone Special logo on matching headstock, 2 humbuckers, no trem, black.

2005-2010		$450	$600

Jaguar Classic Player Special
2009-2019. Classic Player series, classic Jag look, tremolo, 2 single-coils.

2009-2019		$525	$675

Jaguar Classic Player Special HH
2009-2019. Classic Player series. 2 humbucker version.

2009-2019		$525	$675

Jaguar FSR Classic '66 Reissue
2008-2010. Fender Special Run, '66 specs, block inlays, black logo, custom colors, limited edition.

2008-2010		$950	$1,250

Jaguar FSR Thinline
2012. Limited Edition, semi-hollowbody with f-hole, 2 vintage-style single-coil pickups.

2012		$1,100	$1,425

Jaguar Special Edition HH
2005-2014. 2 humbuckers, matching headstock, no trem.

2005-2014		$500	$650

Johnny Marr Signature Jaguar
2012-2019. Artist series, based on Marr's '65 Jaguar, maple neck, rosewood 'board.

2012-2019		$1,000	$1,300

Kurt Cobain Signature Jaguar
2011-present. Artist Series, based on Cobain's '65 Jaguar.

2011-2019		$1,000	$1,300

Modern Player Jaguar
2012-2014. Mahogany body, maple neck, rosewood 'board, 2-color chocolate burst, trans red or trans black.

2012-2014		$290	$375

Pawn Shop Jaguarillo
2012-2013. Alder body, maple neck, rosewood 'board, HSS pickups, various colors.

2012-2013		$475	$625

Player Jaguar
2018-present. Humbucker and single-coil pickups.

2018-2019		$375	$500

Jazzmaster
1958-1980. Contoured body, 2 pickups, rosewood 'board, clay dot inlay, reintroduced as Japanese-made Jazzmaster '62 in '94. Custom color Fenders can be forged and bogus finishes have been a problem. As the value of custom color Fenders has increased, so has the problem of bogus non-original finishes. The prices in the Guide are for factory original finishes in excellent condition. Please refer to the Fender Guitar Intro Section for details on Fender color options.

1958	Sunburst	$7,200	$9,500
1958	Sunburst, maple 'board	$6,900	$9,100
1959	Custom color, includes rare	$11,000	$18,000
1959	Sunburst	$6,600	$8,700
1960	Common color	$10,000	$13,000
1960	Rare color	$13,000	$17,000
1960	Sunburst	$6,200	$8,000
1961	Common color	$8,000	$10,500
1961	Rare color	$10,500	$14,000
1961	Sunburst	$5,700	$7,200
1962	Common color	$7,600	$10,000
1962	Rare color	$10,000	$13,000
1962	Sunburst, curved 'board	$4,800	$6,200
1963	Common color	$5,000	$8,000
1963	Rare color	$8,000	$12,000
1963	Sunburst	$4,800	$6,200
1964	Common color	$4,800	$7,500
1964	Rare color	$7,500	$11,000
1964	Sunburst	$4,800	$6,200
1965	Common color	$4,500	$6,500
1965	Rare color	$6,500	$8,700
1965	Sunburst	$4,350	$5,600
1966	Common color	$4,000	$5,500
1966	Rare color	$5,500	$7,500

1966 Fender Jaguar
Patrick McHaffie

1966 Fender Jazzmaster
Phill Fesser

*2011 Fender Blacktop
Jazzmaster HS*

Imaged by Heritage Auctions, HA.com

1985 Fender Katana

MODEL YEAR	FEATURES	EXC. COND. LOW	HIGH
1966	Sunburst	$4,100	$5,300
1967-1969	Common color	$4,000	$5,500
1967-1969	Rare color	$5,100	$7,000
1967-1969	Sunburst	$4,100	$5,300
1970	Common color	$4,000	$5,500
1970	Rare color	$5,100	$7,000
1970-1980	Sunburst	$2,750	$3,600
1971-1974	Custom color	$3,000	$4,000
1975-1980	Custom color	$2,600	$3,500

Roadworn '60s Jazzmaster
2015-present. '60s style with aged/worn alder body and maple neck, worn nitro-lacquer finish.

| 2015-2019 | | $500 | $650 |

Jazzmaster '62
1986-2012. Japanese-made reintroduction of Jazzmaster, basswood body, rosewood 'board, from '99 U.S.-made American Vintage series, various colors.

| 1986-1998 | Import | $850 | $1,100 |
| 1999-2012 | USA | $1,200 | $1,575 |

Jazzmaster '65
2013-2018. American Vintage series, alder body, maple neck, mid-'60s neck profile, rosewood 'board.

| 2013-2018 | | $1,375 | $1,800 |

Jazzmaster '69
1986-1990s. Made in Japan.

| 1986-1989 | | $850 | $1,100 |
| 1990-1999 | | $750 | $975 |

American Ultra Jazzmaster
2019-present. Alder or ash body, maple neck, rosewood 'board, 2 pickups.

| 2019 | | $1,050 | $1,375 |

Blacktop Jazzmaster HS
2010-2014. Stripped-down electronics with a single-coil and a humbucker, 1 volume, 1 tone, single 3-way switch, maple neck, rosewood 'board, black or sunburst.

| 2010-2014 | | $325 | $425 |

Classic Player Jazzmaster Special
2008-2019. Alder body, maple neck, rosewood 'board, 2 single-coils, 3-color sunburst or black.

| 2008-2019 | | $525 | $675 |

Elvis Costello Jazzmaster
2008-2010. Artist series, walnut stain, '70s neck, vintage style tremolo.

| 2008-2010 | | $1,300 | $1,725 |

J Mascis Jazzmaster
2007-2009. Artist series, purple sparkle finish, matching headstock, Adjusto-Matic bridge, reinforced tremolo arm.

| 2007-2009 | | $1,000 | $1,325 |

Pinup Girl Jazzmaster (Custom Shop)
1997. Custom Shop Limited Edition, pinup girl art on body, figured maple neck, 3 pickups, certificate of authenticity.

| 1997 | | $2,000 | $2,600 |

Select Jazzmaster
2012-2013. Chambered alder body with a carved flame maple top, Fender Select headstock medallion, various finish options.

| 2012-2013 | | $1,700 | $2,250 |

Sonic Youth Signature Jazzmaster
2009-2014. Lee Ranaldo and Thurston Moore Signature models based on their modified Jazzmasters which basically removed the standard control layout and replaced it with a 3-way switch.

| 2009-2014 | Lee Ranaldo | $1,200 | $1,600 |
| 2009-2014 | Thurston Moore | $1,200 | $1,600 |

The Ventures Limited Edition Jazzmaster
1996. Japanese-made, ash body, 2 pickups, block inlay, transparent purple/black.

| 1996 | | $1,000 | $1,300 |

Troy Van Leeuwen Jazzmaster
2014-present. Alder body, maple neck, Oxblood finish, red tortoiseshell 'guard, matching headstock.

| 2014-2019 | | $750 | $1,000 |

White Opal Jazzmaster HH
2016. Special Edition, made in Mexico, white opal body and headstock, pearloid 'guard, 2 humbuckers.

| 2016 | | $350 | $450 |

JZM Deluxe
2007-2009. Electracoustic Series, acoustic/electric, Jazzmaster/Jaguar body styling, Fishman and Tele pickups, sunburst or trans amber.

| 2007-2009 | | $325 | $425 |

Katana
1985-1986. Japanese-made wedge-shaped body, 2 humbuckers, set neck, triangle inlays, black.

| 1985-1986 | | $625 | $825 |

King
1963-1965. Full-size 15 5/8" wide acoustic, natural. Renamed Kingman in '65.

| 1963-1965 | Brazilian rosewood option | $2,250 | $2,900 |
| 1963-1965 | Indian, Zebra, Vermillion | $1,150 | $1,500 |

Kingman ASCE
2008-2017. Cutaway acoustic-electric, mahogany back and sides.

| 2008-2017 | | $300 | $400 |

Kingman SCE
2008-2017. Cutaway acoustic-electric, mahogany back and sides.

| 2008-2017 | | $275 | $375 |

Kingman USA Pro Custom
2013-2014. US-made, Custom Shop Pro series, limited run of 50, AA sitka spruce top, maple back/sides/neck, Firemist Gold finish.

| 2013-2014 | | $950 | $1,200 |

Kingman USA Select
2012. All solid woods, rosewood 'board, 3-color sunburst, Fishman electronics.

| 2012 | COA | $975 | $1,275 |

Kingman USA Select C
2012. Custom Shop limited edition of 150, Engelmann spruce top, mahogany back and sides, vintage C-shaped maple neck, rosewood 'board, Fiesta Red.

| 2012 | COA | $1,000 | $1,300 |

Kingman/Elvis Kingman
2012-2013. Wildwood model as used by Elvis Presley in the '67 film 'Clambake', spruce top, mahogany back

MODEL		EXC. COND.	
YEAR	FEATURES	LOW	HIGH

and sides, rosewood 'board, natural.

| 2012-2013 | | $275 | $375 |

Lead I

1979-1982. Double-cut solidbody with 1 humbucker, maple or rosewood 'board, black or brown.

| 1979-1982 | | $525 | $675 |

Lead II

1979-1982. Lead with 2 pickups, black or brown.

| 1979-1982 | | $700 | $900 |

Lead III

1982. Lead with 2 split-coil humbuckers, 2 3-way switches, various colors.

| 1982 | | $700 | $900 |

Player Lead II

2020-present. Reintroduced using late-70s and updated model features.

| 2020 | | $350 | $450 |

Player Lead III

2020-present. Reintroduced using late-70s and updated model features.

| 2020 | | $350 | $450 |

LTD

1969-1975. Archtop electric, single-cut, gold-plated hardware, carved top and back, 1 pickup, multi-bound, bolt-on neck, sunburst.

| 1969-1975 | | $2,500 | $3,300 |

Malibu

1965-1971. Flat-top, spruce top, mahogany back and sides, black, mahogany or sunburst. Later version is import.

| 1965-1971 | | $550 | $750 |

Malibu (California Series)

1983-1995. Made first in Japan, then Korea in '85.

| 1983-1995 | | $170 | $230 |

Malibu SCE

2006-2013. Imported single-cut acoustic/electric, solid spruce top, laminated mahogany back and sides, block inlays.

| 2006-2013 | | $175 | $235 |

Marauder

1965 only. The Marauder has 3 pickups, and some have slanted frets, only 8 were made, thus it is very rare. 1st generation has hidden pickups, 2nd has exposed.

| 1965 | 1st generation | $8,000 | $10,500 |
| 1965 | 2nd generation | $5,500 | $7,500 |

Marauder (Modern Player Series)

2011-2014. Jazzmaster-type body, 1 Jazzmaster pickup and 1 Triple Bucker, rosewood 'board.

| 2011-2014 | | $300 | $400 |

Mod Shop

2016-present. Models designed by customer by choosing options from a menu and built by Fender, 4 models offered – Jazz Bass, Precision Bass, Stratocaster and Telecaster. Values should be determined on case-by-case basis.

| 2016-2019 | | $1,500 | $2,000 |

Montara (California Series)

1990-1995. Korean-made single-cut acoustic/electric flat-top, natural, sunburst or black. Maple with flamed sides starting '92.

| 1990-1995 | | $350 | $475 |

Montego I/II

1968-1975. Electric archtop, single-cut, bolt-on neck, 1 pickup (I) or 2 pickups (II), chrome-plated hardware, sunburst.

| 1968-1975 | I | $2,000 | $2,700 |
| 1968-1975 | II | $2,200 | $2,900 |

Musiclander

1969-1972. Also called Swinger and Arrow, solidbody, 1 pickup, arrow-shaped headstock, no model name on peghead, red, white, and blue. Fender used '66-'68 dated necks but final assembly did not begin until '69.

| 1969-1972 | | $2,000 | $2,600 |

Musicmaster

1956-1980. Solidbody, 1 pickup, short-scale (3/4) neck, Desert Sand ('56-'61), sunburst ('61-'63), red, white or blue after. Regular-scale necks were optional and are called Musicmaster II from '64 to '69, after '69 II is dropped and Musicmaster continues with regular-scale neck.

1956-1959	Blond	$1,475	$1,975
1960-1964	Blond	$1,175	$1,575
1964-1965	Nitro, red, white, blue	$1,175	$1,575
1966-1968	Nitro, red, white, blue	$1,075	$1,450
1969-1972	Poly, red, white, blue	$975	$1,300
1973-1980	Red, white, blue	$975	$1,300

Musicmaster II

1964-1969. Solidbody, 1 pickup, long regular-scale neck version of Musicmaster, red, white, or blue.

| 1964-1965 | | $1,175 | $1,575 |
| 1966-1969 | | $950 | $1,450 |

Mustang

1964-1982, 1997-1998, 2016-present. Solidbody, 2 pickups. Reissued as '69 Mustang in 1990s, name changed back to Mustang '97-'98. Dakota Red, Daphne Blue and Olympic White with Competition Red, Blue and Orange finishes with a racing stripe on the front of the body added '69-'73 (with matching headstock for '69-'70).

1964-1965	Red, white or blue	$1,750	$2,300
1966-1969	Red, white or blue	$1,600	$2,100
1969-1970	Competition color	$1,600	$2,100
1970-1979	Contour body, poly	$1,450	$1,875
1978-1980	Antigua	$1,500	$2,000
1980-1982	Various colors	$1,050	$1,350

Mustang '65 Reissue

2006-2016. Made in Japan, Classic Series.

| 2006-2016 | | $500 | $650 |

Mustang '69 Reissue

1986-1998, 2005. Japanese-made, blue or white.

| 1986-1998 | | $500 | $650 |

Mustang 90/Player Mustang 90

2016-present. Made in Mexico, 2 MP-90 pickups. Named to Player series in '20.

| 2016-2019 | | $300 | $400 |

American Special Mustang

2017-2018. FSR model, 2 humbucking pickups, ash body with natural finish or alder Olympic White Pearl.

| 2017-2018 | | $650 | $850 |

1980 Fender Lead II
Tom Pfeifer

1965 Fender Mustang
Robbie Keene

GUITARS

Ca. 1969 Fender Newporter
Rivington Guitars

1985 Fender Performer
Franklin Amiano

MODEL YEAR	FEATURES	EXC. COND. LOW	HIGH
Kurt Cobain Mustang			
2012-2016. Artist Series, rosewood 'board, Fiesta Red finish.			
2012-2016		$525	$700
Newporter			
1965-1971. Acoustic flat-top, mahogany back and sides. Reissued as import.			
1965-1968	Spruce top	$475	$625
1968-1971	Mahogany top	$425	$575
Newporter (California Series)			
1983-1995. Made first in Japan, then Korea in '85.			
1983-1995		$125	$170
Newporter (Custom Shop USA)/USA Select Newporter			
2013-2014. Fishman electronics, 150 offered, certificate of authenticity.			
2013-2014		$1,400	$1,800
Newporter Classic			
2018-present. Spruce top, matching headstock, natural mahogany back and sides, pau ferro 'board.			
2018-2019		$425	$550
Palomino			
1968-1971. Acoustic flat-top, spruce top, mahogany back and sides, triple-bound, black or mahogany.			
1968-1971		$625	$850
Pawn Shop Series			
2011-2014. All-new designs with diverse Fender components and the philosophy "guitars that never were but should have been".			
2011-1014	Various models	$450	$600
Performer			
1985-1986. Imported Swinger-like body design, 2 slanted humbuckers.			
1985-1986		$1,200	$1,550
Prodigy			
1991-1993. US-made, electric solidbody, double-cut, chrome-plated hardware, 2 single-coil and 1 humbucker pickups, blue or black.			
1991-1993		$675	$875
Redondo			
1969-1970. Mid-size flat-top, 14 3/8" wide, replaces Newport spruce top model.			
1969-1970		$425	$575
Redondo (California Series)			
1983-1995. Made first in Japan, then Korea in '85.			
1983-1995		$135	$180
Robben Ford			
1989-1994. Symmetrical double-cut, 2 pickups, glued-in neck, solidbody with tone chambers, multi-bound, gold-plated hardware, sunburst. After '94 made in Fender Custom Shop.			
1989-1994		$1,400	$1,850
1995	Custom Shop	$2,350	$3,100
San Luis Rey (California Series)			
1990-1995. Acoustic flat-top, solid spruce top, rosewood back and sides.			
1990-1995		$225	$300
San Miguel (California Series)			
1990-1995. Acoustic cutaway flat-top, spruce top, mahogany back and sides.			
1990-1995		$160	$215

MODEL YEAR	FEATURES	EXC. COND. LOW	HIGH
Santa Maria (California Series)			
1988-1995. Acoustic flat-top 12-string, spruce top, mahogany back and sides.			
1988-1995		$160	$215
Santa Marino (California Series)			
1990-1995. Acoustic flat-top, solid spruce top, mahogany back and sides.			
1990-1995		$170	$225
Sergio Vallin Signature			
2015-2017. New offset double-cut body shape, HSS pickups.			
2015-2017		$400	$525
Shenandoah 12-String			
1965-1971. Acoustic flat-top, spruce top, mahogany back and sides.			
1965-1971	Antigua	$1,100	$1,425
1965-1971	Blond	$800	$1,075
Showmaster (Import)			
2003-2007. Off-set double-cut solidbody, set neck, various models.			
2003	Celtic, 1 bridge humbucker	$350	$475
2003-2007	HH, 2 humbuckers	$350	$475
2004-2006	3 single coils	$350	$475
Showmaster FMT (Custom Shop)			
2000-2007. Bound figured maple top (FMT), 2 single-coil pickups and a bridge position humbucker, maple neck, Custom Shop certificate.			
2000-2007		$1,550	$2,050
Sonoran SCE (California Series)			
2006-2018. Cutaway flat-top acoustic, 6-on-a-side tuners, spruce top, laminated mahogany back and sides, rosewood 'board, electronics options.			
2006-2018		$175	$225

Squier Series

The following are all Squier Series instruments from Fender, listed alphabetically. Fender Japan was established in '82 with Squier production beginning that same year. Production was shifted to Korea in '87 and later allocated to China, India (Squier II '89-'90), Mexico and other countries.

MODEL YEAR	FEATURES	EXC. COND. LOW	HIGH
Squier '51			
2004-2006. Korean-made, Strat-style body with a Tele-style neck, various colors.			
2004-2006		$75	$100
Squier Bullet			
1983-1988, 1995-1996, 2000-2011. Strat style, early with Tele headstock, 1980s' models include H-2 ('83-'86, 2 humbuckers), S-3 ('83-'86, 3 single-coils), S-3T ('83-'88, 3 single-coils, vibrato). Name revived in 1995 (3 SC, vib.) and in 2000 on various models with 3 SC or 2 HB pickups.			
1983-1984	H-2	$375	$500
1983-1984	S-3, T	$375	$500
1985-1986	H-2	$300	$400
1985-1988	S-3, T	$300	$400
2000-2011		$85	$105
Squier Duo-Sonic '50s (Classic Vibe Series)			
2008-2010. Made in China.			
2008-2010		$190	$250

The *Vintage Guitar Price Guide* shows low to high values for items in all-original excellent condition, and, where applicable, with original case or cover.

MODEL YEAR	FEATURES	EXC. COND. LOW	HIGH

Squier Katana
1985-1987. Wedge-shaped body, 1 humbucker, bolt neck, dot inlays.

1985-1987		$550	$750

Squier Showmaster Series
2002-2005. Made in China, various pickup configs.

2002-2005	Various models	$125	$175

Squier Stagemaster HH
1999-2002. 2 humbuckers, reverse headstock, 6- or 7-string.

1999-2002		$125	$175

Squier Standard Double Fat Strat
1999-2007. 2 humbucker pickups.

1999-2007		$90	$125

Squier Standard Fat Strat
1996-2006. Hum/single/single pickups. Replaced by the HSS.

1996-2006		$90	$125

Squier Standard Floyd Rose Stratocaster
1992-1996. Floyd Rose tailpiece, black, white or foto flame finish, Fender and Squier headstock logos.

1992-1996		$275	$375

Squier Standard Stratocaster
1982-2019. Standard Series represent the classic designs.

1982-1983	1st logo, JV serial	$950	$1,275
1984	1st logo, JV serial	$875	$1,175
1985-1989	2nd logo, SQ serial	$425	$600
1990-1999	Mexico	$275	$375
2000-2019	Indonesia	$100	$165

Squier II Stratocaster
1988-1992. Squier II models were targeted at a lower price point than regular Squier series. Mainly built in Korea but some early ones from India. Line was replaced by other models under regular Squier instruments.

1988-1992		$155	$225

Squier Stratocaster (Affinity Series)
1997-present. Lower priced version, made in China.

1997-2019		$75	$125

Squier Stratocaster '50s (Classic Vibe Series)
2008-present. Alder body, maple 'board, white pickguard, 2-tone sunburst, Lake Placid Blue or Oly White.

2008-2019		$200	$275

Squier Stratocaster '60s (Classic Vibe Series)
2008-present. As '50s Classic Vibe but with rosewood 'board, tortoise pickguard, 3-tone sunburst or candy apple red.

2008-2019		$200	$275

Squier Stratocaster Pro-Tone
1996-1998. Korean-made, higher-end Squier series with solid ash bodies, one-piece maple necks, alnico single-coils.

1996-1998		$350	$475

Squier Tom Delonge Stratocaster
2002-2003. Hardtail, 1 humbucker.

2002-2003		$250	$325

Squier Standard Telecaster
1982-2019. Standard Series represent the classic designs.

1982-1984	1st logo, JV serial	$950	$1,275
1985-1989	2nd logo, SQ serial	$425	$600
1990-1999	Mexico	$275	$375
2000-2019	Indonesia	$90	$125

Squier Standard Telecaster Special
2004-2007. Made in Indonesia, 1 humbucker, 1 single-coil.

2004-2007		$90	$125

Squier Telecaster (Affinity Series)
1998-present. Lower priced version, made in China.

1998-2019		$50	$85

Squier Telecaster Custom/Custom II
2003-2012. 2 humbuckers, Custom II has 2 soapbar single-coils. Changed to Vintage Modified series in '12.

2003-2012		$90	$125

Squier J5 (John 5) Telecaster (Artist Series)
2009-present. Black with chrome hardware or Frost Gold with gold hardware (introduced '14), matching headstock.

2014-2019	Frost Gold	$225	$300

Squier Telecaster Thinline (Classic Vibe Series)
2014-present. Semi-hollow mahogany body with f-hole.

2004-2019		$190	$250

Squier Venus
1997-1998. Offset double-cut solidbody, 2 pickups, co-designed by Courtney Love, also offered as 12-string.

1997-1998		$375	$500

Squier Vintage Modified Series
2012-present. Imported, various models, large script Squier logo and small Fender logo on headstock.

2012-2016	Jazzmaster Special	$160	$210
2012-2016	Surf Stratocaster	$160	$210
2012-2016	Telecaster Special	$160	$210
2012-2019	'70s Stratocaster	$160	$210
2012-2019	Stratocaster HSS	$160	$210

Starcaster
1974-1980, 2014. Offset double-cut, thinline semi-hollowbody, arched maple top and back, 2 humbuckers, 5 knobs (2 tone, 2 volume, 1 master volume), originally offered in tobacco sunburst, natural, walnut, black, white or custom blond finish. Model revived in Modern Player Series in '14 without master volume. Fender also used the Starcaster name as a brand on a line of budget guitars in the 2000s.

1974-1980	Various colors	$3,275	$4,275
2014	Modern Player	$500	$650

Starcaster by Fender
2000s. Fender used the Starcaster brand on a line of budget versions of the Strat, Tele, and J- and P-Bass. They also offered small solid state amps and guitar packages with nylon- or steel-string acoustic or a Strat/amp combo. Sold in Costco and other discounters.

2000s	Acoustic	$65	$125

Fender Squier J5 Telecaster

Fender Squire Vintage Modified Surf Stratocaster

GUITARS

Fender Standard Stratacoustic

1954 Fender Stratocaster
Tony Sheedy

MODEL YEAR	FEATURES	EXC. COND. LOW	HIGH
2000s	Electric guitar only	$65	$125
2000s	Pack with guitar, amp, stand	$75	$135

Stratacoustic/Stratacoustic Deluxe/ Stratacoustic Standard

2000-2019. Thinline acoustic/electric, single-cut, spruce top, fiberglass body, various colors. Stratacoustic discontinued '05, Deluxe begins '07 and Standard added in '09.

2002-2005	Stratacoustic	$140	$190
2007-2009	Deluxe	$400	$550
2009-2019	Standard	$200	$300

Stratacoustic Plus/Stracoustic Premier

2014-2017. Standard with Mini USB output added, Premier is 3-color sunburst flame maple, Plus is Inca Silver top with matching head.

2014-2017	Plus	$225	$325
2014-2017	Premier	$250	$350

Stratocaster

The following are all variations of the Stratocaster. The first five listings are for the main American-made models. All others are listed alphabetically after that in the following order:

Stratocaster
Standard Stratocaster (includes "Smith Strat")
American Standard Stratocaster
American Series Stratocaster
American Professional Stratocaster
25th Anniversary Stratocaster
30th Anniversary Guitar Center Strat
35th Anniversary Stratocaster
40th Anniversary 1954 Stratocaster Limited Edition
40th Anniversary American Standard Stratocaster
40th Anniversary Stratocaster Diamond Dealer
40th Anniversary Stratocaster ST62 (Japan)
'50s Stratocaster/Classic Series '50s Stratocaster
American Original '50s Stratocaster
Classic Player '50s Stratocaster
Classic Series '50s Stratocaster Lacquer
Road Worn '50s Stratocaster
50th Anniversary 1954 Stratocaster
50th Anniversary American Deluxe Stratocaster
50th Anniversary American Standard Stratocaster
50th Anniversary Standard Stratocaster
50th Anniversary Stratocaster
50th Anniversary Stratocaster Relic
'54 Stratocaster
'54 Stratocaster FMT
'55 Stratocaster
'55 Dual-Mag Strat Journeyman Relic
'55 Historic 1955 NOS Stratocaster
'55 Journeyman Relic Stratocaster
'55 Rocking Dog Stratocaster
'56 Stratocaster
'56 Journeyman Stratocaster Closet Classic

'56 Stratocaster Heavy Relic
American Vintage '56 Stratocaster
American Vintage '56 Stratocaster Limited Edition Roasted Ash
'57 Special Stratocaster
'57 Stratocaster
'57 Stratocaster (Custom Shop)
'57 Stratocaster (USA)
'57 Time Machine 1957 Relic Stratocaster
'57 Vintage Stratocaster (Japan)
American Vintage '57 Commemorative Stratocaster
Vintage Custom 1957 Stratocaster NOS
Wildwood "10s" 1957 Limited Stratocaster Relic
'58 Journeyman Relic Stratocaster
'58 Limited Edition MIJ Stratocaster
'58 Stratocaster
'58 Stratocaster (Dakota Red)
'58 Time Machine 1958 Heavy Relic Stratocaster
'59 Rocking Dog Stratocaster
'59 Stratocaster (Custom Shop)
'59 Time Machine 1959 Heavy Relic Stratocaster
'59 Time Machine 1959 Relic Stratocaster
American Vintage '59 Pine Stratocaster
American Vintage '59 Stratocaster
Wildwood "10s" 1959 Limited Stratocaster Relic
'60 FMT Stratocaster
'60 Stratocaster
'60s Stratocaster/'60 Stratocaster
American Original '60s Stratocaster
Custom 1960 Stratocaster
'60s Stratocaster/Classic Series '60s Stratocaster
Classic Player '60s Stratocaster
Classic Series '60s Stratocaster Lacquer
Limited Edition '60s Daybreak Stratocaster
Road Worn '60s Stratocaster
60th Anniversary '54 Stratocaster (Custom Shop)
60th Anniversary American Stratocaster
60th Anniversary American Vintage 1954 Stratocaster
60th Anniversary Commemorative Stratocaster
'61 Stratocaster
Wildwood "10s" 1961 Limited Stratocaster
'62 Stratocaster (USA)
'62 Commemorative Stratocaster
'62 Vintage Stratocaster (Japan)
'62 Heavy Relic Stratocaster
'62 Stratocaster ST62US Reissue
'62 Vintage Custom 1962 Stratocaster
Dave's Guitar Shop American 1962 Stratocaster
Deluxe Vintage Player '62 Stratocaster
Willcutt Guitars True '62 Stratocaster
'63 Stratocaster
'63 Stratocaster Journeyman Relic
'64 Stratocaster (Custom Shop)
'64 Time Machine Journeyman Relic Stratocaster
'65 Stratocaster (Custom Shop)
'65 Journeyman Closet Classic Stratocaster
'65 Time Machine 1965 Journeyman Relic Stratocaster
American Vintage '65 Stratocaster

Mark Kendrick Master Design '65 Stratocaster
'66 Stratocaster (Custom Shop)
'67 Time Machine 1967 Journeyman Relic Aged Stratocaster
'67 Time Machine 1967 Journeyman Relic Custom Top Stratocaster
'68 Heavy Relic Stratocaster
'68 Reverse Strat Special (USA)
'68 Stratocaster (Japan)
'69 Stratocaster (Custom Shop)
Wildwood "10s" 1969 Limited Stratocaster
'70s Stratocaster/Classic Series '70s Stratocaster
American Vintage '70s Stratocaster
'72 Stratocaster (Japan)
'72 Stratocaster Limited Edition (Japan)
Acoustasonic Stratocaster
Aerodyne Stratocaster
Albert Hammond Jr. Signature Stratocaster
Aluminum Stratocaster (Custom Shop)
Aluminum Stratocaster American Standard
American Acoustasonic Stratocaster
American Classic Holoflake Stratocaster
American Classic Stratocaster
American Custom Stratocaster (Custom Shop)
American Deluxe Stratocaster
American Deluxe Stratocaster Designer Series
American Deluxe Stratocaster FMT HSS
American Deluxe Stratocaster HSS Mahogany
American Elite Stratocaster
American Elite Stratocaster Limited Edition
American Longboard Stratocaster HSS
American Performer Stratocaster
American Special Stratocaster
American Standard Stratocaster Limited Edition
American Ultra Stratocaster
Ancho Poblano Journeyman Relic Stratocaster
Ancho Poblano Limited Edition Roasted Stratocaster Relic
Antigua Stratocaster
Artisan Series Stratocaster (Custom Shop)
Big Apple Stratocaster
Big Block Stratocaster
Big Head Stratocaster
Bill Carson Stratocaster
Billy Corgan Stratocaster
Blackie Stratocaster (Custom Shop 1987)
Blackie Stratocaster (Custom Shop)
Blacktop Stratocaster
Mahogany Blacktop Stratocaster Limited Edition
Blue Flower Stratocaster
Bonnie Raitt Stratocaster
Bowling Ball/Marble Stratocaster
Buddy Guy Standard Stratocaster
Buddy Guy Stratocaster (Signature)
Buddy Holly Tribute Stratocaster
California Stratocaster/California Fat Stratocaster
Carved Top Stratocaster HSS (Custom Shop)
Classic Player Stratocaster
Classic Player Stratocaster HH
Collector's Edition Stratocaster ('62 Reissue)

Contemporary Stratocaster
Contemporary Stratocaster (Import)
Crash Stratocaster
Custom Classic Stratocaster
Custom Deluxe Stratocaster
Dave Murray Stratocaster
David Gilmour Signature Stratocaster
Deluxe Lone Star Stratocaster
Deluxe Players Special Edition Stratocaster
Deluxe Players Stratocaster
Deluxe Roadhouse Stratocaster
Deluxe Stratocaster
Deluxe Stratocaster HSS Plus Top IOS
Deluxe Stratocaster Plus
Dick Dale Stratocaster
Elite Stratocaster
EOB (Ed O'Brien) Sustainer Stratocaster
Eric Clapton Gold Leaf Stratocaster
Eric Clapton Signature Journeyman Relic Stratocaster
Eric Clapton Signature Stratocaster
Eric Clapton Stratocaster
Eric Clapton Stratocaster (Custom Shop)
Eric Johnson 1954 "Virginia" Stratocaster
Eric Johnson Signature Stratocaster Thinline
Eric Johnson Stratocaster
Floyd Rose Classic Relic Stratocaster
Floyd Rose Classic Stratocaster (Strat HSS) (Strat HH)
Ford Shelby GT Stratocaster
Foto Flame Stratocaster
Freddy Tavares Aloha Stratocaster
FSR Stratocaster
George Fullerton 50th Anniversary '57 Strat Ltd. Ed. Set
Gold Stratocaster
Gold Elite Stratocaster
Gold Stratocaster (Custom Shop)
GT11 Stratocaster
Hank Marvin Stratocaster
Hank Marvin 40th Anniversary Stratocaster
Harley-Davidson 90th Anniversary Stratocaster
Highway One Stratocaster/HSS
HM Strat (USA/Import)
HM Strat Limited Edition
Homer Haynes HLE Stratocaster
Hot Wheels Stratocaster
HRR Stratocaster/ Floyd Rose HRR (Japan)
Ike Turner Tribute Stratocaster
Jeff Beck Signature Stratocaster (CS)
Jeff Beck Stratocaster
Jerry Donahue Hellecaster Stratocaster
Jim Root Stratocaster
Jimi Hendrix Limited Edition Stratocaster (Custom Shop)
Jimi Hendrix Monterey Pop Stratocaster
Jimi Hendrix Monterey Stratocaster
Jimi Hendrix Stratocaster
Jimi Hendrix Tribute Stratocaster
Jimi Hendrix Voodoo 29th Anniversary Stratocaster
Jimi Hendrix Voodoo Child Journeyman Relic Stratocaster

1956 Fender Stratocaster (lefty)
HI Guitars

1958 Fender Stratocaster
Andrew Yanis

GUITARS

1961 Fender Stratocaster
Marty Fab

1964 Fender Stratocaster
Mario Vilas

Jimi Hendrix Voodoo Child Stratocaster
Jimi Hendrix Voodoo Stratocaster
Jimmie Vaughan Tex-Mex Stratocaster
John Jorgenson Hellecaster Stratocaster
John Mayer Limited Edition Black1 Stratocaster
John Mayer Stratocaster
Kenny Wayne Shepherd Stratocaster
Koa Stratocaster
Kon Tiki Stratocaster
Lenny Stratocaster
Lincoln Brewster Signature Stratocaster
Lite Ash Stratocaster Special Edition
Lone Star Stratocaster
Mark Knopfler Stratocaster
Masterbuilt Custom Shop Stratocaster
Masterbuilt Dennis Galuszka Fat '50s Strato-
    caster
Matthias Jabs Signature Stratocaster
Michael Landau Signature Relic Stratocaster
    1963/1968
Milonga Deluxe Stratocaster
MLB Major League Baseball Stratocaster
Mod Shop Stratocaster
Modern Player Stratocaster HSH/HSS
Moto Limited Edition Stratocaster
Moto Set Stratocaster
Orange Krush Limited Edition Stratocaster
Paisley Stratocaster
Parallel Universe Volume II Jazz Stratocaster
Playboy 40th Anniversary Stratocaster
Player Series Stratocaster
Post Modern Stratocaster (CS)
Post Modern Stratocaster Closet Classic (Cus-
    tom Shop)
Post Modern Stratocaster Journeyman Relic
    (Custom Shop)
Post Modern Stratocaster NOS (Custom Shop)
Powerhouse/Powerhouse Deluxe Stratocaster
Proud Stratocaster
Rarities Stratocaster
Richie Sambora Stratocaster
Ritchie Blackmore Stratocaster
Ritchie Blackmore Tribute Stratocaster
Roadhouse Stratocaster
Roasted Journeyman Relic Tomatillo Strato-
    caster
Robert Cray Signature Stratocaster
Robert Cray Stratocaster (Mexico)
Robin Trower Signature Stratocaster
Rory Gallagher Tribute Stratocaster
Sandblasted Stratocaster
Select Stratocaster
Set-Neck Stratocaster
Short-Scale (7/8) Stratocaster
So-Cal Custom Shop J.W. Black Stratocaster
So-Cal Speed Shop Stratocaster
Special Edition David Lozeau Art Stratocaster
Special Edition Stratocaster
Special Edition Stratocaster (Matching Head-
    stock)
Special Edition White Opal Stratocaster
Splatter Stratocaster
Standard Roland Ready Stratocaster

Standard Stratocaster (Japan)
Standard Stratocaster Satin Finish
Standard Stratocaster (Mexico)
Standard Stratocaster Plus Top
Stevie Ray Vaughan Signature Stratocaster
    (Custom Shop)
Stevie Ray Vaughan Signature Stratocaster
    Relic (Custom Shop)
Stevie Ray Vaughan Stratocaster
Stevie Ray Vaughan Tribute #1 Stratocaster
Strat Plus
Stratocaster Junior
Stratocaster Pro Closet Classic (Custom Shop)
Stratocaster Pro NOS (Custom Shop)
Stratocaster Special
Stratocaster XII
Strat-o-Sonic
Sub Sonic Stratocaster
Super Stratocaster
Tanqurey Tonic Stratocaster
Texas Special Stratocaster
The Edge Stratocaster
The Strat
Tie-Dye Stratocaster
Tom Delonge Stratocaster
Tom Morello Soul Power Stratocaster
Tree of Life Stratocaster
Turquoise Sparkle Stratocaster
U.S. Ultra / Ultra Plus Stratocaster
Ventures Limited Edition Stratocaster
VG Stratocaster
Vintage Hot Rod Stratocaster
Vintera Series Stratocaster
Walnut Elite Stratocaster
Walnut Stratocaster
Western Stratocaster
Whiteguard Stratocaster Limited Edition
Yngwie Malmsteen Signature Stratocaster
Yngwie Malmsteen Stratocaster

Stratocaster

1954-1981. Two-tone sunburst until '58, 3-tone after. Custom color finishes were quite rare in the '50s and early-'60s and are much more valuable than the standard sunburst finish. By the '70s, color finishes were much more common and do not affect the value near as much. In '75 Fender dropped the optional custom colors and started issuing the guitars in a variety of standard colors (sunburst, blond, white, natural, walnut and black).

Custom color Fenders can be forged and bogus finishes have been a problem. As the value of custom color Fenders has increased, so has the problem of bogus non-original finishes. The prices in the Guide are for factory original finishes in excellent condition. One color, Shell Pink, is notable because many vintage authorities wonder if a Shell Pink Strat even exists? An ultra-rare custom color should have strong documented provenance and be verifiable by at least one (preferable two or more) well-known vintage authorities. Please refer to the Fender Guitar Intro Section for details on Fender color options.

Three-bolt neck '72-'81, otherwise 4-bolt. Unless noted, all Stratocasters listed have the Fender tremolo system.

Non-tremolo models (aka hardtails) typically sell for less. Many guitarists feel the tremolo block helps produce a fuller range of sound. On average, many more tremolo models were made. One year, '58, seems to be a year where a greater percentage of non-tremolo models were made. Tremolo vs. non-tremolo valuation should be taken on a brand-by-brand basis; for example, a pre-'65 Gibson ES-335 non-tremolo model is worth more than a tremolo equipped model.

From '63-'70, Fender offered both the standard Brazilian rosewood fretboard and an optional maple fretboard. Prices listed here, for those years, are for the rosewood 'board models. Currently, the market considers the maple 'board to be a premium, so guitars with maple, for those years, are worth 10% to 15% more than the values shown.

Renamed Standard Stratocaster for '82-'84 (see following listings), American Standard Stratocaster for '86-2000, the American Series Stratocaster for '00-'07, and the American Standard Stratocaster (again) for '08-'16. Currently called the American Professional Stratocaster.

MODEL YEAR	FEATURES	EXC. COND. LOW	HIGH
1954	Very first '54, rare features	$104,000	$135,000
1954	Early-mid '54, typical features	$63,000	$82,000
1954	Sunburst, later production	$43,000	$56,000
1955	Late-'55, blond, nickel hw	$44,000	$57,000
1955	Sunburst, ash body	$30,000	$41,000
1956	Blond, nickel hw	$33,000	$43,000
1956	Mary Kaye, gold hw	$54,000	$70,000
1956	Sunburst, alder body	$28,000	$36,000
1956	Sunburst, ash body	$29,500	$38,000
1956	Sunburst, non-trem	$17,300	$22,500
1957	Blond, nickel hw	$33,000	$43,000
1957	Mary Kaye, gold hw	$54,000	$70,000
1957	Sunburst	$28,000	$36,000
1957	Sunburst, non-trem	$17,300	$22,500
1958	Blond, nickel hw	$31,000	$40,000
1958	Mary Kaye, gold hw	$52,600	$68,300
1958	Sunburst 2-tone, maple	$26,000	$33,700
1958	Sunburst 2-tone, non-trem	$17,300	$22,500
1958	Sunburst 3-tone, maple	$24,400	$31,700
1958	Sunburst 3-tone, non-trem	$16,600	$21,600
1959	Blond, nickel hw, maple 'board	$31,000	$40,000
1959	Blond, nickel hw, slab 'board	$29,800	$38,800

MODEL YEAR	FEATURES	EXC. COND. LOW	HIGH
1959	Custom color	$44,000	$57,000
1959	Mary Kaye, gold hw, maple	$52,000	$68,300
1959	Mary Kaye, gold hw, slab	$48,000	$62,000
1959	Sunburst, maple	$24,400	$31,700
1959	Sunburst, non-trem, slab	$16,600	$21,600
1959	Sunburst, slab, 1-ply 'guard	$20,800	$27,000
1959	Sunburst, slab, 3-ply 'guard	$18,500	$24,000
1960	Common color	$24,000	$31,000
1960	Rare color	$31,000	$45,000
1960	Sunburst	$19,000	$25,000
1961	Common color	$24,000	$31,000
1961	Rare color	$31,000	$45,000
1961	Sunburst	$17,000	$22,000
1962	Common color, early slab	$22,000	$29,000
1962	Common color, late curve	$19,200	$25,000
1962	Rare color, early slab	$29,000	$45,000
1962	Rare color, late curve	$25,000	$40,000
1962	Sunburst, early slab	$17,000	$22,000
1962	Sunburst, late curve	$16,000	$20,000
1963	Common color	$17,000	$23,000
1963	Rare color	$23,000	$40,000
1963	Sunburst	$16,000	$20,000
1964	Common color	$17,000	$23,000
1964	Rare color	$23,000	$40,000
1964	Sunburst, spaghetti logo	$15,000	$19,000
1964	Sunburst, transition logo	$14,000	$18,000
1965	Common color	$15,400	$20,000
1965	Rare color	$20,000	$28,500
1965	Sunburst, F-plate	$9,600	$12,500
1965	Sunburst, green 'guard	$13,000	$17,000
1965	Sunburst, white 'guard	$12,000	$16,000
1966	Common color	$13,000	$17,500
1966	Rare color	$17,900	$24,000
1966	Sunburst, block markers	$13,500	$17,500
1966	Sunburst, dot markers	$9,500	$12,500
1967	Common color	$13,000	$17,500
1967	Rare color	$17,900	$24,000
1967	Sunburst	$9,500	$12,500
1968	Common color, nitro	$13,000	$17,500
1968	Common color, poly	$9,000	$12,000
1968	Common color, poly body, nitro neck	$9,500	$12,300

1965 Fender Stratocaster

1968 Fender Stratocaster

Daniel Hess

To get the most from this book, be sure to read "Using *The Guide*" in the introduction.

1975 Fender Stratocaster
Carter Vintage Guitars

1979 Fender Stratocaster
Robbie Keene

MODEL YEAR	FEATURES	EXC. COND. LOW	HIGH
1968	Rare color, nitro	$17,900	$24,000
1968	Rare color, poly	$12,000	$16,500
1968	Rare color, poly body, nitro neck	$12,300	$18,400
1968	Sunburst, nitro	$9,500	$12,500
1968	Sunburst, poly	$7,800	$10,100
1968	Sunburst, poly body, nitro neck	$8,200	$10,700
1969	Common color, all nitro	$10,000	$15,000
1969	Common color, poly	$9,000	$12,000
1969	Rare color, poly	$12,000	$16,500
1969	Rare colors, all nitro	$15,000	$20,000
1969	Sunburst, all nitro	$8,300	$11,100
1969	Sunburst, poly	$7,800	$10,100
1970	Common color, poly	$7,800	$10,200
1970	Rare color, poly	$10,300	$13,300
1970	Sunburst, poly	$7,100	$9,200
1971	Common color, 4-bolt	$7,800	$10,200
1971	Early-mid '71, sunburst, 4-bolt	$7,100	$9,200
1971	Late '71, sunburst, 3-bolt	$2,850	$3,700
1971	Rare color, 4-bolt	$10,300	$13,300
1972	Common color, 3-bolt	$4,000	$5,200
1972	Rare color, 3-bolt	$5,000	$6,500
1972	Sunburst, 3-bolt	$2,850	$3,700
1973	Common color	$3,300	$4,300
1973	Natural	$2,350	$3,050
1973	Rare color	$4,300	$5,500
1973	Sunburst	$2,600	$3,400
1973	Walnut	$2,500	$3,250
1974	Black, blond, white (white parts)	$3,000	$3,875
1974	Natural	$2,350	$3,050
1974	Sunburst (white parts)	$2,600	$3,400
1974	Walnut	$2,500	$3,250
1975	Black, blond, white (black parts)	$2,575	$3,350
1975	Black, blond, white (white parts)	$3,000	$3,875
1975	Early-'75, sunburst (white parts)	$2,500	$3,300
1975	Late-'75, sunburst (black parts)	$1,900	$2,500
1975	Natural	$2,050	$2,650
1975	Walnut (black parts)	$1,900	$2,450
1976-1979	Various colors	$1,800	$2,300
1980	Antigua	$1,800	$2,300
1980	Black, white, wine	$1,800	$2,300
1980	International colors, 3-bolt	$2,000	$2,600
1980	Natural	$1,800	$2,300
1980	Sunburst	$1,800	$2,300

MODEL YEAR	FEATURES	EXC. COND. LOW	HIGH
1981	Black, white, wine	$1,550	$2,050
1981	International colors	$2,000	$2,600
1981	Sunburst	$1,550	$2,050

Standard Stratocaster (includes "Smith Strat")

1981-1984. Replaces the Stratocaster. Renamed the American Standard Stratocaster for '86-'00 (see next listing). Renamed American Series Stratocaster in '00. From '81/'82 to mid-'83, 3 knobs same as regular Strat but with 4-bolt neck. In August '81, Dan Smith was hired by Bill Schultz and Fender produced an alder body, 4-bolt neck, 21-fret, small headstock Standard Stratocaster that has been nicknamed the Smith Strat (made from Dec. '81-'83). Mid-'83 to the end of '84 2 knobs and 'guard mounted input jack. Not to be confused with current Standard Stratocaster, which is made in Mexico.

1981-1983		$1,550	$2,050
1983-1984	Sunburst, 2-knob	$875	$1,125
1983-1984	Various colors, 2-knob	$875	$1,125

American Standard Stratocaster

1986-2000, 2008-2016. Fender's new name for the American-made Strat when reintroducing it after CBS sold the company. The only American-made Strats made in 1985 were the '57 and '62 models. See Stratocaster and Standard Stratocaster for earlier models. Name used again for '08-'16, various pickup options including SSS, HH, HSH, HSS, Fat and HSS plus. Renamed American Series Stratocaster in 2000 and again renamed the American Professional Series Stratocaster in 2017.

1986-2000	Various colors & options	$750	$1,000
2008-2016	Various colors & options	$750	$1,000

American Series Stratocaster

2000-2007. Ash or alder body, rosewood or maple 'board, dot markers, various pickup options including HSS and HH, 5-way switch, hand polished fret edges. Renamed the American Standard Stratocaster again in '08.

2000-2007	Various colors & options	$750	$1,000
2004	50th Anniversary	$750	$1,000

American Professional Stratocaster

2017-present. Model replaces American Standard Series Strat, redesign includes new V-Mod pickups, narrow-tall frets, new 'deep C' neck profile, genuine bone nut, various colors. Also available left-hand model.

2017-2019	High-end features	$900	$1,200
2017-2019	Low-end features	$750	$1,000

25th Anniversary Stratocaster

1979-1980. Has ANNIVERSARY on upper body horn, silver metallic or white pearlescent finish.

1979-1980		$1,775	$2,300

30th Anniversary Guitar Center Strat

1994. Commemorates Guitar Center's opening in '64, 250 made, 30th Anniversary Limited Edition Guitar Center logo on neck plate, quilted top, sunburst.

1994		$875	$1,150

GUITARS

MODEL YEAR	FEATURES	EXC. COND. LOW	HIGH

35th Anniversary Stratocaster

1989-1991. Custom Shop model, 500 made, figured maple top, Lace Sensor pickups, Eric Clapton preamp circuit.

1989-1991		$1,775	$2,300

40th Anniversary 1954 Stratocaster Limited Edition

1994. Standard production (not Custom Shop), 1,954 made, "40th Anniversary STRATOCASTER 1994" neck plate, serial number series xxxx of 1954, spaghetti logo, tremolo, Kluson tuners, solid maple neck, 2-tone sunburst semi-transparent finish on ash body.

1994		$1,775	$2,300

40th Anniversary American Standard Stratocaster

1994 only. US-made, American Standard model (not Custom Shop), plain top, appearance similar to a '54 maple-neck Strat, sunburst, 2 neck plates offered "40th Anniversary" and "40th Anniversary and still rockin'".

1994		$900	$1,150

40th Anniversary Stratocaster Diamond Dealer

1994 only. Custom Shop model, 150 made, 40th Anniversary headstock inlay, flamed maple top on ash body, '54-'94 inlay at 12th fret, gold etched 'guard, gold hardware, sunburst.

1994		$2,700	$3,500

40th Anniversary Stratocaster ST62 (Japan)

1994 only. Made in Japan, '62 reissue specs.

1994		$900	$1,150

'50s Stratocaster/Classic Series '50s Stratocaster

1985-2019. 'Made in Japan' logo until 'Crafted in Japan' logo mid-'97, basswood body, then mid-'99 made in Mexico with poplar or alder body. Foto-Flame finish offered '92-'94.

1985-1996	Made in Japan	$600	$800
1997-1999	Crafted in Japan	$550	$725
1999-2019	Mexico	$425	$575

American Original '50s Stratocaster

2018-present. Vintage-style appointments, 3 pickups, alder or ash body (White Blonde only), 2-color sunburst or Aztec Gold.

2018-2019		$1,100	$1,425

Classic Player '50s Stratocaster

2006-2019. U.S.-made components but assembled in Mexico, alder body, maple neck and 'board, vintage-style pickups.

2006-2019		$475	$625
2014	50th Anniversary	$525	$700

Classic Series '50s Stratocaster Lacquer

2014-2019. Candy Apple Red nitro-lacquer finish.

2014-2019		$475	$625

Road Worn '50s Stratocaster

2009-present. Maple 'board, '50s specs, aged finish.

2009-2019		$500	$650

50th Anniversary 1954 Stratocaster

2004-2005. Custom Shop, celebrates 50 years of the Strat, 1954 specs and materials, replica form-fit case, certificate, Fender took orders for these up to December 31, 2004.

2004-2005		$3,000	$4,000

50th Anniversary American Deluxe Stratocaster

2004-2005. Deluxe series features, engraved neck plate, tweed case.

2004-2005		$1,050	$1,350

50th Anniversary American Standard Stratocaster

2004. Engraved neck plate, '54 replica pickups, tweed case.

2004		$850	$1,125

50th Anniversary Standard Stratocaster

2004. Made in Mexico, Aztec gold finish, no logo on guitar to indicate 50th Anniv., CE on neck plate to indicate import.

2004		$450	$575

50th Anniversary Stratocaster

1995-1996. Custom Shop model, flame maple top, 3 vintage-style pickups, gold hardware, gold 50th Anniversary (of Fender) coin on back of the headstock, sunburst, 2500 made.

1995-1996		$1,250	$1,600

50th Anniversary Stratocaster Relic

1995-1996. Custom Shop Relic model, aged played-in feel, diamond headstock inlay, Shoreline Gold finish, 200 units planned.

1995-1996		$2,600	$3,400

'54 Stratocaster

1992-1998. Custom Shop Classic reissue, ash body, Custom '50s pickups, gold-plated hardware.

1992-1998	Various options	$1,900	$2,450

'54 Stratocaster FMT

1992-1998. Custom Classic reissue, Flame Maple Top, also comes in gold hardware edition.

1992-1998		$1,800	$2,300

'55 Stratocaster

2006, 2013. Custom Shop model, 1st version is Limited Edition of 100 Relics with 2-tone sunburst; 2nd version is CS Closet Classic. Both include certificate of authenticity.

2006	Relic	$1,900	$2,450
2013	Closet Classic	$1,750	$2,300

'55 Dual-Mag Strat Journeyman Relic

2017-2019. Custom Shop Limited Edition, certificate of authenticity.

2017-2019		$2,400	$3,100

'55 Historic 1955 NOS Stratocaster

2018-present. Custom Shop NOS, certificate of authenticity.

2018-2020		$2,050	$2,650

'55 Journeyman Relic Stratocaster

2017. Custom Shop, vintage-correct appointments, certificate of authenticity.

2017		$1,900	$2,450

'55 Rocking Dog Stratocaster

2007. Custom Shop, various colors.

2007		$2,100	$2,700

1994 Fender 40th Ann. 1954 Stratocaster Limited Edition

Craig Brody

Fender Classic Series '50s Stratocaster

*Fender American Vintage
'56 Stratocaster*

2003 Fender '57 Stratocaster
Rivington Guitars

'56 Stratocaster
1996-2016. Custom Shop model, most detailed replica (and most expensive to date) of '56 Strat, including electronics and pickups, offered with rosewood or maple 'board, gold hardware is +$100.

MODEL YEAR	FEATURES	EXC. COND. LOW	HIGH
1996-1998	Cunetto built Relic	$2,150	$2,800
1997-1998	Cunetto era (staff built)	$2,075	$2,700
1999-2010	Closet Classic	$1,750	$2,300
1999-2010	NOS	$1,750	$2,300
1999-2014	Relic	$1,900	$2,450
2014-2016	Heavy relic	$2,000	$2,600

'56 Journeyman Stratocaster Closet Classic
2020. Custom Shop, certificate of authenticity.

2020		$2,200	$2,850

'56 Stratocaster Heavy Relic
2020. Custom Shop, certificate of authenticity.

2020		$2,250	$2,950

American Vintage '56 Stratocaster
2013-2018. Vintage '56 style, maple 'board, black, Shell Pink or aged white blonde.

2013-2018		$1,075	$1,450

American Vintage '56 Stratocaster Limited Edition Roasted Ash
2017. Roasted ash body, roasted maple neck and 'board, nitro lacquer finish.

2017		$1,375	$1,775

'57 Special Stratocaster
1992-1993. Custom Shop model, flamed maple top, birdseye maple neck, run of 60 made, sunburst.

1992-1993		$2,000	$2,600

'57 Stratocaster
1994-1996. Custom Shop model, replaced by the more authentic, higher-detailed '56 Custom Shop Stratocaster by '99, Custom Shop models can be distinguished by the original certificate that comes with the guitar.

1994-1996	Various colors	$2,000	$2,600

'57 Stratocaster (Custom Shop)
2007, 2010-2016. Heavy Relic (2007, '15-'16), Closet Classic ('10-'13), NOS Dealer Select program ('13-'16) where models are built for specific dealers.

2007	Relic	$1,900	$2,450
2010-2013	Closet Classic	$1,750	$2,300
2013-2016	NOS	$1,750	$2,300
2015-2016	Heavy relic	$2,000	$2,600

'57 Stratocaster (USA)
1982-2012. U.S.-made at the Fullerton, California plant ('82-'85) and at the Corona, California plant ('85-'12), American Vintage series.

1982-1984		$2,550	$3,300
1986-1989		$1,225	$1,600
1986-1989	Rare color	$1,500	$1,900
1990-1999		$1,225	$1,600
1990-1999	Rare color	$1,475	$1,950
2000-2012	Various colors	$1,100	$1,450

'57 Time Machine 1957 Relic Stratocaster
2020. Custom Shop Time Machine series, certificate of authenticity.

2020		$1,800	$2,350

'57 Vintage Stratocaster (Japan)
1982-1998. Made in Japan logo, JV serial numbers '82-'84, E serial '84-'87, Crafted in Japan logo by '98, various colors.

1982-1984	MIJ logo, JV serial	$1,250	$1,600
1998	CIJ logo	$850	$1,100

American Vintage '57 Commemorative Stratocaster
2007. Limited production, 1957-2007 Commemorative logo neckplate.

2007-2012		$1,075	$1,450

Vintage Custom 1957 Stratocaster NOS
2019-present. Custom Shop, maple 'board, aged white blonde with gold hardware.

2019-2020		$2,050	$2,650

Wildwood "10s" 1957 Limited Stratocaster Relic
2014-2015. Custom Shop Dealer Select model for Wildwood Music, '57 specs with 3 single coil or HSS pickups, certificate of authenticity.

2014-2015		$1,900	$2,450

'58 Journeyman Relic Stratocaster
2016. Custom Shop, vintage-correct appointments, certificate of authenticity.

2016		$1,900	$2,450

'58 Limited Edition MIJ Stratocaster
2013. Made in Japan logo, 252 offered.

2013		$725	$950

'58 Stratocaster
1996-1999. Custom Shop, ash body, Fat '50s pickups, chrome or gold hardware (gold is +$100.), Custom Shop models have certificate of authenticity.

1996-1999	Various colors	$2,000	$2,600

'58 Stratocaster (Dakota Red)
1996. Custom Shop model, run of 30 made in Dakota Red with matching headstock, maple neck, Texas special pickups, gold hardware.

1996		$2,000	$2,600

'58 Time Machine 1958 Heavy Relic Stratocaster
2020. Custom Shop Time Machine series, certificate of authenticity.

2020		$2,400	$3,100

'59 Rocking Dog Stratocaster
2007. Custom Shop, commissioned by Garrett Park Guitars, based on '59 rosewood 'board Strat, various colors.

2007		$2,150	$2,800

'59 Stratocaster (Custom Shop)
2010-2013. Relic or Heavy Relic, rosewood 'board, certificate of authenticity.

2010-2013	Relic	$1,900	$2,450
2013	Heavy Relic	$2,000	$2,600

'59 Time Machine 1959 Heavy Relic Stratocaster
2020. Custom Shop Time Machine series, certificate of authenticity.

2020		$2,400	$3,100

'59 Time Machine 1959 Relic Stratocaster
2020. Custom Shop Time Machine series, certificate of authenticity.

2020		$1,800	$2,350

The ***Vintage Guitar Price Guide*** shows low to high values for items in all-original excellent condition, and, where applicable, with original case or cover.

The Official Vintage Guitar magazine Price Guide 2021   **Fender** American Vintage '59 Pine Strat — '62 Strat (USA)   **113**

GUITARS

MODEL YEAR	FEATURES	EXC. COND. LOW	HIGH

American Vintage '59 Pine Stratocaster
2017. Limited Edition neck plate, pine body built from re-claimed 100-year-old wood, 3 vintage '59 single-coil pickups.

2017		$1,300	$1,650

American Vintage '59 Stratocaster
2013-2018. Maple or slab rosewood 'board.

2012-2018		$1,075	$1,450

Wildwood "10s" 1959 Limited Stratocaster Relic
2011-2017. Custom Shop, quartersawn maple neck, Brazilian rosewood 'board, 3 pickups, faded 3-color sunburst. Limited Edition neck plate, decal, and certificate of authenticity.

2011	Maple 'board	$1,900	$2,450
2011-2017	Brazilian	$3,500	$4,600

'60 FMT Stratocaster
1997-1999. Custom Shop model, flame maple top.

1997-1999		$2,000	$2,600

'60 Stratocaster
1992-1999. Custom Shop, 3 Texas Special pickups, various colors, optional gold hardware is +$100, with certificate of authenticity. In 2000 the '60 Stratocaster name was applied to the Time Machine model (see following).

1992-1999		$2,000	$2,600

'60s Stratocaster/'60 Stratocaster
1996-present. Custom Shop Relic/Time Machine. For '96-'99 was called the '60s Stratocaster, in 2000, name was changed to '60 Stratocaster. Heavy Relic began late-'15. Optional gold hardware is +$100. Vince Cunetto and company did the aging of the guitars to mid-1999. The price includes the original Certificate of Authenticity, a guitar without the original certificate is worth less than the values shown.

1996-1998	Cunetto built Relic	$2,200	$2,800
1997-1999	Cunetto era (staff built)	$2,100	$2,700
1999-2010	Closet Classic	$1,750	$2,300
1999-2010	NOS	$1,750	$2,300
1999-2015	Relic	$1,900	$2,450
2015-2020	Heavy relic	$2,000	$2,600

American Original '60s Stratocaster
2018-present. Vintage-style appointments, 3 pickups, alder body, 3-color sunburst. Candy Apple Red or Olympic White.

2018-2019		$1,075	$1,400

Custom 1960 Stratocaster
1994. Short run of 20 custom ordered and specified instruments that have 1960 specs along with other specs such as a pearloid 'guard, came with Certificate of Authenticity, matching headstock color.

1994		$2,000	$2,600

'60s Stratocaster/Classic Series '60s Stratocaster
1985-2019. 'Made in Japan' logo until 'Crafted in Japan' logo mid-'97, basswood body, then mid-'99 made in Mexico with poplar or alder body. Foto-Flame finish offered '92-'94.

1985-1996	Made in Japan	$600	$800
1997-1999	Crafted in Japan	$550	$725
1999-2019	Mexico	$425	$575

Classic Player '60s Stratocaster
2006-2019. U.S.-made components but assembled in Mexico, alder body, maple neck, rosewood 'board, vintage-style pickups.

2006-2019		$475	$625

Classic Series '60s Stratocaster Lacquer
2014-2019. Made in Mexico, 3-color sunburst nitro-lacquer finish.

2014-2019		$475	$625

Limited Edition '60s Daybreak Stratocaster
2019-2020. Traditional series, made in Japan, Olympic White with matching headstock, gold hardware.

2019-2020		$500	$650

Road Worn '60s Stratocaster
2009-present. Rosewood 'board, '60s specs, aged finish.

2009-2019		$500	$650

60th Anniversary '54 Stratocaster (Custom Shop)
2014. Heavy relic, certificate of authenticity, 60th guitar case.

2014		$1,900	$2,450

60th Anniversary American Stratocaster
2006-2007. Celebrates Fender's 60th, US-made, 'Sixty Years' decal logo on headstock, engraved 60th Anniversary neck plate, Z-series serial number, coin on back of headstock, sunburst only, paperwork.

2006-2007	American flag logo	$800	$1,025

60th Anniversary American Vintage 1954 Stratocaster
2014-2016. 1,954 built, came with reproduction 1954 paperwork and 1954 Anniversary Strat Certificate.

2014-2016		$1,075	$1,400

60th Anniversary Commemorative Stratocaster
2014. Celebrates the Strat's 60th, US-made, 60th Anniversary neckplate, 60th medallion on back of headstock, gold hardware, special case, commemorative book.

2014		$750	$1,000

'61 Stratocaster
2001-2012. Custom Shop model, certificate of authenticity.

2001-2012		$1,900	$2,450

Wildwood "10s" 1961 Limited Stratocaster
2010-present. Custom Shop, NOS, relic or heavy relic, quartersawn maple and AA flame maple necks, 3 pickups, "faded" thin nitro finishes in multiple colors.

2010-2016	NOS	$1,750	$2,300
2010-2019	Relic	$1,900	$2,450

'62 Stratocaster (USA)
1982-2012. Made at Fullerton plant ('82-'85) then at Corona plant ('86-present), American Vintage series.

1982-1984	SN: V series	$2,700	$3,500
1986-1989		$1,225	$1,600
1986-1989	Rare color	$1,450	$1,900
1990-1999	Common color	$1,225	$1,600
1990-1999	Rare color	$1,450	$1,900
2000-2012	Common color	$1,075	$1,450

2013 Fender '60s Stratocaster
Bernunzio Uptown Music

1982 Fender '62 Stratocaster
Imaged by Heritage Auctions, HA.com

GUITARS

2005 Fender '69 Stratocaster (Custom Shop)
Rivington Guitars

1994 Fender Aluminum Stratocaster American Standard

MODEL YEAR	FEATURES	EXC. COND. LOW	HIGH

'62 Commemorative Stratocaster
2007. Limited production, part of American Vintage Series, 1957-2007 Commemorative logo neckplate.
| 2007 | | $1,050 | $1,400 |

'62 Vintage Stratocaster (Japan)
1982-1984. Made in Japan, JV serial numbers, various colors.
| 1982-1984 | | $1,250 | $1,700 |

'62 Heavy Relic Stratocaster
2007-2010. Custom Shop Dealer Select series, extreme Relic work.
| 2007-2010 | | $2,000 | $2,600 |

'62 Stratocaster ST62US Reissue
2008-2012. Made by Fender Japan for that market, US-made 'vintage' pickups.
| 2008-2012 | | $525 | $700 |

'62 Vintage Custom 1962 Stratocaster
2019-present. Custom Shop Limited Edition, NOS finish, alder body, maple neck and 'board, 3-color sunburst.
| 2019 | | $2,050 | $2,650 |

Dave's Guitar Shop American 1962 Stratocaster
2019-2020. Limited Edition, various colors with nitro lacquer finish.
| 2019-2020 | | $1,200 | $1,575 |

Deluxe Vintage Player '62 Stratocaster
2005-2006. Limited Edition, vintage and modern features based upon '62 specs, 3 Samarium Cobalt Noiseless pickups, Deluxe American Standard electronics, Olympic White or Ice Blue Metallic.
| 2005-2006 | | $1,125 | $1,500 |

Willcutt Guitars True '62 Stratocaster
2016-present. Custom Shop, limited run for Bob Willcutt Guitars, 4 models; 'V' neck, '59 'C' neck, '60s 'C' neck and large 'C' neck.
| 2016-2019 | | $2,000 | $2,600 |

'63 Stratocaster
2015-2018. Custom Shop Time Machine series, Relic in '15-'17, Heavy Relic '18.
| 2015-2017 | Relic | $1,900 | $2,450 |
| 2018 | Heavy Relic | $1,900 | $2,450 |

'63 Stratocaster Journeyman Relic
2015. Custom Shop, vintage-correct appointments, alder body, bird's-eye maple neck, rosewood 'board, 3 single-coil pickups, certificate of authenticity.
| 2015 | | $2,000 | $2,600 |

'64 Stratocaster (Custom Shop)
Certificate of authenticity.
| 2009-2012 | Relic | $1,900 | $2,450 |
| 2011-2014 | Closet Classic | $1,750 | $2,300 |

'64 Time Machine Journeyman Relic Stratocaster
2018-present. Custom Shop Time Machine series, vintage-correct appointments, certificate of authenticity.
| 2018-2019 | | $2,050 | $2,650 |

'65 Stratocaster (Custom Shop)
1998-1999, 2003-2006, 2010 (no Closet Classic). Custom Shop model, '65 small-headstock specs, rosewood or maple cap 'board, transition logo, offered in NOS, Relic, or Closet Classic versions.
1998-1999	Cunetto era (staff built)	$2,100	$2,700
2003-2006	Closet Classic	$1,750	$2,300
2003-2010	NOS	$1,750	$2,300
2003-2010	Relic	$1,900	$2,450

'65 Journeyman Closet Classic Stratocaster
2019. Custom Shop, vintage-correct appointments, certificate of authenticity.
| 2019 | | $2,200 | $2,850 |

'65 Time Machine 1965 Journeyman Relic Stratocaster
2010. Custom Shop Time Machine series, vintage-correct appointments, certificate of authenticity.
| 2010 | | $2,150 | $2,775 |

American Vintage '65 Stratocaster
2013-2017. V serial number, flash coat finish, various colors, some with matching headstock.
| 2013-2017 | | $1,100 | $1,450 |

Mark Kendrick Master Design '65 Stratocaster
2004. Custom Shop Limited Edition, run of 65, alder body, maple neck, African rosewood 'board, Lake Placid Blue over Olympic White.
| 2004 | | $2,800 | $3,800 |

'66 Stratocaster (Custom Shop)
2004-2008. Custom Shop model, offered in Closet Classic, NOS or Relic versions.
2004-2008	Closet Classic	$1,750	$2,300
2004-2008	NOS	$1,750	$2,300
2004-2008	Relic	$1,900	$2,450

'67 Time Machine 1967 Journeyman Relic Aged Stratocaster
2020. Custom Shop Time Machine series, vintage-correct appointments.
| 2020 | | $2,200 | $2,850 |

'67 Time Machine 1967 Journeyman Relic Custom Top Stratocaster
2020. Custom Shop Time Machine series, vintage-correct appointments.
| 2020 | | $2,150 | $2,775 |

'68 Heavy Relic Stratocaster
2007-2010. Custom Shop, Dealer Select model, extreme Relic work.
| 2007-2010 | | $2,000 | $2,600 |

'68 Reverse Strat Special (USA)
2001-2002. With special reverse left-hand neck, large headstock (post-CBS style).
| 2001-2002 | | $2,000 | $2,600 |

'68 Stratocaster (Japan)
1996-1999, 2013. '68 specs including large headstock, part of Collectables Series, sunburst, natural, Olympic White.
| 1996-2013 | | $800 | $1,050 |

'69 Stratocaster (Custom Shop)
1997-2012, 2016. Large headstock, U-shaped maple neck with rosewood or maple cap options, '69-style finish, gold hardware is +$100, since 2000, offered in NOS, Relic, or Closet Classic (no CC after '08) versions. Heavy Relic in '16.
| 1997-1999 | Cunetto era (staff built) | $2,100 | $2,700 |
| 2000-2008 | Closet Classic | $1,750 | $2,300 |

MODEL YEAR	FEATURES	EXC. COND. LOW	HIGH
2000-2009	NOS	$1,750	$2,300
2000-2012	Relic	$1,900	$2,450
2016	Heavy Relic	$2,000	$2,600

Wildwood "10s" 1969 Limited Stratocaster
2014. Custom Shop, Relic, Jimi Hendrix specs, certificate of authenticity.

| 2014 | | $1,900 | $2,450 |

'70s Stratocaster/Classic Series '70s Stratocaster
1999-2019. Made in Mexico, large headstock, white pickups and knobs, rosewood 'board.

| 1999-2019 | | $525 | $700 |

American Vintage '70s Stratocaster
2009-2012. Large '70s headstock, early '70s white pickups and knobs, 3-bolt neck.

| 2009-2012 | | $1,075 | $1,425 |

'72 Stratocaster (Japan)
1985-1996. Basswood body, maple 'board, large headstock, various colors (does not include the Paisley '72).

| 1985-1986 | | $1,000 | $1,300 |
| 1987-1996 | | $900 | $1,200 |

'72 Stratocaster Limited Edition (Japan)
2013. Made in Japan for US domestic sales, 144 made, large headstock, bullet truss rod, 3-bolt maple neck, 21 frets, 3 Alnico pickups.

| 2013 | | $550 | $700 |

Acoustasonic Stratocaster
2003-2009. Hollowed out alder Strat body with braceless graphite top, 3 in-bridge Fishman piezo pickups, acoustic sound hole.

| 2003-2009 | | $575 | $725 |

Aerodyne Stratocaster
2004-2009. Import Strat with Aerodyne body profile, bound body, black.

| 2004-2009 | | $575 | $725 |

Albert Hammond Jr. Signature Stratocaster
2018-present. Made in Mexico, styled after his 1985 reissue of a '72 Strat.

| 2018-2019 | | $475 | $625 |

Aluminum Stratocaster (Custom Shop)
1994. Custom Shop aluminum bodies, chrome body with black 'guard, black body with chrome 'guard, or green with black lines and red swirls. There are also several Custom Shop one-offs with aluminum bodies.

| 1993-1994 | Chrome | $1,800 | $2,300 |

Aluminum Stratocaster American Standard
1994-1995. Aluminum-bodied American Standard with anodized finish in blue marble, purple marble or red, silver and blue stars and stripes. Some with 40th Anniversary designation. There is also a Custom Shop version.

| 1994-1995 | Various patterns & options | $1,500 | $1,950 |

American Acoustasonic Stratocaster
2020-present. Solid A sitka spruce top, mahogany back and sides, ebony 'board, various colors.

| 2020 | | $1,050 | $1,400 |

American Classic Holoflake Stratocaster
1992-1993. Custom Shop model, splatter/sparkle finish, pearloid 'guard.

| 1992-1993 | | $1,650 | $2,150 |

American Classic Stratocaster
1992-1999. Custom Shop version of American Standard, 3 pickups, tremolo, rosewood 'board, nickel or gold-plated hardware, various colors.

| 1992-1999 | Various options | $1,650 | $2,150 |

American Custom Stratocaster (Custom Shop)
2020. Custom Shop American Custom series, various woods and colors.

| 2020 | | $2,400 | $3,100 |

American Deluxe Stratocaster
1998-2016. Premium alder or ash body, maple neck, various pickup options including SSS, HSS, HSH, HSS Plus, Fat and Shawbucker, various colors.

| 1998-2016 | Various options | $950 | $1,225 |

American Deluxe Stratocaster Designer Series
2004-2015. Limited production, various upgrades such as flamed maple top, mahogany, etc.

| 2004-2015 | | $1,100 | $1,425 |

American Deluxe Stratocaster FMT HSS
2004-2009. Flame maple top version of the HSS.

| 2004-2009 | | $1,100 | $1,425 |

American Deluxe Stratocaster HSS Mahogany
2015-2016. Limited Edition 10 for 15 series, 2-piece mahogany body.

| 2015-2016 | | $900 | $1,200 |

American Elite Stratocaster
2016-2019. Alder body, 3 single-coil pickups or HSS with Shawbucker.

| 2016-2019 | | $1,050 | $1,350 |

American Elite Stratocaster Limited Edition
2016. Various color options with matching headstock.

| 2016 | | $1,075 | $1,400 |

American Longboard Stratocaster HSS
2015. Part of Fender's limited edition 10 for 15 series, vintage surfboard laminate top design.

| 2015 | | $800 | $1,050 |

American Performer Stratocaster
2018-present. Made in US, new features include 3 Yosemite single-coil pickups, Greasebucket tone system, various colors.

| 2018-2019 | | $650 | $850 |

American Special Stratocaster
2010-2018. Limited Edition, '70s headstock with post-CBS black Stratocaster logo, Texas Special pickups (SSS or HSS), satin (early were gloss) finish.

| 2010-2018 | | $650 | $850 |

American Standard Stratocaster Limited Edition
1990s-2019. American Standard series, various limited edition models.

| 1995-1996 | Matching hdstk | $1,000 | $1,300 |
| 2001 | Standard hdstk, white | $1,000 | $1,300 |

Fender American Deluxe Stratocaster

2018 Fender American Elite Stratocaster
Carter Vintage Guitars

*1992 Fender Bill Carson
Stratocaster*

Bob Moreland

*1984 Fender Bowling Ball/
Marble Stratocaster*

MODEL YEAR	FEATURES	EXC. COND. LOW	HIGH
2009	Matching hdstk, Seafoam/		
	Surf Green	$1,000	$1,300
2014-2017	Channel Bound	$750	$975
2015	Blackout		
	(Mystic Black)	$775	$1,000
2015-2016	Mystic Aztec Gold	$750	$975
2015-2016	Oiled Ash	$775	$1,000
2015-2016	Vintage White	$775	$1,000
2017	Rosewood neck		
	& hdstk	$750	$1,000
2019	Pale Moon Quilt	$1,100	$1,400

American Ultra Stratocaster

2019-present. Various options and colors.

2019-2020		$1,100	$1,425

Ancho Poblano Journeyman Relic Stratocaster

2019. Custom Shop Limited Edition series.

2019		$2,000	$2,625

Ancho Poblano Limited Edition Roasted Stratocaster Relic

2019-2020. Custom Shop Limited Edition series, roasted alder body with relic lacquer finish.

2019-2020		$2,100	$2,700

Antigua Stratocaster

2004. Made in Japan, limited-edition reissue, '70s features and antigua finish.

2004		$600	$800

Artisan Series Stratocaster (Custom Shop)

2015-present. Features distinctively figured woods, gold hardware, hand-rubbed oil finishes, certificate of authenticity, various models: Okoume, Claro Walnut, Figured Rosewood, Spalted Maple, Tamo Ash, Thinline Koa.

2015	Okoume	$1,950	$2,500
2016-2019	Spalted Maple	$2,100	$2,700
2016-2019	Tamo Ash	$2,100	$2,700
2020	Maple Burl	$2,000	$2,800

Big Apple Stratocaster

1997-2000. Two humbucking pickups, 5-way switch, rosewood 'board or maple neck, non-tremolo optional.

1997-2000	Various colors	$725	$950

Big Block Stratocaster

2005-2006. Pearloid block markers, black with matching headstock, 2 single coils (neck, middle) 1 humbucker (bridge), vintage style tremolo.

2005-2006		$550	$700

Big Head Stratocaster

2020. Custom Shop Limited Edition series.

2020		$1,975	$2,600

Bill Carson Stratocaster

1992. Based on the '57 Strat, birdseye maple neck, Cimarron Red finish, 1 left-handed and 100 right-handed produced, serial numbers MT000-MT100, made in Fender Custom Shop, and initiated by The Music Trader (MT) in Florida.

1992		$1,650	$2,150

Billy Corgan Stratocaster

2008-2012. US-made, 3 DiMarzio pickups, string-thru hardtail bridge.

2008-2012		$950	$1,225

Blackie Stratocaster (Custom Shop 1987)

1987. 12 made, includes Certificate of Authenticity.

1987		$2,225	$2,875

Blackie Stratocaster (Custom Shop)

November 2006. Blackie tribute, 185 instruments for U.S. market, 90 made for export, original retail price $24,000.

2006		$8,300	$10,700

Blacktop Stratocaster

2011-2015. Alder body, maple neck, rosewood or maple 'board, various pickup options including HH and HSH, various finish options. Floyd Rose version also available.

2011-2015		$325	$425

Mahogany Blacktop Stratocaster Limited Edition

2019. 2 or 3 Alnico humbuckers, mahogany body, black headstock, Oly White, black, or crimson red, chrome or gold hardware.

2019		$440	$575

Blue Flower Stratocaster

1984-1997, 2002-2004. Made in Japan, '72 Strat reissue with a '68 Tele Blue Floral finish.

1984-1987	1st issue	$1,000	$1,300
1988-1994		$900	$1,175
1995-1997		$800	$1,025
2002-2004	2nd issue	$600	$800

Bonnie Raitt Stratocaster

1995-2001. Alder body, often in blueburst, Bonnie Raitt's signature on headstock.

1995-2001		$1,500	$2,000

Bowling Ball/Marble Stratocaster

1984. Standard Strat with 1 tone and 1 volume control, jack on 'guard, called Bowling Ball Strat due to the swirling, colored finish.

1984	All colors	$2,800	$3,700

Buddy Guy Standard Stratocaster

1996-present. Made in Mexico, maple neck, polka-dot finish.

1996-2019		$475	$625

Buddy Guy Stratocaster (Signature)

1995-2009. Maple neck, 3 Gold Lace Sensor pickups, ash body, signature model, blond or sunburst.

1995-2009		$725	$925

Buddy Holly Tribute Stratocaster

2014. Custom Shop model, 50 made, '55 specs, with certificate of authenticity.

2014		$5,500	$7,200

California Stratocaster/California Fat Stratocaster

1997-1999. Made in the U.S., painted in Mexico, 3 single coils, Fat has HSS, various colors.

1997-1999	SSS or HSS	$550	$700

Carved Top Stratocaster HSS (Custom Shop)

1995-1998. Carved figured maple top, HSS (HH offered in '98), certificate of authenticity, various colors.

1995-1998		$1,700	$2,200

Classic Player Stratocaster

2000. Custom Shop model, Standard Stratocaster with useful 'player-friendly features' such as noiseless

The Official Vintage Guitar magazine Price Guide 2021   **Fender** Classic Player Strat HH — Eric Clapton Strat (CS)   **117**

GUITARS

MODEL YEAR	FEATURES	EXC. COND. LOW	HIGH

stacked single-coil pickups and factory Sperzel locking tuners, black, gold anodized 'guard.

| 2000 | | $1,150 | $1,500 |

Classic Player Stratocaster HH
2015-2016. Alder body, maple neck, bound rosewood 'board, 2 humbuckers, dark Mercedes Blue gloss finish with matching headstock.

| 2015-2016 | | $475 | $625 |

Collector's Edition Stratocaster ('62 Reissue)
1997. Pearl inlaid '97 on 12th fret, rosewood 'board, alder body, gold hardware, tortoise 'guard, nitro finish, sunburst, 1997 made.

| 1997 | | $1,050 | $1,350 |

Contemporary Stratocaster
1989-1998. Custom Shop model, 7/8 scale body, hum/single/single pickups, various colors.

| 1989-1998 | | $1,200 | $1,550 |

Contemporary Stratocaster (Import)
1985-1987. Import model used while the new Fender reorganized, black or natural headstock with silver-white logo, black or white 'guard, 2 humbucker pickups or single-coil and humbucker, 2 knobs and slider switch.

| 1985-1987 | | $525 | $700 |

Crash Stratocaster
2005-2007. Master Built Custom Shop model, hand painted by John Crash Matos, approximately 50, comes with certificate, the prices shown include the original certificate.

| 2005-2007 | | $3,050 | $3,975 |

Custom Classic Stratocaster
2000-2008. Custom Shop version of American Standard Strat.

| 2000-2008 | | $1,800 | $2,400 |

Custom Deluxe Stratocaster
2009-2014. Custom Shop, birdseye maple neck, rosewood or maple 'board, certificate. Model also available with flame maple top.

| 2009-2014 | | $2,400 | $3,100 |

Dave Murray Stratocaster
2009-present. Alder body, maple neck, rosewood 'board, 3 pickups, 2-color sunburst.

| 2009-2019 | | $575 | $750 |

David Gilmour Signature Stratocaster
2008-2019. Custom Shop, NOS or Relic, based on Gilmour's '70 black Stratocaster, certificate of authenticity.

| 2008-2019 | | $2,200 | $3,300 |

Deluxe Lone Star Stratocaster
2007-2016. Reissue of Lone Star Strat, made in Mexico, 1 humbucker and 2 single-coils, rosewood 'board.

| 2007-2016 | | $350 | $450 |

Deluxe Players Special Edition Stratocaster
2007. Made in Mexico, Special Edition Fender oval sticker on back of headstock along with 60th Anniversary badge.

| 2007 | | $350 | $475 |

Deluxe Players Stratocaster
2004-2016. Made in Mexico, 3 noiseless single-coils, push-button switching system.

| 2004-2016 | | $375 | $500 |

Deluxe Roadhouse Stratocaster
2008-present. Deluxe series reissue, Texas Special pickups.

| 2008-2019 | | $450 | $600 |

Deluxe Stratocaster
2016-present. Mexico-made, ck and 'board, 3 vintage noiseless single-coils. Becomes American Deluxe Strat.

| 2016-2019 | SSS and HSS | $450 | $600 |

Deluxe Stratocaster HSS Plus Top With IOS Connectivity
2014-2016. Deluxe series, plugs into iOS devices.

| 2014-2016 | | $350 | $450 |

Deluxe Stratocaster Plus
1987-1998. Alder (poplar earlier) with ash veneer front and back, 3 Lace Sensor pickups, Floyd Rose, various colors. Becomes American Deluxe Strat Plus.

| 1987-1998 | | $800 | $1,050 |

Dick Dale Stratocaster
1994-present. Custom Shop signature model, alder body, reverse headstock, sparkle finish.

| 1994-present | | $1,600 | $2,100 |

Elite Stratocaster
1983-1984. The Elite Series feature active electronics and noise-cancelling pickups, push buttons instead of 3-way switch, Elite script logo on 4-bolt neck plate, various colors. Also see Gold Elite Stratocaster and Walnut Elite Stratocaster.

| 1983-1984 | | $2,000 | $2,600 |

EOB (Ed O'Brien) Sustainer Stratocaster
2017-present. Alder body, maple neck and 'board, 3 pickups (Sustainer in neck position), custom "Flower of Life" neck plate, gloss poly white finish.

| 2017-2019 | | $600 | $800 |

Eric Clapton Gold Leaf Stratocaster
2004. Custom Shop model, special build for Guitar Center, 50 made, 23k gold leaf finish/covering.

| 2004 | | $3,800 | $4,900 |

Eric Clapton Signature Journeyman Relic Stratocaster
2020-present. Custom Shop, Clapton's signature on the headstock, 2-color sunburst or aged white blonde.

| 2020 | | $2,850 | $3,675 |

Eric Clapton Signature Stratocaster
2019-present. Custom Shop model, alder body, maple neck, three Vintage Noiseless pickups, Clapton's signature on headstock, black or Mercedes Blue.

| 2019-2020 | | $2,500 | $3,300 |

Eric Clapton Stratocaster
1988-present. U.S.-made, '57 reissue features, had Lace Sensor pickups until '01, when switched to Vintage Noiseless. Black versions have added "Blackie" decal on headstock.

| 1988-2019 | | $900 | $1,200 |

Eric Clapton Stratocaster (Custom Shop)
2004-2016. Custom Shop model, standard non-active single-coil pickups, black or blue finish.

| 2004-2016 | | $1,725 | $2,200 |

Fender Deluxe Lone Star Stratocaster

2004 Fender Eric Clapton Stratocaster
Robbie Keene

To get the most from this book, be sure to read "Using **The Guide**" in the introduction.

GUITARS

2017 Fender Eric Johnson Stratocaster

1997 Fender Jerry Donahue Hellecaster Stratocaster
Stoeffu Vogt

MODEL YEAR	FEATURES	EXC. COND. LOW	HIGH

Eric Johnson 1954 "Virginia" Stratocaster
2020. Stories Collection, limited numbers offered from both Custom Shop and Corona production.

2020	Custom Shop	$1,400	$1,800
2020	Fender Corona	$1,400	$1,800

Eric Johnson Signature Stratocaster Thinline
2018-present. Alder body, maple neck and 'board, 3 single-coil pickups, 2-color sunburst or vintage white.

2017-2019		$925	$1,225

Eric Johnson Stratocaster
2005-present. '57 spec body and 1-piece maple soft-v-neck, or, for '09 to '15, rosewood 'board, special design pickups, vintage tremolo with 4 springs, EJ initials and guitar-player figure engraved neck plate. Also listed as Eric Johnson Stratocaster Maple or Rosewood.

2005-2019	Maple or rosewood	$1,075	$1,400

Floyd Rose Classic Relic Stratocaster
1998. Custom Shop model, late '60s large headstock, 1 humbucker and 1 Strat pickup.

1998		$1,900	$2,450

Floyd Rose Classic Stratocaster (Strat HSS) (Strat HH)
1992-2002. Two single-coils, bridge humbucker, Floyd Rose tremolo, becomes Floyd Rose Classic Strat HSS or HH (2 humbuckers) in '98.

1992-2002		$1,000	$1,350

Ford Shelby GT Stratocaster
2007. 200 made, black with silver Shelby GT racing stripe.

2007	200 made	$1,900	$2,500

Foto Flame Stratocaster
1994-1996, 2000. Japanese-made Collectables model, alder and basswood body with Foto Flame (simulated woodgrain) finish on top cap and back of neck.

1994-2000		$600	$775

Freddy Tavares Aloha Stratocaster
1993-1994. Custom Shop model, hollow aluminum body with hand engraved Hawaiian scenes, custom inlay on neck, 153 made.

1993-1994		$4,200	$5,400

FSR Stratocaster
2012-2019. Factory Special Run models might be 'dealer exclusive' or open to all dealers as limited run. FSR have a special set of appointments that are not standard to the core lineup.

2012	Antigua Strat	$500	$675
2013	Hot Rod Strat	$400	$525
2013-2017	Special Ed Classic '60s Strat Laq Surf Green	$575	$775
2015-2016	Amer Std '54 Strat	$700	$925
2017-2019	Special Ed '50s Strat	$500	$650
2018-2019	MIJ Traditional '50s Strat	$475	$625

George Fullerton 50th Anniversary '57 Strat Ltd. Ed. Set
2007. 150 made, '57 Strat with matching relic Pro Junior tweed amp, certificates of authenticity signed by Fullerton, commemorative neck plate.

2007		$2,800	$3,800

Gold Stratocaster
1981-1983. Gold metallic finish, gold-plated brass hardware, 4-bolt neck, maple 'board, skunk strip, trem.

1981-1983		$2,100	$2,800

Gold Elite Stratocaster
1983-1984. The Elite series feature active electronics and noise-cancelling pickups, the Gold Elite has gold hardware and pearloid tuner buttons, also see Elite Stratocaster and Walnut Elite Stratocaster.

1983-1984		$2,000	$2,600

Gold Stratocaster (Custom Shop)
1989. Custom Shop, 500 made, gold finish with gold anodized and white 'guards included.

1989		$2,100	$2,800

GT11 Stratocaster
2019-2020. Custom Shop, exclusive models for Sweetwater, relic and heavy relic.

2019-2020	Heavy relic	$2,100	$2,800
2019-2020	Relic	$2,100	$2,700

Hank Marvin Stratocaster
1995-1996. Custom Shop model, Feista Red.

1995-1996		$1,800	$2,350

Hank Marvin 40th Anniversary Stratocaster
1998. Custom Shop logo with '40 Years 1958-1998' marked on back of headstock, Fiesta Red, only 40 made, Custom Shop certificate.

1998		$4,600	$6,000

Harley-Davidson 90th Anniversary Stratocaster
1993. Custom Shop, 109 total made, Harley-Davidson and Custom Shop V logo on headstock (Diamond Edition, 40 units), 9 units produced for the Harley-Davidson company without diamond logo, 60 units were not Diamond Edition, chrome-plated engraved metal body, engraved 'guard, Custom Shop Certificate important attribute.

1993		$8,100	$10,500

Highway One Stratocaster/HSS
2002-2014. U.S.-made, alder body, satin lacquer finish, HSS version has humbucker/single/single pickups.

2002-2014		$600	$750

HM Strat (USA/Import)
1988-1992 ('88 Japanese-made, '89-'90 U.S.- and Japanese-made, '91-'92 U.S.-made). Heavy Metal Strat, Floyd Rose, regular or pointy headstock, black hardware, H, HH, SH, or SSH pickup options. Later models have choice of SHH or SSH.

1988-1990	Import	$700	$900
1989-1992	USA	$700	$900

HM Strat Limited Edition
2020-present. '88-'92 HM specs, available in era-correct Day-Glo colors, Frozen Yellow, Flash Pink, Ice Blue and Bright White.

2020		$650	$850

Homer Haynes HLE Stratocaster
1988-1989. Custom Shop model, limited edition of 500, '59 Strat basics with gold finish, gold anodized guard and gold hardware.

1988-1989		$1,900	$2,450

MODEL YEAR	FEATURES	EXC. COND. LOW	HIGH

Hot Wheels Stratocaster
2003. Custom Shop model commissioned by Hot Wheels, 16 made, orange flames over blue background, large Hot Wheels logo.

| 2003 | | $1,350 | $1,775 |

HRR Stratocaster/ Floyd Rose HRR (Japan)
1990-1994. Japanese-made, hot-rodded vintage-style Strat, Floyd Rose tremolo system, H/S/S pickups, maple neck, sunburst or colors. Called the Floyd Rose HRR for '92-'94 (with optional Foto Flame finish).

| 1990-1994 | | $700 | $925 |

Ike Turner Tribute Stratocaster
2005. Custom Shop model, 100 made, replica of Ike Turner's Sonic Blue Strat.

| 2005 | | $2,400 | $3,100 |

Jeff Beck Signature Stratocaster (CS)
2004-present. Custom Shop, 3 Noiseless dual-coils, Olympic White or Surf Green.

| 2004-2019 | | $1,450 | $1,900 |
| 2020 | | $2,400 | $3,100 |

Jeff Beck Stratocaster
1991-present. Alder body, originally 4 Lace Sensors (H/S/S) changing to 3 Noiseless dual-coils in '01, rosewood 'board, Olympic White and Surf Green (Midnight Purple until '02).

1991	1st issue, larger hdsk	$1,800	$2,350
1992-1993	1st issue, larger hdsk	$1,450	$1,900
1994-2009		$900	$1,200
2010-2019	Artist Series	$900	$1,200

Jerry Donahue Hellecaster Stratocaster
1997. Made in the Fender Japan Custom Shop as one part of the 3-part Hellecasters Series, limited edition, Seymour Duncan pickups, maple, blue with blue sparkle guard.

| 1997 | | $700 | $900 |

Jim Root Stratocaster
2010-present. Artist series, mahogany body, ebony or maple 'board, 2 active pickups, black hardware, black or white finish.

| 2010-2019 | | $800 | $1,075 |

Jimi Hendrix Limited Edition Stratocaster (Custom Shop)
2019-present. Custom Artist series, designed from Hendrix's modified '68 Strat used at Woodstock ('69), aged Olympic White.

| 2019-2020 | | $3,850 | $5,000 |

Jimi Hendrix Monterey Pop Stratocaster
1997-1998. Custom Shop model, near replica of Monterey Pop Festival sacrifice guitar, red psychedelic-style finish.

| 1997-1998 | | $8,400 | $11,200 |

Jimi Hendrix Monterey Stratocaster
2017-2018. Body art like Hendrix's hand-painted original that he destroyed at Monterey Pop Festival, custom neck plate, signature on headstock rear.

| 2017-2018 | | $450 | $600 |

Jimi Hendrix Stratocaster
2015-present. Reverse headstock, silhouette and engraved 'Authentic Hendrix' on neckplate.

| 2015-2018 | | $500 | $650 |

Jimi Hendrix Tribute Stratocaster
1997-2000. Left-handed guitar strung right-handed, maple cap neck, Olympic White. Fender headstock logo positioned upside down, made for right-handed player to look as if they are playing a left-handed guitar flipped over.

| 1997-2000 | | $1,650 | $2,150 |

Jimi Hendrix Voodoo 29th Anniversary Stratocaster
1993. Fender Custom Shop made only 35 for Guitar Center, large 'Guitar Center 29th Anniversary' logo on neckplate, right-handed body with reverse left-handed headstock and reversed Fender headstock logo, purple sparkle finish.

| 1993 | | $2,000 | $2,700 |

Jimi Hendrix Voodoo Child Journeyman Relic Stratocaster
2020. Custom Shop, Olympic White or black with aged relic finish.

| 2020 | | $2,750 | $3,550 |

Jimi Hendrix Voodoo Child Stratocaster
2020. Custom Shop, Olympic White or black with NOS finish.

| 2020 | NOS | $2,500 | $3,300 |

Jimi Hendrix Voodoo Stratocaster
1997-2002. Right-handed body with reverse peghead, maple neck, sunburst, Olympic White, or black.

| 1997-2002 | | $1,650 | $2,150 |

Jimmie Vaughan Tex-Mex Stratocaster
1997-present. Poplar body, maple 'board, signature on headstock, 3 Tex-Mex pickups, various colors.

| 1997-2019 | | $475 | $625 |

John Jorgenson Hellecaster Stratocaster
1997. Fender Japan Custom Shop, part of the 3-part Hellecasters Series, limited edtion, Seymour Duncan pickups, gold sparkle 'guard, gold hardware, split single-coils, rosewood 'board.

| 1997 | | $875 | $1,125 |

John Mayer Limited Edition Black1 Stratocaster
2010. Custom Shop, 83 made, black finish NOS or extreme relic option, JC serial number, Custom Shop/ John Cruz logo on back of headstock includes personal letter from John Mayer.

| 2010 | NOS | $2,450 | $3,200 |

John Mayer Stratocaster
2005-2014. Alder body, special scooped mid-range pickups, special design gigbag with pocket for laptop computer.

| 2005-2014 | | $925 | $1,200 |

Kenny Wayne Shepherd Stratocaster
2009-2016. Based on Shepherd's '61, rosewood 'board, jumbo frets, Artic White with cross, black with racing stripes or 3-color sunburst.

| 2009-2016 | | $500 | $675 |

Koa Stratocaster
2006-2008. Made in Korea, Special Edition series, sunburst over koa veneer top, plain script Fender logo, serial number on back of headstock with.

| 2006-2008 | | $400 | $550 |

Fender Jim Root Stratocaster

1997 Fender Jimi Hendrix Voodoo Stratocaster

Craig Brody

2007 Fender Lenny Stratocaster
Imaged by Heritage Auctions, HA.com

*2017 Fender Michael
Landau 1968 Stratocaster*

MODEL YEAR	FEATURES	EXC. COND. LOW	HIGH

Kon Tiki Stratocaster
2003. Custom Shop model, limited run of 25, Tiki Green including Tiki 3-color art work on headstock.

| 2003 | | $2,000 | $2,600 |

Lenny Stratocaster
Introduced Dec. 12, 2007 by Guitar Center stores, Custom Shop model, 185 guitars made, initial product offering price was 17K.

| 2007 | | $6,700 | $8,800 |

Lincoln Brewster Signature Stratocaster
2019-present. Ash body, 1-piece maple neck, 3 single-coil pickups, gold with lacquer finish.

| 2019-2020 | | $1,100 | $1,425 |

Lite Ash Stratocaster Special Edition
2004-2007. Korea, light ash body, birds-eye maple neck.

| 2004-2007 | | $400 | $525 |

Lone Star Stratocaster
1996-2001. Alder body, 1 humbucker and 2 single-coil pickups, rosewood 'board or maple neck, various colors.

| 1996 | 50th Anniv Badge | $700 | $925 |
| 1997-2001 | | $700 | $925 |

Mark Knopfler Stratocaster
2003-2013. '57 body with '62 maple neck.

| 2003-2013 | | $1,025 | $1,325 |

Masterbuilt Custom Shop Stratocaster
2006-present. Various models and builders, specific identification to builder, must include certificate of authenticity.

| 2006-2020 | Various models | $3,000 | $6,300 |

Masterbuilt Dennis Galuszka Fat '50s Stratocaster
2020. Alder Body, Brazilian rosewood neck and 'board, 3 Fat '50s single-coil pickups, Aged Sherwood Green.

| 2020 | | $4,300 | $5,675 |

Matthias Jabs Signature Stratocaster
1998. Made in Japan, 200 offered, Candy Apple Red.

| 1998 | | $850 | $1,100 |

Michael Landau Signature Relic Stratocaster 1963/1968
2014-present. Custom Shop Artist series, Relic, alder body, rosewood 'board, '63 is worn Fiesta Red over 3-color sunburst, '68 is black or bleached 3-color sunburst.

| 2014-2019 | 1963 Relic | $2,000 | $2,600 |
| 2014-2019 | 1968 Relic | $2,000 | $2,600 |

Milonga Deluxe Stratocaster
2005. Special Edition made in Mexico, Vintage Noiseless pickups, rosewood 'board, Olympic White, gold hardware.

| 2005 | | $350 | $450 |

MLB Major League Baseball Stratocaster
2014. Official team logos and imagery unique to each, licensed by Major League Baseball Properties.

| 2014 | Various models | $450 | $575 |

Mod Shop Stratocaster
2017-present. Mod Shop allows you to create your own factory-customized electric guitar or bass.

| 2017-2020 | | $1,500 | $2,000 |

Modern Player Stratocaster HSH/HSS
2013-2015. Made in China, hum-single-hum or hum-single-single.

| 2013-2015 | | $290 | $375 |

Moto Limited Edition Stratocaster
1995. Custom Shop model, pearloid cover in various colors, includes Certificate of Authenticity, not to be confused with white pearloid Moto Strat which is part of a guitar and amp set (as listed below).

| 1995 | | $1,965 | $2,550 |

Moto Set Stratocaster
1995-1996. Custom Shop set including guitar, case, amp and amp stand, white pearloid finish.

| 1995-1996 | Red (few made) | $3,125 | $4,075 |
| 1995-1996 | White | $3,125 | $4,075 |

Orange Krush Limited Edition Stratocaster
1995. Custom Shop, 25 made, based on '57 Strat, orange finish with matching headstock, certificate of authenticity.

| 1995 | | $1,750 | $2,300 |

Paisley Stratocaster
1984-1997, 2003-2004, 2008. Japanese-made '72 Strat reissue with a reissue '68 Tele Pink Paisley finish, large headstock until mid-'94, 'Made in Japan' logo used until early-'97, 'Crafted in Japan' after.

1984-1987	1st issue	$1,200	$1,600
1988-1994		$1,100	$1,500
1995-1997		$1,000	$1,300
2003-2004		$675	$875
2008	2nd issue, 200 made	$675	$875

Parallel Universe Volume II Jazz Stratocaster
2019-present. Parrallel Universe Volume II series, limited edition, alder body, 2 pickups, Mystic Surf Green with nitro lacquer finish.

| 2019-2020 | | $1,100 | $1,425 |

Playboy 40th Anniversary Stratocaster
1994. Custom Shop model, nude Marilyn Monroe graphic on body. 175 built.

| 1994 | | $12,500 | $16,200 |

Player Series Stratocaster
2017-present. Models include Player, Player HSS, Player HSH, Player Plus Top, Player Plus Top HSS, and Player Floyd Rose HSS.

2017-2020	Player	$375	$500
2018-2020	Player Floyd Rose	$440	$575
2018-2020	Player Plus Top	$400	$525

Post Modern Stratocaster (CS)
2015-2019. Custom Shop, offered in Journeyman Relic, NOS, and lush Closet Classic finishes.

2015-2017	NOS	$1,750	$2,300
2016-2019	Journeyman Relic	$2,000	$2,600
2019	Closet Classic	$1,750	$2,300

Post Modern Stratocaster Closet Classic (Custom Shop)
2019. Custom Shop, made exclusive for Sweetwater, certificate.

| 2019 | Aged natural | $2,150 | $2,775 |

MODEL YEAR	FEATURES	EXC. COND. LOW	HIGH

Post Modern Stratocaster Journeyman Relic (Custom Shop)
2019. Custom Shop, made exclusive for Sweetwater, alder or ash, certificate.

2019	Alder	$2,225	$2,875
2019	Ash	$2,150	$2,775

Post Modern Stratocaster NOS (Custom Shop)
2019. Custom Shop, made exclusive for Sweetwater, certificate.

2019	Aged natural	$2,100	$2,700

Powerhouse/Powerhouse Deluxe Stratocaster
1997-2010. Made in Mexico, Standard Strat configuration with pearloid 'guard, various colors.

1997-2010		$350	$475
2005	Powerbridge, TRS stereo	$375	$500

Proud Stratocaster
2003. Custom Shop, 3 made to commemorate United Way and Rock & Roll Hall of Fame project, body painted in detail by Fender's artist.

2003		$2,250	$2,900

Rarities Stratocaster
2019-present. Rarities series, limited edition, models include; Flame Maple Top, Flame KOA Top, Quilt Maple Top.

2019-2020	Various models	$1,450	$1,850

Richie Sambora Stratocaster
1993-2002. Alder body, Floyd Rose tremolo, maple neck, U.S. and Mexico models offered.

1993-2002	USA	$2,100	$2,700
1994-2002	Mexico	$400	$500
1995-1997	Mexico, swirl color	$525	$675

Ritchie Blackmore Stratocaster
2009-present. Based on Blackmore's '70s large headstock model, scalloped rosewood 'board, Duncan Quarter Pound Flat pickups, Olympic White.

2009-2019		$675	$875

Ritchie Blackmore Tribute Stratocaster
2014. Custom Shop model, '68 specs, maple neck.

2014		$3,000	$4,000

Roadhouse Stratocaster
1997-2000. U.S.-made, poplar body, tortoise shell 'guard, maple 'board, 3 Texas Special pickups, various colors.

1997-2000		$575	$775

Roasted Journeyman Relic Tomatillo Stratocaster
2018-2019. Custom Shop Limited Edition series, roasted alder body and flame maple neck, various aged colors with lacquer finish.

2018-2019		$2,400	$3,100

Robert Cray Signature Stratocaster
1991-present. Custom Shop, rosewood 'board, chunky neck, lighter weight, non-trem, alder body, gold-plated hardware, various colors.

1991-2019		$1,900	$2,500

Robert Cray Stratocaster (Mexico)
1996-present. Artist series, chrome hardware.

1996-2019		$500	$650

Robin Trower Signature Stratocaster
2004-present. Custom Shop Custom Artist series, 100 made, large headstock (post '65-era), with '70s logo and 3-bolt neck, bullet truss rod, white.

2004-2019		$1,800	$2,350

Rory Gallagher Tribute Stratocaster
2004-present. Custom Shop, based on Gallagher's '61 model, heavily distressed, price includes the original certificate.

2005-2019		$2,500	$3,200

Sandblasted Stratocaster
2014-2015. Limited Edition series, ash body, sandblasted finish.

2014-2015		$625	$825

Select Stratocaster
2012-2015. Select Series, figured top, rear-headstock 'Fender Select' medallion, gloss-lacquer finish, various colors.

2012-2015		$1,475	$1,925

Set-Neck Stratocaster
1992-1999. Custom Shop model, mahogany body and figured maple top, 4 pickups, glued-in neck, active electronics, by '96 ash body.

1992-1999		$1,600	$2,075

Short-Scale (7/8) Stratocaster
1989-1995. Similar to Standard Strat, but with 2 control knobs and switch, 24" scale vs. 25" scale, sometimes called a mini-Strat, Japanese import, various colors.

1989-1995		$500	$675

So-Cal Custom Shop J.W. Black Stratocaster
2000-2001. So-Cal logo art on body, 20 offered.

2000-2001		$1,500	$1,950

So-Cal Speed Shop Stratocaster
2005-2006. Limited Edition for Musician's Friend, red, white, and black So-Cal paint job, basswood body, rosewood 'board, 1 humbucker, So-Cal Speed Shop decal.

2005-2006		$475	$625

Special Edition David Lozeau Art Stratocaster
2015-2016. Finishes include orange Tree of Life, blue Dragon, yellow Rose Tattoo and red Sacred Heart, etched David Lozeau neck plate.

2015-2016		$350	$475

Special Edition Stratocaster
2004-2009. Import model, Special Edition oval logo on back of headstock, various styles offered, '50s or '60s vintage copy specs, maple 'board, ash or koa body, see-thru or opaque finish.

2004-2009		$350	$450

Special Edition Stratocaster (Matching Headstock)
2016-2017. Made in Mexico, various colors with matching headstock.

2016-2017		$350	$450

Special Edition White Opal Stratocaster
2016. Made in Mexico, white opal body and headstock, pearloid 'guard, 3 humbuckers.

2016		$350	$450

2007 Fender Stratocaster Powerhouse Deluxe

Lew Campbell

2001 Fender Richie Sambora Stratocaster

Imaged by Heritage Auctions, HA.com

1995 Fender Strat Plus
Rivington Guitars

2005 Fender Tie-Dye Stratocaster
Imaged by Heritage Auctions, HA.com

MODEL YEAR	FEATURES	EXC. COND. LOW	HIGH
Splatter Stratocaster			
2003. Made in Mexico, splatter paint job, various color combinations, with gig bag.			
2003		$525	$675
Standard Roland Ready Stratocaster			
1998-2011. Made in Mexico, built-in Roland pickup system and 3 single-coils.			
1998-2011		$350	$450
Standard Stratocaster (Japan)			
1985-1989. Interim production in Japan while the new Fender reorganized, standard pickup configuration and tremolo system, 3 knobs with switch, traditional style input jack, traditional shaped headstock, offered in black, red or white.			
1985-1989		$700	$900
Standard Stratocaster Satin Finish			
2003-2006. Basically Mexico-made Standard with satin finish.			
2003-2006		$225	$300
Standard Stratocaster (Mexico)			
1990-2018. Made in Mexico, renamed Player Series in '18. Not to be confused with the American-made Standard Stratocaster of '81-'84. Various models and colors, high-end range includes a hard guitar case, while low-end includes only a gig bag.			
1990-2018	Various models	$300	$400
Standard Stratocaster Plus Top			
2014-2018. Made in Mexico, alder body with flamed maple top. Renamed Player Series Plus Top in '18.			
2014-2018		$350	$450
Stevie Ray Vaughan Signature Stratocaster (Custom Shop)			
2019-present. Custom Artist series, 3-color sunburst with NOS lacquer finish.			
2019-2020	NOS	$2,500	$3,300
Stevie Ray Vaughan Signature Stratocaster Relic (Custom Shop)			
2019-present. Custom Artist series, aged 3-color sunburst with relic lacquer finish.			
2019-2020	Relic	$2,800	$3,600
Stevie Ray Vaughan Stratocaster			
1992-present. U.S.-made, alder body, sunburst, gold hardware, SRV 'guard, lefty tremolo, Brazilian rosewood 'board (pau ferro by '93).			
1992-2019		$925	$1,225
Stevie Ray Vaughan Tribute #1 Stratocaster			
2004. Custom Shop model limited edition recreation of SRV's #1 made by Master Builder John Cruz in the Custom Shop, 100 made, $10,000 MSRP, includes flight case stenciled "SRV - Number One," and other goodies.			
2004		$19,000	$25,000
Strat Plus			
1987-1999. Three Lace Sensor pickups, alder (poplar available earlier) body, tremolo, rosewood 'board or maple neck, various colors. See Deluxe Strat Plus for ash veneer version.			
1987-1999	Various colors	$900	$1,200
Stratocaster Junior			
2004-2006. Import, short 22.7" scale, Alder body, non-trem hardtail bridge.			
2004-2006		$250	$350

MODEL YEAR	FEATURES	EXC. COND. LOW	HIGH
Stratocaster Pro Closet Classic (Custom Shop)			
2006-2013. Ash body, early '60s neck, rosewood or maple board, solid or sunburst finish.			
2006-2013		$1,750	$2,300
Stratocaster Pro NOS (Custom Shop)			
2012-2016. Ash body, maple neck, rosewood 'board, solid or 3-tone sunburst.			
2012-2016		$1,450	$1,900
Stratocaster Special			
1993-1995. Made in Mexico, a humbucker and a single-coil pickup, 1 volume, 1 tone.			
1993-1995		$300	$400
Stratocaster XII			
1988-1997, 2003-2010. 1st version Japanese-made, alder body, 22-fret rosewood 'board. 2nd version is 21-fret Classic Series model for 2 years then Classic Series.			
1988-1997		$675	$875
2003-2010		$700	$925
Strat-o-Sonic			
2003-2006. American Special Series, Stratocaster-style chambered body, includes Strat-o-Sonic Dove I (1 pickup, '03 only), Dove II/DV II (2 black P-90s, '03-'06) and HH (2 humbuckers, '05-'06).			
2003	Dove I	$625	$825
2003-2006	Dove II/DV II	$725	$950
2003-2006	HH	$725	$950
Sub Sonic Stratocaster			
2000-2001. Baritone model, offered in 2 production models - HH (2 humbuckers, 2000-'01), HSS (hum-single-single, '01) - and in a Custom Shop version of the HSS (2000-'01).			
2000-2001		$725	$950
2000-2001	Custom Shop, COA	$1,900	$2,500
Super Stratocaster			
1997-2003. Deluxe series, made in Mexico, 3 Super Fat single-coils, Super Switching gives 2 extra pickup options, gold tremolo.			
1997-2003		$375	$500
Tanqurey Tonic Stratocaster			
1988. Made for a Tanqurey Tonic liquor ad campaign giveaway in '88, Tanqurey Tonic Green; many were given to winners around the country, ads said that they could also be purchased through Tanqurey, but that apparently didn't happen.			
1988		$1,125	$1,450
Texas Special Stratocaster			
1991-1992. Custom Shop model, 50 made, state of Texas map stamped on neck plate, Texas Special pickups, maple fretboard, sunburst.			
1991-1992		$1,725	$2,250
The Edge Stratocaster			
2016-2020. U2 guitarist The Edge signature on large '70s-style headstock, alder body, 1-piece quartersawn maple neck and 'board, 3 pickups, black.			
2016-2020		$1,025	$1,325
The Strat			
1980-1983. Alder body, 4-bolt neck, large STRAT on painted peghead, gold-plated brass hardware, various colors.			
1980-1983		$1,050	$1,375

MODEL YEAR	FEATURES	EXC. COND. LOW	HIGH

Tie-Dye Stratocaster
2004-2005. Single-coil neck and humbucker bridge pickups, Band of Gypsies or Hippie Blue tie-dye pattern poly finish.

2004-2005		$375	$475

Tom Delonge Stratocaster
2001-2004. 1 humbucker, rosewood back and sides. Also in Squier version.

2001-2004		$525	$675

Tom Morello Soul Power Stratocaster
2020-present. Alder body, rosewood 'board, black with white 'guard. Shipped with "Soul Power" decal for face of guitar.

2020		$750	$1,000

Tree of Life Stratocaster
1993. Custom Shop model, 29 made, tree of life fretboard inlay, 1-piece quilted maple body.

1993		$4,200	$5,400

Turquoise Sparkle Stratocaster
2001. Custom Shop model, limited run of 75 for Mars Music, turquoise sparkle finish.

2001		$1,100	$1,425

U.S. Ultra / Ultra Plus Stratocaster
1990-1997. Alder body with figured maple veneer on front and back, single Lace Sensor pickups in neck and middle, double Sensor at bridge, ebony 'board, sunburst.

1990-1997		$1,400	$1,850

Ventures Limited Edition Stratocaster
1996. Japanese-made tribute model, matches Jazzmaster equivalent, black.

1996		$1,000	$1,300

VG Stratocaster
2007-2009. American Series, modeling technology using Roland's VG circuitry, 5 guitar tone banks deliver 16 sounds.

2007-2009		$825	$1,100

Vintage Hot Rod Stratocaster
2007-2014. Vintage styling with modern features, '07-'13 named '57 Strat and '62 Strat, in '14 changed to '50s and '60s.

2007-2014	All models	$1,100	$1,450

Vintera Series Stratocaster
2019-present. Modified 50s, 60s and 70s Strat models, various options and colors.

2019-2020	All models	$500	$675

Walnut Elite Stratocaster
1983-1984. The Elite Series features active electronics and noise-cancelling pickups, Walnut Elite has a walnut body and neck, gold-plated hardware and pearloid tuner buttons. Also see Elite Stratocaster and Gold Elite Stratocaster.

1983-1984		$2,000	$2,600

Walnut Stratocaster
1981-1983. American black walnut body and 1-piece neck and 'board.

1981-1983		$1,550	$2,000

Western Stratocaster
1995. Custom Shop model, only 5 made, featured in Fender Custom Shop book from the 1990s.

1995		$6,300	$8,100

Whiteguard Stratocaster Limited Edition
2018. Limited Edition neck plate, ash body, Tele hardware and white 'guard, 2 single-coil pickups, lacquer finish.

2018		$900	$1,200

Yngwie Malmsteen Signature Stratocaster
2020. Custom Shop Custom Artist series, 2-piece select alder body, flat sawn maple neck, various color nitro lacquer finish.

2020		$3,000	$3,900

Yngwie Malmsteen Stratocaster
1988-present. U.S.-made, maple neck, scalloped 'board, 3 single-coil pickups, blue, red, white.

1988-2019		$950	$1,250

Swinger
1969-1972. See listing for Musiclander.

SX Series
1992-1995. Dreadnought and jumbo acoustics, ply or solid spruce tops with various wood options on back and sides, E models with electronics.

1992-1994	1200sx	$400	$530
1992-1994	1300sx	$525	$700
1992-1994	1500sx	$450	$600
1992-1994	1505sx	$500	$665
1992-1995	1000sx	$275	$365
1992-1995	1100sx	$325	$430
1992-1995	1105sxe	$375	$500
1993-1994	1600sxe	$525	$700
1994-1995	600sx	$125	$165
1994-1995	800sx	$150	$200

T-Bucket 300CE
2016-2018. Acoustic/electric, D-size, cutaway.

2016-2018		$175	$235

TC-90/TC-90 Thinline
2004. Made in Korea, semi-hollow thinline, double-cut.

2004		$425	$575

Telecaster
The following are all variations of the Telecaster. Broadcaster and Nocaster models are under Broadcaster. The first five listings are for the main American-made models. All others are listed alphabetically after that in the following order:

Telecaster
Standard Telecaster
American Standard Telecaster
American Series Telecaster
American Professional Telecaster
30th Anniversary Guitar Center Tree of Life Telecaster
40th Anniversary Telecaster
'50 Custom Telecaster
'50s Telecaster/Classic Series '50s Telecaster
Road Worn '50s Telecaster
50th Anniversary Spanish Guitar Set Custom Shop
50th Anniversary Telecaster
'52 Telecaster/American Vintage '52 Telecaster

1993 Fender U.S. Ultra Stratocaster

Keith Myers

1969 Fender Swinger

GUITARS

1952 Fender Telecaster
Trey Rabinek

1963 Fender Telecaster
Kevin Rush

American Vintage '52 Telecaster Korina
   (U.S.A.)
'52 Telecaster (Custom Shop)
'52 Vintage Telecaster (Japan)
'54 Telecaster (Custom Shop)
'58 Telecaster (Custom Shop)
American Vintage '58 Telecaster (U.S.A.)
'60s Telecaster Custom
'60s Telecaster/Classic Series '60s Telecaster
'60 Telecaster Custom
60th Anniversary American Telecaster
60th Anniversary Telecaster Limited Edition
60th Anniversary Telecaster (U.S.A.)
'61 Telecaster Custom
'62 Telecaster Custom (Import)
'62 Telecaster Custom (U.S.A.)
'62 Mod Squad Custom Telecaster
'62 Telecaster Reissue (Japan)
Junkyard Dog 1962 Telecaster Relic
'63 Telecaster
'63 Telecaster Custom Relic LTD
'64 Telecaster Limited Relic
American Vintage '64 Telecaster
'67 Telecaster (CS)
'68 Telecaster Rosewood
'69 Tele/Telecaster Thinline (Import)
'69 Telecaster Thinline (Custom Shop)
'72 Telecaster Custom/Classic Series '72 Telecaster Custom
'72 Telecaster Deluxe/Classic Series '72 Telecaster Deluxe
'72 Telecaster Thinline American Vintage
'72 Telecaster Thinline/Classic Series Telecaster
   Thinline
1972 Closet Classic Telecaster Custom (CS)
1998 Collectors Edition Telecaster
'90s Telecaster Deluxe (Foto-Flame)
'90s Telecaster Thinline
Aerodyne Telecaster
Albert Collins Telecaster
Aluminum Telecaster
American Acoustasonic Telecaster
American Classic Holoflake Telecaster
American Classic Telecaster
American Deluxe HH Telecaster
American Deluxe Power Telecaster
American Deluxe Telecaster
American Elite Telecaster Thinline
American Nashville B-Bender Telecaster
American Professional Telecaster Deluxe
   Shawbucker
American Special Telecaster
American Standard B-Bender Telecaster
American Standard Telecaster Channel Bound
American Standard Telecaster Special Edition
American Ultra Telecaster
Andy Summers Masterbuilt Tribute Telecaster
Antigua Telecaster
Big Block Telecaster
Bigsby Telecaster
Blacktop Telecaster Series
Blue Flower Telecaster
Bowling Ball/Marble Telecaster

Brown's Canyon Redwood Telecaster
Buck Owens Limited Edition Telecaster
Cabronita Telecaster (American Standard)
Cabronita Telecaster (Classic Player)
California Fat Telecaster
California Telecaster
Chambered Mahogany Telecaster
Clarence White Telecaster (Custom Shop)
Classic Player Baja Telecaster
Collector's Edition Telecaster
Contemporary Telecaster (Import)
Custom Classic Telecaster
Custom Deluxe Telecaster
Custom Telecaster
Danny Gatton Signature Telecaster
Deluxe Nashville Power Telecaster
Deluxe Nashville Telecaster (Mexico)
Deluxe Telecaster (U.S.A.)
Elite Nashville Telecaster
Elite Telecaster
Fat Telecaster
Foto Flame Telecaster
G.E. Smith Telecaster
Graham Coxon Special Run Telecaster
Highway One Telecaster/Texas Telecaster
HMT Telecaster (Import)
J5 Triple Telecaster Deluxe
James Burton Standard Telecaster
James Burton Telecaster
Jerry Donahue JD Telecaster
Jerry Donahue Telecaster
Jim Adkins JA-90 Telecaster Thinline
Jim Root Telecaster
Jimmy Bryant Tribute Telecaster
Jimmy Page Mirror Telecaster
Joe Strummer Telecaster
John Jorgenson Telecaster
Jr. Telecaster
La Cabronita Especial Telecaster
Masterbuilt Custom Shop Telecaster
Matched Set Telecaster
Merle Haggard Signature Telecaster
Mod Shop Telecaster
Moto Limited Edition Telecaster
Muddy Waters Signature Telecaster Custom
Muddy Waters Tribute Telecaster
Nashville Telecaster
NHL Premier Edition Telecaster
Nokie Edwards Telecaster
Old Pine Telecaster
Paisley Telecaster
Parallel Universe Troublemaker Telecaster
Parallel Universe Volume II Tele Mágico
Player Telecaster
Rosewood Telecaster
Rosewood Telecaster (Japan)
Rosewood Telelcaster Limited Edition
Select Telecaster
Select Telecaster Thinline
Set-Neck Telecaster
Snakehead Telecaster (Custom Shop)
Sparkle Telecaster
Special Edition Deluxe Ash Telecaster

MODEL YEAR	FEATURES	EXC. COND. LOW	HIGH
	Special Edition Koa Telecaster		
	Special Edition White Opal Telecaster		
	Special Telecaster/Telecaster Special		
	Standard Telecaster (Japan)		
	Standard Telecaster (Mexico)		
	Telecaster (Japanese Domestic)		
	Telecaster Custom		
	Telecaster Custom (Japan)		
	Telecaster Custom FMT HH (Korea)		
	Telecaster Stratocaster Hybrid		
	Telecaster Thinline		
	Tele-Sonic		
	Texas Special Telecaster		
	Twisted Telecaster Limited Edition		
	Two-Tone Telecaster Thinline		
	Vintage Hot Rod Telecaster		
	Waylon Jennings Tribute Telecaster		
	Will Ray Signature Jazz-A-Caster		
	Will Ray Signature Mojo Telecaster		

Telecaster

1951-1982. See Standard Telecaster (following listing) for '82-'85, American Standard Telecaster for '88-'00, the American Series Telecaster for '00-'07. and the American Standard Telecaster (again) for '08-'16. Currently called the American Professional Telecaster.

In the late '60s and early '70s Fender began to increase their use of vibrato tailpieces. A vibrato tailpiece for this period is generally worth about 13% less than the values shown. Please refer to the Fender Guitar Intro Section for details on Fender color options. The "rare color" listing have a wide range due to the various colors included in that category.

From '63-'70, Fender offered both the standard Brazilian rosewood fretboard and an optional maple fretboard. Prices listed here, for those years, are for the rosewood 'board models. Currently, the market considers the maple 'board to be a premium, so guitars with maple, for those years, are worth 10% to 15% more than the values shown.

MODEL YEAR	FEATURES	EXC. COND. LOW	HIGH
1951	Blond, black 'guard	$36,000	$47,000
1952	Blond, black 'guard	$34,000	$44,000
1953	Blond, black 'guard	$32,000	$41,000
1954	Blond, black 'guard	$29,000	$37,000
1954	Blond, white 'guard	$21,500	$28,000
1955	Blond, white 'guard	$20,000	$26,000
1956	Blond	$18,000	$24,000
1957	Blond, backloader	$18,000	$24,000
1958	Blond, backloader	$17,000	$22,000
1958	Blond, top loader	$16,000	$21,000
1958	Sunburst, backloader	$18,000	$24,000
1958	Sunburst, top loader	$17,500	$23,000
1959	Blond, maple	$14,500	$19,000
1959	Blond, slab	$13,000	$17,000

MODEL YEAR	FEATURES	EXC. COND. LOW	HIGH
1959	Custom color	$30,000	$39,000
1959	Sunburst, maple	$17,000	$22,000
1959	Sunburst, slab	$16,500	$21,400
1960	Blond, slab	$14,000	$18,300
1960	Common color	$22,700	$29,500
1960	Rare color	$29,500	$37,700
1960	Sunburst, slab	$16,500	$21,400
1961	Blond, slab	$13,300	$17,300
1961	Common color	$18,100	$23,500
1961	Rare color	$23,500	$30,600
1961	Sunburst, slab	$15,300	$19,900
1962	Blond, curved	$10,600	$13,800
1962	Blond, slab	$11,800	$15,300
1962	Common color	$18,100	$23,500
1962	Rare color	$23,500	$30,600
1962	Sunburst, curve	$13,750	$17,850
1962	Sunburst, slab	$14,550	$18,900
1963	Blond	$10,600	$13,800
1963	Common color	$18,100	$23,500
1963	Rare color	$23,500	$30,600
1963	Sunburst	$13,750	$17,850
1963-1964	Mahogany, see-thru cherry	$21,175	$27,500
1964	Blond	$9,800	$12,750
1964	Common color	$15,700	$20,400
1964	Rare color	$20,400	$26,500
1964	Sunburst	$12,150	$15,800
1965	Blond	$8,250	$10,700
1965	Common color	$12,500	$16,300
1965	Early '65, Sunburst	$10,000	$13,000
1965	Late '65, Sunburst	$8,200	$10,700
1965	Rare color	$16,300	$25,500
1966	Blond	$6,900	$8,975
1966	Common color	$7,850	$10,200
1966	Rare color	$10,200	$14,300
1966	Sunburst	$7,500	$9,800
1967	Blond	$6,900	$8,975
1967	Blond, smuggler	$7,900	$10,200
1967	Common color	$7,850	$10,200
1967	Rare color	$10,200	$14,300
1967	Sunburst	$7,500	$9,800
1968	Blond	$5,800	$7,500
1968	Blue Flora	$13,600	$17,700
1968	Common color	$7,850	$10,200
1968	Pink Paisley	$12,500	$16,300
1968	Rare color	$10,200	$14,300
1968	Sunburst	$7,500	$9,800
1969	Blond, poly	$5,100	$6,600
1969	Blue Flora	$13,600	$17,700
1969	Common color	$6,800	$9,200
1969	Pink Paisley	$12,550	$16,320
1969	Rare color	$9,200	$13,000
1969	Sunburst	$6,625	$8,775
1970	Blond	$4,225	$5,500
1970	Common color	$6,700	$8,700
1970	Rare color	$8,700	$12,000
1970	Sunburst	$4,225	$5,500
1971	Blond	$3,100	$4,100
1971	Common color	$5,200	$6,700
1971	Rare color	$6,700	$9,200

1964 Fender Telecaster

1967 Fender Telecaster
Robbie Keene

1972 Fender Telecaster
John Hosford

1978 Fender Telecaster
Robbie Keene

MODEL YEAR	FEATURES	EXC. COND. LOW	HIGH
1971	Sunburst	$3,100	$4,100
1972	Blond	$2,700	$3,500
1972	Common color	$3,500	$4,600
1972	Natural	$2,500	$3,200
1972	Rare color	$4,600	$6,000
1972	Sunburst	$2,700	$3,500
1973	Black, white	$2,700	$3,500
1973	Blond	$2,700	$3,500
1973	Natural	$2,500	$3,200
1973	Rare color	$3,500	$4,300
1973	Sunburst	$2,700	$3,500
1973	Walnut	$2,500	$3,200
1974	Blond, black, white	$2,700	$3,500
1974	Natural	$2,500	$3,200
1974	Sunburst	$2,700	$3,500
1974	Walnut	$2,500	$3,200
1975	Blond, black, white	$2,700	$3,500
1975	Natural	$2,500	$3,200
1975	Sunburst	$2,700	$3,500
1975	Walnut	$2,500	$3,200
1976	Blond, black, white	$1,800	$2,300
1976	Natural	$1,800	$2,300
1976	Sunburst	$1,800	$2,300
1976	Walnut	$1,800	$2,300
1977	Antigua	$1,800	$2,300
1977	Black, blond, white	$1,800	$2,300
1977	Natural	$1,800	$2,300
1977	Sunburst	$1,800	$2,300
1977	Walnut	$1,800	$2,300
1978	Antigua	$1,800	$2,300
1978	Black, blond, white, wine	$1,800	$2,300
1978	Natural	$1,800	$2,300
1978	Sunburst	$1,800	$2,300
1978	Walnut	$1,800	$2,300
1979	Antigua	$1,800	$2,300
1979	Black, blond, white, wine	$1,800	$2,300
1979	Natural	$1,800	$2,300
1979	Sunburst	$1,800	$2,300
1979	Walnut	$1,800	$2,300
1980	Antigua	$1,550	$2,050
1980	Black, blond, white, wine	$1,550	$2,050
1980	International color	$2,000	$2,600
1980	Natural	$1,550	$2,050
1980	Sunburst	$1,550	$2,050
1981	Black and Gold	$1,550	$2,050
1981	Black, blond, white, wine	$1,550	$2,050
1981	International color	$2,000	$2,600
1981	Sunburst	$1,550	$2,050

Standard Telecaster

1982-1984. See Telecaster for '51-'82, and American Standard Telecaster (following listing) for '88-2000. Not to be confused with the current Standard Telecaster, which is made in Mexico.

1982	Blond, sunburst	$1,550	$2,050
1983-1984	Blond, sunburst	$875	$1,125

MODEL YEAR	FEATURES	EXC. COND. LOW	HIGH

American Standard Telecaster

1988-2000, 2008-2016. Name used when Fender reissued the standard American-made Tele after CBS sold the company. The only American-made Tele available for '86 and '87 was the '52 Telecaster. See Telecaster for '51-'81, and Standard Telecaster for '82-'84. All '94 models have a metal 40th Anniversary pin on the headstock, but should not be confused with the actual 40th Anniversary Telecaster model (see separate listing), all standard colors. Renamed the American Series Telecaster in 2000, then back to American Standard Series Telecaster in '08. Becomes American Professional in '17.

1988-2000		$750	$1,000
2008-2016		$750	$1,000

American Series Telecaster

2000-2007. See Telecaster for '51-'81, Standard Telecaster for '82-'84, and American Standard for '88-'99. Renamed American Standard again in '08.

2000-2007		$750	$1,000

American Professional Telecaster

2017-present. Model replaces American Standard Tele, redesign includes 2 V-Mod pickups, narrow-tall frets, new 'deep C' neck profile, various colors. Also available left-hand model.

2017-2019		$750	$1,000

30th Anniversary Guitar Center Tree of Life Telecaster

1994. Limited Edition, produced for 30th anniversary of Guitar Center, engraved neckplate with GC logo, tree-of-life 'board inlay.

1994		$3,700	$4,800

40th Anniversary Telecaster

1988, 1999. Custom Shop model limited edition run of 300, 2-piece flamed maple top, gold hardware ('88), flamed maple top over ash body, gold hardware ('99).

1988	1st run, high-end	$4,000	$5,200
1999	2nd run, plain top	$3,000	$4,000

'50 Custom Telecaster

1997. Custom Shop, limited run of 10, humbucker neck pickup, standard unbound body, highly figured maple neck, blackguard specs.

1997		$1,750	$2,300

'50s Telecaster/Classic Series '50s Telecaster

1990-2019. Made in Japan (basswood body) until mid '99, then in Mexico with ash body. Foto-Flame finish offered in '94 (see separate listing).

1990-1999	Japan	$600	$800
1999-2019	Mexico	$450	$600

Road Worn '50s Telecaster

2009-2019. Maple 'board, '50s specs, aged finish.

2009-2019		$500	$650

50th Anniversary Spanish Guitar Set Custom Shop

1996. 50 sets made, Tele Prototype reproduction with similar era copy of woodie amp.

1996		$4,000	$5,200

50th Anniversary Telecaster

1995-1996. Custom Shop model, flame maple top, 2 vintage-style pickups, gold hardware, sunburst,

The **Vintage Guitar Price Guide** shows low to high values for items in all-original excellent condition, and, where applicable, with original case or cover.

MODEL YEAR	FEATURES	EXC. COND. LOW	HIGH

gold 50th Anniversary coin on back of the headstock, 1250 made.

1995-1996		$1,375	$1,800

'52 Telecaster/American Vintage '52 Telecaster

1982-1984, 1986-2017. Ash body, maple neck or rosewood 'board, blond. Replaced by the American Original '50s Telecaster.

1982-1984		$1,950	$2,550
1986-1999		$1,200	$1,600
1990-1999	Copper (limited)	$1,200	$1,600
2000-2017		$1,100	$1,450

American Vintage '52 Telecaster Korina (U.S.A.)

2015. Part of Fender's limited edition 10 for 15 series, Korina body, '52 specs.

2015		$1,300	$1,700

'52 Telecaster (Custom Shop)

2004-2018. Custom Shop Dealer Select model, NOS, Relic and Closet Classic offered, changed to Heavy Relic in '15.

2004-2012	NOS	$1,750	$2,300
2004-2014	Relic	$1,900	$2,450
2010-2011	Closet Classic	$1,750	$2,300
2015-2018	Heavy relic	$2,000	$2,600

'52 Vintage Telecaster (Japan)

1982-1984. Made in Japan, JV serial numbers.

1982-1984		$1,250	$1,600

'54 Telecaster (Custom Shop)

1997-1998, 2013-2016. Relic, Closet Classic available with more recent model.

2013-2016	Relic	$1,900	$2,450

'58 Telecaster (Custom Shop)

2008. Custom Shop, relic and heavy relic.

2008	Heavy relic	$2,000	$2,600
2008	NOS	$1,750	$2,300
2008	Relic	$1,900	$2,450

American Vintage '58 Telecaster (U.S.A.)

2013-2018. Ash body, white 'guard, Aged White Blonde.

2013-2018		$1,075	$1,400

'60s Telecaster Custom

1997-1999. Custom Shop, bound alder body, sunburst, black or custom colors, nickel or gold hardware.

1997-1999		$1,900	$2,450

'60s Telecaster/Classic Series '60s Telecaster

1992-2019. Made in Japan (basswood body) until mid '99, then in Mexico with ash body. Foto-Flame finish offered in '94 (see separate listing). '06 version may have 60th Anniversary Badge on back of headstock.

1992-1996	Made in Japan	$600	$800
1997-1999	Crafted in Japan	$550	$750
1999-2019	Mexico	$425	$575

'60 Telecaster Custom

2003-2004. Custom Shop Time Machine, bound alder body, offered in NOS, Closet Classic and Relic versions and in sunburst, CA Red and Sonic Blue.

2003-2004	Closet Classic	$1,750	$2,300
2003-2004	NOS	$1,750	$2,300
2003-2004	Relic	$1,900	$2,450

60th Anniversary American Telecaster

2006-2007. Special Edition commemorating Fender's 60th year, banner headstock 60th logo, neck plate reads Diamond Anniversary 1946-2006, made in U.S.A., rosewood 'board, sunburst.

2006-2007		$800	$1,025

60th Anniversary Telecaster Limited Edition

2006. Limited Edition of 1,000, 60 Diamond Anniversary 1946-2006 logo engraved in neck plate, American Flag logo on pickguard, '51 NoCaster pickup layout, 60 wood inlay on the face below bridge, clear nitro finish on natural ash body, silver guitar case with Fender 60 logo on inside lid.

2006		$1,350	$1,750

60th Anniversary Telecaster (U.S.A.)

2011-2012. Celebrating 60 years of the Tele, commemorative chrome neck plate, ash body, blonde thin-skin finish.

2011-2012		$800	$1,025

'61 Telecaster Custom

2010-2012. Custom Shop Dealer Select model, bound body Custom, NOS, Relic or Heavy Relic.

2010-2012	Closet Classic	$1,750	$2,300
2010-2012	NOS	$1,750	$2,300
2010-2012	Relic	$1,900	$2,450

'62 Telecaster Custom (Import)

1985-1999. Made in Japan, bound top and back, rosewood 'board, sunburst or red.

1985-1989		$1,050	$1,350
1990-1999		$800	$1,050

'62 Telecaster Custom (U.S.A.)

1999-2012. American Vintage Series, rosewood board.

1999-2012		$750	$975

'62 Mod Squad Custom Telecaster

2013. Custom Shop, Broadcaster bridge pickup and Duncan neck humbucker.

2013		$2,175	$2,825

'62 Telecaster Reissue (Japan)

1989-1990, 2005-2006. Made by Fender Japan.

1989-1990		$925	$1,250
2005-2006		$825	$1,100

Junkyard Dog 1962 Telecaster Relic

2014-2015. Custom Shop Dealer Select series, ash body, rosewood neck and 'board, white guard, Vintage Blonde.

2014-2015		$2,125	$2,750

'63 Telecaster

1999-2010, 2018-2019. Custom Shop, alder body (or blond on ash), original spec pickups, C-shaped neck, rosewood 'board. Relic offered in '07 and later heavy relic in '18.

1999-2010	Closet Classic	$1,750	$2,300
1999-2010	NOS	$1,750	$2,300
2007	Relic	$1,900	$2,450
2018-2019	Heavy relic	$1,900	$2,450

'63 Telecaster Custom Relic LTD

2006. Custom Shop, Limited Edition.

2006		$1,900	$2,450

1982 Fender American Vintage '52 Telecaster

Billy White Jr.

2006 Fender 60th Anniversary Telecaster Limited Edition

Imaged by Heritage Auctions, HA.com

Fender '72 Telecaster Thinline American Vintage

2017 Fender American Elite Telecaster Thinline

MODEL YEAR / FEATURES	EXC. COND. LOW	HIGH

'64 Telecaster Limited Relic
2009. Custom Shop, rosewood 'board, thin nitro finish, 50 each of black, aged white, and 3-tone chocolate sunburst.

| 2009 | $1,900 | $2,450 |

American Vintage '64 Telecaster
2013-2018. Ash body, mid-'60s 'C' neck profile, rounded rosewood 'board, 2 vintage single-coil pickups, White Blonde.

| 2013-2018 | $1,075 | $1,400 |

'67 Telecaster (CS)
2005-2008, 2010-2011. Custom Shop, alder body, rosewood or maple 'board, Relic, NOS or Closet Classic, 2010 and later is rosewood 'board, Relic or NOS.

2005-2008	Closet Classic	$1,750	$2,300
2005-2011	NOS	$1,750	$2,300
2005-2011	Relic	$1,900	$2,450

'68 Telecaster Rosewood
Custom Shop, rosewood body.

| 2007 | NOS | $1,750 | $2,300 |

'69 Tele/Telecaster Thinline (Import)
1986-2015. Import, Classic Series, 2 Tele pickups.

1986-1989	$825	$1,075
1990-1999	$675	$900
2000-2015	$575	$775

'69 Telecaster Thinline (Custom Shop)
2005-2006. Semi-hollow mahoganhy body, maple neck with maple 'board.

| 2005-2006 | $1,750 | $2,300 |

'72 Telecaster Custom/Classic Series '72 Telecaster Custom
1986-2019. Import, 1 humbucker and 1 single-coil, 2 humbuckers after '99.

1986-1989	Japan	$1,050	$1,350
1990-1999	Japan	$900	$1,200
2000-2019	Mexico	$475	$600

'72 Telecaster Deluxe/Classic Series '72 Telecaster Deluxe
2004-2019. Made in Mexico, alder body, large Deluxe 'guard, 2 humbuckers.

| 2004-2019 | $350 | $450 |

'72 Telecaster Thinline American Vintage
2012-2013. US-made, American Vintage FSR model, f-hole, 2 humbuckers.

| 2012-2013 | $1,150 | $1,500 |

'72 Telecaster Thinline/Classic Series Telecaster Thinline
1986-2019. Import, 2 humbuckers, f-hole.

| 1986-1999 | Japan | $800 | $1,050 |
| 2000-2019 | Mexico | $375 | $500 |

1972 Closet Classic Telecaster Custom (CS)
2013. Custom Shop, ash body, maple neck and 'board, 2 pickups, black finish.

| 2013 | $1,750 | $2,300 |

1998 Collectors Edition Telecaster
1998. 1,998 made, 1998 logo inlay on 'board, maple, gold hardware.

| 1998 | $1,050 | $1,350 |

'90s Telecaster Deluxe (Foto-Flame)
1995-1998. Import, 1 Tele-style bridge pickup and 2 Strat-style pickups, rosewood 'board, Foto Flame '95-'97 and standard finishes '97-'98.

| 1995-1997 | Foto-Flame | $600 | $775 |
| 1997-1998 | Standard finish | $600 | $775 |

'90s Telecaster Thinline
1998-2001. Bound semi-hollow ash body, f-hole, white or brown shell 'guard, 2 single-coils, sunburst, black, natural, or transparent crimson.

| 1998-2001 | $1,525 | $2,000 |

Aerodyne Telecaster
2004-2009. Imported Tele with Aerodyne body profile, bound body, black.

| 2004-2009 | $575 | $725 |

Albert Collins Telecaster
1990-2018. Custom Shop signature model, bound swamp ash body, humbucker pickup in neck position, natural or silver sparkle.

| 1990-2018 | $1,900 | $2,500 |

Aluminum Telecaster
1994-1995. Aluminum-bodied American Standard with anodized finish in blue marble, purple marble or red, silver and blue stars and stripes.

| 1994-1995 | Marble patterns | $1,500 | $1,950 |
| 1994-1995 | Red-silver-blue flag option | $1,500 | $1,950 |

American Acoustasonic Telecaster
2019-present. Solid A sitka spruce top, mahogany back, sides and neck, various colors.

| 2019-2020 | $1,050 | $1,125 |

American Classic Holoflake Telecaster
1996-1999. Custom Shop model, splatter/sparkle finish, pearloid 'guard.

| 1996-1999 | $1,650 | $2,150 |

American Classic Telecaster
1996-1999. Custom Shop model, handcrafted version of American Standard, thin lacquer-finished ash body, maple or rosewood 'board, various options and colors, earlier versions had gold hardware and custom-color options.

| 1996-1999 | $1,650 | $2,150 |

American Deluxe HH Telecaster
2004-2006. Rosewood, maple top, 2 humbucker pickups.

| 2004-2006 | $950 | $1,225 |

American Deluxe Power Telecaster
1999-2001. Made in USA, with Fishman power bridge piezo pickups.

| 1999-2001 | $950 | $1,225 |

American Deluxe Telecaster
1998-2017. Premium ash or alder body with see-thru finishes.

| 1998-2017 | $950 | $1,225 |

American Elite Telecaster Thinline
2016-2019. Single-cut semi-hollow ash body, maple neck and 'board, 2 single-coil pickups, various colors.

| 2016-2019 | $950 | $1,225 |

American Nashville B-Bender Telecaster
1998-2015. US-made, alder body, added Texas Special Strat pickup in middle position, white

MODEL YEAR	FEATURES	EXC. COND. LOW	HIGH

pearloid 'guard, Parsons-Fender B-string bender, 5-way switch.

| 1998-2015 | | $1,300 | $1,675 |

American Professional Telecaster Deluxe Shawbucker
2017-2018. With 2 ShawBucker humbucking pickups, various colors.

| 2017-2018 | | $750 | $975 |

American Special Telecaster
2010-2018. Alder body, gloss finish, Texas Special pickups.

| 2010-2018 | | $650 | $850 |

American Standard B-Bender Telecaster
1995-1997. US-made, alder body, maple neck, Parsons-Fender B-string bender.

| 1995-1997 | | $1,200 | $1,550 |

American Standard Telecaster Channel Bound
2014-2015. Limited Edition, channel-bound compound-radius fingerboard.

| 2014-2015 | | $750 | $975 |

American Standard Telecaster Special Edition
2009. Surf Green, Fiesta Red or Daphne Blue with matching headstock.

| 2009 | | $1,000 | $1,300 |

American Ultra Telecaster
2019-present. Alder or ash body, upgrades include 2 Ultra Noiseless Vintage Tele single-coil pickups and 7 new colors with gloss poly finish.

| 2019-2020 | | $1,050 | $1,375 |

Andy Summers Masterbuilt Tribute Telecaster
2009. Custom shop, based on Summer's '61 Tele, heavy relic, 250 made, custom electronics rear-mounted overdrive unit controlled by a third knob, includes DVD, strap and Andy Summer's logo travel guitar case.

| 2009 | | $4,700 | $6,100 |

Antigua Telecaster
2004. Made in Japan, limited edition (400 made) reissue, '70s features and antigua finish.

| 2004 | | $600 | $800 |

Big Block Telecaster
2005-2006. Pearloid block markers, black with matching headstock, 3 single-coils with center pickup reverse wound.

| 2005-2006 | | $550 | $700 |

Bigsby Telecaster
2003. Made in Mexico, standard Tele specs with original Fender-logo Bigsby tailpiece.

| 2003 | | $525 | $675 |

Blacktop Telecaster Series
2012-2015. Includes 2 humbucker HH and hum-single-single Baritone.

| 2012-2015 | Various models | $325 | $425 |

Blue Flower Telecaster
1985-1993, 2003-2004. Import, Blue Flower finish.

| 1985-1993 | 1st issue | $650 | $850 |
| 2003-2004 | 2nd issue | $500 | $650 |

Bowling Ball/Marble Telecaster
1984. Standard Tele, called Bowling Ball Tele due to the swirling color, blue, red or yellow.

| 1984 | | $2,800 | $3,700 |

Brown's Canyon Redwood Telecaster
2011. For Fender's 60th anniversary in 2011, they released 12 limited edition U.S.-made Tele-bration Telecasters, including this one with body made from 1890s California redwood.

| 2011 | | $1,200 | $1,575 |

Buck Owens Limited Edition Telecaster
1998-1999. Red, white and blue sparkle finish, 250 made, gold hardware, gold 'guard, rosewood 'board.

| 1998-1999 | | $1,325 | $1,725 |

Cabronita Telecaster (American Standard)
2011. For Fender's 60th anniversary in 2011, American Standard series, they released 12 limited edition U.S.-made Tele-bration Telecasters, including this one with 2 TV Jones Filter'Trons.

| 2011 | | $850 | $1,100 |

Cabronita Telecaster (Classic Player)
2014-2015. Mexico version, Classic Player series.

| 2014-2015 | | $300 | $400 |

California Fat Telecaster
1997-1998. Alder body, maple fretboard, Tex-Mex humbucker and Tele pickup configuration.

| 1997-1998 | | $550 | $700 |

California Telecaster
1997-1998. Alder body, maple fretboard, sunburst, Tex-Mex Strat and Tele pickup configuration.

| 1997-1998 | | $550 | $700 |

Chambered Mahogany Telecaster
2006. U.S.-made, chambered mahogany body, Delta Tone System.

| 2006 | | $875 | $1,125 |

Clarence White Telecaster (Custom Shop)
1994-2000. Parsons-White B-Bender and Scruggs-style tuners on both E strings, sunburst.

| 1994-2000 | | $6,000 | $7,800 |

Classic Player Baja Telecaster
2007-2019. Made in Mexico, Custom Shop designed neck plate logo, thin gloss poly blond finish.

| 2007-2019 | | $550 | $700 |

Collector's Edition Telecaster
1998. Mid-1955 specs including white 'guard, offered in sunburst with gold hardware (which was an option in '55), 1,998 made.

| 1998 | | $1,050 | $1,350 |

Contemporary Telecaster (Import)
1985-1987. Japanese-made while the new Fender reorganized, 2 or 3 pickups, vibrato, black chrome hardware, rosewood 'board.

| 1985-1987 | | $475 | $625 |

Custom Classic Telecaster
2000-2008. Custom Shop, maple or rosewood 'board, certificate of authenticity.

| 2000-2008 | | $1,800 | $2,400 |

Fender American Ultra Telecaster

Fender Antigua Telecaster

GUITARS

2008 Fender G.E. Smith Telecaster

Fender James Burton Telecaster

MODEL YEAR	FEATURES	EXC. COND. LOW	HIGH

Custom Deluxe Telecaster
2009-2014. Custom Shop model, ash body, AA birds-eye maple neck, rosewood or maple 'board, abalone dot inlays, 2 pickups, certificate, black Bakelite 'guard, Aged White Blonde, Dakota Red or faded 2-color sunburst.

2009-2014		$2,400	$3,100

Custom Telecaster
1972-1981. One humbucking and 1 Tele pickup, standard colors, see Telecaster Custom for 2 Tele pickup/bound body version.

1972-1981		$2,725	$3,525

Danny Gatton Signature Telecaster
1990-2018. Custom Shop model, like '53 Telecaster, maple neck, 2 humbuckers.

1990-1999	Frost Gold	$2,750	$3,600
2000-2018	Various colors	$1,800	$2,350

Deluxe Nashville Power Telecaster
1999-2014. Like Deluxe Nashville, but with piezo transducer in each saddle.

1999-2014		$425	$550

Deluxe Nashville Telecaster (Mexico)
1997-present. Tex-Mex Strat and Tele pickup configuration, various colors.

1997-2019		$425	$550

Deluxe Telecaster (U.S.A.)
1972-1981. Two humbuckers, various colors. Mexican-made version offered starting in 2004.

1972-1974	Common color	$2,400	$3,200
1972-1975	Less common color	$3,200	$4,600
1975	Common color	$2,100	$2,800
1976-1979	Common color	$1,800	$2,300
1980-1981	Common color	$1,550	$2,050

Elite Nashville Telecaster
Limited Edition, ash body, 3 pickups, Antique Cherry Burst.

2016		$1,300	$1,700

Elite Telecaster
1983-1985. Two active humbucker pickups, 3-way switch, 2 volume knobs, 1 presence and filter controls, chrome hardware, various colors.

1983-1985		$2,275	$2,950

Fat Telecaster
1999-2001. Humbucker pickup in neck, Tele bridge pickup.

1999-2001		$600	$775

Foto Flame Telecaster
1994-1996. Import, sunburst or transparent.

1994-1996		$600	$775

G.E. Smith Telecaster
2007-2014. Swamp ash body, vintage style hardware, U-shaped neck, oval and diamond inlays.

2007-2014		$975	$1,250

Graham Coxon Special Run Telecaster
2011, 2013-2014. Blond, Tele bridge and humbucker neck pickup, rosewood 'board, limited run in 2011.

2011-2014		$875	$1,125

Highway One Telecaster/Texas Telecaster
2003-2011. U.S.-made, alder body, satin lacquer finish, Texas version (introduced in '04) has ash body and Hot Vintage pickups.

2003-2011		$600	$750

HMT Telecaster (Import)
1990-1993. Japanese-made Heavy Metal Tele, available with or without Floyd Rose tremolo, 1 Fender Lace Sensor pickup and 1 DiMarzio bridge humbucker pickup, black.

1990-1993		$350	$450

J5 Triple Telecaster Deluxe
2007-2017. John 5 model, made in Mexico, 3 humbuckers, medium jumbo frets.

2007-2017		$550	$725

James Burton Standard Telecaster
1995-2016. Mexico, 2 Texas Special Tele pickups, standard colors (no paisley).

1995-2016		$450	$575

James Burton Telecaster
1990-present. Ash body, 3 Fender Lace pickups, available in black with Gold Paisley, black with Candy Red Paisley, Pearl White, and Frost Red until '05. In '06 in black with red or blue flame-shaped paisley, or Pearl White.

1990-2005	Black & gold paisley, gold hw	$1,400	$1,825
1990-2005	Black & red paisley, black hw	$1,100	$1,425
1990-2010	Frost Red or Pearl White	$825	$1,075
2006-2019	Paisley flames	$825	$1,075

Jerry Donahue JD Telecaster
1993-1999. Made in Japan, Custom Strat neck pickup and Custom Tele bridge pickup, basswood body, special "V" shaped maple neck.

1993-1999		$1,000	$1,300

Jerry Donahue Telecaster
1992-2001. Custom Shop model designed by Donahue, Tele bridge pickup and Strat neck pickup, birdseye maple neck, top and back, gold hardware, passive circuitry, sunburst, transparent Crimson Red or Sapphire Blue. There was also a Japanese-made JD Telecaster.

1992-2001		$1,400	$1,825

Jim Adkins JA-90 Telecaster Thinline
2008-present. Rosewood 'board, vintage-style P-90 soapbars.

2008-2019		$450	$600

Jim Root Telecaster
2007-present. Made in Mexico, black hardware, mahogany body.

2007-2019		$525	$675

Jimmy Bryant Tribute Telecaster
2004-2005. Custom Shop model, hand-tooled leather 'guard overlay with JB initials.

2004-2005		$2,050	$2,650

Jimmy Page Mirror Telecaster
2019-present. Ash body, 2 single-coil pickups, white blonde lacquer finish, vintage-style tweed case, shipped with eight round mirrors.

2019-2020		$1,400	$1,800

Joe Strummer Telecaster
2007-2009. Limited edition, heavily relic'd based on Strummer's '66 Tele, Fender offered a limited edition art customization kit as part of the package.

2007	Limited Edition	$800	$1,050
2007-2009	Standard edition	$800	$1,050

MODEL YEAR	FEATURES	EXC. COND. LOW	HIGH

John Jorgenson Telecaster
1998-2001. Custom Shop, korina body, double-coil stacked pickups, sparkle or black finish.

1998-2001	Sparkle	$1,950	$2,550

Jr. Telecaster
1994, 1997-2000. Custom Shop model, transparent blond ash body, 2 P-90-style pickups, set neck, 11 tone chambers, 100 made in '94, reintroduced in '97.

1994		$2,050	$2,650
1997-2000		$2,050	$2,650

La Cabronita Especial Telecaster
2009-2010. Custom Shop relics, 1 or 2 TV Jones pickups. In '09, 10 each with 1 pickup in black or Shoreline Gold and 20 each with 2 pickups in black or Shoreline Gold. In '10, 10 each with 1 pickup in Candy Apple Red or Sonic Blue and 20 each with 2 pickups in Candy Apple Red or Sonic.

2009-2010	Various colors	$3,050	$3,975

Masterbuilt Custom Shop Telecaster
2006-present. Various models and builders, specific identification to builder, must include certificate of authenticity.

2006-2019	Various models	$3,000	$6,000

Matched Set Telecaster
1994. Matching Tele and Strat Custom Shop models, model name on certificate is "Matched Set Telecaster", 3 sets were built, each set has serial number 1, 2, or 3.

1994		$3,150	$4,075

Merle Haggard Signature Telecaster
2009-2018. Custom Shop, figured maple body and neck, maple 'board, 2-color sunburst.

2009-2018		$2,675	$3,475

Mod Shop Telecaster
2017-present. Mod Shop allows you to create your own factory-customized electric guitar or bass.

2017-2020		$1,500	$2,000

Moto Limited Edition Telecaster
1990s. Custom Shop model, pearloid cover in various colors. There were also Strat and Jag versions.

1990s		$1,965	$2,550

Muddy Waters Signature Telecaster Custom
2001-2009. Mexico, Fender amp control knobs, Telecaster Custom on headstock, Muddy Waters signature logo on neck plate, Candy Apple Red.

2001-2009		$600	$800

Muddy Waters Tribute Telecaster
2000. Custom Shop, 100 made, Fender amp control knobs, rosewood 'board, relic Candy Apple Red finish, certificate of authenticity.

2000		$2,500	$3,300

Nashville Telecaster
1995. Custom Shop model, 3 pickups.

1995		$1,550	$2,000

NHL Premier Edition Telecaster
1999-2000. Limited edition of 100 guitars with NHL hockey art logo on the top.

1999-2000	All models	$825	$1,075

Nokie Edwards Telecaster
1996. Made in Japan, limited edition, book matched flamed top, multi-lam neck, Seymour Duncan pickups, gold hardware, zero fret, tilted headstock.

1996		$1,100	$1,500

Old Pine Telecaster
2011. For Fender's 60th anniversary in 2011, they released 12 limited edition U.S.-made Tele-bration Telecasters, including this one with 100-year-old pine body, 300 made.

2011		$1,200	$1,550

Paisley Telecaster
1986-1998, 2003-2004, 2008. Import, 'Made in Japan' logo used until '98, 'Crafted in Japan' after, Pink Paisley finish.

1986-1998		$650	$850
2003-2004		$500	$650
2008	600 made	$500	$650

Parallel Universe Troublemaker Telecaster
July 2018. Parallel Universe series, limited edition, mahogany body, maple top, custom Cabronita 'guard, 2 ShawBucker (1T and 2T) humbucking pickups. Bigsby optional.

2018		$1,325	$1,725
2018	with Bigsby	$1,275	$1,650

Parallel Universe Volume II Tele Mágico
2020. Parallel Universe Volume II series, limited edition, ash body, flame maple neck and 'board, Daphane Blue or Surf Green.

2020		$1,375	$1,800

Player Telecaster
2018-present. Alder body, maple neck, 2 SS or HH pickups, various colors with gloss finish.

2018-2019		$375	$500

Rosewood Telecaster
1969-1972. Rosewood body and neck.

1969-1972		$10,000	$13,000

Rosewood Telecaster (Japan)
1986-1996. Japanese-made reissue, rosewood body and neck.

1986-1996		$1,800	$2,375

Rosewood Telelcaster Limited Edition
2014. Custom Shop, Limited Edition neck plate, based on George Harrison's rosewood Tele.

2014		$3,150	$4,100

Select Telecaster
2012-2013. Select Series, figured maple top, rear-headstock 'Fender Select' medallion, gloss-lacquer finish, chrome or gold hardware.

2012-2013		$1,475	$1,925

Select Telecaster Thinline
2012-2013. Select Series, figured maple top, rear-headstock 'Fender Select' medallion, gloss-lacquer finish, chrome or gold hardware.

2012-2013		$1,600	$2,100

Set-Neck Telecaster
1990-1996. Glued-in neck, Custom Shop, 2 humbucking pickups, Set-Neck CA (Country Artist) has 1 humbucker and 1 Tele pickup, various colors.

1990-1996		$1,600	$2,075

Fender Merle Haggard Signature Telecaster

1986 Fender Paisley Telecaster

1972 Fender Telecaster Custom
John Rutherford

1974 Fender Telecaster Thinline

Snakehead Telecaster (Custom Shop)
Custom Shop Limited Edition, 45 offered.

MODEL YEAR	FEATURES	EXC. COND. LOW	HIGH
2010		$3,800	$5,000

Sparkle Telecaster
1993-1995. Custom Shop model, poplar body, white 'guard, sparkle finish: champagne, gold, silver.

1993-1995		$1,650	$2,150

Special Edition Deluxe Ash Telecaster
2009-2016. Mexico, butterscotch finish, ash body, 1-piece maple neck.

2009-2016		$350	$450

Special Edition Koa Telecaster
2006-2008. Made in Korea, standard Tele specs, koa veneer top over basswood body, pearloid 'guard, sunburst.

2006-2008		$350	$450

Special Edition White Opal Telecaster
2016. Made in Mexico, white opal body and headstock, pearloid 'guard.

2016		$350	$450

Special Telecaster/Telecaster Special
2004-2008. Made in Mexico, Special Edition logo with star logo sticker on back of headstock, special features like 6-way bridge and modern tuners.

2004-2008		$350	$450

Standard Telecaster (Japan)
1985-1989. In '85, the only Teles were interim production in Japan while the new Fender reorganized, no serial number, Japan headstock logo in '85, back of neck '86-'89.

1985-1989		$700	$900

Standard Telecaster (Mexico)
1990-2018. Guitar production at the Mexico facility started in '90. High end of range includes a hard guitar case, while the low end of the range includes only a gig bag, various colors. Replaced by Player Series.

1990-2018		$300	$400

Telecaster (Japanese Domestic)
1982-1997. Made in Japan for Japanese domestic market (not for export), suffix serial numbers JV5 ('82-'84) and A6 through V6 ('84-'97).

1982-1984	JV serial	$875	$1,125
1985-1997		$600	$775

Telecaster Custom
1959-1972. Body bound top and back, rosewood 'board, 2 Tele pickups, see Custom Telecaster for the 1 Tele/1 humbucker version. Please refer to the Fender Guitar Intro Section for details on Fender color options.

1959	Sunburst, maple	$20,400	$26,500
1960	Custom color	$21,850	$39,900
1960	Sunburst	$21,175	$27,500
1961	Custom color	$20,900	$38,950
1961	Sunburst	$20,400	$26,500
1962	Custom color	$18,050	$36,100
1962	Sunburst, curve	$18,100	$23,500
1962	Sunburst, slab	$18,850	$24,500
1963	Custom color	$18,000	$33,000
1963	Sunburst	$17,700	$23,500
1964	Custom color	$16,000	$28,000
1964	Sunburst	$15,775	$20,500

MODEL YEAR	FEATURES	EXC. COND. LOW	HIGH
1965	Custom color	$15,000	$26,000
1965	Sunburst	$13,200	$17,100
1966	Custom color	$12,000	$21,000
1966	Sunburst	$10,000	$13,000
1967	Custom color	$10,000	$17,000
1967	Sunburst	$10,000	$13,000
1968	Custom color	$10,000	$17,000
1968	Sunburst	$10,000	$13,000
1969	Custom color	$10,000	$17,000
1969	Sunburst	$10,000	$13,000
1970	Custom color	$8,000	$14,000
1970	Sunburst	$7,800	$10,200
1971	Custom color, 4-bolt	$7,600	$12,800
1971	Sunburst, 3-bolt	$3,450	$4,475
1971	Sunburst, 4-bolt	$7,200	$9,375
1972	Custom color, 3-bolt	$5,100	$6,625
1972	Sunburst, 3-bolt	$3,450	$4,475

Telecaster Custom (Japan)
1985. Made in Japan during the period when Fender suspended all USA manufacturing in '85, Tele Custom specs including bound body.

1985		$900	$1,175

Telecaster Custom FMT HH (Korea)
2003-present. Part of Special Edition, Korean-made, flamed maple top, 2 humbuckers.

2003-2019		$600	$775

Telecaster Stratocaster Hybrid
2006. Custom Shop model, Tele body shape, Strat pickup system and wiring, Strat headstock shape, dot markers on rosewood board, reissue tremolo, includes Custom Shop Certificate that reads "Telecaster Stratocaster Hybrid".

2006		$1,725	$2,250

Telecaster Thinline
1968-1980. Semi-hollowbody, 1 f-hole, 2 Tele pickups, ash or mahogany body, in late-'71 the tilt neck was added and the 2 Tele pickups were switched to 2 humbuckers. Please refer to the Fender Guitar Intro Section for details on Fender color options.

1968	Common color	$10,200	$13,250
1968	Natural ash	$6,675	$8,675
1968	Natural mahogany	$6,675	$8,675
1968	Rare color	$12,550	$16,300
1968	Sunburst	$7,475	$9,700
1969	Common color	$8,625	$11,200
1969	Natural ash	$5,900	$7,650
1969	Natural mahogany	$5,900	$7,650
1969	Rare color	$11,200	$14,600
1969	Sunburst	$6,600	$8,575
1970	Common color	$7,250	$9,425
1970	Natural ash	$5,025	$6,525
1970	Natural mahogany	$5,025	$6,525
1970	Rare color	$9,400	$12,200
1970	Sunburst	$5,675	$7,350
1971	Color option, 3-bolt, hums	$4,700	$6,125
1971	Color option, 4-bolt, singles	$8,625	$11,200
1971	Natural ash, 3-bolt	$3,000	$3,875

GUITARS

MODEL YEAR	FEATURES	EXC. COND. LOW	HIGH
1971	Natural ash, 3-bolt, hums	$3,000	$3,875
1971	Natural ash, 4-bolt, singles	$3,375	$4,375
1971	Natural mahogany, 3-bolt	$3,000	$3,875
1971	Natural mahogany, 3-bolt, hums	$3,000	$3,875
1971	Natural mahogany, 4-bolt, singles	$3,375	$4,375
1971	Sunburst, 3-bolt, hums	$3,150	$4,075
1971	Sunburst, 4-bolt, singles	$3,900	$5,100
1972	Color option	$4,700	$6,125
1972	Mahogany	$2,625	$3,425
1972	Natural ash	$2,625	$3,425
1972	Sunburst	$2,750	$3,575
1973	Color option	$4,300	$5,600
1973	Mahogany	$2,600	$3,400
1973	Natural ash	$2,600	$3,400
1973	Sunburst	$2,600	$3,400
1974	Color option	$4,300	$5,600
1974	Mahogany	$2,600	$3,400
1974	Natural ash	$2,600	$3,400
1974	Sunburst	$2,750	$3,575
1975	Color option	$4,300	$5,600
1975	Natural ash	$2,600	$3,400
1975	Sunburst	$2,600	$3,400
1976	Color option	$3,300	$4,275
1976	Natural ash	$2,550	$3,300
1976	Sunburst	$2,600	$3,400
1977	Color option	$3,300	$4,275
1977	Natural ash	$2,550	$3,300
1977	Sunburst	$2,600	$3,400
1978	Color option	$3,075	$4,000
1978	Natural ash	$2,275	$2,950
1978	Sunburst	$2,350	$3,050

Tele-Sonic
1998-2000. U.S.A., chambered Telecaster body, 2 DeArmond pickups, dot markers, upper bass bout 3-way toggle switch.

1998-2000		$850	$1,100

Texas Special Telecaster
1991-1992. Custom Shop model, 60 made, state of Texas outline on the 'guard, ash body with Texas Orange transparent finish, large profile maple neck, with certificate of authenticity.

1991-1992		$1,725	$2,250

Twisted Telecaster Limited Edition
2005. Custom Shop, 50 built by Master Builder Yuriy Shishkov, 100 built by the Custom Shop team, top loaded Bigsby.

2005	Shishkov built	$2,700	$3,500
2005	Team built	$1,900	$2,500

Two-Tone Telecaster Thinline
2019. Limited Edition, alder body, various top color with matching headstock and white back and sides.

2019		$1,050	$1,375

Vintage Hot Rod Telecaster
2007-2014. Vintage styling with modern features, '07-'13 named '52 Tele and '62 Tele, in '14 changed to '50s, and '60s.

2007-2014	All models	$1,100	$1,450

Waylon Jennings Tribute Telecaster
1995-2003. Custom Shop, black with white leather rose body inlays.

1995-2003		$5,000	$6,500

Will Ray Signature Jazz-A-Caster
1997. Made in Fender Japan Custom Shop as one part of the three part Hellecasters Series, limited edition, Strat neck on a Tele body with 2 soap-bar Seymour Duncan Jazzmaster-style pickups, gold leaf finish.

1997		$1,000	$1,300

Will Ray Signature Mojo Telecaster
1998-2001. Custom Shop, ash body, flamed maple Strat neck, locking tuners, rosewood 'board, skull inlays, double coil pickups, optional Hipshot B bender.

1998-2001		$2,300	$3,000

Telecoustic/Telecoustic Deluxe/ Telecoustic Standard
2000-2016. Thinline acoustic/electric, single-cut, spruce top, fiberglass body, various colors. Telecoustic discontinued '05, Deluxe begins '07 and Standard added in '09.

2002-2005	Telecoustic	$150	$200
2007-2009	Deluxe	$400	$600
2009-2016	Standard	$225	$300

Telecoustic Plus/Telecoustic Premier
2014-2016. Standard with Mini USB output added, Premier is 3-color sunburst flame maple, Plus is Sherwood Green top with matching head.

2014-2016	Plus	$250	$325
2014-2016	Premier	$275	$360

Toronado/Toronado Deluxe/HH/ Highway/GT
1998-2006. Deluxe Series made in Mexico, various models.

1998-2006		$500	$675

Villager 12-String
1965-1969, 2011-2017. Acoustic flat-top, spruce top, mahogany back and sides, 12 strings, natural. Reintroduced in '11 (California Series) with on-board Fishman System, made in China.

1965-1969		$625	$850
2011-2017	Reintroduced	$250	$350

Violin - Electric
1958-1976, 2013. Violin-shape, solidbody, sunburst is the standard finish.

1958-1976		$1,600	$2,200
2013		$475	$625

Wildwood
1963-1971. Acoustic flat-top with Wildwood dyed top.

1966-1971	Various (unfaded)	$1,575	$2,050

1972 Fender Telecaster Thinline

Fender 2000 Will Ray Signature Mojo Telecaster
Jimmy James

GUITARS

2006 First Act Volkswagen Garagemaster
Billy White Jr.

1975 Framus Jan Akkerman
Larry Cramer

MODEL		EXC. COND.	
YEAR	FEATURES	LOW	HIGH

Fenix
Late 1980s-mid 1990s. Brand name of Korean manufacturer Young Chang, used on a line of original-design and copy acoustic, electric and bass guitars. They also built Squier brand guitars for Fender during that period.

Fenton-Weill
See info under Burns-Weill.

Fernandes
1969-present. Established in Tokyo. Early efforts were classical guitars, but they now offer a variety of intermediate grade, production, imported guitars and basses.

Fina
Production classical and steel-string guitars and acoustic basses built in Huiyang City, Guang Dong, China.

Finck, David
1986-present. Luthier David Finck builds his production/custom, professional and premium grade, acoustic guitars, presently in Valle Crucis, North Carolina. In the past, he has built in Pittsburg, Kansas and Reader, West Virginia.

Fine Resophonic
1988-present. Professional and premium grade, production/custom, wood and metal-bodied resophonic guitars (including reso-electrics) built by luthiers Mike Lewis and Pierre Avocat in Vitry Sur Seine, France. They also build ukes and mandolins.

First Act
1995-present. Budget and professional grade, production/custom, acoustic, solid and semi-hollow body guitars built in China and in their Custom Shop in Boston. They also make basses, violins, and other instruments.

Firth Pond & Company
1822-1867. An east coast retail distributor that sold Martin and Ashborn private brand instruments. The company operated as Firth and Hall from 1822-1841 (also known as Firth, Hall & Pond) in New York City and Litchfield, Connecticut. Most instruments were small parlor size (11" lower bout) guitars, as was the case for most builders of this era. Sometimes the inside back center seam will be branded Firth & Pond. Brazilian rosewood sides and back instruments fetch considerably more than most of the other tone woods and value can vary considerably based on condition. Guitars from the 1800s are sometimes valued more as antiques than working vintage guitars. In 1867 Firth & Sons sold out to Oliver Ditson Company.

Flammang Guitars
1990-present. Premium grade, custom/production, steel string guitars built by luthier David Flammang in Greene, Iowa and previously in East Hampton and Higganum, Connecticut.

Flaxwood
2004-present. Professional grade, production/custom, solid and semi-hollow body guitars built in Finland, with bodies of natural fiber composites.

Fleishman Instruments
Introduced in 1974, premium and presentation grade, custom flat-tops made by luthier Harry Fleishman in Sebastopol, California. He also offers basses and electric uprights. Fleishman is the director of Luthiers School International.

Fletcher Brock Stringed Instruments
1992-present. Custom flat-tops and archtops made by luthier Fletcher Brock originally in Ketchum, Idaho, and currently in Seattle, Washington. He also builds mandolin family instruments.

Flowers Guitars
1993-present. Premium grade, custom, archtop guitars built by luthier Gary Flowers in Baltimore, Maryland.

Floyd Rose
2004-2006. Floyd Rose, inventor of the Floyd Rose Locking Tremolo, produced a line of intermediate and professional grade, production, solidbody guitars from '04 to '06. They continue to offer bridges and other accessories.

Foggy Mountain
Intermediate grade, production, steel and nylon string acoustic and acoustic/electric guitars imported from China.

Fontanilla Guitars
1987-present. Luthier Allan Fontanilla builds his premium grade, production/custom, classical guitars in San Francisco, California.

Fouilleul
1978-present. Production/custom, classical guitars made by luthier Jean-Marie Fouilleul in Cuguen, France.

Fox Hollow Guitars
2004-present. Luthier Don Greenough builds his professional and premium grade, custom, acoustic and electric guitars in Eugene, Oregon. He also builds mandolins.

Fox or Rocking F
1983-present. Premium grade, custom, steel string acoustic guitars built in Seattle, Washington by luthier Cat Fox.

MODEL YEAR	FEATURES	EXC. COND. LOW	HIGH

Foxxe

1990-1991. Short-lived brand of solidbodies offered by the same company that produced Barrington guitars, Korean-made.

Frame Works

1995-present. Professional grade, production/custom, steel- and nylon-string guitars built by luthier Frank Krocker in Burghausen, Germany. The instruments feature a neck mounted on a guitar-shaped frame. Krocker has also built traditional archtops, flat-tops, and classicals.

Framus

1946-1977, 1996-present. Professional and premium grade, production/custom, guitars made in Markneukirchen, Germany. They also build basses, amps, mandolins and banjos. Frankische Musikindustrie (Framus) founded in Erlangen, Germany by Fred Wilfer, relocated to Bubenreuth in '54, and to Pretzfeld in '67. Begun as an acoustic instrument manufacturer, Framus added electrics in the mid-'50s. Earliest electrics were mostly acoustics with pickups attached. Electric designs begin in early-'60s. Unique feature was a laminated maple neck with many thin plies. By around '64-'65 upscale models featured the organtone, often called a spigot, a spring-loaded volume control that allowed you to simulate a Leslie speaker effect. Better models often had mutes and lots of switches.

In the '60s, Framus instruments were imported into the U.S. by Philadelphia Music Company. Resurgence of interest in ca. '74 with the Jan Akkermann hollowbody followed by original mid-'70s design called the Nashville, the product of an alliance with some American financing.

The brand was revived in '96 by Hans Peter Wilfer, the president of Warwick, with production in Warwick's factory in Germany.

Amateur

Early-1960s to mid-1970s. Model 5/1, small flat-top, early without pickguard, plain, dot markers.

1960s-70s	Model 5/1	$175	$225

Atilla Zoller AZ-10

Early-1960s-early-1980s. Single-cut archtop, 2 pickups, neck glued-in until the '70s, bolt-on after, sunburst. Model 5/65 (rounded cutaway, made until late '60s) and Model 5/67 (sharp cutaway).

1960s	Model 5/65	$600	$775
1960s-70s	Model 5/67	$600	$775

Atlantic

Ca. 1965-ca. 1970. Model 5/110, single-cut thin body electric archtop, 2 pickups, tremolo optional.

1965-1970	Model 5/110	$525	$675

Atlantic (08000) Elec-12

Mid- to late-1960s. Model 5/011 and 5/013, double cut semi-hollow, 2 pickups, 12-string.

1960s	Model 5/013	$525	$675

Big 18 Doubleneck

Late-1960s. Model 5/200 is a solidbody and Model 5/220 is acoustic.

1960s	Model 5/200	$675	$875
1960s	Model 5/220	$675	$875

Caravelle

Ca.1965-ca. 1975. Double-cut archtop, tremolo, model 5/117-52 has 2 pickups and 5/117-54 has 3.

1965-1975		$575	$750

Gaucho

Late-1960s to mid-1970s. Lower grade flat-top, concert size, spruce top, mahogany sides and back, rosewood bridge and 'board, sunburst or natural finish.

1960s-70s	Model 5/194	$180	$235

Guitar-Banjo 6/76 Dixi, SL-76

Ca.1957-early 1970s. Banjo body, guitar neck, silver hardware.

1950s-1970s		$400	$575

Hollywood

1960s. Double-cut, 3 pickups, red sunburst.

1960s	Model 5/132	$715	$925

Jan Akkerman

1974-1977. Single-cut semi-hollowbody, 2 pickups, gold hardware.

1974-1977		$310	$400

Jumbo

1963 to late-1970s. Models earlier 5/97, later 5/197, jumboflat-top, mahogany or maple sides and back.

1960s-70s		$450	$585

Jumbo 12-String

Late-1960s to mid-1970s. 12-string version.

1960s-70s	Model 5/297	$450	$585

Missouri (E Framus Missouri)

Ca.1955-ca. 1975. Originally non-cut acoustic archtop until early '60s when single-cut archtop with 1 or 2 pickups added.

1960s	Model 5/60	$470	$610

New Sound Series

1960s. Double-cut semi-hollowbody, model 5/116-52 has 2 pickups and 5/116-54 has 3.

1960s		$635	$825

Sorella Series

Ca.1955 to mid-1970s. Single-cut, Model 5/59 is acoustic archtop (with or without single pickup), 5/59-50 is 1-pickup electric archtop, 5/59-52 is electric 2-pickup.

1955-1975	Model 5/59	$550	$700
1965-1972	Model 5/59-50	$600	$775
1965-1972	Model 5/59-52	$625	$800

Sorento

Ca.1963-ca. 1970. Thinline archtop, single-cut, 2 pickups, organ effect, f-holes.

1963-1970	Model 5/112-53	$600	$775

Sorento 12

Ca.1963-ca. 1970. 12-string version.

1963-1970	Model 5/012	$685	$890

Sport

Early 1950s-mid-1970s. Small beginner flat-top, plain appointments, dot markers.

1950s-70s	Model 50/1	$180	$230

1960s Framus Missouri Model 5/60

Imaged by Heritage Auctions, HA.com

1962 Framus Sorella Model 5/59-50

Rivington Guitars

Franklin Guitar Company OM

*Fritz Brothers Roy
Buchanan Bluesmaster*

MODEL YEAR	FEATURES	EXC. COND. LOW	HIGH

Strato de Luxe 12 String
Ca. 1963-ca. 1970. Model 5/067(metal pickguard) and 5/068 (wood grain pickguard and large gold cover plates), 2 pickups, tremolo.

| 1963-1970 | Model 5/068 | $600 | $775 |

Strato de Luxe Series
Ca.1964-ca. 1970. 1, 2 (5/155, 5/167-52, 5/168-52) or 3 (5/167-54, 5/168-54) pickups, some models have gold hardware.

| 1960s | 2 pickups | $515 | $665 |
| 1960s | 3 pickups | $600 | $775 |

Strato Super
Early- to late-1960s. Offset double-cut, 2 pickups.

| 1960s | Model 5/155-52 | $600 | $775 |

Studio Series
Late-1950s to mid-1970s. Model 5/51 (a.k.a. 030) is non-cut acoustic archtop (some with pickup - 5/51E), 5/108 is electric archtop, 1 pickup.

| 1960s-70s | Model 5/51 | $200 | $260 |
| 1960s-70s | Model 5/51E | $250 | $325 |

Television Series
Early- to late-1960s. Model 5/118-52 2 pickups and 5/118-54 3 pickups, offset double-cut thinline hollowbody.

| 1960s | Model 5/118-52 | $535 | $700 |
| 1960s | Model 5/118-54 | $635 | $825 |

Texan Series
Late-1960s to early-1980s. Model 5/196, 5/196E (with pickup) and 5/296 12-string flat-top, mahogany back and sides. 6-string ends in late '70s.

| 1960s-70s | 6-string | $260 | $335 |
| 1960s-80s | 12-string | $260 | $335 |

Western
1960s. Model 5/195, grand concert size, lower grade flat-top, spruce top, maple sides and back.

| 1960s | Model 5/195 | $200 | $260 |

Franklin Guitar Company
1974-present. Premium and presentation grade, custom, flat-top steel string guitars built first in Franklin, Michigan and since 2003 in Rocheport, Missouri by luthier Nick Kukich. He also built in Idaho, Washington and Oregon.

Fraulini
2001-present. Luthier Todd Cambio builds his professional and premium grade, primarily custom, early 20th century style guitars, in Madison, Wisconsin.

FreeNote
Intermediate to professional grade, the innovative FreeNote 12-Tone Ultra Plus provides two frets for every traditional fret placement which provides an unlimited number of playable notes.

Fresher
1973-1985. The Japanese-made Fresher brand models were mainly copies of popular brands and limited numbers were imported into the U.S. They also made basses.

MODEL YEAR	FEATURES	EXC. COND. LOW	HIGH

Solidbody Electric
1970s. Import from Japan, various models.

| 1970s | | $100 | $300 |

Fret-King
2008-present. Luthier Trev Wilkinson builds professional and premium grade, production, solidbody and semi-hollow electric guitars and basses in Yorkshire, U.K., and also offers a line imported from Korea.

Fritz Brothers
1988-present. Premium grade, production/custom, acoustic, semi-hollow, and solidbody guitars and basses built by luthier Roger Fritz, originally in Mobile, Alabama, then in Mendocino, California. In 2013 he again relocated to Mobile.

Froggy Bottom Guitars
1974-present. Luthier Michael Millard builds his premium and presentation grade, production/custom flat-tops in Newfane, Vermont (originally in Hinsdale, New York, and until '84 production was in Richmond, New Hampshire).

Frudua Guitar Works
1988-present. Luthier Galeazzo Frudua builds his intermediate to premium grade, production/custom, electric guitars, basses and amps in Imola, Italy.

Fukuoka Musical Instruments
1993-present. Custom steel- and nylon-string flat-tops and archtops built in Japan.

Furch
See listing for Stonebridge.

Furnace Mountain Guitar Works
1995-1999. Instruments built by luthier Martin Fair in New Mexico. He currently builds under the Fairbuilt Guitar Co. brand.

Fury
1962-2017. Founded by Glenn McDougall in Saskatoon, Saskatchewan, Fury offered production, hollow, semi-hollow and solidbody electric guitars and basses. McDougall died in early '17.

Futurama
1957-mid to late 1960s. Futurama was a brand name used by Selmer in the United Kingdom. Early instruments made by the Drevokov Cooperative in Czechoslovakia, models for '63-'64 made by Sweden's Hagstrom company. Some later '60s instruments may have been made in Japan. Beatles fans will recognize the brand name as Beatle George Harrison's first electric.

MODEL YEAR	FEATURES	EXC. COND. LOW	HIGH

Futurama/II/III
1957-1969. Offset double-cut, 2- or 3-pickup versions available, large Futurama logo on headstock with the reverse capital letter F. George Harrison purchased his Futurama in '59; maple neck, 3 pickups, 3 push button levels, 2 knobs, Futurama logo on 'guard. The price shown for the Harrison model assumes an all-original, excellent condition that exactly matches his '59 model.

1959	III, Harrison, maple	$1,500	$4,300
1959	III, rosewood	$800	$1,025

Fylde Guitars
1973-present. Luthier Roger Bucknall builds his professional and premium grade, production/custom acoustic guitars, basses, mandolins, mandolas, bouzoukis, and citterns in Penrith, Cumbria, UK.

G & L
1980-present. Intermediate and professional grade, production/custom, solidbody and semi-hollowbody electric guitars made in the U.S. and overseas. They also make basses. Founded by Leo Fender and George Fullerton following the severance of ties between Fender's CLF Research and Music Man. Company sold to John MacLaren and BBE Sound, when Leo Fender died in '91. In '98 they added their Custom Creations Department. In '03 G & L introduced the Korean-made G & L Tribute Series. George Fullerton died in July, '09.

ASAT
1986-1998. Called the Broadcaster in '85. Two or 3 single-coil or 2 single-coil/1 humbucker pickup configurations until early-'90s, 2 single-coils after.

1986		$900	$1,200
1987	Leo sig on headstock	$1,100	$1,450
1988-1991	Leo sig on body	$1,000	$1,325
1992-1998	BBE era	$750	$975

ASAT 20th Anniversary
2000. Limited Edition run of 50, ash body, tinted birdseye maple neck, 2-tone sunburst.

2000		$1,100	$1,450

ASAT '50
1999. Limited edition of 10.

1999		$1,100	$1,450

ASAT Bluesboy Limited Edition
1999. Limited edition of 20.

1999		$1,000	$1,325

ASAT Bluesboy Semi-Hollow Limited Edition
1999. Limited edition of 12, thin semi-hollow.

1999		$900	$1,200

ASAT Classic
1990-present. Two single-coil pickups, individually adjustable bridge saddles, neck-tilt adjustment and tapered string posts.

1990-1991	Leo sig on body	$950	$1,225
1992-1997	3-bolt neck	$850	$1,125
1997-2019	4-bolt neck	$850	$1,125

ASAT Classic B-Bender
1997. 12 made with factory-original B-Bender.

1997		$1,100	$1,450

ASAT Classic Bluesboy
2001-present. Humbucker neck pickup, single-coil at bridge.

2001-2019		$750	$975

ASAT Classic Bluesboy Rustic
2010-2015. Classic Bluesboy with Rustic aging and refinements.

2010-2015		$1,300	$1,700

ASAT Classic Bluesboy Semi-Hollow
1997-present. Chambered Classic with f-hole.

1997-2019		$900	$1,150

ASAT Classic Commemorative
1991-1992. Leo Fender signature and birth/death dating.

1991-1992	Australian lacewood, 6 made	$4,800	$6,300

ASAT Classic Custom
1996-1997, 2002-2013. Large rectangular neck pickup, single-coil bridge pickup.

1996-1997	1st version	$900	$1,200
2002-2013	2nd version, 4-bolt neck	$900	$1,200

ASAT Classic Custom Semi-Hollow
2002-2013. Custom with f-hole.

2002-2013		$875	$1,150

ASAT Classic S
2007. Limited run of 50, certificate, swamp ash body, 3 single-coil pickups, Nashville pickup configuration.

2007		$925	$1,200

ASAT Classic Semi-Hollow
1997-present. With f-hole.

1997-2019		$925	$1,200

ASAT Classic Three
1998. Limited Edition run of 100.

1998		$1,225	$1,575

ASAT Custom
1996. No pickguard, 25 to 30 made.

1996		$900	$1,175

ASAT Deluxe
1997-present. Flamed maple top, bound body, 2 humbuckers.

1997	3-bolt neck	$1,100	$1,450
1997-1999	4-bolt neck	$1,100	$1,450
2000-2019	4-bolt neck	$1,000	$1,350

ASAT Deluxe Semi-Hollow
1997-2018. Two humbuckers.

1997-2018		$1,100	$1,450

ASAT III
1988-1991, 1996-1998. Single-cut body, 3 single-coil pickups.

1988-1991	1st version, Leo era, 150 made	$1,150	$1,500
1996-1998	Post Leo era	$1,100	$1,450

ASAT JD-5/Jerry Donahue JD-5
2004-2007. Jerry Donahue model, single-cut, 2 single-coils, special wired 5-way switch.

2004-2007		$1,100	$1,450

1993 G & L ASAT Classic
Rivington Guitars

G & L ASAT Classic Custom Semi-Hollow

1980 G & L F-100

1989 G & L Interceptor

MODEL YEAR	FEATURES	EXC. COND. LOW	HIGH
ASAT Junior			
1998-1999. Limited Edition run of 250, single-cut semi-hollowbody, 2 single-coils.			
1998-1999		$1,125	$1,450
ASAT S-3			
1998-2000. Three soap-bar single-coil pickups, limited production.			
1998-2000		$725	$1,025
ASAT Special			
1992-present. Like ASAT, but with 2 larger P-90-type pickups, chrome hardware, various colors.			
1992-1997	3-bolt neck	$725	$1,025
1997-2019	4-bolt neck	$725	$1,025
ASAT Special Semi-Hollow			
1997-2018. Semi-hollow version of ASAT Special.			
1997-2018		$725	$1,025
ASAT Special Deluxe			
2001-2015. No 'guard version of the Special with figured maple top.			
2001-2015		$950	$1,250
ASAT Z-2 Limited Edition			
1999. Limited run of 10, semi-hollow construction, natural ash, tortoise bound, engraved neckplate.			
1999		$1,100	$1,500
ASAT Z-3			
1998-present. Three offset-style Z-3 high output pickups, sunburst.			
1998-2019		$725	$1,025
ASAT Z-3 Semi-Hollow			
1998-present. F-hole version of Z-3.			
1998-2019		$725	$1,025
Broadcaster			
1985-1986. Solidbody, 2 single-coils with adjustable polepieces act in humbucking mode with selector switch in the center position, black parts and finish, name changed to ASAT in early-'86.			
1985-1986	Kahler	$800	$1,025
1985-1986	Signed by Leo, ebony 'board	$1,700	$2,200
1985-1986	Signed by Leo, maple 'board	$1,700	$2,200
Cavalier			
1983-1986. Offset double-cut, 2 humbuckers, 700 made, sunburst.			
1983-1986		$925	$1,200
Climax			
1992-1996. Offset double-cut, bolt maple neck, six-on-a-side tuners, double locking vibrato, blue.			
1992-1996		$800	$1,050
Climax Plus			
1992-1996. Two humbuckers replace single-coils of the Climax, plus 1 single-coil.			
1992-1996		$725	$950
Climax XL			
1992-1996. Two humbuckers only.			
1992-1996		$725	$950
Comanche V			
1988-1991. Solidbody, 3 Z-shaped single-coil humbuckers, maple neck in choice of 3 radii, rosewood 'board, vibrato, fine tuners, Leo Fender's signature on the body, sunburst.			
1988-1991		$1,000	$1,300

MODEL YEAR	FEATURES	EXC. COND. LOW	HIGH
Comanche VI			
1990-1991. Leo Fender's signature on the body, 6 mini-toggles.			
1990-1991		$1,000	$1,300
Comanche (Reintroduced)			
1998-present. Reissue with either swamp ash or alder body, bolt-on maple neck, 3 Z-coil pickups, standard or premium finish options.			
1998-2019	Premium finish, flame top	$925	$1,200
1998-2019	Standard finish	$850	$1,100
Commemorative			
1992-1997. About 350 made, Leo Fender signature on upper bass bout.			
1991	Cherryburst	$1,900	$2,500
1992-1997	Sunburst	$1,700	$2,300
F-100 (Model I and II)			
1980-1986. Offset double-cut solidbody, 2 humbuckers, natural. Came in a I and II model - only difference is the radius of the 'board.			
1980-1986		$750	$975
F-100 E (Model I and II)			
1980-1982. Offset double-cut solidbody, 2 humbuckers, active electronics, pre-amp, natural. Came in a I and II model - only difference is the radius of the 'board.			
1980-1982		$800	$1,025
Fallout			
2013-present. SC-2 body style, P-90 and humbucker, swamp ash body on premier and alder on standard finishes, maple neck, maple or rosewood 'board.			
2013-2019		$725	$950
G-200			
1981-1982. Mahogany solidbody, maple neck, ebony 'board, 2 humbucking pickups, coil-split switches, natural or sunburst, 209 made.			
1981-1982		$1,750	$2,300
GBL-LE (Guitars by Leo Limited Edition)			
1999. Limited edition of 25, semi-hollowbody, 3 pickups.			
1999		$1,050	$1,350
George Fullerton Signature			
1995-2007. Double-cut solidbody, sunburst.			
1995-1997	3-bolt neck	$925	$1,200
1997-2007	4-bolt neck	$925	$1,200
HG-1			
1982-1983. Offset double-cut, 1 humbucker, dot inlays. Very rare as most were made into HG-2s.			
1982-1983		$1,425	$1,900
HG-2			
1982-1984. 2-humbucker HG, body changes to classic offset double-cut in '84.			
1982-1983	Mustang-body	$1,200	$1,550
1984	S-body	$1,200	$1,550
Interceptor			
1983-1991. To '86 an X-shaped solidbody, either 3 single-coils, 2 humbuckers, or 1 humbucker and 2 single-coils, '87-'89 was an offset double-cut solidbody.			
1983-1985	1st X-body, 70 made	$2,200	$2,900

MODEL YEAR	FEATURES	EXC. COND. LOW	HIGH
1985-1986	2nd X-body, 12 made	$2,200	$2,900
1987-1991	Double-cut	$1,200	$1,600

Invader

1984-1991, 1998-2018. Double-cut solidbody, 2 single-coil and 1 humbucker pickups.

1984-1991	1st version	$750	$1,000
1998-2018	2nd version	$750	$1,000

Invader Plus

1998-2018. Two humbuckers and single blade pickup in the middle position.

1998-2018		$675	$900

Invader XL

1998-2018. Fancy top, 2 humbuckers.

1998-2018		$875	$1,175

John Jorgenson Signature Model ASAT

1995. About 190 made, Silver Metalflake finish.

1995		$1,050	$1,350

Legacy

1992-present. Classic double-cut configuration, USA logo, 3-bolt neck until '97, 4-bolt after, various colors.

1992-1994	3-bolt neck, Duncan SSLs	$675	$875
1995-1997	3-bolt neck, Alnicos	$675	$875
1998-2019	4-bolt neck, Alnicos	$675	$875

Legacy Deluxe

2001-2015. No 'guard, figured maple top.

2001-2015		$775	$1,000

Legacy HH

2001-present. Two humbucker pickups.

2001-2019		$675	$875

Legacy HSS

2001-present. One humbucker pickup at bridge position plus 2 single-coil pickups.

2001-2019		$675	$875

Legacy Special

1993-present. Legacy with 3 humbuckers, various colors.

1992-1997	3-bolt neck	$675	$875
1998-2019	4-bolt neck	$675	$875

25th Anniversary Limited Edition

2006. G&L Custom Creations, 250 made, combines appearance of '81 F-100 with contours and control layout of ASAT Super, single-cut mahogany body, 2 custom wound MFD humbuckes, custom blend 'root beer' finish.

2006		$900	$1,200

Nighthawk

1983. Offset double-cut solidbody, 3 single-coil pickups, 269 made, sunburst, name changed to Skyhawk in '84.

1983		$725	$950

Rampage

1984-1991. Offset double-cut solidbody, hard rock maple neck, ebony 'board, 1 bridge-position humbucker pickup, sunburst. Currently available as Jerry Cantrell Signature Model.

1984-1991	Common color	$950	$1,250
1984-1991	Rare color	$1,425	$1,850

MODEL YEAR	FEATURES	EXC. COND. LOW	HIGH

Rampage (Reissue)

2000. Limited Edition run of 70, supplied with gig bag and not hard case, ivory finish.

2000		$600	$775

S-500

1982-present. Double-cut mahogany or ash solidbody, maple neck, ebony or maple 'board, 3 single-coil pickups, vibrato.

1982-1987		$925	$1,225
1988-1991	Mini-toggle, Leo sig on body	$825	$1,100
1992-1997	3-bolt neck	$675	$900
1997-2019	4-bolt neck	$675	$900

S-500 Deluxe

2001-2015. Deluxe Series features, including no 'guard and flamed maple top, natural.

2001-2015	Flame & solid tops	$850	$1,100

SC-1

1982-1983. Offset double-cut solidbody, 1 single-coil pickup, tremolo, sunburst, 250 made.

1981-1982		$725	$950

SC-2

1982-1983, 2010-2018. Offset double-cut solidbody, 2 MFD soapbar pickups, about 600 made in original run, reissue maple or rosewood 'board.

1982-1983	Shallow cutaway	$950	$1,250
1983	Deeper, pointed cutaway	$950	$1,250
2010-2018	Reissue	$525	$675

SC-3

1982-1991. Offset double-cut solidbody, 3 single-coil pickups, tremolo.

1982-1983	Shallow cutaway	$800	$1,050
1984-1987	Deeper cutaway, no 'guard	$800	$1,050
1988-1991	Deeper cutaway, 'guard	$725	$950

Skyhawk

1984-1991. Renamed from Nighthawk, offset double-cut, 3 single-coils, signature on headstock '84-'87, then on body '88-'91.

1984-1987	Dual-Fulcrum or saddle lock	$800	$1,025
1984-1987	Kahler	$625	$800
1988-1991	Dual-Fulcrum or saddle lock	$625	$800
1988-1991	Kahler	$575	$750

Superhawk

1984-1987. Offset double-cut, maple neck, ebony 'board, G&L or Kahler tremolos, 2 humbuckers, signature on headstock.

1984-1987		$700	$900

Tribute Series

2003-present. Import versions of regular models.

2003-2019	Various models	$200	$500

Trinity

2006. Only 25 made, ASAT-style with 3 new style single-coils, designed by Tim Page of Buffalo Brothers, the last G&L to have COA signed by George Fullerton.

2006		$1,350	$1,800

G & L S-500

1987 G & L SC-3

Carter Vintage Guitars

G & L Will Ray Signature Model

2017 Gallagher G-70

MODEL YEAR	FEATURES	EXC. COND. LOW	HIGH

Will Ray Signature Model
2002-2018. Will Ray signature on headstock, 3 Z-coil pickups, Hipshot B-Bender.

| 2002-2018 | | $650 | $850 |

G.L. Stiles

1960-1994. Built by Gilbert Lee Stiles primarily in the Miami, Florida area. First solidbody, including pickups and all hardware, built by hand in his garage. Stiles favored scrolls, fancy carving and walnut fingerboards. His later instruments were considerably fancier and more refined. He moved to Hialeah, Florida by '63 and began making acoustic guitars and other instruments. Only his solidbodies had consecutive serial numbers. Stiles, who died in '94, made approximately 1000 solidbodies and 500 acoustics.

Gadotti Guitars

1997-present. Luthier Jeanfranco Biava Gadotti builds his premium grade, custom/production, nylon- and steel-string, carved, chambered solidbodies in Orlando, Florida.

Gadow Guitars

2002-2019. Luthier Ryan Gadow built his professional and premium grade, custom/production, solid and semi-hollow body guitars and basses in Durham, North Carolina.

Gagnon

Luthier Bill Gagnon began building his premium and presentation grade, production/custom, archtop guitars in Beaverton, Oregon, starting in 1998.

Galanti

Ca.1962-ca.1967. Electric guitars offered by the longtime Italian accordion maker, some built by Zero Sette. They may have also offered acoustics.

Electric
1962-1967. Solidbody or hollowbody.

| 1962-1967 | Fancy features | $500 | $750 |
| 1962-1967 | Plain features | $250 | $500 |

Galiano

New Yorkers Antonio Cerrito and Raphael Ciani offered guitars under the Galiano brand during the early part of the last century. They used the brand both on guitars built by them and others, including The Oscar Schmidt Company. They also offered mandolins.

Gallagher

1965-present. Professional and premium grade, production/custom, flat-top guitars built in Wartrace, Tennessee. J. W. Gallagher started building Shelby brand guitars in the Slingerland Drum factory in Shelbyville, Tennessee in '63. In '65 he and his son Don made the first Gallagher guitar, the G-50. Doc Watson began using Gallagher guitars in '68. In '76, Don assumed operation of the business when J. W. semi-retired. J. W. died in '79.

MODEL YEAR	FEATURES	EXC. COND. LOW	HIGH

71 Special
1970s-2015. Rosewood back and sides, spruce top, herringbone trim, bound ebony 'board, natural.

| 1970s-2015 | | $1,625 | $2,100 |

72 Special
1977-2016. Rosewood back and sides, spruce top, abalone trim, bound ebony 'board, natural.

| 1977-2016 | | $2,900 | $3,800 |

A-70 Ragtime Special
1978-2015. Smaller auditorium/00 size, spruce top, mahogany back and sides, G logo, natural.

| 1978-2015 | | $1,175 | $1,475 |

Custom 12-String
Introduced in 1965-present. Mahogany, 12-fret neck, natural.

| 1965 | | $1,200 | $1,550 |

Doc Watson
1968-present. Spruce top, mahogany back and sides, scalloped bracing, ebony 'board, herringbone trim, natural.

| 1968-2019 | | $2,200 | $2,850 |

Doc Watson (Cutaway)
1975-2010. Spruce top, mahogany back and sides, scalloped bracing, ebony 'board, herringbone trim, natural.

| 1975-2010 | | $2,300 | $2,950 |

Doc Watson 12-String
1995-2000. Natural.

| 1995-2000 | | $1,850 | $2,400 |

Doc Watson Signature
2000-present. Signature inlay 12th fret.

| 2000-2019 | | $2,300 | $2,950 |

G-45
1970-2008. Mahogany back and sides, spruce top, ebony 'board, natural.

| 1970-1979 | | $1,300 | $1,650 |
| 1980-2008 | | $1,100 | $1,400 |

G-50
1960s-2015. Mahogany back and sides, spruce top, ebony 'board, natural.

| 1960s | | $1,900 | $2,450 |
| 1970-2015 | | $1,425 | $1,850 |

G-65
1980s-2015. Rosewood back and sides, spruce top, ebony 'board, natural.

| 1980s-2015 | | $1,475 | $1,950 |

G-70
1978-present. Rosewood back and sides, herringbone purfling on top and soundhole, mother-of-pearl diamond 'board inlays, bound headstock, natural.

| 1978-2019 | | $1,500 | $1,900 |

G-71
1970s. Indian rosewood, gold tuners.

| 1970s | | $1,800 | $2,225 |

Gallagher, Kevin

1996. Kevin Gallagher, luthier, changed name brand to Omega to avoid confusion with J.W. Gallagher. See Omega listing.

MODEL YEAR	FEATURES	EXC. COND. LOW	HIGH

Gallotone

1950s-1960s. Low-end foreign brand similar to 1950s Stellas, the Gallotone Champion, a 3/4 size student flat-top, is associated with John Lennon as his early guitar.

Galloup Guitars

1994-present. Luthier Bryan Galloup builds his professional and premium grade, production/custom flat-tops in Big Rapids, Michigan. He also operates the Galloup School of Lutherie and The Guitar Hospital repair and restoration business.

Galveston

Budget and intermediate grade, production, imported acoustic, acoustic/electric, resonator and solidbody guitars. They also offer basses and mandolins.

Gamble & O'Toole

1978-present. Premium grade, custom classical and steel string guitars built by luthier Arnie Gamble in Sacramento, California, with design input and inlay work from his wife Erin O'Toole.

Ganz Guitars

1995-present. Luthier Steve Ganz builds his professional grade, production/custom classical guitars in Bellingham, Washington.

Garcia

Made by luthier Federico Garcia in Spain until late-1960s or very early-'70s when production moved to Japan.

Classical

1960s-1970s. Mid-level, '60s model is solid spruce top with solid mahogany, rosewood or walnut back and sides, '70s model is Spanish pine top with walnut back and sides.

1960s	Mahogany	$225	$300
1960s	Rosewood	$300	$400
1960s	Walnut	$225	$300
1970s	Spanish pine/ Brazilian rosewood	$450	$700
1970s	Spanish pine/walnut	$225	$300

Garrison

2000-2007. Intermediate and professional grade, production, acoustic and acoustic/electric guitars designed by luthier Chris Griffiths using his Active Bracing System (a single integrated glass-fiber bracing system inside a solid wood body). He started Griffiths Guitar Works in 1993 in St. John's, Newfoundland, and introduced Garrison guitars in 2000. In '07, the Garrison facility was acquired by Gibson.

Gary Kramer

2005-present. Gary Kramer, the founder of the original Kramer brand, started a new business in 2005. The initial line was based upon a half-moon

shaped model called the USA Delta Wing. Later import models were added.

Gauge Guitars

2002-present. Luthier Aaron Solomon builds custom, professional and premium grade, solidbody and semi-solid electric guitars in New Jersey.

Gemelli

Early 1960s-ca. 1966. European-made (likely Italian) guitars. Similar to Bartolini guitars, so most likely from same manufacturer. Originally plastic covered, they switched to paint finishes by around '65.

Gemunder

1870s-1910s. New York shop that specialized in reproduction-aged violins, but also made parlor-sized guitars that were similar to Martin guitars of the era. An original label on the inside back identifies August Gemunder and Sons, New York.

Parlor

1870s-1910s. Style 28 appointments, rosewood body, spruce top.

1870-1910s		$1,150	$1,500

George

See listing under Chris George.

German Guitars

2001-present. Luthier Greg German builds his premium grade, custom/production, acoustic archtop guitars in Broomfield, Colorado.

Giannini

1900-present. Classical, acoustic, and acoustic/electric guitars built in Salto, SP, Brazil near Sao Paolo. They also build violas, cavaquinhos and mandolins. Founded by guitar-builder Tranquillo Giannini, an Italian who traveled to Brazil in 1890 and discovered the exotic woods of Brazil. The company was producing 30,000 instruments a year by '30. They began exporting their acoustic instruments to the U.S. in '63. They added electric guitars in '60, but these weren't imported as much, if at all. Gianninis from this era used much Brazilian Rosewood.

Classical

Early-1970s. Nylon string import, small body.

1970s	Brazilian rosewood	$300	$400
1970s	Pau ferro, mahogany	$150	$200

CraViolia

1972-1974, 2004-present. Kidney bean-shaped rosewood body, acoustic, natural, line included a classical, a steel string, and a 12-string.

1972-1974		$450	$575

CraViolia 12-String

1972-1974, 2004-present. Kidney bean-shaped body, 12 strings.

1972-1974		$450	$575
2004-2019		$150	$200

1965 Giannini 8141 Model #4 Classical
Craig Brody

2017 Giannini GSCRA12-SPC CEQ

1938 Gibson Advanced Jumbo

*2005 Gibson B.B. King
80th Birthday Lucille*

Imaged by Heritage Auctions, HA.com

MODEL YEAR	FEATURES	EXC. COND. LOW	HIGH

Gibson

1890s (1902)-present. Intermediate, professional, and premium grade, production/custom, acoustic and electric guitars made in the U.S. They also build basses, mandolins, amps, and banjos. Gibson also offers instruments under the Epiphone, Kramer, Steinberger, Dobro, Tobias, Valley Arts, Garrison, Slingerland (drums), Baldwin (pianos), Trace Elliot, Electar (amps), Maestro, Gibson Labs, Oberheim, and Echoplex brands.

Founded in Kalamazoo, Michigan by Orville Gibson, a musician and luthier who developed instruments with tops, sides and backs carved out of solid pieces of wood. Early instruments included mandolins, archtop guitars and harp guitars. By 1896 Gibson had opened a shop. In 1902 Gibson was bought out by a group of investors who incorporated the business as Gibson Mandolin-Guitar Manufacturing Company, Limited. The company was purchased by Chicago Musical Instrument Company (CMI) in '44. In '57 CMI also purchased the Epiphone guitar company, transferring production from Philadelphia to the Gibson plant in Kalamazoo. Gibson was purchased by Norlin in late-'69 and a new factory was opened in Nashville, Tennessee in '74. The Kalamazoo factory ceased production in '84. In '85, Gibson was sold to a group headed by Henry Juskewiscz. Gibson purchased the Flatiron Company in '87 and built a new factory in '89, moving acoustic instrument production to Bozeman, Montana. In '18 Gibson went into Chapter 11 bankruptcy, emerging later in the year with KKR as new majority owner and James "JC" Curleigh as CEO.

The various models of Firebirds, Flying Vs, Les Pauls, SGs, and Super 400s are grouped together under those general headings. Custom Shop and Historic instruments are listed with their respective main model (for example, the '39 Super 400 Historical Collection model is listed with the Super 400s).

Model specifications can cross model years. For example, it is possible that an early '60 Gibson guitar might have a specification, such as a wider-rounder neck, which is typically a '59 spec. In that case it is possible for the early '60 model to be valued more closely to the late '59 model than to a mid to late '60 model with a thinner-flatter neck profile.

Orville Gibson

1894-1902. Hand-made and carved by Orville Gibson, various models and sizes most with standard printed white rectangle label "O.H. Gibson" with photo of Orville Gibson and lyre-mandolin. Prices are for fully functional original or refurbished examples. It is almost expected that a black Orville Gibson instrument has been refinished, and most of those were done by Gibson.

1894-1902	Basic plain model	$4,200	$39,000
1894-1902	Fancy rare model	$22,000	$49,000
1894-1902	Very rare, historical	$27,000	$69,000

335 S Custom

1980-1981. Solidbody, 335-shaped, mahogany body, unbound rosewood 'board, 2 exposed Dirty Finger

humbuckers, coil-tap, TP-6 tailpiece. Also available in natural finish, branded headstock Firebrand version.

1980-1981		$1,025	$1,325

335 S Deluxe

1980-1982. Same as 335 S Custom but with bound ebony 'board, brass nut.

1980-1982		$1,025	$1,325

335 S Limited Run

2011-2013. Maple body and neck, rosewood 'board, nitro-finish sunburst.

2011-2013		$875	$1,150

335 S Standard

1980-1981. Same as 335 S Custom except stop tailpiece, no coil-tap. Also available in natural finish, branded headstock Firebrand version.

1980-1981		$1,025	$1,325

Advanced Jumbo

1936-1940. Dreadnought, 16" wide, round shoulders, Brazilian rosewood back and sides, sunburst, reintroduced '90-'97.

1936-1940		$52,500	$67,500

Advanced Jumbo (Reissue)

1990-1999, 2002-2018. Issued as a standard production model, but soon available only as a special order for most of the '90s; currently offered as standard production. Renamed 1936 Advanced Jumbo for 1997-1998. There were also some limited-edition Ajs offered during the '90s.

1990-1999	Reissue	$1,625	$2,100
1994	Machiche	$1,625	$2,100
2002-2018	Reintroduced	$1,625	$2,100

Advanced Jumbo 12

2015. 12-fret neck.

2015		$2,025	$2,625

Advanced Jumbo 75th Anniversary

2011-2012. 75th Anniversary label, 2nd edition 75 made with on-board electronics.

2011	1st edition	$1,875	$2,425
2012	2nd edition	$1,875	$2,425

1935 Advanced Jumbo

2013. Limited run of 35, Adirondack red spruce top, Indian rosewood back and sides, Vintage Sunburst.

2013		$3,850	$4,950

Advanced Jumbo Koa (CS)

2006. Custom Shop model, koa back and sides, Adirondack top.

2006		$2,025	$2,625

Advanced Jumbo Luthier's Choice (CS)

2000-2005, 2008. Custom Shop model.

2000-2005	Brazilian	$5,000	$6,500
2008	Cocobolo	$2,800	$3,700

Advanced Jumbo Pro

2011-2013. Guitar Center model, Baggs pickup, Sitka top, solid rosewood back and sides.

2011-2013		$1,150	$1,500

Advanced Jumbo Red Spruce/AJ Red Spruce

2013. Limited edition, Adirondack red spruce top, rosewood back and sides.

2013		$1,600	$2,100

The Official Vintage Guitar magazine Price Guide 2021   **Gibson** Advanced Jumbo Supreme — Barney Kessel Standard   **143**

GUITARS

MODEL YEAR	FEATURES	EXC. COND. LOW	HIGH

Advanced Jumbo Supreme (CS)
2007. Custom Shop model, Madagascar rosewood back and sides, Adirondack spruce top.

2007		$2,025	$2,625

Iron Mountain Advanced Jumbo (CS)
2014. Custom Shop model, limited run of 65, Adirondack red spruce top, Birdseye maple back and sides, Honeyburst finish.

2014		$2,025	$2,625

Randy Scruggs Advanced Jumbo Limited Edition
2010-2018. Sitka spruce top, East Indian rosewood body, king's crown headstock logo on, crown markers, Fishman pickup, vintage sunburst.

2010-2018		$1,900	$2,500

All American II
1996. Solidbody electric with vague double-cut Melody Maker body style, 2 pickups.

1996		$450	$600

B.B. King Custom
1980-1988. Lucille on peghead, 2 pickups, multi-bound, gold-plated parts, Vari-tone, cherry or ebony, renamed B.B. King Lucille in '88.

1980-1988		$2,200	$2,900

B.B. King Lucille
1988-2019. Introduced as B.B. King Custom, renamed B.B. King Lucille. Lucille on peghead, 2 pickups, multi-bound, gold-plated parts, Vari-tone, cherry or ebony. In '07 B.B. King logo and large king's crown on headstock with Lucille logo on truss rod cover.

1988-2019		$2,200	$2,900
2007-2009	King logo	$2,200	$2,900

B.B. King Standard
1980-1985. Like B.B. King Custom, but with stereo electronics and chrome-plated parts, cherry or ebony.

1980-1985		$1,900	$2,500

B.B. King 80th Birthday Lucille
2005. Custom Shop, limited run of 80, 'guard engraved with crown and signature, headstock engraved with artwork from King's birthday tribute album.

2005		$3,900	$5,100

B.B. King Super Lucille
2002-2004. Signed guard, abalone inlays, custom black sparkle finish.

2002-2004		$3,100	$4,100

B-15
1967-1971. Mahogany, spruce top, student model, natural finish.

1967-1971		$675	$875

B-20
1971-1972. 14.5" flat-top, mahogany back and sides, dot markers, decal logo, strip in-line tuners with small buttons.

1971-1972		$900	$1,200

B-25 3/4 / B-25 N 3/4
1962-1968. Short-scale version, flat-top, mahogany body, cherry sunburst (natural finish is the B-25 3/4 N).

1962	Wood bridge	$1,100	$1,425
1963-1964	Plastic bridge	$950	$1,225
1965		$850	$1,100
1966-1968		$775	$1,000

B-25/B-25 N
1962-1977, 2008-2012. Flat-top, mahogany, bound body, upper belly on bridge (lower belly '68 on), cherry sunburst or black (natural finish is B-25 N). Reissued in '08.

1962	Wood bridge	$1,800	$2,400
1963-1964	Plastic bridge	$1,700	$2,200
1965		$1,400	$1,800
1966-1968	Above belly bridge	$1,300	$1,700
1968	Black, white 'guard	$2,400	$3,100
1968	Red, white 'guard	$2,100	$2,700
1969	Below belly bridge	$1,100	$1,400
1970-1977		$1,000	$1,300
2008-2012	Reissue, black	$1,150	$1,500

B-25-12/B-25-12 N
1962-1977. Flat-top 12-string version, mahogany, bound body, cherry sunburst (natural finish is the B-25-12 N).

1962-1964	No tailpiece	$1,500	$1,950
1965	Trapeze tailpiece	$1,200	$1,600
1966-1968	Trapeze tailpiece	$1,150	$1,500
1969	Below belly bridge	$1,000	$1,300
1970-1977		$900	$1,200

B-45-12/B-45-12 N
1961-1979. Flat-top 12-string, mahogany, round shoulders for '61, square after, sunburst (natural finish is the B-45-12 N).

1961-1962	Round shoulder	$1,700	$2,200
1962-1963	Square shoulder	$1,550	$2,000
1964	No tailpiece	$1,550	$2,000
1965	Trapeze tailpiece	$1,250	$1,650
1966-1968		$1,200	$1,550
1969	Below belly bridge	$1,050	$1,350
1970-1979		$950	$1,250

B-45-12 Limited Edition
1991-1992. Limited edition reissue with rosewood back and sides, natural.

1991-1992		$950	$1,250

Barney Kessel Custom
1961-1973. Double-cut archtop, 2 humbuckers, gold hardware, cherry sunburst.

1961	PAFs	$5,750	$7,500
1962	Black finish	$4,475	$5,875
1962-1964	Pat #	$4,475	$5,875
1965-1969		$4,000	$5,175
1970-1973		$3,000	$3,900

Barney Kessel Standard
1961-1974. Double-cut archtop, 2 humbuckers, nickel hardware, cherry sunburst.

1961	PAFs	$5,500	$7,100
1962-1964	Pat #	$4,200	$5,500
1965		$3,800	$4,900
1966-1969		$3,600	$4,700
1970-1973		$2,700	$3,500

1964 Gibson B-25-12 N
Ted Wulfers

1968 Gibson Barney Kessel Custom
Jeff Marshall

1957 Gibson Byrdland

1967 Gibson C-O Classical

Imaged by Heritage Auctions, HA.com

Blue Ridge
1968-1979, 1989-1990. Flat-top, dreadnought, laminated rosewood back and sides, natural finish, reintroduced for '89-'90.

Model Year	Features	EXC. COND. LOW	EXC. COND. HIGH
1968-1969		$1,025	$1,325
1970-1979		$925	$1,175

Blue Ridge 12
1970-1978. Flat-top, 12 strings, laminated rosewood back and sides, natural finish.

1970-1978		$925	$1,175

Blues King
2012-2013. Acoustic/electric, non-cut, bubinga back and sides, dot inlays.

2012-2013		$1,350	$1,800

Blueshawk
1996-2006. Small single-cut, f-holes, 2 single-coil hum cancelling Blues 90 pickups, 6-way Varitone dial, gold hardware, Bigsby option starts '98.

1996-2006		$800	$1,050

B-SJ Blue Ridge
1989. Model name on label is B-SJ, truss rod covers logo is Blue Ridge, SJ appointments but with narrow peghead shape.

1989		$1,225	$1,575

Byrdland
1955-1992. Thinline archtop, single-cut (rounded until late-'60, pointed '60-late-'69, rounded after '69, rounded or pointed '98-present), 2 pickups, now part of the Historic Collection.

Model Year	Features	EXC. COND. LOW	EXC. COND. HIGH
1956-1957	Natural, Alnicos	$7,200	$9,500
1956-1957	Sunburst, Alnicos	$5,600	$7,400
1958-1959	Natural, PAFs	$10,400	$13,800
1958-1959	Sunburst, PAFs	$7,300	$9,500
1960-1962	Natural, PAFs	$8,800	$11,700
1960-1962	Sunburst, PAFs	$7,000	$9,200
1963-1964	Natural, pat #	$5,600	$7,400
1963-1964	Sunburst, pat #	$4,900	$6,500
1965	Natural	$4,800	$6,300
1965	Sunburst	$4,800	$6,300
1966-1969	Natural	$4,700	$6,200
1966-1969	Sunburst	$4,700	$6,200
1970-1992	Various colors	$3,700	$4,800

Byrdland Historic Collection
1993-2018. Custom shop, various colors.

1993-2018		$4,600	$6,000

C-0 Classical
1962-1971. Spruce top, mahogany back and sides, bound top, natural.

1962-1964		$550	$725
1965		$475	$625
1966-1971		$450	$575

C-1 Classical
1957-1971. Spruce top, mahogany back and sides, bound body, natural.

1957-1959		$600	$775
1960-1964		$550	$725
1965		$500	$650
1966-1971		$450	$575

C-1 D Laredo
1963-1971. Natural spruce top, mahogany sides and back, upgrade to standard C-1.

1963-1965		$550	$725

C-1 E Classical Electric
1960-1967. C-1 with ceramic bridge pickup, catalog notes special matched amplifier that filters out fingering noises.

Model Year	Features	EXC. COND. LOW	EXC. COND. HIGH
1960-1964		$550	$725
1965		$500	$650
1966-1967		$450	$575

C-1 S Petite Classical
1961-1966. Petite 13 1/4" body, natural spruce top, mahogany back and sides.

1961-1964		$550	$725
1965		$500	$650
1966-1967		$450	$575

C-2 Classical
1960-1971. Maple back and sides, bound body, natural.

1960-1964		$625	$825
1965		$575	$750
1966-1971		$525	$675

C-4 Classical
1962-1968. Maple back and sides, natural.

1962-1964		$650	$850
1965		$600	$775
1966-1968		$550	$725

C-6 Classical/Richard Pick
1958-1971. Rosewood back and sides, gold hardware, natural.

1958-1959	Brazilian	$1,350	$1,750
1960-1964	Brazilian	$1,250	$1,600
1965	Brazilian	$1,125	$1,450
1966-1969	Brazilian	$1,025	$1,325
1970-1971	Indian	$625	$825

C-8 Classical
1962-1969. Rosewood back and sides, natural.

1962-1964		$1,225	$1,600
1965		$1,125	$1,450
1966-1969		$1,025	$1,325

C-100 Classical
1971-1972. Slotted peghead, spruce top, mahogany back and sides, ebony 'board, Gibson Master Model label, non-gloss finish.

1971-1972		$450	$575

C-200 Classical
1971-1972. C-100 with gloss finish.

1971-1972		$525	$675

C-300 Classical
1971-1972. Similar to C-100, but with rosewood 'board, wood binding, wider soundhole ring.

1971-1972		$525	$675

C-400 Classical
1971-1972. Rosewood sides and back, spruce top, high-end appointments, chrome hardware.

1971-1972		$550	$725

C-500 Classical
1971-1972. C-400 with gold hardware.

1971-1972		$625	$825

CF-100
1950-1958. Flat-top, pointed cutaway, mahogany back and sides, bound body, sunburst finish.

1950-1958		$3,700	$4,825

The **Vintage Guitar Price Guide** shows low to high values for items in all-original excellent condition, and, where applicable, with original case or cover.

MODEL YEAR	FEATURES	EXC. COND. LOW	HIGH

CF-100 E
1951-1958, 2009. CF-100 with a single-coil pickup. Also offered in '94 1950 CF-100 E limited edition and in '07 as a Custom Shop model.

1950-1958		$3,800	$4,925

CF-100 E Reissue (Custom Shop)
2007. Custom Shop, all maple body, ebony 'board, 24 made.

2007		$1,900	$2,500

Challenger I
1983-1985. Single-cut Les Paul-shaped solidbody, 1 humbucker, bolt-on maple neck, rosewood 'board, dot markers, silver finish standard.

1983-1985		$425	$575

Challenger II
1983-1985. 2 humbucker version.

1983-1985		$450	$600

Challenger III
1984. 3 single-coil version, never cataloged so could be very limited.

1984		$475	$625

Chet Atkins CE
1981-2005. CE stands for Classical Electric, single-cut, multi-bound body, rosewood 'board until '95, then ebony, standard width nut, gold hardware, various colors.

1981-2005		$1,200	$1,550

Chet Atkins CEC
1981-2005. Same as CE, but with ebony 'board and 2" classical width nut, black or natural.

1981-2005		$1,200	$1,550

Chet Atkins Country Gentleman
1986-2005. Thinline archtop, single rounded cutaway, 2 humbuckers, multi-bound, gold hardware, Bigsby. Part of Gibson's Custom line.

1986-2005		$2,100	$2,700

Chet Atkins SST
1987-2006. Steel string acoustic/electric solidbody, single-cut, bridge transducer pickup, active bass and treble controls, gold hardware.

1987-1993	White	$1,575	$2,025
1987-2006	Black	$1,575	$2,025
1987-2006	Natural	$1,025	$1,325
1993	Red Wine or Antique	$1,575	$2,025
1994	Cherry Sunburst	$1,575	$2,025

Chet Atkins SST Celebrity
1991-1993. Gold hardware, 200 made, black body with unique white 'guard.

1991-1993		$1,750	$2,275

Chet Atkins SST-12
1990-1994. 12-string model similar to 6-string, mahogany/spruce body, preamp circuit controls single transducer pickup, natural or ebony finish.

1990-1994		$1,025	$1,325

Chet Atkins Super 4000 (Custom Shop)
1997-2000. Figured curly maple back and sides, orange amber finish, 25 built, COA.

1997-2000		$16,500	$21,000

Chet Atkins Tennessean
1990-2005. Single rounded cutaway archtop, 2 humbuckers, f-holes, bound body. Part of Gibson's Custom line.

1990-2005		$1,250	$1,625

Chicago 35
1994-1995. Flat-top dreadnought, round shoulders, mahogany back and sides, prewar script logo.

1994-1995		$900	$1,150

Citation
1969-1971. 17" full-depth body, single-cut archtop, 1 or 2 floating pickups, fancy inlay, natural or sunburst. Only 8 shipped for '69-'71, reissued the first time '79-'83 and as part of the Historic Collection in '93.

1969-1971	Sunburst, natural	$14,000	$18,000

Citation (1st Reissue)
1979-1983. Reissue of '69-'71 model, reintroduced in '93 as part of Gibson's Historic Collection.

1979-1983	Sunburst, natural	$14,000	$18,000

Citation (2nd Reissue)
1993-2018. Limited production via Gibson's Historic Collection, natural or sunburst.

1994-2018	Various colors	$11,000	$14,000

Citation Custom Shop Vanderbilt Rose
2015. Vanderbilt Rose lacquer finish with matching maple 'guard.

2015		$6,500	$8,400

CJ-165/CJ-165 Modern Classic
2006-2008. Called J-165 in first year of production, classic small body non-cutaway flat-top, solid spruce top, maple or rosewood back and sides.

2006-2008		$1,200	$1,600

CJ-165 EC Modern Classic
2007-2009. As above, but with single-cut, electronics, maple or rosewood back and sides.

2007-2009		$1,350	$1,750

CL-10 Standard
1997-1998. Flat-top, solid spruce top, laminated mahogany back and sides.

1997-1998		$800	$1,025

CL-20 Standard Plus
1997-1998. Flat-top, laminated back and sides, 4-ply binding with tortoiseshell appointments, abalone diamond inlays.

1997-1998		$950	$1,225

CL-30 Deluxe
1997-1998. J-50 style dreadnought, solid spruce top, bubinga back and sides, factory electronics.

1997-1998		$975	$1,250

CL-35 Deluxe
1998. Single cutaway CL-30.

1998		$1,025	$1,350

CL-40 Artist
1997-1998. Flat-top, gold hardware, rosewood back and sides.

1997-1998		$1,375	$1,800

CL-45 Artist
1997-1998. Single cutaway CL-40.

1997-1998		$1,475	$1,900

CL-50
1997-1999. Custom Shop model, D-style body, higher-end appointments, offered with Brazilian rosewood.

1997-1999		$2,900	$3,800

1983 Gibson Challenger II
Gary Klinger

1958 Gibson CF-100 E

1969 Gibson Crest Silver
Gary's Classic Guitars

Gibson CS-336
Emmitt Omar

MODEL YEAR	FEATURES	EXC. COND. LOW	HIGH

Corvus I
1982-1984. Odd-shaped solidbody with offset V-type cut, bolt maple neck, rosewood 'board, 1 humbucker, standard finish was silver gloss, but others available at an additional cost.

1982-1984		$750	$1,000

Corvus II
1982-1984. Same as Corvus I, but with 2 humbuckers, 2 volume controls, 1 master tone control.

1982-1984		$850	$1,100

Corvus III
1982-1984. Same as Corvus I, but with 3 single-coil pickups, master volume and tone control, 5-way switch.

1982-1984		$950	$1,250

Crest Gold
1969-1971. Double-cut thinline archtop, Brazilian rosewood body, 2 pickups, bound top and headstock, bound f-holes, gold-plated parts. The Crest name was also used on a few (3-6) custom guitars based on the L-5CT built in 1959-'61.

1969-1971		$4,500	$6,000

Crest Silver
1969-1972. Silver-plated parts version of Crest.

1969-1972		$4,100	$5,400

CS Series
2002-2017. Scaled down ES-335 body style, made in Custom Shop.

2002-2003	CS-356 (plain top)	$1,900	$2,500
2002-2012	CS-336F (figured top)	$2,200	$2,900
2002-2014	CS-356F (figured top)	$2,500	$3,300
2002-2017	CS-336 (plain top)	$2,100	$2,700

Dave Grohl DG-335
2007-2008. Inspired By Series, Trini Lopez Standard specs, Certificate of Authenticity, Pelham Blue or black finish.

2007-2008		$5,200	$6,800

Dove
1962-1996, 1999-2013. Flat-top acoustic, maple back and sides, square shoulders.

1962-1964	Natural or Sunburst	$4,200	$5,500
1965	Natural, early '65	$3,900	$5,000
1965	Natural, late '65	$3,000	$4,000
1965	Sunburst, early '65	$3,900	$5,000
1965	Sunburst, late '65	$2,800	$3,600
1966-1969	Natural or Sunburst	$2,400	$3,100
1970-1979	Various colors	$1,800	$2,300
1980-1984	Double X	$1,725	$2,225
1985-1988	Single X	$1,575	$2,025
1989	New specs	$1,575	$2,025
1990-1996	Various colors	$1,725	$2,225
1999-2013	Reissue model	$1,725	$2,225

'60s Dove
1997-2004. Spruce top, maple back and sides, Dove appointments.

1997-2004		$2,100	$2,725

'60s Dove Limited Edition
2014. Sitka spruce top, flame maple back and sides, Indian rosewood 'board, Vintage Cherryburst finish.

2014		$2,000	$2,575

Dove Artist
1999-2005. Sitka spruce, Indian rosewood.

1999-2005		$1,575	$2,025

Dove Commemorative
1994-1996. Commemorates Gibson's 100th anniversary, Heritage or Antique Cherry finish, 100 built.

1994-1996		$2,100	$2,725

Dove In Flight Limited Edition (CS)
1996-1997. Custom Shop, 250 made, figured maple sides and back, Adirondack top, Certificate of Authenticity, dove inlays on headstock.

1996-1997		$3,400	$4,500

Doves In Flight (Brazilian)
2003. Custom Shop, only 2 made.

2003		$8,500	$11,000

Doves In Flight (Production Model)
1996-present. Gibson Custom model, maple back and sides, doves in flight inlays.

1996-2019		$3,050	$4,000

Dove Elvis Presley Signature
2008-2010. Artist Series, Certificate of Authenticity, black.

2008-2010		$2,100	$2,725

Super Dove
2009-2012. Cutaway, on-board electronics, sold through certain retailers.

2009-2012		$2,200	$2,850

Duane Eddy Signature
2004-2009. Single rounded cut, flamed maple top and back, 2 single-coils and piezo, pearl 'moustache' markers, signature engraved on 'guard, Bigsby, Rockabilly Brown finish.

2004-2009		$3,500	$4,500

EAS Deluxe
1992-1994. Single-cut flat-top acoustic/electric, solid flamed maple top, bound rosewood 'board, trapezoid inlays, 3-band EQ, Vintage Cherry Sunburst.

1992-1994		$875	$1,125

EAS Standard/Classic
1992-1995. Like EAS Deluxe, but with spruce top, unbound top, dot inlays, called EAS Classic for '92.

1992-1995		$775	$1,000

EBS(F)-1250 Double Bass
1962-1968. Double-cut SG-type solidbody, double-neck with bass and 6-string, originally introduced as the EBSF-1250 because of a built-in fuzztone, which was later deleted, only 22 made.

1962-1964	Various colors	$16,200	$21,000
1965	Various colors	$12,000	$16,000
1966-1968	Various colors	$11,700	$15,200

EC-10 Standard
1997-1998. Jumbo single-cut, on-board electronics, solid spruce top, maple back and sides.

1997-1998		$775	$1,000

MODEL YEAR	FEATURES	EXC. COND. LOW	HIGH

EC-20 Starburst
1997-1998. Jumbo single-cut, on-board electronics, solid spruce top, maple back and sides, renamed J-185 EC in '99.

1997-1998		$1,275	$1,650

EC-30 Blues King Electro (BKE)
1997-1998. Jumbo single-cut, on-board electronics, solid spruce top, maple back and sides, double parallelogram inlays, renamed J-185 EC in '99.

1997-1998		$1,350	$1,800

EDS-1275 Double 12
1958-1967, 1977-1990. Double-cut doubleneck with one 12- and one 6-string, thinline hollowbody until late-'62, SG-style solidbody '62 on.

1958-1961	Custom order	$30,000	$40,000
1962-1964	SG body	$27,000	$35,000
1965	SG body	$21,000	$27,000
1966-1967	SG body	$15,000	$20,000
1977-1979	Various colors	$4,300	$5,700
1977-1979	White	$4,300	$5,700
1980-1989	Various colors	$3,200	$4,200
1990	Various colors	$2,550	$3,300

EDS-1275 Double 12 (Historic Collection)
1991-2018. Custom Shop Historic Collection reissue.

1991-2018	Various colors	$2,550	$3,300

EDS-1275 Double 12 Centennial
1994. Guitar of the Month (May), gold medallion on back of headstock, gold hardware.

1994	Cherry	$2,650	$3,400

EDS-1275 Double 12 Jimmy Page VOS Signature
2008. Custom Shop model with Certificate of Authenticity, 250 made.

2008		$6,400	$8,200

EDS-1275 Double Neck Alex Lifeson
2015. Custom Shop model based on Lifeson's '70s Gibson, limited run of 100, first 25 signed and played by Alex, aged Arctic White.

2015		$4,200	$5,500

EMS-1235 Double Mandolin
1958-1963, 1965-1967. Double-cut, doubleneck with 1 regular 6-string and 1 short 6-string (the mandolin neck), thinline hollowbody until late-1962, SG-style solidbody '62-'68, black, sunburst or white, total of 61 shipped.

1958-1961	Custom order	$27,000	$35,000
1962-1963	SG body	$25,000	$32,000
1965	SG body	$21,000	$27,000
1966-1967	SG body	$20,000	$26,000

ES-5/ES-5N
1949-1955. Single-cut archtop, 3 P-90 pickups, sunburst or natural (5N). Renamed ES-5 Switchmaster in '55.

1949-1955	Natural	$6,800	$8,800
1949-1955	Sunburst	$6,000	$7,800

ES-5 Switchmaster/ES-5N Switchmaster
1956-1962. Renamed from ES-5, single-cut (rounded until late-'60, pointed after) archtop, 3 P-90s until end of '57, humbuckers after, switchmaster control.

1956-1957	Natural, P-90s	$8,000	$10,400
1956-1957	Sunburst, P-90s	$7,400	$9,600
1957-1960	Natural, hums	$13,000	$17,000
1957-1960	Sunburst, hums	$12,300	$16,000
1960-1962	Pointed Florentine cutaway	$9,500	$12,300

ES-5/ES-5 Switchmaster Custom Shop Historic
1995-2006. Historic Collection.

1995-2002	ES-5, sunburst, P-90s	$3,500	$4,500
1995-2002	Switchmaster, sunburst, hums	$3,500	$4,500
1995-2002	Switchmaster, Wine Red, hums	$3,200	$4,200
1995-2006	Switchmaster, natural, hums	$3,500	$4,500

ES-100
1938-1941. Archtop, 1 pickup, bound body, sunburst, renamed ES-125 in '41.

1938-1941		$1,425	$1,825

ES-120 T
1962-1970. Archtop, thinline, 1 f-hole, bound body, 1 pickup, sunburst.

1962-1964		$1,150	$1,475
1965		$1,075	$1,400
1966-1970		$1,050	$1,350

ES-125
1941-1943, 1946-1970. Archtop, non-cut, 1 pickup, sunburst, renamed from ES-100.

1941-1943	Blade pickup	$1,925	$2,500
1947-1949	1st non-adj, P-90s	$1,925	$2,500
1950	1st non-adj, P-90s	$1,800	$2,350
1951-1959	Adj P-90s with poles	$1,800	$2,350
1960-1964		$1,300	$1,700
1965		$1,200	$1,550
1966-1970		$1,025	$1,325

ES-125 C
1966-1970. Wide body archtop, single pointed cutaway, 1 pickup, sunburst.

1965		$1,375	$1,775
1966-1970		$1,275	$1,650

ES-125 CD
1966-1970. Wide body archtop, single-cut, 2 pickups, sunburst.

1965		$1,850	$2,400
1966-1970		$1,700	$2,200

ES-125 D
1957. Limited production (not mentioned in catalog), 2 pickup version of thick body ES-125, sunburst.

1957		$2,025	$2,625

ES-125 T
1956-1968. Archtop thinline, non-cut, 1 pickup, bound body, sunburst.

1956-1959		$1,700	$2,200
1960-1964		$1,450	$1,900
1965		$1,350	$1,750
1966-1968		$1,200	$1,600

ES-125 T 3/4
1957-1968. Archtop thinline, short-scale, non-cut, 1 pickup, sunburst.

1957-1960		$1,700	$2,200
1961-1964		$1,450	$1,900

1968 Gibson Dove

1955 Gibson ES-5 Switchmaster
Jim King

GUITARS

1961 Gibson ES-125 TC

Jim King

1957 Gibson ES-140 3/4

Robbie Keene

MODEL YEAR	FEATURES	EXC. COND. LOW	HIGH
1965		$1,350	$1,750
1966-1968		$1,200	$1,600

ES-125 TC

1960-1970. Archtop thinline, single pointed cutaway, bound body, 1 P-90 pickup, sunburst.

1960-1964		$1,700	$2,200
1965		$1,550	$2,000
1966-1970		$1,475	$1,900

ES-125 TD

1957-1963. Archtop thinline, non-cut, 2 pickups, sunburst.

1957-1963		$2,200	$2,900

ES-125 TDC or ES-125 TCD

1960-1971. Archtop thinline, single pointed cutaway, 2 P-90 pickups, sunburst.

1960-1964		$2,800	$3,625
1965	Early '65	$2,700	$3,525
1965	Late '65	$2,325	$3,025
1966-1971		$2,325	$3,025

ES-130

1954-1956. Archtop, non-cut, 1 pickup, bound body, sunburst, renamed ES-135 in '56.

1954-1956		$2,025	$2,625

ES-135

1956-1958. Renamed from ES-130, non-cut archtop, 1 pickup, sunburst, name reused on a thin body in the '90s.

1957-1959		$2,025	$2,625

ES-135 (Thinline)

1991-2003. Single-cut archtop, laminated maple body, 2 humbuckers or 2 P-90s, chrome or gold hardware, sunburst.

1991-2003	Stop tail	$1,025	$1,325
1991-2003	Trapeze	$1,025	$1,325

ES-137 Classic

2002-2015. Thin-body electric single cut, trapezoid inlays, 2 humbuckers, f-holes, gold hardware.

2002-2015		$1,300	$1,700

ES-137 Custom

2002-2011. Like Classic, but with split-diamond inlays and varitone.

2002-2011		$1,300	$1,700

ES-137 P (Premier)

2002-2005. Like Classic, but with exposed humbuckers, chrome hardware and very small trapezoid inlays.

2002-2005		$1,050	$1,350

ES-139

2013-2016. Semi-hollow Les Paul style body, 2 humbuckers, Guitar Center model.

2013-2016		$775	$1,000

ES-140 (3/4) or ES-140N (3/4)

1950-1956. Archtop, single-cut, 1 pickup, bound body, short-scale, sunburst or natural option (140N).

1950-1956	Natural option	$2,100	$2,800
1950-1956	Sunburst	$2,000	$2,600

ES-140 (3/4) T or ES-140N (3/4) T

1957-1968. Archtop thinline, single-cut, bound body, 1 pickup, short-scale, sunburst or natural option (140N).

1956-1958	Natural option	$2,100	$2,800

MODEL YEAR	FEATURES	EXC. COND. LOW	HIGH
1956-1959	Sunburst	$2,000	$2,600
1960-1964	Sunburst	$1,800	$2,400
1965	Sunburst	$1,675	$2,200
1966-1968	Sunburst	$1,500	$2,000

ES-150

1936-1942, 1946-1956. Historically important archtop, non-cut, bound body, Charlie Christian bar pickup from '36-'39, various metal covered pickups starting in '40, sunburst.

1936-1939	Charlie Christian pu	$4,700	$6,100
1940-1942	Metal covered pu	$4,700	$6,100
1946-1949	P-90 pickup	$1,950	$2,550
1950-1956	P-90 pickup	$1,850	$2,400

ES-150 DC

1969-1975. Archtop, double rounded cutaway, 2 humbuckers, multi-bound.

1969-1975	Cherry, natural, walnut	$2,300	$3,300

ES-165 Herb Ellis

1991-2011. Single pointed cut hollowbody, 1 humbucker, gold hardware.

1991-2011		$1,650	$2,150

ES-175 or ES-175N

1949-1971. Archtop, single pointed cutaway, 1 pickup (P-90 from '49-early-'57, humbucker early-'57-'71), multi-bound, sunburst or natural option (175N).

1949-1956	Natural, P90	$4,000	$5,300
1949-1956	Sunburst, P-90	$3,750	$4,900
1957-1959	Natural, hum	$6,400	$8,300
1957-1963	Sunburst, PAF	$6,100	$7,900
1964	Sunburst, pat #	$4,200	$5,500
1965	Sunburst, hum	$3,300	$4,275
1966-1969	Sunburst, pat #	$2,700	$3,475
1967-1969	Black	$2,700	$3,475
1970-1971	Various colors	$2,400	$3,100

ES-175 CC

1978-1979. 1 Charlie Christian pickup, sunburst or walnut.

1978-1979		$2,400	$3,100

ES-175 D or ES-175N D

1952-2016. Archtop, single-cut, 2 pickups (P-90s from '53-early-'57, humbuckers early-'57 on), sunburst or natural option (175N D). Humbucker pickups were converted from PAF-stickers to Pat. No.-stickers in '62. Different models were converted at different times. An ES-175 model, made during the transitional time, with PAFs, will fetch more. In some of the electric-archtop models, the transition period may have been later than '62. Cataloged as the ES-175 Reissue in the '90s, Currently as the ES-175 under Gibson Memphis.

1952-1956	Natural, P-90s	$5,400	$7,000
1952-1956	Sunburst, P-90s	$4,000	$5,200
1957-1963	Natural, PAFs	$10,000	$13,000
1957-1963	Sunburst, PAFs	$7,500	$10,000
1964	Natural, pat #	$5,400	$7,000
1964	Sunburst, pat #	$4,700	$6,100
1965	Natural, pat #	$4,600	$6,000
1965	Sunburst, hums	$4,100	$5,300
1966	Natural, pat #	$3,800	$4,900
1966	Sunburst, hums	$3,200	$4,200
1967-1969	Black	$3,200	$4,200

MODEL YEAR	FEATURES	EXC. COND. LOW	HIGH
1967-1969	Various colors	$3,200	$4,200
1970-1979	Various colors	$2,600	$3,350
1980-2016	Various colors	$2,400	$3,100

ES-175 D Tenor

1966. Rare custom ordered tenor version, sunburst.

1966		$3,100	$4,000

ES-175 D-AN

1999-2000. Limited run, P-90s, Antique Natural finish.

1999-2000		$2,500	$3,200

ES-175 SP

2006. Single humbucker version, sunburst.

2006		$2,300	$3,000

ES-175 Steve Howe

2001-2007. Maple laminate body, multi-bound top, sunburst.

2001-2007		$2,600	$3,400

ES-175 T

1976-1980. Archtop thinline, single pointed cutaway, 2 humbuckers, various colors.

1976-1980		$2,600	$3,350

ES-225 T or ES-225N T

1955-1959. Thinline, single pointed cutaway, 1 P-90 pickup, bound body and neck, sunburst or natural option (225N T).

1955-1959	Natural	$2,900	$3,850
1955-1959	Sunburst	$2,150	$2,850

ES-225 TD or ES-225N TD

1956-1959. Thinline, single-cut, 2 P-90s, bound body and neck, sunburst or natural option (225N TD).

1956-1959	Natural	$4,300	$5,700
1956-1959	Sunburst	$3,200	$4,200

1959 ES-225 Historic

2014-2016. Single-cut TD reissue with 2 P-90s, sunburst.

2014-2016		$2,100	$2,700

ES-235 Gloss

2019-present. Semi-hollow single-cut, maple neck, rosewood 'board, 2 pickups.

2019		$975	$1,250

ES-250 or ES-250N

1939-1940. Archtop, carved top, special Christian pickup, multi-bound, high-end appointments, sunburst or natural option (250N).

1939	Natural, stairstep hs	$21,500	$28,100
1939	Sunburst, stairstep hs	$13,500	$17,600
1940	Natural, standard hs	$21,500	$28,100
1940	Sunburst, standard hs	$13,500	$17,600

ES-295

1952-1958. Single pointed cutaway archtop, 2 pickups (P-90s from '52-late-'57, humbuckers after), gold finish, gold-plated hardware.

1952-1957	P-90s	$5,700	$7,500
1957-1958	Humbuckers	$12,800	$16,600

ES-295 Reissue

1990-1993. Gold finish, 2 P-90 pickups, Bigsby.

1990-1993		$2,600	$3,400

ES-295 Historic Collection

1990-2000. Antique Gold finish, 2 P-90 pickups, Bigsby.

1990-2000		$2,600	$3,400

ES-295 '52 Historic Collection (CS)

2013-2015. Custom Shop. Limited VOS Vintage Cherry offered in '15.

2013-2015		$2,600	$3,400
2015	Limited Cherry	$2,600	$3,400

ES-295 Scotty Moore Signature

1999. Custom Shop, 15 produced, 12 with Scotty's actual signature on lower bout, Bullion Gold, trapeze tailpiece.

1999		$5,700	$7,500

ES-300 or ES-300N

1940-1942, 1945-1953. Archtop, non-cut, f-holes, had 4 pickup configurations during its run, sunburst or natural (300N).

1940	Natural, oblong diagonal pu	$4,200	$5,500
1940	Sunburst, oblong diagonal pu	$3,500	$4,600
1941-1942	Natural, 1 pu	$4,200	$5,500
1941-1942	Sunburst, 1 pu	$3,500	$4,600
1945	Black, 1 pu	$3,200	$4,200
1945-1949	Sunburst, 1 pu	$2,900	$3,800
1945-1953	Natural, 1 pu	$3,200	$4,200
1949-1953	Natural, 2 pus	$3,700	$4,800
1949-1953	Sunburst, 2 pus	$3,400	$4,400

ES-320 TD

1971-1974. Thinline archtop, double-cut, 2 single-coil pickups, bound body, cherry, natural, or walnut.

1971-1974		$1,400	$1,825

ES-325 TD

1972-1978. Thinline archtop, double-cut, 2 mini-humbuckers, 1 f-hole, bound body, top mounted control panel, cherry or walnut.

1972-1978		$1,625	$2,125

ES-330 L

2009-2015. Custom Shop, classic 330 design, 2 dog-ear P-90 pickups, sunburst or black. 2015 model has humbuckers.

2009-2015	P-90s	$2,100	$2,725

ES-330 T or ES-330N T

1959-1963. Double rounded cutaway, thinline, 1 pickup, bound body and neck, sunburst, cherry or natural option (330N T). In the '60s came with either an original semi-hard case (better than chip board) or a hardshell case. Prices quoted are for hardshell case; approximately $100 should be deducted for the semi-hard case.

1959-1961	Natural	$7,000	$9,000
1959-1963	Cherry	$3,850	$5,000
1959-1963	Sunburst	$3,850	$5,000

ES-330 TD or ES-330N TD

1959-1972. Double rounded cutaway, thinline, 2 pickups, bound body and neck, sunburst, cherry or natural option (330N TD). In the '60s came with either an original semi-hard case (better than chip board) or a hardshell case. Prices noted for the hardshell case; approximately $100 should be deducted for the semi-hard case.

1959-1961	Natural	$9,000	$11,500

1952 Gibson ES-150
Frank Manno

1970s Gibson ES-175D
Bernunzio Uptown Music

GUITARS

1967 Gibson ES-330 TD
Tyler Willison

1966 Gibson ES-335 TD
Bernunzio Uptown Music

MODEL YEAR	FEATURES	EXC. COND. LOW	HIGH
1959-1962	Cherry, dots	$5,200	$6,700
1959-1962	Sunburst, dots	$5,200	$6,700
1963-1964	Cherry, blocks	$4,300	$5,600
1963-1964	Sunburst, blocks	$4,300	$5,600
1965	Sunburst, cherry	$3,800	$4,900
1966-1968	Sunburst, cherry	$3,400	$4,500
1967-1968	Burgundy Metallic (unfaded)	$3,600	$4,700
1968	Walnut option	$3,600	$4,700
1969-1972	Various colors, long neck	$3,600	$4,700

ES-330 TDC
1998-2000. Custom Shop model, block markers.

MODEL YEAR	FEATURES	EXC. COND. LOW	HIGH
1998-2000		$2,100	$2,725

ES-330 VOS
2012-2016. Custom Shop, Bigsby tailpiece, late '50s specs and VOS finish in sunburst, natural or cherry.

MODEL YEAR	FEATURES	EXC. COND. LOW	HIGH
2012-2016	All colors	$2,100	$2,725

Wildwood Spec 1959 ES-330
2015. Figured top, natural, certificate.

MODEL YEAR	FEATURES	EXC. COND. LOW	HIGH
2015		$2,450	$3,200

1964 ES-330 Historic
2015-2017. Vintage specs, P-90 pickups, trapeze tailpiece.

MODEL YEAR	FEATURES	EXC. COND. LOW	HIGH
2015-2017		$2,100	$2,725

ES-333
2002-2005. Economy ES-335, no 'guard, no headstock inlay, exposed coils, stencil logo, satin finish.

MODEL YEAR	FEATURES	EXC. COND. LOW	HIGH
2002-2005		$1,250	$1,650

ES-335 TD or ES-335N TD
1958-1981. The original design ES-335 has dot 'board inlays and a stop tailpiece, sunburst, cherry or natural option (335N). Block inlays replaced dots in mid-'62, in late-'64 the stop tailpiece was replaced with a trapeze tailpiece. Replaced by the ES-335 DOT in '81.

MODEL YEAR	FEATURES	EXC. COND. LOW	HIGH
1958	Natural, bound neck	$68,000	$90,000
1958	Natural, bound neck, Bigsby	$52,000	$67,000
1958	Natural, unbound neck	$68,000	$90,000
1958	Natural, unbound neck, Bigsby	$52,000	$67,000
1958	Sunburst, bound neck	$29,000	$37,000
1958	Sunburst, bound neck, Bigsby	$24,000	$31,000
1958	Sunburst, unbound neck	$29,000	$37,000
1958	Sunburst, unbound neck, Bigsby	$24,000	$31,000
1959	Cherry (early), stop tail	$27,000	$35,000
1959	Natural, bound neck	$77,000	$102,000
1959	Natural, bound neck, Bigsby	$65,000	$85,000
1959	Sunburst, bound neck	$35,000	$45,000
1959	Sunburst, bound neck, Bigsby	$26,000	$34,000

MODEL YEAR	FEATURES	EXC. COND. LOW	HIGH
1960	Cherry, factory Bigsby	$20,000	$26,200
1960	Cherry, factory stop tail	$25,000	$32,000
1960	Natural, factory Bigsby	$40,000	$52,500
1960	Natural, factory stop tail	$49,000	$64,000
1960	Sunburst, factory Bigsby	$20,000	$26,000
1960	Sunburst, factory stop tail	$24,000	$32,000
1961	Cherry, factory Bigsby	$17,200	$22,150
1961	Cherry, factory stop tail	$21,000	$27,000
1961	Sunburst, factory Bigsby	$17,200	$22,150
1961	Sunburst, factory stop tail	$21,000	$27,000
1962	Cherry, blocks, PAFs	$17,000	$22,000
1962	Cherry, blocks, pat#	$14,000	$18,000
1962	Cherry, dots, PAFs	$21,000	$27,000
1962	Cherry, vibrola, pat#	$11,500	$15,000
1962	Sunburst, blocks, PAFs	$17,000	$22,000
1962	Sunburst, blocks, pat#	$14,000	$18,000
1962	Sunburst, dots, PAFs	$21,000	$27,000
1962	Sunburst, dots, pat#	$14,000	$18,000
1962	Sunburst, vibrola, pat#	$11,500	$15,000
1963-1964	Cherry, factory Bigsby	$11,500	$15,000
1963-1964	Cherry, factory Maestro	$11,500	$15,000
1963-1964	Cherry, factory stop tail	$14,000	$18,000
1963-1964	Sunburst, factory Bigsby	$11,500	$15,000
1963-1964	Sunburst, factory Maestro	$11,500	$15,000
1963-1964	Sunburst, factory stop tail	$14,000	$18,000
1965	Early '65, wide neck	$7,500	$9,800
1965	Mid '65, narrow neck	$4,900	$6,300
1966	Cherry, sunburst	$4,300	$5,600
1966	Pelham Blue	$10,000	$13,100
1966	Sparkling Burgundy	$5,900	$7,600
1967	Black	$7,325	$9,500
1967	Cherry, sunburst	$4,700	$6,100
1967	Pelham Blue	$10,000	$13,100

The *Vintage Guitar Price Guide* shows low to high values for items in all-original excellent condition, and, where applicable, with original case or cover.

MODEL YEAR	FEATURES	EXC. COND. LOW	HIGH
1967	Sparkling Burgundy	$5,900	$7,600
1968	Cherry, sunburst	$4,500	$5,900
1968	Pelham Blue	$10,000	$13,100
1968	Sparkling Burgundy	$7,300	$9,500
1969	Cherry, sunburst	$4,100	$5,300
1969	Walnut finish option	$3,500	$4,500
1970-1976	Cherry, sunburst	$3,100	$4,100
1970-1976	Walnut finish option	$2,700	$3,500
1977-1979	All colors, coil tap	$2,400	$3,200
1980-1981	All colors	$2,150	$2,800

ES-335 Dot

1981-1990. Reissue of '60 ES-335 and replaces ES-335 TD. Name changed to ES-335 Reissue. Various color options including highly figured wood.

1981	Black	$2,800	$3,700
1981-1990	Cherry, sunburst	$2,500	$3,300
1982-1984	Natural	$3,100	$4,000
1985-1990	Natural	$2,500	$3,200

ES-335 Dot CMT (Custom Shop)

1983-1985. Custom Shop ES-335 Dot with curly maple top and back, full-length center block, 2 PAF-labeled humbuckers, natural or sunburst.

1983-1985		$3,000	$3,900

ES-335 Reissue/ES-335 '59 Dot Reissue/ES-335

1991-present. Replaced the ES-335 DOT, dot inlays, various color options including highly figured wood. Renamed the 1959 ES-335 Dot Reissue in '98 and currently just ES-335 followed by options - Dot, Block (added in '98), Fat Neck (added in '08), Figured (added in '06), Plain, Satin (added in '06).

1991-2019	Cherry, sunburst, walnut, black	$1,800	$2,350
1991-2019	Natural	$1,950	$2,525
2006-2017	Satin	$1,475	$1,925

ES-335 Dot P-90

2007. Custom Shop limited edition with black dog-ear P-90s, stop tailpiece.

2007		$1,800	$2,350

ES-335-12

1965-1971. 12-string version of the 335.

1965-1968		$2,550	$3,300

ES-335 '59 Dot Historic Collection (CS)

1999-2000, 2002-2016. Custom Shop model, Historical Series based upon 1959 ES-335 dot neck, figured maple top on early series, plain on later, nickel hardware.

1999-2016	Figured top	$2,900	$3,750
2002-2016	Plain top	$2,650	$3,450

1959 ES-335 Dot Reissue Limited Edition

2009-2017. Custom Shop, plain laminated maple top/back/sides, rounded '59 neck profile, '57 Classic humbuckers, Certificate of Authenticity, 250 each to be made in Antique Vintage Sunburst or Antique Natural (standard gloss or V.O.S. treatments).

2009-2017		$2,900	$3,750

ES-335 '60s Block Inlay

2004-2007. Made in Memphis facility, plain maple top, small block markers.

2004-2007		$1,850	$2,425

50th Anniversary 1960 ES-335 (Custom Shop)

2009-2010. Dot markers, natural.

2009-2010		$2,700	$3,500

50th Anniversary 1963 Block ES-335TD/ES-335TDC (Custom Shop)

2010-2013. Block markers, double-ring vintage-style tuners, Antique Vintage Sunburst (TD), Antique Faded Cherry (TDC).

2010-2013	TD, sunburst	$2,650	$3,450
2010-2013	TDC, cherry	$2,650	$3,450

ES-335 '63 Block Historic Collection (CS)

1998-2000, 2002-2018. Custom Shop model, Historical Series based upon 1963 ES-335 with small block markers, figured maple top on early series, plain on later, nickel hardware.

1998-2000	1st release, figured top	$2,900	$3,750
2002-2018	2nd release, figured top	$2,900	$3,750
2002-2018	Plain top	$2,650	$3,450

ES-335 Alvin Lee

2006-2007. Custom Division Nashville, 50 made, features reflect Alvin Lee's Big Red ES-335 complete with decal art, cherry red, includes certificate of authenticity (if missing value is reduced). There is also an unlimited version without certificate.

2006-2007	With certificate	$3,750	$5,000

ES-335 Andy Summers

2002. Custom Shop, 50 made, script signature on 'guard, early dot neck specs, nitro cherry finish, certificate of authenticity.

2007	With certificate	$2,700	$3,500

ES-335 Artist

1981. Off-set dot markers, large headstock logo, metal truss rod plate, gold hardware, 3 control knobs with unusual toggles and input specification.

1981		$2,500	$3,300

ES-335 Canadian Custom

2007. Custom Shop Canadian exclusive run of 50, maple leaf 'Limited Edition' decal on back of headstock, 'Custom Made' engraved plate on guitar front, solid mahogany neck, pearloid block inlays, antique cherry finish with aged binding.

2007		$1,950	$2,500

ES-335 Centennial

1994. Centennial edition, gold medallion in headstock, diamond inlay in tailpiece, cherry.

1994		$2,550	$3,325

ES-335 Chris Cornell

2012-2016. Olive Drab Green or black.

2012-2016		$2,600	$3,400

ES-335 CRR/CRS

1979. Country Rock Regular with standard wiring and CRR logo. Country Rock Stereo with stereo wiring and CRS logo, 300 of each built, 2 pickups, coil-tap.

1979	CRR	$2,400	$3,200
1979	CRS	$2,600	$3,300

2017 Gibson ES-335

1967 Gibson ES-335-12
Carter Vintage Guitars

GUITARS

1979 Gibson ES-335 Pro
Michael Campbell

*2014 Gibson ES-335
Rich Robinson*
Michael Alonzi

MODEL YEAR	FEATURES	EXC. COND. LOW	HIGH
ES-335 Diamond Edition			
2006. Trini Lopez style diamond f-holes, Bigsby tailpiece option, gold hardware, Pelham Blue, pearl white or black pearl.			
2006		$2,200	$2,975
ES-335 Eric Clapton Crossroads '64 Reissue			
2005. Reissue of EC's, with certificate of authenticity.			
2005		$8,500	$11,000
ES-335 Goldtop			
2013-2016. Gibson Memphis, limited edition, 2 Burstbucker humbuckers, gold finish.			
2013-2016		$1,800	$2,350
ES-335 Gothic			
1998-1999. Gothic appointments including ebony 'board and black satin finish.			
1998-1999		$1,100	$1,425
ES-335 Government Series			
2015-2016. Made from guitar bodies, necks and 'boards returned from Federal Government after '11 raid on Gibson, special run of 300 built, each with Certificate of Authenticity.			
2015		$1,600	$2,100
ES-335 Jim Beam Limited Edition			
1999. Promotional Custom Shop model, approximately 18 made, large Jim Beam notation on body, comes with certificate.			
1999		$1,800	$2,325
ES-335 Jimmy Wallace Reissue			
Special order by Texas Gibson dealer Jimmy Wallace.			
1980	Blond	$2,700	$3,500
ES-335 Joe Bonamassa Signature			
2012. Based on Joe's '61 335, VOS sunburst.			
2012		$3,000	$3,900
ES-335 King of the Blues			
2006. Offered through Guitar Center, 150 made, based on B.B.'s Lucille.			
2006		$2,200	$2,900
ES-335 Larry Carlton			
2002-2016. Mr. 335 logo on truss rod cover, block neck like Larry's guitar, vintage (faded) sunburst.			
2002-2016		$2,700	$3,500
ES-335 Lee Ritenour			
2008. Custom Shop, COA, 50 signed and 100 unsigned, Antique Cherry finish.			
2008		$2,700	$3,500
ES-335 Limited Edition			
2001. ES-335 style crown inlay on headstock, P-90 pickups.			
2001		$1,950	$2,525
ES-335 Nashville			
1994. All serial numbers begin with 94, first year Custom Shop run (not the Centennial).			
1994		$2,700	$3,400
ES-335 Pro			
1979-1981. Two humbucking pickups with exposed coils, bound 'board, cherry or sunburst.			
1979-1981		$1,925	$2,500

MODEL YEAR	FEATURES	EXC. COND. LOW	HIGH
ES-335 Rich Robinson			
2014-2016. Bigsby, small blocks, Cherry VOS finish.			
2014-2016		$2,725	$3,525
ES-335 Roy Orbison			
2006. About 70 made, RO serial number, black finish.			
2006		$2,800	$3,650
ES-335 Rusty Anderson			
2013. Figured maple, natural, dot neck specs.			
2013		$2,900	$3,775
ES-335 Showcase Edition			
1988. Guitar of the Month series, limited production, black gothic-style hardware, EMG pickups, transparent white/beige finish.			
1988		$2,200	$2,900
ES-335 Studio			
1986-1991, 2013-present. Bound body, 2 Dirty Finger humbuckers, cherry or ebony. Reissued in '13 by Gibson Memphis using '58 specs but with Vintage Sunburst or ebony finish.			
1986-1991		$1,325	$1,725
2013-2019	Memphis	$800	$1,050
ES-335 Warren Haynes			
2013-2015. Custom Shop model.			
2013-2015	500 made	$2,700	$3,500
2014	1961 Ltd Ed	$2,700	$3,500
ES-336			
1996-1998. Custom Shop smaller sized ES-335 with smaller headstock, dot markers.			
1996-1998	All options	$1,800	$2,350
ES-339			
2007-present. Smaller-sized bound 335 body, 2 humbuckers, block inlays.			
2007-2019	All options	$1,750	$2,250
ES-339 Studio			
2013-2018. Stripped-down 339, no binding or pickguard, dot inlays.			
2013-2018		$800	$1,050
ES-340 TD			
1968-1973. The 335 with a laminated maple neck, master volume and mixer controls, various colors.			
1968-1973	Natural, Walnut	$2,500	$3,250
ES-345 TD or ES-345 TDSV			
1959-1983. The 335 with Vari-tone, stereo, 2 humbuckers, gold hardware, double parallelogram inlays, stop tailpiece '59-'64 and '82-'83, trapeze tailpiece '65-'82. Cataloged as ES-345 TDSV by '80.			
1959	Cherry, Bigsby	$17,000	$22,000
1959	Cherry, stud tail	$22,000	$28,000
1959	Natural, Bigsby	$28,000	$36,000
1959	Natural, stud tail	$43,000	$56,000
1959	Sunburst, Bigsby	$17,000	$22,000
1959	Sunburst, stud tail	$22,000	$28,000
1960	Cherry, Bigsby	$15,000	$20,000
1960	Cherry, stud tail	$20,000	$26,000
1960	Natural, Bigsby	$26,000	$34,000
1960	Natural, stud tail	$40,000	$53,000
1960	Sunburst, Bigsby	$15,000	$20,000
1960	Sunburst, stud tail	$20,000	$26,000
1961	Cherry, Bigsby	$12,000	$16,000

MODEL YEAR	FEATURES	EXC. COND. LOW	HIGH
1961	Cherry, stud tail	$16,000	$21,000
1961	Sunburst, Bigsby	$12,000	$16,000
1961	Sunburst, stud tail	$16,000	$21,000
1962	Bigsby, PAF	$12,000	$16,000
1962	Stud tail, PAF	$13,000	$17,000
1963-1964	Bigsby, pat #	$9,800	$13,000
1963-1964	Stud tail, pat #	$11,500	$15,000
1965	Early '65 wide neck	$6,500	$8,500
1965	Mid '65 narrow neck	$4,200	$5,500
1966-1969	Various colors	$3,550	$4,600
1970-1979	Various colors	$2,750	$3,600
1980-1983	TDSV, Various colors	$2,400	$3,100

ES-345 Historic Collection
1998-1999. Custom Shop, stopbar, Bigsby or Maestro tailpiece, Viceroy Brown, Vintage Sunburst, Faded Cherry or natural.

1998-1999		$2,900	$3,750

ES-345 Reissue
2002-2010. ES-345 features with 6-position Varitone selector, gold hardware, stop tailpiece, various colors.

2002-2010		$2,000	$2,600

1959 ES-345 TD
2014-2015. Period-correct '59 specs with VOS aged look, certificate of authenticity, Historic Burst or natural (TDN) finish.

2014	'59 reissue	$2,500	$3,300
2015	VOS aged	$2,800	$3,700

ES-346 Paul Jackson Jr.
1997-2006. Custom Shop, 335-like with figured or plain maple top, rosewood 'board, double-parallelogram inlays.

1997-2006		$2,400	$3,125

ES-347 TD or ES-347 S
1978-1985, 1987-1993. 335-style with gold hardware, tune-o-matic bridge, 2 Spotlight double-coil pickups, coil-tap, bound body and neck, S added to name in '87.

1978-1984	TD	$2,450	$3,175
1987-1993	S	$2,450	$3,175

ES-350 or ES-350N
1947-1956. Originally the ES-350 Premier, full body archtop, single-cut, 1 P-90 pickup until end of '48, 2 after, sunburst or natural (350N).

1947-1948	Natural, 1 pu	$4,900	$6,350
1947-1948	Sunburst, 1 pu	$4,300	$5,700
1949-1956	Natural, 2 pu	$5,200	$6,800
1949-1956	Sunburst, 2 pu	$4,800	$6,300

ES-350 Centennial
1994. Guitar of the Month, sunburst, gold hardware, gold medallion on back of headstock, diamond accents, 101 made with serial numbers from 1984-1994. Included a gold signet ring.

1994		$3,000	$3,925

ES-350 T or ES-350N T
1955-1963, 1977-1981, 1992-1993. Called the ES-350 TD in early-'60s, thinline archtop, single-cut (round '55-'60 and '77-'81, pointed '61-'63), 2 P-90 pickups '55-'56, humbuckers after, gold hardware. Limited runs were done in 1992-1993.

1956	Natural, P-90s	$5,700	$7,350

MODEL YEAR	FEATURES	EXC. COND. LOW	HIGH
1956	Sunburst, P-90s	$4,500	$5,850
1957-1959	Natural, PAFs	$9,000	$12,000
1957-1959	Sunburst, PAFs	$8,200	$10,800
1960-1963	Natural, PAFs	$8,000	$10,500
1960-1963	Sunburst, PAFs	$7,500	$9,800
1977-1981	Natural, sunburst	$2,650	$3,450

ES-350 T (Custom Shop)
1998-2000. Historic Collection reissue.

1998-2000		$2,900	$3,775

Chuck Berry 1955 ES-350 T
2019. Limited to 55, antique natural with VOS finish.

2019		$9,000	$11,000

ES-355 TD
1958-1970. 335-style with large block inlays, multi-bound body and headstock, 2 humbuckers, the 355 model was standard with a Bigsby, sideways or Maestro vibrato, non-vibrato models were an option. The prices shown assume a vibrato tailpiece, a factory stop tailpiece was considered an advantage and will fetch more. Early examples have factory Bigsby vibratos, early '60s have sideways vibratos, and late '60s have Maestro vibratos, cherry finish was the standard finish.

1958-1959	Cherry, PAFs, Bigsby vibrato	$18,000	$24,000
1959	Cherry, PAFs, stop tail	$19,000	$24,500
1960-1962	Cherry, PAFs, Bigsby vibrato	$16,000	$21,000
1962	Cherry, PAFs, side-pull vibrato	$16,000	$21,000
1963-1964	Cherry, pat #, Bigsby vibrato	$11,000	$14,300
1965	Early '65 wide neck	$8,000	$10,300
1965	Mid '65 narrow neck	$5,300	$6,900
1966-1968	Cherry or sunburst	$4,950	$6,400
1966-1968	Sparkling Burgundy	$8,000	$10,300
1969-1970	Cherry or sunburst	$4,300	$5,500

ES-355 TDSV
1959-1982. Stereo version of ES-355 with Vari-tone switch, a mono version was available but few were made, the 355 model was standard with a Bigsby, sideways or Maestro vibrato, non-vibrato models were an option. The prices shown assume a vibrato tailpiece. A factory stop tailpiece was considered an advantage and will fetch more, early examples have factory Bigsby vibratos, early-'60s have sideways vibratos and late-'60s have Maestro vibratos, cherry finish was standard, walnut became available in '69.

1959	Bigsby	$15,500	$20,200
1960	Bigsby	$14,500	$19,000
1961-1963	Sideways, late PAFs	$14,500	$19,000
1962	Maestro, late PAFs	$14,500	$19,000
1963-1964	Maestro, pat #	$11,000	$14,300
1965	Early '65 wide neck	$7,900	$10,300

1969 Gibson ES-345 TDSV
Craig Brody

1998 Gibson ES-350 T (Custom Shop)
Bernunzio Uptown Music

Gibson ES-359

2001 Gibson ES-446 S
Greg Perrine

MODEL YEAR	FEATURES	EXC. COND. LOW	HIGH
1965	Mid '65 narrow neck	$5,300	$6,900
1966	Sparkling Burgundy	$8,000	$10,300
1966-1967	Cherry or sunburst, Maestro	$4,800	$6,200
1968	Various colors, Maestro	$4,800	$6,200
1969	Various colors, Bigsby	$4,300	$5,500
1970-1982	Various colors, Bigsby	$3,850	$5,000

ES-355/ES-355 TD (Custom Shop)
1994, 1997, 2006-2010. Mono, Bigsby or stop tail.

1994-2010		$2,900	$3,750

ES-355 Alex Lifeson
2008-2010. Custom Shop Inspired By series.

2008-2010		$3,800	$4,900

ES-355 Centennial
1994. Guitar of the Month, sunburst, gold hardware, gold medallion on back of headstock, diamond accents, 101 made with serial numbers from 1984-1994. Included a gold signet ring.

1994		$2,900	$3,750

ES-355 Curly Maple Limited Edition
2010-2012. Figured flamed maple top, stop tailpiece, natural finish.

2010-2012		$3,000	$4,000

ES-355 Limited Edition VOS
2015-2018. Gibson Memphis, Bigsby, gold hardware, various colors with VOS finish.

2015-2018		$3,300	$4,300

ES-355 Summer Jam Series
2011. Custom Shop Summer Jam series, 25 made in Bourbon Burst.

2011		$2,900	$3,800

ES-359
2008-2016. Custom Shop, ES-335/ES-339 style with LP Custom style appointments, minor-figured top and back, sunburst.

2008-2016		$1,850	$2,400

ES-369
1981-1982. A 335-style with 2 exposed humbucker pickups, coil-tap, sunburst.

1981-1982		$2,000	$2,600

ES-390
2014-2018. Memphis model, thinline hollow-body, rosewood 'board, 2 P-90s, Vintage Dark Burst finish.

2014-2018		$1,675	$2,200

ES-446
1999-2003. Single cut semi-hollow, 2 humbuckers, Bigsby, Custom Shop.

1999-2003	Various colors	$2,175	$2,825

ES-775
1990-1993. Single-cut hollowbody, 2 humbuckers, gold hardware, ebony, natural or sunburst.

1990-1993		$2,175	$2,825

ES-Artist
1979-1985. Double-cut thinline, semi-hollowbody, no f-holes, 2 humbuckers, active electronics, gold hardware, ebony, fireburst or sunburst. Moog electronics includes 3 mini-switches for compressor, expander and bright boost.

1979-1985		$2,600	$3,375

EST-150 (Tenor)
1937-1939. Tenor version of ES-150, Charlie Christian pickup, sunburst, renamed ETG-150 in '40.

1937-1939		$2,800	$3,600

ETG-150 (Tenor)
1940-1942, 1947-1971. Renamed from EST-150, tenor version of ES-150, 1 metal-covered pickup '40-'42, P-90 after, sunburst.

1940-1942		$2,600	$3,400
1947-1959		$1,550	$2,000
1960-1964		$1,400	$1,800
1965		$1,300	$1,700
1966-1971		$1,225	$1,600

Everly Brothers
1962-1972. Jumbo flat-top, huge double 'guard, star inlays, natural is optional in '63 and becomes the standard color in '68, reintroduced as the J-180 Everly Brothers in '86.

1962-1964	Black	$10,000	$13,000
1963	Natural option	$10,000	$13,000
1965	Early '65, black, large neck	$8,500	$11,000
1965	Late '65, black, small neck	$6,500	$8,500
1966-1967	Black	$5,800	$7,500
1968-1969	Natural replaces black	$4,500	$5,800
1970-1972	Natural	$3,800	$4,900

Explorer
1958-1959, 1963. Some '58s shipped in '63, korina body, 2 humbuckers. The Explorer market is a very specialized and very small market, with few genuine examples available and a limited number of high-end buyers. The slightest change to the original specifications can mean a significant drop in value. The narrow price ranges noted are for all original examples that have the original guitar case.

1958-1959		$490,000	$700,000
1963		$225,000	$300,000

Explorer (Mahogany)
1975-1982. Mahogany body, 2 humbuckers, black, white or natural.

1975-1982	Black or white	$2,800	$3,700
1975-1982	Natural	$2,800	$3,700

Explorer I
1981-1982. Replaces Explorer (Mahogany), 2 Dirty Finger humbuckers, stoptail or Kahler vibrato, becomes Explorer 83 in '83.

1981-1982		$825	$1,075

Explorer 83 or Explorer (Alder)
1983-1989. Renamed Explorer 83 from Explorer I, changed to Explorer in '84, alder body, 2 humbuckers, maple neck, ebony 'board, dot inlays, triangle knob pattern.

1983-1984		$1,400	$1,850
1985-1989	Custom color, limited run	$1,250	$1,600
1985-1989	Standard finishes	$1,100	$1,425

The *Vintage Guitar Price Guide* shows low to high values for items in all-original excellent condition, and, where applicable, with original case or cover.

MODEL YEAR	FEATURES	EXC. COND. LOW	HIGH

Explorer II (E/2)
1979-1983. Five-piece maple and walnut laminate body sculptured like V II, ebony 'board with dot inlays, 2 humbuckers, gold-plated hardware, natural finish.

1978-1983	Figured top	$2,500	$3,250
1979-1983	Various colors	$2,400	$3,100

Explorer III
1984-1985. Alder body, 3 P-90 pickups, 2 control knobs, chrome or black hardware ('85 only), optional locking trem.

1984-1985	All options	$950	$1,250

Explorer '76/X-plorer/Explorer
1990-2014, 2019-present. Mahogany body and neck, rosewood 'board, dot inlays, 2 humbucking pickups, name changed to X-plorer in 2002 and to Explorer in '09. Reintroduced in '19.

1990-2001	Various colors	$950	$1,250
2002-2014	Various colors	$900	$1,200

Explorer 90 Double
1989-1990. Mahogany body and neck, 1 single-coil and 1 humbucker, strings-thru-body.

1989-1990		$1,225	$1,600

Explorer Baritone
2011-2013. 28"-scale, 2 exposed humbuckers.

2011-2013		$1,350	$1,775

Explorer Centennial
1994 only. Les Paul Gold finish, 100 year banner inlay at 12th fret, diamonds in headstock and gold-plated knobs, Gibson coin in rear of headstock, only 100 made.

1994		$3,900	$5,000

Explorer CMT/The Explorer
1981-1984. Flamed maple body, bound top, exposed-coil pickups, TP-6 tailpiece.

1981-1984		$2,400	$3,100

Explorer Custom Shop
2003-2012. Custom Shop model with Certificate of Authenticity, Korina body, gold hardware.

2003-2012		$4,200	$5,500

Explorer Designer Series
1983-1985. Custom paint finish.

1983-1985		$1,300	$1,700

Explorer Gothic
1998-2003. Gothic Series with black finish and hardware.

1998-2003		$775	$1,000

Explorer Government Series
2013-2016. Made from guitar bodies, necks and 'boards returned from Federal Government after '11 raid on Gibson, special run of 300 built, each with Certificate of Authenticity.

2013		$900	$1,175

Explorer Heritage
1983. Reissue of '58 Explorer, korina body, gold hardware, inked serial number, limited edition.

1983	Black, white, red	$3,000	$3,900
1983	Natural	$4,200	$5,500

Explorer (Limited Edition Korina)
1976. Limited edition korina body replaces standard mahogany body, natural.

1976		$5,300	$7,000

Explorer (Limited Edition Mahogany)
1999. Mahogany with natural finish.

1999		$1,400	$1,800

Explorer Korina
1982-1984. Korina body and neck, 2 humbucking pickups, gold hardware, standard 8-digit serial (versus the inked serial number on the Heritage Explorer of the same era).

1982-1984		$4,200	$5,500

Explorer 1958 Korina/Split Headstock
1994. Split headstock, 50 made.

1994		$6,000	$8,000

Explorer 50th Anniversary '58 Korina
2007-2008. Custom Shop model, natural korina, includes custom colors.

2007-2008		$6,000	$8,000

Explorer 50-Year Brimstone Commemorative
2008. Guitar of the month Oct. '08, solid mahogany body, AA figured maple top, higher-end appointments, 50th logo on truss rod cover, Brimstone Burst finish.

2008		$2,100	$2,800

Explorer 120
2014. 120th Anniversary inlay at 12th fret, mahogany body, cherry or black.

2014		$1,100	$1,425

Explorer Pro
2002-2005, 2007-2008. Explorer model updated with smaller, lighter weight mahogany body, 2 humbuckers, ebony or natural.

2002-2008		$1,100	$1,425

Dethklok "Thunderhorse" Explorer
2011-2012. Limited Edition of 400, Thunderhorse logo on truss rod cover, silverburst finish.

2011-2012		$1,550	$2,000

Explorer Robot
2008-2012. Announced Sept. '08, Robot Tuning System, trapezoid markers, 2 exposed humbuckers, red finish.

2008-2012		$1,025	$1,325

Explorer Split Headstock Collection
2001. Custom Shop model, 25 made, Explorer body with V-split headstock.

2001		$2,600	$3,350

Explorer T
2016-2018. Mahogany body, rosewood 'board, white 'guard, ebony or cherry finish.

2016-2018		$1,000	$1,300

Explorer Voodoo
2002-2004. Juju finish, red and black pickup coils.

2002-2004		$975	$1,275

Explorer XPL
1985. Gibson Custom Shop logo on back of headstock, factory Gibson Kahler tremolo, extra cutaway on lower treble bout.

1985		$950	$1,200

Holy Explorer
2009-2011. Explorer body 7 routed holes, 1 knob, 2 exposed humbuckers, Limited Run Series certificate of authenticity, 350 made.

2009-2011		$900	$1,150

1983 Gibson Explorer Heritage
Steve Evans

1983 Gibson Explorer Korina
Bo Belaski

1976 Gibson Firebird 76

Imaged by Heritage Auctions, HA.com

1963 Gibson Firebird III

Reverse Explorer

2008. Guitar of the Month Sept. '08, 1,000 made, Antique Walnut finish, includes custom guitar case.

MODEL YEAR	FEATURES	EXC. COND. LOW	HIGH
2008		$1,175	$1,525

Sammy Hagar Signature Explorer

2011-2013. Mahogany with Red Rocker finish, ghosted Chickenfoot logo on back.

2011-2013		$1,500	$2,000

Shred X Explorer

2008. Guitar of the Month June '08, 1,000 made, ebony finish, black hardware, 2 EMG 85 pickups, Kahler.

2008		$925	$1,200

Tribal Explorer

2009-2011. Black tribal graphics on white body. Limited run of 350.

2009-2011		$875	$1,100

X-Plorer/X-Plorer V New Century

2006-2007. Full-body mirror 'guard, mahogany body and neck, 2 humbuckers, mirror truss rod cover.

2006-2007		$925	$1,200

Firebird I

1963-1969. Reverse body and 1 humbucker '63-mid-'65, non-reversed body and 2 P-90s mid-'65-'69.

1963	Sunburst, reverse, hardtail	$10,000	$13,300
1963	Sunburst, reverse, trem	$6,500	$8,500
1964	Cardinal Red, reverse	$10,500	$13,700
1964	Sunburst, reverse, hardtail	$9,500	$12,500
1964	Sunburst, reverse, trem	$5,400	$7,000
1965	Cardinal Red, reverse	$8,700	$11,300
1965	Custom color, non-reverse	$7,300	$9,500
1965	Sunburst, non-reverse, 2 P-90s	$3,000	$3,900
1965	Sunburst, reverse	$4,800	$6,300
1966	Custom color, non-reverse	$5,400	$7,000
1966	Sunburst, non-reverse	$3,000	$3,900
1967	Custom color, non-reverse	$5,400	$7,000
1967	Sunburst, non-reverse	$3,000	$3,900
1968-1969	Sunburst, non-reverse	$3,000	$3,900

Firebird I 1963 Reissue Historic Collection

2000-2006. Neck-thru, reverse body, Firebird logo on 'guard, various colors including sunburst and Frost Blue.

2000-2006	Various colors	$2,000	$2,625

Firebird I Custom Shop

1991-1992. Limited run from Custom Shop, reverse body, 1 pickup, gold-plated, sunburst.

1991-1992		$1,925	$2,525

Firebird 76

1976-1978. Reverse body, gold hardware, 2 pickups.

MODEL YEAR	FEATURES	EXC. COND. LOW	HIGH
1976	Bicentennial	$2,400	$3,125
1976	Black	$2,400	$3,125
1976	Sunburst, red/white/ blue guard logo	$2,400	$3,100
1977-1978	Sunburst	$2,250	$2,925
1977-1978	White	$2,250	$2,925

Firebird I/ Firebird 76

1980-1982. Reintroduced Firebird 76 but renamed Firebird I.

1980-1982		$2,250	$2,925

Firebird II/Firebird 2

1981-1982. Maple body with figured maple top, 2 full size active humbuckers, TP-6 tailpiece.

1981-1982		$2,400	$3,125

Firebird III

1963-1969. Reverse body and 2 humbuckers '63-mid-'65, non-reversed body and 3 P-90s mid-'65-'69.

1963	Cardinal Red	$10,000	$13,000
1963	Golden Mist	$10,000	$13,000
1963	Polaris White	$9,200	$12,000
1963	Sunburst	$7,500	$9,700
1964	Cardinal Red, reverse	$10,000	$13,050
1964	Golden Mist, reverse	$10,000	$13,050
1964	Pelham Blue	$10,000	$13,050
1964	Polaris White, reverse	$8,500	$11,050
1964	Sunburst, reverse	$7,500	$9,750
1965	Cherry, non-reverse, 3 P-90s	$4,200	$5,525
1965	Cherry, reverse	$7,500	$9,750
1965	Frost Blue, non-reverse	$7,700	$10,050
1965	Frost Blue, reverse	$9,000	$12,000
1965	Inverness Green, non-reverse	$7,700	$10,050
1965	Iverness Green, reverse	$9,000	$12,000
1965	Sunburst, non-reverse, 2 P-90s	$3,600	$4,650
1965	Sunburst, non-reverse, 3 P-90s	$3,700	$4,850
1965	Sunburst, reverse, 2 P-90s	$5,300	$7,000
1965	Sunburst, reverse, mini hums	$5,700	$7,500
1966	Polaris White	$7,000	$9,050
1966-1967	Frost Blue	$7,700	$10,050
1966-1969	Pelham Blue	$7,700	$10,050
1966-1969	Sunburst	$3,600	$4,650
1967	Cherry	$3,700	$4,850

Firebird III 1964 Reissue (Custom Shop)

2000-2013. Maestro, mini-humbuckers, sunburst or color option.

2000-2013		$2,400	$3,125

MODEL YEAR	FEATURES	EXC. COND. LOW	HIGH

Firebird Non-Reverse
2002-2004. Non-reverse body, 2 humbuckers, standard finishes. There was also a limited edition in '02 with swirl finishes.

2002-2004		$1,150	$1,500

Firebird Studio Non-Reverse
2011-2012. Non-reverse body, 3 tapped P-90 pickups, 5-way pickup selector switch, dot markers, vintage sunburst or Pelham Blue nitro finish.

2011-2012		$850	$1,125

Firebird Studio Tribute/Studio T
2012-2017. Reverse mahogany body, '70s profile maple neck, 2 mini-humbuckers.

2012-2017		$850	$1,125

Firebird Studio/Firebird III Studio
2004-2010. Two humbuckers, dot markers, tune-o-matic and bar stoptail, reverse body, dark cherry finish.

2004-2010		$850	$1,125

Firebird V
1963-1969. Two humbuckers, reverse body '63-mid-'65, non-reversed body mid-'65-'69.

1963	Sunburst, reverse	$11,500	$15,100
1963-1964	Pelham Blue, reverse	$16,000	$21,100
1964	Cardinal Red, reverse	$14,500	$19,100
1964	Sunburst, reverse	$10,300	$13,600
1965	Cardinal Red, reverse	$13,000	$17,100
1965	Sunburst, non-reverse	$4,500	$5,800
1965	Sunburst, reverse	$7,700	$10,100
1966-1967	Cardinal Red, non-reverse	$8,500	$11,000
1966-1969	Sunburst	$4,400	$5,700

Firebird V/Firebird V Reissue/Firebird V 2010
1986-1987, 1990-2018. Based on Firebird V specs, reverse body, 2 pickups, tune-o-matic bridge, vintage sunburst, classic white or ebony with Cardinal Red optional in '91. Called Reissue for '90-'93, renamed V in '94, then V 2010 in '10.

1986-1987	Sunburst, white, black	$2,075	$2,725
1990	Sunburst, white, black	$1,850	$2,400
1991	Cardinal Red	$1,750	$2,300
1991-1999	Sunburst, white, black	$1,250	$1,625
2000-2018	Sunburst, white, black	$1,125	$1,450

Firebird V-12
1966-1967. Non-reverse Firebird V-style body with standard six-on-a-side headstock and split diamond headstock inlay (like ES-335-12 inlay), dot markers, special twin humbucking pickups (like mini-humbuckers).

1966-1967	Custom color	$8,400	$11,000
1966-1967	Sunburst	$3,900	$5,100

Firebird V 1963 Aged (Custom Shop)
2016. Reverse body, Vintage Sunburst, aged hardware.

2016		$2,700	$3,550

Firebird V 1963 Johnny Winter
2008. Johnny Winter script logo, certificate of authenticity.

2008		$4,500	$6,000

Firebird V 1965 Reissue (Custom Shop)
2000-2013. Reverse body, 2 mini-humbuckers, Maestro tremolo, certificate, sunburst or colors.

2000-2013		$2,200	$2,900

Firebird V 50th Anniversary
2013. Gold hardware, '50th Anniversary 1963-2013' on 'guard, gold finish.

2013		$1,325	$1,725

Firebird V Celebrity Series
1990-1993. Reverse body, gold hardware, 2 humbuckers, various colors.

1990-1993		$2,200	$2,875

Firebird V Guitar Trader Reissue
1982. Guitar Trader commissioned Firebird reissue, only 15 made, sunburst or white.

1982		$2,700	$3,550

Firebird V Limited Edition Zebrawood
2007. Limited edition from Gibson USA, Guitar of the Week #12, 400 made, zebrawood reverse body.

2007		$1,500	$1,950

Firebird V Medallion
1972-1973. Reverse body, 2 humbuckers, Limited Edition medallion mounted on body.

1972-1973		$4,500	$5,900

Firebird V Zebra Wood
2007. Limited to 400, zebra wood body, guitar of the week series.

2007		$1,800	$2,350

Firebird VII
1963-1969. Three humbuckers, reverse body '63-mid-'65, non-reversed body mid-'65-'69, sunburst standard.

1963-1964	Sunburst, reverse	$12,000	$15,500
1964	Custom color, reverse	$18,000	$24,000
1965	Custom color, non-reverse	$12,200	$16,000
1965	Custom color, reverse	$15,000	$20,000
1965	Sunburst, non-reverse	$4,850	$6,400
1965	Sunburst, reverse	$8,700	$11,500
1966-1967	Custom color, non-reverse	$10,000	$13,000
1966-1967	Sunburst, non-reverse	$4,600	$6,100
1968	Custom color	$10,000	$13,000
1968-1969	Sunburst	$4,600	$6,100

Firebird VII (Reissued)
2002-2007. Various production models, reverse and non-reverse, 3 pickups, block markers, vibrola, various color options with matching headstock finish.

2002-2007	All colors	$1,575	$2,050

2002 Gibson Firebird V Reissue
Johnny Zapp

1967 Gibson Firebird V-12
Carter Vintage Guitars

GUITARS

1982 Gibson Flying V Heritage
Steve Evans

1982 Gibson Flying V II

MODEL YEAR	FEATURES	EXC. COND. LOW	HIGH

Firebird VII 1965 Historic Collection (Custom Shop)
1998-2013. Custom Shop/Historic Collection, 3 mini-humbuckers, Vintage Sunburst or solid colors.

1998-2013	Vintage Sunburst	$2,200	$2,900

20th Anniversary 1965 Firebird VII Reissue
2014. Custom Shop, '65 specs, gold hardware, Golden Mist finish, certificate of authenticity.

2014		$3,000	$3,900

Firebird VII Centennial
1994 only. Headstock medallion, sunburst.

1994		$2,900	$3,800

Firebird X Limited Edition Robot
2011-2018. 1800 to be made, lightweight swamp ash body, 1-piece maple neck, curly maple 'board, 3 pickups, robot electronics, nitro lacquer finish in Redolution or Bluevolution.

2011-2018		$2,275	$2,975

Elliot Easton "Tikibird" Firebird
2013-2018. Reverse body, mahogany, rosewood 'board, 2 pickups, Tiki graphic on 'guard, signature on headstock back, Gold Mist Poly finish.

2013-2018		$1,400	$1,825

Firebird Custom Acoustic
2004-2018. Sitka spruce top, quilted maple back and sides, ebony 'board, mother-of-pearl headstock logo with MOP and abalone flames inlay, antique natural finish.

2004-2018		$2,500	$3,300

Firebird Zero
2016-2018. S Series, new body design, 2 pickups, poplar body, maple neck, rosewood 'board, various colors.

2016-2018		$365	$480

Flamenco 2
1963-1967. Natural spruce top, 14 3/4", cypress back and sides, slotted headstock, zero fret.

1963-1967		$1,100	$1,450

Flying V
1958-1959, 1962-1963. Only 81 shipped in '58 and 17 in '59, guitars made from leftover parts and sold in '62-'63, natural korina body, string-thru-body design. Original case with oxblood interior adds $2,500.

As with any ultra high-end instrument, each instrument should be evaluated on a case-by-case basis. The Flying V market is a very specialized market, with few untouched examples available, and a limited number of high-end buyers. The price ranges noted are for all-original, excellent condition guitars with the original Flying V case. The slightest change to the original specifications can mean a significant drop in value.

1958-1959		$240,000	$340,000

Flying V (Mahogany)
1966-1970, 1975-1981. Mahogany body, around 200 were shipped for '66-'70. Gibson greatly increased production of Flying Vs in '75. See separate listing for the '71 Medallion V version.

1966	Cherry, sunburst	$21,000	$27,500
1967-1970	Cherry, sunburst	$16,500	$21,500
1975-1981	Various colors	$3,500	$4,550
1979-1981	Silverburst	$3,600	$4,750

MODEL YEAR	FEATURES	EXC. COND. LOW	HIGH

Flying V (Mahogany String-through-body)
1982. Mahogany body, string-thru-body design, only 100 made, most in white, some red or black possible.

1982	All colors	$2,000	$2,600

Flying V Heritage
1981-1982. Limited edition based on '58 specs, korina body, 4 colors available.

1981-1982	Natural	$4,200	$5,500
1981-1982	Various colors	$3,000	$3,950

Flying V I/V '83/Flying V (no pickguard)
1981-1988. Introduced as Flying V I, then renamed Flying V '83 in 1983, called Flying V from '84 on. Alder body, 2 exposed humbuckers, maple neck, ebony 'board, dot inlays, black rings, no 'guard, ebony or ivory finish, designed for lower-end market.

1981-1988		$1,400	$1,800

Flying V Korina
1983. Name changed from Flying V Heritage, korina body, various colors.

1983		$4,200	$5,500

Flying V Reissue/'67/Factor X/Flying V
1990-2014. Mahogany body, called Flying V Reissue first year, then '67 Flying V '91-'02, V Factor X '03-'08, Flying V '09-'14.

1990-2014	Various colors	$850	$1,125

Flying V II
1979-1982. Five-piece maple and walnut laminate sculptured body (1980 catalog states top is either walnut or maple), ebony 'board with dot inlays, 2 V-shaped pickups (2 Dirty Fingers humbuckers towards end of run), gold-plated hardware, natural.

1979-1982		$2,400	$3,100
1982	Silverburst	$2,400	$3,100

Flying V 50th Anniversary
2008. Built as replica of '58 square shoulder V, 100 made, natural finish on korina body and neck, rosewood 'board, 8-series serial number, price includes original certificate.

2008		$4,800	$6,250

Flying V '58 Historic Collection (Custom Shop)
1991-2013. Historic Collection, based on '58 Flying V, gold hardware, natural korina.

1991-1999		$4,500	$5,900
2000-2013		$4,000	$5,200

Flying V '67 Historic Collection (Custom Shop)
1997-2004. Historic Collection, '67 Flying V specs, korina body, natural or opaque colors.

1997-2004		$2,100	$2,700

Flying V '84 Silverburst
2007. Limited Edition Guitar of the Week,

2007		$850	$1,100

Flying V '90 Double
1989-1990. Mahogany body, stud tailpiece, 1 single-coil and 1 double-coil humbucker, Floyd Rose tremolo, ebony, silver or white.

1989-1990		$1,350	$1,800

Flying V '98
1998. Mahogany body, '58 style controls, gold or chrome hardware.

1998		$1,350	$1,800

MODEL YEAR FEATURES	EXC. COND. LOW	HIGH

Flying V (Custom Shop)
2004-2008. A few made each year, figured maple top, options include standard point-headstock or split-headstock.

2004-2008	$3,500	$4,500

Flying V 120
2014. Mahogany body and neck, 120th Anniversary inlay at 12th fret, rosewood 'board, 2 BurstBucker pickups, ebony, classic white or Heritage Cherry.

2014	$850	$1,125

Flying V 50-Year Commemorative
2008. Guitar of the Month March '08, 1,000 made, AA flamed maple top, higher-end appointments, 50th logo on truss rod cover, Brimstone Burst finish.

2008	$1,500	$2,000

Flying V Brendon Small Snow Falcon
2013. Snow Falcon decal on headstock back, 2 Burstbucker pickups, chrome hardware, Snow Burst finish, limited run.

2013	$1,350	$1,750

Flying V Centennial
1994 only. 100th Anniversary Series, all gold, gold medalion, other special appointments.

1994	$3,900	$5,000

Flying V CMT/The V
1981-1985. Maple body with a curly maple top, 2 pickups, stud tailpiece, natural or sunburst.

1981-1985	$2,800	$3,700

Flying V Custom (Limited Edition)
2002. Appointments similar to Les Paul Custom, including black finish, only 40 made.

2002	$4,000	$5,200

Flying V Designer Series
1983-1984. Custom paint finish.

1983-1984	$1,300	$1,700

Flying V Faded
2002-2012. Worn cherry finish.

2002-2012	$575	$750

Flying V Gothic/'98 Gothic
1998-2003. Satin black finish, black hardware, moon and star markers.

1998-2003	$775	$1,000

Flying V Government Series
2012-2016. Made from guitar bodies, necks and 'boards returned from Federal Government after '11 raid on Gibson, special run of 300 built, each with Certificate of Authenticity.

2013	$900	$1,175

Flying V Hendrix Hall of Fame
Late-1991-1993. Limited Edition (400 made), numbered, black.

1991-1993	$2,100	$2,700

Flying V Hendrix Psychedelic
2005-2006. Hand-painted 1967 Flying V replica, 300 made, includes certificate, instruments without the certificate are worth less than the amount shown.

2005-2006	$5,500	$7,200

Flying V Lenny Kravitz
2002. Custom Shop, 125 made.

2002	$2,600	$3,400

Flying V Lonnie Mack
1993-1995. Mahogany body with Lonnie Mack-style Bigsby vibrato, cherry.

1993-1995	$3,000	$4,000

Flying V LTD
2001. Limited Edition, certificate of authenticity.

2001	$875	$1,125

Flying V Medallion
1971. Mahogany body, stud tailpiece, numbered Limited Edition medallion on bass side of V, 350 made in '71 (3 more were shipped in '73-'74).

1971-1974	$10,800	$14,000

Flying V New Century
2006-2007. Full-body mirror 'guard, mahogany body and neck, 2 humbuckers, Flying V style neck profile, mirror truss rod cover.

2006-2007	$925	$1,200

Flying V Primavera
1994. Primavera (light yellow/white mahogany) body, gold-plated hardware.

1994	$1,500	$1,925

Flying V Robot
2008-2011. Robot Tuning System.

2008-2011	$1,025	$1,325

Flying V T
2016-2017. Mahogany body, thicker 1-piece 'board.

2016-2017	$900	$1,175

Flying V The Holy V
2009. Guitar of the month for Jan. '09, large triangular cutouts in bouts, split diamond markers, 1 humbucker, 1 control knob.

2009	$900	$1,150

Flying V Voodoo
2002-2003. Black finish, red pickups.

2002-2003	$1,000	$1,300

Limited Edition Flying V
2016. Dirty Fingers, faded amber finish, gig bag.

2016	$450	$575

Reverse Flying V
2006-2008. Introduced as part of Guitar of the Week program, reintroduced by popular demand in a '07 limited run, light colored solid mahogany body gives a natural Korina appearance or opaque white or black, V-shaped reverse body, traditional Flying V neck profile.

2006-2008	$900	$1,175

Rudolph Schenker Flying V
1993. Only 103 made, black and white body and headstock, signature on 'guard.

1993	$1,400	$1,825

Shred V
2008. Guitar of the Month, 1000 made, EMG humbuckers, Kahler, black.

2008	$900	$1,175

Tribal V
2009-2011. Black tribal graphics on white body. Limited run of 350.

2009-2011	$875	$1,100

F-25 Folksinger
1963-1971. 14-1/2" flat-top, mahogany body, most have double white 'guard, natural.

1963-1964	$875	$1,125

Gibson Flying V Hendrix Psychedelic

2002 Gibson Flying V Voodoo

Imaged by Heritage Auctions, HA.com

1983 Gibson Futura
Imaged by Heritage Auctions, HA.com

*1977 Gibson Howard
Roberts Custom*
Bernunzio Uptown Music

MODEL YEAR	FEATURES	EXC. COND. LOW	HIGH
1965		$800	$1,025
1966-1971		$725	$950

FJN Folk Singer
1963-1967. Jumbo flat-top, square shoulders, natural finish with deep red on back and sides.

1963-1964		$1,700	$2,225
1965		$1,550	$2,025
1966-1967		$1,450	$1,925

Futura
1982-1984. Deep cutout solidbody, 2 humbucker pickups, gold hardware, black, white or purple.

1982-1984		$1,500	$2,000

Historic Korina Futura
1998-1999. Explorer body with V headstock.

1998-1999		$6,000	$8,000

GB Series Guitar Banjos
See listings in Banjo section of the Price Guide.

GGC-700
1981-1982. Slab single-cut body, 2 exposed humbuckers, dots.

1981-1982		$600	$800

GK-55 Active
1979-1980. LP body style, 2 exposed Dirty Fingers humbuckers, bolt neck, dot markers.

1979-1980		$575	$750

Gospel
1973-1979. Flat-top, square shoulders, laminated maple back and sides, arched back, Dove of Peace headstock inlay, natural.

1973-1979		$825	$1,075

Gospel Reissue
1992-1997. Laminated mahogany back and sides, natural or sunburst (walnut added in '94, blue and red in '95), changes to old-style script logo and headstock ornamentation in '94.

1992-1993	Reissue specs	$1,025	$1,325
1994-1997	Old-style specs	$1,025	$1,325

GS-1 Classical
1950-1956. Mahogany back and sides.

1950-1956		$600	$775

GS-2 Classical
1950-1956. Maple back and sides.

1950-1959		$625	$825

GS-5 Custom Classic/C-5 Classical
1954-1960. Brazilian rosewood back and sides, renamed C-5 Classical in '57.

1954-1960		$1,350	$1,750

GS-35 Classical/Gut String 35
1939-1942. Spruce top, mahogany back and sides, only 39 made.

1939-1942		$1,425	$1,850

GS-85 Classical/Gut String 85
1939-1942. Brazilian rosewood back and sides.

1939-1942		$2,800	$3,600

GY (Army-Navy)
1918-1921. Slightly arched top and back, low-end budget model, Sheraton Brown.

1918-1921		$600	$775

Harley Davidson LTD
1994-1995. Limited Edition, 16" wide body, flat-top, Harley Davidson in script and logo, black, 1500 sold through

Harley dealers to celebrate 100th Anniversary of Harley.

1994-1995		$1,600	$2,100

Heritage
1965-1982. Flat-top dreadnought, square shoulders, rosewood back and sides (Brazilian until '67, Indian '68 on), bound top and back, natural finish.

1965-1967	Brazilian	$1,800	$2,350
1968	Indian	$825	$1,100
1969-1982	Indian	$900	$1,175

Heritage-12
1968-1971. Flat-top dreadnought, 12 strings, Indian rosewood back and sides, bound top and back, natural finish.

1968-1971		$900	$1,175

HG-00 (Hawaiian)
1932-1942. Hawaiian version of L-00, 14 3/4" flat-top, mahogany back and sides, bound top, natural.

1932-1947		$4,000	$5,200

HG-20 (Hawaiian)
1929-1933. Hawaiian, 14 1/2" dreadnought-shaped, maple back and sides, round soundhole and 4 f-holes.

1929-1933		$4,000	$5,200

HG-22 (Hawaiian)
1929-1932. Dreadnought, 14", Hawaiian, round soundhole and 4 f-holes, white paint logo, very small number produced.

1929-1932		$4,200	$5,600

HG-24 (Hawaiian)
1929-1932. 16" Hawaiian, rosewood back and sides, round soundhole plus 4 f-holes, small number produced.

1929-1932		$5,500	$7,300

HG-Century (Hawaiian)
1937-1938. Hawaiian, 14 3/4" L-C Century of Progress, pearloid 'board.

1937-1938		$3,800	$5,000

Howard Roberts Artist
1976-1980. Full body single-cut archtop, soundhole, 1 humbucking pickup, gold hardware, ebony 'board, various colors.

1976-1980		$2,050	$2,700

Howard Roberts Artist Double Pickup
1979-1980. Two pickup version of HR Artist.

1979-1980		$2,200	$2,900

Howard Roberts Custom
1975-1981. Full body single-cut archtop, soundhole, 1 humbucking pickup, chrome hardware, rosewood 'board, various colors.

1975-1981		$2,100	$2,800

Howard Roberts Fusion/Fusion II/Fusion III
1979-2009. Single-cut, semi-hollowbody, 2 humbucking pickups, chrome hardware, ebony 'board (unbound until '78), TP-6 tailpiece, various colors, renamed Howard Roberts Fusion II in late-'88, and Howard Roberts Fusion III in '91.

1979-2009		$1,850	$2,450

HP-415 W
2017-2018. High Performance series, slimmer round shoulder cutaway, sitka spruce top, walnut back and sides.

2017-2018		$825	$1,050

MODEL YEAR	FEATURES	EXC. COND. LOW	HIGH

Hummingbird

1960-present. Flat-top acoustic, square shoulders, mahogany back and sides, bound body and neck.

1960	Cherry Sunburst	$4,600	$6,000
1961-1964	Cherry Sunburst	$4,400	$5,700
1963-1965	Natural	$4,700	$6,100
1965	Cherry Sunburst, early '65	$3,200	$4,200
1965	Cherry Sunburst, late '65	$2,800	$3,700
1966	Cherry Sunburst	$2,700	$3,500
1966	Natural	$2,800	$3,700
1967-1968	Natural, screwed 'guard	$2,800	$3,700
1967-1968	Sunburst, screwed 'guard	$2,700	$3,500
1969	Natural, screwed 'guard	$2,300	$3,000
1969	Sunburst, screwed 'guard	$2,300	$3,000
1970-1971	Natural, sunburst	$2,150	$2,800
1972-1979	Double X, block markers	$2,150	$2,800
1980-1985	Double X, block markers	$1,850	$2,400
1985-1988	Single X	$1,450	$1,900
1989	25 1/2" scale	$1,775	$2,300
1990-2019		$1,700	$2,250
1994	100 Years 1894-1994 label	$1,700	$2,250
2019	Black	$2,300	$3,000

Hummingbird Historic Collection
2005-2006. Limited run, Vintage Honeyburst.

2005-2006		$1,850	$2,400

50th Anniversary 1960 Hummingbird
2010-2012. 200 made, 50th Anniversary logo on truss rod cover.

2010-2012		$3,000	$3,900

Hummingbird 12 (Custom Shop)
2005-2011. 12-string, vintage sunburst.

2005-2011		$2,000	$2,600

Hummingbird Artist
2007-2011. Plain (no Hummingbird) small 'guard, L.R. Baggs Element, sold through Guitar Center.

2007-2011		$1,275	$1,650

Hummingbird Custom Koa
2004, 2009-2018. Highly flamed koa back and sides, spruce top, gloss finish.

2004-2018		$3,000	$4,000

Hummingbird Limited Edition
1993-1994. Only 30 made, quilted maple top and back.

1993-1994		$2,300	$3,000

Hummingbird Madagascar Honeyburst
2009. Limited run of 20, figured Madagascar rosewood back and sides, factory electronics, certificate of authenticity.

2009		$2,700	$3,500

Hummingbird Modern Classic
2010-2012. Cherry sunburst or ebony finish, L.R. Baggs Element Active pickup system.

2010-2012		$1,775	$2,300

Hummingbird Pro
2010-2013. Non-cut, plain (no Hummingbird) small 'guard, L.R. Baggs Element, Guitar Center.

2010-2013		$1,125	$1,450

Hummingbird Pro EC
2010-2013. Cutaway version, Fishman Prefix Plus-T, Guitar Center.

2010-2013		$1,200	$1,550

Hummingbird Quilt Series (Custom Shop)

2007-2014		$2,300	$3,000

Hummingbird Studio
2019-present. Slim body, on-board electronics, Antique Natural or Walnut Burst.

2019		$1,300	$1,700

Hummingbird True Vintage
2007-2013. Sitka spruce top, Madagascar rosewood bridge and 'board, special '60s Heritage Cherry or sunburst finish.

2007-2013		$2,500	$3,250

Invader
1983-1988. Single cutaway solid mahogany body, two humbucker pickups, four knobs with three-way selector switch, stop tailpiece, bolt-on maple neck.

1983-1988	All colors	$575	$750

J-15
2014-present. Acoustic-electric dreadnought, slope shoulder, walnut back and sides, antique natural.

2014-2019		$1,000	$1,275

J-25
1983-1985. Flat-top, laminated spruce top, synthetic semi-round back, ebony 'board, natural or sunburst.

1983-1985		$425	$550

J-29 Rosewood
2014-2016. Sitka spruce top, solid rosewood back and sides.

2014-2016		$1,200	$1,550

J-30
1985-1993. Dreadnought-size flat-top acoustic, mahogany back and sides, sunburst, Renamed J-30 Montana in '94.

1985-1993		$1,250	$1,600

J-30 Cutaway
1990-1995. Cutaway version of J-30, transducer pickup.

1990-1995		$1,300	$1,650

J-30 Montana
1994-1997. Renamed from J-30, dreadnought-size flat-top acoustic, mahogany back and sides, sunburst.

1994-1997		$1,250	$1,600

J-30 RCA Limited Edition
1991. Limited edition for RCA Nashville, RCA logo on headstock.

1991		$1,250	$1,600

J-35
2012-2018. Sitka spruce top, mahogany back, sides and neck, rosewood 'board.

2012-2018		$1,125	$1,450

J-40
1971-1982. Dreadnought flat-top, mahogany back and sides, economy satin finish.

1971-1982		$875	$1,125

1963 Gibson Hummingbird
Craig Brody

2012 Gibson J-35
Bernunzio Uptown Music

GUITARS

1968 Gibson J-45
KC Cormack

1957 Gibson J-50
Skip Crum

MODEL YEAR	FEATURES	EXC. COND. LOW	HIGH

J-45

1942-1982, 1984-present. Dreadnought flat-top, mahogany back and sides, round shoulders until '68 and '84 on, square shoulders '69-'82, sunburst finish (see J-50 for natural version) then natural finish also available in '90s, renamed J-45 Western in '94, renamed Early J-45 in '97 then renamed J-45 in '99. The prices noted are for all-original crack free instruments. A single professionally repaired minor crack that is nearly invisible will reduce the value only slightly. Two or more, or unsightly repaired cracks will devalue an otherwise excellent original acoustic instrument. Repaired cracks should be evaluated on a case-by-case basis.

MODEL YEAR	FEATURES	LOW	HIGH
1942-1945	Banner logo, Adirondack	$7,500	$9,700
1942-1945	Banner logo, mahogany	$6,500	$8,500
1945	Banner logo, sitka	$6,000	$7,800
1946-1948	Script logo, sitka	$6,000	$7,800
1949	Small 'guard	$5,500	$7,000
1950-1954		$5,000	$6,500
1955-1959	Big 'guard	$4,200	$5,500
1960-1964	Round shoulders	$3,200	$4,200
1965	Early '65, wide nut	$2,800	$3,700
1965	Late '65, slim nut	$2,300	$3,000
1966-1967	Round shoulders	$2,100	$2,800
1968	Black, Cherry	$3,500	$4,500
1968	Blue, Green	$4,500	$5,800
1968-1969	Sunburst, Gibson 'guard	$2,100	$2,800
1969	Square D-shape, late '69	$1,775	$2,300
1970	Square, sunburst	$1,500	$2,000
1971-1982	Sunburst	$1,300	$1,700
1984-1993	Various colors	$1,300	$1,700
1994-1997	Western	$1,300	$1,700
1997-1998	Early J-45	$1,300	$1,700
1999-2019	Standard	$1,300	$1,700

J-45 1942 Legend
2006-2014. Early J-45 specs, Adirondack red spruce body, mahogany back/sides/neck, rosewood 'board, Vintage Sunburst finish, certificate of authenticity.
| 2006-2014 | | $3,100 | $4,100 |

J-45 1968 Reissue Limited Edition
2004-2007. Special run using '68 specs including Gibson logo 'guard, black or cherry finish.
| 2004-2007 | | $1,300 | $1,700 |

J-45 Brad Paisley
2010-2016. Adirondack red spruce top, mahogany back and sides, cherry sunburst.
| 2010-2016 | | $2,150 | $2,800 |

J-45 Buddy Holly Limited Edition
1995-1996. 250 made.
| 1995-1996 | | $2,150 | $2,800 |

J-45 Celebrity
1985. Acoustic introduced for Gibson's 90th anniversary, spruce top, rosewood back and sides, ebony 'board, binding on body and 'board, only 90 made.
| 1985 | | $1,350 | $1,750 |

J-45 Custom
1999-present. Custom logo on truss rod, maple, mahogany or rosewood body, abalone trim, fancy headstock inlay.
| 1999-2019 | Various woods | $1,500 | $3,000 |

J-45 Custom Vine
1999-2010. Custom Shop, Indian rosewood back and sides, fancy pearl and abalone vine inlay in ebony 'board, pearl Gibson logo and crown, natural gloss finish.
| 1999-2010 | | $2,500 | $3,200 |

J-45 Elite Mystic
2014. Figured back, limited edition, rosewood back and sides.
| 2014 | | $1,925 | $2,500 |

J-45 Heart of Texas Rosewood
2004. Custom Shop, soundhole label signed by Master Luthier Ren Ferguson, Indian rosewood back and sides, abalone top trim.
| 2004 | | $2,750 | $3,600 |

J-45 Historic
2005. Limited edition, 670 made, Historic Collection logo rear headstock, sunburst.
| 2005 | | $1,600 | $2,100 |

J-45 John Hiatt
2010-2011. Signature on truss rod cover, 100 offered, Tri Burst top with Tobacco Brown back and sides.
| 2010-2011 | | $2,000 | $2,600 |

J-45 Natural Anniversary Limited Edition
2009. Custom Shop decal on headstock back, 20 made, spruce top, maple neck, zebrawood back and sides, natural finish.
| 2009 | | $2,000 | $2,600 |

J-45 Red Spruce Edition
2007. Custom Shop limited edition, only 50 made.
| 2007 | | $2,200 | $2,850 |

J-45 Rosewood
1999-2006. Indian rosewood body, spruce top.
| 1999-2006 | | $1,300 | $1,700 |

J-45 True Vintage/J-45 Vintage
2007-2019. Part of Vintage Series, vintage sunburst finish. True dropped from name in '19.
| 2007-2019 | | $1,850 | $2,400 |

J-45 Walnut Limited Edition
2015. Adirondack, flamed walnut.
| 2015 | | $2,000 | $2,600 |

Working Man 45 (J-45)
1998-2005. Soft shoulder J-45 style, gloss finish spruce top, satin finish mahogany back and sides, dot markers, natural.
| 1998-2005 | | $975 | $1,250 |

J-50
1942, 1945-1981, 1990-1995, 1998-2008 (present). Dreadnought flat-top, mahogany back and sides, round shoulders until '68, square shoulders after, natural finish (see J-45 for sunburst version). Though not labeled J-50, the J-45 Standard is now also available in natural finish.
1945	Banner logo	$6,000	$7,800
1946-1949		$5,100	$6,600
1950-1954	Small 'guard	$4,200	$5,400

MODEL YEAR	FEATURES	EXC. COND. LOW	HIGH
1955	Big 'guard	$3,800	$5,000
1956-1959	Standard fixed bridge	$3,700	$4,800
1960-1964	Round shoulders	$3,100	$4,000
1965	Early '65, wide nut	$2,800	$3,600
1965	Late '65, slim nut	$2,800	$3,600
1966-1968	Round shoulders	$2,000	$2,600
1969	Round shoulders	$1,850	$2,400
1969	Square D-shape, late '69	$1,600	$2,100
1970-1981	Square shoulders	$1,325	$1,700
1990-2008		$1,325	$1,700

J-55 (Jumbo 55) Limited Edition
1994 only. 16" flat-top, spruce top, mahogany back and sides, 100 made, sunburst.

1994		$1,400	$1,825

J-55 (Reintroduced)
1973-1982. Flat-top, laminated mahogany back and sides, arched back, square shoulders, sunburst. See Jumbo 55 listing for '39-'43 version.

1973-1982		$950	$1,225

J-60 Curly Maple
1993 and 1996. Curly maple back and sides, limited edition from Montana shop, natural.

1993,1996		$1,525	$2,000

J-60/J-60 Traditional
1992-1999. Solid spruce top dreadnought, square shoulders, Indian rosewood back and sides, ebony 'board, multiple bindings, natural or sunburst.

1992-1999		$1,200	$1,550

J-100/J-100 Custom
1970-1974, 1985-1997. Flat-top jumbo, multi-bound top and back, black 'guard, dot inlays, mahogany back and sides, '80s version has maple back and sides, dot inlays and tortoise shell 'guard, '90s model has maple back and sides, no 'guard, and J-200 style block inlays.

1970-1974	Mahogany	$1,150	$1,500
1985-1997	Maple	$1,150	$1,500

J-100 Xtra
1991-1997, 1999-2004. Jumbo flat-top, mahogany back and sides, moustache bridge, dot inlays, various colors, J-100 Xtra Cutaway also available, reintroduced in '99 with maple back and sides and single-bound body.

1991-2004		$1,150	$1,500

J-150/SJ-150 Maple
1999-2008. Super jumbo body, solid spruce top, figured maple back and sides (rosewood in '05), MOP crown inlays, moustache bridge with transducer. Renamed SJ-150 in 2006.

1999-2005	J-150	$1,500	$1,950
2006-2008	SJ-150	$1,500	$1,950

J-160E
1954-1979. Flat-top jumbo acoustic, 1 bridge P-90 pickup, tone and volume controls on front, sunburst finish, reintroduced as J-160 in '90.

1954-1964		$4,200	$5,400
1965		$3,200	$4,200
1966-1969		$2,800	$3,700
1970-1979		$1,700	$2,200

J-160E Reissue/Standard/VS
1990-1997, 2003-2008. Reintroduced J-160E with solid spruce top, solid mahogany back and sides.

1990-2008		$1,525	$2,000

J-160E John Lennon Peace
2003-2013. J-160E with tortoise 'guard, natural, signature on truss rod cover.

2003-2013		$1,750	$2,300

J-160E John Lennon Peace Limited Edition
2009. Certificate of authenticity, 750 made.

2009		$1,900	$2,475

J-160E Montana Special
1995 only.

1995		$1,525	$2,000

J-160 VS/John Lennon 70th
2010. Commemorative edition for John Lennon's 70th birthday, 500 made, vintage sunburst gloss finish.

2010		$1,700	$2,200

J-165 (Maple)
See CJ-165 listing.

J-180/Everly Brothers/The Everly Brothers
1986-2005. Reissue of the '62-'72 Everly Brothers model, renamed The Everly Brothers ('92-'94), then The Everly ('94-'96), then back to J-180, black.

1986-2005		$1,775	$2,300

J-180 Billy Jo Armstrong
2011. Certificate of authenticity, 300 made.

2011		$2,000	$2,600

J-180 Special Edition
1993. Gibson Bozeman, only 36 made, Everly Brother specs, large double white pearloid 'guard.

1993		$2,100	$2,700

J-185/J-185N
1951-1959. Flat-top jumbo, figured maple back and sides, bound body and neck, sunburst (185) or natural (185N).

1951-1959	Natural, sunburst	$11,000	$14,500

J-185 Reissue
1990-1995, 1999-2018. Flat-top jumbo, figured maple back and sides, bound body and neck, natural or sunburst, limited run of 100 between '91-'92.

1990-2018		$1,675	$2,200

1951 J-185 (Centennial Model)
1994-1995. Oct. '94 Centennial model, limited run of 100.

1994-1995		$2,800	$3,650

J-185 Custom Vine
2004-2012. J-185 with abalone and mother-of-pearl vine 'board inlay.

2004-2012		$2,100	$2,700

J-185 EC
1999-2018. Acoustic/electric, rounded cutaway, maple back and sides. Replaced EC-30 Blues King.

1999-2018		$1,550	$2,000

J-185 EC Custom
2005. Limited Edition, 200 made, spruce top, figured maple sides and back, pearl double parallelogram markers, Fishman Prefix Plus on-board electronics.

2005		$1,550	$2,000

1999 Gibson J-150
Ted Wulfers

2007 Gibson J-185 Reissue

To get the most from this book, be sure to read "Using *The Guide*" in the introduction.

1967 Gibson J-200
Bernunzio Uptown Music

*Gibson Johnny A
Signature Series*

Imaged by Heritage Auctions, HA.com

MODEL YEAR	FEATURES	EXC. COND. LOW	HIGH

J-185 EC Quilt
2002. Quilted maple top, flamed maple body.

| 2002 | | $2,300 | $3,000 |

J-185 EC Rosewood
2006-2018. Acoustic/electric, rounded cutaway, Indian rosewood back and sides.

| 2006-2018 | | $1,550 | $2,000 |

J-185-12
2001-2004. 12-string J-185, flamed maple sides and back.

| 2001-2004 | | $1,675 | $2,200 |

J-190 EC Super Fusion
2001-2004. Jumbo single cut acoustic/electric, spruce top, curly maple back and sides, neck pickup and Fishman Piezo.

| 2001-2004 | | $1,500 | $2,000 |

J-200/SJ-200/J-200N/SJ-200N
1946-present. Labeled SJ-200 until ca.'54. Super Jumbo flat-top, maple back and sides, see Super Jumbo 200 for '38-'42 rosewood back and sides model, called J-200 Artist for a time in the mid-'70s, renamed '50s Super Jumbo 200 in '97 and again renamed SJ-200 Reissue in '99. Currently again called the SJ-200. 200N indicates natural option.

1946-1949	Natural, sunburst	$10,500	$14,000
1950-1959	Natural, sunburst	$9,500	$12,500
1960-1964	Natural, sunburst	$8,000	$10,500
1965	Natural, sunburst	$5,700	$7,400
1966	Natural, sunburst	$4,900	$6,400
1967-1969	Natural, sunburst	$5,000	$6,500
1970-1979	Natural, sunburst	$2,800	$3,600
1972	Artist (label)	$2,800	$3,600
1980-1989	Natural, sunburst	$2,550	$3,300
1990-1999	Natural, sunburst	$2,550	$3,300
2000-2019	Natural, sunburst	$2,550	$3,300

J-200 Celebrity
1985-1987. Acoustic introduced for Gibson's 90th anniversary, spruce top, rosewood back, sides and 'board, binding on body and 'board, sunburst, only 90 made.

| 1985-1987 | | $2,450 | $3,200 |

J-200 Custom
2009-2013. Additional abalone trim, gold hardware, sunburst or natural. Model name also used in 1993 on J-200 with tree-of-life fingerboard inlay.

| 2009-2013 | | $2,700 | $3,500 |

J-200 Deluxe Rosewood
1993-1996. Rosewood back and sides, abalone trim, gold hardware, sunburst or natural.

| 1993-1996 | | $3,400 | $4,400 |

J-200 E
1986-1987. Built in Nashville, on-board volume control, sunburst.

| 1986-1987 | | $2,550 | $3,300 |

J-200 Elvis Presley Signature
2002. 250 made, large block letter Elvis Presley name on 'board, figured maple sides and back, gloss natural spruce top, black and white custom designed 'guard after one of Presley's personal guitars.

| 2002 | | $3,000 | $3,900 |

J-200 Jr.
1991-1996, 2002. Smaller 16" body, sunburst, natural, black or cherry.

| 1991-1996 | | $1,550 | $2,000 |

J-200 Koa
1994-2013. Figured Hawaiian Koa back and sides, spruce top, natural.

| 1994-2013 | | $2,450 | $3,200 |

J-200 M Trophy 75th Anniversary
2012-2013. Quilt maple back and sides, rosewood 'board, abalone crown inlays, antique natural or vintage sunburst nitrocellulose finish.

| 2012-2013 | | $2,450 | $3,200 |

J-200 Montana Gold Flame Maple
1998-2012. SJ-200 design, AAA Sitka spruce top with Eastern curly maple back and sides, ebony 'board, Custom Montana Gold banner peghead logo, antique natural.

| 1998-2012 | | $2,450 | $3,200 |

J-200 Montana Western Classic Supreme
2016. Spruce top, rosewood back and sides, maple neck, Sunset Burst finish.

| 2016 | | $3,300 | $4,300 |

J-200 Rose
1994-1995. Centennial Series model, based on Emmylou Harris' guitar, black finish, rose 'guard, gold tuners, 100 built.

| 1994-1995 | | $3,500 | $4,500 |

J-200 Rosewood
1991, 1994-1996. Made in Bozeman, rosewood back and sides.

| 1991-1996 | | $3,000 | $4,000 |

J-200 Studio
2009-2018. Studio logo on truss rod cover, unbound 'board, plain 'guard.

| 2009-2018 | | $2,000 | $2,600 |

J-200 Western Classic Pre-War
1999-2012. Indian rosewood.

| 1999-2012 | | $2,450 | $3,200 |

J-200 Western Classic Pre-War 200 Brazilian
2003. Based on Ray Whitley's 1937 J-200, Custom Shop, limited production, Brazilian rosewood back and sides.

| 2003 | | $5,700 | $7,500 |

J-200/SJ-200 Ron Wood
1997. Based on a '57 SJ-200 with Wood's oversized double 'guard on either side of the sound hole, flame-pattern fretboard inlays, script signature inlay on headstock, natural.

| 1997 | | $3,200 | $4,200 |

J-250 Monarch/SJ-250 Monarch
1995-2018. Rosewood back and sides, maple neck, ebony 'board, abalone trim, certificate of authenticity.

| 1995-2018 | | $10,000 | $13,000 |

J-250 R
1972-1973, 1976-1978. A J-200 with rosewood back and sides, sunburst, only 20 shipped from Gibson.

| 1972-1978 | | $2,800 | $3,600 |

MODEL YEAR	FEATURES	EXC. COND. LOW	HIGH

J-1000/SJ-1000

1992-1994. Jumbo cutaway, spruce top, rosewood back and sides, on-board electronics, diamond-shape markers and headstock inlay.

1992-1994		$1,825	$2,350

J-1500

1992. Jumbo cutaway flat-top, higher-end appointments including Nick Lucas-style position markers, sunburst.

1992		$1,900	$2,450

J-2000/J-2000 Custom/J-2000 R

1986, 1992-1999. Cutaway acoustic, rosewood back and sides (a few had Brazilian rosewood or maple bodies), ebony 'board and bridge, Sitka spruce top, multiple bindings, sunburst or natural. Name changed to J-2000 Custom in '93 when it became available only on a custom-order basis.

1986-1999	All models	$3,100	$4,000

Jackson Browne Signature

2011-2016. Based on '30s Jumbo style with increased body depth and upgraded tonewoods, Model 1 without pickup, Model A with pickups, Adirondack red spruce top, English walnut back and sides, nitro lacquer sunburst finish.

2011-2016	Model 1	$2,900	$3,800
2011-2016	Model A	$2,900	$3,800

JG-0

1970-1972. Economy square shouldered jumbo, follows Jubilee model in '70.

1970-1972		$750	$975

JG-12

1970. Economy square shouldered jumbo 12-string, follows Jubilee-12 model in '70.

1970		$750	$975

Johnny A Signature Series

2004-2013. Thinline semi-hollow, sharp double-cut, flamed maple top, humbuckers, gold hardware, Bigsby, sunburst, includes certificate of authenticity.

2004-2013	Includes rare color option	$2,550	$3,350

Johnny Smith/Johnny Smith Double

1961-1989. Single-cut archtop, 1 or 2 humbucker pickups, gold hardware, multiple binding front and back, natural or sunburst. By '80 cataloged as JS and JSD models.

1961-1964		$9,200	$12,000
1965		$5,800	$7,500
1966-1969		$5,500	$7,000
1970-1989		$5,000	$6,700

Jubilee

1969-1970. Flat-top, laminated mahogany back and sides, single bound body, natural with black back and sides.

1969-1970		$750	$975

Jubilee Deluxe

1970-1971. Flat-top, laminated rosewood back and sides, multi-bound body, natural finish.

1970-1971		$750	$975

Jubilee-12

1969-1970. Flat-top, 12 strings, laminated mahogany back and sides, multi-bound, natural.

1969-1970		$750	$975

Jumbo

1934-1936. Gibson's first Jumbo flat-top, mahogany back and sides, round shoulders, bound top and back, sunburst, becomes the 16" Jumbo 35 in late-'36.

1934	Unbound	$17,700	$23,000
1935-1936	Bound	$13,100	$17,000

Jumbo 35/J-35

1936-1942. Jumbo flat-top, mahogany back and sides, silkscreen logo, sunburst, reintroduced as J-35, square-shouldered dreadnought, in '83.

1936-1938	Sunburst, 3 tone bars	$10,500	$13,500
1939	Natural, 3 tone bars	$10,100	$13,100
1939	Sunburst, 3 tone bars	$10,100	$13,100
1940-1942	Sunburst, 2 tone bars	$7,700	$10,000

Jumbo 55/J-55

1939-1943. Flat-top dreadnought, round shoulders, mahogany back and sides, pearl inlaid logo, sunburst, reintroduced in '73 as J-55.

1939-1940	Stairstep	$11,500	$15,000
1941-1943	Non-stairstep	$9,500	$12,300

Jumbo Centennial Special

1994. Reissue of 1934 Jumbo, natural, 100 made.

1994		$2,000	$2,600

Junior Pro

1987-1989. Single-cut, mahogany body, KB-X tremolo system 1 humbucker pickup, black chrome hardware, various colors.

1987-1989		$425	$550

Kalamazoo Award Model

1978-1981. Single-cut archtop, bound f-holes, multibound top and back, 1 mini-humbucker, gold-plated hardware, woodgrain 'guard with bird and branch abalone inlay, highly figured natural or sunburst.

1978-1981	Natural	$10,500	$13,500
1978-1981	Sunburst	$10,500	$13,500

Keb' Mo' Royale

2016. Limited to 50, aged Adirondack red spruce top, vintage sunburst finish, label signed by artist, includes certificate of authenticity.

2016		$2,100	$2,700

Keb' Mo' Signature Bluesmaster

2010-2015. Limited run of 300, small-bodied flat-top acoustic, Baggs pickup, soundhole-mounted volume control, vintage sunburst or antique natural finish.

2010-2015		$1,900	$2,450

Kiefer Sutherland KS-336

2007. Custom Shop model inspired by Artist Series.

2007		$2,800	$3,600

KZ II

1980-1981. Double-cut solidbody, 2 humbuckers, 4 knob and toggle controls, tune-o-matic, dot markers, stencil Gibson logo on headstock, KZ II logo on truss rod cover, walnut stain finish.

1980		$750	$975

1960s Gibson Johnny Smith Double
Freedom Guitars

1980 Gibson Kalamazoo Award Model

GUITARS

1933 Gibson L-00
Bernunzio Uptown Music

Gibson L-1 Robert Johnson

MODEL YEAR	FEATURES	EXC. COND. LOW	HIGH
L-0			
1926-1933, 1937-1942. Acoustic flat-top, maple back and sides '26-'27, mahogany after.			
1926-1928	135", maple	$3,700	$4,800
1928-1930	135", mahogany	$3,700	$4,800
1931-1933	1475"	$3,900	$5,000
1937-1942	Reissue, spruce top	$3,900	$5,000
L-00			
1932-1946. Acoustic flat-top, mahogany back and sides, bound top to '36 and bound top and back '37 on.			
1932-1946		$3,900	$5,000
L-00 1937 Legend			
2006-2016. Part of the Vintage Series.			
2006-2016		$2,800	$3,650
L-00 Standard			
2016-present. Small body, sitka spruce top, mahogany back and sides, Vintage Sunburst nitro finish.			
2016-2019		$1,925	$2,500
L-00 Sustainable			
2018-present. Sitka spruce top, richlite 'board and bridge made from recycled trees pulp, Antique Natural.			
2018-2019		$1,100	$1,400
L-00/Blues King			
1991-1997, 1999-2019. Reintroduced as L-00, called Blues King L-00 for '94-'97, back as L-00 for '99-'02, called Blues King '03-present.			
1991-1997	L-00/Blues King	$1,350	$1,800
2003-2019	Blues King	$1,350	$1,800
L-1 (Archtop)			
1902-1925. Acoustic archtop, single-bound top, back and soundhole, name continued on flat-top model in '26.			
1902-1907	125"	$1,500	$1,950
1908-1919	135"	$1,500	$1,950
1920-1925	135", Loar era	$1,500	$1,950
L-1 (Flat-Top)			
1926-1937. Acoustic flat-top, maple back and sides '26-'27, mahogany after.			
1926-1929	135", 12-fret	$3,600	$4,700
1930-1931	1475", 13-fret	$3,600	$4,700
1932-1937	14-fret	$3,900	$5,000
L-1 1928 Blues Tribute			
2014-2018. Adirondack red spruce top, mahogany back and sides, rosewood 'board, faded Vintage Sunburst.			
2014-2018		$2,050	$2,700
L-1 Robert Johnson			
2007-2016. 1926 specs, Robert Johnson inlay at end of 'board.			
2007-2016		$1,425	$1,850
L-1 Special			
2016. Adirondack red spruce top, limited edition of 75.			
2016		$1,900	$2,450
L-2 (Archtop)			
1902-1926. Round soundhole archtop, pearl inlay on peghead, 1902-'07 available in 3 body sizes: 12.5" to 16", '24-'26 13.5" body width.			
1902-1907	125"	$1,500	$1,950
1924-1926	135"	$1,500	$1,950

MODEL YEAR	FEATURES	EXC. COND. LOW	HIGH
L-2 (Flat-Top)			
1929-1935. Acoustic flat-top, rosewood back and sides except for mahogany in '31, triple-bound top and back, limited edition model in '94.			
1929-1933	Brazilian	$11,000	$14,300
1931-1932	Mahogany	$8,800	$11,500
L-2 1929 Reissue			
1994 only. Spruce top, Indian rosewood back and sides, raised 'guard.			
1994		$1,800	$2,325
L-3 (Archtop)			
1902-1933. Acoustic archtop, available in 3 sizes: 12.5", 13.5", 16".			
1902-1907	125", round hole	$1,900	$2,500
1908-1919	135", round hole	$1,900	$2,500
1920		$1,900	$2,500
1921-1926	Loar era	$1,900	$2,500
1927-1928	135", oval hole	$1,900	$2,500
1929-1933	135", round hole	$1,900	$2,500
L-4			
1912-1956. Acoustic archtop, 16" wide.			
1912-1919	12-fret, oval hole	$2,150	$2,850
1920		$2,150	$2,850
1921-1924	Loar era	$2,150	$2,850
1925-1927	12-fret, oval hole	$2,150	$2,850
1928-1934	14-fret, round hole	$2,250	$3,000
1935-1946	Fleur-de-lis, f-holes	$2,650	$3,500
1947-1949	Crown, double-parallel	$2,650	$3,500
1950-1956		$2,475	$3,300
L-4 A/L-4 A EC			
2003-2008. 15 3/4" lower bout, mid-size jumbo, rounded cutaway, factory electronics with preamp.			
2003-2008		$1,350	$1,750
L-4 C/L-4 CN			
1949-1971. Single-cut acoustic archtop, sunburst or natural (CN).			
1949-1959	Natural	$4,200	$5,500
1949-1959	Sunburst	$3,900	$5,000
1960-1964	Natural	$3,900	$5,000
1960-1964	Sunburst	$3,300	$4,300
1965	Natural	$2,800	$3,600
1965	Sunburst	$2,500	$3,200
1966-1969	Natural, sunburst	$1,925	$2,500
1970-1971	Natural, sunburst	$1,400	$1,825
L-4 CES/L-4 CES Mahogany			
1958, 1969, 1986-2018. Single pointed cutaway archtop, 2 humbuckers, gold parts, natural or sunburst, maple back and sides '58 and '69, mahogany laminate back and sides for '86-'93, became part of Gibson's Historic Collection with laminated maple back and sides for '94, renamed L-4			
CES Mahogany with solid mahogany back and sides in '04, Custom Shop model.			
1958	Natural, PAF hums	$9,800	$12,700
1958	Sunburst, PAF hums	$9,000	$11,700
1969	Natural, sunburst	$3,100	$4,000
1986-1993	Laminate mahogany	$2,400	$3,100

MODEL YEAR	FEATURES	EXC. COND. LOW	HIGH
1994-2003	Laminate maple	$2,400	$3,100
2004-2018	Solid mahogany	$2,400	$3,100

L-4 Special Tenor/Plectrum

Late-1920s. Limited edition 4-string flat-top.

1929		$1,850	$2,400

L-5 '34 Non-Cutaway Historic

1994. 1934 specs including block pearl inlays, bound snakehead peghead, close grained solid spruce top, figured solid maple sides and back, Cremona Brown sunburst finish, replica Grover open back tuners.

1994		$4,200	$5,400

L-5 Premier/L-5 P

1939-1947. Introduced as L-5 Premier (L-5 P) and renamed L-5 C in '48, single rounded cutaway acoustic archtop.

1939-1947	Sunburst	$10,700	$14,000

L-5 Premier/L-5 P/L-5 PN

1939-1947. Introduced as L-5 Premier (L-5 P) and renamed L-5 C in '48, single rounded cutaway acoustic archtop, sunburst or natural option (PN).

1939-1947	Natural option	$12,400	$16,100

L-5/L-5N

1924-1958. Acoustic archtop, non-cut, multiple bindings, Lloyd Loar label in '24, 17" body by '35, Master Model label until '27, sunburst with natural option later.

MODEL YEAR	FEATURES	EXC. COND. LOW	HIGH
1924	Loar era, '24 ship date	$43,000	$55,000
1925	According to specs, early '25 ship date	$42,000	$54,000
1925	According to specs, late '25 ship date	$30,000	$50,000
1926	According to specs, '26 ship date	$30,000	$50,000
1927	According to specs, '27 ship date	$30,000	$50,000
1928-1929	Values vary according to specs	$20,000	$30,000
1930-1932	Values vary according to specs	$15,000	$30,000
1933-1939	16" body, values vary according to specs	$5,500	$10,000
1935-1940	17" body, values vary according to specs	$4,000	$8,200
1939-1940	Natural option, values per specs	$6,500	$9,200
1946-1949	Natural option, values per specs	$5,500	$10,000
1946-1949	Sunburst, values per specs	$4,000	$7,000
1950-1958	Natural	$5,000	$6,700
1950-1958	Sunburst	$3,700	$6,500

L-5 C/L-5 CN

1948-1982. Renamed from L-5 Premier (L-5 P), single rounded cutaway acoustic archtop, sunburst or natural option (CN)

MODEL YEAR	FEATURES	EXC. COND. LOW	HIGH
1948-1949	Natural	$11,000	$14,400
1948-1949	Sunburst	$9,500	$12,400
1950-1959	Natural	$9,500	$12,400
1950-1959	Sunburst	$8,300	$10,800
1960-1964	Natural	$8,300	$10,900
1960-1964	Sunburst	$7,000	$9,100
1965	Natural	$6,400	$8,400
1965	Sunburst	$5,700	$7,500
1966-1969	Natural	$5,300	$7,000
1966-1969	Sunburst	$5,000	$6,500
1970-1982	Natural, sunburst	$3,900	$5,000

L-5 CES/L-5 CESN

1951-2018. Electric version of L-5 C, single round cutaway (pointed mid-'60-'69), archtop, 2 pickups (P-90s '51-'53, Alnico Vs '54-mid-'57, humbuckers after), sunburst or natural (CESN), now part of Gibson's Historic Collection.

MODEL YEAR	FEATURES	EXC. COND. LOW	HIGH
1951-1957	Natural, single coils	$15,200	$19,800
1951-1957	Sunburst, single coils	$13,100	$17,000
1958-1959	Natural, PAFs	$19,200	$24,800
1958-1959	Sunburst, PAFs	$16,000	$20,500
1960-1962	Natural, PAFs	$17,000	$22,500
1960-1962	Sunburst, PAFs	$15,000	$19,500
1963-1964	Natural, pat #	$12,000	$17,000
1963-1964	Sunburst, pat #	$9,000	$14,000
1965	Natural	$8,500	$11,000
1965	Sunburst	$8,500	$11,000
1966-1969	Natural	$6,700	$8,700
1966-1969	Sunburst	$6,000	$7,700
1970-1979	Natural, sunburst	$5,000	$6,500
1980-1984	Kalamazoo made	$5,000	$6,500
1985-1992	Nashville made	$5,000	$6,500

L-5 CES (Custom Shop/Historic Collection)

1994-1997. Historic Collection series, sunburst or natural.

MODEL YEAR	FEATURES	EXC. COND. LOW	HIGH
1994	100th Anniv, black	$5,000	$6,500
1994-1996	Natural, highly figured	$5,000	$6,500
1994-1996	Sunburst	$5,000	$6,500
1997	Wine Red	$5,000	$6,500

L-5 CT (George Gobel)

1959-1961. Single-cut, thinline archtop acoustic, some were built with pickups, cherry.

1959-1961		$15,500	$20,000

L-5 CT Reissue

1998-2007. Historic Collection, acoustic and electric versions, natural, sunburst, cherry.

1998-2007		$4,600	$6,000

L-5 S

1972-1985, 2004-2005. Single-cut solidbody, multibound body and neck, gold hardware, 2 pickups (low impedance '72-'74, humbuckers '75 on), offered in natural, cherry sunburst or vintage sunburst. 1 humbucker version issued in '04 from Gibson's Custom, Art & Historic division.

1972-2005	All options	$3,700	$4,800

1917 Gibson L-3
Frank Manno

1939 Gibson L-5N
Dr. Jazz

GUITARS

1975 Gibson L-6 S
Keith Myers

1967 Gibson L-7 CN
Imaged by Heritage Auctions, HA.com

MODEL YEAR	FEATURES	EXC. COND. LOW	HIGH

L-5 S Ron Wood
2015. Custom Shop, limited run of 250 with 1st 50 signed by Ron, certificate of authenticity, 2 Burstbucker pickups, ebony gloss finish.

2015		$3,700	$4,800

L-5 Signature
2001-2004. Carved spruce top, AAA maple back, tangerineburst or vintage sunburst.

2001-2004		$4,700	$6,100

L-5 Studio
1996-2000. Normal L-5 dual pickup features, marble-style 'guard, translucent finish, dot markers.

1996-2000		$2,100	$2,700

L-5 Wes Montgomery Custom Shop
1993-2018. Various colors.

1993-2018		$5,000	$6,500

L-6 S
1973-1975. Single-cut solidbody, 2 humbucking pickups, 6 position rotary switch, stop tailpiece, cherry or natural. Renamed L-6 S Custom in '75.

1973-1975		$1,000	$1,300

L-6 S Custom
1975-1980. Renamed from the L-6 S, 2 humbucking pickups, stop tailpiece, cherry or natural.

1975-1980		$1,000	$1,300
1978-1980	Silverburst option	$1,000	$1,300

L-6 S Deluxe
1975-1981. Single-cut solidbody, 2 humbucking pickups, no rotary switch, strings-thru-body design, cherry or natural.

1975-1981		$1,125	$1,450

L-6 S Reissue
2011-2012. With rotary switch, 2 humbuckers, natural or silverburst.

2011-2012		$700	$925

L-7/L-7N
1932-1956. Acoustic archtop, bound body and neck, fleur-de-lis peghead inlay, 16" body '32-'34, 17" body X-braced top late-'34, sunburst or natural (N).

1932-1934	16" body	$3,000	$3,900
1935-1939	17" body, X-braced	$3,000	$3,900
1940-1949	Natural	$2,900	$3,800
1940-1949	Sunburst	$2,500	$3,300
1950-1956	Natural	$2,700	$3,500
1950-1956	Sunburst	$2,400	$3,100

L-7 C/L-7 CN
1948-1972, 2002-2013. Single-cut acoustic archtop, triple-bound top, sunburst or natural (CN). Gibson revived the L-7 C name for a new acoustic archtop in 2002.

1948-1949	Natural	$3,900	$5,200
1948-1949	Sunburst	$3,300	$4,400
1950-1959	Natural	$3,500	$4,700
1950-1959	Sunburst	$3,000	$4,000
1960-1964	Natural	$3,100	$4,200
1960-1964	Sunburst	$2,900	$3,900
1965	Natural	$2,900	$3,900
1965	Sunburst	$2,700	$3,600
1966-1972	Natural	$2,800	$3,700
1966-1972	Sunburst	$2,400	$3,200

L-7 Custom Electric
1936. L-7 with factory Christian-style pickup, limited production, often custom ordered.

1936		$7,400	$10,000

L-7 E/L-7 CE
1948-1954. L-7 and L-7 C with "McCarty" assembly of pickguard-mounted pickups (1 or 2), sunburst only.

1948-1954	L-7 CE	$4,000	$5,200
1948-1954	L-7 E	$3,300	$4,300

L-7 C Custom Shop
2006. Custom Shop logo, Certificate of Authenticity.

2006		$3,300	$4,400

L-10
1923-1939. Acoustic archtop, single-bound body and 'board, black or sunburst (added in '35).

1923-1934	16", F-holes	$4,100	$5,400
1935-1939	17", X-braced	$4,100	$5,400

L-12
1930-1955. Acoustic archtop, single-bound body, 'guard, neck and headstock, gold-plated hardware, sunburst.

1930-1934	16"	$4,500	$5,900
1935-1939	17", X-braced	$4,500	$5,900
1940-1941	Parallel top braced	$4,500	$5,900
1946-1949	Post-war	$2,800	$3,600
1950-1955		$2,600	$3,400

L-12 Premier/L-12 P
1947-1950. L-12 with rounded cutaway, sunburst.

1947-1950		$3,800	$4,900

L-20 20th Anniversary Limited Edition
2009. Custom Shop, 20 made, "20th Anniversary" logo on back of headstock and on label, Certificate of Authenticity.

2009		$2,625	$3,400

L-20 Special/L-20 K International Special
1993-1994. Rosewood or mahogany back and sides (koa on the K), ebony 'board, block inlays, gold tuners, multi-bound.

1993-1994	L-20, mahogany	$1,625	$2,100
1993-1994	L-20, rosewood	$1,625	$2,100
1993-1994	L-20K, koa	$1,625	$2,100

L-30
1935-1943. Acoustic archtop, single-bound body, black or sunburst.

1935-1943		$950	$1,225

L-37
1937-1941. 14-3/4" acoustic archtop, flat back, single-bound body and 'guard, sunburst.

1937-1941		$1,000	$1,300

L-47
1940-1942. Acoustic archtop.

1940-1942		$1,100	$1,425

L-48
1946-1971. 16" acoustic archtop, single-bound body, mahogany sides, sunburst.

1946-1949		$1,125	$1,450
1950-1959		$1,025	$1,325
1960-1964		$1,075	$1,400
1965		$800	$1,050
1966-1969		$700	$900
1970-1971		$625	$800

The ***Vintage Guitar Price Guide*** shows low to high values for items in all-original excellent condition, and, where applicable, with original case or cover.

MODEL YEAR	FEATURES	EXC. COND. LOW	HIGH

L-50

1932-1971. 14.75" acoustic archtop, flat or arched back, round soundhole or f-holes, pearl logo pre-war, decal logo post-war, maple sides, sunburst, 16" body late-'34.

1932-1934	1475" body	$1,750	$2,300
1934-1943	16" body	$1,750	$2,300
1946-1949	16", trapezoids	$1,675	$2,200
1950-1959		$1,400	$1,850
1960-1964		$1,350	$1,750
1965		$1,100	$1,450
1966-1969		$925	$1,200
1970-1971		$850	$1,100

L-75

1932-1939. 14.75" archtop with round soundhole and flat back, size increased to 16" with arched back in '35, small button tuners, dot markers, lower-end style trapeze tailpiece, pearl script logo, sunburst.

1932	1475", dot neck	$1,900	$2,450
1933-1934	1475", pearloid	$1,900	$2,450
1935-1939	16" body	$1,900	$2,450

L-130

1999-2005. 14 7/8" lower bout, small jumbo, solid spruce top, solid bubinga back and sides, rosewood 'board, factory electronics with preamp.

1999-2005		$1,025	$1,325

L-140

1999-2005. Like L-130 but with rosewood back and sides, ebony 'board.

1999-2005		$1,150	$1,500

L-200 Emmylou Harris

2001-2016. Smaller and thinner than standard 200, flamed maple sides and back, gold hardware, crest markers, natural or sunburst.

2001-2016		$1,900	$2,450

L-C Century

1933-1939. Curly maple back and sides, bound body, white pearloid 'board and peghead (all years) and headstock (until '38), sunburst.

1933-1938	Pearloid	$4,800	$6,300
1939		$4,400	$5,700

L-C Century Elvis Costello Limited

2016. Signed custom label, pearloid 'board, Adirondack red spruce top, AAA flamed maple back and sides, 300 made.

2016		$3,800	$4,900

L-C Century Reissue

1994. Pearloid headstock and 'board.

1994		$2,050	$2,650

LC-1 Cascade

2002-2006. LC-Series acoustic/electric, advanced L-00-style, solid quilted maple back and sides.

2002-2006		$1,275	$1,650

LC-2 Sonoma

2002-2006. Released November '02, LC-Series acoustic/electric, advanced L-00-style, solid walnut back and sides.

2002-2006		$1,525	$1,975

MODEL YEAR	FEATURES	EXC. COND. LOW	HIGH

LC-3 Caldera

2003-2004. 14 3/4" flat-top, soft cutaway, solid cedar top, solid flamed Koa back and sides, fancy appointments.

2003-2004		$1,625	$2,075

Le Grande

1993-2010. Electric archtop, 17", formerly called Johnny Smith.

1993-2010		$5,000	$6,700

Les Paul

Following are models bearing the Les Paul name, beginning with the one that started it all, the original Les Paul Model. All others are then listed pretty much alphabetically as follows:

Les Paul Model
'52 Les Paul Goldtop
'52 Les Paul Tribute
'54 Les Paul Goldtop
'54 Les Paul Wildwood
'55 Les Paul Goldtop Hot-Mod Wraptail
'56 Les Paul Goldtop
'57 Les Paul Goldtop
'57 Les Paul Goldtop (R-7 wrap-around)
1957 Les Paul Junior Single Cut (VOS)
'58 Les Paul Figured Top
'58 Les Paul Plaintop (VOS)
1958 Les Paul Junior Double Cut (VOS)
'59 Les Paul Flametop/Reissue/Standard
'59 Les Paul Burst Brothers
'59 Les Paul Plaintop (VOS)
True Historic 1959 Les Paul
'60 Les Paul Corvette
'60 Les Paul Flametop/Standard '60s
'60 Les Paul Plaintop (VOS)
'60 Les Paul Junior
'60 Les Paul Special
True Historic 1960 Les Paul
Les Paul 10th Anniversary Chambered '58 Reissue
Les Paul 25/50 Anniversary
Les Paul 30th Anniversary
Les Paul 40th Anniversary (from 1952)
Les Paul 40th Anniversary (from 1959)
Les Paul 50th Anniversary (Historic Custom Shop)
Les Paul 50th Anniversary 1956 Les Paul Standard
Les Paul 50th Anniversary 1957 Les Paul Standard Goldtop
Les Paul 50th Anniversary 1959 Les Paul Standard
Les Paul 50th Anniversary 1960 Les Paul Standard
Les Paul 50th Anniversary DaPra
Les Paul 50th Anniversary Korina Tribute
Les Paul 50th Anniversary Les Paul Standard (Sweetwater)
Les Paul 55
Les Paul (All Maple)
Les Paul Ace Frehley "Budokan" LP Custom

1937 Gibson L-37
Robbie Keene

2016 Gibson L-C Century Elvis Costello Limited

GUITARS

1952 Gibson Les Paul Model
Imaged by Heritage Auctions, HA.com

1953 Gibson Les Paul Model

Les Paul Ace Frehley Signature
Les Paul Artisan and Artisan/3
Les Paul Artist/L.P. Artist/Les Paul Active
Les Paul Axcess Alex Lifeson
Les Paul Axcess Dave Amato
Les Paul Axcess Standard
Les Paul BFG
Les Paul Billy F. Gibbons Goldtop
Les Paul Bird's-Eye Standard
Les Paul Carved Series
Les Paul Catalina
Les Paul Centennial ('56 LP Standard Goldtop)
Les Paul Centennial ('59 LP Special)
Les Paul Class 5
Les Paul Classic
Les Paul Classic 1960 Mars Music
Les Paul Classic Antique Mahogany
Les Paul Classic Custom
Les Paul Classic H-90
Les Paul Classic Limited Edition
Les Paul Classic Mark III/MIII
Les Paul Classic Plus
Les Paul Classic Premium Plus
Les Paul Classic Premium Plus Custom Shop
Les Paul Classic Tom Morgan Limited Edition
Les Paul Cloud 9 Series
Les Paul Collector's Choice Series
Les Paul Custom
Les Paul Custom 20th Anniversary
Les Paul Custom 25
Les Paul Custom 25th Anniversary
Les Paul Custom 35th Anniversary
Les Paul Custom '54
Les Paul Custom Historic '54
Les Paul Custom Historic '57 Black Beauty
Les Paul Custom Historic '68
Les Paul Custom Jimmy Page
Les Paul Custom Lite
Les Paul Custom Lite (Show Case Edition)
Les Paul Custom Mick Ronson '68
Les Paul Custom Music Machine
Les Paul Custom Peter Frampton Signature
Les Paul Custom Plus
Les Paul Custom Showcase Edition
Les Paul Custom Silverburst
Les Paul Dale Earnhardt
Les Paul Dale Earnhardt Intimidator
Les Paul Dark Fire
Les Paul Dark Knight Quilt Top
Les Paul DC AA
Les Paul DC Classic
Les Paul DC Pro
Les Paul DC Standard (Plus)
Les Paul DC Studio
Les Paul Deluxe
Les Paul Deluxe 30th Anniversary
Les Paul Deluxe '69 Reissue
Les Paul Deluxe Hall of Fame
Les Paul Deluxe Limited Edition
Les Paul Deluxe Limited Edition AMS
Les Paul Deluxe Reissue
Les Paul Deluxe #1 Pete Townshend
Les Paul Deluxe #3 Pete Townshend

Les Paul Deluxe #9 Pete Townshend
Les Paul Dickey Betts Goldtop
Les Paul Dickey Betts Red Top
Les Paul Don Felder Hotel California 1959
Les Paul Duane Allman (Custom Shop)
Les Paul Duane Allman Hot 'Lanta (Custom Shop)
Les Paul Dusk Tiger
Les Paul Elegant
Les Paul Elegant Streak Silver
Les Paul Eric Clapton 1960
Les Paul ES-Les Paul
Les Paul Florentine Plus
Les Paul Supreme Florentine
Les Paul Futura
Les Paul Gary Moore BFG
Les Paul Gary Moore Signature
Les Paul Gary Rossington Signature
Les Paul Goddess
Les Paul Government Series II
Les Paul GT
Les Paul Guitar Trader Reissue
Les Paul HD.6-X Pro Digital
Les Paul Heritage 80
Les Paul Heritage 80 Award
Les Paul Heritage 80 Elite
Les Paul Heritage 80/Standard 80
Les Paul Hot Rod Magazine '58 Standard
Les Paul Indian Motorcycle
Les Paul Jeff Beck 1954 Oxblood
Les Paul Jim Beam (Custom Shop)
Les Paul Jimmy Page "Number Two"
Les Paul Jimmy Page (Custom Authentic)
Les Paul Jimmy Page Signature
Les Paul Jimmy Page Signature Custom Shop
Les Paul Jimmy Wallace Reissue
Les Paul Joe Bonamassa Aged Goldtop
Les Paul Joe Bonamassa Bonabyrd
Les Paul Joe Bonamassa Skinnerburst 1959
Les Paul Joe Bonamassa 'Tomato Soup Burst' Limited Edition
Les Paul Joe Perry 1959 Custom Shop
Les Paul Joe Perry Signature
Les Paul Jumbo
Les Paul Junior
Les Paul Junior 3/4
Les Paul Junior Billie Joe Armstrong Signature
Les Paul Junior DC Hall of Fame
Les Paul Junior Double Cutaway
Les Paul Junior Faded
Les Paul Junior John Lennon LTD
Les Paul Junior Lite
Les Paul Junior Special
Les Paul Junior Special Robot
Les Paul Junior Tenor/Plectrum
Les Paul 2016 Limited Run Series
Les Paul Katrina
Les Paul KM (Kalamazoo Model)
Les Paul Korina (Custom Shop)
Les Paul Leo's Reissue
Les Paul Limited Edition (3-tone)
Les Paul Lou Pallo Signature
Les Paul LP-295 Goldtop

MODEL YEAR	FEATURES	EXC. COND. LOW	HIGH
Les Paul DC Standard (Plus)			
1998-1999, 2001-2006. Offset double-cut, highly flamed maple top, translucent lacquer finishes in various colors, reintroduced as Standard Lite in '99 but without Les Paul designation on headstock or truss rod cover.			
1998-1999		$1,125	$1,475
2001-2006		$1,125	$1,475
Les Paul DC Studio			
1997-1999. DC Series double-cut like late '50s models, carved maple top, 2 humbucker pickups, various colors.			
1997-1999		$625	$825
Les Paul Deluxe			
1969-1985. In 1969, the Goldtop Les Paul Standard was renamed the Deluxe. Two mini-humbuckers (regular humbuckers optional in mid-'70s). Mid-'70s sparkle tops are worth more than standard finishes. The market slightly favors the Goldtop finish, but practically speaking condition is more important than finish, such that all finishes fetch about the same amount (with the exception of the sparkle finish). Initially, the Deluxe was offered only as a Goldtop and the first year models are more highly prized than the others. Cherry sunburst was offered in '71, cherry in '71-'75, walnut in '71-'72, brown sunburst in '72-'79, natural in '75, red sparkle in '73-'75 only, blue sparkle in '73-'77, wine red/see-thru red offered '75-'85. In '99, the Deluxe was reissued for its 30th anniversary.			
1969	Goldtop	$4,650	$6,050
1970	Goldtop	$3,800	$4,900
1971-1975	Goldtop	$3,000	$4,000
1971-1975	Natural	$2,300	$3,000
1971-1975	Red (solid)	$2,300	$3,000
1971-1975	Sunburst	$2,300	$3,000
1971-1975	Wine	$2,300	$3,000
1973-1975	Red sparkle, fewer made	$3,500	$4,600
1973-1977	Blue sparkle, more made	$3,200	$4,200
1976-1979	All other colors	$2,000	$2,800
1976-1979	Goldtop	$2,800	$3,600
1976-1979	Natural	$2,300	$3,000
1976-1979	Sunburst	$2,300	$3,000
1980-1985	Various colors	$2,000	$2,800
Les Paul Deluxe 30th Anniversary			
1999. Limited Edition logo on the lower back of the headstock, Deluxe logo on truss rod cover, Wine Red.			
1999		$1,100	$1,500
Les Paul Deluxe '69 Reissue			
2000-2005. Mini-humbuckers, gold top			
2000-2005		$1,300	$1,675
Les Paul Deluxe Hall of Fame			
1991. All gold finish.			
1991		$1,550	$2,000
Les Paul Deluxe Limited Edition			
1999-2002. Limited edition reissue with Les Paul Standard features and Deluxe mini-humbuckers, black.			
1999-2002		$1,350	$1,750

MODEL YEAR	FEATURES	EXC. COND. LOW	HIGH
Les Paul Deluxe Limited Edition AMS			
2014. Limited edition chocolate finish, offered only by American Musical Supply.			
2014		$400	$525
Les Paul Deluxe Reissue			
2012. Mini-humbuckers, chambered body.			
2012		$1,675	$2,200
Les Paul Deluxe #1 Pete Townshend			
2006. Limited to 75, red.			
2006		$5,100	$6,600
Les Paul Deluxe #3 Pete Townshend			
2006. Limited to 75, goldtop.			
2006		$5,100	$6,600
Les Paul Deluxe #9 Pete Townshend			
2006. Limited to 75, cherry burst.			
2006		$5,100	$6,600
Les Paul Dickey Betts Goldtop			
2001-2003. Aged gold top.			
2001-2003		$5,100	$6,600
Les Paul Dickey Betts Red Top			
2003. Transparent red, gold hardware.			
2003		$3,600	$4,700
Les Paul Don Felder Hotel California 1959			
2010. Custom Shop, '59 sunburst specs, 50 Murphy aged and signed by Felder, 100 aged, and 150 in VOS finish.			
2010	Aged, signed	$6,100	$7,900
2010	Aged, unsigned	$5,500	$7,200
2010	VOS	$4,700	$6,100
Les Paul Duane Allman (Custom Shop)			
2013. Custom Shop certificate, Murphy Aged or VOS, 150 made of each.			
2013	Aged	$6,400	$8,300
2013	VOS	$4,900	$6,300
Les Paul Duane Allman Hot 'Lanta (Custom Shop)			
2003. "DUANE" spelled out in fret wire on back, Custom Shop certificate, 55 made.			
2003		$16,500	$21,500
Les Paul Dusk Tiger			
Late-2009-2012. Limited edition, 1000 to be made, features Gibson's Robot Technology, Burstbucker bridge, P-90H neck and 6 Piezo pickups.			
2009-2012		$1,675	$2,175
Les Paul Elegant			
1996-2004. Custom Shop, highly flamed maple top, abalone crown markers and Custom Shop headstock inlay.			
1996-2004		$2,500	$3,250
Les Paul Elegant Streak Silver			
1999. Custom Shop, Flow Silver finish, made for Mars Music.			
1999		$1,850	$2,400
Les Paul Eric Clapton 1960			
2011. Nicknamed the Beano Burst, '60 thinner 'Clapton' neck profile, Custom Bucker pickups, nickel-plated Grover kidney button tuners, lightly figured maple cap, traditional 17-degree angled headstock, total of 500 made; 55 Murphy Aged and signed by Clapton, 95 unsigned Murphy Aged, 350 finished with Gibson's VOS treatment.			
2011	Aged	$6,400	$8,300
2011	Aged, signed	$15,500	$20,500
2011	VOS	$5,200	$6,800

1973 Gibson Les Paul Deluxe
Rich Goldman

1976 Gibson Les Paul Deluxe
Ted Wulfers

GUITARS

Gibson Les Paul Gary Moore BFG

1982 Gibson Les Paul Heritage 80
Sam Gabriel

MODEL YEAR	FEATURES	EXC. COND. LOW	HIGH

Les Paul ES-Les Paul
2014-2018. Semi-hollow Les Paul body with f-holes, 3-ply maple/basswood/maple top and back, mahogany neck with maple spline, dark rosewood 'board, 2 pickups, light burst or black.

2014-2018		$1,575	$2,050

Les Paul Florentine Plus
1997-2001. Custom Shop model, hollowbody with f-holes, higher-end appointments.

1997-2001		$2,600	$3,400

Les Paul Supreme Florentine
2009-2015. Les Paul Standard with sharp Florentine cutaway, 350 made, Bigsby tailpiece, chambered mahogany body, highly figured maple top and back, Caribbean Blue finish.

2009-2015		$2,150	$2,800

Les Paul Futura
2014-2015. Light weight, unbound, Min-Etune, various bright colors.

2014-2015		$675	$875

Les Paul Gary Moore BFG
2009-2012. Plain appointment BFG specs, P-90 neck pickup and Burstbucker 3 bridge pickup.

2009-2012		$1,025	$1,325

Les Paul Gary Moore Signature
2000-2002. Signature Series model, Gary Moore script logo on truss rod cover, flamed maple top.

2000-2002		$2,225	$2,875

Les Paul Gary Rossington Signature
2002. GR serial number, replica of his '59 LP Standard, Custom Shop, aged finish, 250 made, includes display case with backdrop photo of Rossington, price includes certificate with matching serial number.

2002		$6,900	$8,900

Les Paul Goddess
2006-2007. Maple carved top, trapezoid inlays, smaller body, 2 humbuckers, 2 controls, tune-a-matic bridge.

2007		$1,000	$1,300

Les Paul Government Series II
2014-2018. 2 Dirty Fingers pickups, certificate of authenticity, Government Tan finish.

2013-2018		$900	$1,175

Les Paul GT
2007. Includes over/under dual truss rods, GT logo on truss rod cover, several specs designed to add durability during heavy professional use.

2007		$1,300	$1,675

Les Paul Guitar Trader Reissue
1982-1983. Special order flametop Les Paul by the Guitar Trader Company, Redbank, New Jersey. Approximately 47 were built, the first 15 guitars ordered received original PAFs, all were double black bobbins (except 1 Zebra and 1 double white), 3 of the guitars were made in the '60-style. The PAF equipped models were based on order date and not build date. The serial number series started with 9 1001 and a second serial number was put in the control cavity based upon the standard Gibson serial number system, which allowed for exact build date identification. Gibson's pickup designer in the early-'80s was Tim Shaw and

the pickups used for the last 32 guitars have been nicknamed Shaw PAFs. After Gibson's short run for Guitar Trader, 10 non-Gibson replica Les Pauls were made. These guitars have a poorly done Gibson logo and other telltale issues.

1982-1983	Actual PAFs installed	$9,000	$11,700
1982-1983	Shaw PAFs, highly flamed	$4,000	$5,200
1982-1983	Shaw PAFs, low flame	$3,500	$4,600

Les Paul HD.6-X Pro Digital
2008-2009. Digital sound system, hex pickups.

2008-2009		$1,900	$2,500

Les Paul Heritage 80
1980-1982. Copy of '59 Les Paul Standard, curly maple top, mahogany body, rosewood 'board, nickel hardware, sunburst. In '80 cataloged as Les Paul Standard-80 without reference to Heritage, the catalog notes that the guitar has Heritage Series truss rod cover.

1980-1982	Figured top	$3,750	$4,850
1980-1982	Plain top	$2,925	$3,825

Les Paul Heritage 80 Award
1982. Ebony 'board, 1-piece mahogany neck, gold-plated hardware, sunburst.

1982	Figured	$4,425	$5,750
1982	Highly figured	$5,425	$7,050

Les Paul Heritage 80 Elite
1980-1982. Copy of '59 Les Paul Standard, quilted maple top, mahogany body and neck, ebony 'board, chrome hardware, sunburst. In '80 cataloged as Les Paul Standard-80 Elite without reference to Heritage, the catalog notes that the guitar has the distinctive Heritage Series truss rod cover.

1980-1982		$4,100	$5,350

Les Paul Heritage 80/Standard 80
1982. Based on '57 Les Paul Standard Goldtop, Heritage Series Standard 80 logo on truss rod cover.

1982		$3,150	$4,125

Les Paul Hot Rod Magazine '58 Standard
2008. Custom Shop, Hot Rod inspired flames over a figured-maple top, Hot Rod truss rod cover.

2008		$3,000	$4,000

Les Paul Indian Motorcycle
2002. 100 made, has Indian script logo on fretboard and chrome cast war bonnet on the body, crimson red and cream white.

2002		$3,000	$4,000

Les Paul Jeff Beck 1954 Oxblood
2009. Custom Shop, limited run of 150, 1st 50 aged, hand-signed and played by Beck, next 100 VOS, mahogany body, carved maple top, rosewood 'board, Burstbucker humbucking pickups, Oxblood finish.

2009		$4,000	$5,200

Les Paul Jim Beam (Custom Shop)
Ca. 2002-2003. JBLP serial number series, several versions of Jim Beam logo art on top of guitar, award-ribbon-style B Bean logo on headstock, around 75 made.

2002-2003		$1,325	$1,725

The **VINTAGE GUITAR Price Guide** shows low to high values for items in all-original excellent condition, and, where applicable, with original case or cover.

MODEL YEAR	FEATURES	EXC. COND. LOW	HIGH

Les Paul Jimmy Page "Number Two"

2009-2010. Custom Shop, 1st 25 aged and signed, 100 aged and unsigned, 200 VOS.

2009-2010		$9,000	$12,000

Les Paul Jimmy Page (Custom Authentic)

2004-2006. Custom Shop, includes certificate.

2004-2006		$6,500	$8,400

Les Paul Jimmy Page Signature

1995-1999. Jimmy Page signature on 'guard, mid-grade figured top, push-pull knobs for phasing and coil-tapping, Grover tuners, gold-plated hardware. This is not the '04 Custom Shop Jimmy Page Signature Series Les Paul (see separate listing).

1995	1st year, highly figured	$5,000	$6,500
1995	1st year, low figure	$4,100	$5,300
1995	1st year, moderate figure	$4,400	$5,700
1996-1999	Highly figured	$4,100	$5,300
1996-1999	Low figure	$2,700	$3,500
1996-1999	Moderate figure	$3,450	$4,400

Les Paul Jimmy Page Signature Custom Shop

2004. January '04 NAMM Show, 175 planned production, the first 25 were personally inspected, played-in, and autographed by Jimmy Page. Initial retail price for first 25 was $25,000, the remaining 150 instruments had an initial retail price of $16,400. Cosmetically aged by Tom Murphy to resemble Page's No. 1 Les Paul in color fade, weight, top flame, slab cut attribution on the edges, neck size and profile.

2004	1st 25 made	$13,500	$17,500
2004	26-150	$10,500	$13,500

Les Paul Jimmy Wallace Reissue

1978-1997. Les Paul Standard '59 reissue with Jimmy Wallace on truss rod cover, special order by dealer Jimmy Wallace, figured maple top, sunburst.

1978-1983	Kalamazoo-made, high flame	$3,500	$4,600
1978-1983	Kalamazoo-made, low flame	$2,900	$3,800
1983-1989	Nashville-made	$2,900	$3,800
1990-1997		$2,900	$3,800

Les Paul Joe Bonamassa Aged Goldtop

2008. Inspired By Series, LP Standard aged goldtop with black trim (including black pickup rings), serial number starts with BONAMASSA.

2008		$2,350	$3,050

Les Paul Joe Bonamassa Bonabyrd

2015-2016. Limited Edition, 100 made each signed by Joe, plain maple top, retro Firebird headstock, Indian rosewood 'board, 2 Custom Bucker pickups, Antique Pelham Blue finish.

2015-2016		$4,600	$6,000

Les Paul Joe Bonamassa Skinnerburst 1959

2014. Custom Shop, recreation of '59 Les Paul, 150 Murphy aged (first 50 signed by Joe) and 150 VOS, faded Dirty Lemon finish.

2014	All options	$5,500	$8,500

Les Paul Joe Bonamassa 'Tomato Soup Burst' Limited Edition

2016. Limited run of 150, AAA flamed maple top, mahogany back and neck, rosewood 'board, Tomato Soup Burst finish.

2016		$2,900	$3,800

Les Paul Joe Perry 1959 Custom Shop

2013. Custom Shop, recreation of '59 Les Paul, 150 Murphy aged (first 50 signed by Perry) and 150 VOS, faded Tobacco Sunburst finish.

2013		$8,500	$11,000

Les Paul Joe Perry Signature

1997-2001. Unbound slab body with push-pull knobs and Joe Perry signature below bridge, Bone-Yard logo model with typical Les Paul Standard bound body, configuration and appointments.

1997-2001	Bone-Yard option with logo	$1,525	$1,975
1997-2001	Unbound standard model	$1,525	$1,975

Les Paul Jumbo

1969-1970. Single rounded cutaway, flat-top dreadnought acoustic/electric, 1 pickup, rosewood back and sides, natural.

1969-1970		$2,600	$3,400

Les Paul Junior

1954-1963, 1986-1992, 2001-2002, 2005-2013. One P-90 pickup, single-cut solidbody '54-mid-'58, double-cut '58-early-'61, SG body '61-'63, renamed SG Jr. in '63, reintroduced as single-cut for '86-'92, reissued as the 1957 Les Paul Jr. Single Cutaway in '98. Headstock repair reduces the value by 40%-50%. Reinstalled tuners reduces the value by 5% to 10%. Replaced tuner buttons reduces the value by 5% to 10%.

1954-1958	Sunburst, single-cut	$4,800	$6,200
1958-1961	Cherry, double-cut	$4,600	$6,000
1961-1963	Cherry, SG body	$3,000	$4,000
1986-1992	Sunburst, single-cut, tune-o-matic	$600	$800
1998-2013	Sunburst, single-cut, stop tail	$600	$800

Les Paul Junior 3/4

1956-1961. One P-90 pickup, short-scale, single-cut solidbody '54-mid-'58, double-cut '58-early-'61.

1956-1958	Sunburst, single-cut	$2,400	$3,100
1958-1961	Cherry, double-cut	$2,100	$2,700

Les Paul Junior Billie Joe Armstrong Signature

2006-2013. 1956 LP Junior specs.

2006-2013		$950	$1,225

Les Paul Junior DC Hall of Fame

1990-1992. Part of Hall of Fame Series, limited run of LP Junior Double Cutaway but with P-100 pickup.

1990-1992		$600	$800

Les Paul Junior Double Cutaway

1986-1992, 1995-1996. Copy of '50s double-cut Jr., cherry or sunburst, reissued as the 1958 Les Paul Jr. Double Cutaway in '98.

1986-1989		$600	$800

2002 Gibson Les Paul Indian Motorcycle

1957 Gibson Les Paul Junior

Frank Thoubboron

GUITARS

2010 Gibson Les Paul Michael Bloomfield 1959 Standard

2005 Gibson Les Paul Neal Schon Signature

Wayne Stephens

MODEL YEAR	FEATURES	EXC. COND. LOW	HIGH
Les Paul Junior Faded			
2010-2012. Single-cut, faded cherry finish.			
2010-2012		$525	$700
Les Paul Junior John Lennon LTD			
2008. Custom Shop, 300 made, Charlie Christian neck pickup and P-90 bridge as per Lennon's modified Junior, aged-relic finish, certificate, book and New York t-shirt.			
2008		$3,000	$3,900
Les Paul Junior Lite			
1999-2002. Double-cut, Tune-o-matic, 2 P-100 pickups, stop tail, mini-trapezoid markers, burnt cherry gloss finish.			
1999-2002		$575	$750
Les Paul Junior Special			
1999-2004. LP Jr. single-cut slab body with 2 P-90s (making it a Special) instead of the standard single P-90, double pickup controls, cherry, tinted natural or sunburst.			
1999-2004		$625	$825
Les Paul Junior Special Robot			
2008. P-90s, TV Yellow.			
2008		$650	$850
Les Paul Junior Tenor/Plectrum			
Late-1950s. Four string neck on Junior body, cherry.			
1959		$3,400	$4,400
Les Paul 2016 Limited Run Series			
Various limited edition models released in 2016.			
2016-2018	LP Fort Knox	$2,450	$3,200
2016-2018	LP Pete Townshend Deluxe	$2,450	$3,200
2016-2018	LP Redwood	$2,450	$3,200
2016-2018	LP Standard Figured Walnut	$2,450	$3,200
2016-2018	LP Sunken Treasure	$2,450	$3,200
2016-2018	Mahogany Limited	$2,450	$3,200
Les Paul Katrina			
2005. 300 made in cooperation with Music Rising Foundation and the Edge U2.			
2005		$2,100	$2,700
Les Paul KM (Kalamazoo Model)			
1979. Regular Les Paul Standard with 2 exposed humbuckers, KM on headstock, sunburst, approximately 1500 were made in the Kalamazoo plant.			
1979		$2,400	$3,100
Les Paul Korina (Custom Shop)			
1999. Limited run with figured Korina top, Custom Shop logo on back of headstock.			
1999		$2,425	$3,125
Les Paul Leo's Reissue			
1980-1985. Special order from Gibson's Nashville facility for Leo's Music, Oakland, California. Identified by serial number with L at the beginning, flamed maple top. About 800 guitars were made, with about 400 being exported to Japan. Kalamazoo-made Leo's have a 2nd serial number in the control cavity, Nashville-made Leo's do not have a 2nd serial number.			
1980-1983	Kalamazoo-made, high flame	$4,200	$5,600

MODEL YEAR	FEATURES	EXC. COND. LOW	HIGH
1980-1983	Kalamazoo-made, low flame	$3,200	$4,300
1983-1985	Nashville-made	$3,000	$4,300
Les Paul Limited Edition (3-tone)			
1997. Limited Edition stamped on the back of the headstock, Les Paul Standard configuration with cloud inlay markers, 2-piece 3-tone sunburst finish over non-figured maple top.			
1997		$1,825	$2,400
Les Paul Lou Pallo Signature			
2010. Maple top, mahogany back and neck, rosewood 'board, 2 pickups, ebony finish.			
2010		$1,525	$2,000
Les Paul LP-295 Goldtop			
2008. Guitar of the Month (April, '08), limited run of 1000, Les Paul body style, goldtop, 2 humbuckers, ES-295 appointments such as 'guard and fretboard markers, Bigsby tailpiece option.			
2008		$1,950	$2,550
Les Paul Marc Bolan			
2011. Artist model with certificate of authenticity, limited run of 100 hand aged and 350 VOS, Bolan Chablis finish.			
2011		$3,600	$4,800
Les Paul Menace			
2006-2007. Carved mahogany body, 2 humbucker pickups.			
2006-2007		$500	$650
Les Paul Michael Bloomfield 1959 Standard			
2009-2011. Custom Shop, limited production of 100 Murphy-aged and 200 VOS, matching certificate of authenticity.			
2009-2011		$5,400	$7,000
Les Paul Modern			
2017-present. New light-weight features, mahogany body with maple top, back is natural finish, top with faded pelham blue, sparkling burgundy or graphite black.			
2017-2020		$1,500	$3,000
Les Paul Music Machine 25th Anniversary			
2002. Custom run for dealer Music Machine with special serial number series, 14 flame top and 14 quilt top instruments were produced, Music Machine 25th Anniversary logo on truss rod cover, special cherry sunburst finish.			
2002	Flame top	$4,100	$5,400
2002	Quilt top	$3,700	$4,800
Les Paul Music Machine Brazilian Stinger			
2003. Custom run for dealer Music Machine with special serial number series, Brazilian rosewood 'board, black stinger paint on back of neck-headstock, '59 or '60 reissue body and neck profile options, highly figured flame or quilt top options, other reissue options available.			
2003	'54, '56 or '58, figured flame or quilt	$8,800	$11,500
2003	'54, '56 or '58, goldtop	$5,500	$8,500
2003	'59 or '60, figured flame or quilt	$9,000	$12,000
2003	'59 or '60, plain top	$7,900	$10,500

MODEL YEAR	FEATURES	EXC. COND. LOW	HIGH

Les Paul Neal Schon Signature
2005. Custom Shop, 80 made, Floyd Rose tremolo, signature on truss rod cover, COA, black.

| 2005 | | $8,000 | $10,500 |

Les Paul Old Hickory
1998 only. Limited run of 200, tulip poplar body wood from The Hermitage, Custom-style trim.

| 1998 | | $3,200 | $4,200 |

Les Paul Paul Kossoff 1959 Standard
2012-2013. Custom Shop, 100 aged and 250 VOS made, green lemon finish, certificate of authenticity.

| 2012-2013 | Aged | $4,600 | $6,000 |
| 2012-2013 | VOS | $4,200 | $5,500 |

Les Paul Peace
2014-2015. AA top, rosewood 'board, 2 pickups, various color finishes.

| 2014-2015 | | $1,400 | $1,800 |

Les Paul Personal
1969-1972. Two angled, low impedance pickups, phase switch, gold parts, walnut finish.

| 1969-1972 | | $1,550 | $2,050 |

Les Paul Pro Deluxe
1978-1982. Chrome hardware, 2 P-90s, various colors. Les Pauls could vary significantly in weight during the '70s and '80s and lighter-weight examples may be worth up to 25% more than these values.

| 1978-1982 | | $1,850 | $2,450 |

Les Paul Pro Showcase Edition
1988. Goldtop 1956 specs, Showcase Edition decal, 200 made.

| 1988 | | $2,275 | $2,950 |

Les Paul Professional
1969-1971, 1977-1979. Single-cut, 2 angled, low impedance pickups, carved top, walnut or white.

| 1969-1971 | Walnut | $1,775 | $2,300 |
| 1969-1971 | White | $2,425 | $3,150 |

Les Paul Recording
1971-1979. Two angled, low impedance pickups, high/low impedance selector switch, walnut '71-'77, white added '75, natural, ebony and sunburst added '78.

1971-1977	Walnut	$1,775	$2,300
1975-1979	White	$2,425	$3,150
1978-1979	Black, Natural, Sunburst	$1,875	$2,425

Les Paul Reissue Flametop
1983-1990. Flame maple top, 2 humbuckers, thicker '59-style neck, sunburst finish, renamed '59 Les Paul Flametop in '91.

| 1983-1990 | Highly figured | $3,800 | $5,000 |

Les Paul Reissue Goldtop
1983-1991. Goldtop finish, 2 P-100 pickups, renamed '56 Les Paul Goldtop in '91.

| 1983-1991 | | $2,200 | $2,900 |

Les Paul Richard Petty LTD
2003. Richard Petty's image on front and back, 'The King' inlay on fretboard.

| 2003 | | $2,225 | $2,900 |

Les Paul SG '61 Reissue
1993-2003. Renamed the Les Paul SG '61 Reissue from SG '62 Reissue, early '60s Les Paul Standard SG specs with small guard, trapezoid markers, heritage cherry finish, by 2003 the Les Paul script marking was not on the truss rod cover, renamed to SG '61 Reissue.

| 1993-2003 | Stud Tail | $1,325 | $1,700 |

Les Paul SG Standard Authentic
2005. SG '61 specs, small guard, Les Paul truss rod logo, stud tailpiece.

| 2005 | | $1,750 | $2,300 |

Les Paul SG Standard Reissue
2000-2004. Reissue of early-'60s specs including Deluxe Maestro vibrato with lyre tailpiece (stop bar tp offered), small 'guard, holly head veneer, standard color faded cherry, available in Classic White or TV Yellow, becomes the SG Standard Reissue by '05.

| 2000-2004 | Maestro | $1,750 | $2,300 |

Les Paul Signature "T"
2014-2018. Chambered solidbody, 2 exposed split-coil humbuckers, "Les Paul" signature on 'guard, Min-Etune.

| 2014-2018 | | $1,375 | $1,800 |

Les Paul Signature/L.P. Signature
1973-1978. Thin semi-hollowbody, double-cut, 2 low impedance pickups, f-holes, various colors. The Price List refers to it as L.P. Signature.

| 1973-1978 | | $2,650 | $3,450 |

Les Paul Silver Streak
1982. Custom Shop decal, silver finish.

| 1982 | | $2,150 | $2,850 |

Les Paul Slash Appetite
2010-2012. Figured maple top, Slash artwork headstock logo, 2 Alnico II Pro Slash pickups, Appetite Amber finish.

| 2010-2012 | | $3,650 | $4,725 |

Les Paul Slash Appetite For Destruction
2010-2011. Custom Shop, figured maple top, 2 Duncan Slash pickups, butterscotch finish available as VOS or Aged.

| 2010-2011 | VOS | $7,100 | $9,225 |

Les Paul Slash Signature
2008. Slash logo on truss rod, Darkburst, SL serial number series.

| 2008 | | $2,425 | $3,150 |

Les Paul Slash Signature Goldtop
2008. Limited Edition, 1000 made, LP Standard model, Slash logo truss rod cover, Limited Edition logo back of headstock, certificate of authenticity.

| 2008 | | $2,425 | $3,150 |

Les Paul Slash Signature VOS
2008-2010. Inspired By Series, Slash hat logo on body and signature logo on guitar case, plain maple top with faded VOS finish.

| 2008-2010 | | $3,000 | $3,900 |

Les Paul Slash Snakepit
1997. Custom Art Historic, highly figured top, cobra inlay neck, snake and hat on body.

| 1997 | | $20,000 | $26,000 |

Les Paul SM
1980. Solid mahogany, single-cut with coil-tap, Les Paul SM truss rod logo, burgundy or silverburst finish.

| 1980 | Various wood & finish | $1,100 | $2,050 |

1969 Gibson Les Paul Professional
Pete Pensec

1976 Gibson Les Paul Recording Guitar
Craig Brody

GUITARS

1994 Gibson Les Paul Special Centennial

Imaged by Heritage Auctions, HA.com

1958 Gibson Les Standard

Gary's Classic Guitars

MODEL YEAR	FEATURES	EXC. COND. LOW	HIGH
Les Paul SmartWood Exotic			
1998-2001. Full-depth Les Paul-style built with eco-friendly woods, Muiracatiara (or Muir) top, mahogany back, Preciosa 'board, pearloid dots.			
1998-2001		$800	$1,050
Les Paul SmartWood Standard			
1996-2002. Smartwood Series, figured maple top, mahogany body, Smartwood on truss rod cover, antique natural.			
1996-2002		$800	$1,050
Les Paul SmartWood Studio			
2002-2006. Muiracatiara (Muir) top and mahogany back, Preciosa (Prec) 'board, Studio appointments including pearl-style dot markers.			
2002-2006		$700	$900
Les Paul Southern Rock Tribute 1959			
2014-2018. Limited Edition, commemorative medallion on switch-cavity cover, first 50 aged and signed by Southern Rock Ambassadors (Dickey Betts, Charlie Daniels, Gary Rossington, Jimmy Hall), remainder are VOS, reverse burst finish.			
2014-2016	Aged	$4,775	$6,200
2014-2018	VOS	$4,000	$5,150
Les Paul Special			
1955-1959. Slab solidbody, 2 pickups (P-90s in '50s, P-100 stacked humbuckers on later version), single-cut until end of '58, double in '59, the '89 reissue is a single-cut, renamed SG Special in late-'59.			
1955-1959	TV Yellow	$9,000	$11,500
1959	Cherry	$7,100	$9,400
Les Paul Special (Reissue)			
1989-1998, 2002-2006. Briefly introduced as Les Paul Junior II but name changed to Special in the first year, single-cut, 2 P-100 stacked humbuckers, TV Yellow, in '90 there was a run of 300 with LE serial number, renamed Special SL in '98.			
1989-1998	P-100s	$650	$850
2002-2006	Humbuckers	$650	$850
Les Paul Special 100/100 Special			
2015-2016. Reissue double-cut slab body, 2 P-90s, 'Les Paul 100' birthday signature on headstock.			
2015-2016		$625	$825
Les Paul Special 3/4			
1959. Slab solidbody, 2 P-90 pickups, double-cut, short-scale, cherry finish, renamed SG Special 3/4 in late-'59.			
1959		$4,000	$5,150
Les Paul Special Centennial			
1994 only. 100 made, double-cut, cherry, 100 year banner at the 12th fret, diamonds in headstock and in gold-plated knobs, gold-plated Gibson coin in back of headstock.			
1994		$2,700	$3,500
Les Paul Special Double Cutaway			
1976-1979, 1993-1994. Double-cut, 2 P-90s, 1990s version was made in Custom Shop and was reintroduced as the '60 Les Paul Special Historic in '98.			
1976-1979		$1,725	$2,250
1993-1994	Custom Shop	$975	$1,275

MODEL YEAR	FEATURES	EXC. COND. LOW	HIGH
Les Paul Special Faded			
2005-2012. Double- or single-cut, dot markers, 2 P-90s, Special logo on truss rod cover, faded TV limed mahogany or cherry finish.			
2005-2012		$525	$700
Les Paul Special New Century			
2006-2008. Full-body mirror 'guard, 2 exposed humbuckers, single-cut LP Special body, mirror truss rod cover.			
2006-2008		$825	$1,075
Les Paul Special Robot			
2008. Two P-90 pickups, various colors.			
2008	TV Yellow	$775	$1,000
Les Paul Special Tenor			
1959. Four-string electric tenor, LP Special body, TV Yellow.			
1959		$3,600	$4,700
Les Paul Special Worn Cherry			
2003-2006. Single-cut, non-bound LP Special with 2 humbuckers.			
2003-2006		$525	$700
Les Paul Spider-Man			
2002. Custom Shop, superhero depicted on the body, red spider logo, gold hardware, Standard appointments. 15 guitars were produced as a Gibson/Columbia TriStar Home Entertainment/Tower Records promotion, while a larger batch was sold at retail.			
2002		$2,575	$3,350
Les Paul Spotlight Special			
1983-1984. Curly maple and walnut top, 2 humbuckers, gold hardware, multi-bound top, Custom Shop Edition logo, natural or sunburst.			
1983-1984	Figured top	$4,800	$6,200
Les Paul Standard (Sunburst)			

1958-1960, special order 1972-1975. Les Paul Sunbursts from '58-'60 should be individually valued based on originality, color and the amount and type of figure in the maple top, changed tuners or a Bigsby removal will drop the value. Approximately 15% came with the Bigsby tailpiece. The noted price ranges are guidance valuations. Each '58-'60 Les Paul Standard should be evaluated on a case-by-case basis. As is always the case, the low and high ranges are for an all original, excellent condition, undamaged guitar. About 70% of the '58-'60 Les Paul Standards have relatively plain maple tops. The majority of '58-'60 Les Paul Standards have moderate or extreme color fade.

Wider fret wire was introduced in early-'59. White bobbins were introduced in early- to mid-'59. Double ring Kluson Deluxe tuners were introduced in late-'60. It has been suggested that all '58-'60 models have 2-piece centerseam tops. This implies that 1-piece tops, 3-piece tops and off-centerseam tops do not exist.

The terminology of the 'Burst includes: arching medullary grain, swirling medullary grain, ribbon-curl, chevrons, Honey-Amber, receding red aniline, pinstripe, bookmatched, double-white bobbins, zebra bobbins, black bobbins, fiddleback maple, sunburst finish, Honeyburst, lemon drop, quarter sawn, blistered figure, width of gradation, flat sawn, Teaburst, Bigsby-shadow, rift sawn, heel size, aged clear lacquer, 3-dimensional figure, intense fine flame, tag-shadow, red pore filler, Eastern maple fleck, medium-thick flame, shrunk tuners, wave and flame, flitch-matched, elbow discoloration, ambered top coat, natural gradation, grain orientation, script oxidation, asymmetrical figure Tangereneburst, Greenburst, and birdseye.

The bobbins used for the pickup winding were either black or white. The market has determined that white bobbin PAFs are the most highly regarded. Generally speaking, in '58 bobbins were black, in '59 the bobbin component transitioned to white and some guitars have 1 white and 1 black bobbin (aka zebra). In '60, there were zebras and double blacks returned.

Rather than listing separate line items for fade and wood, the Guide lists discounts and premiums as follows. The price ranges shown below are for instruments with excellent color, excellent wood, with the original guitar case. The following discounts and premiums should be considered.

An instrument with moderate or total color fade should be discounted about 10%.

One with a factory Bigsby should be discounted about 10%-15%.

Original jumbo frets are preferred over original small frets and are worth +10%.

MODEL YEAR	FEATURES	EXC. COND. LOW	HIGH
1958	Highly figured	$255,000	$332,000
1958	Minor figured	$190,000	$247,000
1958	Plain top, no figuring	$128,000	$166,000
1959	Highly figured	$322,000	$418,000
1959	Minor figured	$227,000	$295,000
1959	Plain top, no figuring	$146,000	$190,000
1960	Early '60, fat neck, highly figured	$219,000	$285,000
1960	Early '60, fat neck, minor figured	$172,000	$224,000
1960	Early '60, fa neck, plain top	$117,000	$152,000
1960	Late '60, flat neck, highly figured	$209,000	$271,000
1960	Late '60, flat neck, minor figured	$152,000	$198,000
1960	Late '60, flat neck, plain top	$109,000	$142,000

Les Paul Standard (SG body)

1961-1963 (SG body those years). Renamed SG Standard in late-'63.

MODEL YEAR	FEATURES	EXC. COND. LOW	HIGH
1961-1963	Cherry, side vibrola, PAFs	$10,800	$14,000
1962	Cherry, Bigsby, 1 pat #, 1 PAF	$8,500	$11,000
1962-1963	Cherry, side vibrola, pat #	$7,800	$10,100
1962-1963	Ebony block, SG, PAFs, dlx vibrola	$11,700	$15,200
1962-1963	Ebony block, SG, pat #, dlx vibrola	$9,600	$12,500

Les Paul Standard (reintroduced then renamed)

1968-1969. Comes back as a goldtop with P-90s for '68-'69 (renamed Les Paul Deluxe, '69), available as special order Deluxe '72-'76.

MODEL YEAR	FEATURES	EXC. COND. LOW	HIGH
1968	P-90s, small hdsk, no volute	$12,300	$16,000
1968-1969	P-90s, large hdsk	$9,300	$12,000

Les Paul Standard (reintroduced)

1976-July 2008, 2012-2018. Available as special order Deluxe '72-'76, reintroduced with 2 humbuckers '76-present. The '75 Price List shows a Les Paul Standard (B) model which is equipped with a Bigsby tailpiece versus a wraparound, also shows a Les Paul Standard (B) with palm pedal. Replaced by Les Paul Standard 2008 in August '08. Name revived in '12 on chambered-body version with tapped Burstbucker pickups, available in AAA tops, black, Gold Top or Blue Mist finishes.

MODEL YEAR	FEATURES	EXC. COND. LOW	HIGH
1971	Early special order goldtop, P-90s	$7,300	$9,500
1972-1974	Special order goldtop, P-90s	$5,200	$6,800
1972-1974	Special order sunburst, P-90s	$4,475	$5,825
1974-1975	Special order, hums	$4,475	$5,825
1976	Sunburst, 4-piece pancake body	$2,575	$3,350
1976	Wine Red or natural	$2,100	$2,725
1977	Other colors	$2,100	$2,725
1977	Sunburst	$2,575	$3,350
1978	Natural	$2,100	$2,725
1978	Other colors	$2,100	$2,725
1978	Sunburst	$2,575	$3,350
1979	Brown Sunburst	$2,575	$3,350
1979	Cherry Sunburst	$2,575	$3,350
1979	Goldtop	$2,575	$3,350
1979	Natural	$2,100	$2,725
1979	Wine Red	$2,100	$2,725
1980-1986	Black, natural, Wine Red	$2,150	$2,850
1980-1986	Sunburst	$2,150	$2,850
1980-1989	White (RRhoads)	$2,150	$2,850
1981-1982	Goldtop	$2,150	$2,850
1982	Candy Apple Red, gold hw, LD	$2,150	$2,850
1987-1989	Various colors	$2,150	$2,850
1990-1993	Ltd Ed colors with sticker	$2,150	$2,850
1990-1999	White (RRhoads)	$1,700	$2,200
1990-2018	Figured top	$1,900	$2,500
1990-2018	Plain top	$1,600	$2,100
2000-2018	Opague solid color	$1,600	$2,100

Les Paul Standard '50s

2019-present. Mahogany body with maple top, '50s neck profile, 2 Burstbucker pickups, Goldtop, Heritage Cherry Sunburst or Tobacco Burst finish.

MODEL YEAR	FEATURES	EXC. COND. LOW	HIGH
2019-2020		$1,200	$1,550

1959 Gibson Les Paul Standard
Keith Nelson

1962 Gibson Les Paul Standard (SG body)

GUITARS

Gibson Les Paul Studio '60s Tribute

Gibson Les Paul Standard Faded
Ted Mottor

MODEL YEAR	FEATURES	EXC. COND. LOW	HIGH

Les Paul Standard '60s
2019-present. Mahogany body with figured maple top, slim '60s neck profile, 2 Burstbucker pickups, Iced Tea, Bourbon Burst or Unburst finish.

2019-2020		$1,200	$1,550

Les Paul Standard '82
1982. Standard 82 on truss rod cover, made in Kalamazoo, Made in USA stamp on back of the headstock, generally quilted maple tops.

1982		$2,150	$2,850

Les Paul Standard 2008
August 2008-2012. 2008 added to name, chambered mahogany body, new asymmetrical neck profile, locking grovers, plain or AA flamed maple top, Ebony, Gold Top, various sunbursts.

2008-2012	Figured top	$1,900	$2,500
2008-2012	Gold top	$1,700	$2,200
2008-2012	Plain top	$1,600	$2,100

Les Paul Standard 2010 Limited
2010. Robot tuning technology, 2 pickups, scripted "Limited Edition" logo on headstock, Fireball finish.

2010		$1,575	$2,075

Les Paul Standard Billy Gibbons 'Pearly Gates'
2009-2011. Aged - 50 made, Aged and signed - 50 made, V.O.S. - 250 made.

2009-2011	Aged	$8,000	$10,500
2009-2011	VOS	$7,500	$10,000

Les Paul Standard Faded
2005-2008. Figured top, exposed humbuckers, faded satin finish.

2005-2008		$1,600	$2,100

Les Paul Standard Lite
1999-2001. DC body-style, renamed from DC Standard in '99, reintroduced as Les Paul Standard DC Plus in 2001, various translucent finishes, available in 2004 under this name also.

1999-2001		$1,100	$1,425

Les Paul Standard Lite Limited Edition
2014. Thin body LP, Burstbuckers, 3 knobs, coil tap switch, "120th Anniversary" on 12th fret, highly figured flame top or plain top offered.

2014	Plain top	$825	$1,100

Les Paul Standard Mike McCready 1959
2010-2016. Custom Shop, limited to 50 aged and signed, 100 VOS finish.

2010-2016	Aged, signed	$6,100	$7,900
2010-2016	VOS	$5,300	$6,900

Les Paul Standard Plus
1995-2008. Gibson USA model, figured maple top, Vintage Sunburst, Heritage Cherry Sunburst or Honeyburst finish.

1995-2008		$2,000	$2,600

Les Paul Standard Premium Plus
1999-2007. Premium plus flamed maple top.

1999-2007		$2,100	$2,700

Les Paul Standard Raw Power
2000-2001, 2006-2007. Natural gloss finish on maple top, appears to have been a Musician's Friend version in '06-'07.

2000-2001		$1,425	$1,850

Les Paul Standard Rick Nielsen 1959 Aged
2016-2017. Custom Shop, first 50 aged and signed, figured maple top, mahogany back and neck, Indian rosewood 'board, aged or vintage gloss finish.

2016-2017	Signed, first 50	$5,400	$7,300
2016-2017	Unsigned, SNs after 50	$4,200	$5,400

Les Paul Standard Robot
2007. Blueburst finish, robot tuning.

2007		$900	$1,200

Les Paul Standard Showcase Edition
1988. Showcase Edition logo on back of neck, Guitar of the Month, silverburst.

1988		$2,725	$3,550

Les Paul Standard Sparkle
2001. Sparkle holoflake top, reflective back, Standard logo on truss rod.

2001		$1,825	$2,375

Les Paul Strings and Things Standard
1975-1978. Special order flamed maple top Les Paul Standard model, built for Chris Lovell, owner of Strings and Things, a Gibson dealer in Memphis, approximately 28 were built, sunburst. Authentication of a Strings and Things Les Paul is difficult due to no diffinitive attributes, valuation should be on a case-by-case basis.

1975-1978	Figured 2-piece top	$5,900	$7,700
1975-1978	Plain 2-piece top	$4,700	$6,100
1975-1978	Plain 3-piece top	$3,200	$4,200

Les Paul Studio
1983-present. Non bound mahogany body, (early models have alder body), 2 humbuckers, various colors.

1983-2019		$825	$1,075
2009-2012	Silverburst	$825	$1,075

Les Paul Studio 120th Anniversary
2014. Figured maple top, 120th Anniversary badge on 12th fret, vintage gloss finish on various colors.

2014		$825	$1,075

Les Paul Studio '50s Tribute
2010-2016. '56 LP Goldtop specs, P-90s, '50s neck, Tune-o-matic, stopbar tailpiece, chambered unbound body.

2010-2016		$600	$775

Les Paul Studio '60s Tribute
2011-2016. Similar to '50s Tribute except for '60 slim taper neck.

2011-2016		$600	$775

Les Paul Studio '70s Tribute
2012-2016. Similar to '50s Tribute except for '70s neck profile with volute.

2012-2016		$600	$775

Les Paul Studio Baritone
2004-2012. 28" baritone scale, maple top, mahogany back and neck, 2 pickups, nitro gloss honeyburst finish.

2004-2012		$850	$1,100

Les Paul Studio BFD
2007. Studio specs but with BFD electronics.

2007		$550	$725

MODEL YEAR	FEATURES	EXC. COND. LOW	HIGH

Les Paul Studio Custom
1981-1985. 2 humbucking pickups, multi-bound top, gold-plated hardware, various colors.

1981-1985		$1,100	$1,425

Les Paul Studio Deluxe '60s
2010-2012. Exposed pickups, Deluxe logo on truss rod cover, sunburst.

2010-2012		$825	$1,075

Les Paul Studio Faded Vintage Mahogany
2007-2010. Vintage mahogany with faded satin.

2007-2010		$575	$750

Les Paul Studio Faded/Les Paul Studio Pro Faded
2005-2012. Faded sunburst tops. Name changes to Studio Pro Faded in '12, then ends production.

2005-2012		$575	$750

Les Paul Studio Gem
1996-1998. Limited edition with Les Paul Studio features, but using P-90 pickups instead of humbucker pickups, plus trapezoid markers and gold hardware.

1996-1998		$825	$1,075

Les Paul Studio Gothic
2000-2001. Orville Gibson image on back of headstock, single Gibson crescent and star neck marker, Gothic Black with black hardware.

2000-2001		$700	$900

Les Paul Studio Gothic Morte
2011-2012. All-mahogany body, African Obeche 'board, 2 humbuckers, satin ebony finish.

2011-2012		$700	$900

Les Paul Studio Joe Bonamassa
2011-2013. Maple top, mahogany back and neck, 2 Alnico II pickups, goldtop finish.

2011-2013		$1,100	$1,425

Les Paul Studio Limited Edition
1997. P-100 pickups, black.

1997		$700	$900

Les Paul Studio Lite
1987-1998. Carved maple top, mahogany back and neck, 2 humbucker pickups, various colors.

1987-1998		$825	$1,075

Les Paul Studio Lite Mark III/M3/M III
1991-1994. HSH pickup configuration, trans finishes.

1991-1994		$825	$1,075

Les Paul Studio MLB Baseball
2008. Major League Baseball graphics on body, only 30 made, satin finish, dot markers.

2008		$1,150	$1,500

Les Paul Studio Platinum
2004-2006. 2 Humbuckers, no position markers, brushed metal hardware, body, neck and headstock in satin platinum finish, matching platinum hardshell case.

2004-2006		$825	$1,075

Les Paul Studio Platinum Plus
2004-2006. Same as Platinum but with trapezoid markers and black hardshell case.

2004-2006		$825	$1,075

Les Paul Studio Plus
2002-2007. Two-piece AA flamed unbound top, gold hardware, Desert Burst or see-thru black.

2002-2007		$875	$1,125

Les Paul Studio Premium Plus
2006-2008. AAA flamed-maple top.

2006-2008		$1,150	$1,500

Les Paul Studio Raw Power
2009-2012. Unbound maple top, chambered maple body, 2 humbuckers, dots, satin finishes.

2009-2012		$825	$1,075

Les Paul Studio Robot
2007-2011. Robot tuning, trapezoid inlays, silverburst, fireburst, wine red, black, red metallic, green metallic.

2007-2011	All colors	$775	$1,000

Les Paul Studio Robot Limited Edition
2012. 'Chameleon' tone circuit.

2012		$775	$1,000

Les Paul Studio Roland Synthesizer
1985. With Roland 700 synth.

1985		$775	$1,000

Les Paul Studio Shred
2012. Unbound body, trapazoid markers, 2 humbuckers. Floyd Rose, high-gloss ebony nitro finish.

2012		$825	$1,075

Les Paul Studio Standard
1984-1987. Cream top and neck binding, dots.

1984-1987		$1,275	$1,655

Les Paul Studio Swamp Ash
2004-2012. Studio model with swamp ash body.

2004-2012		$825	$1,075

Les Paul Studio USA Anniversary Flood
2011. Commemorating the Nashville flood of May, 2010, blue or green swirl.

2011		$925	$1,200

Les Paul Supreme
2003-2018. Highly figured AAAA maple top and back on translucent finishes only, custom binding, deluxe pearl markers, chambered mahogany body, globe logo or "Supreme" on headstock, solid colors available by '06.

2003-2018	Various tops & colors	$2,150	$2,800

Les Paul Tie Dye (St. Pierre)
1996-1997. Hand colored by George St. Pierre, just over 100 made.

1996-1997		$1,900	$2,500

Les Paul Tie Dye Custom Shop
2002. Limited series of one-off colorful finishes, Custom Shop logo.

2002		$1,900	$2,500

Les Paul Traditional Pro/Pro II
2010-2014. Exposed tapped coil humbuckers, sunbursts, goldtop, ebony or wine red.

2010-2014		$1,350	$1,750

Les Paul Traditional/Plus
2008-2019. Traditional on truss rod, '80s styling with weight-relief holes in an unchambered body, standard appointments. Figured maple (Plus) or opaque color top.

2008-2014	Various	$1,450	$1,900
2008-2019	Plus	$1,550	$2,000

2019 Gibson Les Paul Traditional

1996 Gibson Les Paul Tie Dye (St. Pierre)
Rivington Guitars

To get the most from this book, be sure to read "Using *The Guide*" in the introduction.

GUITARS

1998 Gibson Les Paul Ultima
Imaged by Heritage Auctions, HA.com

2017 Gibson Les Paul J

MODEL YEAR	FEATURES	EXC. COND. LOW	HIGH
Les Paul TV			
1954-1959. Les Paul Jr. with limed mahogany (TV Yellow) finish, single-cut until mid-'58, double-cut after, renamed SG TV (see that listing for more) in late-'59.			
1954-1958	Single-cut	$8,800	$11,500
1958-1959	Double-cut	$8,000	$10,500
Les Paul TV 3/4			
1954-1957. Limed mahogany (TV Yellow) Les Paul Jr. 3/4, short-scale, single-cut.			
1954-1957		$4,050	$5,250
Les Paul Ultima			
1996-2007. Custom Shop, flame or quilt sunburst, abalone and mother-of-pearl tree of life, harp, or flame fingerboard inlay, multi abalone bound body.			
1996-2007		$5,800	$7,500
Les Paul Ultra-Aged 1959 Murphy			
2012. Custom Shop, Bigsby optional, aged by Tom Murphy.			
2012		$4,100	$5,300
Les Paul Vixen			
2006-2007. Les Paul Special single-cut slab body, dot markers, 2 humbuckers, 2 controls, wrap-around bridge.			
2006-2007	Various colors	$700	$925
Les Paul Voodoo/Voodoo Les Paul			
2004-2005. Single-cut, swamp ash body, 2 exposed humbuckers, black satin finish.			
2004-2005		$1,200	$1,600
Les Paul Warren Haynes Standard			
2007. Gibson Custom, Inspired by Artist series.			
2007		$2,450	$3,200
Les Paul XR-I/XR-II/XR-III			
1981-1983. No frills model with Dirty Finger pickups, dot markers, Les Paul stencil logo on headstock, goldburst, silverburst and cherryburst finishes.			
1981-1983	XR-I, goldburst	$825	$1,075
1981-1983	XR-II	$825	$1,075
1981-1983	XR-III	$825	$1,075
Les Paul Zakk Wylde Signature			
1999, 2003-2016. Custom shop, black and antique-white bullseye graphic finish. Green Camo option.			
1999-2016	Various options & colors	$2,600	$5,000
Les Paul Zebra Wood			
2007. Zebrawood top, mahogany back and neck, rosewood 'board, 2 '57 Classic pickups, natural satin zebrawood finish.			
2007		$1,600	$2,100
LPJ/Les Paul J			
2013-2018. Mahogany body with carved maple top, '50s profile maple neck, rosewood 'board, 2 Modern Classics humbucking pickups, various finishes.			
2013-2018		$450	$600
The Les Paul			
1976-1979. Figured maple top, 2 humbuckers, gold hardware, rosewood binding, 'guard, 'board, knobs, cover plates, etc., natural or rosewood finishing, natural only by '79.			
1976-1979	Natural or rosewood	$7,300	$9,500

MODEL YEAR	FEATURES	EXC. COND. LOW	HIGH
The Paul			
1978-1982. Offered as The Paul Standard with solid walnut body and The Paul Deluxe with solid mahogany body, 2 exposed humbuckers.			
1978-1982	Walnut or mahogany	$950	$1,250
The Paul Firebrand Deluxe			
1980-1982. Single-cut mahogany solidbody, rough natural finish, Gibson branded in headstock, 2 exposed humbuckers.			
1980-1982	Black	$875	$1,150
1980-1982	Pelham Blue	$875	$1,150
1980-1982	Rough natural	$875	$1,150
The Paul II			
1996-1998. Mahogany body, 2 humbucking pickups, rosewood dot neck, renamed The Paul SL in '98.			
1996-1998		$600	$800
LG-0			
1958-1974. Flat-top acoustic, mahogany, bound body, rosewood bridge '58-'61 and '68-'74, plastic bridge '62-'67, natural.			
1958-1961	Rosewood bridge	$900	$1,175
1962-1964	Plastic bridge	$775	$1,000
1965	Plastic bridge	$700	$900
1966	Plastic bridge	$575	$750
1967-1969	Rosewood bridge	$575	$750
1970-1974		$500	$650
LG-1			
1943-1968. Flat-top acoustic, spruce top, mahogany back and sides, bound body, rosewood bridge '43-'61, plastic bridge after, examples seen to '74, sunburst.			
1943-1949		$1,450	$1,900
1950-1959	Rosewood bridge	$1,450	$1,900
1960-1961	Rosewood bridge	$1,350	$1,800
1962-1964	Plastic bridge	$1,200	$1,550
1965		$1,150	$1,475
1966-1968		$1,100	$1,450
LG-2			
1942-1962. Flat-top acoustic, spruce top, mahogany back and sides (some with maple '43-'46), banner headstock '42-'46, bound body, X-bracing, sunburst finish, replaced by B-25 in '62.			
1942-1945	Banner, mahogany	$2,700	$3,500
1942-1945	Banner, spruce	$3,500	$4,500
1946-1949	Sitka	$3,100	$4,100
1950-1959		$2,700	$3,500
1960-1961	Rosewood bridge	$2,150	$2,800
1962	Adjustable bridge	$2,000	$2,600
LG-2 3/4			
1949-1962. Short-scale version of LG-2 flat-top, wood bridge, sunburst.			
1949	Rosewood bridge	$1,750	$2,300
1950-1959	Rosewood bridge	$1,550	$2,000
1960-1961	Rosewood bridge	$1,400	$1,800
1962	Adjustable bridge	$1,250	$1,600
LG-2 3/4 Arlo Guthrie			
2003, 2005-2018. Vintage replica finish.			
2003-2018		$1,300	$1,675

MODEL YEAR	FEATURES	EXC. COND. LOW	HIGH
LG-2 American Eagle			
2013-2018. Sitka top, mahogany back and sides, L.R. Baggs.			
2013-2018		$1,000	$1,325
LG-2 Banner			
2013. All mahogany, only 50 made.			
2013		$1,500	$1,950
LG-2 H			
1945-1955. Flat-top, Hawaiian, natural or sunburst.			
1944-1945		$2,900	$3,700
1946-1949		$2,250	$2,900
1950-1955		$1,950	$2,550
LG-3			
1942-1964. Flat-top acoustic, spruce top, mahogany back and sides, bound body, natural finish, replaced by B-25 N.			
1942-1945	Banner	$3,500	$4,500
1946-1949		$3,200	$4,200
1950-1959		$2,550	$3,300
1960-1961	Last wood bridge	$2,150	$2,800
1962-1964	Plastic bridge	$2,000	$2,600
L-Jr.			
1918-1927. Archtop, solid carved spruce top, carved figured birch back, Sheraton Brown or natural finish.			
1918-1927		$1,600	$2,100
Longhorn Double Cutaway			
2008. Guitar of the Month for July '08, AA figured maple top, 2 active pickups, piezo pickup, sunburst or transparent finishes.			
2008		$1,325	$1,725
M III Series			
1991-1996, 2013-2018. Double-cut solidbody with extra long bass horn, six-on-a-side tuners on a reverse pointy headstock, dot markers, reverse Gibson decal logo. Reissued in '13 with natural finish on 'board and choice of Cosmic Cobalt, Electric Lime, Vibrant Red, or Orange Glow.			
1991-1992	Deluxe	$1,125	$1,500
1991-1996	Standard	$900	$1,200
2013-2018	Reissue	$825	$1,100
M IV Series			
1993-1995. M III with Steinberger vibrato.			
1993-1995	S Deluxe	$1,125	$1,500
1993-1995	S Standard	$900	$1,200
Mach II			
1990-1991. Renamed from U-2, offset double-cut, 2 single coils and 1 humbucking pickup.			
1990-1991		$700	$925
Map Guitar			
1983, 1985. Body cutout like lower 48, 2 humbuckers, limited run promotion, '83 version in natural mahogany or red, white and blue, '85 version red, white and blue stars and stripes on a white background. This model can often be found in better than excellent condition because the instrument is as much a show piece as it is a player guitar, and the price range reflects that.			
1983	Natural	$2,300	$2,900
1983	Red, white & blue	$2,500	$3,100

MODEL YEAR	FEATURES	EXC. COND. LOW	HIGH
Marauder			
1975-1980. Single-cut solidbody, pointed headstock, 2 pickups, bolt-on neck, various colors.			
1975-1980		$750	$1,000
Marauder Custom			
1976-1977. Marauder with 3-way selector switch, bound 'board, block markers, bolt-on neck, Marauder logo on truss rod cover, sunburst.			
1976-1977		$1,100	$1,450
Melody Maker			
1959-1971, 1986-1993. Slab solidbody, 1 pickup, single-cut until '61, double '61-'66, SG body '66-'71, reintroduced as single-cut in '86-'93. A single-cut Les Paul Melody Maker was offered from '03-'06.			
1959-1961	Sunburst, single-cut	$1,000	$1,300
1962-1964	Sunburst or cherry, double-cut	$875	$1,150
1965-1966	Cherry, double cut	$800	$1,050
1966-1971	Various colors, SG body	$1,000	$1,300
1986-1993	Reintroduced as single-cut	$550	$700
Melody Maker 3/4			
1959-1963. Short-scale version.			
1959-1963		$950	$1,250
Melody Maker D			
1960-1970. Two pickup version of Melody Maker, reintroduced as Melody Maker Double in '77.			
1960-1961	Sunburst, single-cut	$1,550	$2,000
1961-1964	Sunburst, cherry, double-cut	$1,400	$1,800
1965-1966	Sunburst, cherry, double-cut	$1,175	$1,500
1966-1970	Various colors, SG body	$1,200	$1,550
Melody Maker Double			
1977-1983. Reintroduction of Melody Maker D, double-cut solidbody, 2 pickups, cherry or sunburst.			
1977-1983	Bolt-on	$575	$750
1977-1983	Set-neck	$725	$950
Melody Maker III			
1967-1971. SG-style double-cut solidbody, 3 pickups, various colors.			
1967-1971		$1,275	$1,650
Melody Maker 12			
1967-1971. SG-style solidbody, 12 strings, 2 pickups, red, white or Pelham Blue.			
1967-1971		$1,150	$1,500
Melody Maker Faded			
2003. Les Paul Jr. styling, single-cut, 1 P-90 style pickup, Nashville tune-o-matic bridge, black satin finish.			
2003		$325	$425
Les Paul Melody Maker			
2003-2008. Slab single-cut solidbody, one P-90, tune-o-matic bridge, dot markers, 2 knobs. Revised in '07 with 1 single-coil (2 also offered), wrap around tailpiece, 1 knob, pickguard mounted jack.			
2003-2006	1 pickup	$325	$425
2007-2008	1 pickup, revised specs	$325	$425
2007-2008	2 pickup option	$325	$425

1958 Gibson LG-0
Ted Wulfers

1967 Gibson Melody Maker D
Tim McClutchy

Gibson Melody Maker Joan Jett Signature Blackheart

Gibson Midtown Standard P-90

MODEL YEAR	FEATURES	EXC. COND. LOW	HIGH

Melody Maker Joan Jett Signature
2008-2012. Double-cut, worn-white (til '11), 1 Burstbucker 3. Blackheart version in black with red dots starts '10.

2008-2012		$700	$900

Midnight Special
1974-1975. L-6S body style, maple 'board, dot markers, 2 humbucker pickups, custom colors.

1974-1975		$1,000	$1,300

Midtown Custom
2012-2014. 335-style semi-hollow, 2 humbuckers, block markers.

2012-2014		$975	$1,275

Midtown Standard P-90
2012-2014. Like Midtown Custom, but with dots, P-90s.

2012-2014		$975	$1,275

MK-35
1975-1978. Mark Series flat-top acoustic, mahogany back and sides, black-bound body, natural or sunburst, 5226 made.

1975-1978		$525	$675

MK-53
1975-1978. Mark Series flat-top acoustic, maple back and sides, multi-bound body, natural or sunburst, 1424 made.

1975-1978		$600	$775

MK-72
1975-1978. Mark Series flat-top acoustic, rosewood back and sides, black-bound body, chrome tuners, natural or sunburst, 1229 made.

1975-1978		$625	$825

MK-81
1975-1978. Mark Series flat-top acoustic, rosewood back and sides, multi-bound body, gold tuners, high-end appointments, natural or sunburst, 431 made.

1975-1978		$800	$1,050

Moderne
2012. Limited run, mahogany body and neck, dual '57 Classic humbuckers, trans amber or ebony finish.

2012		$1,200	$1,550

Moderne Heritage
1981-1983. Limited edition, korina body, 2 humbucking pickups, gold hardware, natural, black or white.

1981-1983	All colors	$4,600	$6,000

Nick Lucas
1926-1937. Though they were shipped into '41, the last year of production was '37. Mahogany 13 ½" L-1 body ('26-'29), 14 ¾" L-00 body ('30-'41), parallel bracing '26-'27, X-braced '28-'41, 12 frets early (13 and 14 later), banjo tuners early (guitar style later), black (rare) or sunburst finish. Reintroduced in '91.

1928-1929	Standard		
	Lucas inlay	$9,800	$12,700
1928-1929	Trap-door inlay	$12,700	$16,500
1930	14 ¾" begins	$12,000	$15,500
1931-1932		$14,300	$18,500
1933-1934		$32,600	$42,000
1935-1937	Sunburst	$31,000	$40,000

MODEL YEAR	FEATURES	EXC. COND. LOW	HIGH

Nick Lucas Reissue Limited Edition
1991-1992. 100 made, label signed by Ren Ferguson.

1991-1992		$1,800	$2,350

Nick Lucas Tenor
1928-1938. 14 ¾", 12-fret, early models have mahogany, later maple, The Gibson headstock logo.

1928-1930	Mahogany	$6,000	$7,800
1934-1938	Maple	$6,600	$8,600

Nick Lucas Elite
1999-2002. Ebony 'board, abalone inlay and inlays.

1999-2002		$2,650	$3,450
2001	Elite Custom	$2,650	$3,450

Nick Lucas Grande
2015-2016. Limited Edition of 50, sitka spruce top, English walnut back and sides, COA, Honeyburst finish.

2015-2016		$2,400	$3,100

Nick Lucas Koa Elite
2015. Limited to 50, Adirondack and koa, COA.

2015		$2,400	$3,100

Nick Lucas Supreme
2015. Limited to 40, Adirondack red spruce top, AAA flame koa back and sides, abalone trim, certificate of authenticity, Honeyburst finish.

2015		$2,650	$3,450

Nighthawk 2009 Limited
2009. Limited series, AAA figured maple top, mahogany body, Translucent Amber finish.

2009		$950	$1,250

Nighthawk Custom
1993-1998. Flame maple top, ebony 'board, gold hardware, fireburst, single/double/mini pickups.

1993-1998		$950	$1,250

Nighthawk Special
1993-1998. Single-cut solidbody, figured maple top, double-coil and mini-pickup or with additional single-coil options, dot marker inlay, cherry, ebony or sunburst.

1993-1998		$750	$1,000

Nighthawk Standard
1993-1998. Single-cut solidbody, figured maple top, 2 or 3 pickups, double-parallelogram inlay, amber, fireburst or sunburst.

1993-1998		$875	$1,150

Nighthawk Standard 2010 Limited
2010-2012. Limited Run series, AAA quilted maple top, chambered poplar body, 3 pickups, Memphis Mojo, St. Louis Sauce or Chicago Blue finishes.

2010-2012		$950	$1,250

Nighthawk Studio
2011-2012. AAA quilted maple top, dots.

2011-2012		$525	$675

Nouveau NV6T-M
1986-1987. Hybrid USA/Japan, a line of Gibson flat-tops with imported parts assembled and finished in the U.S., acoustic dreadnought, bound maple body, natural.

1986-1987		$385	$500

MODEL YEAR / FEATURES	EXC. COND. LOW	HIGH

NR-336F
2012. Custom Shop, 25 made, double-cut, non-reverse (NR) Firebird headstock, flamed maple top, rosewood 'board, antique sunburst top, cherry back.
2012 $1,950 $2,550

OP-25
1991-1992. Acoustic-electric, limited production run, synthetic back.
1991-1992 $600 $775

Original Jumbo (Custom Shop)
2003. 16" jumbo body, Adirondack top, mahogany sides and back, butterbean tuner buttons, deep sunburst finish on complete body, Custom Art Historic.
2003 $1,900 $2,450

Pat Martino Custom/Signature
1999-2006. Sharp single-cut thinline, f-holes, 2 humbuckers, flamed cherry sunburst maple top, small snakehead style headstock, Pat Martino logo on truss rod cover.
1999-2006 $2,100 $2,750

PG-00
1932-1937. Plectrum neck, flat-top.
1932-1937 $1,500 $1,900

PG-1
1928-1938. Plectrum neck, flat-top.
1929 $1,400 $1,800

PG-175
1950. Acoustic/electric with ES-175 bobdy and 4-string plectrum neck, bow-tie markers, sunburst.
1950 $2,700 $3,500

Q-100
1985-1986. Offset double-cut solidbody, Kahler trem, 6-on-a-side tuners, 1 humbucker, black hardware.
1985-1986 $575 $750

Q-200/Q2000
1985-1986. Like Q-100, but with 1 single and 1 hum, black or chrome hardware. Name changed to 2000 late '85.
1985-1986 $650 $850

Q-300/Q3000
1985-1986. Like Q-100, but with 3 single-coils, black or chrome hardware. Name changed to 3000 late '85.
1985-1986 $725 $925

Q-3000 Custom Shop
1985. Limited Custom production, 3 single-coil pickups.
1985 $1,025 $1,325

Q-400/Q4000
Late-1985-1987. Limited custom production, like Q-100, but with 2 singles and 1 hum, black hardware, Name changed to 400 late '85. Ferrari Red or Pink Panther finish as 4000, ebony as 400.
1985-1987 $1,025 $1,325

RD Artist CMT
1981. Figured top.
1981 $1,850 $2,400

RD Artist/77
1980. The 77 model has a 25.5" scale versus 24.75".
1980 $1,575 $2,075

RD Artist/79
1978-1982. Double-cut solidbody, 2 humbuckers, TP-6 tailpiece, active electronics, ebony 'board, block inlays, gold-plated parts, various colors, called just RD (no Artist) in '81 and '82.
1978-1982 $1,650 $2,150

RD Custom
1977-1979. Double-cut solidbody, 2 humbuckers, stop tailpiece, active electronics, dot inlays, maple 'board, chrome parts, natural or walnut.
1977-1979 $1,650 $2,150

RD Standard
1977-1979. Double-cut solidbody, 2 humbuckers, stop tailpiece, rosewood 'board, dot inlays, chrome parts, natural, sunburst or walnut.
1977-1979 $1,650 $2,150

RD Standard Reissue
2007, 2009, 2011. 400 Silverburst made in '07. Black or Trans Amber Red versions offered as limited run in '09 in Japan and in U.S. in '11.
2007-2011 Various colors $850 $1,100

Roy Smeck Radio Grande Hawaiian
1934-1939. Dreadnought acoustic flat-top, rosewood back and sides, bound body and neck, natural.
1934-1939 Brazilian $11,000 $14,300

Roy Smeck Radio Grande Hawaiian Limited
1994. Centennial Guitar of the Month in '94, 100 made, Indian rosewood.
1994 $1,900 $2,500

Roy Smeck Radio Grande Hawaiian Reissue
1996. Part of SmartWood Series, Grenadillo back and sides.
1996 $1,900 $2,500

Roy Smeck Stage Deluxe Hawaiian
1934-1942. Dreadnought acoustic flat-top, mahogany back and sides, bound body, natural.
1934-1942 $6,400 $8,300

S-1
1976-1980. Single-cut solidbody, pointed headstock, 3 single-coil pickups, similar to the Marauder, various colors.
1976-1980 $850 $1,100

SG
Following are models, listed alphabetically, bearing the SG name.

SG I
1972-1978. Double-cut, mahogany body, 1 mini-humbucker (some with SG Jr. P-90), wraparound bridge/tailpiece, cherry or walnut.
1972-1978 $650 $850

SG II
1972-1979. SG I with 2 mini-humbuckers (some in '75 had regular humbuckers), 2 slide switches, cherry or walnut.
1972-1979 $800 $1,050

SG III
1972-1977. SG II with sunburst and tune-o-matic.
1972-1977 $850 $1,100

1975 Gibson MK-35
Craig Brody

1982 Gibson Moderne Heritage
Steve Evans

1971 Gibson SG 200

Imaged by Heritage Auctions, HA.com

1970 Gibson SG Custom

Garrett Park

MODEL YEAR	FEATURES	EXC. COND. LOW	HIGH

SG-3

2007-2008. SG styling, SG Standard appointments, 3 gold humbuckers or 3 single coils, 1 rotor switch, 2 knobs, stop tail.

| 2007-2008 | 3 humbuckers | $850 | $1,100 |
| 2007-2008 | 3 single coils | $600 | $775 |

SG '61 Reissue

2003-2015. Renamed from Les Paul SG '61 Reissue, no Les Paul script on truss rod, small 'guard, stop bar tailpiece (no Deluxe Maestro vibrato), '60 slim-taper neck profile.

| 2003-2015 | | $1,300 | $1,700 |

SG '62 Reissue/SG Reissue

1986-1991. Trapezoid markers, stop bar, 2 humbuckers, called SG Reissue '86-'87, SG '62 Reissue '88-'91. Reintroduced as Les Paul SG '61 Reissue for '93-'03 and SG '61 Reissue '03-present, cherry.

| 1986-1991 | | $1,300 | $1,700 |

SG '62 Reissue Showcase Edition

1988. Guitar of the Month, bright blue opaque finish, 200 made.

| 1988 | | $1,375 | $1,800 |

Les Paul '63 Corvette Sting Ray

1995-1997. Custom Shop SG-style body carved to simulate split rear window on '63 Corvette, Sting Ray inlay, 150 made, offered in black, white, silver or red.

| 1995-1997 | | $3,800 | $4,900 |

SG-90 Double

1988-1990. SG body, updated electronics, graphite reinforced neck, 2 pickups, cherry, turquoise or white.

| 1988-1990 | | $650 | $850 |

SG-90 Single

1988-1990. SG body, updated electronics, graphite reinforced neck, 1 humbucker pickup, cherry, turquoise or white.

| 1988-1990 | | $650 | $850 |

SG-100

1971-1972. Double-cut solidbody, 1 pickup, cherry or walnut.

1971-1972	Melody Maker pickup	$850	$1,125
1971-1972	P-90 pickup option	$850	$1,125
1971-1972	Sam Ash model	$850	$1,125

SG-200

1971-1972. Two pickup version of SG-100 in black, cherry or walnut finish, replaced by SG II.

| 1971-1972 | Melody Maker pickups | $950 | $1,250 |

SG-250

1971-1972. Two-pickup version of SG-100 in cherry sunburst, replaced by SG III.

| 1971-1972 | Melody Maker pickups | $1,000 | $1,300 |

SG-400/SG Special 400

1985-1987. SG body with 3 toggles, 2 knobs (master volume, master tone), single-single-humbucker pickups, available with uncommon opaque finishes.

| 1985-1987 | | $750 | $1,000 |

SG Angus Young

2010-2016. Like Angus Signature but with small guard, stop tailpiece and tune-o-matic, Aged Cherry.

| 2010-2016 | | $1,425 | $1,850 |

SG Angus Young Signature

2000-2009. Late-'60s Std specs with large 'guard, Deluxe Maestro lyre vibrato with Angus logo, aged cherry finish.

| 2000-2009 | | $1,425 | $1,850 |

SG Baritone

2013-2016. Longer 27" scale, 2 exposed humbuckers, ebony 'board, Alpine White finish.

| 2013-2016 | | $900 | $1,150 |

SG Carved Top - Autumn Burst

2009. Limited run of 350, highly flamed carved maple top, rosewood 'board, certificate of authenticity.

| 2009 | | $1,375 | $1,800 |

SG Classic/SG Classic Faded

1999-2001, 2003-2013. Late '60s SG Special style, Classic on truss rod cover, large 'guard, black soapbar single-coil P-90s, dot markers, stop bar tailpiece, cherry or ebony stain.

| 1999-2013 | | $725 | $950 |

SG Custom

1963-1980. Renamed from Les Paul Custom, 3 humbuckers, vibrato, made with Les Paul Custom plate from '61-'63 (see Les Paul Custom), white finish until '68, walnut and others after.

1963-1964	White, pat #, Maestro	$11,200	$14,500
1965	Early '65, white, large neck	$9,200	$12,000
1965	Late '65, white, small neck	$8,500	$11,000
1966-1968	White, large 'guard	$6,000	$8,000
1969	Walnut, lyre, 1-piece neck	$5,000	$6,600
1969	Walnut, lyre, 3-piece neck	$3,600	$4,800
1969	White, lyre, 1 piece neck	$5,000	$6,600
1969	White, lyre, 3 piece neck	$3,600	$4,800
1970	Walnut, lyre	$3,000	$4,000
1970	White, lyre	$3,000	$4,000
1970-1973	Walnut, Bigsby	$2,300	$3,100
1970-1973	White option, Bigsby	$3,000	$3,900
1974-1975	Brown, dark cherry	$1,700	$2,200
1974-1975	White option	$2,500	$3,200
1976-1979	Brown, dark cherry	$1,500	$1,950
1976-1979	White option	$2,300	$3,000
1980	Various colors	$1,600	$2,100

SG Custom '67 Reissue/Les Paul SG '67 Custom

1991-1993. The SG Custom '67 Reissue has a wine red finish, the Les Paul SG '67 Custom ('92-'93) has a wine red or white finish.

| 1991-1993 | | $1,925 | $2,500 |

SG Custom Elliot Easton Signature

2006-2007. Custom Shop, SG Custom specs, Maestro deluxe vibrola, Pelham Blue or white, includes Certificate of Authenticity.

| 2006-2007 | | $2,600 | $3,400 |

The ***Vintage Guitar Price Guide*** shows low to high values for items in all-original excellent condition, and, where applicable, with original case or cover.

MODEL YEAR	FEATURES	EXC. COND. LOW	HIGH

SG Deluxe
1971-1972, 1981-1985, 1998-1999, 2013-2018. The '70s models were offered in cherry, natural or walnut finishes, reintroduced in '98 with 3 Firebird mini-humbucker-style pickups in black, red or Ice Blue finishes, in 2013 with 3 '57 Classic humbuckers in Cobalt Fade, Lime Burst, Orange Burst or Red Fade.

1971-1972	Cherry	$1,225	$1,600
1971-1972	Natural, walnut	$1,225	$1,600
1981-1985	Various colors	$1,025	$1,325
1998-1999	Various colors	$925	$1,200
2013-2018	New specs, all colors	$1,300	$1,700

SG Diablo
2008. Guitar of the Month for Dec. '08, 1,000 made, '61 specs, metallic silver finish with matching headstock, 1 volume, 1 tone knob, 3-way toggle, 24 frets.

2008		$1,000	$1,300

SG Diablo Premium Plus
2012-2013. AAA maple top.

2012-2013		$1,000	$1,300

SG Diablo Tremolo
2012-2013. Diablo with Floyd Rose.

2012-2013		$1,000	$1,300

SG Dickey Betts
2012. Custom, 75 hand-aged made include a leather certificate of authenticity signed by Betts, 250 VOS include unsigned COA, Vintage Red finish.

2012	Aged	$4,400	$5,700
2012	VOS	$2,600	$3,400

SG Elegant
2004-2013. Custom Shop, quilt maple top, gold hardware, Blue Burst, Firemist and Iguana Burst finishes.

2004-2013		$2,150	$2,850

SG Elite
1987-1989. SG Custom specs, 3 humbuckers, gold hardware, ebony 'board, various colors.

1987-1989		$1,500	$1,950

SG Exclusive
1979. SG with humbuckers, coil-tap and rotary control knob, block inlay, pearl logo (not decal), black/ebony finish.

1979		$1,550	$2,000

SG Firebrand
1980-1982. Double-cut mahogany solidbody, rough natural finish, Gibson branded in headstock, 2 exposed humbuckers, Firebrand logo on The SG (Standard) model.

1980-1982		$675	$875

SG Frank Zappa "Roxy"
2013. 400 offered, Maestro vibrola, 2 exposed-coil humbuckers.

2013		$1,625	$2,150

SG Futura
2013-2014. Mahogany body, maple neck, rosewood 'board, 2 pickups, various colors.

2013-2014		$600	$775

SG Goddess
2007. SG Goddess logo on truss rod cover, only 2 control knobs versus standard 4, exposed humbuckers.

2007		$675	$875

SG Gothic
2000-2003. SG Special with satin black finish, moon and star marker on 12th fret, black hardware.

2000-2003		$700	$900

SG Gothic Morte
2011-2012. Solid mahogany body, African Obeche 'board, 2 pickups, satin ebony finish

2011-2012		$350	$475

SG Government Series
2013-2016. Made from guitar bodies, necks and 'boards returned from Federal Government after '11 raid on Gibson, with Certificate of Authenticity.

2013-2016		$900	$1,175

SG GT
2006-2007. '61 specs with racing stripes paint job and removable tailpiece hood scoop, locking tuners, Candy Apple Red, Daytona Blue, or Phantom Black.

2006-2007		$1,800	$2,400

SG Jeff Tweedy Signature
2012. SG Standard with Maestro vibrola, mahogany body and neck, rosewood 'board, Blue Mist.

2012		$1,850	$2,450

SG Judas Priest Signature
2003. Custom Shop, 30 made, dot markers, exposed '57 classic humbucker and EMG58 pickups, black, large chrome metal 'guard, also sold as a set with Flying V Judas Priest, includes certificate of authenticity.

2003		$1,750	$2,300

SG Judas Priest Signature Set With Flying V
2003. Custom Shop, 30 sets made.

2003		$3,800	$5,000

SG Junior
1963-1971, 1991-1994. One pickup, solidbody. Prices are for an unfaded finish, cherry finish faded to brown reduces the value by 30%.

1963-1964	Cherry	$2,700	$3,500
1964	White	$3,100	$4,100
1965	Early-'65, cherry	$2,500	$3,300
1965	Late-'65, cherry	$1,950	$2,600
1965	Pelham Blue	$3,850	$5,000
1965	White	$2,600	$3,400
1966-1968	White	$2,450	$3,200
1966-1969	Cherry	$1,725	$2,300
1970-1971	Cherry or walnut	$1,600	$2,100
1991-1994	Various colors	$650	$825

SG Junior Limited
2018. Double-cut, mahogany body and neck, rosewood 'board, 1 single-coil pickup, Vintage Cherry.

2018		$800	$1,050

SG Junior P-90
2006-2007. Single P-90 pickup, large 'guard, stop tail, cherry finish.

2006-2007		$625	$850

SG Les Paul '61 Custom Reissue
1997-2005. 1961 specs, SG body style, 3 humbuckers, Deluxe Maestro vibrato or stud with tune-o-matic bridge, white or silver option.

1997-2005		$1,750	$2,300

SG Les Paul '62 Custom
1986-1990. 1962 specs, 3 humbuckers.

1986-1990		$1,750	$2,300

2014 Gibson SG Government Series

2001 Gibson SG '61 Reissue
Bernunzio Uptown Music

GUITARS

1980 Gibson SG Firebrand

1963 Gibson SG Special
Dave's Guitar Shop

MODEL YEAR	FEATURES	EXC. COND. LOW	HIGH

SG Les Paul '62 Custom (Custom Shop)
2003. Custom Shop, Maestro vibrato, small 'guard, white.

2003		$1,750	$2,300

SG Les Paul '90 Custom
1990-1992. 1962 specs, 3 humbuckers.

1990-1992		$1,750	$2,300

SG Les Paul Custom 30th Anniversary
1991. SG body, 3 humbuckers, gold hardware, TV Yellow finish, 30th Anniversary on peghead.

1991		$2,150	$2,800

SG Menace
2006-2007. Carved mahogany body, 2 exposed humbuckers, flat black finish, black hardware, single brass knuckle position marker, gig bag.

2006-2007		$600	$800

SG Music Machine Stinger
2003. Custom run for dealer Music Machine, special serial number series, SG Custom with 2 pickups and SG Standard models available, black stinger paint job on neck/headstock, various colors.

2003	SG Custom	$2,150	$2,800
2003	SG Standard	$2,000	$2,600

SG Original
2013-2019. Mahogany body, slim '60s neck profile, Lyre vibrato, '57 classic pickups, Vintage Cherry. Replaced by SG Standard '61 Maestro Vibrola in '19.

2013-2019		$1,450	$1,900

SG Pete Townshend Signature
2001. Signature on back of headstock.

2001		$1,200	$1,550

SG Pete Townshend Signature (Custom Shop)
2000. SG Special with '69 specs, large 'guard, 2 cases, cherry red, COA, limited edition of 250.

2000	Includes certificate	$1,200	$1,550

SG Platinum
2005. A mix of SG Special and SG Standard specs, platinum paint on the body, back of neck, and headstock, no crown inlay, Gibson stencil logo, exposed humbucker pickups, large plantium-finish 'guard, special plantinum colored Gibson logo guitar case.

2005		$575	$750

SG Pro
1971-1974. Tune-o-matic bridge, vibrato, 2 P-90 pickups, cherry, mahogany or walnut.

1971-1974		$1,150	$1,500

SG R1/SG Artist
1980-1982. Active RD-era electronics. SG style but thicker body, no 'guard, ebony 'board, black finish, dot markers, renamed SG Artist in '81.

1980	SG-R1	$1,000	$1,300
1981-1982	SG Artist	$1,000	$1,300

SG Raw Power
2009-2012. All maple body, neck and 'board, 2 exposed-coil humbuckers, offered in 9 satin finishes, including natural.

2009-2012		$725	$950

SG Select
2007. Made in Nashville, TN, carved solid bookmatched AAA flame maple, 3-piece flamed maple neck, described as the most exquisite SG offered to date, 2 humbuckers, gold hardware.

2007		$1,600	$2,100

SG Special
1959-1978. Rounded double-cut for '59-'60, switched to SG body early-'61, 2 P-90s '59-'71, 2 mini-humbuckers '72-'78, 2 regular humbuckers on current version, redesigned in '85. Prices are for an unfaded finish, cherry finish faded to brown reduces the value by 20%-30%. Instruments with stop tailpieces vs. Maestro tailpiece have the same value.

1959	Cherry, slab, high neck pu	$6,800	$9,000
1960	Cherry, slab, lower neck pu	$6,800	$9,000
1961-1962	Cherry, SG body	$4,700	$6,200
1962	White, SG body	$5,700	$7,400
1963-1964	Cherry, Maestro or stop	$4,700	$6,200
1963-1964	White	$5,700	$7,400
1965	Cherry, Maestro or stop	$3,100	$4,100
1965	White	$4,500	$6,000
1966	Cherry, large 'guard	$2,750	$3,650
1966	Cherry, small 'guard	$2,750	$3,650
1966	White, large 'guard	$3,600	$4,750
1966	White, small 'guard	$3,900	$5,200
1967	Cherry, large 'guard	$2,850	$3,700
1967	White, large 'guard	$3,600	$4,750
1968-1969	Cherry, large 'guard	$2,750	$3,650
1970-1971	Cherry, large 'guard	$2,350	$3,100
1972-1978	Mini-hums	$1,125	$1,475

SG Special (redesigned)
1985-1996. In mid-'85 Gibson introduced a redesigned SG Special model with 2 control knobs (1 pickup) or 3 control knobs (2 pickups) versus the previously used 4-knob layout.

1985-1986	1 pu, 2 knobs	$500	$650
1985-1989	2 pus, 3 knobs	$575	$750
1990-1996	2 pus, 3 knobs	$525	$675

SG Special (reintroduced)
1996-present. In '96 Gibson reintroduced the original 4-knob layout, 2 humbucker pickups, dot markers.

1996-2019		$550	$700

SG Special 3/4
1961. Only 61 shipped.

1961		$2,400	$3,100

SG Special '60s Tribute
2011-2018. '60s specs including small guard, dot markers, dual P-90s, Slim Taper '60s neck profile, 4 worn-finish options.

2011-2018		$550	$700

MODEL YEAR	FEATURES	EXC. COND. LOW	HIGH

SG Special Faded (3 pickups)
2007. Made in Nashville, TN, 3 exposed 490 hum-buckers, dot markers, stop tail, SG initials on truss rod cover, 2 knobs and 6-position selector switch, hand-worn satin finish.

2007		$550	$700

SG Special Faded/Faded SG Special
2002-2018. Aged worn cherry finish.

2002-2005	Half moon markers	$525	$675
2003-2018	Dot markers	$525	$675

SG Special I
1983-1985. Dot markers, 1 exposed-coil humbucker pickup with 2 knobs, called by various names includ-ing Gibson Special ('83), Special I, and SG Special I.

1983-1985		$525	$675

SG Special II
1983-1985. Dot markers, 2 exposed-coil humbucker pickups with 3 knobs, called by various names includ-ing Gibson Special ('83), Special II, SG Special II.

1983-1985		$550	$700

SG Special II EMG
2007. EMG humbucker pickups, no position mark-ers, standard 4-knob and 3-way toggle switch SG format, black satin finish over entire guitar, black hardware.

2007		$575	$750

SG Special New Century
2006-2008. Full-body mirror 'guard, 2 exposed humbuckers, SG body, mirror truss rod cover.

2006-2008		$750	$975

SG Special Robot
2008-2012. Dot markers, robot tuning.

2008-2012		$750	$975

SG Special Robot Limited
2008. Limited run with trapezoid markers, robot tuning.

2008		$950	$1,250

SG Special Robot Limited Silverburst
2008. Limited run of 400.

2008		$1,000	$1,300

SG Special VOS Reissue
2006-2013. Custom Shop, mahogany body and neck, bound rosewood 'board, dot inlays, 2 P-90s, certificate, white, TV yellow, or faded cherry finish.

2006-2013		$1,700	$2,200

SG Standard
1963-1981, 1983-present. Les Paul Standard changes to SG body, 2 humbuckers, some very early models have optional factory Bigsby. Prices are for an unfaded finish, a cherry finish faded to brown reduces the value by 30% or more.

1963-1964	Cherry, small 'guard, deluxe vibrato	$9,600	$12,600
1964	Pelham Blue, small 'guard, dlx vibrato	$13,300	$17,600
1965	Cherry, small 'guard, dlx vibrato, large neck	$8,000	$11,000
1965	Cherry, small 'guard, dlx vibrato, small neck	$7,300	$10,000
1965	Pelham Blue, small 'guard, dlx vibrato	$12,000	$16,300
1966	Early '66 cherry, small 'guard, dlx vibrato	$7,000	$9,200
1966	Late '66, cherry, large 'guard	$5,300	$6,800
1967	Burgundy Metallic	$5,700	$7,300
1967	Cherry	$5,300	$6,800
1967	White	$5,700	$7,300
1968	Cherry, engraved lyre	$4,600	$6,000
1969	Engraved lyre, 1-piece neck	$4,600	$6,000
1969	Engraved lyre, 3-piece neck	$3,700	$4,800
1970	Walnut, non-lyre tailpiece	$2,000	$2,600
1970-1971	Cherry, non-lyre tailpiece	$2,100	$2,800
1970-1971	Engraved lyre, 3-piece neck	$2,800	$3,600
1972-1979	Blocks, mini 'guard, top mount	$1,550	$2,000
1980-1986	New colors, small blocks	$1,400	$1,800
1992-1999	New specs	$850	$1,125
2000-2019	Standard colors	$850	$1,125
2006-2012	Silverburst, 400 made	$1,000	$1,300

SG Standard '61 Reissue
2004-2008. Small 'guard, stop tail, Nashville tune-o-matic bridge, Gibson Deluxe Keystone tuners, standard Gibson logo and crown inlay, no Les Paul logo, Vintage Original Spec aging optional from '06. Reintroduced in '19.

2004-2008		$1,200	$1,550

SG Standard '61
2019-present. Classic '61 design, 3 models offered - Maestro vibrola, Sideways or Stop Bar, mahogany body and neck, rosewood 'board, vintage cherry finish.

2019-2020	Maestro vibrola	$1,150	$1,500
2019-2020	Sideways vibrola	$1,150	$1,500
2019-2020	Stop Bar vibrola	$1,000	$1,300

SG Standard 24 50th Anniversary
2011. Limited run, mother-of-pearl Gibson logo with gold 50th Anniversary silkscreen, 2 '57 classic pickups, antique ebony finish.

2011		$900	$1,175

SG Standard (ETune)
2014-2018. Min-Etune robot tuners, Etune logo on truss rod.

2014-2018		$850	$1,100

SG Standard Brian Ray '63 (Custom Shop)
2015. Silver Fox finish, Bigsby, certificate of au-thenticity.

2015		$2,450	$3,250

2017 Gibson SG Special Faded

1972 Gibson SG Standard
Paul Thomason

To get the most from this book, be sure to read "Using **The Guide**" in the introduction.

2017 Gibson SG Standard High Performance

1960 Gibson SJ
David Stone

MODEL YEAR	FEATURES	EXC. COND. LOW	HIGH

SG Standard Celebrity Series
1991-1992. SG Standard with large 'guard, gold hardware, black finish.

| 1991-1992 | | $1,300 | $1,700 |

SG Standard Gary Rossington Signature
2004. '63-'64 SG Standard specs with Deluxe Maestro vibrola, '60 slim taper neck, limited edition, faded cherry aged by Tom Murphy.

| 2004 | | $3,800 | $4,900 |

SG Standard High Performance
2016-2019. Solid mahogany body and neck, AA figured maple top, 2 pickups, different colors offered each year.

| 2016-2019 | | $1,100 | $1,400 |

SG Standard Korina (Custom Shop)
2008-2009. Custom Shop limited reissue of '60s SG Standard, 2 BurstBucker pickups, black.

| 2008-2009 | | $1,850 | $2,400 |

SG Standard Korina Limited Edition
1993-1994. Korina version of SG Standard, limited run, natural.

| 1993-1994 | | $2,300 | $3,000 |

SG Standard Limited Edition
2000. Limited Edition logo back of headstock, 2 humbuckers, large pearloid guard, gold hardware, dark opaque finish.

| 2000 | | $850 | $1,100 |

SG Standard Limited Edition (3 pickups)
2007. Guitar of the Week, 400 made, 3 single-coil blade pickups, 6-position rotator switch with chickenhead knob, SG logo on truss rod cover, large 'guard, satin finish.

| 2007 | | $775 | $1,000 |

SG Standard Reissue
2004-2018. Reissue of near '63-'64 specs with Deluxe Maestro lyre vibrato and small 'guard, also offered with stop bar tailpiece, cherry finish, '60 slim taper neck, smooth neck heel joint, trapezoid markers, unmarked truss rod cover without Les Paul designation, formerly called Les Paul SG Standard Reissue, by 2005 part of Gibson's 'Vintage Original Spec' Custom Shop series, certificate of authenticity.

2004-2007	VOS, Maestro	$1,650	$2,200
2007-2018	VOS, stoptail	$1,750	$2,300
2008-2009	Maestro, LP logo	$1,750	$2,300

SG Standard VOS Historic
2003-2014. Custom Shop, Vintage Original Specs.

| 2003-2014 | | $1,750 | $2,300 |

SG Standard Robby Krieger
2009. Custom Shop model, Inspired By series, based on Krieger's '67 SG, limited run of 150 with 50 aged and signed, 100 with V.O.S. finish treatment, certificate of authenticity.

| 2009 | Aged, signed | $3,100 | $4,100 |
| 2009 | VOS | $2,500 | $3,300 |

SG Standard Robby Krieger 50th Anniversary
2012. Mahogany body and neck, rosewood 'board, 2 '57 classic Alnico II pickups, Maestro tailpiece, Heritage Cherry finish.

| 2012 | | $1,300 | $1,700 |

SG Supreme
2004-2007. '57 humbuckers, flamed maple top, split-diamond markers, various colors.

| 2004-2007 | | $1,400 | $1,825 |

SG Tony Iommi Signature (Historic/Custom Shop)
2001-2003. Custom Shop higher-end, signature humbuckers without poles, cross inlays, ebony or Wine Red.

| 2001-2003 | | $3,400 | $4,400 |

SG Tony Iommi Signature (Production)
2002-2003. Standard production model.

| 2002-2008 | | $1,600 | $2,075 |

SG TV
1961-1963. Name changed from Les Paul TV, SG body, 1 pickup, white finish. In '64 called SG Jr. White.

| 1961-1963 | White, SG body | $3,500 | $4,600 |

SG Voodoo/Voodoo SG
2002-2004. Carved top, black hardware, voodoo doll inlay at 5th fret, Juju finish (black with red wood filler).

| 2002-2004 | | $875 | $1,125 |

SG-X (All American I)
1995-2000. Renamed the SG-X in '98, previously part of the All American series, SG body with single bridge humbucker, various colors.

| 1995-1999 | | $500 | $650 |

SG-X Tommy Hilfiger
1998. Hilfiger logo on front, dot markers, plain headstock like a SG Special, dark blue finish, 100 made.

| 1998 | | $450 | $575 |

SG Zoot Suit
2007-2010. Body of individual dyed strips of birch.

| 2007-2010 | | $1,250 | $1,625 |

SG-Z
1998. Z-shaped string-thru tailpiece, 2 humbuckers, split diamond markers.

| 1998 | | $1,150 | $1,475 |

The SG
1979-1983. Offered as The SG Standard (walnut body) and The SG Deluxe (mahogany), ebony 'board, 2 humbuckers.

| 1979-1983 | Walnut or mahogany | $650 | $850 |

Sheryl Crow Signature
2001-2018. Artist Series, based on Sheryl Crow's 1962 Country and Western with Hummingbird influences.

| 2001-2018 | | $1,700 | $2,300 |

Sheryl Crow Southern Jumbo Special Edition
2013-2018. Adirondack red spruce top, mahogany back and sides, rosewood 'board, with signed certificate of authenticity, Montana Sunsetburst finish. Limited production in '13.

| 2013-2018 | | $2,300 | $3,000 |

SJ (Southern Jumbo)
1942-1969,1991-1996. Flat-top, sunburst standard, natural optional starting in '54 (natural finish version called Country-Western starting in '56), round shoulders (changed to square in '62), catalog name changed to SJ Deluxe in '70, refer to that listing.

| 1942-1944 | Banner, Adirondack | $11,000 | $14,500 |

The Official Vintage Guitar magazine Price Guide 2021   **Gibson** SJ Deluxe (Southern Jumbo) — SJ-200 Elvis Presley   **195**

GUITARS

MODEL YEAR	FEATURES	EXC. COND. LOW	HIGH
1942-1944	Banner, mahogany	$8,400	$11,000
1945	Script, Sitka	$8,800	$11,700
1946	Script, Sitka	$7,900	$10,500
1947	Script, Sitka	$7,200	$9,500
1948	Script, Sitka	$6,500	$8,600
1949	Script, Sitka	$5,700	$7,600
1950-1953		$4,300	$5,600
1954-1956	Natural option	$4,300	$5,600
1954-1959	Sunburst	$4,300	$5,600
1960-1962	Round shoulder (ends)	$4,200	$5,600
1962-1964	Square shoulder (begins)	$3,800	$5,000
1965	Cherry Sunburst	$2,600	$3,500
1965	Tobacco Sunburst	$3,100	$4,100
1966	Tobacco Sunburst	$3,000	$4,000
1966-1968	Cherry Sunburst	$2,500	$3,300
1969	Below belly bridge	$2,000	$2,650

SJ Deluxe (Southern Jumbo)
1970-1978. SJ name changed to SJ Deluxe in catalog, along with a series of engineering changes.

1970-1971	Non-adj saddle	$1,600	$2,100
1972-1973	Unbound 'board	$1,600	$2,100
1974-1978	4-ply to binding	$1,600	$2,100

SJN (Country-Western)
1956-1969. Flat-top, natural finish version of SJ, round shoulders '56-'62, square shoulders after, called the SJN in '60 and '61, the SJN Country Western after that, catalog name changed to SJN Deluxe in '70, refer to that listing.

1956-1959		$4,800	$6,300
1960-1962	Round shoulder (ends)	$4,200	$5,500
1962-1964	Square shoulder (begins)	$3,800	$4,900
1965		$2,900	$3,800
1966-1968		$2,500	$3,200
1969	Below belly bridge, SJN logo	$1,900	$2,500

SJN Deluxe (Country-Western Jumbo)
1970-1978. SJN name changed to SJN Deluxe in catalog, along with a series of engineering changes.

1970-1971	Non-adj saddle	$1,600	$2,100
1972-1973	Unbound 'board	$1,600	$2,100
1974-1978	4-ply to binding	$1,600	$2,100

SJ 1942 Reissue (Southern Jumbo)
2000. Custom Shop, mahogany back and sides, '42 SJ appointments, 'Only A Gibson is Good Enough' banner logo.

2000		$2,100	$2,800

SJ Reissue (Southern Jumbo)
2003-2007. Sunburst.

2003-2007		$1,500	$2,000

SJ Hank Williams Jr. Hall of Fame (Southern Jumbo)
1997. Custom Shop, mahogany back and sides, SJ appointments.

1997		$2,100	$2,800

MODEL YEAR	FEATURES	EXC. COND. LOW	HIGH

SJ Kristofferson (Southern Jumbo)
2009-2012. Limited run of 300, AAA Sitka top, mahogany back and sides, Indian rosewood 'board, aged vintage sunburst.

2009-2012		$1,800	$2,400

SJ True Vintage (Southern Jumbo)
2007-2008. "Only A Gibson Is Good Enough" headstock banner, sitka spruce top, dark mahogany back and sides, dual parallelogram markers.

2007-2008		$2,000	$2,600

SJ Woody Guthrie (Southern Jumbo)
2003-2018. Single-bound round shoulder body, mahogany back and sides, parallelogram inlays.

2003-2018		$1,750	$2,300

SJ-100
2008. Jumbo body, dot markers, crown headstock inlay, inlaid Gibson logo, natural.

2008		$1,000	$1,350

SJ-100 1939 Centennial
1994. Acoustic flat-top, limited edition, sunburst.

1994		$1,800	$2,300

SJ-100 1941
2013-2018. Sitka spruce top, mahogany back, sides and neck, rosewood 'board, Vintage Sunburst or Antique Natural.

2013-2018		$1,700	$2,200

SJ-200 Bob Dylan Autographed Collector's Edition
2015-2018. Exact replica of Dylan's personal highly-customized SJ-200, Indian rosewood, Sitka spruce, Dylan eye logo inlaid on headstock, abalone inlay on 'guard, label signed by Bob Dylan, 175 made, case with embroidered eye logo.

2015-2018		$7,800	$10,000

SJ-200 Bob Dylan Player's Edition
2015-2018. Adirondack red spruce, flamed maple, eye logo headstock inlay, LR Baggs Anthem pickup.

2015-2018		$3,500	$4,500

SJ-200 Centennial Limited Edition
1994. Made in Bozeman, Montana, 100 made, 'guard specs based on '38 design, inside label "Gibson 100 Years 1894-1994", includes certificate of authenticity.

1994		$2,400	$3,200

SJ-200 Custom Rosewood
2007. Custom shop, certificate of authenticity.

2007		$3,100	$4,000

SJ-200 Elite
1998-2007. Gibson Custom Shop Bozeman, maple sides and back.

1998-2007		$2,800	$3,600

SJ-200 Elite Custom Koa
2004. Figured koa, ebony board with abalone crown inlays, Antique Natural.

2004		$3,000	$3,900

SJ-200 Elvis Presley
2007. Custom Shop, 250 made, kings crown logo and facsimile signature of Presley on truss rod cover, certificate of authenticity, black finish.

2007		$2,900	$3,750

Gibson SJ Kristofferson (Southern Jumbo)

2017 Gibson SJ-200 Bob Dylan Player's Edition

To get the most from this book, be sure to read "Using **The Guide**" in the introduction.

2011 Gibson SJ-200 True Vintage
Johnny Zapp

1982 Gibson Sonex-180 Deluxe
Imaged by Heritage Auctions, HA.com

MODEL YEAR	FEATURES	EXC. COND. LOW	HIGH
SJ-200 Pete Townshend Limited			
2004-2012. Gibson Custom Shop Bozeman, maple sides and back.			
2004	Signed 1st 50 made	$4,000	$5,500
2004-2012		$2,450	$3,200
SJ-200 Ray Whitley/J-200 Custom Club			
1994-1995. Based on Ray Whitley's late-1930s J-200, including engraved inlays and initials on the truss rod cover, only 37 made, one of the limited edition models the Montana division released to celebrate Gibson's 100th anniversary.			
1994-1995		$10,800	$14,000
SJ-200 Sea Green Limited Edition			
2016. Bozeman Custom Shop, 40 made, Sitka spruce top, AAA flamed maple back and sides, mother-of-pearl crown inlays.			
2016		$2,700	$3,500
SJ-200 Summer Jam Koa			
2006. Custom Shop, only 6 made, offered to attendees of Gibson Guitar Summer Jam, highly figured koa back/sides.			
2006		$3,700	$4,800
SJ-200 True Vintage/SJ-200 Vintage			
2007-2019. AAA Adirondack red spruce top, AAA Eastern curly maple back and sides, rosewood 'board, tortoise 'guard, nitrocellulose finish. True dropped from name in '19.			
2007-2019		$3,000	$3,900
SJ-200 Vine			
2002-2018. Custom Shop, Sitka spruce top, Eastern curly maple back/sides, abalone vine inlay in 'board, abalone body trim. Limited Edition in '15, 30 made.			
2002-2014		$4,700	$6,000
2015-2018		$3,900	$5,000
SJ-200 Vintage			
2017-2019. Aged red spruce top, 2-piece maple neck, rosewood 'board, VOS finish in Vintage Sunburst.			
2017-2019		$3,300	$4,300
SJ-300			
2007-2010. Super Jumbo with Indian rosewood back and sides, ebony 'board, abalone crown inlays and rosette, gold imperial tuners, active transducer.			
2007-2010		$2,600	$3,400
Sonex Artist			
1981-1985. Active electronics, 3 mini switches, 2 humbuckers.			
1981-1985		$550	$725
Sonex-180 Custom			
1980-1982. Two Super humbuckers, coil-tap, maple neck, ebony 'board, single-cut, body of Multi-Phonic synthetic material, black or white.			
1980-1982		$550	$725
Sonex-180 Deluxe			
1980-1984. Hardwood neck, rosewood 'board, single-cut, body of Multi-Phonic synthetic material, 2 pickups, no coil-tap, various colors.			
1980-1984		$550	$725
Sonex-180 Standard			
1980. Dirty-fingers pickups, rosewood 'board, ebony finish.			
1980		$550	$725

MODEL YEAR	FEATURES	EXC. COND. LOW	HIGH
Songbird Deluxe			
1999-2002. Solid rosewood back, sides and 'board, on-board electronics. Renamed Songwriter Deluxe.			
1999-2002		$1,100	$1,450
Songwriter			
2003-present. Sitka spruce top, rosewood back, sides and 'board, mahogany neck, Antique Natural or Rosewood Burst.			
2003-2019		$1,500	$2,000
Songwriter Deluxe			
2003-2011. Solid rosewood back and sides, trapezoid inlays, cutaway or non-cutaway, on-board electronics.			
2003-2011		$1,300	$1,725
Songwriter Deluxe 12-String			
2006-present. 12-string version, non-cut.			
2006-2019		$1,300	$1,725
Songwriter Deluxe Koa			
2009. Custom Shop, all koa, cutaway.			
2009		$1,850	$2,400
Songwriter Deluxe Standard			
2009-2012. Solid rosewood back and sides, bound ebony 'board, diamond and arrows inlays, cutaway or non-cutaway.			
2009-2012		$1,550	$2,000
Songwriter Deluxe Studio			
2009-2018. Like Standard, but with bound rosewood 'board and double parallelogram inlays, cutaway or non-cutaway.			
2009-2018		$1,150	$1,500
Songwriter Special			
2007. Mahogany sides and back, dark opaque finish.			
2007		$1,050	$1,400
Songwriter Special Deluxe			
2003. Custom Shop, Brazilian rosewood.			
2003		$1,650	$2,100
Songwriter Studio			
2003-2019. Non-cutaway or cutaway.			
2003-2019		$1,400	$1,875
Special 400			
1985. Double-cut SG body, exposed humbucker and 2 single-coils, Kahler locking tremolo, coil tap.			
1985		$525	$700
Spirit I			
1982-1987. Double rounded cutaway, 1 pickup, chrome hardware, various colors.			
1982-1987		$950	$1,275
Spirit I XPL			
1985-1986. Spirit I with 6-on-a-side Explorer-style headstock.			
1985-1986		$950	$1,275
Spirit II			
1982-1987. Spirit I with 2 pickups, bound top.			
1982-1987		$1,050	$1,400
Spirit II XPL			
1985-1986. 2 pickup version.			
1985-1986		$1,050	$1,400
SR-71			
1987-1989. Floyd Rose tremolo, 1 humbucker, 2 single-coil pickups, various colors, Wayne Charvel designed.			
1987-1989		$1,050	$1,400

GUITARS

MODEL YEAR	FEATURES	EXC. COND. LOW	HIGH
Star			
1992. Star logo on headstock, star position markers, single sharp cutaway flat-top, sunburst.			
1991-1992		$1,200	$1,600
Starburst Standard/Flame			
1992-1994. Single-cut acoustic/electric, star inlays, figured maple back and sides.			
1992-1994		$1,200	$1,600
Style O			
1902-1925. Acoustic archtop, oval soundhole, bound top, neck and headstock, various colors.			
1902-1906	Paddle headstock	$4,500	$6,000
1902-1906	Paddle headstock, fancy	$5,800	$7,500
1906-1908	Slotted headstock	$5,400	$7,000
1908-1913	Solid headstock	$5,400	$7,000
1914-1921	Scroll variation	$5,400	$7,000
1922-1924	Loar era	$5,600	$7,500
1925	Scroll, truss rod	$5,600	$7,500
Style O-1			
1902. Acoustic archtop, celluloid binding.			
1902		$6,400	$8,500
Style O-2			
1902. Acoustic archtop, pearl/ebony binding.			
1902		$6,400	$8,500
Style O-3			
1902. Acoustic archtop, green/white binding.			
1902		$6,400	$8,500
Style R Harp Guitar			
1902-1907. Acoustic 6-string, with 6 sub-bass strings, walnut back and sides, bound soundhole.			
1902-1907		$4,100	$5,300
Style R-1 Harp Guitar			
1902. Style R with fancier pearl and ivory rope pattern binding.			
1902		$4,100	$5,300
Style U Harp Guitar			
1902-1939. Acoustic 6-string, with 10 or 12 sub-bass strings, walnut (until about '07) or birch back and sides, bound soundhole, black.			
1902-1939		$4,400	$5,700
Style U-1 Harp Guitar			
1902-1907, 1915, 1917. Slightly fancier Style U.			
1902-1917		$4,800	$6,300
Super 300			
1948-1955. Acoustic archtop, non-cut, bound body, neck and headstock, sunburst.			
1948-1949		$3,600	$4,800
1950-1955		$3,400	$4,500
Super 300 C			
1954-1958. Acoustic archtop, rounded cutaway, bound body, neck and headstock, sunburst with natural option.			
1954-1958	Sunburst	$4,100	$5,400
Super 400			
1935-1941, 1947-1955. Introduced early '35 as Super L-5 Deluxe. Acoustic archtop, non-cut, multi-bound, f-holes, sunburst (see Super 400 N for natural version).			
1935	Early, L-5 Deluxe, highly flamed maple	$12,000	$16,000

MODEL YEAR	FEATURES	EXC. COND. LOW	HIGH
1935	Early, L-5 Deluxe, plain maple	$10,000	$13,000
1935	Late, 400, highly flamed maple	$10,000	$13,000
1935	Late, 400, plain maple	$7,500	$10,000
1936-1941	Highly flamed maple	$8,500	$11,500
1936-1941	Plain maple	$6,400	$8,500
1947-1949	Highly flamed maple	$5,300	$7,000
1947-1949	Plain maple	$4,100	$5,500
1950-1955		$3,800	$5,000
Super 400 N			
1940, 1948-1955. Natural finish version of Super 400, highly flamed, non-cut, acoustic archtop.			
1940		$10,000	$13,000
1948-1949		$7,300	$9,700
1950-1955		$6,400	$8,500
Super 400 P (Premier)			
1939-1941. Acoustic archtop, single rounded cutaway, '39 model 'board rests on top, sunburst finish.			
1939-1941		$15,000	$20,000
Super 400 PN (Premier Natural)			
1939-1940. Rounded cutaway, '39 'board rests on top, natural finish.			
1939-1940		$21,000	$28,000
Super 400 C			
1948-1982. Introduced as Super 400 Premier, acoustic archtop, single-cut, sunburst finish (natural is called Super 400 CN).			
1948-1949		$10,000	$13,000
1950-1959		$9,000	$12,000
1960-1964		$8,000	$10,500
1965		$6,000	$8,000
1966-1969		$5,300	$7,000
1970-1982		$3,800	$5,000
Super 400 CN			
1950-1987. Natural finish version of Super 400 C.			
1950-1959		$10,000	$13,500
1960-1964		$9,000	$12,000
1965		$8,300	$11,000
1966-1969		$7,200	$9,500
Super 400 CES			
1951-2018. Electric version of Super 400 C, archtop, single-cut (round '51-'60 and '69-present, pointed '60-'69), 2 pickups (P-90s '51-'54, Alnico Vs '54-'57, humbuckers '57 on), sunburst (natural version called Super 400 CESN), now part of Gibson's Historic Collection.			
1951-1953	P-90s	$11,500	$15,000
1954-1957	Alnico Vs	$11,500	$15,000
1957-1960	PAFs	$15,000	$20,000
1961-1962	PAFs, sharp cut begins	$14,500	$19,000
1963-1964	Pat #	$10,500	$14,000
1965		$7,000	$9,000
1966-1969		$6,100	$8,000
1970-1979		$5,400	$7,100
1980-2018		$5,400	$7,100

2019 Gibson Songwriter

1948 Gibson Super 400

1962 Gibson Tal Farlow

Gibson Traveling Songwriter EC

MODEL YEAR	FEATURES	EXC. COND. LOW	HIGH
Super 400 CESN			
1952-2016. Natural version of Super 400 CES, now part of Gibson's Historic Collection.			
1952-1953	P-90s	$11,500	$15,000
1954-1956	Alnico Vs	$11,500	$15,000
1957-1960	PAFs	$14,500	$19,000
1961-1962	PAFs, sharp cut begins	$14,000	$18,300
1963-1964	Pat #	$9,700	$12,700
1965		$8,500	$11,000
1966-1969		$7,300	$9,500
1970-1979		$5,000	$6,700
1980-2016		$5,000	$6,700
Super 400 Custom Shop			
2009. Non-cutaway, natural.			
2009		$7,000	$9,000
'39 Super 400			
1993-1997. Historic Collection, reissue of non-cut '39 version, various colors.			
1993-1997		$5,500	$7,500
Super 4000 Chet Atkins			
2000. Limited run of 25. AAA sitka spruce carved top, highly figured carved maple back, antique natural and faded cherry sunburst.			
2000		$16,000	$21,000
Super Jumbo 100			
1939-1943. Jumbo flat-top, mahogany back and sides, bound body and neck, sunburst, reintroduced as J-100 with different specs in '84.			
1939-1940		$25,000	$33,000
1941	Early '41	$25,000	$33,000
1941	Late '41	$21,000	$28,000
1942		$21,000	$28,000
1943		$21,000	$28,000
Super Jumbo/Super Jumbo 200			
1938-1942. Initially called Super Jumbo in '38 and named Super Jumbo 200 in '39. Name then changed to J-200 (see that listing) by '47 (with maple back and sides) and SJ-200 by the '50s. Named for super large jumbo 16 7/8" flat-top body, double braced with rosewood back and sides, sunburst finish.			
1938		$94,000	$122,000
1939-1940		$92,000	$120,000
1941	Early '41	$90,000	$116,000
1941	Late '41	$81,000	$107,000
1942		$81,000	$107,000
Super V BJB			
1978-1983. A Super V CES but with a single floating pickup.			
1978-1983		$4,200	$5,400
Super V CES			
1978-1993. Archtop, L-5 with a Super 400 neck, 2 humbucker pickups, natural or sunburst.			
1978-1993		$4,200	$5,400
Tal Farlow			
1962-1971, 1993-2018. Full body, single-cut archtop, 2 humbuckers, triple-bound top, reintroduced '93 as part of Gibson's Historic Collection.			
1962-1964	Viceroy Brown	$5,200	$6,800
1965	Viceroy Brown	$4,800	$6,300

MODEL YEAR	FEATURES	EXC. COND. LOW	HIGH
1966-1971	Viceroy Brown	$4,300	$5,600
1993-2018	Various colors	$3,000	$3,900
TG-0			
1927-1933. Acoustic tenor based on L-0, mahogany body, light amber.			
1927-1933		$1,500	$2,000
1960-1964		$775	$1,025
1965		$600	$775
1966-1969		$525	$700
1970-1974		$500	$650
TG-00			
1932-1943. Tenor flat-top based on L-00.			
1932-1943		$1,500	$2,000
TG-1/L-1 Tenor/L-4 Tenor			
1927-1937. Acoustic flat-top, tenor or plectrum guitar based on L-1, mahogany back and sides, bound body, sunburst.			
1927-1937		$1,500	$2,000
1928-1932	Rare Lucas/ Johnson body	$2,400	$3,200
TG-2/L-2 Tenor			
1929-1930. Acoustic tenor guitar.			
1929-1930		$3,600	$4,700
TG-7			
1934-1940. Tenor based on the L-7, sunburst.			
1934-1940		$2,700	$3,500
TG-25/TG-25 N			
1962-1970. Acoustic flat-top, tenor guitar based on B-25, mahogany back and sides, sunburst or natural (25 N).			
1962-1964		$775	$1,000
1965		$675	$875
1966-1969		$600	$775
1970		$450	$600
TG-50			
1934-1940, 1947-1961, 1963. Acoustic archtop, tenor guitar based on L-50, mahogany back and sides, sunburst.			
1934-1940		$1,050	$1,400
1947-1963		$975	$1,300
Traveling Songwriter EC			
2005-2015. Solid spruce top, solid mahogany sides and back, soft cutaway, on-board electronics and EQ.			
2005-2015		$1,450	$1,900
Trini Lopez Standard			
1964-1970. Double rounded cutaway, thinline archtop, 2 humbuckers, tune-o-matic bridge, trapeze tailpiece, single-bound, cherry, Sparkling Burgundy and Pelham Blue finishes.			
1964	Cherry	$6,300	$8,200
1965	Cherry	$6,000	$7,700
1965	Pelham Blue	$6,600	$8,500
1965	Sparkling Burgundy	$6,000	$7,700
1966-1970	Cherry	$5,800	$7,500
1966-1970	Sparkling Burgundy	$5,800	$7,500
1970	Pelham Blue	$6,100	$8,000

MODEL YEAR FEATURES	EXC. COND. LOW	HIGH

Trini Lopez Standard (Custom Shop)

2010-2011. Custom Shop reissue of thinline Trini Lopez Standard, diamond f-holes, 6-on-a-side tuners, trapeze tailpiece, Certificate of Authenticity, cherry red.

2010-2011	$2,400	$3,100

Trini Lopez Deluxe

1964-1970. Double pointed cutaway archtop, 2 humbuckers, triple-bound, sunburst.

1964	$5,400	$7,000
1965	$5,200	$6,700
1966-1969	$5,000	$6,500
1970	$4,600	$6,000

U-2

1987-1989. Double-cut, 1 humbucker and 2 single-coil pickups, ebony or red, renamed Mach II in '90-'91.

1987-1991	$775	$1,000

U-2 Showcase Edition

1988. November 1988 Guitar of the Month series, 250 made.

1988	$775	$1,000

US-1/US-3

1986-1991. Double-cut maple top with mahogany back, 3 humbucker pickups (US-1), or 3 P-90s (US-3), standard production and Custom Shop.

1986-1991	$775	$1,000

Vegas Standard

2006-2007. Flat-top semi-hollowbody thinline, slim neck, 2 humbuckers, f-holes, split diamond inlays.

2006-2007	$950	$1,225

Vegas High Roller

2006-2007. Upgraded version, AAA maple top, gold hardware and frets, block inlays.

2006-2007	$1,125	$1,450

Victory MV II (MV 2)

1981-1984. Asymetrical double-cut with long horn, 3-way slider, maple body and neck, rosewood 'board, 2 pickups.

1981-1984	$825	$1,075

Victory MV X (MV 10)

1981-1984. 3 humbuckers, 5-way switch, various colors.

1981-1984	$825	$1,075

WRC

1987-1988. Designed for Gibson by Wayne R. Charvel (WRC), earlier models had Kahler trem, later Floyd Rose, offered in red, black or white.

1987-1988	$675	$875

XPL Custom

1985-1986. Explorer-like shape, exposed humbuckers, locking tremolo, bound maple top, sunburst or white.

1985-1986	$1,000	$1,300

Y2K Dwight Yoakam Signature

2005. Limited run of 200, small body jumbo, spruce top, highly figured maple sides and back, 2-piece flamed maple neck, double 'guard, gloss natural finish.

2005	$1,650	$2,150

Zakk Wylde ZV Buzzsaw

2008. Custom Shop Inspired By series, limited run of 50, Flying V wings with SG horns, 2 humbuckers.

2008	$2,450	$3,200

MODEL YEAR FEATURES	EXC. COND. LOW	HIGH

Gibson Baldwin

2005-ca. 2013. Entry-level electric and acoustic guitars, basses, amps and accessories made in China for discount store market and sold under the Signature, Maestro, Echelon, and Genesis brand names. Models include Les Paul and SG copies. Guitars have Music-Gibson logo on neckplate and brand logo on headstock.

Giffin

1977-1988, 1997-present. Professional and premium grade, production/custom, hollow-, semi-hollow-, and solidbody guitars built by luthier Roger Giffin in West San Fernando Valley, California. For '77-'88, Giffin's shop was in London. From '88 to '93, he worked for the Gibson Custom Shop in California as a Master Luthier. In '97, Giffin set up shop in Sweden for a year, moving back to California in the Spring of '98. He also built small numbers of instruments during '67-'76 and '94-'96 (when he had a repair business).

Gigliotti

2000-present. Premium grade, production/custom, electric guitars with a metal plate top and tone chambers and designed by Patrick Gigliotti in Tacoma, Washington.

Gila Eban Guitars

Premium grade, custom, classical guitars built by luthier Gila Eban in Riverside, Connecticut, starting in 1979.

Gilbert Guitars

1965-present. Custom classical guitars by luthiers John Gilbert and William Gilbert in Paso Robles, California. Son William has handled all production since '91. John died early 2012.

Gilchrist

1977-present. Currently known more for his mandolins, luthier Steve Gilchrist, of Warrnambool, Australia, has also built premium and presentation grade, custom, guitars.

Acoustic Archtop

1990s-present. Very limited production.

1990s-2019	$17,500	$22,500

Gilet Guitars

1976-present. Luthier Gerard Gilet builds production/custom, premium grade, acoustic, classical, flamenco, and wooden bodied resonator guitars in Botany, Sydney, New South Wales, Australia. He also builds lap steels.

Girl Brand Guitars

1996-2012. Premium-grade, production/custom, guitars built by luthier Chris Larsen in Tucson, Arizona. Larson now builds under the Larsen Guitar Mfg. name.

1965 Gibson Trini Lopez Standard

Matt Carleson

2008 Gibson Zakk Wylde ZV Buzzsaw

GUITARS

Godin A6 Ultra (A Series)

2017 Godin 5th Avenue

MODEL YEAR	FEATURES	EXC. COND. LOW	HIGH

Gitane

2003-present. Intermediate and professional grade, production, classic Selmer-Maccaferri style jazz guitars made in China for Saga.

Gittler

1974-ca.1985. Minimalistic electric guitar designed by Allan Gittler, consisting basically of a thin rod with frets welded to it. A total of 560 were built, with Gittler making the first 60 in the U.S. from '74 to the early '80s. The remainder were made around '85 in Israel by the Astron corporation under a licensing agreement. Three Gittler basses were also built. Gittler emigrated to Israel in the early '80s and changed his name to Avraham Bar Rashi. He died in 2002. A U.S.-made Gittler is the only musical instrument in the Museum of Modern Art in New York.

Metal Skeleton

1971-1999.

1971-1982		$2,600	$3,200
1982-1999		$2,300	$2,900

Giulietti

1962-1965. The Giulietti Accordion Company, New York, offered guitars and amps in the '60s.

GJ2

Gold Jackson Enterprises LLC, a partnership between luthier Grover Jackson and Jon Gold, established 2012, builds professional and premium grade, production/custom, solidbody electric guitars in Laguna Hills, California.

Glendale

2004-present. Professional grade, production/custom, solidbody guitars built by luthier Dale Clark in Arlington, Texas.

GLF

1991-1997. Solidbody electric guitars built by luthier Kevin Smith in Minnesota. In '97 he started building his ToneSmith line of guitars.

Glick Guitars

Premium grade, production/custom, acoustic and electric archtop, and acoustic guitars built in Santa Barbara, California by luthier Mike Glick, starting in '96.

Global

Late-1960s-1970s. Budget copy models, not unlike Teisco, imported from Asia for the student market. They also offered amps.

Electric Solidbody

Late-1960s-1970s.

1968		$85	$165

GMP

1990-2005. Professional and premium grade solidbody electric guitars built by GM Precision Products, Inc. of San Dimas, California. Original owners were Gary and Cameron Moline, Dave Pearson and Glenn Matjezel. Many guitars featured fancy tops or custom graphics. They also made basses. Overall production is estimated at 1120 guitars and basses. GMP reopened in '10 under new ownership (see following).

GMP (Genuine Musical Products)

2010-present. The GMP brand was acquired by Dan and Kim Lawrence in '08. Since '10, Dan along with fellow luthiers Glenn Matjezel and William Stempke build professional and premium grade, production/custom, electric guitars in San Dimas, California. They also build basses.

GMW

1998-present. Professional grade, production/custom, solidbody guitars from Lee Garver's GMW Guitarworks of Glendora, California.

Godin

1987-present. Intermediate and professional grade, production, solidbody electrics and nylon and steel string acoustic/electrics from luthier Robert Godin. They also build basses and mandolins. Necks and bodies are made in La Patrie, Quebec with final assembly in Berlin, New Hampshire. Godin is also involved in the Seagull, Norman, Richmond, Art & Lutherie, and Patrick & Simon brand of guitars. SA on Godin models stands for Synth Access.

5th Avenue Kingpin

2008-present. Full-size non-cut electric archtop, 1 or 2 P-90 pickups, plain or highly flamed top, premium price for highly flamed.

2008-2019		$575	$750

5th Avenue Uptown

2012-present. Archtop cutaway with Bigsby, f-holes, Canadian wild cherry top, back and sides, silver leaf maple neck, various colors.

2012-2019		$575	$750

A Series

1990s-present. Multiac-style body.

1990s-2019	A-12, 12-string	$425	$550
1990s-2019	A-6, 6-string	$400	$525

Acousticaster (6)

1987-present. Thin line single-cut chambered maple body, acoustic/electric, maple neck, 6-on-a-side tuners, spruce top.

1987-2019		$375	$500

Acousticaster 6 Deluxe

1994-2008. Acousticaster 6 with mahogany body.

1994-2008		$450	$575

Artisan ST I/ST I

1992-1998. Offset double-cut solidbody, birdseye maple top, 3 pickups.

1992-1998		$275	$375

Flat Five X

2002-2004. Single-cut, semi-hollow with f-holes, 3-way pickup system (magnetic to transducer).

2002-2004		$575	$750

The Official Vintage Guitar magazine Price Guide 2021   **Godin** Freeway Classic — **Goodall** Concert Jumbo Cutaway   **201**

GUITARS

MODEL YEAR	FEATURES	EXC. COND. LOW	HIGH

Freeway Classic/Freeway Classic SA
2004-2015. Offset double-cut solidbody, birdseye maple top on translucent finishes, hum-single-hum pickups.

2004-2015		$375	$500

G-1000/G-2000/G-3000
1993-1996. Offset double-cut solidbody, extra large bass horn, various pickup options.

1993-1996		$200	$275

Glissentar A11
2000-2017. Electric/acoustic nylon 11-string, solid cedar top, chambered maple body, fretless, natural.

2000-2017		$525	$700

Jeff Cook Signature
1994-1995. Quilted maple top, light maple back, 2 twin rail and 1 humbucker pickups.

1994-1995		$500	$650

L.R. Baggs Signature
1990s. Single-cut chambered thinline electric, spruce top, mahogany body, EQ.

1990s		$375	$500

LG/LGT
1995-2011. Single-cut carved slab mahogany body, 2 Tetrad Combo pickups ('95-'97) or 2 Duncan SP-90 pickups ('98-present), various colors, satin lacquer finish. LGT with tremolo.

1995-2011		$275	$375

LGX/LGXT/LGX-SA
1996-2018. Single-cut maple-top carved solidbody, 2 Duncan humbuckers, various quality tops offered. LGXT with tremolo.

1996-2018	Standard top	$525	$675
1997-2018	SA synth access	$750	$975
1998-2018	AA top	$750	$975
1998-2018	AAA top	$825	$1,075

Montreal
2004-present. Chambered body carved from solid mahogany, f-holes, 2 humbuckers, saddle transducer, stereo mixing output.

2004-2019		$650	$825

Multiac Series
1994-present. Single-cut, thinline electric with solid spruce top, RMC Sensor System electronics, available in either nylon string or steel string versions, built-in EQ, program up/down buttons.

1994-2019	Various models	$800	$1,300

Radiator
1999-2013. Single-cut, dual pickup, pearloid top, dot markers.

1999-2013		$215	$290

Redline Series
2007-2015. Maple body and neck, rosewood 'board, Redline 1 has 1 pickup, 2 and 3 have 2 pickups (3 has Floyd Rose), various colors.

2007-2011	Redline 1	$275	$360
2008-2015	Redline 3	$300	$400

SD Series
1990s-2012.

1990-2012	SD 22, SD 24	$190	$250

Solidac - Two Voice
2000-2009. Single-cut, 2-voice technology for electric or acoustic sound.

2000-2009		$250	$325

TC Signature
1987-1999. Single-cut, quilted maple top, 2 Tetrad Combo pickups.

1987-1999		$375	$500

Velocity
2007-2011. Offset double-cut, hum/single/single.

2007-2011		$375	$500

Gold Tone
1993-present. Wayne and Robyn Rogers build their intermediate and professional grade, production/custom guitars and basses in Titusville, Florida. They also build lap steels, mandolins, ukuleles, banjos and banjitars.

Goldbug Guitars
1997-present. Presentation grade, production/custom, acoustic and electric guitars built by luthier Sandy Winters in Delavan, Wisconsin.

Golden Hawaiian
1920s-1930s. Private branded lap guitar most likely made by one of the many Chicago makers for a small retailer, publisher, cataloger, or teaching studio.

Guitars
1920-1930s	Sunburst	$375	$500

Goldentone
1960s. Guitars made by Ibanez most likely in the mid to late '60s. Often have a stylized I (for Ibanez) on the tailpiece or an Ibanez logo on the headstock.

Goldon
German manufacturer of high-quality archtops and other guitars before and shortly after WW II. After the war, they were located in East Germany and by the late 1940s were only making musical toys.

Goodall
1972-present. Premium grade, custom flat-tops and nylon-strings, built by luthier James Goodall originally in California and, since '92, in Kailua-Kona, Hawaii.

Classical
1986. Brazilian and cedar.

1986	BC425	$5,000	$6,600

Concert Jumbo
1998-present. Various woods.

2007-2019	Red cedar/ Indian rosewood	$2,400	$3,200
2007-2019	Sitka/figured koa	$2,400	$3,200

Concert Jumbo Cutaway
2004-2018. Rosewood.

2004-2018		$2,900	$3,800

Godin Redline Series
Bernunzio Uptown Music

Goodall Concert Jumbo

1962 Gower G-55-2
Craig Brody

1960s Goya Rangemaster
Imaged by Heritage Auctions, HA.com

MODEL YEAR	FEATURES	EXC. COND. LOW	HIGH
Jumbo KJ			
1995-2011. Sitka, koa.			
1995-2011		$2,400	$3,200
RS Rosewood Standard			
1989-1997. Indian rosewood back and sides.			
1989-1997		$2,100	$2,700
Standard			
1980s-present. Jumbo-style with wide waist, mahogany back and sides, sitka spruce top.			
1980s-2019		$1,900	$2,500

Goodman Guitars

1975-present. Premium grade, custom/production, archtop, flat-top, classical, and electric guitars built by luthier Brad Goodman in Brewster, New York. He also builds mandolins.

Goran Custom Guitars

1998-present. Luthier Goran Djuric builds his professional and premium grade, custom, electric guitars in Belgrade, Serbia. He also builds effects.

Gordon-Smith

1979-present. Intermediate and professional grade, production/custom, semi-hollow and solidbody guitars built by luthier John Smith in Partington, England.

Gower

1955-1960s. Built in Nashville by Jay Gower, later joined by his son Randy. Gower is also associated with Billy Grammer and Grammer guitars.

MODEL YEAR	FEATURES	EXC. COND. LOW	HIGH
G-55-2 Flat-Top			
1960s. Square shoulder-style flat-top, triple abalone rosette, abalone fretboard trim, small block markers, natural.			
1960s		$725	$950
G-65 Flat-Top			
1960s. Square shoulder-style flat-top, lower belly bridge with pearl dots on bridge, dot markers, sunburst.			
1960s		$550	$725
G-100 Flat-Top			
1960s	Brazilian rosewood	$775	$1,025
Solidbody Electric			
1960s. Mosrite influenced odd-shaped body, 2 single-coils, bolt neck, Bigsby bridge.			
1960s		$600	$800

Goya

1952-1996. Brand initially used by Hershman Musical Instrument Company of New York City, New York, in mid-'50s for acoustic guitars made in Sweden by Levin, particularly known for its classicals. From '58 to '61 they imported Hagstrom- and Galanti-made electrics labeled as Goya; in '62 they offered electrics made by Valco. In '67 they again offered electrics, this time made by Zero Sette in Castelfidardo, Italy. By '63 the company had become the Goya Musical Instrument Corporation, marketing primarily Goya acoustics. In '67 they again offered electrics, this time made by Zero Sette in Castelfidardo, Italy. Goya was purchased by Avnet, Inc., prior to '66, when Avnet purchased Guild Guitars. In '69, Goya was purchased by Kustom which offered the instruments until '71. Probably some '70s guitars were made in Japan. The brand name was purchased by C.F. Martin in '76, with Japanese-made acoustic guitars, solidbody electric guitars and basses, banjos and mandolins imported in around '78 and continuing into the '90s.

MODEL YEAR	FEATURES	EXC. COND. LOW	HIGH
Classical			
1950s-1980s. Various models.			
1955-60s	G Series	$100	$1,000
1980s	Japan	$350	$450
Flamenco			
1955-1960s. Various models.			
1955-60s	FL Series	$300	$500
Folk			
1950s-1980s. Various models.			
1955-60s	F Series	$300	$500
Model 80/Model 90			
1959-1962. Single-cut body, replaceable modular pickup assembly, sparkle top.			
1959-1962		$750	$1,000
Panther S-3			
1967-1968. Double-cut solidbody, 3 pickups, Panther S-3 Goya logo, volume and tone knobs with 6 upper bass bout switches, bolt-on neck.			
1967-1968		$750	$1,000
Rangemaster			
1967-1968. Wide variety of models.			
1967-1968		$600	$800
Steel			
1955-1960s. Various models.			
1955-60s	M and S Series	$100	$250

Graf

See listing under Oskar Graf Guitars.

Grammer

1965-1971. Acoustic guitars built in Nashville. Founded by country guitarist Bill Grammer, music store owner Clyde Reid and luthier J.W. Gower (who also built his own line). Grammer sold the company to Ampeg in '68 who sold it again in '71, but it quickly ceased business. Originally the Grammer headstock logo had an upper-case G, Ampeg-made instruments have a lower-case one.

MODEL YEAR	FEATURES	EXC. COND. LOW	HIGH
G-10			
1965-1970. Solid Brazilian rosewood back and sides, solid spruce top, large crown-shaped bridge, pearl dot markers, natural.			
1965-1967	Grammer era	$1,250	$1,650
1968-1970	Ampeg era	$1,100	$1,450
G-20			
1965-1970. Natural.			
1965-1967	Grammer era	$1,250	$1,650
1968-1970	Ampeg era	$1,100	$1,450
G-30			
1965-1970. Natural.			
1965-1967	Grammer era	$1,250	$1,650
1968-1970	Ampeg era	$1,100	$1,450

MODEL YEAR	FEATURES	EXC. COND. LOW	HIGH

G-50
1965-1970. Top-of-the-line Grammer, Brazilian rosewood back and sides, Adirondack spruce top.

1965-1967	Grammer era	$1,700	$2,200
1968-1970	Ampeg era	$1,500	$2,000

S-30
1965-1970. Solid spruce top, solid ribbon mahogany back and sides.

1965-1967	Grammer era	$950	$1,250
1968-1970	Ampeg era	$800	$1,050

Granada
Late 1960s-1980s. Japanese-made acoustic, electric solid, semi-hollow and hollowbody guitars, many copies of classic American models. They also offered basses.

Acoustic
1970-1979. Import from Japan, various copy models.

1970-1979		$110	$150

Electric
1970-1979. Import from Japan, various copy models.

1970-1979		$150	$200

Granata Guitars
1989-present. Luthier Peter Granata builds his professional grade, custom, flat-top and resonator guitars in Oak Ridge, New Jersey.

Graveel
Production/custom, solidbody guitars built by luthier Dean Graveel in Indianapolis, Indiana.

Grazioso
1950s. Grazioso was a brand name used by Selmer in England on instruments made in Czechoslovakia. They replaced the brand with their Futurama line of guitars.

GRD
1978-1982. High-end acoustic and electric guitars produced in Charles Fox's Guitar Research & Design Center in Vermont. GRD introduced the original thin-line acoustic-electric guitar to the world at the '78 Winter NAMM show.

Great Divide Guitars
2009-2011. Budget and intermediate grade, production, flat-top guitars imported from China, designed by luthier Tom Bedell, Dan Mills and Sophia Yang. They also offer Bedell Guitars.

Greco
1960s-present. Brand name used in Japan and owned by Kanda Shokai. Fuji Gen Gakki, maker of many Hoshino/Ibanez guitars, also made many Greco models during the '70s; thus often Greco guitars are similar to Ibanez. During the '70s the company sold many high-quality copies of American designs, though by '75 they offered many weird-shaped original designs, including the Iceman and carved people shapes. By the late-'70s they were

offering neck-through-body guitars. Currently offering solidbody, hollowbody and acoustic guitars and basses, including models licensed by Zemaitis.

Green, Aaron
1990-present. Premium and presentation grade, custom, classical and flamenco guitars built by luthier Aaron Green in Waltham, Massachusetts.

Greene & Campbell
2002-2005. Luthier Dean Campbell built his intermediate and professional grade, production/custom, solidbody guitars in Westwood, Massachusetts. Founding partner Jeffrey Greene left the company in '04; Greene earlier built guitars under his own name. In '05, Campbell changed the name to Campbell American Guitars.

Greene, Jeffrey
2000-2002. Professional grade, production/custom, electric solidbody guitars built by luthier Jeffrey Greene in West Kingston, Rhode Island. He went to work with Dean Campbell building the Greene & Campbell line of guitars.

Greenfield Guitars
1996-present. Luthier Michael Greenfield builds his production/custom, presentation grade, acoustic steel string, concert classical and archtop guitars in Montreal, Quebec.

Gretsch
1883-present. Currently Gretsch offers intermediate, professional, and premium grade, production, acoustic, solidbody, hollowbody, double neck, resonator and Hawaiian guitars. They also offer basses, amps and lap steels. In 2012 they again started offering mandolins, ukuleles and banjos.

Previous brands included Gretsch, Rex, 20th Century, Recording King (for Montgomery Ward), Dorado (Japanese imports). Founded by Friedrich Gretsch in Brooklyn, New York, making drums, banjos, tambourines, and toy instruments which were sold to large distributors including C. Bruno and Wurlitzer. Upon early death of Friedrich, son Fred Gretsch, Sr. took over business at age 15. By the turn of the century the company was also making mandolins. In the '20s, they were distributing Rex and 20th Century brands, some made by Gretsch, some by others such as Kay. Charles "Duke" Kramer joined Gretsch in '35. In '40 Gretsch purchased Bacon & Day banjos. Fred Gretsch, Sr. retired in '42 and was replaced by sons Fred, Jr. and Bill. Fred departs for Navy and Bill runs company until his death in '48, when Fred resumes control. After the war the decision was made to promote the Gretsch brand rather than selling to distributors, though some jobbing continues. Kramer becomes Chicago branch manager in '48.

In '67 Baldwin of Cincinnati bought Gretsch. During '70-'72 the factory relocated from Brooklyn

Granata Resonator

1980 Greco Goldtop
Jon Way

1961 Gretsch Bikini (6025)
Randy Barnett

Gretsch Billy-Bo Jupiter
Thunderbird (6199)

to Booneville, Arkansas and company headquarters are moved to Cincinnati. A '72 factory fire drastically reduced production for next two years. In '78 Baldwin bought Kustom amps and sold Gretsch to Kustom's Charlie Roy, and headquarters are moved to Chanute, Kansas. Duke Kramer retired in '80. Guitar production ends '80-'81. Ca. '83 ownership reverted back to Baldwin and Kramer was asked to arrange the sale of the company. In '84 Fred Gretsch III was contacted and in '85 Gretsch guitars came back to the Gretsch family and Fred Gretsch Enterprises, Ltd (FGE). Initial Gretsch Enterprise models were imports made by Japan's Terada Company. In '95, some U.S.-made models were introduced. In 2003, Gretsch granted Fender the rights to develop, produce, market and distribute Gretsch guitars worldwide, including development of new products.

Binding rot can be a problem on 1950s models and prices shown are for fully original, unrestored bindings.

12-String Electric Archtop (6075/6076)
1967-1972. 16" double-cut, 2 Super Tron pickups, 17" body option available, sunburst (6075) or natural (6076).

MODEL YEAR	FEATURES	EXC. COND. LOW	HIGH
1967-1972	Natural or sunburst	$1,675	$2,225

12-String Flat-Top (6020)
1969-1972. 15 1/5" body, mahogany back and sides, spruce top, slotted headstock, dot markers.

1969-1972		$800	$1,050

Anniversary (6124/6125)
1958-1972, 1993-1999. Single-cut hollowbody archtop, 1 pickup (Filtron '58-'60, Hi-Lo Tron '61 on), bound body, named for Gretsch's 75th anniversary. 6125 is 2-tone green with 2-tone tan an option, 6124 sunburst. Model numbers revived in '90s.

1958-1959	Green 2-tone	$2,250	$2,900
1958-1959	Sunburst	$1,550	$2,000
1960-1961	2-tone green or tan	$2,125	$2,750
1960-1961	Sunburst	$1,350	$1,750
1962-1964	2-tone green or tan	$1,700	$2,200
1962-1964	Sunburst	$1,225	$1,600
1965-1966	Various colors	$1,225	$1,600
1967-1969	Various colors	$1,050	$1,350
1970-1972	Various colors	$925	$1,200

Anniversary Tenor (6124)
1958-1971. Gretsch offered many models with the 4-string tenor option and also made small batches of tenors, with the same colors and pickups as standard models.

1958-1971		$1,200	$1,550

Anniversary Reissue (6124/6125)
1993-1999. 1 pickup Anniversary reissue, 6124 in sunburst, 6125 2-tone green.

1993-1999		$1,100	$1,425

Anniversary Reissue (6117/6118)
1993-present. 2 pickup like Double Anniversary, 6118 in 2-tone green with (T) or without Bigsby, 6117 is sunburst.

1993-2015	6117	$1,300	$1,725
1993-2019	6118	$1,300	$1,725

Astro-Jet (6126)
1965-1967. Solidbody electric, double-cut, 2 pickups, vibrato, 4/2 tuner arrangement, red top with black back and sides.

MODEL YEAR	FEATURES	EXC. COND. LOW	HIGH
1965-1967		$1,300	$1,700

Atkins Axe (7685/7686)
1976-1980. Solidbody electric, single pointed cutaway, 2 pickups, ebony stain (7685) or red rosewood stain (7686), called the Super Axe with added on-board effects.

1976-1980		$1,025	$1,325

Atkins Super Axe (7680/7681)
1976-1981. Single pointed cutaway solidbody with built-in phaser and sustain, five knobs, three switches, Red Rosewood (7680) or Ebony (7681) stains.

1976-1981		$1,550	$2,000

Bikini (6023/6024/6025)
1961-1962. Solidbody electric, separate 6-string and bass neck-body units that slide into 1 of 3 body butterflies - 1 for the 6-string only (6023), 1 for bass only (6024), 1 for double neck (6 and bass - 6025). Components could be purchased separately.

1961-1962	6023/6024, single neck	$775	$1,000
1961-1962	6025, double neck	$1,575	$2,050

Billy-Bo Jupiter Thunderbird (6199)
2005-present. Billy Gibbons and Bo Diddley influenced, chambered mahogany body, laminate maple top, 2 pickups.

2005-2019		$1,700	$2,200

Black Falcon (6136BK/TBK/DSBK)
1992-1997, 2003-2015. Black version of Falcon, single-cut, 2.75" body, oversize f-holes, G tailpiece, DSBK with DynaSonic pickups replaces Filter'Tron BK in '06. Had the Limited Edition 1955 designation for '96-'97. Bigsby-equipped TBK offered '04-present.

1992-2015		$1,825	$2,350

Black Falcon (7594BK)
1992-1998. Black version of G7594 Falcon, double-cut, 2" thick body, Bigsby.

1992-1998		$1,825	$2,350

Black Falcon I (7593BK)
1993-1998, 2003-2005. G63136BK with Bigsby and standard f-holes. Came back in '03 as Black Falcon I with wire handle Gretsch Bigsby tailpiece.

1993-1998		$1,825	$2,350

Black Hawk (6100/6101)
1967-1972. Hollowbody archtop, double-cut, 2 pickups, G tailpiece or Bigsby vibrato, bound body and neck, sunburst (6100) or black (6101).

1967-1969	6100, sunburst	$1,900	$2,475
1967-1969	6101, black	$1,900	$2,475
1970-1972	6100, sunburst	$1,900	$2,475
1970-1972	6101, black	$1,900	$2,475

Black Penguin (6134B)
2003-2015. Jet black version.

2003-2015		$1,825	$2,350

Bo Diddley (1810/5810)
2000-2015. Korean-made version.

2000-2015		$175	$225

MODEL YEAR	FEATURES	EXC. COND. LOW	HIGH

Bo Diddley (6138)

1999-present. Reproduction of rectangle-shaped, semi-hollow guitar originally made for Diddley by Gretsch, Firebird Red.

1999-2019		$1,125	$1,450

Broadkaster (Hollowbody)

1975-1980. Double-cut archtop, hollowbody, 2 pickups, natural or sunburst.

1975-1977	7603, Bigsby, natural	$725	$950
1975-1977	7604, Bigsby, sunburst	$725	$950
1975-1977	7607, G tailpiece, natural	$725	$950
1975-1977	7608, G tailpiece, sunburst	$725	$950
1977-1980	7609, red	$725	$950

Broadkaster (Solidbody)

1975-1979. Double-cut, maple body, 2 pickups, bolt-on neck, natural (7600) or sunburst (7601).

1975-1979		$650	$850

BST 1000 Beast

1979-1980. Single-cut solidbody, bolt-on neck, mahogany body, available with 1 pickup in walnut stain (8210) or red stain (8216) or 2 pickups in walnut (7617, 8215, 8217) or red stain (8211).

1979-1980		$500	$650

BST 2000 Beast

1979. Symmetrical double-cut solidbody of mahogany, 2 humbucking pickups, bolt-on neck, walnut stain (7620 or 8220) or red stain (8221).

1979		$575	$750

BST 5000 Beast

1979-1980. Asymmetrical double-cut solidbody, neck-thru, walnut and maple construction, 2 humbucker pickups, stud tailpiece, natural walnut/maple (8250).

1979-1980		$650	$850

Burl Ives (6004)

1949-1955. Flat-top acoustic, mahogany back and sides, bound body, natural top (6004).

1949-1955		$625	$825

Chet Atkins Country Gentleman (6122/7670)

1957-1981. Hollowbody, single-cut to late-'62 and double after, 2 pickups, painted f-holes until '72, real after, mahogany finish (6122). Model number changes to 7670 in '71. Guitars made during and after '64 might have replaced body binding which reduces the value shown by about 10% or more.

1957-1959		$7,500	$9,900
1960		$5,000	$6,500
1961		$4,500	$6,000
1962-1963	George Harrison specs	$3,500	$4,600
1964		$3,000	$3,900
1965		$2,700	$3,500
1966-1970		$2,250	$2,850
1971-1981	7670	$2,000	$2,600

Chet Atkins Country Gentleman (6122-1958)

2007-2015. Single-cut reissue of '58.

2007-2015		$1,500	$1,975

Chet Atkins Country Gentleman (6122-1962)

2007-2015. Double-cut reissue of '62, double muffler (mutes) system, Filter'Trons.

2007-2015		$1,500	$1,975

Chet Atkins Hollowbody (6120)

1954-1966, 2007-2015. Archtop electric, single-cut to '61, double after, 2 pickups, vibrato, f-holes (real to '61 and fake after), cactus and cows engraved block inlays '54-early '56, G brand on top '54-'56, orange finish (6120). Renamed Chet Atkins Nashville in '67. Reissued single-cut in '07.

1954-1955	G brand, Western	$9,600	$12,500
1955-1956	Non-engraved, amber red	$8,400	$11,000
1957-1959	No G-brand	$7,400	$9,600
1960-1961	Single-cut	$5,700	$7,500
1961-1965	Double-cut	$2,700	$3,500
1966	Double-cut	$2,650	$3,500
2007-2015	Single-cut	$1,400	$1,800

Chet Atkins Nashville (6120/7660)

1967-1980. Replaced Chet Atkins Hollowbody (6120), electric archtop, double-cut, 2 pickups, amber red (orange). Renumbered 7660 in '72, reissued in '90 as the Model 6120 Nashville.

1967-1969	6120	$1,875	$2,450
1970-1971	6120	$1,575	$2,075
1972-1980	7660	$1,425	$1,875

Chet Atkins Hollowbody (6120W-1957)

2007-2009. Western Maple Stain, western block inlays, Bigsby.

2007-2009		$1,500	$1,975

Brian Setzer Black Phoenix (6136-SLBP)

2005-2015. Artist Signature Series, nitro gloss black.

2005-2015		$1,825	$2,350

Brian Setzer Hot Rod (6120SHx)

1999-present. Like SSL, but with only pickup switch and 1 master volume control.

1999-2019		$1,200	$1,600

Brian Setzer Nashville (6120SSL, etc.)

1993-present. Hollowbody electric, double-cut, 2 Alnico PAF Filtertron pickups, based on the classic Gretsch 6120.

1993-2019	Western Orange	$1,825	$2,350

Chet Atkins Junior

1970. Archtop, single-cut, 1 pickup, vibrato, open f-holes, double-bound body, orange stain.

1970		$875	$1,150

Duane Eddy (6210DE)

1997-2003. 6120 style, 2 DeArmond single coils, Bigsby, orange.

1997-2003		$1,500	$1,975

Duane Eddy Signature Hollow Body (6120DE)

2011-present. Single-cut, Western Orange stain lacquer finish.

2011-2019		$1,500	$1,975

Eddie Cochran Signature Hollow Body (6120)

2011-present. Artist Signature Edition, maple body, rosewood 'board, Bigsby, Western maple stain.

2011-2019		$1,500	$1,975

1970 Gretsch BST 1000 Beast

1960 Gretsch Chet Atkins Hollowbody 6120

Paul Harbinson

Gretsch Chet Atkins Tennessean (6119/7655)

Darien Zalefsky,

Gretsch Duane Eddy Signature Hollow Body (6120DE)

MODEL YEAR	FEATURES	EXC. COND. LOW	HIGH
Keith Scott Nashville (6120KS)			
1999-2013. Hump-back inlays, gold hardware, metallic gold finish.			
1999-2013		$1,500	$1,975
Nashville Double Neck 6/12 (6120)			
1997-2002. Built in Japan, few made, all gold hardware, necks are maple with ebony 'boards, orange finish.			
1997-2002		$2,150	$2,800
Nashville Jr. (6120-JR/JR2)			
1998-2004. Orange, 2 pickups.			
1998-2004		$950	$1,225
New Nashville (6120N)			
2001-2003. Single-cut, humptop inlays, gold hardware.			
2001-2003		$1,500	$1,975
Reverend Horton Heat (6120RHH)			
2005-present. Cows and cactus inlays, TV jones pickups.			
2005-2019		$1,500	$1,975
Chet Atkins Solidbody (6121)			
1955-1963. Solidbody electric, single-cut, maple or knotty pine top, 2 pickups, Bigsby vibrato, G brand until '57, multi-bound top, brown mahogany, orange finish (6121).			
1955-1956		$8,000	$10,500
1957	G brand	$6,800	$8,800
1957-1959	No G brand	$6,000	$7,800
1960	Single-cut	$5,500	$7,200
1961-1963	Double-cut	$4,500	$5,800
Chet Atkins Tennessean (6119/7655)			
1958-1980. Archtop electric, single-cut, 1 pickup until '61 and 2 after, vibrato. Renumbered as the 7655 in '71.			
1958-1959	1 Filter-Tron	$2,100	$2,700
1960-1961	1 Hi-Lo	$1,900	$2,500
1961-1964	2 Hi-Lo	$2,200	$2,800
1965-1967	2 pickups	$2,100	$2,700
1968-1970	2 pickups	$1,900	$2,500
1971-1980	7655	$1,900	$2,500
Chet Atkins Tennessee Rose (6119-1959, 1962)			
1995-2015. Import, 16" maple body, maple neck, dual FilterTron pickups.			
1995-2015		$1,500	$1,975
Clipper (6185/6186/6187/7555)			
1958-1975. Archtop electric, single-cut, sunburst, 1 pickup (6186) until '72 and 2 pickups (6185) from '72-'75, also available in 1 pickup natural (6187) from '59-'61.			
1958-1961	6186	$825	$1,075
1959-1961	6187	$900	$1,175
1962-1967	6186	$800	$1,025
1968-1971	6186	$750	$950
1972-1975	7555	$925	$1,200
Committee (7628)			
1977-1980. Neck-thru electric solidbody, double-cut, walnut and maple body, 2 pickups, 4 knobs, natural.			
1977-1980		$725	$925
Constellation			
1955-1960. Renamed from Synchromatic 6030 and			

MODEL YEAR	FEATURES	EXC. COND. LOW	HIGH
6031, archtop acoustic, single-cut, G tailpiece, humped block inlay.			
1955-1960		$1,375	$1,800
Convertible (6199)			
1955-1958. Archtop electric, single-cut, 1 pickup, multi-bound body, G tailpiece, renamed Sal Salvador in '58.			
1955-1958		$1,800	$2,350
Corsair			
1955-1960. Renamed from Synchromatic 100, archtop acoustic, bound body and headstock, G tailpiece, available in sunburst (6014), natural (6015) or burgundy (6016).			
1955-1960		$800	$1,025
Corvette (Hollowbody)			
1955-1959. Renamed from Electromatic Spanish, archtop electric, 1 pickup, f-holes, bound body, Electromatic on headstock, non-cut, sunburst (6182), natural or Jaguar Tan (6184), and ivory with rounded cutaway (6187).			
1955-1959	6182, sunburst	$900	$1,150
1955-1959	6184, Jaguar Tan	$1,175	$1,525
1955-1959	6184, natural	$1,175	$1,525
1957-1959	6187, ivory	$1,175	$1,525
Corvette (Solidbody)			
1961-1972, 1976-1978. Double-cut slab solidbody. Mahogany 6132 and cherry 6134 1 pickup for '61-'68. 2 pickup mahogany 6135 and cherry 7623 available by '63-'72 and '76-'78. From late-'61 through '63 a Twist option was offered featuring a red candy stripe 'guard. Platinum Gray 6133 available for '61-'63 and the Gold Duke and Silver Duke sparkle finishes were offered in '66.			
1961-1962	Mahogany, cherry	$825	$1,075
1961-1963	Platinum Gray	$1,275	$1,650
1961-1963	Twist 'guard	$1,275	$1,650
1963-1965	Custom color, 1 pu	$1,275	$1,650
1963-1965	Custom color, 2 pus	$1,525	$2,000
1963-1965	Mahogany, cherry, 1 pu	$650	$850
1963-1965	Mahogany, cherry, 2 pus	$900	$1,200
1966	Gold Duke	$1,275	$1,650
1966	Silver Duke	$1,275	$1,650
1966-1968	Mahogany, cherry, 1 pu	$525	$675
1966-1972	Mahogany, cherry, 2 pus	$875	$1,125
1976-1978	7623, 2 pus	$700	$925
Corvette/CVT (5135)			
2006-2018. Like double-cut solidbody Corvette, 2 Mega'Tron pickups, Bigsby, becomes the CVT in '10.			
2006-2018		$525	$675
Country Classic I/II (6122 Reissue)			
1989-2006. Country Gentleman reissue in '58 (I) and '62 (II) specs. Also cataloged as G6122-1958 and G6122-1962 Country Classic.			
1989-2006	'58, single-cut	$1,500	$1,975
1989-2006	'62, double-cut	$1,500	$1,975

GUITARS

MODEL YEAR	FEATURES	EXC. COND. LOW	HIGH

Country Classic II Custom Edition (6122)

2005. Reissue of George Harrison's 2nd 6122 Country Gentleman, the Custom Edition has TV Jones Filtertron pickups.

2005		$1,500	$1,975

Country Club

1954-1981. Renamed from Electro II Cutaway, archtop electric, single-cut, 2 pickups (Filter Trons after '57), G tailpiece, multi-bound, various colors.

1954-1956	Sunburst	$3,000	$4,000
1954-1959	Cadillac Green	$4,000	$5,100
1954-1959	Natural	$3,525	$4,625
1957-1959	Sunburst	$3,025	$4,025
1960-1961	Sunburst	$2,400	$3,100
1960-1962	Cadillac Green	$3,150	$4,100
1960-1962	Natural	$2,400	$3,100
1962-1964	Sunburst	$2,100	$2,700
1964	Cadillac Green	$2,900	$3,800
1965-1969	Sunburst or walnut	$1,600	$2,075
1970-1981	Various colors	$1,650	$2,150

Country Club 1955 Reissue (6196-1955) (FGE)

1995-1999. U.S.-made reissue of Country Club, single-cut, 2 DeArmond pickups, hand-rubbed lacquer finish.

1995-1999		$1,500	$1,975

Country Club (6196, etc.)

2001-present. Includes Cadillac Green (G6196, '01-present), sunburst (G6192, '03-'08), amber natural (G6193,'03-'08), Bamboo Yellow (G6196TSP-BY, '09-'13), and smoky gray and violet 2-tone (G6196TSP-2G, '09-'12), G6196T-59GE Golden Era Edition ('16-present), T means Bigsby.

2001-2019	Cadillac Green	$1,500	$1,975
2009-2013	Bamboo Yellow	$1,500	$1,975

Country Roc (7620)

1974-1978. Single-cut solidbody, 2 pickups, belt buckle tailpiece, western scene fretboard inlays, G brand, tooled leather side trim.

1974-1978		$1,650	$2,150

Custom (6117)

1964-1968. Limited production, smaller thinner version of Double Anniversary model, 2 pickups, cat's eye soundholes, red or black finish.

1964		$2,300	$3,000
1965-1966		$2,000	$2,600
1967-1968		$1,800	$2,300

Deluxe Chet (7680/7681)

1972-1974. Electric archtop with rounded cutaway, Autumn Red (7680) or brown walnut (7681) finishes.

1972-1974		$1,850	$2,400

Deluxe Flat-Top (7535)

1972-1978. 16" redwood top, mahogany back and sides.

1972-1978		$1,450	$1,900

Double Anniversary Mono (6117/6118)

1958-1976. Archtop electric, single-cut, 2 pickups, stereo optional until '63, sunburst (6117) or green 2-tone (6118). Reissued in '93 as the Anniversary 6117 and 6118.

1958-1959	Green 2-tone	$2,250	$2,975
1958-1959	Sunburst	$1,625	$2,150
1960-1961	Green 2-tone	$1,825	$2,425
1960-1961	Sunburst	$1,475	$1,950
1962-1964	Green 2-tone or tan	$1,800	$2,400
1962-1964	Sunburst	$1,475	$1,950
1965-1966	Various colors	$1,075	$1,425
1967-1969	Various colors	$900	$1,175
1970-1976	Various colors	$800	$1,050

Double Anniversary Stereo (6111/6112)

1961-1963. One stereo channel/signal per pickup, sunburst (6111) or green (6112).

1961-1963	Green	$1,625	$2,150
1961-1963	Sunburst	$1,300	$1,700

Duo-Jet (6128)

1953-1971. Solidbody electric, single-cut until '61, double after, 2 pickups, block inlays to late '56, then humptop until early '58, then thumbprint inlays, black (6128) with a few special order Cadillac Green, sparkle finishes were offered '63-'66, reissued in '90.

1953-1956	Black, single-cut	$4,900	$6,400
1956-1958	Black, humptop	$5,500	$7,100
1956-1958	Cadillac Green	$6,700	$8,600
1958-1960	Black, thumbprint	$3,900	$5,100
1961-1964	Black, double-cut	$3,200	$4,200
1963-1964	Sparkle, double-cut	$3,900	$5,100
1965-1966	Sparkle, double-cut	$3,200	$4,200
1965-1971	Black	$2,675	$3,450

Duo-Jet (6128TCG)

2005-2016. Cadillac Green, gold hardware, Bigsby.

2005-2016		$1,500	$1,975

Duo-Jet Reissue (6128/6128T)

1990-present. Reissue of the '50s solidbody, optional Bigsby (G6128T).

1990-2019		$1,350	$1,750

Duo-Jet Tenor

1959-1960. Electric tenor, 4 strings, block inlays, black.

1959-1960		$2,600	$3,400

Duo-Jet Vintage Select Edition '59 (6128T-59)

2017-present. Bigsby, TV Jones Filter'Trons, black.

2017-2020		$1,500	$1,975

Elliot Easton Signature Duo-Jet (6128TEE)

2000-2005. Bigsby, gold hardware, Cadillac Green (TEE), red (TREE), black (TBEE).

2000-2005		$1,500	$1,975

Eldorado (6040/6041)

1955-1970, 1991-1997. This is the larger 18" version, renamed from Synchromatic 400, archtop acoustic, single-cut, triple-bound fretboard and peghead, sunburst (6040) or natural (6041). Reintroduced in '91, made by Heritage in Kalamazoo, as the G410 Synchromatic Eldorado in sunburst or natural (G410M).

1955-1959	Natural	$2,200	$2,900
1955-1959	Sunburst	$1,800	$2,300
1960-1963	Natural	$1,600	$2,100
1960-1963	Sunburst	$1,450	$1,900
1964	Natural	$1,400	$1,800
1964	Sunburst	$1,300	$1,700
1965-1997	Natural, sunburst	$1,150	$1,500

1961 Gretsch Country Club
Geoff Parsons

1964 Gretsch Double Anniversary Mono (6117/6118)
Guitar Maniacs

GUITARS

1955 Gretsch Fleetwood (6039)
Bernunzio Uptown Music

1959 Gretsch Jet Firebird (6131)

MODEL YEAR	FEATURES	EXC. COND. LOW	HIGH
Eldorado (6038/6039)			
1959-1968. The smaller 17" version, named Fleetwood from '55 to '58, sunburst (6038) or natural (6039), also available as a full body non-cutaway.			
1959-1964	Natural, sunburst	$1,100	$1,425
1965-1968	Natural, sunburst	$900	$1,175
Electro Classic (6006/6495)			
1969-1973. Classical flat-top with piezo pickup.			
1969-1970	6006	$550	$700
1971-1973	6495	$550	$700
Electro II Cutaway (6192/6193)			
1951-1954. Archtop electric, single-cut, Melita bridge by '53, 2 pickups, f-holes, sunburst (6192) or natural (6193). Renamed Country Club in '54.			
1951-1954	6192, sunburst	$2,500	$3,300
1951-1954	6193, natural	$2,725	$3,550
Electro II Non-Cutaway (6187/6188)			
1951-1954. 16" electric archtop, 2 DeArmonds, large f-holes, block markers, 6187 sunburst, 6188 natural, label is Model 6187-8, vertical Electromatic logo on headstock.			
1951-1954	6187, sunburst	$875	$1,125
1951-1954	6188, natural	$975	$1,250
Electromatic (5420T)			
2013-present. Hollowbody, single-cut, Bigsby.			
2013-2019		$525	$675
Electromatic (5422-12)			
2013-present. 12-string 5422.			
2013-2019		$475	$625
Electromatic (5422T)			
2013-present. Hollowbody, double-cut, Bigsby.			
2013-2019		$475	$625
Electromatic Hollow Body (5120/5125-29/5420)			
2005-present. Single-cut, 2 dual-coils, Bigsby, black, Aspen Green, sunburst or orange. With Filter'Tron pickups in '13 (5420).			
2005-2019		$525	$675
Electromatic Hollow Body (5122/5422)			
2009-present. Double-cut version of G5120, 2 dual-coils, Bigsby, black, trans red or walnut. With Filter'Tron pickups in '13 (5422).			
2009-2019		$525	$675
Tim Armstrong Signature Electromatic (5191BK)			
2010-present. Hollow body, single-cut, all maple, 2 Filter'Tron pickups, black.			
2010-2019		$525	$675
Electromatic Spanish (6185/6185N)			
1940-1955. Hollowbody, 17" wide, 1 pickup, sunburst (6185) or natural (6185N). Renamed Corvette (hollowbody) in '55.			
1940-1949	Sunburst	$1,050	$1,325
1950-1955	Natural	$1,050	$1,325
1950-1955	Sunburst	$950	$1,225
Fleetwood (6038/6039)			
1955-1958. Named Synchromatic prior to '55, single-cut, sunburst (6038) or natural (6039). Renamed Eldorado in '59, available by custom order.			
1955-1958	Natural	$2,500	$3,250
1955-1958	Sunburst	$2,000	$2,600

MODEL YEAR	FEATURES	EXC. COND. LOW	HIGH
Folk/Folk Singing (6003/7505/7506)			
1963-1975. Lower-model of Gretsch flat-tops, 14 1/4", mahogany back and sides. Renamed from Jimmie Rodgers model, renamed Folk Singing in '63.			
1963-1964		$575	$750
1965-1969		$500	$650
1970-1975		$425	$550
Golden Classic (Hauser Model/Model 6000)			
1961-1969. Grand Concert body size, nylon-string classical, 14 1/4" spruce top, mahogany back and sides, multiple inlaid sound hole purfling, inlaid headstock.			
1961-1969		$385	$500
Grand Concert (6003)			
1955-1959. Lower-model of Gretsch flat-tops, 14 1/4", mahogany back and sides. Renamed from Model 6003 and renamed Jimmie Rodgers in '59.			
1955-1959		$475	$625
Guitar-Banjo			
1920s. 6-string guitar neck on banjo body, slotted headstock, open back.			
1920s		$500	$650
Jet 21			
Late-1940s. 16" acoustic archtop, Jet 21 engraved logo on headstock, bound top and back, white 'guard, jet black finish.			
1947-1948		$460	$600
Jet Firebird (6131)			
1955-1971. Solidbody electric, single-cut until '61, double '61-'71, 2 pickups, black body with red top, block inlays to late '56, then humptop until early '58, then thumbprint inlays.			
1955-1958	Single-cut	$5,200	$6,800
1959-1960	Single-cut	$4,500	$5,800
1961-1964	Double-cut	$3,700	$4,800
1965-1967		$3,000	$3,900
1968-1971	Super Trons	$3,000	$3,900
Jet Firebird Reissue/Power Jet Firebird (6131/6131T)			
1989-1997, 2003-2019. Single-cut '58 specs, red top, 2 FilterTrons, thumbprint markers, gold hardware for '91-'05, currently chrome. Bigsby available (T). Non-Bigsby 6131 ends in '05. DynaSonic-equipped TDS starts in '05 and TV Jones PowerTrons (TVP) in '06.			
2003-2019		$1,100	$1,425
Jimmie Rodgers (6003)			
1959-1962. 14" flat-top with round hole, mahogany back and sides, renamed from Grand Concert and renamed Folk Singing in '63.			
1959-1962		$600	$775
Jumbo Synchromatic (125F)			
1947-1955. 17" flat-top, triangular soundhole, bound top and back, metal bridge anchor plate, adjustable wood bridge, natural top with sunburst back and sides or optional translucent white-blond top and sides.			
1947-1955	Natural	$1,700	$2,200
1947-1955	White-blond	$1,900	$2,450
Malcom Young Signature Jet (6131-MY)			
2018-present. Professional Collection series, double-cut mahogany body, maple top, aged white binding, semi-gloss natural finish.			
2018-2020		$1,600	$2,100

MODEL YEAR	FEATURES	EXC. COND. LOW	HIGH

Model 25 (Acoustic)
1933-1939. 16" archtop, no binding on top or back, dot markers, sunburst.

1933-1939		$500	$650

Model 30 (Acoustic)
1939-1949. 16" archtop, top binding, dot markers, sunburst.

1939-1949		$575	$750

Model 35 (Acoustic)
1933-1949. 16" archtop, single-bound top and back, dot markers, sunburst.

1933-1949		$625	$825

Model 40 Hawaiian (Acoustic)
1936-1949. Flat-top, bound top and neck, diamond inlays.

1936-1949		$725	$925

Model 50/50R (Acoustic)
1936-1949. Acoustic archtop, f-holes. Model 50R (1936-'39) has round soundhole.

1936-1939	TG-50 Tenor	$525	$700
1936-1949	50/50R	$800	$1,050

Model 65 (Acoustic)
1933-1939. Archtop acoustic, bound body, amber.

1933-1939		$875	$1,150

Model 75 Tenor (Acoustic)
1933-1949. 4-string tenor.

1933-1949		$575	$750

Model 6003
1951-1955. 14 1/4", mahogany back and sides, renamed Grand Concert in '55.

1951-1954		$600	$775

Monkees
Late 1966-1968. Hollowbody electric, double-cut, 2 pickups, Monkees logo on 'guard, bound top, f-holes and neck, vibrato, red.

1966-1968		$2,550	$3,300

New Yorker
Ca.1949-1970. Archtop acoustic, f-holes, sunburst.

1949-1959		$800	$1,025
1960-1964		$700	$900
1965-1969		$600	$775
1970		$500	$650

New Yorker Tenor (6050)
1950s. 4-string tenor version.

1950s		$475	$625

Ozark/Ozark Soft String (6005)
1965-1968. 16" classical, rosewood back and sides.

1965-1968		$450	$575

Princess (6106)
1963. Corvette-type solidbody double-cut, 1 pickup, vibrato, gold parts, colors available were white/grape, blue/white, pink/white, or white/gold, often sold with the Princess amp.

1963		$1,425	$1,850

Rally (6104/6105)
1967-1969. Archtop, double-cut, 2 pickups, vibrato, racing stripe on truss rod cover and pickguard, Rally Green (6104) or Bamboo Yellow (6105).

1967-1969	6104 or 6105	$1,700	$2,200

Rambler (6115)
1957-1961. Small body electric archtop, single-cut, 1 DeArmond pickup '57-59, then 1 Hi-Lo 'Tron '60-'61, G tailpiece, bound body and headstock.

1957-1959	DeArmond	$1,100	$1,425
1960-1961	Hi-Lo 'Tron	$950	$1,225

Rancher
1954-1980. Flat-top acoustic, triangle soundhole, Western theme inlay, G brand until '61 and '75 and after, Golden Red (orange), reissued in '90.

1954-1957	G brand	$3,800	$4,950
1958-1961	G brand	$3,400	$4,450
1962-1964	No G brand	$2,700	$3,550
1965-1969	No G brand	$2,200	$2,850
1970-1974	No G brand	$1,800	$2,350
1975-1980	G brand	$1,800	$2,350

Roc I/Roc II (7635/7621)
1974-1976. Electric solidbody, mahogany, single-cut, Duo-Jet-style body, 1 pickup (7635) or 2 pickups (7621), bound body and neck.

1974-1976	Roc I	$1,050	$1,375
1974-1977	Roc II	$1,225	$1,575

Roc Jet
1970-1980. Electric solidbody, single-cut, 2 pickups, adjustamatic bridge, black, cherry, pumpkin or walnut.

1970-1980		$1,375	$1,800

Round-Up (6130)
1954-1960. Electric solidbody, single-cut, 2 pickups, G brand, belt buckle tailpiece, maple, pine, knotty pine or orange. Reissued in '90.

1954-1956	Knotty pine (2 knots)	$9,900	$12,900
1954-1956	Knotty pine (4 knots)	$11,200	$14,500
1954-1956	Mahogany (few made)	$9,100	$11,800
1954-1956	Maple	$9,100	$11,800
1954-1956	Pine	$9,900	$12,900
1957-1960	Orange	$9,100	$11,800

Round-Up Reissue (6121/6121W)
1989-1995, 2003-2006. Based on the '50s model, Bigsby, Western Orange.

1989-2006		$1,400	$1,800

Round-Up Western Leather Trim (6130)
2006-2007. Higher-end reissue of '55 Round-Up, G brand, tooled leather around edge.

2006-2007		$1,500	$1,975

Round-Up Knotty Pine (6130KPW)
2008-2010. Like '06 6130 but with belt buckle tailpiece and knotty pine top.

2008-2010		$2,500	$3,300

Sal Fabraio (6117)
1964-1968. Double-cut thin electric archtop, distinctive cats-eye f-holes, 2 pickups, sunburst, ordered for resale by guitar teacher Sal Fabraio.

1964-1968		$1,550	$2,025

Sal Salvador (6199)
1958-1968. Electric archtop, single-cut, 1 pickup, triple-bound neck and headstock, sunburst.

1958-1959		$1,875	$2,450
1960-1962		$1,650	$2,150
1963-1964		$1,350	$1,775
1965-1968		$1,200	$1,575

2019 Gretsch Malcom Young Signature Jet (6131-MY)

1954 Gretsch Round-Up (6130)

Gretsch Sparkle Jet 6129TL
Angelo Guarini

1972 Gretsch Super Chet
KC Cormack

MODEL YEAR	FEATURES	EXC. COND. LOW	HIGH

Sho Bro (Hawaiian/Spanish)
1969-1978. Flat-top acoustic, multi-bound, resonator, lucite fretboard, Hawaiian version non-cut, square neck and Spanish version non- or single-cut, round neck.

| 1969-1978 | Hawaiian | $625 | $825 |
| 1969-1978 | Spanish | $600 | $775 |

Sierra Jumbo (3700)
1999-2005. Historic series, single-cut jumbo body, triangular soundhole, sunburst finish.

| 1999-2005 | | $365 | $475 |

Silver Classic (Hauser Model/Model 6001)
1961-1969. Grand Concert body size, nylon-string classical. Similar to Golden Classic but with less fancy appointments.

| 1961-1969 | | $300 | $400 |

Silver Falcon (6136SL) (1955) (T)
1995-1999, 2003-2005. Black finish, silver features, single cut, G tailpiece available until '05, T for Bigsby available starting '05. Had the 1955 designation in the '90s.

| 1995-1999 | | $1,500 | $1,975 |

Silver Falcon (7594SL)
1995-1999. Black finish and silver features, double-cut, 2" thick body.

| 1995-1999 | | $1,500 | $1,975 |

Silver Jet (6129)
1954-1963. Solidbody electric, single-cut until '61, double '61-'63, 2 pickups, Duo-Jet with silver sparkle top, reissued in '89. Optional sparkle colors were offered but were not given their own model numbers; refer to Duo-Jet listing for optional colors.

| 1954-1960 | Single-cut | $5,000 | $6,475 |
| 1961-1963 | Double-cut | $3,700 | $4,900 |

Silver Jet 1957 Reissue (6129-1957)
1989-2019. Reissue of single-cut '50s Silver Jet, silver sparkle. '1957' added to name in '94.

| 1989-2019 | | $1,150 | $1,500 |

Silver Jet 1962 Reissue (6129-1962)
1996-2009. Reissue of '60s double-cut Silver Jet, silver sparkle.

| 1996-2009 | | $1,150 | $1,500 |

Songbird (Sam Goody 711)
1967-1968. Standard body thinline double cutaway with G soundholes, offered by Sam Goody of New York.

| 1967-1968 | | $1,850 | $2,400 |

Southern Belle (7176)
1983. Electric archtop, walnut, parts from the late-'70s assembled in Mexico and U.S., 5 made with all original parts, several others without pickguard and case.

| 1983 | | $900 | $1,200 |

Sparkle Jet (6129/6129T/6129TG)
1995-2019. Duo-Jet with sparkle finishes other than Silver, single-cut, 2 pickups. Many different colors offered over the years.

| 1995-2019 | | $1,150 | $1,500 |

Streamliner Single Cutaway (6189/6190/6191)
1955-1959. Electric archtop, single-cut, maple top, G tailpiece, 1 pickup, multi-bound, Jaguar Tan (6189), sunburst (6190), or natural (6191), name reintroduced as a double-cut in '68.

1955-1959	6189	$2,000	$2,600
1955-1959	6190	$1,400	$1,850
1955-1959	6191	$1,800	$2,400

Streamliner Center Block Jr. (2655T)
2016-present. Double-cut, spruce center block, Bigsby, black, walnut stain or Golddust.

| 2016-2019 | | $350 | $450 |

Streamliner Double Cutaway (6102/6103)
1968-1973. Reintroduced from single-cut model, electric archtop, double-cut, 2 pickups, G tailpiece, cherry or sunburst.

| 1968-1973 | | $1,150 | $1,500 |

Sun Valley (6010/7515/7514)
1959-1977. Flat-top acoustic, laminated Brazilian rosewood back and sides, multi-bound top, natural or sunburst.

1959-1964	6010	$750	$975
1965-1970	6010	$600	$775
1971-1972	7515	$550	$725
1973-1977	7514	$550	$725

Super Chet (7690/7690-B/7691/7691-B)
1972-1980. Electric archtop, single rounded cutaway, 2 pickups, gold hardware, mini control knobs along edge of 'guard, Autumn Red or walnut.

| 1972-1980 | | $2,225 | $2,925 |

Supreme (7545)
1972-1978. Flat-top 16", spruce top, mahogany or rosewood body options, gold hardware.

| 1972-1978 | Mahogany | $1,150 | $1,500 |
| 1972-1979 | Rosewood | $1,425 | $1,850 |

Synchromatic (6030/6031)
1951-1955. 17" acoustic archtop, becomes Constellation in '55.

| 1951-1955 | 6030 or 6031 | $950 | $1,225 |

Synchromatic (6038/6039)
1951-1955. 17" acoustic archtop, single-cut, G tailpiece, multi-bound, sunburst (6038) or natural (6039), renamed Fleetwood in '55.

| 1951-1955 | 6038 or 6039 | $1,050 | $1,375 |

Synchromatic 75
1939-1949. Acoustic archtop, f-holes, multi-bound, large floral peghead inlay. Tenor available.

| 1939-1949 | | $675 | $875 |
| 1939-1949 | Tenor | $425 | $550 |

Synchromatic Jr. (3900)
2000-2003. Historic Series, 15" single-cut archtop acoustic.

| 2000-2003 | | $775 | $1,000 |

Synchromatic 100 (6014/6015)
1939-1955. Renamed from No. 100F, acoustic archtop, double-bound body, amber, sunburst (6014) or natural (6015), renamed Corsair in '55.

1939-1949	Natural	$625	$825
1939-1949	Sunburst	$550	$725
1950-1955	Natural	$575	$750

MODEL YEAR	FEATURES	EXC. COND. LOW	HIGH

Synchromatic 160 (6028/6029)

1939-1943, 1947-1951. Acoustic archtop, cats-eye soundholes, maple back and sides, triple-bound, natural or sunburst.

1939-1943	Sunburst	$900	$1,200
1947-1951	Sunburst	$800	$1,050
1948-1951	Natural	$900	$1,200

Synchromatic 200

1939-1949. Acoustic archtop, cats-eye soundholes, maple back and sides, multi-bound, gold-plated hardware, amber or natural.

1939-1949		$1,000	$1,300

Synchromatic 300

1939-1955. Acoustic archtop, cats-eye soundholes until '51 and f-holes after, multi-bound, natural or sunburst.

1939-1949	Natural	$1,800	$2,400
1939-1949	Sunburst	$1,600	$2,100
1950-1955	Natural	$1,600	$2,100
1950-1955	Sunburst	$1,500	$1,950

Synchromatic 400

1940-1955. Acoustic archtop, cats-eye soundholes until '51 and f-holes after, multi-bound, gold hardware, natural or sunburst.

1940-1949	Natural	$3,600	$4,700
1940-1949	Sunburst	$3,300	$4,300
1950-1955	Natural	$3,300	$4,300
1950-1955	Sunburst	$4,000	$5,200

Synchromatic 400F/6042 Flat-Top

1947-1955. 18" flat-top, renamed 6042 in the late '40s.

1947-1948	400F	$3,600	$4,675
1949-1955	6042	$3,600	$4,675

Synchromatic G400/400C

1990-2008. Acoustic archtop, full-body, non-cut (400) or single-cut (C), sunburst.

1990-2008	G400	$925	$1,200
1990-2008	G400C	$925	$1,200

Synchromatic Limited (450/450M)

1997. Acoustic archtop, hand carved spruce (G450) or maple (G450M) top, floating pickup, sunburst, only 50 were to be made.

1997	Maple	$1,000	$1,300
1997	Spruce	$900	$1,175

Synchromatic Sierra

1949-1955. Renamed from Synchromatic X75F (see below), acoustic flat-top, maple back and sides, triangular soundhole, sunburst.

1949-1955		$1,100	$1,425

Synchromatic X75F

1947-1949. Acoustic flat-top, maple back and sides, triangular soundhole, sunburst, renamed Synchromatic Sierra in '49.

1947-1949		$1,100	$1,425

TK 300 (7624/7625)

1977-1981. Double-cut maple solidbody, 1 humbucker, bolt-on neck, six-on-a-side tuners, hockey stick headstock, Autumn Red or natural.

1977-1981		$525	$675

Town and Country (6021)

1954-1959. Renamed from Jumbo Synchromatic 125 F, flat-top acoustic, maple back and sides, triangular soundhole, multi-bound.

1954-1959		$1,700	$2,200

Traveling Wilburys (TW300T)

1988-1990. Promotional guitar, solidbody electric, single-cut, 1 and 2 pickups, 6 variations, graphics.

1988-1990		$375	$500

Van Eps 6-String (6081/6082)

1968-1971. Electric archtop, single-cut, 2 pickups, 6 strings.

1968-1971		$2,500	$3,200

Van Eps 7-String (6079/6080/7580/7581)

1968-1978. 7 string version, sunburst (6079) or walnut (6080), model numbers change to 7580 (sunburst) and 7581 (walnut) in '72.

1968-1971	6079 or 6080	$2,500	$3,200
1972-1978	7580 or 7581	$2,300	$3,000

Viking

1964-1975. Archtop, double-cut, 2 pickups, vibrato, sunburst (6187), natural (6188) or Cadillac Green (6189). Re-designated 7585 (sunburst) and 7586 (natural) in '72.

1964	Cadillac Green	$3,500	$4,500
1964	Natural	$3,100	$4,000
1964	Sunburst	$2,150	$2,800
1965-1968	Cadillac Green	$2,550	$3,300
1965-1971	Natural	$2,450	$3,200
1965-1971	Sunburst	$1,775	$2,300
1972-1975	Sunburst, natural	$1,625	$2,100

Wayfarer Jumbo (6008)

1969-1971. Flat-top acoustic dreadnought, non-cut, maple back and sides, multi-bound, Wayfarer and sailing ship logo on 'guard.

1969-1971		$750	$975

White Falcon Mono (6136/7594)

1955-1981. Includes the single-cut 6136 of '55-'61, the double-cut 6136 of '62-'70, and the double-cut 7594 of '71-'81.

1955-1961	6136, single-cut	$19,100	$24,900
1962-1964	6136, double-cut	$9,100	$11,800
1965-1969		$6,200	$8,000
1970		$5,500	$7,100
1971-1972	7594	$4,600	$5,900
1973-1981		$4,400	$5,700

White Falcon Stereo (6137/7595)

1958-1981. Features Project-O-Sonic Stereo, includes the single-cut 6137 of '58-'61, the double-cut 6137 of '62-'70, and the double-cut 7595 of '71-'81.

1958-1961	6137, single-cut	$19,100	$24,900
1962-1964	6137, double-cut	$9,100	$11,800
1965-1969		$6,200	$8,000
1970		$5,500	$7,100
1971-1972	7595	$4,600	$5,900
1973-1981		$3,500	$4,500

White Falcon (Import)

1989-present. Various imported models.

1989-2019	Various models	$2,150	$2,800

1988 Gretsch Traveling Wilburys (TW300T)
Ted Wulfers

1958 Gretsch White Falcon Mono

GUITARS

1956 Gretsch White Penguin (6134)

1967 Gruggett

MODEL YEAR	FEATURES	EXC. COND. LOW	HIGH

White Falcon Custom U.S.A. (6136-1955)
1995-1999. U.S.-made, single-cut, DynaSonic pick-ups, gold sparkle appointments, rhinestone embedded knobs, white. In '04, Current U.S. model called G6136CST is released. The import White Falcon has sometimes been listed with the 1955 designation and is not included here.

1995-1999		$2,650	$3,450

White Penguin (6134)
1955-1962. Electric solidbody, single-cut until '61, double '61-'62, 2 pickups (DeArmond until '58 then Filter Tron), fewer than 100 made, white, gold sparkle bound, gold-plated parts. More than any other model, there seems a higher concern regarding forgery.

1956-1962		$100,000	$135,000

White Penguin (G6134)
1993, 2003-2018. White, single-cut, metalflake binding, gold hardware, jeweled knobs, Cadillac G tailpiece.

2003-2018		$1,600	$2,100

Greven
1969, 1975-present. Luthier John Greven builds his premium grade, production/custom, acoustic guitars in Portland, Oregon.

Griffin String Instruments
1976-present. Luthier Kim Griffin builds his professional and premium grade, production/custom, parlor, steel-string, and classical guitars in Greenwich, New York.

Grimes Guitars
1972-present. Premium and presentation grade, custom, flat-tops, nylon-strings, archtops, semi-hollow electrics made by luthier Steve Grimes originally in Port Townsend, Washington, and since '82 in Kula, Hawaii. He also made mandolins early on.

Grinnell
Late 1930s-early 1940s. Private brand made by Gibson for Grinnell Music of Detroit and Southeast Michigan, which at the time, was the largest music chain in the Detroit area.

KG-14
1940. Gibson-made L-00 flat-top style with maple sides and back, tortoise-style binding on top and back, ladder bracing.

1940		$1,650	$2,150

Groehsl
1890-1921. Chicago's Groehsl Company made guitars for Wards and other mass-marketers. In 1921 the company became Stromberg-Voisinet, which in turn became the Kay Musical Instrument Company.

Groove Tools
2002-2004. Korean-made, production, intermediate grade, 7-string guitars that were offered by Conklin Guitars of Springfield, Missouri. They also offered basses.

Grosh
1993-present. Professional and premium grade, production/custom, solid and semi-hollow body guitars and basses built by luthier Don Grosh originally in Santa Clarita, California and, since '05 in Broomfield, Colorado. He also builds basses. Grosh worked in production for Valley Arts from '84-'92. Guitars generally with bolt necks until '03 when set-necks were added to the line.

Classical Electric
1990s. Single-cut solidbody with nylon strings and piezo-style hidden pickup, highly figured top.

1990s		$1,200	$1,550

Custom S Bent Top/Bent Top Custom
2003-2019. Offset double-cut, figured maple carved top, 2 pickups.

2003-2019		$1,200	$1,550

Custom T Carve Top
2003-2012. Single-cut, figured maple carved top, 2 pickups.

2003-2012		$1,200	$1,550

ElectraJet Custom
2009-present. Modified offset double-cut, 2 P-90s, 2 hums, or single-single-hum pickups.

2009-2019		$1,200	$1,550

Retro Classic
1993-present. Offset double-cut, 3 pickups.

1993-2019		$1,200	$1,550

Retro Classic Vintage T
1993-present. Single-cut, black 'guard.

1993-2019		$1,200	$1,550

Gruen Acoustic Guitars
Luthier Paul Gruen builds professional grade, custom steel-string guitars, starting in 1999, in Chapel Hill, North Carolina.

Gruggett
Mid 1960s-2012. In the 1960s, luthier Bill Gruggett worked with Mosrite and Hallmark guitars as well as building electric guitars under his own name in Bakersfield, California. He continued to make his Stradette model for Hallmark guitars until his death in October, 2012.

Guernsey Resophonic Guitars
Production/custom, resonator guitars built by luthier Ivan Guernsey in Marysville, Indiana, starting in 1989.

Guild
1952-present. Professional and premium grade, production/custom, acoustic and acoustic/electric guitars. They have built solid, hollow and semi-hollowbody guitars in the past. Founded in New York City by jazz guitarist Alfred Dronge, employing many ex-Epiphone workers. The company was purchased by Avnet, Inc. in '66 and the Westerly, Rhode Island factory was opened in '68. Hoboken factory closed in '71 and headquarters

MODEL YEAR	FEATURES	EXC. COND. LOW	HIGH

moved to Elizabeth, New Jersey. Company was in bankruptcy in '88 and was purchased by Faas Corporation, New Berlin, Wisconsin. The brand was purchased by Fender in '95 and production was moved from Westerly to the Fender plant in Corona, California in 2001. In '05, Fender moved Guild production to their newly-acquired Tacoma plant in Washington. In '08, production moved to the Ovation/Hamer plant in New Hartford, Connecticut. With the 2001 move to the Fender Corona plant, Bob Benedetto and Fender veteran Tim Shaw (who previously ran the Nashville-based custom shop) created a line of Guild acoustic guitars that were primarily based on vintage Guild Hoboken designs.

Designs of Tacoma-built Guild product were nothing like Tacoma guitars. The new Guilds were dovetail neck based with nitrocellulose finishes. Later, FMIC Guild introduced the Contemporary Series giving the Tacoma factory another line in addition to the vintage-based F and D model Traditional Series. In '14 Fender sold Guild to Cordoba Music Group, manufacturer of Cordoba acoustic guitars who moved production to Oxnard, California.

A-50
1994-1996. Original A-50 models can be found under the Cordoba A-50 listing, the new model drops the Cordoba name, size 000 flat-top, spruce top, Indian rosewood body.

1994-1996		$875	$1,125

Aragon F-30
1954-1986. Acoustic flat-top, spruce top, laminated maple arched back (mahogany back and sides by '59), reintroduced as just F-30 in '98.

1954-1959		$1,600	$2,100
1960-1986		$1,475	$1,925

Aragon F-30 NT
1959-1985. Natural finish version of F-30.

1959-1985		$1,725	$2,275

Aragon F-30 R
1973-1995. Rosewood back and sides version of F-30, sunburst.

1973-1979		$1,825	$2,375

Aristocrat M-75
1954-1963. Electric archtop, routed semi-hollow single-cut body, 2 pickups, sunburst, natural (added '59) or cherry (added '61), reintroduced as Bluesbird M-75 in '67.

1954-1959		$3,425	$4,450
1960-1963		$3,200	$4,150

Aristocrat M-75 Tenor
Mid-late 1950s. Tenor version of 6-string Aristocrat electric, dual soapbar pickups, 4 knobs.

1950s		$2,300	$3,000

Artist Award
1961-1999. Renamed from Johnny Smith Award, single-cut electric archtop, floating DeArmond pickup (changed to humbucker in '80), multi-bound, gold hardware, sunburst or natural.

1961-1969		$5,250	$6,825
1970-1999		$4,200	$5,475

Bluegrass D-25/D-25 M
1968-1999. Flat-top, mahogany top until '76, spruce after, mahogany back and sides, various colors, called Bluegrass D-25 M in late-'70s and '80s, listed as D-25 in '90s.

1968-1979		$525	$700
1980-1999		$525	$700

Bluegrass D-25-12
1987-1992, 1996-1998. 12-string version of D-25.

1987-1998		$500	$650

Bluegrass D-35
1966-1988. Acoustic flat-top, spruce top and mahogany back and sides, rosewood 'board and bridge, natural.

1966-1988		$900	$1,150

Bluegrass F-40/Valencia F-40
1954-1963, 1973-1983. Acoustic flat-top, spruce top, maple back and sides, rosewood 'board and bridge, natural or sunburst.

1954-1963	Valencia F-40	$2,400	$3,125
1973-1983	Bluegrass F-40	$1,125	$1,475

Bluegrass F-47
1963-1976. 16" narrow-waist style, mahogany sides and back, acoustic flat-top, spruce top, mahogany back and sides, bound rosewood 'board and bridge, natural.

1963-1969	Horses-art 'guard	$2,000	$2,600
1970-1976		$2,000	$2,600

Bluegrass Jubilee D-40
1963-1992. Acoustic flat-top, spruce top, mahogany back and sides, rosewood 'board and bridge, natural. Has been reissued.

1963-1969		$1,475	$1,900
1970-1992		$1,300	$1,700

Bluegrass Jubilee D-40 C
1975-1991. Acoustic flat-top, single Florentine cutaway, mahogany back and sides, rosewood 'board and bridge, natural.

1975-1991		$1,350	$1,775

Bluegrass Jubilee D-44
1965-1972. Acoustic flat-top, spruce top, pearwood back and sides, ebony 'board, rosewood bridge.

1965-1972		$1,300	$1,700

Bluegrass Jubilee D-44 M
1971-1985. Acoustic flat-top, spruce top, maple back & sides, ebony fingerboard, rosewood bridge.

1971-1985		$1,300	$1,700

Bluegrass Special D-50
1963-1993. Acoustic flat-top, spruce top, rosewood back and sides, ebony fretboard, multi-bound.

1963-1968	Brazilian rosewood	$3,600	$4,600
1969-1979	Indian rosewood	$1,500	$2,000
1980-1993	Indian rosewood	$1,475	$1,950

Bluegrass Special D-50 (Reissue)/D-50
1999-2004, 2006-2014. Also available with pickup system, initially listed as D-50.

1999-2014		$1,350	$1,750

Blues 90
2000-2002. Bluesbird single-cut, chambered body, unbound rosewood board, dots, 2 Duncan 2 P-90s.

2000-2002		$950	$1,250

1961 Guild Aristocrat M-75
Carter Vintage Guitars

1971 Guild Bluegrass D-35
Imaged by Heritage Auctions, HA.com

1970 Guild Bluesbird M-75

1995 Guild Brian May Pro
Rivington Guitars

MODEL YEAR	FEATURES	EXC. COND. LOW	HIGH

Bluesbird M-75 (Hollowbody)
1967-1970. Reintroduced from Aristocrat M-75, thinbody electric archtop of maple, spruce ('67) or mahogany, single-cut, 2 pickups, Deluxe has gold hardware, Standard chrome. A solidbody Bluesbird was also introduced in '70.

1967-1970		$2,175	$2,800

Bluesbird M-75 (Solidbody)
1970-1978. Solidbody version of Bluesbird M-75, mahogany body, rounded cutaway, 2 pickups.

1970-1978	CS, plain top, chrome hdw	$1,775	$2,325
1970-1978	GS, flamed top, gold hdw	$2,175	$2,800

Bluesbird M-75 (Solidbody) Reintroduced
1984-1988.

1984-1985	3 single-coil pus	$950	$1,250
1986	EMG pickups	$950	$1,250
1987-1988	DiMarzio pickups	$950	$1,250

Bluesbird (Reintroduced)
1994-2003. Single-cut chambered solidbody, 2 humbuckers, block inlays, available with AAA flamed top.

1994-2003		$1,175	$1,525
2001	Fender Custom Shop	$1,800	$2,325

Bluesbird
2011-2012. Single-cut solidbody, Chesterfield headstock logo, flame maple top, block markers, 2 humbuckers, natural finish.

2011-2012		$1,175	$1,525

Brian May BHM-1
1984-1987. Electric solidbody, double-cut, vibrato, 3 pickups, bound top and back, red or green, Brian May Pro, Special and Standard introduced in '94.

1984-1987		$2,500	$3,200

Brian May Pro
1994-1995. Electric solidbody, double-cut, vibrato, 3 pickups, bound top and back, various colors.

1994-1995		$2,500	$3,200

Brian May Signature Red Special
1994. Signature initials on truss rod cover, script signature on back of headstock, BM serial number, dot markers, custom Duncan pickups, custom vibrola, red special finish.

1994		$2,500	$3,200

CA-100 Capri
1956-1973. Acoustic archtop version of CE-100, sharp Florentine cutaway, solid spruce top, laminated maple back and sides, rosewood 'board and bridge, nickel-plated metal parts, natural or sunburst.

1956-1959		$1,575	$2,025
1960-1973		$1,400	$1,825

Capri CE-100
1956-1985. Electric archtop, single Florentine cutaway, 1 pickup (2 pickups by '83), maple body, Waverly tailpiece, sunburst, in '59-'82 CE-100 D listed with 2 pickups.

1956-1959		$1,625	$2,100
1960-1985		$1,475	$1,900

Capri CE-100 D
1956-1982. Electric archtop, single Florentine cutaway, 2 pickups, maple body, sunburst, Waverly tailpiece (D dropped, became the Capri CE-100 in '83).

1956-1959		$1,900	$2,475
1960-1982		$1,750	$2,250

Capri CE-100 T Tenor
1950s. Electric-archtop Capri 4-string tenor guitar, sunburst.

1956		$1,400	$1,800

CO-1/CO-1C
2006-2008. Vintage F-30 style, red cedar top, solid mahogany neck/back/sides, rosewood 'board, natural. CO-1C with soft cutaway.

2006-2008	CO-1	$750	$975
2006-2008	CO-1C	$775	$1,025

CO-2/CO-2C
2008. As CO-1 but with red spruce top, ebony 'board, and offered in blonde, Antique Burst or Ice Tea Burst. CO-2C with soft cutaway.

2008	CO-2	$750	$975
2008	CO-2C	$775	$1,025

Cordoba A-50
1961-1972. Acoustic archtop, lowest-end in the Guild archtop line, named Granada A-50 prior to '61.

1961-1965		$900	$1,175
1966-1972		$825	$1,075

Cordoba T-50 Slim
1961-1973. Thinbody version of Cordoba X-50.

1961-1965		$950	$1,250
1966-1969		$875	$1,150
1970-1972		$800	$1,050

Cordoba X-50
1961-1970. Electric archtop non-cut, laminated maple body, rosewood 'board, 1 pickup, nickel-plated parts.

1961-1965		$975	$1,275
1966-1970		$900	$1,175

CR-1 Crossroads Single E/Double E
1993-2000. Single-cut solidbody acoustic, humbucker (S2 in '93) neck pickup and Piezo bridge, 97 single necks (Single E, '93-'97) and very few 6/12 double necks (Double E, '93, '98-'00) made by Guild custom shop.

1993-1997	Single neck	$1,225	$1,600
1993-2000	Double neck	$3,000	$3,900

Custom F-412 12-String
1968-1986. Special order only from '68-'74, then regular production, 17" wide body 12-string version of F-50 flat-top, spruce top, maple back and sides, arched back, 2-tone block inlays, gold hardware, natural finish.

1968-1969		$1,650	$2,150
1970-1979		$1,500	$1,950
1980-1986		$1,400	$1,800

Custom F-512 12-String
1968-1986, 1990. Rosewood back and sides version of F-412. See F-512 for reissue.

1968-1969	Indian rosewood	$1,800	$2,400
1970-1979	Indian rosewood	$1,700	$1,250
1980-1986	Indian rosewood	$1,550	$2,100

MODEL YEAR	FEATURES	EXC. COND. LOW	HIGH

Custom F-612 12-String
1972-1973. Acoustic 12-string, similar to Custom F-512, but with 18" body, fancy mother-of-pearl inlays, and black/white marquee body, neck and headstock binding.

| 1972-1973 | Brazilian rosewood | $3,100 | $4,000 |
| 1972-1973 | Indian rosewood | $1,575 | $2,025 |

Custom Shop 45th Anniversary
1997. Built in Guild's Nashville Custom Shop, all solid wood, spruce top, maple back and sides, high-end appointments, gold hardware, natural.

| 1997 | | $2,000 | $2,600 |

CV-1/CV-1C
2006-2008. F-40 style, solid Indian rosewood back/sides, rosewood 'board. CV-1C with sharp cutaway.

| 2006-2008 | CV-1 | $750 | $975 |
| 2006-2008 | CV-1C | $775 | $1,025 |

CV-2/CV-2C
2008. As CV-1 but with flamed maple back/sides, ebony 'board. CV-2C with sharp cutaway.

| 2008 | CV-2 | $750 | $975 |
| 2008 | CV-2C | $775 | $1,025 |

D-4 Series
1991-2002. Dreadnought flat-top, mahogany sides, dot markers.

| 1991-2002 | 6-String | $490 | $635 |
| 1992-1999 | 12-String | $490 | $635 |

D-6 (D-6 E/D-6 HG/D-6 HE)
1992-1995. Flat-top, 15 3/4", mahogany back and sides, natural satin non-gloss finish, options available.

| 1992-1995 | | $490 | $635 |

D-15 Mahogany Rush
1983-1988. Dreadnought flat-top, mahogany body and neck, rosewood 'board, dot inlays, stain finish.

| 1983-1988 | | $475 | $625 |

D-15 12-String
1983-1985. 12-string version of Mahogany Rush D-15.

| 1983-1985 | | $475 | $625 |

D-16 Mahogany Rush
1984-1986. Like D-15, but with gloss finish.

| 1984-1986 | | $600 | $775 |

D-17 Mahogany Rush
1984-1988. Like D-15, but with gloss finish and bound body.

| 1984-1988 | | $625 | $825 |

D-25/D-25 M
2003. Solid mahogany body. Refer to Bluegrass D-25 for earlier models. Reintroduced in '06 as GAD-25.

| 2003 | | $650 | $850 |

D-26 (Guitar Center)
1995. Made for Guitar Center, spruce top, mahogany back and sides, natural finish.

| 1995 | | $650 | $850 |

D-30
1987-1999. Acoustic flat-top, spruce-top, laminated maple back and solid maple sides, rosewood 'board, multi-bound, various colors.

| 1987-1999 | | $900 | $1,175 |

D-40
1999-2007. Solid spruce top, mahogany back and sides, rosewood 'board. See earlier models under Bluegrass Jubilee D-40.

| 1999-2007 | | $1,025 | $1,325 |

D-40 Bluegrass Jubilee
2006-2014. Indian rosewood, red spruce top, mahogany back and sides, 3-piece neck (mahogany/walnut/mahogany).

| 2006-2014 | No pickup | $1,025 | $1,325 |
| 2006-2014 | With Duncan D-TAR | $1,075 | $1,400 |

D-40 Richie Havens
2003-2014. Richie Havens signature logo on truss rod cover, mahogany sides and back, Fishman Matrix, natural.

| 2003-2014 | | $1,075 | $1,400 |

D-40C NT
1975-1991. Pointed cutaway version.

| 1975-1991 | | $1,150 | $1,500 |

D-46
1980-1985. Dreadnought acoustic, ash back, sides and neck, spruce top, ebony 'board, ivoroid body binding.

| 1980-1985 | | $725 | $950 |

D-55
See TV Model.

D-55 50th Anniversary
2003. Brazilian rosewood, 1953-2003 Anniversary logo.

| 2003 | | $3,700 | $4,800 |

D-60
1987-1990, 1998-2000. Renamed from D-66, rosewood back and sides ('87-'90), maple ('98-'00), scalloped bracing, multi-bound top, slotted diamond inlay, G shield logo.

| 1987-1990 | Rosewood | $1,825 | $2,375 |
| 1998-1999 | Maple | $1,825 | $2,375 |

D-64
1984-1986. Maple back and side, multi-bound body, notched diamond inlays, limited production.

| 1984-1986 | | $1,825 | $2,375 |

D-66
1984-1987. Amber, rosewood back and sides, 15 3/4", scalloped bracing, renamed D-60 in '87.

| 1984-1987 | | $1,825 | $2,375 |

D-70
1981-1985. Dreadnought acoustic, spruce top, Indian rosewood back and sides, multi-bound, ebony 'board with mother-of-pearl inlays.

| 1981-1985 | | $2,350 | $3,100 |

D-70-12E
1981-1985. Only 2 made, 12-string version, Fishman electronics.

| 1981-1985 | | $2,350 | $3,100 |

D-80
1983-1987. Non-carved heel.

| 1983-1987 | | $2,350 | $3,100 |

D-100
1990-1998. Top-of-the-line dreadnought-size acoustic, spruce top, rosewood back and sides, scalloped bracing.

| 1990-1998 | | $2,350 | $3,100 |

1977 Guild Capri CE-100 D
Greg Gagliono

1975 Guild D-50
Daniel Malone

GUITARS

1963 Guild Duane Eddy DE-300
Earl Ward

*2002 Guild F-47 RCE
Grand Auditorium*
Imaged by Heritage Auctions, HA.com

MODEL YEAR	FEATURES	EXC. COND. LOW	HIGH

D-125
2011-2014. All mahogany with Indian rosewood 'board, natural or cherry red.

2011-2014		$375	$500

D-212 12-String
1981-1983. 12-string version of D-25, laminated mahogany back and sides, natural, sunburst or black, renamed D-25-12 in '87, reintroduced as D-212 '96-present.

1981-1983		$500	$650

D-412 12-String
1990-1997. Dreadnought, 12 strings, mahogany sides and arched back, satin finished, natural.

1990-1997		$900	$1,175

DC-130
1994-1995. US-made, limited run, D-style cutaway, flamed maple top/back/sides.

1994-1995		$2,100	$2,800

DCE True American
1993-2000. Cutaway flat-top acoustic/electric, 1 with mahogany back and sides, 5 with rosewood.

1993-2000	DCE1, DCE1 TA	$525	$700
1994-2000	DCE5	$625	$800

Del Rio M-30
1959-1964. Flat-top, 15", all mahogany body, satin non-gloss finish.

1959		$1,650	$2,125
1960-1964		$1,550	$2,025

Detonator
1987-1990. Electric solidbody, double-cut, 3 pickups, bolt-on neck, Guild/Mueller tremolo system, black hardware.

1987-1990		$395	$515

DK-70 Peacock Limited Edition
1995-1996. Limited run of 50, koa, peacock 'guard.

1995-1996		$2,800	$3,600

Duane Eddy Deluxe DE-500
1962-1974, 1984-1987. Electric archtop, single rounded cutaway, 2 pickups (early years and '80s version have DeArmonds), Bigsby, master volume, spruce top with maple back and sides, available in blond (BL) or sunburst (SB).

1962	Sunburst	$3,800	$4,925
1962-1963	Natural	$4,800	$6,325
1963	Sunburst	$3,700	$4,825
1964	Natural	$4,700	$6,225
1964	Sunburst	$3,600	$4,825
1965	Natural	$3,800	$5,025
1965	Sunburst	$3,400	$4,425
1966	Natural	$3,500	$4,625
1966	Sunburst	$3,200	$4,225
1967-1969	Various colors	$3,100	$4,125
1970-1974	Various colors	$2,825	$3,725
1984-1987	Various colors	$2,400	$3,125

Duane Eddy Standard DE-400
1963-1974. Electric archtop, single rounded cutaway, 2 pickups, vibrato, natural or sunburst, less appointments than DE-500 Deluxe.

1963	Natural, cherry (option)	$3,100	$4,125
1963	Sunburst	$2,700	$3,525

MODEL YEAR	FEATURES	EXC. COND. LOW	HIGH
1964	Natural, cherry (option)	$2,900	$3,825
1964	Sunburst	$2,400	$3,125
1965	Natural	$2,700	$3,525
1965	Sunburst	$2,200	$2,925
1966	Natural	$2,400	$3,125
1966	Sunburst	$2,000	$2,625
1967-1969	Various colors	$1,900	$2,525
1970-1974	Various colors	$1,700	$2,225

DV Series
1992-1999, 2007-2011. Acoustic flat-top, mahogany or rosewood back and sides, ebony or rosewood 'board, satin or gloss finish.

1992-2001	DV-52S, rosewood, satin	$1,100	$1,450
1993-1994	DV-76	$2,800	$3,600
1993-1995	DV-62, rosewood, HB trim	$1,225	$1,600
1994-1995	DV-72, rosewood, HB trim, fancy	$2,300	$3,000
1994-1995	DV-73, rosewood	$2,300	$3,000
1995-1996	DV-74 Pueblo, LE, Western motif	$2,800	$3,600
1995-1999	DV-6, mahogany, satin	$625	$800
1999-2000	DV-25, mahogany, satin	$800	$1,050
1999-2001	DV-4, mahogany, satin	$500	$650

Economy M-20
1958-1965, 1969-1973. Mahogany body, acoustic flat-top, natural or sunburst satin finish.

1958-1959		$1,450	$1,875
1960-1969		$1,375	$1,775
1970-1973		$1,224	$1,575

F-4 CEHG
1992-2002. High Gloss finish, single-cut flat-top, acoustic/electric.

1992-2002		$510	$660

F-5 CE
1992-2001. Acoustic/electric, single cutaway, rosewood back and sides, dot inlays, chrome tuners.

1992-2001		$500	$650

F-30
1990-2001. Formerly the Aragon F-30, made in Westerly, Rhode Island.

1990-2001		$850	$1,100

F-30 R-LS
1990s. Custom Shop model, other F-30 models are listed under Aragon F-30 listing, rosewood sides and back, bearclaw spruce top, limited production.

1990s		$1,100	$1,425

F-44
1984-1987. Acoustic flat-top, maple, designed by George Gruhn.

1984-1987		$1,500	$2,000

F-45 CE
1983-1992. Acoustic/electric, single cutaway, mahogany or maple back and sides, rosewood 'board, natural.

1983-1984	Laminated mahogany	$625	$825
1985-1992	Flamed maple	$725	$950

The *Vintage Guitar Price Guide* shows low to high values for items in all-original excellent condition, and, where applicable, with original case or cover.

MODEL YEAR	FEATURES	EXC. COND. LOW	HIGH

F-46 NT
1984. Jumbo body style flat-top, designed for Guild by George Gruhn.

| 1984 | | $1,500 | $2,000 |

F-47 M/F-47 MC
2007-2016. Made in USA, solid flamed maple sides and back, MC with cutaway.

| 2007-2016 | F-47 M | $1,300 | $1,700 |
| 2007-2016 | F-47 MC | $1,400 | $1,800 |

F-47 R/F-47 RC
2008-2014. Solid rosewood sides and back, available with electronics, RC with cutaway.

| 2008-2014 | | $1,300 | $1,700 |

F-47 RCE Grand Auditorium
1999-2003. Cutaway acoustic/electric, rosewood back and sides, block inlays.

| 1999-2003 | | $1,300 | $1,700 |

F-50/F-50 R
2002-2016. Jumbo, solid spruce top, solid maple sides, arched laminated maple back, abalone rosette. See Navarre F-50/F-50 for earlier models.

| 2002-2016 | F-50, maple | $1,550 | $2,000 |
| 2002-2016 | F-50R, rosewood | $1,550 | $2,000 |

F-65 CE
1992-2001. Acoustic/electric, single cutaway, rosewood back and sides, block inlay, gold tuners.

| 1992-2001 | | $1,500 | $1,950 |

F-212 12-String
1964-1982. Acoustic flat-top jumbo, 12 strings, spruce top, mahogany back and sides, 16" body.

| 1964-1982 | | $1,075 | $1,400 |

F-212 XL 12-String
1966-1986, 1998-2000. Acoustic flat-top, 17" body, 12 strings, spruce top, mahogany back and sides, ebony fingerboard.

| 1966-1986 | | $1,075 | $1,400 |
| 1998-2000 | F-212 | $950 | $1,225 |

F-312 Artist 12-String
1964-1973. Flat-top, rosewood back and sides, spruce top, no board inlay (but some in '72 may have dots).

| 1964-1968 | Brazilian rosewood | $3,200 | $4,175 |
| 1969-1973 | Indian rosewood | $1,600 | $2,100 |

F-412
2002-2016. Solid spruce top, solid maple back and sides, block inlays, 12-string. See Custom F-412 for earlier models.

| 2002-2016 | | $1,475 | $1,900 |

F-512
2002-present. Solid spruce top, rosewood back and sides, 12-string. See Custom F-512 for earlier models.

| 2002-2019 | | $1,650 | $2,150 |

Freshman M-65
1958-1973. Electric archtop, single-cut, mahogany back and sides, f-holes, 1 single-coil (some with 2), sunburst or natural top.

1958-1959		$1,400	$1,825
1960-1969		$1,200	$1,550
1970-1973		$1,125	$1,475

Freshman M-65 3/4
1958-1973. Short-scale version of M-65, 1 pickup.

1958-1959		$1,200	$1,550
1960-1969		$1,000	$1,300
1970-1973		$975	$1,250

FS-20 CE
1986-1987. Solidbody acoustic, routed mahogany body.

| 1986-1987 | | $550 | $700 |

FS-46 CE
1983-1986. Flat-top acoustic/electric, pointed cutaway, mahogany, black, natural or sunburst.

| 1983-1986 | | $625 | $800 |

G-5 P
1988-ca.1989. Handmade in Spain, cedar top, gold-plated hardware.

| 1988-1989 | | $775 | $1,000 |

G-37
1973-1986. Acoustic flat-top, spruce top, laminated maple back and sides, rosewood 'board and bridge, sunburst or natural top.

| 1973-1986 | | $775 | $1,000 |

G-41
1974-1978. Acoustic flat-top, spruce top, mahogany back and sides, rosewood 'board and bridge, 20 frets.

| 1975-1978 | | $775 | $1,000 |

G-45 Hank Williams Jr.
1982-1986, 1993-1996. Hank Williams Jr. logo on 'guard, flat-top.

| 1982-1996 | | $950 | $1,250 |

G-75
1975-1977. Acoustic flat-top, 3/4-size version of D-50, spruce top, rosewood back and sides, mahogany neck, ebony 'board and bridge.

| 1975-1977 | | $775 | $1,000 |

G-212 12-String
1974-1983. Acoustic flat-top 12-string version of D-40, spruce top, mahogany back and sides, natural or sunburst.

| 1974-1983 | | $775 | $1,000 |

G-212 XL 12-String
1974-1983. Acoustic flat-top, 12 strings, 17" version of G-212.

| 1974-1983 | | $775 | $1,000 |

G-312 12-String
1974-1987. Acoustic flat-top 12-string version of the D-50, spruce top, rosewood back and sides.

| 1974-1987 | | $925 | $1,200 |

GAD (Guild Acoustic Design) Series
2004-2014. Imported, all models begin with GAD.

| 2004-2014 | | $350 | $800 |

George Barnes AcoustiLectric
1962-1972. Electric archtop, single-cut, solid spruce top, curly maple back and sides, multi-bound, 2 humbuckers, gold-plated hardware, sunburst or natural finish.

| 1962-1972 | | $3,450 | $4,500 |

George Barnes Guitar in F
1963-1973. Smaller electric archtop at 13.5", 2 humbuckers, chrome hardware.

| 1963-1973 | | $3,450 | $4,500 |

1975 Guild F-112 NT
Garrett Park

Guild George Barnes AcoustiLectric

1964 Guild Jet Star S-50
Todd Bauer

Late-1950s Guild Johnny Smith Award

MODEL YEAR	FEATURES	EXC. COND. LOW	HIGH
GF-25			
1987-1992. Acoustic flat-top, mahogany back and sides.			
1987-1992		$675	$875
GF-25 C			
1988-1991. Cutaway GF-25.			
1988-1991		$775	$1,025
GF-30			
1987-1991. Acoustic flat-top, maple back/sides/neck, multi-bound.			
1987-1991		$925	$1,200
GF-40			
1987-1991. Mahogany back and sides, multi-bound.			
1987-1991		$1,050	$1,350
GF-50			
1987-1991. Acoustic flat-top, rosewood back and sides, mahogany neck, multi-bound.			
1987-1991		$1,150	$1,500
GF-55			
1990-1991. Jumbo acoustic, spruce top, rosewood back and sides, natural.			
1990-1991		$1,500	$2,000
GF-60			
1987-1989. Jumbo size, rosewood or maple sides and back, diamond markers.			
1987-1989	GF-60M, maple	$1,925	$2,500
1987-1989	GF-60R, rosewood	$1,925	$2,500
GF-60 C			
1987-1989. Cutaway GF-60.			
1987-1989		$2,050	$2,675
Granada A-50 (Acoustic Archtop)			
1956-1960. Lowest-end acoustic archtop in the Guild line, renamed Cordoba A-50 in '61.			
1956-1960		$1,050	$1,350
Granada X-50			
1954-1961. Electric archtop, non-cut, laminated all maple body, rosewood 'board and bridge, nickel-plated metal parts, 1 pickup, sunburst. Renamed Cordoba X-50 in '61.			
1955-1959		$1,200	$1,575
1960-1961		$1,075	$1,425
GV Series			
1993-1995. Flat-top, rosewood back and sides, various enhancements.			
1993-1995	GV-52, gloss	$1,075	$1,400
1993-1995	GV-52, satin	$875	$1,125
1993-1995	GV-70, abalone, gloss	$1,125	$1,450
1993-1995	GV-72, herringbone, gloss	$1,125	$1,450
Jet Star S-50			
1963-1970. Electric solidbody, double-cut, mahogany or alder body, 1 pickup, vibrato optional by '65, asymmetrical headstock until '65, reintroduced as S-50 in '72-'78 with body redesign.			
1963-1965	3-on-side	$1,375	$1,800
1966-1969	6-in-line	$1,050	$1,350
1970		$975	$1,275
JF-4 NT			
1992-1995. Jumbo flat-top, mahogany, natural.			
1992-1995		$575	$750

MODEL YEAR	FEATURES	EXC. COND. LOW	HIGH
JF-30			
1987-2004. Jumbo 6-string acoustic, spruce top, laminated maple back, solid maple sides, multi-bound.			
1987-2004		$950	$1,250
JF-30 E			
1994-2004. Acoustic/electric version.			
1994-2004		$1,025	$1,350
JF-30-12			
1987-2004. 12-string version of the JF-30.			
1987-2004		$950	$1,250
JF-50 R			
1987-1988. Jumbo 6-string acoustic, rosewood back and sides, multi-bound.			
1987-1988		$950	$1,250
JF-55			
1989-2000. Jumbo flat-top, spruce top, rosewood body.			
1989-2000		$1,275	$1,650
JF-55-12			
1991-2000. 12-string JF-55.			
1991-2000		$1,275	$1,650
JF-65			
1987-1994. Renamed from Navarre F-50, Jumbo flat-top acoustic, spruce top, R has rosewood back and sides and M has maple.			
1987-1994	JF-65M, maple	$1,500	$2,000
1987-1994	JF-65R, rosewood	$1,500	$2,000
JF-65-12			
1987-2001. 12-string, version of JF-65.			
1987-2001	JF-65M-12, maple	$1,500	$2,000
1987-2001	JF-65R-12, rosewood	$1,500	$2,000
JF-100			
1992-1995. Jumbo, maple top, rosewood back and sides, abalone trim, natural.			
1992-1995		$2,350	$3,100
JF-100-12			
1992-1995. Jumbo 12-string version.			
1992-1995		$2,350	$3,100
Johnny Smith Award			
1956-1961. Single-cut electric archtop, floating DeArmond pickup, multi-bound, gold hardware, sunburst or natural, renamed Artist Award in '61.			
1956-1961		$6,525	$8,500
Johnny Smith Award Benedetto			
2004-2006. 18 custom made instruments under the supervision of Bob Benedetto, signed by Johnny Smith, with certificate of authenticity signed by Smith and Benedetto.			
2004-2006	18 made	$5,025	$6,525
JV-72			
1993-1999. Jumbo acoustic, custom turquoise inlay.			
1993-1999		$2,150	$2,800
Liberator Elite			
1988. Limited Edition, set-neck, offset double-cut solidbody, figured maple top, mahogany body, rising-sun inlays, 3 active pickups, last of the Guild solidbodies.			
1988		$850	$1,100

MODEL YEAR	FEATURES	EXC. COND. LOW	HIGH

M-80 CS/M-80
1975-1984. Solidbody, double-cut, 2 pickups, introduced as M-80 CS with bound rosewood 'board and block inlays, shortened to M-80 in '80 with unbound ebony 'board and dots.

1975-1980		$1,100	$1,450

Manhattan X-170 (Mini-Manhattan X-170)
1985-2002. Called Mini-Manhattan X-170 in '85-'86, electric archtop hollowbody, single rounded cutaway, maple body, f-holes, 2 humbuckers, block inlays, gold hardware, natural or sunburst.

1985-2002		$1,325	$1,725

Manhattan X-175 (Sunburst)
1954-1985. Electric archtop, single rounded cutaway, laminated spruce top, laminated maple back and sides, 2 pickups, chrome hardware, sunburst. Reissued as X-160 Savoy.

1954-1959		$1,775	$2,300
1960-1969		$1,600	$2,100
1970-1985		$1,500	$1,950

Manhattan X-175 B (Natural)
1954-1976. Natural finish X-175.

1954-1959		$1,775	$2,300
1960-1969		$1,600	$2,100
1970-1976		$1,500	$1,950

Mark I
1961-1972. Classical, Honduras mahogany body, rosewood 'board, slotted headstock.

1961-1969		$325	$425
1970-1973		$290	$375

Mark II
1961-1987. Like Mark I, but with spruce top and body binding.

1961-1969		$475	$625
1970-1979		$365	$475
1980-1987		$275	$365

Mark III
1961-1987. Like Mark II, but with Peruvian mahogany back and sides and floral soundhole design.

1961-1969		$500	$650
1970-1979		$450	$600
1980-1987		$365	$475

Mark IV
1961-1985. Like Mark III, but with flamed pearwood back and sides (rosewood offered in '61, maple in '62).

1961-1969	Pearwood	$550	$725
1970-1979	Pearwood	$500	$650
1980-1985	Pearwood	$420	$550

Mark V
1961-1987. Like Mark III, but with rosewood back and sides (maple available for '61-'64).

1961-1968	Brazilian rw	$1,100	$1,450
1969-1979	Indian rw	$550	$725
1980-1987	Indian rw	$420	$550

Mark VI
1962-1973. Rosewood back and sides, spruce top, wood binding.

1962-1968	Brazilian rw	$1,450	$1,875
1969-1973	Indian rw	$725	$950

Mark VII Custom
1968-1973. Special order only, spruce top, premium rosewood back and sides, inlaid rosewood bridge, engraved gold tuners.

1962-1968	Brazilian rw	$1,650	$2,150
1969-1973	Indian rw	$825	$1,075

Navarre F-48
1972-1975. 17", mahogany, block markers.

1972-1975		$1,100	$1,450

Navarre F-50/F-50
1954-1986, 1994-1995. Acoustic flat-top, spruce top, curly maple back and sides, rosewood 'board and bridge, 17" rounded lower bout, laminated arched maple back, renamed JF-65 M in '87. Reissued in '94 and again in '02 as the F-50.

1954-1956		$3,550	$4,600
1957-1962	Pearl block markers	$3,550	$4,600
1963-1969	Ebony 'board	$3,325	$4,325
1970-1995		$1,750	$2,300

Navarre F-50 R/F-50 R
1965-1987. Rosewood back and side version of F-50, renamed JF-65 R in '87. Reissued in '02 as F-50R.

1965-1968	Brazilian rw	$4,375	$5,675
1969-1987	Indian rw	$1,750	$2,300

Nightbird
1985-1987. Single-cut solidbody, tone chambers, 2 pickups, multi-bound, black or gold hardware, renamed Nightbird II in '87.

1985-1987		$1,750	$2,250

Nightbird I
1987-1988. Like Nightbird but with chrome hardware, less binding and appointments.

1987-1988		$1,750	$2,250

Nightbird II
1987-1992. Renamed from Nightbird, with black hardware, renamed Nightbird X-2000 in '92.

1987-1992		$1,750	$2,250

Nightbird X-2000
1992-1996. Renamed from Nightbird II.

1992-1996		$1,750	$2,250

Park Ave X-180
2005. Cutaway acoustic archtop, 2 pickups, block markers.

2005		$1,400	$1,825

Peregrine
1999-2005. Solidbody acoustic, cutaway, Fishman.

1999-2005	Custom	$850	$1,100
1999-2005	Flamed maple	$925	$1,200
1999-2005	S7CE, (CS)	$925	$1,200
1999-2005	S7CE, (CS), quilted	$925	$1,200
1999-2005	Standard	$775	$1,000

Polara S-100
1963-1970. Double-cut mahogany or alder solidbody, rosewood 'board, 2 single coils, built-in stand until '70, asymmetrical headstock, in '70 Polara dropped from title (see S-100), renamed Polara S-100 in '97.

1963-1970	2 or 3 pickups	$1,350	$1,775

1975 Guild Mark III
Rivington Guitars

1986 Guild Nightbird
Earl Bell

GUITARS

1976 Guild S-100
Willie Moseley

1978 Guild S-300A
Tom Pfeifer

MODEL YEAR	FEATURES	EXC. COND. LOW	HIGH
Roy Buchanan T-200			
1986. Single-cut solidbody, 2 pickups, pointed six-on-a-side headstock, poplar body, bolt-on neck, gold and brass hardware.			
1986		$525	$675
S-50			
1972-1978. Double-cut solidbody, 1 single-coil (switched to humbucker in '74), dot inlay.			
1972-1978		$825	$1,100
S-60/S-60 D			
1976-1981. Double-cut solidbody with long bass horn, 1 humbucker (60) or 2 single-coils (60 D), mahogany body, rosewood 'board.			
1976-1981		$750	$975
S-65 D			
1980-1981. S-60 but with 1 DiMarzio Super Distortion pickup.			
1980-1981		$750	$975
S-70 D/S-70 AD			
1979-1981. Solidbody (mahogany D, ash AD), rosewood 'board, 3 single-coils.			
1979-1981	S-70AD, ash	$900	$1,175
1979-1981	S-70D, mahogany	$825	$1,075
S-90			
1972-1977. Double-cut SG-like body, 2 humbuckers, dot inlay, chrome hardware.			
1972-1977		$875	$1,150
S-100			
1970-1978, 1994-1996. S-100 Standard is double-cut solidbody, 2 humbuckers, block inlays. Deluxe of '72-'75 had added Bigsby. Standard Carved of '74-'77 has acorns and oakleaves carved in the top.			
1970-1978	Standard	$1,350	$1,775
1972-1975	Deluxe	$1,350	$1,775
1974-1977	Standard Carved	$1,350	$1,775
S-100 Reissue			
1994-1997. Renamed Polara in '97.			
1994-1997		$675	$875
S-250			
1981-1983. Double-cut solidbody, 2 humbuckers.			
1981-1983		$395	$515
S-261			
Ca.1985. Double-cut, maple body, black Kahler tremolo, 1 humbucker and 2 single-coil pickups, rosewood 'board.			
1985		$395	$515
S-270 Runaway			
1985. Offset double-cut solidbody, 1 humbucker, Kahler.			
1985		$395	$515
S-271 Sprint			
1986. Replaced the S-270.			
1986		$395	$515
S-275			
1982-1983. Offset double-cut body, 2 humbuckers, bound figured maple top, sunburst or natural.			
1982-1983		$395	$515
S-280 Flyer			
1983-1984. Double-cut poplar body, 2 humbuckers or 3 single-coils, maple or rosewood neck, dot markers.			
1983-1984		$395	$515

MODEL YEAR	FEATURES	EXC. COND. LOW	HIGH
S-281 Flyer			
1983-1988. Double-cut poplar body S-280 with locking vibrato, optional pickups available.			
1983-1988		$395	$515
S-284 Starling/Aviator			
1984-1988. Starling (early-'84) and Aviator (late-'84-'88), double-cut, 3 pickups.			
1984	Starling	$395	$515
1984-1988	Aviator	$395	$515
S-285 Aviator			
1986. Deluxe Aviator, bound 'board, fancy inlays.			
1986		$395	$515
S-300 Series			
1976-1983. Double-cut mahogany solidbody with larger bass horn and rounded bottom, 2 humbuckers. S-300 A has ash body, D has exposed DiMarzio humbuckers.			
1976-1983	S-300	$675	$875
1977-1982	S-300D	$675	$875
1977-1983	S-300A	$675	$875
S-400/S-400 A			
1980-1981. Double-cut mahogany (400) or ash (400 A) solidbody, 2 humbuckers.			
1980-1981		$750	$1,000
Savoy A-150			
1958-1973, 2013-present. Acoustic archtop version of X-150, available with floating pickup, natural or sunburst finish. Reissued in 2013.			
1958-1961	Natural	$2,000	$2,575
1958-1961	Sunburst	$1,800	$2,350
2013-2019		$925	$1,200
Savoy X-150			
1954-1965. Electric archtop, single rounded cutaway, spruce top, maple back and sides, rosewood 'board and bridge, 1 single-coil pickup, sunburst, blond or sparkling gold finish. Reissued in '98 as X-150 Savoy.			
1954	Sunburst	$1,975	$2,575
1955-1959	Sunburst	$1,875	$2,450
1960-1965	Sunburst	$1,725	$2,225
Slim Jim T-100			
1958-1973. Electric archtop thinline, single-cut, laminated all-maple body, rosewood 'board and bridge, Waverly tailpiece, 1 pickup, natural or sunburst.			
1958-1959		$1,550	$2,000
1960-1964		$1,475	$1,900
1965-1969		$1,275	$1,650
1970-1973		$1,175	$1,525
Slim Jim T-100 D			
1958-1973. Semi-hollowbody electric, single Florentine cutaway, thinline, 2-pickup version of the T-100, natural or sunburst.			
1958-1959		$1,700	$2,200
1960-1964		$1,550	$2,000
1965-1969		$1,475	$1,900
1970-1973		$1,225	$1,600
Songbird S Series			
1984-1991. Designed by George Gruhn, flat-top, mahogany back, spruce top, single pointed cutaway, pickup with preamp, multi-bound top, black, natural or white. Renamed S-4 later in run.			
1984-1991		$800	$1,025

The *Vintage Guitar Price Guide* shows low to high values for items in all-original excellent condition, and, where applicable, with original case or cover.

MODEL YEAR	FEATURES	EXC. COND. LOW	HIGH

Standard (STD) Series
2010-2014. Imported flat-top acoustics based on classic Guild models, various models.
| 2010-2014 | F-30 STD | $1,025 | $1,325 |

Standard F-112 12-String
1968-1982. Acoustic flat-top, spruce top, mahogany back, sides and neck.
1968-1969		$775	$1,025
1970-1979		$650	$850
1980-1982		$615	$800

Starfire I
1960-1964. Electric archtop, single-cut thinline, laminated maple or mahogany body, bound body and neck, 1 pickup.
| 1960-1961 | Starfire Red | $950 | $1,250 |
| 1962-1964 | | $875 | $1,150 |

Starfire II
1960-1976, 1997-2001. Electric archtop, single-cut thinline, laminated maple or mahogany body, bound body and rosewood neck, 2 pickups.
1960-1961	Sunburst	$1,625	$2,100
1962	Emerald Green	$1,625	$2,150
1962-1966	Special color options	$1,750	$2,400
1962-1966	Sunburst, Starfire Red	$1,450	$1,900
1967-1975	Sunburst, Starfire Red	$1,350	$1,900
1997-2001	Reissue model	$1,025	$1,325

Starfire III
1960-1974, 1997-2005, 2013-present. Electric archtop, single-cut thinline, laminated maple or mahogany body, bound body and rosewood neck, 2 pickups, Guild or Bigsby vibrato, Starfire Red. Reintroduced under Newark St. Collection in '13.
1960-1961		$1,875	$2,450
1962-1966		$1,775	$2,350
1967-1974		$1,650	$2,150
1997-2005	Reissue model	$800	$1,050
2013-2019	Newark St	$675	$900

Starfire IV
1963-1987, 1991-2005. Thinline, double-cut semi-hollowbody, laminated maple or mahogany body, f-holes, 2 humbuckers, rosewood 'board, cherry or sunburst.
1963-1966		$1,900	$2,500
1967-1975		$1,750	$2,300
1976-1979		$1,500	$2,000
1980-1987		$1,450	$1,900
1991-2005	Reissue model	$850	$1,125

Starfire IV Special (Custom Shop)
2001-2002. Nashville Custom Shop.
| 2001-2002 | | $1,300 | $1,700 |

Starfire V
1963-1973, 1999-2001. Same as Starfire IV but with block markers, Bigsby and master volume, natural or sunburst finish, reissued in '99.
1963-1966		$2,000	$2,600
1967-1973		$1,950	$2,550
1999-2001	Reissue model	$950	$1,225

Starfire VI
1964-1979. Same as Starfire IV but with higher appointments such as ebony 'board, pearl inlays, Guild/Bigsby vibrato, natural or sunburst.
1964-1966		$2,000	$2,600
1967-1975		$1,950	$2,550
1976-1979		$1,800	$2,350

Starfire XII
1966-1973. Electric archtop, 12-string, double-cut, maple or mahogany body, set-in neck, 2 humbuckers, harp tailpiece.
| 1966-1969 | | $1,300 | $1,700 |
| 1970-1973 | | $1,200 | $1,600 |

Stratford A-350
1956-1973. Acoustic archtop, single rounded cutaway, solid spruce top with solid curly maple back and sides, rosewood 'board and bridge (changed to ebony by '60), sunburst.
1956-1959		$1,950	$2,525
1960-1965		$1,850	$2,375
1966-1969		$1,750	$2,275
1970-1973		$1,650	$2,150

Stratford A-350 B
1956-1973. A-350 in blond/natural finish option.
1956-1959		$2,200	$2,850
1960-1965		$2,050	$2,675
1966-1969		$1,950	$2,550
1970-1973		$1,850	$2,425

Stratford X-350
1954-1965. Electric archtop, single rounded cutaway, laminated spruce top with laminated maple back and sides, rosewood 'board, 6 push-button pickup selectors, sunburst finish (natural finish is X-375).
| 1954-1959 | | $2,575 | $3,375 |
| 1960-1965 | | $2,375 | $3,125 |

Stratford X-375/X-350 B
1953-1965. Natural finish version of X-350, renamed X-350 B in '58.
| 1953-1958 | X-375 | $2,775 | $3,600 |
| 1959-1965 | X-350B | $2,250 | $2,975 |

Stuart A-500
1956-1969. Acoustic archtop single-cut, 17" body, A-500 sunburst, available with Guild logo, floating DeArmond pickup.
| 1956-1965 | | $2,300 | $3,000 |
| 1966-1969 | | $2,100 | $2,800 |

Stuart A-550/A-500 B
1956-1969. Natural blond finish version of Stuart A-500, renamed A-500 B in '60.
1956-1959		$2,500	$3,200
1960-1965		$2,300	$3,000
1966-1969		$2,200	$2,900

Stuart X-500
1953-1995. Electric archtop, single-cut, laminated spruce top, laminated curly maple back and sides, 2 pickups, sunburst.
1953-1959		$2,800	$3,600
1960-1965		$2,600	$3,400
1966-1969		$2,400	$3,200
1970-1995		$2,200	$2,300

1957 Guild Savoy X-150
Carter Vintage Guitars

1966 Guild Starfire V
Angelo Guarini

GUITARS

1963 Guild, Thunderbird S-200
Ben Blazz

1962 Guild Troubadour F-20
Imaged by Heritage Auctions, HA.com

MODEL YEAR	FEATURES	LOW	HIGH
Stuart X-550/X-500 B			
1953-1995. Natural blond finish Stuart X-500, renamed X-500 B in '60.			
1953-1959		$2,800	$3,600
1960-1964		$2,600	$3,400
1965-1969		$2,400	$3,200
1970-1995		$2,200	$3,000
Studio 301/ST301			
1968-1970. Thinline, semi-hollow archtop Starfire-style but with sharp horns, 1 pickup, dot inlays, cherry or sunburst.			
1968-1969	Single-coil	$775	$1,025
1970	Humbucker	$900	$1,200
Studio 302/ST302			
1968-1970. Like Studio 301, but with 2 pickups.			
1968-1969	Single-coils	$1,025	$1,350
1970	Humbuckers	$1,025	$1,350
Studio 303/ST303			
1968-1970. Like Studio 301, but with 2 pickups and Guild/Bigsby.			
1968-1969	Single-coils	$1,225	$1,600
1970	Humbuckers	$1,225	$1,600
Studio 402/ST402			
1969-1970. Inch thicker body than other Studios, 2 pickups, block inlays.			
1969-1970	Humbuckers	$1,500	$1,950
1969-1970	Single-coils	$1,500	$1,950
T-250			
1986-1988. Single-cut body and pickup configuration with banana-style headstock.			
1986-1988		$450	$575
Thunderbird S-200			
1963-1968. Electric solidbody, offset double-cut, built-in rear guitar stand, AdjustoMatic bridge and vibrato tailpiece, 2 humbucker pickups until changed to single-coils in '66.			
1963-1965	Humbuckers	$3,000	$4,000
1966-1968	Single-coils	$2,650	$3,500
Troubadour F-20			
1956-1987. Acoustic flat-top, spruce top with maple back and sides (mahogany '59 and after), rosewood 'board and bridge, natural or sunburst.			
1956-1964		$1,525	$1,975
1965-1969		$1,450	$1,900
1970-1979		$1,225	$1,600
1980-1987		$1,125	$1,450
TV Model D-55/D-65/D-55			
1968-1987, 1990-present (special order only for 1968-1973). Dreadnought acoustic, spruce top, rosewood back and sides, scalloped bracing, gold-plated tuners, renamed D-65 in '87. Reintroduced as D-55 in '90.			
1968-1969		$1,950	$2,525
1970-1975		$1,850	$2,375
1976-1979		$1,750	$2,250
1980-1987		$1,650	$2,150
1988-1989	D-65	$1,525	$2,000
1990-1999		$1,525	$2,000
2000-2019	D-55	$1,550	$2,000

MODEL YEAR	FEATURES	LOW	HIGH
Willy Porter Signature			
2007-2008. AAA sitka spruce top, solid flamed maple sides and back, special appointments, Fishman Ellipse system.			
2007-2008		$1,050	$1,350
X-79 Skyhawk			
1981-1986. Four-point solidbody, 2 pickups, coil-tap or phase switch, various colors.			
1981-1986		$775	$1,000
X-80 Skylark/Swan			
1982-1985. Solidbody with 2 deep cutaways, banana-style 6-on-a-side headstock, renamed Swan in '85.			
1982-1985		$775	$1,000
X-82 Nova/Starfighter			
1981-1986. Solidbody, XR-7 humbuckerss, also available with 3 single-coil pickups, Quick Change SP-6 tailpiece, Adjusto-Matic bridge, Deluxe tuning machine.			
1981-1983	Nova	$775	$1,000
1984-1986	Starfighter	$775	$1,000
X-88 D Star			
1984-1987. 2 humbucker version X-88.			
1984-1987		$775	$1,000
X-88 Flying Star Motley Crue			
1984-1986. Pointy 4-point star body, rocketship meets spearhead headstock on bolt neck, 1 pickup, optional vibrato.			
1984-1986		$775	$1,000
X-92 Citron			
1984. Electric solidbody, detachable body section, 3 pickups.			
1984		$675	$875
X-100/X-110			
1953-1954. Guild was founded in 1952, so this is a very early model, 17" non-cut, single-coil soapbar neck pickup, X-100 sunburst, X-110 natural blond.			
1953-1954	X-100	$1,175	$1,550
1953-1954	X-110	$1,400	$1,825
X-100 Bladerunner			
1985-1987. 4-point body with large cutouts, 1 humbucker, Kahler, script Guild logo on body, cutout headstock.			
1985-1987		$2,000	$2,600
X-150 D Savoy			
1998-2003. Savoy with 2 humbuckers.			
1998-2003		$1,000	$1,300
X-150 Savoy			
1998-2005	1 pickup	$900	$1,150
X-160 Savoy			
1989-1993. No Bigsby, black or sunburst.			
1989-1993		$1,250	$1,625
X-161/X-160B Savoy			
1989-1994. X-160 Savoy with Bigsby, sunburst or black.			
1989-1994		$1,250	$1,625
X-200/X-220			
1953-1954. Electric archtop, spruce top, laminated maple body, rosewood 'board, non-cut, 2 pickups. X-200 is sunburst and X-220 blond.			
1953-1954	X-200	$1,575	$2,050
1953-1954	X-220	$1,725	$2,250

MODEL YEAR	FEATURES	EXC. COND. LOW	HIGH
X-300/X-330			

1953-1954. No model name, non-cut, 2 pickups, X-300 is sunburst and X-330 blond. Becomes Savoy X-150 in '54.

MODEL YEAR	FEATURES	EXC. COND. LOW	HIGH
1953-1954	X-300	$1,575	$2,050
1953-1954	X-330	$1,725	$2,250
X-400/X-440			

1953-1954. Electric archtop, single-cut, spruce top, laminated maple body, rosewood 'board, 2 pickups, X-400 in sunburst and X-440 in blond. Becomes Manhattan X-175 in '54.

1953-1954	X-400	$2,100	$2,750
1953-1954	X-440	$2,325	$3,050
X-600/X-660			

1953. No model name, single-cut, 3 pickups, X-600 in sunburst and X-660 in blond. Becomes Stratford X-350 in '54.

1953	X-600	$2,825	$3,650
1953	X-660	$3,250	$4,175
X-700			

1994-1999. Rounded cutaway, 17", solid spruce top, laminated maple back and sides, gold hardware, natural or sunburst.

1994-1999		$1,775	$2,300

Guillermo Roberto Guitars

Professional grade, solidbody electric bajo quintos made in San Fernando, California starting in the year 2000.

Guitar Company of America

1971-present. Professional grade, production, acoustic guitars built by luthier Dixie Michell. Originally built in Tennessee, then Missouri; currently being made in Tulsa, Oklahoma. She also offers mandolins.

Guitar Mill

2006-2011. Luthier Mario Martin built his production/custom, professional grade, semi-hollow and solidbody guitars and basses in Murfreesboro, Tennessee. He also built basses. In '11, he started branding his guitars as Mario Martin.

Gurian

1965-1981. Luthier Michael Gurian started making classical guitars on a special order basis, in New York City. In '69, he started building steel-string guitars as well. 1971 brought a move to Hinsdale, Vermont, and with it increased production. In February, '79 a fire destroyed his factory, stock, and tools. He reopened in West Swanzey, New Hampshire, but closed the doors in '81. Around 2,000 Gurian instruments were built. Dealers have reported that '70s models sometimes have notable wood cracks which require repair.

MODEL YEAR	FEATURES	EXC. COND. LOW	HIGH
CL Series			

1970-1981. Classical Series, mahogany (M), Indian rosewood (R), or Brazilian rosewood (B).

1970-1981	CLB, Brazilian rosewood	$2,700	$3,500
1970-1981	CLM, mahogany	$1,300	$1,700
1970-1981	CLR, Indian rosewood	$1,500	$1,900
FLC			

1970-1981. Flamenco guitar, yellow cedar back and sides, friction tuning pegs.

1970-1981		$1,600	$2,100
JB3H			
1970-1981	Brazilian rosewood	$3,000	$3,900
JM/JMR			

1970-1981. Jumbo body, mahogany (JM) or Indian rosewood (JMR), relatively wide waist (versus D-style or SJ-style).

1970-1981	JM	$1,500	$2,000
1970-1981	JMR	$1,500	$2,000
JR3H			

1970-1981. Jumbo, Indian rosewood sides and back, 3-piece back, herringbone trim.

1970-1981		$1,875	$2,450
S2B3H			
1970-1981	Brazilian rosewood	$3,000	$4,000
S2M			

1970-1981. Size 2 guitar with mahogany back and sides.

1970-1981		$1,450	$1,900
S2R/S2R3H			

1970-1981. Size 2 with Indian rosewood sides and back, R3H has 3-piece back and herringbone trim.

1970-1981	S2R	$1,500	$2,000
1970-1981	S2R3H	$1,600	$2,100
S3B3H			
1981	Brazilian rosewood	$3,000	$4,000
S3M			
1970-1981	Mahogany	$1,500	$2,000
S3R/S3R3H			

1970-1981. Size 3 with Indian Rosewood, S3R3H has 3-piece back and herringbone trim.

1970-1981	S3R	$1,600	$2,100
1970-1981	S3R3H	$1,700	$2,200

Guyatone

1933-present. Made in Tokyo by Matsuki Seisakujo, founded by Hawaiian guitarists Mitsuo Matsuki and Atsuo Kaneko (later of Teisco). Made Guya brand Rickenbacker lap steel copies in '30s. After a hiatus for the war ('40-'48), Seisakujo resumes production of laps and amps as Matsuki Denki Onkyo Kenkyujo. In '51 the Guyatone brand is first used on guitars and basses, and in '52 they changed the company name to Tokyo Sound Company. Guyatones are among the earliest U.S. imports, branded as Marco Polo, Winston, Kingston and Kent. Other brand names included LaFayette and Bradford. Production and exports slowed after '68.

1975 Guild TV Model D-55
Peter Busch

Ca.1968 Guyatone LG-350T Sharp 5
Rivington Guitars

GUITARS

1965 Hagstrom Corvette
Guitar Maniacs

1966 Hagstrom Model I

MODEL YEAR	FEATURES	EXC. COND. LOW	HIGH

Hagenlocher, Henner

1996-present. Luthier Henner Hagenlocher builds his premium grade, custom, nylon-string guitars in Granada, Spain.

Hagstrom

1958-1983, 2004-present. Intermediate, professional, and premium grade, production/custom, solid-body, semi-hollowbody and acoustic guitars made in the U.S. and imported. Founded by Albin Hagström of Älvdalen, Sweden, who began importing accordions in 1921 and incorporated in '25. The name of the company was changed to A.B. Hagström, Inc. in '38, and an American sales office was established in '40. Electric guitar and bass production began in '58 with plastic-covered hollowbody De Luxe and Standard models. The guitars were imported into the U.S. by Hershman Music of New York as Goya 90 and 80 from '58-'61. Bass versions were imported in '61. Following a year in the U.S., Albin's son Karl-Erik Hagström took over the company as exclusive distributor of Fender in Scandinavia; he changed the U.S. importer to Merson Musical Instruments of New York (later Unicord in '65), and redesigned the line. The company closed its doors in '83. In 2004 American Music & Sound started manufacturing and distributing the Hagstrom brand under license from A.B. Albin Hagstrom. In 2009 U.S. Music became involved via its acqustion of JAM, and the 'new' Hagstrom established a Swedish office. A new line of instruments under the Vintage Series (made in China) included classic '60s models. Later the Northen series was introduced with instruments made entirely in Europe.

Corvette/Condor
1963-1967. Offset double-cut solidbody, 3 single-coils, multiple push-button switches, spring vibrato, called the Condor on U.S. imports.

1963-1967		$775	$1,000

D'Aquisto Jimmy
1969-1975, 1976-1979. Designed by James D'Aquisto, electric archtop, f-holes, 2 pickups, sunburst, natural, cherry or white. The '69 had dot inlays, the later version had blocks. From '77 to '79, another version with an oval soundhole (no f-holes) was also available.

1969-1975	1st design	$1,000	$1,300
1976-1979	2nd design	$1,000	$1,300

Deluxe Series
2004-2008. Carved single-cut mahogany body, set-neck, 2 humbuckers, sparkle tops or sunburst.

2004-2008	Various models	$175	$325

F Series (China)
2004-2015 Offset double-cut basswood body, 2 or 3 pickups.

2004-2015	Various models	$175	$325

H-12 Electric/Viking XII
1965-1967. Double-cut, 2 pickups, 12 strings.

1965-1967		$375	$475

H-22 Folk
1965-1967 Flat-top acoustic.

1965-1967		$275	$350

MODEL YEAR	FEATURES	EXC. COND. LOW	HIGH

Impala
1963-1967. Two-pickup version of the Corvette, sunburst.

1963-1967		$575	$775

Kent
1962-1967. Offset double-cut solidbody, 2 pickups.

1962-1967		$375	$500

Model I
1965-1971. Small double-cut solidbody, 2 single-coils, early models have plastic top.

1965-1969	Rare finish, 6-in-line	$575	$750
1965-1969	Standard finish, 6-in-line	$325	$425
1970-1971	3-on-a-side	$300	$400

Model II/F-200 Futura/H II
1965-1972, 1975-1976. Offset double-cut slab body with beveled edge, 2 pickups, called F-200 Futura in U.S., Model II elsewhere, '75-'76 called H II. F-200 reissued in 2004.

1965-1970	Rare finish, 6-in-line	$600	$800
1965-1970	Standard finish, 6-in-line	$400	$600
1970-1972	3-on-a-side	$325	$450

Model III/F-300 Futura/H III
1965-1972, 1977. Offset double-cut slab body with beveled edge, 3 pickups, called F-300 Futura in U.S., Model III elsewhere, '77 called H III.

1965-1969		$600	$800
1970-1977		$325	$425

Swede
1970-1982, 2004-present. Bolt-on neck, single-cut solidbody, black, cherry or natural, '04 version is set-neck.

1979-1982		$675	$875

Super Swede
1979-1983, 2004-present. Glued-in neck upgrade of Swede, '04 version is maple top upgrade of Swede.

1979-1983		$700	$900
1979-1983	Custom color	$900	$1,200
2004-2019	Reissue	$260	$335

Viking/V1
1965-1975, 1978-1979, 2004-present. Double-cut thinline, 2 f-holes, 2 pickups, chrome hardware, dot inlays, also advertised as the V-1. '60s had 6-on-side headstock, '70s was 3-and-3, latest version back to 6-on-side.

1965-1979		$800	$1,025
2004-2019	Reissue	$260	$335

Viking Deluxe/V2
1967-1968, 2004-present. Upscale version, gold hardware, block inlays, bound headstock and f-holes. Current version upgrades are blocks and flame maple.

1967-1968		$825	$1,075
2004-2019	Reissue	$260	$335

Hahn

2007-present. Professional and premium grade, custom electric guitars built by luthier Chihoe Hahn in Garnerville, New York.

MODEL YEAR	FEATURES	EXC. COND. LOW	HIGH

Haight

1989-present. Premium and presentation grade, production/custom, acoustic (steel and classical) guitars built in Scottsdale, Arizona by luthier Norman Haight. He also builds mandolins.

Halfling Guitars and Basses

Luthier Tom Ribbecke builds premium grade, production/custom, pin bridge, thinline and jazz guitars and basses, starting in 2003, in Healdsburg, California.

Hallmark

1965-1967, 2004-present. Imported and U.S.-made, intermediate and premium grade, production/custom, guitars and basses from luthiers Bob Shade and Bill Gruggett, and located in Greenbelt, Maryland. They also make basses. The brand was originally founded by Joe Hall in Arvin, California, in '65. Hall had worked for Semie Moseley (Mosrite) and had also designed guitars for Standel in the mid-'60s. Bill Gruggett, who also built his own line of guitars, was the company's production manager. Joe Hall estimates that less than 1000 original Hallmark guitars were built. The brand was revived by Shade in '04.

Sweptwing

1965-1967. Pointed body, sorta like a backwards Flying V.

1965-1967		$1,525	$2,000

Hamblin Guitars

Luthier Kent Hamblin built his premium grade, production/custom, flat-top acoustic guitars in Phoenix, Arizona and Telluride, Colorado, and presently builds in Colorado Springs. He began building in 1996.

Hamer

1974-2012, 2017-present. Intermediate grade, production, electric guitars. Hamer previously made basses and the Slammer line of instruments. Founded in Arlington Heights, Illinois, by Paul Hamer and Jol Dantzig. Prototype guitars built in early-'70s were on Gibson lines, with first production guitar, the Standard (Explorer shape), introduced in '75. Hamer was puchased by Kaman Corporation (Ovation) in '88. The Illinois factory was closed and the operations were moved to the Ovation factory in Connecticut in '97. On January 1, '08, Fender acquired Kaman Music Corporation and the Hamer brand. In '90, they started the Korean-import Hamer Slammer series which in '97 became Hamer Import Series (no Slammer on headstock). In '05 production was moved to China and name changed to XT Series (in '07 production moved to Indonesia). The U.S.-made ones have U.S.A. on the headstock. The less expensive import Slammer brand (not to be confused with the earlier Slammer Series) was introduced in '99 (see that listing). Fender suspended production of the Hamer brand at the end of 2012, later selling

KMC (and Hamer brand) to Jam Industries, which relaunched Hamer in '17.

Artist/Archtop Artist/Artist Custom

1995-2012. U.S.-made, similar to Sunburst Archtop with semi-solid, f-hole design, sunburst, named Archtop Artist, then renamed Artist (with stop tailpiece)/Artist Custom in '97.

1995-2012	Higher-end specs	$1,300	$1,725
1995-2012	Standard specs	$900	$1,200

Artist 25th Anniversary Edition

1998. Made in USA, 25th Anniversary Edition script logo on headstock.

1998		$900	$1,200

Artist Korina

2001-2012. Double-cut, bass f-hole, korina (limba) body and neck, 2 P-90s or 2 humbuckers (HB), natural gloss finish.

2001-2012		$1,225	$1,625

Artist Ultimate

1998-2012. Figured maple top, deluxe binding, gold hardware.

1998-2012		$2,000	$2,600

Blitz

1982-1984 (1st version), 1984-1990 (2nd version). Explorer-style body, 2 humbuckers, 3-on-a-side peghead, dot inlays, choice of tremolo or fixed bridge, second version same except has angled 6-in-line peghead and Floyd Rose tremolo.

1982-1984	3-on-a-side	$1,150	$1,500
1984-1990	6-in-line	$900	$1,175

Californian

1987-1997. Made in USA, solidbody double cut, bolt neck, 1 humbucker and 1 single-coil, Floyd Rose tremolo.

1987-1989		$1,800	$2,400
1990-1997		$1,600	$2,100

Californian Custom

1987-1997. Made in USA, downsized contoured body, offset double-cut, neck-thru-body, optional figured maple body, Duncan Trembucker and Trem-single pickups.

1987-1989		$1,700	$2,200
1990-1997		$1,500	$1,900

Californian Elite

1987-1997. Made in USA, downsized contoured body, offset double-cut, optional figured maple body, bolt-on neck, Duncan Trembucker and Trem-single pickups.

1987-1989		$1,700	$2,200
1990-1997		$1,500	$1,900

Centaura

1989-1995. Alder or swamp ash offset double-cut, bolt-on neck, 1 humbucker and 2 single-coils, Floyd Rose, sunburst.

1989-1995		$750	$975

Chaparral

1985-1987 (1st version), 1987-1994 (2nd version). Offset double-cut, glued neck, angled peghead, 1 humbucker and 2 single-coils, tremolo, second version has bolt neck with a modified peghead.

1985-1987	Set-neck	$850	$1,100
1987-1994	Bolt-on neck	$750	$950

1972 Hagstrom Swede
Rivington Guitars

1967 Hagstrom Viking Deluxe
Imaged by Heritage Auctions, HA.com

GUITARS

Hamer Diablo

Hamer Newport
Bernunzio Uptown Music

MODEL YEAR	FEATURES	EXC. COND. LOW	HIGH
Daytona			
1993-1997. Offset double-cut, bolt neck, dot inlay, 3 single-coils, Wilkinson tremolo.			
1993-1997		$875	$1,150
Diablo			
1992-1997. Offset double-cut, bolt neck, rosewood 'board, dot inlays, reversed peghead '92-'94, 2 pickups, tremolo.			
1992-1997		$725	$925
DuoTone			
1993-2003. Semi-hollowbody, double-cut, bound top, glued-in neck, rosewood 'board, 2 humbuckers, EQ.			
1993-2003		$575	$750
Echotone/Echotone Custom			
2000-2002. Thinline semi-hollow archtop, f-holes, 2 humbuckers, trapezoid inlays, gold hardware.			
2000-2002		$300	$385
Eclipse			
1994-1996. Asymmetrical double-cut slab mahogany body, glued neck, rosewood 'board, 2 Duncan Mini-Humbuckers, cherry.			
1994-1996		$600	$800
Eclipse (Import)			
1997-1999. Import version.			
1997-1999		$250	$325
Eclipse 12-String			
1994-1996. 12-string version of Eclipse.			
1995		$600	$800
FB I			
1986-1987. Reverse Firebird-style body, glued-in neck, reverse headstock, 1 pickup, rosewood 'board with dot inlays, also available in non-reverse body.			
1986-1987		$575	$750
FB II			
1986-1987. Reverse Firebird-style, glued-in neck, ebony 'board with boomerang inlays, angled headstock, 2 humbuckers, Floyd Rose tremolo, also available as a 12-string.			
1986-1987		$600	$800
Korina Standard			
1995-1996. Limited run, Korina Explorer-type body, glued-in neck, angled peghead, 2 humbuckers.			
1995-1996		$1,400	$1,800
Maestro			
1990. Offset double-cut, 7 strings, tremolo, bolt-on maple neck, 3 Seymour Duncan rail pickups.			
1990		$950	$1,225
Mirage			
1994-1998. Double-cut carved figured koa wood top, transparent flamed top, initially with 3 single-coil pickups, dual humbucker option in '95.			
1994-1998		$900	$1,150
Newport Series			
1999-2012. USA, double-cut thinline, center block, f-holes, 2 humbuckers (Newport 90 has P-90s), wraparound bridge tailpiece.			
1999-2012	Newport	$1,025	$1,350
1999-2012	Newport Pro	$1,125	$1,450
Phantom A5			
1982-1884, 1985-1986 (2nd version). Offset double-cut, glued neck, 3-on-a-side peghead, 1 triple-coil and			

MODEL YEAR	FEATURES	EXC. COND. LOW	HIGH
1 single-coil pickup, second version same but with 6-in-line peghead and Kahler.			
1982-1984		$900	$1,175
Phantom GT			
1984-1986. Contoured body, offset double-cut, glued-in fixed neck, 6-in-line peghead, 1 humbucker, single volume control.			
1984-1986		$875	$1,125
Prototype			
1981-1985. Contoured mahogany body, double-cut with 1 splitable triple-coil pickup, fixed bridge, three-on-a-side peghead, Prototype II has extra pickup and tremolo.			
1981-1985		$975	$1,250
Scarab I			
1984-1986. Multiple cutaway body, 6-in-line peghead, 1 humbucker, tremolo, rosewood or ebony 'board, dot inlays.			
1984-1986		$975	$1,250
Scarab II			
1984-1986. Two humbucker version of the Scarab.			
1984-1986		$1,050	$1,350
Scepter			
1986-1990. Futuristic-type body, ebony 'board with boomerang inlays, angled 6-in-line peghead, Floyd Rose tremolo.			
1986-1990		$1,100	$1,400
Slammer Series			
1990-1997. Various models imported from Korea, not to be confused with Hamer's current Slammer budget line started in '98.			
1990-1997		$200	$425
Special Series			
1980-1983 (1st version), 1984-1985 (Floyd Rose version), 1992-1997 (2nd version), 2017-present. Double-cut solidbody, flame maple top, glued neck, 3-on-a-side peghead, 2 humbuckers, Rose version has mahogany body with ebony 'board, the 2nd version is all mahogany and has tune-o-matic bridge, stop tailpiece and Duncan P-90s, cherry red.			
1980-2019	Various models	$1,200	$1,600
Standard			
1974-1985, 1995-2005. Futuristic body, maple top, bound or unbound body, glued neck, angled headstock, either unbound neck with dot inlays or bound neck with crown inlays, 2 humbuckers. Reissued in '95 with same specs but unbound mahogany body after '97. Higher dollar Standard Custom still available.			
1974-1975	Pre-production, about 20 made	$7,500	$10,000
1975-1977	Production, about 50 made, PAFs	$6,500	$8,500
1977-1979	Dimarzio PAF-copies	$4,200	$5,500
1980-1985		$3,000	$4,000
1995-1999		$2,300	$3,000
2000-2005	USA, flamed top	$1,900	$2,500
Standard (Import, XT)			
1998-2012. Import version, 2 humbuckers.			
1998-2012		$250	$325

MODEL YEAR	FEATURES	EXC. COND. LOW	HIGH
Standard Custom GSTC			
2007-2012. Made in USA, flamed maple top, mahogany neck, rosewood 'board.			
2007-2012		$2,600	$3,400
Stellar 1			
1999-2000. Korean import, double-cut, 2 humbuckers.			
1999-2000		$125	$170
Steve Stevens I			
1984-1992. Introduced as Prototype SS, changed to Steve Stevens I in '86, contoured double-cut, 6-in-line headstock, dot or crown inlays, 1 humbucker and 2 single-coil pickups.			
1984-1992		$750	$975
Steve Stevens II			
1986-1987. One humbucker and 1 single-coil version.			
1986-1987		$750	$975
Studio			
1993-2012. Double-cut, flamed maple top on mahogany body, 2 humbuckers, cherry or natural.			
1993-2012		$800	$1,025
Studio Custom			
1997-2012. Carved figured maple, humbuckers, tune-o-matic bridge, stop tailpiece, sunburst.			
1997-2012		$1,200	$1,600
Sunburst			
1977-1983, 1990-1992, 2018-present. Double-cut bound solidbody, flamed maple top, glued-in neck, bound neck and crown inlays optional, 3-on-a-side headstock, 2 humbuckers.			
1977-1983		$2,300	$3,000
1990-1992		$1,600	$2,100
Sunburst (Import, XT)			
1997-2012. Import version of Sunburst, flat-top or archtop, 2 pickups.			
1997-2012		$180	$230
Sunburst Archtop			
1991-1997. Sunburst model with figured maple carved top, 2 humbuckers, offered under various names: Standard - unbound neck and dot inlays, tune-o-matic and stop tailpiece '91-'93 (replaced by the Studio). Custom - bound neck and crown inlays '91-'93, which became the Archtop for '94-'97 (replaced by the Studio Custom). Archtop GT - Gold top with P-90 soapbar-style pickups '93-'97.			
1991-1997	Various models	$1,300	$1,650
T-51			
1993-1997. Classic single-cut southern ash body, 2 single-coils.			
1993-1997		$650	$850
T-62			
1991-1995. Classic offset double-cut solidbody, tremolo, pau ferro 'board, Lubritrak nut, locking tuners, 3-band active EQ, various colors.			
1991-1995		$650	$850
TLE			
1986-1992. Single-cut mahogany body, maple top, glued neck, 6-in-line headstock, rosewood 'board, dot inlays, 3 pickups.			
1986-1992		$825	$1,050

MODEL YEAR	FEATURES	EXC. COND. LOW	HIGH
TLE Custom			
1986-1992. Bound, single-cut solidbody with maple top, glued-in neck, angled headstock, ebony 'board with boomerang inlays, 3 pickups.			
1986-1992		$825	$1,050
Vector			
1982-1985. V-style body (optional flame maple top), 3-on-a-side peghead, rosewood 'board, 2 humbuckers, Sustain Block fixed bridge (Kahler or Floyd Rose tremolos may also be used).			
1982-1985		$1,500	$2,000
Vector Limited Edition Korina			
1997. 72 built in Hamer's Arlington Heights, Illinois shop, price includes original Hamer certificate of authenticity with matching serial number, Flying-V Vector style body, gold hardware, natural finish.			
1997		$2,200	$2,800

Hanson

2009-present. Founders John and Bo Pirruccello import intermediate grade, electric guitars which are set up in Chicago, Illinois.

Harden Engineering

1999-present. Professional grade, custom, solidbody guitars built by luthier William Harnden in Chicago, Illinois. He also builds effects pedals.

Harmony

1892-1976, late 1970s-present. Huge, Chicago-based manufacturer of fretted instruments, mainly budget models under the Harmony name or for many other American brands and mass marketers. Harmony was at one time the largest guitar builder in the world. In its glory days, Harmony made over one-half of the guitars built in the U.S., with '65 being their peak year. But by the early-'70s, the crash of the '60s guitar boom and increasing foreign competition brought an end to the company. The Harmony brand appeared on Asian-built instruments starting in the late '70s to the '90s with sales mainly through mass-retail stores. In 2000, the Harmony brand was distributed by MBT International. In '02, former MBT marketing director Alison Gillette launched Harmony Classic Reissue Guitars and Basses and in '09 the trademark was acquired by Westheimer Corporation. Many Harmony guitars have a factory order number on the inside back of the guitar which often contains the serial number. Most older Harmony acoustics and hollowbodies have a date ink-stamped inside the body. DeArmond made most of the electronic assemblies used on older Harmony electrics, and they often have a date stamped on the underside.

Amplifying Resonator Model 27

1930s. Dobro-licensed with Dobro metal resonator, wood body.

1930s		$525	$700

Archtone H1215/H1215 Tenor

1950s. Lower-end archtop, sunburst.

1950-1960s	4-string tenor	$190	$250
1950-1960s	6-string	$200	$260

Hamer Vector
Imaged by Heritage Auctions, HA.com

Harden Engineering Switchblade

GUITARS

1950s Harmony Broadway H954
Imaged by Heritage Auctions, HA.com

1960 Harmony Meteor H71
Tom Pfeifer

MODEL YEAR	FEATURES	EXC. COND. LOW	HIGH

Bob Kat H14/H15
1968. Replaces Silhouette solidbody, H14 has single pickup and 2 knobs, H15 has 2 pickups. When vibrato is added it becomes the H16 model.

| 1968 | H14 | $250 | $325 |
| 1968 | H15 | $350 | $450 |

Brilliant Cutaway H1310/H1311
1962-1965. 16 1/2" body (Grand Auditorium), acoustic archtop cutaway, block markers, sunburst.

| 1962-1965 | | $425 | $550 |

Broadway H954
1930s-1971. 15-3/4" body, acoustic archtop, dot markers, sunburst.

| 1930s-1971 | | $175 | $225 |

Buck Owens
1969. Acoustic flat-top, red, white and blue. The price shown is for a guitar that has an unblemished finish, paint-wear will reduce the price, prices vary considerable due to the condition of the finish.

| 1969 | | $1,500 | $2,000 |

Cremona
1930s-1952. Full-size archtop line, Harmony and Cremona logo on headstock, natural. Cutaways became available in '53.

| 1940-1952 | | $220 | $285 |

D Series (Electric)
Late-1980s-Early-1990s. Classic electric copy models including offset double- and single-cut solidbody and double-cut thin hollowbody (D720), 1 to 3 pickups. All models begin with D, some models part of Harmony Electric series and others the Harmony Igniter series.

| 1980s-90s | Various models | $60 | $80 |

Espanada H63
1950s-1965. Thick body, single-cut, jazz-style double pickups, black finish with white appointments, by early '60s 'Espanada' logo on lower bass bout.

| 1950s-1965 | | $1,050 | $1,375 |

Folk H162
1950s-1971. Grand concert size acoustic, spruce top, mahogany body.

| 1950s-1971 | | $325 | $425 |

Folk H165/H6365
1958-1974. Square-shouldered flat-top, all mahogany body. Renamed the H6365 in '72.

| 1958-1974 | | $290 | $375 |

Grand Concert H165
1948-1957. Flat-top, all mahogany body. Body changed to square-shoulder in '58 (see Folk H165).

| 1948-1957 | | $250 | $325 |

H/HG Series (Electric)
Late-1980s-Early-1990s. Classic electric copy models including offset double-cut, single-cut and double-cut semi-hollow, 1 to 3 pickups, with or without tremolo. All models begin with H or HG, some models part of Harmony Electric series and others the Harmony Igniter series.

| 1980s-90s | Various models | $45 | $85 |

H60 Double Cutaway Hollowbody
1968-1970. Thinline double-cut, 2 pickups, trapeze tailpiece, sunburst.

| 1968-1970 | | $800 | $1,050 |

H62 Blond
1950s-1965. Thin body, dual pickup archtop, curly maple back and sides, spruce top, block markers, blond.

| 1950s-1965 | | $1,075 | $1,400 |

H62VS (Reissue)
2000s. H62 with sunburst finish.

| 2000s | | $650 | $850 |

H64 Double Cutaway Electric
1968-1970. Factory Bigsby, dot markers, sunburst.

| 1968-1970 | | $975 | $1,275 |

H68 Deep Body Electric
1968-1971. Full-body single-cut electric archtop, 2 pickups, trapeze bridge, block markers.

| 1968-1971 | | $975 | $1,275 |

H72/H72V Double Cutaway Hollowbody
1966-1971. Multiple bindings, 2 pickups, cherry red, H72V has Bigsby.

| 1966-1971 | | $975 | $1,275 |

H74 Neo-Cutaway
1961-1967. Modified double-cut, 2 pickups, Bigsby, 3-part F-holes, dot inlays.

| 1961-1967 | | $1,050 | $1,375 |

H75 Double Cutaway Hollowbody
1960-1970. Three pickups, multi-bound body, 3-part f-holes, block inlays, bolt neck, brown sunburst.

| 1960-1970 | | $1,050 | $1,375 |

H76 Double Cutaway Hollowbody
1960-1962. H75 with Bigsby.

| 1960-1962 | | $1,050 | $1,375 |

H77 Double Cutaway Hollowbody
Late-1960s. Same as H75, but in cherry sunburst.

| 1960s | | $1,050 | $1,375 |

H78 Double Cutaway Hollowbody
Late-1960s. H78 with Bigsby.

| 1960s | | $1,050 | $1,375 |

H79 Double Cutaway Hollowbody 12-String
1966-1970. Unique slotted headstock, cherry finish.

| 1966-1970 | | $975 | $1,275 |

H910 Classical
1970s. Beginner guitar, natural.

| 1970s | | $50 | $65 |

H1200 Auditorium Series
1948-1975. Moderately-priced acoustic archtop, treble-clef artwork on headstock, model 1213 & 1215 (shaded brown sunburst) and 1214 (blond ivory, ends in '64). Model 1215 was renamed H6415 in '72 and lasted until '75.

| 1948-1975 | Various models | $190 | $250 |

H1270 12-String Flat-Top
1965. 16" deluxe acoustic 12-string flat-top, spruce top, mahogany sides and back, dot markers.

| 1965 | | $350 | $450 |

H1310 Brilliant Cutaway
1953-1973. Grand Auditorium acoustic archtop, single rounded cutaway, block inlays, sunburst. Called H6510 in '72.

| 1953-1973 | | $450 | $575 |

H1311 Brilliant Cutaway
1953-1962. As H 1310, but in blond.

| 1953-1963 | | $625 | $800 |

The *Vintage Guitar Price Guide* shows low to high values for items in all-original excellent condition, and, where applicable, with original case or cover.

MODEL YEAR	FEATURES	EXC. COND. LOW	HIGH

H4101 Flat-Top Tenor
1950s-1970s. Mahogany body, 4-string.

1950-1970s		$225	$300

Holiday Rocket
Mid-1960s. Similar to H59 Rocket III but with push-button controls instead of rotary selector switch, 3 Goldentone pickups, pickup trim rings, Holiday logo on 'guard, higher model than standard Rocket.

1960s		$875	$1,150

Hollywood H37
1960-1961. Electric archtop, auditorium size 15.75" body, 1 pickup, Harmony and Hollywood logo on headstock, 2-tone gold metallic finish.

1960-1961		$425	$550

Hollywood H39
1960-1965. Like H37 but with sunburst.

1960-1965		$290	$375

Hollywood H41
1960-1965. Like H37 but with 2 pickups, sunburst.

1960-1965		$375	$475

Igniter Series (D/H/HG)
Late-1980s to early-1990s. Pointy-headstock electric copy models, offset double-cut, all models begin with D, H, or HG.

1980s-90s	Various models	$90	$115

Lone Ranger
1950-1951. Lone Ranger headstock stencil, Lone Ranger and Tonto stencil on brown body. This model was first introduced in 1936 as the Supertone Lone Ranger with same stencil on a black body.

1950-1951		$225	$300

Master H945
1965-1966. 15" (Auditorium) acoustic archtop, block markers, music note painted logo on headstock, sunburst.

1965-1966		$200	$250

Meteor H70/H71
1958-1966. Single rounded cutaway 2" thin body, 2 pickups, 3-part f-holes, block inlays, bolt neck, H70 sunburst, H71 natural (ended '65), lefty offered '65-'66, reintroduced as H661 and H671 (without Meteor name) in '72-'74.

1958-1965	H71, natural	$1,050	$1,350
1958-1966	H70, sunburst	$1,050	$1,350

Modern Trend H65
1956-1960. Short-scale electric thin body archtop, 1 single-coil, block inlays, sherry blond finish on curly maple grain.

1956-1960		$700	$925

Monterey H950/H952/H1325/H1456/H1457/H6450
1930s-1974. Line of Auditorium and Grand Auditorium acoustic archtop models.

1950s	H952 Colorama	$270	$350
1950s-60s	Other models	$175	$225
1970s	H6450	$115	$150

Patrician (1407/1414/1418)
1932-1973. Model line mostly with mahogany bodies and alternating single/double dot markers (later models with single dots), introduced as flat-top, changed to archtop in '34. In '37 line expanded to 9 archtops (some with blocks) and 1 flat-top. Flat-tops disappeared in the '40s, with various archtops offered up to '73.

1932-1973		$290	$375

Professional H1252 Hawaiian
1940. Hawaiian acoustic jumbo, high-end appointments, vertical Professional logo on front of headstock, figured koa or mahogany back and sides, spruce top, Brazilian rosewood fretboard, various-shaped fretboard markers.

1940		$1,775	$2,350

Rebel H81
1968-1971. Single pickup version of Rebel, brown sunburst.

1968-1971		$275	$350

Rebel H82/H82G
Listed as a new model in 1971. Thin body, hollow tone chamber, double-cut, 2 pickups, H82 sunburst, H82G greenburst avacado shading (renumbered as H682 and H683 in '72).

1970s	H82	$450	$575
1970s	H82G	$450	$575

Rocket I H53
1959-1973. Single-cut, f-holes, 1 pickup, trapeze, 2-tone brown sunburst ('59-'62) or red sunburst ('63 on).

1959-1969		$375	$475
1970-1973		$290	$375

Rocket II H54
1959-1973. Same as H53 but with 2 pickups.

1959-1969		$625	$800
1970-1973		$375	$475

Rocket III H59
1960-1973. Same as H53 but with 3 pickups.

1960-1969		$800	$1,050
1970-1973		$725	$950

Roy Rogers H600
1954-1958. 3/4 size, stencil, sold through Sears.

1954-1958		$225	$350

Roy Smeck Artiste H1442
1939-ca. 1942. Grand auditorium acoustic archtop, Roy Smeck Artiste logo on headstock, split rectangle markers, black, white guard.

1939-1942		$390	$500

Roy Smeck H73
1963-1964. Electric hollowbody, single neck silver bar-style pickup or 2 Harmony pickups.

1963-1964		$850	$1,100

Roy Smeck Vita Standard H1250
1928-1931. Pear shaped body, seal-shaped sound holes.

1928-1331		$600	$800

Silhouette De Luxe Double H19
1965-1969. Double-cut solidbody, deluxe pickups, block markers, advanced vibrato, sunburst.

1965-1969		$575	$750

Silhouette H14/H15/H17
1963-1967. Double-cut solidbody, H14 single pickup, H15 dual pickup, H17 dual with vibrato (offered until '66).

1963-1967	H14	$250	$325
1963-1967	H15	$350	$450
1963-1967	H17	$425	$550

1955 Harmony Patrician
Edward Sparks

1960 Harmony Rocket III H59
Imaged by Heritage Auctions, HA.com

GUITARS

1970 Harmony Sovereign
Edward Sparks

1960 Harmony Stratotone Mars
Larry Krauss

MODEL YEAR	FEATURES	EXC. COND. LOW	HIGH

Singing Cowboys H1057
1950s. Western chuck-wagon scene stencil top, Singing Cowboys stenciled on either side of upper bouts, brown background versus earlier Supertone version that had black background.

| 1950s | | $250 | $325 |

Sovereign Jumbo Deluxe H1266
1960s-1970s. Jumbo nearly D-style, 16" wide body with out-size 'guard, natural.

| 1960s | | $350 | $450 |
| 1970s | | $290 | $375 |

Sovereign Jumbo H1260
1960s-1970s. Jumbo shape, 16" wide body, natural.

| 1960s | | $475 | $625 |
| 1970s | | $325 | $425 |

Sovereign Western Special Jumbo H1203
1960s-1970s. 15" wide body, 000-style.

| 1960s | | $375 | $475 |

Stratotone Deluxe Jupiter H49
1958-1965. Single-cut, tone chamber construction, 2 pickups, bound spruce top, curly maple back and 6 control knobs, blond finish.

| 1958-1965 | | $750 | $1,000 |

Stratotone Doublet H88
1954-1957. Basically 2 pickup H44.

| 1954-1957 | | $1,150 | $1,500 |

Stratotone H44
1953-1957. First edition models had small bodies and rounded cutaway, 1 pickup with plain cover using 2 mounting rivets, sometimes called Hershey Bar pickup, '60s models had slightly larger bodies and sharp cutaways, some with headstock logo Harmony Stratotone with atomic note graphic.

| 1953-1957 | | $1,150 | $1,500 |

Stratotone Mars Electric H45/H46
1958-1968. Single-cut, tone chamber construction, sunburst finish, H45 with 1 pickup, H46 with 2 pickups.

| 1960s | H45 | $400 | $525 |
| 1960s | H46 | $525 | $700 |

Stratotone Mercury Electric H47/H48
1958-1968. Single-cut, tone chamber construction, H47 with 1 pickup, block inlay and curly maple sunburst top, H48 is the same with a blond top.

| 1960s | H47 | $575 | $750 |
| 1960s | H48 | $575 | $750 |

Stratotone Newport H42/1 and H42/2
1957-1958. Brightly colored, single-cut, Newport headstock logo, 1 single-coil. 42/1 in sunshine yellow, /2 in metallic green.

| 1957-1958 | | $1,150 | $1,500 |

TG1201 Tenor
1950s. Spruce top, two-on-a-side tuners, Sovereign model tenor, natural.

| 1950s | | $225 | $300 |

Vibra-Jet H66
1962-1966. Thinline single-cut, 2 pickups, built-in tremolo circuit and control panel knobs and selection dial, sunburst.

| 1962-1966 | | $1,050 | $1,375 |

Harptone
1893-ca. 1975. The Harptone Manufacturing Corporation was located in Newark, New Jersey. They made musical instrument cases and accessories and got into instrument production from 1934 to '42, making guitars, banjos, mandolins, and tiples. In '66 they got back into guitar production, making the Standel line from '67 to '69. Harptone offered flattops and archtops under their own brand until the mid-'70s when the name was sold to the Diamond S company, which owned Micro-Frets.

Acoustic
1966-mid-1970s. Various models.

| 1966-1970s | Deluxe/Custom | $1,400 | $1,825 |
| 1966-1970s | Standard | $975 | $1,300 |

Electric
1966-mid-1970s. Various models.

| 1966-1970s | | $1,300 | $1,700 |

Harrison Guitars
1992-present. Luthier Douglas Harrison builds premium grade, production/custom, archtop and semi-hollowbody jazz guitars in Toronto, Ontario.

Harwood
Harwood was a brand introduced in 1885 by Kansas City, Missouri instrument wholesalers J.W. Jenkins & Sons (though some guitars marked Harwood, New York). May have been built by Jenkins until circa 1905, but work was later contracted out to Harmony.

Parlor
1890s. Slotted headstocks, most had mahogany bodies, some with Brazilian rosewood body, considered to be well made.

| 1890s | Brazilian rosewood | $750 | $1,000 |
| 1890s | Mahogany | $425 | $550 |

Hascal Haile
Late 1960s-1986. Luthier Hascal Haile started building acoustic, classical and solidbody guitars in Tompkinsville, Kentucky, after retiring from furniture making. He died in '86.

Hauver Guitar
2001-present. Professional and premium grade, custom, acoustic guitars, built in Sharpsburg, Maryland by luthier Michael S. Hauver.

Hayes Guitars
Professional and premium grade, production/custom, steel and nylon string guitars made by luthier Louis Hayes in Paonia, Colorado. He began building in 1993.

Hayman
1970-1973. Solid and semi-hollowbody guitars and basses developed by Jim Burns and Bob Pearson for Ivor Arbiter of the Dallas Arbiter Company and built by Shergold in England.

MODEL YEAR	FEATURES	EXC. COND. LOW	HIGH

Haynes
1865-early 1900s. The John C. Haynes Co. of Boston also made the Bay State brand.

Heartfield
1989-1994. Founded as a joint venture between Fender Musical Instrument Corporation (U.S.A.) and Fender Japan (partnership between Fender and distributors Kanda Shokai and Yamano Music) to build and market more advanced designs (built by Fuji Gen-Gakki). First RR and EX guitar series and DR Bass series debut in '90. Talon and Elan guitar series and Prophecy bass series introduced in '91. The brand was dead by '94.

Elan
1989-1994. Carved-style bound double-cut body, flamed top, 2 humbuckers, offset headstock.

1989-1994		$415	$535

EX/EX II
1990-1994. 3 single-coils, Floyd Rose tremolo.

1990-1994		$415	$535

Talon
1989-1994. Offset double-cut, wedge-triangle headstock, dot markers, hum/single/hum pickups.

1989-1994	I, II, III	$330	$425
1989-1994	IV	$390	$510

Heiden Stringed Instruments
1974-present. Luthier Michael Heiden builds his premium grade, production/custom, flat-top guitars in Chilliwack, British Columbia. He also builds mandolins.

Heit Deluxe
Ca. 1967-1970. Imported from Japan by unidentified New York distributor. Many were made by Teisco, the most famous being the Teisco V-2 Mosrite copy. They also had basses.

Acoustic Archtop
1967-1970. Various models.

1967-1970		$130	$200

Electric Solidbody
1967-1970. Various models.

1967-1970		$160	$350

Electric Thinline Hollowbody
1967-1970. Various models.

1967-1970		$190	$350

Hembry Guitars
2002-present. Professional grade, production/custom, solidbody electric guitars built by luthier Scott Hembry in Shelton, Washington. He also builds basses.

Hemken, Michael
1993-present. Luthier Michael Hemken builds his premium grade, custom, archtops in St. Helena, California.

HenBev
Premium grade, production, solid and hollow body electric guitars and basses built by luthier Scotty Bevilacqua in Oceanside, California, starting in the year 2005.

Hendrick
1982-1985. Solidbody guitars built by luthier Kurt Hendrick in Texas, Ohio and Michigan. Less than 100 built, the most popular model was the Generator. Hendrick also worked with Schecter, Fender, Jackson and Epiphone.

Henman Guitars
2010-present. Owners Graham and Paris Henman offer premium grade, production/custom, solidbody and chambered electric guitars and basses built by luthier Rick Turner in Santa Cruz, California.

Heritage
1985-present. Professional, premium, and presentation grade, production/custom, hollow, semi-hollow, and solidbody guitars built in Kalamazoo, Michigan. They have also made banjos, mandolins, flat-tops, and basses in the past.

Founded by Jim Deurloo, Marvin Lamb, J.P. Moats, Bill Paige and Mike Korpak, all former Gibson employees who did not go to Nashville when Norlin closed the original Gibson factory in '84. In 2007, Vince Margol bought out Paige. In '16, a private group of local Kalamazoo investors bought the business with Deurloo, Lamb and Paige remaining active in the company.

Eagle
1986-2009. Single rounded cut semi-hollowbody, mahogany body and neck, bound body, 1 jazz pickup, f-holes, sunburst or natural.

1986-2009		$1,700	$2,200

Eagle Classic
1992-present. Standard Collection, Eagle with maple body and neck, bound neck and headstock, gold hardware, sunburst or natural.

1992-2020		$2,400	$3,100

Gary Moore Model
1989-1991. Single-cut solidbody, 2 pickups, chrome hardware, sunburst.

1989-1991		$1,500	$1,925

Golden Eagle
1985-2019. Single-cut hollowbody, back inlaid with mother-of-pearl eagle and registration number, multi-bound ebony 'board with mother-of-pearl cloud inlays, bound f-holes, gold-plated parts, ebony bridge inlaid with mother-of-pearl, mother-of-pearl truss rod cover engraved with owner's name, 1 Heritage jazz pickup, multi-bound curly maple 'guard.

1985-1999	Floating pickup	$2,200	$2,900
1985-1999	Mounted pickup	$2,200	$2,900

Groove Master
2004-2018. 16" hollow-body, single rounded cutaway, neck pickup, sunburst.

2004-2018		$1,350	$1,775

1966 Harptone

Heritage Eagle Classic

GUITARS

GUITARS

1986 Heritage H-140
Carter Vintage Guitars

Heritage H-357
C.J. Stanley

MODEL YEAR	FEATURES	EXC. COND. LOW	HIGH
H-137			
1980s-present. Standard Collection, single-cut solidbody, 2 P-90s, sunburst, natural lime (early) or TV yellow (later).			
1980s-2018	Sunburst or natural lime	$1,000	$1,300
2019-2020	Sunburst or TV yellow	$1,050	$1,350
H-137 AA			
2018-present. Artisan Aged Collection, sunburst or TV yellow with aged finish.			
2018-2020		$1,050	$1,350
H-140/H-140 CM			
1985-2005, 2007-2016. Single pointed cutaway solidbody, bound curly maple ('85-'04) or solid gold top ('94-'05), 2 humbuckers, chrome parts.			
1985-1996	Black	$1,000	$1,300
1985-2004	CM, curly maple	$1,000	$1,300
1994-2005	Goldtop	$1,000	$1,300
2001	CM, flamed maple	$1,000	$1,300
2007-2016	2nd edition, goldtop	$1,000	$1,300
H-147			
1990-1991. Single-cut solidbody, 2 humbuckers, mahogany body, mother-of-pearl block inlays, black with black or gold hardware.			
1990-1991		$900	$1,175
H-150			
1990s-present. Standard Collection, solid carved figured maple top, mahogany back, various colors.			
1990s-2020		$1,400	$1,800
H-150 AA			
2018-present. Artisan Aged Collection, sunburst, ebony, various colors with aged finish.			
2018-2020		$1,400	$1,800
H-150 C/H-150 CM			
1985-2018. Single rounded cutaway solidbody, curly maple top, 2 pickups, chrome parts, cherry sunburst.			
1985-2018	Flamed	$1,400	$1,800
1985-2018	Goldtop	$1,275	$1,675
H-150 Deluxe Limited Edition			
1992. 300 made.			
1992		$1,350	$1,750
H-157			
1989-2004. Mahogany body with maple top, natural, sunburst or black.			
1989-2004		$1,500	$1,900
H-157 Ultra			
1993-1994. Single-cut solidbody, large block markers, highly figured maple top.			
1993-1994		$1,500	$1,900
H-160			
1986, 2007. Limited production.			
1986		$725	$950
2007	2nd Edition	$800	$1,050
H-170			
1980s-1997. Double-cut solidbody, 2 humbuckers, bound carved top, was also a later curly maple top version (H-170CM).			
1980s-1997		$1,000	$1,300

MODEL YEAR	FEATURES	EXC. COND. LOW	HIGH
H-204 DD			
1986-1989. Single-cut solidbody of mahogany, curly maple top, 1-piece mahogany neck, 22-fret rosewood 'board.			
1986-1989		$500	$650
H-207 DD			
1986-1989. Double-cut solidbody of mahogany, curly maple top, 1-piece mahogany neck, 22-fret rosewood 'board.			
1986-1989		$500	$650
H-357			
1989-1994. Asymmetrical solidbody, neck-thru.			
1989-1994		$1,725	$2,225
H-516 Thin			
1999-2015. Single-cut, thin all maple body, mahogany neck, 2 humbucking pickups, various colors.			
1999-2015		$1,500	$1,950
H-530			
2016-present. Standard Collection, double-cut hollowbody, sunburst, trans cherry or antique natural.			
2016-2020		$1,600	$2,075
H-535			
1987-present. Standard Collection, double-cut semi-hollowbody, curly maple top and back, 2 pickups, various colors.			
1987-2018		$1,475	$1,900
2019-2020		$1,550	$2,000
H-535 AA			
2018-present. Artisan Aged Collection, various colors with aged finish.			
2018-2020		$1,550	$2,000
H-537			
1990. Single-cut, thinline, dots.			
1990		$1,200	$1,550
H-550			
1990-2018. Single-cut hollowbody, laminated maple top and back, multiple bound top, white bound 'guard, f-holes, 2 humbuckers.			
1990-2018		$1,600	$2,100
H-555			
1989-2018. Like 535, but with maple neck, ebony 'board, pearl and abalone inlays, gold hardware.			
1989-2018		$1,600	$2,075
H-575			
1987-present. Standard Collection, sharp single-cut hollowbody, solid maple top and back, cream bound top and back, wood 'guard, f-holes, 2 humbuckers.			
1987-2020		$1,900	$2,500
H-575 AA			
2018-present. Artisan Aged Collection, various colors with aged finish.			
2018-2020		$1,900	$2,500
H-576			
1990-2004. Single rounded cut hollowbody, laminated maple top and back, multiple bound top, single bound back and f-holes and wood 'guard, 2 humbuckers.			
1990-2004		$1,500	$2,000

MODEL YEAR FEATURES	EXC. COND. LOW	HIGH

Henry Johnson (HJ) Signature
2005-2018. Pointed single cut curly maple back and sides hollowbody, 2 humbuckers, block inlays, multi-bound.

2005-2018	$1,300	$1,700

HFT-445
1987-2000. Flat-top acoustic, mahogany back and sides, spruce top, maple neck, rosewood 'board.

1987-2000	$650	$850

Johnny Smith
1989-2001. Custom hand-carved 17" hollowbody, single-cut, f-holes, 1 pickup, various colors.

1989-2001 Various options	$2,400	$3,100

Kenny Burrell (KB) Groove Master
2004-2018. Single-cut 16" hollow body, 1 humbucker, gold hardware, block inlays.

2004-2018	$1,700	$2,200

Millennium Eagle 2000
2000-2009. Single-cut semi-solidbody, multiple bound curly maple top, single-bound curly maple back, f-holes, 2 humbuckers, block inlays.

2000-2009	$1,600	$2,000

Millennium Eagle Custom
2000-2009. Like ME 2000 but with curlier maple, multiple bound neck, split block inlays.

2000-2009	$2,150	$2,750

Millennium SAE
2000-2009. Single-cut semi-solidbody, laminated arch top, single cream bound top and back, f-holes, 2 humbuckers.

2000-2009	$1,000	$1,250

Millennium Ultra/Standard Ultra
2004-2016. Single-cut, ultra curly maple top, mahogany back and sides, 1-piece mahogany neck, f-holes, mother-of-pearl block inlays.

2004-2016	$1,400	$1,800

Parsons Street
1989-1992. Offset double-cut, curly maple top on mahogany body, single/single/hum pickups, pearl block markers, sunburst or natural.

1989-1992	$600	$800

Roy Clark
1992-2018. Thinline, single-cut semi-hollow archtop, gold hardware, 2 humbuckers, block markers, cherry sunburst.

1992-2018	$1,900	$2,500

SAE Custom
1992-2000. Single-cut maple semi-hollowbody, f-holes, 2 humbuckers and 1 bridge pickup.

1992-2000	$1,000	$1,300

Super Eagle
1988-2018. 18" body, single-cut electric archtop, 2 humbuckers.

1989-2018	$2,400	$3,100

Sweet 16
1987-2018. Single-cut maple semi-hollowbody, spruce top, 2 pickups, pearl inlays.

1987-2018	$1,900	$2,500

Hermann Hauser
Born in 1882, Hauser started out building zithers and at age 23 added classical guitars and lutes, most built in his shop in Munich, Germany. He died in 1952. His son and grandson and great-granddaughter, Hermann II and III and Kathrin, continued the tradition. The Hermann Hauser's legacy is based on his innovative approach to bracing and top thickness which gave his instruments their own voice. Hermann I Era instruments are linked with Andres Segovia who used them. Hermann II Era instruments are linked with modern players like Julian Bream. Hermann III builds Segovia style and custom-made instruments. Kathrin Hauser, daughter of Hermann III, is a fourth generation builder. The original Hauser shop in Munich was destroyed by Allied bombing in 1946 and was moved to Reisbach in the Bavaria region, where the shop remains. Hauser instruments used paper labels on the inside back. The labels often stipulate the city of construction as well as the Hermann Hauser name. Labels are easily removed and changed, and an original instrument should be authenticated. Beautiful violin-like clear varnish finish ends in '52, approximately 400 instruments were made by Hermann I. Under Hermann II, nitrocellulose lacquer spray replaces varnish in '52, bracing patterns change in the '60s, which was a welcome change for modern players. Instruments should be evaluated on a case by case basis.

Hermann Hauser II
1952-1988. Born in 1911 and the son of Hermann Hauser I, he built between 500 and 600 classical guitars in Germany during his career. He died in 1988.

Hermann Hauser III
1988-present. Hermann III started build guitars in '74, and took over the family business upon the death of his father in '88. He continues to build Segovia style and custom-made classical guitars in Munich, Germany.

Hess
1872-ca. 1940. Located in Klingenthal, Germany, Hess built acoustic and harp guitars, as well as other stringed instruments and accordians.

Hewett Guitars
1994-present. Luthier James Hewett builds his professional and premium grade, custom/production, steel string, archtop jazz, solidbody and harp guitars in Panorama Village, Texas.

Hill Guitar Company
1972-1980, 1990-present. Luthier Kenny Hill builds his professional and premium grade production/custom, classical and flamenco guitars in Felton, California and Michoacan, Mexico.

Heritage H-530

Hewett Grand Concert

GUITARS

2000 Höfner Jazzica Custom
Bernunzio Uptown Music

Höfner Club Model 50
Rivington Guitars

MODEL YEAR	FEATURES	EXC. COND. LOW	HIGH

Hirade Classical
1968-present. Professional grade, production, solid top, classical guitars built in Japan by Takamine. The late Mass Hirade was the founder of the Takamine workshop. He learned his craft from master luthier Masare Kohno. Hirade represents Takamine's finest craftsmanship and material.

HML Guitars
1997-present. Howard Leese custom-designs premium grade, electric guitars, which are built by luthier Jack Pimentel in Puyallup, Washington.

Hoffman Guitars
1971-present. Premium grade, custom flat-tops and harp guitars built by luthier Charles Hoffman in Minneapolis, Minnesota.

Höfner
1887-present. Budget, intermediate, professional and premium grade, production, solidbody, semi-hollow, archtop, acoustic, and classical guitars built in Germany and the Far East. They also produce basses and bowed-instruments. Founded by Karl Höfner in Schonbach, Germany. The company was already producing guitars when sons Josef and Walter joined the company in 1919 and '21 and expanded the market worldwide. They moved the company to Bavaria in '50 and to Hagenau in '97. The S in Hofner model names usually denotes cutaway.

Beatle Electric Model 459TZ
1966-1967. Violin-shaped 500/1 body, block-stripe position markers, transistor-powered flip-fuzz and treble boost, sunburst.

1966-1967		$1,250	$1,600

Beatle Electric Model 459VTZ
1966-1967. Same as Model 459TZ except with vibrato tailpiece, brown (standard) or blond option.

| 1966-1967 | Blond option | $1,250 | $1,600 |
| 1966-1967 | Brown | $1,050 | $1,400 |

Beatle Electric Model G459TZ Super
1966-1967. Deluxe version of Model 459TZ, flamed maple sides, narrow grain spruce top, gold hardware, elaborate inlays and binding, natural blond.

| 1966-1967 | | $1,300 | $1,700 |

Beatle Electric Model G459VTZ Super
1966-1967. Same as G459TZ Super but with vibrato tailpiece.

| 1966-1967 | | $1,400 | $1,850 |

Club Model 40 John Lennon Limited Edition
2008. Limited run of 120, single-cut, spruce top, maple back and sides, neck pickup, vertical Höfner logo on headstock, Lennon signature on 'guard.

| 2008 | | $1,450 | $1,900 |

Club Model 50
1959-1962. Mid-level of the late '50s 'Club Series', single-cut, 2 pickups, sunburst.

| 1959-1962 | | $1,225 | $1,625 |

Club Model 60
1959. Highest model of late '50s 'Club Series', single-cut, 2 black bar pickups, 2 knobs and 2 slider switches on control panel, highest-end split-diamond style markers, natural blond finish.

| 1959 | | $1,375 | $1,825 |

Club Model 126
1954-1970. Mid-sized single-cut solidbody, dot markers, flamed maple back and sides, spruce top, sunburst. Listed with Höfner Professional Electric Series.

| 1954-1958 | | $800 | $1,075 |

Committee Model 4680 Thin Electric
1961-1968. Thinline single-cut archtop, 2 pickups, split-arrowhead markers, no vibrato, sunburst.

| 1961-1968 | | $725 | $975 |

Deluxe Model 176
1964-1983. Double-cut, 3 pickups, polyester varnished sunburst finish, vibrola tailpiece, similar to Model 175 polyester varnished red and gold version.

| 1964-1969 | | $350 | $475 |
| 1970-1983 | | $300 | $400 |

Galaxy Model 175
1963-1966. Double-cut, 3 pickups, red and gold vinyl covering, fancy red-patch 'guard, vibrola, similar to Model 176 polyester varnished sunburst version.

| 1963-1966 | Red & gold vinyl | $575 | $750 |
| 1963-1966 | Sunburst | $500 | $650 |

Golden Höfner
1959-1963. Single-cut archtop, blond, 2 pickups, f-holes.

| 1959-1963 | | $4,850 | $6,450 |

Jazzica Custom
2000-2010. Full body, single soft cutaway, acoustic/electric archtop, carved German spruce top, sunburst.

| 2000-2010 | | $1,300 | $1,700 |

Model 165
1975-1976. Offset double-cut, S-style body, 2 single-coil pickups, bolt-on neck.

| 1975-1976 | | $275 | $375 |

Model 171
1975-1976. Copy of Tele-Thinline.

| 1975-1976 | | $250 | $325 |

Model 172 II (R) (S) (I)
1962-1963. Double-cut body, polyester varnished wood (S) or scuff-proof red (R) or white (I) vinyl, 2 pickups, vibrato.

| 1962-1963 | | $300 | $400 |

Model 173 II (S) (I)
1962-1963. Double-cut body, polyester varnished wood (S) or scuffproof vinyl (I), 3 pickups, vibrato.

| 1962-1963 | Gold foil vinyl | $350 | $450 |
| 1962-1963 | White vinyl | $350 | $450 |

Model 178
1967-ca. 1969. Offset double-cut solidbody, 2 pickups with an array of switches and push button controls, fancy position markers, vibrola, sunburst. 178 used on different design in the '70s.

| 1967-1969 | | $375 | $475 |

MODEL YEAR	FEATURES	EXC. COND. LOW	HIGH

Model 180 Shorty Standard
1982. Small-bodied travel guitar, single-cut, solid-body, 1 pickup, travel, the Shorty Super had a built-in amp and speaker.

1982		$200	$275

Model 450S Acoustic Archtop
Mid-1960s. Economy single-cut acoustic archtop in Hofner line, dot markers, Höfner logo on 'guard, sunburst.

1960s		$350	$450

Model 455/S
1950s-1970. Archtop, single-cut, block markers.

1959		$425	$575

Model 456 Acoustic Archtop
1950s-1962. Full body acoustic archtop, f-holes, laminated maple top, sides, back, large pearloid blocks, two color pearloid headstock laminate.

1950s-1962		$450	$600

Model 457 President
1959-1972. Single-cut thinline archtop, 2 pickups, non-vibrato.

1959-1972		$550	$725

Model 457/12 12-String Electric
1969-1970. Comfort-thin cutaway archtop, shaded brown.

1969-1970		$425	$575

Model 462 Acoustic Archtop
Ca. 1952-1960s. Single-cut archtop, bound cat's-eye soundholes, 3-piece pearloid headstock overlay, 3-piece large block inlays. Also offered with fingerboard mounted pickup with no controls (EG) and by mid '50s with 1, 2, or 3 pickups with volume and tone knobs/switches (462S/E1, 2, or 3).

1952-1960s	462S	$400	$525
1952-1960s	462SEG	$600	$800

Model 463
1958-1960. Archtop electric, 2 or 3 pickups.

1958-1960		$725	$975

Model 470SE2 Electric Archtop
1961-1994. Large single rounded cutaway electric archtop on Höfner's higher-end they call "superbly flamed maple (back and sides), carved top of best spruce," 2 pickups, 3 control knobs, gold hardware, pearl inlay, natural finish only.

1961-1994		$600	$800

Model 471SE2 Electric Archtop
1969-1977. Large single pointed cutaway electric archtop, flamed maple back and sides, spruce top, black celluloid binding, ebony 'board, pearl inlays, sunburst version of the 470SE2.

1969-1977		$600	$800

Model 490 Acoustic
Late 1960s. 16" body, 12-string, spruce top, maple back and sides, dot markers, natural.

1960s		$175	$225

Model 490E Acoustic Electric
Late 1960s. Flat-top 12-string with on-board pickup and 2 control knobs.

1960s		$250	$325

Model 491 Flat-Top
1960s-1970s. Slope shoulder body style, spruce top, mahogany back and sides, shaded sunburst.

1970s		$250	$325

Model 492 Acoustic
Late 1960s. 16" body, 12-string, spruce top, mahogany back and sides, dot markers.

1960s		$225	$300

Model 492E Acoustic Electric
Late 1960s. Flat-top 12-string with on-board pickup and 2 control knobs.

1960s		$225	$300

Model 496 Jumbo Flat-Top
1960s. Jumbo-style body, selected spruce top, flamed maple back and sides, gold-plated hardware, vine pattern 'guard, sunburst.

1960s		$375	$500

Model 514-H Classical Concert
1960s. Concert model, lower-end of the Höfner classical line, natural.

1960s		$100	$150

Model 4500 Thin Electric
Late-1960s-early-1970s. Thinline archtop, single-cut, 3 options, laminated maple top and back, dot markers, top mounted controls, brown sunburst.

1960s-70s	E1, 1 pickup	$375	$500
1960s-70s	E2, 2 pickups	$450	$600
1960s-70s	V2, 2 pickups, vibrato	$475	$625

Model 4560 Thin Electric
Late-1960s-early-1970s. Thinline archtop, single-cut, 2 options, laminated maple top and back, 2-color headstock, large block markers, top mounted controls, brown sunburst.

1960s-70s	E2	$475	$625
1960s-70s	V2, vibrato	$525	$675

Model 4574VTZ Extra Thin
Late-1960s-early-1970s. Extra thinline acoustic, 2 pickups.

1960s-70s		$500	$675

Model 4575VTZ Extra Thin
Late-1960s-early-1970s. Extra-thinline acoustic, double-cut with shallow rounded horns, 3 pickups, vibrato arm, treble boost and flip-fuzz, straight-line markers.

1960s-70s		$575	$750

Model 4578TZ President
1959-1970. Double-cut archtop. 'President' dropped from name by late-'60s and renamed Model 4578 Dual Cutaway, also added sharp horns.

1959-1965		$525	$675
1966-1970		$450	$600

Model 4600 Thin Electric
Late-1960s-early-1970s. Thinline acoustic, double-cut, 2 pickups, dot markers, sunburst, V2 with vibrato.

1960s-70s	E2	$450	$600
1960s-70s	V2, vibrato	$500	$650

Model 4680 Thin Electric
Late-1960s-early-1970s. Single-cut thinline electric, 2 pickups, 3-in-a-line control knobs, ornate inlays, spruce top, brown sunburst, V2 with vibrato.

1960s-70s	E2	$675	$900
1960s-70s	V2, vibrato	$725	$975

1961 Hofner 173 II (S)
Imaged by Heritage Auctions, HA.com

1967 Höfner Model 457 President
Clay Harrell

1980s Hohner Professional Series - TE Prinz
Imaged by Heritage Auctions, HA.com

1980s Hondo H-790 Lazer
Imaged by Heritage Auctions, HA.com

MODEL YEAR	FEATURES	EXC. COND. LOW	HIGH
Model 4700 Thin Electric			
Late-1960s-early-1970s. Deluxe version of Model 4680, gold plated appointments and natural finish, V2 with vibrato.			
1960s-70s	E2	$800	$1,050
1960s-70s	V2, vibrato	$875	$1,125
Senator Acoustic Archtop			
1958-1960s. Floating pickup option available, full body archtop, f-holes, made for Selmer, London.			
1958-1960		$325	$425
Senator E1			
1961. Senator full body archtop with single top mounted pickup and controls.			
1961		$475	$625
Verythin Standard			
2001-2008. Update of the 1960s Verythin line, 2 humbuckers, f-holes, dot inlays.			
2001-2008		$800	$1,050

Hohner

1857-present. Budget and intermediate grade, production, acoustic and electric guitars and basses. They also have mandolins, banjos and ukuleles. Matthias Hohner, a clockmaker in Trossingen, Germany, founded Hohner in 1857, making harmonicas. Hohner has been offering guitars and basses at least since the early '70s. HSS was founded in 1986 as a distributor of guitars and other musical products. By 2000, Hohner was also offering the Crafter brands of guitars.

MODEL YEAR	FEATURES	EXC. COND. LOW	HIGH
Alpha Standard			
1987. Designed by Klaus Scholler, solidbody, stereo outputs, Flytune tremolo.			
1987		$175	$250
G 2T/G 3T Series			
1980s-1990s. Steinberger-style body, 6-string, neck-thru, locking tremolo.			
1980s-90s		$250	$325
Jacaranda Rosewood Dreadnought			
1978. Flat-top acoustic.			
1978		$125	$175
Jack			
1987-1990s. Mate for Jack Bass. Headless, tone circuit, tremolo, 2 single-coils and 1 humbucker.			
1987-1992		$250	$325
L 59/L 75 Series			
Late-1970s-1980s. Classic single-cut solidbody, 2 humbuckers, glued neck, sunburst, 59 has upgrade maple body with maple veneer top.			
1970s-80s		$250	$325
	Miller Beer Guitar		
1985. Solidbody, shaped like Miller beer logo.			
1985		$175	$250
Professional			
1980s. Single-cut solidbody, maple neck, extra large 'guard, natural.			
1980s		$250	$325
Professional Series - TE Custom			
1980s-1990s. Single-cut solidbody, bolt neck.			
1980s-90s		$550	$750

MODEL YEAR	FEATURES	EXC. COND. LOW	HIGH
Professional Series - TE Prinz			
Late 1980s-early 1990s. Based on Prince's No. 1 guitar, 2 single-coils, bolt neck, Professional The Prinz headstock logo, natural.			
1989-1990		$550	$750
SE 35			
1989-mid-1990s. Semi-hollow thinline, 2 humbuckers, natural.			
1989		$250	$325
SG Lion			
1980s-1990s. Offset double-cut, pointy headstock, glued neck.			
1980s-90s		$175	$250
ST Series			
1986-1990s. Includes the bolt neck ST 57, ST Special, ST Special S, Viper I, Viper II (snakeskin finish option), ST Victory, ST Metal S, and the ST Custom.			
1986-1992		$200	$300
Standard Series - EX Artist			
1970s-1980s. Solidbody, 2 humbuckers, gold hardware, neck-thru, solid maple body, rosewood 'board, tremolo.			
1970s-80s		$200	$300
Standard Series - RR Custom			
1970s-1980s. Randy Rhoads V body, 2 humbuckers, chrome hardware, glued neck, mahogany body, rosewood 'board, tremolo.			
1970s-80s		$200	$300
Standard Series - SR Heavy			
1970s-1980s Hybrid body, 2 humbuckers, neck-thru, solid maple body, rosewood 'board, tremolo.			
1970s-80s		$200	$300

Holiday

1960s. Electric, acoustic and bass guitars sold by Aldens, a Chicago catalog company. Most models built by Harmony. They also offered mandolins and banjos.

MODEL YEAR	FEATURES	EXC. COND. LOW	HIGH
Silhouette Bobcat			
1964-1967. Solidbody electric made by Harmony, similar to Harmony Silhouette, offset double-cut, 2 pickups, 4-in-a-row control knobs.			
1964-1967		$370	$460

Hollenbeck Guitars

1970-2008. Luthier Bill Hollenbeck built his premium grade, production/custom, hollow and semi-hollow body acoustics and electric guitars in Lincoln, Illinois. Bill passed away in '08.

Hollingworth Guitars

1995-present. Luthier Graham Hollingworth builds his production/custom, premium grade, electric, acoustic and archtop guitars in Mermaid Beach, Gold Coast, Queensland, Australia. He also builds lap steels.

Holman

1966-1968. Built by the Holman-Woodell guitar factory in Neodesha, Kansas. The factory was started to build guitars for Wurlitzer, but that fell through by '67.

MODEL YEAR	FEATURES	EXC. COND. LOW	HIGH

Holst

1984-present. Premium grade, custom, archtop, flat-top, semi-hollow, and classical guitars built in Creswell, Oregon by luthier Stephen Holst. He also builds mandolins. Until '01 he was located in Eugene, Oregon.

Holzapfel (Holzapfel & Beitel)

1898-1930s. Carl C. Holzapfel and Clemence Beitel built guitars, banjos, and mandolins in Baltimore, but are best-known as early innovators of the 12-string guitar. Beitel left the company in 1905 and Holzapfel continued to build instruments up to the depression. He, and later his son, Carl M., mainly repaired instruments after that (up to 1988), but still would do custom builds.

Hondo

1969-1987, 1991-2005. Budget grade, production, imported acoustic, classical and electric guitars. They also offered basses, banjos and mandolins. Originally imported by International Music Corporation (IMC) of Fort Worth, Texas, founded by Jerry Freed and Tommy Moore and named after a small town near San Antonio, Texas. Early pioneers of Korean guitarmaking, primarily targeted at beginner market. Introduced their first electrics in '72. Changed brand to Hondo II in '74. Some better Hondos made in Japan '74-'82/'83. In '85 IMC purchases major interest in Jackson/Charvel, and the Hondo line was supplanted by Charvels. 1987 was the last catalog before hiatus. In '88 IMC was sold and Freed began Jerry Freed International and in '91 he revived the Hondo name. Acquired by MBT International in '95, currently part of Musicorp.

Acoustic Flat-Top
1969-1987, 1991-2005.

1969-2005		$75	$125

Electric Hollowbody
1969-1987, 1991-2005.

1969-2005		$150	$450

Electric Solidbody
1969-1987, 1991-2005.

1969-1987		$150	$450
1991-1999		$150	$250
2000-2005		$50	$150

Longhorn 6/12 Doubleneck Copy
1970s-1980s. Copy of Danelectro Longhorn 6/12 Doubleneck guitar, Dano coke bottle-style headstock, white sunburst.

1970s-80s		$550	$725

Longhorn Copy
Ca. 1978-1980s. Copy of Danelectro Long Horn guitar, Dano Coke bottle-style headstock, brown-copper.

1978-80s		$400	$525

M 16 Rambo-Machine Gun
1970s-1980s. Machine gun body-style, matching machine gun-shaped guitar case, black or red. Price includes original case with form-fit interior; deduct as much as 40% less for non-original case.

1970s-80s		$400	$525

Hopf

1906-present. Intermediate, professional, premium, and presentation grade, production/custom, classical guitars made in Germany. They also make basses, mandolins and flutes.

The Hopf family of Germany has a tradition of instrument building going back to 1669, but the modern company was founded in 1906. Hopf started making electric guitars in the mid-'50s. Some Hopf models were made by others for the company. By the late-'70s, Hopf had discontinued making electrics, concentrating on classicals.

Explorer Standard
1960s. Double-cut semi-hollow, sharp horns, center block, 2 mini-humbuckers.

1960s		$450	$600

Saturn Archtop
1960s. Offset cutaway, archtop-style soundholes, 2 pickups, white, says Saturn on headstock.

1960s		$575	$750

Super Deluxe Archtop
1960s. Archtop, 16 3/4", catseye soundholes, carved spruce top, flamed maple back and sides, sunburst.

1960s		$600	$800

Hopkins

1998-present. Luthier Peter Hopkins builds his presentation grade, custom, hand-carved archtop guitars in British Columbia.

Horabe

Classical and Espana models made in Japan.

Classical

1960-1980s	Various models	$300	$600

Hottie

In 2009, amp builders Jean-Claude Escudie and Mike Bernards added production/custom, professional and premium grade, solidbody electric guitars built by luthier Saul Koll in Portland, Oregon.

House Guitars

2004-present. Luthier Joshua House builds his production/custom, premium grade, acoustic guitars and guitar-bouzoukis in Goderich, Ontario.

Howe-Orme

1897-ca. 1910. Elias Howe and George Orme's Boston-based publishing and distribution buisness offered a variety of mandolin family instruments and guitars and received many patents for their designs. Many of their guitars featured detachable necks.

Hoyer

1874-present. Intermediate grade, production, flat-top, classical, electric, and resonator guitars. They also build basses. Founded by Franz Hoyer, building classical guitars and other instruments. His son, Arnold, added archtops in the late-1940s, and solidbodies in the '60s. In '67, Arnold's son,

Holst

Hopkins Monarch Regal

Ibanez AM-225 Artist
Imaged by Heritage Auctions, HA.com

1983 Ibanez AR-100 Artist
Craig Brody

MODEL YEAR	FEATURES	EXC. COND. LOW	HIGH

Walter, took over, leaving the company in '77. The company changed hands a few times over the following years. Walter started building guitars again in '84 under the W.A. Hoyer brand, which is not associated with Hoyer.

Acoustic
1960s. Acoustic archtop or flat-top.

1960s		$200	$500

Junior
Early-1960s. Solidbody with unusual sharp horn cutaway, single neck pickup, bolt-on neck, dot markers, Arnold Hoyer logo on headstock, shaded sunburst.

1960s		$525	$675

Soloist Electric
1960-1962. Single-cut archtop, 2 pickups, teardrop f-holes, sunburst.

1960-1962		$525	$675

Special 24
1950s-1960s. Single-cut acoustic archtop, Hoyer Special script logo on headstock, pickups added in '60s. SL was deluxe version.

1950s	Acoustic	$1,100	$1,500

Huerga
Introduced in 1995, professional to presentation grade, production/custom, archtop, flat-top, and metal-front solidbody electric guitars built by luthier Diego Huerga in Buenos Aires, Argentina.

Humming Bird
1947-ca.1975. Japanese manufacturer offering acoustics and electrics. By 1968 making pointy Mosrite inspirations. Probably not imported into the U.S.

Electric Solidbody
1950s		$150	$225

Humphrey, Thomas
1970-2008. Premium and presentation grade, custom, nylon-string guitars built by luthier Thomas Humphrey in Gardiner, New York. In 1996 Humphrey began collaborating with Martin Guitars, resulting in the Martin C-TSH and C-1R. Often the inside back label will indicate the year of manufacture. Humphrey died in April, 2008.

Classical
1976-1984. Brazilian or Indian rosewood back and sides, spruce top, traditionally-based designs evolved over time with Millenium becoming a benchmark design in 1985, values can increase with new designs. Valuations depend on each specific instrument and year and type of construction, price ranges are guidance only; each instrument should be evaluated on a case-by-case basis.

1976-1984		$4,700	$6,000

Millennium (Classical)
1985-2008. Professional performance-grade high-end classical guitar with innovative taper body design and elevated 'board, tops are generally spruce (versus cedar) with rosewood back and sides.

1995-2008		$8,500	$11,000

Steel String
1974. D-style, only 4 made.

1974		$2,700	$3,500

Huss and Dalton Guitar Company
1995-present. Luthiers Jeff Huss and Mark Dalton build their professional and premium grade flat-tops and banjos in Staunton, Virginia.

Hutchins
2006-present. Gary Hutchins in Sussex, U.K. imports intermediate and professional grade, production, acoustic and electric guitars and basses from China, Germany and Korea.

Ian A. Guitars
1991-present. In the early 1990s luthier Ian Anderson built guitars under his name, in 2005 he began using the Ian A. brand. He builds premium grade, production/custom, solidbody electric guitars in Poway, California.

Ibanez
1932-present. Budget, intermediate, and professional grade, production/custom, acoustic and electric guitars. They also make basses, amps, mandolins, and effects.

Founded in Nagoya, Japan, by Matsujiro Hoshino as book and stationary supply, started retailing musical instruments in 1909, importing them by '21. The company's factories were destroyed during World War II, but the business was revived in '50. The Ibanez name in use by 1957. Junpei Hoshino, grandson of founder, became president in '60; a new factory opened called Tama Seisakusho (Tama Industries). Brand names by '64 included Ibanez, Star, King's Stone, Jamboree and Goldentone, supplied by 85 factories serving global markets. Sold acoustic guitars to Harry Rosenblum of Elger Guitars ('59-ca.'65) in Ardmore, Pennsylvania, in early-'60s. Around '62 Hoshino purchased 50% interest in Elger Guitars, and ca. '65 changed the name to Ibanez.

Jeff Hasselberger headed the American guitar side beginning '73-'74, and the company headquarters were moved to Cornwells Heights, Pennsylvania in '74. By '75 the instruments are being distributed by Chesbro Music Company in Idaho Falls, Idaho, and Harry Rosenblum sells his interest to Hoshino shortly thereafter. Ca. '81, the Elger Company becomes Hoshino U.S.A. An U.S. Custom Shop was opened in '88.

Most glued-neck guitars from '70s are fairly rare. Dating: copy guitars begin ca. '71. Serial numbers begin '75 with letter (A-L for month) followed by 6 digits, the first 2 indicating year, last 4 sequential (MYYXXXX). By '88 the month letter drops off. Dating code stops early-'90s; by '94 letter preface either F for Fuji or C for Cort (Korean) manufacturer followed by number for year and consecutive

MODEL YEAR	FEATURES	EXC. COND. LOW	HIGH

numbers (F4XXXX=Fuji, C4XXXX=Cort, 1994).

Pickups on Asian import electric guitars from the '50s-'70s are often considered to be the weakest engineering specification on the instrument. Old Ibanez pickups can become microphonic and it is not unusual to see them replaced.

AE (Acoustic Electric) Series
1983-present. Models include AE, AEF, AEL flat-tops (no archtops).

1983-2019	Various models	$100	$400

AH10 (Allan Holdsworth)
1985-1987. Offset double-cut solidbody, bolt neck, bridge humbucker, dots, various colors.

1985-1987	1 pickup	$300	$400

AH20 (Allan Holdsworth)
1986. As AH10 but with 2 humbuckers.

1986	2 pickups	$325	$425

AM Series
1985-1991. Small body archtops, models include AM70, 75, 75T, 100, 225. Becomes Artstar in '92.

1985-1991	Various models	$400	$700

AM Stagemaster Series
1983-1984, 1989-1990. Made in Japan, small double-cut semi-hollow body, 2 humbuckers, models include AM50, 100, 205, 255. Model name used again, without Stagemaster in '89-'90.

1983-1984	Various models	$400	$700

AR50 "Jr. Artist"
1979-1983. Double-cut solidbody, dot markers, 2 humbuckers.

1979-1983		$400	$525

AR100 Artist
1979-1984. Double-cut solidbody, set neck, maple top, 2 humbuckers.

1979-1984		$750	$950

AR300 Artist
1979-1982. Symmetrical double-cut, carved maple top.

1979-1982		$825	$1,050

AR500 Artist
1979-1982. 2 humbuckers, EQ.

1979-1982		$825	$1,050

Artcore Series
2002-present. Made in China, hollowbody electric, models include AF, AG, AK, AM, AS and TM.

2002-2019	Various models	$150	$600

AS50 Artist
1980-1981. Made in Japan, semi-acoustic.

1980-1981		$450	$575

AS50 Artstar
1998-1999. Laminated maple body, bound rosewood 'board, dot inlays, 2 humbuckers.

1998-1999		$450	$575

AS80 Artstar
1994-2002. Made in Korea, double cut semi-hollow body, dots, 2 humbuckers.

1994-2002		$450	$575

AS100 Artist
1979-1981. Set neck, gold hardware.

1979-1981		$575	$750

AS180 Artstar
1997-1999. Double cut semi-hollow body, plain top, dots, 2 humbuckers.

1997-1999		$575	$750

AS200 Artist
1979-1986. Double-cut semi-acoustic, flamed maple, block markers, gold hardware, 2 humbuckers, replaced Artist 2630. Artist dropped from name when model becomes hollowbody archtop in '82.

1979-1986		$900	$1,200

AS200 Artstar
1992-2000. Flame maple top, gold hardware, 2 humbuckers, block inlays.

1992-2000		$775	$1,000

AW Artwood Series
1979-present. Electric/acoustics, various models.

1979-2019	Various models	$150	$500

BL Blazer Series
1980-1982, 1997-1998. Offset double-cut, 10 similar models in the '80s with different body woods and electronic configurations. Series name returns on 3 models in late '90s.

1980-1998	Various models	$200	$600

Bob Weir Model 2681
1975-1980, 1995. Double-cut ash solidbody, ebony 'board, tree-of-life inlay, gold-plated pickups, limited numbers. Reintroduced as a limited run in '95.

1975-1980		$1,800	$2,300

Bob Weir Standard Model 2680
1976-1980. Standard production model of 2681.

1976-1980		$1,250	$1,600

Bob Weir Model One BWM1 (Cowboy Fancy)
2005. Double-cut swamp ash solidbody, ebony 'board, pearl vine inlay down neck and part way around body, 30 made.

2005		$2,500	$3,300

Challenger 2552ASH
1977-1978. T-style ash solidbody.

1977-1978		$400	$525

CN100 Concert Standard
1978-1979. Double-cut solidbody, set neck, 2 humbuckers, chrome hardware, dot markers.

1978-1979		$400	$525

CN200 Concert Custom
1978-1979. Carved maple top, mahogany body, 7 layer black/white binding, bolt-on neck, gold hardware, block inlays, 2 Super 80 pickups.

1978-1979		$450	$600

CN250 Concert
1978-1979. Like CN200 but with vine inlay.

1978-1979		$575	$750

DG350 Destroyer II
1986-1987. X Series, modified X-shaped basswood body, flame maple top, 2 humbuckers, trem.

1986-1987		$275	$375

DT50 Destroyer II
1980-1982. Modified alder Explorer body, 6-in-line headstock, bolt neck, 2 humbuckers, thick paint.

1980-1982		$450	$575

Ibanez AS200 Artist

1982 Ibanez BL Blazer
Carter Vintage Guitars

To get the most from this book, be sure to read "Using *The Guide*" in the introduction.

GUITARS

1979 Ibanez George Benson GB10
Bernunzio Uptown Music

*1979 Ibanez Iceman
PS10 Paul Stanley*
Craig Brody

MODEL YEAR	FEATURES	EXC. COND. LOW	HIGH
DT150 Destroyer II			
1982-1984. Like DT50 but birch/basswood, 1 humbucker.			
1982-1984		$450	$575
DT155 Destroyer II			
1982-1984. Like DT150 but with 3 humbuckers.			
1982-1984		$750	$975
DT350 Destroyer II			
1984-1985. X Series, opaque finish, 1 humbucker, trem.			
1984-1985		$350	$450
DT400 Destroyer II			
1980-1982. Modified mahogany Explorer body, flame maple top, 6-in-line headstock, set-neck, 2 humbuckers, cherry sunburst. Model changed to DT500 in '82.			
1980-1982		$450	$575
DT500 Destroyer II			
1982-1984. Replaced the DT400, flame maple top.			
1982-1984		$450	$575
DT555 Destroyer II Phil Collen			
1983-1987. Bound basswood solidbody, 3 humbuckers, vibrato, black.			
1983-1987		$1,800	$2,300
DTX120 Destroyer			
2000-2004. X Series, known as the Millennium Destroyer, 2 humbuckers.			
2000-2004		$225	$300
EX Series			
1988-1993. Double-cut solidbodies with long thin horns.			
1988-1993	Various models	$150	$300
FA (Full Acoustic) Series			
1978-1982. Single-cut full body jazz-style.			
1978-1982	Various models	$950	$1,225
FG-100			
1982-1987. Single-cut archtop, maple top, 2 humbuckers.			
1982-1987		$950	$1,225
GAX Series			
1998-2009. Symmetrical double-cut (Gibson SG style) with 2 humbuckers, lower cost of the AX line.			
1998-2009	Various models	$90	$175
George Benson GB10			
1977-present. Single-cut, laminated spruce top, flame maple back and sides, 2 humbuckers, 3-piece set-in maple neck, ebony 'board.			
1977-1979	Sunburst	$1,700	$2,200
1977-1989	Blond	$1,700	$2,200
1980-1989	Sunburst	$1,450	$1,900
1990-2007	Sunburst	$1,150	$1,500
1990-2019	Blond	$1,450	$1,900
2004	Blond	$1,250	$1,600
George Benson GB15			
2006-2010. Like GB10, but with 1 humbucker.			
2006-2010		$1,600	$2,100
George Benson GB20			
1978-1982. Larger than GB10, laminated spruce top, flame maple back and sides.			
1978-1982		$2,200	$2,900

MODEL YEAR	FEATURES	EXC. COND. LOW	HIGH
George Benson GB100 Deluxe			
1993-1996. GB-10 with flamed maple top, pearl binding, sunburst finish 'guard, pearl vine inlay tailpiece, gold hardware.			
1993-1996		$2,400	$3,100
GSA Series			
2000-2011. Offset double-cut body.			
2000-2011	GSA20/GSA60	$85	$125
Iceman 2663/2663 TC/2663 SL			
1975-1978. The original Iceman Series models, called the Flash I, II and III respectively, I has 2 humbuckers, II (TC) and III (SL) have 1 triple-coil pickup.			
1975-1978		$900	$1,200
Iceman PS10 Paul Stanley			
1978-1981. Limited edition Paul Stanley model, abalone trim, Stanley's name engraved at 21st fret, reissued in '95 with upgraded model names.			
1978-1981	Korina finish	$1,700	$2,200
1978-1981	Sunburst or black	$1,400	$1,800
Iceman PS10 II Paul Stanley			
1995-1996. Reissue of original PS-10.			
1995-1996	Black	$1,300	$1,750
Iceman PS10 LTD Paul Stanley			
1995-1996. Limited edition, gold mirror appointments, gold hardware, black pearl metalflake finish.			
1995-1996		$2,150	$2,800
Iceman Series			
1975-2010. Ibanez unique body styles with hooked lower treble horn body.			
1978	IC210	$875	$1,150
1978-1979	IC250	$875	$1,150
1978-1979	IC300 (Korina)	$875	$1,150
1978-1982	IC400	$900	$1,200
1978-1990	IC200	$700	$900
1979-1980	IC50	$700	$900
1981-1982	IC400 CS	$800	$1,050
1994	IC500	$800	$1,050
1994-2003	IC300	$300	$400
1995-1996	IC350	$300	$400
IMG-2010 Guitar Controller MIDI			
1985-1987. Similar to Roland GR-707, slim triangle-wedge body with treble horn.			
1985-1987	Guitar only	$500	$650
JEM 7 Series			
1988-2010. Basswood or alder body, various models, alder 7V offered until '10.			
1988-2010	Various models	$1,400	$2,000
JEM 77 Series			
1988-1999, 2003-2010. Basswood body, monkey grip handle, 3 pickups, 'board with tree of life or pyramids inlay, finishes include floral pattern or multicolor swirl. Current version has dot inlays and solid finish. The JEM 77BRMR Bad Horsie was introduced in '05 with a mirror finish.			
1980-2010	Various models	$1,900	$2,900
JEM 555			
1994-2000. Basswood, dots and vine inlay, 3 pickups.			
1994-2000		$475	$625

MODEL		EXC. COND.	
YEAR	FEATURES	LOW	HIGH

JEM 777 Series
1987-1996. Basswood body, monkey grip 3 pickups, pyramids or vine inlay.

1987-1996	Various models	$1,900	$3,500

JEM 10th Anniversary
1996. Limited Edition signature Steve Vai model, bolt neck, vine metal 'guard, vine neck inlays and headstock art.

1996		$3,900	$5,100

JEM 20th Anniversary
2007. Steve Vai 20th Anniversary JEM model, green acrylic illuminating body, celebrates the 20th year (1987-2007) of the Ibanez JEM series, limited edition.

2007		$3,200	$4,500

JEM 90th Anniversary
1997. Limited Edition signature Steve Vai model, textured silver finish, chrome 'guard.

1997		$1,400	$2,000

JEM Y2KDNA (Limited Edition)
2000. Red Swirl marble finish using Steve Vai's blood in the paint.

2000		$2,700	$3,500

Joe Pass JP20
1981-1990. Full body, single-cut, 1 pickup, abalone and pearl split block inlay, JP inlay on headstock.

1981-1990	Sunburst	$1,550	$2,000

Joe Satriani JS6
1993. Limited production, lightweight mahogany body, non-gloss finish, JS Series headstock logo.

1993		$1,000	$1,400

Joe Satriani JS100
1994-2014. Offset double cut basswood body, 2 humbuckers, vibrato, red, black, white or custom finish.

1994-2014	Custom finish	$450	$625
1994-2014	Standard finish	$350	$450

Joe Satriani JS1000
1994-1996, 1998-2012. 2 DiMarzio humbuckers, lightweight body.

1994-2012	Various colors	$700	$1,000

Joe Satriani JS1200
2004-2016. Candy Apple Red.

2004-2016		$800	$1,100

Joe Satriani JS 10th Anniversary
1998. Chrome-metal body, Satriani Anniversary script on back cover plate.

1998		$2,100	$2,800

Joe Satriani JS 20th Anniversary
2008. Opaque finish with alien surfer graphic.

2008		$2,100	$2,800

Joe Satriani Y2K
2000. Clear see-thru plexi-style body.

2000		$1,700	$2,200

John Petrucci JPM100 P2
1996. Offset double-cut solidbody, 2 pickups, multi-color graphic.

1996		$1,650	$2,150

John Petrucci JPM100 P3
1997. As P2 but with same graphic in black and white.

1997		$1,650	$2,150

John Petrucci JPM100 P4
1998. As P2 but with same graphic in camo colors.

1998		$1,650	$2,150

John Scofield JSM100
2001-present. Double-cut semi hollow body, 2 humbuckers, ebony 'board, gold hardware.

2001-2019		$1,625	$2,100

Lee Ritenour LR10
1981-1987. Flame maple body, bound set neck, Quick Change tailpiece, 2 pickups, dark red sunburst, foam-filled body to limit feedback.

1981-1987		$1,625	$2,100

M310
1982. D-size flat-top, maple back and sides, rosewood 'board.

1982		$150	$200

M340
1978-1979. D-size flat-top, flamed maple back and sides, maple 'board. 'board.

1978-1979		$200	$300

Maxxas
1987-1988. Solidbody (MX2) or with internal sound chambers (MX3, '88 only), 2 pickups, all-access neck joint system.

1987-1988	MX2	$900	$1,200
1988	MX3	$1,000	$1,300

MC Musician Series
1978-1982. Solidbodies, various models.

1978-1980	MC500, carved top	$1,100	$1,500
1978-1980	Neck-thru body	$800	$1,100
1978-1982	Bolt neck	$650	$850

Mick Thompson MTM-1
2006. Seven logo on fretboard, MTM1 logo on back of headstock.

2006		$625	$825

Model 600 Series
1974-1978. Copy era acoustic flat-tops with model numbers in the 600 Series, basically copies of classic American square shoulder dreadnoughts. Includes the 683, 684, 693 and the 6-in-line 647; there were 12-string copies as well.

1974-1978		$550	$725

Model 700 Series
1974-1977. Upgraded flat-top models such as the Brazilian Scent 750, with more original design content than 600 Series.

1974-1977		$550	$725

Model 900 Series
1963-1964. Offset double-cut solidbody with sharp curving horns, Burns Bison copy.

1963-1964	901, 1 pickup	$250	$350
1963-1964	992, 2 pickups	$275	$375

Model 1453
1971-1973. Copy of classic single-cut hollowbody, replaced by Model 2355 in '73.

1971-1973		$1,200	$1,600

Model 1800 Series
1962-1963. Offset double-cut solidbody (Jazzmaster-style), models came with bar (stud) or vibrato tailpiece, and 2, 3 or 4 pickups.

1962-1963	Various models	$250	$350

1979 Ibanez M340
Tom Pfeifer

1977 Ibanez Model 684 Concord
Imaged by Heritage Auctions, HA.com

GUITARS

1975 Ibanez Model 2355M
Michael Wright

1974 Ibanez Model 2375W Strato
Michael Wright

MODEL YEAR	FEATURES	EXC. COND. LOW	HIGH

Model 1912
1971-1973. Double-cut semi-hollow body, sunburst finish.

| 1971-1973 | | $700 | $1,200 |

Model 2020
1970. Initial offering of the copy era, offset double-cut, 2 unusual rectangular pickups, block markers, raised nailed-on headstock logo, sunburst.

| 1970 | | $600 | $800 |

Model 2240M
Early 1970s. Thick hollowbody electric copy, single pointed cutaway, double-parallelogram markers, 2 humbuckers, natural finish.

| 1971-1973 | | $1,200 | $1,600 |

Model 2336 Les Jr.
1974-1976. Copy of classic slab solidbody, TV Lime.

| 1974-1976 | | $450 | $600 |

Model 2340 Deluxe '59er
1974-1977. Copy of classic single-cut solidbody, Hi-Power humbuckers, opaque or flametop.

| 1974-1977 | Flametop | $550 | $750 |
| 1974-1977 | Opaque | $550 | $750 |

Model 2341 Les Custom
1974-1977. Copy of classic single-cut solidbody.

| 1974-1977 | | $550 | $750 |

Model 2342 Les Moonlight/Sunlight Special
1974-1977. Copy of classic slab solidbody, black (Moonlight) or ivory (Sunlight).

| 1974-1977 | | $500 | $675 |

Model 2343 FM Jr.
1974-1976 Copy of LP TV Jr

| 1974-1976 | | $500 | $675 |

Model 2343 Jr.
1974-1976. Copy of classic Jr., cherry mahogany.

| 1974-1976 | | $500 | $675 |

Model 2344
1974-1976. Copy of classic double-cut solidbody.

| 1974-1976 | | $350 | $450 |

Model 2345
1974-1976. Copy of classic sharp double-cut solidbody, set neck, walnut or white, vibrato, 3 pickups.

| 1974-1976 | | $550 | $750 |

Model 2346
1974. Copy of classic sharp double-cut solidbody, vibrato, set neck, 2 pickups.

| 1974 | | $550 | $750 |

Model 2347
1974-1976. Copy of classic sharp double-cut solidbody, set-neck, 1 pickup.

| 1974-1976 | | $450 | $600 |

Model 2348 Firebrand
1974-1977. Copy of classic reverse solidbody, mahogany body, bolt neck, 2 pickups.

| 1974-1977 | | $700 | $925 |

Model 2350 Les
1971-1977. Copy of classic single-cut solidbody, bolt neck, black, gold hardware, goldtop version (2350G Les) also available. A cherry sunburst finish (2350 Les Custom) was offered by '74.

| 1971-1977 | | $600 | $775 |

Model 2351 Les
1974-1977. Copy of classic single-cut solidbody, gold top, 2 pickups.

| 1974-1977 | | $550 | $750 |

Model 2351DX
1974-1977. Copy of classic single-cut solidbody, gold top, 2 mini-humbuckers.

| 1974-1977 | | $550 | $750 |

Model 2351M Les
1974-1977. LP Standard style, sunburst.

| 1974-1977 | | $550 | $750 |

Model 2352 Telly
1974-1978. Copy of early classic single-cut solidbody, 1 bridge pickup, white finish.

| 1974-1978 | | $550 | $750 |

Model 2352CT
1974-1978. Copy of classic single-cut solidbody, single-coil bridge and humbucker neck pickup.

| 1974-1978 | | $550 | $750 |

Model 2352DX Telly
1974-1978. Copy of classic single-cut solidbody, 2 humbuckers.

| 1974-1978 | | $550 | $750 |

Model 2354
1974-1977. Copy of classic sharp double-cut solidbody, 2 humbuckers, vibrato.

| 1974-1977 | | $550 | $750 |

Model 2354S
1972-1977. Stop tailpiece version of 2354.

| 1972-1977 | | $550 | $750 |

Model 2355/2355M
1973-1977. Copy of classic single-cut hollowbody, sunburst or natural maple (M).

| 1973-1977 | | $1,000 | $1,300 |

Model 2356
1973-1975. Copy of classic double pointed cutaway hollowbody, bowtie markers, sunburst. There was another Model 2356 in '74, a copy of a different hollowbody.

| 1973-1975 | | $800 | $1,050 |

Model 2363R
1973-1974. Cherry finish copy of classic varitone double-cut semi-hollow body.

| 1973-1974 | | $850 | $1,150 |

Model 2364 Ibanex
1971-1973. Dan Armstrong see-thru Lucite copy, 2 mounted humbuckers.

| 1971-1973 | | $650 | $900 |

Model 2368 Telly
1973-1978. Copy of classic single-cut thinline, chambered f-hole body, single coil pickup, mahogany body.

| 1973-1978 | | $550 | $700 |

Model 2368F
1973-1974. Classic single-cut black 'guard copy.

| 1973-1974 | | $550 | $750 |

Model 2370
1972-1977. Sunburst version of Model 2363R.

| 1972-1977 | | $850 | $1,150 |

MODEL YEAR	FEATURES	EXC. COND. LOW	HIGH

Model 2372 Les Pro/2372DX Les Pro
1972-1977. Copy of classic single-cut solidbody, bolt neck, low impedance pickups, DX with gold hardware available for '73-'74.
1972-1977 $550 $750

Model 2374 Crest
1974-1976. Copy of classic double-cut semi-hollow body, walnut finish.
1974-1976 $800 $1,100

Model 2375 Strato
1971-1978. Strat copy, 3 single-coils, sunburst.
1971-1978 $575 $750

Model 2375 Strato 6/12
1974-1975. Double neck, 6 and 12 strings.
1974-1975 $1,125 $1,475

Model 2375ASH Strato
1974-1978. 2375 with ash body.
1974-1978 $575 $750

Model 2375WH/N/BK Strato
1974-1978. 2375 in white (WH), natural (N), and black (BK) finishes.
1974-1978 $675 $875

Model 2377
1974-1975. Copy of classic double sharp-cut solid-body, short production run, dot markers.
1974-1975 $450 $600

Model 2380
1973-1977. Copy of LP Recording, single-cut solid-body, low impedence pickups, small block markers.
1973-1977 $550 $750

Model 2383
1974-1976. Copy of classic double sharp cut solid-body, white or walnut, 3 humbuckers, gold hardware.
1974-1976 $475 $650

Model 2384 Telly
1974-1976. Copy of classic single-cut, f-holes, 2 humbuckers, ash body.
1974-1976 $550 $750

Model 2387 Rocket Roll/Rocket Roll Sr.
1975-1977. Copy of classic v-shaped solidbody, bolt-neck (2387) or set-neck (2387DX/2387CT), dot markers, gold-covered pickups.
1975-1977   All models $1,300 $1,725

Model 2390
1974-1976. Copy of classic double-cut semi-hollow body, maple 'board, walnut finish.
1974-1976 $850 $1,150

Model 2394
Ca. 1974-ca. 1976. SG style, 2 humbuckers, maple 'board, black block inlays.
1974-1976 $550 $750

Model 2395
1974-1976. Natural finished 2390.
1974-1976 $850 $1,150

Model 2397
1974-1976. Double-cut semi-hollow body, low imped-ance electronics, trapezoid markers, goldtop.
1974-1976 $850 $1,150

Model 2399DX Jazz Solid
1974-1976. Single-cut solidbody, sunburst, set-neck, gold hardware.
1974-1976 $850 $1,150

Model 2401 Signature
1974-1976. Double-cut semi-hollow archtop, gold top, bolt neck.
1974-1976 $850 $1,150

Model 2402/2402DX Double Axe
1974-1977. Double sharp cut solidbody 6/12 double-neck, cherry or walnut, DX model has gold hardware and white finish.
1974-1977   All models $1,125 $1,475

Model 2404 Double Axe
1974-1977. Double sharp cut solidbody guitar/bass doubleneck copy, walnut, white available '75 only.
1974-1977 $1,125 $1,475

Model 2405 Custom Agent
1974-1977. Single-cut solidbody, set neck, scroll headstock, pearl body inlay, 2 humbuckers.
1974-1977 $825 $1,075

Model 2406 Double Axe
1974-1977. Double sharp cut solidbody doubleneck, two 6-strings, cherry or wlanut.
1974-1977 $825 $1,075

Model 2407 Stratojazz 4/6
1974-1975. Half Strat, half Jazz bass, all rock and roll!
1974-1975 $825 $1,075

Model 2451
1974-1977. Single-cut solidbody, maple 'board, black or natural, set neck.
1974-1977 $850 $1,150

Model 2453 Howie Roberts
1974-1977. Single-cut archtop, round soundhole, maple body, set neck, rosewood 'board, block mark-ers, 1 pickup, gold hardware, burgundy or sunburst.
1974-1977 $1,200 $1,550

Model 2454
1974-1977. Copy of classic double-cut semi-hollow body, set-neck, small block markers, cherry finish over ash.
1974-1977 $850 $1,150

Model 2455
1974-1977. L-5 copy, sharp single-cut archtop, blocks, natural.
1974-1977 $1,850 $2,400

Model 2459 Destroyer
1975-1977. Korina finished mahogany body.
1975-1977 $1,850 $2,400

Model 2460
1975-1977. L-5 copy, rounded cut laminated archtop, blocks, natural.
1975-1977 $1,850 $2,400

Model 2461
1975-1977. Copy of classic single-cut archtop, laminated spruce top, curly maple body, set-neck, ebony 'board, pearl blocks, 2 pickups, gold hardware, sunburst or natural.
1975-1977 $1,850 $2,400

1975 Ibanez Model 2402
John DeSilva

1975 Ibanez Model 2404 Double Axe
Greg Perrine

GUITARS

1975 Ibanez Model 2453 Howie Roberts
Carter Vintage Guitars

1976 Ibanez Model 2671 Randy Scruggs
Greg Perrine

MODEL YEAR	FEATURES	EXC. COND. LOW	HIGH
Model 2464			
1975-1977. Byrdland copy, rounded single-cut, blocks, natural.			
1975-1977		$1,850	$2,400
Model 2469 Futura			
1976-1977. Korina finished furturistic model copy.			
1976-1977		$1,850	$2,400
Model 2601 Artist			
1976-1978. D-style flat-top with fancy appointments.			
1976-1978		$300	$500
Model 2612 Artist			
1974-1975. Rounded double-cut solidbody, black finish, birch top, gold hardware, bound rosewood 'board, 2 humbuckers, fleur-de-lis inlay.			
1974-1975		$800	$1,025
Model 2613 Artist			
1974-1975. Natural version of 2612.			
1974-1975		$800	$1,025
Model 2616 Artist Jazz			
1974-1975. Single-cut curly maple hollow body, f-holes, fleur-de-lis, 2 humbuckers.			
1974-1975		$1,400	$1,850
Model 2617 Artist			
1976-1980. Pointed double-cut natural ash solidbody, set-neck, German carved top, spilt block inlays, bound ebony 'board, 2 humbuckers, later would evolve into the Professional model.			
1976-1980		$1,250	$1,600
Model 2618 Artist			
1976-1979. Like 2617, but with maple and mahogany body and dot markers. Becomes AR200 in '79.			
1976-1979		$800	$1,025
Model 2619 Artist			
1976-1979. Like 2618, but with split block markers. Becomes AR300 in '79.			
1976-1979		$800	$1,025
Model 2622 Artist EQ			
1977-1979. EQ, Steve Miller model. Becomes AR500 in '79.			
1977-1979		$950	$1,250
Model 2630 Artist Deluxe			
1976-1979. Double cut semi-hollow body, sunburst, name changed to AS200 in '79.			
1976-1979		$1,150	$1,500
Model 2640 Artist/AR1200 Doubleneck			
1977-1984. Double-cut solidbody, set 6/12 necks, 4 humbuckers, gold hardware. Called 2640 until '79 when changed to AR1200.			
1977-1984		$1,175	$1,525
Model 2662 Super Cutaway			
1974-1976. Solidbody, set neck, two dramatic cutaways, block inlays, 2 humbuckers.			
1974-1976		$800	$1,025
Model 2671 Randy Scruggs			
1976-1978. Single-cut solidbody, tree-of-life inlay, German-carve top.			
1976-1978		$1,150	$1,500
Model 2700 Artist Custom			
1977-1978. Cutaway, dot markers, gold hardware, natural, black, antique violin or dark satin finish.			
1977-1978		$1,300	$1,700

MODEL YEAR	FEATURES	EXC. COND. LOW	HIGH
Model 2710 Artist Custom			
1978. Like Model 2700 with exotic wood and anvil case.			
1978		$1,350	$1,750
Model 2800 Andorra Series			
1974-1979. Classical nylon-string guitars, part of Ibanez Andorra Series, all with 2800-2899 model numbers.			
1974-1979		$150	$400
Model 2900 Andorra Professional Series			
1974-1979. Steel-string dreadnought models with solid spruce tops, all with 2909-2912 model numbers.			
1974-1979		$150	$400
Pat Metheny PM			
1996-present. Acoustic-electric archtops, single or single/half cutaway, 1 or 2 humbuckers.			
1996-2010	PM100	$1,125	$1,500
1997-1999	PM20	$850	$1,125
2000-2015	PM120	$1,350	$1,750
Paul Gilbert PGM			
1992-2011. Superstrat body style, painted f-holes, appointments vary with model numbers.			
1997-2011	PGM300 WH	$1,100	$1,400
1998	PGM 90th	$1,200	$1,600
1998	PGM200 FB	$1,200	$1,600
PF Performer Series Acoustics			
1987-present. Mostly dreadnought size flat-tops.			
1987-2019	Various models	$75	$300
PF100 Performer Standard			
1978-1979. Single-cut solidbody, plain birch top, mahogany body, bolt neck, dot inlays, 2 humbuckers.			
1978-1979		$350	$475
PF200 Performer Custom			
1978-1979. Maple top PF100.			
1978-1979		$475	$625
PF300 Performer			
1978-1980. Single-cut solidbody, maple top, mahogany body, set neck, 2 humbuckers, Tri-Sound.			
1978-1980		$475	$625
PF400 Performer			
1978-1979. Single cut solidbody, flame maple top, alder body, set neck, block inlays, 2 humbuckers, Tri-Sound.			
1978-1979		$525	$675
PL Pro Line Series			
1985-1987. Pro Line models begin with PL or PR.			
1985-1987	Various models	$300	$900
PR Pro Line Series			
1985-1987. Pro Line models begin with PL or PR.			
1985-1987	Various models	$300	$900
Reb Beach Voyager RBM1			
1991-1996. Unusual cutaway lower bout, extreme upper bout cutaways, RBM Series logo on headstock.			
1991-1996		$950	$1,225
RG/RS Roadster/Roadstar Series			
1992-present. A large family of guitars whose model identification starts with RG or RS prefix, includes the Roadstar Standard and Roadstar Deluxe models.			
1992-2019	Higher-range	$500	$700
1992-2019	Highest-range	$700	$1,400
1992-2019	Low to mid-range	$250	$350

MODEL YEAR	FEATURES	EXC. COND. LOW	HIGH
1992-2019	Lower-range	$150	$250
1992-2019	Mid-range	$350	$500

Roadstar II Series
1982-1985. Various offset double-cut solidbodies, 'Roadstar II Series' on headstock, 3 single-coils or 2 humbuckers. Over 40 models appeared in this line, offered in Standard, Deluxe and Custom forms.

1982-1985	RS1010SL S Lukather	$450	$600
1982-1985	Various models	$300	$550

Rocket Roll II RR550
1982-1984. Flying V body, six-on-side headstock, pearloid blocks, cherry sunburst, maple top, set neck.

1982-1984		$1,000	$1,300

RT Series
1992-1993. Offset double-cut, bolt neck, rosewood 'board, dot markers.

1992-1993	Various models	$250	$400

RX Series
1994-1997. Offset double-cut, solidbodies.

1994-1997	Various models	$80	$150

S Models
1987-present. In '87 Ibanez introduced a new line of highly tapered, ultra-thin body, offset double-cut guitars that were grouped together as the S Models. Intially the S Models were going to be called the Sabre models but that name was trademarked by Music Man and could not be used. The S models will carry an S suffix or S prefix in the model name.

1987-2019	Various models	$275	$600

ST Studio Series
1978-1982. Double-cut solidbodies, lots of natural finishes, various models, even a doubleneck.

1979-1981	Various models	$275	$500

STW Double
1999. Double neck with 7-string and 6-string neck, limited edition.

1999		$1,626	$2,100

TC/TV Talman Series
1994-1998. Softer double-cut solidbodies.

1994-1998	Various models	$200	$475

Universe UV7/UV7P/UV77 Series
1990-1997. Basswood 7-strings, hum/single/hum pickups. The '90-'93 white 7P and multi-colored 77 have pyramid inlays, the black '90-'97 7 has dots.

1990-1997	Various models	$1,200	$4,000

Universe UV777 Series
1998-2012. Basswood 7-string, pyramid inlays, maple 'board, hum/single/hum pickups.

1991-2012	Various models	$1,200	$2,000

USRG U.S.A. Custom Series
1994-1995. RG style guitars built in the U.S. by PBC Guitar Technology.

1994-1995	Various models	$1,000	$1,300

V300 Vintage Series
1978-1991. Vintage Series acoustic dreadnought, spruce top, mahogany back and sides, sunburst or various colors.

1978-1991		$150	$200

Xiphos Series
2007-2015. Part of the X Series, various XP and XPT models, X-shaped solidbody electric, neck-thru construction. Replaced by Iron Label (XPIR) series in '15.

2007-2015	Various models	$600	$800

XV500
1985-1987. Sharply pointed X-body with scalloped bottom.

1985-1987		$300	$400

Ibanez, Salvador
1875-1920. Salvador Ibanez was a Spanish luthier who operated a small guitar-building workshop. In the early 1900s he founded Spain's largest guitar factory. In 1929 Japan's Hoshino family began importing Salvador Ibanez guitars. Demand for the Salvador Ibanez guitars became so great that the Hoshino family began building their own guitars, which ultimately became known as the Ibanez brand. Guitars from 1875-1920 were mostly classical style and often can be identified by a label on the inside back which stipulates Salvador Ibanez.

Ignacio Rozas
1987-present. Luthier Ignacio M. Rozas builds his classical and flamenco guitars in Madrid, Spain. He also offers factory-made guitars built to his specifications.

Illusion Guitars
1992-present. Luthier Jeff Scott builds his premium grade, production/custom, solidbody guitars in Fallbrook, California.

Imperial
Ca.1963-ca.1970. Imported by the Imperial Accordion Company of Chicago, Illinois. Early guitars made in Italy by accordion builder Crucianelli. By ca. '66 switched to Japanese guitars. They also made basses.

Electric Solidbody
1963-1968. Italian-made until '66, then Japanese-made, includes the Tonemaster line.

1963-1968		$200	$275

Imperial (Japan)
1957-1960. Early, budget grade, Japanese imports from the Hoshino company which was later renamed Ibanez.

Infeld
2003-2005. Solidbody guitars and basses offered by string-maker Thomastik-Infeld of Vienna.

Infinox
1980s. Infinox by JTG, of Nashville, offered a line of 'the classic shapes of yesterday and the hi tech chic of today'. Classic shapes included copies of many classic American solidbody designs with the block letter Infinox by JTG logo on headstock, special metallic grafteq paint finish, space-age faux

1985 Ibanez PR1440
Imaged by Heritage Auctions, HA.com

1990 Ibanez Universe UV7P
Bas van de Weijer

GUITARS

Island Atoll

Italia Mondial

MODEL		EXC. COND.	
YEAR	FEATURES	LOW	HIGH

graphite-feel neck, Gotoh tuning machines, Gotoh locking nut tremolo with fine tuners, all models with 1 or 2 humbucker pickups.

Interdonati

1920s-1930s. Guitars built by luthier Philip Interdonati, in New York City, originally professional grade. He also built mandolins.

Size 000 Flat-Top
1920s-1930s.

1920s-30s	Less fancy	$2,500	$3,500
1920s-30s	More fancy	$3,500	$7,000

Isana

1951-1974. Acoustic and electric archtop guitars built by luthier Josef Sandner in Nauheim, Germany. Elvis played one while in the army in Germany.

Acoustic Archtop

1951-1974	Various models	$350	$1,300

Island Instruments

2010-present. Luthier Nic Delisle builds professional and premium grade, production/custom, small-bodied acoustic and electric guitars in Montreal, Quebec. He also builds basses.

Italia

1999-present. Intermediate grade, production, solid, semi-solid, and hollow body guitars and basses designed by Trevor Wilkinson and made in Korea.

J Backlund Design

2008-present. Professional and premium grade, custom, electric guitars and basses designed by J. Backlund in Hixson, Tennessee. He also imports Korean-made guitars under the Retronix brand.

J Burda Guitars

Flat-top guitars built by luthier Jan Burda in Berrien Springs, Michigan.

J. Frog Guitars

1978-present. Professional and premium grade, production/custom, solidbody guitars made by Ed Roman Guitars.

J.B. Player

1980s. Budget and intermediate grade, production, imported acoustic, acoustic/electric, and solidbody guitars and basses. They also offer banjos and mandolins. Founded in United States. Moved production of guitars to Korea but maintained a U.S. Custom Shop. MBT International/Musicorp took over manufacture and distribution in '89, then Kamen acquired MBT in 2005.

J.R. Zeidler Guitars

1977-2002. Luthier John Zeidler built premium and presentation grade, custom, flat-top, 12-string, and archtop guitars in Wallingford, Pennsylvania. He also built mandolins. He died in '02 at age 44.

MODEL		EXC. COND.	
YEAR	FEATURES	LOW	HIGH

J.S. Bogdanovich

1996-present. Production/custom, premium grade, classical and steel string guitars built by luthier John S. Bogdanovich in Swannanoa, North Carolina.

J.T. Hargreaves Basses & Guitars

1995-present. Luthier Jay Hargreaves builds his premium grade, production/custom, classical and steel string guitars and basses in Seattle, Washington.

Jack Daniel's

2004-2017. Acoustic and electric guitars and basses, some with Jack Daniel's artwork on the body and headstock, built by Peavey for the Jack Daniel's Distillery. There is also an amp model.

Jackson

1980-present. Currently Jackson offers intermediate, professional, and premium grade, production, electric guitars. They also offer basses. In '78 Grover Jackson bought out Charvel Guitars and moved it to San Dimas. Jackson made custom-built bolt-on Charvels. In '82 the pointy, tilt-back Jackson headstock became standard. The Jackson logo was born in '80 and used on a guitar designed as Randy Rhoad's first flying V. Jacksons were neck-through construction. The Charvel trademark was licensed to IMC in '85. IMC moved the Jackson factory to Ontario, California in '86. Grover Jackson stayed with Jackson/Charvel until '89 (see Charvel). On October 25, 2002, Fender Musical Instruments Corp (FMIC) took ownership of Jackson/Charvel Manufacturing Inc.

Dinky Reverse DR2
1996-1998. US-made, reverse headstock, no inlay, 2 Duncan humbuckers, ebony 'board.

1996-1998		$650	$850

Dinky Reverse DR3/DR5
1992-2001. Import, reverse headstock, 2 humbuckers, dots (DR5) or sharkfin inlays (DR3), locking trem.

1992-1997	Dots	$275	$400
1995-2001	Sharkfin	$350	$450

DX Series
2000-2007. Standard offset double-cut body, reverse headstock.

2000-2007		$175	$300

Fusion Pro
Late 1980s-early 1990s. Import from Japan.

1980s-90s		$450	$600

Fusion U.S.A.
1992-1994. Jackson with Made In USA logo on headstock, graphics.

1992-1994		$750	$975

Jenna II RX1OD Rhoads
2009. Limited production, Rhoads body style, named after performer Jenna Jameson.

2009		$450	$600

MODEL YEAR	FEATURES	EXC. COND. LOW	HIGH

JSX94
1994-1995. Offset double-cut solidbody, single/single/hum, rosewood 'board, dot markers.

1994-1995		$260	$340

JTX
1993-1995. Partial offset double-cut, single-coil neck pickup, humbucker bridge pickup, Jackson-Rose double lock vibrato, bolt-on neck, dot markers on maple fretboard, JTX truss rod cover logo.

1993-1995		$300	$400

Kelly Custom
1984-early 1990s. Solidbody, Kahler tremolo, 2 humbuckers, ebony 'board with shark's tooth inlays, bound neck and headstock.

1984-1993		$1,300	$1,800

Kelly Pro
1994-1995. Pointy-cut solidbody, neck-thru, 2 humbuckers, bound ebony 'board, sharkfin inlays.

1994-1995		$600	$800

Kelly Standard
1993-1995. Pointy cutaway solidbody, bolt neck, 2 humbuckers, dot markers.

1993-1995		$450	$600

Kelly U.S.A. (KE2)
1998-present. Alder solidbody, flame maple top, neck-thru.

1998-2019		$1,100	$1,500

Kelly XL
1994-1995. Pointy cutaway solidbody, bolt neck, 2 humbuckers, bound rosewood 'board, sharkfin inlays.

1994-1995		$525	$675

King V (KV2)
2003-present. King V Pro reissue, neck-thru, shark-fin markers, Floyd Rose, U.S.-made.

2003-2019		$600	$775

King V Pro
1993-1995. Soft V-shaped neck-thru solidbody, sharkfin markers, 2 humbuckers.

1993-1995		$525	$675

King V STD
1993-1995. Bolt neck version of King V.

1993-1995		$275	$350

Phil Collen
1989-1991, 1993-1995. Offset double-cut maple neck-thru solidbody, 6-in-line tuners, 1 volume, bound ebony 'board, U.S.-made, early version has poplar body, 1 humbucker; later version with basswood body, 1 single-coil and 1 humbucker.

1993-1995		$1,150	$1,500

Phil Collen PC1 (U.S.A.)
1996-present. Quilt maple top, bolt-on maple neck, maple board, koa body '96-'00, mahogany body '01-present, 1 humbucker and 1 single coil '96-'97, humbucker, stacked humbucker, and single coil '98-present.

1996-2019		$1,300	$1,700

Phil Collen PC3 (Import)
1996-2001. Downscale version of Collen model, poplar body, bolt neck, humbucker\single\single.

1996-2001		$425	$575

PS Performers Series
1994-2003. Some with PS model number on truss rod cover.

1994-2003	Various models	$275	$350

Randy Rhoads (Import)
1992-2011. Bolt neck import version.

1992-2011		$300	$500

Randy Rhoads Limited Edition
1992 only. Shark fin-style maple neck-thru body, gold hardware, white with black pinstriping, block inlays, 6-in-line tuners, U.S.-made, only 200 built.

1992		$4,000	$6,000

Randy Rhoads Pro Series RR3 and RR5
1995-2012. Made in Japan, various finishes.

1995-2012	RR3, bolt-on	$300	$500
2001-2011	RR5, neck-thru	$400	$600

Randy Rhoads Relic Tribute
2010-2011. Custom Shop limited edition to celebrate the 30th anniversary of the Randy Rhoads Concorde, 60 made, exacting dimension and design of Rhoads' original custom-made Concorde guitar, relic-treatment to mimic the original.

2010-2011		$5,200	$6,900

Randy Rhoads U.S.A./RR Series
1983-present. V-shaped (also referred to as concorde-shaped) neck-thru solidbody, 2 humbuckers, originally made at San Dimas plant, serial numbers RR 0001 to RR 1929, production moved to the Ontario plant by '87, serial numbers RR 1930 to present in sequential order.

1983	Early serial #, no trem	$3,500	$5,000
1983	Mid serial #, no trem	$2,500	$3,500
1983-1986	Late serial #, Kahler trem	$1,700	$2,500
1983-1986	Rose trem or string-thru	$1,700	$2,500
1987-1989	Early Ontario-built	$1,500	$2,000
1990-1992	Early '90s vintage	$1,300	$1,800
1993-1999		$1,300	$1,800
2000-2002		$1,300	$1,800
2002-2019	RR5	$850	$1,100
2005	RR1	$1,300	$1,800

RX Series
2000-2011. Bolt-on, shark fin inlays.

2000-2008	RX10D Rhoads	$175	$250

San Dimas Serialized Plated
1980-1982. Various custom-built solidbody models, values vary depending on each individual instrument. The values are true for so-called "Serialized Plated" with Jackson neck plate, Jackson logo and serial number.

1980-1982		$3,100	$4,100

Soloist Custom
1993-1995. Double-cut, neck-thru solidbody, 1 humbucker and 2 single-coils, bound ebony 'board, shark's tooth inlays, U.S.-made.

1993-1995		$1,300	$1,800

1997 Jackson Dinky Reverse DR2

1999 Jackson Randy Rhoads
Randy Schleyhahn

James Tyler Mongoose Special

*Jason Z. Schroeder
The Chopper TL*

MODEL YEAR	FEATURES	EXC. COND. LOW	HIGH
Soloist Pro			
1990-1995. Import version of Soloist, with, shark's tooth inlays.			
1990-1995		$600	$800
Soloist Shannon			
1998. Shark fin inlays, single-single-hum pickups, Rose, signed by Mike Shannon.			
1998		$1,300	$1,800
Soloist Student J1 (U.S.A.)			
1984-1999. Double-cut neck-thru solidbody, Seymour Duncan single-single-hum pickups, rosewood 'board, dot inlays, no binding.			
1984-1986	San Dimas-built	$1,075	$1,400
1986-1999	Ontario-built	$1,075	$1,400
Soloist/Soloist USA/SL Series			
1984-present. U.S.-made, double-cut, neck-thru, string-thru solidbody, 2 humbuckers, bound rosewood 'board, standard vibrato system on Soloist is Floyd Rose locking vibrato, a guitar with Kahler vibrato is worth less. Replaced by the Soloist USA in '90.			
1984-1986	Custom order, Floyd Rose	$1,500	$2,000
1984-1986	Custom order, Kahler	$1,400	$2,300
1984-1986	San Dimas-built, Floyd Rose	$1,500	$2,000
1984-1986	San Dimas-built, Kahler	$1,500	$2,000
1986-1990	Custom order features	$1,500	$2,000
1986-1990	Ontario-built	$1,500	$2,000
1990-2020	Various models, includes SL1 & SL2	$1,300	$1,800
Stealth EX			
1992-late 1990s. Offset double-cut, pointed headstock, H/S/S pickups, offset dot markers, tremolo, Jackson Professional logo.			
1990s		$350	$475
Stealth HX			
1992-1995. 3 humbucker version of Stealth, string-thru body.			
1992-1995		$350	$475
Stealth XL			
1993. Stealth XL truss rod cover logo, 1 humbucker, 2 single-coils, left edge dot markers.			
1993		$350	$475
Surfcaster SC1			
1998-2001. Jackson logo on headstock, Charvel Surfcaster styling.			
1998-2001		$875	$1,125
Warrior Pro (Import)			
1990-1992. Japanese version.			
1990-1992		$300	$400
Warrior U.S.A.			
1990-1992. Four point neck-thru solidbody, 1 humbucker and 1 single-coil, triangle markers, active electronics, U.S.-made, the Warrior Pro was Japanese version.			
1990-1992	Red	$825	$1,075

MODEL YEAR	FEATURES	EXC. COND. LOW	HIGH
Y2KV Dave Mustaine Signature			
2000-2002. V-shaped body, shark tooth markers, neck-thru, 2 humbuckers.			
2000-2002		$2,000	$2,600

Jackson-Guldan/Jay G Guitars

1920s-1960s. The Jackson-Guldan Violin Company, of Columbus, Ohio, mainly built inexpensive violins, violas, cellos, etc. but also offered acoustic guitars in the 1950s and early '60s, some of which were distributed by Wards. Their sales flyers from that era state - Made in America by Jackson-Guldan Craftsman. Very similar to small (13"-14") Stella economy flat-tops. Jay G name with quarter-note logo is sometimes on the headstock. They also offered lap steels and small tube amps early on.

Jacobacci

1930s-1994. Founded in France by Italian Vincent Jacobacci and originally building basso-guitars, banjos, and mandolins. Sons Roger and Andre joined the company and encouraged pop to add lapsteels and electric and regular acoustic guitars around '52. The guitars are sometimes labeled as Jaco and, from ca. '54 to ca. '66, as Jaco Major. In '58 the company introduced aluminum neck models, and in '59 their first solidbodies. In the '60s they also made instruments branded Royal, Texas, Ohio, Star and made instruments for Major Conn and other companies. By the mid '60s, they were producing mainly jazz style guitars.

Jamboree

1960s. Guitar brand exported by Japan's Hoshino (Ibanez).

James Einolf Guitars

1964-2017. Production/custom, professional grade, flat-top guitars built first in Denver, then Castle Rock, Colorado by luthier James Einolf.

James R. Baker Guitars

1996-present. Luthier James R. Baker builds his premium grade, custom, archtops in Shoreham, New York.

James Trussart

1980-present. Luthier James Trussart builds his premium grade, custom/production, solid and semi-hollow body electric guitars and basses in Los Angeles, California.

James Tyler

Early 1980s-present. Luthier James Tyler builds his professional and premium grade, custom/production, solidbody guitars and basses in Van Nuys, California, and also has a model built in Japan.

MODEL YEAR	FEATURES	EXC. COND. LOW	HIGH

Janofsky Guitars

Production classical and flamenco guitars built by luthier Stephen Janofsky in Amherst, Massachusetts starting in 1978.

Jaros

Beginning 1995 these professional and premium grade, production/custom, solidbody and acoustic/electric guitars were originally built by father and son luthiers Harry and Jim Jaros in Rochester, Pennsylvania. In '01 Ed Roman in Las Vegas, bought the brand. He sold it in '04 to Dave Weiler in Nashville. Serial numbers under 1000 were made by the Jaros', numbers 1001-2000 were made by Ed Roman, over 2000 made by Dave Weiler.

Jasmine

1994-2019. Budget and intermediate grade, production, steel and classical guitars offered by Takamine Jasmine or Jasmine by Takamine. Student level instruments.

Jason Z. Schroeder Guitars

1994-present. Luthier Jason Schroeder builds professional and premium grade, production/custom, electric guitars in Redding, California.

Jay Turser

1997-present. Budget and intermediate grade, production, imported acoustic, acoustic/electric, electric and resonator guitars and basses. They also amps. Designed and developed by Tommy Rizzi for Music Industries Corp.

JBG (Joe Bochar Guitars)

2009-present. Production/custom, professional grade, solidbody electric guitars built by luthier Joe Bochar in Santa Clarita, California.

JD Bluesville

John Schappell and luthier Davis Millard build their professional grade, custom/production, solidbody electric guitars in Allentown, Pennsylvania. They began in 2005.

Jeff Traugott Guitars

1991-present. Premium and presentation grade, custom, flat-top, nylon-string, and acoustic/electric guitars built by luthier Jeff Traugott, in Santa Cruz, California.

Jeremy Locke Guitars

Premium grade, production/custom, classical and flamenco guitars built by luthier Jeremy Locke in Coomera, South East Queensland, Australia, starting in 1985.

Jeronimo Pena Fernandez

1967-present. Luthier Jeronimo Pena Fernandez started building classical guitars in Marmolejo, Spain, in the '50s. In '67, he went full-time and soon

became well-known for his fine work. He is now retired, but still builds a few guitars a year. Prices can vary depending on model specs, each instrument should be evaluated on a case-by-case basis.

Jerry Jones

1981-2011. Intermediate grade, production, semi-hollowbody electric guitars and sitars from luthier Jerry Jones, built in Nashville, Tennessee. They also built basses. Jones started building custom guitars in '81, and launched his Danelectro-inspired line in '87. He retired in 2011.

Electric Models

Various models include Baritone 6-string ('89-'11); Electric Sitar ('90-'11) with buzz-bar sitar bridge, individual pickup for sympathetic strings and custom color gator finish; Longhorn Guitarlin ('89-'00, '05-'11) with large cutaway Guitarlin-style body, 24 frets in '89 and 31 after;and the Neptune 12-string ('81-'11) single-cut with 3 pickups.

1981-2011	Neptune 12-string	$1,000	$1,300
1981-2011	Neptune 6/12 Double Neck	$1,925	$2,500
1989-2011	Baritone 6-string	$1,275	$1,675
1989-2011	Longhorn Guitarlin	$1,000	$1,300
1990-2011	Baby Sitar	$1,000	$1,300
1990-2011	Shorthorn	$950	$1,250
1990-2011	Sitar	$1,000	$1,300
1990-2011	U-3, 3 pickups	$950	$1,250

Jersey Girl

1991-present. Premium grade, production/custom, solidbody guitars made in Japan. They also build effects.

JET

1998-present. Premium grade, custom/production, chambered solidbody electric guitars built by luthier Jeffrey Earle Terwilliger in Raleigh, North Carolina.

Jewel

1920s. Instruments built by the Oscar Schmidt Co. and possibly others. Most likely a brand made for a distributor.

JG Guitars

1991-present. Luthier Johan Gustavsson builds his premium and presentation grade, production/custom, solidbody electric guitars in Malmö, Sweden.

Jim Dyson

Intermediate, professional and premium grade, production/custom electric guitars and basses built by luthier Jim Dyson in Torquay, Southern Victoria, Australia, starting in 1972. He also builds lap steels.

Jim Redgate Guitars

1992-present. Luthier Jim Redgate builds his premium grade, custom, nylon-string classical guitars in Belair, Adelaide, South Australia.

Jeff Traugott Model R

Jersey Girl Letter To Nowhere

GUITARS

Jon Kammerer

*2011 JY Jeffrey Yong
JJ Seismic I*

John Le Voi Guitars

1970-present. Production/custom, gypsy jazz, flat-top, and archtop guitars built by luthier John Le Voi in Lincolnshire, United Kingdom. He also builds mandolin family instruments.

John Page Guitars and John Page Classic

2006-present. Luthier John Page builds his custom, premium grade, chambered and solidbody electric guitars in Sunny Valley, Oregon.

John Price Guitars

1984-present. Custom classical and flamenco guitars built by luthier John Price in Australia.

Johnson

Mid-1990s-present. Budget, intermediate and professional grade, production, acoustic, classical, acoustic/electric, resonator and solidbody guitars and basses imported by The Music Link, Brisbane, California. Johnson also offers amps, mandolins, ukuleles and effects.

Jon Kammerer Guitars

1997-present. Luthier Jon Kammerer builds his professional and premium grade, custom/ production, solidbody, chambered, hollowbody, and acoustic guitars and basses in Keokuk, Iowa.

Jones

See TV Jones listing.

Jordan

1981-present. Professional and premium grade, custom, flat-top and archtop guitars built by luthier John Jordan in Concord, California. He also builds electric violins and cellos.

Jose Oribe

1962-present. Presentation grade, production, classical, flamenco, and steel-string acoustic guitars built by luthier Jose Oribe in Vista, California.

Jose Ramirez

See listing under Ramirez, Jose.

Juliett

1960s. Guitars built by Zerosette (or Zero-Sette), an accordion builder near Castelfidardo, Italy.

JY Jeffrey Yong Guitars

2003-present. Professional and premium grade, production/custom, classical, acoustic and electric guitars and basses and harp guitars built by Jeffrey Yong in Kuala Lumpur, Malaysia.

K & S

1992-1998. Hawaiian-style and classical guitars distributed by George Katechis and Marc Silber and handmade in Paracho, Mexico. A few 16" wide

Leadbelly Model 12-strings were made in Oakland, California by luthier Stewart Port. K & S also offered mandolins, mandolas and ukes. In '98, Silber started marketing guitars under the Marc Silber Guitar Company brand and Katechis continued to offer instruments under the Casa Montalvo brand.

Kakos, Stephen

Luthier Stephen Kakos builds his premium grade, production/custom, classical guitars in Mound, Minnesota starting in 1972.

Kalamazoo

1933-1942, 1965-1970. Budget brand built by Gibson. Made flat-tops, solidbodies, mandolins, lap steels, banjos and amps. Name revived for a line of amps, solidbodies and basses in '65-'67. Playability and string tension will affect values of '60s electrics.

KG-1/KG-1 A

1965-1969. Offset double-cut (initial issue) or SG-shape (second issue), 1 pickup, Model 1 A with spring vibrato, red, blue or white.

1965-1969	$350	$475

KG-2/KG-2 A

1965-1970. Offset double-cut (initial shape) or SG-shape, 2 pickups, Model 2 A with spring vibrato, red, blue or white.

1965-1970	$375	$500

KG-11

1933-1941. Flat-top, all mahogany, 14" with no 'guard, sunburst.

1933-1941	$1,000	$1,300

KTG-11 Tenor

1936-1940. Tenor version of 11.

1936-1940	$525	$675

KG-12

1940-1941. Rare model, L-00, sunburst.

1940-1941	$1,600	$2,100

KG-14/KG-14 N

1936-1940. Flat-top L-0-size, mahogany back and sides, with 'guard, sunburst or natural (N).

1936-1940	$1,600	$2,100

KTG-14 Tenor

1936-1940. Tenor version of 14.

1936-1940	$700	$900

KG-16

1939-1940. Gibson-made archtop, small body, f-hole.

1939-1940	$775	$1,025

KG-21

1936-1941. Early model 15" archtop (bent, not curved), dot markers, bound top, sunburst.

1936-1941	$775	$1,025

KTG-21 Tenor

1935-1939. Tenor version of 21.

1935-1939	$525	$675

KG-22

1940-1942. Early model 16" archtop.

1940-1942	$950	$1,225

MODEL YEAR	FEATURES	EXC. COND. LOW	HIGH

KG-31
1935-1940. Archtop L-50-size, 16" body, non-carved spruce top, mahogany back and sides.

1935-1940		$950	$1,225

KG-32
1939-1942. Archtop, 16" body.

1939-1942		$1,000	$1,300

KG Senior
1933-1934. Senior Model logo, firestripe guard, bound top and bottom, rope rose.

1933-1934		$1,475	$1,900

KG Sport
1937-1942. Small body, ¾ size.

1937-1942		$1,475	$1,900

KGN-12 Oriole
1940-1941. Flat-top, same body as KG-14, but with maple back and sides, stencil Oriole picture on headstock, natural.

1940-1941		$1,600	$2,100

KGN-32 Oriole
1940-1941. Archtop, maple back and sides, stencil Oriole picture on headstock, natural.

1940-1941		$1,600	$2,100

KHG Series
1936-1941. Acoustic Hawaiian guitar (HG), some converted to Spanish set-up.

1936-1940	KHG-11	$1,000	$1,275
1936-1941	KHG-14	$1,600	$2,100

Kamico
1947-1951. Flat-top acoustic guitars. Low-end budget brand made by Kay Musical Instrument Company and sold through various distributors. They also offered lap steel and amp sets.

K Stratotone Thin Single
1950s. Similar to Kay Stratotone-style neck-thru solidbody, single slim-tube pickup.

1950s		$900	$1,200

Kapa
Ca. 1962-1970. Begun by Dutch immigrant and music store owner Koob Veneman in Hyattsville, Maryland whose father had made Amka guitars in Holland. Kapa is from K for Koob, A for son Albert, P for daughter Patricia, and A for wife Adeline. Crown shield logo from Amka guitars. The brand included some Hofner and Italian imports in '60. Ca. '66 Kapa started offering thinner bodies. Some German Pix pickups ca. '66. Thinlines and Japanese bodies in '69. Kapa closed shop in '70 and the parts and equipment were sold to Micro-Frets and Mosrite. Later Veneman was involved with Bradley copy guitars imported from Japan. Approximately 120,000 Kapa guitars and basses were made.

Electric
1962-1970. Various models include Challenger with 3-way toggle from '62-'66/'67 and 2 on/off switches after; Cobra with 1 pickup; Continental and Continental 12-string; Minstrel and Minstrel 12-string with teardrop shape, 3 pickups; and the Wildcat, mini offset double-cut, 3 pickups and mute.

1962-1970	Various models	$200	$625

Karol Guitars
2001-present. Luthier Tony Karol builds his custom, premium grade, acoustic and electric guitars in Mississauga, Ontario.

Kasha
1967-1997. Innovative classical guitars built by luthier Richard Schneider in collaboration with Dr. Michael Kasha. Schneider also consulted for Gibson and Gretsch. Schneider died in '97.

Kathy Wingert Guitars
1996-present. Luthier Kathy Wingert builds her premium grade, production/custom, flat-tops in Rancho Palos Verdes, California.

Kawai
1927-present. Kawai is a Japanese piano and guitar maker. They started offering guitars around '56 and they were imported into the U.S. carrying many different brand names, including Kimberly and Teisco. In '67 Kawai purchased Teisco. Odd-shaped guitars were offered from late-'60s through the mid-'70s. Few imports carrying the Kawai brand until the late-'70s; best known for high quality basses. By '90s they were making plexiglass replicas of Teisco Spectrum 5 and Kawai moon-shaped guitar. Kawai quit offering guitars and basses around 2002.

Acoustic
1956-2002		$240	$340

Electric
1956-2002	Common model	$200	$375
1956-2002	Rare model	$400	$625

Kay
Ca. 1931 (1890)-present. Originally founded in Chicago, Illinois as Groehsl Company (or Groehsel) in 1890, making bowl-backed mandolins. Offered Groehsl, Stromberg, Kay Kraft, Kay, Arch Kraft brand names, plus made guitars for S.S.Maxwell, Old Kraftsman (Spiegel), Recording King (Wards), Supertone (Sears), Silvertone (Sears), National, Dobro, Custom Kraft (St.Louis Music), Hollywood (Shireson Bros.), Oahu and others.

In 1921 the name was changed to Stromberg-Voisinet Company. Henry Kay "Hank" Kuhrmeyer joined the company in '23 and was secretary by '25. By the mid-'20s the company was making many better Montgomery Ward guitars, banjos and mandolins, often with lots of pearloid. First production electric guitars and amps are introduced with big fanfare in '28; perhaps only 200 or so made. Last Stromberg instruments seen in '32. Kuhrmeyer becomes president and the Kay Kraft brand was introduced in '31, probably named for Kuhrmeyer's middle name, though S-V had used Kay brand on German Kreuzinger violins '28-'36. By '34, if not earlier, the company is changed to the Kay Musical Instrument Company. A new factory was built at 1640 West Walnut Street in '35. The Kay Kraft

Karol

1960s Kawai

GUITARS

1965 Kay K100 Vanguard
Carter Vintage Guitars

1950s Kay K161 Thin Twin
Bernunzio Uptown Music

MODEL YEAR	FEATURES	EXC. COND. LOW	HIGH

brand ends in '37 and the Kay brand is introduced in late-'36 or '37.

Violin Style Guitars and upright acoustic basses debut in '38. In '40 the first guitars for Sears, carrying the new Silvertone brand, are offered. Kamico budget line introduced in '47 and Rex flat-tops and archtops sold through Gretsch in late-'40s. Kuhrmeyer retires in '55 dies a year later. New gigantic factory in Elk Grove Village, Illinois opens in '64. Seeburg purchased Kay in '66 and sold it to Valco in '67. Valco/Kay went out of business in '68 and its assets were auctioned in '69. The Kay name went to Sol Weindling and Barry Hornstein of W.M.I. (Teisco Del Rey) who began putting Kay name on Teisco guitars. By '73 most Teisco guitars are called Kay. Tony Blair, president of Indianapolis-based A.R. Musical Enterprises Inc. (founded in '73) purchased the Kay nameplate in '79 and currently distributes Kay in the U.S. Currently Kay offers budget and intermediate grade, production, acoustic, semi-hollow body, solidbody, and resonator guitars. They also make amps, basses, banjos, mandolins, ukes, and violins.

K11/K8911 Rhythm Special
1953-1961. Single-cut 17" acoustic archtop, "eighth note" headstock logo, large position markers, white 'guard, became K8911 in '57, sunburst or blond (B).

1953-1961	Blond	$800	$1,050
1953-1961	Sunburst	$750	$1,000

K20 Super Auditorium
1939-1942. 16" archtop, solid spruce top, maple back and sides, sunburst.

1939-1942		$250	$325

K20T
1970s. Japanese-made solidbody, 2 pickups, tremolo, model number on neck plate, circle-capital K logo on headstock.

1970s		$120	$155

K21/K21B Cutaway Professional
1952-1956. Single-cut 17" acoustic archtop, split block markers, sunburst or blond (B).

1952-1956	Blond	$1,000	$1,300
1952-1956	Sunburst	$925	$1,200

K22 Artist Spanish
1947-1956. Flat-top similar to Gibson J-100 17", spruce top, mahogany back and sides.

1947-1956		$500	$650

K26 Artist Spanish
1947-1951. Flat-top, block markers, natural.

1947-1951		$550	$725

K27 Jumbo
1952-1956. 17" Jumbo flat-top, fancy appointments.

1952-1956		$975	$1,250

K37T Spanish Tenor
1952-1956. Mahogany bodied archtop, tenor.

1952-1956		$200	$265

K39 Super Grand Auditorium
1947-1951. Full size acoustic archtop, faux rope binding on top, Kay script logo.

1947-1951		$300	$400

MODEL YEAR	FEATURES	EXC. COND. LOW	HIGH

K44 Artist Archtop
1947-1951. Non-cut archtop, solid spruce top, 17" curly maple veneered body, block markers, sunburst.

1947-1951		$375	$485

K45 Professional Master Size Archtop
1952-1954. Non-cut archtop, 17" body, engraved tortoiseshell-celluloid headstock, large block markers, natural.

1952-1954		$450	$600

K45 Travel Guitar
1981. Made in Korea, known as the 'rifle guitar', 'travel guitar', or 'Austin-Hatchet copy', circle K logo.

1981		$285	$375

K46 Master Size Artist Archtop
1947-1951. Non-cut archtop, solid spruce top, 17" curly maple-veneered body, double-eighth note headstock inlay, sunburst.

1947-1951		$450	$575

K48 Master Size Artist Archtop
1947-1951. Non-cut archtop, 17" solid spruce top with figured maple back and sides, split block inlays, sunburst or black.

1947-1951		$700	$900

K48/K21 Jazz Special
Late-1960s. Slim solidbody with 3 reflective pickups, garden spade headstock, fancy position Circle K headstock logo, white.

1968		$400	$525

K100 Vanguard
1961-1966. Offset double-cut slab solidbody, genuine maple veneered top and back over hardwood body, sunburst.

1961-1966		$250	$325

K102 Vanguard
1961-1966. Double pickup version of the K100, sunburst.

1961-1966		$275	$365

K136 (aka Stratotone)
1955-1957. Small single-cut slab solidbody electric, similar to Harmony Stratotone style, set neck, 1 pickup, trapeze tailpiece, triangle paint graphic in Spring Green and White Mist, matching green headstock, attractive finish adds value to this otherwise lower-end student model.

1955-1957		$900	$1,175

K142 (aka Stratotone)
1955-1957. Small slab solidbody, introduced in '55 along with the K136, offered with 1 pickup or 2 pickups (more rare), trapeze tailpiece, copper finish.

1955-1957	1 pickup	$700	$925
1955-1957	2 pickups	$825	$1,100

K161 Thin Twin/Jimmy Reed
1952-1958. Single-cut semi-hollow body, 2 pickups.

1952-1958		$900	$1,200

K161V Thin Twin
2009-present. Vintage Reissue series, single-cut hollowbody, 2 pickups.

2009-2019		$600	$800

MODEL YEAR	FEATURES	EXC. COND. LOW	HIGH

K300 Double Cutaway Solid Electric
1962-1966. Two single-coils, block inlays, some with curly maple top and some with plain maple top, natural.

1962-1966		$365	$475

K360 Apollo/K365 Apollo II
1965-1968. Solidbody, 2 pickups, block inlays, vibrato.

1965-1968		$700	$1,000

K535
1961-1965. Thinline double-cut, 2 pickups, vibrato, sunburst.

1961-1965		$425	$550

K550 Dove
1970s. Square shoulder D-style, 2 Dove-style 'guards, capital K logo.

1970s		$100	$130

K571/K572/K573 Speed Demon
1961-1965. Thinline semi-acoustic/electric, single pointed cutaway, some with Bigsby vibrato, with 1 (K571), 2 (K572) or 3 (K573) pickups. There was also a Speed Demon solidbody.

1961-1965	571, 1 pickup	$290	$375
1961-1965	572, 2 pickups	$350	$450
1961-1965	573, 3 pickups	$365	$475

K580 Galaxy
1961-1966. Thinline, single-cut, 1 pickup.

1961-1966		$400	$525

K592 Double Cutaway Thinline
1962-1966. Thinline semi-acoustic/electric, double Florentine cut, 2 or 3 pickups, Bigsby vibrato, pie-slice inlays, cherry.

1962-1966		$400	$525

K672/K673 Swingmaster
1961-1965. Single rounded cutaway semi-hollowbody, with 2 (K672) or 3 (K673) pickups.

1961-1965	672, 2 pickups	$800	$1,050
1961-1965	673, 3 pickups	$875	$1,150

K682 Galaxie II
1966-1968. Hollowbody, 2 pickups, vibrato tailpiece.

1966-1968		$400	$525

K775/K776 Jazz II
1961-1966. Electric thinline archtop, double-cut, standard Bigsby vibrato, 2 Gold K pickups, 4 knobs with toggle controls. Replaces Barney Kessel series as top-of-the-line model.

1961-1966	775, shaded	$1,150	$1,500
1961-1966	776, blond	$1,150	$1,500

K797 Acoustic Archtop
1930s. Full size student-intermediate acoustic archtop, 3-on-a-strip tuners, dot markers, sunburst.

1935-1937		$210	$275

K1160 Standard
1957-1964. Small 13" (standard) flat-top, laminated construction.

1957-1964		$40	$55

K1452 Aristocrat
1952. Acoustic-electric archtop, 2 pickups, sunburst.

1952		$620	$800

K1700/K1701 Barney Kessel Pro
1957-1960. 13" hollowbody, single-cut, Kelvinator headstock, ebony 'board with pearl inlays, white binding, 1 (K1701) or 2 (K1700) pickups, sunburst.

1957-1960	1700, 2 pickups	$1,500	$2,000
1957-1960	1701, 1 pickup	$1,400	$1,800

K1961/K1962/K1963 Value Leader
1960-1965. Part of Value Leader line, thinline single-cut, hollowbody, identified by single chrome-plated checkered, body-length guard on treble side, laminated maple body, maple neck, dot markers, sunburst, with 1 (K1961), 2 (K1962) or 3 (K1963) pickups.

1960-1965	1961, 1 pickup	$300	$400
1960-1965	1962, 2 pickups	$350	$450
1960-1965	1963, 3 pickups	$400	$525

K1982/K1983 Style Leader/Jimmy Reed
1960-1965. Part of the Style Leader mid-level Kay line. Sometimes dubbed Jimmy Reed of 1960s. Easily identified by the long brushed copper dual guardplates on either side of the strings. Brown or gleaming golden blond (natural) finish, laminated curly maple body, simple script Kay logo, with 2 (K1982) or 3 (K1983) pickups.

1960-1965	1982, 2 pickups	$440	$575
1960-1965	1983, 3 pickups	$510	$675

K3500 Studio Concert
1966-1968. 14 1/2" flat-top, solid spruce top, laminated maple back and sides.

1966-1968		$70	$90

K5113 Plains Special
1968. Flat-top, solid spruce top, laminated mahogany back and sides.

1968		$115	$150

K5160 Auditorium
1957-1965. Flat-top 15" auditorium-size, laminated construction.

1957-1965		$115	$150

K6100 Country
1950s-1960s. Jumbo flat-top, spruce x-braced top, mahogany back and sides, natural.

1957-1962		$300	$400

K6116 Super Auditorium
1957-1965. Super Auditorium-size flat-top, laminated figured maple back and sides, solid spruce top.

1957-1965		$175	$225

K6120 Western
1960s. Jumbo flat-top, laminated maple body, pinless bridge, sunburst.

1962		$150	$200

K6130 Calypso
1960-1965. 15 1/2" flat-top with narrow waist, slotted headstock, natural.

1960-1965		$215	$276

K6533/K6535 Value Leader
1961-1965. Value Leader was the budget line of Kay, full body archtop, with 1 (K6533) or 2 (K6535) pickups, sunburst.

1961-1965	6533, 1 pickup	$300	$400
1961-1965	6535, 2 pickups	$350	$450

1961 Kay K776 Jazz
Jim Bame

1960s Kay K1983 Style Leader
Richard Kregear

GUITARS

1950s Kay K8990 Upbeat
Curt Huettner

Kiesel Delos

MODEL YEAR	FEATURES	EXC. COND. LOW	HIGH

K6700/K6701 Barney Kessel Artist
1956-1960. Single-cut, 15 1/2" body, 1 (K6701) or 2 (K6700) pickups, Kelvinator headstock, sunburst or blond.

| 1956-1960 | 6700, 2 pickups | $2,100 | $2,800 |
| 1956-1960 | 6701, 1 pickup | $1,900 | $2,500 |

K6878 Style Leader
1966-1968. Full size (15.75) acoustic archtop, circle K logo on 'guard, sunburst.

| 1966-1968 | | $200 | $260 |

K7000 Artist
1960-1965. Highest-end of Kay classical series, fan bracing, spruce top, maple back and sides.

| 1960-1965 | | $290 | $375 |

K7010 Concerto
1960-1965. Entry level of Kay classical series.

| 1960-1965 | | $70 | $90 |

K7010 Maestro
1960-1965. Middle level of Kay classical series.

| 1960-1965 | | $175 | $225 |

K8110 Master
1957-1960. 17" master-size flat-top which was largest of the series, laminated construction.

| 1957-1960 | | $125 | $160 |

K8127 Solo Special
1957-1965. Kay's professional grade flat-top, narrow waist jumbo, block markers.

| 1957-1965 | | $350 | $450 |

K8700/K8701 Barney Kessel Jazz Special
1956-1960. Part of the Gold K Line, top-of-the-line model, 17" single-cut archtop, 1 (K8701) or 2 (K8700) pickups, 4 controls and toggle, Kelvinator headstock with white background, natural or shaded sunburst, Barney Kessel signature logo on acrylic scalloped 'guard, no signature logo on '60 model.

| 1956-1960 | 8700, 2 pickups | $2,100 | $2,800 |
| 1956-1960 | 8701, 1 pickup | $1,900 | $2,500 |

K8990/K8995 Upbeat
1956/1958-1960. Less expensive alternative to Barney Kessel Jazz Special, 2 (K8990) or 3 (K8995) pickups, Gold K Line, Kelvinator headstock, sunburst.

| 1956-1960 | 8990, 2 pickups | $1,100 | $1,400 |
| 1958-1960 | 8995, 3 pickups | $1,200 | $1,550 |

Wood Amplifying Guitar
1934. Engineered after Dobro/National metal resonator models except the resonator and chamber on this model are made of wood, small production.

| 1934 | | $1,600 | $2,100 |

Kay Kraft
1927-1937. First brand name of the Kay Musical Instrument Company as it began its transition from Stromberg-Voisinet Company to Kay (see Kay for more info).

Recording King

| 1931-1937 | | $450 | $600 |

Venetian Archtop
1930s. Unique Venetian cutaway body style, acoustic with round soundhole, flower-vine decal art on low bout.

| 1930s | | $825 | $1,100 |

MODEL YEAR	FEATURES	EXC. COND. LOW	HIGH

KB
1989-present. Luthier Ken Bebensee builds his premium grade, custom, acoustic and electric guitars and basses in North San Juan, California. He was located in San Luis Obispo from '89-'01. He also builds mandolins.

Kel Kroydon (by Gibson)
1930-1933. Private branded budget level instruments made by Gibson. They also had mandolins and banjos. The name has been revived on a line of banjos by Tom Mirisola and made in Nashville.

KK-1
1930-1933. 14 3/4" L-0 sytle body, colorful parrot stencils on body.

| 1930-1933 | | $3,375 | $4,500 |

Keller Custom Guitars
Professional grade, production/custom, solidbody guitars built by luthier Randall Keller in Mandan, North Dakota. He began in 1994.

Keller Guitars
1975-present. Premium grade, production/custom, flat-tops made by luthier Michael L. Keller in Rochester, Minnesota.

Kelly Guitars
1968-present. Luthier Rick Kelly builds professional grade, custom, solidbody electric guitars in New York, New York.

Ken Franklin
2003-present. Luthier Ken Franklin builds his premium grade, production/custom, acoustic guitars in Ukiah, California.

Kendrick
1989-present. Premium grade, production/custom, solidbody guitars built in Texas. Founded by Gerald Weber in Pflugerville, Texas and currently located in Kempner, Texas. Mainly known for their handmade tube amps, Kendrick added guitars in '94 and also offers speakers and effects.

Kenneth Lawrence Instruments
1986-present. Luthier Kenneth Lawrence builds his premium grade, production/custom, electric solidbody and chambered guitars and basses in Arcata, California.

Kent
1961-1969. Imported from Japan by Buegeleisen and Jacobson of New York, New York. Manufacturers unknown but many early guitars and basses were made by Guyatone and Teisco.

Acoustic Flat-Top
1962-1969. Various models.

| 1962-1969 | | $120 | $150 |

MODEL YEAR	FEATURES	EXC. COND. LOW	HIGH

Acoustic/Electric
1962-1969. Various models.

1962-1969		$145	$180

Electric 12-String
1965-1969. Thinline electric, double pointy cutaways, 12 strings, slanted dual pickup, sunburst.

1965-1969		$250	$350

Semi-Hollow Electric
1962-1969. Thinline electric, offset double pointy cutaways, slanted dual pickups, various colors.

1962-1969		$250	$350

Solidbody Electric
1962-1969. Models include Polaris I, II and III, Lido, Copa and Videocaster.

1962-1969	Common model	$125	$250
1962-1969	Rare model	$250	$350

Kevin Ryan Guitars
1989-present. Premium grade, custom, flat-tops built by luthier Kevin Ryan in Westminster, California.

KeyKord
Ca. 1929-mid 1930s.. Keykord offered guitars, ukes and banjos that had a push-button mechanism mounted over the fingerboard that "fingered" a different chord for each button. The guitars were built by Chicago's Stromberg-Voisinet (Kay).

Tenor
1920s-1930s. Venetian mahogany body, 4-string, pearloid headstock overlay.

1920s-30s		$475	$600

Kiesel
1946-present. Founded by Lowell C. Kiesel in '46. Refer to Carvin listing for more info regarding the early years. Prior to his death in 2009, L.C. had turned the business over to his sons and it was located in several different California cities over the years.

In 2015, son Mark and grandson Jeff Kiesel began the new independent Kiesel Custom Guitars. They build professional and premium grade, acoustic and electric guitars and basses in Escondido, California.

Kimbara
1970s-1980s. Japanese line of guitars and basses mainly imported into the U.K. Models were the same as the Fresher brand.

Kimberly
Late-1960s-early-1970s. Private branded import made in the same Japanese factory as Teisco. They also made basses.

Longhorn
1960s. S-style, deep double-cut, 2 pickups.

1960s		$250	$325

May Queen
1960s. Same as Teisco May Queen with Kimberly script logo on headstock and May Queen Teisco on the 'guard.

1960s		$400	$525

Kinal
1969-present. Production/custom, professional and premium grade, solid body electric and archtop guitars and basses built and imported by luthier Michael Kinal in Vancouver, British Columbia.

King's Stone
1960s. Guitar brand exported by Japan's Hoshino (Ibanez).

Kingsley
1960s. Early Japanese imports, Teisco-made.

Soldibody Electric
1960s. Four pickups with tremolo.

1960s		$275	$350

Kingslight Guitars
1980-2015. Luthier John Kingslight built his premium grade, custom/production, steel string guitars and basses in Portage, Michigan (in Taos, New Mexico for '80-'83).

Kingston
Ca. 1958-1967. Guitars and basses imported from Japan by Jack Westheimer and Westheimer Importing Corporation of Chicago, Illinois. Early examples made by Guyatone and Teisco. They also offered mandolins and banjos.

Electric
1958-1967. Various models include: B-1, soldibody, 1 pickup; B-2T/B-3T/B-4T, solidbodies, 2/3/4 pickups and tremolo; SA-27, thin hollowbody, 2 pickups, tremolo.

1958-1967	Common model	$125	$250
1958-1967	Rare model	$250	$350

Kinscherff Guitars
1990-present. Luthier Jamie Kinscherff builds his premium grade, production/custom, flat-top guitars in Austin, Texas.

Kleartone
1930s. Private brand made by Regal and/or Gibson.

Small Flat-Top

1930s		$500	$650

Klein Acoustic Guitars
1972-present. Luthiers Steve Klein and Steven Kauffman build their production/custom, premium and presentation grade flat-tops and basses outside Sonoma, California.

Klein Electric Guitars
1988-2007. Steve Klein added electrics to his line in '88. In '95, he sold the electric part of his business to Lorenzo German, who continued to produce professional grade, production/custom, solidbody guitars and basses in Linden, California.

Kinal Standard MT

1969 Kent Model 741
Greg Perrine

GUITARS

Knaggs Steve Stevens Signature

Koll Duo Glide

MODEL YEAR	FEATURES	EXC. COND. LOW	HIGH

K-Line Guitars

2005-present. Professional grade, production/custom, T-style and S-style guitars and basses built by luthier Chris Kroenlein in St. Louis, Missouri. He also builds basses.

Klira

1887-1980s. Founded by Johannes Klira in Schoenbach, Germany, mainly made violins, but added guitars in the 1950s. The guitars of the '50s and '60s were original designs, but by the '70s most models were similar to popular American models. The guitars of the '50s and '60s were aimed at the budget market, but workmanship improved with the '70s models. They also made basses.

Electric

1960s	Common model	$300	$450
1960s	Rare model	$450	$650

Knaggs

2010-present. Luthiers Joseph Knaggs and Peter Wolf build premium and presentation grade, production/custom, acoustic and electric guitars and basses in Greensboro, Maryland.

Knox

Early-mid-1960s. Budget grade guitars imported from Japan, script Knox logo on headstock.

Electric Solidbody

1960s. Student models, 2 pickups, push buttons.

1960s		$100	$350

Knutsen

1890s-1920s. Luthier Chris J. Knutsen of Tacoma and Seattle, Washington, experimented with and perfected Hawaiian and harp guitar models. He moved to Los Angeles, California around 1916. He also made steels, mandolins and ukes. Dealers state the glue used on Knutsen instruments is prone to fail and instruments may need repair.

Convertible

1909-1914. Flat-top model with adjustable neck angle that allowed for a convertible Hawaiian or Spanish setup.

1909-1914		$3,100	$4,000

Harp Guitar

1900s. Normally 11 strings with fancy purfling and trim.

1900-1910		$1,800	$2,400

Knutson Luthiery

1981-present. Professional and premium grade, custom, archtop and flat-top guitars built by luthier John Knutson in Forestville, California. He also builds basses, lap steels and mandolins.

Kohno

1960-present. Luthier Masaru Kohno built his classical guitars in Tokyo, Japan. When he died in '98, production was taken over by his nephew, Masaki Sakurai.

Koll

1990-present. Professional and premium grade, custom/production, solidbody, chambered, and archtop guitars and basses built by luthier Saul Koll, originally in Long Beach, California, and since '93, in Portland, Oregon.

Kona

1910s-1920s. Acoustic Hawaiian guitars sold by C.S. Delano and others, with later models made by the Herman Weissenborn Co. Weissenborn appointments are in line with style number, with thicker body and solid neck construction. Kona name currently used on an import line.

Style 2

1927-1928		$2,600	$3,400

Style 3

1920s	Koa	$3,300	$4,300

Style 4

1920s	Hawaiian	$3,600	$4,700
1920s	Spanish	$3,400	$4,500

Kona Guitar Company

2000-present. Located in Fort Worth, Texas, Kona imports budget and intermediate grade, production, nylon and steel string acoustic and solid and semi-hollow body electric guitars and basses. They also offer amps, mandolins and ukes.

Koontz

1970-late 1980s. Luthier Sam Koontz started building custom guitars in the late '50s. Starting in '66 Koontz, who was associated with Harptone guitars, built guitars for Standel. In '70, he opened his own shop in Linden, New Jersey, building a variety of custom guitars. Koontz died in the late '80s. His guitars varied greatly and should be valued on a case-by-case basis.

Kopp String Instruments

2000-present. Located in Republic, Ohio from 2000-2004, luthier Denny Kopp presently builds his professional and premium grade, production/custom, semi-hollow archtop electric and hand-carved archtop jazz guitars in Catawba Island, Ohio.

Kopy Kat

1970s. Budget copy-era solidbody, semi-hollow body and acoustic guitars imported from Japan. They also made basses and mandolins.

Acoustic

1970s	J-200 copy	$125	$175

Kragenbrink

Premium grade, production/custom, steel string acoustic guitars built by luthier Lance Kragenbrink in Vandercook Lake, Michigan, starting in the year 2001.

MODEL		EXC. COND.	
YEAR	FEATURES	LOW	HIGH

Kramer

1976-1990, 1995-present. Currently Kramer offers budget and intermediate grade, production, imported acoustic, acoustic/electric, semi-hollow and solidbody guitars. They also offer basses, amps and effects.

Founded by New York music retailer Dennis Berardi, ex-Travis Bean partner Gary Kramer and ex-Norlin executive Peter LaPlaca. Initial financing provided by real estate developer Henry Vaccaro. Parent company named BKL Corporation (Berardi, Kramer, LaPlaca), located in Neptune City, New Jersey. The first guitars were designed by Berardi and luthier Phil Petillo and featured aluminum necks with wooden inserts on back to give them a wooden feel. Guitar production commenced in late-'76. Control passed to Guitar Center of Los Angeles for '79-'82, which recommended a switch to more economical wood necks. Aluminum necks were phased out during the early-'80s, and were last produced in '85. In '84 they added their first import models, the Japanese-made Focus line, followed by the Korean-made Striker line. By 1986 Kramer was the top American electric guitarmaker. In '89, a new investment group was brought in with James Liati as president, hoping for access to Russian market, but the company went of business in late-'90. In '95 Henry Vaccaro and new partners revived the company and designed a number of new guitars in conjunction with Phil Petillo. However, in '97 the Kramer brand was sold to Gibson. In '98, Henry Vaccaro released his new line of aluminum-core neck, split headstock guitars under the Vacarro brand. From 1997 to 2009, sales of Kramer instruments was only through Gibson's MusicYo website. In 2010, Gibson began to distribute the brand through traditional music retail channels with new issues and 1980s legacy models. Non-U.S.-made models include the following lines: Aerostar, Ferrington, Focus, Hundred (post-'85 made with 3 digits in the 100-900), Showster, Striker, Thousand (post-'85 made with 4 digits in the 1000-9000), XL (except XL-5 made in '80s).

Serial numbers for import models include:

Two alpha followed by 4 numbers: for example AA2341 with any assortment of letters and numbers.

One alpha followed by 5 numbers: for example B23412.

Five numbers: for example 23412.

Model number preceding numbers: for example XL1-03205.

The notation "Kramer, Neptune, NJ" does indicate U.S.A.-made production.

Most post-'85 Kramers were ESP Japanese-made guitars. American Series were ESP Japanese components that were assembled in the U.S.

The vintage/used market makes value distinctions between U.S.-made and import models.

Headstock and logo shape can help identify U.S. versus imports as follows:

Traditional or Classic headstock with capital K as Kramer: U.S.A. '81-'84.

Banana (soft edges) headstock with all caps KRAMER: U.S.A. American Series '84-'86.

Pointy (sharp cut) headstock with all caps KRAMER: U.S.A. American Series '86-'87.

Pointy (sharp cut) headstock with downsized letters Kramer plus American decal: U.S.A. American Series '87-'94.

Pointy (sharp cut) headstock with downsized letters Kramer but without American decal, is an import.

1984 Reissue

2003-2007. Made in the U.S., based on EVH's Kramer, single Gibson humbucker, Rose tremolo, various colors.

2003-2007		$525	$700

250-G Special

1977-1979. Offset double-cut, tropical woods, aluminum neck, dot markers, 2 pickups.

1977-1979		$550	$725

350-G Standard

1976-1979. Offset double-cut, tropical woods, aluminum neck, tuning fork headstock, ebonol 'board, zero fret, 2 single coils, dot inlays. The 350 and 450 were Kramer's first models.

1976-1979		$750	$1,000

450-G Deluxe

1976-1980. Like 350-G, but with block inlays, 2 humbuckers. Became the 450G Deluxe in late '77 with dot inlays.

1976-1980		$850	$1,100

650-G Artist

1977-1980. Aluminum neck, ebonol 'board, double-cut solidbody, 2 humbuckers.

1977-1980		$950	$1,250

Baretta

1984-1990. Offset double-cut, banana six-on-a-side headstock, 1 pickup, Floyd Rose tremolo, black hardware, U.S.A.-made.

1984	Non-tilt hdstk	$2,500	$4,000
1984-1985	2nd style, angled hdstk	$800	$1,075
1984-1985	With graphics	$900	$1,200
1985-1987	3rd style, ESP neck	$475	$625
1985-1987	With graphics	$575	$775
1988-1990	Standard opaque	$475	$625
1988-1990	With graphics	$575	$775
1990	Baretta III hybrid	$425	$550

Baretta '85 Reissue

2006. Made in the U.S., based on 1985 banana headstock model, Rose tremolo.

2006		$600	$800

Baretta II/Soloist

1986-1990. Soloist sleek body with pointed cutaway horns.

1986-1990		$450	$600

1978 Kramer 450-G Deluxe
Carter Vintage Guitars

1988 Kramer Baretta
Abalone Vintage

GUITARS

Late-1980s Kramer Ferrington
Imaged by Heritage Auctions, HA.com

1983 Kramer Pacer

MODEL YEAR	FEATURES	EXC. COND. LOW	HIGH

Classic Series

1986-1987. Solidbody copies of the famous Southern California builder, including offset contoured double-cut (Classic I) and slab body single-cut designs (Classic II and Classic III).

1986-1987	Classic I	$400	$525
1986-1987	Classic II	$625	$825
1986-1987	Classic III	$625	$825

Condor

1985-1986. Futuristic 4-point body with large upper bass horn and lower treble horn.

1985-1986		$475	$625

DMZ Custom Series

1978-1981. Solidbody double-cut with larger upper horn, bolt-on aluminum T-neck, slot headstock, models include the 1000 (super distortion humbuckers), 2000 (dual-sound humbuckers), 3000 (3 SDS single-coils), 6000 (dual-sound humbuckers, active DBL).

1978-1981	DMZ-1000	$775	$1,025
1978-1981	DMZ-2000	$800	$1,050
1978-1981	DMZ-3000	$1,050	$1,425
1978-1981	DMZ-6000	$1,200	$1,600

Duke Custom/Standard

1981-1982. Headless aluminum neck, 22-fret neck, 1 pickup, Floyd Rose tremolo.

1981-1982		$350	$450

Duke Special

1982-1985. Headless aluminum neck, two pickups, tuners on body.

1982-1985		$375	$500

Elliot Easton Pro I

1987-1988. Designed by Elliot Easton, offset double-cut, six-on-a-side headstock, Floyd Rose tremolo, 2 single-coils and 1 humbucker.

1987-1988		$600	$800

Elliot Easton Pro II

1987-1988. Same as Pro I, but with fixed-bridge tailpiece, 2 single-coils.

1987-1988		$525	$700

Ferrington

1985-1990. Acoustic-electric, offered in single- and double-cut, bolt-on electric-style neck, transducers, made in Korea.

1985-1990		$225	$300

Floyd Rose Signature Edition

1983-1984. Four pointed-bout body with deep cutawaybelow tremolo assembly, Floyd Rose vibrato system.

1983-1984		$600	$800

Focus/F Series (Import)

1983-1989. Kramer introduced the Focus series as import copies of their American-made models like the Pacer, Baretta, Vanguard (Rhoads-V), and Voyager (star body). Model numbers were 1000-6000, plus the Focus Classic I, II, and III. Most models were offset, double-cut solidbodies. In '87 the Focus line was renamed the F-Series. In '88 a neck-through body design, which is noted as NT, was introduced for a short time. The Classic series was offered with over a dozen color options.

1983-1989	Various models	$200	$425

Gene Simmons Axe

1980-1981. Axe-shaped guitar, aluminum neck, 1 humbucker, slot headstock, stop tailpiece, 25 were made.

1980-1981		$4,200	$6,500

Gorky Park (Import)

1986-1989. Triangular balalaika, bolt-on maple neck, pointy droopy six-on-a-side headstock, 1 pickup, Floyd Rose tremolo, red with iron sickle graphics, tribute to Russian rock, reissued in late-'90s.

1986-1989		$225	$300

Hundred Series

1988-1990. Import budget line, most with offset double-cut 7/8th solidbody.

1988-1990	Various models	$200	$350

Jersey Star

2004-2007. A reissue of the Richie Sambora model.

2004-2007		$700	$925

Liberty '86 Series

1986-1987. Offset double cut arched-top solidbody, pointy head, 2 humbuckers, black, white or flame-maple bound body.

1986-1987	Black or white	$575	$750
1986-1987	Flame maple	$625	$825

Metalist/Showster Series

1989-1990. Korean-made offset double-cut solidbody, metal trim in body design, pointy droopy six-on-a-side headstock, various pickup options, Floyd Rose.

1989-1990		$350	$475

Night Rider

2000-2007. Inexpensive import double-cut semi-hollow, 2 humbuckers.

2000-2007		$70	$95

Nightswan

1987-1990. Offset double-cut, six-on-a-side headstock, 2 Duncan humbuckers, Floyd Rose tremolo, blue metallic.

1987-1990		$1,000	$1,300
1987-1990	Custom color or finish	$1,100	$1,425

Pacer Series

1981-1987. Offset double-cut, six-on-a-side headstock, various pickup options, bolt-on maple neck.

1981-1982	Pacer, 2 pus, soft hdstk	$675	$900
1982	Imperial, soft hdstk	$600	$800
1982	Special, 1 pu	$525	$700
1982-1984	Carerra, 2 pus, classic hdstk	$500	$650
1982-1984	Pacer, 2 pus, classic hdstk	$450	$600
1983-1984	Custom, classic hdstk	$500	$650
1983-1984	Deluxe, classic hdstk	$600	$800
1983-1984	Imperial, classic hdstk	$600	$800
1984	Pacer, 2 pus, banana hdstk	$450	$600
1985	Carerra USA, 2 pus, banana hdstk	$500	$650

The ***Vintage Guitar Price Guide*** shows low to high values for items in all-original excellent condition, and, where applicable, with original case or cover.

MODEL YEAR	FEATURES	EXC. COND. LOW	HIGH
1985	Custom USA, banana hdstk	$500	$650
1985	Deluxe USA, banana hdstk	$600	$800
1985	Imperial USA, banana hdstk	$600	$800
1986	Carerra Japan, 2 pus, pointy hdstk	$500	$650
1986-1987	Custom Japan, pointy hdstk	$500	$650
1986-1987	Deluxe USA/Japan, pointy hdstk	$600	$800
1986-1987	Imperial USA/ Japan, pointy hdstk	$600	$800
1987	Custom II	$500	$650

Paul Dean

1986-1988. Offset double cut, neck-thru, hum/single/single pickups, droopy pointy head.

1986-1988		$635	$825

ProAxe (U.S.A.)

1989-1990. U.S.A.-made, offset double-cut, sharp pointy headstock, dot markers, 2 or 3 pickups, smaller 7/8ths size body, 3 models offered with slightly different pickup options. The model was discontinued when Kramer went out of business in 1990.

1989-1990	Deluxe	$700	$900
1989-1990	Special	$675	$875
1989-1990	Standard	$650	$850

Richie Sambora

1987-1989. Designed by Sambora, mahogany offset double-cut, maple neck, pointy droopy 6-on-a-side headstock, gold hardware, Floyd Rose, 3 pickups, 2 coil-taps.

1987-1989		$900	$1,200

Ripley Series

1984-1987. Offset double-cut, banana six-on-a-side headstock, 22 frets, hexophonic humbucking pickups, panpots, dual volume, Floyd Rose tremolo, black hardware, stereo output, pointy droopy headstock in '87.

1984-1987		$800	$1,050

Savant/Showster Series

1989-1990. Offset double-cut solidbody, pointy headstock, various pickup options.

1989-1990		$265	$350

Stagemaster Deluxe (U.S.A.)

1981. U.S.-made version.

1981		$1,300	$1,700

Stagemaster Series (Import)

1983-1987. Offset double-cut neck-thru solidbody models, smaller 7/8th body, built by ESP in Japan.

1983-1987	Custom/Custom I	$800	$1,050
1983-1987	Deluxe/Deluxe I	$700	$925
1983-1987	Imperial	$575	$750
1983-1987	Special	$500	$650
1983-1987	Standard/Standard I	$575	$750
1987	Deluxe II	$625	$825

Striker Series (Import)

1984-1989. Korean imports, offset double-cut, various pickup options, series included Striker 100, 200, 300, 400, 600 and 700 Bass.

1984-1989	Various models	$175	$300

Sustainer

1989. Offset double-cut solidbody, reverse pointy headstock, Floyd Rose tremolo.

1989		$650	$850

Vanguard Series

1981-1986. U.S.-made or American Series (assembled in U.S.). V shape, 1 humbucker, aluminum (Special '81-'83) or wood (Custom '81-'83) neck. Added for '83-'84 were the Imperial (wood neck, 2 humbuckers) and the Headless (alum neck, 1 humbucker). For '85-'86, the body was modified to a Jackson Randy Rhoads style V body, with a banana headstock and 2 humbuckers. In '99 this last design was revived as an import.

1981-1983	Custom	$825	$1,100
1981-1983	Special	$825	$1,100
1983-1984	Imperial	$825	$1,100
1985-1986	Rhoads V-body	$550	$725

Vanguard (Reissue)

1999-2014. 2 humbuckers, pointy headstock, licensed Floyd Rose.

1999-2014		$225	$300

Voyager

1982-1985. Wood neck, classic headstock, rosewood 'board, 1 pickup (2 optional), Floyd Rose tremolo, black.

1982-1985	Imperial	$700	$950

XKG-10

1980-1981. Aluminum neck, V-shaped body.

1980-1981		$650	$850

XKG-20

1980-1981. More traditional double-cut body with small horns.

1980-1981		$650	$850

XL Series

1980-1981, 1987-1990. The early-'80s U.S.-made models had aluminum necks and were completely different than the late-'80s wood neck models, which were inexpensive imports.

1980-1981	Aluminum neck	$650	$850
1987-1990	Wood neck	$150	$225

ZX Aero Star Series (Import)

1986-1989. Offset double-cut solidbodies, pointy six-on-a-side headstock. Models include the 1 humbucker ZX-10, 2 humbucker ZX-20, 3 single coil ZX-30, and hum/single/single ZX-30H.

1986-1989		$130	$175

Kramer-Harrison, William

1977-present. Luthier William Kramer-Harrison builds his premium grade, custom, classical and flat-top guitars in Kingston, New York.

KSM

Luthier Kevin S. Moore, starting in 1988, premium grade, custom/production, solidbody electric guitars in Logan, Utah.

Kubicki

1973-present. Kubicki is best known for their Factor basses, but did offer a few guitar models in the early '80s. See Bass section for more company info.

1982 Kramer Vanguard
Imaged by Heritage Auctions, HA.com

1980 Kramer XL5

MODEL YEAR	FEATURES	EXC. COND. LOW	HIGH

Kustom

1968-present. Founded by Bud Ross in Chanute, Kansas, and best known for the tuck-and-roll amps, Kustom also offered guitars from '68 to '69. See Amp section for more company info.

Electric Hollowbody

1968-1969. Hollowed-out 2-part bodies; includes the K200A (humbucker, Bigsby), the K200B (single-coils, trapeze tailpiece), and the K200C (less fancy tuners), various colors.

1968-1969		$900	$1,200

Kwasnycia Guitars

1997-present. Production/custom, premium grade, acoustic guitars built by luthier Dennis Kwasnycia in Chatham, Ontario.

Kyle, Doug

Premium grade, custom, Selmer-style guitars made by luthier Doug Kyle in the U.K., starting in 1990.

L Benito

Professional grade, steel and nylon string acoustics from luthier Lito Benito and built in Chile starting in 2001.

La Baye

1967. Designed by Dan Helland in Green Bay, Wisconsin and built by the Holman-Woodell factory in Neodesha, Kansas. Introduced at NAMM and folded when no orders came in. Only 45 prototypes made. A few may have been sold later as 21st Century. They also had basses.

2x4 6-String

1967. Narrow plank body, controls on top, 2 pickups, tremolo, 12-string version was also made.

1967		$1,150	$1,500

La Mancha

Professional and premium grade, production/custom, classical guitars made in Mexico under the supervision of Kenny Hill and Gil Carnal and distributed by Jerry Roberts of Nashville, Tennessee. They began in 1996.

La Patrie

Production, classical guitars. Founded by luthier Robert Godin, who also has the Norman, Godin, Seagull, and Patrick & Simon brands of instruments.

La Scala

Ca. 1920s-1930s. La Scala was another brand of the Oscar Schmidt Company of New Jersey, and was used on guitars, banjos, and mandolins. These were often the fanciest of the Schmidt instruments. Schmidt made the guitars and mandolins; the banjos were made by Rettberg & Lang.

1990 Larrivee C-10 Deluxe
Carter Vintage Guitars

Lace Music Products

1979-present. Intermediate and professional, production, electric guitars from Lace Music Products of Cypress, California, a division of Actodyne General Inc. which was founded by Don Lace Sr., inventor of the Lace Sensor Pickup. In '96, Lace added amplifiers, followed by guitars in 2001 and Rat Fink guitars in '02.

Lacey Guitars

1974-present. Luthier Mark Lacey builds his premium and presentation archtops and flat-tops in Nashville, Tennessee.

Lado

1973-present. Founded by Joe Kovacic, Lado builds professional and premium grade, production/custom, solidbody guitars and basses in Lindsay, Ontario. Some model lines are branded J. K. Lado.

Lafayette

Ca. 1963-1967. Sold through Lafayette Electronics catalogs. Early Japanese-made guitars and basses from pre-copy era, generally shorter scale beginner instruments. Many made by Guyatone, some possibly by Teisco.

Acoustic Thinline Archtop

1963-1967. Various models.

1963-1967		$325	$400

Laguna

2008-present. Guitar Center private label, budget and intermediate grade, production, imported electric and acoustic guitars price range.

Lakeside (Lyon & Healy)

Early-1900s. Mainly catalog sales of guitars and mandolins from the Chicago maker. Marketed as a less expensive alternative to the Lyon & Healy Washburn product line.

Harp Guitar

Early-1900s. Spruce top, rosewood finished birch back and sides, two 6-string necks with standard tuners, 1 neck is fretless without dot markers, rectangular bridge.

1900s	Various models	$1,800	$2,400

Lakewood

1986-present. Luthier Martin Seeliger builds his professional and premium grade, production/custom, steel and nylon string guitars in Giessen, Germany. He has also built mandolins.

Langdon Guitars

1997-present. Luthier Jeff Langdon builds his professional and premium grade, production/custom, flat-top, archtop, and solidbody guitars in Eureka, California.

MODEL YEAR	FEATURES	EXC. COND. LOW	HIGH

Langejans Guitars

1971-2016. Premium grade, production/custom, flat-top, 12-string, and classical guitars built by luthier Delwyn Langejans in Holland, Michigan. He retired in '16.

Larrivee

1968-present. Professional and premium grade, production/custom, acoustic, acoustic/electric, and classical guitars built in Vancouver, British Columbia and, since '01, in Oxnard, California. They also offered several acoustic and a few electric basses over the years as well as ukes. Founded by Jean Larrivee, who apprenticed under Edgar Monch in Toronto. He built classical guitars in his home from '68-'70 and built his first steel string guitar in '71. Moved company to Victoria, BC in '77 and to Vancouver in '82. In '83, he began building solid-body electric guitars until '89, when focus again returned to acoustics.

Up to 2002, Larrivee used the following model designations: 05 Mahogany Standard, 09 Rosewood Standard, 10 Deluxe, 19 Special, 50 & 60 Standard (unique inlay), 70 Deluxe, and 72 Presentation. Starting in '03 designations used are: 01 Parlor, 03 Standard, 05 Select Mahogany, 09 Rosewood Artist, 10 Rosewood Deluxe, 19 California Anniv. Special Edition Series, 50 Traditional Series, 60 Traditional Series, E = Electric, R = Rosewood.

Larrivee also offers Limited Edition, Custom Shop, and Custom variations of standard models although the model name is the same as the standard model. These Custom models are worth more than the values shown.

0-60
2005. Small fancy rosewood.
2005		$1,400	$1,900

00-05
1996. 14.25", all mahogany.
| 1996 | | $950 | $1,250 |

00-09
| 2000s | | $1,000 | $1,300 |

00-10
2000s. 00-size 14" lower bout, spruce top, rosewood back and sides, gloss finish.
| 2000s | | $1,100 | $1,500 |

000-50
2008-present. Mahogany back and sides.
| 2008-2019 | | $1,200 | $1,600 |

000-60
2006-present. Traditional Series, Indian rosewood.
| 2006-2019 | | $1,200 | $1,600 |

000-60K
Traditional Series, figured koa.
| 2012 | | $2,000 | $2,600 |

C-10 Deluxe
Late-1980s-1990s. Sitka spruce top, Indian rosewood back and sides, sharp cutaway, fancy binding.
| 1980s | | $1,300 | $1,700 |

C-72 Presentation
1990s. Spruce top, Indian rosewood back and sides, non-cut Style D, ultra-fancy abalone and pearl hand-engraved headstock.
| 1990s | Jester headstock | $2,200 | $2,900 |

C-72 Presentation Cutaway
1990s. Spruce top, Indian rosewood back and sides, sharp cutaway, ultra-fancy abalone and pearl hand-engraved headstock.
| 1990s | Mermaid headstock | $2,500 | $3,300 |

D-03E
2008-present. Solid mahogany back and sides, spruce top, satin finish.
| 2008-2019 | | $700 | $900 |

D-03R
2002-present. Rosewood.
| 2002-2019 | | $700 | $900 |

D-03RE
2010-present. Rosewood, on-board electronics.
| 2010-2019 | | $750 | $975 |

D-04E
2000-2004, 2013-2014. mahogany, on-board electronics.
| 2013-2014 | | $900 | $1,200 |

DV-03 K
Koa back and sides, Venetian cutaway.
| 2000s | | $1,200 | $1,600 |

D-05-12E
2008-2013. 12 strings.
| 2008-2013 | | $900 | $1,200 |

D-09
2001-present. Rosewood, spruce top, gloss finish.
| 2001-2012 | Indian or walnut | $1,100 | $1,425 |
| 2001-2019 | Brazilian | $2,400 | $3,100 |

D-10 Deluxe
1990s-present. Spruce top, rosewood, abalone top and soundhole trim.
| 1995-2019 | | $1,575 | $2,050 |

D-50
2003-present. Traditional Series, mahogany back and sides.
| 2003-2019 | | $1,200 | $1,600 |

D-60
2003-present. Rosewood back and sides.
| 2000s | Brazilian rosewood | $2,400 | $3,100 |
| 2003-2019 | Indian rosewood | $1,100 | $1,425 |

D-70
Horsehead headstock inlay, ebony 'board, rosewood back and sides.
| 1992-1995 | | $1,500 | $2,000 |

D-Style Classical
1970s. Rosewood body, unicorn inlays.
| 1970s | | $1,300 | $1,700 |

J-05-12
2000s. Jumbo acoustic-electric 12-string, spruce top, mahogany back and sides.
| 2000s | | $1,050 | $1,350 |

J-09
Jumbo, rosewood back and sides, sitka spruce top.
| 2000s | | $1,200 | $1,600 |

Larrivee D-40R Legacy

Larrivee D-09

GUITARS

2015 Larrivee OM-2
Bernunzio Uptown Music

Leach VG Franconia

MODEL YEAR	FEATURES	EXC. COND. LOW	HIGH
J-09-12K			
Jumbo 12-string, rosewood back and sides.			
2000s		$1,500	$2,000
J-70			
1990s. Jumbo, sitka spruce top, solid Indian rosewood back and sides, presentation grade fancy appointments, limited production.			
1990s		$1,600	$2,050
JV-05 Mahogany Standard			
Mahogany back and sides, Venetian cutaway.			
2000s		$900	$1,200
L Series			
1990s-2000s.			
1990s	L-50	$1,300	$1,700
1990s	L-72 Presentation Custom	$2,500	$3,300
2000s	L-30 (Classical)	$950	$1,250
L-0 Standard Series			
1980s-present. Models include L-03 (satin finish), L-05 (mahogany) and L-09 (Indian rosewood).			
1980s-2019	L-05	$950	$1,250
1983-2019	L-09	$1,050	$1,350
1990s-2019	L-03	$650	$850
2000s	L-01	$500	$650
2000s	L-03-12R, 12-string	$650	$850
2008-2012	L-03K, koa	$900	$1,175
2008-2019	L-03R, rosewood	$650	$850
2008-2019	L-03RE	$700	$900
LS Series			
1990s-2011.			
1998	LS-05, mahogany	$1,100	$1,150
2008-2011	LS-03R, rosewood	$900	$1,200
LV Series			
1990s-present. Various models.			
1990s-2019	LV-05, LV-05E	$1,100	$1,400
1990s-2019	LV-09	$1,200	$1,550
2002	LV-19 Special Vine	$3,000	$3,700
2007-2019	LV-03, LV-03E	$900	$1,200
2007-2019	LV-10, LV-10E	$1,900	$2,600
OM Series			
1990s-present. Various models.			
1990-2000s	OM-02	$600	$800
1990-2000s	OM-09R, rosewood	$1,050	$1,400
1990s-2019	OM-03, mahogany, satin	$750	$1,000
1990s-2019	OM-10 Deluxe, rosewood	$1,650	$2,200
1999-2019	OM-05, mahogany	$1,050	$1,400
2000-2019	OM-03R, rosewood	$750	$1,000
2000-2019	OM-40, mahogany	$1,300	$1,700
2000-2019	OM-50, mahogany	$1,050	$1,400
2000s	OM-09K, koa	$1,500	$1,900
2008-2019	OM-60 Bluegrass	$1,150	$1,500
OMV Series			
1990s-2019. Various models.			
2000s	OMV-50	$1,500	$2,000
2003	OMV-09	$1,050	$1,400
2009	OMV-60	$1,600	$2,100
Parlor Walnut			
Early 2000s. Spruce top, solid walnut back and sides.			
2002		$500	$700

MODEL YEAR	FEATURES	EXC. COND. LOW	HIGH
PV Series			
2007-present. Various Parlor models.			
2007	PV-09, maple	$1,050	$1,350
2007-2019	PV-09, Brazilian	$2,200	$2,900
RS-2 Ventura			
2010-2015. Mahogany solidbody, rosewood 'board, 1 or 2 pickups, satin finish various colors.			
2010-2015		$650	$900
RS-4 CM Carved Top			
1988-1989. Carved top solidbody, curly maple top, single-single-humbucker pickups, sunburst or translucent finishes.			
1988-1989		$1,000	$1,300
SD Series			
2008-present. Various models.			
2008	SD-03R	$1,100	$1,400
2008-2019	SD-50, mahogany	$1,500	$1,900
2008-2019	SD-60, SD-60E	$1,150	$1,500

Larry Alan Guitars
2003-present. Professional and premium grade, production/custom, acoustic and electric guitars and basses, built by luthier Larry Alan Daft in Lansing, Michigan. He also builds effects pedals.

Larson Brothers
1900-1944. Chicago's Carl and August Larson bought Maurer & Company in 1900 where they built guitars and mandolin family instruments until 1944. Their house brands were Maurer, Prairie State and Euphonon and they also built for catalog companies Wm. C. Stahl and W. J. Dyer & Bro., adding brands like Stetson, a house brand of Dyer. See brand listings for more information.

Laskin
1973-present. Luthier William "Grit" Laskin builds his premium and presentation grade, custom, steel-string, classical, and flamenco guitars in Toronto, Ontario. Many of his instruments feature extensive inlay work.

Laurie Williams Guitars
1983-present. Luthier Laurie Williams builds his premium and presentation grade, custom/production, steel string, classical and archtop guitars on the North Island of New Zealand. He also builds mandolins.

Leach Guitars
1980-present. Luthier Harvey Leach builds his professional and premium grade, custom, flat-tops, archtops, and solidbody electrics, travel guitars and basses in Cedar Ridge, California.

Lehmann Stringed Instruments
1971-present. Luthier Bernard Lehmann builds his professional and premium grade, production/custom, flat-top, archtop, classical and Gypsy guitars in Rochester, New York. He also builds lutes, vielles and rebecs.

MODEL		EXC. COND.	
YEAR	FEATURES	LOW	HIGH

Lehtela
1993-present. Professional and premium grade, custom/production, acoustic, acoustic/electric, archtop, and solidbody guitars and basses built by luthier Ari Lehtela in Newell, North Carolina.

Lentz
1975-present. Luthier Scott Lentz builds his professional, premium, and presentation grade, custom/production, solidbody electric guitars in San Marcos, California.

Les Stansell Guitars
1980-present. Luthier Les Stansell builds his premium grade, custom, nylon-string guitars in Pistol River, Oregon.

Levin
1900-1973. Founded by Herman Carlson Levin and located in Gothenburg, Sweden, Levin was best known for their classical guitars, which they also built for other brands, most notably Goya from ca. 1955 to the mid '70s. They also built mandolins and ukes.

Levy-Page Special
1930s. Acoustic guitars likely built by Gibson, having many features of Kalamzoo guitars of the era. Possibly made for a distributor.

Lewis
1981-present. Luthier Michael Lewis builds his premium and presentation grade, custom/production, archtop guitars in Grass Valley, California. He also builds mandolins. He also built guitars under the D'Angelico name.

Linc Luthier
1991-present. Professional and premium grade, custom/production, electric and acoustic guitars, basses and double-necks built by luthier Linc Luthier in Upland, California.

Lindberg
Ca. 1950s. Line of guitars produced by Hoyer for Germany's Lindberg music store.

Lindert
1986-2002. Luthier Chuck Lindert made his intermediate and professional grade, production/custom, Art Deco-vibe electric guitars in Chelan, Washington.

Line 6
1996-present. Professional grade, production, imported solidbody and acoustic modeling guitars able to replicate the tones of a variety of instruments. Line 6 also builds effects and amps.

Lion
1960s. One of the brand names of guitars built for others by Egmond in Holland.

Lipe Guitars USA
1983-1989, 2000-present. Luthier Michael Lipe built custom, professional grade, guitars and basses in Sun Valley, California. He died Dec. 2018.

Liscombe
1992-2013. Professional grade, production and limited custom, chambered electric guitars built by luthier Ken Liscombe in Burlington, Ontario.

Loar (The)
2005-present. Professional grade, production, imported archtop acoustic guitars designed by Greg Rich for The Music Link, which also has Johnson and other brands of instruments. They also offer mandolins.

Lollar
1979-present. Luthier Jason Lollar builds his premium grade, production/custom, solidbody and archtop guitars in Vashon, Washington.

Lopez, Abel Garcia
Luthier Abel Garcia Lopez builds his premium grade, custom, classical guitars in Mexico starting in 1985.

Loprinzi
1972-present. Professional and premium grade, production/custom, classical and steel-string guitars built in Clearwater, Florida. They also build ukes. Founded by Augustino LoPrinzi and his brother Thomas in New Jersey. The guitar operations were taken over by AMF/Maark Corp. in '73. LoPrinzi left the company and again started producing his own Augustino Guitars, moving his operations to Florida in '78. AMF ceased production in '80, and a few years later, LoPrinzi got his trademarked name back.

Classical
1970s. Various models.

1970s	Brazilian rosewood	$1,550	$2,000
1970s	Indian rosewood	$900	$1,200
1970s	Mahogany	$750	$1,000

Lord
Mid-1960s. Acoustic and solidbody electric guitars imported by Halifax.

Acoustic or Electric Soldibody

1960s	Various models	$80	$150

Lotus
Late-1970s-2004. Budget grade acoustic and electric guitars and basses imported originally by Midco International, of Effingham, Illinois, and most recently by Musicorp. They also offered banjos and mandolins.

Lehmann Manouche

1985 Lotus
Tom Pfeifer

GUITARS

Lowden Jazz Series

1920 Lyon & Healy Thornward
Bernunzio Uptown Music

MODEL		EXC. COND.	
YEAR	FEATURES	LOW	HIGH

Louis Panormo

Early to mid-1800s. Spanish guitars made in London, England by luthier Louis (Luis) Panormo. He was born in Paris in 1784, and died in 1862.

Lowden

1973-present. Luthier George Lowden builds his premium and presentation grade, production/custom, steel and nylon string guitars in Downpatrick, Northern Ireland. From '80 to '85, he had some models made in Japan.

Flat-Top

1980s-present. Standard models include D, F, O, and S sizes and models 10 thru 32.

1980s-2019 Various models	$2,000	$2,900

LsL Instruments

2008-present. Luthier Lance Lerman builds his production, professional grade, solidbody electric guitars and basses in Los Angeles, California.

LSR Headless Instruments

1988-present. Professional and premium grade, production/custom, solidbody headless guitars and basses made by Ed Roman Guitars.

LTD

1995-present. Intermediate grade, production, Korean-made solidbody guitars and basses offered by ESP.

Lucas Custom Instruments

1989-present. Premium and presentation grade, production/custom, flat-tops built by luthier Randy Lucas in Columbus, Indiana.

Lucas, A. J.

1990-present. Luthier A. J. Lucas builds his production/custom, classical and steel string guitars in Lincolnshire, England.

Luis Feu de Mesquita

2000-present. Professional and premium grade, custom, acoustic and flat-top guitars including Spanish, classical and flamenco built in Toronto, Ontario by luthier Luis Feu de Mesquita.

Luna Guitars

2005-present. Located in Tampa, Florida, Yvonne de Villiers imports her budget to professional grade, production, acoustic and electric guitars and basses from Japan, Korea and China. She also added ukuleles in '09 and amps in '10.

Luttrell Guitars

1993-present. Professional and premium grade, production/custom, acoustic, electric and resonator guitars built by luthier Ralph H. Luttrell in Sandy Springs, Georgia.

MODEL		EXC. COND.	
YEAR	FEATURES	LOW	HIGH

Lyle

Ca. 1969-1980. Imported by distributor L.D. Heater of Portland, Oregon. Generally higher quality Japanese-made copies of American designs by unknown manufacturers, but some early ones, at least, were made by Arai and Company. They also had basses and mandolins.

Lyon & Healy

1864-present. Founded by George Washburn Lyon and Patrick Joseph Healy, Lyon & Healy was an industry giant, operating a chain of music stores, and manufacturering harps (their only remaining product), pianos, Washburn guitars and a line of brass and wind instruments. See Washburn, American Conservatory, Lakeside, and College brands.

Lyon by Washburn

1990s-2000s. Budget grade, production, solidbody guitars and basses sold by mass merchandisers such as Target.

Lyra

1920s. Instruments built by the Oscar Schmidt Co. and possibly others. Most likely a brand made for a distributor.

Lyric

Luthier John Southern started building his professional and premium grade, custom, semihollow and solidbody and basses guitars in Tulsa, Oklahoma in 1996.

M. Campellone Guitars

See listing under Campellone Guitars

M.Zaganin and N.Zaganin

1989-present. Luthier Márcio Zaganin began his career using the M.Zaganin brand, in 2004 it was changed to N. He builds professional and premium grade, production/custom, semi-hollow and solidbody electric guitars in São Paulo, Brazil. He also builds basses.

Maccaferri

1923-1990. Built by luthier and classical guitarist Mario Maccaferri (b. May 20, 1900, Cento, Italy; d. 1993, New York) in Cento, Italy; Paris, France; New York, New York; and Mount Vernon, New York. Maccaferri was a student of Luigi Mozzani from '11 to '28. His first catalog was in '23, and included a cutaway guitar. He also made mandolins. His Europe-era instruments are very rare. He designed Selmer guitars in '31. Maccaferri invented the plastic clothespin during World War II and used that technology to produce plastic ukes starting in '49 and Dow Styron plastic guitars in '53. He made several experimental plastic electrics in the '60s and plastic violins in the late-'80s.

MODEL YEAR	FEATURES	EXC. COND. LOW	HIGH

Plastic (Dow Styron)
1950s. Plastic construction, models include Deluxe (archtop, crown logo), Islander (Islander logo), TV Pal (4-string cutaway) and Showtime (Showtime logo).

1950s	Deluxe	$175	$225
1950s	Islander	$150	$200
1950s	Romancer	$150	$200
1950s	Showtime	$150	$200
1950s	TV Pal	$115	$150

Madeira
1973-ca. 1984, ca. 1990. Imported Budget and intermediate grade acoustic and electric guitars distributed by Guild. The Japanese-made electrics were basically copies of Gibson, Fender and Guild models, the acoustics originally copies of Martin. The electrics only offered first year or so during the '70s run. Name revived again around '90 on imported acoustics and electrics. They also offered mandolins and banjos.

Madrid
1996-present. Luthier Brandon Madrid builds his production/custom, professional and premium grade, acoustic and solidbody electric guitars, in San Diego, California. Prior to 2009 he built in Portland, Oregon.

Maestro
1950s-1970s, 2001-2012. Maestro is a brand name Gibson first used on 1950s accordian amplifiers. The first Maestro effects were introduced in the early-'60s and they used the name until the late-'70s. In 2001, Gibson revived the name for a line of effects, banjos and mandolins. Those were dropped in '09, when imported budget and intermediate, production, acoustic and electric guitars and amps were added. By '12 the brand is no longer listed with Gibson.

Electric
2009-2012. Various student models, Maestro headstock logo, 'By Gibson' logo on truss rod cover.

2009-2012		$55	$95

Magnatone
Ca.1937-1971, 2013-present. Founded as Dickerson Brothers in Los Angeles, California and known as Magna Electronics from '47, with Art Duhamell president. Brands include Dickerson, Oahu (not all), Gourley, Natural Music Guild, Magnatone. In '59 Magna and Estey merged and in '66 the company relocated to Pennsylvania. In '71, the brand was taken over by a toy company. Between 1957 and '67, the company produced four different model lines of Spanish electrics. In 2013, Ted Kornblum revived the Magnatone name on a line of tube amps built in St. Louis, Missouri.

Cyclops
1930s. Dobro-made resonator guitar.

1930s	Round neck	$1,200	$1,550
1930s	Square neck	$1,200	$1,550

MODEL YEAR	FEATURES	EXC. COND. LOW	HIGH

Mark Artist Series
1959-1961	More common	$900	$1,150
1959-1961	Rare	$1,150	$1,500

Mark Series
1955-1960. Solidbody series made by Paul Bigsby in small quantities, then taken over by Paul Barth at Magnatone in '59.

1955-1959	Mark IV	$2,100	$2,700
1955-1959	Mark V	$2,100	$2,700

Model Series
1962	Model 100	$300	$385
1962	Model 150	$300	$385
1962	Model 200, 2 pickups	$300	$385

X-5 Zephyr
1965-1966. Double-cut with 2 DeArmond single-coil pickups, vibrato, metallic finish.

1965-1966		$550	$725

X-15 Tornado
1965-1966. Offset double-cut body, 2 pickups, various options.

1965-1966		$825	$1,075

X-20 Typhoon
1965-1966. Double-cut solidbody, 3 pickups, various options.

1965-1966		$925	$1,225

Magno-Tone
1930s. Brand most likely used by a music studio (or distributor) on instruments made by others, including Regal-built resonator instruments.

Mai Kai
1910s. Line of Hawaiian guitars built in Los Angeles, California by the Shireson Brothers.

Mako
1985-1989. Line of budget to lower-intermediate solidbody guitars from Kaman (Ovation, Hamer). They also offered basses and amps.

Solidbody
1985-1989	Various models	$100	$400

Mal n' Sal
See listing for Alternative Guitar and Amplifier Company.

Malinoski
1986-present. Luthier Peter Malinoski builds his production/custom, professional and premium grade, solidbody electric guitars and basses in Hyattsville, Maryland.

Mann
Ca. 1971-ca. 1985. A brand name used in Canada by Japan's Hoshino company on some of the same acoustic and electric models as their Ibanez guitars.

Manne
1987-present. Professional and premium grade, production/custom, semi-acoustic and electric guitars and basses built by luthier Andrea Ballarin in Italy.

1965 Magnatone x-5 Zephyr
Rivington Guitars

1966 Magnatone X-15 Tornado
Imaged by Heritage Auctions, HA.com

GUITARS

Marchione 16" Archtop

1967 Martin 0-16 NY
Imaged by Heritage Auctions, HA.com

MODEL		EXC. COND.	
YEAR	FEATURES	LOW	HIGH

Manson Guitar Works

1979-present. Premium grade, production/custom, electric guitars built by luthiers Hugh Manson and Adrian Ashton in Exeter, Devon UK. They also offer a line of professional grade, guitars crafted in the Czech Republic and assembled in UK. They also build basses.

Manuel & Patterson

1993-present. Luthiers Joe Manuel and Phil Patterson build professional, premium and presentation grade, production/custom, flat-top, archtop and solidbody electric guitars in Abita Springs, Louisiana. They also offer mandolins.

Manuel Contreras

1962-1994. Luthier Manuel Gonzalez Contreras worked with José Ramírez III, before opening his own shop in Madrid, Spain, in '62.

Manuel Contreras II

1986-present. Professional grade, production/custom, nylon-string guitars made in Madrid, Spain, by luthier Pablo Contreras, son of Manuel.

Manuel Ramirez

See listing under Ramirez, Manuel.

Manuel Rodriguez and Sons, S.L.

1905-present. Professional, premium, and presentation grade, custom flat-top and nylon-string guitars from Madrid, Spain.

Manuel Velázquez

1933-2014. Luthier Manuel Velázquez (d. 2014) built his classical guitars in Puerto Rico ('72-'82), New York City, Virginia, and Florida. His son Alfredo continues to build guitars.

Manzanita Guitars

1993-present. Custom, steel-string, Hawaiian, and resonator guitars built by luthiers Manfred Pietrzok and Moritz Sattler in Rosdorf, Germany.

Manzer Guitars

1976-present. Luthier Linda Manzer builds her premium and presentation grade, custom, steel-string, nylon-string, and archtop guitars in Toronto, Ontario.

Maple Lake

2003-present. Intermediate grade, production, flat-top and acoustic/electric imported guitars from luthier Abe Wechter. Wechter also builds guitars under his own name.

MapleTree Guitars Canada

2011-present. Steve Maric, owner and luthier from Toronto, Canada, works with luthier Fulu Wang, Beijing, China to build production/custom, professional grade, acoustic guitars.

MODEL		EXC. COND.	
YEAR	FEATURES	LOW	HIGH

Mapson

1995-present. Luthier James L. Mapson builds his premium and presentation grade, production/custom, archtops in Santa Ana, California.

Marc Silber Guitar Company

1998-present. Intermediate and professional grade, production, flat-top, nylon-string, and Hawaiian guitars designed by Marc Silber and made in Mexico. These were offered under the K & S Guitars and/or Silber brands for 1992-'98. Silber also has ukuleles.

Marchione Guitars

1993-present. Premium and presentation grade, custom, archtops and solidbodies built by Stephen Marchione originally in New York City, but currently in Houston, Texas.

Marcia

1920s. Instruments built by the Oscar Schmidt Co. and possibly others. Most likely a brand made for a distributor.

Marco Polo

1960-ca. 1964. Imported from Japan by Harry Stewart and the Marco Polo Company of Santa Ana, California. One of the first American distributors to advertise inexpensive Japanese guitars and basses. Manufacturers unknown, but some acoustics by Suzuki, some electrics by Guyatone.

Acoustic Hollowbody

1960-1964	Various models	$75	$250

Mario Martin Guitars

2011-present. Luthier Mario Martin builds his production/custom, professional grade, semi-hollow and solidbody guitars and basses in Murfreesboro, Tennessee. From 2006 to '11, he built guitars under the Guitar Mill brand name.

Mark Wescott Guitars

Premium grade, custom, flat-tops, built by luthier Mark Wescott in Somers Point, New Jersey starting in 1980.

Marling

Ca. 1975. Budget line guitars and basses marketed by EKO of Recanati, Italy; probably made by them, although possibly imported.

Acoustic

1975. Includes the steel-string S.110, and the dreadnoughts W.354 Western, and W.356 Western.

1975		$75	$250

Electric Soldibody

1975. Includes the E.400 (semi-acoustic/electric), E.490 (solidbody), E.480 (single-cut-style), and the 460 (Manta-style).

1975		$75	$250

MODEL YEAR	FEATURES	EXC. COND. LOW	HIGH

Martelle

1934. Private brand attributed to Gibson and some to Kay.

De Luxe

1934. Gibson 12-fret round shoulder Jumbo construction, laminate maple or mahogany back and sides, sunburst, Hawaiian or Spanish option.

1934		$6,400	$8,300

Martin

1833-present. Intermediate, professional, premium, and presentation grade, production/custom, acoustic, acoustic/electric, archtop and resonator guitars. Founded in New York City by Christian Frederick Martin, former employee of J. Staufer in Vienna, Austria. Moved to Nazareth, Pennsylvania in 1839. Early guitars were made in the European style, many made with partners John Coupa, Charles Bruno and Henry Schatz. Scalloped X-bracing was introduced in the late-1840s. The dreadnought was introduced in 1916 for the Oliver Ditson Company, Boston; and Martin introduced their own versions in 1931.

Martin model size and shape are indicated by the letter prefix (e.g., 0, 00, 000, D, etc.); materials and ornamentation are indicated by number, with the higher the number, the fancier the instrument (e.g., 18, 28, 35, etc.). Martin offered electric thinline guitars from '61-'68 and electric solidbodies from '78-'82. The Martin Shenandoah was made in Asia and assembled in U.S. Japanese Martin Sigma ('72-'73) and Korean Martin Stinger ('85 on) imported solidbodies.

Most Martin flat-top guitars, particularly Style 18 and above, came with a standard natural finish, therefore Martin guitar finish coloring is generally not mentioned because it is assumed to be see-through natural. Conversely, Gibson's standard finish for their flat-tops during their Golden Era was sunburst. Martin introduced their shaded (sunburst) finish as an option on their Style 18 in 1934 and their Style 28 in 1931. Values for a shaded finish should be considered on a case-by-case basis. Braced for steel strings specifications described under certain models are based on current consensus information and data provided by the late Martin employee-historian Mike Longworth, and is for guidance only. Variations from these specs have been found, so "bracing" should be considered on a case-by-case basis.

0-15

1935, 1940-1943, 1948-1961. Maple or birch in '35, all mahogany after, unbound rosewood 'board, slotted peghead and 12-fret neck until '34, solid peghead and 14-fret neck thereafter, natural mahogany.

1935	Maple or birch	$2,600	$3,400
1940-1949	Mahogany begins	$2,600	$3,400
1950-1959		$2,400	$3,100
1960-1961		$2,050	$2,650

0-15 H

1940. Hawaiian neck, all mahogany.

1940		$2,600	$3,400

MODEL YEAR	FEATURES	EXC. COND. LOW	HIGH

0-15 M Elderly Instruments 40th Anniversary Limited Editions

2011-2012. Only 10 offered, solid mahogany body and neck, special appointments, inside label signed by Elderly Instruments president Stan Werbin and Martin CEO Chris Martin.

2011-2012		$950	$1,225

0-15 T

1960-1963. Tenor with Style 15 appointments, natural mahogany.

1960-1963		$900	$1,200

0-16

1961 only. Six made.

1961		$1,750	$2,275

0-16 NY

1961-1977, 1979-1992, 1994. Mahogany back and sides, 12 frets, slotted peghead, unbound extra-wide rosewood 'board, natural.

1961-1969		$1,750	$2,275
1970-1979		$1,475	$1,900
1980-1989		$1,250	$1,625
1990-1994		$1,250	$1,625

0-17

1906-1917, 1929-1948, 1966-1968. First version has mahogany back and sides, 3 black soundhole rings, rosewood bound back, unbound ebony 'board, 12 frets, slotted peghead. Second version ('29 and on) is all mahogany, 3 white-black-white soundhole rings, top bound until '30, thin black backstripe, 12 frets and slotted peghead until '34, solid peghead and 14 frets beginning in '33, natural mahogany.

1906-1917	Gut	$1,925	$2,500
1929-1933	Steel, 12-fret	$2,625	$3,400
1933-1934	Flat natural, 14-fret	$3,325	$4,300
1934-1938	Gloss dark, 14-fret	$3,325	$4,300
1939	Early '39, 175 neck	$3,325	$4,300
1939	Later '39, 168 neck	$3,325	$4,300
1940-1948		$3,025	$3,900
1966-1968	Special order	$1,900	$2,450

0-17 H

1930, 1935-1940. Hawaiian, mahogany back and sides, 12 frets clear of body, natural.

1930	12-fret	$2,800	$3,600
1935-1940	14-fret	$3,100	$4,025

0-17 S

Early 1930s. Limited production style 17 with spruce top, unique 'guard.

1931		$4,350	$5,600

0-17 T

1932-1960. Mahogany back and sides, tenor, natural.

1932-1933		$1,125	$1,425
1934-1939		$1,625	$2,100
1940-1949		$1,250	$1,625
1950-1960		$1,000	$1,300

0-18

1898-1994, 2017-present. Rosewood back and sides until 1917, mahogany back and sides after, Adirondack spruce top until 1946, slotted peghead and 12 frets until 1934, solid peghead and 14 frets after 1934, braced for steel strings in 1923, improved neck in late-1934,

1936 Martin 0-17
KC from Larryville Ga.

1950 Martin 0-18
Dave Kyle

1919 Martin 0-18
David Stone

1956 Martin 0-18
Bernunzio Uptown Music

MODEL YEAR	FEATURES	EXC. COND. LOW	HIGH

non-scalloped braces appear late-'44, natural. Reintroduced '17, sitka spruce, mahogany.

1898-1917	Brazilian	$3,200	$4,150
1918-1922	Mahogany, gut	$2,100	$2,725
1923-1934	12-fret, steel	$4,425	$5,750
1932-1938	14-fret	$4,850	$6,300
1939	Early '39, 175 neck	$4,850	$6,300
1939	Later '39, 168 neck	$4,300	$5,600
1940-1944		$3,925	$5,100
1945-1949		$2,975	$3,850
1950-1959		$2,850	$3,700
1960-1964		$2,500	$3,200
1965		$2,350	$3,050
1966-1969		$2,075	$2,700
1970-1979		$1,750	$2,300
1980-1989		$1,550	$2,000
1990-1994		$1,550	$2,000
2017-2019	Reintroduced	$1,450	$1,875

0-18 G

1960s. Special order classical nylon-string model, natural.

1961		$1,650	$2,150

0-18 K

1918-1935 Hawaiian, all koa wood, T-frets and steel T-bar neck in late-1934, natural

1918-1933		$3,500	$4,500
1934-1935	14-fret	$4,600	$6,000

0-18 KH

1927-1928. Hawaiian, koa.

1927-1928		$4,200	$5,500

0-18 T

1929-1932, 1936-1989, 1991-1992, 1994-1995. Mahogany body, spruce top, tenor, natural.

1929-1939		$1,825	$2,350
1940-1949		$1,550	$2,000
1950-1959		$1,325	$1,725
1960-1969		$1,150	$1,500
1970-1979		$975	$1,275
1980-1989		$825	$1,075
1991-1995		$825	$1,075

0-18 T Nick Reynolds

2010-2011. Custom Artist Edition, mahogany.

2010-2011		$2,000	$2,625

0-18 TE

1959, 1962. Only 2 made, tenor, 1 pickup.

1959, 1962		$4,200	$5,425

0-18 VS Elderly Instruments 40th Anniversary Limited Edition

2012-2014. Mahogany body, sitka spruce top, slotted headstock, 12-fret neck, inside label signed by C. F. Martin IV and Elderly founder Stan Werbin.

2012-2014		$1,625	$2,125

0-20

1850-1859		$4,425	$5,750

0-21

1898-1931, 1934-1938, 1941, 1944, 1946-1948. Rosewood back and sides, Adirondack spruce top until 1946, 12 frets, T-frets and steel T-bar neck in late-1934, non-scalloped braces in late-1944, natural.

1898-1926		$4,650	$6,000
1927-1930		$6,500	$8,500

MODEL YEAR	FEATURES	EXC. COND. LOW	HIGH
1930	14-fret (only year)	$6,500	$8,500
1931-1938		$6,500	$8,500
1941		$6,200	$8,100
1944	Non-scalloped	$5,600	$7,300
1946-1948		$4,500	$5,800

0-21 K

1919-1929. Koa top, back and sides.

1919-1929		$6,500	$8,500

0-21 T

1929-1930, 1935, 1961.

1929-1935		$3,600	$4,600
1961		$1,950	$2,500

0-26

1850-1890. Rosewood back and sides, ivory-bound top, rope-style purfling.

1850-1890		$5,700	$7,400

0-27

1850s-1890s. Rosewood back and sides, ivory-bound top.

1850s	Antique market value	$6,800	$8,900
1890s		$5,400	$7,100

0-28

1874-1931, 1937 (6 made), 1969 (1 made). Brazilian rosewood back and sides, herringbone binding until 1937, natural.

1874-1895		$5,150	$6,700
1896-1897	Dark orange (rare)	$5,150	$6,700
1898-1923		$5,150	$6,700
1924-1927	Gut	$5,150	$6,700
1925-1927	Steel option	$7,300	$9,500
1928-1929	Steel (standard)	$7,300	$9,500
1930-1931	Belly bridge, 12-fret	$7,900	$10,300
1937	Belly bridge, 14-fret	$10,000	$13,000
1969	Brazilian	$4,500	$5,900

0-28 H

1927-1928. One made each year, Hawaiian, koa.

1927-1928		$7,300	$9,500

0-28 IA Ian Anderson

2004. Limited Edition 87 made, adirondack spruce top, Indian rosewood sides and back, slotted headstock, can be converted from nylon to light steel strings.

2004		$2,850	$3,700

0-28 K

1917-1931, 1935. Hawaiian, all koa wood, braced for steel strings in '23, natural.

1917-1924		$6,500	$8,500
1925-1929		$7,300	$9,500
1930-1935		$7,900	$10,300

0-28 T

1930-1931, 1941. Tenor neck.

1930-1931	Steel option	$4,000	$5,200
1941		$3,200	$4,200

0-28 VS

2009-2019. Rosewood back and sides, slotted head, 12 fret neck.

2009-2019		$2,200	$2,850

The *Vintage Guitar Price Guide* shows low to high values for items in all-original excellent condition, and, where applicable, with original case or cover.

MODEL YEAR	FEATURES	EXC. COND. LOW	HIGH

0-30
1899-1921. Brazilian rosewood back and sides, ivory-bound body, neck and headstock.

1899-1921		$5,500	$7,100

0-34
1885, 1898-1899, 1907. Brazilian rosewood.

1885-1907		$5,800	$7,600

0-40
1860s-1898, 1912-1913. Indian rosewood.

1880-1913		$7,300	$9,500

0-42
1870s-1924, 1926-1930, 1 each in '34, '38,'42. Brazilian rosewood back and sides, 12 frets, natural.

1890-1924		$10,700	$14,000
1926-1927	Gut	$10,700	$14,000
1928-1942	Steel	$16,000	$21,000

0-44 Soloist/Olcott-Bickford Artist
1911-1931. Vahdah Olcott-Bickford Artist Model, run of 17 style-44 guitars made, Brazilian rosewood, ivory or faux-ivory-bound ebony 'board.

1911-1931		$15,000	$19,500

0-45
1904-1908, '11, '13, '15, '17-'20, '22-'24, '26-'30, '39. Brazilian rosewood back and sides, natural, special order only for '31-'39.

1904-1927	Gut	$25,000	$32,000
1927-1939	Steel	$34,000	$45,000

0-45 JB Joan Baez
1998. Indian rosewood, 59 made.

1998		$3,500	$4,500

0-45 S Stephen Stills
2007. 91 made, Madagascar rosewood sides and back, Adirondack spruce top.

2007		$5,800	$7,600

0-X1 E
2020-present. Concert size, figured mahogany laminate, Fishman electronics.

2020		$375	$475

00-1
1995-2002. Grand Concert, mahogany.

1995-2002		$650	$825

00-1 R
1995-1999. Rosewood version.

1995-1999		$650	$825

00-15
1999-2010. Sapele/mahogany.

1999-2010		$800	$1,025

00-15 E Retro
2017-2018. Solid mahogany top, back and sides, electronics.

2017-2018		$1,075	$1,400

00-15 M
2009-present. All mahogany.

2009-2019		$800	$1,025

00-15 M Custom Elderly Instruments
2010-2014. All mahogany, diamond and square inlays, custom-made for Elderly Instruments, about 10 offered each year.

2010-2014		$825	$1,075

00-15 M Elderly Instruments 40th Anniversary Limited Edition
2012. Only 12 made, mahogany body and neck, label signed by Elderly's president Stan Werbin and Martin CEO Chris Martin.

2012		$825	$1,075

00C-15 AE
2000-2002. Built in electronics, natural finish.

2000-2002		$750	$1,000

00-16 C
1962-1977, 1980-1981. Classical, mahogany back and sides, 5-ply bound top, satin finish, 12 frets, slotted peghead, natural.

1962-1969		$1,000	$1,300
1970-1977		$850	$1,100
1980-1981	2 made	$700	$925

00-16 DBFM
2006. Women and Music series, deep body (DB), flamed maple (FM), slotted headstock.

2001-2003		$1,150	$1,500

00-16 DBM
2000-2005. Women and Music series, deep body (DB), mahogany (M), slotted headstock, gloss finish.

2000-2005		$1,150	$1,500

00-16 DBR
1998-2000. Women and Music series, deep body (DB), rosewood ®, 14-fret slotted headstock, gloss natural finish.

1998-2000		$1,150	$1,500

00C-16 DB
1999-2002. Women in Music series, cutaway, deep body (DB), mahogany, slotted headstock.

1999-2002		$1,300	$1,725

00C-16 DBRE
2005-2007. Women and Music series, rounded cutaway, deep body (DB), rosewood (R), electronics (E).

2005-2007		$1,375	$1,800

00-17
1908-1917, 1930-1960, 1982-1988, 2001-2004. Mahogany back and sides, 12 frets and slotted headstock until '34, solid headstock and 14 frets after '34, natural mahogany, reissued in 2001 with a high gloss finish.

1908-1917	Gut	$2,400	$3,100
1930-1933	Steel, 12-fret	$3,500	$4,500
1934	14-fret, flat natural	$3,800	$4,900
1935-1938	14-fret, gloss dark	$3,800	$4,900
1939	Early '39, 175 neck	$3,800	$4,900
1939	Later '39, 168 neck	$3,500	$4,500
1940-1944		$3,500	$4,500
1945-1949		$2,800	$3,600
1950-1960		$2,350	$3,050
1982-1988		$1,400	$1,800
2001-2004	Reissue	$1,400	$1,800

00-17 Authentic 1931
2018-present. Mahogany top, back and sides, Brazilian rosewood 'board, vintage gloss finish.

2018-2020		$3,000	$3,900

00-17 H
1934-1935. Hawaiian set-up, mahogany body, no binding.

1934-1935		$3,800	$4,900

1903 Martin 0-28
California Vintage

1998 Martin 0-45 JB Joan Baez

GUITARS

1959 Martin 00-18
Bernunzio Uptown Music

1999 Martin 00-18
SH Steve Howe

00-17 S Black Smoke/Whiskey Sunset
2015-present. Sitka spruce top, mahogany back and sides, rosewood 'board and bridge, on-board electronics (E) optional.

		LOW	HIGH
2015-2019	No electronics	$950	$1,250
2016-2019	With electronics	$1,125	$1,475

00-17 SO Sing Out!
2000. Limited Edition, 50 made for 50th anniversary of Sing Out! Magazine, folk era logo inlays, SING OUT inlay on 20th fret, mahogany body.

	LOW	HIGH
2000	$1,275	$1,650

00L-17 Black Smoke/Whiskey Sunset
2016-2019. Sitka spruce top. Mahogany back and sides, on-board electronics (E) optional.

		LOW	HIGH
2016-2019	No electronics	$1,075	$1,400
2016-2019	With electronics	$1,200	$1,525

00-18
1898-1995, 2016-present. Rosewood back and sides until 1917, mahogany after, braced for steel strings in '23, improved neck in late-'34, war-time design changes '42-'46, non-scalloped braces in late-'44, Adirondack spruce top until '46, natural. Reissued 2016 with sitka spruce top and mahogany back and sides.

		LOW	HIGH
1898-1917	Brazilian	$3,600	$4,700
1918-1922	Mahogany	$3,100	$4,100
1923-1929		$4,800	$6,200
1930-1932	12-fret	$6,600	$8,600
1933	14-fret, bar fret	$6,900	$9,000
1934-1937	14-fret	$7,200	$9,400
1938	175 neck	$7,200	$9,400
1939	Early '39, 175 neck	$7,200	$9,400
1939	Later '39, 168 neck	$6,300	$8,200
1940-1941		$6,200	$8,100
1942-1944	Scalloped	$6,200	$8,100
1944-1949	Non-scalloped	$4,800	$6,200
1950-1959		$3,500	$4,500
1960-1964		$3,200	$4,200
1965		$3,100	$4,000
1966-1969		$2,800	$3,600
1970-1979		$2,000	$2,600
1980-1989		$1,700	$2,200
1990-1995		$1,700	$2,200
2016-2019		$1,400	$1,800

00-18 Authentic 1931
2016-2018. Adirondack spruce top, mahogany back and sides, ebony 'board, Vintage Tone System (VTS), natural finish.

	LOW	HIGH
2016-2018	$3,300	$4,300

00-18 C
1962-1995. Renamed from 00-18 G in '62, mahogany back and sides, classical, 12 frets, slotted headstock, natural.

	LOW	HIGH
1962-1969	$1,400	$1,800
1970-1979	$1,000	$1,300
1980-1989	$850	$1,100
1990-1995	$850	$1,100

00-18 CTN Elizabeth Cotton
2001. Commemorative Edition, 76 made.

	LOW	HIGH
2001	$1,925	$2,500

00-18 Custom
2008. Custom Shop run of 75 or more made.

	LOW	HIGH
2008	$1,925	$2,500

00-18 E
1959-1964. Flat-top Style 18, single neck pickup and 2 knobs, heavier bracing, natural.

	LOW	HIGH
1959-1964	$4,100	$5,300

00-18 G
1936-1962. Mahogany back and sides, classical, natural, renamed 00-18 C in '62.

	LOW	HIGH
1936-1939	$2,100	$2,700
1940-1949	$1,500	$1,950
1950-1959	$1,425	$1,850
1960-1962	$1,400	$1,800

00-18 Gruhn Limited Edition
1995. Sitka spruce top, C-shaped neck profile, 25 made.

	LOW	HIGH
1995	$1,675	$2,200

00-18 H
1935-1941. Hawaiian, mahogany back and sides, 12 frets clear of body, natural. The Price Guide is generally for all original instruments. The H conversion is an exception, because converting from H (Hawaiian-style) to 00-18 specs is considered by some to be a favorable improvement and something that adds value.

	LOW	HIGH
1935-1938	$6,000	$7,800

00-18 H Geoff Muldaur
2006-2011. Solid Adirondack spruce top, solid mahogany sides and back, sunburst.

	LOW	HIGH
2006-2011	$2,300	$3,000

00-18 K
1918-1925, 1934. All koa wood.

	LOW	HIGH
1918-1921	$3,100	$4,000
1922-1925	$4,400	$5,700
1934	$6,000	$7,800

00-18 S John Mellencamp
2009-2010. Slotted, 12-fret.

	LOW	HIGH
2009-2010	$2,550	$3,300

00-18 SH Steve Howe
1999-2000. Limited edition run of 250.

	LOW	HIGH
1999-2000	$1,775	$2,275

00-18 T
1931, 1936, 1938-1940. Tenor version.

	LOW	HIGH
1931	$2,500	$3,300
1936-1939	$3,000	$3,900
1940	$2,700	$3,500

00-18 Tim O'Brien Limited Edition Signature
2008-2011. 25.5" scale, label signed by O'Brien.

	LOW	HIGH
2008-2011	$3,100	$4,000

00-18 V
1984, 2003-2016. Vintage Series, mahogany back and sides, spruce top.

		LOW	HIGH
1984	9 made	$1,700	$2,200
2003-2016		$1,700	$2,200

00-18 V/VS Elderly Instruments 40th Anniversary
2012-2013. Limited Edition, solid (V) or slotted (VS) headstock, 12-fret, low profile.

		LOW	HIGH
2012-2013	V	$1,625	$2,100
2013	VS	$1,625	$2,100

The *Vintage Guitar Price Guide* shows low to high values for items in all-original excellent condition, and, where applicable, with original case or cover.

MODEL YEAR	FEATURES	EXC. COND. LOW	HIGH

00-21

1898-1996. Brazilian rosewood back and sides, changed to Indian rosewood in 1970, dark outer binding, unbound ebony 'board until 1947, rosewood from 1947, slotted diamond inlays until '44, dot after, natural.

1898-1926	Gut bracing	$4,825	$6,225
1927-1939	Steel bracing	$10,000	$13,000
1940-1943	Scalloped	$9,500	$12,500
1944-1949	Non-scalloped	$7,700	$10,000
1950-1959		$6,400	$8,400
1960-1964		$5,050	$6,600
1965		$3,900	$5,100
1966-1969	Brazilian	$3,700	$4,800
1970-1979	Indian	$2,100	$2,700
1980-1989	Indian	$1,775	$2,300
1990-1996	Indian	$1,775	$2,300

00-21 Custom

2005-2006. Custom order size 00 style 21, Brazilian rosewood sides and back.

2005-2006		$3,000	$4,000

00-21 G

1937-1938. Gut string, Brazilian rosewood sides and back.

1937-1938		$2,300	$3,000

00-21 Golden Era

1998. Limited edition, Adirondack spruce top, scalloped braces, rosewood back and sides.

1998-2000		$1,950	$2,500

00-21 H

Hawaiian, special order, limited production.

1914	1 made	$5,000	$6,500
1934		$10,000	$13,000
1952, 1955	1 made each year	$6,400	$8,400

00-21 Kingston Trio LTD

2007. 50th Anniversary of the Kingston Trio, inspired by Dave Guard's 00-21, 100 made, 12-fret, Indian rosewood, Kingston Trio label and notation "In Memory of Dave Guard 1934-1991".

2008-2009		$2,700	$3,500

00-21 LE

1987. Guitar of the Month, 19 made.

1987		$2,100	$2,700

00-21 NY

1961-1965. Brazilian rosewood back and sides, no inlay, natural.

1961-1964		$4,800	$6,300
1965		$4,200	$5,500

00-21 S

1968. Slotted headstock, Brazilian rosewood sides and back.

1968		$4,200	$5,500

00-21 T

1934. Tenor, Brazilian rosewood back and sides, only 2 made.

1934		$3,700	$4,900

00-25 K

1980, 1985, 1988. Spruce top, koa back and sides.

1980-1988		$1,925	$2,500

00-25 K2

1980, 1982-1984, 1987-1989. Koa top, back and sides.

1980-1989		$1,925	$2,500

00-28

1898-1931, 1934, 1936-1941, 1958 (1 made), 1977 (1 made), 1984 (2 made), 2017-present. Brazilian rosewood back and sides, changed to Indian rosewood in 1977, herringbone purfling through 1941, white binding and unbound 'board after 1941, no inlays before 1901, diamond inlays from 1901-'41, dot after, natural. Reintroduced 2017, sitka spruce top, modified low oval neck.

1898-1924	Gut	$7,800	$10,000
1925-1931	Steel	$14,000	$18,000
1934-1941	Few made	$20,000	$26,000
1958	Special order	$8,300	$11,000
1977	Special order	$2,000	$2,600
1984	Special order	$1,700	$2,200
2017-2019	Reissue	$1,700	$2,200

00-28 C

1966-1995. Renamed from 00-28 G, Brazilian rosewood back and sides, changed to Indian rosewood in '70, classical, 12 frets, natural.

1966-1969	Brazilian	$2,700	$3,600
1970-1979	Indian	$1,325	$1,750
1980-1989		$1,150	$1,525
1990-1995		$1,150	$1,525

00-28 G

1936-1962. Brazilian rosewood back and sides, classical, natural, reintroduced as 00-28 C in '66.

1936-1939		$4,200	$5,500
1940-1946		$3,800	$5,000
1947-1949		$3,400	$4,500
1950-1959		$2,900	$3,800
1960-1962		$2,700	$3,600

00-28 K

1919-1921, 1926, 1928-1931, 1933. Hawaiian, koa back and sides.

1919-1921	34 made	$9,200	$12,000
1926-1933	1 made per year	$15,000	$19,000

00-28 T

1931, 1940. Tenor, Brazilian rosewood back and sides, tenor 4-string neck, only 2 made.

1931, 1940		$5,400	$7,100

00-28 VS

2009-2019. Rosewood back and sides.

2009-2019		$2,200	$2,850

00-28 VS Custom Shop

2009-2013. Various Custom Shop options.

2009-2013		$2,500	$3,200

00-30

1890s-1921. Rosewood .

1899-1921		$9,400	$12,300

00-34

1898-1899. 6 made.

1898-1899		$10,600	$13,800

00-37 K2 Steve Miller

2001. Flamed koa back and sides, solid Engelmann spruce top, limited edition run of 68.

2001		$4,000	$5,100

1947 Martin 00-21
Imaged by Heritage Auctions, HA.com

1925 Martin 00-28
Izzy Miller

To get the most from this book, be sure to read "Using *The Guide*" in the introduction.

1930 Martin 00-42
Imaged by Heritage Auctions, HA.com

1975 Martin 00-45
Imaged by Heritage Auctions, HA.com

MODEL YEAR	FEATURES	EXC. COND. LOW	HIGH
00-40	*1913, 1917. 4 made.*		
1913	Brazilian	$20,000	$26,000
1917	Koa	$20,000	$26,000

00-40 H
1928-1939. Hawaiian, Brazilian rosewood back and sides, 12 frets clear of body, natural. H models are sometimes converted to standard Spanish setup, in higher-end models this can make the instrument more valuable to some people.

1928-1929	Pyramid bridge	$20,000	$26,000
1930-1939	Belly bridge	$20,000	$26,000

00-40 K
Few were made (only 6), figured koa, natural.

1918	1 made	$20,000	$26,000
1930	5 made	$20,000	$26,000

00-40 Martin Stauffer
1997. Rosewood/spruce, 35 made.

1997		$5,000	$6,400

00-41 Custom Shop
2005. Custom Shop model.

2005		$3,300	$4,300

00-42
1898-1943, 1973 (1 made). Brazilian rosewood back and sides, Indian rosewood in 1973, pearl top borders, 12 frets, ivory bound peghead until 1918, ivoroid binding after 1918, natural.

1898-1927	Pyramid bridge	$14,000	$18,000
1927-1943	Steel bracing	$27,000	$35,000
1973	1 made	$3,100	$4,100

00-42 G
1936-1939. Gut string slotted headstock classical, only 3 made.

1936-1939	3 made	$8,000	$10,500

00-42 JM-C John Mayer Crossroads
2219. Limited run of 50 for Guitar Center, designed by John Mayer to benefit Crossroads Centre in Antigua, Sitka spruce top, Cocobolo back and sides, gloss finish.

2019		$5,500	$7,200

00-42 K
1919. Koa body, only 1 made.

1919	1 made	$23,000	$30,000

00-42 K2 Robbie Robertson
2008-2009. Limited Edition, all koa body (K2), 00-12 fret style, high-end appointments.

2008-2009		$4,200	$5,500

00-42 Linda Ronstadt Limited Edition
2009-2010. Madagascar rosewood, slotted headstock.

2009-2010		$5,100	$6,600

00-42 SC John Mayer
2012-2019. Sitka spruce top, cocobolo back, sides and headplate, ebony 'board.

2012-2019		$4,500	$6,000

00-44 G
1938. Set up with gut strings, 1 made.

1938		$23,000	$30,000

00-44 Soloist/Olcott-Bickford Artist
1913-1939. Custom-made in small quantities, Brazilian rosewood, ivory or faux-ivory-bound ebony 'board.

1913-1939	6 made	$32,000	$41,000

00-45
1904-1929, 1970-1982, 1984-1987, 1989-1990, 1992-1993. Brazilian rosewood back and sides, changed to Indian rosewood in '70, 12 frets and slotted headstock until '34 and from '70 on 14 frets, and solid headstock from '34-'70, natural.

1904-1927	Gut	$32,000	$42,000
1927-1929	Steel	$65,000	$85,000
1970-1979	Reintroduced	$4,200	$5,400
1980-1993		$3,700	$4,800

00-45 K
1919. Koa body, 1 made.

1919		$46,000	$60,000

00-45 S
1970. Slotted headstock.

1970		$4,600	$5,900

00-45 S Limited Edition
2002. 1902 vintage-pattern with fancy inlays, 00 size style 45, 50 made.

2002		$9,000	$11,700

00-45 SC John Mayer
2012-2013. Limited Edition, 25 made, slotted headstock, cocobolo.

2012-2013		$8,100	$10,500

00-45 ST Stauffer Commemorative
1997-1998. Limited Edition, 25 made, six-on-a-side headstock, 45-style appointments, 00 body, Sitka top, Brazilian rosewood back and sides.

1997-1998		$8,200	$10,700

00-55
1935. 12 made for Rudnick's Music of Akron, Ohio.

1935		$6,500	$8,500

00CMAE
1999-2001. Single-cut acoustic-electric flat-top, laminate back and sides, made in U.S.

1999-2001		$525	$675

00CXAE
2000-2013. Single-cut acoustic-electric flat-top, composite laminate back and sides, made in U.S.

2000-2013	Various colors	$400	$525

00L Fly Fishing
2019-present. Limited Edition, run of 100, artwork by William Matthews, sitka spruce top, Goncalo Alves back and sides, gloss finish.

2019-2020		$2,400	$3,100

00LX1AE
2017-2019. Sitka spruce top, mahogany laminate back and sides, Fishman electronics, natural. Replaced by 00L-X2E in '20.

2017-2019		$325	$425

00L-X2E
2020-present. Sitka spruce top, figured mahogany laminate back and sides, Fishman electronics, natural finish.

2020		$450	$575

00X1AE
2015-2019. Non-cut, acoustic-electric, HPL mahogany back and sides. Replaced by 00-X2E in '20.

2015-2019		$325	$425

MODEL YEAR	FEATURES	EXC. COND. LOW	HIGH

00-X2E
2020-present. Sitka spruce top, figured mahogany laminate back and sides, Fishman electronics, natural finish.
| 2020 | | $450 | $575 |

00-DB Jeff Tweedy Signature
2011-2019. Custom Shop Signature Edition with solid FSC® Certified Mahogany and mahogany burst finish.
| 2011-2019 | | $1,400 | $1,850 |

000-1
1994-2005. Solid spruce top with laminated mahogany back and sides.
| 1994-2005 | | $625 | $800 |

000-1 E
1994-2005. 000-1 with electronics.
| 1994-2005 | | $650 | $850 |

000-1 R
1994-2003. 000-1 with back and sides.
| 1994-2003 | | $625 | $800 |

000-10 E
2019-present. Road Series, updated version of 000RS1, sapele top, back and sides, satin finish.
| 2019-2020 | | $425 | $550 |

000-12 E Koa
2019-present. Road Series, sitka spruce top, koa veneer back and sides, Fishman electronics, gloss finish.
| 2019-2020 | | $900 | $1,150 |

000-13 E
2017-2018. Road Series, updated version of 000RSG, sitka spruce top, siris back and sides, Fishman electronics, natural gloss.
| 2017-2018 | | $600 | $775 |

000-15 M
2010-present. All mahogany.
| 2010-2019 | | $750 | $975 |

000-15 M Burst
2016-2018. Solid mahogany, 14-fret, satin finish with added burst to top.
| 2016-2018 | | $775 | $1,000 |

000-15 M Elderly Instruments 40th Anniversary
2011-2012. 10 made, mahogany body and neck, label signed by Elderly Instruments president Stan Werbin and Martin CEO Chris Martin
| 2011-2012 | | $1,050 | $1,350 |

000-15 M StreetMaster
2017-present. Same specs as 000-15M but with distressed mahogany satin finish.
| 2017-2019 | | $750 | $975 |

000-15 SM
2011-present. Solid mahogany, slotted headstock, 12-fret neck, satin finish.
| 2011-2019 | | $900 | $1,200 |

000-15 Special
2016-present. Sitka spruce top, mahogany back and sides, satin finish.
| 2016-2019 | | $850 | $1,100 |

000-15/000-15 S
1999-2009. Mahogany body, headstock is solid or slotted (S, first offered in '00). Renamed 000-15 M with solid headstock in '10.
| 1999-2009 | 000-15 | $800 | $1,050 |
| 2000-2009 | 000-15 S | $925 | $1,200 |

000-16 Series
1989-present. Mahogany back and sides, diamonds and squares inlay, sunburst, name changed to 000-16 T Auditorium with higher appointments in '96, in 2000-2005 slotted (000-16 S) and gloss finish (000-16 SGT) were offered. Various models continue to be added to this series.
1989	000-16 M	$900	$1,200
1989-1995	000-16	$900	$1,200
1989-2019	000-16 GT	$750	$1,000
1995-1998	000-16 T	$775	$1,000
1996	000-16 TR	$775	$1,000
1996-2002	000-16 R	$900	$1,200
2001-2005	000-16 RGT	$750	$1,000
2002-2003	000-16 SRGT	$825	$1,050
2003-2004	000-16 SGT	$825	$1,050
2019-2020	000-16 E	$1,200	$1,575

000-17
1911, 1952. Mahogany back and sides, 1 made in 1911, 25 more in '52.
| 1911 | | $7,000 | $9,000 |
| 1952 | | $3,500 | $4,500 |

000-17 Black Smoke/Whiskey Sunset
2016-present. Sitka spruce top, mahogany back and sides, rosewood 'board and bridge, on-board electronics optional.
| 2016-2019 | No electronics | $950 | $1,250 |
| 2016-2019 | With electronics | $1,125 | $1,475 |

000-17 S
2002-2004. All mahogany, slotted headstock, 12 fret neck.
| 2002-2004 | | $1,075 | $1,400 |

000-17 SM
2013-2015. Sitka spruce top, mahogany back and sides, East Indian rosewood headplate, vintage slotted headstock.
| 2013-2015 | | $1,075 | $1,400 |

000-18
1906, 1911-present (none in 1932-1933). Maple back and sides in '06, then rosewood until '17, and mahogany since, longer scale in '24-'34, 12-fret neck until '33, changed to 14 in '34. Improved neck late-'34, war-time changes '41-'46, non-scalloped braces in late-'44, switched from Adirondack spruce to Sitka spruce top in '46 (though some Adirondack tops in '50s and '60s), natural. Now called the 000-18 Auditorium.
1906	Maple	$7,600	$10,000
1911-1917		$7,600	$10,000
1920-1922	Gut, mahogany	$6,800	$9,000
1923-1931	Steel, 12-fret	$9,600	$12,500
1934	Early '34,		
	long scale	$12,300	$16,000
1934-1938	14-fret	$12,300	$16,000
1939	Early '39 175 neck	$11,500	$15,000
1939	Late '39, 168 neck	$9,200	$12,000

1937 Martin 000-18
Doug Brazzell

1972 Martin 000-18
Rivington Guitars

1948 Martin 000-21
Carter Vintage Guitars

1936 Martin 000-28
M. Mattingly

MODEL YEAR	FEATURES	LOW	HIGH
1940-1941		$8,500	$11,000
1942-1943	Scalloped braces	$8,500	$11,000
1944	Scalloped braces	$7,600	$9,800
1944-1949	Non-scalloped	$5,400	$7,000
1950-1953		$4,200	$5,500
1954-1959		$3,850	$5,000
1960-1964		$3,550	$4,600
1965		$3,375	$4,400
1966-1969		$2,875	$3,725
1970-1979		$2,000	$2,600
1980-1989		$1,700	$2,200
1990-1999		$1,700	$2,200
2000-2013		$1,400	$1,800
2014-2019		$1,450	$1,900

000-18 Authentic 1937
2008-2011. Natural or sunburst, high-X bracing.

2008-2011		$3,300	$4,300

000-18 E Retro
2012-2019. Sitka spruce top, mahogany back and sides.

2012-2019		$1,525	$2,000

000-18 G
1955. Classical, 1 made.

1955		$3,100	$4,100

000-18 Golden Era 1934 Special Edition
2007. Adirondack red spruce top, scalloped and forward shifted X-bracing, 14-fret V-shaped mahogany neck, 20-fret ebony 'board, old style decal logo.

2007		$2,200	$2,850

000-18 Golden Era 1937
2006-2014. Natural or sunburst. 1937 dropped from name in '12.

2006-2014		$2,250	$2,900

000-18 Golden Era Sunburst
2006-2014. Sunburst version.

2006-2014		$2,250	$2,900

000-18 Kenny Sultan
2007-2009. Flamed mahogany sides, diamond and squares inlays, label signed by Sultan.

2007-2009		$2,200	$2,850

000-18 Norman Blake Signature
2006-2011. 12 fret neck on 14-fret body.

2006-2011		$2,200	$2,850

000-18 P
1930. Plectrum neck.

1930		$4,000	$5,200

000-18 S
1976-1977. Slotted, 12-fret.

1976-1977		$2,300	$3,000

000-18 T
1930, '34, '36, '38, '41. Tenor.

1930		$4,100	$5,400
1934-1938		$7,700	$10,000
1941		$4,600	$6,000

000-18 V/VS Elderly Instruments 40th Anniversary
2012-2013. Limited Edition, solid (V) or slotted (VS) headstock, Sitka top, label signed by C.F. Martin IV and Stan Werbin, includes matching wood guitar stand.

2012-2013	V	$1,950	$2,550
2013	VS	$1,950	$2,550

000-18 WG Woody Guthrie
1999. Signed label including artwork and model identification.

1999		$2,100	$2,725

000-21
1902-1923 (22 made over that time), 1931(2), 1938-1959, 1965 (1), 1979 (12). Brazilian rosewood back and sides, changed to Indian rosewood in '79, natural.

1902-1913		$11,000	$14,500
1918-1923		$12,000	$15,500
1931	12-fret	$13,800	$18,000
1938-1939	Early '39, 175 neck	$20,700	$27,500
1939	Late '39, 168 neck	$16,200	$21,500
1940-1941		$13,700	$18,200
1942-1945		$12,000	$16,000
1946		$8,500	$11,000
1947-1949		$7,100	$9,200
1950-1959		$6,400	$8,400
1965	Brazilian	$5,050	$6,600
1979	Indian	$2,100	$2,700

000-21 10-String/Harp Guitar
1902. Only 2 made, 10 strings, Brazilian rosewood back and sides.

1902		$4,300	$5,500

000-28
1902-present. Brazilian rosewood back and sides, changed to Indian rosewood in '70, herringbone purfling through '41, white binding and unbound 'board after '41, no inlays before '01, slotted diamond inlays from '01-'44, dot after, 12 frets until '32, 14 frets '31 on (both 12 and 14 frets were made during '31-'32), natural through '93, sunburst or natural after.

1902-1927	Gut	$13,500	$17,500
1925-1927	Steel	$25,000	$33,000
1928	12-fret	$25,000	$33,000
1929	Pyramid bridge, 12-fret	$25,000	$33,000
1930	Belly bridge, 12-fret	$25,000	$33,000
1931-1933	12 fret	$25,000	$33,000
1934	Early '34 long scale	$42,000	$56,000
1934-1937	14-fret	$38,000	$51,000
1938-1939	Early '39, 175 neck	$35,000	$46,000
1939	Late '39, 168 neck	$30,000	$39,000
1940-1941		$26,000	$35,000
1942-1944	Scalloped, herringbone	$22,000	$29,000
1944-1946	Non-scalloped, herringbone	$17,500	$23,000
1947-1949	Non-herringbone	$12,000	$15,500
1950-1952		$9,500	$12,500
1953-1955	Kluson	$9,500	$12,500
1956-1958	Early '58 Kluson	$8,300	$11,000
1958-1959	Late '58 Grover	$8,300	$11,000
1960-1962		$6,000	$8,000
1964		$6,300	$8,300
1965-1966	Early '66, Tortoise 'guard	$4,950	$6,550
1967-1969		$4,750	$6,250
1970-1979		$2,000	$2,600

MODEL YEAR	FEATURES	EXC. COND. LOW	HIGH
1980-1989		$1,725	$2,225
1990-1999		$1,725	$2,225
2000-2009		$1,725	$2,225
2010-2019		$1,725	$2,225

000-28 C
1962-1967. Classical, Brazilian rosewood back and sides, slotted peghead, natural.

1962-1967		$3,500	$4,600

000-28 E Modern Deluxe
2020-present. Sitka spruce top with Vintage Tone System (VTS), East Indian rosewood back and sides, Fishman electronics, gloss finish.

2020		$3,200	$4,150

000-28 EC
1996-present. Custom Signature Edition, Eric Clapton specs, sitka spruce top, Indian rosewood back and sides, herringbone trim, natural or sunburst.

1996-2019	Natural	$1,950	$2,550
1996-2019	Sunburst	$1,950	$2,550

000-28 EC Eric Clapton Crossroads Madagascar
2013. Limited to 150 in collaboration with Guitar Center, soundhole label hand-signed by Clapton and Chris Martin, Crossroads symbol inlaid (mother-of-pearl) into bridge, Clapton signature between 19th-20th frets, Clapton signature case and strap.

2013		$3,500	$4,600

000-28 ECB Eric Clapton
2002-2003. Limited edition, EC 000-28 with Brazilian rosewood, certificate of authenticity, label hand-signed by Eric Clapton and Chris Martin.

2002-2003		$6,000	$7,800

000-28 F
1964-1967. Folk, 12-fret, slotted.

1964		$6,300	$8,300
1965-1966		$5,100	$6,800
1967		$4,900	$6,500

000-28 G
1937, 1939-1940, 1946-1947, 1949-1950, 1955. Special order classical guitar, very limited production.

1937, 1939		$6,400	$8,500
1940		$5,800	$7,700
1946-1949		$4,500	$6,000
1950, 1955		$4,100	$5,500

000-28 Golden Era
1996 only. Sitka spruce top, rosewood back and sides, scalloped braces, herringbone trim, 12-fret model, natural.

1996		$3,000	$4,000

000-28 H
2000-2017. Herringbone top trim, production model for '00-'02, Custom Shop model made for Elderly Instruments after that (stamped Custom on neck block).

2000-2002		$1,700	$2,200
2003-2017	Custom Shop	$1,850	$2,450

000-28 HB Brazilian 1937 Reissue
1997. Pre-war specs including scalloped bracing, Brazilian rosewood.

1997		$5,400	$7,000

000-28 K
1921. Non-catalog special order model, only 2 known to exist, koa top, back and sides.

1921	Rare model	$25,000	$33,000

000-28 K Authentic 1921
2014-2015. Slotted, 12-fret, highly figured koa body.

2014-2015		$3,300	$4,350

000-28 LSH/LSH Custom
2008. Large sound hole (LSH), style 28 appointments, wild grain East Indian sides and back.

2008		$1,900	$2,500

000-28 M Eric Clapton
2009. Limited Edition run of 461, Madagascar rosewood back and sides, Carpathian spruce top, signature between 19th and 20th frets, interior label hand-signed by Clapton, natural or sunburst.

2009		$4,200	$5,500

000-28 Martin/Mandolin Brothers 25th Anniversary
1997-1998. Limited Edition, 25 made, mandolin 12th fret inlay, signed label.

1997-1998		$2,400	$3,100

000-28 Modern Deluxe
2019-present. Sitka spruce top, Vintage Tone System, Indian rosewood back and sides.

2019		$2,000	$2,600

000-28 Norman Blake
2004-2008. Signature Edition, 12-fret neck on 14-fret body, B version is Brazilian rosewood.

2004-2008	Brazilian	$5,500	$7,200
2004-2008	Indian	$2,850	$3,750

000-28 NY
1962. 2 made.

1962		$6,200	$7,600

000-28 Perry Bechtel
2007. East Indian rosewood back and sides, 29 made.

2007		$3,500	$4,500

000-28 S
1974-1977. Slotted headstock, 12-fret neck.

1974-1977		$2,000	$2,600

000-28 SO Sing Out! 40th Anniversary
1990. Limited Edition, 40 made for 40th Anniversary of Sing Out! Magazine.

1990		$2,200	$2,900

000-28 VS
1999-2019. Vintage Series, spruce top with aging toner, scalloped bracing, rosewood sides and back, slotted diamond markers, herringbone top trim.

1999-2019		$2,200	$2,850

000-30 Authentic 1919
2017-2018. Adirondack spruce top, Vintage Tone System, Madagascar rosewood back and sides.

2017-2018		$4,000	$5,200

000-38
1980. Rosewood back and sides, 3 made.

1980		$1,900	$2,500

000-40
1909. Ivoroid bound top and back, snowflake inlay, 1 made.

1909		$25,000	$32,000

2009 Martin 000-28 M Eric Clapton
Carter Vintage Guitars

Martin 000-28 VS

1943 Martin 000-42
Imaged by Heritage Auctions, HA.com

*2019 Martin 000-42
Authentic 1939*

MODEL YEAR	FEATURES	EXC. COND. LOW	HIGH

000-40 PR Peter Rowan
2001. Mahogany back and sides, slotted headstock, 12-fret, phases of the moon inlays.

2001		$2,400	$3,100

000-40 Q2GN Graham Nash
2003. Limited edition of 147 guitars, quilted mahagony top/back/sides, flying-heart logo on headstock, Graham Nash signature on frets 18-20.

2003		$2,900	$3,800

000-41
1975, 1996. Custom shop style 000-41.

1975		$3,100	$4,100
1996		$2,700	$3,500

000-42
1918, 1921-1922, 1925, 1930, 1932, 1934, 1938-1943, 2004-present. Brazilian rosewood back and sides, natural. The 1918-1934 price range is wide due to the variety of specifications.

1918-1925	Limited production	$30,000	$39,000
1930, 1932	2 made, 14 fret	$47,000	$60,000
1934	1 made	$60,000	$77,000
1938	27 made	$54,000	$69,000
1939	Early '39,175 neck	$54,000	$69,000
1939	Later '39, 168 neck	$50,000	$64,000
1940-1943	Last pearl border	$41,000	$52,000
2004-2019		$3,000	$4,000

000-42 Authentic 1939
2017-2019. Adirondack spruce top with Vintage Tone System (VTS), Madagascar rosewood back and sides, ebony 'board and bridge.

2017-2019		$6,700	$8,700

000-42 EC Eric Clapton
1995. Style 45 pearl-inlaid headplate, ivoroid bindings, Eric Clapton signature, 24.9" scale, flat-top, sunburst top price is $8320 ('95 price), only 461 made; 433 natural, 28 sunburst.

1995		$5,400	$7,000

000-42 ECB Eric Clapton
2000-2001. With Brazilian rosewood, 200 made.

2000-2001		$10,000	$13,000

000-42 EC-Z Eric Clapton Crossroads
2019-present. Ziricote back and sides, 50 made to benefit Crossroads Centre.

2019-2020		$8,500	$11,300

000-42 M Eric Clapton Limited Edition
2008-2009. Limited Edition, 250 made, Madagascar rosewood sides and back, Carpathian spruce top.

2008-2009		$5,300	$6,900

000-42 Marquis
2007-2009. Indian rosewood.

2007-2009		$3,900	$5,100

000-42 SB
2004. 1935 style with sunburst finish, Indian rosewood back and sides.

2004		$3,100	$4,000

000-44 Soloist/Olcott-Bickford Artist
1917-1919. Style 44 guitars were made for guitarist Vahdah Olcott-Bickford, rosewood back and sides, 3 made.

1917-1919		$34,000	$44,500

000-45
1906, 1911-1914, '17-'19, '22-'29, '34-'42, '70-'94. Brazilian rosewood back and sides, changed to Indian rosewood in '70, 12-fret neck and slotted headstock until '34 (but 7 were made in '70 and 1 in '75), 14-fret neck and solid headstock after '34, natural.

1906-1919		$44,000	$57,000
1922-1927	Gut	$44,000	$57,000
1926-1929	Steel	$91,000	$119,000
1930-1931	000-45 designated	$91,000	$119,000
1934	Early '34, long scale	$130,000	$170,000
1934	Late '34, short scale	$125,000	$160,000
1935-1937	14 fret, CFM inlay	$125,000	$160,000
1938	Early '38	$125,000	$160,000
1938	Late '38	$112,000	$148,000
1940-1942	168 neck	$94,000	$122,000
1970-1977		$4,600	$6,000
1980-1989		$4,400	$5,800
1990-1994		$4,400	$5,800

000-45 7-String
1911, 1929, 1931. 1 made each year.

1911-1931		$29,000	$38,000

000-45 B
1985. Brazilian rosewood, 2 made.

1985		$10,500	$13,700

000-45 EC Eric Clapton Crossroads Brazilian
2013. Limited to 18 in collaboration with Guitar Center, Brazilian rosewood, Crossroads symbol inlaid both ends of bridge, Crossroads case and strap.

2013		$26,000	$34,000

000-45 EC Eric Clapton Crossroads Madagascar
2013. Limited to 55 in collaboration with Guitar Center, Crossroads symbol inlaid both ends of bridge, Crossroads case and strap.

2013		$7,700	$10,000

000-45 H
1937. Brazilian rosewood, Hawaiian, 2 made.

1937		$128,000	$170,000

000-45 JR Jimmie Rodgers
1997-1998. Adirondack spruce top, Brazilian rosewood back and sides, scalloped high X-braces, abalone trim, natural, 52 made.

1997-1998		$11,200	$14,800

000-45 S
1974-1976. 12-fret.

1974-1976		$5,000	$6,500

000-45 S Stephen Stills
2005. Only 91 made, Indian rosewood.

2005		$7,800	$10,300

000C David Gray Custom
2005-2006. Custom Artist Edition, 000-size cutaway, Italian spruce top, mahogany back and sides, interior label signed by David Gray.

2005-2006		$1,900	$2,450

MODEL YEAR	FEATURES	EXC. COND. LOW	HIGH

000C DB Dion The Wanderer
2002. Cutaway acoustic/electric, 57 made, scalloped bracing, mahogany sides and back, slotted diamond and square markers, Dion logo on headstock, gloss black finish.

2002		$3,300	$4,400

000C DG Doug Greth Commemorative Edition
2011. Nylon string cutaway, slotted headstock, mahogany back and sides, 48 made.

2011		$1,450	$1,900

000C Nylon
2012-2018. Cutaway, 12-fret, sitka spruce top, sapele back and sides, slotted headstock, Fishman.

2012-2018		$1,200	$1,550

000C Steve Miller Pegasus
2005-2006. Cutaway, mahogany back and sides, Pegasus logo.

2005-2006		$2,200	$2,850

000C-1 E Auditorium
1997-1999. Cutaway, mahogany back and sides, transducer pickup.

1997-1999		$775	$1,025

000C12-16 E Nylon
2020-present. Gloss sitka spruce top, satin mahogany back and sides, Fishman electronics.

2020		$1,400	$1,800

000C-15 E
1999-2002. Cutaway, mahogany back and sides, Fishman.

1999-2002		$875	$1,150

000C-16 (T Auditorium)
1990-1998. Cutaway acoustic, mahogany back and sides, diamonds and squares inlay, name changed to 000-C16T Auditorium in '96.

1990-1998		$1,000	$1,325

000C-16 GTE
1999-2003. Cutaway, mahogany.

1999-2003		$1,075	$1,400

000C-16 GTE Premium
2003-2009. Mahogany back and sides.

2003-2009		$1,200	$1,550

000C-16 RB (Baby Face)
2000-2002. Cutaway acoustic, East Indian rosewood back and sides.

2000-2002		$1,425	$1,850

000C-16 RGTE
2000-2010. Cutaway, rosewood back and sides.

2000-2010		$925	$1,200

000C-16 SGTNE
2003-2006. Classical nylon string, cutaway, mahogany body, 12-fret cedar neck, slotted headstock.

2003-2006		$1,050	$1,350

000C-16 SRNE
2003-2005. Classical cutaway, rosewood body, 12-fret cedar neck, slotted headstock.

2003-2005		$1,050	$1,350

000C-16 T
1996-1997. Sitka spruce top, mahogany back, sides and neck, rosewood 'board.

1996-1997		$750	$1,000

000C-28 Andy Summers
2006. Cutaway, rosewood back and sides, Buddhist Mudra inlays.

2006		$2,900	$3,700

000C-28 SMH Merle Haggard
2001-2002. Cutaway, 12-fret neck, Blue Yodel No. 13 inlay.

2001-2002		$3,100	$4,000

000CJr-10 E
2019-present. Junior Series, 000Jr-10 model with Fishman electronics.

2019-2020		$450	$575

000CME
1999-2002. Laminate back and sides, on-board electronics, satin finish.

1999-2002		$650	$850

000CXE Black
2003-2013. Acoustic-electric, cutaway, laminated body, black finish.

2003-2013		$425	$550

000E Black Walnut Ambertone
2020. Limited Edition, run of 125, sitka spruce top with gloss amber burst finish, satin black walnut back and sides, Fishman electronics.

2020		$1,300	$1,725

000-ECHF Bellezza Bianca
2005-2006. Eric Clapton and Hiroshi Fujiwara White Beauty model, Engleman spruce top, flamed Pacific big-leaf maple back and sides, model name logo on 20th fret, white finish, all-white case, 410 made. This and the Nera are examples of a 'collectible guitar' that is often found in near mint condition. High-end of price range shown is for near mint, nearly unplayed condition.

2005-2006		$2,250	$2,900

000-ECHF Bellezza Nera
2004-2005. Eric Clapton and Hiroshi Fujiwara Black Beauty Model, 476 made, Italian Alpine spruce top, Indian rosewood back and sides, black finish.

2004-2005		$3,000	$3,900

000-JBP Jimmy Buffett Pollywog
2003. Model name and number on label inside back, 168 made.

2003		$2,450	$3,200

000Jr-10
2019-present. Junior Series, sitka spruce top, sapele back and sides, satin finish.

2019-2020		$375	$500

000-M
1997-2009. Road Series, mahogany or sapele back and sides.

1997-2009		$550	$700

000-MMV Custom
2005-2018. Guitar Center model, spruce, rosewood, gloss finish.

2005-2018		$1,125	$1,450

000RS1
2014-2018. Road Series, made in Mexico, sapele top, back and sides, Fishman Sonitone electronics. Replaced by 000-10E in '19.

2014-2018		$425	$550

1997 Martin 000-45 JR Jimmie Rodgers
Carter Vintage Guitars

1990s Martin 000C-16

1930 Martin 1-17P

Bernunzio Uptown Music

1890s Martin 1-21

Imaged by Heritage Auctions, HA.com

MODEL YEAR	FEATURES	EXC. COND. LOW	EXC. COND. HIGH
000RS2			
2014-2015. Road Series as above with spruce top.			
2014-2015		$425	$550
000RS25 Navojoa 25th Anniversary			
2014-2016. Made in Mexico, celebrates 25th Anniversary of Martin's Navojoa facility, headstock Anniversary logo, sitka spruce top, sapele back and sides, East Indian rosewood 'board.			
2014-2016		$450	$600
000X Hippie			
2007. Limited Edition of 200, celebrates the 40th Anniversary of the 'Summer of Love'.			
2007		$1,125	$1,475
000X1			
2000-2010. Mahogany grained HPL (high pressure laminate) back and sides, solid spruce top.			
2000-2010		$300	$400
000X1 AE			
2010-2019. 000X1 with electronics. Replaced by 000-X2E in '20.			
2010-2019		$325	$425
000-X2 E			
2020-present. X Series, sitka spruce top, figured mahogany laminate back and sides, Fishman electronics.			
2020		$450	$575
000XE Black			
2002-2005. Black satin finish.			
2002-2005		$325	$425
000XM Auditorium			
1999-2002. Spruce top, Indian rosewood back and sides, natural finish.			
1999-2002		$325	$425
0000-1			
1997-2001. 0000-size, mahogany.			
1997-2001		$625	$800
0000-18 Custom/Custom 0000-18 (Gruhn 35th Anniversary)			
2005-2009. Commissioned for Gruhn Guitars 35th Anniversary, 1st year models have signed Anniversary labels, 16" lower bout, high X-brace, mahogany back and sides.			
2005-2009		$2,000	$2,600
0000-21 S Custom (Gruhn 45th Anniversary)			
2015. Commissioned for Gruhn Guitars 45th Anniversary, label signed by CF Martin IV and George Gruhn, Adirondack spruce top, Cocobolo or Guatemalan rosewood back and sides.			
2015		$4,600	$5,900
0000-28 Series			
1997-2011. Several models, jumbo-size 0000 cutaway body, models include; H (herringbone trim, sitka spruce top), Custom (Indian rosewood, sitka), H-AG (Arlo Guthrie 30th anniversary, Indian rosewood back and sides, only 30 made), HA (herringbone trim, Adirondack).			
1997-2000	0000-28 H	$1,700	$2,200
1998-2006	0000-28 Custom	$1,700	$2,200
1999	0000-28 H-AG	$2,150	$2,800
2011	0000-28 HA	$2,150	$2,800

MODEL YEAR	FEATURES	EXC. COND. LOW	EXC. COND. HIGH
0000-38 (M-38)			
1997-1998. Called M-38 in '77-'97 and '07-present (see that listing), 0000-size, Indian rosewood back and sides, multi-bound.			
1997-1998		$2,000	$2,600
1/4 - 28			
1973, 1979. 14 made.			
1973, 1979		$4,500	$6,000
1-17			
1906-1917 (1st version), 1931-1934 (2nd version). First version has spruce top, mahogany back and sides, second version has all mahogany with flat natural finish.			
1906-1917		$1,900	$2,450
1931-1934		$1,900	$2,450
1-17 P			
1928-1931, 1939. Mahogany back and sides, plectrum neck, 272 made.			
1928-1931		$1,150	$1,500
1939	5-string (special)	$1,150	$1,500
1-18			
1899-1903, 1906-1907, 1909-1921, 1923-1927. Brazilian rosewood or mahogany back and sides.			
1899-1917	Brazilian	$2,750	$3,550
1918-1921	Mahogany	$2,000	$2,550
1923-1927	Steel, 12-fret	$2,000	$2,550
1-18 H			
1918. Hawaiian, only 3 made.			
1918		$2,000	$2,550
1-18 K			
1917-1919. Koa.			
1917-1919		$3,300	$4,300
1-18 P			
1929. 5-string plectrum, 1 made.			
1929		$1,850	$2,400
1-18 T			
1927. Tenor 5-string, only 3 made.			
1927		$1,850	$2,400
1-20			
1860s. Parlor guitar, rosewood back and sides.			
1867		$3,800	$4,900
1-21			
1860s-1907, 1911, 1913-1921, 1925-1926. Initially offered in size 1 in the 1860s, ornate soundhole rings. A beautiful crack-free instrument is worth twice as much as a worn model with repaired cracks.			
1860s-1926		$3,800	$4,900
1-21 P			
1930. Plectrum.			
1930		$2,000	$2,600
1-22			
1850s. Antique market value.			
1850s		$5,400	$7,100
1-26			
1850s-1880s. Rosewood back and sides, ivory-bound top, rope-style purfling, antique market value.			
1850s-80s		$5,400	$7,100
1-27			
1880s-1907, 1911, 1913-1921, 1925-1926. Antique market value.			
1880-1926		$5,400	$7,100

MODEL YEAR	FEATURES	EXC. COND. LOW	HIGH
1-28			
1880s-1904, 1906-1907, 1909, 1911-1920, 1923. Style 28 appointments including Brazilian rosewood back and sides, antique market value.			
1880s-1923		$5,400	$7,100
1-28 P			
1928-1930. Plectrum.			
1928-1930		$2,500	$3,300
1-30			
1860s-1904, 1906-1907, 1911-1914, 1916-1917, 1919. Size 1 Style 30 with pearl soundhole trim, cedar neck, antique market value.			
1860s-1919		$6,000	$7,700
1-42			
1858-1919. Rosewood back and sides, ivory-bound top and 'board.			
1858-1919		$7,300	$9,500
1-45			
1904-1905, 1911-1913, 1919. Only 6 made, slotted headstock and Style 45 appointments.			
1904-1919		$15,000	$20,000
2-15			
1939-1964. All mahogany body, dot markers.			
1939-1964		$1,750	$2,300
2-17			
1910, 1922-1934, 1936-1938. 1910 version has spruce top, mahogany back and sides. '22 on, all mahogany body, no body binding after '30.			
1867	Gut	$2,300	$3,000
1910	Gut, 6 made	$1,800	$2,350
1922-1938	Steel	$2,500	$3,300
2-17 H			
1927-1929, 1931. Hawaiian, all mahogany, 12 frets clear of body.			
1927-1931		$2,500	$3,300
2-17 T			
1927-1928. Tenor, 45 made.			
1927-1928		$1,250	$1,650
2-18			
1857-1900, 1902-1903, 1907, 1925, 1929, 1934, 1938. Rosewood back and sides, changed to mahogany from 1917, dark outer binding, black back stripe, no dot inlay until 1902.			
1870s-80s		$2,600	$3,400
2-18 T			
1928-1930. Tenor.			
1928-1930		$1,250	$1,650
2-20			
1855-1897. Rare style only offered in size 2.			
1855-1897		$3,200	$4,200
2-21			
1850s-1900, 1903-1904, 1909, 1925, 1928-1929. Rosewood back and sides, herringbone soundhole ring.			
1885-1929		$2,600	$3,400
2-21 T			
1928. Tenor.			
1928		$1,300	$1,700
2-24			
1857-1898. Antique market value.			
1857-1898		$4,400	$5,700

MODEL YEAR	FEATURES	EXC. COND. LOW	HIGH
2-27			
1857-1880s, 1898-1900, 1907. Brazilian rosewood back and sides, pearl ring, zigzag back stripe, ivory bound ebony 'board and peghead.			
1857-1907		$5,300	$7,000
2-28			
Brazilian rosewood back and sides, slot head.			
1880		$5,300	$7,000
2-28 T			
1928-1929. Tenor neck, Brazilian rosewood back and sides, herringbone top purfling.			
1928-1929		$3,200	$4,300
2-30			
1874, 1902-1904, 1909-1910, 1921. Similar to 2-27, only 7 made.			
1874-1921		$5,300	$7,000
2-34			
1850s-1898. Similar to 2-30.			
1850s-1898		$5,700	$7,400
2-40			
1850s-1898, 1909.			
1850s-1898		$6,000	$7,800
2-42			
1858-1900.			
1874		$7,100	$9,500
2-44			
1930. Style 44, Olcott-Bickford Soloist custom order, only 4 made.			
1930		$11,700	$15,300
2-45 T			
1927-1928. Tenor style 45, 2 made.			
1927-1928		$7,000	$9,000
2 1/2-17			
1856-1897, 1909, 1911-1914. The first Style 17s were small size 2 1/2 and 3, these early models use Brazilian rosewood.			
1856-1897		$2,600	$3,400
1909-1914		$2,500	$3,300
2 1/2-18			
1865-1898, 1901, 1909-1914, 1916-1923. Parlor-size body with Style 18 appointments.			
1865-1898	Antique market value	$2,400	$3,200
1901-1917	Brazilian	$2,400	$3,200
1918-1923	Mahogany	$2,200	$2,900
2 1/2-21			
1880s, 1909, 1911-1913, 1917-1921. Brazilian rosewood back and sides.			
1880s-1921		$2,500	$3,300
2 1/2-42			
1880s, 1911. Style 42 size 2 1/2 with Brazilian rosewood. Only 1 made 1911.			
1880s-1911		$7,000	$9,400
3-17			
1856-1897, 1908 (1 made). The first Style 17s were small size 2 1/2 and 3. The early models use Brazilian rosewood, spruce top, bound back, unbound ebony 'board.			
1856-1870s	Brazilian	$2,200	$2,900
1880s-1897		$1,700	$2,200
1908	1 made	$1,700	$2,200

1917 Martin 1-28

1930 Martin 2-17

Imaged by Heritage Auctions, HA.com

1953 Martin 5-15T
Bernunzio Uptown Music

1929 Martin 5-17T
Craig Brody

MODEL YEAR	FEATURES	EXC. COND. LOW	HIGH
3-21			
1885. Brazilian rosewood.			
1885		$2,500	$3,300
3-24			
1860. Brazilian rosewood.			
1860		$4,300	$5,600
3-34			
1860. Brazilian rosewood.			
1860		$5,600	$7,300
5-15			
2003-2007. Sapele or mahogany body, shorter scale.			
2003-2007		$900	$1,175
5-15 T			
1949-1963. Tenor neck, all mahogany, non-gloss finish.			
1927-1930		$1,100	$1,475
1949-1963		$850	$1,150
5-16			
1962-1963. Mahogany back and sides, unbound rosewood 'board.			
1962-1963		$1,600	$2,100
5-17			
1912-1914, 1916, 1927-1928, 1930-1931, 1933-1943. Special order 1912-'36, standard production '37-'43.			
1912-1916		$1,600	$2,100
1927-1928		$2,000	$2,600
1930-1939		$2,000	$2,600
1940-1943		$1,800	$2,400
5-17 T			
1949-1958. Tenor neck, all mahogany.			
1949-1958		$1,150	$1,525
5-18			
1898-1899, 1912-1914, 1917, 1919-1921, 1923-1924, 1926-1932, 1934-1937, 1940-1941, 1943-1962, 1965, 1968-1977, 1979-1981, 1983-1989. Rosewood back and sides (changed to mahogany from 1917 on), 12 frets, slotted headstock.			
1898-1917		$2,500	$3,300
1919-1921	Gut	$1,800	$2,400
1923-1937	Steel	$3,300	$4,400
1940-1949		$3,200	$4,200
1950-1959		$2,650	$3,500
1960-1962		$2,200	$2,900
1965		$2,000	$2,600
1966-1969		$1,700	$2,200
1970-1979		$1,450	$1,850
1980-1989		$1,250	$1,650
5-18 Marty Robbins			
2009-2011. Custom Edition, 12-fret, Adirondack top, mahogany back and sides.			
2009-2011		$1,500	$2,000
5-18 T			
1940, 1954, 1960-1961. Tenor, only 1 made each year.			
1940		$1,200	$1,600
1954		$1,025	$1,350
1960-1961		$875	$1,150
5-21			
1890s, 1902, 1912-1914, 1916-1920, 1927, 1977. Rosewood back and sides.			
1890s-1977		$2,500	$3,300

MODEL YEAR	FEATURES	EXC. COND. LOW	HIGH
5-21 T			
1927-1928. Tenor guitar with 21-styling.			
1927-1928		$1,300	$1,700
5-28			
1901-1902, 1904, 1918, 1920-1921, 1923, 1935, 1939, 1969-1970, 1977, 1980-1981, 1988, 2001-2002. Special edition, 1/2-size parlor guitar, rosewood back and sides.			
1901-1923	Gut	$2,600	$3,400
1935-1939	Steel	$4,500	$5,900
1969-1970	Brazilian	$2,800	$3,800
1977	Indian	$2,100	$2,800
1980-1981		$1,800	$2,400
2001-2002		$1,750	$2,250
7-28			
1980-1995, 1997-2002. 7/8-body-size of a D-model, Style 28 appointments.			
1980-2002		$1,575	$2,100
7-37 K			
1980-1987. 7/8-size baby dreadnought acoustic, koa back and sides, spruce top, oval soundhole.			
1980-1987		$1,600	$2,200
Alternative II Resophonic			
2004-2007. Textured aluminum top, matching headstock overlay, high pressure laminate sides and back, spun aluminum cone resonator, Fishman pickup.			
2004-2007		$550	$725
Alternative X			
2001-2013. OO-Grand Concert body shape, textured aluminum top, matching headstock overlay, spun aluminum cone resonator, Fishman pickup.			
2001-2013		$550	$725
Alternative X Midi			
2003-2004. Roland GK Midi pickup with 13-pin output, additional Fishman Prefix Pro pickup and preamp system, requires Roland GA-20 interface.			
2003-2004		$575	$775
Alternative XT			
2002-2005. Alternative with DiMarzio humbucker, volume & tone controls, coil tap, Bigsby.			
2003-2005		$550	$725
America's Guitar 175th Anniversary			
2008. D-style, 14-fret, Adirondack spruce top, Madagascar rosewood sides and back, 175 made, 'America's Guitar' headstock inlay, '175th Anniversary 1833-2008'.			
2008		$4,000	$5,200
ASD-41 Australian Series			
2005. Tasmanian Blackwood sides and back, Sitka spruce top, Australian theme appointments and label.			
2005		$2,800	$3,700
Backpacker			
1992-present. Small-bodied travel guitar, nylon called Classic Backpacker.			
1992-2019	Steel strings	$105	$140
1994-2019	Nylon strings	$105	$140
Backpacker 25th Anniversary			
2017 only. Sapele.			
2017		$150	$195

MODEL YEAR	FEATURES	EXC. COND. LOW	HIGH

C-1

1931-1942. Acoustic archtop, mahogany back and sides, spruce top, round hole until '33 (449 made), f-holes appear in '32 (786 made), bound body, sunburst.

| 1931-1933 | Round hole | $2,100 | $2,700 |
| 1932-1942 | F-hole | $2,000 | $2,600 |

C-1 P

1931-1933, 1939. Archtop, plectrum.

| 1931-1933 | Round hole | $1,400 | $1,900 |
| 1939 | F-hole | $1,400 | $1,900 |

C-1 R Humphrey

1997-2000. Solid cedar top, laminated rosewood back and sides, satin finish.

| 1997-2000 | | $750 | $1,000 |

C-1 T

1931-1934, 1936-1938. Archtop, tenor, round hole (71 made) or f-hole (83 made).

| 1931-1933 | Round hole | $1,400 | $1,900 |
| 1933-1938 | F-hole | $1,300 | $1,700 |

C-1-12

1932. Only 1 made, 12-string version.

| 1932 | | $2,000 | $2,600 |

C-2

1931-1942. Acoustic archtop, Brazilian rosewood back and sides, carved spruce top, round hole until '33 (269 made), f-holes appear in '32 (439 made), zig-zag back stripe, multi-bound body, slotted-diamond inlay, sunburst.

1931-1933	Round hole	$2,900	$3,800
1932-1942	F-hole	$2,300	$3,000
1939	Maple	$2,300	$3,000

C-2 P

1931. Archtop, plectrum, round hole, 2 made.

| 1931 | | $2,100 | $2,800 |

C-2 T

1931-1936. Archtop, tenor, round or f-hole.

| 1931-1934 | Round hole | $2,000 | $2,700 |
| 1934-1936 | F-hole | $1,500 | $2,000 |

C-2-12

1932. Only 1 made, 12-string version.

| 1932 | | $2,500 | $3,300 |

C-3

1931-1934. Archtop, Brazilian rosewood back and sides, round soundhole until early '33 (53 made), f-holes after (58 made).

| 1931-1933 | Round hole | $4,300 | $5,700 |
| 1933-1934 | F-hole | $3,400 | $4,500 |

C-3 T

1933. Archtop, tenor, 1 made.

| 1933 | | $3,100 | $4,100 |

Car Talk Special Edition

2008-2010. D-size, East Indian rosewood back and sides, car parts and tools inlay, Car Talk credits on 'guard.

| 2008-2010 | | $2,950 | $3,800 |

CEO Series

1997-present. Chief Executive Officer (C.F. Martin IV), Special Edition (CEO-1 through CEO-6) and Custom Signature Edition (CEO-7 through CEO-9), various woods and specs. CEO-1/1R ('97-'98), 2 ('98), 3 ('99-'00), 4 ('01-'04), 4R ('02-'10), 5 ('01-'04), 6 ('11-'13),

7 ('15-present), 8 ('15-'17), 8.2/E ('17-'18), 9 ('19-present).

1997-2013	CEO-1 to CEO-6	$1,575	$2,050
2015-2017	CEO-8, Sig Ed	$3,500	$4,500
2015-2019	CEO-7, Sig Ed	$1,575	$2,050
2017-2018	CEO-82, Sig Ed	$1,850	$2,400
2017-2018	CEO-82E, Sig Ed	$2,000	$2,600

CF-1 American Archtop

2004-2009. 17", solid maple sides, laminated maple back, ebony 'board, dot markers, 1 pickup, sunburst, natural or black.

| 2004-2009 | | $2,100 | $2,700 |

CF-2 American Archtop

2004-2009. CF-1 with 2 humbuckers, sunburst, natural or black.

| 2004-2009 | | $2,200 | $2,800 |

Claire's Guitar

2005-2006. Made to celebrate the birth of Claire Frances Martin, limited to 100, small parlor size, sitka spruce top, Brazilian rosewood back and sides, fancy appointments, comes with pink-lined hard case.

| 2005-2006 | | $3,400 | $4,400 |

Concept III

2003. U.S.-made, solid spruce top, solid mahogany back and sides, cutaway, on-board electronics, sparkle-mist finish.

| 2003 | | $1,275 | $1,650 |

Cowboy 2015 Limited Edition/LE Cowboy 2015

2015. Limited to number sold in '15, 000, 12-fret, sitka spruce top, solid Goncalo Alves back and sides, cowboy on horse artwork by William Matthews.

| 2015 | | $2,200 | $2,850 |

Cowboy 2016 Limited Edition/LE Cowboy 2016

2016. Limited to number sold in '16, auditorium, 12-fret, sitka spruce top, mahogany back and sides, cowboy on bucking bronco artwork by William Matthews.

| 2016 | | $2,200 | $2,850 |

Cowboy Series

2000-2009. Models include Cowboy X (2000, 250 made), Cowboy II ('01, 500 made), Cowboy III ('03, 750 made), and Cowboy IV ('05-'06, 250 made), Cowboy V ('06-'09, 500 made).

| 2001-2009 | Various models | $500 | $1,000 |

CS-21-11

2011. Limited Edition, 171 made, Madagascar rosewood.

| 2011 | | $2,850 | $3,700 |

CS-Bluegrass-16

2016-present. Limited to 100, Adirondack spruce top, Guatemalan rosewood back and sides, vintage gloss finish.

| 2016-2019 | | $3,900 | $5,100 |

CS-CF Martin Outlaw-17

2017-present. Limited to 100 made, Adirondack spruce top, mahogany back and sides, natural gloss finish.

| 2017-2019 | | $3,600 | $4,800 |

1950 Martin 5-18
David Stone

Martin Backpacker

GUITARS

1993 Martin D-1
Imaged by Heritage Auctions, HA.com

Martin D-15 M

MODEL YEAR	FEATURES	EXC. COND. LOW	HIGH

CSN (Gerry Tolman Tribute)
2007-2009. CSN logo on headstock, D-style, high-end appointments, East Indian rosewood back and sides. Tolman was CSN's longtime manager and was killed in car wreck in '06.

2007-2009		$1,950	$2,500

C-TSH (Humphrey/Martin)
1997-2002. Designed by classical guitar luthier Thomas Humphrey, based on his Millenium model, arched Englemann spruce top, rosewood back and sides.

1997-2002		$1,750	$2,275

Custom 15
1991-1994. Renamed HD-28V Custom 15 in ca. 2001.

1991-1994		$1,950	$2,525

Custom D Classic Mahogany
2006-2014. D body, spruce top, mahogany back and sides.

2006-2014		$625	$800

Custom D Classic Rosewood
2006-2011. D body, spruce top, rosewood back and sides.

2006-2011		$625	$800

Custom Shop 18 Style 0000
2019. Adirondack, Sinker mahogany back and sides. 12-fret Sinker is old growth from 1900-1920.

2019	12-fret	$2,500	$3,200
2019	14-fret	$2,100	$2,800

Custom Shop 18 Style Dreadnought
2019. Adirondack, Sinker mahogany back and sides.

2019		$2,150	$2,850

D-1 (D-18)
1931. Name first used for the prototype of the D-18, made in 1931.

1931		$61,000	$80,000

D-1
1992-2005, 2009. Current model with mahogany body, A-frame bracing, available as an acoustic/electric.

1992-2005		$650	$825
2009	Reintroduced	$650	$825

D12-1
1996-2001. Mahogany, satin finish, 12-string.

1996-2001		$650	$825

D-1 Authentic 1931
2016-2019. Adirondack spruce top, dark mahogany back and sides, Vintage Gloss finish.

2016-2019		$3,200	$4,200

D-1 E
1994-1998, 2009. Acoustic/electric version, current model solid sitka with sapele.

1994-1998		$700	$900
2009		$700	$900

D-1 GT
2011-2014. Double bound body, gloss finish top, satin back and sides.

2011-2014		$650	$825

D-1 R
1994-2003, 2012. D-1 with laminated rosewood back and sides.

1994-2003		$650	$825
2012	Reintroduced	$650	$825

D-1 RE
1994-1995, 1998. D-1R with various electronics.

1994-1998		$700	$900

D-2
1931-1932, 1934. Earliest version of the D-28, Brazilian rosewood.

1931-1934		$186,000	$240,000

D-2 R
1996-2002. Style 28 appointments, laminated rosewood back and sides, natural satin finish.

1996-2002		$650	$825

D-3 R
1996-2002. Style 35 appointments, laminated rosewood back and sides, natural satin finish.

1996-2002		$700	$900

D-3-18
1991. Sitka spruce top, 3-piece mahogany back, 80-piece limited edition.

1991		$1,300	$1,675

D-10 E
2019-present. Road Series, updated version of DSR1/DSR2, sitka spruce or sapele top, sapele back and sides, Fishman electronics, satin finish.

2019-2020		$425	$550

D-11 E

2019		$550	$725

D-12 E
2019-present. Sitka spruce top, sapele back and sides, Fishman.

2019		$600	$800

D-12 E Koa
2020. Sitka spruce top, koa veneer back and sides, gloss finish.

2020		$900	$1,150

D12 David Crosby
2009-2011. D-size 12-string, quilted mahogany body, Carpathian spruce top.

2009-2011		$2,700	$3,500

D-13 E
2019-present. Updated version of DRSG, sitka spruce top, siris back and sides, Fishman.

2019		$625	$825

D-15/D-15 M
1997-present. Body is all mahogany up to 2002, mahogany or sapele (which is like mahogany) up to '10. Becomes the all-mahogany D-15M in '11.

1997-2010		$725	$950
2011-2019	M	$725	$950

D-15 M Burst
2015-2018. Shaded mahogany top, back and sides, satin finish.

2015-2018		$775	$1,000

D-15 M Elderly Instruments 40th Anniversary
2012. Only 10 made, solid mahogany body, special appointments, label signed by Elderly president Stan Werbin and Chris Martin.

2012		$825	$1,100

D-15 M StreetMaster
2017-present. Distressed mahogany satin finish.

2017-2019		$825	$1,100

MODEL YEAR	FEATURES	EXC. COND. LOW	HIGH

D-15 S
2001-2009. Slotted headstock D-15, body is solid sapele or mahogany.

| 2001-2009 | | $725 | $950 |

D-16 A
1987-1990. North American ash back and sides, scalloped bracing.

| 1987-1990 | | $1,050 | $1,375 |

D-16 Adirondack
2009-2013. Adirondack spruce top, mahogany back and sides.

| 2009-2013 | | $1,325 | $1,725 |

D-16 E
2017-present. Gloss sitka spruce top, satin sycamore back and sides, Fishman electronics.

| 2017-2019 | | $1,150 | $1,500 |
| 2020 | | $1,125 | $1,475 |

D-16 E Burst
2019-present. Mahogany burst ovangkol gloss top, satin ovangkol back and sides, Fishman electronics.

| 2019-2020 | | $1,300 | $1,725 |

D-16 E Rock The Vote
2019-present. Special Edition, designed by David Crosby, custom artwork by Robert F. Goetzl, sitka spruce gloss top, satin sycamore back and sides, Fishman electronics.

| 2019-2020 | | $1,500 | $2,000 |

D-16 E Rosewood
2019-present. Gloss sitka spruce top, satin East Indian rosewood back and sides, Fishman electronics.

| 2019-2020 | | $1,225 | $1,575 |

D-16 GT
1999-2019. D-16 with gloss top.

| 1999-2019 | | $775 | $1,025 |

D-16 GTE
1999-2015. D-16 GT with Fishman electronics.

| 1999-2015 | | $850 | $1,100 |

D-16 H (1991, 1992, 1993)
1990-1994. D-16 with herringbone soundhole ring, replaced by D-16 T in '94.

| 1990-1994 | | $850 | $1,100 |

D-16 K
1986. Koa D-16.

| 1986 | | $1,100 | $1,450 |

D-16 Lyptus
2003-2005. Lyptus back and sides.

| 2003-2005 | | $900 | $1,200 |

D-16 M Mahogany
1986-1990. Mahogany back and sides.

| 1986-1990 | | $900 | $1,200 |

D-16 O Oak
1999. Red oak or white oak, 4 made.

| 1999 | | $900 | $1,200 |

D-16 R/D-16 TR/D-16 TRG
1995-2009. Spruce top, Indian rosewood back and sides, satin finish (R) or gloss (TRG).

| 1995-2009 | | $775 | $1,025 |

D-16 RGT
1999-2019. D-16 T specs with rosewood back and sides, gloss finish.

| 1999-2019 | | $775 | $1,025 |

D-16 RGT Ryman Auditorium
2007. Custom designed by George Gruhn, oak 'guard, headplate and fret markers made from original Ryman Auditorium pews, laser-etched image of Ryman on headplate, spruce top, Indian rosewood back and sides, special Ryman label.

| 2007 | | $2,025 | $2,600 |

D-16 T/D-16 TG
1994-1998. Mahogany back and sides, satin finish or gloss (TG).

| 1994-1998 | | $775 | $1,025 |

D-16 W Walnut
1987, 1990. Walnut back and sides.

| 1987, 1990 | | $775 | $1,025 |

D-17
2001-2005. All solid mahogany back, sides and top, natural brown mahogany finish.

| 2001-2005 | | $775 | $1,025 |

D-17 E
2002-2003. With on-board electronics.

| 2002-2003 | | $775 | $1,025 |

D-17 M
2013-2016. Shaded spruce top, solid mahogany back and sides.

| 2013-2016 | | $775 | $1,025 |

D-18
1931-present. Standard Series, mahogany back and sides, spruce top, black back stripe, 12-fret neck, changed to 14 frets in '34.

1931-1934	12-fret	$51,000	$66,000
1934	14-fret, dark top	$45,000	$59,000
1934-1937	14-fret	$45,000	$59,000
1938	Early '38, Advanced X	$40,000	$52,000
1938	Late '38, Rear X	$30,000	$40,000
1939	Early '39, 175 neck	$27,000	$35,000
1939	Late '39, 168 neck	$25,000	$33,000
1940-1941		$20,400	$26,500
1942-1944	Scalloped	$18,500	$24,000
1944-1945	Non-scalloped	$13,400	$17,500
1946-1947		$9,300	$12,000
1948-1949		$7,000	$9,000
1950-1953		$5,300	$6,900
1954-1959		$5,000	$6,600
1960-1964		$3,700	$4,900
1965		$3,375	$4,400
1966-1969		$2,850	$3,700
1970-1979		$2,100	$2,700
1980-1989		$1,700	$2,200
1983	50th Ann 1833-1983	$1,700	$2,200
1990-1999		$1,700	$2,200
2000-2019		$1,475	$1,900

D12-18
1973-1995. Mahogany back and sides, 12 strings, 14 frets clear of body, solid headstock.

1973-1979		$1,325	$1,700
1980-1989		$1,125	$1,450
1990-1995		$1,125	$1,450

1988 Martin D-16
Bernunzio Uptown Music

1952 Martin D-18
Ian Gilmour

2002 Martin D-18 DC
David Crosby
Imaged by Heritage Auctions, HA.com

1972 Martin D-28
Bernunzio Uptown Music

MODEL YEAR	FEATURES	EXC. COND. LOW	HIGH

CS-D18-12
2012. Custom Shop, based on 1929 Ditson 111 (12-string), 75 made, 12-fret mahogany neck, Adirondack spruce top, Madagascar rosewood binding.
| 2012 | | $3,200 | $4,200 |

D-18 1955 CFM IV
2010. Celebrates C. F. Martin IV birthday, 55 made.
| 2010 | | $2,600 | $3,400 |

D-18 75th Anniversary Edition
2009. '75th Anniversary Edition 1934-2009' noted on label and headstock stencil.
| 2009 | | $2,300 | $3,000 |

D-18 Andy Griffith
2003. Bear claw spruce top, Andy's script signature on 18th fret.
| 2003 | | $1,950 | $2,500 |

D-18 Authentic 1937
2006-2012. Authentic pre-war specs, Adirondack spruce, forward X-brace and scalloped Adirondack bracing, 14-fret neck.
| 2006-2012 | | $3,800 | $4,900 |

D-18 Authentic 1939
2013-present. Adirondack spruce top, mahogany back, sides and neck, ebony 'board, vintage gloss finish.
| 2013-2020 | | $3,800 | $4,900 |
| 2019-2020 | VTS Aged | $3,850 | $5,050 |

D-18 Custom Adirondack
2016. Adirondack spruce top, mahogany back and sides.
| 2016 | | $2,200 | $2,900 |

D-18 CW Clarence White Commemorative Edition
2001. Rare Appalachian spruce top, 2-piece quilted mahogany back and sides, Clarence White's signature between 19th - 20th frets, aged gloss lacquer finish.
| 2001 | | $2,300 | $2,950 |

D-18 D
1975. Frap pickup.
| 1975 | | $1,600 | $2,100 |

D-18 DC David Crosby
2002. David Crosby signature at 20th fret, Engelmann spruce top, quilted mahogany back and sides, 250 made.
| 2002 | | $2,100 | $2,750 |

D-18 Del McCourey 50th Anniversary
2008. Adirondack spruce top, mahogany sides and back, interior label signed by Del McCourey, 50 made.
| 2008 | | $2,400 | $3,150 |

D-18 E
1958-1959. D-18 factory built with DeArmond pickups which required ladder bracing (reducing acoustic volume and quality).
| 1958-1959 | | $4,400 | $5,700 |

D-18 E 2020
2020. Limited Edition, 2,020 offered, sitka spruce top, mahogany back and sides, electronics, gloss finish.
| 2020 | | $2,000 | $2,600 |

D-18 E Modern Deluxe
2020-present. With Fishman electronics.
| 2020 | | $2,800 | $3,600 |

D-18 E Retro
2012-2019. Sitka spruce top, mahogany back and sides.
| 2012-2019 | | $1,525 | $2,000 |

D-18 GE Golden Era
1995, 2000-2016. 1995 version is a copy of a '37 D-18, 272 made. The current model is based on '34 model. Natural or sunburst.
1995		$2,200	$2,850
2000-2016	Natural	$2,200	$2,850
2000-2016	Sunburst	$2,200	$2,850

D-18 Golden Era Special Edition 1934
1999-2012. Specs from '34 D-18, red Adirondack spruce top, mahogany back and sides, aged finish.
| 1999-2012 | | $2,200 | $2,850 |

D-18 H
1934-1935. Hawaiian.
| 1934-1935 | | $46,000 | $60,000 |

D-18 H Huda
1966. Huda wood, Hawaiian, 2 made.
| 1966 | | $2,850 | $3,700 |

D-18 LE
1986-1987. Limited Edition, quilted or flamed mahogany back and sides, scalloped braces, gold tuners with ebony buttons.
| 1986-1987 | | $1,700 | $2,200 |

D-18 MB
1990. Limited Edition Guitar of the Month, flame maple binding, Engelmann spruce top signed by shop foremen, X-brace, total of 99 sold.
| 1990 | | $1,700 | $2,200 |

D-18 Modern Deluxe
2019-present. Sitka spruce top with Vintage Tone System (VTS), mahogany back and sides, gloss finish.
| 2019 | | $1,700 | $2,200 |

D-18 P
2010-2011. Fishman electronics.
| 2010-2011 | | $1,525 | $1,950 |

D-18 S
1967-1994. Mahogany back and sides, 12-fret neck, slotted headstock, majority of production before '77, infrequent after that.
1967-1969		$3,300	$4,250
1970-1979		$2,300	$3,000
1980-1989		$1,950	$2,525
1990-1994		$1,950	$2,525

D-18 Special
1989. Guitar of the Month, 28 made, first Martin to use rosewood for binding, heel cap and endpiece since 1932, scalloped top, mahogany back and sides, slotted-diamond markers.
| 1989 | | $1,850 | $2,450 |

D-18 SS
2009-2012. 24.9" short scale.
| 2009 | | $1,500 | $2,000 |

D-18 V/D-18 Vintage
1985 (V), 1992 (Vintage). Low-profile neck, scalloped braces, bound, total of 218 sold, Guitar of the Month in '85, Vintage Series in '92.
| 1985 | V | $1,850 | $2,450 |
| 1992 | Vintage | $1,850 | $2,450 |

MODEL YEAR	FEATURES	EXC. COND. LOW	HIGH
D-18 VE			
2004-2007. D-18 V with Fishman Ellipse.			
2004-2007		$1,850	$2,375
D-18 VM/D-18 V/D-18 VO			
1995-2011. Vintage Series, 14-fret, mahogany (M) back and sides, tortoise binding, V-neck. M dropped from name in '99. Natural finish. 48 sunburst (D-18 VO) made in '95.			
1995	D-18VO	$1,750	$2,250
1995-1998	D-18VM	$1,750	$2,250
1999-2011	D-18V	$1,750	$2,250
D-18 VMS/D-18 VS			
1996-2011. Vintage Series, 12-fret version of D-18 VM/V, M dropped from name in '99.			
1996-1999	D-18VS	$1,750	$2,250
1999-2011	D-18VMS	$1,750	$2,250
D-19			
1977-1988. Deluxe mahogany dreadnought, optional mahogany top, multi-bound but unbound rosewood 'board.			
1977-1979		$1,700	$2,200
1980-1988		$1,450	$1,900
D12-20			
1964-1991. Mahogany back and sides, 12 strings, 12 frets clear of body, slotted headstock.			
1964-1969		$1,500	$1,950
1970-1979		$1,275	$1,650
1980-1991		$1,075	$1,400
D-21			
1955-1969. Brazilian rosewood back and sides, rosewood 'board, chrome tuners.			
1955-1959		$6,275	$8,400
1960-1964		$5,700	$7,700
1965		$5,100	$6,700
1966-1969		$4,700	$6,300
D-21 JC Jim Croce			
1999-2000. Jim Croce signature and 1973 dime inlaid on neck, Indian rosewood back and sides, 73 made.			
1999-2000		$3,200	$4,200
D-21 JCB Jim Croce			
1999-2001. Same as above but with Brazilian rosewood back and sides.			
1999-2001		$6,400	$8,300
D-21 LE			
1985. Limited Edition, 75 made.			
1985		$1,650	$2,150
D-21 Special/D-21 S			
2008-present. Indian rosewood back and sides, herringbone soundhole.			
2008-2019		$1,600	$2,075
D-25 K			
1980-1989. Dreadnought-size, koa back and sides, spruce top.			
1980-1989		$1,725	$2,250
D-25 K2			
1980-1989. Same as D-25K, but with koa top and black 'guard.			
1980-1989		$1,725	$2,250

MODEL YEAR	FEATURES	EXC. COND. LOW	HIGH
D-28			
1931-present. Brazilian rosewood back and sides (changed to Indian rosewood in '70), '36 was the last year for the 12-fret model, '44 was the last year for scalloped bracing, '47 was the last year herringbone trim was offered, natural. Ultra high-end D-28 Martin guitar (pre-'47) valuations are very sensitive to structural and cosmetic condition. Finish wear and body cracks for ultra high-end Martin flat-tops should be evaluated on a case-by-case basis. Small variances within the 'excellent condition' category can lead to notable valuation differences.			
1931-1935	12-fret	$163,000	$215,000
1934-1937	14-fret	$95,000	$125,000
1938	Early '38, Advanced X	$95,000	$125,000
1938	Late '38, Rear X	$90,000	$120,000
1939	Early '39, 175 neck	$89,000	$118,000
1939	Late '39, 168 neck	$78,000	$102,000
1940-1941		$57,000	$74,000
1942	Scalloped	$47,000	$61,000
1943	Scalloped	$43,000	$56,000
1944	Scalloped, herringbone	$38,000	$50,000
1944-1946	Herringbone, non-scalloped	$22,500	$29,000
1947	Early '47, herringbone, non-scalloped	$22,500	$29,000
1947-1949	Late '47, non-herringbone	$10,600	$14,000
1950-1952		$9,000	$11,700
1953	Klusons	$9,000	$11,700
1954-1958		$8,500	$11,100
1959	Grover	$8,500	$11,100
1960-1961		$6,400	$8,500
1962		$6,400	$8,500
1963-1964		$6,400	$8,500
1965		$5,300	$6,900
1966-1968		$4,700	$6,100
1969	Brazilian	$4,700	$6,100
1970-1979	Indian	$2,400	$3,200
1980-1989		$1,600	$2,100
1990-1999		$1,600	$2,100
2000-2017	Early '17, Standard X	$1,600	$2,100
2017-2019	Late '17, Forward X	$1,600	$2,100
D12-28			
1970-2018. Indian rosewood back and sides, 12 strings, 14 frets clear of body, solid headstock.			
1970-1979		$1,700	$2,200
1980-1989		$1,550	$2,000
1990-1999		$1,550	$2,000
2000-2019		$1,550	$2,000
D-28 1935 Special			
1993. Guitar of the Month, 1935 features, Indian rosewood back and sides, peghead with Brazilian rosewood veneer.			
1993		$2,100	$2,750

1952 Martin D-28
Bernunzio Uptown Music

Martin D12-28

GUITARS

1998 Martin D-28 LF Lester Flatt

1974 Martin D12-35

Peter Van Wagner

MODEL YEAR	FEATURES	EXC. COND. LOW	HIGH
D-28 1955 CFM IV			
2009-2010. Limited Edition, 55 made celebrating Chris Martin IV birthyear 1955, Madagascar rosewood.			
2009-2010		$3,200	$4,200
D-28 50th Anniversary			
1983. Stamped inside '1833-1983 150th Anniversary', Indian rosewood back and sides.			
1983		$1,650	$2,150
D-28 75th Anniversary			
2009 only. Limited production celebrating 1934 to 2009, Madagascar rosewood back and sides, Adirondack spruce top.			
2009		$3,700	$4,800
D-28 75th Anniversary Brazilian			
1983. Brazilian rosewood back and sides.			
1983		$4,900	$6,400
D-28 150th Anniversary			
1983-1985. Limited production of 268, only '83 vintage have the anniversary stamp, Brazilian rosewood sides and back.			
1983	150th stamp	$4,900	$6,400
1984-1985	No stamp	$4,900	$6,400
D-28 Authentic 1931			
2013-2015. Adirondack spruce top, Madagascar rosewood back and sides, authentic '31 appointments, vintage gloss finish.			
2013-2015		$3,950	$5,150
D-28 Authentic 1937			
2007-2009, 2014-present. '37 specs, 50 made of first Brazilian rosewood batch. Reintroduced '14 with Madagascar rosewood and Vintage Tone System (VTS).			
2007-2009	Brazilian	$12,500	$16,000
2014-2019	Madagascar	$4,300	$5,700
2020	VTS aged	$4,300	$5,700
D-28 Authentic 1941			
2013-2016. Adirondack, Madagascar rosewood.			
2013-2016		$4,300	$5,700
D-28 Custom			
1984. Guitar of the Month Nov. '84, double bound D-body, multi-ring rosette, rosewood back/sides, spruce top, 43 made.			
1984		$2,400	$3,100
D-28 CW/CWB Clarence White			
2003-2014. CW has Indian rosewood back and sides, the CWB Brazilian, only 150 CWBs were to be built.			
2003-2004	CWB	$5,600	$7,200
2003-2014	CW	$2,800	$3,600
D-28 D			
1975. Frap pickup.			
1975		$2,100	$2,700
D-28 Dan Tyminski			
2010-2013. Custom Artist limited edition, Indian rosewood back and sides, Adirondack spruce top, other bracing specs.			
2010-2013		$2,200	$2,900
D-28 DM Del McCourey Signature			
2003. Limited edition of 115, natural.			
2003		$2,300	$3,000

MODEL YEAR	FEATURES	EXC. COND. LOW	HIGH
D-28 E			
1959-1964. Electronics, Brazilian rosewood back and sides, 2 DeArmond pickups, natural.			
1959-1964		$5,200	$6,800
D-28 E Modern Deluxe			
2020-present. Sitka spruce VTS aged top, East Indian rosewood back and sides, Fishman electronics, gloss finish.			
2020		$3,200	$4,150
D-28 Elvis Presley			
2008-2010. Carpathian spruce top, East Indian rosewood back and sides.			
2008-2010		$3,000	$3,900
D-28 Elvis Presley CVR			
2008-2010. Carpathian spruce top, East Indian rosewood back and sides, tooled leather cover.			
2008-2010		$3,800	$4,900
D-28 M Elvis Presley			
2008-2010. Limited Edition, 175 made, Madagascar rosewood back and sides, Adirondack top, tooled leather cover.			
2008-2010		$4,900	$6,400
D-28 GE Golden Era			
1999-2005. GE Golden Era, Brazilian rosewood, herringbone trim.			
1999-2005		$6,000	$7,800
D-28 HW Hank Williams			
1998. Limited Edition, 150 made, replica of Hank Williams' 1944 D-28, Brazilian rosewood sides and back, scalloped braces, herringbone.			
1998		$5,500	$7,000
D-28 John Lennon			
2017-2018. Sitka spruce top with Vintage Tone System, East Indian rosewood back and sides, back inlaid with a peace sign, Lennon's self-portrait illustration beneath Martin logo on headstock.			
2017-2018		$2,400	$3,100
D-28 John Lennon 75th Anniversary			
2016. Limited Edition to commemorate Lennon's 75th birthday, 75 made, Adirondack spruce top, Madagascar rosewood back and sides, headplate includes Lennon's famous self-portrait illustration.			
2016		$6,000	$8,000
D-28 John Prine			
2017-present. Only 70 offered, Engelmann spruce top, Madagascar rosewood back and sides, inlaid pearl angel wings on headstock.			
2017-2019		$3,200	$4,200
D-28 KTBS Bob Shane			
2003. Bob Shane of the Kingston Trio, Signature Edition with 51 offered, sitka spruce top, East Indian rosewood back and sides, The Kingston Trio logo between 11th-13th frets, Shane's pearl signature 19th-20th frets.			
2003		$2,700	$3,500
D-28 LF Lester Flatt			
1998. Limited Edition, 50 made, Brazilian rosewood.			
1998		$5,500	$7,000

MODEL YEAR	FEATURES	EXC. COND. LOW	HIGH

D-28 Louvin Brothers
2015-present. Limited run of 50, sitka spruce top, East Indian rosewood back and sides, printed Louvin Brothers artwork from "Satan is Real" album.

2015-2019		$2,100	$2,700

D-28 LSH
1991. Guitar of the Month, Indian rosewood back and sides, herringbone trim, snowflake inlay, zigzag back stripe.

1991		$2,200	$2,850

D-28 LSV
1999-2005. Large soundhole model.

1999-2005		$1,900	$2,450

D-28 M Merle Travis
2008-2010. 100 made, Adirondack top, Madagascar rosewood back and sides, curly maple neck, 6-on-a-side Bigsby-style headstock, heart-diamond-spade-club inlays.

2008-2010		$3,600	$4,700

D-28 M The Mamas and The Papas
2012-2014. 100 made, Madagascar rosewood back and sides.

2012-2014		$2,100	$2,750

D-28 Marquis
2004-2017. Golden Era appointments, Adirondack top, Indian rosewood, natural or sunburst.

2004-2017	Natural	$2,375	$3,100
2004-2017	Sunburst	$2,375	$3,100
2007-2009	Madagascar option	$2,375	$3,100

D-28 Modern Deluxe
2019-present. Sitka spruce top with Vintage Tone System (VTS), East Indian rosewood back and sides, gloss finish.

2019		$2,300	$3,000

D-28 P
1988-1990, 2011-2012. P indicates low-profile neck, Indian rosewood back and sides. Reintroduced 2011 with high performance neck.

1988-1990		$1,550	$2,000
2011-2012		$1,550	$2,000

D-28 S
1954-1994. Rosewood back and sides, 12-fret neck.

1954-1959	Special order	$9,000	$11,500
1960-1964	Special order	$7,000	$9,000
1965	Special order	$6,300	$7,900
1966-1969	Brazilian	$5,700	$7,300
1970-1979	Indian	$2,300	$3,000
1980-1989		$1,800	$2,350
1990-1994		$1,800	$2,350

D-28 SW Wurlitzer
1962-1965, 1968. Made for the Wurlitzer Co.

1962-1964		$7,000	$9,000
1965		$6,300	$7,900
1968		$5,700	$7,300

D-28 V
1983-1985. Limited Edition, Brazilian rosewood back and sides, herringbone trim, slotted diamond inlay.

1983-1985		$4,900	$6,400

D-35
1965-present. Brazilian rosewood sides and 3-piece back, changed to Brazilian wings and Indian center in '70, then all Indian rosewood in '71, natural with sunburst option. For a brief time, on the back side, the center panel was Brazilian and the two side panels were Indian.

1965-1970	Brazilian	$5,000	$6,600
1970	Center panel only Brazilian	$2,600	$3,400
1970-1979	Indian	$2,250	$2,925
1980-1989		$1,700	$2,250
1983	150th center strip	$1,700	$2,250
1990-1999		$1,700	$2,250
2000-2019		$1,700	$2,250
2015	50th Anniv Label	$1,700	$2,250

D12-35
1965-1995. Brazilian rosewood back and sides, changed to Indian rosewood in '70, 12 strings, 12 frets clear of body, slotted headstock.

1965-1969	Brazilian	$3,700	$4,800
1970-1979	Indian	$1,600	$2,100
1980-1989		$1,550	$2,000
1990-1995		$1,550	$2,000

D12-35 50th Anniversery Limited Edition
2015-2016. Limited to 183 (the quantity of 1st production run in '65), European spruce top, 3-piece East Indian rosewood back and sides, natural gloss finish.

2015-2016		$3,300	$4,300

D-35 30th Anniversery
1995. Limited Edition, D-35 with '1965-1995' inlay on 20th fret, gold hardware, limited edition of 207 instruments.

1995		$2,700	$3,500

D-35 E Retro
2012-2019. Sitka spruce top, East Indian rosewood back and sides.

2012-2019		$2,000	$2,575

D-35 Ernest Tubb
2003. Indian rosewood back and sides, special inlays, 90 built.

2003		$2,300	$3,000

D-35 JC Johnny Cash
2006-present. Rosewood back and sides.

2006-2019		$2,700	$3,500

D-35 MP
2011-2012. Madagascar rosewood back and sides, high performance neck.

2011-2012		$1,575	$2,050

D-35 P
1986-1990. P indicates low-profile neck.

1986-1990		$1,600	$2,100

D-35 S
1966-1993. Brazilian rosewood back and sides, changed to Indian rosewood in '70, 12-fret neck, slotted peghead.

1966-1969	Brazilian	$6,000	$7,600
1970-1979	Indian	$2,400	$3,100
1980-1989		$1,850	$2,400
1990-1993		$1,850	$2,400

1965 Martin D-35
Greg Perrine

1966 Martin D-35 S
Carter Vintage Guitars

Martin D-42

1941 Martin D-45

Imaged by Heritage Auctions, HA.com

MODEL YEAR	FEATURES	EXC. COND. LOW	HIGH
D-35 Seth Avett			
2013-2019. Swiss spruce top, East Indian rosewood/ flamed koa back, copper snowflake inlay.			
2013-2019		$1,950	$2,550
D-35 SW Wurlitzer			
1966, 1968. Made for the Wurlitzer Co., Brazilian rosewood.			
1966, 1968		$6,000	$7,600
D-35 V			
1984. Limited Edition, 10 made, Brazilian rosewood back and sides.			
1984		$5,200	$6,700
D-37 K			
1980-1994. Dreadnought-size, koa back and sides, spruce top.			
1980-1994		$2,150	$2,800
D-37 K2			
1980-1994. Same as D-37 K, but has a koa top and black 'guard.			
1980-1994		$2,150	$2,800
D-37 W Lucinda Williams			
2003. Only 4 made, never put into production, Aztec pearl inlay favored by Lucinda Williams, quilted mahogany sides and back.			
2003		$3,250	$4,200
D-40			
1997-2005. Indian rosewood back and sides, hexagon inlays.			
1997-2005		$1,850	$2,400
D-40 BLE			
1990. Limited Edition Guitar of the Month, Brazilian rosewood back and sides, pearl top border except around 'board.			
1990		$5,800	$7,500
D-40 DM Don McLean			
1998. Only 50 made, Englemann spruce top.			
1998		$4,500	$5,800
D-40 FMG			
1995-1996. Figured mahogany back and sides, 150 made.			
1995-1996		$3,200	$4,200
D-40 FW Limited Edition			
1996. Figured claro walnut sides and back, 'Limited Edition D-40 FW' label, 148 made.			
1996		$2,200	$2,800
D-40 QM Limited Edition			
1996. Limited Edition, 200 made, quilted maple body.			
1996		$2,200	$2,800
D-41			
1969-present. Brazilian rosewood back and sides for the first ones in '69 then Indian rosewood, bound body, scalloped braces, natural.			
1969	Brazilian	$16,000	$21,000
1970-1979	Indian	$3,000	$3,900
1980-1989		$2,700	$3,500
1990-1999		$2,700	$3,500
2000-2017		$2,700	$3,500
2018-2019	New specs	$2,750	$3,550

MODEL YEAR	FEATURES	EXC. COND. LOW	HIGH
D12-41			
1970-1994. Very few made, special order after '93, 12-string, 14-fret.			
1970-1994		$3,500	$4,500
D-41 A Turbo Mandolin Brothers			
2011, 2013. Two Custom Shop models made for Mandolin Bros., Adirondack top. Similar except 10 40th Anniversary models which have abalone and pearl mandolin 12th-fret inlay and label signed by Stan Jay and Chris Martin.			
2011		$2,850	$3,700
D-41 BLE			
1989. Limited Edition Guitar of the Month, Brazilian rosewood back and sides, pearl top border except around 'board.			
1989		$5,400	$7,000
D-41 DF Dan Fogelberg			
2001. 141 made, East Indian rosewood back and sides, hexagon 'board inlays, pearl snowflakes inlaid on bridge.			
2001		$4,000	$5,200
D-41 E			
1971. Indian rosewood.			
1971		$3,000	$3,900
D-41 GJ George Jones			
2001. Style 41 appointments, limited edition of 100, label signed by the Opossum.			
2001		$2,900	$3,700
D-41 K Purple Martin			
2013-present. Limited to 50 with labels signed by C.F. Martin IV, highly flamed koa back and sides, purple martin-inspired inlay on 'board, bridge, and 'guard.			
2013-2019		$6,300	$8,200
D-41 Porter Wagoner			
2008-2011. Custom Artist series, Indian rosewood back and sides.			
2008-2011		$2,400	$3,100
D-41 S/SD-41 S			
1970-1994. Sunburst, Indian rosewood, 12-fret neck, slotted peghead.			
1970-1976		$3,400	$4,500
1977-1994		$3,000	$3,900
D-41 Special			
2004-2011. D-41 with snowflake inlays.			
2004-2011		$2,600	$3,400
D-42			
1996-present. Dreadnought, Indian rosewood back and sides, spruce top, pearl rosette and inlays, snowflake 'board inlays, gold tuners, gloss finish.			
1996-2019		$3,100	$4,000
D-42 E			
1996-2008. With Fishman Ellipse VT pickup system.			
1996-2008		$3,250	$4,200
D-42 Amazon Rosewood			
2007. Limited Edition, 35 offered, Amazon rosewood is similar to Brazilian rosewood but a different species.			
2007		$3,350	$4,400

MODEL YEAR	FEATURES	EXC. COND. LOW	HIGH

D-42 AR (Amazon Rosewood)
2002-2003. Limited to 30 made, Amazon rosewood is similar to Brazilian rosewood but a different species.

2002-2003		$3,350	$4,400

D-42 Flamed Mahogany
2006. Adirondack, figured mahogany, 30 made with tree-of-life inlay.

2006		$5,100	$6,600

D-42 JC Johnny Cash
1997. Rosewood back and sides, gloss black lacquer on body and neck, Cash signature inlaid at 19th fret, have label signed by Cash and C.F. Martin IV, 80 sold.

1997		$3,900	$5,100

D-42 K Limited Edition
1998. 150 made, highly flamed koa back and sides, sitka top with aging toner, high X-brace design, 45-style abalone snowflake inlays.

1998		$3,000	$3,900

D-42 K/D-42 K2
1998-2006. K has koa back and sides, the all koa body K2 was discontinued in '05.

1998-2006	D-42 K	$3,000	$3,900
2000-2005	D-42 K2	$3,000	$3,900

D-42 LE
1988 only. Limited Edition (75 sold), D-42-style, scalloped braces, low profile neck.

1988		$3,000	$3,900

D-42 Peter Frampton
2006-2007. Indian rosewood back and sides, Style 45 features.

2006-2007		$4,000	$5,200

D-42 Purple Martin Flamed Myrtle
2018-present. Flamed myrtle back and sides, limted to 100 made.

2018-2020		$8,200	$10,700

D-42 SB
2006-2007. Sunburst finish, sitka spruce top, 45-style appointments.

2006-2007		$3,000	$4,000

D-42 V
1985. Vintage Series, 12 made, Brazilian rosewood, scalloped braces.

1985		$5,800	$7,500

D-45
1933-1942 (96 made), 1968-present. Brazilian rosewood back and sides, changed to Indian rosewood during '69. The pre-WW II D-45 is one of the holy grails. A pre-war D-45 should be evaluated on a case-by-case basis. The price ranges are for all-original guitars in excellent condition and are guidance pricing only. These ranges are for a crack-free guitar. Unfortunately, many older acoustics have a crack or two and this can make ultra-expensive acoustics more difficult to evaluate than ultra-expensive solidbody electrics. Technically, a repaired body crack makes a guitar non-original, but the vintage market generally considers a professionally repaired crack to be original. Crack width, length and depth can vary, therefore extra attention is suggested.

1936-1938		$335,000	$435,000
1939	Early, wide neck	$335,000	$435,000
1939	Late, thin neck	$285,000	$375,000
1940-1942		$260,000	$340,000
1968		$29,000	$38,000
1969	Brazilian	$29,000	$38,000
1970-1979		$5,400	$7,000
1980-1989		$4,900	$6,400
1990-1999		$4,750	$6,150
2000-2017		$4,750	$6,150
2018-2019	New specs	$4,800	$6,250

D12-45
1970s-1987. Special order instrument, not a standard catalog item, with D-45 appointments, Indian rosewood.

1970-1979		$4,000	$5,200
1980-1987		$3,800	$5,000

D-45 100th Anniversary LE
1996. Limited Edition, '1896-1996 C.F. Martin Commemorative Anniversary Model' label.

1996		$4,800	$6,200

D-45 150th Anniversary
1983. Brazilian rosewood back and sides, sitka spruce top, '150th' logo stamp.

1983		$9,200	$12,000

D-45 CFM CMR Sr. (200th Anniversary, Brazilian)
1996. Commemorating the 200th Anniversary of C.F. Martin Sr. birthday, Brazilian rosewood back and sides, style 45 Deluxe pearl bordering, fossilized ivory nut and saddle, 14-fret neck, gold hardware.

1996		$9,200	$12,000

D-45 CFM CMR Sr. (200th Anniversary, East Indian)
1996. Commemorating the 200th Anniversary of C.F. Martin Sr. birthday, Indian rosewood back and sides, style 45 pearl bordering, bone nut and saddle, 14-fret neck, gold hardware.

1996		$4,700	$6,100

D-45 (1939 Reissue Mandolin Brothers)
1990. Commissioned by Mandolin Brothers, 5 made, figured Brazilian rosewood. Original name "The Reissue 1939 Martin D-45." Said to be the first reissue of the era and the seed for the '90s Martin Custom Shop.

1990		$9,600	$12,500

D-45 (1939 Reissue)
1992. High-grade spruce top, figured Brazilian rosewood back and sides, high X and scalloped braces, abalone trim, natural, gold tuners.

1992		$9,600	$12,500

D-45 B Brazilian
1994. Brazilian rosewood.

1994		$9,200	$12,000

D-45 Celtic Knot
2004-2005. Brazilian rosewood, Celtic knot 'board inlays, 30 built.

2004-2005		$15,500	$20,000

D-45 Custom Shop
1984, 1991-1992. Various options and models, Indian rosewood back and sides in '84, then Brazilian rosewood.

1984	Indian	$4,700	$6,200
1991-1992	Brazilian	$10,500	$13,500

Martin D-42 Purple
Martin Flamed Myrtle

1968 Martin D-45
Wayne Stephens

1991 Martin D-45 KLE

Martin DCPA4 Siris

MODEL YEAR	FEATURES	EXC. COND. LOW	HIGH

D-45 Deluxe
1993 only. Guitar of the Month, Brazilian rosewood back and sides, figured spruce top, inlay in bridge and 'guard, tree-of-life inlay on 'board, pearl borders and back stripe, gold tuners with large gold buttons, total of 60 sold.

1993		$12,300	$16,000

D-45 Deluxe Commemorative 200th Anniversary
1996. Commemorating the 200th Anniversary of C.F. Martin Sr. birthday, 91 made, Brazilian rosewood back and sides, style 45 Deluxe pearl bordering, fossilized-ivory nut and saddle, 14-fret neck, gold hardware.

1996		$9,600	$12,500

D-45 E Aura
2010. With Fishman Electronics Ellipse Aura technology.

2010		$4,700	$6,100

D-45 E Retro
2013-2019. East Indian rosewood, Fishman.

2013-2019		$5,400	$7,000

D-45 GE Golden Era
2001-2004. 167 made, '37 specs, Brazilian rosewood.

2001-2004		$15,000	$19,800

D-45 Gene Autry
1994 only. Gene Autry inlay (2 options available), natural.

1994	Gene Autry 'board	$14,000	$19,000
1994	Snowflake 'board option	$14,000	$19,000

D-45 K
2006-2008. Flamed koa back and sides.

2006-2008		$5,400	$7,000

D-45 KLE
1991. Limited Edition koa, Engelmann, bear claw, 54 made.

1991		$5,700	$7,400

D-45 LE
1987. Limited Edition, 44 made, Guitar of the Month, September '87.

1987		$12,000	$15,500

D-45 Mike Longworth Commemorative Edition
2004-2006. East Indian rosewood back and sides, Adirondack spruce top, 91 made, label signed by Mike's wife Sue and C.F. Martin IV.

2004-2006		$5,800	$7,500

D-45 S Authentic 1936
2013-present. Adirondack spruce top, Vintage Tone System, Brazilian rosewood back and sides, '36 style appointments and specs.

2013-2019		$31,000	$40,000

D-45 S Deluxe
1992. Limited Edition, 50 made, Indian rosewood, spruce top, high-end appointments.

1992		$6,000	$7,800

D-45 S/SD-45 S
1969-1994. Brazilian rosewood back and sides in '69, Indian rosewood after, 12-fret neck, S means slotted peghead, only 50 made.

1969	Brazilian	$33,000	$43,000
1970-1979	Indian	$6,100	$8,000
1980-1994	Indian	$5,600	$7,300

D-45 SS Steven Stills
1998. Brazilian rosewood back and sides, 91 made.

1998		$20,000	$26,000

D-45 V Brazilian
1983. Brazilian rosewood back and sides, scalloped braces, snowflake inlay, natural.

1983		$9,600	$12,500

D-45 VR/D-45 V
1997-present. Vintage specs, Indian rosewood back and sides, vintage aging toner, snowflake inlay. Name changed to D-45 V in '99 (not to be confused with Brazilian rosewood D-45 V of the '80s).

1997-1998	VR	$5,300	$6,800
1999-2019	V	$5,300	$6,800

D-45 Woodstock 50th Anniversary
2019-2020. Limited Edition, run of 50, East Indian rosewood back and sides, abalone inlay, Woodstock dove on headstock, '1969-2019' on 'board, peace sign on heelcap.

2019-2020		$7,500	$10,000

D-50 Deluxe/D-50 DX
2001-2003. Deluxe limited edition, 50 made, one of the most ornate Martin models ever made, Brazilian rosewood back and sides, highly ornate pearl inlay.

2001-2003		$27,000	$34,000

D-50 K Deluxe/D-50 K2 Deluxe
2003-2006. As D-50 Deluxe with ornate pearl inlay and highly flamed koa back and sides (K, 45 made) or highly flamed koa top, back and sides (K2, 5 made).

2003-2006	K Deluxe	$22,000	$28,000
2003-2006	K2 Deluxe	$22,000	$28,000

D-60
1989-1995. Birdseye maple back and sides, snowflake inlays, tortoiseshell binding and 'guard.

1989-1995		$1,700	$2,200

D-62
1987-1995. Flamed maple back and sides, chrome-plated enclosed Schaller tuners.

1987-1995		$1,400	$1,800

D-62 LE
1986. Limited Edition, Guitar of the Month October '86, flamed maple back and sides, spruce top, snowflake inlays, natural.

1986		$1,500	$1,950

D-76 Bicentennial Limited Edition
1975-1976. Limited to 200 made in '75 and 1,976 made in '76, Indian rosewood back and sides, 3-piece back, herringbone back stripe, pearl stars on 'board, eagle on peghead.

1975-1976		$2,700	$3,500

D-93
1993. Mahogany, spruce, 93 pertains to the year, not a style number.

1993		$1,550	$2,000

D-100 Deluxe
2004. Limited Edition, guitars have the first 50 sequential serial numbers following the millionth Martin guitar (1,000,001 to 1,000,050), fancy pearl inlay on back, 'guard, headstock, 'board and bridge.

MODEL YEAR	FEATURES	EXC. COND. LOW	HIGH

Herringbone top and rosette inlay, Adirondack spruce top, Brazilian rosewood back and sides.

| 2004 | | $27,000 | $35,000 |

D-200 Deluxe
2017-present. Celebration of Martin's two-millionth serial number, limited to 50 offered, watch-themed highly decorative, comes with renowned watchmaker Roland G Murphy watch with matching serial no., premium case has built-in hygrometer.

| 2017-2019 | | $75,000 | $95,000 |

D-222 100th Anniversary
2016. Commemorates 100th anniversary of the dreadnought, limited to 100, sitka spruce top, mahogany back and sides, ivoroid binding, slotted headstock.

| 2016 | | $2,800 | $3,600 |

D-420
2017-2019. Top with custom legal weed illustration by artist Robert Goetzl, mahogany back and sides.

| 2017-2019 | | $1,400 | $1,800 |

D Jr.
2017-2018. Dreadnought Junior, sitka spruce top, sapele back and sides.

| 2017-2018 | | $275 | $350 |

D Jr. E
2015-2018. Dreadnought Junior with Fishman electronics.

| 2015-2018 | | $325 | $425 |

DC Series
1980s-2019. Dreadnought cutaway versions, E models have electronics, GT is gloss top, R means rosewood back and sides. Replaced by DC-X Series starting in '20.

1981-1997	DC-28	$1,775	$2,300
1996-2000	DC-1	$550	$700
1996-2010	DC-1E	$600	$775
1997-2000	DCM	$525	$675
1997-2005	DC-1M	$575	$700
1997-2006	DCME	$550	$725
1998	DCXM	$400	$525
1998-2001	DCXME	$400	$525
1998-2010	DC-15E	$600	$775
1999-2000	DC-1R	$550	$700
2000	DCRE	$550	$725
2000-2013	DCX1E	$400	$525
2001-2005	DCXE Black	$400	$525
2002-2003	DC-16RE	$625	$825
2003-2005	DC-16GTE Premium	$900	$1,150
2003-2016	DC-16GTE	$800	$1,050
2003-2019	DC-16E	$800	$1,050
2004-2013	DCX1KE	$400	$525
2004-2013	DCX1RE	$400	$525
2005	DC Trey Anastasio	$3,400	$4,400
2005	DC-16RE Aura	$650	$850
2005	DC-16RGTE Aura	$926	$1,200
2005-2007	DC-16E Koa	$850	$1,100
2005-2008	DC-16RGTE	$875	$1,150
2005-2010	DC-Aura	$1,700	$2,200
2006-2019	DC-28E	$1,850	$2,400

2009-2016	DCPA1/ DCPA1 Plus	$1,650	$2,150
2011	DCPA2/DCPA3	$900	$1,175
2011-2016	DCPA4 Shaded	$900	$1,200
2011-2017	DCPA4 Rosewood	$950	$1,250
2013-2016	DCPA5	$400	$500
2013-2016	DCPA5 Black	$400	$500
2013-2016	DCPA5K Koa	$400	$500
2016-2019	DC-15ME	$600	$775
2016-2019	DC-35E	$1,900	$2,450
2017-2018	DCRSG	$500	$650
2017-2019	DC-18E	$1,775	$2,300
2017-2019	DCPA4	$850	$1,100
2017-2019	DCX1AE/ DCX1AE Macassar	$375	$500
2017-2019	DCX1RAE	$400	$525
2019	DC-13E	$500	$650

DC-X Series
2020-present. New spec models to replace the DC Series. Various options and finishes.

| 2020 | DC-X2E | $500 | $650 |

Ditson Dreadnaught 111
2007-2009. Based on 1929 Ditson 111, 12-fret neck, slot head, mahogany back and sides, Brazilian rosewood binding.

| 2007-2009 | | $2,650 | $3,400 |

DM
1996-2009. Solid sitka spruce top, laminated mahogany back and sides, dot markers, natural satin.

| 1996-2009 | | $475 | $600 |

DM-12
1996-2009. 12-string DM.

| 1996-2009 | | $475 | $600 |

DM3 MD Dave Matthews
1999-2001. Englemann top, 3-piece Indian rosewood back, African padauk center wedge, 234 made.

| 1999-2001 | | $3,700 | $4,700 |

Doobie-42 Tom Johnston Signature Edition
2007. D-42 style, 35 made, solid Indian rosewood back and sides, abalone and catseye markers, other special appointments.

| 2007 | | $3,400 | $4,450 |

DR
1997-2008. Road Series Dreadnought, rosewood back and sides.

| 1997-2008 | | $525 | $675 |

DR Centennial
2016-present. Limited Edition celebrates '100 Years of the Dreadnought', Adirondack, East Indian rosewood, antique white binding, satin finish.

| 2016-2019 | | $1,300 | $1,650 |

DRS1 (Road/1 Series)
2011-2019. D-size, sapele top, back and sides, satin finish, Fishman. Replaced by D-10E in '19.

| 2011-2019 | | $425 | $550 |

DRS2 (Road/1 Series)
2012-2018. DRS1 with spruce top. Replaced by D-10E in '19.

| 2012-2018 | | $450 | $600 |

2017 Martin D-200 Deluxe

Martin DC-X2E

GUITARS

2002 Martin DX121
Johnny Zapp

1962 Martin F-65
Bill Ruxton

MODEL YEAR	FEATURES	EXC. COND. LOW	HIGH

DRSG
2017-2018. Sitka spruce top, siris back and sides, Fishman Sonitone.

2017-2018		$650	$850

DRSGT
2014-2015. Sitka spruce top, sapele back and sides, Fishman with USB port.

2014-2015		$500	$650

DSR Sugar Ray
2003. Limited Edition of 57 made, D-17 style, all mahogany, signed by C.F. Martin IV and all members of Sugar Ray band.

2003		$2,900	$3,800

DSS-17
2018-present. Slope-shoulder dreadnought, sitka spruce top, mahogany back and sides with antique white binding, satin Black Smoke or Whiskey Sunset Burst.

2018-2019	Black Smoke	$875	$1,150
2019-2020	Whiskey Sunset	$875	$1,150

DVM Veterans
2002-2008. D-style, spruce top, rosewood back and sides, special veterans ornamentation.

2002-2008		$1,550	$2,000

Dwight Yoakam DD28
2017-2018. Custom Signature Edition, sitka spruce top, East Indian rosewood back and sides, inlaid mother-of-pearl and recon stone playing cards.

2017-2018		$2,500	$3,200

DX 175th Anniversary
2008. Rosewood HPL back and sides, founder's picture on top.

2008		$375	$475

DX Johnny Cash
2019-present. D-sized, Jett black HPL top, back and sides, custom 'board inlaid with stars and CASH logo, Cash's signature on rosette and label, Fishman electronics.

2019-2020		$450	$575

DX Series
1996-2019. D-size, high pressure wood laminate (HPL) backs and sides, exterior wood-grain image with gloss finish. M is for mahogany wood-grain, R rosewood and K koa. A 1 indicates a solid spruce top with Series 1 bracing, otherwise top is wood-patterned HPL. C indicates cutaway and E Fishman Presys Plus and AE Fishman Sonitone. Replaced by D-X Series starting in '20.

1996-2009	DXM/DMX	$325	$425
1998-2012	DXME	$325	$425
1999-2000	D12XM 12-String	$325	$425
1999-2020	DXMAE	$325	$425
2000-2013	DX1	$300	$400
2000-2019	DX1AE	$325	$425
2001-2009	DX1R	$325	$425
2002-2009	DXK2	$325	$425
2004-2009	DX1K	$325	$425
2008-2010	D12X1 12-String	$325	$425
2010-2020	DX1KAE	$325	$425
2011-2019	D12X1AE 12-String	$375	$475
2013	DX1E	$325	$425

MODEL YEAR	FEATURES	EXC. COND. LOW	HIGH
2014-2019	DXAE Black	$325	$425
2014-2019	DXK2AE	$325	$425
2015-2019	DX1RAE	$325	$425
2017	DX420	$775	$1,025
2017-2019	DX2AE Macassar	$325	$425

D-X Series
2020-present. New spec dreadnought models to replace the DX Series. Various options and finishes.

2020	D-X1E	$375	$475
2020	D-X2E	$450	$575
2020	D-X2E 12-String	$450	$575

E-18
1979-1983. Offset double-cut, maple and rosewood laminate solidbody, 2 DiMarzio pickups, phase switch, natural.

1979-1983		$1,050	$1,350

E-28
1980-1983. Double-cut electric solidbody, carved top, ebony 'board, 2 humbuckers.

1980-1983		$1,150	$1,500

EM-18
1979-1983. Offset double-cut, maple and rosewood laminate solidbody, 2 exposed-coil humbucking pickups, coil split switch.

1979-1983		$1,050	$1,350

EMP-1
1998-1999. Employee series designed by Martin employee team, cutaway solid spruce top, ovangkol wood back and sides with rosewood middle insert (D-35-style insert), on-board pickup.

1998-1999		$1,500	$1,950

EMP-2 Limited Edition
1999. D size, tzalam body, flying saucer inlays.

1999		$1,500	$1,950

F-1
1940-1942. Archtop, mahogany back and sides, carved spruce top, multi-bound, f-holes, sunburst, 91 made.

1940-1942		$1,475	$1,900

F-1-12
1941. F-1 12 string.

1941		$1,600	$2,075

F-2
1940-1942. Carved spruce top, maple or rosewood back and sides, multi-bound, f-holes, 46 made.

1940-1942		$1,700	$2,200

F-5
1940. 2 made.

1940		$3,100	$4,000

F-7
1935-1939, 1941-1942. Brazilian rosewood back and sides, f-holes, carved top, back arched by braces, multi-bound, sunburst top finish.

1935-1942		$4,300	$5,600

F-9
1935-1942. Highest-end archtop, Brazilian rosewood, Martin inlaid vertically on headstock, 7-ply top binding, 45-style back strip, sunburst.

1935-1942		$9,100	$11,800

MODEL YEAR	FEATURES	EXC. COND. LOW	HIGH

F-50
1961-1965. Single-cut thinline archtop with laminated maple body, 1 pickup.

1961-1965		$1,025	$1,325

F-55
1961-1965. Single-cut thinline archtop with laminated maple body, 2 pickups.

1961-1965		$1,900	$2,500

F-65
1961-1965. Electric archtop, double-cut, f-holes, 2 pickups, square-cornered peghead, Bigsby, sunburst.

1961-1965		$1,900	$2,500

Felix The Cat
2004-2010. Felix the Cat logo art, Don Oriolo logo, red body, Felix gig bag.

2004	Felix I, 756 made	$425	$550
2005-2006	Felix II, 625 made	$425	$550
2007-2010	Felix III, 1000 made	$425	$550

GCD-16 CP (Guitar Center)
1998. 15 5/8" Style D.

1998		$1,575	$2,050

GPC Series
2010-present. Standard Series (GPC-), Performing Artist (GPCPA) and X Series (GPCX), Grand Performance size, cutaway, acoustic/electric, various woods.

2010-2016	GPCPA1/Plus	$1,650	$2,100
2011	GPCPA2	$1,175	$1,500
2011-2012	GPCPA3	$1,175	$1,500
2012-2016	GPCPA5K Koa	$400	$500
2013-2016	GPCPA5	$400	$500
2013-2016	GPCPA5 Black	$400	$500
2013-2019	GPC12PA4 12-string	$900	$1,150
2013-2019	GPCPA4 Rosewood	$900	$1,200
2013-2019	GPCPA4 Sapele	$925	$1,200
2016-2018	GPC-35E	$1,950	$2,525
2016-2019	GPC-28E	$1,900	$2,475
2016-2020	GPC-18E	$1,775	$2,300
2017-2018	GPC-15ME	$950	$1,250
2017-2018	GPCRSG	$700	$900
2017-2018	GPCRSGT	$525	$700
2017-2018	GPCXAE Black	$350	$475
2017-2019	GPCX1AE	$375	$500
2017-2019	GPCX1RAE	$375	$500
2017-2019	GPCX2E Macassar	$375	$500
2019-2020	GPC-11E (Road Series)	$650	$850
2019-2020	GPC-13E (Road Series)	$700	$900
2020	GPC-16E	$1,125	$1,475
2020	GPC-16E Rosewood	$1,225	$1,575
2020	GPC-X2E	$500	$650

Grand J12-40 E Special
2009-2011. J12-40 with D-TAR Multi-source electronics.

2009-2011		$2,250	$2,900

Grand J-28 LSE
2011-2014. Baritone.

2011-2014		$1,800	$2,350

MODEL YEAR	FEATURES	EXC. COND. LOW	HIGH

Grand J-35 E
2009-2011. Grand jumbo size, rosewood back and sides.

2009-2011		$1,800	$2,350

Grand Ole Opry/HDO Grand Ole Opry
1999-2007. Custom Shop Limited Edition, 650 made, 'Grand Ole Opry 75th Anniversary' on neck block, WSM microphone headstock logo, off-white Micarta fingerboard, sitka spruce top, East Indian rosewood back and sides.

1999-2007		$2,100	$2,750

GT-70
1965-1966. Electric archtop, bound body, f-holes, single-cut, 2 pickups, tremolo, burgundy or black finish.

1965-1966		$2,000	$2,600

GT-75
1965-1967. Electric archtop, bound body, f-holes, double-cut, 2 pickups, tremolo, burgundy or black finish. There is also a 12-string version.

1965-1967		$2,000	$2,600

Hawaiian X
2002-2004. Hawaiian scene painted on top, similar to the Cowboy guitar model, limited edition of 500.

2002-2004		$575	$725

HD-7 Roger McGuinn
2005-2008. Rosewood back and sides, herringbone top trim, 7-string with double G.

2005-2008		$2,300	$3,000

HD-16 R Adirondack
2008-2016. Rosewood back and sides, Adirondack top.

2010-2016		$1,350	$1,750

HD-16 R LSH
2007-2013. Indian rosewood (R), large sound hole (LSH).

2007-2013		$1,350	$1,750

HD-18 JB Jimmy Buffett
1998. 424 made, solid mahogany back and sides, herringbone trim, palm tree headstock logo, Style 42 markers, Buffett pearl signature.

1998		$4,200	$5,500

HD-18 LE
1987. Indian rosewood.

1987		$1,625	$2,125

HD-28
1976-present. Standard Series, Indian rosewood back and sides, scalloped bracing, herringbone purfling.

1976-1979		$2,525	$3,325
1980-1989		$1,750	$2,250
1990-1999		$1,750	$2,250
2000-2017	Last Standard X	$1,750	$2,250
2018-2019	Forward X	$1,750	$2,250

HD-28 1935 Special
1993. 'HD-28 1935 Special' model name on label.

1993		$2,075	$2,700

HD-28 2R
1991, 1993-1997. 2R specification for 2 herringbone soundhole rings, larger soundhole.

1991-1997		$1,750	$2,250

1967 Martin GT-75
Greg Perrine

1989 Martin HD-28
Steve Zuckerman

GUITARS

1990 Martin HD-28 BLE
Carter Vintage Guitars

Martin HD-28 VR

MODEL YEAR	FEATURES	EXC. COND. LOW	HIGH

HD-28 AWB Custom
2008-2013. Elderly Instruments Custom model, Adirondack spruce top, rosewood back and sides, white-bound body, gloss natural finish.

| 2008-2013 | | $2,250 | $2,900 |

HD-28 BLE
1990. Guitar of the Month, 100 made, Brazilian rosewood back and sides, herringbone soundhole ring, low profile neck (LE), chrome tuners, aging toner finish.

| 1990 | | $5,000 | $6,500 |

HD-28 BSE
1987-1999. Brazilian rosewood, 93 made.

| 1987-1999 | | $5,000 | $6,500 |

HD-28 CTB
1992. Guitar of the Month, mahogany back and sides, slotted peghead, herringbone back stripe, gold tuners, custom tortoise bound.

| 1992 | | $1,950 | $2,550 |

HD-28 Custom 150th Anniversary
1983. 150th Anniversary, Martin Custom Shop, Indian rosewood sides and back, '1833-1983 150th Year' stamped on inside backstrip.

| 1983 | | $2,450 | $3,200 |

HD-28 Custom/Custom HD-28
1994. Custom Shop model.

| 1994-1995 | | $1,950 | $2,550 |

HD-28 E Retro
2013-2019. Solid sitka spruce top, East Indian rosewood back and sides.

| 2013-2019 | | $2,000 | $2,575 |

HD-28 GM
1989. Grand Marquis, Guitar of the Month, scalloped braced Sitka spruce top with 1930s-era bracing pattern that replaced the X-brace below the soundhole, herringbone top purfling, soundhole ring and back stripe, gold tuners.

| 1989 | | $2,600 | $3,375 |

HD-28 GM LSH
1994. Grand Marquis, Guitar of the Month, rosewood back and sides, large soundhole with double herringbone rings, snowflake inlay in bridge, natural (115 made) or sunburst (36 made).

| 1994 | Natural | $2,600 | $3,375 |
| 1994 | Sunburst | $2,600 | $3,375 |

HD-28 KM Keb Mo
2001-2002. Signature Edition, Hawaiian koa back and sides, 252 made.

| 2001-2002 | | $2,100 | $2,750 |

HD-28 LE
1985. Limited Edition, Guitar of the Month, rosewood back and sides, scalloped bracing, herringbone top purfling, diamonds and squares 'board inlay, V-neck.

| 1985 | | $2,375 | $3,100 |

HD-28 LSV
1997-2005. Vintage Series, large soundhole, patterned after Clarence White's modified '35 D-28.

| 1997-2005 | | $2,100 | $2,750 |

HD-28 M
1988. Standard profile.

| 1988 | | $1,700 | $2,200 |

HD-28 MP
1990-1991, 2011-2012. Bolivian rosewood back and sides, herringbone top trim, low profile neck. Reissued in 2011 with Madagascar rosewood and modern-style neck.

| 1990-1991 | | $1,625 | $2,100 |
| 2011-2012 | | $1,625 | $2,100 |

HD-28 P
1987-1989. Rosewood back and sides, scalloped braces, herringbone, low profile neck (P), zigzag back stripe.

| 1987-1989 | | $1,625 | $2,100 |

HD-28 PSE
1988. Signature Edition, Guitar of the Month, rosewood back and sides, signed by C.F. Martin IV and foremen, scalloped braces, herringbone top purfling, low profile neck, squared peghead, ebony tuner buttons.

| 1988 | | $1,950 | $2,525 |

HD-28 S Custom
1995. Slotted headstock.

| 1995 | | $1,950 | $2,525 |

HD-28 SB/HD-28 Ambertone/HD-28 SB-AMB
2016-2017. Various wood and finish options for HD-28.

| 2016-2017 | | $1,925 | $2,500 |

HD-28 SE
1986-1987. Signature Edition, rosewood back and sides, signed by C. F. Martin and foremen/supervisors, '87 model was a Guitar of the Month and had Brazilian rosewood.

| 1986 | | $1,950 | $2,525 |
| 1987 | Brazilian | $4,500 | $5,800 |

HD-28 SO Sing Out!
1996. Limited edition, 45 made, Indian rosewood back and sides.

| 1996 | | $2,200 | $2,800 |

HD-28 V Custom
2007-2012. Indian rosewood back and sides, Adirondack top, wide nut, Elderly Instruments special issue.

| 2007-2012 | | $2,450 | $3,150 |

HD-28 V/HD-28 VR
1996-2019. 14-fret, Indian rosewood body, R dropped from name in '99.

| 1996-1999 | HD-28 VR | $2,175 | $2,825 |
| 2000-2019 | HD-28 V | $2,175 | $2,825 |

HD-28 VAW Custom
2007-2017. Custom for Elderly Instruments, Indian rosewood back and sides, herringbone trim, diamond and square inlays, aged gloss finish.

| 2007-2017 | | $2,500 | $3,300 |

HD-28 VE
2004-2006. HD-28 V with Fishman Ellipse Blend system.

| 2004-2006 | | $2,275 | $2,925 |

HD-28 VS
1996-2016. Slotted headstock, 12-fret, spruce top with aging toner, Indian rosewood sides and back.

| 1996-2016 | | $2,300 | $3,000 |

MODEL YEAR	FEATURES	EXC. COND. LOW	HIGH

HD-35
1978-present. Indian rosewood back and sides, herringbone top trim, zipper back stripe.

1978-1979		$2,400	$3,100
1980-1989		$1,825	$2,375
1990-1999		$1,825	$2,375
2000-2019		$1,825	$2,375

HD-35 CFM IV 60th
2016-present. Celebrates C.F. Martin IV's 60th birthday, limited to 60, European spruce top, 3-piece back of siris wings and East Indian rosewood wedge, personally signed label.

| 2016-2019 | | $4,700 | $6,100 |

HD-35 Custom
2009. Custom Designed on neck block, Adirondack spruce top, East Indian rosewood sides and back.

| 2009 | | $2,000 | $2,575 |

HD-35 Nancy Wilson
2006-2007. Englemann spruce top, 3-piece back with bubinga center wedge, 101 made.

| 2006-2007 | | $2,500 | $3,225 |

HD-35 P
1987-1989. HD-35 with low profile neck.

| 1987-1989 | | $1,875 | $2,400 |

HD-35 SJC Judy Collins
2002. 50 made, Collins signature headstock logo, wildflower headstock inlay, East Indian rosewood, 3-piece back with figured maple center.

| 2002 | | $2,400 | $3,075 |

HD-40 MK Mark Knopfler
2001-2002. Limited Edition of 251 made, Mark Knopfler signature inlay 20th fret, herringbone trim, fancy marquetry soundhole rings.

| 2001-2002 | | $3,000 | $3,900 |

HD-40 MS Marty Stuart
1996. Indian rosewood, 250 made, pearl/abalone inlay.

| 1996 | | $3,000 | $3,900 |

HD-40 Tom Petty SE
2004-2006. Signature Edition, Indian rosewood sides and back, high-end appointments, 274 made, inside label with signature.

| 2004-2006 | | $4,000 | $5,100 |

HD-282 R
1992-1996. Large soundhole with 2 herringbone rings, zigzag backstripe.

| 1992-1996 | | $1,900 | $2,450 |

HD Dierks Bentley
2013-2014. Rosewood.

| 2013-2014 | | $2,700 | $3,500 |

HD Elliot Easton Custom Edition
2006-2008. Limited Edition, Adirondack spruce top with aging tone, Fishman Ellipse Aura pickup available on HDE.

| 2006-2008 | | $2,275 | $2,950 |

HDN Negative Limited Edition
2003. Limited to 135 made, unusual appointments include pearloid headstock and black finish, HDN Negative Limited Edition notation on the inside label.

| 2003 | | $2,500 | $3,250 |

HJ-28
1992, 1996-2000. Limited Edition, Guitar of the Month in '92, regular production started in '96. Jumbo, non-cut, spruce top, Indian rosewood sides and back, herringbone top purfling, with or without on-board electronics.

| 1992 | LE 69 made | $2,000 | $2,600 |
| 1996-2000 | | $2,000 | $2,600 |

HJ-28 M
1994. Mahogany/spruce, herringbone top purfling, Guitar of the Month, 72 made.

| 1994 | | $2,100 | $2,700 |

HJ-38 Stefan Grossman
2008-2011. Custom Edition, Madagascar rosewood back and sides.

| 2008-2011 | | $2,500 | $3,250 |

HM Ben Harper
2008-2009. Special Edition, M-style width, 000-style depth, solid Adirondack spruce top, solid East Indian rosewood sides and back, onboard Fishman Ellipse Matrix Blend.

| 2008-2009 | | $2,600 | $3,350 |

HOM-35
1989. Herringbone Orchestra Model, Guitar of the Month, scalloped braces, 3-piece Brazilian rosewood back, bookmatched sides, 14-fret neck, only 60 built.

| 1989 | | $3,700 | $4,800 |

HPD-41
1999-2001. Like D-41, but with herringbone rosette, binding.

| 1999-2001 | | $2,600 | $3,350 |

HTA Kitty Wells 'Honky Tonk Angel'
2002. D-size with 000-size depth, Indian rosewood back and sides, Queen of Country Music inlay logo on headstock (no Martin headstock logo).

| 2002 | | $1,800 | $2,300 |

J-1 Jumbo
1997-2001. Jumbo body with mahogany back and sides.

| 1997-2001 | | $685 | $875 |

J12-15
2000-2008. 12-string version of J-15.

| 2000-2008 | | $685 | $875 |

J12-16 GT
2000-2013. 16" jumbo 12-string, satin solid mahogany back and sides, gloss solid spruce top.

| 2000-2013 | | $850 | $1,075 |

J12-16 GTE
2014-2015. Jumbo 12-string, Fishman.

| 2014-2015 | | $900 | $1,150 |

J12-40/J12-40 M
1985-1996. Called J12-40M from '85-'90, rosewood back and sides, 12 strings, 16" jumbo size, 14-fret neck, solid peghead, gold tuners.

| 1985-1990 | J12-40M | $2,100 | $2,700 |
| 1991-1996 | J12-40 | $2,100 | $2,700 |

J12-65
1985-1995. Called J12-65M for '84-'90, 12-string, figured maple back and sides.

| 1985-1995 | | $1,725 | $2,250 |

1981 Martin HD-35
Imaged by Heritage Auctions, HA.com

1996 Martin HD-40 MS Marty Stuart
Imaged by Heritage Auctions, HA.com

1996 Martin J-40
Bernunzio Uptown Music

2006 Martin JC Buddy Guy
Imaged by Heritage Auctions, HA.com

MODEL YEAR	FEATURES	EXC. COND. LOW	HIGH
J-15			
1999-2010. Jumbo 16" narrow-waist body, solid mahogany top, sides, and back, satin finish.			
1999-2010		$800	$1,025
J-15 E			
2000-2001. Acoustic/electric J-15.			
2000-2001		$850	$1,075
J-18/J-18 M			
1987-1996. J-size body with Style 18 appointments, natural, called J-18M for '87-'89.			
1987-1989	J-18M	$1,450	$1,900
1990-1996	J-18	$1,450	$1,900
J-21 MC			
1986. J cutaway, oval soundhole.			
1986		$1,550	$2,000
J-21/J-21 M			
1985-1996. Called J-21M prior to '90, Indian rosewood back and sides, black binding, rosewood 'board, chrome tuners.			
1985-1989	J-21 M	$1,450	$1,900
1990-1996	J-21	$1,450	$1,900
J-40			
1990-present. Called J-40 M from '85-'89, Jumbo, Indian rosewood back and sides, triple-bound 'board, hexagonal inlays.			
1990-2019		$2,100	$2,700
J-40 BK			
1990-1997. Black finish and 'guard, gold hardware.			
1990-1997		$2,100	$2,700
J-40 Custom			
1993-1996. J-40 with upgrades including abalone top trim and rosette.			
1993-1996		$2,000	$2,600
J-40 M/J-40 MBK			
1985-1989. Jumbo, Indian rosewood back and sides, triple-bound 'board, hexagonal inlays, MBK ('88-'89) indicates black, name changed to J-40 in '90.			
1985-1989	J-40 M	$2,100	$2,700
1988-1989	J-40 MBK	$2,100	$2,700
J-40 MBLE			
1987. Brazilian rosewood, Style 45 snowflakes, 17 made.			
1987		$3,850	$5,000
J-40 MC			
1987-1989. Rounded Venetian cutaway version of J-40 M, oval soundhole, gold-plated enclosed tuners. Becomes JC-40 in '90.			
1987-1989		$2,150	$2,750
J-41 Special			
2004-2007. East Indian rosewood back and sides, Style 45 snowflake inlays.			
2004-2007		$2,100	$2,700
J-45 M Deluxe			
1986. Guitar of the Month, East Indian rosewood back and sides, tortoise-colored binding, mother-of-pearl and abalone, gold tuners with ebony buttons.			
1986		$2,800	$3,600
J-65 Custom/J-65 FM			
1993-1996. White binding, herringbone. Available with MEQ electronics.			
1993-1996		$1,825	$2,400
1993-1996	With MEQ	$1,825	$2,400

MODEL YEAR	FEATURES	EXC. COND. LOW	HIGH
J-65/J-65 E/J-65 M			
1985-1995. Jumbo, maple back and sides, gold-plated tuners, scalloped bracing, ebony 'board, tortoise shell-style binding.			
1985-1995		$1,725	$2,250
JC Buddy Guy			
2006-2007. Only 36 made, rosewood back and sides.			
2006-2007		$2,500	$3,250
JC-1 E			
1999-2002. Jumbo, mahogany, cutaway, pickup.			
1999-2002		$825	$1,075
JC-16 GTE			
2000-2003. Jumbo, cutaway, mahogany back and sides, gloss top, Fishman.			
2000-2003		$925	$1,175
JC-16 GTE Premium			
2003-2005. Fishman Prefix Stereo Blender pickup system.			
2003-2005		$1,000	$1,300
JC-16 KWS Kenny Wayne Shepherd Signature			
2001-2002. Cutaway, blue lacquer top, back and sides in gloss black, on-board electronics, 198 made.			
2001-2002	198 made	$1,125	$1,450
JC-16 ME Aura			
2006-2009. JC-16 with maple back and sides, Fishman Aura.			
2006-2009		$1,400	$1,800
JC-16 RE Aura			
2006-2011. Like ME, but with rosewood back and sides.			
2006-2011		$1,400	$1,800
JC-16 RGTE Aura			
2000-2003. Like RE Aura, but with gloss top.			
2000-2003		$925	$1,175
JC-16 WE			
2002-2003. Jumbo cutaway, solid walnut sides and back, solid sitka spruce top.			
2002-2003		$975	$1,225
JC-40			
1990-1997. Renamed from J-40 MC, cutaway flat-top, oval sound hole.			
1990-1997		$2,150	$2,750
JSO! Sing Out 60th Pete Seeger			
2011. Triangular soundhole, Sitka top, East Indian rosewood back and sides, 2 'guards, 120 made. There was also a 12-string model (J12SO!).			
2011		$2,300	$3,000
LE-HMSD 2015 (HMS Dreadnought Battleship)			
2015. Limited Edition, HMS Dreadnought Battleship (British Royal Navy) illustrated by artist Robert Goetzl is printed on the sitka spruce top, dark mahogany back and sides, ebony 'board.			
2015		$2,800	$3,550
LX Series			
2003-present. The LX series is the Little Martin models, featuring small bodies with high pressure wood laminate (HPL) backs and sides with an exterior wood-grain image with a gloss finish. M is for mahog-			

MODEL YEAR	FEATURES	EXC. COND. LOW	HIGH

any wood-grain, R for rosewood and K for koa. They are also offered in all solid-colors. A 1 indicates a HPL spruce top, 2 is HPL koa top. E indicates electronics.

MODEL YEAR	FEATURES	LOW	HIGH
2003-2019	LXM	$180	$235
2004-2020	LX1	$190	$250
2004-2020	LXK2	$180	$235
2009	LX Elvis Presley	$320	$415
2009-2020	LX1E	$240	$315
2013-2014	LX1E Ed Sheeran	$300	$395
2013-2019	LXME	$230	$300
2017-2020	LX Black	$180	$235
2019-2020	LX1R	$265	$350
2019-2020	LX1RE	$300	$400

M2C-28
1988. Double-cut, Guitar of the Month, 22 made.

1988		$1,800	$2,350

M-3 H Cathy Fink
2005. M 0000-size body, gloss finish, rosewood sides, 3-piece back with flamed koa center panel, torch headstock inlay, herringbone top trim, no Martin logo on headstock.

2005		$1,900	$2,450

M-3 M George Martin
2005-2006. M Model, Style 40 appointments with Style 42 snowflake inlays, 127 made.

2005-2006		$3,000	$3,850

M-3 SC Shawn Colvin
2002-2003. M 0000-size body, 120 made, mahogany sides, 3-piece mahogany/rosewood back, Fishman, Shawn Colvin & C.F.M. III signed label.

2002-2003		$1,700	$2,150

M-16 GT
2001-2003. M-size single cut, gloss top, mahogany sides and back.

2001-2003		$750	$975

M-18
1984-1988. M size, mahogany.

1984-1988		$1,700	$2,200

M-21
December 1984. Guitar of the Month, low profile neck M-Series, Indian rosewood back and sides, special ornamentation.

1984		$1,650	$2,150

M-21 Steve Earle
2008-2011. East Indian rosewood back and sides, Italian Alpine spruce top.

2008-2011		$2,100	$2,725

M-30 Jorma Kaukonen
2010-2013. Custom Artist Edition, M 0000-size body, Style 30 appointments, East Indian rosewood back and sides, Maltese diamond/square inlays, optional electronics.

2010-2013		$3,200	$4,200

M-35/M-36
1978-1997, 2007-present. First 26 labeled as M-35, Indian rosewood back and sides, bound 'board, low profile neck, multi-bound, white-black-white back stripes.

1978	M-35, 26 made	$1,750	$2,250
1978-1979		$1,750	$2,250
1980-1997		$1,575	$2,100
2007-2019		$1,575	$2,100
2008	M-36 175th Anniv	$1,575	$2,100

M-36 B
1985. Brazilian rosewood.

1985		$3,200	$4,200

M-38 (0000-38)
1977-1997, 2007-2011. Called 0000-38 (see that listing) in '97-'98, 0000-size, Indian rosewood back and sides, multi-bound.

1977-1979		$2,250	$2,900
1980-1989		$2,000	$2,600
1990-1997		$2,000	$2,600
2007-2011		$2,000	$2,600

M-38 B
1985. Brazilian rosewood.

1985		$3,700	$4,800

M-42 David Bromberg
2006. 0000-14 body, rosewood back and sides, snowflakes, 83 made.

2006		$3,000	$3,900

M-64
1985-1996. Flamed maple back and sides, tortoiseshell-style 'guard and binding. The 11 made in '85 were labeled M-64R.

1985-1996		$1,575	$2,100

MC12-41 Richie Sambora
2006. 12-string version of OMC-41 Richie Sambora, planned 200 made combined models.

2006		$3,000	$3,900

MC-16 GTE
2002-2004. M-16 GT with single-cut and Fishman.

2002-2004		$850	$1,100

MC-16 GTE Premium
2003-2005. Fishman Prefix Stereo Blender pickup system.

2003-2005		$1,025	$1,325

MC-28
1981-1996. Rosewood back and sides, single-cut, oval soundhole, scalloped braces.

1981-1996		$1,775	$2,300

MC-37 K
1981-1982, 1987-1994. Cutaway, koa back and sides.

1981-1994		$1,925	$2,500

MC-38 Steve Howe
2009-2011. Indian rosewood back and sides, cutaway, slot headstock.

2009-2011		$4,300	$5,600

MC-68/MC-68 R/MC-68+
1985-1996. Auditorium-size, single-cut, maple back and sides, scalloped bracing, verticle logo, natural or sunburst. In '85 called the MC-68 R (for adjustable truss-rod), 7 with sunburst shaded top option called MC-68+.

1985	MC-68	$1,725	$2,225
1985-1996	MC-68+	$1,825	$2,325
1986-1996	MC-68 R	$1,725	$2,225

MC-DSM
2007-2010. Limited Edition of 100, cutaway, designed by District Sales Manager (DSM), spruce top, figured koa back and sides.

2007-2010		$2,500	$3,200

Martin M-30 Jorma Kaukonen

1979 Martin M-38
Gantt Kushner

1996 Martin MTV-1 Unplugged Edition

Martin OM-18 Authentic 1933

MODEL YEAR	FEATURES	EXC. COND. LOW	HIGH
Mini-Martin Limited Edition			
1999-2009. Size 5 Terz body, solid sitka spruce top, rosewood sides and back, vintage style Martin Geib case with green interior.			
1999-2009		$1,475	$1,900
MMV			
2008-2012. D-style, rosewood sides and back, nitro finish.			
2008-2012		$1,000	$1,300
Model American 1			
2018. Limited Edition D-body, United States sourced woods, Adirondack spruce top, sycamore back and sides, cherry neck, black walnut 'board, gloss finish.			
2018		$1,650	$2,200
MTV-1 Unplugged			
1996. Body is 1/2 rosewood and 1/2 mahogany, scalloped bracing, MTV logo on headstock, gloss (588 sold) or satin (73 sold) finish.			
1996	Gloss finish	$1,225	$1,600
1996	Satin finish	$1,150	$1,500
MTV-2 Unplugged			
2003-2004. Body is 1/2 rosewood and 1/2 maple, scalloped bracing, MTV logo on headstock.			
2003-2004		$1,150	$1,500
N-10			
1968-1993. Classical, mahogany back and sides, fan bracing, wood marquetry soundhole ring, unbound rosewood 'board, 12-fret neck and slotted peghead from '70.			
1968-1970	Short-scale	$1,500	$1,950
1970-1979	Long-scale	$1,400	$1,825
1980-1993	Long-scale	$1,200	$1,550
N-20			
1968-1992. Classical, Brazilian rosewood back and sides (changed to Indian rosewood in '69), multi-bound, 12-fret neck, solid headstock (changed to slotted in '70), natural.			
1968-1969	Brazilian, short-scale	$5,200	$6,800
1969	Prismatone pu & Baldwin C-1 Amp	$7,000	$9,200
1970	Indian, short-scale	$2,600	$3,400
1970-1979	Indian, long-scale	$2,600	$3,400
1980-1992	Long-scale	$2,600	$3,400
N-20 B			
1985-1986. Brazilian rosewood N-20.			
1985-1986		$4,800	$6,200
OM-1			
1999-2002, 2009-2010. Sitka spruce top, sapele back and sides, East Indian rosewood 'board, natural satin finish.			
1999-2010		$650	$825
OM-1 GT			
2011-2014. OM-1 with gloss top.			
2011-2014		$650	$825
OM-15			
2001-2003. Mahogany body, cutaway.			
2001-2003		$800	$1,025

MODEL YEAR	FEATURES	EXC. COND. LOW	HIGH
OM-15 M			
2015. All mahogany, natural satin finish.			
2015		$800	$1,025
OM-16 GT			
2001-2005. Spruce top, mahogany back, sides and neck, natural gloss finish.			
2001-2005		$775	$1,025
OM-18			
1930-1934. Orchestra Model, mahogany back and sides, 14-fret neck, solid peghead, banjo tuners (changed to right-angle in '31).			
1930-1931	Banjo tuners, small 'guard	$24,000	$31,000
1931	Standard tuners, small 'guard	$18,000	$24,000
1932-1933	Standard tuners, large 'guard	$15,000	$19,500
OM-18 Authentic 1933			
2013-2019. Period-correct (1933) appointments, Vintage Tone System, vintage gloss finish.			
2013-2019		$3,000	$3,900
OM-18 Golden Era			
2003-2009. Mahogany back and sides, Brazilian rosewood purfling and binding.			
2003-2009		$2,000	$2,600
OM-18 P			
1930-1931. Plectrum.			
1930-1931		$7,100	$9,200
OM-18 Special			
2012. Custom Shop model.			
2012		$1,950	$2,500
OM-18 V			
1999-2009. Vintage features.			
1999-2009		$1,750	$2,250
OM-18 VLJ Laurence Juber			
2002, 2008-2010. Cutaway, Adirondack spruce top.			
2002-2009		$2,650	$3,400
OM-21			
1994-present. Indian rosewood back and sides, herringbone back stripe and soundhole ring, 14-fret neck, chrome tuners, natural or sunburst.			
1994-2019		$1,550	$2,000
OM-21 Special			
1991, 2007-2011. Upgrade to ebony 'board, rosewood bindings.			
1992-2011		$1,750	$2,300
OM-21 Special Limited Edition			
1991. Custom Shop, prototype to '92 production.			
1991	36 made	$1,750	$2,300
OM-28			
1929-1933, 1990-1997, 2015-present. Brazilian rosewood back and sides, 14-fret neck, solid peghead, banjo tuners (changed to right-angle in '31), reintroduced with Indian rosewood for '90-'97 and again in 2015.			
1929	Banjo pegs, small 'guard, pyramid end bridge	$73,000	$94,000
1930	Early '30, banjo tuners, small 'guard, pyramid	$64,000	$83,000

MODEL YEAR	FEATURES	EXC. COND. LOW	HIGH
1930	Late '30, banjo tuners, small 'guard, belly bridge	$58,000	$75,000
1931	Early '31, banjo tuners, small 'guard, belly bridge	$58,000	$75,000
1931	Late '31, standard tuners, large 'guard	$48,000	$62,000
1931	Mid '31, banjo tuners, large 'guard	$55,000	$71,000
1932-1933	Standard tuners, full-size 'guard	$48,000	$62,000
1990-1997		$1,750	$2,300
2015-2019		$1,750	$2,300

OM-28 Authentic 1931
2015-2019. Adirondack spruce top, Madagascar rosewood back and sides, Vintage Tone System (VTS).

2015-2019		$4,300	$5,700

OM-28 E Modern Deluxe
2020. Sitka spruce VTS top, East Indian rosewood back and sides, flamed maple binding, gloss finish.

2020		$3,200	$4,150

OM-28 E Retro
2012-2019. Sitka top, Indian rosewood back and sides, herringbone binding, Fishman.

2012-2019		$2,000	$2,575

OM-28 Golden Era
2003-2004. Brazilian rosewood back and sides, Adirondack spruce top.

2003-2004		$6,000	$7,800

OM-28 Golden Era Guatemalan Rosewood
2015. Custom Shop model, Guatemalan rosewood back and sides.

2015		$3,500	$4,600

OM-28 JM John Mayer
2003. Limited Edition, 404 made.

2003		$6,000	$8,000

OM-28 LE
1985. Limited Edition only 40 made, Guitar of the Month, Indian rosewood back and sides, herringbone top binding, V-neck.

1985		$2,350	$3,050

OM-28 M Roseanne Cash
2008. Signature Edition, Madagascar rosewood back and sides, 100 made.

2008		$3,400	$4,400

OM-28 Marquis
2005-2015. Pre-war appointments, Adirondack top, East Indian rosewood back, sides and headplate.

2005-2015		$2,375	$3,100

OM-28 Marquis Adirondack
2011-2013. Adirondack spruce top.

2011-2013		$2,375	$3,100

OM-28 Marquis Madagascar
2007-2008. Madagascar rosewood.

2007-2008		$2,375	$3,100

OM-28 Modern Deluxe
2019-present. Sitka spruce top with Vintage Tone System (VTS), East Indian rosewood back and sides, '30s style script logo on headstock.

2019		$2,000	$2,600

OM-28 PB Perry Bechtel
1993. Guitar of the Month, signed by Perry Bechtel's widow Ina, Indian rosewood back and sides, zigzag back stripe, chrome tuners, V-neck, 50 made.

1993		$3,200	$4,200

OM-28 SO Sing Out!
1985. For Sing Out! Magazine's 35th anniversary, label signed by Pete Seeger.

1985		$2,250	$2,900

OM-28 V Custom Shop Brazilian and Adirondack
2000-2001. Brazilian rosewood back and sides, Adirondack "red" spruce top, ca. 1933 prewar features including Martin gold headstock decal logo.

2000-2001		$5,700	$7,400

OM-28 VR/OM-28 V
1984-1990, 1999-2014. VR suffix until '99, then just V (Vintage Series), rosewood back and sides.

1984-1999	VR	$2,100	$2,800
1999-2014	V	$2,100	$2,800

OM-35
2003-2007. 000-size body, Indian rosewood sides and 3-piece back, spruce top, gloss natural finish.

2003-2007		$1,800	$2,300

OM-40 BLE
1990. Limited Edition, 50 made, Brazilian rosewood back and sides.

1990		$6,000	$7,750

OM-40 LE
1994. Limited Edition, Guitar of the Month, Indian rosewood back and sides, double pearl borders, snowflake inlay on 'board, gold tuners, natural (57 sold) or sunburst (29 sold).

1994		$3,000	$3,900

OM-40 Rory Block
2004. Limited Edition, 38 made, 000-size, Indian rosewood back and sides, Englemann spruce top, 'the road' inlay markers, vintage-auto inlay on headstock.

2004		$2,400	$3,075

OM-41 Special
2005-2006. Rosewood back and sides, Style 45 snowflake inlays.

2005-2006		$2,500	$3,250

OM-42
1930, 1999-present. Indian rosewood back and sides, Style 45 snowflake inlays, there were 2 guitars labeled OM-42 built in 1930.

1930	2 made		$77,000	$100,000
1999-2019			$3,100	$4,000

OM-42 Flamed Mahogany
2006. Limited Edition, 30 made, flamed mahogany back and sides, vines.

2006		$5,000	$6,500

OM-42 Koa
2005-2008. Koa sides and back.

2006-2008		$3,000	$3,900

2015 Martin OM-21
Rivington Guitars

1930 Martin OM-28
Bernunzio Uptown Music

GUITARS

*2002 Martin OM-45
GE Golden Era*

Carter Vintage Guitars

*2016 Martin CS-OM
True North-16*

MODEL YEAR	FEATURES	EXC. COND. LOW	HIGH

OM-42 PS Paul Simon
1997. Bookmatched sitka spruce top, Indian rosewood back and sides, 42- and 45-style features, low profile PS neck, 500 planned but only 223 made.

1997		$3,000	$3,900

OM-45
1930-1933. OM-style, 45 level appointments. Condition is critically important on this or any ultra high-end instrument, minor flaws are critical to value.

1930	Banjo pegs, 19 made	$211,000	$275,000
1931	10 made	$154,000	$200,000
1932	5 made	$154,000	$200,000
1933	6 made	$145,000	$200,000

OM-45/SOM-45/Special OM-45
1977-1994. First batch labeled SOM-45, 2 labeled OM-45 N in '94 that had square tube bar in neck and without scalloped braces.

1977-1979		$5,400	$7,000
1980-1989		$4,900	$6,400
1990-1994		$4,700	$6,100
1994	OM-45 N option	$4,700	$6,100

OM-45 Custom Deluxe
1998-1999. Limited custom shop run of 14, Adirondack spruce and typical Style 45 appointments.

1998-1999		$12,000	$15,400

OM-45 Deluxe
1930. Only 14 made, Brazilian rosewood back and sides, zipper pattern back stripe, pearl inlay in 'guard and bridge. Condition is critically important on this or any ultra high-end instrument, minor flaws are critical to value.

1930		$253,000	$330,000

OM-45 Deluxe (Special)
1999. 4 made on special order, highly figured Brazilian rosewood.

1999		$15,000	$20,000

OM-45 Deluxe Golden Era
1998. Brazilian, few made.

1998		$15,000	$20,000

OM-45 GE Golden Era
1999, 2001-2005. Red spruce top, Brazilian rosewood.

1999-2005		$15,000	$20,000

OM-45 Tasmanian Blackwood
2005. Limited Edition, 29 made, Tasmanian Blackwood (koa-family) back and sides with curly grain, 000-size, OM and 45 style appointments.

2005		$5,500	$7,000

OM-45/OM-45B Roy Rogers
2006. Limited Edition, based on Roy's 1930 OM-45 Deluxe, Indian rosewood (84 made) or Brazilian rosewood (45B, 14 made).

2006	Brazilian	$15,600	$20,500
2006	Indian	$6,900	$8,900

OM 1833 Custom Shop Limited Edition
2006. Italian alpine spruce top, flamed claro walnut back and sides, 000-size, low profile 14-fret neck, fancy inlay and appointments, natural gloss finish.

2006		$2,800	$3,600

MODEL YEAR	FEATURES	EXC. COND. LOW	HIGH

CS-OM True North-16
2016. Custom Shop Limited Edition, 50 made, Adirondack spruce top, figured koa back and sides, back features a compass design inlaid with flamed jarrah, Claro walnut, waterfall bubinga and Paua pearl, ebony headplate has True North design inlaid with mother of pearl.

2016		$7,400	$9,600

OM Chris Hillman
2009-2010. Adirondack top, Indian rosewood back and sides, sunburst.

2009-2010		$2,200	$2,900

OM Jeff Daniels
2012-2013. Based on Daniels 1934 C-2 archtop conversion, Adirondack, Madagascar rosewood back and sides, sunburst.

2012-2013		$2,200	$2,900

OM Negative
2007-2008. Limited Edition, 60 made, black body and white 'board, black inside label signed Dick Boak, gloss finish.

2007-2008		$2,600	$3,400

OMC Aura
2004-2011. OM size, cutaway, rosewood back and sides, Fishman Aura.

2004-2011		$1,850	$2,400

OMC Cherry
2008-2013. Sustainable wood program, solid cherry back and sides, solid rescued spruce top, 000 body, cutaway, Fishman.

2008-2013		$1,500	$1,950

OMC Fingerstyle 1
2005-2008. Cutaway, Spanish cedar back and sides, no inlays.

2005-2008		$1,600	$2,100

OMC Red Birch
2005-2009. Sustainable Series.

2005-2009		$1,650	$2,100

OMC-1 E
2009-2010. Style 28 appointments, cutaway, on-board Fishman.

2009-2010		$625	$800

OMC-15 E
2001-2007. All solid mahogany body.

2001-2007		$850	$1,125

OMC-15 ME
2016-present. Mahogany top, back and sides, East Indian rosewood 'board, Fishman electronics.

2016-2019		$950	$1,225

OMC-16 E Burst
2019-present. Mahogany burst ovangkol gloss top, satin ovangkol back and sides, Fishman electronics.

2019-2020		$1,300	$1,725

OMC-16 E Koa
2005-2009. Koa back and sides, on-board electronics.

2005-2009		$1,250	$1,600

OMC-16 E Maple
2005-2009. Maple, on-board electronics.

2005		$1,150	$1,500

MODEL YEAR	FEATURES	EXC. COND. LOW	HIGH

OMC-16 E/E Premium

2003-2007, 2017-2019. Sitka spruce top, sapele back and sides, on-board electronics. Premium model with Prefix Premium Blend electronics. Reintroduced '17 with cherry back and sides and Fishman® Matrix VT.

2003-2007		$1,250	$1,600
2017-2019	16E, Reintroduced	$1,250	$1,600

OMC-16 GTE

2010-2013. Gloss top, satin sapele back and sides.

2010-2013		$1,000	$1,300

OMC-16 RE Aura

2005-2009. East Indian rosewood back and sides, gloss body.

2005-2009		$1,400	$1,800

OMC-16 RE/RE Premium

2003-2005. Solid rosewood back and sides, on-board electronics.

2003-2005		$1,250	$1,600

OMC-16 WE

2002-2003. Walnut back and sides.

2002-2003		$1,125	$1,450

OMC-18 E

2017-2019. Sitka spruce top, mahogany back and sides, ebony 'board, Fishman electronics.

2017-2019		$1,750	$2,300

OMC-18 LJ Laurence Juber

2008-2010. Cutaway 000, Adirondack spruce top.

2008-2010		$2,300	$3,000

OMC-28

1990. Guitar of the Month, 81 made, Indian rosewood, low profile neck, label signed by C.F. Martin IV.

1990		$1,750	$2,300

OMC-28 BLJ Laurence Juber

2004. Brazilian rosewood, 50 made.

2004		$5,300	$6,900

OMC-28 E

2006-2009, 2017-2019. OMC-28 with Fishman Ellipse. Reintroduced '17 with Fishman Aura.

2006-2009		$1,900	$2,475
2017-2019		$1,900	$2,475

OMC-28 Laurence Juber

2004-2005. OM size, cutaway, Indian rosewood.

2004-2005		$2,200	$2,850

OMC-28 M Laurence Juber

2006-2011. Madagascar rosewood.

2006-2011		$2,600	$3,400

OMC-35 E

2016. Sitka spruce top, East Indian rosewood back & sides, ebony 'board and 'guard, Fishman electronics.

2016		$1,950	$2,550

OMC-41 Richie Sambora

2006-2009. Madagascar rosewood sides and back, combination Style 45 and 41 appointments, 12-string is MC12-41 Richie Sambora, planned 200 made combined models.

2006-2009		$3,400	$4,400

OMC-LJ Pro Laurence Juber

2013. Custom Artist Edition, Adirondack spruce top, flamed maple back and sides.

2013		$2,300	$3,000

OMCPA Series

2010-2019. Performing Artist Series, OM size, cutaway, acoustic/electric, various woods.

2010-2016	OMCPA1/1 Plus	$1,650	$2,150
2011	OMCPA2	$900	$1,175
2011-2013	OMCPA3	$1,150	$1,500
2011-2019	OMCPA4 Sapele	$925	$1,200
2012-2019	OMCPA4 Rosewood	$925	$1,200
2013-2016	OMCPA5 Black	$400	$500

OMCRE

2008-2009. Carpathian spruce top, East Indian rosewood sides and back, Babicz adjustable neck joint, Fishman, gloss finish.

2008-2009		$1,650	$2,100

OMC-X1E Black

2020-present. Replaces OMCXAE Black. Jett black HPL top, back and sides, Fishman electronics.

2020		$375	$500

OMCXK2E

2006-2009. Hawaiian Koa HPL (high pressure laminate) textured finish.

2006-2009		$475	$625

OMJM John Mayer

2003-present. Indian rosewood sides and back.

2003-2019		$1,925	$2,500

OMM

2000-2003. Solid spruce top, mahogany back and sides.

2000-2003		$550	$700

OMM John Renbourne

2011-2013. Madagascar rosewood sides and back.

2011-2013		$2,475	$3,200

OMXAE Black

2014-2019. Black HPL back and sides, black Richlite 'board.

2014-2019		$325	$425

POW MIA

2006-2010. POW MIA logo position marker lettering on fretboard, D-style body, dark finish.

2006-2010		$2,175	$2,825

PS2 Paul Simon Signature

2003. Paul Simon signature logo at bottom of fretboard, 200 made.

2003		$2,100	$2,700

R-15

1934. Archtop, sunburst.

1934	2 made	$1,175	$1,525

R-17

1934-1942. All mahogany, arched top and back, 3-segment f-holes (changed to 1-segment in '37).

1934-1942	940 made	$1,175	$1,525

R-18 P

1934-1936. Only 4 made, plectrum neck.

1934-1936		$1,200	$1,600

R-18 S/R-18

1932-1942. Spruce arched top (carved top by 1937), mahogany back and sides, bound top, sunburst.

1932-1942	1,928 made	$1,600	$2,100

Martin OM Jeff Daniels

1937 Martin R-18
Frank Manno

GUITARS

2016 Martin SS-OMVine-16

Martin SWOMGT

R-18 T

1934-1941. Tenor archtop, 14 3/8" lower bout, 2 f-holes, dot markers, sunburst.

MODEL YEAR	FEATURES	EXC. COND. LOW	HIGH
1934-1941		$1,200	$1,600

R-21

1938. 000 body archtop, 1 made.

1938		$3,300	$4,300

SC-13 E

2020-present. Sitka spruce top, koa veneer back and sides, patent-pending Sure Align neck system, Fishman electronics.

2020		$1,050	$1,375

Schoenberg Soloist by C.F. Martin

1987-1994. Designed by Eric Schoenberg with help from luthier Dana Bourgeois, OM body, Brazilian rosewood back and sides.

1987-1994		$4,500	$5,800

Shenandoah Series

1983-1993. Bodies and necks were built in Japan with final assembly and finishing in Nazareth and a Thinline piezo added, styled after U.S. models with a 32 added to the model name.

1983-1993	Various models	$600	$1,000

SP000 Series

1996-2002. Special Edition 000-size, spruce top with aging toner, scalloped bracing, rosewood or mahogany body.

1996-1997	SP000C-16TR	$1,075	$1,375
1996-2002	SP000-16	$1,025	$1,325
1996-2002	SP000-16R	$1,025	$1,325
1996-2002	SP000-16T	$1,025	$1,325
1996-2002	SP000-16TR	$1,025	$1,325
1997-2002	SP000C-16R	$1,075	$1,375
1999-2002	SP000C-16	$1,075	$1,375
1999-2002	SP000C-16E	$1,125	$1,450
2003	SP000C-16R Custom Shop	$1,800	$2,300

SP00-16 RST Stauffer

2000-2002. Stauffer 6-on-a-side headstock, 12-fret neck, rosewood back and sides.

2000-2002		$1,050	$1,350

SPD12-16 R

1997-2004. 12-string, solid rosewood body, abalone soundhole ring, Style-45 backstripe.

1999-2000		$1,000	$1,300

SPD-16 Series

1997-2004. D-16 Series Special models.

1996-1999	SPD-16TR	$1,025	$1,325
1997-2004	SPD-16	$1,025	$1,325
1997-2004	SPD-16T	$1,025	$1,325
1999-2001	SPD-16B Black	$1,025	$1,325
1999-2002	SPD-16M Maple	$950	$1,225
1999-2002	SPD-16W Walnut	$975	$1,250
2000	SPD-16E	$1,050	$1,350
2000-2002	SPD-16R	$1,025	$1,325
2000-2005	SPD-16K	$1,450	$1,850
2000-2005	SPD-16K2	$1,450	$1,850

SPDC-16 Series

1997-2001. Cutaway version of SPD-16.

MODEL YEAR	FEATURES	EXC. COND. LOW	HIGH
1997-1999	SPDC-16TR	$1,025	$1,325
1997-2001	SPDC-16RE Rosewood	$1,075	$1,400
2000-2002	SPDC-16R	$1,025	$1,325

SPJC-16 RE

2000-2003. Single-cut, East Indian rosewood body, 000-size, on-board electronics.

2000-2003		$1,075	$1,400

SPOM-16

1999-2001. Mahogany.

1999-2001		$1,075	$1,400

SS-0041GB-17

2017-present. Limited Edition of 50, Grand Concert 12-fret, European spruce top with Vintage Tone System (VTS), Guatemalan rosewood back and sides, gloss finish.

2017-2019		$4,700	$6,100

SS-00L41-16

2016-present. Limited Edition, Adirondack spruce top with Vintage Tone System (VTS), moabi back and sides, mahogany neck, hand-rubbed finish.

2016-2019		$2,800	$3,600

SS-OMVine-16

2016. Limited Edition of 35, NAMM show special, figured English walnut, aluminum vine inlay on ebony 'board.

2016		$7,300	$9,500

Stauffer

1830s-ca.1850s. One of C.F. Martin's earliest models, distinguished by the scrolled, six-on-a-side headstock, ornamentation varies. Each instrument should be evaluated on a case-by-case basis, those in truly original excellent condition may be worth more than the values shown.

1835	Fancy (2nd highest)	$22,000	$28,900
1835	Fancy (highest)	$28,900	$99,000
1835	Mid-level	$15,100	$19,900
1835	Plain (2nd lowest)	$10,500	$14,500
1835	Plain (lowest)	$7,200	$9,800

Sting Mini

2006. 100 made, Size 5, Western red cedar top, Solomon padauk body.

2005-2006		$1,625	$2,100

Stinger

1980s-1990s. Import copy offset S-style electric solidbody.

1980s-90s		$150	$200

SW00-D8 Machiche

2006-2007. Smartwood Limited Edition, 125 made, rescued solid spruce top, sustainable machiche sides and back.

2006-2007		$1,000	$1,300

SWC

1998. Smartwood 'The Sting Signature Classical Model', machiche wood body.

1998		$1,000	$1,300

MODEL YEAR	FEATURES	EXC. COND. LOW	HIGH

SWD
1998-2001. Smartwood D-size, built from wood material certified by the Forest Stewardship Council, sitka top, cherry back and sides, natural satin finish.

1998-2001		$850	$1,100

SWD Red Birch
2003-2005. Red Birch.

2003-2005		$850	$1,100

SWDGT
2001-2016. Gloss top SWD.

2001-2016		$850	$1,100

SWDTG
2000-2007. Cherry back and sides, gloss finish.

2000-2007		$850	$1,100

SWMGT
2002-2003. M size, cherry back and sides, gloss finish.

2002-2003		$850	$1,100

SWOM
2000-2001. Sustainable Woods Series.

2000-2001		$850	$1,100

SWOMGT
2001-2018. Smartwood OM, rescued solid sitka spruce top, sustainable cherry sides and back, gloss finish.

2001-2018		$850	$1,100

Yuengling 180th Anniversary Custom
2008. Celebrating 180th company anniversary, limited production, large company logo on top of body, fancy D-41 style appointments, certificate.

2008		$2,500	$3,200

Maruha
1960s-1970s. Japanese-made acoustic, classical, archtop and solidbody guitars, often copies of American brands. Probably not imported into the U.S.

Marvel
1950s-mid-1960s. Brand name used for budget guitars and basses marketed by Peter Sorkin Company in New York, New York. Sorkin manufactured and distributed Premier guitars and amplifiers made by its Multivox subsidiary. Marvel instruments were primarily beginner-grade. Brand disappears by mid-'60s. The name was also used on archtop guitars made by Regal and marketed by the Slingerland drum company in the 1930s to early 1940s.

Electric
1940s-1950s. Various models.

1940s-50s		$175	$425

Marveltone by Regal
1925-1930. Private branded by Regal, Marveltone pearl style logo on headstock.

Guitar
1925-1930. 14" Brazilian rosewood.

1925-1930		$2,000	$2,600

Masaki Sakurai
See Kohno brand.

Mason
1936-1939. Henry L. Mason on headstock, wholesale distribution, similar to Gibson/Cromwell, pressed wood back and sides.

Student/Intermediate Student
1936-1939. Various flat-top and archtop student/ budget models.

1936-1939		$475	$850

Mason Bernard
1990-1991. Founded by Bernie Rico (BC Rich founder). During this period BC Rich guitars were licensed and controlled by Randy Waltuch and Class Axe. Most Mason models were designs similar to the BC Rich Assassin, according to Bernie Rico only the very best materials were used, large MB logo on headstock. Around 225 guitars were built bearing this brand.

Maton
1946-present. Intermediate and professional grade, production/custom, acoustic, acoustic/electric, hollowbody and solidbody guitars built in Box Hill, Victoria, Australia. Founded by Bill May and his brother Reg and still run by the family. Available in USA since '82.

Matsuda Guitars
See listing for Michihiro Matsuda.

Matsuoka
1970s. Ryoji Matsuoka from Japan built intermediate grade M series classical guitars that often featured solid tops and laminated sides and back.

Matt Pulcinella Guitars
1998-present. Production/custom, professional grade, electric guitars and basses built in Chadds Ford, Pennsylvania by luthier Matt Pulcinella.

Mauel Guitars
Luthier Hank Mauel builds his premium grade, custom, flat-tops in Auburn, California. He began in 1995.

Maurer
Late 1880s-1944. Robert Maurer built guitars and mandolins in the late 1880s under the Maurer and Champion brands in his Chicago shop. Carl and August Larson bought the company in 1900 and retained the Maurer name. The Larsons also built under the Prairie State, Euphonon, W. J. Dyer and Wm. C. Stahl brands.

Max B
2000-present. Luthier Sebastien Sulser builds professional grade, production/custom, electric guitars and basses in Kirby, Vermont.

1962 Maton EG240SE

Maton Fyrebird 12
Ben Rogers

GUITARS

McCurdy The Moderna

Late-1970s MCI B-35 Guitorgan

Tom Pfeifer

MODEL YEAR	FEATURES	EXC. COND. LOW	HIGH

May Bell

1923-1940s. Brand of flat-top guitars, some with fake resonators, marketed by the Slingerland Company. Most were made by Regal.

Maya

See El Maya.

McAlister Guitars

1997-present. Premium grade, custom, flat-tops built by luthier Roy McAlister in Watsonville, California.

McCollum Guitars

1994-2009. Luthier Lance McCollum builds his premium grade, custom, flat-top and harp guitars in Colfax, California. McCollum died in 2009.

McCurdy Guitars

1983-present. Premium grade, production/ custom, archtops built by luthier Ric McCurdy originally in Santa Barbara, California and, since '91, New York, New York.

McElroy

1995-present. Premium grade, custom, classical and flat-top steel string acoustic guitars built by luthier Brent McElroy in Seattle, Washington.

McGill Guitars

1976-present. Luthier Paul McGill builds his premium grade, production/custom, classical, resonator, and acoustic/electric guitars in Nashville, Tennessee.

McGlincy

Ca. 1974-ca. 1978. Custom flat-tops built by luthier Edward McGlincy in Toms River, New Jersey. Only 12 instruments made and owners included Gordon Lightfoot and David Bromberg. He later offered uke and guitar kits. He also operated Ed's Musical Instruments. McGlincy died in '97.

McGlynn Guitars

2005-2007. Luthier Michael J. McGlynn built his premium and presentation grade, custom, solidbody guitars in Henderson, Nevada. McGlynn died in '07.

McGowan Guitars

Luthier Brian McGowan builds his production/ custom, premium grade, steel-string acoustic guitars in Hampton, Virginia. He began in 2004.

MCI, Inc

1967-1988. MusiConics International (MCI), of Waco, Texas, introduced the world to the Guitorgan, invented by Bob Murrell. Later, they also offered effects and a steel guitar. In the '80s, a MIDI version was offered. MCI was also involved with the Daion line of guitars in the late '70s and early '80s. MCI also built a double-neck lap steel.

MODEL YEAR	FEATURES	EXC. COND. LOW	HIGH

GuitOrgan B-35

1970s (ca. 1976-1978?). Duplicated the sounds of an organ and more. MCI bought double-cut semi-hollow body guitars from others and outfitted them with lots of switches and buttons. Each fret has 6 segments that correspond to an organ tone. There was also a B-300 and B-30 version, and the earlier M-300 and 340.

1970s	Fully functional	$900	$1,300

McInturff

1996-present. Professional and premium grade, production/custom, solidbody guitars built by luthier Terry C. McInturff originally in Holly Springs, North Carolina, and since '04, in Moncure, North Carolina. McInturff spent 17 years doing guitar repair and custom work before starting his own guitar line.

McKnight Guitars

1992-present. Luthier Tim McKnight builds his custom, premium grade, acoustic steel string guitars in Morral, Ohio.

McPherson Guitars

1981-present. Premium grade, production, flat-tops built by luthier Mander McPherson in Sparta, Wisconsin.

Mean Gene

1988-1990. Heavy metal style solidbodies made by Gene Baker, who started Baker U.S.A. guitars in '97, and Eric Zoellner in Santa Maria, California. They built around 30 custom guitars. Baker currently builds b3 guitars.

Megas Guitars

1989-present. Luthier Ted Megas builds his premium grade, custom, archtop and solidbody guitars, originally in San Francisco, and currently in Portland, Oregon.

Melancon

1995-present. Professional and premium grade, custom/production, solid and semi-hollow body guitars and basses built by luthier Gerard Melancon in Thibodaux, Louisiana.

Mello, John F.

1973-present. Premium grade, production/custom, classical and flat-top guitars built by luthier John Mello in Kensington, California.

Melophonic

1960s. Brand built by the Valco Company of Chicago, Illinois.

Resonator Guitar

1965. Valco-made.

1965		$750	$975

MODEL YEAR	FEATURES	EXC. COND. LOW	HIGH

Melville Guitars

1988-present. Luthier Christopher Melville builds his premium grade, custom, flat-tops in Milton, Queensland, Australia.

Memphis

One of the many guitar brands built by Japan's Matsumoku company.

Mercurio

2002-2005. Luthier Peter Mercurio built his custom/production solidbody guitars, featuring his interchangeable PickupPak system to swap pickups, in Chanhassen, Minnesota.

Mermer Guitars

1983-present. Luthier Richard Mermer builds his premium grade, production/custom, steel-string, nylon-string, and Hawaiian guitars in Sebastian, Florida.

Merrill Brothers

Premium grade, production/custom, steel-string and harp guitars built by luthiers Jim and Dave Merrill in Williamsburg, Virginia, starting in 1998.

Mesrobian

1995-present. Luthier Carl Mesrobian builds his professional and premium grade, custom, archtop guitars in Salem, Massachusetts.

Messenger

1967-1968. Built by Musicraft, Inc., originally of 156 Montgomery Street, San Francisco, California. The distinguishing feature of the Messengers is a metal alloy neck which extended through the body to the tailblock, plus mono or stereo outputs. Sometime before March '68 the company relocated to Astoria, Oregon. Press touted "improved" magnesium neck, though it's not clear if this constituted a change from '67. Brand disappears after '68. They also made basses.

Electric Hollowbody Archtop

1967-1968. Symmetrical double-cut body shape, metal neck with rosewood 'boards, stereo.

1967-1968		$1,600	$2,100

Metropolitan

1995-2008. Professional and premium grade, production/custom, retro-styled solidbodies designed by David Wintz reminiscent of the '50s National Res-o-glas and wood body guitars. They featured full-scale set-neck construction and a wood body instead of Res-o-glas. Wintz also made Robin and Alamo brand instruments.

Electric Solidbody

1995-2008	Various models	$1,200	$1,600

Meyers Custom Guitars

Professional grade, custom, solidbody electric guitars built by luthier Donald Meyers in Houma, Louisiana, beginning 2005.

Miami

1920s. Instruments built by the Oscar Schmidt Co. and possibly others. Most likely a brand made for a distributor.

Michael Collins Custom Guitars

Premium grade, custom/production, classical, flamenco and steel string guitars built in Argyle, New York, by luthier Michael Collins, starting in 1975.

Michael Collins Guitars

2002-present. Luthier Michael Collins builds his professional and premium grade, custom, Selmer style, archtop and flat-top guitars in Keswick, Ontario. He also builds mandolins.

Michael Cone

1968-present. Presentation grade, production/custom, classical guitars built previously in California and currently in Kihei Maui, Hawaii by luthier Michael Cone. He also builds ukuleles.

Michael Dunn Guitars

Luthier Michael Dunn begins in 1968, builds production/custom Maccaferri-style guitars in New Westminster, British Columbia. He also offers a harp uke and a Weissenborn- or Knutsen-style Hawaiian guitar, and has built archtops.

Michael Kelly

1999-present. Founded by Tracy Hoeft and offering intermediate and professional grade, production, acoustic, solidbody and archtop guitars. The brand was owned by the Hanser Music Group from 2004-'15. They also offer mandolins and basses.

Michael Lewis Instruments

1992-present. Luthier Michael Lewis builds his premium and presentation grade, custom, archtop guitars in Grass Valley, California. He also builds mandolins.

Michael Menkevich

Luthier Michael Menkevich builds his professional and premium grade, production/custom, flamenco and classical guitars in Elkins Park, Pennsylvania, starting in 1970.

Michael Silvey Custom Guitars

2003-ca. 2007. Solidbody electric guitars built by Michael Silvey in North Canton, Ohio.

Michael Thames

1972-present. Luthier Michael Thames builds his premium grade, custom/production, classical guitars in Taos, New Mexico.

1968 Messenger
Jamsy

*1997 Metropolitan
Westport Custom*

GUITARS

Michihiro Matsuda OM

Microfrets Plainsman
Michael Kellum

MODEL YEAR	FEATURES	EXC. COND. LOW	HIGH

Michael Tuttle

2003-present. Professional and premium grade, custom, solid and hollowbody guitars and basses built by luthier Michael Tuttle in Saugus, California.

Michihiro Matsuda

1997-present. Presentation grade, production/custom, steel and nylon string acoustic guitars built by luthier Michihiro Matsuda in Oakland, California. He also builds harp guitars.

Microfrets

1967-1975, 2004-2005. Professional grade, production, electric guitars built in Myersville, Maryland. They also built basses. Founded by Ralph S. Jones, Sr. in Frederick, Microfrets offered over 20 models of guitars that sported innovative designs and features, with pickups designed by Bill Lawrence. The brand was revived, again in Frederick, by Will Meadors and Paul Rose in '04.

Serial numbers run from about 1000 to about 3800. Not all instruments have serial numbers, particularly ones produced in '75. Serial numbers do not appear to be correlated to a model type, but are sequential by the general date of production.

Instruments can be identified by body styles as follows; Styles 1, 1.5, 2, and 3. An instrument may be described as a Model Name and Style Number (for example, Covington Style 1). Style 1 has a wavey-shaped pickguard with control knobs mounted below the guard and the 2-piece guitar body has a particle board side gasket. Style 1.5 has the same guard and knobs, but no side body gasket. Style 2 has an oblong pickguard with top mounted control knobs and a pancake style seam between the top and lower part of the body. Style 3 has a seamless 2-piece body and a Speedline neck.

Baritone Signature
1971. Baritone version of Signature Guitar, sharply pointed double-cut, with or without f-holes, single- or double-dot inlays.

1971		$1,100	$1,400

Baritone Stage II
1971-ca. 1975. Double-cut, 2 pickups.

1971-1975		$1,100	$1,400

Calibra I
1969-1975. Double-cut, 2 pickups, f-hole.

1969-1975		$950	$1,250

Covington
1967-1969. Offset double-cut, 2 pickups, f-hole.

1967-1969		$1,400	$1,850

Golden Comet
1969. Double-cut, 2 pickups, f-hole, name changed to Wanderer.

1969		$1,200	$1,600

Golden Melody
1969, 2004-2005. Offset double-cut, 2 pickups, f-hole, name changed to Stage II in '69.

1969-1971		$1,325	$1,750

Huntington
1969-1975. Double-cut, 2 pickups.

1969-1975		$1,400	$1,850

Orbiter
1967-1969. Odd triple cutaway body, thumbwheel controls on bottom edge of 'guard.

1967-1969		$1,400	$1,850

Plainsman
1967-1969. Offset double-cut, 2 pickups, f-hole, thumbwheel controls on bottom edge of 'guard.

1967-1969		$1,500	$1,975

Signature
1967-1969. Double-cut, 2 pickups.

1967-1969		$1,400	$1,850

Spacetone
1969-1971, 2004-2005. Double-cut semi-hollow body, 2 pickups.

1969-1971		$1,400	$1,850

Stage II
1969-1975. Renamed from Golden Melody, offset double-cut, 2 pickups.

1969-1975		$1,325	$1,750

Swinger
1971-1975. Offset double-cut, 2 pickups.

1971-1975		$1,400	$1,850

Voyager/The Voyager
1967-1968. Early model, less than a dozen made, Voyager headstock logo (no Microfrets logo), 2 DeArmond-style single-coils, offset double-cut body, FM transmitter on upper bass bout facilitates wireless transmission to Microfrets receiver or FM radio.

1967-1968		$2,500	$3,300

Wanderer
1969-1971. Renamed from Golden Comet, double-cut, 2 pickups.

1969-1971		$1,200	$1,600

Mike Lull Custom Guitars

1995-present. Professional and premium grade, production/custom, guitars and basses built by luthier Mike Lull in Bellevue, Washington.

Milburn Guitars

1990-present. Luthiers Orville and Robert Milburn build their premium grade, custom, classical guitars in Sweet Home, Oregon.

Miller

1960s. One of the brand names of guitars built for others by Egmond in Holland.

Minarik

Luthier M.E. Minarik builds his professional and premium grade, custom/production, solid and chambered body guitars in Van Nuys, California.

Minerva

1930s. Resonator and archtop guitars sold through catalog stores, likely made by one of the big Chicago builders of the era.

MODEL YEAR	FEATURES	EXC. COND. LOW	HIGH

Mirabella

1997-present. Professional and premium grade, custom archtops, flat-tops, hollowbody, and solid-body guitars and basses built by luthier Cristian Mirabella in Babylon, New York. He also builds mandolins and ukes.

Miranda Guitars

2002-present. Owner Phil Green uses components made by various shops in California to assemble and set-up, professional grade, full-size travel/silent-practice guitars in Palo Alto, California.

Mitre

1983-1985. Bolt neck, solidbody guitars and basses made in Aldenville (or East Longmeadow), Massachusetts, featuring pointy body shapes, 2 humbuckers, active or passive electronics.

MJ Guitar Engineering

1993-present. Professional and premium grade, production/custom, hollowbody, chambered and solidbody guitars and basses built by luthier Mark Johnson in Rohnert Park, California.

Mobius Megatar

2000-2019. Professional grade, production, hybrid guitars designed for two-handed tapping, built in Mount Shasta, California. Founded by Reg Thompson, Henri Dupont, and Traktor Topaz in '97, they released their first guitars in '00.

Modulus

1978-2013. Founded by Geoff Gould in the San Francisco area, and later built in Novato, California. Modulus built professional grade, production/custom, solidbody electric guitars up to '05.

Genesis 2/2T

1996-2005. Double-cut, extended bass horn alder body, bolt-on carbon fiber/red cedar neck, hum-single-single pickups, locking vibrato (2T model).

1996-2005		$1,200	$1,600

Moll Custom Instruments

1996-present. Luthier Bill Moll builds his professional and premium grade, archtops in Springfield, Missouri. He has also built violins, violas and cellos.

Monrad, Eric

1993-present. Premium, custom, flamenco and classical guitars built by luthier Eric Monrad in Healdsburg, California.

Monroe Guitars

Luthier Matt Handley builds his custom, professional grade, solidbody electric guitars and basses in State Center, Iowa. He started in 2004.

Montalvo

See listing under Casa Montalvo.

Montaya

Late 1970s-1980s. Montaya Hyosung 'America' Inc., Korean acoustic and electric import copies.

Monteleone

1976-present. Presentation grade, production/custom, archtop guitars built by Luthier John Monteleone in Islip, New York. He also builds mandolins. Instruments should be evaluated on a case-by-case basis.

Montgomery Ward

The mail-order and retail giant offered a variety of instruments and amps from several different U.S. and overseas manufacturers.

Model 8379/H44 Stratotone

Mid-1950s. Private branded Harmony Stratotone, some without logo but with crown-style stencil/painted logo on headstock, many with gold-copper finish, 1 pickup.

1957		$750	$1,000

Monty

1980-present. Luthier Brian Monty builds his professional, premium and presentation grade, production/custom, archtop, semi-hollow, solidbody, and chambered electric guitars originally in Lennoxville, Quebec, and currently in Anne de Prescott, Ontario.

Moog

1964-present. Moog introduced its premium grade, production, Harmonic Control System solidbody guitar in 2008. They also offer guitar effects.

Moon (Japan)

1979-present. Professional and premium grade, production/custom, guitars and basses made in Japan.

Moon (Scotland)

1979-present. Intermediate, professional and premium grade, production/custom, acoustic and electric guitars built by luthier Jimmy Moon in Glasgow, Scotland. They also build mandolin family instruments.

Moonstone

1972-present. Professional, premium, and presentation grade production/custom flat-top, solid and semi-hollow electric guitars, built by luthier Steve Helgeson in Eureka, California. He also builds basses. Higher unit sales in the early-'80s. Some models have an optional graphite composite neck built by Modulus.

Eclipse Standard

1979-1983. Figured wood body, offset double-cut, neck-thru, dot markers, standard maple neck, natural finish.

1979-1983		$1,500	$1,950
1979-1983	XII	$1,500	$1,950

1969 Microfrets Signature

Miranda Travel Guitar

1980 Moonstone Vulcan Deluxe

1967 Mosrite Celebrity 3
Imaged by Heritage Auctions, HA.com

MODEL YEAR	FEATURES	EXC. COND. LOW	HIGH

Exploder
1980-1983. Figured wood solidbody, neck-thru, standard maple neck, natural finish.

1980-1983		$1,750	$2,300

Flaming V
1980-1984. Figured wood body, V-shaped, neck-thru, standard maple neck, natural finish.

1980-1984		$1,750	$2,300

M-80
1980-1984. Figured wood double-cut semi-hollow body, standard maple or optional graphite neck, natural finish.

1980s	Maple or graphite	$2,400	$3,200

Vulcan Deluxe
1979-1983. Figured maple carved-top body, offset double-cut, diamond markers, standard maple or optional graphite neck, natural finish.

1979-1983	Maple or graphite	$2,400	$3,200

Vulcan Standard
1979-1983. Mahogany carved-top body, offset double-cutaway, dot markers, standard maple or optional graphite neck, natural finish.

1979-1983	Maple or graphite	$2,200	$2,900

Morales
Ca.1967-1968. Guitars and basses made in Japan by Zen-On, not heavily imported into the U.S., if at all.

Solidbody Electric
1967-1968	Various models	$125	$275

More Harmony
1930s. Private branded by Dobro for Dailey's More Harmony Music Studio. Private branding for catalog companies, teaching studios, publishers, and music stores was common for the Chicago makers. More Harmony silk-screen logo on the headstock.

Dobro
1930s. 14" wood body with upper bout f-holes and metal resonator, sunburst.

1930s		$800	$1,050

Morgaine Guitars
Luthier Jorg Tandler builds his professional and premium grade, production/custom electrics in Germany, starting in 1994.

Morgan Monroe
1999-present. Intermediate grade, production, acoustic, acoustic/electric and resonator guitars and basses made in Korea and distributed by SHS International of Indianapolis, Indiana. They also offer mandolins and banjos.

Morris
1967-present. Intermediate, professional and premium grade, production, acoustic guitars imported by Moridaira of Japan. Morris guitars were first imported into the U.S. from the early '70s to around '90. They are again being imported into the

U.S. starting in 2001. They also offered mandolins in the '70s.

000 Copy
1970s. Brazilian rosewood laminate body.

1970s		$350	$450

Acoustic-Electric Archtop
1970s. Various models.

1970s		$450	$600

D-45 Copy
1970s. Brazilian laminate body.

1970s		$400	$525

Mortoro Guitars
1992-present. Luthier Gary Mortoro builds his premium grade, custom, archtop guitars in Miami, Florida.

Mosrite
The history of Mosrite has more ups and downs than just about any other guitar company. Founder Semie Moseley had several innovative designs and had his first success in 1954, at age 19, building doubleneck guitars for super picker Joe Maphis and protégé Larry Collins. Next came the Ventures, who launched the brand nationally by playing Mosrites and featuring them on album covers. At its '60s peak, the company was turning out around 1,000 guitars a month. The company ceased production in '69, and Moseley went back to playing gospel concerts and built a few custom instruments during the '70s.

In the early-'80s, Mosrite again set up shop in Jonas Ridge, North Carolina, but the plant burned down in November '83, taking about 300 guitars with it. In early-'92, Mosrite relocated to Booneville, Arkansas, producing a new line of Mosrites, of which 96% were exported to Japan, where the Ventures and Mosrite have always been popular. Semie Moseley died, at age 57, on August 7, '92 and the business carried on until finally closing its doors in '93. The Mosrite line has again been revived, offering intermediate and premium grade, production, reissues.

Throughout much of the history of Mosrite, production numbers were small and model features often changed. As a result, exact production dates are difficult to determine.

Balladeer
1964-1965. Mid-size flat-top, slope shoulder, natural or sunburst.

1964-1965		$1,075	$1,400

Brass Rail
1970s. Double-cut solidbody, has a brass plate running the length of the 'board.

1970s		$1,000	$1,300

Celebrity 1
Late-1960s-1970s. Thick hollowbody, 2 pickups, sunburst.

1960s-70s		$1,000	$1,300

The Official Vintage Guitar magazine Price Guide 2021   **Mosrite** Celebrity 2 Standard — **Mossman** Great Plains   **309**

GUITARS

MODEL YEAR	FEATURES	EXC. COND. LOW	HIGH

Celebrity 2 Standard
Late-1960s-1970s. Thin hollowbody, 2 pickups, in the '70s, it came in a Standard and a Deluxe version.

1960s-70s		$1,000	$1,300

Celebrity 3
Late-1960s-1970s. Thin hollowbody, double-cut, 2 pickups, f-holes.

1960s-70s		$1,000	$1,300

Combo Mark 1
1966-1968. Bound body, 1 f-hole.

1966-1968		$1,500	$1,975

Custom-Built
1952-1962. Pre-production custom instruments hand-built by Semie Moseley, guidance pricing only, each instrument will vary. A wide variety of instruments were made during this period. Some were outstanding, but others, especially those made around '60, could be very basic and of much lower quality. Logos would vary widely and some '60 logos looked especially homemade.

1952-1959	Rare, higher-end	$9,500	$13,000
1960-1962	Common, lower-end	$1,500	$2,000

D-40 Resonator
1960s. Symmetrical double-cut thinline archtop-style body with metal resonator in center of body, 2 pickups, 2 control knobs and toggle switch.

1960s		$1,100	$1,450

D-100 Californian
1960s. Double-cut, resonator guitar with 2 pickups.

1967		$1,100	$1,450

Gospel
1967. Thinline double-cut, f-hole, 2 pickups, vibrato, Gospel logo on headstock.

1967	Sunburst	$1,400	$1,850
1967	White	$1,950	$2,550

Joe Maphis Doubleneck
1963-1968. Limited Edition reissue of the guitar Semie Moseley made for Maphis, with the smaller octave neck, sunburst.

1963-1968	Octave 6/standard 6	$3,600	$4,800
1963-1968	Standard 6/12	$3,600	$4,800

Joe Maphis Mark 1
1959-1972. Semi-hollow double-cut, 2 single-coils, spruce top, walnut back, rosewood 'board, natural.

1959-1972		$1,600	$2,100

Joe Maphis Mark XVIII
1960s. 6/12 doubleneck, double-cut, 2 pickups on each neck, Moseley tremolo on 6-string.

1960s		$2,800	$3,600

Mosrite 1988
1988-early-1990s. Has traditional Mosrite body styling, Mosrite pickups and bridge.

1988		$550	$725

Octave Guitar
1963-1965. 14" scale, 1 pickup, Ventures Mosrite body style, single neck pickup, very few made.

1963-1965		$4,100	$5,400

Stereo 350
1974-1975. Single-cut solidbody, 2 outputs, 2 pickups, 4 knobs, slider and toggle, black.

1974-1975		$1,100	$1,475

Ventures Model
1963-1968. Double-cut solidbody, triple-bound body '63, no binding after, Vibramute for '63-'64, Moseley tailpiece '65-'68.

1963	Blue or red, bound	$5,725	$7,425
1963	Sunburst, bound	$4,775	$6,150
1964	Blue or red, Vibramute	$4,250	$5,500
1964	Sunburst, Vibramute	$3,925	$5,100
1965	Moseley (2 screws)	$3,100	$4,000
1965	Vibramute (3 screws)	$3,700	$4,800
1966-1968	Moseley	$2,600	$3,400

Ventures (Jonas Ridge/Boonville)
1982-1993. Made in Jonas Ridge, NC or Booneville, AR, classic Ventures styling.

1982-1993		$1,625	$2,100

Ventures Mark V
1963-1967. Double-cut solidbody.

1963-1967		$1,350	$1,775

Ventures Mark XII (12-String)
1966-1967. Double-cut solidbody, 12 strings.

1966-1967		$2,400	$3,100

Mossman

Professional and premium grade, production/custom, flat-top guitars built in Sulphur Springs, Texas, starting in 1965. They have also built acoustic basses. Founded by Stuart L. Mossman in Winfield, Kansas. In '75, fire destroyed one company building, including the complete supply of Brazilian rosewood. They entered into an agreement with C.G. Conn Co. to distribute guitars by '77. 1200 Mossman guitars in a Conn warehouse in Nevada were ruined by being heated during the day and frozen during the night. A disagreement about who was responsible resulted in cash flow problems for Mossman. Production fell to a few guitars per month until the company was sold in '86 to Scott Baxendale. Baxendale sold the company to John Kinsey and Bob Casey in Sulphur Springs in '89.

Flint Hills
1970-1979. Flat-top acoustic, Indian rosewood back and sides.

1970-1979	Indian rosewood	$1,400	$1,800

Flint Hills Custom

1970-1979	Indian rosewood	$1,950	$2,550

Golden Era
1970-1977. D-style, vine inlay and other high-end appointments, Brazilian rosewood back and sides until '76, then Indian rosewood.

1970-1975	Brazilian rosewood	$3,200	$4,100
1976-1977	Indian rosewood	$2,100	$2,700

Golden Era Custom

1970-1975	Brazilian rosewood	$4,400	$5,700

Great Plains
1970-1979. Flat-top, Brazilian rosewood until '76 then Indian rosewood, herringbone trim.

1970-1975	Brazilian rosewood	$2,400	$3,100
1976-1979	Indian rosewood	$1,600	$2,075

Mosrite Joe Maphis Doubleneck

1975 Mossman Great Plains
David Stone

1976 Mossman Southwind

MotorAve Guitars McQueen

MODEL YEAR	FEATURES	EXC. COND. LOW	HIGH
Great Plains Custom			
1970-1975	Brazilian rosewood	$3,375	$4,375
Southwind			

1976-ca. 1986, mid-1990s-2002. Flat-top, abalone trim top.

1976-1979	Indian rosewood	$1,850	$2,400
Tennessee			

1972-1979. D-style, spruce top, mahogany back and sides, rope marquetry purfling, rope binding.

1972-1979	Mahogany	$1,075	$1,375
Tennessee 12-String			
1975-1979	Mahogany	$1,075	$1,375
Timber Creek			

1976-1979. D-style, Indian rosewood back and sides, spruce top.

1976-1979	Indian rosewood	$1,700	$2,200
Winter Wheat			

1976-1979, mid-1990s-2000s. Flat-top, Indian rosewood back and sides, abalone trim, natural finish.

1976-1979	Indian rosewood	$1,825	$2,375
Winter Wheat 12-String			

1976-1979. 12-string version of Winter Wheat, natural.

1976-1979	Indian rosewood	$1,825	$2,375

MotorAve Guitars

2002-present. Luthier Mark Fuqua builds his professional and premium grade, production, electric guitars originally in Los Angeles, California, and currently in Durham, North Carolina.

Mouradian

1983-present. Luthiers Jim and Jon Mouradian build their professional and premium grade, production/custom, electric guitars and basses in Winchester, Massachusetts.

Mozart

1930s. Private brand made by Kay.

Hawaiian (Square Neck)

1930s. Spruce top, solid mahogany sides and back, pealoid overlay on peghead with large Mozart inscribed logo, small jumbo 15 1/2" body.

1935-1939		$775	$1,025

Mozzani

Built in shops of Luigi Mozzani (b. March 9, 1869, Faenza, Italy; d. 1943) who opened lutherie schools in Bologna, Cento and Rovereto in 1890s. By 1926 No. 1 and 2 Original Mozzani Model Mandolin (flat back), No. 3 Mandola (flat back), No. 4 6-String Guitar, No. 5 7-, 8-, and 9-String Guitars, No. 6 Lyre-Guitar.

M-Tone Guitars

2009-present. Professional and premium grade, production/custom, solidbody electric guitars built in Portland, Oregon by luthier Matt Proctor.

MODEL YEAR	FEATURES	EXC. COND. LOW	HIGH

Muiderman Guitars

1997-present. Custom, premium grade, steel string and classical guitars built by luthier Kevin Muiderman currently in Grand Forks, North Dakota, and previously in Beverly Hills, Michigan, 1997-2001, and Neenah, Wisconsin, '01-'07. He also builds mandolins.

Murph

1965-1967. Mid-level electric semi-hollow and solidbody guitars built by Pat Murphy in San Fernado, California. Murph logo on headstock. They also offered basses and amps.

Electric Solidbody

1965-1967		$900	$1,175
Electric XII			
1965-1967		$900	$1,175

Music Man

1972-present. Professional grade, production, solidbody guitars built in San Luis Obispo, California. They also build basses. Founded by ex-Fender executives Forrest White and Tom Walker in Orange County, California. Music Man originally produced guitar and bass amps based on early Fender ideas using many former Fender employees. They contracted with Leo Fender's CLF Research to design and produce a line of solidbody guitars and basses. Leo Fender began G & L Guitars with George Fullerton in '80. In '84, Music Man was purchased by Ernie Ball and production was moved to San Luis Obispo.

Albert Lee Signature

1993-present. Swamp ash body, figured maple neck, 3 pickups, white pearloid 'guard, Pinkburst.

1993-1996	Pinkburst	$1,000	$1,300
1996-2019	Tremolo option	$900	$1,200
Axis			

1996-present. Offset double-cut solidbody, figured maple top, basswood body, 2 humbucker pickups, Floyd Rose.

1996-2019		$900	$1,200
Axis Sport			

1996-2002. Two P-90s.

1996-2002		$900	$1,200
Axis Super Sport			

2003-present. Figured top.

2003-2019		$900	$1,200
Edward Van Halen			

1991-1995. Basswood solidbody, figured maple top, bolt-on maple neck, maple 'board, binding, 2 humbuckers, named changed to Axis.

1991-1995		$1,775	$2,300

John Petrucci 6/JP-6

2008-present. Standard model, basswood body, maple neck, rosewood 'board, various colors with high gloss finish.

2008-2019		$1,300	$1,700

MODEL YEAR	FEATURES	EXC. COND. LOW	HIGH

John Petrucci BFR

2011-present. Ball Family Reserve (BFR).

| 2011-2019 | | $1,500 | $2,000 |

Reflex

2011-2017. Referred to as The Game Changer, patent-pending pickup switching system, maple or rosewood neck with matching headstock, black finish.

| 2011-2017 | | $1,100 | $1,450 |

S.U.B 1

2004-2006. Offset double-cut solidbody.

| 2004-2005 | | $400 | $525 |

Sabre I

1978-1982. Offset double-cut solidbody, maple neck, 2 pickups, Sabre I comes with a flat 'board with jumbo frets.

| 1978-1982 | | $900 | $1,200 |

Sabre II

1978-1982. Same as Sabre I, but with an oval 7 1/2" radius 'board.

| 1978-1982 | | $900 | $1,200 |

Silhouette

1986-present. Offset double-cut, contoured beveled solidbody, various pickup configurations.

| 1986-2019 | | $900 | $1,200 |
| 2006 | 20th Anniversary | $900 | $1,200 |

Silhouette 6/12 Double Neck

2009-2014. Alder body, maple or rosewood 'boards, 4 humbuckers.

| 2009-2014 | | $1,450 | $1,900 |

Silhouette Special

1995-present. Silhouette with Silent Circuit.

| 1995-2019 | | $900 | $1,200 |

Steve Morse Signature

1987-present. Solidbody, 4 pickups, humbuckers in the neck and bridge positions, 2 single-coils in the middle, special pickup switching, 6-bolt neck mounting, maple neck.

| 1987-2019 | | $1,250 | $1,650 |

Stingray I

1976-1982. Offset double-cut solidbody, flat 'board radius.

| 1976-1982 | | $900 | $1,200 |

Stingray II

1976-1982. Offset double-cut solidbody, rounder 'board radius.

| 1976-1982 | | $900 | $1,200 |

Musicvox

1996-2001, 2011-present. Intermediate grade, production, imported retro-vibe guitars and basses from Matt Eichen of Cherry Hill, New Jersey.

Myka

2003-present. Luthier David Myka builds his professional and premium grade, custom/production, solidbody, semi-hollowbody, hollowbody, archtop, and flat-top guitars in Seattle, Washington. Until '07 he was located in Orchard Park, New York.

Nady

1976-present. Wireless sound company Nady Systems offered guitars and basses with built-in wireless systems for 1985-'87. Made by Fernandes in Japan until '86, then by Cort in Korea.

Lightning/Lightning I

1985-1987. Double-cut, neck-thru, solidbody, 24 frets, built-in wireless, labeled as just Lightning until cheaper second version came out in '86.

| 1985 | Fernandes | $300 | $375 |
| 1986-1987 | Cort | $275 | $350 |

Lightning/Lightning II

1986-1987. Cheaper, bolt-neck version of the Lightning I.

| 1986-1987 | Cort | $250 | $325 |

Napolitano Guitars

Luthier Arthur Napolitano began in 1993 to build professional and premium grade, custom, archtop guitars in Allentown, New Jersey.

NashGuitars

2001-present. Luthier Bill Nash builds his professional grade, production/custom, aged solidbody electric guitars and basses in Olympia, Washington.

Nashville Guitar Company

1985-present. Professional and premium grade, custom, flat-top guitars built by luthier Marty Lanham in Nashville, Tennessee. He has also built banjos.

National

Ca. 1927-present. Founded in Los Angeles, California as the National String Instrument Corporation by John Dopyera, George Beauchamp, Ted Kleinmeyer and Paul Barth. In '29 Dopyera left to start the Dobro Manufacturing Company with Rudy and Ed Dopyera and Vic Smith. The Dobro company competed with National until the companies reunited. Beauchamp and Barth then left National to found Ro-Pat-In with Adolph Rickenbacker and C.L. Farr (later becoming Electro String Instrument Corporation, then Rickenbacher). In '32 Dopyera returns to National and National and Dobro start their merger in late-'33, finalizing it by mid-'34. Throughout the '30s, National and Dobro maintained separate production, sales and distribution. National Dobro moved to Chicago, Illinois in '36. In Chicago, archtop and flat-top bodies are built primarily by Regal and Kay; after '37 all National resonator guitar bodies made by Kay. L.A. production is maintained until around '37, although some assembly of Dobros continued in L.A. (primarily for export) until '39 when the L.A. offices are finally closed. By ca. '39 the Dobro brand disappears.

In '42, the company's resonator production ceased and Victor Smith, Al Frost and Louis Dopyera buy the company and change name to Valco Manufacturing Company. Post-war production resumes in '46.

1979 Musicman Sabre II
Tom Pfeifer

Nash Guitars '63 S
John Rutherford

GUITARS

1970s National Big Daddy LP-457-2

Imaged by Heritage Auctions, HA.com

1936 National Duolian

BobTekippe

Valco is purchased by treasurer Robert Engelhardt in '64. In '67, Valco bought Kay, but in '68 the new Valco/Kay company went out of business. In the Summer of '69 the assets, including brand names, were auctioned off and the National and Supro names were purchased by Chicago-area distributor/importer Strum 'N Drum (Noble, Norma brands). The National brand is used on copies in early- to mid-'70s, and the brand went into hiatus by the '80s.

In '88 National Resophonic Guitars is founded in San Luis Obispo, California, by Don Young, with production of National-style resonator guitars beginning in '89 (see following). In the '90s, the National brand also resurfaces on inexpensive Asian imports.

National Resonator guitars are categorized by materials and decoration (from plain to fancy): Duolian, Triolian, Style 0, Style 1, Style 2, Style 3, Style 4, Don #1, Style 97, Don #2, Don #3, Style 35.

National guitars all have serial numbers which provide clues to date of production. This is a complex issue. This list combines information included in George Gruhn and Walter Carter's Gruhn's Guide to Vintage Guitars, which was originally provided by Bob Brozman and Mike Newton, with new information provided by Mike Newton.

Pre Chicago numbers:
A101-A450 1935-1936.

Chicago numbers:
A prefix (some may not have the prefix) 1936-mid-1997. B prefix Mid-1937-1938. C prefix Late-1938-1940. G prefix up to 200 Ea. 1941-ea. 1942. G suffix under 2000 Ea. 1941-ea. 1942. G suffix 2000-3000s (probably old parts) 1943-1945. G suffix 4000s (old parts) Late 1945-mid-1947. V100-V7500 1947. V7500-V15000 1948. V15000-V25000 1949. V25000-V35000 1950. V35000-V38000 1951. X100-X7000 1951. X7000-X17000 1952. X17000-X30000 1953. X30000-X43000 1954. X43000-X57000 1955. X57000-X71000 1956. X71000-X85000 1957. X85000-X990001958. T100-T5000 1958. T5000-T25000 1959. T25000-T50000 1960. T50000-T75000 1961. T75000-T90000 1962. G100-G5000 1962. T90000-T99000 1963. G5000-G15000 1963. G15000-G40000 1964. 1 prefix 1965-ea. 1968. 2 prefix Mid-1968.

Aragon De Luxe
1939-1942. Archtop with resonator (the only archtop resonator offered), spruce top and maple back and sides, light brown.

MODEL YEAR	FEATURES	EXC. COND. LOW	HIGH
1939-1942		$5,000	$6,500

Big Daddy LP-457-2
1970s. Strum & Drum import, single-cut, LP-style, 2 pickups, gold hardware, black.

1970s		$225	$300

Bluegrass 35
1963-1965. Acoustic, non-cut single-cone resonator, Res-O-Glas body in Arctic White.

1963-1965		$1,150	$1,550

Bobbie Thomas
Ca.1967-1968. Double-cut thinline hollowbody, bat-shaped f-holes, 2 pickups, Bobbie Thomas on 'guard, vibrato.

MODEL YEAR	FEATURES	EXC. COND. LOW	HIGH
1967-1968		$500	$675

Cameo
1957-1958. Renamed from Model 1140 in '57, full-body acoustic archtop with carved top.

1957-1958		$600	$775

Collegian
1942-1943. Metal body resonator similar to Duolian, 14-fret round or square neck, yellow.

1942-1943		$975	$1,275

Don Style 1
1934-1936. Plain body with engraved borders, pearl dot inlay, 14 frets, single-cone, silver (nickel-plated).

1934-1936		$5,100	$6,800

Don Style 2
1934-1936. Geometric Art Deco body engraving, 14 frets, single-cone, fancy square pearl inlays and pearloid headstock overlay, silver (nickel-plated).

1934-1936		$6,000	$7,700

Don Style 3
1934-1936. Same as Style 2 but more elaborate floral engravings, fancy pearl diamond inlays, 14 frets, single-cone, silver (nickel-plated), only a very few made.

1934-1936		$10,500	$13,800

Duolian
1930-1939. Acoustic steel body, frosted paint finish until '36, mahogany-grain paint finish '37-'39, round neck, square neck available in '33, 12-fret neck until '34 then 14-fret.

1930-1934	Round neck, 12 or 14 frets	$3,000	$4,000

EG 685 Hollow Body Electric
1970s. Strum & Drum distributed, double-cut hollowbody copy, 2 pickups.

1970s		$260	$335

El Trovador
1933 only. Wood body, 12 frets.

1933		$1,575	$2,075

Electric Spanish
1935-1938. 15 1/2" archtop with Pat. Appl. For bridge pickup, National crest logo, fancy N-logo 'guard, black and white art deco, sunburst, becomes New Yorker Spanish '39-'58.

1935-1938		$875	$1,150

Estralita
1934-1942. Acoustic with single-cone resonator, f-holes, multi-bound, 14-fret, mahogany top and back, shaded brown.

1934-1942		$650	$850

Glenwood 95
1962-1964. Glenwood 98 without third bridge-mount pickup, Vermillion Red or Flame Red.

1962-1964		$2,400	$3,100

Glenwood 98
1964-1965. USA map-shaped solidbody of molded Res-O-Glas, 2 regular and 1 bridge pickup, vibrato, 3 tailpiece options, Pearl White.

1964-1965		$2,500	$3,300

MODEL YEAR	FEATURES	EXC. COND. LOW	HIGH

Glenwood 99
1962-1965. USA map-shaped solidbody of molded Res-O-Glas, 2 regular and 1 bridge pickups, butterfly inlay.

| 1962-1963 | Snow White | $2,500 | $3,300 |
| 1964-1965 | Green/Blue | $4,600 | $6,000 |

Glenwood Deluxe
1959-1961. Renamed from Glenwood 1105, Les Paul-shaped solidbody, wood body, not fiberglass, multi-bound, 2 pickups, factory Bigsby, vibrato, natural.

| 1959-1961 | | $1,450 | $1,900 |

Havana
1938-1942. Natural spruce top, sunburst back and sides.

| 1938-1942 | Round neck | $650 | $850 |
| 1938-1942 | Square neck | $425 | $550 |

Model 1100 California
1949-1955. Electric hollowbody archtop, multibound, f-holes, trapeze tailpiece, 1 pickup, natural.

| 1949-1955 | | $725 | $950 |

Model 1104 Town and Country
1954-1958. Model just below Glenwood 1105, dots, 2 or 3 pickups, plastic overlay on back, natural finish.

| 1954-1958 | 2 pickups | $1,375 | $1,800 |
| 1954-1958 | 3 pickups | $1,525 | $2,000 |

Model 1105 Glenwood
1954-1958. Les Paul-shaped solidbody, wood body, not fiberglass, single-cut, multi-bound, 2 pickups, natural, renamed Glenwood Deluxe with Bigsby in '59.

| 1954-1958 | | $1,675 | $2,200 |

Model 1106 Val-Trol Baron
1959-1960. Single-cut solidbody, 2 pickups, 1 piezo, block inlays, black.

| 1959-1960 | | $1,050 | $1,375 |

Model 1107 Debonaire
1953-1960. Single rounded-cutaway full-depth 16" electric archtop, single neck pickup, Debonaire logo on 'guard (for most models), large raised National script logo on headstock, sunburst.

| 1953-1960 | | $625 | $800 |

Model 1109/1198 Bel-Aire
1953-1960. Single pointed cut archtop, 2 (1109) pickups until '57, 3 (1198) after, master tone knob and jack, bound body, sunburst.

| 1953-1957 | 1109, 2 pickups | $850 | $1,100 |
| 1958-1960 | 1198, 3 pickups | $925 | $1,200 |

Model 1110/1111 Aristocrat
1941-1954. Electric full body non-cut archtop, 1 pickup, 2 knobs, early model with triple backslash markers, later with block markers, National-crest headstock inlaid logo, natural finish only until model numbers added to name in '48, shaded sunburst finish (1110) and natural (1111).

1941-1948	Natural	$675	$875
1948-1955	1110, shaded sunburst	$850	$1,100
1948-1955	1111, natural	$850	$1,100

Model 1120 New Yorker
1954-1958. Renamed from New Yorker Spanish, 16.25" electric archtop, 1 pickup on floating 'guard, dot markers, blond.

| 1954-1958 | | $600 | $775 |

Model 1122 Cosmopolitan
1954-1957. Small wood non-cutaway solidbody, dot markers, 1 pickup, 2 knobs on mounted 'guard.

| 1954-1957 | | $525 | $675 |

Model 1122 Val-Trol Junior
1959-1960. Single-cut solidbody, 1 pickup and 1piezo, dot inlays, ivory.

| 1959-1960 | | $800 | $1,050 |

Model 1123 Bolero
1954-1957. Les Paul-shape, control knobs mounted on 'guard, single pickup, trapeze tailpiece, sunburst.

| 1954-1957 | | $600 | $775 |

Model 1124/1124B/1134 Avalon
1954-1957. Small wood solidbody, 2 pickups, 4 control knobs and switch on top-mounted 'guard, block markers, short trapeze bridge, sunburst (1124) or blond (1124B).

| 1954-1957 | 1124, sunburst | $900 | $1,200 |
| 1954-1957 | 1124B/1134, blond | $1,000 | $1,300 |

Model 1125 Dynamic
1951-1959. Full body 15.5" acoustic-electric archtop, sunburst version of New Yorker 1120 with some appointments slightly below the New Yorker, dot markers, 1 pickup, sunburst.

| 1951-1959 | | $525 | $675 |

Model 1135 Acoustic Archtop
1948-1954. 17.25" full body acoustic archtop, carved top, split pearl markers.

| 1948-1954 | | $675 | $875 |

Model 1140 Acoustic Archtop
1948-1957. 15.5" full body acoustic archtop, carved top, dot markers.

| 1948-1957 | | $500 | $650 |

Model 1150 Flat-Top Auditorium
1951-1958. Auditorium-size flat-top, 14.25" narrow-waist, dot markers.

| 1951-1958 | | $525 | $675 |

Model 1155 Jumbo
1948-1961. Flat-top acoustic with Gibson Jumbo body, mahogany back and sides, bolt-on neck.

| 1948-1961 | | $1,500 | $2,700 |

Model 1170 Club Combo
1952-1955, 1959-1961. Electric hollowbody archtop, 2 pickups, rounded cutaway.

| 1952-1961 | | $925 | $1,225 |

N600 Series
1968. Offset double-cut solidbody, 1, 2, and 3 pickup models, with and without vibrato.

1968	N624, 1 pickup	$375	$525
1968	N634, 2 pus, vibrato	$500	$650
1968	N644, 3 pus, vibrato	$600	$800
1968	N654, 12-string	$500	$650

N700 Series
1968. Flat-top, 700/710 dreadnoughts, 720/730 jumbos.

1968	N700 Western	$500	$650
1968	N710	$275	$375
1968	N720 Western	$325	$425
1968	N730 Deluxe	$450	$600

1958 National Model 1125 Dynamic
www.guitarswest.net

1959 National Model 1155 Jumbo
Craig Brody

1936 National Style 0

1930 National Style 0
Bernunzio Uptown Music

MODEL YEAR	FEATURES	EXC. COND. LOW	HIGH

N800 Series
1968. Double-cut semi-hollow body, various models with or without Bigsby.

1968	No Bigsby	$475	$625
1968	With Bigsby	$525	$725

New Yorker Spanish
1939-1953. Electric archtop, 15.5" body until '47 then 16.25", 1 neck pickup, dot-diamond markers, sunburst or natural. Renamed New Yorker 1120 in '54.

1939-1946	15.5"	$1,150	$1,500
1947-1953	1625"	$1,150	$1,500

Newport 82
1963-1965. Renamed from Val-Pro 82, USA map-shaped Res-O-Glas, 1 pickup, Pepper Red finish.

1963-1965		$1,225	$1,600

Newport 84
1963-1965. Renamed from Val-Pro 84, USA map-shaped Res-O-Glas, 1 regular and 1 bridge pickup, Sea Foam Green finish.

1963-1965		$2,300	$3,000

Newport 88
1963-1965. Renamed from Val-Pro 88, USA map-shaped Res-O-Glas, 2 regular and 1 bridge pickup, Raven Black finish.

1963-1965		$1,525	$2,000

Reso-phonic
1956-1964. Pearloid-covered, single-cut semi-solidbody acoustic, single resonator, maroon or white, also a non-cut, square neck version was offered, which is included in these values.

1956-1964	Round neck, common finish	$1,075	$1,400
1956-1964	Round neck, rare finish	$1,200	$1,550
1956-1964	Square neck	$925	$1,200

Rosita
1933-1939. Plywood body by Harmony, plain metal resonator, plain appointments.

1933-1939		$650	$850

Silvo (Electric Hawaiian)
1937-1941. Nickel-plated metal body flat-top, small upper bout, f-holes, square neck, multiple straight line body art over dark background, Roman numeral parallelogram markers, National badge headstock logo, Silvo name on coverplate.

1937-1941	Silver	$1,875	$2,450

Studio 66
1961-1964. Electric solidbody of Res-O-Glas, single-cut, 1 pickup, renamed Varsity 66 in '65.

1961-1962	Sand Buff, bridge pu	$825	$1,100
1963-1964	Jet Black, neck pu	$825	$1,100

Style 0
1930-1942. Acoustic single-cone brass body (early models had a steel body), Hawaiian scene etching, 12-fret neck '30-'34, 14-fret neck '35 on, round (all years) or square ('33 on) neck.

1930-1934	Round neck, 12-fret, common etching	$2,500	$3,200
1930-1934	Round neck, 12-fret, rare etching	$3,000	$4,000
1933-1942	Square neck, common etching	$1,100	$1,400

MODEL YEAR	FEATURES	EXC. COND. LOW	HIGH

1933-1942	Square neck, rare etching	$2,100	$2,700
1935-1942	Round, 14-fret (Mark Knophler assoc)	$4,800	$6,200
1935-1942	Round, 14-fret, common etching	$2,100	$2,700
1935-1942	Round, 14-fret, rare etching	$3,000	$4,000

Style 0 Tenor
1929-1930. Tenor, 4 strings, single-cone brass body, Hawaiian scene etching.

1929-1930		$800	$1,050

Style 1 Tricone
1927-1943. German silver body tricone resonator, ebony 'board, mahogany square (Hawaiian) or round (Spanish) neck, plain body, 12-fret neck until '34, 14-fret after.

1927-1943	Round neck	$4,000	$5,200
1928-1943	Square neck	$2,600	$3,400

Style 1 Tricone Plectrum
1928-1935. 26" scale versus the 23" scale of the tenor.

1928-1935		$1,300	$1,700

Style 1 Tricone Tenor
1928-1935. Tenor, 4 strings, 23" scale, square neck is Hawaiian, round neck is Spanish.

1928-1935		$1,300	$1,700

Style 1.5 Tricone
1930s. A "1/2" style like the 1.5 represents a different engraving pattern.

1930s	Round neck	$6,100	$8,000
1930s	Square neck	$2,150	$2,750

Style 2 Tricone
1927-1942. German silver body tricone resonator, wild rose engraving, square (Hawaiian) or round (Spanish) neck, 12-fret neck until '34, 14-fret after.

1927-1942	Round neck	$8,500	$11,000
1927-1942	Square neck	$2,700	$3,500

Style 2 Tricone Plectrum
1928-1935. 26" scale versus the 23" scale of the tenor.

1928-1935		$1,250	$1,600

Style 2 Tricone Tenor
1928-1935. Tenor.

1928-1935		$1,250	$1,600

Style 2.5 Tricone
1927-1928. Collector term for Style 2 with additional rose engravings on coverplate, bound ebony fretboard.

1927-1928		$5,000	$6,600

Style 3 Tricone
1928-1941. German silver body tricone resonator, lily-of-the-valley engraving, square (Hawaiian) or round (Spanish) neck, 12-fret neck until '34, 14-fret after, reintroduced with a nickel-plated brass body in '94.

1928-1939	Round neck	$9,400	$12,000
1928-1941	Square neck	$3,200	$4,200

Style 3 Tricone Plectrum
1928-1935. 26" scale versus the 23" scale of the tenor.

1928-1935		$2,300	$3,000

Style 3 Tricone Tenor
1928-1939. Tenor version.

1928-1939		$2,300	$3,000

The *Vintage Guitar Price Guide* shows low to high values for items in all-original excellent condition, and, where applicable, with original case or cover.

MODEL YEAR	FEATURES	EXC. COND. LOW	HIGH
Style 4 Tricone			
1928-1940. German silver body tricone resonator, chrysanthemum etching, 12-fret neck until '34, 14-fret after, reissued in '95 with same specs.			
1928-1940	Round neck	$13,000	$17,000
1928-1940	Square neck	$3,200	$4,200
Style 35			
1936-1942. Brass body tricone resonator, sandblasted minstrel and trees scene, 12 frets, square (Hawaiian) or round (Spanish) neck.			
1936-1942	Round neck	$20,000	$26,000
1936-1942	Square neck	$6,500	$8,300
Style 97			
1936-1940. Nickel-plated brass body tricone resonator, sandblasted scene of female surfrider and palm trees, 12 frets, slotted peghead.			
1930s	Early '30s	$6,700	$8,600
1930s	Late '30s	$4,600	$6,000
1930s	Round neck	$21,000	$27,000
Style N			
1930-1931. Nickel-plated brass body single-cone resonator, plain finish, 12 frets.			
1930-1931		$3,000	$4,000
Triolian			
1928-1941. Single-cone resonator, wood body replaced by metal body in '29, 12-fret neck and slotted headstock '28-'34, changed to 14-fret neck in '35 and solid headstock in '36, round or square ('33 on) neck available.			
1928-1936	Various colors	$2,300	$3,000
1936-1937	Fake rosewood grain	$2,150	$2,800
Triolian Tenor			
1928-1936. Tenor, metal body.			
1928-1936		$850	$1,100
Trojan			
1934-1942. Single-cone resonator wood body, f-holes, bound top, 14-fret round neck.			
1934-1942		$1,050	$1,350
Val-Pro 82			
1962-1963. USA map-shaped Res-O-Glas, 1 pickup, Vermillion Red finish, renamed Newport 82 in '63.			
1962-1963		$975	$1,275
Val-Pro 84			
1962-1963. USA map-shaped Res-O-Glas, 1 regular and 1 bridge pickup, snow white finish, renamed Newport 84 in '63.			
1962-1963		$1,100	$1,425
Val-Pro 88			
1962-1963. USA map-shaped Res-O-Glas, 2 regular and 1 bridge pickup, black finish, renamed Newport 88 in '63.			
1962-1963		$1,825	$2,375
Varsity 66			
1964-1965. Renamed from Studio 66 in '64, molded Res-O-Glas, 1 pickup, 2 knobs, beige finish.			
1964-1965		$825	$1,100
Westwood 72			
1962-1964. USA map-shaped solid hardwood body (not fiberglass), 1 pickup, Cherry Red.			
1962-1964		$1,375	$1,800

MODEL YEAR	FEATURES	EXC. COND. LOW	HIGH
Westwood 75			
1962-1964. USA map-shaped solid hardwood body (not fiberglass), 1 regular and 1 bridge pickup, cherry-to-black sunburst finish.			
1962-1964		$1,375	$1,800
Westwood 77			
1962-1965. USA map-shaped solid hardwood body (not fiberglass), 2 regular and 1 bridge pickup.			
1962-1965	Blond-Ivory	$1,375	$1,800

National Reso-Phonic

1989-present. Professional and premium grade, production/custom, single cone, acoustic-electric, and tricone guitars (all with resonators), built in San Luis Obispo, California. They also build basses, mandolins and ukuleles. McGregor Gaines and Don Young formed the National Reso-Phonic Guitar Company with the objective of building instruments based upon the original National designs. Replicon is the aging process to capture the appearance and sound of a vintage National.

MODEL YEAR	FEATURES	EXC. COND. LOW	HIGH
Collegian			
2010-present. Thin gauge steel body, 9.5" cone, biscuit bridge, aged ivory finish.			
2010-2019		$1,250	$1,600
Delphi			
1993-2010. Single cone, steel body.			
1993-2010		$1,425	$1,850
Dueco			
2012-present. Gold or Silver crystalline finish.			
2012-2019		$1,775	$2,300
El Trovador			
2010-present. Wood body Dobro-style, single cone, biscuit bridge.			
2010-2019		$1,900	$2,500
Estralita Deluxe			
2006-present. Single cone, walnut body, figured maple top, koa offered in '03.			
2006-2019	Maple or koa	$1,600	$2,050
Estralita Harlem Slim			
2010. Laminate maple.			
2010		$1,125	$1,450
Model 97			
2002-2009. Nickel-plated tricone resonator, female surfrider and palm trees scene.			
2002-2009		$2,400	$3,100
Model D			
2003-2010. Laminate wood body, spruce top, walnut back and sides, spun cone and spider bridge. Replaced by Smith and Young Model 1 (metal body) and Model 11 (wood body).			
2003-2010		$1,300	$1,700
Reso Rocket			
2005-present. Single-cut steel body, Tricone style grill.			
2005-2019		$2,250	$2,900
Reso Rocket N			
2009-present. Highly polished nickel-plated finish.			
2009-2019		$2,250	$2,900

1928 National Style 2 Tricone Tenor

National Reso-Phonic ResoLectric

GUITARS

Nik Huber Dolphin II

1960s Norma Sparkle-Top

MODEL YEAR	FEATURES	EXC. COND. LOW	HIGH

Resoelectric Jr./Jr. II
2005-2010. Basic model of ResoLectric with painted body, Jr. with P-90, Jr. II with Lollar lipstick-tube. Replaced by the ResoTone.

2005-2010		$725	$925

ResoLectric
1992-present. Single-cut electric resonator, maple (flamed maple since '96), single biscuit, 1 regular pickup (lipstick-tube up to '95, P-90 since) and 1 under-saddle.

1992-1995	Lipstick pickup	$1,500	$1,925
1996-2019	P-90	$1,400	$1,800

Style M-1/M-2
1990-1994, 2003-2010. Bound mahogany body single-cone, M-1 with ebony 'board, M-2 with bound rosewood 'board.

1990-2010		$1,400	$1,800

Style N
1993-2005. Nickel-plated brass body single-cone resonator, plain mirror finish, 12 fret neck.

1993-2005		$2,100	$2,700

Style O/O Deluxe
1992-present. Nickel-plated brass body, Hawaiian palm tree etched. Deluxe has upgrades like figured-maple neck and mother-of-pearl diamond inlays.

1992-2019		$1,600	$2,100

Tricone
1994-present. Nickel-plated brass body, bound ebony 'board.

1994-2019	Style 1	$1,800	$2,400
1994-2019	Style 1.5	$2,200	$2,900
1995	Style 3, Lily of the Valley	$3,900	$5,100

Triolian
2009-present. Steel body with f-holes, sieve-hole coverplate, maple neck, 12 or 14 fret neck, ivoroid-bound rosewood 'board, mother-of-pearl markers, hand painted walnut-burst.

2009-2019	12 fret	$1,400	$1,825
2009-2019	14 fret	$1,400	$1,825

Navarro Custom
1986-present. Professional and premium grade, production/custom, electric guitars and basses built in San Juan, Puerto Rico by luthier Mike Navarro.

Neubauer
1966-1990s. Luthier Helmut Neubauer built his acoustic and electric archtop guitars in Bubenreuth, Germany.

New Era Guitars
See listing under ARK - New Era Guitars.

New Orleans Guitar Company
1992-present. Luthier Vincent Guidroz builds his premium grade, production/custom, solid and semi-hollow body guitars in New Orleans, Louisiana.

Nickerson Guitars
1983-present. Luthier Brad Nickerson builds his professional and premium grade, production/custom, archtop and flat-top guitars in Northampton, Massachusetts.

Nielsen
2004-present. Premium grade, custom/production, archtop guitars built by luthier Dale Nielsen in Duluth, Minnesota.

Nik Huber Guitars
1997-present. Premium grade, production/custom, electric guitars built in Rodgau, Germany by luthier Nik Huber.

Nioma
1932-1952. NIOMA, the National Institute of Music and Arts, was founded in Seattle but soon had schools across the western U.S. and Canada. By '35 they added guitar instruction, offering their own branded Spanish, resonator and lap steel (with matching amps) guitars, made by Regal, Harmony, Dickerson.

Noble
Ca. 1950-ca. 1969. Instruments made by others and distributed by Don Noble and Company of Chicago. Plastic-covered guitars made by EKO debut in '62. Aluminum-necked Wandré guitars added to the line in early-'63. By ca. '65-'66 the brand is owned by Chicago-area importer and distributor Strum 'N Drum and used mainly on Japanese-made solidbodies. Strum 'N Drum bought the National brand name in '69 and imported Japanese copies of American designs under the National brand and Japanese original designs under Norma through the early '70s.

The Noble brand disappears at least by the advent of the Japanese National brand, if not before. They also offered amps.

NoName Guitars
1999-present. Luthier Dan Kugler builds his production/custom, professional and premium grade, acoustic guitars and basses in Conifer, Colorado.

Nordy (Nordstrand Guitars)
2003-present. Professional and premium grade, production/custom, electric guitars and basses built by luthier Carey Nordstrand in Yucaipa, California.

Norma
Ca.1965-1970. Imported from Japan by Strum 'N Drum, Inc. of Chicago (see Noble brand info). Early examples were built by Tombo, most notably sparkle plastic covered guitars and basses.

Electric Solidbody
1965-1970s. Type of finish has affect on value. Various models include; EG-350 (student double-cut, 1 pickup), EG-403 (unique pointy cutaway, 2 pickups),

MODEL YEAR	FEATURES	EXC. COND. LOW	HIGH

EG-400 (double-cut, 2 pickups), EG-450 (double-cut, 2 split-coil pickups), EG-421 (double-cut, 4 pickups), EG-412-12 (double-cut, 12-string).

| 1965-1968 | Blue, red, gold sparkle | $300 | $600 |
| 1965-1970s | Non-sparkle | $195 | $250 |

Norman

1972-present. Intermediate grade, production, acoustic and acoustic/electric guitars built in LaPatrie, Quebec. Norman was the first guitar production venture luthier Robert Godin was involved with. He has since added the Seagull, Godin, and Patrick & Simon brands of instruments.

Normandy Guitars

2008-present. Jim Normandy builds professional grade, production, aluminum archtop and electric guitars and basses in Salem, Oregon.

Northworthy Guitars

Professional and premium grade, production/custom, flat-top and electric guitars and basses built by luthier Alan Marshall in Ashbourne, Derbyshire, U.K., starting in 1987. He also builds mandolins.

Norwood

1960s. Budget guitars imported most likely from Japan.

Electric Solidbody

1960s. Offset double-cut body, 3 soapbar-style pickups, Norwood label on headstock.

| 1960s | | $155 | $200 |

Novax Guitars

1989-present. Luthier Ralph Novak builds his fanned-fret professional and premium grade, production/custom, solidbody and acoustic guitars and basses, originally in San Leandro, California, and since May '06, in Eugene, Oregon.

Noyce

1974-present. Luthier Ian Noyce builds his production/custom, professional and premium grade, acoustic and electric guitars and basses in Ballarat, Victoria, Australia.

Nyberg Instruments

1993-present. Professional grade, custom, flat-top and Maccaferri-style guitars built by luthier Lawrence Nyberg in Hornby Island, British Columbia. He also builds mandolins, mandolas, bouzoukis and citterns.

Oahu

1926-1985, present. The Oahu Publishing Company and Honolulu Conservatory, based in Cleveland, Ohio was active in the sheet music and student instrument business in the '30s. An instrument, set of instructional sheet music, and lessons were offered as a complete package. Lessons were often given to large groups of students. Instruments, lessons, and sheet music could also be purchased by mail order. The Oahu Publishing Co. advertised itself as The World's Largest Guitar Dealer. Most '30s Oahu guitars were made by Kay with smaller numbers from the Oscar Schmidt Company.

Guitar Models from the Mid-'30s include: 71K (jumbo square neck), 72K (jumbo roundneck), 68B (jumbo, vine body decoration), 68K (deluxe jumbo square neck), 69K (deluxe jumbo roundneck), 65K and 66K (mahogany, square neck), 64K and 67K (mahogany, roundneck), 65M (standard-size, checker binding, mahogany), 53K (roundneck, mahogany), 51 (black, Hawaiian scene, pearlette 'board), 51K (black, pond scene decoration), 52K (black, Hawaiian scene decoration), 50 and 50K (student guitar, brown).

The brand has been revived on a line of tube amps.

Graphic Body

1930s. 13" painted artwork bodies, includes Styles 51 and 52 Hawaiian scene.

| 1930s | Floral, higher appointments | $275 | $375 |
| 1930s | Hawaiian scene | $275 | $375 |

Round Neck 14" Flat-Top

1930s. Spruce top, figured maple back and sides, thin logo.

| 1932 | | $725 | $950 |

Style 50K Student

1930s. Student-size guitar, brown finish.

| 1935 | | $175 | $225 |

Style 52K

1930s. 13" with fancy Hawaiian stencil, slotted headstock.

| 1930s | | $275 | $350 |

Style 65M

1933-1935. Standard-size mahogany body, checker binding, natural brown.

| 1933-1935 | | $475 | $625 |

Style 68K De Luxe Jumbo

1930s. Hawaiian, 15.5" wide, square neck, Brazilian back and sides, spruce top, fancy pearl vine inlay, abalone trim on top and soundhole, rosewood pyramid bridge, fancy pearl headstock inlay, butterbean tuners, ladder-braced, natural. High-end model made for Oahu by Kay.

| 1934-1935 | | $3,100 | $4,100 |

Style 71K Hawaiian

1930s. Hawaiian, gold vine pattern on bound sunburst top, dot inlays.

| 1930s | | $875 | $1,150 |

Ochoteco Guitars

1979-present. Production/custom steel- and nylon-stringed guitars built by luthier Gabriel Ochoteco in Germany until '84 and in Brisbane, Australia since.

Normandy Alumicaster

1930s Oahu
Bernunzio Uptown Music

1981 O'Hagan Twenty-Two
Christopher Tritschler

Oskar Graf No. 4/11

MODEL YEAR	FEATURES	EXC. COND. LOW	HIGH

Odessa

1981-1990s. Budget guitars imported by Davitt & Hanser (BC Rich). Mainly acoustics in the '90s, but some electrics early on.

O'Hagan

1979-1983. Designed by clarinetist and importer Jerol O'Hagan in St. Louis Park, Minnesota. Primarily neck-thru construction, most with German-carved bodies. In '81 became Jemar Corporation and in '83 it was closed by the I.R.S., a victim of recession. SN=YYM(M)NN (e.g., 80905, September '80, 5th guitar); or MYMNNN (e.g., A34006, April 1983, 6th guitar). Approximately 3000 total instruments were made with the majority being Night-Watches (approx. 200 Twenty Twos, 100-150 Sharks, 100 Lasers; about 25 with birdseye maple bodies).

Electric

1979-1983. Models include; Laser (solidbody, double-cut, maple or walnut body, set-thru neck, 3 single-coil Schaller pickups), Shark (Explorer-looking solidbody) and Twenty Two (V, 2 humbuckers).

1979-1983		$525	$700

Ohio

1959-ca. 1965. Line of electric solidbodies and basses made by France's Jacobacci company, which also built under its own brand. Sparkle finish, bolt-on aluminum necks, strings-thru-body design.

Old Kraftsman

Ca. 1930s-ca. 1960s. Brandname used by the Spiegel catalog company for instruments made by other American manufacturers, including Regal, Kay and even Gibson. The instruments were of mixed quality, but some better grade instruments were comparable to those offered by Wards.

Archtop

1930s-1960s. Various models.

1930s	17", Stauffer-style hdstk	$300	$400
1950s-60s		$225	$300

Flat-Top

1930s-1960s. Various models.

1950s	Prairie Ramblers (stencil)	$225	$300

Jazz II K775

1960-1963. Kay 775 with Old Kraftsman logo on large headstock, small double-cut thinline, 2 pickups, Bigsby, natural.

1960-1963		$850	$1,100

Sizzler K4140

1959. Single-cut, single neck pickup, Sizzler logo on body with other art images.

1959		$385	$500

Thin Twin Jimmy Reed

1952-1958		$1,000	$1,300

Value Leader

1961-1965. Electric single-cut semi-solid, 1 pickup, Kay Value Leader series.

1961-1965		$300	$400

OLP (Officially Licensed Product)

2001-2009. Intermediate grade, production, imported guitars and basses based on higher dollar guitar models officially licensed from the original manufacturer. OLP logo on headstock.

Olson Guitars

1977-present. Luthier James A. Olson builds his presentation grade, custom, flat-tops in Circle Pines, Minnesota.

Olympia by Tacoma

1997-2006. Import acoustic guitars and mandolins from Tacoma Guitars.

OD Series

1997-2006	Various models	$75	$275

Omega

1996-2010. Luthier Kevin Gallagher built his premium grade, custom/production acoustic guitars in East Saylorsburg, Pennsylvania. He died in '10.

Oncor Sound

1980-ca. 1981. This Salt Lake City, Utah-based company made both a guitar and a bass synthesizer.

Optek

1980s-present. Intermediate grade, production, imported Fretlight acoustic/electric and electric guitars. Located in Reno, Nevada.

Fretlight

1989-present. Double-cut, 126 LED lights in fretboard controlled by a scale/chord selector.

1989-2019		$275	$375

Opus

1972-Mid 1970s. Acoustic and classical guitars, imported from Japan by Ampeg/Selmer. In '75-'76, Harmony made a line of acoustics with the Opus model name.

Original Senn

2004-present. Luthier Jeff Senn builds his professional and premium grade, production/custom, solidbody electric guitars and basses in Nashville, Tennessee.

Ormsby Guitars

2003-present. Luthier Perry Ormsby builds his custom, professional and premium grade, solid and chambered electric guitars in Perth, Western Australia.

Orpheum

1897-1942, 1944-late 1960s, 2001-2006. Intermediate grade, production, acoustic and resonator guitars. They also offered mandolins. Orpheum originally was a brand of Rettberg and Lange, who made instruments for other companies as well. William Rettberg and William Lange bought the facilities of New York

MODEL YEAR	FEATURES	EXC. COND. LOW	HIGH

banjo maker James H. Buckbee in 1897. Lange went out on his own in '21 to start the Paramount brand. He apparently continued using the Orpheum brand as well. He went out of business in '42. In '44 the brand was acquired by New York's Maurice Lipsky Music Co. who used it primarily on beginner to medium grade instruments, which were manufactured by Regal, Kay, and United Guitar (and maybe others). In the early '60s Lipsky applied the brand to Japanese and European (by Egmond) imports. Lipsky dropped the name in the early '70s. The brand was revived for '01 to '06 by Tacoma Guitars.

Auditorium Archtop 835/837
1950s. Acoustic archtop, auditorium size, dot markers, Orpheum shell headpiece, white celluloid 'guard, model 835 with spruce top/back/sides, 837 with mahogany.

1950s		$250	$350

Orpheum Special (Regal-made)
1930s. Slot head, Dobro-style wood body, metal resonator, sunburst.

1930s		$675	$900

President
1940s. 18" pro-level acoustic archtop, Orpheum block logo and President script logo on headstock, large split-block markers, sunburst.

1940s		$1,275	$1,700

Style B
1940s. Acoustic archtop, Style B logo on headstock, block markers, sunburst.

1940s		$500	$675

Thin Twin Jimmy Reed 865E
1950s. Model 865E is the Orpheum version of the generically named Thin Twin Jimmy Reed style electric Spanish cutaway thin solidbody, hand engraved shell celluloid Orpheum headpiece, described as #865E Cutaway Thin Electric Guitar in catalog.

1950s		$1,000	$1,475

Ultra Deluxe Professional 899
1950s. 17" cutaway, 2 pickups, 2 knobs, maple back and sides, top material varies, dot markers, finishes as follows: E-C copper, E-G gold, E-G-B gold-black sunburst, E-B blond curly maple, E-S golden orange sunburst.

1950s	All finishes	$1,100	$1,475

Orville
1984-1993. Orville by Gibson and Orville guitars were made by Japan's Fuji Gen Gakki for Gibson. See following listing for details. Guitars listed here state only Orville (no By Gibson) on the headstock.

Electric

1990s	CE Atkins	$725	$925
1990s	ES-335	$1,025	$1,350
1990s	Les Paul Custom	$850	$1,125
1990s	Les Paul Standard	$900	$1,200

Orville by Gibson
1984-1993. Orville by Gibson and Orville guitars were made by Japan's Fuji Gen Gakki for Gibson. Basically the same models except the Orville by Gibson guitars had real Gibson USA PAF '57 Clas-

sic pickups and a true nitrocellulose lacquer finish. The Orville models used Japanese electronics and a poly finish. Some Orvilles were made in Korea and are of a lower quality. These Korean guitars had the serial number printed on a sticker. Prices here are for the Orville by Gibson models.

Acoustic-Electric
1984-1993. On-board electronics.

1984-1993	Dove	$1,200	$1,550
1984-1993	J-160E	$1,200	$1,550
1984-1993	J-200NE	$1,200	$1,550

Electric
1984-1993. Various models.

1984-1993	ES-175	$1,225	$1,600
1984-1993	ES-335	$1,225	$1,600
1984-1993	Explorer	$1,050	$1,375
1984-1993	Firebird V	$900	$1,175
1984-1993	Firebird VII	$900	$1,175
1984-1993	Flying V	$1,050	$1,375
1984-1993	Les Paul Custom	$850	$1,125
1984-1993	Les Paul Jr	$525	$675
1984-1993	Les Paul Standard	$900	$1,500
1984-1993	Les Paul Studio JP	$800	$1,025
1984-1993	MM/Les Paul Jr	$425	$550
1984-1993	SG Les Paul Custom	$850	$1,125
1984-1993	SG LP Standard	$750	$975

Osborne Sound Laboratories
Late 1970s. Founded by Ralph Scaffidi and wife guitarist Mary Osborne; originally building guitar amps, they did also offer solidbody guitars.

Oscar Schmidt
1879-1938, 1979-present. Budget and intermediate grade, production, acoustic, acoustic/electric, and electric guitars and basses distributed by U.S. Music Corp. (Washburn, Randall, etc.). They also offer mandolins, banjos, ukuleles and the famous Oscar Schmidt autoharp.

The original Oscar Schmidt Company, Jersey City, New Jersey, offered banjo mandolins, tenor banjos, guitar banjos, ukuleles, mandolins and guitars under their own brand and others (including Sovereign and Stella). By the early 1900s, the company had factories in the U.S. and Europe producing instruments producing instruments under their own brand as well as other brands for mail-order and other distributors. Oscar Schmidt was also an early contributor to innovative mandolin designs and the company participated in the '00-'30 mandolin boom. The company hit hard times during the Depression and was sold to Harmony by the end of the '30s. In '79, Washburn acquired the brand and it is now part of U.S. Music.

Oskar Graf Guitars
1970-present. Premium and presentation grade, custom, archtop, acoustic and classical guitars and basses built in Clarendon, Ontario, by luthier Oskar Graf. He also builds lutes.

1940s Orpheum President
Imaged by Heritage Auctions, HA.com

1993 Orville Les Paul Standard
Stoeffu Vogt

GUITARS

1976 Ovation Adamas
Sam Stathakis

1981 Adamas II Model
Rivington Guitars

MODEL YEAR	FEATURES	EXC. COND. LOW	HIGH

Otwin

1950s-1960s. A brand used on electric guitars made by the Musima company of East Germany. Musima also produced guitars under their own brand.

Outbound Instruments

1990-2002. Intermediate grade, production, travel-size acoustics from the Boulder, Colorado-based company.

Ovation

1966-present. Intermediate and professional grade, production, acoustic and acoustic/electric guitars. They also build basses and mandolins. Until 2014, they also had U.S. production.

Helicopter manufacturer Kaman Corporation, founded in 1945 by jazz guitarist and aeronautical engineer Charles Huron Kaman in Bloomfield, Connecticut, decided to use their helicopter expertise (working with synthetic materials, spruce, high tolerances) and designed, with the help of employee and violin restorer John Ringso, the first fiberglass-backed (Lyracord) acoustic guitars in '65. Production began in '66 and the music factory moved to New Hartford, Connecticut, in '67. Early input was provided by fingerstyle jazz guitarist Charlie Byrd, who gave Kaman the idea for the name Ovation. Kaman Music purchased Hamer Guitars in '88, and Trace Elliot amplifiers (U.K.) in '90. In '08, Fender acquired Kaman Music Corporation and the Ovation brand; in '14 U.S. production ceased and the brand was sold to Drum Workshop, Inc., who re-opened the Hartford, CT plant in late '15.

Adamas 1581-KK Kaki King
2011-2014. Deep bowl cutaway, rosewood 'board, 12th-fret crown inlay, OP-Pro preamp, Kaki personally signs the label on each guitar.

2011-2014		$2,350	$3,000

Adamas 1587
1979-1998. Carbon top, walnut, single-cut, bowl back, binding, mini-soundholes.

| 1979-1998 | Black Sparkle | $1,300 | $1,700 |

Adamas 1597
1998-2003. Carbon birch composite top, on-board electronics.

| 1998-2003 | Black | $725 | $975 |

Adamas 1598-MEII Melissa Etheridge
2001-2014. Mid-depth cutaway, ebony 'board, 'ME' maple symbol at 12th fret, OP-Pro preamp, Melissa personally signs the label on each guitar.

| 2001-2014 | 12-string | $1,100 | $1,500 |

Adamas 1687
1977-1998. Acoustic/electric, carbon top, non-cut, bowl back, mini-soundholes.

| 1977-1998 | Sunburst | $1,300 | $1,700 |

Adamas CVT W591
2000. Crossweave fiber top, mid-depth body, on-board electronics.

| 2000 | | $850 | $1,100 |

Adamas II 1881 NB-2
1993-1998. Acoustic/electric, single-cut, shallow bowl, brown.

| 1993-1998 | | $1,225 | $1,600 |

Adamas Millenium
2000. Limited edition, 75 made, planet inlays, Cobalt Blue.

| 2000 | | $1,800 | $2,400 |

Anniversary Electric 1657
1978. Deep bowl, abalone inlays, gold-plated parts, for Ovation's 10th anniversary. They also offered an acoustic Anniversary.

| 1978 | | $325 | $425 |

Balladeer 1111
1968-1983, 1993-2000. Acoustic, non-cut with deep bowl, bound body, natural top, later called the Standard Balladeer.

| 1976-1983 | | $300 | $400 |

Balladeer Artist 1121
1968-1990. Acoustic, non-cut with shallow bowl, bound body.

| 1968-1969 | Early production | $400 | $525 |
| 1970-1990 | | $300 | $400 |

Balladeer Classic 1122
1970s. Classical shallow-bowl version of Concert Classic, nylon strings, slotted headstock.

| 1970s | | $275 | $375 |

Balladeer Custom 1112
1976-1990. Acoustic, deep bowl, diamond inlays.

| 1976-1990 | | $375 | $475 |

Balladeer Custom Electric 12-String 1655/1755
1982-1994. 12-string version of Balladeer Custom Electric.

| 1982-1994 | | $325 | $425 |

Balladeer Custom Electric 1612/1712
1976-1990. Acoustic/electric version of Balladeer Custom, deep bowl.

| 1976-1990 | | $400 | $525 |

Balladeer Standard 1561/1661/1761/1861
1982-2000. Acoustic/electric, deep bowl, rounded cutaway.

| 1982-2000 | | $375 | $500 |

Balladeer Standard 1771 LX
2008-2010. Acoustic/electric, mid-depth bowl, rosewood, sitka spruce top.

| 2008-2010 | | $450 | $575 |

Balladeer Standard 12-String 6751 LX
2008-2010. Acoustic/electric, 12 strings, rosewood, spruce top.

| 2008-2010 | | $525 | $675 |

Breadwinner 1251
1971-1983. Axe-like shaped single-cut solidbody, 2 pickups, textured finish, black, blue, tan or white.

| 1971-1983 | | $700 | $900 |

Celebrity CC-48
2007-2013. Acoustic/electric, super shallow, laminated spruce top, white bound rosewood 'board with abalone dot inlays.

| 2007-2013 | | $200 | $275 |

MODEL YEAR	FEATURES	EXC. COND. LOW	HIGH

Celebrity CC-57
1990-1996. Laminated spruce top, shallow bowl, mahogany neck.

| 1990-1996 | | $200 | $275 |

Celebrity CC-63
1984-1996. Classical, deep bowl, piezo bridge pickup.

| 1984-1996 | | $200 | $275 |

Celebrity CK-057
2002-2004. Acoustic/electric rounded cutaway, shallow back.

| 2002-2004 | | $275 | $350 |

Celebrity CS-257
1992-2005, 2010. Made in Korea, super shallow bowl back body, single-cut, Adamas soundholes, alternating dot and diamond markers.

| 1992-2005 | Celebrity | $325 | $425 |
| 2010 | Celebrity Deluxe | $375 | $475 |

Classic 1613/1713
1971-1993. Acoustic/electric, non-cut, deep bowl, no inlay, slotted headstock, gold tuners, natural.

| 1971-1993 | | $375 | $500 |

Classic 1663/1763
1982-1998. Acoustic/electric, single-cut, deep bowl, cedar top, EQ, no inlay, slotted headstock, gold tuners.

| 1982-1998 | | $450 | $600 |

Classic 1863
1989-1998. Acoustic/electric, single-cut, shallow bowl, no inlay, cedar top, EQ, slotted headstock, gold tuners.

| 1989-1998 | | $450 | $600 |

Collectors Series
1982-2008. Limited edition, different model featured each year and production limited to that year only, the year designation is marked at the 12th fret, various colors (each year different).

| 1982-2008 | Common models | $450 | $600 |
| 1982-2008 | Rare models | $650 | $1,200 |

Concert Classic 1116
1974-1990. Deep-bowl nylon string classical, slotted headstock.

| 1974-1990 | | $275 | $350 |

Contemporary Folk Classic Electric 1616
1974-1990. Acoustic/electric, no inlay, slotted headstock, natural or sunburst.

| 1974-1990 | | $275 | $350 |

Country Artist Classic Electric 6773
1995-2011. Classic electric, soft-cut, solid spruce top, slotted headstock, Ovation pickup system.

| 1995-2011 | | $425 | $550 |

Country Artist Electric 1624
1971-1990. Nylon strings, slotted headstock, standard steel-string sized neck to simulate a folk guitar, on-board electronics.

| 1971-1990 | | $450 | $600 |

Custom Ballader 1762
1992. Rounded cutaway, higher-end specs.

| 1992 | | $600 | $800 |

Custom Elite Guitar Center 30th Anniversary
1994. 50 made.

| 1994 | | $950 | $1,275 |

Custom Legend 1117
1970s. Non-electrical 2nd generation Ovation, higher-end with abalone inlays and gold hardware, open V-bracing pattern. Model 1117-4, natural.

| 1970s | | $550 | $725 |

Custom Legend 1569
1980s. Rounded cutaway acoustic/electric, super shallow bowl, gloss black finish.

| 1980s | | $500 | $650 |

Custom Legend 1619/1719
1970s. Acoustic/electric 2nd generation Ovation, electric version of model 1117, higher-end with abalone inlays and gold hardware, open V-bracing pattern.

| 1970s | | $550 | $725 |

Custom Legend 1759
1984-2004. Single-cut acoustic/electric.

| 1984-2004 | | $550 | $725 |

Custom Legend 1769
1982, 1993, 1996-1999. Single-cut acoustic/electric.

| 1982-1999 | | $825 | $1,100 |

Custom Legend 1869
1994, 2003. Acoustic/electric, cutaway, super shallow bowl.

| 1994, 2003 | | $625 | $825 |

Custom Legend 6759

| 2003 | | $1,250 | $1,650 |

Deacon 1252
1973-1980. Axe-shaped solidbody electric, active electronics, diamond fret markers.

| 1973-1980 | | $850 | $1,100 |

Deacon 12-String 1253
1975. Axe-shaped solidbody, diamond inlay, 2 pickups. only a few made.

| 1975 | | $850 | $1,100 |

Eclipse
1971-1973. Thinline double cut acoustic-electric archtop, 2 pickups.

| 1971-1973 | | $650 | $850 |

Elite 1718
1982-1997. Acoustic/electric, non-cut, deep bowl, solid spruce top, Adamas-type soundhole, volume and tone controls, stereo output.

| 1982-1997 | | $625 | $825 |

Elite 1758
1990-1998. Acoustic/electric, non-cut, deep bowl.

| 1990-1998 | | $625 | $825 |

Elite 1768
1990-1998. Acoustic/electric, cutaway, deep bowl.

| 1990-1998 | | $525 | $675 |

Elite 1858 12-String
1993-2004. 12-string acoustic/electric, ebony 'board and bridge.

| 1993-2004 | | $625 | $825 |

Elite 1868
1983-2004. Acoustic/electric, cutaway, shallow bowl.

| 1983-2004 | | $475 | $625 |

Elite 5858
1991. Super shallow bowl, single cutaway, Adamas-style soundhole, gold hardware, on-board factory OP24 pickup.

| 1991 | | $525 | $675 |

1994 Ovation Collectors Series Model 1994-7

1980 Ovation Deacon 1252
Jon Way

GUITARS

*1974 Ovation Glen Campbell
12-String 1118 (K-1118)*

Imaged by Heritage Auctions, HA.com

1987 Ovation Legend 1717

Bernunzio Uptown Music

MODEL YEAR	FEATURES	EXC. COND. LOW	HIGH
Elite Doubleneck			
1989-1990s. Six- and 12-string necks, can be ordered with a variety of custom options.			
1989		$675	$900
Elite Standard 6868			
1994-1999. Elite Standard with cutaway shallow bowl.			
1994-1999		$500	$650
Elite T/TX 1778			
2002-2018. Acoustic/electric, cutaway, U.S. T replaced by import TX in '08.			
2002-2008	T, original version	$625	$825
2008-2018	TX, Import	$200	$300
Folklore 1614			
1972-1983. Acoustic/electric, 12-fret neck on full-size body, wide neck, on-board electronics.			
1972-1983		$450	$600
GCXT			
2008. Acoustic-electric, single-cut, flamed paint graphic, made for Guitar Center.			
2008		$525	$700
Glen Campbell 12-String 1118 (K-1118)			
1968-1982. Acoustic, 12 strings, shallow bowl version of Legend, gold tuners, diamond inlay.			
1968-1982		$500	$650
Glen Campbell Artist 1627			
2006. Glen Campbell 40th Anniversary model, diamond inlay, gold tuners.			
2006		$875	$1,150
Glen Campbell Artist Balladeer 1127			
1968-1990. Acoustic, shallow bowl, diamond inlay, gold tuners, natural.			
1968-1990		$500	$650
Hurricane 12-String K-1120			
1968-1969. ES-335-style electric semi-hollowbody, double-cut, 12 strings, f-holes, 2 pickups.			
1968-1969		$625	$825
Josh White 1114			
1967-1970, 1972-1983. Wide 12-fret neck, dot markers, classical-style tuners.			
1967-1970		$550	$700
1972-1983		$450	$600
Legend 1117			
1972-1999. Deep bowl acoustic, 5-ply top binding, gold tuners, various colors (most natural).			
1972-1999		$400	$550
Legend 1567/1867			
1984-2004. Acoustic/electric, shallow bowl, single-cut, gold tuners.			
1984-2004		$450	$600
Legend 12-String 1866			
1989-2007. Acoustic/electric, cutaway, 12 strings, shallow bowl, 5-ply top binding, black.			
1989-2007		$450	$600
Legend 1717			
1990-2008. Acoustic/electric, 5-ply top binding, various colors.			
1990-2008		$425	$575
Legend 1767			
1990s. Acoustic/electric, deep bowl, single-cut, black.			
1990s		$425	$575

MODEL YEAR	FEATURES	EXC. COND. LOW	HIGH
Legend Cutaway 1667			
1982-1996. Acoustic/electric, cutaway, deep bowl, abalone, gold tuners.			
1982-1996		$475	$625
Legend Electric 1617			
1972-1998. Acoustic/electric, deep bowl, abalone, gold tuners, various colors.			
1972-1998		$400	$550
Pacemaker 12-String 1115/1615			
1968-1982. Originally called the K-1115 12-string, Renamed Pacemaker in '72.			
1968-1982		$450	$600
Patriot Bicentennial			
*1976. Limited run of 1776 guitars, Legend Custom model with drum and flag decal and 1776*1976 decal on lower bout.*			
1976		$775	$1,000
Pinnacle			
1990-1992. Spruce or sycamore top, broad leaf pattern rosette, mahogany neck, piezo bridge pickup, sunburst.			
1990-1992		$400	$525
Pinnacle Shallow Cutaway			
1990-1994. Pinnacle with shallow bowl body and single-cut, sunburst.			
1990-1994		$400	$525
Preacher 1281			
1975-1982. Solidbody, mahogany body, double-cut, 2 pickups.			
1975-1982		$550	$725
Preacher Deluxe 1282			
1975-1982. Double-cut solidbody, 2 pickups with series/parallel pickup switch and mid-range control.			
1975-1982		$550	$725
Preacher 12-String 1285			
1975-1983. Double-cut solidbody, 12 strings, 2 pickups.			
1975-1983		$550	$725
Thunderhead 1460			
1968-1972. Double-cut, 2 pickups, gold hardware, phase switch, master volume, separate tone controls, pickup balance/blend control, vibrato.			
1968-1972	Natural or rare color	$1,100	$1,500
1968-1972	Sunburst	$825	$1,100
Tornado 1260			
1968-1973. Same as Thunderhead without phase switch, with chrome hardware.			
1968-1973		$600	$800
UK II 1291			
1980-1982. Single-cut solidbody, 2 pickups, body made of Urelite on aluminum frame, bolt-on neck, gold hardware.			
1980-1982		$725	$925
Ultra GS/GP Series			
1984. Korean solidbodies and necks assembled in U.S., DiMarzio pickups, offset double-cut (GS) with 1 hum, or hum/single/single or LP style (GP) with 2 humbuckers. There was also a bass.			
1984		$325	$425

The **Vintage Guitar Price Guide** shows low to high values for items in all-original excellent condition, and, where applicable, with original case or cover.

MODEL YEAR	FEATURES	EXC. COND. LOW	HIGH

Ultra Series
1970s-2000s. Various Ultra model acoustic/electrics.

1970-2000s		$200	$600

Viper 1271
1975-1982. Single-cut, 2 single-coil pickups.

1975-1982		$575	$750

Viper EA 68
1994-2008. Thin acoustic/electric, single-cut mahogany body, spruce top over sound chamber with multiple upper bout soundholes, black.

1994-2008		$400	$525

Viper III 1273
1975-1982. Single-cut, 3 single-coil pickups.

1975-1982		$575	$750

VXT Hybrid
2007-2009. Single-cut solidbody, 2 Seymour Duncan '59 humbuckers, Fishman Power Bridge.

2007-2009		$625	$800

Overture Guitars
Luthier Justin Hoffman began building in the year 2008, professional to presentation grade, custom/production, solidbody guitars and basses in Morton, Illinois.

P. W. Crump Company
1975-present. Luthier Phil Crump builds his custom flat-top guitars in Arcata, California. He also builds mandolin-family instruments.

Palen
1998-present. Premium grade, production/custom, archtop guitars built by luthier Nelson Palen in Beloit, Kansas.

Palmer
Early 1970s-present. Budget and intermediate grade, production acoustic, acoustic/electric and classical guitars imported from Europe and Asia. They also have offered electrics.

Panache
2004-2008. Budget grade, production, solidbody electric and acoustic guitars imported from China.

PANaramic
1961-1963. Guitars and basses made in Italy by the Crucianelli accordion company and imported by PANaramic accordion. They also offered amps made by Magnatone.

Acoustic-Electric Archtop
1961-1963. Full body cutaway, 2 pickups.

1961-1963		$850	$1,100

Paolo Soprani
Early 1960s. Italian plastic covered guitars with pushbutton controls made by the Polverini Brothers.

Paramount
1921-1942, Late 1940s. The William L. Lange Company began selling Paramount banjos, guitar banjos and mandolin banjos in the early 1920s, and added archtop guitars in '34. The guitars were made by Martin and possibly others. Lange went out of business by '42; Gretsch picked up the Paramount name and used it on acoustics and electrics for a time in the late '40s.

GB
1920s-1930s. Guitar banjo.

1920s		$900	$1,200

Style C
1930s. 16" acoustic archtop, maple back and sides.

1930s		$400	$525

Style L
1930s. Made by Martin, limited to about 36 instruments, small body with resonator, Brazilian rosewood.

1930s	Spanish 6-string	$5,000	$6,500
1930s	Tenor 4-string	$3,600	$4,700

Parker
1992-2016. U.S.-made and imported intermediate, professional, and premium grade, production/custom, solidbody guitars featuring a thin skin of carbon and glass fibers bonded to a wooden guitar body. In '05, they added wood body acoustic/electrics. They also build basses. Originally located northwest of Boston, Parker was founded by Ken Parker and Larry Fishman (Fishman Transducers). Korg USA committed money to get the Fly Deluxe model into production in July '93. Parker added a Custom Shop in '03 to produce special build instruments and non-core higher-end models that were no longer available as a standard product offering. In early '04, Parker was acquired by U.S. Music Corp. and moved USA production from the Boston area to Chicago. U.S. Music was acquired by Jam Industries in '09 and production of Parker Guitars was ceased in '16.

Concert
1997 only. Solid sitka spruce top, only piezo system pickup, no magnetic pickups, transparent butterscotch.

1997		$1,350	$1,800

Fly
1993-1994. There are many Parker Fly models, the model simply called Fly is similar to the more common Fly Deluxe, except it does not have the Fishman piezo pickup system.

1993-1994		$1,350	$1,800

Fly Artist
1998-1999. Solid sitka spruce top, vibrato, Deluxe-style electronics, transparent blond finish.

1998-1999		$1,500	$2,000

Fly Classic
1996-1998, 2000-2011. One-piece Honduras mahogany body, basswood neck, electronics same as Fly Deluxe.

1996-2011		$1,350	$1,800

1970 Ovation Tornado 1260
Imaged by Heritage Auctions, HA.com

Ovation Ultra GP
Sam Stathakis

2017 Parkwood P810

*Patrick James Eggle
Guitars Macon Junior*

MODEL YEAR	FEATURES	EXC. COND. LOW	HIGH

Fly Classic Maple
2000. Classic with maple body (vs. mahogany), transparent butterscotch.

2000		$1,350	$1,800

Fly Deluxe
1993-2016. Poplar body, basswood neck, 2 pickups, Fishman bridge transducer, '93-'96 models were offered with or without vibrato, then non-vibrato discontinued. The Deluxe normally came with a gig bag, but also offered with a hardshell case, which would add about $50 to the values listed.

1993-2016		$1,350	$1,800

Fly Supreme
1996-1999. One-piece flame maple body, electronics same as the Fly Deluxe, highly flamed butterscotch, includes hard molded case.

1996-1999		$1,900	$2,500

MaxxFly PDF Series
2013-2016. PDF is import line of more traditionally-shaped Maxx solidbodies, various models.

2013	PDF60	$275	$350
2013	PDF70	$325	$425
2013-2016	PDF30	$250	$325

Mojo
2003-2010. Fly either single-cut or double-cut.

2003-2005	Single-cut	$900	$1,200
2003-2010	Double-cut	$1,300	$1,725

NiteFly Series
1996-2009. Two single-coil and 1 humbucker pickup NiteFly, Fishman piezo system, bolt neck, maple body for '96-'98, ash for '99-present. Called the NiteFly in '96, NiteFly NFV2 ('97-'98), NiteFly NFV4 ('98), NiteFly NFV6 ('99), NiteFly SA ('00-present).

1996-2009	Various models	$675	$975

P Series
2000-2009. Various models include P-38 (ash body, bolt maple neck, rosewood 'board, vibrato, piezo bridge pickup and active Parker Alnico humbucker and 2 single-coils, gig bag); P-40 (as P-38, but with pickups mounted on body, no 'guard); P-44 (mahogany body, flamed maple top, piezo bridge pickup and 2 special Parker humbuckers).

2000-2009		$275	$525

Tulipwood Limited Edition
1998. Limited build of 35, standard Deluxe features with tulipwood body.

1998		$1,325	$1,750

Parkwood

2007-present. Intermediate grade, acoustic and acoustic-electric guitars, Parkwood logo on headstock.

Patrick Eggle Guitars

1991-present. Founded by Patrick Eggle and others in Birmingham, England, building solid and semi-solidbody electric guitars and basses. In '95, Eggle left the company to build acoustics.

Patrick James Eggle

2001-present. Eggle co-founded the Patrick Eggle Guitar company in '91 building solidbodies. In '95, he left to do repairs and custom work. In '01 he opened a new workshop in Bedforshire, England, building professional and premium grade, production/custom, archtop and flatop guitars. For a short time he relocated to Hendersonville, North Carolina, but in '05 returned to England and opened a shop in Oswestry.

Paul Berger

1972-2015. Acoustic guitars built by luthier Paul Berger in St. Augustine, Florida. He died in '15.

Paul H. Jacobson

1974-present. Premium grade, production/ custom, classical guitars built by luthier Paul H. Jacobson in Cleveland, Missouri.

Paul Reed Smith

1985-present. Intermediate, professional and premium grade, production/custom, solid, semi-hollow body, and acoustic guitars made in the U.S. and imported. They also build basses. Paul Reed Smith built his first guitar in '75 as an independent study project in college and refined his design over the next 10 years building custom guitars. After building two prototypes and getting several orders from East Coast guitar dealers, Smith was able to secure the support necessary to start PRS in a factory on Virginia Avenue in Annapolis, Maryland. On '95, they moved to their current location on Kent Island in Stevensville. In 2001 PRS introduced the Korean-made SE Series. Acoustics were added in '08.

10th Anniversary
1995. 200 made, mother-of-pearl inlays, abalone purfling, gold pickups, either wide-fat or wide-thin neck, 10th Anniversary logo, price includes certificate of authenticity.

1995	With certificate	$3,250	$4,200

305
2010-2013. Alder body, maple neck and 'board, birds, 3 single-coils.

2010-2013		$1,025	$1,325

305 25th Anniversary
2010. 305 made, 3 single-coils, wide-fat or wide-thin, 25th Anniversary logo.

2010		$1,075	$1,400

513 Rosewood
Dec.2003-2006. Brazilian rosewood neck, newly developed PRS pickup system with 13 sound settings, hum-single-hum pickups.

2003-2006		$2,000	$2,600

513 Swamp Ash
2010. Figured ash, natural.

2010		$1,225	$1,600

513 25th Anniversary
2010. Carved figured maple top, 25th Anniversary shadow birds inlay.

2010		$1,825	$2,375

MODEL YEAR	FEATURES	EXC. COND. LOW	HIGH
Al Di Meola Prism			
2008-2014. Curly maple 10 top, 22-fret, prism multicolor finish.			
2008-2014		$1,550	$2,000
Artist/Artist I/Artist 24			
1991-1994. Carved maple top, offset double-cut, 24-fret neck, bird markers, less than 500 made. A different Custom 24 Artist package was subsequently offered in the 2000s.			
1991-1994		$2,775	$3,600
Angelus Cutaway			
2009-present. Flat-top, on-board electronics, European spruce top, figured mahogany back and sides, flamed maple binding. Listed under Private Stock in '20, with select wood options.			
2009-2019		$2,450	$3,200
Artist II/Artist 22			
1993-1995. Curly maple top, maple purfling on rosewood 'board, inlaid maple bound headstock, abalone birds, 22 frets, gold hardware, short run of less than 500.			
1993-1995		$1,825	$2,375
Artist III			
1996-1997. Continuation of the 22-fret neck with some changes in materials and specs, figured maple tops, short run of less than 500 instruments.			
1996-1997		$2,025	$2,650
Artist IV			
1996. Continuation of the 22-fret neck with some upgrades in materials and specs, short run of less than 70 instruments.			
1996		$2,900	$3,800
Artist Limited			
1994-1995. Like the Artist II with 14-carat gold bird inlays, abalone purfling on neck, headstock and truss rod cover, Brazilian rosewood 'board, 165 made.			
1994-1995		$2,900	$3,800
CE 22			
1994-2000, 2005-2008. Double-cut carved alder body (1995), mahogany '96-'00 and '05-'07, back to alder in '08, bolt-on maple neck with rosewood 'board, dot inlays, 2 humbuckers, chrome hardware, translucent colors, options include vibrato and gold hardware and custom colors.			
1994-1995	Alder	$1,025	$1,325
1996-2000	Mahogany	$1,025	$1,325
2005-2008	Reintroduced	$1,025	$1,325
CE 22 Maple Top			
1994-2008. CE 22 with figured maple top, upgrade options included gold hardware, custom colors or 10 top.			
1994-2008		$1,025	$1,325
CE 24 (Classic Electric, CE)			
1988-2000, 2005-2008. Double-cut, alder body to '95, mahogany '96-'00 and '05-'07, back to alder in '08, carved top, 24-fret bolt-on maple neck, 2 humbuckers, dot inlays, upgrade options included gold hardware, custom colors or 10 top.			
1988-2008		$1,025	$1,325

MODEL YEAR	FEATURES	EXC. COND. LOW	HIGH
CE 24 Maple Top (CE Maple Top)			
1989-2008. CE 24 with figured maple top, upgrade options may include any or all the following: gold hardware, custom colors or 10 top.			
1989-2008		$1,025	$1,325
Chris Henderson Signature			
2007-2012. Single-cut, 3 exposed humbucker pickups, carved flame maple top on mahogany body, wide flat neck profile, 22 frets.			
2007-2012		$1,025	$1,325
Corvette			
2005-2006. Custom 22 with Velcity Yellow finish, Standard 22 red finish, Z06 inlays, Corvette logo on body.			
2005	Custom 22, yellow	$1,025	$1,325
2006	Standard 22, red	$1,025	$1,325
Custom (Custom 24/PRS Custom)			
1985-present. Double-cut solidbody, curly maple top, mahogany back and neck, pearl and abalone moon inlays, 24 frets, 2 humbuckers, tremolo, options include quilted or 10 Top, bird inlays, and gold hardware. 1985 Customs should be evaluated on a case by case basis.			
1985		$3,000	$17,000
1986		$3,000	$6,500
1987		$2,700	$3,500
1988		$2,300	$3,000
1989		$1,600	$2,100
1990		$1,300	$1,700
1991-2019		$1,400	$1,800
Custom 22			
1993-2009, 2013-present. Custom 22 with flamed or quilted maple top on mahogany body, 22-fret set-neck, upgrade option is gold hardware, normally the quilt top is higher than flamed top.			
1993-2019		$1,425	$1,900
Custom 22 (Brazilian)			
2003-2004. Limited run of 500 with Brazilian rosewood 'board, figured 10 top, pearl bird inlays.			
2003-2004		$2,400	$3,100
Custom 22 20th Anniversary			
2005. Abalone 20th Anniversary birds inlay, 20th engraved on truss rod cover.			
2005		$1,700	$2,200
Custom 22 Soapbar			
1998-2002. 3 Seymour Duncan soapbar single-coils.			
1998-2002		$1,300	$1,700
Custom 22/12			
December 2003-2009. 12-string version, flame or quilt maple top, hum/single/hum pickups.			
2003-2009		$1,800	$2,400
Custom 24 (Brazilian)			
2003-2004. Limited run with Brazilian rosewood 'board, figured 10 top, pearl bird inlays.			
2003-2004		$2,700	$3,500
Custom 24 (Walnut)			
1992. Seamless matched walnut over mahogany, 3 made.			
1992		$2,400	$3,100
Custom 24 20th Anniversary			
2005. Abalone 20th Anniversary birds inlay, 20th engraved on truss rod cover.			
2005		$1,800	$2,400

2004 PRS CE-22
Robbie Keene

2003 PRS Custom 22
Bernunzio Uptown Music

GUITARS

1985 PRS Custom 24

1983 PRS Dragon II

MODEL YEAR	FEATURES	EXC. COND. LOW	HIGH

Custom 24 25th Anniversary
2010. Carved figured maple top, 25th Anniversary shadow birds inlay.

| 2010 | | $1,800 | $2,400 |

Custom 24 30th Anniversary
2015. Figured maple top, 30th Anniversary on headstock, birds in flight neck inlay.

| 2015 | | $1,800 | $2,400 |

Dave Navarro Signature
2005-2014. Carved maple top, bird inlays, tremolo, white.

| 2005-2014 | | $1,425 | $1,850 |

DC3
2010-2013. Double-cut contoured body, bolt-on neck, 3 special single-coils.

| 2010-2013 | | $975 | $1,275 |

DGT David Grissom Trem
2007-present. Based on the McCarty Tremolo model with an added volume control, a nitro topcoat, vintage colors, large frets designed for .011 gauge strings.

| 2007-2019 | | $1,800 | $2,300 |

Dragon I
1992. Fingerboard inlay of a dragon made of 201 pieces of abalone, turquoise and mother-of-pearl, gold hardware, 50 made. The Dragon model collector requires an instrument to be truly mint and pristine with no play wear. The values shown here are for pristine instruments. Any issue whatsoever may dramatically reduce the high-side price shown. Price includes the certificate of authenticity.

| 1992 | Amber quilt, amber flame | $13,800 | $18,000 |
| 1992 | Teal black | $12,300 | $16,000 |

Dragon II
1993. Fingerboard inlay of a dragon made of 218 pieces of gold, coral, abalone, malachite, onyx and mother-of-pearl, 100 made.

| 1993 | | $7,500 | $10,000 |

Dragon III
1994. Fingerboard inlay of a dragon made of 438 pieces of gold, red and green abalone, mother-of-pearl, mammoth ivory, and stone, 100 made.

| 1994 | | $7,500 | $10,000 |

Dragon 2002
2002. Limited edition of 100 guitars, ultra-inlay work depicting dragon head on the guitar body.

| 2002 | | $6,500 | $8,500 |

Dragon 25th Anniversary
2009-2010. Multi-material dragon fingerboard inlay, green ripple abalone Modern Eagle headstock, body shape and electronics are modeled after an early company PRS guitar, 60 made.

| 2009-2010 | | $8,000 | $10,500 |

Dragon Doubleneck
2005. Limited edition 20th Anniversary model, about 50 made.

| 2005 | | $15,000 | $20,000 |

Dragon Millenium/Dragon 2000
1999-2000. Three-D dragon inlay in body versus neck inlay of previous models, limited production of 50 guitars.

| 1999-2000 | Black cherry | $9,600 | $12,500 |
| 1999-2000 | Rare color | $11,500 | $15,000 |

MODEL YEAR	FEATURES	EXC. COND. LOW	HIGH

EG II
1991-1995. Double-cut solidbody, bolt-on neck, 3 single-coils, single-single-hum, or hum-single-hum pickup options, opaque finish.

| 1991-1995 | | $775 | $1,000 |

EG II Maple Top
1991-1995. EG II with flamed maple top, chrome hardware.

| 1991-1995 | | $1,000 | $1,300 |

EG 3
1990-1991. Double-cut solidbody, bolt-on 22-fret neck, 3 single-coil pickups.

1990-1991	Flamed 10 top	$975	$1,250
1990-1991	Opaque finish	$775	$1,000
1990-1991	Plain top, sunburst	$775	$1,000

EG 4
1990-1991. Similar to EG 3 with single-single-hum pickup configuration, opaque finish.

| 1990-1991 | | $775 | $1,000 |

Golden Eagle
1997-1998. Very limited production, eagle head and shoulders carved into lower bouts, varied high-end appointments.

| 1997-1998 | | $11,000 | $14,000 |

Johnny Hiland
2006-2009. Maple fretboard.

| 2006-2009 | | $1,300 | $1,700 |

KL-33 Korina
2008. Double-cut solid korina body, rosewood 'board, PRS Mira pickups, limited run of 100.

| 2008 | | $1,400 | $1,800 |

KQ-24 Custom 24 (Killer Quilt)
2009. Limited Edition of 120, quilted maple top over korina body, 24 frets.

| 2009 | | $1,500 | $2,000 |

Limited Edition
1989-1991, 2000. Double-cut, semi-hollow mahogany body, figured cedar top, gold hardware, less than 300 made. In '00, single-cut, short run of 5 antique white and 5 black offered via Garrett Park Guitars.

| 1989-1991 | Tune-o-matic | $2,900 | $3,800 |
| 2000 | | $2,900 | $3,800 |

Limited Edition Howard Leese Golden Eagle
2009. Private Stock, curly maple top, old style mother of pearl birds, 100 made.

| 2009 | | $3,600 | $4,700 |

LTD Experience (Limited Experience)
2007. 200 built to commemorate PRS 2007 Experience Open House, 24 frets, matching headstock, maple top with mahogany body.

| 2007 | | $1,450 | $1,900 |

Mark Tremonti Model
2001-2007. Single-cut, 2 humbuckers, black or platinum finish.

| 2001-2007 | | $1,275 | $1,675 |

Mark Tremonti Signature Model
2007-present. Single-cut, 2 humbuckers, figured maple top (10 top upgrade offered), various finishes.

| 2007-2019 | 10 top upgrade | $1,700 | $2,200 |
| 2007-2019 | Standard figured top | $1,500 | $1,950 |

MODEL YEAR FEATURES	EXC. COND. LOW	HIGH

Mark Tremonti Tribal
2004-2006. With Tribal artwork, 100 made.

| 2004-2006 | $1,625 | $2,100 |

McCarty Model
1994-2007. Mahogany body with figured maple top, upgrade options may include a 10 top, gold hardware, bird inlays. Replaced by McCarty II.

| 1994-1999 | $1,500 | $2,000 |
| 2000-2007 | $1,500 | $2,000 |

McCarty II
2008-2009. Replaced the McCarty, featured new MVC (Mastering Voice Control) circuitry for switching between a single-coil voice to a heavy-metal voice, opaque finish.

| 2008-2009 | $1,500 | $2,000 |

McCarty 1957/2008 Limited
2008. "1957/2008" logo on truss rod cover, 08 serial number series, 150 made.

| 2008 | $1,925 | $2,500 |

McCarty 58/MC-58
2009-2011. "MC-58" logo on truss rod cover, similar to other McCarty models except for new neck shape, 57/08 humbucker pickups and V12 finish.

| 2009-2011 | $2,025 | $2,650 |

McCarty Archtop (Spruce)
1998-2000. Deep mahogany body, archtop, spruce top, 22-fret set-neck.

| 1998-2000 | $1,700 | $2,250 |

McCarty Archtop Artist
1998-2002. Highest grade figured maple top and highest appointments, gold hardware.

| 1998-2002 | $2,900 | $3,800 |

McCarty Archtop II (Maple)
1998-2000. Like Archtop but with figured maple top.

| 1998-2000 Flamed or quilt | $2,100 | $2,750 |

McCarty Hollowbody I/Hollowbody I
1998-2009. Medium deep mahogany hollowbody, maple top, 22-fret set-neck, chrome hardware. McCarty dropped from name in '06.

| 1998-2009 | $2,000 | $2,600 |

McCarty Hollowbody II/Hollowbody II
1998-2017. Like Hollowbody I but with figured maple top and back. McCarty dropped from name in '06.

| 1998-2017 | $2,000 | $2,600 |

McCarty Hollowbody/Hollowbody Spruce
2000-2009. Similar to Hollowbody I with less appointmentsm spruce top. McCarty dropped from name in '06.

| 2000-2009 | $1,600 | $2,050 |

McCarty Model/McCarty Brazilian
2003-2004. Limited run of 250, Brazilian rosewood 'board, Brazilian is printed on headstock just below the PRS script logo.

| 1999 | $2,700 | $3,500 |
| 2003-2004 | $2,400 | $3,100 |

McCarty Rosewood
2004-2005. PRS-22 fret with Indian rosewood neck.

| 2004-2005 | $1,700 | $2,200 |

McCarty Soapbar (Korina)
2008-2009. Korina body, 2 Duncan soapbar pickups.

| 2008-2009 | $1,400 | $1,825 |

McCarty Soapbar (Maple)
1998-2007. Soapbar with figured maple top option, nickel hardware.

| 1998-2007 | $1,300 | $1,725 |

McCarty Soapbar/Soapbar Standard
1998-2009. Solid mahogany body, P-90-style soapbar pickups, 22-fret set-neck, nickel-plated hardware, upgrade options may include gold hardware and bird inlays.

| 1998-2009 | $1,300 | $1,725 |

McCarty Standard
1994-2006. McCarty Model with carved mahogany body but without maple top, nickel-plated hardware, upgrade options may include gold hardware and bird inlays.

| 1994-2006 | $1,300 | $1,725 |

Metal
1985. Solid mahogany body with custom 2-color striped body finish and graphics, 24-fret set-neck, nickel hardware, 2 humbuckers.

| 1985 | $5,000 | $8,000 |

Metal '85 Reissue (Private Stock)
2008. With certificate of authenticity.

| 2008 | $3,000 | $4,000 |

Mira
2007-2013. 2 exposed-coil humbuckers, abalone moon inlays, various opaque finishes. Replaced by S2 Mira in '14.

| 2007-2013 | $700 | $925 |

Mira 25th Anniversary
2010. 2 soapbar single-coils, shadow bird inlays.

| 2010 | $700 | $925 |

Mira Korina
2007-2009. Korina body and neck version, natural.

| 2007-2009 | $800 | $1,075 |

Mira Maple Top (MT)
2008-2009. Figured maple, moon or bird inlays.

| 2008-2009 | $925 | $1,200 |

Modern Eagle
2004-2007. Higher-end model based on Private Stock innovations, satin nitrocellulose finish, Brazilian rosewood neck.

| 2004-2007 | $3,500 | $4,500 |

Modern Eagle II/MEII
2008-2009. Curly maple top, black rosewood neck and 'board.

| 2008-2009 | $2,800 | $3,600 |

Modern Eagle Quatro/ME Quatro
2010-2012. Updated version of Modern Eagle, 53/10 humbucker pickups, select upgraded woods.

| 2010-2012 | $2,100 | $2,700 |

NF3
2010-2013. 3 Narrowfield pickups on top-mounted 1-piece assembly, double-cut contoured body, bolt-on neck.

| 2010-2013 | $900 | $1,150 |

P22
2012-2016. Carved figured maple top, birds, rosewood 'board, 10-top flame optional.

| 2012-2016 | $2,500 | $3,200 |

1998 PRS McCarty Archtop Artist
Imaged by Heritage Auctions, HA.com

1985 PRS Metal
Ian Gilmour

GUITARS

1989 PRS Standard
Imaged by Heritage Auctions, HA.com

2001 PRS Singlecut
Craig Brody

MODEL YEAR	FEATURES	EXC. COND. LOW	HIGH

P245
2015. Semi-hollow electric, single-cut, 2 humbuckers and a piezo.

| 2015 | | $2,200 | $2,800 |

Paul's Dirty 100
2010. Private Stock run of 100, highly figured curly maple top, moon inlays, 'Paul's Dirty 100' logo on back of headstock, black gold finish, paisley hard case.

| 2010 | | $3,000 | $4,000 |

Paul's Guitar
2013-present. Carved figured maple top, mahogany back and neck, Hondouran rosewood 'board with brushstroke birds, various colors. Artist package and other options offered.

| 2013-2019 | | $2,100 | $2,700 |

Private Stock Program
April 1996-present. Custom instruments based around existing PRS models. Values may be somewhat near regular production equivalent models or higher. The Private Stock option was reintroduced by 2003. That year a standard production offering might retail at about $7,500, but a '03 Santana I Private Stock might retail at over $15,000, so each guitar should be evaluated on a case-by-case basis.

| 1996-2019 | Various models | $3,600 | $6,000 |

PRS Guitar
1975-1985. About 75 to 100 guitars were built by Paul Smith himself or with a team of others, from '75 to '85, before he formed the current PRS company. Each guitar from this era should be evaluated on a case-by-case basis and the values shown are for guidance only. Authentication is highly recommended; these guitars do not have a PRS serial number. Some of these went to celebrity players and, as such, may command values higher than shown here because of that connection.

1975-1983	Mahogany	$5,000	$21,000
1975-1983	Maple	$7,000	$44,000
1984-1985	Preproduction with provenance	$5,000	$21,000
1985-1986	Team-built	$3,000	$8,000

Rosewood Limited
1996. Mahogany body with figured maple top, 1-piece rosewood neck with ultra-deluxe tree-of-life neck inlay, gold hardware.

| 1996 | | $6,100 | $8,000 |

Santana
1995-1998, 2011-present. Limited production special order, figured maple top, 24-fret, symmetric Santana headstock, unique body purfling, chrome and nickel-plated hardware, yellow is most popular color, followed by orange, quality of top will affect price.

| 1995 | 1st 100 signed | $4,400 | $5,700 |
| 1995-1998 | | $3,400 | $4,400 |

Santana II
1998-2007. Three-way toggle replaces former dual mini-switches, special order, Brazilian 'board.

| 1998-2007 | | $3,400 | $4,400 |

Santana III
2001-2006. Less ornate version of Santana II.

| 2001-2006 | | $1,500 | $2,000 |

MODEL YEAR	FEATURES	EXC. COND. LOW	HIGH

Santana (Brazilian)
2003. Quilted maple top, Brazilian rosewood neck and fretboard, eagle inlay on headstock, Santana Brazilian logo on back cover plate, 200 made.

| 2003 | | $5,000 | $6,500 |

Santana 25th Anniversary Santana II
2010. Figured maple top, rosewood 'board, eagle inlay on headstock, 25th Anniversary shadow birds.

| 2010 | | $1,900 | $2,450 |

SC 58 Artist
2011-2012. Artist grade figured maple top, rosewood 'board, MOP/Paua birds.

| 2011-2012 | | $2,075 | $2,700 |

SC 245
2007-2010. Single-cut 22-fret, 2 humbuckers, bird markers, SC 245 logo on truss rod cover.

| 2007 | Flamed top | $1,700 | $2,200 |
| 2007-2010 | Solid color top | $1,350 | $1,750 |

SC 250
2007-2010. Figured maple top, 2 humbuckers, 25" scale and locking tuners.

| 2007-2010 | | $1,400 | $1,800 |

SC-J Thinline
2008. Large full-scale single-cut hollowbody, originally part of Private Stock program until made in limited run of 300, select grade maple top and back over a mahogany middle body section, SC-J logo on truss rod cover.

| 2008 | | $3,600 | $4,700 |

SE Series
2001-present. PRS import line, solidbody and semi-hollow.

| 2001-2019 | Higher-end models | $400 | $550 |
| 2001-2019 | Most models | $225 | $400 |

Signature/PRS Signature
1987-1991. 1,000 made, solid mahogany body, figured maple top, hand-signed signature on headstock, Vintage Yellow is most valuable color and will fetch more, orange is second, quilt top is more valuable than flametop. Each guitar should be evaluated on a case-by-case basis.

| 1987 | Various colors | $3,000 | $8,000 |
| 1988-1991 | Various colors | $2,500 | $6,000 |

Signature (Private Stock)
2011. Limited run by Private Stock, 100 made, 408 humbucker pickups (8 tonal configurations), special signature headstock and fretboard inlays.

| 2011 | | $4,600 | $6,000 |

Singlecut
2000-2004, 2005-early 2008. Single-cut mahogany body, maple top, 22-fret 'board, upgrade options include 10 top flamed maple, gold hardware, bird inlays. Replaced by SC 245 and SC 250.

2000-2007	Various specs	$1,200	$1,700
2001	Brazilian neck/'board	$1,900	$2,500
2006-2007	Artist 20th Anniv, Brazilian	$1,900	$2,500
2006-2007	Standard 20th Anniv, Indian	$1,200	$1,575
2007-2008	Ltd Ed, Indian	$1,300	$1,675

The Official Vintage Guitar magazine Price Guide 2021 | **PRS** Singlecut Hollowbody II — **Peavey** Destiny Custom | **329**

GUITARS

MODEL YEAR	FEATURES	EXC. COND. LOW	HIGH

Singlecut Hollowbody II CB 25th Anniversary
2010. Semi-hollow (CB means center block), f-holes, 10 maple top, bird inlays.

2010		$1,750	$2,300

Singlecut Hollowbody Standard
2008-2009. Mahogany body.

2008-2009		$1,750	$2,300

Singlecut Standard Satin
2006-2007. Thinner solid mahogany body, thin nitro cellulose finish, humbuckers or soapbars.

2006-2007		$1,000	$1,300

Special
1987-1990, 1991-1993. Similar to Standard with upgrades, wide-thin neck, 2 HFS humbuckers. From '91-'93, a special option package was offered featuring a wide-thin neck and high output humbuckers.

1987-1990	Solid color finish	$1,750	$2,300
1991-1993	Special order only	$2,000	$2,600

Standard
1987-1998. Set-neck, solid mahogany body, 24-fret 'board, 2 humbuckers, chrome hardware. Originally called the PRS Guitar from '85-'86 (see that listing), renamed Standard 24 from '98.

1987-1989	Sunburst & optional colors	$4,000	$5,200
1990-1991	Last Brazilian 'board	$2,100	$2,700
1992-1995		$1,075	$1,400
1995-1998	Stevensville	$1,075	$1,400

Standard 22
1994-2009. 22-fret Standard.

1994-1995		$1,075	$1,400
1995-1999	Stevensville	$1,075	$1,400
2000-2009		$1,075	$1,400

Standard 24
1998-2009. Renamed from Standard, solid mahogany body, 24-fret set-neck.

1998-2009		$1,075	$1,400

Starla
2008-2013. Single-cut solidbody with retro-vibe, glued neck, 2 chrome humbuckers. Replaced by S2 Starla in '14.

2008-2013		$700	$925

Studio
1988-1991, 2011-2013. Standard model variant, 24-fret set-neck, chrome and nickel hardware, single-single-hum pickups. The Studio package of pickups was offered until '96 on other models. Reissued in '11 with 22 frets, flamed maple top.

1988-1991		$1,550	$2,000
2011-2013	Reintroduced	$1,550	$2,000

Studio Maple Top
1990-1991. Mahogany solidbody, bird inlays, 2 single-coils and 1 humbucker, tremolo, transparent finish.

1990-1991		$1,550	$2,000

Swamp Ash Special
1996-2009. Solid swamp ash body, 22-fret bolt-on maple neck, 3 pickups, upgrade options available.

1996-2009		$1,125	$1,475

Swamp Ash Special 25th Anniversary
2010. Swamp ash body, bolt-on neck, 25th Anniversary shadow bird inlays.

2010		$1,125	$1,475

Tonare Grand
2009-2016. Full-body flat-top, European/German spruce top, rosewood back and sides, optional Adirondack red spruce top or AAAA grade top, onboard Acoustic Pickup System.

2009-2016		$2,450	$3,200

West Street/1980 West Street Limited
2008. 180 made for US market, 120 made for export market, faithful replica of the model made in the original West Street shop, Sapele top.

2008		$2,000	$2,600

Pawar
1999-2010. Founded by Jay Pawar, Jeff Johnston and Kevin Johnston in Willoughby Hills, Ohio, Pawar built professional and premium grade, production/custom, solidbody guitars.

PBC Guitar Technology
See Bunker Guitars for more info.

Pearl
1971-ca.1974. Acoustic and electric guitars sold by Pearl Musical Instrument Co. (Pearl drums), and built by other Japanese builders.

Peavey
1965-present. Headquartered in Meridan, Mississippi, Peavey builds budget, intermediate, professional, and premium grade, production/custom, acoustic and electric guitars. They also build basses, amps, PA gear, effects and drums. Hartley Peavey's first products were guitar amps. He added guitars to the mix in '78.

Axcelerator/AX
1994-1998. Offset double-cut swamp ash or poplar body, bolt-on maple neck, dot markers, AX with locking vibrato, various colors.

1994-1998		$300	$400

Cropper Classic
1995-2005. Single-cut solidbody, 1 humbucker and 1 single coil, figured maple top over thin mahogany body, transparent Onion Green.

1995-2005		$325	$400

Defender
1994-1995. Double-cut, solid poplar body, 2 humbuckers and 1 single-coil pickup, locking Floyd Rose tremolo, metallic or pearl finish.

1994-1995		$150	$185

Destiny
1989-1992. Double-cut, mahogany body, maple top, neck-thru-bridge, maple neck, 3 integrated pickups, double locking tremolo.

1989-1992		$225	$300

Destiny Custom
1989-1992. Destiny with figured wood and higher-end appointments, various colors.

1989-1992		$325	$425

PRS SE Custom 24
Martin Secrest

2018 PRS SE Standard 24
Michael Mitchell

GUITARS

Peavey EVH Wolfgang

1984 Peavey Razer

MODEL YEAR	FEATURES	EXC. COND. LOW	HIGH

Detonator AX
1995-1998. Double-cut, maple neck, rosewood 'board, dot markers, hum/single/hum pickups, black.

1995-1998		$170	$210

EVH Wolfgang
1996-2004. Offset double-cut, arched top, bolt neck, stop tailpiece or Floyd Rose vibrato, quilted or flamed maple top upgrade option.

1996	Pat pending		
	early production	$2,000	$2,500
1997-1998	Pat pending	$1,500	$1,900
1999-2004	Flamed maple top	$1,350	$1,700
1999-2004	Standard top	$1,000	$1,250

EVH Wolfgang Special
1997-2004. Offset double-cut lower-end Wolfgang model, various opaque finishes, flamed top optional.

1996-2004	Standard top, D-Tuna	$550	$725
1997-2004	Flamed maple top	$600	$800
1997-2004	Standard basswood	$500	$675

Falcon/Falcon Active/Falcon Custom
1987-1992. Double-cut, 3 pickups, passive or active electronics, Kahler locking vibrato.

1987-1992	Custom color	$300	$350
1987-1992	Standard color	$200	$250

Firenza
1994-1999. Offset double-cut, bolt-on neck, single-coil pickups.

1994-1999		$275	$325

Firenza AX
1994-1999. Upscale Firenza Impact with humbucking pickups.

1994-1999		$300	$375

Generation Custom EX
2006-2008. Single-cut solidbody, 2 humbuckers, 5-way switch.

2006-2008		$175	$225

Generation S-1/S-2/S-3
1988-1994. Single-cut, maple cap on mahogany body, bolt-on maple neck, six-on-a-side tuners, active single/hum pickups, S-2 with locking vibrato system.

1988-1994		$200	$400

Horizon/Horizon II
1983-1985. Extended pointy horns, angled lower bout, maple body, rear routing for electronics, 2 humbucking pickups. Horizon II has added blade pickup.

1983-1985		$200	$275

HP Special USA
2008-2011. Offset cutaway, 2 humbuckers.

2008-2011		$500	$625

Hydra Doubleneck
1985-1989. Available as a custom order, 6/12-string necks each with 2 humbuckers, 3-way pickup select.

1985-1989		$550	$675

Impact 1/Impact 2
1985-1987. Offset double-cut, Impact 1 has higher-end synthetic 'board, Impact 2 with conventional rosewood 'board.

1985-1987		$200	$275

MODEL YEAR	FEATURES	EXC. COND. LOW	HIGH

Mantis
1984-1989. Hybrid X-shaped solidbody, 1 humbucking pickup, tremolo, laminated maple neck.

1984-1989		$200	$275

Milestone 12-String
1985-1986. Offset double-cut, 12 strings.

1985-1986		$125	$160

Milestone/Milestone Custom
1983-1986. Offset double-cut solidbody.

1983-1986		$100	$125

Mystic
1983-1989. Double-cut, 2 pickups, stop tailpiece initially, later Power Bend vibrato, maple body and neck.

1983-1989		$250	$350

Nitro I Active
1988-1990. Active electronics.

1988-1990		$200	$250

Nitro I/II/III
1986-1989. Offset double-cut, banana-style headstock, 1 humbucker (I), 2 humbuckers (II), or single/single/hum pickups (III).

1986-1989	Nitro I	$125	$160
1986-1989	Nitro II	$150	$200
1986-1989	Nitro III	$175	$250

Odyssey
1990-1994. Single-cut, figured carved maple top on mahogany body, humbuckers.

1990-1994		$375	$475

Odyssey 25th Anniversary
1990. Single-cut body, limited production.

1990		$500	$625

Omniac JD USA
2005-2010. Jerry Donahue-designed single-cut solidbody, 2 single-coils.

2005-2010		$650	$775

Patriot
1983-1987. Double-cut, single bridge humbucker.

1983-1987		$175	$225

Patriot Plus
1983-1987. Double-cut, 2 humbucker pickups, bi-laminated maple neck.

1983-1987		$200	$275

Patriot Tremolo
1986-1990. Double-cut, single bridge humbucker, tremolo, replaced the standard Patriot.

1986-1990		$200	$275

Predator Plus 7ST
2008-2010. 7-string.

2008-2010		$225	$275

Predator Series
1985-1988, 1990-2016. Double-cut poplar body, 2 pickups until '87, 3 after, vibrato.

1985-2016		$125	$175

Raptor Series
1997-present. Offset double-cut solidbody, 3 pickups.

1997-2019		$60	$85

Razer
1983-1989. Double-cut with arrowhead point for lower bout, 2 pickups, 1 volume and 2 tone controls, stop tailpiece or vibrato.

1983-1989		$300	$375

MODEL YEAR	FEATURES	EXC. COND. LOW	HIGH

Reactor
1993-1999. Classic single-cut style, 2 single-coils.
| 1993-1999 | | $260 | $325 |

Rockmaster II Stage Pack
2000s. Student solidbody Rockmaster electric guitar and GT-5 amp pack.
| 2000 | | $40 | $50 |

Rotor Series
2004-2010. Classic futuristic body, elongated upper treble bout/lower bass bout, 2 humbuckers.
| 2004-2008 | Rotor EXP | $225 | $280 |
| 2004-2010 | Rotor EX | $195 | $240 |

T-15
1981-1983. Offset double-cut, bolt-on neck, dual ferrite blade single-coil pickups, natural. Amp-in-case available.
| 1981-1983 | Amp-in-case | $200 | $250 |
| 1981-1983 | Guitar only | $150 | $185 |

T-25
1979-1985. Synthetic polymer body, 2 pickups, cream 'guard, sunburst finish.
| 1979-1985 | | $250 | $350 |

T-25 Special
1979-1985. Same as T-25, but with super high output pickups, phenolic 'board, black/white/black 'guard, ebony black finish.
| 1979-1985 | | $250 | $350 |

T-26
1982-1986. Same as T-25, but with 3 single-coil pickups and 5-way switch.
| 1982-1986 | | $250 | $350 |

T-27
1981-1983. Offset double-cut, bolt-on neck, dual ferrite blade single-coil pickups.
| 1981-1983 | | $300 | $400 |

T-30
1982-1985. Short-scale, 3 single-coil pickups, 5-way select, by '83 amp-in-case available.
| 1982-1985 | Guitar only | $250 | $325 |
| 1983-1985 | Amp-in-case | $325 | $425 |

T-60
1978-1988. Contoured offset double-cut, ash body, six-in-line tuners, 2 humbuckers, thru-body strings, by '87 maple bodies, various finishes.
| 1978-1988 | | $425 | $550 |

T-1000 LT
1992-1994. Double-cut, 2 single-coils and humbucker with coil-tap.
| 1992-1994 | | $225 | $275 |

Tracer Custom
1989-1990. Tracer with 2 single humbuckers and extras.
| 1989-1990 | | $170 | $210 |

Tracer/Tracer II
1987-1994. Offset scooped double-cut with extended pointy horns, poplar body, 1 pickup, Floyd Rose.
| 1987-1994 | | $170 | $210 |

Vandenberg Quilt Top
1989-1992. Vandenberg Custom with quilted maple top, 2 humbuckers, glued-in neck, quilted maple top, mahogany body and neck.
| 1989-1992 | | $875 | $1,150 |

Vandenberg Signature
1988-1992. Double-cut, reverse headstock, bolt-on neck, locking vibrato, various colors.
| 1988-1992 | | $500 | $650 |

Vortex I/Vortex II
1986. Streamlined Mantis with 2 pickups, 3-way, Kahler locking vibrato. Vortex II has Randy Rhoads Sharkfin V.
| 1986 | | $275 | $340 |

V-Type Series
2004-2007. Offset double-cut solidbody, pointed reverse 6-on-a-side headstock, 2 humbuckers.
| 2004-2007 | | $250 | $310 |

Pederson Custom Guitars
2009-present. Luthier Kevin Pederson builds his premium grade, production/custom, hollowbody and solidbody guitars in Forest City, Iowa. From 1997-2009 he produced guitars under the Abyss brand name.

Pedro de Miguel
1991-present. Luthiers Pedro Pérez and Miguel Rodriguez build their professional and premium grade, custom/production, classical guitars in Madrid, Spain. They also offer factory-made instruments built to their specifications.

Pedulla
1975-2019. Known for basses, Pedulla did offer a few solidbody guitar models into the early 1980s.

MVP
1981-1984. Double-cut solidbody, 2 humbuckers, dot markers, 4 knobs with main toggle and 3 mini-toggle switches, stencil Pedulla logo, MVP serial number series.
| 1981-1984 | | $1,075 | $1,400 |

Peekamoose
1983-present. Production/custom, premium grade, solidbody, chambered, and archtop electric guitars built in New York City, New York by luthier Paul Schwartz.

Pegasus Guitars and Ukuleles
1977-present. Premium grade, custom steel-string guitars built by luthier Bob Gleason in Kurtistown, Hawaii, who also builds ukulele family instruments.

Penco
Ca. 1974-1978. Generally high quality Japanese-made copies of classic American acoustic, electric and bass guitars. Imported by Philadelphia Music Company of Limerick, Pennsylvania during the copy era. Includes dreadnought acoustics with laminated woods, bolt-neck solidbody electric guitars and basses, mandolins and banjos.

Acoustic Flat-Top
1974-1978. Various models.
| 1974-1978 | | $100 | $275 |

1978 Peavey T-60

1988 Peavey Vandenberg

GUITARS

Petros African Rose Dwende

1939 Prairie State 18 3/4"

MODEL YEAR	FEATURES	EXC. COND. LOW	HIGH
Electric			
1974-1978. Various copies.			
1974-1978	Solidbody	$150	$325
1974-1978	Thinline Archtop	$150	$325

Penn

1950s. Archtop and acoustic guitars built by made by United Guitar Corporation in Jersey City, New Jersey, which also made Premier acoustics. Penn was located in L.A.

Pensa (Pensa-Suhr)

1982-present. Premium grade, production/custom, solidbody guitars and basses built in the U.S. Rudy Pensa, of Rudy's Music Stop, New York City, New York, started building Pensa guitars in '82. In '85 he teamed up with John Suhr to build Pensa-Suhr instruments. Name changed back to Pensa in '96.

Classic

1992-Ca. 1998. Offset double-cut, 3 single-coils, gold hardware.

1992-1998	Various models	$1,600	$2,100

MK 1 (Mark Knopfler)

1985-2018. Offset double-cut solidbody, carved flamed maple bound top, 3 pickups, gold hardware, dot markers, bolt-on neck.

1985-2018		$1,600	$2,100

Suhr Custom

1985-1989. Two-piece maple body, bolt-on maple neck with rosewood 'board, custom order basis with a variety of woods and options available.

1985-1989	Various options	$1,600	$2,100

Suhr Standard

1985-1991. Double-cut, single/single/hum pickup configuration, opaque solid finish normally, dot markers.

1985-1991		$1,425	$1,900

Perlman Guitars

1976-present. Luthier Alan Perlman builds his premium grade, custom, steel-string and classical guitars in San Francisco, California.

Perri Ink.

Custom, professional grade, solidbody electric guitars built by luthier Nick Perri in Los Angeles, California, starting in 2009.

Perry Guitars

1982-present. Premium grade, production/custom, classical guitars built by luthier Daryl Perry in Winnipeg, Manitoba. He also builds lutes.

Petillo Masterpiece Guitars

1965-present. Intermediate, professional and premium grade, custom, steel-string, nylon-string, 12-string, resonator, archtop, and Hawaiian guitars in Ocean, New Jersey, originally by father and son luthiers Phillip J. "Doc" and David Petillo. Doc died in August, 2010.

Petros Guitars

1992-present. Premium grade, production/custom, flat-top, 12-string, and nylon-string guitars built by father and son luthiers Bruce and Matthew Petros in Kaukauna, Wisconsin.

PH Guitars

2006-present. Luthier Paul A. Hartmann builds professional and premium grade, custom, acoustic archtop and electric guitars in Hyde Park, New York.

Phantom Guitar Works

1992-present. Intermediate grade, production/custom, classic Phantom, and Teardrop shaped solid and hollowbody guitars and basses assembled in Clatskanie, Oregon. They also offer the Mando-Guitar. Phantom was established by Jack Charles, former lead guitarist of the band Quarterflash. Some earlier guitars were built overseas.

Pheo

Luthier Phil Sylvester, began building in 1996, unique premium grade, production/custom, electric and acoustic guitars in Portland, Oregon.

Phoenix Guitar Company

1994-present. Luthiers George Leach and Diana Huber build their premium grade, production/custom, archtop and classical guitars in Scottsdale, Arizona.

Pieper

Premium grade, custom, solidbody guitars and basses built by luthier Robert Pieper in New Haven, Connecticut starting in 2005.

Pignose

1972-present. The original portable amp company also offers intermediate grade, production, dreadnaught and amplified electric guitars. They also offer effects. Refer to Amps section for more company info.

Pilgrim

1970's-late-1980s, 2010-present. Built in the U.K., luthier Paul Tebbutt introduced the brand back in the '70s and his guitars were available until late '80s. His designs are now used on intermediate grade, production, electric acoustic guitars, built in the Far East and distributed by John Hornby Skewes & Co. Ltd. They also offer mandolins, ukuleles and banjos.

Pimentel and Sons

1951-present. Luthiers Lorenzo Pimentel and sons build their professional, premium and presentation grade, flat-top, jazz, cutaway electric, and classical guitars in Albuquerque, New Mexico.

MODEL YEAR	FEATURES	EXC. COND. LOW	HIGH

Player

1984-1985. Player guitars featured interchangable pickup modules that mounted through the back of the guitar. They offered a double-cut solidbody with various options and the pickup modules were sold separately. The company was located in Scarsdale, New York.

Pleasant

Late 1940s-ca.1966. Solidbody electric guitars, obviously others, Japanese manufacturer, probably not imported into the U.S.

Electric Solidbody

1940s-1966. Various models.

1940s-1966		$100	$200

Potvin

2003-present. Production/custom, professional and premium grade, chambered, hollowbody and solidbody electric guitars built by luthier Mike Potvin in Ontario.

Prairie State

1927-ca.1940. A Larson Brothers brand, basically a derivative of Maurer & Company. The Prairie State models were slightly more expensive than the equivalent Maurer models. They featured a patented steel rod mechanism to strengthen the body, which ran from the end block to the neck block. The model usually had Brazilian rosewood back and sides, laminated necks and X-bracing. Some later models were built with figured maple.

Prairiewood

2005-present. Luthier Robert Dixon of Fargo, North Dakota builds professional grade, production/custom, hollowbody archtop and solidbody guitars.

Premier

Ca.1938-ca.1975, 1990s-2010. Brands originally offered by Premier include Premier, Multivox, Marvel, Belltone and Strad-O-Lin. Produced by Peter Sorkin Music Company in Manhattan, New York City, New York, who began in Philadelphia, relocating to NYC in '35. First radio-sized amplifiers and stick-on pickups for acoustic archtops were introduced by '38. After WWII, they set up the Multivox subsidiary to manufacture amplifiers ca. '46. First flat-top with pickup appeared in '46.

Most acoustic instruments made by United Guitar Corporation in Jersey City, New Jersey. Ca. '57 Multivox acquires Strad-O-Lin. Ca.'64-'65 their Custom line guitars are assembled with probably Italian bodies and hardware, Japanese electronics, possibly Egmond necks from Holland. By ca. '74-'75, there were a few Japanese-made guitars, then Premier brand goes into hiatus. The brand reappears on Asian-made budget and intermediate grade, production, solidbody guitars and basses beginning in the '90s.

Bantam Custom

1950s-1960s. Single-cut archtop, dots, earlier with white potted pickups, then metal-covered pickups, and finally Japanese-made pickups (least valued).

1950s-60s		$625	$825

Bantam Deluxe

1950s-1960s. Single-cut archtop, fully bound, sparkle knobs, earlier with white potted pickups, then metal-covered pickups, and finally Japanese-made pickups (least valued), block markers, 1 or 2 pickups (deduct $100 for 1 pickup).

1950s-60s	Blond, sunburst	$1,225	$1,625

Bantam Special

1950s-1960s. Single-cut archtop, dots, early models with white potted pickups, then metal-covered pickups, and finally Japanese-made pickups (least valued), 1 or 2 pickups (deduct $100 for 1 pickup).

1950s-60s		$625	$825

Custom Solidbody

1958-1970. Notable solidbody bass scroll cutaway, various models with various components used, finally import components only.

1958-1970	1 pickup	$350	$475
1958-1970	2 pickups	$400	$550
1958-1970	3 pickups	$575	$775

Deluxe Archtop

1950s-1960s. Full body 17 1/4" archtop, square block markers, single-cut, early models with white potted pickups, later '60s models with metal pickups.

1950s-60s	Blond, sunburst	$1,000	$1,300

E-727

1958-1962. E-scroll style solidbody with scroll bass bout, 3 single-coil pickups, Premier headstock logo, made by the Multivox factory in New York.

1958-1962		$500	$675

Semi-Pro 16" Archtop

1950s-early-1960s. Thinline electric 16" archtop with 2 1/4" deep body, acoustic or electric.

1950s-60s	*Acoustic*	*$500*	*$675*
1950s-60s	Electric	$575	$775

Semi-Pro Bantam Series

1960s. Thinline electric archtop with 2 3/4" deep body, offered in cutaway and non-cut models.

1960s		$250	$325

Special Archtop

1950s-1960s. Full body 17 1/4" archtop, less fancy than Deluxe, single-cut, early models with white potted pickups, '60s models with metal pickups.

1950s-60s		$675	$875

Studio Six Archtop

1950s-early-1960s. 16" wide archtop, single pickup, early pickups white potted, changed later to metal top.

1950s-60s		$400	$525

Prenkert Guitars

1980-present. Premium and presentation grade, production/custom, classical and flamenco guitars built in Sebastopol, California by luthier Richard Prenkert.

1959 Premier Custom Solidbody

1959 Premier A-300
Rivington Guitars

GUITARS

1996 R.C. Allen Leader
Imaged by Heritage Auctions, HA.com

1966 Jose Ramirez 1A
Carter Vintage Guitars

MODEL YEAR	FEATURES	EXC. COND. LOW	HIGH

Prestige

2003-present. Intermediate, professional, and premium grade, production/custom, acoustic, solidbody and hollowbody guitars and basses from Vancouver, British Columbia.

PST Guitars

Ca. 2000-present. Professional and premium grade, custom, electric guitars and basses, built by luthier P. Scott Tucker, in King George, Virginia. He has also built acoustic guitars.

Queen Shoals Stringed Instruments

1972-ca. 2010. Luthier Larry Cadle builds his production/custom, flat-top, 12-string, and nylon-string guitars in Clendenin, West Virginia.

Queguiner, Alain

1982-present. Custom flat-tops, 12 strings, and nylon strings built by luthier Alain Queguiner in Paris, France.

Quest

1982-ca. 1986. Originally labeled Quest by Vantage, these solidbody guitars and basses were built in Japan, mostly by Chushin Gakki.

R.C. Allen

1951-2014. Luthier R. C. "Dick" Allen built professional and premium grade, custom hollowbody and semi-hollowbody guitars in El Monte, California. He has also built solidbody guitars. He passed away in '14.

Rahan

1999-present. Professional grade, production/custom, solidbody guitars built by luthiers Mike Curd and Rick Cantu in Houston, Texas.

Rahbek Guitars

2000-present. Professional and premium grade, production/custom, solidbody electrics built by luthier Peter Rahbek in Copenhagen, Denmark.

Raimundo

1970s-present. Intermediate, professional and premium grade flamenco and classical guitars made in Valencia, Spain, by luthiers Antonio Aparicio and Manual Raimundo.

RainSong

1991-present. Professional grade, production, all-graphite and graphite and wood acoustic guitars built originally in Maui, and currently in Woodinville, Washington. Developed by luthier engineer John Decker with help from luthier Lorenzo Pimentel, engineer Chris Halford, and sailboard builder George Clayton.

RAM Guitars

2007-present. Luthier Ron Mielzynski builds his professional grade, production/custom, solidbody, chambered and archtop electric guitars in Fox River Grove, Illinois.

Rambler

See Strobel Guitars listing.

Ramirez, Jose

1882-present. Professional, premium, and presentation grade, custom/production, classical guitars built in Madrid, Spain. Founded by Jose Ramirez (1858-1923) who was an apprentice at the shop of Francisco Gonzales. Jose opened his own workshop in 1882 working with his younger brother, Manuel. Manuel split with Jose and opened his own, competing workshop. Jose's business was continued by Jose's son Jose Ramirez II (1885-1957), grandson Jose III (1922-1995), and great grandchildren Jose IV (1953-2000) and Amalia Ramirez. In the 1930's a larger body instrument with improved fan bracing was developed to meet the needs for more power and volume. Other refinements were developed and the Ramirez 1A Tradicional was soon introduced which found favor with Andres Segovia. The Ramirez company has produced both student and professional instruments, but in the classical guitar field, like the old-master violin business, a student model is often a very fine instrument that is now valued at $2,000 or more. In the 1980s Ramirez offered the E Series student guitar line that was built for, but not by, Ramirez. In 1991 the company offered the even more affordable R Series which was offered for about $1,300. As is typically the case, Ramirez classical guitars do not have a name-logo on the headstock. The brand is identified by a Ramirez label on the inside back which also may have the model number listed.

A/1A

1960s-2000s. Classical, Brazilian or Indian rosewood.

1960s	Brazilian	$4,500	$5,900
1970-2000s	Indian	$1,700	$2,200
1970s	Brazilian	$4,000	$5,200
1980s	Brazilian	$3,100	$4,000

A/2A

1970s-80s	Indian	$1,800	$2,350

AE Estudio

2004		$1,400	$1,800

De Camera

1980s. Classical, cedar top, Brazilian rosewood back and sides.

1980s		$2,150	$2,800

E/1E/Estudio

1988-1990s. Intermediate level.

1988-1990s		$950	$1,225

E/2E

1990s-2000s. Red cedar top, Indian rosewood back and sides, Spanish cedar neck, ebony 'board.

1990-2000s		$1,000	$1,300

MODEL YEAR	FEATURES	EXC. COND. LOW	HIGH

E/3E/Estudio
1990s. Cedar, rosewood.

| 1990s | | $1,150 | $1,500 |

E/4E/Estudio
1980s-2000s. Top of the E Series line, solid red cedar top, solid Indian rosewood back and sides.

| 1980-2000s | | $1,600 | $2,100 |

Flamenco
1920s-1979. European spruce top, cyprus back and sides.

1920s-50s		$3,000	$3,900
1960-1969		$2,150	$2,800
1970-1979		$2,100	$2,700

R1
1991-2014. Red cedar top, mahogany sides and back, Spanish cedar neck, ebony 'board. Replaced by RA series in '14.

| 1991-2014 | | $500 | $650 |

R2
1991-2014. Red cedar top, Indian rosewood back and sides, cedar neck, ebony 'board. Replaced by RA series in '14.

| 1991-2014 | | $875 | $1,125 |

R3
1998. Cedar, rosewood.

| 1998 | | $875 | $1,125 |

R4 Classical
1995-2014. All solid wood, Western red cedar top, rosewood back and sides. Replaced by RB series in '14.

| 1995-2014 | | $1,150 | $1,500 |

S/S1
2005-2007. Solid German spruce top, African mahogany sides and back, most affordable in Estudio line.

| 2005-2007 | | $525 | $700 |

Segovia
Cedar, Indian rosewood.

| 1966 | | $4,500 | $5,800 |
| 1974-1978 | | $3,150 | $4,100 |

SP Series
2002-2018. Semi-professional level designed to be between the company's 'concert/professional' series and 'student' series.

| 2002-2018 | | $3,600 | $4,800 |

Ramirez, Manuel

1890-1916. Brother of Jose Ramirez, and a respected professional classical guitar builder from Madrid, Spain. His small shop left no heirs so the business was not continued after Manuel's death in 1916. Manuel was generally considered to be more famous during his lifetime than his brother Jose, and while his business did not continue, Manuel trained many well known Spanish classical guitar luthiers who prospered with their own businesses. During Manuel's era his shop produced at least 48 different models, with prices ranging from 10 to 1,000 pesetas, therefore vintage prices can vary widely. Guitars made prior to 1912 have a label with a street address of Arlaban 10, in 1912 the shop moved to Arlaban 11.

Randy Reynolds Guitars

1996-2018. Luthier Randy Reynolds builds his premium grade, production/custom classical and flamenco guitars in Colorado Springs, Colorado. Reynolds announced his retirement January 1, 2019.

Randy Wood Guitars

1968-present. Premium grade, custom/production, archtop, flat-top, and resonator guitars built by luthier Randy Wood in Bloomingdale, Georgia. He also builds mandolins.

Rarebird Guitars

1978-present. Luthier Bruce Clay builds his professional and premium grade, production/custom, guitars and basses, originally in Arvada, Colorado, and currently in Hoehne, Colorado.

Rat Fink

2002-2005. Lace Music Products, the makers of the Lace Sensor pickup, offered the intermediate grade, production, guitars and basses, featuring the artwork of Ed "Big Daddy" Roth until '05.

Rayco

2002-present. Professional and premium grade, custom, resonator and Hawaiian-style acoustic guitars built in British Columbia, by luthiers Mark Thibeault and Jason Friesen.

Recco

1960s. Electric guitar imports made by Teisco, pricing similar to Teisco models, Recco logo on headstock, upscale solidbodies can have four pickups with several knobs and four switches.

Electric Solidbody

| 1960s | 4 pickups | $375 | $475 |

Recording King

1929-1943. Brand name used by Montgomery Ward for instruments made by various American manufacturers, including Kay, Gibson and Gretsch. Generally mid-grade instruments. M Series are Gibson-made archtops.

Carson Robison/Model 1052
1938-1939. Made by Gibson, flat-top, 16", sunburst.

| 1938-1939 | | $1,900 | $2,500 |

Kay 17" Flat-Top

| 1940-1941 | | $725 | $950 |

M-2
1936-1941. Gibson-made archtop with carved top and f-holes, maple back and sides.

| 1936-1941 | | $525 | $700 |

M-3
1936-1941. Gibson-made archtop, f-holes, maple back and sides, carved top.

| 1936-1941 | | $650 | $850 |

Randy Wood Custom

1938 Recording King Carson Robison
Imaged by Heritage Auctions, HA.com

GUITARS

1978 Rennaissance SPG
Rivington Guitars

1978 Renaissance T-200G
Craig Brody

MODEL YEAR	FEATURES	EXC. COND. LOW	HIGH

M-4

1937-1940. Gibson-made archtop, f-holes, maple back and sides, rope-checkered binding, flying bat wing markers.

| 1937-1940 | | $800 | $1,050 |

M-5

1936-1941. Gibson-made archtop with f-holes, maple back and sides, trapeze tailpiece, checkered top binding.

| 1936-1938 | 16" body | $1,050 | $1,375 |
| 1939-1941 | 17" body | $1,125 | $1,475 |

M-6

1938-1939. M-5 with upgraded gold hardware.

| 1938-1939 | | $1,150 | $1,525 |

Model 1124

1937. 16" acoustic archtop, body by Gibson, attractive higher-end appointments, block-dot markers, sunburst.

| 1937 | | $1,425 | $1,850 |

Model 681

Mid-1930s. Small flat top by Gibson, ladder-braced.

| 1930s | | $1,050 | $1,375 |

Ray Whitley

1939-1940. High-quality model made by Gibson, round shoulder flat-top, mahogany (Model 1028) or Brazilian rosewood (Model 1027) back and sides, 5-piece maple neck, Ray Whitley stencil script peghead logo, pearl crown inlay on peghead, fancy inlaid markers.

| 1939-1940 | Brazilian | $20,000 | $26,000 |
| 1939-1940 | Mahogany | $10,000 | $13,000 |

Roy Smeck

1938-1940. 16.25" electric archtop, large Recording King badge logo, Roy Smeck stencil logo, bar pickup, 2 control knobs on upper bass bout, dot markers.

| 1938-1940 | | $1,100 | $1,425 |

Recording King (TML)

2005-present. Budget grade, production, acoustic cowboy stenciled guitars designed by Greg Rich for The Music Link, which also offers Johnson and other brand instruments. They also have banjos and ukes.

Redentore

2007-present. Luthier Mark Piper builds professional and premium grade, production/custom, archtop jazz, acoustic flat-top, carve-top and semi-hollow electric guitars in Columbia, Tennessee.

RedLine Acoustics and RedLine Resophonics

2007-present. Professional and premium grade, production, acoustic and resophonic guitars built in Hendersonville, Tennessee by luthiers Steve Smith, Jason Denton, Christian McAdams and Ryan Futch. They also build mandolins and plan to add lap steels.

Regal

Ca. 1895-1966, 1987-present. Intermediate and professional grade, production, acoustic and wood and metal body resonator guitars and basses. Originally a mass manufacturer founded in Indianapolis, Indiana, the Regal brand was first used by Emil Wulschner & Son. After 1900, new owners changed the company name to The Regal Manufacturing Company. The company was moved to Chicago in '08 and renamed the Regal Musical Instrument Company. Regal made brands for distributors and mass merchandisers as well as marketing its own Regal brand. Regal purchased the Lyon & Healy factory in '28. Regal was licensed to co-manufacture Dobros in '32 and became the sole manufacturer of them in '37 (see Dobro for those instruments). Most Regal instruments were beginner-grade; however, some very fancy archtops were made during the '30s. The company was purchased by Harmony in '54 and absorbed. From '59 to '66, Harmony made acoustics under the Regal name for Fender. In '87 the Regal name was revived on a line of resonator instruments by Saga.

Acoustic Hawaiian

1930s. Student model, small 13" body, square neck, glued or trapeze bridge.

| 1930s | Faux grain painted finish | $275 | $375 |
| 1930s | Plain sunburst, birch, trapeze | $175 | $225 |

Concert Folk H6382

1960s. Regal by Harmony, solid spruce top, mahogany back and sides, dot markers, natural.

| 1960s | | $200 | $250 |

Deluxe Dreadnought H6600

1960s. Regal by Harmony, solid spruce top, mahogany back and sides, bound top and back, rosewood 'board, dot markers, natural.

| 1960s | | $200 | $250 |

Dreadnought 12-String H1269

1960s. Regal by Harmony, solid spruce top, 12-string version of Deluxe, natural.

| 1960s | | $200 | $250 |

Esquire

1940s. 15 1/2" acoustic archtop, higher-end appointments, fancy logo art and script pearl Esquire headstock logo and Regal logo, natural.

| 1940s | | $800 | $1,000 |

Meteor

1960s. Single-cut acoustic-electric archtop, 2 pickups.

| 1960s | | $925 | $1,200 |

Model 27

1933-1942. Birch wood body, mahogany or maple, 2-tone walnut finish, single-bound top, round or square neck.

| 1933-1942 | | $800 | $1,000 |

Model 45

1933-1937. Spruce top and mahogany back and sides, bound body, square neck.

| 1933-1937 | | $1,300 | $1,700 |

MODEL YEAR	FEATURES	EXC. COND. LOW	HIGH

Model 46
1933-1937. Round neck.

1933-1937		$1,300	$1,700

Model 55 Standard
1933-1934. Regal's version of Dobro Model 55 which was discontinued in '33.

1933-1934		$800	$1,000

Model 75
1939-1940. Metal body, square neck.

1939-1940		$1,500	$1,900

Model TG 60 Resonator Tenor
1930s. Wood body, large single cone biscuit bridge resonator, 2 upper bout metal ports, 4-string tenor.

1930s		$1,200	$1,500

Parlor
1920s. Small body, slotted headstock, birch sides and back, spruce top.

1920s		$200	$275

Prince
1930s. High-end 18" acoustic archtop, fancy appointments, Prince name inlaid in headstock along with Regal script logo and strolling guitarist art.

1930s		$1,475	$1,900

Spirit Of '76
1976. Red-white-blue, flat-top.

1976		$375	$475

Reliance

1920s. Instruments built by the Oscar Schmidt Co. and possibly others. Most likely a brand made for a distributor.

Relixx

2001-2013. Intermediate and professional grade, production/custom, aged vintage-style solidbody guitars built in Sanborn, New York by luthier Nick Hazlett. He discontinued complete guitars in '13 and now offers only vintage parts.

Renaissance

1978-1980. Plexiglass solidbody electric guitars and basses. Founded in Malvern, Pennsylvania, by John Marshall (designer), Phil Goldberg and Daniel Lamb. Original partners gradually leave and John Dragonetti takes over by late-'79. The line is redesigned with passive electronics on guitars, exotic shapes, but when deal with Sunn amplifiers falls through, company closes. Brandname currently used on a line of guitars and basses made by Rick Turner in Santa Cruz, California.

Fewer than 300 of first series made, plus a few prototypes and several wooden versions; six or so prototypes of second series made. SN=M(M) YYXXXX: month, year, consecutive number.

Electric Plexiglas Solidbody
1978-1980. Models include the SPG ('78-'79, DiMarzio pickups, active electronics), T-200G ('80, Bich-style with 2 passive DiMarzio pickups), and the S-200G ('80, double-cut, 2 DiMarzio pickups, passive electronics).

1978-1980		$625	$800

Renaissance Guitars

1994-present. Professional grade, custom, semi-acoustic flat-top, nylon-string and solidbody guitars and basses built by luthier Rick Turner in Santa Cruz, California. He also builds ukes.

Republic Guitars

2006-present. Intermediate grade, production, reso-phonic and Weissenborn-style guitars imported by American Folklore, Inc. of Austin, Texas. They also offer mandolins and ukes.

Retronix

2013-present. Korean-made solidbody guitars designed and imported by J. Backlund. They also build J. Backlund guitars.

Reuter Guitars

1984-present. Professional and premium grade, custom, flat-top, 12-string, resonator, and Hawaiian guitars built by luthier John Reuter, the Director of Training at the Roberto-Venn School of Luthiery, in Tempe, Arizona.

Reverend

1996-present. Intermediate grade, production, guitars and basses from luthier Joe Naylor, designed and setup by Reverend first in Warren, and since '10 in Livonia, Michigan, and manufactured in South Korea. There were also earlier U.S. production guitars built in Warren. Reverend has built amps and effects in the past. Naylor also founded Naylor Amps, Armor Gold Cables, Stringdog, and Railhammer Pickups.

Rex

1920s-1940s, 1950s-1960s. Generally beginner-grade guitars made by Kay and sold through Fred Gretsch distributors. In the '50s and '60s, the Lamberti Brothers Company in Melbourne, Australia built electrics bearing the Rex brand that were not distributed by Gretsch. They also had built amps.

Ribbecke Guitars

Premium and presentation grade, custom thinline, flat-top, and archtop guitars built by luthier Tom Ribbecke, starting in 1973, in Healdsburg, California.

Rice Custom Guitars

1998-present. Father and son luthiers, Richard Rice and Christopher Rice, build professional and premium grade, custom, solidbody, semi-hollow and hollowbody electric guitars and basses in Arlington Heights, Illinois.

Rich and Taylor

1993-1996. Custom acoustic and electric guitars, mandolins and banjos from luthiers Greg Rich and Mark Taylor (Crafters of Tennessee).

Reverend Volcano
Christopher Tritschler

Rick Hayes Instruments

MODEL YEAR	FEATURES	EXC. COND. LOW	HIGH

2000 Rick Turner Model 1 LB
Craig Brody

1986 Rickenbacker 320
Jeff DiPaola

Richard Schneider
1960s-1997. Luthier Richard Schneider built his acoustic guitars in Washington state. Over the years, he collaborated with Dr. Michael A. Kasha on many guitar designs and innovations. Originally from Michigan, he also was involved in designing guitars for Gretsch and Gibson. He died in early '97.

Richmond
2008-present. Luthiers Robert Godin (Godin Guitars) and Daniel Fiocco build intermediate and professional grade, production, chambered and solidbody electric guitars in Richmond, Quebec.

Richter Mfg.
1930s. One of many Chicago makers of the era, the company allegedly bought already-made guitars from other manufacturers, painted and decorated them to their liking and resold them.
Small 13"
1930s. Typical small 13" lower bout body, slotted headstock, decalmania art over black finish, single dot markers.

1930s		$250	$350

Rick Hayes Instruments
2006-present. Owned by Rick and Lyn Hayes and offering professional and premium grade, production/custom, dreadnought acoustic and electric guitars, and mandolins built by Rick and Steve Hogsed in Goshen, Ohio.

Rick Turner
1979-1981, 1990-present. Rick Turner has a long career as a luthier, electronics designer and innovator. He also makes the Renaissance line of guitars in his shop in Santa Cruz, California. The guitars and basses built in 1979-'81 were numbered sequentially in the order they were completed and shipped with the second part of the serial number indicating the year the instrument was built. Turner estimates that approximately 200 instruments were made during that period.

Rickenbacker
1931-present. Professional and premium grade, production/custom, acoustic and electric guitars built in California. They also build basses. Founded in Los Angeles as Ro-Pat-In by ex-National executives George Beauchamp, Paul Barth and National's resonator cone supplier Adolph Rickenbacher. Rickenbacher was born in Basel, Switzerland in 1886, emigrated to the U.S. and moved to Los Angeles in 1918, opening a tool and die business in '20.

In the mid-'20s, Rickenbacher began providing resonator cones and other metal parts to George Beauchamp and Louis Dopyera of National String Instrument Corporation and became a shareholder in National. Beauchamp, Barth and Harry Watson came up with wooden "frying pan" electric Hawaiian lap steel for National in '31; National was not interested, so Beauchamp and Barth joined with Rickenbacher as Ro-Pat-In (probably for ElectRO-PATent-INstruments) to produce Electro guitars. Cast aluminum frying pans were introduced in '32. Some Spanish guitars (flat-top, F-holes) with Electro pickups were produced beginning in '32. Ro-Pat-In changes their name to Electro String Instrument Corporation in '34, and brand becomes Rickenbacher Electro, soon changed to Rickenbacker, with a "k." Beauchamp retires in '40. There was a production hiatus during World War II.

In '53, Electro was purchased by Francis Cary Hall (born 1908), owner of Radio and Television Equipment Company (Radio-Tel) in Santa Ana, California (founded in '20s as Hall's Radio Service, which began distributing Fender instruments in '46). The factory was relocated to Santa Ana in '62 and the sales/distribution company's name is changed from Radio-Tel to Rickenbacker Inc. in '65.

1950s serial numbers have from 4 to 7 letters and numbers, with the number following the letter indicating the '50s year (e.g., NNL8NN would be from '58). From '61 to '86 serial numbers indicate month and year of production with initial letter A-Z for the year A=1961, Z=1986) followed by letter for the month A-M (A=January) plus numbers as before followed by a number 0-9 for the year (0=1987; 9=1996). To avoid confusion, we have listed all instruments by model number. For example, the Combo 400 is listed as Model 400/Combo 400. OS and NS stands for Old Style and New Style. On the 360, for example, Ric changed the design in 1964 to their New Style with more rounded body horns and rounded top edges and other changes. But they still offered the Old Style with more pointed horns and top binding until the late 1960s. Ric still sometimes uses the two designations on some of their vintage reissues.

Electro ES-16
1964-1971. Double-cut, set neck, solidbody, 3/4 size, 1 pickup. The Electro line was manufactured by Rickenbacker and distributed by Radio-Tel. The Electro logo appears on the headstock.

1964-1971		$775	$1,025

Electro ES-17
1964-1975. Cutaway, set neck, solidbody, 1 pickup.

1964-1975		$850	$1,125

Electro Spanish (Model B Spanish)
1935-1943. Small guitar with a lap steel appearance played Spanish-style, hollow black bakelite body augmented with 5 chrome plates (white enamel in '40), 1 octagon knob (2 round-ridged in '38), called the Model B ca. '40.

1935-1937	Chrome, 1 knob	$2,750	$3,600
1935-1937	Tenor 4-string, 1 knob	$2,750	$3,600
1938-1939	Chrome, 2 knobs	$2,750	$3,600
1940-1943	White, 2 knobs	$2,450	$3,150

Electro-Spanish Ken Roberts
1935-1939. Mahogany body, f-holes in lower bout, horseshoe pickup, Kauffman vibrato.

1935-1939		$3,425	$4,500

MODEL YEAR	FEATURES	EXC. COND. LOW	HIGH
Model 220 Hamburg			
1992-1997. Solidbody.			
1992-1997		$725	$950
Model 230 GF Glenn Frey			
1992-1997. Glenn Frey Limited Edition, solidbody, 2 high output humbuckers, black hardware, chrome 'guard.			
1992-1997		$1,450	$1,850
Model 230 Hamburg			
1983-1991. Solidbody, offset double-cut, 2 pickups, dot inlay, rosewood 'board, chrome-plated hardware.			
1983-1991		$850	$1,100
Model 250 El Dorado			
1983-1991. Deluxe version of Hamburg, gold hardware, white binding.			
1983-1991		$775	$1,000
Model 260 El Dorado			
1992-1997. Replaces 250.			
1992-1997		$775	$1,000
Model 310			
1958-1970, 1981-1985. Two-pickup version of Model 320.			
1958-1960	Capri, thick body	$6,900	$9,000
1961-1969	Thinner body	$4,400	$5,700
1981-1985	Reintroduced	$1,300	$1,700
Model 315			
1958-1974. Two-pickup version of Model 325.			
1958-1960	Capri, thick body	$6,900	$9,000
1960-1969	Thinner body	$4,400	$5,700
1970-1973		$2,600	$3,400
1974		$2,300	$3,000
Model 320			
1958-1992. Short-scale hollowbody, 3 pickups, f-holes optional in '61 and standard in '64 and optional again in '79.			
1958-1960	Capri, thick body	$9,000	$11,700
1960-1969		$6,500	$8,400
1970-1973		$2,600	$3,400
1974-1979		$2,100	$2,700
1980-1992		$1,700	$2,200
Model 320/12V63			
1986. Short run for Japanese market.			
1986		$2,200	$2,800
Model 325			
1958-1975, 1985-1992. This was a low production model, with some years having no production. In the mid-'60s, the 325 was unofficially known as the John Lennon Model due to his guitar's high exposure on the Ed Sullivan Show and in the Saturday Evening Post.			
1958	John Lennon specs, 8 made	$31,000	$40,000
1959-1960		$14,000	$18,000
1961-1963		$11,000	$14,300
1964-1966	Fireglo or black	$5,500	$7,200
1966	Mapleglo	$5,500	$7,200
1967-1969		$5,500	$7,200
1970-1975		$2,850	$3,700
Model 325 B			
1983-1984. Reissue of early '60s model.			
1983-1984		$1,725	$2,250

MODEL YEAR	FEATURES	EXC. COND. LOW	HIGH
Model 325 JL			
1989-1993. John Lennon Limited Edition, 3 vintage Ric pickups, vintage vibrato, maple body; 3/4-size rosewood neck, a 12-string and a full-scale version are also available.			
1989-1993		$1,800	$2,300
Model 325 S			
1964-1967. F-holes.			
1964-1967		$6,900	$9,000
Model 325/12			
1985-1986, 1999. Based on John Lennon's one-of-a-kind '64 325/12.			
1985-1986		$2,100	$2,700
1999		$2,100	$2,700
Model 325C58			
2002-2014. Copy of the '58 model that John Lennon saw in Germany.			
2002-2014		$1,800	$2,300
Model 325C64			
2002-present. Copy of the famous '64 model.			
2002-2019		$1,800	$2,300
Model 325V59			
1984-2001. Reissue of John Lennon's modified '59 325, 3 pickups, short-scale.			
1984-2001		$2,000	$2,600
Model 325V63			
1984-2001. Reissue of John Lennon's '63 325.			
1984-2001		$2,000	$2,600
Model 330			
1958-present. Thinline hollowbody, 2 pickups, slash soundhole, natural or sunburst.			
1958-1960	Capri, thick body	$6,300	$8,200
1961-1969	Thinner body	$3,400	$4,400
1970-1973		$2,400	$3,150
1974-1979		$2,200	$2,900
1980-2019		$1,400	$1,825
Model 330 F			
1958-1969. F-style.			
1958-1960	Thick version	$6,500	$8,400
1961-1969	Thin version	$3,400	$4,400
Model 330/12			
1965-present. Thinline, 2 pickups, 12-string version of Model 300.			
1964	Only 1 made	$3,400	$4,400
1965-1969	330-style body	$3,400	$4,400
1970-1979		$2,250	$2,900
1980-1989		$1,400	$1,850
1990-1999		$1,300	$1,700
2000-2019		$1,200	$1,600
Model 330S/12			
1964 (1 made)-1965 (2 made).			
1964-1965		$4,300	$5,600
Model 331 Light Show			
1970-1975. Model 330 with translucent top with lights in body that lit up when played, needed external transformer. The first offering's design, noted as Type 1, had heat problems and a fully original one is difficult to find. The 2nd offering's design, noted as Type 2, was a more stable design and is more highly valued in the market.			
1970-1971	Type 1 1st edition	$7,700	$10,000
1972-1975	Type 2 2nd edition	$9,200	$12,000

1990 Rickenbacker Model 325
Carter Vintage Guitars

1981 Rickenbacker Model 330
Angelo Guarini

GUITARS

1991 Rickenbacker Model 355 JL

Craig Brody

1960 Rickenbacker 360F

MODEL YEAR	FEATURES	EXC. COND. LOW	HIGH
Model 335			
1958-1977. Thinline, 330-style body, 2 pickups, vibrato, Fireglo. Called the 330VB from '85-'97.			
1958-1960	Capri, thick body	$6,300	$8,350
1961-1969	Thinner body	$2,600	$3,400
1970-1973		$2,450	$3,150
1974-1977		$2,250	$2,975
Model 335 F			
1958-1969. F-style.			
1958-1961	Thick version	$6,300	$8,350
1961-1969	Thin version	$2,700	$3,600
Model 336/12			
1966-1974. Like 300-12, but with 6-12 converter comb, 330-style body.			
1966-1969		$2,700	$3,600
1970-1974		$2,250	$2,975
Model 340			
1958-2014. Thin semi-hollowbody, thru-body maple neck, 2 single-coil pickups, sharp point horns, very limited production '58-'65, with first notable volume of 45 units starting in '66.			
1958-1960	Capri, thick body	$6,300	$8,350
1961-1969	Thinner body	$2,600	$3,400
1970-1973		$2,450	$3,150
1974-1979		$2,250	$2,975
1980-2014		$1,350	$1,800
Model 340 F			
1958-1969. F-style.			
1958-1960	Thick version	$6,300	$8,350
1961-1969	Thin version	$2,700	$3,600
Model 340/12			
1980-2014. 12-string version, 330-style body.			
1980-2014		$1,525	$2,000
Model 345			
1961-1974. Thinline 330-345 series, version with 3 pickups and vibrato tailpiece.			
1958-1960	Capri, thick body	$6,300	$8,350
1961-1969	Thinner body	$2,700	$3,600
1970-1973		$2,450	$3,150
1974		$2,250	$2,975
Model 345 F			
1958-1969. F-style.			
1958-1960	Thick version	$6,300	$8,350
1961-1969	Thin version	$2,700	$3,600
Model 345 Reissue			
2002. Low production, 3 pickups.			
2002		$1,800	$2,300
Model 350 Liverpool			
1983-1997. Thinline, 3 pickups, vibrato, no soundhole.			
1983-1997		$1,650	$2,150
Model 350 SH			
1988-1990. Susanna Hoffs Limited Edition.			
1988-1990		$2,850	$3,700
Model 350/12V63 Liverpool			
1994-2014. Vintage Series, 12-string 350V63.			
1994-2014		$1,800	$2,350
Model 350V59			
1988. Very low production.			
1988		$1,650	$2,150

MODEL YEAR	FEATURES	EXC. COND. LOW	HIGH
Model 350V63 Liverpool			
1994-present. Vintage Series, like 355 JL, but without signature.			
1994-2019		$1,650	$2,150
Model 355 JL			
1989-1993. John Lennon model, signature and drawing on 'guard.			
1989-1993		$2,400	$3,200
Model 355/12 JL			
1989-1993. 12-string 355 JL, limited production.			
1989-1993		$2,450	$3,200
Model 360/360 VB			
1958-1991, 2000-present. Deluxe thinline, 2 pickups, slash soundhole, bound body until '64.			
1958-1960	Capri, thick body	$6,500	$8,400
1961-1967		$3,200	$4,200
1968-1969		$3,000	$4,000
1970-1973	360, no vibrato	$2,600	$3,350
1974-1989	360 VB, vibrato	$1,500	$1,950
1990-2019		$1,300	$1,700
Model 360V64			
1991-2003. Reissue of '64 Model 360 old style body without vibrola, has binding with full length inlays.			
1991-2003		$2,000	$2,600
Model 360 CW			
2000. Carl Wilson Limited Edition, 6-string, includes certificate, 500 made.			
2000		$2,150	$2,800
Model 360 DCM 75th Anniversary			
2006. 360 with 75th Anniversary dark cherry metallic finish, 75 made.			
2006		$2,150	$2,800
Model 360 F			
1959-1972. F-style.			
1959-1960	Thick version	$6,400	$8,400
1961-1969	Thin version	$2,900	$3,800
1970-1972	Thin version	$2,450	$3,200
Model 360 SF			
1968-ca. 1972. Slanted frets (SF), standard on some models, an option on others.			
1968-1972		$3,850	$5,000
Model 360 Tuxedo			
1987 only. Tuxedo option included white body, white painted fretboard, and black hardware.			
1987		$1,550	$2,000
Model 360 WB			
1984-1998. Double bound body, 2 pickups, vibrato optional (VB).			
1984-1990		$1,725	$2,200
1991-1998	WB, no vibrato	$1,550	$2,000
1991-1998	WBVB, vibrato	$1,725	$2,200
Model 360/12			
1964-present. Deluxe double-cut thinline, 2 pickups, triangle inlays. The 360/12 was offered in both the Old Style (OS) body with double-bound body and pointed horns, and the New Style (NS) body with rounded top edges and rounder horns. George Harrison's original 360/12 had the OS body in a Fireglo finish. Production of the OS and NS bodies overlapped.			
1964	OS, Fireglo, pointed horns,		

MODEL YEAR	FEATURES	EXC. COND. LOW	HIGH
	Harrison	$24,000	$31,000
1964-1969	NS, Fireglo, rounded horns	$3,100	$4,050
1964-1969	NS, Mapleglo, rounded horns	$3,300	$4,250
1964-1969	OS, Mapleglo, pointed horns	$13,000	$17,000
1965-1969	OS, Fireglo, pointed horns	$15,500	$20,000
1970-1973		$3,000	$3,900
1974-1979		$2,500	$3,300
1980-2009		$1,550	$2,000
2010-2019		$1,500	$1,950

Model 360/12 CW
2000. Carl Wilson, 12-string version of 360 CW.

2000		$2,500	$3,250

Model 360/12 RCA
1992. Limited edition made for RCA Nashville as gifts for their artists, has RCA dog-and-gramophone logo on pickguard.

1992		$2,200	$2,800

Model 360/12 Tuxedo
1987 only. 12-string version of 360 Tuxedo.

1987		$2,200	$2,800

Model 360/12 VP
2004. VP is vintage pickup.

2004		$2,000	$2,600

Model 360/12 WB
1984-1998. 12-string version of 360 WB.

1984-1998		$2,200	$2,800

Model 360/12C63
2004-present. More exact replica of the Harrison model.

2004-2019		$2,200	$2,800

Model 360/12V64
1985-2003. Deluxe thinline with '64 features, 2 pickups, 12 strings, slanted plate tailpiece.

1985-2003		$2,200	$2,800

Model 362/12
1975-1992. Doubleneck 6 & 12, 360 features.

1975-1992		$2,000	$2,600

Model 365
1958-1974. Deluxe thinline, 2 pickups, vibrato, called Model 360 WBVB from '84-'98.

1958-1960	Capri, thick body	$6,500	$8,400
1961-1969		$3,000	$3,900
1970-1973		$2,750	$3,600
1974		$2,600	$3,400

Model 365 F
1959-1972. Thin full-body (F designation), 2 pickups, Deluxe features.

1959-1960	Capri, thick body	$6,500	$8,400
1961-1969	Thin version	$2,900	$3,800
1970-1972		$2,750	$3,600

Model 366/12 Convertible
1966-1974. Two pickups, 12 strings, comb-like device that converts it to a 6-string, production only noted in '68, perhaps available on custom order basis.

1966-1968	OS	$3,850	$5,000

Model 370
1958-1990, 1994-2007. Deluxe thinline, 3 pickups. Could be considered to be a dealer special order item from '58-'67 with limited production.

1958-1960	Capri, thick body	$6,500	$8,400
1961-1969	Thin version	$3,000	$3,950
1970-1973		$2,750	$3,600
1974-1979		$2,600	$3,400
1980-1999		$1,550	$2,000
2000-2007		$1,550	$2,000

Model 370 F
1959-1972. F-style, 3 pickups, Deluxe features.

1959-1961	Thick version	$6,500	$8,400
1961-1969	Thin version	$3,000	$3,950
1970-1972		$2,750	$3,600

Model 370 VP
2006-2007. Limited run with special specs including vintage toaster pickups (VP).

2006-2007		$2,500	$3,200

Model 370 WB
1984-1998. Double bound body, 3 pickups, vibrato optional (VB).

1984-1998		$1,375	$1,800

Model 370/12
1966-1990, 1994-present. Not regular production until '80, deluxe thinline, 3 pickups, 12 strings. Could be considered to be a dealer special order item in the '60s and '70s with limited production.

1966		$6,900	$9,000
1967-2019		$1,750	$2,300

Model 370/12 RM
1988. Limited Edition Roger McGuinn, 1000 made, higher-quality appointments.

1988-1989		$3,900	$5,100

Model 375
1958-1974. Deluxe thinline, 3 pickups, vibrato, called Model 370 WBVB from '84-'98.

1958-1960	Capri, thick body	$6,500	$8,400
1961-1969	Thin version	$3,100	$4,000
1970-1973		$2,800	$3,600
1974		$2,700	$3,500

Model 375 F
1959-1972. F-style, 2 pickups.

1959-1960	Thick version	$6,500	$8,400
1961-1969	Thin version	$3,100	$4,000
1970-1972		$2,800	$3,600

Model 380 L Laguna
1996-2005. Semi-hollow, oil-finished walnut body, Maple neck and 'board, 2 humbuckers, PZ saddle pickups optional.

1996-2005		$1,550	$2,000
1996-2005	PZ option	$1,550	$2,000

Model 381
1958-1963, 1969-1974. Double-cut archtop, 2 pickups, slash soundhole, solid 'guard, reintroduced in '69 with double split-level 'guard.

1958-1963	Low production	$6,500	$8,400
1969	Various colors, some rare	$3,100	$4,000
1970-1975		$2,800	$3,600

1992 Rickenbacker Model 370
Carter Vintage Guitars

1981 Rickenbacker Model 370/12
Craig Brody

1960 Rickenbacker Model 450
Carter Vintage Guitars

Rickenbacker Model 450V63
Ron O'Keefe

Model 381 JK John Kay
1988-1997. John Kay Limited Edition, 250 made, 2 humbucking pickups, active electronics, stereo and mono outputs, Jetglo black.

Year	Features	Low	High
1988-1997		$2,350	$3,050

Model 381/12V69
1987-present. Reissue of 381/12, deep double-cut body, sound body cavity, catseye soundhole, triangle inlays, bridge with 12 individual saddles. Finishes include Fireglo, Mapleglo and Jetglo.

Year	Features	Low	High
1987-2019	Figured top	$2,350	$3,050

Model 381V69
1991-present. Reissue of vintage 381.

Year	Features	Low	High
1987-2019		$2,350	$3,050

Model 382
1958-1963, 1969-1974. 381 with vibrato unit. Very light production.

Year	Features	Low	High
1958-1963	Low production	$6,500	$8,400
1969-1974	Various colors, some rare	$2,900	$3,800

Model 383
1958-1963, 1969-1974. 381 with 3 pickups. Very light production.

Year	Features	Low	High
1958-1963	Low production	$6,500	$8,400
1969-1974	Various colors, some rare	$2,900	$3,800

Model 384
1958-1963, 1969-1974. 381 with 3 pickups and vibrato unit. Very light production.

Year	Features	Low	High
1958-1963	Low production	$6,500	$8,400
1969-1974	Various colors, some rare	$2,900	$3,800

Model 400/Combo 400
1956-1958. Double-cut tulip body, neck-thru, 1 pickup, gold anodized 'guard, 21 frets, replaced by Model 425 in '58. Available in black (216 made), blue turquoise (53), Cloverfield Green (53), Montezuma Brown (41), and 4 in other custom colors.

Year	Features	Low	High
1956-1958		$3,075	$4,000

Model 420
1965-1983. Non-vibrato version of Model 425, single pickup.

Year	Features	Low	High
1965-1968		$1,200	$1,600
1969-1983		$1,000	$1,350

Model 425/Combo 425
1958-1973. Double-cut solidbody, 1 pickup, sunburst.

Year	Features	Low	High
1958-1959	425 Cresting Wave	$2,500	$3,250
1960		$1,800	$2,300
1961-1964		$1,375	$1,800
1965-1968		$1,200	$1,575
1969-1973		$1,000	$1,300

Model 425/12V63
1999-2000. 136 made.

Year	Features	Low	High
1999-2000		$1,300	$1,700

Model 425V63
1999-2000. Beatles associated model, 145 JG black made, 116 BG burgundy transparent made, originally custom ordered by Rickenbacker collectors and they were not part of Rickenbacker's sales literature in the late '90s.

Year	Features	Low	High
1999-2000		$1,200	$1,550

Model 430
1971-1982. Style 200 body, natural.

Year	Features	Low	High
1971-1982		$650	$850

Model 450/Combo 450
1957-1984. Replaces Combo 450, 2 pickups (3 optional '62-'77), tulip body shape '57-'59, cresting wave body shape after.

Year	Features	Low	High
1957-1958	450 Tulip body (Combo)	$3,100	$4,000
1958-1959	450 Cresting Wave	$2,600	$3,300
1960	Cresting Wave, flat body	$1,800	$2,300
1961-1966	Cresting Wave, super slim	$1,550	$2,000
1970-1979	Includes rare color	$1,250	$1,625
1980-1984		$925	$1,200

Model 450/12
1964-1985. Double-cut solidbody, 12-string version of Model 450, 2 pickups.

Year	Features	Low	High
1964-1966		$1,550	$2,000
1967-1969		$1,450	$1,900
1970-1979	Includes rare color	$1,300	$1,700
1980-1985		$1,000	$1,300

Model 450V63
1999-2001. Reissue of '63 450.

Year	Features	Low	High
1999-2001		$1,100	$1,450

Model 456/12 Convertible
1968-1978. Double-cut solidbody, 2 pickups, comb-like device to convert it to 6-string.

Year	Features	Low	High
1968-1969		$1,935	$2,525
1970-1978		$1,625	$2,075

Model 460
1961-1985. Double-cut solidbody, 2 pickups, neck-thru-body, deluxe trim.

Year	Features	Low	High
1961-1965		$2,075	$2,700
1966-1969		$1,800	$2,350
1970-1979	Includes rare color	$1,550	$2,000
1980-1985		$1,100	$1,450

Model 480
1973-1984. Double-cut solidbody with long thin bass horn in 4001 bass series style, 2 pickups, cresting wave body and headstock, bolt-on neck.

Year	Features	Low	High
1973-1979		$1,900	$2,500
1980-1984		$1,750	$2,300

Model 481
1973-1983. Cresting wave body with longer bass horn, 2 humbuckers (3 optional), angled frets.

Year	Features	Low	High
1973-1979		$1,900	$2,500
1980-1983		$1,750	$2,300

Model 483
1973-1983. Cresting wave body with longer bass horn, 3 humbuckers.

Year	Features	Low	High
1973-1979		$2,050	$2,700
1980-1983		$1,850	$2,400

Model 600/Combo 600
1954-1958. Modified double-cut, horseshoe pickup.

Year	Features	Low	High
1954-1957	Blond/white	$3,400	$4,400
1956-1958	OT/Blue Turquoise	$3,400	$4,400

MODEL YEAR	FEATURES	EXC. COND. LOW	HIGH

Model 610
1985-1991. Cresting-wave cutaway solidbody, 2 pickups, trapeze R-tailpiece, Jetglo.

1985-1991		$725	$950

Model 610/12
1988-1997. 12-string version of Model 610.

1988-1997		$825	$1,050

Model 615
1962-1966, 1969-1977. Double-cut solidbody, 2 pickups, vibrato.

1962-1965		$1,550	$2,000
1966-1969		$1,400	$1,800
1970-1977		$1,400	$1,800

Model 620
1974-present. Double-cut solidbody, deluxe binding, 2 pickups, neck-thru-body.

1974-1979		$1,500	$1,900
1980-2019		$1,250	$1,625

Model 620/12
1981-present. Double-cut solidbody, 2 pickups, 12 strings, standard trim.

1981-2019		$1,300	$1,725

Model 625
1962-1977. Double-cut solidbody, deluxe trim, 2 pickups, vibrato.

1962-1965		$4,400	$5,800
1966-1969		$2,800	$3,600
1970-1977		$2,200	$2,900

Model 650/Combo 650
1957-1959. Standard color, 1 pickup.

1957-1959		$3,400	$4,400

Model 650 A Atlantis
1992-2003. Double cut cresting wave solidbody, maple body wings, neck-thru, 2 pickups, chrome hardware, turquoise.

1992-2003		$1,000	$1,300

Model 650 C Colorado
1993-2017. Like Atlantis but with balck finish.

1993-2017		$1,000	$1,300

Model 650 D Dakota
1993-2017. Like Atlantis but with walnut body wings and oil-satin finish.

1993-2017		$1,000	$1,300

Model 650 E Excalibur/F Frisco
1991-2003. Like Atlantis but with brown vermilion body wings and gold hardware. Name changed to Frisco in '95.

1991-2003		$1,000	$1,300

Model 650 S Sierra
1993-2017. Like Dakota but with gold hardware.

1993-2017		$1,000	$1,300

Model 660
1998-present. Cresting wave maple body, triangle inlays, 2 pickups.

1998-2019		$1,600	$2,100

Model 660 DCM 75th Anniversary
2006-2007. 75th 1931-2006 Anniversary pickguard logo.

2006-2007		$1,750	$2,300

Model 660/12
1998-present. 12-string 660.

1998-2019		$1,900	$2,450

Model 660/12 TP
1991-1998. Tom Petty model, 12 strings, cresting wave body, 2 pickups, deluxe trim, limited run of 1000, certificate of authenticity.

1991-1998	With certificate	$3,600	$4,700

Model 800/Combo 800
1954-1959. Offset double-cut, 1 horseshoe pickup until late-'57, second bar type after.

1954-1957	Blond/white, 1 pickup	$4,700	$6,100
1954-1957	Blue or green, 1 pickup	$4,700	$6,100
1957-1959	Blond/white, 2 pickups	$4,700	$6,100
1957-1959	Blue or green, 2 pickups	$4,700	$6,100

Model 850/Combo 850
1957-1959. Extreme double-cut, 1 pickup until '58, 2 after, various colors, called Model 850 in the '60s.

1957-1959	Various colors	$4,700	$6,100

Model 900
1957-1980. Double-cut tulip body shape, 3/4 size, 1 pickup. Body changes to cresting wave shape in '69.

1957-1966		$1,400	$1,800

Model 950/Combo 950
1957-1980. Like Model 900, but with 2 pickups, 21 frets. Body changes to cresting wave shape in '69.

1957-1964		$1,600	$2,100
1965-1980		$1,400	$1,825

Model 1000
1957-1970. Like Model 900, but with 18 frets. Body does not change to cresting wave shape.

1956-1966		$1,200	$1,575
1967-1970		$1,100	$1,450

Model 1993/12 RM
1964-1967. Export 'slim-line' 12-string model made for English distributor Rose-Morris of London, built along the lines of the U.S. Model 360/12 but with small differences that are considered important in the vintage guitar market.

1964	Flat tailpiece	$4,275	$5,600
1965-1967	R tailpiece	$4,275	$5,600

Model 1996 RM
1964-1967. Rose-Morris import, 3/4 size built similarly to the U.S. Model 325.

1964-1967		$7,000	$9,000

Model 1996 RM Reissue
2006. Reissue of the Rose-Morris version of Model 325, this reissue available on special order in 2006.

2006		$2,600	$3,400

Model 1997 PT
1987-1988. Pete Townshend Signature Model, semi-hollowbody, single f-hole, maple neck, 21-fret rosewood 'board, 3 pickups, Firemist finish, limited to 250 total production.

1987-1988		$2,600	$3,400

Model 1997 RM
1964-1967. Export 'slim-line' model made for English distributor Rose-Morris of London, built along the lines of the U.S. Model 335, but with small differences that are considered important in the vintage guitar market,

1958 Rickenbacker Model 600 Combo
Larry Wassgren

Rickenbacker Model 660/12
Ron O'Keefe

Robertson Guitars Dreadnought

Robinson Small Jumbo

MODEL YEAR	FEATURES	EXC. COND. LOW	HIGH

2 pickups, vibrola tailpiece. Rose-Morris export models sent to the USA generally had a red-lined guitar case vs. the USA domestic blue-lined guitar case.

| 1964-1967 | | $3,050 | $4,000 |

Model 1997 RM Reissue

1987-1995. Reissue of '60s Rose-Morris model, but with vibrola (VB) or without.

| 1987-1995 | | $1,800 | $2,350 |

Model 1997 SPC

1993-2002. 3 pickup version of reissue.

| 1993-2002 | | $1,375 | $1,800 |

Model 1998 RM

1964-1967. Export 'slim-line' model made for English distributor Rose-Morris of London, built along the lines of a U.S. Model 345 but with small differences that are considered important in the vintage guitar market, 3 pickups, vibrola tailpiece.

| 1964-1967 | | $3,050 | $4,000 |

Rickenbacker Spanish/Spanish/SP

1946-1949. Block markers.

| 1946-1949 | | $1,500 | $1,950 |

S-59

1940-1942. Arch top body built by Kay, horseshoe magnet pickup.

| 1940-1942 | | $1,400 | $1,800 |

Rigaud Guitars

1978-present. Luthier Robert Rigaud builds his premium grade, custom, parlor to jumbo acoustic guitars in Greensboro, North Carolina. He also builds ukuleles under the New Moon brand.

Ritz

1989. Solidbody electric guitars and basses produced in Calimesa, California, by Wayne Charvel, Eric Galletta and Brad Becnel, many of which featured cracked shell mosiac finishes.

RKS

Professional and premium grade, production/custom, electric hollowbody and solidbody guitars and basses designed by Ravi Sawhney and guitarist Dave Mason and built in Thousand Oaks, California. They began in 2003.

Robert Cefalu

Luthier Robert Cefalu built his professional grade, production/custom, acoustic guitars in Buffalo, New York. The guitars have an RC on the headstock.

Robert Guitars

1981-present. Luthier Mikhail Robert builds his premium grade, production/custom, classical guitars in Summerland, British Columbia.

Robertson Guitars

1995-present. Luthier Jeff Robertson builds his premium grade, production/custom flat-top guitars in South New Berlin, New York.

MODEL YEAR	FEATURES	EXC. COND. LOW	HIGH

Robin

1982-2010. Professional and premium grade, production/custom, guitars from luthier David Wintz and built in Houston, Texas. Most guitars were Japanese-made until '87; American production began in '88. Most Japanese Robins were pretty consistent in features, but the American ones were often custom-made, so many variations in models exist. They also made Metropolitan ('96-'08) and Alamo ('00-'08) brand guitars.

Avalon Classic

1994-2010. Single-cut, figured maple top, 2 humbuckers.

| 1994-2010 | Various options | $1,250 | $1,650 |

Medley Pro

1990s. Solidbody with 2 extreme cutaway horns, hum-single-single.

| 1990s | US-made | $725 | $975 |

Medley Special

1992-1995. Ash body, maple neck, rosewood 'board, 24 frets, various pickup options.

| 1992-1995 | | $450 | $600 |

Medley Standard

1985-2010. Offset double-cut swamp ash solidbody, bolt neck, originally with hum-single-single pickups, but now also available with 2 humbuckers.

| 1985-1987 | Japan-made | $400 | $525 |
| 1988-2010 | US-made | $800 | $1,075 |

Octave

1982-1990s. Tuned an octave above standard tuning, full body size with 15 1/2" short-scale bolt maple neck. Japanese-made production model until '87, U.S.-made custom shop after.

| 1990s | With original case | $600 | $775 |

Raider I/Raider II/Raider III

1985-1991. Double-cut solidbody, 1 humbucker pickup (Raider I), 2 humbuckers (Raider II), or 3 single-coils (Raider III), maple neck, either maple or rosewood 'board, sunburst.

1985-1991	1 pickup	$350	$450
1985-1991	2 pickups	$375	$500
1985-1991	3 pickups	$425	$550

Ranger

1982. First production model with 2 single-coil pickups in middle and neck position, reverse headstock, dot markers.

| 1982 | | $775 | $1,025 |

Ranger Custom

1982-1986, 1988-2010. Swamp ash bound body, bolt-on maple neck, rosewood or maple 'board, 2 single coils and 1 humbucker, orange, made in Japan until '86, U.S.-made after.

| 1982-1986 | Japan-made | $400 | $525 |
| 1988-2010 | US-made | $775 | $1,025 |

RDN-Doubleneck Octave/Six

1982-1985. Six-string standard neck with 3 pickups, 6-string octave neck with 1 pickup, double-cut solidbody.

| 1982-1985 | With original case | $875 | $1,125 |

MODEL YEAR	FEATURES	EXC. COND. LOW	HIGH

Savoy Deluxe/Standard
1995-2010. Semi-hollow thinline single cut archtop, 2 pickups, set neck.

| 1996-2010 | | $1,200 | $1,625 |

Soloist/Artisan
1982-1986. Mahogany double-cut solidbody, carved bound maple top, set neck, 2 humbuckers. Renamed Artisan in '85. Only about 125 made in Japan.

| 1982-1986 | | $575 | $775 |

Wedge
1985-ca. 1988. Triangle-shaped body, 2 humbuckers, Custom with set neck and triangle inlays, Standard with bolt neck and dots, about 200 made.

| 1980s | | $775 | $1,025 |

Wrangler
1995-2002. Classic '50s single-cut slab body, 3 Rio Grande pickups, opaque finish.

| 1995-2002 | | $575 | $775 |

Robinson Guitars

2002-present. Premium and presentation grade, custom/production, steel string guitars built by luthier Jake Robinson first in Kalamazoo, and since '08 in Hoxeyville, Michigan.

RockBeach Guitars

2005-present. Luthier Greg Bogoshian builds his custom, professional grade, chambered electric guitars and basses in Rochester, New York.

Rockinbetter

2011-2014. Intermediate grade, production electric guitars and basses, copies of Rickenbacker models, made in China.

Rocking F

See listing under Fox.

Rockit Guitar

Luthier Rod MacKenzie builds his premium grade, custom, electric guitars and basses in Everett, Washington, starting in 2006.

Rogands

Late 1960s. Produced by France's Jacobacci company and named after brothers Roger and Andre. Short-lived brand; the brothers made instruments under several other brands as well.

Roger

Guitars built in Germany by luthier Wenzel Rossmeisl and named for his son Roger. Roger Rossmeisl would go on to work at Rickenbacker and Fender.

Rogue

2001-present. Budget and intermediate grade, production, acoustic, resonator, electric and sitar guitars and basses. They also offer mandolins, banjos, ukuleles, and lap steels. They previously offered effects and amps. Fender offered instruments branded Rogue by Squire for a short period starting in '99.

Roland

Best known for keyboards, effects, and amps, Roland offered synthesizer-based guitars and basses from 1977 to '97.

GR-707 Synth Guitar
1983-1986. Slab-wedge asymmetrical body, bass bout to headstock support arm, 2 humbucker pickups, multi-controls.

| 1983-1986 | Silver | $700 | $900 |

GS-500 Synth Guitar/Module
1977-1986. Snyth functions in a single-cut solidbody guitar. The GS-300 was the same electronics in a classic offset double-cut body.

| 1977-1986 | Sunburst | $700 | $900 |

Rolando

1916-ca. 1919. Private branded instruments made for the Southern California Music Company of Los Angeles, by Martin. There were three models.

00-28K/1500

| 1916-1919 | | $6,900 | $9,000 |

Rolf Spuler

1981-2014. Presentation grade, custom, hybrid electric-acoustic guitars, built by luthier Rolf Spuler in Gebenstorf, Switzerland. He also built basses. He passed away in '14.

Roman & Lipman Guitars

1989-2000. Production/custom, solidbody guitars and basses made in Danbury, Connecticut by Ed Roman Guitars.

Roman Abstract Guitars

1989-present. Professional and premium grade, production/custom, solidbody guitars made by Ed Roman Guitars.

Roman Centurion Guitars

2001-present. Premium and presentation grade, custom guitars made by Ed Roman Guitars.

Roman Pearlcaster Guitars

1999-present. Professional and premium grade, production/custom, solidbody guitars made Ed Roman Guitars.

Roman Quicksilver Guitars

1997-present. Professional and premium grade, production/custom, solid and hollow-body guitars made by Ed Roman Guitars.

Roman RVC Guitars

1999-present. Professional and premium grade, production/custom, solidbody guitars made by Ed Roman Guitars.

Roman Vampire Guitars

2004-present. Professional and premium grade, production/custom, solidbody guitars made by Ed Roman Guitars. Special orders only since about '13.

1960 Roger Super Cutaway
Alf Tengs-Pedersen

1978 Roland GS-500

GUITARS

1976 S.D. Curlee Standard

Saga Blueridge

MODEL YEAR	FEATURES	EXC. COND. LOW	HIGH

Rono

In 1967 luthier Ron Oates began building professional and premium grade, production/custom, flat-top, jazz, Wiesenborn-style, and resonator guitars and basses in Boulder, Colorado. He also built mandolins.

Ro-Pat-In

See Rickenbacker.

Rosetti

1950s-1960s. Guitars imported into England by distributor Rosetti, made by Holland's Egmond, maybe others.

Solid 7

1960s. Symmetrical cutaway electric semi-hollow, large 'guard with top-mounted dual pickups, 4 control knobs, value is associated with Paul McCartney's use in '60, value dependent on completely original McCartney specs.

1960s	McCartney model	$1,000	$2,000
1960s	Various other	$425	$575

Roudhloff

1810s-1840s. Luthier Francois Roudhloff built his instruments in France. Labels could state F. Roudhloff-Mauchand or Roudhloff Brothers. Valuation depends strongly on condition and repair. His sons built guitars under the D & A Roudhloff label.

Rowan

Professional and premium grade, production/custom, solidbody and acoustic/electric guitars built by luthier Michael Rowan in Garland, Texas.

Royal

Ca. 1954-ca. 1965. Line of jazz style guitars made by France's Jacobacci company, which also built under its own brand.

Royal (Japan)

1957-1960s. Early budget level instruments made by Tokyo Sound Company and Gakki and exported by Japan's Hoshino (Ibanez).

Royden Guitars

Professional grade, production/custom, flat-tops and solidbody electrics built by luthier Royden Moran in Peterborough, Ontario, starting in 1996.

RS Guitarworks

1994-present. Professional grade, production/custom, solid and hollowbody guitars built by luthier Roy Bowen in Winchester, Kentucky.

Rubio, German Vasquez

1993-present. Luthier German Vasquez Rubio builds his professional and premium grade, production/custom classical and flamenco guitars in Los Angeles, California.

MODEL YEAR	FEATURES	EXC. COND. LOW	HIGH

Ruck, Robert

1966-2018. Premium grade, custom classical and flamenco guitars built by luthier Robert Ruck originally in Kalaheo, Hawaii, then in Eugene, Oregon. Ruck died in '18.

Running Dog Guitars

1994-present. Luthier Rick Davis builds his professional and premium grade, custom flat-tops in Seattle, Washington. He was originally located in Richmond, Vermont.

Ruokangas

1995-present. Luthier Juha Ruokangas builds his premium and presentation grade, production/custom, solidbody and semi-acoustic electric guitars in Hyvinkaa, Finland.

Rustler

1993-ca. 1998. Solidbody electrics with hand-tooled leather bound and studded sides and R branded into the top, built by luthier Charles Caponi in Mason City, Iowa.

RWK

1991-present. Luthier Bob Karger builds his intermediate grade, production/custom, solidbody electrics and travel guitars in Highland Park, Illinois.

Ryder

1963. Made by Rickenbacker, the one model with this brand was the same as their solidbody Model 425.

S. Walker Custom Guitars

2002-present. Luthier Scott Walker builds his premium grade, production/custom, solid and semi hollow body electric guitars in Santa Cruz, California.

S. Yairi

Ca. 1960-1980s. Steel string folk guitars and classical nylon string guitars by master Japanese luthier Sadao Yairi, imported by Philadelphia Music Company of Limerick, Pennsylvania. Early sales literature called the brand Syairi. Most steel string models have dreadnought bodies and nylon-string classical guitars are mostly standard grand concert size. All models are handmade. Steel string Jumbos and dreadnoughts have Syairi logo on the headstock, nylon-classical models have no logo. The Model 900 has a solid wood body, others assumed to have laminate bodies.

S.B. Brown Guitars

Custom flat-tops made by luthier Steve Brown in Fullerton, California.

MODEL YEAR	FEATURES	EXC. COND. LOW	HIGH

S.B. MacDonald Custom Instruments

1988-present. Professional and premium grade, custom/production, flat-top, resonator, and solid-body guitars built by luthier Scott B. MacDonald in Huntington, New York.

S.D. Curlee

1975-1982. Founded in Matteson, Illinois by music store owner Randy Curlee, after an unsuccessful attempt to recruit builder Dan Armstrong. S.D. Curlee guitars were made in Illinois, while S.D. Curlee International instruments were made by Matsumoku in Japan. The guitars featured mostly Watco oil finishes, often with exotic hardwoods, and unique neck-thru-bridge construction on American and Japanese instruments. These were the first production guitars to use a single-coil pickup at the bridge with a humbucker at the neck, and a square brass nut. DiMarzio pickups. Offered in a variety of shapes, later some copies. Approximately 12,000 American-made basses and 3,000 guitars were made, most of which were sold overseas. Two hundred were made in '75-'76; first production guitar numbered 518.

Electric Solidbody

1975-1982. Models include the '75-'81 Standard I, II and III, '76-'81 International C-10 and C-11, '80-'81 Yankee, Liberty, Butcher, Curbeck, Summit, Special, and the '81-'82 Destroyer, Flying V.

1975-1982		$325	$425

S.L. Smith Guitars

Professional grade, production/custom, acoustic guitars built by Steven Smith in Brant Lake, New York beginning in 2007.

S.S. Stewart

The original S.S. Stewart Company (1878-1904), of Philadelphia, Pennsylvania is considered to be one of the most important banjo manufacturers of the late 19th century. Samuel Swaim Stewart died in 1988 and his family was out of the company by the early 1900s, and the brand was soon acquired by Bugellsein & Jacobsen of New York. The brand name was used on guitars into the 1960s.

Flat-Top

1930s. Gibson L-2 style body.

1932		$7,000	$9,000

S101

Budget and intermediate grade, production, classical, acoustic, resonator, solid and semi-hollow body guitars and basses imported from China by America Sejung Corp. They also offer mandolins, and banjos.

Sadowsky

1980-present. Professional and premium grade, production/custom, solidbody, semi-hollowbody, archtop, and electric nylon-string guitars built by luthier Roger Sadowsky in Brooklyn, New York. He also builds basses and amps. In '96, luthier Yoshi Kikuchi started building Sadowsky Tokyo instruments in Japan.

Saga

Saga Musical Instruments, of San Francisco, California distributes a wide variety of instruments and brands, occasionally including their own line of solidbody guitars called the Saga Gladiator Series (1987-'88, '94-'95). In the 2000s, Saga also offered component kits ($90-$130) that allowed for complete assembly in white wood.

Sahlin Guitars

Luthier Eric Sahlin hs built his premium grade, custom, classical and flamenco guitars in Spokane, Washington since 1975.

Samick

1958-2001, 2002-present. Budget, intermediate and professional grade, production, imported acoustic and electric guitars and basses. They also offer mandolins, ukes and banjos and distribute Abilene and Silvertone brand instruments.

Samick started out producing pianos, adding guitars in '65 under other brands. In '88 Samick greatly increased their guitar production. The Samick line of 350 models was totally closed out in 2001. A totally new line of 250 models was introduced January 2002 at NAMM. All 2002 models have the new compact smaller headstock and highly styled S logo.

Sammo

1920s. Labels in these instruments state they were made by the Osborne Mfg. Co. with an address of Masonic Temple, Chicago, Illinois. High quality and often with a high degree of ornamentation. They also made ukes and mandolins.

Sand Guitars

1979-present. Luthier Kirk Sand opened the Guitar Shoppe in Laguna Beach, California in 1972 with James Matthews. By '79, he started producing his own line of premium grade, production/custom-made flat-tops.

Sandoval Engineering

1979-present. Luthier Karl Sandoval builds his premium grade, custom, solidbody guitars in Santa Fe Springs, California.

Sano

1944-ca. 1970. Sano was a New Jersey-based accordion company that imported Italian-made solid and semi-hollow body guitars for a few years, starting in 1966; some, if not all, made by Zero Sette. They also built their own amps and reverb units.

1996 Samick Charlie Christian

Sandoval Engineering Original Sandoval Dot V

GUITARS

2017 Santa Cruz D 12-Fret
Bernunzio Uptown Music

2017 Santa Cruz H/13
Bernunzio Uptown Music

MODEL YEAR	FEATURES	EXC. COND. LOW	HIGH

Santa Cruz

1976-present. Professional, premium and presentation grade, production/custom, flat-top, 12-string, and archtop guitars from luthier Richard Hoover in Santa Cruz, California. They also build a mandocello and ukuleles. Founded by Hoover, Bruce Ross and William Davis. Hoover became sole owner in '89. Custom ordered instruments with special upgrades may have higher values than the ranges listed here.

OO 12-Fret
1997-present. Indian rosewood.

1997-2019		$2,200	$2,900

OOO 12-Fret
1994-present. 000 size, 12-fret body, Indian rosewood back and sides, ebony 'board, ivoroid binding.

1994-2019	Indian rosewood	$2,200	$2,900
2011	Brazilian rosewood	$4,300	$5,600

Archtop
Early 1980s-2010. Originally the FJZ, by mid-'90s, called the Archtop, offering 16", 17" and 18" cutaway acoustic/electric models, often special order. Curly maple body, ebony 'board, floating pickup, f-holes, sunburst or natural. Many custom options available.

1980s-90s		$2,800	$3,700

Bob Brozman Baritone
1998-2019. Flat-top acoustic, mahogany body, spruce top.

1998-2019		$2,800	$3,600

D 12-Fret
1994-present. 12-fret neck, slotted headstock, round shoulders, mahogany back and sides, notch diamond markers, herringbone trim. Special orders vary in value and could exceed the posted range.

1994-2019		$2,200	$2,900

D Koa
1980s-1990s. Style D with koa back and sides.

1980s-90s		$2,200	$2,900

D/HR
Style D with Indian rosewood back and sides, Brazilian rosewood headstock overlay.

2000		$2,200	$2,900

D/PW Pre-War
2001-present. Pre-war D-style.

2001-2019	Various models	$2,200	$2,900

F
1979-present. 15 7/8" scale with narrow waist, sitka spruce top, Indian rosewood back and sides, natural.

1979-2019		$2,600	$3,400

F46R
1980s. Brazilian rosewood, single-cut.

1980s		$3,000	$3,900

Firefly
2009-present. Premium quality travel/parlor guitar, cedar top, flamed maple sides and back.

2009-2019		$2,200	$2,900

FS (Finger Style)
1988-present. Single-cut, cedar top, Indian rosewood back and sides, mahogany neck, modified X-bracing.

1988-2019		$2,400	$3,100

H
1977-present. Parlor size, originally a 13-fret neck, but soon changed to 14, Indian rosewood back and sides. The H A/E ('92-'04) added electronics and cutaway.

1977-2019	Indian rosewood	$2,400	$3,100
1994	Flamed koa	$3,200	$4,200
2005	Brazilian rosewood	$3,900	$5,100

H/13
2004-present. Like H, but with 13-fret neck, mahogany back and sides and slotted headstock.

2004-2019	Mahogany	$2,600	$3,400
2005	Flamed koa	$3,200	$4,200

H91
1990s. 14 5/8", flamed koa.

1990s		$3,200	$4,200

Model 1929 OO
2010-present. 00-size, all mahogany, 12-fret neck.

2010-2019		$2,200	$2,900

OM (Orchestra Model)
1987-present. Orchestra model acoustic, sitka spruce top, Indian rosewood (Brazilian optional) back and sides, herringbone rosette, scalloped braces.

1987-2019	Brazilian rosewood	$4,000	$5,300
1987-2019	Indian rosewood	$2,400	$3,100
1995	Koa	$3,000	$4,000
2010	Italian spruce	$4,000	$5,300

OM/PW Pre-War
1999-present. Indian rosewood, advanced X and scalloped top bracing.

1999-2019		$2,200	$2,900

PJ
1990s-present. Palor-size, Indian rosewood back and sides, 24" scale, 12-fret neck.

1990s		$2,500	$3,300

Tony Rice
1976-present. Dreadnought, Indian rosewood body (Brazilian optional until Tony Rice Professional model available), sitka spruce top, solid peghead, zigzag back stripe, pickup optional.

1976-2019		$2,600	$3,400

Tony Rice Professional
1997-present. Brazilian rosewood back and sides, carved German spruce top, zigzag back stripe, solid peghead.

1997-2019		$4,800	$6,200

Vintage Artist
1992-present. Mahogany body, sitka spruce top, zigzag back stripe, solid peghead, scalloped X-bracing, pickup optional.

1992-2019		$2,400	$3,100

Vintage Artist Custom
1992-2004. Martin D-42 style, mahogany body, Indian rosewood back and sides, sitka spruce top, zigzag back stripe, solid peghead, scalloped X-bracing, pickup optional.

1992-2004		$2,500	$3,300

VJ (Vintage Jumbo)
2000-present. 16" scale, round shouldered body, sitka spruce, figured mahogany back and sides, natural.

2000-2019		$2,300	$3,000

MODEL		EXC. COND.	
YEAR	FEATURES	LOW	HIGH

Santos Martinez

Ca. 1997-present. Intermediate grade, production, acoustic and electro-acoustic classical guitars, imported from China by John Hornby Skewes & Co. in the U.K.

Sardonyx

1978-1979. Guitars and basses built by luthier Jeff Levin in the back of Matt Umanov's New York City guitar shop, industrial looking design with 2 aluminum outrigger-style tubes extended from the rectangle body. Very limited production.

Saturn

1960s-1970s. Imported, most likely from Japan, solid and semi-hollow body electric guitars and basses. Large S logo with Saturn name inside the S. Many sold through Eaton's in Canada.

Saturn
1960s-1970s. Solidbody, 4 pickups.

1960s-70s		$325	$425

Sawchyn Guitars

1972-present. Professional and premium grade, production/custom, flat-top and flamenco guitars and mandolins built by luthier Peter Sawchyn in Regina, Saskatchewan.

Schaefer

1997-2014. Premium grade, production/custom, flat-top acoustic guitars built by luthier Edward A. Schaefer in Austin, Texas. He previously built archtops, basses and mandolins. He retired in '14.

Schecter

1976-present. Intermediate, professional and premium grade, production/custom, acoustic and electric guitars and basses. Guitar component manufacturer founded in California by four partners (David Schecter's name sounded the best), started offering complete instruments in '79. The company was bought out and moved to Dallas, Texas in the early '80s. By '88 the company was back in California and in '89 was purchased by Hisatake Shibuya. Schecter Custom Shop guitars are made in Burbank, California and their intermediate grade Diamond Series is made in South Korea.

Scheerhorn

1989-present. Professional and premium grade, custom, resonator and Hawaiian guitars built by luthier Tim Scheerhorn in Kentwood, Michigan. Around 2010, Scheerhorn becomes a division of National Reso-Phonic.

Schoenberg

1986-present. Premium grade, production/custom, flat-tops offered by Eric Schoenberg of Tiburon, California. From '86-'94 guitars made to Schoenberg's specifications by Martin. From '86-'90 constructed by Schoenberg's luthier and from '90-'94 assembled by Martin but voiced and inlaid in the Schoenberg shop. Current models made to Schoenberg specs by various smaller shops.

Schon

1986-1991. Designed by guitarist Neal Schon, early production by Charvel/Jackson building about 200 in the San Dimas factory. The final 500 were built by Larrivee in Canada. Leo Knapp also built custom Schon guitars from '85-'87, and '90s custom-made Schon guitars were also available.

Standard (Canadian-made)
1987-1991. Made in Canada on headstock.

1987-1991		$500	$650

Standard (U.S.A.-made)
1986 only. San Dimas/Jackson model, single-cut, pointy headstock shape, Made in U.S.A. on headstock.

1986		$1,200	$1,550

Schramm Guitars

1990-present. Premium grade, production/custom, classical and flamenco guitars built by luthier David Schramm in Clovis, California.

Schroder Guitars

Luthier Timothy Schroeder (he drops the first e in his name on the guitars) builds premium grade, production/custom, archtops in Northbrook, Illinois. He began in 1993.

Schulte

1950s-2000. Luthier C. Eric Schulte made solidbody, semi-hollow body, hollow body and acoustic guitars, both original designs and copies, covering a range of prices, in the Philadelphia area.

Custom Copy
1982. Single-cut solidbody, figured maple top.

1982		$600	$800

Schulz

Ca. 1903-1917. Luthier August Schulz built harp guitars and lute-guitars in Nuremberg, Germany.

Harp Guitar

1906		$775	$1,000

Schwartz Guitars

1992-present. Premium grade, custom, flat-top guitars built by luthier Sheldon Schwartz in Concord, Ontario.

ScoGo

Professional and premium grade, production/custom, solidbody guitars built by luthier Scott Gordon in Parkesburg, Pennsylvania starting in 2001.

Scorpion Guitars

1998-2014. Professional and premium grade, custom, solidbody guitars made by Ed Roman Guitars.

Schaefer FTG

Schoenberg The Quartet

GUITARS

Seagull Maritime SWS Concert Hall SG

Sekova Single Cut

Scott French

2004-present. Professional grade, production/custom, electric guitars and basses built by luthier Scott French in Auburn, California. In '12 he discontinued offering custom built.

Scott Walker Custom Guitars

Refer to S. Walker Custom Guitars.

SeaGlass Guitars USA

2011-present. Professional grade, production/custom, electric guitars, built by luthier Roger Mello in Groton, Massachusetts.

Seagull

1982-present. Intermediate grade, production, acoustic and acoustic/electric guitars built in Canada. Seagull was founded by luthier Robert Godin, who also has the Norman, Godin, and Patrick & Simon brands of instruments.

Sebring

1980s-mid-1990s. Entry level Korean imports distributed by V.M.I. Industries.

Seiwa

Early 1980s. Entry-level to mid-level Japanese electric guitars and basses, logo may indicate Since 1956.

Sekova

Mid-1960s-mid-1970s. Entry level instruments imported by the U.S. Musical Merchandise Corporation of New York.

Selmer

1932-1952. France-based Selmer & Cie was primarily a maker of wind instruments when they asked Mario Maccaferri to design a line of guitars for them. The guitars, with an internal sound chamber for increased volume, were built in Mantes-la-Ville. Both gut and steel string models were offered. Maccaferri left Selmer in '33, but guitar production continued, and the original models are gradually phased out. In '36, only the 14 fret oval model is built. Production is stopped for WWII and resumes in '46, finally stopping in '52. Less than 900 guitars are built in total.

Classique
1942. Solid Rosewood back and sides, no cutaway, solid spruce top, round soundhole, classical guitar size, possibly only 2 built.

MODEL YEAR FEATURES	EXC. COND. LOW	HIGH
1942	$3,900	$5,000

Concert
1932-1933. For gut strings, cutaway, laminated Indian rosewood back and sides, internal resonator, spruce top with D hole, wide walnut neck, ebony 'board, only a few dozen built.

1932	$8,850	$11,500
1933	$12,300	$16,000

Eddie Freeman Special
1933. For steel strings, 4 strings, laminated Indian rosewood back and sides, cutaway, no internal resonator, solid spruce top, D hole, black and white rosette inlays, walnut 12 fret neck, ebony 'board, 640mm scale, approx. 100 made.

1933	$4,200	$5,500

Espagnol
1932. For gut strings, laminated Indian rosewood back and sides, no cutaway, internal resonator, solid spruce top, round soundhole, wide walnut neck, ebony 'board, only a few made.

1932	$6,000	$7,800

Grand Modele 4 Cordes
1932-1933. For steel strings, 4 string model, laminated back and sides, cutaway, internal resonator, solid spruce top, D hole, walnut neck, ebony 'board, 12 fret, 640mm scale, 2 or 3 dozen made.

1932-1933	$8,800	$11,500

Harp Guitar
1933. For gut strings, solid mahogany body, extended horn holding 3 sub bass strings, 3 screw adjustable neck, wide walnut neck, ebony 'board, only about 12 built.

1933	$8,800	$11,500

Hawaienne
1932-1934. For steel strings, 6 or 7 strings, laminated back and sides, no cutaway, internal resonator, solid spruce top, D hole, wide walnut neck, ebony 'board, 2 or 3 dozen built.

1932-1934	$19,000	$24,500

Modele Jazz
1936-1942, 1946-1952. For steel strings, laminated Indian rosewood back and sides (some laminated or solid mahogany), cutaway, solid spruce top, small oval soundhole, walnut neck, ebony 'board (latest ones with rosewood necks), 14 fret to the body, 670mm scale. Production interrupted for WWII.

1936-1952	$24,000	$31,000

Modeles de Transition
1934-1936. Transition models appearing before 14 fret oval hole model, some in solid maple with solid headstock, some with round soundhole and cutaway, some 12 fret models with oval hole.

1934-1936	$14,200	$18,500

Orchestre
1932-1934. For steel strings, laminated back and sides, cutaway, internal resonator, solid spruce top, D hole, walnut neck, ebony 'board, about 100 made.

1932-1934	$25,500	$33,000

Tenor
1932-1933. For steel strings, 4 strings, laminated back and sides, internal resonator, solid spruce top, D hole, walnut neck, ebony 'board, 12 fret, 570mm scale, 2 or 3 dozen built.

1932-1933	$3,550	$4,600

Serenghetti

2007-present. Luthier Ray Patterson builds professional and premium grade, production/custom, 1-piece and neck-thru guitars and basses in Ocala, Florida.

MODEL YEAR	FEATURES	EXC. COND. LOW	HIGH
814 Series			

1993-present. Grand Auditorium, Indian rosewood back and sides, sitka spruce top. Non-cut offered again in '13 along with 814e version.

MODEL YEAR	FEATURES	EXC. COND. LOW	HIGH
1993-1998	814	$1,500	$2,000
1996-1998	814c	$1,550	$2,050
1998-2017	814ce	$1,650	$2,200
2000	814-BE (Brazilian/ Englemann)	$2,500	$3,200
2018-2019	814ce V-Class braces	$2,100	$2,700

814ce-LTD

2012. Spring Limited Edition, cocobolo back and sides, sitka spruce top.

2012		$1,900	$2,500

815 Series

1970s-2011. Jumbo, Indian rosewood back and sides, sitka spruce top.

1970s-2006	815	$1,775	$2,350
1993-1998	815c	$1,825	$2,400
1997	815c-BR (Brazilian)	$2,500	$3,200
1998-2011	815ce	$1,875	$2,450

816 Series

2008-2019. Grand Symphony, sitka spruce top, Indian rosewood back and sides.

2008-2014	816e	$1,825	$2,400
2008-2019	816ce	$1,875	$2,450
2013-2016	816	$1,775	$2,350

818 Series

2014-present. Grand Orchestra, sitka spruce, Indian rosewood.

2014-2019	818e	$1,850	$2,425

854ce-LTD

2002		$1,900	$2,500

855 Series

1981-2011. Jumbo 12-string, Indian rosewood back and sides, sitka spruce top.

1981-2011		$1,600	$2,100

856 Series

2013-2019. Grand Symphony 12-string, sitka spruce, Indian rosewood.

2013-2019	856ce	$1,700	$2,200

910 Series

1977-2017. Dreadnought, maple back and sides, changed to Brazilian rosewood in '86, wide abalone-style rosette. Non-cut offered again in '13 along with 910e version, Indian rosewood back and sides, sitka spruce top.

1977-1985	910 Maple	$2,300	$3,100
1986-2006	910 Brazilian	$3,900	$5,200
1998-2016	910ce	$2,400	$3,200

912 Series

1993-present. Grand Concert, Indian rosewood back and sides, Engelmann spruce top, abalone. Non-cut offered in '13 along with 912e version.

1993-2002	912c	$2,350	$3,150
1993-2019	912ce	$2,400	$3,200

914 Series

1990s-present. Grand Concert, Indian rosewood back and sides, Engelmann spruce top. Non-cut offered in '13 along with 914e version.

2002-2019	914ce	$2,400	$3,200

914ce-L1

2003. Fall Limited Edition, Indian rosewood back and sides, Engelmann spruce top, abalone leaf and vine inlays.

2003		$2,400	$3,200

914ce-L7

2004. Sitka spruce top, Brazilian rosewood back and sides, abalone rosette.

2004		$3,750	$5,000

916ce

2008-2019. Grand Symphony, Indian rosewood back and sides.

2008-2019		$2,400	$3,200

918 Series

2013-2014. Grand Orchestra, sitka spruce top, Indian rosewood back and sides.

2013-2014	918e	$2,400	$3,200

955

1970s-2006. Jumbo 12 string, rosewood back and sides, spruce top.

1970s-2006		$2,400	$3,200

Baby Taylor

1996-present. 3/4-size Dreadnought, mahogany laminated back and sides until '99, sapele laminate after, various tops.

1996-2019	BT1, sitka spruce	$185	$240
1998-2019	BT2, mahogany	$185	$240
2000-2003	BT3, maple	$185	$240
2016-2019	BTe-Koa	$250	$325
2010-2019	TSBT Taylor Swift	$185	$240

Baby Rosewood

2000-2003. Laminated Indian rosewood back and sides Baby.

2000-2003		$185	$240

Baritone 6

2010-2013. 6-string Grand Symphony, Indian rosewood or mahogany back and sides.

2010-2013		$1,750	$2,300

Baritone 8/GT-8

2010-2013. 8-string Grand Symphony, Indian rosewood or mahogany back and sides.

2010-2014		$2,100	$2,800

Big Baby BBT

2000-present. 15/16-size Dreadnought, sapele laminate back and sides, sitka spruce top.

2000-2019		$225	$300

Builder's Reserve (BR)

A series of special limited guitars built using Taylor's private wood reserves accumulated 30-plus years.

2008	BR VII	$1,750	$2,300

CPSM Chris Proctor Signature

2001. Limited edition, 100 made, Indian rosewood body, Engelmann spruce top.

2001		$1,650	$2,125

CUJO Model

1997. Dreadnought (CUJO-10) or Grand Auditorium (CUJO-14), made from 100+ year old black walnut tree appearing in famous Stephen King movie "Cujo" (1983). Robert Taylor purchased the tree when it was dying of old age. The DN has spruce top, GA has cedar,

Taylor 914ce

Taylor 814ce

Baby Taylor

2014 Taylor K-22ce
Craig Brody

MODEL YEAR	FEATURES	EXC. COND. LOW	HIGH

both have elaborate appointments and are signed by Taylor and King. Only 125 made of each.

| 1997 | CUJO-10, CUJO-14 | $1,425 | $1,850 |

Custom Shop
2008-present. Custom shop models - some are one-offs, others are series ordered by specific dealers. Previously called Taylor's Build To Order program.

Custom Dreadnought/Custom DN
| 2008-2017 | AA+ Indian/ Adirondack | $2,000 | $2,600 |

Custom Grand Auditorium
2008-2017	Adirondack/ mahogany	$2,000	$3,200
2008-2019	Figured koa	$3,500	$4,500
2008-2019	Spruce/maple	$2,000	$3,200

Custom Grand Concert
| 2008-2017 | Rosewood/ ovangkol | $2,000 | $3,200 |

Custom TF
Acoustic-electric, mahogany back and sides.
| 2011 | | $1,750 | $2,300 |

DCSM Dan Crary Signature
1986-2000. Dreadnought, Venetian cutaway, thin spruce top, Indian rosewood back and sides, Crary signature on headstock.
| 1986-2000 | | $1,475 | $1,900 |

DDAD Doyle Dykes Signature Anniversary
2005. Indian rosewood back and sides, soft cutaway, on-board transducer.
| 2005 | | $2,400 | $3,100 |

DDSM Doyle Dykes Signature
2000-2012. Grand auditorium cutaway acoustic/electric, figured maple body.
| 2000-2012 | | $2,400 | $3,100 |

DMSM Dave Matthews Signature
2010-2012. Limited Edition based on 914ce, Taylor Expression pickup system.
| 2010-2012 | | $3,600 | $4,600 |

DN Series
2007-2012. Dreadnought Series, various woods.
2007-2011	DNK (koa)	$1,750	$2,300
2007-2012	DN3	$750	$950
2007-2012	DN5	$1,050	$1,400
2007-2012	DN8	$1,150	$1,500

GA Limited Editions
1995. Grand Auditorium Limited Editions. GA-BE has Brazilian rosewood back and sides with Engelmann spruce top, KC has koa/cedar, KS koa/spruce, MC mahogany/cedar, RS Indian rosewood/spruce, and WS walnut/spruce.
1995	GA-BE, 50 made	$3,700	$4,800
1995	GA-KC	$2,300	$3,000
1995	GA-MC	$2,000	$2,600
1995	GA-RS, 300 made	$2,000	$2,600
1995	GA-WS	$2,200	$2,800

GA Series
2007-2012. Grand Auditorium Series, various woods.
2007-2012	GA3, sapele	$750	$950
2007-2012	GA3-12	$750	$950
2007-2012	GA4, ovangkol	$800	$1,050
2007-2012	GA5, mahogany	$1,075	$1,400

MODEL YEAR	FEATURES	EXC. COND. LOW	HIGH
2007-2012	GA6, maple	$1,225	$1,575
2007-2012	GA6-12, maple	$1,250	$1,600
2007-2012	GA7, rosewood	$1,225	$1,575
2007-2012	GA8, rosewood	$1,150	$1,500
2008-2012	GA-K-12, koa	$1,800	$2,300
2012	GA-CE	$1,700	$2,200
2013	GA-MC	$1,700	$2,200

GC Series
2007-2012. Grand Concert Series, various woods.
2007-2012	GC3, sapele	$750	$950
2007-2012	GC4, ovangkol	$800	$1,400
2007-2012	GC5, mahogany	$1,075	$1,400
2007-2012	GC6, maple	$1,225	$1,575
2007-2012	GC7, rosewood	$1,225	$1,575
2007-2012	GC8, rosewood	$1,150	$1,500
2011	GC-LTD, mahogany	$1,150	$1,500

GS Series
2006-present. Grand Symphony Series, various woods.
2007	GS4E-LTD	$1,075	$1,400
2007-2012	GS3, sapele	$750	$950
2007-2012	GS5, mahogany	$1,075	$1,400
2007-2012	GS5-12, mahogany	$1,175	$1,500
2007-2012	GS6, maple	$1,225	$1,575
2007-2012	GS7, cedar	$1,225	$1,575
2007-2012	GS8, rosewood	$1,150	$1,500
2007-2012	GS8-12, rosewood	$1,250	$1,600
2011-2019	GS Mini, sapele	$275	$350
2019-2020	GS Mini-E, koa	$450	$550
2019-2020	GS Mini-E, mahogany	$350	$450

Hot Rod Limited Edition HR14-LTD/HR15-LTD
2003. Grand Auditorium (HR14) or Jumbo (HR15), 32 of each made, natural finish with red-stained back and sides or gloss black with transparent black.
| 2003 | | $1,900 | $2,500 |

K Series
1983-present. Koa Series, various models with Hawaiian koa.
1983-1992	K20	$1,750	$2,250
1983-2006	K10	$1,450	$1,900
1992-2002	K20c	$1,800	$2,300
1995-1998	K65, 12-string	$2,300	$3,000
1998-2000	K22	$1,850	$2,400
1998-2002	K14c	$1,600	$2,100
1998-2012	K14ce	$1,650	$2,150
2001-2006	K55, 12-string	$2,300	$3,000
2001-2016	K20ce	$1,850	$2,375
2003-2019	K22ce	$2,300	$3,000
2007-2011	K54ce	$2,400	$3,100
2007-2012	K10ce	$1,550	$2,000
2007-2019	K24ce	$2,200	$2,900
2008-2019	K26ce	$2,300	$3,000
2019	K24ce V-Class	$2,200	$2,900

LKSM-6/12 Leo Kottke Signature
1981-2012. Jumbo 17" body, 6- or 12-string, rounded cutaway, sitka spruce top, mahogany back and sides, gloss finish, Leo Kottke signature.
| 1981-2012 | 12-string | $1,850 | $2,450 |
| 1981-2012 | 6-string | $1,850 | $2,450 |

GUITARS

MODEL YEAR	FEATURES	EXC. COND. LOW	HIGH

LTG Liberty Tree L.E.

2002. Limited Edition includes DVD and certificate which are important to instrument's value, solid wood grand concert body, high-end art and appointments. Around 400 made.

2002		$4,500	$5,900

NS Series

2002-2011. Nylon Strung series, various models and woods, models include NS24e/NS24ce (Indian rosewood/spruce), NS32ce/NS34ce (mahogany/spruce), NS42ce/NS44ce (ovangkol), NS52ce/NS54ce (mahogany), NS62ce/NS64ce (maple/Engelmann) and NS72ce/NS74ce (Indian rosewood/cedar). All models were cutaway electric (ce) by '04, until '10 when NS24e was offered.

2002-2006	NS42ce	$750	$975
2002-2006	NS44/NS44ce	$825	$1,100
2002-2006	NS52ce	$850	$1,125
2002-2006	NS54ce	$925	$1,225
2002-2011	NS32ce	$700	$925
2002-2011	NS62ce	$1,175	$1,525
2002-2011	NS64ce	$1,200	$1,550
2002-2011	NS72ce	$1,375	$1,800
2002-2011	NS74/NS74ce	$1,600	$2,100
2004-2011	NS34ce	$725	$950
2010-2011	NS24e/NS24ce	$500	$650

PS Series

1996-present. Presentation Series, various models, Hawaiian koa with Engelmann spruce used early on, followed by Brazilian rosewood, by '07 a variety of woods were offered, values vary depending on specs and appointments.

1996-2019	Various options	$3,800	$6,500

Solidbody Classic

2008-2014. Single- or double-cut, ash body, 2 humbuckers or single-coils, pearl 'guard.

2008-2014		$725	$950

Solidbody Custom

2008-2010. Single- or double-cut, koa top with Tasmanian blackwood body in '08 and mahogany after or walnut top with sapele body, 2 humbuckers, diamond inlays, ivoroid binding.

2008-2010	Various (figured top)	$1,200	$1,900

Solidbody Standard

2008-2014. Single- or double-cut, Tamo ash top ('08-'09) and maple after, sapele body (08-'10) and mahogany after, 2 exposed coil humbuckers, ivoroid binding.

2008-2014		$700	$1,200

T3 Series

2009-present. Semi-hollow thinline, single-cut, figured maple. T3/B with Bigsby.

2009-2019	T3, T3/B	$1,400	$1,800

T5 Series

2005-present. Semi-hollow thinline body, sapele back and sides, spruce, maple, or koa tops, Custom models have gold hardware and Artist inlays, Standard is chrome with micro-dots. Prices will vary depending on type of figured-wood used, figured maple and koa will be more than plain tops.

2005-2019	12-string	$1,500	$2,000
2005-2019	6-string	$1,500	$2,000

Walnut/W Series

1998-2006. Highly figured claro walnut backs and sides with spruce, cedar or walnut tops. Ivoroid, ebony, gold and abalone accents.

1998-2000	W12c	$1,625	$2,125
1998-2006	W10	$1,500	$1,950
2000-2006	W14ce	$1,675	$2,175

WHCM Windham Hill

2003. Commemorative Model, D-size, spruce top, rosewood sides and back, fancy appointments with Windham Hill logo inlay.

2003		$1,400	$1,800

XX 20th Anniversary Series

1994. Limited Edition, grand auditorium, "XX" solid 18 karat gold inlay, mother-of-pearl inlay, abalone rosette, available either mahogany back and sides with cedar top (XX-MC) or Indian rosewood with spruce (XX-RS).

1994	XX-MC	$2,000	$2,700
1994	XX-RS	$2,000	$2,700

XXV 25th Anniversary

1999-2000. Dreadnought (XXV-DR) and grand auditorium (XXV-GA) models, various woods.

1999-2000	XXV-DR, XXV-GA	$1,600	$2,050

XXX 30th Anniversary Series

2004-2005. Limited Edition, grand concert, "XXX" solid 18 karat gold inlay, fancy appointments, XXX-BE has Brazilian rosewood back and sides with Engelmann spruce top, KE has koa/Engelmann spruce, MS maple/spruce and RS Indian rosewood/spruce.

2004-2005	XXX-BE	$3,500	$4,500
2004-2005	XXX-KE	$2,100	$2,800
2004-2005	XXX-MS	$2,000	$2,700
2004-2005	XXX-RS	$2,000	$2,700

XXXV 35th Anniversary Series

2009. Limited Edition, various models and woods, "35" between the 11th and 12th frets. Models include DN (Dreadnought), GC (Grand Concert), GS (Grand Symphony), P (Parlor), TF (12-Fret), 9-string, plus more.

2009	XXXV-9, 9-string	$2,000	$2,700

Taylor/R. Taylor Guitars

2006-2011. Bob Taylor set up the R. Taylor studio with a small group of elite luthiers to handcraft a limited amount of guitars each year, using higher grade materials and offered in a few body styles - essentially custom made models. Each style has a number of options.

Style 1

2006-2009	Various options	$2,400	$3,100

Teisco

Founded in 1946 in Tokyo, Japan by Hawaiian and Spanish guitarist Atswo Kaneko and electrical engineer Doryu Matsuda, the original company name was Aoi Onpa Kenkyujo; Teisco was the instrument name. Most imported into U.S. by Jack Westheimer beginning ca. '60 and Chicago's W.M.I. Corporation beginning around '64, some early ones for New York's Bugeleisen and Jacobson. Brands

Taylor PS14ce

Taylor T5 Standard

1969 Teisco May Queen
Rivington Guitars

1965 Teisco ET 100 Tulip
Jim Edwards

made by the company include Teisco, Teisco Del Rey, Kingston, World Teisco, Silvertone, Kent, Kimberly and Heit Deluxe.

In '56, the company's name was changed to Nippon Onpa Kogyo Co., Ltd., and in '64 the name changed again to Teisco Co., Ltd. In January '67, the company was purchased by Kawai. After '73, the brand was converted to Kay in U.S.; Teisco went into hiatus in Japan until being beifly revived in the early-'90s with plexiglas reproductions of the Spectrum 5 (not available in U.S.). Some older Teisco Del Rey stock continued to be sold in U.S. through the '70s.

Electric

Model Year	Features	Exc. Cond. Low	High
1966-1969	1 pickup	$100	$175
1966-1969	2 pickups	$150	$300
1966-1969	3 pickups	$175	$350
1966-1969	4 pus or sparkle	$350	$600
1966-1969	Spectrum V	$425	$700
1968-1969	May Queen, black	$425	$700
1968-1969	May Queen, red	$425	$700
1968-1969	Phantom	$425	$700

Tele-Star

1965-ca.1972. Imported from Japan by Tele-Star Musical Instrument Corporation of New York, New York. Primarily made by Kawai, many inspired by Burns designs, some in cool sparkle finishes. They also built basses.

Electric

Model Year	Features	Exc. Cond. Low	High
1966-1969	1, 2, or 3 pickups	$100	$375
1966-1969	4 pus or sparkle	$275	$425
1966-1969	Amp-in-case	$250	$325
1969-1970	Double neck 6/4	$525	$675

Tempo

1950s-1970s. Solid and semi-hollow body electric and acoustic guitars, most likely imported by Merson Musical Products from Japan. They also offered basses and amps.

Terada

Japanese guitar manufacturer began producing semi-acoustic and acoustic guitars in the year 1912. They have made guitars for Ibanez, Orville by Gibson, Epiphone Japan, Gretsch, and other well-known brands. At their peak (late '70s to early '90s), they were producing around 10,000 guitars a month using 3 factories. Terada's output is presently about 1/8 of what it was at their peak.

Teuffel

1988-present. Luthier Ulrich Teuffel builds his production/custom, premium and presentation grade electric solidbody guitars in Neu-Ulm, Bavaria, Germany.

Texas

1959-ca. 1965. Line of aluminum neck electric solidbodies and basses made by France's Jacobacci company, which also built under its own brand. One, two, or three pickups.

Teye

2006-present. Luthier Teye Wijterp builds his premium and presentation grade, production/custom, solid and chambered body guitars in Austin, Texas. Some instruments are branded as Electric Gypsy guitars.

Thomas

1960s-1970s. Single, double and triple-neck electrics made by luthier Harvey Thomas in Midway, Washington. Best known for his Maltese cross shaped models, he also offered several other unique shaped designs and one-offs.

Thomas Rein

1972-present. Luthier Thomas Rein builds his premium grade, production/custom, classical guitars in St. Louis, Missouri.

Thompson Guitars

1980-present. Luthier Ted Thompson builds his professional and premium grade, production/custom, flat-top, 12-string, and nylon-string guitars in Vernon, British Columbia.

Thorell Fine Guitars

1994-present. Premium grade, custom/production, archtop, flattop and classical guitars built by luthier Ryan Thorell in Logan, Utah.

Thorn Custom Guitars

2000-present. Professional and premium grade, custom/production, solid and hollowbody electrics built by luthiers Bill Thorn and his sons Bill, Jr. and Ron in Glendale, California. They started Thorn Custom Inlay in the early '90s to do custom inlay work for other builders. In '00, they added their own line of guitars.

Thornward

Ca. 1901-ca. 1910. Line of guitars sold by the Montgomery Ward company and built by others including Lyon & Healy. The name is from a combination of last names of company founder Aaron Montgomery Ward and company manager George Thorne.

Threet Guitars

1990-present. Premium grade, production/custom, flat-tops built by luthier Judy Threet in Calgary, Alberta.

Tilton

1850s-late 1800s. Built by William B. Tilton, of New York City, New York. He was quite an innovator and held several guitar-related patents. He also built banjos.

Parlor

1850s-1890s. Parlor guitar with various woods.

Model Year	Features	Exc. Cond. Low	High
1850s-80s	Brazilian, fancy binding	$1,600	$2,100

MODEL YEAR	FEATURES	EXC. COND. LOW	HIGH
1890s	Diagonal grain spruce, Brazilian	$1,200	$1,600
1890s	Pearl trim, Brazilian	$2,300	$3,000
1890s	Standard grain spruce, Brazilian	$650	$850

Tim Reede Custom Guitars

2004-present. Luthier Tim Reede builds his professional and premium grade, production/custom, archtop, flat-top and electric guitars in Minneapolis, Minnesota.

Timeless Instruments

1980-present. Luthier David Freeman builds his professional, premium and presentation grade, custom, flattop, 12-string, nylon-string, and resonator guitars in Tugaske, Saskatchewan. He also builds mandolins and dulcimers.

Timm Guitars

Professional grade, custom, flat-top, resonator and travel guitars built by luthier Jerry Timm in Auburn, Washington. He started in 1997.

Timtone Custom Guitars

1993-2006. Luthier Tim Diebert built his premium grade, custom, solidbody, chambered-body and acoustic guitars and basses in Grand Forks, British Columbia. He also built lap steels.

Tippin Guitar Co.

1978-present. Professional, premium and presentation grade, production/custom, flat-top guitars built by luthier Bill Tippin in Marblehead, Massachusetts.

Tobias

1977-2019. Known mainly for basses, Tobias did offer guitar models in the '80s. See Bass Section for more company info.

TogaMan GuitarViol

2003-present. Premium grade, production/custom, bow-playable solidbody guitars built by luthier Jonathan Wilson in Sylmar, California.

Tokai

1947-present. Japan's Tokai Company started out making a keyboard harmonica that was widely used in Japanese schools. In '65, they started producing acoustic guitars, followed shortly by electrics. In the late '60s, Tokai hooked up with Tommy Moore, a successful instrument merchandiser from Fort Worth, Texas, and by '70 they were producing private label and OEM guitars, sold in the U.S. under the brands of various importers. By the '70s, the Tokai name was being used on the instruments. Today Tokai continues to offer electrics, acoustics, and electric basses made in Japan and Korea.

MODEL YEAR	FEATURES	EXC. COND. LOW	HIGH
ASD-403 Custom Edition			
1980s. Strat copy, single-single-hum pickups, locking tremolo.			
1980s		$500	$650
AST Series			
Early 1980s. Strat copies, maple board (AST-56) or slab rosewood (AST-62), 3 single-coils.			
1980s	AST-56	$575	$775
1980s	AST-62	$575	$775
ATE Series			
Early 1980s. Tele copies, blond (ATE-52) and pink paisley (ATE-67), 2 single-coils.			
1980s	ATE-52	$575	$775
1980s	ATE-67	$575	$775
Blazing Fire			
1982-1984. Hybrid-shaped solidbody with 2 medium-short pointy horns, cast aluminum body.			
1982-1984		$500	$650
Breezy Sound			
1977-1984. Copy of '60s rosewood board Tele.			
1977-1984		$500	$650
CE-180W Cat's Eyes			
Late-1970s-Early-1980s. D-style flat-top, made by Tokai Gakki, Nyatoh sides and back.			
1979-1980s		$225	$300
CE-250 Cat's Eyes			
Late-1970s-Early-1980s. D-style flat-top.			
1979-1980s		$225	$300
CE-300 Cat's Eyes			
Late-1970s-Early-1980s. D-style flat-top, made by Tokai Gakki, rosewood sides and back.			
1979-1980s		$350	$450
CE-400 Cat's Eyes			
Late-1970s-Early-1980s. D-style flat-top, made by Tokai Gakki, rosewood sides and back.			
1979-1980s		$500	$650
CE-600 Cat's Eyes			
1979-1980. D-style flat-top, rosewood sides and back.			
1979-1980		$500	$650
FV48			
1980s. Flying V copy.			
1980s		$525	$700
Goldstar Sound			
1984. Replica that replaced the Springy Sound, new less pointy headstock shape.			
1984		$500	$650
J-200N			
1979-1980. Gibson J-200 natural copy.			
1979-1980		$500	$650
Les Paul Reborn			
1976-1985. LP copy with Gibson-style Tokai headstock logo and Les Paul Reborn script logo instead of Les Paul Model, renamed Reborn Old in '82, becomes Love Rock in mid-'80s.			
1976-1982	Les Paul Reborn	$700	$925
1982-1985	Reborn Old	$700	$925

1960s Tele-Star
Imaged by Heritage Auctions, HA.com

Thorell Luxurado

GUITARS

1982 Tokai AST-56
Vintage Series

Tony Nobles Baritone

MODEL YEAR	FEATURES	EXC. COND. LOW	HIGH

Love Rock/LS Series
1980s-2000s. Various LP Std copy models (LC are LP Custom copies), 2 humbuckers, sunburst, gold top, black, figured tops at the high end, Love Rock in script logo on headstock.

1980s		$700	$925
2003	LS 75 Love Rock	$700	$925
2003	LS 80 Love Rock	$700	$925

SC Series
Tele copies.

2000s	SC-1	$350	$450

Silver Star
1977-1984. Copy of post-CBS large headstock Strat.

1977-1984		$425	$550

Springy Sound/ST-60
1977-1984. Strat copy, original high-end nitro-finish.

1977-1979	With skunk stripe	$800	$1,025
1979-1984	No skunk stripe	$800	$1,025

Vintage Series EX-55
1980s. Vintage Series, Explorer copies, bolt neck, 1 or 2 humbuckers.

1980s	1 pickup	$500	$650
1980s	2 pickups	$550	$700

Vintage Series TST
Early-1980s. Copy of maple neck (TST-56) and rosewood slab board (TST-62) Strats, 4-bolt neck plate with serial number.

1980s	TST-56	$575	$775
1980s	TST-62	$575	$775

Tom Anderson Guitarworks
1984-present. Professional and premium grade, production/custom, solidbody, semi-solidbody and acoustic guitars built by luthier Tom Anderson in Newbury Park, California.

Solidbody Electric
1984-present. Various models.

1984-2019	Most models	$1,600	$2,400
1984-2019	Private stock or custom models	$2,100	$3,000

TommyHawk
1993-2005. Acoustic travel guitars built by luthier Tom Barth in Succasunna, New Jersey. They also offered a full-scale acoustic/electric model. Barth died in '05.

Toneline
1950s. Student-level private brand built by Chicago builders (Kay, Harmony). Typical '50s Stella brand specs like birch body with painted binding and rosette, pointed Toneline script logo on headstock.

Tonemaster
1960s. Guitars and basses, made in Italy by the Crucianelli Company, with typical '60s Italian sparkle plastic finish and push-button controls, bolt-on neck. Imported into the U.S. by The Imperial Accordion Company. They also offered guitar amps.

Rhythm Tone
1960-1963. Tonemaster headstock logo, Rhythm Tone logo on 'guard, single neck pickup, 3-in-line control knobs, bolt-on neck, black finish.

1960-1963		$700	$925

ToneSmith
1997-present. Luthier Kevin Smith builds his professional and premium grade, production/custom, semi-hollow body guitars and basses in Rogers, Minnesota. He previously built GLF brand guitars and built the line of Vox USA guitars from '98-'01.

Tony Nobles
Professional and premium grade, custom, acoustic and electric guitars built by luthier Tony Nobles in Wimberley, Texas starting in 1990.

Tony Vines Guitars
1989-present. Luthier Tony Vines builds his premium and presentation grade, custom/production, steel string guitars in Kingsport, Tennessee.

Torres (Antonio de Torres Jurado)
19th Century luthier most often associated with the initial development of the Classical Spanish guitar.

Tosca
1950s. Private economy brand made by Valco, possibly for a jobber, mail-order catalog or local department store.

Bolero 1123
1954-1957. Small three-quarter size electric similar to National (Valco) model 1123, single-cut, 1 neck pickup, guard mounted controls.

1954-1957		$600	$775

Toyota
1972-1970s. Imported from Japan by Hershman of New York, New York. At least 1 high-end acoustic designed by T. Kurosawa was ambitiously priced at $650.

Traphagen, Dake
1972-present. Luthier Dake Traphagen builds his premium grade, custom, classical and steel-string guitars in Bellingham, Washington.

Traugott Guitars
1991-present. Premium grade, production/custom, flat-top and acoustic/electric guitars built by luthier Jeff Traugott in Santa Cruz, California.

Traveler Guitar
1992-present. Intermediate grade, production, travel size electric, acoustic, classical and acoustic/electric guitars and basses made in Redlands, California.

Travis Bean

1974-1979, 1999. Aluminum-necked solidbody electric guitars and basses. The company was founded by motorcycle and metal-sculpture enthusiast Travis Bean and guitar repairman Marc McElwee in Southern California; soon joined by Gary Kramer (see Kramer guitars). Kramer left Travis Bean in '75 and founded Kramer guitars with other partners. Guitar production began in mid-'76. The guitars featured carved aluminum necks with three-and-three heads with a T cutout in the center and wooden 'boards. Some necks had bare aluminum backs, some were painted black. A total of about 3,650 instruments were produced. Travis Bean guitar production was stopped in the summer of '79.

Serial numbers were stamped on headstock and were more-or-less consecutive. Original retail prices were $895 to $1195.

The company announced renewed production in '99 with updated versions of original designs and new models, but it evidently never got going.

TB-500

1975-1976. Aluminum neck, T-slotted headstock, double-cut, 2 single coils mounted in 'guard, 2 controls, dot markers, white.

1975-1976	$4,000	$5,200

TB-1000 Artist

1974-1979. Aluminum neck, T-slotted headstock, double-cut archtop, 2 humbuckers, 4 controls, block inlays.

1974-1979	$4,000	$5,200
1974-1979	Rare colors	$4,700	$6,000

TB-1000 Standard

1974-1979. Similar to TB-1000 Artist, but with dot inlays.

1974-1979	$3,700	$4,800

TB-3000 Wedge

1976-1979. Aluminum neck with T-slotted headstock, triangle-shaped body, 2 humbucking pickups, 4 controls, block markers on 'board.

1976-1979	$4,300	$5,600

Tregan Guitars

2007-present. Solidbody electrics including Bison-style sharp curved horns body style, plus other less traditional styles, student and intermediate grade.

Tremblett Archtops

Luthier Mark Tremblett started in the year 2006, he builds professional grade, custom, archtop guitars in Pouch Cove, Newfoundland.

Tremcaster

2008-present. Luthier John Mosconi, along with Robert Gelley and Jeff Russell, builds professional grade, production/custom, electric and acoustic guitars in Akron, Ohio.

Trenier

1998-present. Premium grade, production/custom, archtop guitars built by luthier Bryant Trenier in Seattle, Washington. From '02 to '04 he was located in Prague, Czech Republic.

Triggs

1992-present. Luthiers Jim Triggs and his son Ryan build their professional and premium grade, production/custom, archtop, flat-top, and solidbody guitars originally in Nashville Tennessee, and, since '98, in Kansas City, Kansas. They also build mandolins.

Acoustic/Electric Archtop

1992-present. Various archtop cutaway models.

1992-2009	Byrdland 17"	$1,800	$2,400
1992-2009	Excel 17"	$2,700	$3,600
1992-2009	Jazzmaster	$1,500	$2,000
1992-2009	New Yorker 18"	$4,000	$5,300
1992-2010	Stromberg		
	Master 400	$4,000	$5,300
1997	Trinity 18"	$4,000	$5,300
2006	San Salvador	$2,300	$3,100

Trinity River

Located in Fort Worth, Texas, luthiers Marcus Lawyer and Ross McLeod import their production/custom, budget and intermediate grade, acoustic and resonator guitars and basses from Asia. They also import mandolins and banjos.

True North Guitars

1994-present. Luthier Dennis Scannell builds his premium grade, custom, flat-tops in Waterbury, Vermont.

True Tone

1960s. Guitars, basses and amps retailed by Western Auto, manufactured by Chicago guitar makers like Kay. The brand was most likely gone by '68.

Double Cutaway (K300 Kay)

1962-1966. Made by Kay and similar to their K300, double-cut solidbody, dual pickups and vibrola arm, red.

1962-1966	$365	$475

Double Cutaway Electric Archtop (K592 Kay)

1960s. Made by Kay and similar to their K592 double-cut thinline acoustic, 2 pickups, Bigsby tailpiece, burgundy red.

1960s	$400	$525

Fun Time

Early- to mid-1960s. Student 13" flat-top, painted 5-point 'guard, red sunburst finish.

1960s	$50	$65

Imperial Deluxe

Mid-1960s. Harmony-made (Rocket), 3 pickups, trapeze tailpiece, 6 control knobs, block markers, sunburst.

1960s	$525	$675

Traveler Acoustic AG-105

Triggs Custom

Early 1960s Truetone Speed Master (K6533 Kay)
Tom Pfeifer

1994 Tut Taylor Spider Cone
Bernunzio Uptown Music

MODEL YEAR	FEATURES	EXC. COND. LOW	HIGH
Jazz King (K573 Kay)			
1960s. Kay's K573 Speed Demon, 3 pickups, thinline archtop electric with f-hole, eighth note art on 'guard, sunburst.			
1960s		$365	$475
Rock 'n Roll Electric (K100 Kay)			
1960s. Kay's K100, slab body, single pickup, but with a bright red multiple lacquer finish.			
1960s		$250	$325
Speed Master (K6533 Kay)			
1960s. Made by Kay and similar to their K6533 full-body electric archtop Value Leader line, eighth note art 'guard, sunburst.			
1960s		$300	$400
Western Spanish Auditorium			
Early- to mid-1960s. 15" flat-top, laminate construction, celluloid 'guard, sunburst.			
1960s		$125	$150

Tsunami

Custom, intermediate grade, one-off solidbody electric guitars built by luthier Paul Brzozowski, starting in 2009, in Cleveland, Tennessee.

Tucker

Founded by John N. "Jack" Tucker, John Morrall, and David Killingsworth in 2000, Tucker builds professional and premium grade, production/custom, albizzia wood solidbody guitars and basses in Hanalei, Hawaii.

Tuscany Guitars

2008-2013. Intermediate grade, production, classic model electric guitars imported from Asia and finished by luthier Galeazzo Frudua in San Lazzaro di Savena, Italy.

Tut Taylor

Line of professional and premium grade, production/custom, resophonic guitars built by luthier Mark Taylor of Crafters of Tennessee in Old Hickory, Tennessee. Brand named for his father, dobro artist Tut Taylor. Taylor also builds the Tennessee line of guitars, mandolins and banjos and was part of Rich and Taylor guitars for '93-'96.

TV Jones

1993-present. Professional and premium grade, production/custom, hollow, chambered, and solid body guitars built by luthier Thomas Vincent Jones originally in California, now in Poulsbo, Washington. The instruments have either Jones or TV Jones inlaid on the headstock. He also builds pickups.

U. A. C.

1920s. Instruments built by the Oscar Schmidt Co. and possibly others. Most likely a brand made for a distributor.

Unique Guitars

2003-ca. 2007. Professional and premium grade, production/custom, solidbody guitars and basses built by luthier Joey Rico in California. Joey is the son of Bernie Rico, the founder of BC Rich guitars.

Univox

1964-1978. Univox started out as an amp line and added guitars around '68. Guitars were imported from Japan by the Merson Musical Supply Company, later Unicord, Westbury, New York. Many if not all supplied by Arai and Company (Aria, Aria Pro II), some made by Matsumoku. Univox Lucy ('69) first copy of lucite Ampeg Dan Armstrong. Generally mid-level copies of American designs.

MODEL YEAR	FEATURES	EXC. COND. LOW	HIGH
Acoustic Flat-Top			
1969-1978. Various models.			
1970s		$150	$550
Bicentennial			
1976. Offset double-cut, heavily carved body, brown stain, 3 humbucker-style pickups.			
1976		$675	$875
Deep Body Electric			
1960s-1970s. ES-175 style.			
1960-1970s		$425	$550
Guitorgan FSB C-3000			
1970s. Double-cut semi-hollow body, multiple controls, Guitorgan logo on headstock, footpedal.			
1970s		$775	$1,000
Solid Body Electric			
1960s-1970s. Includes Flying V, Mosrite and Hofner violin-guitar copies.			
1960-1970s	Hi Flier	$475	$625
1960-1970s	Various models	$300	$550
1970s	Effector	$425	$550
Thin Line (Coily)			
1960-1970s	12-string	$425	$550
1960-1970s	6-string	$425	$550

USA Custom Guitars

1999-present. Professional and premium grade, custom/production, solidbody electric guitars built in Tacoma, Washington. USA also does work for other luthiers.

Vaccaro

1997-2002. Founded by Henry Vaccaro, Sr., one of the founders of Kramer Guitars. They offered intermediate and professional grade, production/custom, aluminum-necked guitars and basses designed by Vaccaro, former Kramer designer Phil Petillo, and Henry Vaccaro, Jr., which were made in Asbury Park, New Jersey.

Val Dez

Early-1960s-early-1970s. Less expensive guitars built by Landola in Sweden or Finland; they also made the Espana brand.

MODEL YEAR	FEATURES	EXC. COND. LOW	HIGH

Valco

1942-1968. Valco, of Chicago, was a big player in the guitar and amplifier business. Their products were private branded for other companies like National, Supro, Airline, Oahu, and Gretsch. In '42, National Dobro ceased operations and Victor Smith, Al Frost and Louis Dopyera bought the company and changed the name to Valco Manufacturing Company. Post-war production resumed in '46. Valco was purchased by treasurer Robert Engelhardt in '64. In '67, Valco bought Kay, but in '68 the new Valco/Kay company went out of business.

Valencia

1985-present. Budget grade, production, classical guitars imported first by Rondo Music of Union, New Jersey and presently distributed by others.

Valley Arts

Ca. 1977-2010. Professional and premium grade, production/custom, semi-hollow and solidbody guitars and basses built in Nashville, Tennessee. Valley Arts originally was a Southern California music store owned by partners Al Carness and Mike McGuire where McGuire taught and did most of the repairs. Around '77, McGuire and Valley Arts started making custom instruments on a large scale. By '83, they opened a separate manufacturing facility to build the guitars. In '92 Samick acquired half of the company with McGuire staying on for a year as a consultant. Samick offered made-in-the-U.S. production and custom models under the Valley Arts name. In '02, Valley Arts became a division of Gibson Guitar Corp., which builds the guitars in Nashville. Founders Carness and McGuire were once again involved with the company. They reintroduced the line in January, '03. The brand has been inactive since '10.

Vantage

1977-1998. Budget and intermediate grade, production, acoustic and electric guitars and basses from Japan '77-'90 and from Korea '90-'98.

Vega

1889-1980s, 1989-present. Founded in Boston by the Nelson family, Vega was big in the banjo market into the 1930s, before adding guitars to their line. The company was purchased by C.F. Martin in '70 who built Vega banjos and starting in '76 they also used the brand on imported guitars, first from the Netherlands and later from Japan, with the Japanese Vegas being of higher quality. In '79, Martin sold the Vega trademark to Korea's Galaxy Trading Company. The Deering Banjo Company, in Spring Valley, California acquired the brand in '89 and uses it (and the star logo) on a line of banjos.

C Series Archtop

1933-1950s. Carved-top archtops, '30's models are the 14 5/8" mahogany body C-20 and C-40, 16 1/8" maple body C-60, and the C-70/C75 Vehaphone with

rosewood body and gold parts, and the figured-maple body C-80 with deluxe appointments. By '40 the line was the 14-16" C-19, -26, -46, and -56, and the 17" Professional Series C-66 Professional, C-71 Soloist, C-76 Artist, and C-86 Deluxe. Optional blond finish available by '40.

Year	Model	LOW	HIGH
1933-1939	C-20	$800	$1,050
1933-1939	C-40	$800	$1,050
1933-1939	C-60	$1,200	$1,600
1933-1939	C-70	$1,400	$1,800
1933-1939	C-80	$1,575	$2,025
1938	C-75	$2,400	$3,100
1940-1949	C-19, C-26, C-46	$700	$900
1940-1949	C-56	$1,275	$1,650
1940-1949	C-66 Professional	$1,350	$1,750
1940-1949	C-71 Soloist	$1,425	$1,850
1940-1949	C-76 Artist	$1,550	$2,000
1940-1949	C-86 Deluxe	$1,625	$2,100

Duo-Tron Series Electric Archtops

1947-late 1950s. Various mid-level large body cutaway and non-cut carved-top archtops, 1, 2 or 3 (rare) floating pickups, dot or block markers, natural or sunburst.

Year	Model	LOW	HIGH
1947-50s	Higher end models	$1,825	$2,400
1947-50s	Lower end models	$600	$775
1947-50s	Mid-range models	$875	$1,150

E-201 Electric Archtop

1959. One pickup, sunburst.

1959		$1,400	$1,850

FT-90 Flat-Top

1960s. 15" body with narrow waist, dot markers, Vega logo, natural.

1960s		$325	$420

G-30

1968-ca. 1970. D-style with solid spruce top and solid mahogany sides and back, Vega logo with star on headstock, dot markers, natural finish.

1968-1970		$250	$325

O'Dell

1950s. Full body, single cut, acoustic-electric, 1 pickup, tailpiece controls.

1950s	Sunburst	$850	$1,100

Parlor

Early-1900s-1920s. Small parlor-sized instrument, styles and appointment levels, including binding, purfling and inlays, vary.

1900s	Mahogany	$325	$425
1910-20s	Brazilian, fancy	$1,200	$3,900
1910s	Brazilian	$600	$1,050

Profundo Flat-Top

1930s-1950s. Flat-top D-style body, spruce top, mahogany or rosewood back and sides.

1930s-50s	Mahogany	$1,050	$1,400
1940s-50s	Rosewood	$1,700	$2,200

Solidbody Electric (Import)

1970s-1980s. Solidbody copies of classic designs, Vega script logo on headstock, bolt-on necks.

1970s		$200	$260

Valley Arts Custom Pro

Late-1940s Vega C-26

GUITARS

1982 Veillette-Citron Shark
Micheal Wright

1999 Versoul Henry Solidbody
Kari Nieminen

MODEL YEAR	FEATURES	EXC. COND. LOW	HIGH

Vega Electric Archtop

1939. Full-body electric archtop, figured maple, 1 pickup, 2 control knobs, trapeze bridge, diamond markers, large Vega and star headstock logo, blond.

1939		$875	$1,150

Vega, Charles

1993-2010. Luthier Charles Vega built his premium, production/custom, nylon-string guitars in Baltimore, Maryland.

Veillette

1991-present. Luthiers Joe Veillette (of Veillette-Citron fame) and Martin Keith build their professional grade, production/custom, acoustic, acoustic/electric, electric 6- and 12-string and baritone guitars and basses in Woodstock, New York. They also build mandolins.

Veillette-Citron

1975-1983. Founded by Joe Veillette and Harvey Citron who met at the New York College School of Architecture in the late '60s. Joe took a guitar building course from Michael Gurian and by the Summer of '76, he and Harvey started producing neck-thru solidbody guitars and basses. Veillette and Citron both are back building instruments.

Velázquez

1948-1972. Manuel Velázquez, New York, New York, gained a reputation as a fine repairman in the late 1940s. He opened his 3rd Avenue guitar building shop in the early 1950s. By the mid-1950s he was considered by some as being the finest American builder of classical guitars. Velázquez left New York in 1972 and moved to Puerto Rico. He continued building guitars for the Japanese market. He returned to the United States in 1982. By the 2000s he built instruments with this son and daughter.

Veleno

1967, 1970-1977, 2003-2018. Premium and presentation grade, production/custom, all-aluminum electric solidbody guitars built by luthier John Veleno in St. Petersburg, Florida. First prototype in '67. Later production begins in late-'70 and lasts until '75 or '76. The guitars were chrome or gold-plated, with various anodized colors. The Traveler Guitar was the idea of B.B. King; only 10 were made. Two Ankh guitars were made for Todd Rundgren in '77. Only one bass was made. Approximately 185 instruments were made up to '77 and are sequentially numbered. In 2003, John Veleno reintroduced his brand, he died in '18.

Original (Aluminum Solidbody)
1973-1976. V-headstock, chrome and aluminum.

1973-1976	Rare color	$5,900	$7,800
1973-1976	Standard	$3,400	$4,500

Traveler Guitar
1973-1976. Limited production of about a dozen instruments, drop-anchor-style metal body.

1973-1976		$5,900	$7,800

MODEL YEAR	FEATURES	EXC. COND. LOW	HIGH

Vengeance Guitars & Graphix

2002-present. Luthier Rick Stewart builds his professional and premium grade, custom/production, solidbody guitars and basses in Arden, North Carolina.

Ventura

1970s. Acoustic and electric guitars imported by C. Bruno Company, mainly copies of classic American models. They also offered basses.

Acoustic Flat-Top

1970s		$75	$375

Guitorgan
1970s. Based on MCI Guitorgan, converts standard electric guitar into a Guitorgan through the addition of electronic organ components, multiple switches, large Barney Kessel sharp-horned acoustic-electric style body.

1970s		$700	$900

Hollowbody Electric

1970s		$200	$600

Solidbody Electric

1970s		$200	$600

Verri

Premium grade, production/custom, archtop guitars built by luthier Henry Verri in Little Falls, New York starting in 1992.

Versoul, LTD

1989-present. Premium grade, production/custom steel-string flat-top, acoustic/electric, nylon-string, resonator, solidbody, and baritone guitars, basses and sitars built by luthier Kari Nieminen in Helsinki, Finland.

VibraWood

2012-present. Luthier John J. Slog builds custom, professional and premium grade, vintage-style guitars and basses in Bethlehem, Pennsylvania.

Vicente Tatay

1894-late 1930s. Classical guitars built by luthier Vicente Tatay and his sons in Valencia, Spain.

Victor Baker Guitars

1998-present. Professional and premium grade, custom, carved archtop, flat-top and solidbody electric guitars built by luthier Victor Baker in Philadelphia, Pennsylvania. In '10 he relocated to Brooklyn, New York and is currently in Astoria.

Victor Guitars

2002-2008. Luthiers Edward Victor Dick and Greg German built their premium grade, production/custom, flat-top guitars in Denver, Colorado.

Victoria

Ca. 1902-1920s. Brand name for New York distributor Buegeleisen & Jacobson. Instruments built by the Oscar Schmidt Co. and possibly others. Most likely a brand made for a distributor.

XOX Audio Tools

2007-present. U.S. debut in '08 of premium grade, production/custom, carbon fiber electric guitars built by luthier Peter Solomon in Europe.

Xtone

2003-2014. Semi-hollow body electric, acoustic and acoustic/electric guitars from ESP. Originally branded Xtone on headstock, in '10 the instruments were marketed as a model series under LTD (ESP's other brand) and stated as such on the headstock.

XXL Guitars

2003-present. Luthier Marc Lupien builds his production/custom, professional grade, chambered electric guitars in Montreal, Quebec.

Yamaha

1946-present. Budget, intermediate, professional, and presentation grade, production/custom, acoustic, acoustic/electric, and electric guitars. They also build basses, amps, and effects. The Japanese instrument maker was founded in 1887. Began classical guitar production around 1946. Solidbody electric production began in '66; steel string acoustics debut sometime after that. They began to export guitars into the U.S. in '69. Production shifted from Japan to Taiwan (Yamaha's special-built plant) in the '80s, though some high-end guitars still made in Japan. Some Korean production began in '90s.

Serialization patterns:
Serial numbers are coded as follows:
H = 1, I = 2, J = 3, etc., Z = 12
To use this pattern, you need to know the decade of production.
Serial numbers are ordered as follows:
Year/Month/Day/Factory Order
Example: NL 29159 represents a N=1987 year, L=5th month or May, 29=29th day (of May), 159=159th guitar made that day (the factory order). This guitar was the 159 guitar made on May 29, 1987.

AE Series
1966-2011. Archtop models.

Model Year	Features	Low	High
1966-2011	Higher-end	$700	$1,000
1966-2011	Lower-end	$150	$450
1966-2011	Mid-level	$450	$700

AES Series
1990-2011. Semi-hollowbody models.

Model Year	Features	Low	High
1990-2011	Higher-end	$700	$1,000
1990-2011	Lower-end	$150	$450
1990-2011	Mid-level	$450	$700

AEX1500
1995-2011. Full-body archtop electric, set neck, humbucker and piezo, EQ, multi-bound.

Model Year	Features	Low	High
1995-2011		$700	$1,000

APX Series
1987-present. Acoustic/electric, various features.

Model Year	Features	Low	High
1987-2019	Higher-end	$700	$1,000
1987-2019	Lower-end	$150	$450
1987-2019	Mid-level	$450	$700

CG Series
1984-present. Classical models.

Model Year	Features	Low	High
1984-2019	Higher-end	$250	$400
1984-2019	Lower-end	$50	$150
1984-2019	Mid-level	$150	$250

DW Series
1999-2002. Dreadnought flat-top models, sunburst, solid spruce top, higher-end appointments like abalone rosette and top purfling.

Model Year	Features	Low	High
1999-2002	Higher-end	$250	$400
1999-2002	Lower-end	$50	$150
1999-2002	Mid-level	$150	$250

EG Series
2000-2009. Electric solidbody models.

Model Year	Features	Low	High
2000-2009		$50	$250

Eterna Series
1983-1994. Folk-style acoustics, there were 4 models.

Model Year	Features	Low	High
1983-1994		$50	$175

FG Series
1970s-present. Economy market flat-top models, laminated sides and back, a 12 suffix indicates 12-string, CE indicates on-board electronics, many models are D-style bodies.

Model Year	Features	Low	High
1970-2019	Higher-end	$300	$700
1970-2019	Highest-end	$700	$1,000
1970-2019	Lower-end	$50	$150
1970-2019	Mid-level	$150	$300

G Series
1981-2000. Various Classical models.

Model Year	Features	Low	High
1981-2000		$50	$150

GC Series
1982-present. Classical models, '70s made in Japan, '80s made in Taiwan.

Model Year	Features	Low	High
1982-2019	Higher-end	$700	$1,500
1982-2019	Lower-end	$150	$450
1982-2019	Mid-level	$450	$700

Image Custom
1988-1992. Electric double-cut, Brazilian rosewood 'board, maple top, 2 humbuckers, active circuitry, LED position markers, script Image logo on truss rod cover. The Image was called the MSG in the U.K.

Model Year	Features	Low	High
1988-1992		$700	$1,500

L Series
1984-present. Custom hand-built flat-top models, solid wood.

Model Year	Features	Low	High
1984-2019	Higher-end	$700	$1,500
1984-2019	Lower-end	$350	$450
1984-2019	Mid-level	$450	$700

PAC Pacifica Series
1989-present. Offset double-cut with longer horns, dot markers, large script Pacifica logo and small block Yamaha logo on headstock, various models.

Model Year	Features	Low	High
1989-2019		$100	$500

RGX Series
1988-2011. Bolt-on neck for the 600 series and neck-thru body designs for 1200 series, various models include 110 (1 hum), 211 (hum-single), 220 (2 hums), 312 (hum-single-single), 603 (3 singles), 612 (hum-single-single), 620 (2 hums), 1203S (3 singles), 1212S (hum-single-single), 1220S (2 hums).

Model Year	Features	Low	High
1988-2011	Higher-end	$250	$500

2000 Yamaha AES-1500

2017 Yamaha FG-441S-12

1969 Yamaha SA-30T
Rhoads Music

MODEL YEAR	FEATURES	EXC. COND. LOW	HIGH
1988-2011	Lower-end	$50	$150
1988-2011	Mid-level	$150	$250

RGZ Series
1989-1994. Double-cut solidbodies, various pickups.

1989-1994	Higher-end	$250	$500
1989-1994	Lower-end	$50	$150
1989-1994	Mid-level	$150	$250

SA Series
1966-1994. Super Axe series, full-size and thinline archtop models.

1966-1994	Higher-end	$900	$1,200
1966-1994	Highest-end	$1,200	$1,600
1966-1994	Lower-end	$400	$600
1966-1994	Mid-level	$600	$900

SBG Series
1983-1992. Solidbody models, set necks, model name logo on truss rod cover.

1983-1992	Higher-end	$1,000	$1,300
1983-1992	Highest-end	$1,300	$1,900
1983-1992	Lower-end	$300	$600
1983-1992	Mid-level	$600	$1,000

SE Series
1986-1992. Solidbody electric models.

1986-1992	Higher-end	$350	$500
1986-1992	Lower-end	$150	$200
1986-1992	Mid-level	$200	$350

SF Series
1977-early 1980s. Super Flighter series, double-cut solidbody electrics, 2 humbuckers.

1977-80s	Various models	$575	$750

SG-3
1965-1966. Early double-cut solidbody with sharp horns, bolt neck, 3 hum-single pickup layout, large white guard, rotor controls, tremolo.

1965-1966		$775	$1,025

SG-5/SG-5A
1966-1971. Asymmetrical double-cut solidbody with extended lower horn, bolt neck, 2 pickups, chrome hardware.

1966-1971		$1,025	$1,350

SG-7/SG-7A
1966-1971. Like SG-5, but with gold hardware.

1966-1971		$1,900	$2,500
1993-1996	7A	$1,400	$1,800

SG-7A 20th Anniversary

1986		$1,800	$2,300

SG-20
1972-1973. Bolt-on neck, slab body, single-cut, 1 pickup.

1972-1973		$375	$475

SG-30/SG-30A
1973-1976. Slab katsura wood (30) or slab maple (30A) solidbody, bolt-on neck, 2 humbuckers, dot inlays.

1973-1976		$375	$500

SG-35/SG-35A
1973-1976. Slab mahogany (35) or slab maple (35A) solidbody, bolt-on neck, 2 humbuckers, parallelogram inlays.

1973-1976		$425	$550

SG-40
1972-1973. Bolt-on neck, carved body, single-cut.

1972-1973		$425	$550

SG-45
1972-1976. Glued neck, single-cut, bound flat-top.

1972-1976		$450	$600

SG-50
1974-1976. Slab katsura wood solidbody, glued neck, 2 humbuckers, dot inlays, large 'guard.

1974-1976		$450	$600

SG-60
1972 only. Bolt-on neck, carved body, single-cut.

1972		$450	$600

SG-60T
1973 only. SG-60 with large cast vibrato system.

1973		$450	$600

SG-65
1972-1976. Glued neck, single-cut, bound flat-top.

1972-1976		$550	$725

SG-70
1974-1976. Slab maple solidbody, glued neck, 2 humbuckers, dot inlays, large 'guard.

1974-1976		$550	$725

SG-80
1972 only. Bolt-on neck, carved body, single-cut.

1972		$450	$600

SG-80T
1973. SG-60 with large cast vibrato system.

1973		$500	$650

SG-85
1972-1976. Glued neck, single-cut, bound flat-top.

1972-1976		$550	$725

SG-90
1974-1976. Carved top mahogany solidbody, glued neck, elevated 'guard, bound top, dot inlays, chrome hardware.

1974-1976		$675	$875

SG-175
1974-1976. Carved top mahogany solidbody, glued neck, elevated 'guard, abalone bound top, abalone split wing or pyramid inlays, gold hardware.

1974-1976		$775	$1,000

SG-500
1976-1978. Carved unbound maple top, double pointed cutaways, glued neck, 2 exposed humbuckers, 3-ply bound headstock, bound neck with clay split wing inlays, chrome hardware. Reissued as the SBG-500 (800S in Japan) in '81.

1976-1978		$475	$625

SG-700
1976-1978. Carved unbound maple top, double pointed cutaways, glued neck, 2 humbuckers, 3-ply bound headstock, bound neck with clay split wing inlays, chrome hardware.

1976-1978		$650	$850

SG-700S
1999-2001. Set neck, mahogany body, 2 humbuckers with coil tap.

1999-2001		$650	$850

1973 Yamaha SG-80T

The *Vintage Guitar Price Guide* shows low to high values for items in all-original excellent condition, and, where applicable, with original case or cover.

MODEL		EXC. COND.	
YEAR	FEATURES	LOW	HIGH

SG-800S

1981-1984. Eastern mahogany with maple top, set neck, 2 pickups, blue, tobacco burst or cherry sunburst.

1981-1984		$650	$850

SG-1000/SBG-1000

1976-1983 ('84 in Japan), 2007-2013. Carved maple top, double pointed cutaways, glued neck, 2 humbuckers, 3-ply bound headstock, unbound body, bound neck with clay split wing inlays, gold hardware. Export model name changed to SBG-1000 in '80. SBG-1000 reissued in '07.

1976-1979	SG-1000	$900	$1,200
1980-1983	SBG-1000	$900	$1,200

SG-1500

1976-1979. Carved maple top, double pointed cutaways, laminated neck-thru-body neck, laminated mahogany body wings, 2 humbuckers, 5-ply bound headstock and body, bound neck with dot inlays, chrome hardware. Name used on Japan-only model in the '80s.

1976-1979		$725	$950

SG-2000/SG-2000S

1976-1980 (1988 in Japan). Maple top, double pointed cutaways, neck-thru-body, mahogany body wings, 2 humbuckers, 5-ply bound headstock and body, bound neck with abalone split wing inlays, gold hardware. In '80, the model was changed to the SBG-2000 in the U.S., and the SG-2000S everywhere else except Japan (where it remained the SG-2000). Export model renamed SBG-2100 in '84.

1976-1980		$900	$1,300

SG-2100S

1983. Similar to SG-2000 with upgrades such as the pickups.

1983		$1,150	$1,500

SG-3000/SBG-3000/Custom Professional

1982-1992. SG-2000 upgrade with higher output pickups and abalone purfling on top.

1982-1992		$1,500	$2,000

SGV-300

2000-2006. 1960s SG model features.

2000-2006		$400	$525

SHB-400

1981-1985. Solidbody electric, set-in neck, 2 pickups.

1981-1985		$400	$525

SJ-180

1983-1994. Student Jumbo, entry level Folk Series model, laminated top.

1983-1994		$125	$200

SJ-400S

1983-1994. Student Jumbo Folk Series model, solid wood top.

1983-1994		$225	$300

SL Studio Lord Series

1977-1981. LP-style copy models.

1977-1981		$400	$525

SR Super Rock'n Roller Series

1977-1981. Strat copy models.

1977-1981		$375	$475

SSC Series

1983-1992. Solidbody electric models.

1983-1992	SSC-400/SC-400	$325	$425
1983-1992	SSC-500	$300	$400
1983-1992	SSC-600/SC-600	$425	$550

Weddington Classic

1989-1992. Electric solidbody, redesigned set-in neck/body joint for increased access to the higher frets.

1989-1992		$590	$760

Yanuziello Stringed Instruments

1980-present. Production/custom resonator and Hawaiian guitars built by luthier Joseph Yanuziello, in Toronto, Ontario.

Yosco

1900-1930s. Lawrence L. Yosco was a New York City luthier building guitars, round back mandolins and banjos under his own brand and for others.

Zachary

1996-present. Luthier Alex Csiky builds his professional grade, production, solidbody electric guitars and basses in Windsor, Ontario.

Zanini

2007-2020. Premium grade, production, electric guitars designed by Luca Zanini of Italy and built in the U.S.

Zaukus Guitars

2011-present. Luthier Joseph Zaukus builds his premium grade, production/custom, solidbody electric guitars in Antioch, Tennessee.

Zeiler Guitars

1992-present. Custom flat-top, 12-string, and nylon-string guitars built by luthier Jamonn Zeiler in Aurora, Indiana.

Zemaitis

1960-1999, 2004-present. Professional, premium, and presentation grade, custom/production, electric and acoustic guitars. Tony Zemaitis (born Antanus Casimere Zemaitis) began selling his guitars in 1960. He emphasized simple light-weight construction and was known for hand engraved metal front guitars. The metal front designs were originally engineered to reduce hum, but they became popular as functional art. Each hand-built guitar and bass was a unique instrument. Ron Wood was an early customer and his use of a Zemaitis created a demand for the custom-built guitars. Approximately 6 to 10 instruments were built each year. Tony retired in '99, and passed away in '02 at the age of 67. In '04, Japan's Kanda Shokai Corporation, with the endorsement of Tony Zemaitis, Jr., started building the guitars again. KSC builds the higher priced ones and licenses the lower priced guitars to Greco.

Yamaha SBG-3000

1983 Yamaha SHB400

Imaged by Heritage Auctions, HA.com

GUITARS

Zerberus Nemesis Stone-Top

*Zimnicki Round
Shoulder Jumbo*

MODEL		EXC. COND.	
YEAR	FEATURES	LOW	HIGH

Celebrity association with Zemaitis is not uncommon. Validated celebrity provenance may add 25% to 100% (or more) to a guitar's value. Tony Zemaitis also made so-called student model instruments for customers with average incomes. These had wood tops instead of metal or pearl. Some wood top instruments have been converted to non-Zemaitis metal tops, which are therefore not fully original Zemaitis instruments.

Acoustic instruments are valued more as collectibles and less so for their acoustic sound. Originality and verifiable, documented provenance is required in the Zemaitis market as fake instruments can be a problem.

Zen-On

1946-ca.1968. Japanese manufacturer. By '67 using the Morales brand name. Not heavily imported into the U.S., if at all (see Morales).

Acoustic Hollowbody

1946-1968. Various models.

1950s		$175	$225

Electric Solidbody

1960s. Teisco-era and styling.

1960s		$150	$400

Zerberus

2002-present. Professional and premium grade, production/custom, electric guitars built in Speyer, Germany by luthier Frank Scheucher.

Zeta

1982-2010. Zeta made solid, semi-hollow and resonator guitars, many with electronic and MIDI options, and mandolins in Oakland, California over the years, but mainly offered upright basses, amps and violins.

Ziegenfuss Guitars

2006-present. Luthier Stephen Ziegenfuss builds his professional and premium grade, custom, acoustic and solidbody electric guitars and basses in Jackson, Michigan.

MODEL		EXC. COND.	
YEAR	FEATURES	LOW	HIGH

Zim-Gar

1960s. Imported from Japan by Gar-Zim Musical Instrument Corporation of Brooklyn, New York. Manufacturers unknown. Generally shorter scale beginner guitars.

Electric Solidbody

1960s		$150	$400

Zimnicki, Gary

1980-present. Luthier Gary Zimnicki builds his professional and premium grade, custom, flat-top, 12-string, nylon-string, and archtop guitars in Allen Park, Michigan.

Zion

1980-present. Professional and premium grade, production/custom, semi-hollow and solidbody guitars built by luthier Ken Hoover, originally in Greensboro, North Carolina, currently in Raleigh.

Zolla

Professional grade, production/custom, electric guitars and basses built by luthier Bill Zolla in San Diego, California starting in 1979.

Zon

1981-present. Currently luthier Joe Zon only offers basses, but he also built guitars from '85-'91. See Bass Section for more company info.

Zuni

1993-present. Premium grade, custom, solidbody electric guitars built by luthier Michael Blank in Alto Pass, Illinois and Amasa, Michigan.

ZZ Ryder

Solidbody electric guitars and basses from Stenzler Musical Instruments of Ft. Worth, Texas.

BASSES

1981 Fender Precision Special (U.S.A.). Photo: Willie Moseley.

Alembic Europa

*Alembic Stanley Clarke
Signature Standard Bass*

Bob Moreland

MODEL YEAR	FEATURES	EXC. COND. LOW	HIGH

A Basses

1976-2002. Luthier Albey Balgochian built his professional grade, solidbody basses in Waltham, Massachusetts. Sports the A logo on headstock.

Solidbody Bass

1976-2002		$975	$1,300

Acoustic

Ca. 1965-ca. 1987, 2001-2005, 2008-present. Mainly known for solidstate amps, the Acoustic Control Corp. of Los Angeles, did offer guitars and basses from around '69 to late '74. The brand was revived in '01 by Samick for a line of amps.

Black Widow Bass

1969-1970, 1972-1974. The AC600 Black Widow Bass (fretted and fretless) featured a black double-cut body, German carve, Ebonite 'board, 2 pickups with 1 row of adjustable polepieces, and a protective "spider design" pad on back. Also in the AC650 short-scale. The '72-'74 version had the same body design, but with a rosewood 'board and only 1 pickup with 2 rows of adjustable pole pieces (the '72s had a different split-coil pickup with 4 pole pieces, 2 front and 2 back). Acoustic outsourced the production of the basses, possibly to Japan, but at least part of the final production was by Semie Moseley.

1969-1970		$1,050	$1,400
1972-1974		$900	$1,200

Airline

1958-1968, 2004-present. Brand for Montgomery Ward. Built by Kay, Harmony and Valco. In '04, the brand was revived on a line of reissues from Eastwood guitars.

Electric Solidbody Bass

1958-1968	Various models	$425	$600

Pocket 3/4 Bass (Valco/National)

1962-1968. Airline brand of double-cut Pocket Bass, short-scale, 2 pickups, 1 acoustic bridge and 1 neck humbucker, sunburst and other colors.

1962-1968		$525	$700

Alamo

1947-1982. Founded by Charles Eilenberg, Milton Fink, and Southern Music, San Antonio, Texas. Distributed by Bruno & Sons.

Eldorado Bass (Model 2600)

1965-1966. Solidbody, 1 pickup, angular offset shape, double-cut.

1965-1966		$325	$425

Titan Bass

1963-1970. Hollowbody, 1 pickup, angular offset shape.

1963-1970		$300	$400

Alembic

1969-present. Professional, premium, and presentation grade, production/custom, 4-, 5-, and 6-string basses built in Santa Rosa, California. They also build guitars. Established in San Francisco as one of the first handmade bass builders. Alembic basses come with many options concerning woods

(examples are maple, bubinga, walnut, vermilion, wenge, zebrawood), finishes, inlays, etc., all of which affect the values listed here. These dollar amounts should be used as a baseline guide to values for Alembic.

Anniversary Bass

1989. 20th Anniversary limited edition, walnut and vermillion with a walnut core, 5-piece body, 5-piece neck-thru, only 200 built.

1989		$2,100	$2,800

Custom Shop Built Bass

1969-present. Various one-off and/or custom built instruments. Each instrument should be evaluated individually. Prices are somewhat speculative due to the one-off custom characteristics and values can vary greatly.

1978	Dragon Doubleneck	$7,400	$9,800
2004	Dragon 4-string, 4 made	$3,700	$4,900

Distillate Bass

1981-1991. One of Alembic's early lower-cost models, early ones with 1 pickup, 2 pickups by '82, exotic woods, active electronics.

1981-1991	Distillate 4	$2,000	$2,600
1981-1991	Distillate 5	$2,100	$2,700

Elan Bass

1985-1996. Available in 4-, 5-, 6- and 8-string models, 3-piece thru-body laminated maple neck, solid maple body, active electronics, solid brass hardware, offered in a variety of hardwood tops and custom finishes.

1985-1996	Elan 4	$1,800	$2,400
1985-1996	Elan 5	$1,850	$2,450
1985-1996	Elan 6	$1,950	$2,550

Epic Bass

1993-2015. Mahogany body with various tops, extra large pointed bass horn, maple/walnut veneer set-neck, available in 4-, 5-, and 6-string versions.

1993-2015	4-string	$1,750	$2,350
1993-2015	5-string	$1,800	$2,400
1993-2015	6-string	$1,850	$2,450

Essence Bass

1991-present. Mahogany body with various tops, extra large pointed bass horn, walnut/maple laminate neck-thru.

1991-2019	Essence 4	$1,800	$2,400
1991-2019	Essence 5	$1,850	$2,450
1991-2019	Essence 6	$2,000	$2,600

Europa Bass

1992-present. Mahogany body with various tops, ebony 'board, available as 4-, 5-, and 6-string.

1992-2019		$2,300	$3,050

Excel Bass

1999-present. Solidbody 5-string, set neck, several wood options.

2000s		$2,300	$3,050

Exploiter Bass

1980s. Figured maple solidbody 4-string, neck-thru, transparent finish.

1984-1988		$2,300	$3,050

MODEL YEAR	FEATURES	EXC. COND. LOW	HIGH

Mark King Signature Bass

1989-present. Standard or Deluxe models.

| 1989-2008 | | $4,500 | $6,000 |

Orion Bass

1996-present. Offset double cut solidbody, various figured-wood top, 4, 5, or 6 strings.

| 1996-2019 | | $1,850 | $2,400 |

Persuader Bass

1983-1991. Offset double-cut solidbody, 4-string, neck-thru.

| 1983-1991 | | $1,850 | $2,400 |

Rogue Bass

1996-present. Double-cut solidbody, extreme long pointed bass horn..

| 1996-2019 | | $2,000 | $2,600 |

Series I Bass

1971-present. Mahogany body with various tops, maple/purpleheart laminate neck-thru, active electronics, available in 3 scale lengths and with 4, 5 or 6 strings.

1971-1979	All scales	$3,700	$4,800
1980-1989	All scales	$3,300	$4,300
1990-2019	All scales, highly figured	$3,300	$4,300

Series II Bass

1971-present. Generally custom-made option, each instrument valued on a case-by-case basis, guidance pricing only.

| 1971-1979 | | $3,800 | $5,000 |
| 1980-2019 | | $3,700 | $4,800 |

Spoiler Bass

1981-1999. Solid mahogany body, maple neck-thru, 4, 5 or 6 strings, active electronics, various high-end wood options.

1981-1986	6-string	$2,000	$2,600
1981-1989	5-string	$1,900	$2,500
1981-1999	4-string	$1,800	$2,400

Stanley Clarke Signature Standard Bass

1990-present. Neck-thru-body, active electronics, 24-fret ebony 'board, mahogany body with maple, bubinga, walnut, vermilion, or zebrawood top, 4-, 5-, and 6-string versions.

| 1990-2019 | All scales | $4,300 | $5,600 |

Alleva-Coppolo Basses and Guitars

1995-present. Professional and premium grade, custom/production, solidbody electric basses and guitars built by luthier Jimmy Coppolo in Dallas, Texas for '95-'97, in New York City for '98-2008, and since in Upland, California.

Solidbody Bass

1995-present. Various solidbody 4- and 5-string, various options and materials.

| 1995-2019 | | $3,300 | $4,800 |

Alvarez

1965-present. Imported by St. Louis Music, they offered electric basses from '90 to '02 and acoustic basses in the mid-'90s.

American Showster

1986-2004, 2010-2011. Established by Bill Meeker and David Haines, Bayville, New Jersey. They also made guitars.

AS-57-B Bass

1987-1997. Bass version of AS-57 with body styled like a '57 Chevy tail fin.

| 1987-1997 | | $3,400 | $4,500 |

Ampeg

1949-present. Ampeg was founded on a vision of an amplified bass peg, which evolved into the Baby Bass. Ampeg has sold basses on and off throughout its history. In '08 they got back into basses with the reissue of the Dan Armstrong Plexi Bass.

AEB-1 Bass

1966-1967. F-holes through the body, fretted, scroll headstock, pickup in body, sunburst. Reissued as the AEB-2 for '97-'99.

| 1966-1967 | | $2,900 | $3,800 |

ASB-1 Devil Bass

1966-1967. Long-horn body, fretted or fretless, triangular f-holes through the body, fireburst.

| 1966-1967 | | $4,800 | $6,300 |

AUB-1 Bass

1966-1967. Same as AEB-1, but fretless, sunburst. Reissued as the AUB-2 for '97-'99.

| 1966-1967 | | $3,000 | $4,000 |

AUSB-1 Devil Bass

1966-1967. Same as ASB-1 Devil Bass, but fretless.

| 1966-1967 | | $4,800 | $6,300 |

BB-4 Baby Bass (4-string)

1962-1971. Electric upright slim-looking bass that is smaller than a cello, 4-string, available in sunburst, white, red, black, and a few turquoise. Reissued as the ABB-1 Baby Bass for '97-'99.

| 1962-1971 | Solid color | $2,100 | $2,700 |
| 1962-1971 | Sunburst | $1,750 | $2,250 |

BB-5 Baby Bass (5-string)

1964-1971. Five-string version.

| 1964-1971 | Solid color | $2,200 | $2,900 |
| 1964-1971 | Sunburst | $1,900 | $2,450 |

Dan Armstrong Lucite Bass

1969-1971. Clear solid lucite body, did not have switchable pickups like the Lucite guitar.

| 1969-1971 | Clear | $1,750 | $2,300 |
| 1969-1971 | Smoke | $2,250 | $2,900 |

Dan Armstrong Lucite Reissue/ADA4 Bass

1998-2001, 2008-2009. Lucite body, Dan Armstrong Ampeg block lettering on 'guard. Reissue in '08 as the ADA4.

| 1998-2001 | | $625 | $825 |
| 2008-2009 | Reintroduced | $625 | $825 |

GEB-101 Little Stud Bass

1973-1975. Import from Japan, offset double-cut solidbody, two-on-a-side tuners, 1 pickup.

| 1973-1975 | | $350 | $450 |

GEB-750 Big Stud Bass

1973-1975. Import from Japan, similar to Little Stud, but with 2 pickups.

| 1973-1975 | | $350 | $450 |

Alleva-Coppolo

1968 Ampeg AEB-1
Craig Brody

BASSES

1981 B.C. Rich Mockingbird
Imaged by Heritage Auctions, HA.com

1976 B.C. Rich Eagle
Craig Brody

Wild Dog Bass EB-1
1963-1964. Made by Burns of London, along with the Wild Dog Guitar, offset double cut solidbody, 3 pickups

MODEL YEAR	FEATURES	EXC. COND. LOW	HIGH
1963-1964		$525	$675

Andreas
1995-2004. Aluminium-necked, solidbody guitars and basses built by luthier Andreas Pichler in Dollach, Austria.

Angelica
1967-1975. Student and entry-level basses and guitars imported from Japan.
Electric Solidbody Bass
1970s. Japanese imports.

1970s	Various models	$125	$220

Apollo
Ca. 1967-1972. Entry-level basses imported from Japan by St. Louis Music. They also had guitars and effects.
Electric Hollowbody Bass
1967-1972. Japanese imports.

1967-1972		$425	$575

Arbor
1983-ca. 2013. Budget grade, production, solidbody basses imported by Musicorp (MBT). They also offered guitars.
Electric Bass

1983-2013	Various models	$150	$300

Aria/Aria Pro II
1956-present. Budget and intermediate grade, production, acoustic, acoustic/electric, solidbody, hollowbody and upright basses. They also make guitars, mandolins, and banjos. Originally branded as Aria; renamed Aria Pro II in '75; both names used over the next several year; in '01, the Pro II part of the name was dropped altogether.
Electric Bass

1980s	Various models	$300	$550

Austin Hatchet
Mid-1970s-mid-1980s. Trademark of distributor Targ and Dinner, Chicago, Illinois.
Hatchet Bass

1981	Travel bass	$375	$500

B.C. Rich
1966-present. Budget, intermediate, and premium grade, production/custom, import and U.S.-made basses. They also offer guitars. Many B.C. Rich models came in a variety of colors. For example, in '88 they offered black, Competition Red, metallic red, GlitteRock White, Ultra Violet, and Thunder Blue. Also in '88, other custom colors, graphic features, paint-to-match headstocks, and special inlays were offered.
Bich Bass
1978-1998. Solidbody, neck-thru, 2 pickups.

1978-1979	USA	$1,850	$2,400

MODEL YEAR	FEATURES	EXC. COND. LOW	HIGH
1980-1985		$1,150	$1,500
1986-1989		$800	$1,025
1989-1993	Class Axe era	$800	$1,025
1994-1998	2nd Rico-era	$800	$1,025

Bich Supreme 8-String Bass
Late-1970s-early-1980s.

1978-1982	Painted wood	$3,000	$4,000
1978-1982	Translucent wood	$3,500	$4,500

Eagle Bass (U.S.A. Assembly)
1977-1996. Curved double-cut, solidbody, natural.

1977-1979	Translucent wood	$1,850	$2,400
1977-1996	Painted wood	$1,600	$2,100
1980-1996	Translucent wood	$1,750	$2,300

Gunslinger Bass
1987-1999. Inverted headstock, 1 humbucker.

1987-1989		$550	$750
1989-1993	Class Axe era	$550	$750
1994-1999		$476	$650

Ironbird Bass
1984-1998. Kind of star-shaped, neck-thru, solidbody, 2 pickups, active electronics, diamond inlays.

1984-1989		$850	$1,125
1989-1993	Class Axe era	$775	$1,025
1994-1998	2nd Rico era	$700	$950

Mockingbird Bass
1976-2009. US-made, short horn until '78, long horn after.

1976	Painted	$1,750	$2,300
1976	Translucent	$1,850	$2,400
1977-1978	Painted	$1,600	$2,100
1977-1978	Translucent	$1,750	$2,300
1979-1983	Painted	$1,750	$2,300
1979-1983	Translucent	$1,750	$2,300
1984-1985	End 1st Rico-era	$1,600	$2,100
1986-1989	End 1st Rico era	$1,150	$1,500
1994-2009	New Rico-era	$1,150	$1,500

Mockingbird Heritage Classic Bass
2007-2015. 4-string, neck-thru, quilted maple top, cloud inlay.

2007-2015		$225	$300

Nighthawk Bass
1979-ca.1980. Bolt-neck.

1978-1982		$550	$725

NJ Series Bass
1983-2006. Various mid-level import models include Beast, Eagle, Innovator, Mockingbird, Virgin and Warlock. Replaced by NT Series.

1983-1984	Early, Japan	$250	$450
1985-1986	Japan	$175	$350
1987-2006		$100	$250

Platinum Series Bass
1986-2006. Lower-priced import versions including Eagle, Mockingbird, Beast, Warlock.

1986-1999		$100	$200

Seagull Bass
1973-1975. Solidbody, single cut, changed to Seagull II in '76.

1973		$2,400	$3,200
1974-1975		$2,100	$2,800

MODEL		EXC. COND.	
YEAR	**FEATURES**	**LOW**	**HIGH**

Seagull II Bass
1976-1977. Double-cut version.

1976-1977		$1,800	$2,400

ST-III Bass
1987-1998. Bolt or set neck, black hardware, P-Bass/J-Bass pickup configuration, ebony 'board.

1987-1989	Bolt-on	$500	$650
1987-1989	Neck-thru	$550	$700
1989-1993	Class Axe-era	$500	$650
1994-1998	New Rico-era	$500	$650

Warlock Bass (U.S.A.)
1981-2015. Bolt neck, maple body, rosewood 'board, Badass II low profile bridge by '88.

1981-1985		$975	$1,300
1986-1989		$900	$1,200

Wave Bass
Early 1980s. Double-cut, cresting wave, neck-thru, solid body, 2 pickups, active electronics.

1983		$1,950	$2,600

Baldwin
1965-1970. The giant organ company got into guitars and basses in '65 when it bought Burns Guitars of England and sold those models in the U.S. under the Baldwin name.

Baby Bison Bass
1965-1970. Scroll head, 2 pickups, black, red or white finishes.

1965-1966		$775	$1,025
1966-1970	Model 560	$675	$875

Bison Bass
1965-1970. Scroll headstock, 3 pickups, black or white finishes.

1965-1966		$850	$1,100
1966-1970	Model 516	$750	$975

G.B. 66 Bass
1965-1966. Bass equivalent of G.B. 66 guitar, covered bridge tailpiece.

1965-1966		$600	$775

Jazz Split Sound Bass
1965-1970. Offset double-cut solidbody, 2 pickups, red sunburst.

1965-1966	Long-scale	$775	$1,025
1966-1970	Short-scale	$675	$875

Nu-Sonic Bass
1965-1966. Bass version of Nu-Sonic.

1965-1966		$600	$775

Shadows/Shadows Signature Bass
1965-1970. Named after Hank Marvin's backup band, solidbody, 3 slanted pickups, white finish.

1965-1966	Shadows	$1,225	$1,575
1966-1970	Shadows Signature	$1,150	$1,475

Vibraslim Bass
1965-1970. Thin body, scroll head, 2 pickups, sunburst.

1965-1966		$700	$950
1966-1970	Model 549	$625	$850

Barclay
1960s. Generally shorter-scale, student-level imports from Japan. They also made guitars.

Bass Collection
1985-1992. Mid-level imports from Japan, distributed by Meisel Music of Springfield, New Jersey. Sam Ash Music, New York, sold the remaining inventory from '92 to '94.

Black Jack
1960s. Entry-level and mid-level imports from Japan. They also offered guitars.

Bradford
1960s. House brand of W.T. Grant department store, often imported. They also offered guitars.

Brian Moore
1992-present. Brian Moore added basses in '97. Currently they offer professional grade, production, solidbody basses. They also build guitars and mandolins.

i2000 Bass Series
2000-present. Offset double-cut solidbody with extended bass horn, 2 pickups, 4- (i4) or 5-string (i5), options include piezo (p), fretless (-f), Bartolini pickups (B), and 13-pin mid (.13).

2000-2019		$625	$825

Brice
1985-present. Budget grade, production, electric and acoustic basses imported by Rondo Music of Union, New Jersey.

BSX Bass
1990-present. Luthier Dino Fiumara builds his professional and premium grade, production/custom, acoustic, solidbody, semi-solid upright basses in Aliquippa, Pennsylvania.

Burns
1960-1970, 1974-1983, 1992-present. Intermediate and professional grade, production, basses built in England and Korea. They also build guitars.

Baby Bison Bass
1965-1968. Early version had "V" headstock and long Rez-O-Tube vibrato. Later short Rezo-Tube tailpiece.

1965-1968		$600	$800

Nu-Sonic Bass
1964-1965, 2011-present. Offset double-cut solidbody, 2 pickups.

1964-1965		$750	$1,000

Scorpion Bass
Introduced 1979, 2003-2009. Double-cut scorpion-like solidbody.

2003-2009		$300	$400

Cameo
1960s-1970s. Japanese- and Korean-made electric basses. They also offered guitars.

Electric Bass

1960s-70s	EB-2 style	$225	$300

B.C. Rich ST-III
Ken Kraynak

1965 Baldwin Vibraslim
Guillermo Albino

BASSES

1965 Custom Kraft Bone Buzzer Model 12178

Rivington Guitars

Daion

Carter Vintage Guitars

MODEL YEAR	FEATURES	EXC. COND. LOW	HIGH

Charvel

1976-present. U.S.-made from '78 to '85 and a combination of imports and U.S.-made post-'85. They also build guitars.

Pre-Pro Bass
1980-1981. Pre-mass production basses, made Nov. '80 to '81. Refer to Charvel guitar section for details.

1980-1981	All models	$1,800	$2,400

850 XL Bass
1989. Four-string, neck-thru, active.

1989		$625	$800

CX-490 Bass
1991-1994. Double-cut, 4-string, bolt neck, red or white.

1991-1994		$220	$290

Eliminator Bass
1990-1991. Offset double-cut, active electronics, bolt neck.

1990-1991		$325	$425

Fusion Bass
1989-1991. Active circuitry, 4- and 5-string models.

1989-1991	IV	$400	$525
1989-1991	V	$425	$550

Model 1 Bass
1986-1988. Double-cut, bolt neck, 1 pickup.

1986-1988		$350	$450

Model 2 Bass
1986-1988. Double-cut, bolt neck, 2 pickups.

1986-1988		$350	$450

Model 3 Bass
1986-1988. Neck-thru, 2 single-coils, active, master volume, bass and treble knobs.

1986-1988		$400	$525

Model 4 Bass
1988. Like Model 3, but with bolt neck.

1988		$475	$625

Model 5 Bass
1986-1989. Double-cut, P/J pickups.

1986-1989		$475	$625

San Dimas Serialized Plated Bass
1981-1982. Soft headstock early models.

1981-1982		$1,650	$2,200

SB-4 Bass
1990s. Offset double cut solid, long bass horn, 2 pickups.

1990s		$330	$430

Star Bass
1980-1981. Unique 4-point solidbody, 1 pickup, considered by Charvel collectors to be Charvel's only original early design.

1980-1981		$2,500	$3,300

Surfcaster Bass
1991-1994. Semi-hollow, lipstick tube pickups.

1991-1994		$925	$1,225

Cipher

1960s. Student market basses imported from Japan. They also made guitars.

Electric Solidbody Bass
1960s. Japanese imports.

1960s		$150	$225

Clevinger

1982-present. Established by Martin Clevinger, Oakland, California. Mainly specializing in electric upright basses, but has offered bass guitars as well.

College Line

One of many Lyon & Healy brands, made during the era of extreme design experimentation.

Monster (Style 2089) Bass
Early-1900s. 22" lower bout, flat-top guitar/bass, natural.

1915		$2,300	$3,000

Conrad

Ca.1968-1978. Student and mid-level copy basses imported by David Wexler, Chicago, Illinois. They also offered guitars, mandolins and banjos.

Electric Bass

1970s	Various models	$250	$425

Professional Bison Bass
1970s. Solidbody, 2 pickups.

1970s		$250	$325

Coral

1967-1969. In '66 MCA bought Danelectro and in '67 introduced the Coral brand of guitars, basses and amps. The line included several solid and semi-solidbody basses.

Deluxe D2N4 Bass
1967-1969. Offset double-cut, 2 pickups.

1967-1969	Black	$1,050	$1,400
1967-1969	Sunburst	$975	$1,300

Fiddle FB2B4 Bass
1967-1969. Violin bass hollow body, 2 pickups.

1967-1969		$1,475	$1,900

Firefly F2B4 Bass
1968-1969. 335-style semi-hollow, 2 pickups.

1968-1969	Red	$825	$1,075
1968-1969	Sunburst	$775	$1,025

Long Horn Bass
1968-1969. Standard neck (L2B4) or extended neck (L2LB4), 4 strings.

1968	L2LB4	$1,150	$1,525
1968-1969	L2B4	$1,050	$1,425

Wasp Bass
1967-1969. 4-string (2B4) or 6-string (2B6), black, red or sunburst.

1967-1969	2B4, black or red	$1,050	$1,400
1967-1969	2B4, sunburst	$850	$1,150
1967-1969	2B6, black or red	$1,200	$1,575
1967-1969	2B6, sunburst	$1,050	$1,400

Crestwood

1970s. Imported by La Playa Distributing Company of Detroit. Product line includes copies of the popular classical guitars, flat-tops, electric solidbodies and basses of the era.

Electric Bass
1970s. Includes models 2048, 2049, 2079, 2090, 2092, 2093, and 2098.

1970s		$210	$275

MODEL YEAR	FEATURES	EXC. COND. LOW	HIGH

Crown

1960s. Violin-shaped hollowbody electrics, solidbody electric guitars and basses, possibly others. Imported from Japan.

Electric Solidbody Bass

1960s	Import	$125	$175

Custom Kraft

Late-1950s-1968. A house brand of St. Louis Music Supply, instruments built by Valco and others. They also offered guitars and amps.

Bone Buzzer Model 12178 Bass

Late 1960s. Symmetrical double-cut thin hollow body, lightning bolt f-holes, 4-on-a-side tuners, 2 pickups, sunburst or emerald sunburst.

1968		$425	$575

D'Agostino

1976-early 1990s. Import company established by Pat D'Agostino. Solidbodies imported from EKO Italy '77-'82, Japan '82-'84, and in Korea for '84 on. Overall, about 60% of guitars and basses were Japanese, 40% Korean.

Electric Solidbody Bass

1970s	Various models	$150	$700

Daion

1978-1984. Higher quality copy basses imported from Japan. Original designs introduced in '80s. They also had guitars.

Electric Bass

1978-1984	Higher-end	$450	$900
1978-1984	Lower-end	$150	$450

Danelectro

1946-1969, 1997-present. Danelectro offered basses throughout most of its early history. In '96, the Evets Corporation, of San Clemente, California, introduced a line of Danelectro effects; amps, basses and guitars, many reissues of earlier instruments, soon followed. In early '03, Evets discontinued the guitar, bass and amp lines, but revived the guitar and bass line in '05. Danelectro also built the Coral brand instruments (see Coral).

Dane A Series Bass

1967. Solidbody, 2 pickups, 4-string.

1967		$500	$650

Dane C Series Bass

1967. Semi-solidbody 4- or 6-string, 2 pickups.

1967	4-string	$875	$1,150
1967	6-string	$1,100	$1,400

Dane D Series Bass

1967. Solidbody, 2 pickups, 4- or 6-string.

1967	4-string	$750	$975
1967	6-string	$1,100	$1,400

Dane E Series Bass

1967. Solidbody, 2 pickups, 4-string.

1967	4-string	$750	$975

Hawk Bass

1967. Solidbody, 4-string, 1 pickup.

1967		$850	$1,125

Model 1444L Bass

Ca.1958-ca.1964. Masonite body, single-cut, 2 pickups, copper finish.

1958-1964		$550	$725

Model 3412 Standard (Shorthorn) Bass

1959-1966. Coke bottle headstock, 4- or 6-string, 1 pickup, kidney 'guard through '60, seal 'guard after, copper finish.

1959-1960	Kidney 'guard, 4-string	$750	$950
1959-1960	Kidney 'guard, 6-string	$1,200	$1,500
1961-1966	Seal 'guard, 4-string	$650	$850
1961-1966	Seal 'guard, 6-string	$1,100	$1,400

Model 3612 Standard (Shorthorn) Bass

1959-1966. 6-string version.

1959-1962	Kidney 'guard	$1,200	$1,500
1961-1966	Seal 'guard	$1,100	$1,400

'58 Shorthorn Reissue Bass

1997-2003. Reissues of classic Shorthorn bass.

1997-2003		$225	$300

Model 4423 Longhorn 4-String Bass

1959-1966. Coke bottle headstock, 4-string, 2 pickups, tweed case '59, gray tolex after.

1959	Tweed case	$1,000	$1,300
1960-1966	Gray tolex case	$900	$1,200

Model 4623 Longhorn 6-String Bass

1959-1966, 1969-1970. 6-string version.

1959	Tweed case	$1,200	$1,500
1960-1966	Gray tolex case	$1,100	$1,400
1969-1970		$1,000	$1,300

'58 Longhorn Reissue/Longhorn Pro Bass

1997-2010. Reissues of classic Longhorn bass.

1997-2010		$200	$265

UB-2 6-String Bass

1956-1958. Single-cut, 2 pickups, black, bronze or ivory.

1956-1958		$1,250	$1,600

David J King

1987-present. Production/custom, professional and premium grade, electric basses built by luthier David King first in Amherst, Massachusetts and since '92 in Portland, Oregon.

Dean

1976-present. Intermediate and professional grade, production, solidbody, hollowbody, acoustic, and acoustic/electric, basses made overseas. They also offer guitars, banjos, mandolins, and amps.

Baby ML Bass

1982-1986. Downsized version of ML.

1982-1986	Import	$275	$375

Mach V Bass

1985-1986. U.S.-made pointed solidbody, 2 pickups, rosewood 'board.

1985-1986		$1,050	$1,400

1961 Danelectro Model 3412 Standard (Shorthorn)
Erick Warner

1959 Danelectro Model 4623 Longhorn
Erick Warner

1960s EKO Model 995/2 Violin
Rivington Guitars

1966 Epiphone Embassy Deluxe
Carter Vintage Guitars

MODEL YEAR	FEATURES	EXC. COND. LOW	HIGH
ML Bass			
1977-1986, 2001-2010. Futuristic body style, fork headstock.			
1977-1983	US-made	$1,325	$1,750
1984-1986	Korean import	$350	$450
Rhapsody Series (USA)			
2001-2004. Scroll shaped offset double-cut, various models.			
2001-2004	12-string	$300	$400
2001-2004	8-string	$250	$350
2001-2004	HFB fretless	$200	$250

DeArmond
1999-2004. Electric basses based on Guild models and imported from Korea by Fender. They also offered guitars.
Electric Bass
1999-2004. Various imported models.

1999-2004		$200	$500

Dingwall
1988-present. Luthier Sheldon Dingwall, Saskatoon, Saskatchewan, started out producing guitar bodies and necks, eventually offering complete guitars and basses. Currently Dingwall offers professional to premium grade, production/custom 4-, 5-, and 6-string basses featuring the Novax Fanned-Fret System.

Domino
Ca. 1967-1968. Imported from Japan by Maurice Lipsky Music of New York, mainly copies, but some original designs. They also offered guitars.
Electric Bass
1967-1968. Includes the Beatle Bass and Fireball Bass, a Vox Phantom IV copy.

1967-1968		$250	$450

Dorado
Ca. 1972-1973. Name used briefly by Baldwin/Gretsch on line of Japanese guitar and bass imports.
Electric Solidbody Bass

1970s	Import	$150	$350

Earthwood
1972-1985. Acoustic designs by Ernie Ball with input from George Fullerton and made in Newport Beach, California. One of the first to offer acoustic basses.
Acoustic Bass
1972-1985. Big bodied acoustic bass alternative between Kay double bass and solidbody Fender bass.

1972-1985		$2,000	$3,000

EKO
1959-1985, 2000-present. Built by the Oliviero Pigini Company, Italy. Original importers included LoDuca Brothers, Milwaukee, Wisconsin. Since about 2000, production, acoustic and electric EKO basses are again available and made in Italy and

China. They also make guitars and amps.
Barracuda Bass
1967-1978. Offset double-cut semi-hollow, 2 pickups.

1967-1978		$625	$800

Cobra II Bass
1967-ca.1969. Offset double-cut solidbody, 2 pickups.

1967-1969		$515	$665

Kadett Bass
1967-1978. Red or sunburst.

1967-1978		$625	$800

Model 995/2 Violin Bass
1966-ca.1969.

1966-1969		$850	$1,100

Model 1100/2 Bass
1961-1966. Jaguar-style plastic covered solidbody, 2 pickups, sparkle finish.

1961-1966		$675	$900

Rocket IV/Rokes Bass
1967-early-1970s. Rocket-shape design, solidbody, says Rokes on the headstock, the Rokes were a popular English band that endorsed EKO guitars. Marketed as the Rocket IV in the U.S. and as the Rokes in Europe. Often called the Rok. Sunburst, 1 pickup.

1967-1971		$825	$1,075

Electra
1970-1984, 2013-present. Originally basses imported from Japan by St. Louis Music. They also offered guitars. Currently U.S.-made in Tampa, Florida.
Electric Solidbody Bass
1970s. Japanese imports, various models.

1970s		$450	$650

MPC Outlaw Bass
1970s. Symmetric solidbody with large straight horns, 2 separate plug-in modules for different effects, MPC headstock logo, bowtie markers, sunburst.

1970s		$650	$850

Emperador
1966-1992. Student-level basses imported by Westheimer Musical Instruments. Early models appear to be made by either Teisco or Kawai; later models were made by Cort. They also had guitars.
Electric Solidbody Bass
1960s. Japanese imports, various models.

1960s	Beatle violin bass	$265	$350
1960s	Various models	$135	$180

Engelhardt
Engelhardt specializes in student acoustic basses and cellos and is located in Elk Grove Village, Illinois.

Epiphone
1928-present. Epiphone didn't add basses until 1959, after Gibson acquired the brand. The Gibson Epiphones were American-made until '69, then all imports until into the '80s, when some models were again made in the U.S. Currently Epiphone offers

MODEL YEAR	FEATURES	EXC. COND. LOW	HIGH

intermediate and professional grade, production, acoustic and electric basses.

B-1 Acoustic Bass Viol
1940-1949. Plain maple back and sides, cherry sunburst

1940-1949		$1,450	$1,900

B-2 Acoustic Bass Viol
1940-1949. Mid-level maple back and sides.

1940-1949		$1,600	$2,100

B-3 Acoustic Bass Viol
1940-1949. Higher-level maple back and sides.

1940-1949		$1,700	$2,200

B-4 Acoustic Bass Viol
1940-1949. Highly figured maple back and sides.

1940-1964		$2,100	$2,700

B-5 Artist Acoustic Bass Viol
1941-1964. Highly figured maple back and sides.

1941-1964		$2,700	$3,500

EA/ET/ES Series (Japan)
1970-1979. Production of the Epiphone brand was moved to Japan in '70. Models included the EA (electric thinline) and ET (electric solidbody).

1970-1975	Various models	$400	$700

EB-0/EB-1/EB-3/EBM-4 Bass
1991-present. EB-0 ('98-present), EB-1 ('98-'00), EB-3 ('99-present) and EBM-4 ('91-'98).

1991-2019	Various models	$150	$425

Elitist Series Bass
2003-2005. Higher-end appointments such as set-necks and USA pickups.

2003-2005	EB-3	$650	$875

Embassy Deluxe Bass
1963-1969. Solidbody, double-cut, 2 pickups, tune-o-matic bridge, cherry finish.

1963-1964		$4,300	$5,700
1965		$3,900	$5,200
1966-1969		$3,800	$5,100

Explorer Korina Bass
2000-2001. Made in Korea, Gibson Explorer body style, genuine korina body, set neck, gold hardware.

2000-2001		$325	$425

Genesis Bass
1979-1980. Double-cut solidbody, 2 humbuckers, Made in Taiwan.

1979-1980		$800	$1,100

Jack Cassady Signature Bass
1997-present. Maple body, mahogany neck, rosewood 'board, 1 pickup, metallic gold or ebony finish.

1997-2019		$500	$650

Les Paul Special Bass
1997-2013. LP Jr.-style slab body, single-cut, bolt neck, 2 humbuckers.

1997-2013		$225	$300

Newport EB-6 Bass
1962-1964. 6 strings.

1962-1964		$6,800	$8,800

Newport EBD Bass
1960-1970. Double-cut solidbody, 1 pickup (2 pickups optional until '63), 2-on-a-side tuners until '63, 4-on-a-side after that, cherry.

1960-1964		$1,750	$2,300

MODEL YEAR	FEATURES	EXC. COND. LOW	HIGH
1965		$1,275	$1,675
1966-1970		$1,125	$1,500

Newport EB-SF Bass
1962-1963. Newport with added built-in fuzz, cherry.

1962-1963		$2,600	$3,400

Rivoli Bass (1 Pickup)
1959-1961, 1964-1970, 1994-2000. ES-335-style semi-hollowbody bass, 2-on-a-side tuners, 1 pickup (2 in '70).

1959-1960	Banjo tuners, natural	$5,300	$7,000
1959-1960	Banjo tuners, sunburst	$4,700	$6,100
1961	Standard tuners, natural	$3,000	$4,000
1961	Standard tuners, sunburst	$2,400	$3,200
1964		$2,400	$3,200
1965		$2,100	$2,800
1966-1969		$2,000	$2,600
1967	Sparkling Burgundy	$2,000	$2,600
1970		$2,000	$2,600

Rivoli Bass (2 Pickups)
1970 only. Double pickup Epiphone version of Gibson EB-2D.

1970		$2,100	$2,700

Rivoli II Reissue
1995-2000. Made in Korea, set neck, blond.

1995-2000		$525	$675

Thunderbird IV (Non-Reverse) Bass
1995-1998. Non-reverse-style mahogany body, 2 pickups, 5-string optional.

1995-1998		$300	$400

Thunderbird IV Bass
1997-2019. Reverse-style mahogany body, 2 pickups, sunburst.

1997-2019		$300	$400

Viola Bass
1995-present. Beatle Bass 500/1 copy, sunburst.

1995-2019		$225	$300

ESP
1975-present. Intermediate, professional, and premium grade, production/custom, electric basses. Japan's ESP (Electric Sound Products) made in-roads in the U.S. market with mainly copy styles in the early '80s, mixing in original designs over the years. In the '90s, ESP opened a California-based Custom Shop. They also build guitars.

Electric Bass
1980s-1990s. Various factory production models.

1980s-90s		$625	$800

Essex (SX)
1985-present. Budget grade, production, electric basses imported by Rondo Music of Union, New Jersey. They also offer guitars.

Electric Solidbody Bass

1990s		$75	$125

1966 Epiphone Rivoli
Mike Gutierrez

Epiphone Thunderbird IV

BASSES

1966 Fender Bass V
Fretted Americana

1967 Fender Coronado II
Rivington Guitars

MODEL YEAR	FEATURES	EXC. COND. LOW	HIGH

Estrada

1960s-1970s. Line of classical, acoustic and electric guitars and basses imported from Japan.

Violin Bass

1960s		$375	$500

Fender

1946-present. Intermediate, professional, and premium grade, production/custom, electric and acoustic basses made in the U.S. and overseas. Leo Fender is the father of the electric bass. The introduction of his Precision Bass in late '51 changed forever how music was performed, recorded and heard. Leo followed with other popular models of basses that continue to make up a large part of Fender's production. Please note that all the variations of the Jazz and Precision Basses are grouped under those general headings.

A custom color is worth more than a standard color. The first Precision Bass standard color was blond but changed to sunburst in the late 1950s. The Jazz Bass standard color is sunburst. To understand a custom color, you need to know what the standard color is. Some custom colors are more rare than others. Below is a list of the custom colors offered in 1960 by Fender. They are sorted in ascending order with the most valuable color, Shell Pink, listed last. In the 1960 list, Black and Blond are the least valuable and Shell Pink is the most valuable. A Fiesta Red is typically worth 12% more than a Black or Blond. In the rare color group a Foam Green is normally worth 8% more than a Shoreline Gold. The two very rare colors are often worth 30% more than a Shoreline Gold. In our pricing information we will list the standard color, then the relative value of a common custom color, and then the value of a rare custom color. Remember that the amount of fade also affects the price. These prices are for factory original custom colors with slight or no fade in excellent condition. Fade implies a lighter color, but with custom colors a faded example can also be much darker in color. Blue can fade to dark green. White can fade to deep yellow.

The Price Guide lists the standard color, plus the value of a Common Color and the value of a Rare Color. The list below defines which group a color falls into for 1960, and it is in ascending order so, for example, a Daphne Blue should be considered more valuable than a Lake Placid Blue, assuming they are in equal condition.

Common Color: Black, Blond, Candy Apple Red, Olympic White, Lake Placid Blue, Dakota Red, Daphne Blue, Fiesta Red

Rare Color: Shoreline Gold, Inca Silver, Burgundy Mist, Sherwood Green, Sonic Blue, Foam Green

Rare (Very Rare) Color: Surf Green, Shell Pink

Ashbory Bass

2003-2006. Unique-shaped travel bass, Ashbory logo on body, Fender logo on back of headstock, previously sold under Fender's DeArmond brand.

2005-2006		$260	$350

MODEL YEAR	FEATURES	EXC. COND. LOW	HIGH

Bass V

1965-1970. Five strings, double-cut, 1 pickup, dot inlay '65-'66, block inlay '66-'70. Please refer to the beginning of the Fender Bass Section for details on Fender color options.

1965	Common color	$3,750	$5,000
1965	Rare color	$5,000	$6,600
1965	Sunburst	$3,000	$3,900
1966-1967	Common color	$3,300	$4,400
1966-1967	Rare color	$4,400	$5,700
1966-1967	Sunburst, block inlay	$2,500	$3,300
1966-1967	Sunburst, dot inlay	$2,500	$3,300
1968-1970	Common color	$3,300	$4,400
1968-1970	Rare color	$4,400	$5,700
1968-1970	Sunburst	$2,500	$3,300

Bass VI

1961-1975. Six strings, Jazzmaster-like body, 3 pickups, dot inlay until '66, block inlay '66-'75. Reintroduced as Japanese-made Collectable model '95-'98. Please refer to the beginning of the Fender Bass Section for details on Fender color options.

1961-1962	Common color	$11,500	$15,000
1961-1962	Rare color	$15,000	$20,000
1961-1962	Sunburst	$6,500	$8,500
1963-1964	Common color	$10,500	$14,000
1963-1964	Rare color	$14,000	$18,500
1963-1964	Sunburst	$5,600	$7,400
1965	Common color	$9,400	$12,500
1965	Rare color	$12,500	$16,500
1965	Sunburst	$4,700	$6,200
1966	Common color	$6,600	$8,800
1966	Rare color	$8,800	$11,700
1966	Sunburst, block inlay	$4,000	$5,200
1966	Sunburst, dot inlay	$4,000	$5,200
1967-1969	Common color	$6,600	$8,800
1967-1969	Rare color	$8,800	$11,700
1967-1969	Sunburst	$4,000	$5,200
1970-1971	Custom color	$5,600	$7,500
1970-1971	Sunburst	$3,800	$5,000
1972-1974	Custom color	$5,600	$7,500
1972-1974	Natural	$2,900	$3,800
1972-1974	Sunburst	$3,800	$5,000
1972-1974	Walnut	$3,000	$3,900
1975	Natural	$2,900	$3,800
1975	Olympic White, black, blond	$3,800	$5,000
1975	Sunburst	$3,500	$4,700
1975	Walnut	$3,000	$3,900

Bass VI Reissue (CS)

2006. Custom Shop, 3-tone sunburst, certificate of authenticity.

2006		$1,800	$2,400

Bass VI Reissue (Import)

1995-1998. Import, sunburst.

1995-1998		$1,050	$1,400

Bass VI Reissue (Japan)

Japanese market only, JD serial number.

2014		$825	$1,100

MODEL YEAR	FEATURES	EXC. COND. LOW	HIGH

Bass VI Pawn Shop
2013-2014. Alder body, maple neck, rosewood 'board, 3-color sunburst.

2013-2014		$450	$600

BG Series Bass
1997-2012. Acoustic flat-top basses, single-cut, two-on-a-side tuners, Fishman on-board controls.

1997-2012	Various models	$125	$475

Bullet Bass (B30, B34, B40)
1982-1983. Alder body, 1 pickup, offered in short- and long-scale, red or walnut. U.S.-made, replaced by Japanese-made Squire Bullet Bass.

1982-1983		$550	$725

Bullet Deluxe Bass
1982-1983. Fender logo with Bullet Bass Deluxe on headstock, E-series serial number, small Telecaster-style headstock shape.

1982-1983		$550	$725

Coronado I Bass
1966-1970. Thinline, double-cut, 1 pickup, dot inlay, sunburst and cherry red were the standard colors, but custom colors could be ordered.

1966-1970	Various colors	$1,300	$1,700

Coronado II Bass
1966-1972. Two pickups, block inlay, sunburst and cherry red standard colors, but custom colors could be ordered. Only Antigua finish offered from '70 on.

1966-1969	Various colors	$1,500	$2,000
1966-1969	Wildwood option	$2,200	$2,900
1970-1972	Antigua only	$1,700	$2,250

Coronado Bass Reissue
2014-2016. Reissue of the 2 pickup, block inlay, Coronado II.

2014-2016		$400	$525

Dimension Bass
2004-2006. Made in Mexico, 4- or 5-string, P and J pickups.

2004-2006		$400	$525

HM Bass
1989-1991. Japanese-made, 4 strings (IV) or 5 strings (V), basswood body, no 'guard, 3 Jazz Bass pickups, 5-way switch, master volume, master TBX, sunburst.

1989-1991	IV, 4-string	$625	$825
1989-1991	V, 5-string	$675	$875

Jaguar Bass
2006-2010. Made in Japan, Jaguar Bass logo on headstock.

2006-2010		$750	$1,000

Jaguar Bass Modern Player
2012-2016. Made in China, koto body, maple neck and 'board, black.

2012-2016		$275	$350

Jaguar Baritone Custom Bass
2007. Fender Jaguar Baritone Custom logo on headstock, 6-string.

2007		$900	$1,200

Deluxe Jaguar Bass
2012-2014. Maple neck, rosewood 'board, 2 pickups, 3-color sunburst, Candy Apple Red, Cobalt Blue.

2012-2014		$575	$775

Troy Sanders Jaguar Bass
2014-present. Artist series, alder body, bolt-on maple neck, 2 pickups, silverburst.

2014-2019		$525	$700

Jazz Bass
The following are variations of the Jazz Bass. The first five listings are for the main U.S.-made models. All others are listed alphabetically after that in the following order:
Jazz Bass
Standard Jazz Bass
American Standard Jazz Bass
American Series Jazz Bass
American Professional Jazz Bass
50th Anniversary American Standard Jazz Bass
50th Anniversary Jazz Bass Limited Edition
'60s Jazz Bass (Custom Shop)
'60s Jazz Bass (Import)
Road Worn '60s Jazz Bass
60th Anniversary American Jazz Bass
'62 Jazz Bass
'64 Jazz Bass (Custom Shop)
'64 Jazz Bass (American Vintage)
'66 Jazz Bass Special Limited Edition
'74 Jazz Bass (American Vintage)
'75 Jazz Bass (American Vintage)
Aerodyne Jazz Bass
American Deluxe Jazz/Jazz V Bass
American Deluxe FMT Jazz Bass
American Elite Jazz/Jazz V Bass
American Ultra Jazz Bass
Contemporary Jazz
Custom Classic Jazz/Jazz V Bass
Deluxe Jazz/Jazz V Bass (Active)
Deluxe Power Jazz Bass
Foto Flame Jazz Bass
FSR Standard Special Edition Jazz Bass
Geddy Lee Signature Jazz Bass
Gold Jazz Bass
Highway One Jazz Bass
Jaco Pastorius Jazz Bass
Jazz Plus IV/Jazz Plus V Bass
Jazz Special Bass (Import)
Marcus Miller Signature Jazz Bass
Noel Redding Signature Jazz Bass
Rarities Flame Ash Top Jazz Bass
Reggie Hamilton Jazz Bass
Roscoe Beck Jazz IV/V Bass
Select Jazz Bass
Standard/Player Jazz Bass (Import)
Standard/Player Jazz Fretless Bass (Import)
Ventures Limited Edition Jazz Bass
Victor Baily Jazz Bass

Jazz Bass
1960-1981. Two stack knobs '60-'62, 3 regular controls '62 on. Dot markers '60-'66, block markers from '66 on. Rosewood 'board standard, but maple available from '68 on. With the introduction of vintage reissue models in '81, Fender started calling the American-made version the Standard Jazz Bass.

Fender Jaguar Modern Player

1966 Fender Jazz Bass
Frank Manno

BASSES

1963 Fender Jazz
Craig Brody

1966 Fender Jazz
Carter Vintage Guitars

BASSES

That became the American Standard Jazz Bass in '88, the American Series Jazz Bass in '00, back to the American Standard Jazz Bass in '08, and currently the American Professional Jazz Bass. Post '71 Jazz Bass values are affected more by condition than color or neck option. The Jazz Bass was fitted with a 3-bolt neck or bullet rod in late-'74. Prices assume a 3-bolt neck starting in '75. Please refer to the beginning of the Fender Bass Section for details on Fender color options. Post '71 Jazz Bass values are affected more by condition than color or neck option. The Jazz Bass was fitted with a 3-bolt neck or bullet rod in late-'74. Prices assume a 3-bolt neck starting in '75. Please refer to the beginning of the Fender Bass Section for details on Fender color options.

MODEL YEAR	FEATURES	EXC. COND. LOW	HIGH
1960	Common color	$19,800	$27,000
1960	Rare color	$27,000	$36,000
1960	Sunburst	$18,900	$24,300
1961-1962	Common color, stack knob	$19,800	$27,000
1961-1962	Rare color, stack knob	$27,000	$36,000
1961-1962	Sunburst, stack knob	$18,000	$24,000
1962	Common color, 3 knob, curved	$9,900	$14,400
1962	Common color, 3 knob, slab	$15,300	$20,700
1962	Rare color, 3 knob, curved	$14,400	$24,300
1962	Rare color, knob, slab	$20,700	$31,500
1962	Sunburst, 3 knob, curved	$10,000	$13,300
1962	Sunburst, 3 knob, slab	$10,800	$14,400
1963	Common color	$8,100	$12,600
1963	Rare color	$12,600	$22,500
1963	Sunburst	$9,200	$12,100
1964	Common color	$8,100	$12,600
1964	Rare color	$12,600	$22,500
1964	Sunburst, early '64	$8,000	$10,500
1964	Sunburst, late '64	$7,500	$9,900
1965	Common color	$7,200	$11,700
1965	Rare color	$11,700	$17,000
1965	Sunburst	$5,900	$7,700
1966	Common color	$6,300	$8,600
1966	Rare color	$8,600	$11,500
1966	Sunburst, blocks	$5,100	$6,700
1966	Sunburst, dots	$5,100	$6,700
1967	Custom color	$5,400	$10,000
1967	Sunburst	$5,100	$6,700
1968	Custom color	$5,400	$10,000
1968	Sunburst	$4,900	$6,300
1969	Custom color	$5,000	$9,000
1969	Sunburst	$4,100	$5,400
1970	Custom color	$4,800	$8,600
1970	Sunburst	$3,800	$5,000
1971	Custom color	$3,600	$5,800
1971	Sunburst	$3,000	$4,000
1972	Custom color	$2,400	$4,500

MODEL YEAR	FEATURES	EXC. COND. LOW	HIGH
1972	Natural	$1,800	$2,400
1972	Sunburst	$2,500	$3,300
1973	Custom color	$2,400	$4,500
1973	Natural	$1,800	$2,400
1973	Sunburst	$2,500	$3,300
1973	Walnut	$1,800	$2,400
1974	Custom colors, 3-bolt	$2,200	$2,900
1974	Custom colors, 4-bolt	$2,400	$3,800
1974	Natural, 3-bolt	$1,700	$2,300
1974	Natural, 4-bolt	$1,800	$2,400
1974	Sunburst, 3-bolt, late-'74	$2,200	$2,900
1974	Sunburst, 4-bolt	$2,500	$3,300
1974	Walnut, 3-bolt	$1,700	$2,300
1974	Walnut, 4-bolt	$1,800	$2,400
1975-1977	Black, blond, white, wine, 3-bolt	$2,200	$2,900
1975-1977	Natural, 3-bolt	$1,800	$2,400
1975-1977	Sunburst, 3-bolt	$2,200	$2,900
1975-1977	Walnut, 3-bolt	$1,700	$2,300
1978-1979	Antigua	$1,700	$2,200
1978-1979	Black, blond, white, wine	$1,500	$1,950
1978-1979	Natural	$1,500	$1,950
1978-1979	Sunburst, 3-bolt	$1,500	$1,950
1978-1979	Walnut	$1,500	$1,950
1980	Antigua	$1,700	$2,200
1980	Black, white, wine	$1,500	$1,950
1980	Natural	$1,500	$1,950
1980	Sunburst, 3-bolt	$1,500	$1,950
1981	Black & Gold Collector's Edition	$1,400	$1,900
1981	Black, white, wine	$1,400	$1,900
1981	International colors	$1,900	$2,450
1981	Sunburst	$1,500	$1,950

Standard Jazz Bass

1981-1984. Replaced Jazz Bass ('60-'81) and replaced by the American Standard Jazz Bass in '88. Name now used on import version. Please refer to the beginning of the Fender Bass Section for details on Fender color options.

1981-1984		$775	$1,025

American Standard Jazz Bass

1988-2000, 2008-2016. Replaced Standard Jazz Bass ('81-'88) and replaced by the American Series Jazz Bass in '00, back to American Standard in Jan. '08.

1988-2016		$750	$1,000

American Standard Jazz V Bass

1998-2000, 2008-2016. 5-string version.

1998-2016		$750	$1,000

American Series Jazz Bass

2000-2007. Replaces American Standard Jazz Bass. Renamed American Standard in '08.

2000-2007		$750	$1,000

American Series Jazz V Bass

2000-2007. 5-string version.

2000-2007		$750	$1,000

MODEL YEAR	FEATURES	EXC. COND. LOW	HIGH

American Professional Jazz Bass

2017-present. Redesign includes V-Mod pickups, narrow-tall frets, 'deep C' neck profile, various colors. Also available left-hand model.

| 2017-2019 | | $750 | $1,000 |

50th Anniversary American Standard Jazz Bass

1996. Regular American Standard with gold hardware, 4- or 5-string, gold Fender's 50th Anniversary commemorative neck plate, rosewood 'board, sunburst.

| 1996 | IV | $900 | $1,150 |
| 1996 | V | $925 | $1,175 |

50th Anniversary Jazz Bass Limited Edition

2010. 50th anniversary of the Jazz Bass, nitro Candy Apple Red with matching headstock, mix of vintage and modern specs, rosewood 'board, block markers, 50th Anniversary neck plate.

| 2010 | | $1,550 | $2,000 |

'60s Jazz Bass (Custom Shop)

1994-1998. Early '60s specs, relic for 1996-1998. Replaced by the CS '64 Jazz Bass. Early Relic work was done outside of Fender by Vince Cunetto or his staff.

1994-1995		$2,075	$2,700
1996	Relic (Cunetto)	$2,075	$2,700
1997-1998	Relic (Cunetto staff)	$2,075	$2,700

'60s Jazz Bass (Import)

1991-1994, 2001-2019. Classic series, '60s features, rosewood 'board, Japan-made for first years, Mexico after.

| 1991-1994 | Japan | $525 | $700 |
| 2001-2019 | Mexico | $425 | $575 |

Road Worn '60s Jazz Bass

2009-present. Rosewood 'board, aged finish.

| 2009-2019 | | $475 | $625 |

60th Anniversary American Jazz Bass

2006. Rosewood 'board, 3-tone sunburst.

| 2006 | | $925 | $1,200 |

'62 Jazz Bass

1982-1984, 1986-2012. U.S.A.-made, American Vintage series, reissue of '62 Jazz Bass. Please refer to the beginning of the Fender Bass Section for details on Fender color options.

1982-1984		$2,550	$3,300
1986-1999		$1,225	$1,600
2000-2012		$1,100	$1,450

'64 Jazz Bass (Custom Shop)

1998-2009. Alder body, rosewood 'board, tortoise shell 'guard. From June '95 to June '99 Relic work was done outside of Fender by Vince Cunetto and included a certificate noting model and year built, a bass without the certificate is valued less than shown.

1998-1999	Relic (Cunetto)	$2,075	$2,700
2000-2009	Closet Classic option	$1,750	$2,300
2000-2009	NOS option	$1,750	$2,300
2000-2009	Relic option	$1,900	$2,450

'64 Jazz Bass (American Vintage)

2013-2017. American Vintage series, dot inlays.

| 2013-2017 | | $1,100 | $1,450 |

'66 Jazz Bass Special Limited Edition

2013. Japan, made for retailer Sweetwater, aged Oly White, 132 made for North American distribution.

| 2013 | | $700 | $925 |

'74 Jazz Bass (American Vintage)

2013-2017. American Vintage series, block inlays.

| 2013-2017 | | $1,225 | $1,600 |

'75 Jazz Bass (American Vintage)

1994-2012. American Vintage series, maple neck with black block markers.

| 1994-2012 | | $1,100 | $1,450 |

Aerodyne Jazz Bass

2003-present. Bound basswood body, P/J pickups, Deluxe Series.

| 2003-2019 | | $575 | $725 |

American Deluxe Jazz/Jazz V Bass

1998-2016. U.S., 4 (IV) or 5-string (V), active electronics, alder or ash body. Alder body colors - sunburst or transparent red, ash body colors - white, blond, transparent teal green or transparent purple.

| 1998-2016 | IV or V | $925 | $1,200 |

American Deluxe FMT Jazz Bass

2001-2006. Flame maple top version (FMT), active EQ, dual J pickups.

| 2001-2006 | | $1,000 | $1,300 |

American Elite Jazz/Jazz V Bass

2016-2019. Compound radius 'board, 4 (IV) or 5-string (V), Noiseless pickups, onboard preamp, various colors.

| 2016-2019 | IV or V | $1,125 | $1,475 |

American Ultra Jazz Bass

2019-present. Alder or ash body, 2 Noiseless Vintage pickups, redesigned active/passive preamp, 4- or 5-string, various colors with satin finish.

| 2019-2020 | IV | $1,050 | $1,375 |
| 2019-2020 | V | $1,100 | $1,425 |

Contemporary Jazz

1987. Made in Japan.

| 1987 | | $400 | $525 |

Custom Classic Jazz/Jazz V Bass

2001-2009. Custom Shop, slightly slimmer waist, deeper cutaways, maple or rosewood 'board, block inlays, 4 (IV) or 5-string (V).

| 2001-2009 | IV or V | $1,475 | $1,925 |

Deluxe Jazz/Jazz V Bass (Active)

1995-present. Made in Mexico, active electronics, 4 (IV) or 5-string (V), various colors.

| 1995-2019 | IV or V | $375 | $500 |

Deluxe Power Jazz Bass

2006. Part of Deluxe Series with Fishman piezo power bridge.

| 2006 | | $550 | $725 |

Foto Flame Jazz Bass

1994-1996. Japanese import, alder and basswood body with Foto Flame figured wood image.

| 1994-1996 | | $600 | $775 |

FSR Standard Special Edition Jazz Bass

2007-2009. Made in Mexico, Fender Special Edition logo on back of headstock, ash body with natural finish.

| 2007-2009 | | $350 | $475 |

1979 Fender Jazz
Philip Maciver

Fender Deluxe Jazz V
John Hefty

1998 Fender Roscoe Beck Jazz V

Imaged by Heritage Auctions, HA.com

1978 Fender Musicmaster

Justin Nortillo

MODEL YEAR	FEATURES	EXC. COND. LOW	HIGH
Geddy Lee Signature Jazz Bass			
1998-present. Limited run import in '98, now part of Artist Series, black.			
1998-2019		$600	$800
Gold Jazz Bass			
1981-1984. Gold finish and gold-plated hardware.			
1981-1984		$1,800	$2,400
Highway One Jazz Bass			
2003-2011. U.S.-made, alder body, satin lacquer finish.			
2003-2011		$550	$725
Jaco Pastorius Jazz Bass			
1999-present. Artist Series, standard production model made in Corona, '62 3-color sunburst body without pickup covers.			
1999-2000	Fretted	$1,100	$1,500
1999-2019	Fretless	$1,100	$1,500
Jazz Plus IV/Jazz Plus V Bass			
1990-1994. Alder body, 4-string (IV) or 5-string (V), 2 Lace Sensors, active electronics, rotary circuit selector, master volume, balance, bass boost, bass cut, treble boost, treble cut, various colors.			
1990-1994	Various colors	$700	$975
Jazz Special Bass (Import)			
1984-1991. Japanese-made, Jazz/Precision hybrid, Precision-shaped basswood body, Jazz neck (fretless available), 2 P/J pickups, offered with active (Power) or passive electronics.			
1984-1991		$450	$600
Marcus Miller Signature Jazz Bass			
1998-2014. Artist series.			
1998-2004	Import	$725	$950
2005-2014	US Custom Shop	$1,200	$1,575
Noel Redding Signature Jazz Bass			
1997. Limited Edition import, artist signature on 'guard, sunburst, rosewood 'board.			
1997		$900	$1,175
Rarities Flame Ash Top Jazz Bass			
2019-present. Two-piece alder body with flame ash top, Plasma Red Burst finish.			
2019-2020		$1,450	$1,850
Reggie Hamilton Jazz Bass			
2002-2016. Alder body, passive/active switch and pan control.			
2002-2016		$500	$650
Roscoe Beck Jazz IV/V Bass			
1997-2009. 5-string version offered '97-'06, 4-string '09.			
1997-2009	5-string	$1,350	$1,750
2004-2009	4-string	$1,300	$1,700
Select Jazz Bass			
2012-2013. US-made, figured top, rear-headstock 'Fender Select' medallion.			
2012-2013		$1,600	$2,100
Standard/Player Jazz Bass (Import)			
1985-present. Standard series, Japan-made into '90, Mexico after. Not to be confused with '81-'84 American-made model with the same name.			
1985	Japan	$700	$900
1986-1990	Japan	$675	$875
1991-2019	Mexico	$350	$450

MODEL YEAR	FEATURES	EXC. COND. LOW	HIGH
Standard/Player Jazz Fretless Bass (Import)			
1994-2018. Standard series, fretless version.			
1994-2018	IV or V	$350	$450
Ventures Limited Edition Jazz Bass			
1996. Made in Japan, part of Ventures guitar and bass set, dark purple.			
1996		$1,000	$1,300
Victor Baily Jazz Bass			
2002-2011. Artist series, koa, rosewood and mahogany body, fretless with white fret markers.			
2002-2011		$1,100	$1,425
JP-90 Bass			
1990-1994. Two P/J pickups, rosewood fretboard, poplar body, black or red.			
1990-1994		$375	$500
Kingman Bass			
2011-present. Acoustic, solid spruce top, mahogany back and sides.			
2011-2019		$350	$450
MB Bass			
1994-1995. Made in Japan, offset double-cut, 1 P- and 1 J-style pickup, 4-string (IV) or 5-string (V).			
1994-1995	IV or V	$325	$450
Musicmaster Bass			
1970-1983. Shorter scale, solidbody, 1 pickup. various colors.			
1970-1983		$900	$1,200
Mustang Bass			
1966-1982. Shorter scale, solidbody, 1 pickup, offered in standard colors and, for '69-'73, Competition Red, Blue and Orange with racing stripes on the body (with matching headstock for '69-'70).			
1966-1969		$1,550	$2,000
1969-1970	Competition	$2,025	$2,600
1970-1979		$1,200	$1,600
1978-1980	Antigua finish	$1,500	$1,975
1980-1982		$775	$1,000
Mustang Bass (Japan)			
2002-2018. Alder body, '60s features.			
2002-2018		$500	$650
Parallel Universe '51 Telecaster PJ Bass			
2018. Limited edition, authentic '51 style, mixes elements from both Jazz and Precision Basses.			
2018		$1,100	$1,425
Performer Bass			
1985-1986. Swinger-like body style, active electronics, various colors.			
1985-1986		$1,200	$1,550
Postmodern Bass			
2015-present. Custom Shop, P-Bass body, Jazz Bass neck, at times offered in Relic, Journeyman Relic, NOS, and Lush Closet Classic finishes.			
2015-2019		$1,800	$2,400

Precision Bass

The following are variations of the Precision Bass. The first listings are for the main U.S.-made models. All others are listed alphabetically after that in the following order:

Precision Bass
Standard Precision Bass
American Standard Precision Bass
American Series Precision Bass
American Series Precision V Bass
American Professional Precision Bass
40th Anniversary Precision Bass (Custom Shop)
50th Anniversary American Standard Precision Bass
50th Anniversary Precision Bass
'50s Precision Bass
Road Worn '50s Precision Bass
'51 Precision Bass
'55 Precision Bass (Custom Shop)
'57 Precision Bass
'57 Precision Bass (Custom Shop)
'57 Precision Bass (Import)
'59 Precision Bass (Custom Shop)
60th Anniversary Precision Bass (Mexico)
60th Anniversary Precision Bass (USA)
'61 Precision Bass (Custom Shop)
'62 Precision Bass
'62 Precision Bass (Import)
'63 Precision Bass (U.S.A.)
Adam Clayton Signature Precision Bass
Aerodyne Classic Precision Special Bass
American Deluxe Precision Bass
American Ultra Precision Bass
Big Block Precision Bass
Cabronita Precision Bass
California Precision Bass Special
Deluxe Active Precision Bass Special
Elite Series Precision Bass
Foto Flame Precision Bass
Highway One Precision Bass
Magnificent Seven Limited Edition American Standard PJ Bass
Mark Hoppus Signature Precision Bass
Mike Dirnt Road Worn Precision Bass
Nate Mendel Precision Bass
Precision Bass Jr.
Precision Bass Lyte
Precision Special Bass (U.S.A.)
Precision Special Bass (Mexico)
Pino Palladino Signature Precision Bass
Precision U.S. Plus/Plus Bass
Precision U.S. Deluxe/Plus Deluxe Bass
Roger Waters Precision Bass
Select Precision Bass
Standard/Player Precision Bass (Import)
Sting Precision Bass
Tony Franklin Precision Bass
Walnut Elite Precision Bass
Walnut Precision Special Bass

Precision Bass

1951-1981. Slab body until '54, 1-piece maple neck standard until '59, optional after '69, rosewood 'board standard '59 on (slab until mid-'62, curved after), blond finish standard until '54, sunburst standard after that (2-tone '54-'58, 3-tone after '58). Became the Standard Precision Bass in '81-'85, the American Standard Precision for '88-'00, the American Series Precision Bass in

MODEL YEAR	FEATURES	EXC. COND. LOW	HIGH

'00-'08, and the American Standard Precision again for '08-'16. Currently called the American Professional Precision Bass. Unlike the Jazz and Telecaster Basses, the Precision was never fitted with a 3-bolt neck or bullet rod. Please refer to the beginning of the Fender Bass Section for details on Fender color options.

MODEL YEAR	FEATURES	EXC. COND. LOW	HIGH
1951-1954	Blond, slab	$14,500	$19,000
1955	Blond, contour	$12,500	$16,000
1956	Blond, contour	$10,800	$14,000
1956	Sunburst, contour	$10,000	$13,000
1957	Blond	$10,500	$14,000
1957	Blond, anodized guard	$10,500	$14,000
1957	Sunburst	$9,500	$12,400
1957	Sunburst, anodized guard, late '57	$9,300	$12,000
1958	Blond	$10,500	$14,000
1958	Sunburst, anodized guard	$9,500	$12,400
1959	Blond	$10,500	$14,000
1959	Sunburst, anodized guard	$9,500	$12,400
1959	Sunburst, tortoise guard	$9,500	$12,400
1960	Blond	$10,500	$14,000
1960	Custom color	$18,000	$36,000
1960	Sunburst	$9,000	$11,500
1961	Custom color	$9,000	$26,000
1961	Sunburst	$8,000	$10,500
1962	Custom color, curved	$8,000	$17,000
1962	Custom color, slab	$9,000	$26,000
1962	Sunburst, curved	$6,100	$8,000
1962	Sunburst, slab	$6,800	$9,000
1963	Custom color	$8,000	$17,000
1963	Sunburst	$6,000	$7,800
1964	Custom color	$8,000	$14,000
1964	Sunburst, early '64	$6,000	$7,800
1964	Sunburst, late '64	$5,400	$7,000
1965	Custom color	$7,000	$12,000
1965	Sunburst	$5,100	$6,600
1966	Custom color	$6,000	$11,000
1966	Sunburst	$4,200	$5,400
1967	Custom color	$6,000	$11,000
1967	Sunburst	$4,200	$5,400
1968	Custom color	$6,000	$11,000
1968	Sunburst	$4,200	$5,400
1969	Custom color	$6,000	$11,000
1969	Sunburst	$4,200	$5,400
1970	Custom color	$3,000	$6,500
1970	Sunburst	$2,600	$3,300
1971	Custom color	$3,000	$6,500
1971	Sunburst	$2,200	$2,900
1972	Custom color	$2,300	$5,000
1972	Sunburst	$2,200	$2,900
1973	Custom color	$2,300	$5,000
1973	Natural	$2,000	$2,600
1973	Sunburst	$2,200	$2,900
1973	Walnut	$2,200	$2,900
1974	Black, blond, white	$2,000	$2,700
1974	Natural	$2,000	$2,600

1978 Fender Mustang
Justin Nortillo

1959 Fender Precision
Charlie Faucher

Fender Road Worn '50s Precision

Johnny Zapp

1988 Fender '62 Precision

Jonathan Bell

MODEL YEAR	FEATURES	EXC. COND. LOW	HIGH
1974	Sunburst	$2,200	$2,900
1974	Walnut	$2,200	$2,900
1975-1977	Black, blond, wine, white	$2,100	$2,700
1975-1977	Natural	$2,100	$2,600
1975-1977	Sunburst	$2,100	$2,700
1975-1977	Walnut	$2,100	$2,700
1978-1979	Antigua	$1,700	$2,200
1978-1979	Black, blond, wine, white	$1,500	$1,950
1978-1979	Natural	$1,500	$1,950
1978-1979	Sunburst	$1,500	$1,950
1978-1979	Walnut	$1,500	$1,950
1980	Antigua	$1,700	$2,200
1980	Black, white, wine	$1,400	$1,900
1980	Color withmatching headstk, gold hw	$2,000	$2,575
1980	International colors	$1,900	$2,450
1980	Natural	$1,400	$1,900
1980	Sunburst	$1,400	$1,900
1981	Black & gold	$1,400	$1,900
1981	Black, white, wine	$1,400	$1,900
1981	International colors	$1,900	$2,450
1981	Sunburst	$1,500	$1,950

Standard Precision Bass

1981-1984. Replaces Precision Bass, various colors. Replaced by American Standard Precision '88-'00. The Standard name is used on import Precision model for '88-present.

1981-1984		$775	$1,025

American Standard Precision Bass

1988-2000, 2008-2016. Replaces Standard Precision Bass, replaced by American Series Precision in '00, back to American Standard in Jan. '08.

1988-1989	Blond, gold hw	$750	$1,000
1988-2016	Various colors	$750	$1,000

American Series Precision Bass

2000-2007. Replaces American Standard Precision Bass, various colors. Renamed American Standard in '08.

2000-2007		$750	$1,000

American Series Precision V Bass

2000-2007. 5-string version.

2000-2007		$750	$1,000

American Professional Precision Bass

2017-present. Redesign includes V-Mod pickups, '63 P Bass neck profile, narrow-tall frets, various colors. Also available left-hand model.

2017-2019		$750	$1,000

40th Anniversary Precision Bass (Custom Shop)

1991. 400 made, quilted amber maple top, gold hardware.

1991		$2,000	$2,575

50th Anniversary American Standard Precision Bass

1996. Regular American Standard with gold hardware, 4- or 5-string, gold 50th Anniversary commemorative neck plate, rosewood 'board, sunburst.

1996		$900	$1,150

50th Anniversary Precision Bass

2001. Commemorative certificate with date and serial number, butterscotch finish, ash body, maple neck, black 'guard.

2001	With certificate	$900	$1,150

'50s Precision Bass

1992-1996, 2006-2019. First run made in Japan, currently in Mexico, 1 split-coil, maple neck.

1992-1996	Japan	$450	$600
2006-2019	Mexico	$450	$600

Road Worn '50s Precision Bass

2009-2019. Mexico, 1 split-coil, maple neck, aged finish.

2009-2019		$475	$625

'51 Precision Bass

1994-1997, 2003-2010. Import from Japan, no pickup or bridge covers, blond or sunburst. Offered in Japan in the '90s.

1994-1997	Japan only	$600	$775
2003-2010		$475	$600

'55 Precision Bass (Custom Shop)

2003-2011. 1955 specs including oversized 'guard, 1-piece maple neck/fretboard, preproduction bridge and pickup covers, single-coil pickup. Offered in N.O.S., Closet Classic or highest-end Relic.

2003-2006	NOS	$1,750	$2,300
2003-2006	Relic	$1,900	$2,450
2003-2011	Closet Classic	$1,750	$2,300

'57 Precision Bass

1982-1984, 1986-2012. U.S.-made reissue, American Vintage series, various colors.

1982-1984		$2,550	$3,300
1986-1999		$1,225	$1,600
2000-2012		$1,100	$1,450

'57 Precision Bass (Custom Shop)

2013. Heavy relic.

2013	Heavy relic	$2,000	$2,600

'57 Precision Bass (Import)

1984-1986. Foreign-made, black.

1984-1986		$1,100	$1,400

'59 Precision Bass (Custom Shop)

2003-2010. Custom Shop built with late-'59 specs, rosewood 'board.

2003-2008	Closet Classic	$1,750	$2,300
2003-2010	NOS	$1,750	$2,300
2003-2010	Relic	$1,900	$2,450

60th Anniversary Precision Bass (Mexico)

2005. Made in Mexico, with 60th Anniversary gig bag.

2005		$375	$475

60th Anniversary Precision Bass (USA)

2011. 1951-2011 Anniversary date label.

2011		$925	$1,200

'61 Precision Bass (Custom Shop)

2010-2013. Made for Musician's Friend and Guitar Center.

2010-2013	Closet Classic	$1,750	$2,300
2010-2013	NOS	$1,750	$2,300
2010-2013	Relic	$1,900	$2,450

'62 Precision Bass

1982-1984, 1986-2012. American Vintage series, alder body. No production in '85.

1982-1984		$2,550	$3,300
1986-1989		$1,225	$1,600

The *Vintage Guitar Price Guide* shows low to high values for items in all-original excellent condition, and, where applicable, with original case or cover.

MODEL YEAR	FEATURES	EXC. COND. LOW	HIGH
1990	Mary Kaye Blond	$1,550	$2,000
1990-1999		$1,225	$1,600
2000-2012		$1,100	$1,450

'62 Precision Bass (Import)
1984-1986. Foreign-made, black.

1984-1986		$850	$1,150

'63 Precision Bass (U.S.A.)
2013-2017. American Vintage series.

2013-2017		$1,075	$1,450

Adam Clayton Signature Precision Bass
2011. Custom Shop Limited Edition.

2011		$2,750	$3,600

Aerodyne Classic Precision Special Bass
2006. Made in Japan, labeled Precision and Aerodyne P Bass, figured maple top, matching headstock, P-J pickup.

2006		$575	$725

American Deluxe Precision Bass
1998-2016. U.S., active electronics, 4 (IV) or 5-string (V), alder or ash body. Alder body colors - sunburst or transparent red. Ash body colors - white blond, transparent teal green or transparent purple.

1998-2016	IV or V	$925	$1,200

American Ultra Precision Bass
2019-present. Alder or ash body, 2 Noiseless Vintage pickups, 4-string, various colors with gloss finish.

2019-2020		$1,050	$1,375

Big Block Precision Bass
2005-2009. Pearloid block markers, black finish with matching headstock, 1 double Jazz Bass humbucker, bass and treble boost and cut controls.

2005-2009		$550	$700

Cabronita Precision Bass
2014-2015. One Fideli'Tron pickup, 2 knobs.

2014-2015		$275	$375

California Precision Bass Special
1997. California Series, assembled and finished in Mexico and California, P/J pickup configuration.

1997		$550	$700

Deluxe Active Precision Bass Special
1995-present. Made in Mexico, P/J pickups, Jazz Bass neck.

1995-2019		$350	$450

Elite Series Precision Bass
1983-1985. Active electronics, noise-cancelling pickups, Elite I (ash body, 1 pickup), Elite II (2 pickups), Gold Elite I (gold-plated hardware, 1 pickup), Gold Elite II (2 pickups), various colors.

1983-1985	Various models	$1,550	$2,000

Foto Flame Precision Bass
1994-1996. Made in Japan, simulated woodgrain finish, natural or sunburst.

1994-1996		$600	$775

Highway One Precision Bass
2003-2011. U.S.-made, alder body, satin lacquer finish.

2003-2011		$600	$750

Magnificent Seven Limited Edition American Standard PJ Bass
2016. U.S., P-bass body with Jazz neck, 500 made.

2016		$825	$1,050

Mark Hoppus Signature Precision Bass
2002-2016. Mark Hoppus engraved on neck plate.

2002-2016	Mexico serial no	$475	$625

Mike Dirnt Road Worn Precision Bass
2014-present. '51 era P-Bass style, ash body, maple or rosewood 'board.

2014-2019		$600	$775

Nate Mendel Precision Bass
2013-present. Ash body, rosewood 'board.

2013-2019		$450	$600

Precision Bass Jr.
2004-2006. 3/4 size.

2004-2006		$325	$425

Precision Bass Lyte
1992-2001. Japanese-made, smaller, lighter basswood body, 2 pickups, sunburst.

1992-2001		$525	$700

Precision Special Bass (U.S.A.)
1980-1982. Gold hardware, matching headstock, active electronics, CA Red, LP Blue, Oly White or walnut (see separate listing).

1980-1982	Common color	$1,425	$1,850
1980-1982	Rare color	$1,900	$2,450

Precision Special Bass (Mexico)
1997-1998. 1 P- and 1 J-pickup. chrome hardware.

1997-1998		$400	$525

Pino Palladino Signature Precision Bass
2006-present. Custom Shop, based on '62 used by Palladino, certificate of authenticity, Fiesta Red.

2006		$2,050	$2,650

Precision U.S. Plus/Plus Bass
1989-1992. P-style bass with P- and J-bass pickups.

1989-1992	Standard color	$800	$1,250

Precision U.S. Deluxe/Plus Deluxe Bass
1991-1994. P-style bass with P- and J-bass pickups, active electronics, no 'guard models available.

1991-1994	Standard color	$800	$1,250

Roger Waters Precision Bass
2010-2019. Alder body, maple neck, black.

2010-2019		$500	$650

Select Precision Bass
2012. Alder body, flamed maple top, rear headstock 'Fender Select' medallion.

2012		$1,600	$2,100

Standard/Player Precision Bass (Import)
1985-present. Made in Japan into '90, and Mexico after. Not to be confused with '81-'84 American-made model with the same name.

1985	Japan	$700	$900
1986-1990	Japan	$675	$875
1991-2019	Mexico	$350	$450
2016	Mexico, Custom Art Series	$375	$500

Sting Precision Bass
2001-2013. Made in Japan, 2-tone sunburst, 1 single-coil, Sting's signature.

2001-2013		$475	$625

Tony Franklin Precision Bass
2007-present. Fretless, P and J pickups, 3-way selector, lacquer finish.

2007-2019		$1,100	$1,400

Fender Nate Mendel Precision

Fender Sting Precision

BASSES

BASSES

*1983 Fender Squier
Precision Bass Standard*
Rivington Guitars

1972 Fender Telecaster Bass
Justin Nortillo

Walnut Elite Precision Bass
1983-1985. The Elite Series feature active electronics and noise-cancelling pickups, walnut body, 1 pickup (Elite I) or 2 (Elite II), rosewood 'board, natural.

		LOW	HIGH
1983-1985	Elite I	$1,550	$2,000
1983-1985	Elite II	$1,550	$2,000

Walnut Precision Special Bass
1980-1982. Precision Bass Special with a walnut body, natural.

1980-1982		$1,425	$1,825

Prodigy Active Bass
1992-1995. U.S.-made, poplar body, 1 J- and 1 P-style pickup, active.

1992-1995		$675	$875

Rhodes Piano Bass
1962. Electric keyboard in bass register, Fender-Rhodes sticker, Piano Bass logo, various colors.

1962		$1,300	$1,800

Squier Affinity Jazz Bass
1997-present. Affinity is the lower priced series made in China.

1997-2019		$70	$100

Squier Bronco Bass
1998-present. The lowest priced Squier bass, single coil plastic cover pickup, 3/4 body.

1998-2019		$120	$155

Squier Bullet Bass
1983-2000. Japanese-made, Squier-branded, replaces Bullet Bass, black.

1983-2000		$175	$225

Squier Classic Vibe Bass Series
2009-present. Various models.

2009-2019		$150	$225

Squier HM Bass/HM Bass V
1989-1993. Korean-made, 5-string also offered.

1989-1993		$200	$250

Squier Jazz Bass Standard
1983-2010. Jazz bass import, without cover plates, various colors.

1983-1984	1st logo	$370	$480
1985-1989	2nd logo	$340	$460
1990-1999		$145	$200
2000-2010		$120	$155

Squier Katana Bass
1985-1986. Made in Japan, wedge-shaped, arrow headstock.

1985-1986		$525	$700

Squier Precision Bass Special
1998-2010. Agathis body, P/J pickups, 4-string (IV) or 5-string (V).

1998-2010	IV or V	$95	$125

Squier Precision Bass Standard
1983-2006.

1983-1984	1st logo	$365	$475
1985-1989	2nd logo	$340	$450
1990-1999	Some from Mexico	$145	$200
2000-2006	Indonesia	$120	$150

Squier Vintage Modified Series
2007-2019. Includes Jaguar bass, Jazz and Precision models.

2007-2019	Various models	$125	$200

Stu Hamm Urge Bass (U.S.A.)
1992-1999. Contoured Precision-style body with smaller wide treble cutaway, J and P pickups, 32" scale.

1992-1999		$1,200	$1,600

Stu Hamm Urge II Bass (U.S.A.)
1999-2009. J and P pickups, 34" scale.

1999-2009		$1,200	$1,600

Telecaster Bass
1968-1979. Slab solidbody, 1 pickup, fretless option '70, blond and custom colors available (Pink Paisley or Blue Floral '68-'69). Please refer to the beginning of the Fender Bass Section for details on Fender color options.

1968	Black, nitro	$4,000	$5,200
1968	Black, poly	$3,800	$5,000
1968	Blond, nitro	$2,800	$3,700
1968	Blond, poly	$2,700	$3,600
1968	Blue Floral Paisley	$7,200	$9,400
1968	Lake Placid Blue	$4,500	$6,000
1968	Red (Pink) Paisley	$6,900	$9,000
1969-1972	4-bolt, single-coil	$2,600	$3,400
1973-1974	3-bolt, hum, rare color	$2,500	$3,200
1973-1974	3-bolt, humbucker	$1,900	$2,500
1975-1979	3-bolt, humbucker	$1,750	$2,300

Zone Bass American Deluxe
2001-2006. Smaller lightweight offset double-cut, active humbuckers, exotic tone woods, U.S.-made.

2001-2006		$1,000	$1,300

Fodera
1983-present. Luthiers Vinnie Fodera and Joseph Lauricella build their professional and premium grade, production/custom, solidbody basses in Brooklyn, New York.
High-level Bass
1983-2019	4, 5, 6 strings	$6,000	$8,000
Mid-level Bass
1983-2019	4, 5, 6 strings	$4,000	$6,000
Low-level Bass
1983-2019	4, 5, 6 strings	$3,100	$4,000

Framus
1946-1975, 1996-present. Professional and premium grade, production/custom, basses made in Germany. They also build guitars and amps.
Atlantic Model 5/140 Bass
1960s. Single-cut thinline with f-holes, 2 pickups, sunburst or blackrose.
1960s		$475	$625
Atlantic Model 5/143 Bass
1960s. Offset double-cut thinbody with f-holes, 2 pickups, 4-on-a-side keys.
1960s		$475	$625
Atlantic Model 5/144 Bass
1960s. Double-cut thinbody with f-holes, ES-335 body style, 2 pickups. Becomes Model J/144 in '70s.
1960s		$475	$625

MODEL YEAR	FEATURES	EXC. COND. LOW	HIGH

Charavelle 4 Model 5/153 Bass
1960s. Double-cut thinline with f-holes, 335-style body, 2 pickups, sunburst, cherry red or Sunset.

1960s		$525	$700

De Luxe 4 Model 5/154 Bass
1960s. Double-cut thinline, sharp horns and f-holes, 2 pickups, mute, sunburst or natural/blond.

1960s		$525	$700

Electric Upright Bass
1950s. Full-scale neck, triangular body, black.

1958		$1,500	$1,975

Star Series (Bill Wyman) Bass
1959-1968. Early flyer says, Bill Wyman of the Rolling Stones prefers the Star Bass. The model name was later changed to Framus Stone Bass. Single-cut semi-hollow body, 5/149 (1 pickup) and 5/150 (2 pickups), sunburst.

1959-1965	Model 5/150	$850	$1,100
1960s	Model 5/149	$750	$1,000

Strato De Luxe Star Model 5/165 Bass
Ca. 1964-ca. 1972. Offset double-cut solidbody, 2 pickups, sunburst. There was also a gold hardware version (5/165 gl) and a 6-string (5/166).

1960s		$450	$575

Strato Star Series Bass
Ca. 1963-ca. 1972. Double-cut solidbody, 5/156/50 (1 pickup) or 5/156/52 (2 pickups), beige, cherry or sunburst.

1960s	Model 5/156/50	$450	$575
1960s	Model 5/156/52	$475	$625

T.V. Star Bass
1960s. Offset double-cut thinbody with f-holes, 2 pickups, short-scale, sunburst or cherry red. Most expensive of the '60s Framus basses, although not as popular as the Bill Wyman 5/150 model.

1960s		$450	$600

Triumph Electric Upright Bass
1956-1960. Solidbody bean pole electric bass, small body, long neck, slotted viol peghead, gold or black.

1956-1960		$1,650	$2,150

Fresher
1973-1985. Japanese-made, mainly copies of popular brands and not imported into the U.S., but they do show up at guitar shows. They also made guitars.

Solidbody Electric Bass

1970s		$250	$500

G & L
1980-present. Intermediate and professional grade, production/custom, electric basses made in the U.S. In '03, G & L introduced the Korean-made G & L Tribute Series. A Tribute logo is clearly identified on the headstock. They also build guitars.

ASAT Bass
1989-present. Single-cut, solidbody, active and passive modes, 2 humbuckers, various colors.

1989-1991	About 400 made	$875	$1,150
1992-2019		$750	$975

ASAT Commemorative Bass
1991-1992. About 150 made, 4-string ASAT commemorating Leo Fender's life.

1991-1992		$1,325	$1,725

ASAT Semi-Hollow Bass
2001-present. Semi-hollowbody style on ASAT bass.

2001-2019		$825	$1,075

Climax Bass
1992-1996. Single active humbucker MFD.

1992-1996		$750	$975

El Toro Bass
1983-1989. Double-cut, solidbody, 2 active, smaller, humbuckers, sunburst.

1983-1987		$1,050	$1,375
1988-1989		$875	$1,150

Interceptor Bass
1984-1991. Sharp pointed double-cut, solidbody, 2 active, smaller humbuckers, sunburst.

1984-1986		$1,700	$2,225
1988-1991	Body signature	$1,125	$1,475

JB-2 Bass
2001-2016. Alder body, 2 Alnico V pickups.

2001-2016		$750	$975

L-1000 Bass
1980-1994, 2008. Offset double-cut, solidbody, 1 pickup, various colors. Limited run in '08.

1980-1985	Ash	$750	$1,000
1980-1985	Mahogany	$750	$1,000
1980-1985	Maple	$750	$1,000
1986-1991		$750	$1,000
1992-1999	3-bolt	$750	$1,000
2008	4-bolt	$750	$1,000

L-1500 Bass
1997-2018. Offset double-cut solidbody, 1 MFD humbucker.

1997-2018		$750	$1,000

L-1500 Custom Bass
1997 only.

1997		$750	$1,000

L-1505 Bass
1998-2018. Five-string version, single MFD humbucker.

1998-2018		$800	$1,050

L-2000 30th Anniversary Bass
2010. Pearl Frost with matching headstock.

2010		$1,075	$1,400

L-2000 Bass
1980-present. Offset double-cut solidbody, 2 pickups, active electronics. Originally, the L-2000 was available with active (L-2000E) or passive (L-2000) electronics.

1980-1985	Ash	$1,050	$1,350
1986		$875	$1,150
1987-1991	Leo signature	$875	$1,150
1992-2019		$875	$1,150

L-2000 C.L.F. Centennial
2009-2010. Swamp ash body, blonde, black hardware, planned run of 50, Certificate of Authenticity.

2009-2010	COA, CD	$1,150	$1,500

L-2000 Custom Bass
1997. Ash top, wood-grain binding upgrade.

1997		$850	$1,125

Fodera Emperor Standard Classic

2000's G & L ASAT

1991 G&L SB-1

KC Cormack

1967 Gibson EB-O

Justin Nortillo

BASSES

MODEL YEAR	FEATURES	EXC. COND. LOW	HIGH
L-2000 Fretless Bass			
1980-1998. Fretless version.			
1980-1982		$1,125	$1,450
L-2000(E) Bass			
1980-1982. Offset double-cut, solidbody, 2 pickups, active electronics. Originally, the L-2000 was available with active (L-2000E) or passive (L-2000) electronics.			
1980-1982		$1,125	$1,475
L-2500 Bass			
1997-present. Five-string, dual MFD humbuckers, figured tops can vary.			
1997-2019		$1,125	$1,450
L-2500 Custom Bass			
1997. Ash top, wood-grain binding upgrade.			
1997		$1,125	$1,450
L-5000 Bass			
1988-1993. Offset double-cut, solidbody, G & L Z-shaped split-humbucker, 5 strings, approximately 400 made.			
1988-1992		$750	$975
L-5500 Bass			
1993-1997. Alder body, 5-string.			
1993-1997		$700	$925
L-5500 Custom Bass			
1997. Ash top, wood-grain binding upgrade.			
1997		$700	$925
LB-100 Bass			
1993-present. Follow-up to earlier Legacy Bass.			
1993-2019		$675	$875
Legacy Bass			
1992-1993. Offset double-cut solidbody, 1 split-coil, renamed LB-100 in '93.			
1992-1993		$675	$875
Lynx Bass			
1984-1991. Offset double-cut, solidbody, 2 single-coils, black.			
1984-1991		$675	$875
SB-1 Bass			
1982-2000, 2014-present. Solidbody, maple neck, body and 'board, split-humbucker, 1 tone and 1 volume control. Reappears in '14.			
1982-2000		$550	$700
SB-2 Bass			
1982-present. Maple neck with tilt adjustment, 1 split-coil humbucker and 1 single-coil.			
1982-2019		$700	$900

Garage by Wicked

2004-2010. A line of basses imported from China by luthier Nicholas Dijkman (Wicked) of Montreal, Quebec.

Gibson

1890s (1902)-present. Professional grade, production, U.S.-made electric basses. Gibson got into the electric bass market with the introduction of their Gibson Electric Bass in '53 (that model was renamed the EB-1 in '58 and reintroduced under that name in '69). Many more bass models followed. Gibson's custom colors can greatly increase the value of older instruments. Custom colors offered

MODEL YEAR	FEATURES	EXC. COND. LOW	HIGH
from '63 to '69 are Cardinal Red, Ember Red, Frost Blue, Golden Mist Metallic, Heather Metallic, Inverness Green, Kerry Green, Pelham Blue Metallic, Polaris White, Silver Mist Metallic.			
20/20 Bass			
1987-1988. Designed by Ned Steinberger, slim-wedge Steinberger style solidbody, 2 humbucker pickups, 20/20 logo on headstock, Luna Silver or Ferrari Red finish.			
1987-1988		$1,100	$1,400
Electric Bass (EB-1)			
1953-1958. Introduced as Gibson Electric Bass in '53, but was called the EB-1 by Gibson in its last year of '58, thus, the whole line is commonly called the EB-1 by collectors, reissued in '69 as the EB-1 (see EB-1 listing), brown.			
1953-1958		$4,000	$5,200
EB Bass			
1970, 2013-2019. Renamed from Melody Maker Bass, SG body, 1 humbucker pickup. Reintroduced in '13, 4- or 5-string, 2 pickups			
1970		$1,000	$1,300
2013-2019	Reintroduced	$425	$550
EB-0 Bass			
1959-1979. Double-cut slab body with banjo-type tuners in '59 and '60, double-cut SG-type body with conventional tuners from '61 on, 1 pickup. Faded custom colors are of less value.			
1959-1960	Cherry, slab body	$3,600	$4,700
1961	Cherry, SG body	$1,900	$2,500
1962	Cherry	$1,850	$2,450
1963	Cherry	$1,700	$2,250
1964	Cherry, early raised truss rod	$1,625	$2,150
1964	Cherry, late '64 truss rod	$1,475	$1,950
1965-1966	Cherry	$1,400	$1,850
1965-1966	Pelham Blue	$2,500	$3,275
1967-1968	Cherry	$1,250	$1,625
1967-1968	Pelham Blue	$2,175	$2,800
1968	Black	$1,550	$2,000
1968	Burgundy Metallic	$1,550	$2,000
1969	Cherry, solid head	$1,200	$1,575
1969	Pelham Blue	$2,175	$2,800
1969-1974	Slotted head	$950	$1,250
1975-1979		$950	$1,250
EB-0 F Bass			
1962-1965. EB-0 with added built-in fuzz, cherry.			
1962-1965		$2,800	$3,700
EB-0 L Bass			
1969-1979. 34.5 inch scale version of the EB-0, various colors.			
1969-1979		$1,075	$1,400
EB-1 Bass			
1969-1972. The Gibson Electric Bass ('53-'58) is often also called the EB-1 (see Electric Bass). Violin-shaped mahogany body, 1 pickup, standard tuners.			
1969-1972		$2,800	$3,600
EB-2 Bass			
1958-1961, 1964-1972. ES-335-type semi-hollowbody, double-cut, 1 pickup, banjo tuners '58-'60 and conventional tuners '60 on.			
1958	Sunburst	$4,000	$5,300

MODEL YEAR	FEATURES	EXC. COND. LOW	HIGH
1959	Natural	$4,700	$6,100
1959	Sunburst	$4,100	$5,300
1960	Natural	$4,700	$6,100
1960	Sunburst	$3,900	$5,100
1961	Sunburst, black pu	$2,900	$3,700
1961	Sunburst, brown pu	$3,000	$3,800
1964	Sunburst	$2,200	$2,900
1965	Sunburst	$2,100	$2,800
1966	Cherry, sunburst	$2,050	$2,700
1967-1969	Cherry, sunburst	$2,050	$2,700
1967-1969	Sparkling Burgundy	$2,150	$2,800
1967-1969	Walnut	$1,875	$2,450
1970-1972	Sunburst	$1,875	$2,450

EB-2 D Bass
1966-1972. Two-pickup version of EB-2, cherry, sunburst, or walnut.

MODEL YEAR	FEATURES	EXC. COND. LOW	HIGH
1966-1969	Cherry, sunburst	$2,450	$3,200
1967-1969	Sparkling Burgundy	$2,500	$3,300
1967-1969	Walnut	$2,300	$2,975
1970-1972	Cherry, sunburst	$2,300	$2,975

EB-3 Bass
1961-1979. SG-style solidbody, 2 humbuckers, solid peghead '61-'68 and '72-'79, slotted peghead '69-'71, cherry to '71, various colors after.

MODEL YEAR	FEATURES	EXC. COND. LOW	HIGH
1961-1964		$4,400	$5,750
1965	Early '65, wide nut	$3,500	$4,600
1965	Late '65, narrow nut	$2,475	$3,250
1965	White (rare)	$4,800	$6,200
1966-1968		$2,250	$2,925
1969	Early '69	$1,950	$2,525
1969	Late '69	$1,200	$1,575
1970-1979		$1,200	$1,575

EB-3 L Bass
1969-1972. 34.5" scale version of EB-3, slotted headstock, EB-3L logo on truss rod cover, cherry, natural, or walnut.

MODEL YEAR	FEATURES	EXC. COND. LOW	HIGH
1969-1972		$900	$1,175

EB-4 L Bass
1972-1979. SG-style, 1 humbucker, 34.5" scale, cherry or walnut.

MODEL YEAR	FEATURES	EXC. COND. LOW	HIGH
1972-1979		$775	$1,025

EB-6 Bass
1960-1966. Introduced as semi-hollowbody 335-style 6-string with 1 humbucker, changed to SG-style with 2 pickups in '62.

MODEL YEAR	FEATURES	EXC. COND. LOW	HIGH
1960	Natural, 335-style	$6,400	$8,400
1960-1961	Sunburst, 335-style	$4,800	$6,200
1962-1964	Cherry, SG-style	$8,000	$10,500
1965-1966	Cherry, SG-style	$6,500	$8,500

EB-650 Bass
1991-1993. Semi-acoustic single cut, maple neck, laminated maple body with center block, 2 TB Plus pickups.

MODEL YEAR	FEATURES	EXC. COND. LOW	HIGH
1991-1993	Blond	$3,100	$4,000
1991-1993	Blue	$2,800	$3,600
1991-1993	Other colors	$2,500	$3,200

EB-750 Bass
1991-1993. Like EB-650, but with Bartolini pickups and TCT active EQ.

MODEL YEAR	FEATURES	EXC. COND. LOW	HIGH
1991-1993	Blond	$3,100	$4,000
1991-1993	Blue	$2,800	$3,600
1991-1993	Other colors	$2,500	$3,200

ES-335 Bass
2013. Sunburst or ebony.

MODEL YEAR	FEATURES	EXC. COND. LOW	HIGH
2013		$1,150	$1,500

ES-Les Paul Bass
2015-2018. Semi-solid, 3-ply maple/poplar/maple top, back and sides, rosewood 'board, mother-of-pearl inlay, faded darkburst or gold top finish.

MODEL YEAR	FEATURES	EXC. COND. LOW	HIGH
2015-2018		$1,425	$1,850

Explorer Bass
1984-1987, 2011-2012. Alder body, ebony 'board, dot inlays, 2 humbuckers, various colors. Limited run in '11 in sunburst or silverburst.

MODEL YEAR	FEATURES	EXC. COND. LOW	HIGH
1984-1987	Standard finish	$1,000	$1,300
1985	Designer graphics	$1,075	$1,400
2011-2012	Silverburst	$850	$1,100
2011-2012	Sunburst	$675	$875

Flying V Bass
1981-1982, 2011-2012. Solidbody, Flying V body.

MODEL YEAR	FEATURES	EXC. COND. LOW	HIGH
1981-1982	Blue stain, ebony	$2,600	$3,400
1981-1982	Silverburst	$2,800	$3,600
2011-2012		$1,025	$1,375

Grabber Bass
1974-1982. Double-cut solidbody, 1 pickup, bolt maple neck, maple 'board, various colors.

MODEL YEAR	FEATURES	EXC. COND. LOW	HIGH
1974-1982		$775	$1,000

Grabber III Bass (G-3)
1975-1982. Double-cut solidbody, 3 pickups, bolt maple neck, maple 'board, nickel-plated hardware, various colors.

MODEL YEAR	FEATURES	EXC. COND. LOW	HIGH
1975-1982		$850	$1,100

Gibson IV Bass
1986-1988. Mahogany body and neck, double-cut, 2 pickups, black chrome hardware, various colors.

MODEL YEAR	FEATURES	EXC. COND. LOW	HIGH
1986-1988		$1,150	$1,500

Gibson V Bass
1986-1988. Double-cut, 5 strings, 2 pickups.

MODEL YEAR	FEATURES	EXC. COND. LOW	HIGH
1986-1988		$1,150	$1,500

L9-S Bass
1973. Natural maple or cherry, renamed Ripper Bass in '74.

MODEL YEAR	FEATURES	EXC. COND. LOW	HIGH
1973		$1,200	$1,575

Les Paul Bass
1970-1971. Single-cut solidbody, 2 pickups, walnut finish, renamed Les Paul Triumph Bass '71-'79.

MODEL YEAR	FEATURES	EXC. COND. LOW	HIGH
1970-1971		$1,975	$2,575

Les Paul Money Bass
2007-2008. Solidbody offset double-cut, 2 humbuckers, dot markers, figured maple top over mahogany body, 400 made.

MODEL YEAR	FEATURES	EXC. COND. LOW	HIGH
2007-2008		$975	$1,275

Les Paul Signature Bass
1973-1979. Double-cut, semi-hollowbody, 1 pickup, sunburst or gold (gold only by '76). Name also used on LPB-3 bass in '90s.

MODEL YEAR	FEATURES	EXC. COND. LOW	HIGH
1973-1979	Sunburst or gold	$2,625	$3,400

Les Paul Special LPB-1 Bass
1991-1998. 2 TB-Plus pickups, ebony 'board, dots, slab mahogany body, active electronics, also available as 5-string.

MODEL YEAR	FEATURES	EXC. COND. LOW	HIGH
1991-1998		$675	$875

1967 Gibson EB-2
Izzy Miller

1985 Gibson Explorer Bass "Designer Series"
Craig Brody

1982 Gibson Les Paul Triumph
Craig Brody

1963 Gibson Thunderbird II
Mike Riech

MODEL YEAR	FEATURES	EXC. COND. LOW	HIGH
Les Paul Deluxe Plus LPB-2 Bass			
1991-1998. Upgraded LPB-1, carved maple top, trapezoid inlays, active eq and Bartolini pickups. Flame maple top Premium version offered '93-'98.			
1991-1998		$1,000	$1,300
Les Paul Smartwood Bass			
1998. 2 TB pickups, active electronics, trapezoid inlays.			
1998		$1,200	$1,600
Les Paul Special V Bass			
1993-1996. Single-cut slab body, 5-string, 2 pickups, dot markers, black/ebony.			
1993-1996		$725	$925
Les Paul Standard Bass			
2000-2018. Maple top, chambered mahogany body, trapezoid inlays, 2 pickups.			
2000-2018	Various colors	$1,300	$1,700
Les Paul Standard LPB-3 Bass			
1991-1995. Like Les Paul Deluxe LPB-2 Bass, but with TB Plus pickups. Flame maple top Premium version offered '93-'95.			
1993-1995	Flamed top	$925	$1,200
Les Paul Triumph Bass			
1971-1979. Renamed from Les Paul Bass.			
1971-1979	Various colors	$1,000	$1,300
1973-1974	Optional white	$1,200	$1,600
Melody Maker Bass			
1967-1970. SG body, 1 humbucker pickup.			
1967-1970		$1,000	$1,300
Midtown Standard Bass			
2012-2018. Semi-hollow body, double-cut, baked maple or rosewood board, 2 pickups.			
2012-2018		$975	$1,275
Nikki Sixx Blackbird/Thunderbird Bass			
2000-2003, 2009. Blackbird has black finish and hardware, iron cross inlays.'09 Thunderbird was flamed maple.			
2000-2003		$1,200	$1,550
Q-80 Bass			
1986-1988. Victory Series body shape, 2 pickups, bolt neck, black chrome hardware, renamed Q-90 in '88.			
1986-1988		$650	$825
Q-90 Bass			
1988-1992. Renamed from Q-80, mahogany body, 2 active humbuckers, maple neck, ebony 'board.			
1988-1992		$650	$825
RD Artist Bass			
1977-1982. Double-cut solid maple body, laminated neck, 2 pickups, active electronics, string-thru-body, block inlays, various colors.			
1977-1982		$1,550	$2,000
RD Artist CMT Bass			
1982. Flamed maple top.			
1982		$2,600	$3,400
RD Artist VI Bass			
1980. Only 6 made, 6-string.			
1980		$3,800	$4,900
RD Standard Bass			
1977-1979. Double-cut, solid maple body, laminated neck, 2 pickups, regular electronics, string-thru-body, dot inlays, various colors.			
1977-1979		$1,225	$1,600

MODEL YEAR	FEATURES	EXC. COND. LOW	HIGH
Ripper Bass			
1974-1982. Introduced as L-9 S Bass in '73, double-cut solidbody, glued neck, 2 pickups, string-thru-body, sunburst or natural maple until '76, sunburst only after. Black option '78-'79 and silverburst '80.			
1974-1982	Natural, Sunburst	$1,200	$1,575
1978-1979	Black	$1,200	$1,575
1980	Silverburst	$1,950	$2,500
Ripper II Bass			
2009-2011. Solid maple body, 34" scale, 2 pickups, natural nitro lacquer.			
2009-2011		$900	$1,175
SB Series Bass			
1971-1978. In '71, had oval pickups, replaced mid-model with rectangular pickups. Includes 300 and 350 (30" scale, 1 and 2 pickups), 350 (30", 2 pickups), 400 (34", 1 pickup), 450 (34", 2 pickups). The 450 was special order only.			
1971-1973	SB-300, 400	$525	$700
1972-1974	SB-350, 450	$525	$700
1975-1978	SB-450 special order	$525	$700
SG Reissue/SG Standard Bass			
2005-present. Similar to '60s EB-3, 2 pickups, mahogany body, cherry or white. Renamed SG Standard in '08, various colors.			
2005-2019	Various colors	$825	$1,075
SG Standard Faded Bass			
2013-2018. Solid mahogany body, baked maple 'board, worn cherry or ebony finish.			
2013-2018		$525	$675
SG Supreme Bass			
2007-2008. Made in Nashville, SG body with AAA maple top, 2 pickups.			
2007-2008		$875	$1,150
Thunderbird II Bass			
1963-1969. Reverse solidbody until '65, non-reverse solidbody '65-'69, 1 pickup, custom colors available, reintroduced with reverse body for '83-'84.			
1963	Sunburst, reverse	$7,300	$9,500
1964	Pelham Blue, reverse	$10,800	$14,000
1964	Sunburst, reverse	$5,800	$7,700
1965	Cardinal Red, non-reverse	$6,700	$8,700
1965	Inverness Green, non-reverse	$6,700	$8,700
1965	Sunburst, non-reverse	$3,200	$4,200
1965	Sunburst, reverse	$5,700	$7,600
1966	Cardinal Red, non-reverse	$5,750	$7,650
1966	Pelham Blue	$8,700	$11,300
1966	Sunburst, non-reverse	$3,200	$4,200
1967	Cardinal Red, non-reverse	$5,700	$7,600
1967	Sunburst, non-reverse	$3,075	$4,000
1968	Cardinal Red, non-reverse	$5,700	$7,600

MODEL YEAR	FEATURES	EXC. COND. LOW	HIGH
1968-1969	Sunburst, non-reverse	$3,075	$4,000

Thunderbird III Bass

1979-1982. Reverse body, 2 pickups, Thunderbird logo on 'guard.

1979-1982		$2,300	$2,975

Thunderbird IV Bass

1963-1969. Reverse solidbody until '64, non-reverse solidbody '65-'69, 2 pickups, custom colors available, reintroduced with reverse body for '86-present (see Thunderbird IV Bass Reissue).

1963	Sunburst, reverse	$9,075	$11,800
1964	Frost Blue, reverse	$17,300	$22,500
1964	Pelham Blue, reverse	$17,300	$22,500
1964	Sunburst, reverse	$9,075	$11,800
1965	Cardinal Red, non-reverse	$10,400	$13,500
1965	Inverness Green, non-reverse	$10,400	$13,500
1965	Sunburst, reverse	$8,500	$11,075
1965-1966	Sunburst, non-reverse	$5,100	$6,650
1966	White, non-reverse	$9,700	$12,600
1967-1969	Sunburst, non-reverse	$5,125	$6,650

Thunderbird IV Bass (Reissue)

1987-2016. Has reverse body and 2 pickups, various colors.

1987-2016	Various colors	$1,200	$1,550

Thunderbird IV Bass Zebra Wood Bass

2007. Guitar of the Week (week 11 of '07), limited run of 400, Zebrawood body.

2007		$1,325	$1,725

Thunderbird 50th Anniversary Bass

2013-2018. Mahogany body and neck, rosewood 'board, Bullion Gold finish.

2013-2018		$1,325	$1,725

Thunderbird 76 Bass

1976 only. Reverse solidbody, 2 pickups, rosewood 'board, various colors.

1976		$2,700	$3,500

Thunderbird 79 Bass

1979 only. Reverse solidbody, 2 pickups, sunburst.

1979		$2,700	$3,500

Thunderbird Short Scale Bass

2011-2013. 30.5" scale, 2 pickups, nitro satin ebony finish.

2011-2013		$850	$1,100

Thunderbird Studio/IV Studio Bass

2005-2007. 4- or 5-string versions.

2005-2007		$975	$1,275

Victory Artist Bass

1981-1985. Double-cut, solidbody, 2 humbuckers and active electronics, various colors.

1981-1985		$825	$1,075

Victory Custom Bass

1982-1984. Double-cut, solidbody, 2 humbuckers, passive electronics, limited production.

1982-1984		$825	$1,075

Victory Standard Bass

1981-1986. Double-cut, solidbody, 1 humbucker, active electronics, various colors.

1981-1986		$650	$825

Godin

1987-present. Intermediate and professional grade, production, solidbody electric and acoustic/electric basses from luthier Robert Godin. They also build guitars and mandolins.

A Series Bass

1990s-2000s. Various acoustic/electric, 4- or 5-string.

1990s-2002	A-4, A-5	$450	$600

Freeway A Series Bass

2005-2012. Double-cut solidbodies, 4- or 5-string, passive or active..

2005-2012	Freeway A-4	$400	$525
2005-2012	Freeway A-5	$425	$550

Godlyke

2006-present. Professional and premium grade, production, solidbody basses from effects distributor Godlyke.

Goya

1955-1996. Originally imports from Sweden, brand later used on Japanese and Korean imports. They also offered guitars, mandolins and banjos.

Electric Solidbody Bass

1960s	Various models	$525	$700

Gretsch

1883-present. Intermediate and professional grade, production, solidbody, hollow body, and acoustic/electric basses. Gretsch came late to the electric bass game, introducing their first models in the early '60s. They also build guitars, amps and steels. In 2012 they again offered mandolins, ukes and banjos.

Broadkaster (6119-B) Bass

1991-2013. Single-cut hollowbody, maple top, back and sides.

1991-2013		$1,175	$1,525

Broadkaster (7605/7606) Bass

1975-1979. Double-cut solidbody, 1 pickup, bolt-on maple neck, natural (7605) or sunburst (7606).

1975-1979		$575	$750

Committee (7629) Bass

1977-1980. Double-cut walnut and maple soldibody, neck-thru, 1 pickup, natural.

1977-1980		$600	$775

G6072 Long Scale Hollow Body Bass

1998-2006. Reissue of the '68 double-cut hollowbody, 2 pickups, sunburst, gold hardware.

1998-2006		$825	$1,100

2015 Gibson SG Standard
Rivington Guitars

1976 Gibson Thunderbird 76
Charlie Patty

1968 Gretsch Model 6071
Imaged by Heritage Auctions, HA.com

1999 Guild B-30 E
Carter Vintage Guitars

BASSES

MODEL YEAR	FEATURES	EXC. COND. LOW	HIGH

Model 6070/6072 Bass
1963-1971 (1972 for 6070). Originally listed as the PX6070 Cello Bass, large thinline hollowbody double-cut archtop, fake f-holes, 1 pickup (6070) or 2 (6072), gold hardware.

1963-1964	6070, with endpin	$1,575	$2,050
1965-1972	6070, no endpin, 1 pickup	$1,125	$1,475
1968-1971	6072, 2 pickups	$1,100	$1,425

Model 6071/6073 Bass
1968-1971 (1972 for 6071). Single-cut hollowbody, fake f-holes, 1 pickup (6071) or 2 (6073), padded back, red mahogany.

| 1968-1971 | 6073, 2 pickups | $1,450 | $1,900 |
| 1968-1972 | 6071, 1 pickup | $1,300 | $1,700 |

Model 7615 Bass
1972-1975. Offset double-cut solidbody, slotted bass horn (monkey grip), large polished rosewood 'guard covering most of the body, 2 pickups, dot markers, brown mahogany finish. Only bass offered in Gretsch catalog for this era.

| 1972-1975 | | $750 | $975 |

TK 300 (7626/7627) Bass
1976-1981. Double-cut solidbody, 1 pickup, Autumn Red Stain or natural.

| 1976-1981 | | $475 | $625 |

Guild
1952-present. Guild added electric basses in the mid-'60s and offered them until '02. New owner, Cordoba Music, reintroduced acoustic and electric basses to the line in '15.

Ashbory Bass
1986-1988, 2009. 18" scale, total length 30", fretless, silicone rubber strings, active electronics, low-impedance circuitry.

| 1986-1988 | | $350 | $450 |
| 2009 | Fender Guild reissue | $170 | $225 |

B-4 E Bass
1993-2000. Acoustic/electric single-cut flat-top, mahogany sides with arched mahogany back, multi-bound, gold hardware until '95, chrome after.

| 1993-2000 | | $475 | $625 |

B-30 E Bass
1987-1999. Single-cut flat-top acoustic/electric, mahogany sides, arched mahogany back, multi-bound, fretless optional.

| 1987-1999 | | $850 | $1,125 |

B-50 Acoustic Bass
1975-1987. Acoustic flat-top, mahogany sides with arched mahogany back, spruce top, multi-bound, renamed B-30 in '87.

| 1975-1987 | | $1,000 | $1,300 |

B-301/B-302 Bass
1976-1981. Double-cut solidbody, chrome-plated hardware. Models include B-301 (mahogany, 1 pickup), B-301A (ash, 1 pickup), B-302 (mahogany, 2 pickups), B-302A (ash, 2 pickups), and B-302AF (ash, fretless).

1976-1981	B-301, B-301A	$675	$875
1976-1981	B-302, B-302A	$725	$950
1977-1981	B-302AF	$725	$950

B-401/B-402 Bass
1980-1983. Model 401 with active circuit, 1 pickup. Model 402 passive and active, 2 pickups. A for ash body.

| 1980-1981 | B-401, B-401A | $675 | $875 |
| 1980-1982 | B-402, B402A | $675 | $875 |

B-500 C Acoustic Bass
1992-1993. Acoustic/electric flat-top, round soundhole, single-cut, solid spruce top, maple back and sides, dark stain, limited production.

| 1992-1993 | | $1,025 | $1,350 |

FS-46 Bass
1983. Acoustic-electric flat-top, single-cut, sharp horn fretless.

| 1983 | | $575 | $750 |

Jet Star Bass
1964-1970 (limited production '68-'70). Offset double-cut solidbody, short treble horn, 1 pickup, 2-on-a-side tuners '64-'66 and 4 in-line tuners '66-'70.

| 1964-1966 | 2-on-side tuners | $1,075 | $1,400 |
| 1966-1970 | 4-in-line tuners | $1,075 | $1,400 |

JS I/JS II Bass
1970-1977. Double-cut solidbody, 30" scale, 1 pickup (JS I or 1) or 2 (JS II or 2), carved-top oak leaf design available for '72-'76. 34" long scale (LS) versions offered fretted and fretless for '74-'75.

1970-1977	JS I	$1,100	$1,500
1970-1977	JS II	$1,200	$1,600
1974-1976	JS I, carved	$1,200	$1,600
1974-1976	JS II, carved	$1,300	$1,700

M-85 I/M-85 II Bass (Semi-Hollow)
1967-1972. Single-cut semi-hollowbody, 1 pickup (M-85 I) or 2 (M-85 II).

| 1967-1972 | M-85 I | $1,175 | $1,500 |
| 1967-1972 | M-85 II | $1,250 | $1,625 |

M-85 I/M-85 II BluesBird Bass (Solidbody)
1972-1976. Single-cut solidbody archtop, Chesterfield headstock inlay, cherry mahogany, 1 humbucker pickup (I) or 2 (II).

| 1972-1973 | M-85 I | $1,275 | $1,700 |
| 1972-1976 | M-85 II | $1,350 | $1,800 |

MB-801 Bass
1981-1982. Double-cut solidbody, 1 pickup, dot inlays.

| 1981-1982 | | $550 | $725 |

SB-201/SB-202/SB-203 Bass
1982-1983. Double-cut solidbody, 1 split coil pickup (201), 1 split coil and 1 single coil (202), or 1 split coil and 2 single coils (203).

1982-1983	SB-201	$650	$850
1982-1983	SB-202	$700	$900
1983	SB-203	$725	$925

SB-502 E Bass
1984-1985. Double-cut solidbody, 2 pickups, active electronics.

| 1984-1985 | | $725 | $925 |

SB-600/Pilot Series Bass
1983-1993. Offset double-cut solidbody, bolt-on neck, poplar body. Models include SB-601 (1 pickup), SB-602 (2 pickups or fretless), SB-602 V (2 pickups,

MODEL YEAR	FEATURES	EXC. COND. LOW	HIGH

5-string), SB-604 (2 pickups, offset peghead) and SB-605 (5-string, hipshot low D tuner). Models 604 and 605 are replaced in '93 with Pro4 and Pro5 Pilot.

1983-1989	SB-601	$425	$550
1983-1989	SB-602	$500	$650
1983-1989	SB-602 V	$500	$650
1983-1989	SB-602, fretless	$500	$650
1986-1988	SB-604 Pilot	$500	$650
1986-1993	SB-605	$525	$675

SB-608 Flying Star Motley Crue Bass
1984-1985. Pointy 4-point star body, 2 pickups, E version had EMG pickups.

1984-1985		$875	$1,150

Starfire Bass
1965-1975. Double-cut semi-hollow thinbody, 1 pickup, mahogany neck, chrome-plated hardware, cherry or sunburst.

1965-1969	Single-coil	$1,900	$2,400
1970-1975	Humbucker	$1,900	$2,400

Starfire II Bass
1967-1978. Two-pickup version of Starfire Bass. Single-coils until '69, humbuckers after, sunburst, cherry or very rare black. Starfire II Bass Special had gold hardware.

1967-1969	2 single-coils	$1,950	$2,450
1967-1969	Black	$2,100	$2,700
1970-1978	2 humbuckers	$1,950	$2,450

Starfire II Reissue Bass
1997-present. Reissue of 2 humbucker version.

1997-2019		$800	$1,050

X-701/X-702 Bass
1982-1984. Body with 4 sharp horns with extra long bass horn, 1 pickup (X-701) or 2 (X-702), various metallic finishes.

1982-1984	X-701	$1,000	$1,325
1982-1984	X-702	$1,050	$1,375

GW Basses & Luthiery
2004-present. Professional and premium grade, production/custom, basses built by luthier Grandon Westlund in West Lafayette, Indiana.

Hagstrom
1921-1983, 2004-present. This Swedish guitar company first offered electric basses in '61.

Concord II Deluxe Bass
1967-1970. Bass version of V-IN guitar, 335-style body, 2 pickups, sunburst.

1967-1970		$1,250	$1,650

Coronado IV Bass
1963-1970. Offset double cut, Bi-Sonic pickups.

1963-1970		$875	$1,150

H-8 Bass
1967-1969. Double-cut solidbody, 8 strings, 2 pickups, various colors.

1967-1969		$1,050	$1,400

Kent Bass
1963-1964. 2 single-coils, 4 sliders.

1962-1966		$500	$650

Model I B/F-100 B Bass
1965-1973. Offset double-cut solidbody, 2 single-coils, 5 sliders, 30" scale.

1965-1973		$425	$550

Model II B/F-400 Bass
1965-1970. Like Model I, but with 30.75" scale, red, black, white or blue. Called F-400 in U.S., II B elsewhere.

1965-1970	Various colors	$500	$650

Swede 2000 Bass (With Synth)
1977. Circuitry on this Swede bass connected to the Ampeg Patch 2000 pedal so bass would work with various synths.

1977		$825	$1,100

Swede Bass
1971-1976, 2004-present. Single-cut solidbody, block inlays, bolt neck, 2 humbuckers, 30.75" scale, cherry or black

1971-1976		$800	$1,075

Super Swede Bass
1979-1983, 2004-present. Like Swede, but with neck-thru body, 32" scale, sunburst, mahogany or black.

1979-1983		$800	$1,075

Hamer
1975-2012, 2017-present. Founded in Arlington Heights, Illinois, by Paul Hamer and Jol Dantzig, Hamer was purchased by Kaman in '88. They also built guitars. Fender acquired Hamer in '08 and suspended production in '12. The brand was reintroduced in '17 by Jam Industries.

8-String Short-Scale Bass
1978-1993. Double cut solidbody, 1 or 2 pickups, 30.5" scale.

1978-1993		$1,150	$1,500

12-String Acoustic Bass
1985-2010. Semi-hollow, long scale, single cut, soundhole, 2 pickups. Import XT model added in the 2000s.

1985-2010		$1,500	$1,950

12-String Short-Scale Bass
1978-1996. Four sets of 3 strings - a fundamental and 2 tuned an octave higher, double cut maple and mahogany solidbody, 30.5" scale.

1978-1996		$1,150	$1,500

Blitz Bass
1982-1990. Explorer-style solidbody, 2 pickups, bolt-on neck.

1982-1984	1st edition	$1,100	$1,450
1984-1990		$900	$1,200

Chaparral Bass
1986-1995, 2000-2008. Solidbody, 2 pickups, glued-in neck, later basses have bolt-on neck.

1986-1987	Set-neck	$1,025	$1,325
1987-1995	Bolt-on neck	$925	$1,200

Chaparral 5-String Bass
1987-1995. Five strings, solidbody, 2 pickups, glued-in neck, later basses have 5-on-a-side reverse peghead.

1987-1995		$975	$1,350

1974 Guild M-85 II Bluesbird
Rivington Guitars

1967 Hagstrom H-8
Justin Nortillo

BASSES

Hamer Chaparral 12-String

1964 Höfner 500/1 Beatle
Steve Lee

MODEL YEAR	FEATURES	EXC. COND. LOW	HIGH

Chaparral 12-String Bass
1992-2012. Long 34" scale 12-string, offset double cut. Import XT model added in '01.

1992-2012	USA	$1,500	$1,950
2000-2012	Import	$290	$375

Chaparral Max Bass
1986-1995. Chaparral Bass with figured maple body, glued-in neck and boomerang inlays.

1986-1995		$600	$775

Cruise Bass
1982-1990, 1995-1999. J-style solidbody, 2 pickups, glued neck ('82-'90) or bolt-on neck ('95-'99), also available as a 5-string.

1982-1990	Set-neck	$725	$925
1995-1999	Bolt-on neck	$625	$825

Cruise 5 Bass
1982-1989. Five-string version, various colors.

1982-1989		$650	$950

FBIV Bass
1985-1987. Reverse Firebird shape, 1 P-Bass Slammer and 1 J-Bass Slammer pickup, mahogany body, rosewood 'board, dots.

1985-1987		$575	$775

Monaco 4 Bass
2002-2012. Flamed maple top, rosewood 'board, Tobacco Burst or '59 Burst finish.

2002-2012		$1,775	$2,300

Standard Bass
1975-1984, 2001. US-made, Explorer-style head-stock, 2 humbuckers. Imported in '01.

1975-1979	Flamed top, bound	$3,000	$4,800
1975-1984	Plain top, unbound	$2,100	$2,800
1980-1984	Flamed top, bound	$2,500	$4,300
2001	Import	$265	$350

Velocity 5 Bass
2002-2012. Offset double-cut, long bass horn, active, 1 humbucker.

2002-2012		$175	$225

Harmony
1892-1976, late 1970s-present. Harmony once was one of the biggest instrument makers in the world, making guitars and basses under their own brand and for others.

H Series Bass
Late-1980s-early-1990s. F-style solidbody copies, 1 or 2 pickups, all models begin H.

1980s-90s		$100	$125

H-22 Bass
1959-1972. Single-cut hollowbody, 2-on-a-side, 1 pickup.

1959-1969		$1,000	$1,300
1970-1972		$850	$1,100

H-22 Reissue Bass
2000s. Imported reissue, 1 pickup.

2000s		$265	$350

H-25/Silhouette Bass
1963-1967. Offset double-cut solidbody, 1 pickup (H-25) or 2 (Silhouette).

1963-1967	H-25	$600	$800
1963-1967	Silhouette	$650	$850

H-27 Bass
1968-1972. Double-cut hollowbody, 4-on-a-side, 2 pickups.

1968-1972		$650	$850

Hartke
Hartke offered a line of wood and aluminum-necked basses from 2000 to '03.

Heartfield
1989-1994. Distributed by Fender, imported from Japan. They also offered guitars.

Electric Bass
1989-1994. Double-cut solidbody, graphite rein-forced neck, 2 single-coils, available in 4-, 5- and 6-string models.

1989-1994		$250	$400

Heritage
1985-present. Mainly a builder of guitars, Ka-lamazoo, Michigan's Heritage has offered a few basses in the past.

HB-1 Bass
1987. P-style body, limited production, single-split pick-up, 4-on-a-side tuners, figured maple body, bolt-on neck.

1987		$575	$750

Höfner
1887-present. Professional grade, production, basses. They also offer guitars and bowed instru-ments. Höfner basses, made famous in the U.S. by one Paul McCartney, are made in Germany.

Icon Series
2007-2011. Chinese versions of classic Höfners, often sold without a case or gigbag.

2007-2011		$175	$250

Model (G)5000/1 Super Beatle (G500/1) Bass
1968-2011. Bound ebony 'board, gold-plated hard-ware, natural finish, the version with active circuit is called G500/1 Super Beatle, reissued in '94.

1968-1979	LH	$2,000	$2,700
1968-1979	RH	$1,400	$1,850

Model 172 Series Bass
1968-1970. Offset double-cut, 6-on-a-side tuners, 2 pickups, 2 slide switches, dot markers, 172/S shaded sunburst, 172/R red vinyl covered body, 172/I vinyl covered with white top and black back.

1968-1970	172/I, white	$650	$850
1968-1970	172/R, red	$650	$850
1968-1970	172/S, sunburst	$650	$850

Model 182 Solid Bass
1962-1985. Offset double-cut solidbody, 2 pickups.

1962-1965		$650	$850

Model 185 Solid Bass
1962-ca. 1970. Classic offset double-cut solidbody, 2 double-coil pickups.

1962-1970		$650	$850

Model 500/1 Beatle Bass
1956-present. Semi-acoustic, bound body in violin shape, glued-in neck, 2 pickups, right- or left-handed,

MODEL YEAR	FEATURES	EXC. COND. LOW	HIGH

sunburst. Listed as 500/1 Vintage '58, '59, '62 and '63 in '90s through 2014. Currently named 500/1 Violin Bass.

1956-1960	RH or LH	$5,300	$6,900
1960	LH, McCartney	$4,600	$6,000
1961	LH	$4,600	$6,000
1961	LH, McCartney	$5,800	$7,600
1961	RH	$3,700	$4,800
1962-1963	LH	$3,700	$4,800
1962-1963	RH	$3,300	$4,300
1964	LH	$3,700	$4,800
1964	LH, McCartney	$4,800	$6,200
1964	RH	$3,000	$3,900
1964	RH, McCartney	$3,300	$4,300
1965	LH	$2,300	$3,100
1965	RH	$2,100	$2,800
1966	LH	$2,200	$2,900
1966	RH	$2,000	$2,700
1967	LH	$2,100	$2,700
1967	RH	$1,750	$2,300
1968-1973	LH	$2,000	$2,700
1968-1973	RH	$1,450	$1,900
1974-1979	RH or LH	$1,350	$1,800

'58 Model 500/1 Reissue
2008-2013		$1,350	$1,800

'62 Model 500/1 Beatle Bass Reissue
1990s-2014		$1,350	$1,800

'63 Model 500/1 Beatle Bass Reissue
1994-2010. Right- or left-handed.
1994-2010		$1,350	$1,800

'64 Model 500/1 Beatle Bass Reissue
2015		$1,350	$1,800

Model 500/1 1964-1984 Reissue Bass
1984 '1964-1984' neckplate notation
1984		$1,350	$1,800

Model 500/1 40th Anniversary Bass
1995-1996. Only 300 made.
1995-1996		$2,300	$3,000

Model 500/1 50th Anniversary Bass
2006. Pickguard logo states '50th Anniversary Höfner Violin Bass 1956-2006', large red Höfner logo also on 'guard, 150 made.
2006		$2,300	$3,000

Model 500/1 Cavern Bass
2005. Limted run of 12, includes certificate.
2005		$1,350	$1,800

Model 500/1 Cavern Bass Music Ground
1993. UK commissioned by Music Ground, said to be one of the first accurate reissues, 40 made.
1993		$1,350	$1,800

Model 500/1 Contemporary
2007-2008. Contemporary Series.
2007-2008		$475	$625

Model 500/2 Bass
1965-1970. Similar to the 500/1, but with 'club' body Höfner made for England's Selmer, sunburst. Club Bass has been reissued.
1965-1970		$1,450	$1,900

Model 500/3 Senator Bass
1962-1964. Single-cut thin body, f-holes, 1 511b pickup, sunburst.
1962-1964		$1,350	$1,750

Model 500/5 Bass
1959-1963. Single-cut body with Beatle Bass-style pickups, sunburst. Becomes President Bass in '63.
1959-1963		$2,900	$3,800

Model 500/6 Bass
Late-1960s. Introduced in '67, semi-acoustic, thinline, soft double-cut, 2 pickups, 4 control knobs, dot markers, sunburst.
1967		$1,450	$1,875

Model 500/8BZ / B500/8BZ
Late-1960s. Semi-acoustic, thinline, sharp double-cut, multiple-line position markers, built in flip-fuzz and bass boost, sunburst or natural.
1967	500/8BZ, sunburst	$1,500	$1,950
1967	B500/8BZ, natural	$1,500	$1,950

President Bass
1963-1972. Made for England's Selmer, single-cut archtop, 2 Beatle Bass-style pickups, sunburst.
1963-1965		$2,000	$2,600
1966-1969		$1,575	$2,050
1970-1972		$1,550	$2,000

Hondo
1969-1987, 1991-2005. Budget grade, production, imported acoustic and electric solidbody basses. They also offered guitars, banjos and mandolins.

Electric Solidbody Bass
1969-1987, 1991-2005. Various models.
1969-1999	Rare models	$250	$850
1969-1999	Standard models	$75	$175

Hoyer
1874-present. Intermediate grade, production, electric basses. They also build guitars.

Electric Bass
1960s		$400	$700

Ibanez
1932-present. Intermediate and professional grade, production, solidbody basses. They also have guitars, amps, and effects.

AXB Axstar Series Bass
1986-1987. Various models.
1986-1987		$200	$400

BTB Series Bass
1999-present. Various models.
1999-2019		$200	$500

Challenger Bass
1977-1978. Offered as P-bass or J-bass style, and with ash body option.
1977-1978		$350	$475

DB Destroyer II X Series Bass
1984-1986. Futuristic-style body, P- and J-style pickups, dot markers, bolt neck.
1984-1986		$300	$550

DT Destroyer II Series Bass
1980-1985. Futuristic-style body.
1983-1986		$450	$700

Early-1970s Höfner 501/1 Beatle
Godbold

1963 Höfner 500/2 Club
Larry Wassgren

BASSES

1975 Ibanez Model 2388 B

Jorge Franco Avila

Ibanez SR-300

Rivington Guitars

MODEL YEAR / FEATURES	EXC. COND. LOW	HIGH
ICB Iceman Bass		
1994-1996, 2011. Iceman body, basswood (300) or mahogany (500) body. 300 reissued in '11.		
1994 ICB500, black	$400	$575
1994-1996 ICB300, white	$400	$575
Jet King Bass		
2009-2010. Retro offset double-cut solidbody, bolt neck.		
2009-2010	$175	$300
MC Musician Series Bass		
1978-1988. Various models, solidbody, neck-thru.		
1978-1988	$700	$1,300
Model 2030 Bass		
1970-1973. First copy era bass, offset double-cut, sunburst.		
1970-1973	$550	$750
Model 2353 Bass		
1974-1976. Copy model, offset double-cut, 1 pickup, black.		
1974-1976	$500	$700
Model 2364B Bass		
1971-1973. Dan Armstrong see-thru Lucite copy with 2 mounted humbucker pickups, clear finish.		
1971-1973	$650	$900
Model 2365 Bass		
1974-1975. Copy model, Offset double-cut, rosewood 'board, pearloid block markers, sunburst.		
1974-1975	$550	$750
Model 2366 B/2366 FLB Bass		
1974-1975. Copy model, offset double-cut, 1 split-coil pickup, sunburst, FLB fretless model.		
1974-1975	$500	$700
Model 2385 Bass		
1974-1975. Copy model, offset double-cut, 1 pickup, ash natural finish.		
1974-1975	$500	$700
Model 2388 B Bass		
1974-1976. Ric 4001 copy.		
1974-1976	$500	$700
Model 2452 Bass		
1975. Ripper copy.		
1975	$500	$700
Model 2459 B Destroyer Bass		
1974-1977. Laminated ash body, copy of Korina Explorer-style.		
1974-1977	$1,600	$2,100
Model 2537 DX Bass		
1974-1975. Hofner Beatle copy.		
1974-1975	$550	$700
Model 2609B Black Eagle Bass		
1974-1976. Burns-like bass, offset double-cut solidbody, sharp curving horns.		
1974-1976	$950	$1,120
PL Pro Line Series Bass		
1986-1987. Offset double cut solidbody.		
1986-1987	$200	$475
RB/RS Roadstar Series Bass		
1983-1987. Solidbody basses, various models and colors.		
1983-1987	$250	$500

MODEL YEAR / FEATURES	EXC. COND. LOW	HIGH
Rocket Roll Bass		
1974-1976. Korina solidbody, V-shape, natural.		
1974-1976	$1,700	$2,200
S/SB Series Bass		
1990-1992. Various ultra slim solidbody basses.		
1990-1992	$200	$450
SR Sound Gear Series Bass		
1987-present. Sleek, lightweight designs, active electronics, bolt necks. Model numbers higher than 1000 are usually arched-top, lower usually flat body.		
1987-2019	$200	$450
ST-980 Studio Bass		
1979-1980. Double cut, 8-string, bolt-on neck, walnut-maple-mahogany body.		
1979-1980	$550	$700

Imperial

Ca.1963-ca.1970. Imported by the Imperial Accordion Company of Chicago, Illinois. Early guitars and basses made in Italy, but by ca. '66 Japanese-made.

MODEL YEAR / FEATURES	EXC. COND. LOW	HIGH
Electric Solidbody Bass		
1960s Various models	$150	$400
Hollowbody Bass		
1960s. Hollowbody with sharp double-cuts.		
1960s	$150	$400

Jackson

1980-present. Intermediate, professional, and premium grade, production, solidbody basses. They also offer guitars. Founded by Grover Jackson, who owned Charvel.

MODEL YEAR / FEATURES	EXC. COND. LOW	HIGH
Concert C5P 5-String Bass (Import)		
1998-2000. Bolt neck, dot inlay, chrome hardware.		
1998-2000	$120	$160
Concert Custom Bass (USA)		
1984-1995 Neck-thru Custom Shop bass		
1984-1989	$975	$1,300
1990-1995	$600	$800
Concert EX 4-String Bass (Import)		
1992-1995. Bolt neck, dot inlay, black hardware.		
1992-1995	$200	$275
Concert V 5-String Bass (Import)		
1992-1995. Bound neck, shark tooth inlay.		
1992-1995	$275	$400
Concert XL 4-String Bass (Import)		
1992-1995. Bound neck, shark tooth inlay.		
1992-1995	$225	$325
Kelly Pro Bass		
1994-1995. Pointy-cut bouts, neck-thru solidbody, shark fin marker inlays.		
1994-1995	$600	$800
Piezo Bass		
1986. Piezo bridge pickup, neck-thru, shark tooth inlays. Student model has rosewood 'board, no binding. Custom Model has ebony 'board and binding.		
1986	$1,150	$1,500
Soloist Bass		
1996. Pointy headstock, 4-string.		
1996	$600	$800

MODEL YEAR	FEATURES	EXC. COND. LOW	HIGH

Surfcaster SC1 Bass
1998-2001. Tube and humbucker pickups.
| 1998-2001 | | $850 | $1,125 |

Jerry Jones
1981-2011. Intermediate grade, production, semi-hollow body electric basses from luthier Jerry Jones, and built in Nashville, Tennessee. They also build guitars and sitars. Jones retired in 2011.

Neptune Longhorn 4 Bass
1988-2011. Based on Danelectro longhorn models, 4-string, 2 lipstick-tube pickups, 30" scale.
| 1988-2011 | | $875 | $1,125 |

Neptune Longhorn 6 Bass
1988-2011. 6-string version.
| 1988-2011 | | $1,125 | $1,475 |

Neptune Shorthorn 4 Bass
1988-2011. Danelectro Coke bottle headstock, short horns double cut, 2 pickups.
| 1988-2011 | | $875 | $1,125 |

Juzek
Violin maker John Juzek was originally located in Prague, Czeckoslovakia, but moved to West Germany due to World War II. Prague instruments considered by most to be more valuable. Many German instruments were mass produced with laminate construction and some equate these German basses with the Kay laminate basses of the same era. Juzek still makes instruments.

Kalamazoo
1933-1942, 1965-1970. Kalamazoo was a brand Gibson used on one of their budget lines. They also used the name on electric basses, guitars and amps from '65 to '67.

Electric Bass
| 1965-1970 | | $350 | $500 |

Kapa
Ca. 1962-1970. Kapa was founded by Koob Veneman in Maryland and offered basses and guitars.

Electric Bass
| 1962-1970 | Various models | $200 | $500 |

Kawai
1927-present. Japanese instrument manufacturer Kawai started offering guitars under other brand names around '56. There were few imports carrying the Kawai brand until the late-'70s; best known for high quality basses. Kawai quit offering guitars and basses around 2002.

Electric Bass
| 1970-2002 | Various models | $225 | $525 |

Kay
Ca. 1931-present. Currently, budget and intermediate grade, production, imported solidbody basses. They also make amps, guitars, banjos, mandolins, ukes, and violins. Kay introduced upright acoustic laminate basses and 3/4 viols in '38 and electric basses in '54.

C1 Concert String Bass
1938-1967. Standard (3/4) size student bass, laminated construction, spruce top, figured maple back and sides, shaded light brown.
1938-1949		$1,800	$2,300
1950-1959		$1,700	$2,200
1960-1967		$1,600	$2,100

K-160 Electronic Bass
1955-1956. Same as K-162, but with plain white plastic trim.
| 1955-1956 | | $900 | $1,200 |

K-162 Electronic Bass
1955-1956. Bass version of K-161Thin Twin "Jimmy Reed," single-cut, 1 tube-style pickup.
| 1955-1956 | | $900 | $1,200 |

K-5965 Pro Bass
1954-1965. Single-cut, 1 pickup. named K-5965 Pro by 1961.
| 1954-1965 | | $900 | $1,200 |

K-5970 Jazz Special Electric Bass
1960-1964. Double-cut, pickup, Kelvinator headstock, black or blond.
| 1960-1964 | | $2,000 | $2,575 |

M-1 (Maestro) String Bass
1952-late-1960s. Standard (3/4) size bass, laminated construction, spruce top and curly maple back and sides. Model M-3 is the Junior (1/4) size bass, Model M-1 B has a blond finish, other models include the S-51 B Chubby Jackson Five-String Bass and the S-9 Swingmaster.
| 1952-1967 | | $2,100 | $2,700 |

M-5 (Maestro) String Bass
1957-late-1960s. Five strings.
| 1957-1967 | | $2,300 | $3,000 |

Semi-hollowbody Bass
1954-1966. Single or double cut, 1 or 2 pickups.
| 1954-1966 | 1 pickup | $300 | $400 |
| 1954-1966 | 2 pickups | $350 | $450 |

Solidbody Bass
1965-1968. Single or double cut, 1 or 2 pickups.
| 1965-1968 | 1 pickup | $300 | $400 |
| 1965-1968 | 2 pickups | $350 | $450 |

Ken Smith
See listing under Smith.

Kent
1961-1969. Guitars and basses imported from Japan by Buegeleisen and Jacobson of New York, New York. Manufacturers unknown but many early instruments by Guyatone and Teisco.

Electric Bass
1962-1969. Import models include 628 Newport, 634 Basin Street, 629, and 635.
| 1961-1969 | Common model | $100 | $275 |
| 1961-1969 | Rare model | $275 | $550 |

Kimberly
Late-1960s-early-1970s. Private branded import made in the same Japanese factory as Teisco. They also made guitars.

1997 Jerry Jones Neptune Longhorn 4
Ken Quick

1962 Kay
Dallas Alice Music

BASSES

1979 Kramer 650-B Artist
Imaged by Heritage Auctions, HA.com

1980 Kramer DMZ 6000B
Imaged by Heritage Auctions, HA.com

MODEL YEAR	FEATURES	EXC. COND. LOW	HIGH

Violin Bass
1960s		$400	$550

Kingston
Ca. 1958-1967. Imported from Japan by Westheimer Importing Corp. of Chicago. Early examples made by Guyatone and Teisco. They also offered guitars, mandolins and banjos.
Electric Bass
1960s	Common model	$100	$275
1960s	Rare model	$275	$550

Klira
Founded 1887 in Schoenbach, Germany, mainly making violins, but added guitars and basses in the 1950s. The instruments of the '50s and '60s were aimed at the budget market, but workmanship improved with the '70s models.
Electric Bass
1960s	Beatle Bass copy	$450	$600
1960s	Common model	$300	$450
1960s	Rare model	$450	$600

Kramer
1976-1990, 1995-present. Budget grade, production, imported solidbody basses. They also offer guitars. Kramer's first guitars and basses featured aluminum necks with wooden inserts on back. Around '80 they started to switch to more economical wood necks and aluminum necks were last produced in '85. Gibson acquired the brand in '97.
250-B Special Bass
1977-1979. Offset double-cut, aluminum neck, Ebonol 'board, zero fret, 1 single-coil, natural.
1977-1979		$550	$725
350-B Standard Bass
1976-1979. Offset double-cut, aluminum neck, Ebonol 'board, tropical woods, 1 single-coil, dots. The 350 and 450 were Kramer's first basses.
1976-1979		$750	$1,000
450-B Deluxe Bass
1976-1980. As 350-B, but with 2 single-coils and blocks.
1976-1980		$800	$1,050
650-B Artist Bass
1977-1980. Double-cut, birdseye maple/burled walnut, aluminum neck, zero fret, mother-of-pearl crowns, 2 humbuckers.
1977-1980		$950	$1,250
Deluxe 8 Bass
1980. Multi-piece body, aluminum neck.
1980		$1,025	$1,325
DMB 2000 Bass
1979. Bolt-on aluminum neck, slot headstock.
1979		$725	$950
DMZ 4000 Bass
1978-1982. Bolt-on aluminum neck, slot headstock, double-cut solidbody, active EQ and dual-coil humbucking pickup, dot inlay.
1978-1981		$575	$750
1982	Bill Wyman-type	$575	$750

DMZ 4001 Bass
1979-1980. Aluminum neck, slot headstock, double-cut solidbody, 1 dual-coil humbucker pickup, dot inlay.
1979-1980		$725	$950
DMZ 5000 Bass
1979-1980. Double-cut solidbody, aluminum neck, slotted headstock, 2 pickups, crown inlays.
1979-1980		$925	$1,200
DMZ 6000B Bass
1979-1980. Double-cut, aluminum neck, slotted headstock, 2 pickups, crown inlays.
1979-1980		$925	$1,200
Duke Custom/Standard Bass
1981-1983. Headless, aluminum neck, 1 humbucker.
1981-1983		$375	$490
Duke Special Bass
1982-1985. Headless, aluminum neck, 2 pickups, with frets or fretless.
1982-1985		$375	$490
Ferrington KFB-1/KFB-2 Acoustic Bass
1987-1990. Acoustic/electric, bridge-mounted active pickup, tone and volume control, various colors. KFB-1 has binding and diamond dot inlays; the KFB-2 no binding and dot inlays. Danny Ferrington continued to offer the KFB-1 after Kramer closed in '90.
1987-1990		$200	$260
Focus 7000 Bass
1985-1987. Offset double-cut solidbody, P and double J pickups, Japanese-made.
1985-1987		$190	$245
Focus 8000 Bass
1985-1987. Offset double-cut solidbody, Japanese-made.
1985-1987		$190	$245
Focus K Series Bass
1984-1986. Includes the 1 pickup K 77 and 2 pickup K 88, made in Japan.
1984-1986		$190	$245
Forum Series Bass
1987-1990. Japanese-made double-cut, 2 pickups, neck-thru (I & III) or bolt-neck (II & IV).
1987-1990	Forum I	$380	$490
1987-1990	Forum II	$350	$450
1987-1990	Forum III	$290	$375
1987-1990	Forum IV	$260	$340
Gene Simmons Axe Bass
1980-1981. Axe-shaped body, aluminium neck.
1980-1981		$2,500	$4,200
Hundred Series Bass
1988-1990. Import budget line, 7/8th solidbody.
1988-1990	710	$160	$210
1988-1990	720	$180	$230
Pacer Bass
1982-1984. Offset double-cut solidbody, red.
1982-1984		$550	$700
Pioneer Bass
1981-1986. First wood neck basses, offset double cut, JBX or PBX pickups, dots, '81-'84 models with soft headstocks, later '84 on with banana headstocks.
1981-1986	Double J, 2 JBX	$400	$515
1981-1986	Imperial, JBX & PBX	$375	$485

MODEL YEAR	FEATURES	EXC. COND. LOW	HIGH
1981-1986	Special, 1 PBX	$350	$450
1982-1984	Carrera, JBX & PBX	$400	$515

Ripley Four-String Bass
1985-1987. Four-string version.

1985-1987		$675	$875

Ripley Five-String Bass
1984-1987. Offset double-cut, 5 strings, stereo, pan pots for each string, front and back pickups for each string, active circuitry.

1984-1987		$700	$900

Stagemaster Custom Bass (Import)
1982-1985, 1987-1990. First version had an aluminum neck (wood optional). Later version was neck-thru-body, bound neck, either active or passive pickups.

1982-1985	Imperial	$625	$825
1982-1985	Special	$575	$775
1982-1985	Standard	$625	$825

Stagemaster Deluxe Bass (U.S.A.)
1981. Made in USA, 8-string, metal neck.

1981		$850	$1,125

Striker 700 Bass
1985-1989. Offset double-cut, Korean-import, 1 pickup until '87, 2 after. Striker name was again used on a bass in '99.

1985-1987	1 pickup	$190	$250
1988-1989	2 pickups	$200	$275

Vanguard Bass
1981-1983. V-shaped body, Special (aluminum neck) or Standard (wood neck).

1981-1982	Special	$825	$1,100
1983-1984	Standard	$825	$1,100

Voyager Bass
1982-1983. X-body, headless.

1982-1983		$1,000	$1,325

XKB-10 (Wedge) Bass
1980-1981. Wedge-shaped body, aluminum neck.

1980-1981		$650	$850

XKB-20 Bass
1981. 2nd version, more traditional double cut body.

1981		$550	$725

XL Series Bass
1980-1981. Odd shaped double-cut solidbody, aluminum neck, various models..

1980-1981	XL-9, 4-string	$850	$1,100
1981	XL-24, 4-string	$950	$1,250
1981	XL-8, 8-string	$1,000	$1,300

ZX Aero Star Series Bass (Import)
1986-1989. Various models include ZX-70 (offset double-cut solidbody, 1 pickup).

1986-1989		$135	$175

KSD

2003-present. Intermediate grade, production, imported bass line designed by Ken Smith (see Smith listing).

Kubicki

1973-present. Professional and premium grade, production/custom, solidbody basses built by luthier Phil Kubicki in Santa Barbara, California. Kubicki began building acoustic guitars when he was 15. In '64 at age 19, he went to work with Roger Rossmeisl at Fender Musical Instrument's research and development department for acoustic guitars. Nine years later he moved to Santa Barbara, California, and established Philip Kubicki Technology, which is best known for its line of Factor basses and also builds acoustic guitars, custom electric guitars, bodies and necks, and mini-guitars and does custom work, repairs and restorations. Phil Kubicki died in '13.

Kustom

1968-present. Founded by Bud Ross in Chanute, Kansas, and best known for the tuck-and-roll amps, Kustom also offered guitars and basses from '68 to '69.

Electric Hollowbody Bass

1968-1969	Various models	$900	$1,200

La Baye

1967. Short-lived brand out of Green Bay, Wisconsin and built by the Holman-Woodell factory in Neodesha, Kansas. There was also a guitar model.

Model 2x4 II Bass
1967. Very low production, dual pickups, long-scale, small rectangle solidbody, sometimes referred to as the Bass II.

1967		$1,150	$1,500

Model 2x4 Mini-Bass
1967. Short-scale, 1 pickup, small rectangle solidbody.

1967		$1,150	$1,500

Lakland

1994-present. Professional and premium grade, production/custom, solid and hollowbody basses from luthier Dan Lakin in Chicago, Illinois. Lakland basses are built in the U.S. and overseas (Skyline series).

Electric Bass

1994-2019	Various models	$500	$2,500

Lowrider Basses

2003-2018. Professional grade, production/custom, solidbody basses made by Ed Roman Guitars.

M Basses

2001-present. Production/custom, professional and premium grade, solidbody electric basses built in Terryville, Connecticut by luthier Jon Maghini.

Magnatone

Ca. 1937-1971, 2013-present. Founded as Dickerson Brothers, known as Magna Electronics from '47. Produced instruments under own brand and for many others.

Mark VI/Artist Mark VI Bass
1959. Designed by luthier Paul Barth for Magnatone, double-cut, 4-string, 1 pickup.

1959		$1,100	$1,450

KSD KSD-704

Lakland Skyline Deluxe 2010
Craig Brody

BASSES

BASSES

1982 Martin EB-18
Imaged by Heritage Auctions, HA.com

1969 Microfrets Signature
Rivington Guitars

MODEL YEAR	FEATURES	EXC. COND. LOW	HIGH

X-10 Hurricane Bass
1965-1966. Offset double cut solidbody, 1 single-coil, 4-on-a-side tuners, Magnatone logo on guard and headstock, Hurricane logo on headstock.

| 1965-1966 | | $775 | $1,000 |

Mako
1985-1989. Line of solidbody basses from Kaman (Ovation, Hamer). They also offered guitars and amps.
Electric Solidbody Bass
| 1985-1989 | Various models | $100 | $300 |

Marco Polo
1960-ca.1964. One of the first inexpensive Japanese brands to be imported into the U.S., they also offered guitars.
Solidbody Bass
| 1960s | Various models | $100 | $300 |

Marleaux
1990-present. Luthier Gerald Marleaux builds his custom, premium grade, electric basses in Clausthal-Zellerfeld, Germany.

Marling
Ca. 1975. Budget line instruments marketed by EKO of Recanati, Italy; probably made by them, although possibly imported. They also had guitars.
Electric Solidbody Bass
Models include the E.495 (copy of LP), E.485 (copy of Tele), and the E.465 (Manta-style).
| 1970s | Various models | $100 | $300 |

Martin
1833-present. Professional grade, production, acoustic basses made in the U.S. In 1978, Martin re-entered the electric market and introduced their solidbody EB-18 and EB-28 Basses. In the '80s they offered Stinger brand electric basses. By the late '80s, they started offering acoustic basses.
00C-16GTAE Bass
2006-2011. Mahogany back and sides, Fishman electronics.
| 2006-2011 | | $750 | $1,000 |
B-1/B-1E Acoustic Bass
2002-2006. Mahogany back and sides, E has Fishman electronics.
| 2002-2006 | | $825 | $1,100 |
B-40 Acoustic Bass
1989-1996. Jumbo, rosewood back and sides, built-in pickup and volume and tone controls. The B-40B had a pickup.
| 1989-1996 | B-40B | $1,225 | $1,625 |
| 1989-1996 | Without pickup | $1,075 | $1,425 |
B-65 Acoustic Bass
1989-1993. Like B-40 but with maple back and sides, built-in pickup and volume and tone controls.
| 1989-1993 | | $1,175 | $1,525 |

MODEL YEAR	FEATURES	EXC. COND. LOW	HIGH

BC-15E Acoustic Bass
2000-2006. Single-cut, all mahogany, on-board electronics.
| 2000-2006 | | $925 | $1,225 |
BC-16E Bass
2020-present. Solid sitka spruce top, East Indian rosewood back and sides, built-in Fishman electronics.
| 2020 | | $1,300 | $1,700 |
BC-16GTE Acoustic Bass
2009-2013. Jumbo, cutaway, mahogany back and sides.
| 2009-2013 | | $1,075 | $1,375 |
BCPA4 Acoustic-Electric Bass
2013-present. Performing Artist series, single-cut, sitka spruce top, sapele back and sides.
| 2013-2019 | | $975 | $1,275 |
EB-18 Bass
1979-1982. Electric solidbody, neck-thru, 1 pickup, natural.
| 1979-1982 | | $850 | $1,150 |
EB-28 Bass
1980-1982. Electric solidbody.
| 1980-1982 | | $950 | $1,250 |
SBL-10 Bass
1980s. Stinger brand solidbody, maple neck, 1 split and 1 bar pickup.
| 1980s | | $160 | $230 |

Marvel
1950s-mid-1960s. Brand used for budget guitars and basses marketed by Peter Sorkin Company in New York, New York.
Electric Solidbody Bass
| 1950s | Various models | $100 | $300 |

Messenger
1967-1968. Built by Musicraft, Inc., Messengers featured a neck-thru metal alloy neck. They also made guitars.
Bass
1967-1968. Metal alloy neck. Messenger mainly made guitars - they offered a bass, but it is unlikely many were built.
| 1967-1968 | | $1,600 | $2,100 |

Messenger Upright
Made by Knutson Luthiery, see that listing.

Microfrets
1967-1975, 2004-2005. Professional grade, production, electric basses built in Myersville, Maryland. They also built guitars.
Husky Bass
1971-1974/75. Double-cut, 2 pickups, 2-on-a-side tuners.
| 1971-1975 | | $875 | $1,125 |
Rendezvous Bass
1970. One pickup, orange sunburst.
| 1970 | | $925 | $1,200 |
Signature Bass
1969-1975. Double-cut, 2 pickups, 2-on-a-side tuners.
| 1969-1975 | | $1,325 | $1,725 |

MODEL YEAR	FEATURES	EXC. COND. LOW	HIGH

Stage II Bass
1969-1975. Double-cut, 2 pickups, 2-on-a-side tuners.

1969-1975		$1,300	$1,700

Thundermaster Bass
1967-1975. Double-cut, 2 pickups, 2-on-a-side tuners.

1967-1975		$1,300	$1,700

Modulus

1978-2013. Founded by aerospace engineer Geoff Gould, Modulus offered professional and premium grade, production/custom, solidbody basses built in California. They also built guitars.

Electric Bass
1978-2013. Various standard models.

1978-2013		$1,400	$2,800

Mollerup Basses

In 1984 luthier Laurence Mollerup began building professional grade, custom/production, electric basses and electric double basses in Vancouver, British Columbia. He has also built guitars.

Moonstone

1972-present. Luthier Steve Helgeson builds his premium grade, production/custom, acoustic and electric basses in Eureka, California. He also builds guitars.

Eclipse Deluxe Bass
1980-1984. Double-cut solidbody.

1980-1984		$1,500	$1,950

Exploder Bass
1980-1983. Figured wood body, Explorer-style neck-thru-body.

1980-1983		$1,750	$2,300

Vulcan Bass
1982-1984. Solidbody, flat-top (Vulcan) or carved top (Vulcan II), maple body, gold hardware.

1982-1984		$1,750	$2,300

Morales

Ca.1967-1968. Guitars and basses made in Japan by Zen-On and not heavily imported into the U.S.

Electric Solidbody Bass

1967-1968	Various models	$100	$300

Mosrite

Semie Moseley's Mosrite offered various bass models throughout the many versions of the Mosrite company.

Brut Bass
Late-1960s. Assymetrical body with small cutaway on upper treble bout.

1960s		$500	$650

Celebrity Bass
1965-1969. ES-335-style semi-thick double-cut body with f-holes, 2 pickups.

1965-1966	Custom color	$600	$775
1965-1967	Sunburst	$525	$700
1968-1969	Red	$500	$650
1969	Sunburst	$500	$650

Combo Bass
1966-1968. Hollowbody, 2 pickups.

1966-1968		$1,050	$1,350

Joe Maphis Bass
1966-1969. Ventures-style body, hollow without f-holes, 2 pickups, natural.

1966-1969		$1,100	$1,450

Ventures Bass
1965-1972. Various colors, 1 or 2 pickups.

1965	1 pickup	$1,300	$1,700
1965	2 pickups	$1,450	$1,900
1966	1 pickup	$1,175	$1,550
1966	2 pickups	$1,350	$1,750
1967-1968	1 pickup	$1,050	$1,350
1967-1968	2 pickups	$1,150	$1,500
1969	1 pickup	$975	$1,275
1969	2 pickups	$1,100	$1,450
1970-1972	1 pickup	$900	$1,200
1970-1972	2 pickups	$1,050	$1,350

V-II Bass
1973-1974. Ventures-style, 2 humbuckers, sunburst.

1973-1974		$1,100	$1,450

MTD

1994-present. Intermediate, professional, and premium grade, production/custom, electric basses built by luthier Michael Tobias (who founded Tobias Basses in '77) in Kingston, New York. Since '00, he also imports basses built in Korea to his specifications.

Murph

1965-1967. Mid-level electric solidbody basses built by Pat Murphy in San Fernado, California. Murph logo on headstock. They also offered guitars and amps.

Solidbody Bass

1965-1967		$550	$725

Music Man

1972-present. Intermediate and professional grade, production, electric basses. They also build guitars.

Bongo Bass
2003-present. Double cut solidbody, squared-off horns, 2 pickups, 4-, 5-, and 6-string.

2003-2019	Bongo 4	$900	$1,200
2003-2019	Bongo 5	$1,000	$1,350
2003-2019	Bongo 6	$1,150	$1,500

Cutlass I/Cutlass II Bass
1982-1987. Ash body, graphite neck, string-thru-body.

1982-1984	CLF era Cutlass I	$1,900	$2,500
1982-1984	CLF era Cutlass II	$1,800	$2,350
1984-1987	Ernie Ball era Cutlass I	$1,300	$1,700
1984-1987	Ernie Ball era Cutlass II	$1,400	$1,850

S.U.B. Series Bass
2003-2007. Offset double-cut, 4- or 5-string, 1 humbucker.

2003-2007	IV Bass	$375	$500
2003-2007	V Bass	$425	$550

1982 Moonstone Eclipse Deluxe
Craig Brody

1982 Musicman Cutlass I
Craig Brody

BASSES

1976 Music Man StingRay
Craig Brody

Ovation Magnum I
Imaged by Heritage Auctions, HA.com

BASSES

MODEL YEAR	FEATURES	EXC. COND. LOW	HIGH
Sabre Bass			
1978-ca.1991. Double-cut solidbody bass, 3-and-1 tuning keys, 2 humbucking pickups, on-board preamp, natural.			
1978-1984	CLF era	$1,925	$2,525
1984-1991	Ernie Ball era	$1,075	$1,400
Sterling Bass			
1993-present. Rosewood, 1 pickup, EQ, pearl blue. In '05, additional pickup options available. 5-string introduced in '08.			
1993-2019	4-string	$775	$1,050
2008-2019	5-string	$825	$1,100
StingRay Bass			
1976-present. Offset double-cut solidbody, 1 pickup, 3-and-1 tuners, string-thru until '80, various colors. 5-string introduced in '87. In '05, additional pickup options available.			
1976-1979	CLF era	$2,300	$3,000
1980-1984	CLF era	$1,850	$2,400
1984-1989	Ernie Ball era	$1,075	$1,400
1987-2019	5-string	$1,075	$1,400
1990-2019	4-string	$975	$1,275
StingRay 20th Anniversary Bass			
1996. 1400 made, flamed maple body.			
1996		$1,650	$2,150
StingRay Classic Bass			
2010-present. Ash body, birds-eye or flame maple neck, 4- or 5-string.			
2010-2019		$1,150	$1,500

National

Ca. 1927-present. National offered electric basses in the '60s when Valco owned the brand.

Beatle (Violin) Bass
1970s. Strum & Drum era import, National script logo on headstock, 2 pickups, shaded brown finish.

1970s		$375	$500

EG 700V-2HB German Style Bass
1970s. Strum & Drum era import, Beatle-style violin body, 2 humbuckers, bolt neck.

1970s		$425	$550

N-850 Bass
1967-1968. Semi-hollow double-cut, art deco f-holes, 2 pickups, block markers, bout control knobs, sunburst.

1967-1968		$600	$800

Val-Pro 85 Bass
1961-1962. Res-O-Glas body shaped like the U.S. map, 2 pickups, snow white, renamed National 85 in '63.

1961-1962		$775	$1,000

National Reso-Phonic

1988-present. Professional grade, production/custom, acoustic and acoustic/electric resonator basses built in San Luis Obispo, California. They also build guitars, mandolins and ukuleles.

New York Bass Works

1989-present. Luthier David Segal builds his professional and premium grade, production/custom, electric basses in New York.

Norma

Ca.1965-1970. Guitars and basses imported from Japan by Chicago's Strum and Drum.

Electric Solidbody Bass

1960s	Various models	$100	$275

O'Hagan

1979-1983. Designed by Jerol O'Hagan in St. Louis Park, Minnesota. He also offered guitars.

Electric Solidbody Bass
1979-1983. Models include the Shark Bass, Night-Watch Bass, NightWatch Regular Bass, and the Twenty Two Bass.

1979-1983		$500	$650

Old Kraftsman

1930s-1960s. Brand used by the Spiegel Company. Guitars and basses made by other American manufacturers.

Electric Solidbody Bass

1950s	Various models	$300	$400

Orville by Gibson

1984-1993. Orville by Gibson and Orville guitars were made by Japan's Fuji Gen Gakki for Gibson. Basically the same models except the Orville by Gibson guitars had real Gibson USA pickups and a true nitrocellulose lacquer finish. The Orville models used Japanese electronics and a poly finish. Prices here are for the Orville by Gibson models.

Electric Bass

1984-1993	Thunderbird	$900	$1,175

Ovation

1966-present. Intermediate and professional grade, production, acoustic/electric basses. Ovation offered electric solidbody basses early on and added acoustic basses in the '90s. They also offer guitars and mandolins.

B768/Elite B768 Bass
1990. Single-cut acoustic-electric bass, Elite body style with upper bout soundholes.

1990		$650	$875

Celebrity Series Bass
1990s-2013. Deep bowl back, cutaway, acoustic/electric.

1990s-2013		$275	$350

Magnum Series Bass
1974-1980. Magnum I is odd-shaped mahogany solidbody, 2 pickups, mono/stereo, mute, sunburst, red or natural. Magnum II is with battery-powered preamp and 3-band EQ. Magnum III and IV had a new offset double-cut body.

1974-1980	Various models	$850	$1,150

NSB778 Elite T Bass Nikki Sixx Limited Edition
2005-2013. Made in USA, acoustic-electric 4-string, 1 pickup, solid spruce top, ebony 'board, custom iron cross inlays, red or gray flame finish.

2005-2013		$1,125	$1,450

MODEL YEAR	FEATURES	EXC. COND. LOW	HIGH

Typhoon II/Typhoon III Bass
1968-1971. Ovation necks, but bodies and hardware were German imports. Semi-hollowbody, 2 pickups, red or sunburst. Typhoon II is 335-style and III is fretless.

1968-1971	Typhoon II	$675	$875
1968-1971	Typhoon III	$725	$925

Ultra Bass
1984. Korean solidbodies and necks assembled in U.S., offset double-cut with 1 pickup.

1984		$350	$450

PANaramic
1961-1963. Guitars and basses made in Italy by the Crucianelli accordion company and imported by PANaramic accordion. They also offered amps made by Magnatone.

Electric Bass
1961-1963. Double-cut hollowbody, 2 pickups, dot markers, sunburst.

1961-1963		$850	$1,100

Parker
1992-2016. Premium grade, production/custom, solidbody electric basses. They also built guitars.

Fly Bass
2002-2011. Offered in 4- and 5-string models.

2002-2011		$1,200	$1,600

Paul Reed Smith
1985-present. PRS added basses in '86, but by '92 had dropped the models. In 2000 PRS started again offering professional and premium grade, production, solidbody electric basses. Bird inlays can add $100 or more to the values of PRS basses listed here.

Bass-4
1986-1992, 2007. Set neck, 3 single-coil pickups, hum-cancelling coil, active circuitry, 22-fret Brazilian rosewood 'board. Reintroduced (OEB Series) in 2000s.

1986-1987		$1,700	$2,200
1988-1992		$1,400	$1,800
2007		$1,400	$1,800

Bass-5
1986-1992. Five-string, set-neck, rosewood 'board, 3 single-coil pickups, active electronics. Options include custom colors, bird inlays, fretless 'board.

1986-1987		$1,800	$2,400
1988-1992		$1,500	$2,000

CE Bass-4
1986-1991. Solidbody, maple bolt neck, alder body, rosewood 'board, 4-string.

1986-1987		$1,000	$1,300
1988-1991		$800	$1,050

CE Bass-5
1986-1991. Five-string solidbody, maple bolt neck, alder body, rosewood 'board.

1986-1987		$1,100	$1,400
1988-1991		$900	$1,150

Curly Bass-4
1986-1992. Double-cut solidbody, curly maple top, set maple neck, Brazilian rosewood 'board (ebony on fretless), 3 single-coil and 1 hum-cancelling pickups, various grades of maple tops, moon inlays.

1986-1987		$1,800	$2,400
1988-1992		$1,500	$2,000

Curly Bass-5
1986-1992. Five-string version of Curly Bass-4.

1986-1987		$1,900	$2,500
1988-1992		$1,600	$2,100

Electric Bass
2000-2007. Bolt neck 4-string, offered in regular and maple top versions.

2000-2007	Maple	$1,000	$1,300
2000-2007	Plain	$900	$1,200

Private Stock Program
2010-present. Custom instruments based around existing PRS models.

2010-2019		$3,600	$6,000

Peavey
1965-present. Intermediate and professional grade, production/custom, electric basses. They also build guitars and amps. Hartley Peavey's first products were guitar amps and he added guitars and basses to the mix in '78.

Axcelerator Bass
1994-1998. Offset double-cut, long thin horns, 2 humbuckers, stacked control knobs, bolt neck, dot markers.

1994-1998		$300	$400

Cirrus Series Bass
1998-2012. Offset double-cut, active electronics, in 4-, 5-, 6-string, and custom shop versions.

1998-2009	Cirrus 5	$650	$850
1998-2012	Cirrus 4	$600	$800
1998-2012	Cirrus 6	$725	$950

Dyna-Bass
1987-1993. Double-cut solidbody, active electronics, 3-band EQ, rosewood 'board, opaque finish.

1987-1993		$350	$450

Dyna-Bass Limited
1987-1990. Neck-thru-body, ebony 'board, flamed maple neck/body construction, purple heart strips, mother-of-pearl inlays.

1987-1990		$450	$600

Forum Bass
1994-1995. Double-cut solidbody, rosewood 'board, dot inlays, 2 humbuckers.

1994-1995		$200	$265

Forum Plus Bass
1994. Forum Bass with added active electronics.

1994		$200	$265

Foundation Bass
1984-2002. Double-cut solidbody, 2 pickups, maple neck.

1984-2002		$200	$265

Foundation S Active Bass
1987-1991. Similar to Foundation S Bass with added active circuitry, provides low-impedance output, 2 pickups.

1987-1991		$200	$265

1969 Ovation Typhoon II
Rivington Guitars

1987 PRS Curly Bass-5
Craig Brody

BASSES

Pedulla MVP

1958 Premier Bantam
Izzy Miller

MODEL YEAR	FEATURES	EXC. COND. LOW	HIGH
Foundation S Bass			
1986-1991. Two split-coil pickups, maple body, rosewood 'board, black hardware, black painted headstock.			
1986-1991		$200	$265
Fury Bass			
1983-1999. Double-cut solidbody, rosewood 'board, 1 split-coil humbucker.			
1983-1999		$200	$265
Fury Custom Bass			
1986-1993. Fury Bass with black hardware and narrow neck.			
1986-1993		$200	$265
Fury VI Bass			
2001-2003. 6-string, active electronics, quilt top.			
2001-2003		$275	$365
G-Bass V			
1999-2002. Offset double-cut 5-string, humbucker, 3-band EQ.			
1999-2002		$625	$825
Grind Series Bass			
2001-present. Offset double-cut, neck-thru, long bass horn, 2 pickups, 4, 5, or 6 strings.			
2001-2019	Various models	$200	$325
Liberator JT-84 John Taylor Bass			
2007. 2 humbuckers, black with graphics.			
2007	JT-84	$850	$1,125
Milestone Series Bass			
1994-present. Import offset double cut, Milestone I ('94) replaced by 1 P-style pickup II ('95-'01), split humbucker IV ('99-'04); 2 single-coil III ('99-present) now just called Milestone.			
1994-2019		$85	$125
Millenium Series Bass			
2001-present. Offset double-cut, agathis bodies, maple tops, in 4- or 5-string.			
2001-2019		$150	$600
Patriot Bass			
1984-1988. General J-Bass styling with larger thinner horns, 1 single-coil, maple neck.			
1984-1988		$125	$165
Patriot Custom Bass			
1986-1988. Patriot with rosewood neck, matching headstock.			
1986-1988		$150	$200
RJ-IV Bass			
1990-1993. Randy Jackson Signature model, neck-thru-body, 2 split-coil active pickups, ebony 'board, mother-of-pearl position markers.			
1990-1993		$300	$400
Rudy Sarzo Signature Bass			
1989-1993. Double-cut solidbody, active EQ, ebony 'board, 2 pickups.			
1989-1993		$450	$575
T-20FL Bass			
1980s. Fretless double-cut solidbody, 1 pickup, also available as the fretted T-20 ('82-'83).			
1980s		$200	$265

MODEL YEAR	FEATURES	EXC. COND. LOW	HIGH
T-40/T-40FL Bass			
1978-1987. Double-cut solidbody, 2 pickups. T-40FL is fretless.			
1978-1987	T-40	$425	$550
1978-1987	T-40FL	$425	$550
T-45 Bass			
1982-1986. T-40 with 1 humbucking pickup, and a mid-frequency rolloff knob.			
1982-1986		$300	$400
TL Series Bass			
1988-1998. Neck-thru-body, gold hardware, active humbuckers, EQ, flamed maple neck and body, 5-string (TL-Five) or 6 (TL-Six).			
1988-1998	TL-Five	$500	$650
1989-1998	TL-Six	$550	$725
Zodiac Bass			
2006-2012. Solid alder body, maple neck, 2 pickups.			
2006-2012		$200	$275

Pedulla

1975-2019. Professional and premium grade, production/custom, electric basses made in Rockland, Massachusetts. Founded by Michael Pedulla, and which offered various upscale options that affect valuation, so each instrument should be evaluated on a case-by-case basis. Unless specifically noted, the following listings have standard to mid-level features. High-end options are specifically noted; if not, these options will have a relatively higher value than those shown here. Pedualla announced his retirement in '19.

MODEL YEAR	FEATURES	EXC. COND. LOW	HIGH
Buzz-4/Buzz-5 Bass			
1980-2008. Double-cut neck-thru solidbody, fretless, long-scale, maple neck and body wings, 2 pickups, preamp, some with other active electronics, various colors, 4-, 5-, 6-, 8-string versions.			
1980-1999		$1,150	$1,500
Interceptor Bass			
1980s. Double-cut, maple/walnut laminated neck-thru.			
1980s		$1,000	$1,300
MVP Series Bass			
1984-2019. Fretted version of Buzz Bass, standard or flame top, 4-, 5-, 6-, 8-string versions, MVP II is bolt-on neck version.			
1980s	MVP-6	$1,350	$1,775
1984-1990s	MVP-4 flame top	$1,250	$1,650
1984-1990s	MVP-4 standard top	$1,150	$1,500
1984-1990s	MVP-5	$1,250	$1,650
1990s	MVP II	$800	$1,050
Orsini Wurlitzer 4-String Bass			
Mid-1970s. Body style similar to late-'50s Gibson double-cut slab body SG Special, neck-thru, 2 pickups, natural. Sold by Boston's Wurlitzer music store chain.			
1970s		$1,050	$1,400
Quilt Limited Bass			
Neck-thru-body with curly maple centerstrip, quilted maple body wings, 2 Bartolini pickups, available in fretted or fretless 4- and 5-string models.			
1987		$1,050	$1,400

MODEL YEAR	FEATURES	EXC. COND. LOW	HIGH

Rapture Series Bass
1995-2019. Solidbody with extra-long thin bass horn and extra short treble horn, 4- or 5-string, various colors.

| 1995-2019 | Rapture 4 | $975 | $1,275 |
| 1995-2019 | Rapture 5 | $1,050 | $1,375 |

Series II Bass
1987-1992. Bolt neck, rosewood 'board, mother-of-pearl dot inlays, Bartolini pickups.

| 1987-1992 | | $700 | $900 |

Thunderbass Series Bass
1993-2019. Solidbody with extra-long thin bass horn and extra short treble horn, 4-, 5- or 6-string, standard features or triple A top.

1993-1999	4, AAA top	$1,350	$1,750
1993-1999	4, Standard	$1,050	$1,375
1993-1999	5, AAA top	$1,425	$1,850
1993-1999	5, Standard	$1,175	$1,525
1993-1999	6, AAA top	$1,525	$1,975
1993-1999	6, Standard	$1,250	$1,625
2000-2019	4, AAA top	$1,350	$1,750
2000-2019	5, AAA top	$1,425	$1,850
2000-2019	6, AAA top	$1,525	$1,975

Thunderbolt Series Bass
1994-2019. Similar to Thunderbass Series but with bolt necks, 4-, 5- or 6-string, standard AA or AAA maple or optional 5A or exotic wood (ET) tops.

| 1994-2019 | Thunderbolt 5 | $925 | $1,200 |

Penco
Ca. 1974-1978. Generally high-quality Japanese-made copies of classic American bass guitars. They also made guitars, mandolins and banjos.

Electric Bass

| 1974-1978 | Various models | $150 | $275 |

Premier
Ca.1938-ca.1975, 1990s-2010. Originally American-made instruments, but by the '60s imported parts were being used. 1990s instruments were Asian imports.

Bantam Bass
1950-1970. Small body, single-cut short-scale archtop electric, torch headstock inlay, sparkle 'guard, sunburst.

| 1950-1970 | | $400 | $550 |

Electric Solidbody Bass

| 1960s | Various models | $300 | $400 |

Renaissance
1978-1980. Plexiglass solidbody electric guitars and basses made in Malvern, Pennsylvania.

Plexiglas Bass
1978-1980. Plexiglas bodies and active electronics, models include the DPB bass (double-cut, 1 pickup, '78-'79), SPB (single-cut, 2 pickups, '78-'79), T-100B (Bich-style, 1 pickup, '80), S-100B (double-cut, 1 pickup, '80), and the S-200B (double-cut, 2 pickups, '80).

| 1978-1980 | | $625 | $825 |

Rickenbacker
1931-present. Professional grade, production/custom, electric basses. They also build guitars. Rickenbacker introduced their first electric bass in '57 and has always been a strong player in the bass market.

Electric Upright Bass
1936. Cast aluminum neck and body, horseshoe pickup, extension pole.

| 1936 | | $3,400 | $4,400 |

Model 1999 (Rose-Morris) Bass
1964-1967. Export made for English distributor Rose-Morris of London, built along the lines of the U.S. Model 4000 Bass but with small differences that are considered important in the vintage guitar market.

| 1964-1966 | | $7,300 | $9,500 |
| 1967 | | $6,400 | $8,500 |

Model 2030 Hamburg Bass
1984-1997. Rounded double-cut, 2 pickups, active electronics.

| 1984-1997 | | $650 | $850 |

Model 2030GF (Glenn Frey) Bass
1992-1995. Limited Edition, double-cut, 2 humbuckers, Jetglo finish.

| 1992-1995 | | $1,200 | $1,600 |

Model 2050 El Dorado Bass
1984-1992. Gold hardware, 2 pickups, active.

| 1984-1992 | | $975 | $1,275 |

Model 2060 El Dorado Bass
1992-1997. Gold hardware, 2 pickups, active, double-bound body.

| 1992-1997 | | $1,050 | $1,400 |

Model 3000 Bass
1975-1984. Rounded double-cut, 30" scale, 1 pickup, brown sunburst.

| 1975-1984 | | $1,175 | $1,500 |

Model 3001 Bass
1975-1984. Same as Model 3000 but with longer 33-1/2" scale, Wine Red.

| 1975-1984 | | $1,150 | $1,500 |

Model 3261 (Rose-Morris Slim-Line) Bass
1967. Export model made for English distributor Rose-Morris, built along the lines of a U.S. equivalent Model 4005 Bass.

| 1967 | | $5,100 | $6,600 |

Model 4000 Bass
1958-1985. Cresting wave body and headstock, 1 horseshoe pickup (changed to regular pickup in '64), neck-thru-body.

1958-1962	Plank style	$10,400	$13,500
1963-1966		$7,700	$10,000
1967-1969		$7,000	$9,000
1970-1972		$2,800	$3,600
1973-1985		$1,850	$2,400

Model 4001 Bass
1961-1986. Fancy version of 4000, 1 horseshoe magnet pickup (changed to regular pickup in '64) and 1 bar magnet pickup, triangle inlays, bound neck.

1961-1963	Fireglo	$7,200	$9,500
1963-1966	Mapleglo	$6,500	$8,500
1964-1966	Fireglo	$6,600	$8,800

1979 Renaissance SPB
Craig Brody

1973 Rickenbacker 4000
Craig Brody

1980 Rickenbacker 4003
Bernunzio Uptown Music

*2008 Rickenbacker
Model 4004L Laredo*
Ron O'Keefe

MODEL YEAR	FEATURES	EXC. COND. LOW	HIGH
1967-1969	Various colors	$5,800	$7,500
1970-1972	Various colors	$3,500	$4,500
1973	Early '73 features	$2,950	$3,800
1973	Late '73 features	$2,100	$2,700
1974-1979	Various colors	$2,100	$2,700
1980-1986	Various colors	$1,900	$2,500

Model 4001 C64S Bass
2001-2014. Recreation of Paul McCartney's 4001 featuring changes he made like a reshaped body and zero-fret 'board.

2001-2014		$2,400	$3,100

Model 4001 CS Bass
1991-1997. Chris Squire signature model.

1991-1997	With certificate	$2,400	$3,100

Model 4001 FL Bass
1968-1986. Fretless version of 4001 Bass, special order in '60s, various colors.

1968-1986		$2,400	$3,100

Model 4001 V63 Bass
1984-2000. Vintage '63 reissue of Model 4001S, horseshoe-magnet pickup, Mapleglo.

1984-2000	Figured top	$2,400	$3,200
1984-2000	Plain top	$2,400	$3,100

Model 4001S Bass
1964-1985. Same as Model 4000, but with 2 pickups, export model.

1980-1985		$1,400	$1,800

Model 4002 Bass
1967-1985. Cresting wave body and headstock, 2 humbuckers, black 'guard, checkerboard binding.

1980-1985		$3,700	$4,900

Model 4003 Bass
1979-present. Similar to Model 4001, split 'guard, deluxe features.

1979-2019		$1,350	$1,775

Model 4003 FL Bass
1979-2017. Fretless version.

1979-2017		$1,350	$1,775

Model 4003 Shadow Bass
1986. About 60 made for Guitar Center, all black 'board, inlays and hardware, Jetglo finish.

1986		$2,550	$3,300

Model 4003S Bass
1986-2003, 2012-present. Standard feature version of 4003, 4 strings. Reissued in '12.

1986-2003		$1,450	$1,900
2012-2019	Reissue	$1,175	$1,550

Model 4003S Redneck Bass
1988. Red body, 'board and headstock, black hardware.

1988		$2,350	$3,000

Model 4003S Tuxedo Bass
1987. White body with black 'guard and hardware. 100 made.

1987		$2,350	$3,000

Model 4003S/5 Bass
1986-2003. Model 4003S with 5 strings.

1986-2003		$1,550	$2,025

Model 4003S/8 Bass
1986-2003. Model 4003S with 8 strings.

1986-2003		$2,800	$3,700

MODEL YEAR	FEATURES	EXC. COND. LOW	HIGH

Model 4003S/SPC Blackstar Bass
1989. Black version, black finish, 'board, knobs, and hardware. Also offered as 5-string.

1989		$1,875	$2,450

Model 4003W Bass
2014-present. Solid walnut body, satin natural finish.

2013-2019		$1,250	$1,650

Model 4004C Cheyenne/4004Cii Cheyenne II Bass
1993-2019. Cresting wave, maple neck-thru-body with walnut body and head wings, gold hardware, dot inlay. Replaced by maple top 4004Cii Cheyenne II in '00.

1993-1999	Cheyenne	$1,250	$1,650
2000-2019	Cheyenne II	$1,300	$1,700

Model 4004L Laredo Bass
1993-present. Like Cheyenne but without walnut wings.

1993-2019		$1,150	$1,500

Model 4005 Bass
1965-1984. New style double-cut semi-hollowbody, 2 pickups, R tailpiece, cresting wave headstock.

1965-1966	Fireglo	$9,200	$12,000
1965-1966	Jetglo	$8,000	$10,500
1965-1966	Mapleglo	$9,000	$11,500
1967-1969	Fireglo	$8,400	$11,000
1967-1969	Jetglo	$7,000	$9,200
1967-1969	Mapleglo	$8,000	$10,500
1970-1979	Various colors	$5,700	$7,400
1980-1984	Various colors	$5,300	$6,900

Model 4005 L (Lightshow) Bass
1970-1975. Model 4005 with translucent top with lights in body that lit up when played, needed external transformer.

1970-1971	1st edition	$7,700	$10,100
1972-1975	2nd edition	$8,500	$11,100

Model 4005 WB Bass
1966-1983. Old style Model 4005 with white-bound body, Fireglo.

1966		$8,500	$11,000
1967-1969		$7,500	$10,000
1970-1979		$4,500	$6,000
1980-1983		$4,100	$5,500

Model 4005-6 Bass
1965-1977. Model 4005 with 6 strings.

1965-1969		$8,900	$11,600
1970-1977		$6,000	$8,000

Model 4005-8 Bass
Late-1960s. Eight-string Model 4005, Fireglo or Mapleglo.

1968-1969		$8,500	$11,000

Model 4008 Bass
1975-1983. Eight-string, cresting wave body and headstock.

1975-1979		$1,750	$2,300
1980-1983		$1,550	$2,050

Model 4080 Doubleneck Bass
1975-1992. Bolt-on 6- and 4-string necks, Jetglo or Mapleglo.

1975-1979		$5,000	$6,500
1980-1992		$5,000	$6,500

MODEL YEAR	FEATURES	EXC. COND. LOW	HIGH

Ritter Royal Instruments

Production/custom, solidbody basses built by luthier Jens Ritter in Wachenheim, Germany.

Rob Allen

1997-present. Professional grade, production/custom, lightweight basses made by luthier Robert Allen in Santa Barbara, California.

Robin

1982-2010. Founded by David Wintz and located in Houston, Texas, Robin built basses until 1997. Most basses were Japanese-made until '87; American production began in '88. They also built guitars and also made Metropolitan ('96-'08) and Alamo ('00-'08) brand guitars.

Freedom Bass I

1984-1986. Offset double-cut, active treble and bass EQ controls, 1 pickup.

1984-1986		$525	$700

Freedom Bass I Passive

1986-1989. Non-active version of Freedom Bass, I humbucker. Passive dropped from name in '87.

1986-1989		$525	$700

Medley Bass

1984-1997. Offset deep cutaways, 2 pickups, reverse headstock until '89, then split headstock, back to reverse by '94. Japanese-made until '87, U.S. after.

1984-1987	Japan	$425	$550
1988-1997	USA	$825	$1,100

Ranger Bass

1984-1997. Vintage style body, dot markers, medium scale and 1 pickup from '84 to '88 and long scale with P-style and J-style pickup configuration from '89 to '97.

1984-1987	Japan	$400	$525
1988-1997	USA	$750	$1,000

Rock Bass

2002-2015. Chinese-made, intermediate and professional grade, production, bolt neck solidbody basses from the makers of Warwick basses.

Roland

Best known for keyboards, effects, and amps, Roland offered synthesizer-based guitars and basses from 1977 to '86.

GR-33B (G-88) Bass Guitar Synthesizer

Early-mid 1980s. Solidbody bass with synthesizer in the guitar case, G-88 deluxe bass.

1983-1985		$750	$1,000

Roman & Blake Basses

1977-2003. Professional grade, production/custom, solidbody bass guitars made by Ed Roman Guitars.

Roman USA Basses

Professional grade, production/custom, solidbody basses made by Ed Roman Guitars starting in 2000.

Roscoe Guitars

Early 1980s-present. Luthier Keith Roscoe builds his production/custom, professional and premium grade, solidbody electric basses in Greensboro, North Carolina.

S.D. Curlee

1975-1982. S.D. Curlee guitars and basses were made in Illinois; S.D. Curlee International instruments were made in Japan.

Electric Solidbody Bass

1970s	Various models	$300	$425

Sadowsky

1980-present. Professional and premium grade, production/custom, solidbody basses built by luthier Roger Sadowsky in Brooklyn, New York. He also builds guitars and amps.

Serenader

Mainly known for lap steels this Seattle, Washington brand also built a solidbody bass.

Silvertone

1941-ca.1970, present. Brand used by Sears. Instruments were U.S.-made and imported. Currently, Samick offers a line of acoustic and electric guitars, basses and amps under the Silvertone name.

Model 1376L/1373L 6-String Bass

1956-1959. 2 pickups, 6-string.

1956-1959		$1,250	$1,600

Model 1442 Standard Bass

1966-1968. Solidbody 30" standard size, 1 pickup, dot markers, shaded brown.

1966-1968		$600	$800

Model 1443 Extra Long Bass

1966-1968. Solidbody 34" size, 2 pickups, dot markers, red sunburst.

1966-1968		$750	$1,000

Model 1444 Electric Bass

1959-1965. Bass version of 6-string electric guitar Model 1415 (bronze) and 1416 (black), 4-on-a-side replaces the prior year coke-bottle headstock, 1 pickup on single-cut U-1 style body, black finish.

1959-1965		$700	$900

Simmons

2002-present. Luthier David L. Simmons builds his professional grade, production/custom, 4- and 5-string basses in Hendersonville, North Carolina.

Sinister

2003. A short run of intermediate grade, solidbody basses built for Sinister Guitars by luthier Jon Kammerer.

Smith

1978-present. Professional and premium grade, production/custom, electric basses built by luthier Ken Smith in Perkasie, Pennsylvania. Earlier models had Ken Smith on the headstock, recent models

1984 Robin Freedom II
Rivington Guitars

1966 Silvertone Model 1443 Extra Long Bass
Erick Warner

BASSES

Spector NS-2

1983 Steinberger L2
Carter Vintage Guitars

MODEL YEAR	FEATURES	EXC. COND. LOW	HIGH

have a large S logo. He also designs the imported KSD line of basses.

American-Made Bass

| 1978-2019 | Various models | $1,700 | $3,700 |

Imported Bass

| 1990s | Various models | $450 | $750 |

Soundgear by Ibanez

SDGR Soundgear by Ibanez headstock logo, intermediate grade, production, solidbody electric basses, made in Japan, Korea and Indonesia, starting in 1987.

Spector/Stuart Spector Design

1975-1990 (Spector), 1991-1998 (SSD), 1998-present (Spector SSD). Imtermediate, professional, and premium grade, production/custom, basses made in the U.S., the Czech Republic, Korea, and China. Stuart Spector's first bass was the NS and the company quickly grew to the point where Kramer acquired it in '85. After Kramer went out of business in '90, Spector started building basses with the SSD logo (Stuart Spector Design). In '98 he recovered the Spector trademark.

Squier

See models listed under Squier in Fender section.

Standel

1952-1974, 1997-present. Amp builder Bob Crooks offered instruments under his Standel brand name three different times during the '60s. See Guitar section for production details. See Amp section for more company information.

Custom Deluxe Solidbody 401 Bass

1967-1968. Custom with higher appointments, various colors.

| 1967-1968 | | $900 | $1,200 |

Custom Deluxe Thinbody 402 Bass

1967-1968. Custom with higher appointments, various colors.

| 1967-1968 | | $900 | $1,200 |

Custom Solidbody 501 Bass

1967-1968. Solidbody, 1 pickup, various colors.

| 1967-1968 | | $725 | $950 |

Custom Thinbody 502 Bass

1967-1968. Thin solidbody, 2 pickups, various colors.

| 1967-1968 | | $725 | $950 |

Steinberger

1979-present. Steinberger offers budget and intermediate grade, production, electric basses. They also offer guitars.

H Series

1979-1982. Reinforced molded plastic wedge-shaped body, headless neck, 1 (H1) or 2 (H2) high impedence pickups, black, red or white.

1979-1982	H1, black	$2,150	$2,775
1979-1982	H1, red or white	$3,075	$4,000
1979-1982	H2, black	$2,150	$2,775
1979-1982	H2, red or white	$3,075	$4,000

MODEL YEAR	FEATURES	EXC. COND. LOW	HIGH

L Series

1979-1984. Reinforced molded plastic wedge-shaped body, headless neck, 1 (L1) or 2 (L2) low impedence active pickups, black, red or white. Evolved into XL series.

1979-1984	L1, black	$1,725	$2,300
1979-1984	L1, black, fretless	$1,650	$2,175
1979-1984	L1, red or white	$2,700	$3,550
1979-1984	L2, black	$1,725	$2,300
1979-1984	L2, black, fretless	$1,650	$2,175
1979-1984	L2, red or white	$2,700	$3,550

Q-4 Bass

1990-1991. Composite neck, Double Bass system, headless with traditional-style maple body, low-impedance pickups.

| 1990-1991 | | $1,225 | $1,600 |

Q-5 Bass

1990-1991. Five-string version of Q Bass.

| 1990-1991 | | $1,300 | $1,700 |

XL-2 Bass

1984-1993. Rectangular composite body, 4-string, headless, 2 pickups.

| 1984-1989 | | $1,875 | $2,400 |
| 1990-1993 | | $1,700 | $2,200 |

XL-2GR Bass

1985-1990. Headless, Roland GR synthesizer controller.

| 1985-1990 | | $1,725 | $2,300 |

XM-2 Bass

1986-1992. Headless, double-cut maple body, 4-string, 2 low-impedance pickups, optional fretted, lined fretless or unlined fretless, black, red or white.

| 1986-1992 | | $1,650 | $2,175 |

XT-2/XZ-2 Spirit Bass

1995-present. Headless, rectangular XL body, import.

| 1995-2019 | | $235 | $300 |

Stewart Basses

2000-ca. 2009. Luthier Fred Stewart built his premium grade, custom/production, solidbody basses in Charlton, Maryland. He has also built guitars starting in '94.

Stinger

See Martin listing.

Supro

1935-1968, 2004-present. Supro was a budget brand for the National Dobro Company. Supro offered only two bass models in the '60s. Brand name was revived in '04.

Pocket Bass

1960-1968. Double-cut, neck pickup and bridge mounted pickup, semi-hollow, short-scale, black.

| 1960-1968 | | $575 | $775 |

Taurus Bass

1967-1968. Asymmetrical double-cut, neck pickup and bridge mounted pickup.

| 1967-1968 | | $475 | $650 |

MODEL YEAR	FEATURES	EXC. COND. LOW	HIGH

SX
See listing for Essex.

Tacoma
1995-2009. Professional grade, production, acoustic basses produced in Tacoma, Washington. They also built acoustic guitars and mandolins.

Thunderchief Series Bass
1998-2009. 17 3/4 flat-top, solid spruce top, solid mahogany back, laminated mahogany sides, rounded cutaway, bolt-on neck, dot markers, natural satin finish.

1998-2009	Various models	$775	$1,025

Taylor
1974-present. Professional and premium grade, production, acoustic basses built in El Cajon, California. They presently build guitars.

AB1 Bass
1996-2003. Acoustic/electric, sitka spruce top, imbuia walnut back and sides, designed for 'loose' woody sound.

1996-2003		$1,150	$1,500

AB2 Bass
1996-2003. Acoustic/electric, all imbuia walnut body.

1996-2003		$1,575	$2,050

AB3 Bass
1998-2003. Acoustic/electric, sitka spruce top, maple back and sides.

1998-2003		$1,575	$2,050

Teisco
The Japanese Teisco line started offering basses in the '60s.

Electric Bass
1968-1969. EB-100 (1 pickup, white 'guard), EB-200 (solidbody), EB-200B (semi-hollowbody) and Violin bass.

1968-1969	EB-100	$125	$175
1968-1969	EB-200	$525	$700
1968-1969	EB-200 B	$525	$700
1968-1969	Violin	$525	$700

Tele-Star
1965-ca.1972. Guitars and basses imported from Japan by Tele-Star Musical Instrument Corporation of New York. Primarily made by Kawai, many inspired by Burns designs, some in cool sparkle finishes.

Electric Solidbody Bass

1960s	Various models	$100	$275

Tobias
1977-2019. Founded by Mike Tobias in Orlando, Florida. Moved to San Francisco for '80-'81, then to Costa Mesa, eventually ending up in Hollywood. In '90, he sold the company to Gibson which moved it to Burbank. The first Tobias made under Gibson ownership was serial number 1094. The instruments continued to be made by the pre-Gibson crew until '92, when the company was moved to Nashville. The last LA Tobias/Gibson serial number is 2044. Mike left the company in '92 and started a new business in '94 called MTD where he continues to make electric and acoustic basses. In '99, production of Tobias basses was moved overseas. In late '03, Gibson started again offering U.S.-made Tobias instruments; they are made in Conway, Arkansas, in the former Baldwin grand piano facility. Currently Tobias offers imported and U.S.-made, intermediate and professional grade, production, acoustic and electric basses.

Basic Bass
1984-1999. 30", 32", or 34" scale, neck-thru-body in alder, koa or walnut, 5-piece laminated neck.

1984-1999	Basic B-4	$1,650	$2,150
1984-1999	Basic B-5	$1,750	$2,250

Classic C-4 Bass
1978-1999. One or 2 pickups, active or passive electronics, 2-octave rosewood 'board, available in short-, medium-, and long-scale models.

1978-1999		$1,750	$2,250

Classic C-5 Bass
1985-1999. 30", 32" or 34" scale, alder, koa or walnut body, bookmatched top, ebony or phenolic 'board, hardwood neck.

1985-1999		$1,800	$2,350

Classic C-6 Bass
Ca. 1986-1999. Flamed maple and padauk neck, alder body, padauk top, ebony 'board, active electronics, 32" or 34" scale.

1986-1999		$1,900	$2,450

Growler GR-5 Bass
1996-1999. 5-string, offset double-cut, bolt neck, various colors.

1996-1999		$600	$775

Growler Limited Bass
2009. Natural finish swamp ash body, set-neck.

2009		$675	$875

Killer Bee Bass
1991-1999. Offset double-cut, swamp ash or lacewood body, various colors.

1991-1999	KB-4	$1,500	$2,000
1991-1999	KB-5	$1,600	$2,100
1991-1999	KB-6	$1,700	$2,200

Model T Bass
1989-1991. Line of 4- and 5-string basses, 3-piece maple neck-thru-body, maple body halves, active treble and bass controls. Fretless available.

1989-1991		$1,025	$1,350

Renegade Bass
1998-2001. Offset double-cut, 1 single-coil and 1 humbucker.

1998-2001		$1,400	$1,800

Signature S-4 Bass
1978-1999. Available in 4-, 5-, and 6-string models, chrome-plated milled brass bridge.

1978-1990	Tobias-Burbank	$2,700	$3,500
1990-1992	Gibson-Burbank	$2,150	$2,800

1984 Steinberger XL-2
Justin Nortillo

1960 Teisco EB-200
Carter Vintage Guitars

BASSES

BASSES

Tokai Hard Puncher
Michael Burns

1974 Univox Hi Flier
Greg Boschert

MODEL YEAR	FEATURES	EXC. COND. LOW	HIGH
Standard ST-4 Bass			
1992-1995. Japanese-made, 5-piece maple neck-thru, swamp ash body wings.			
1992-1995		$1,000	$1,300
Toby Deluxe TD-4 Bass			
1994-1996. Offset double-cut, bolt neck.			
1994-1996		$375	$525
Toby Deluxe TD-5 Bass			
1994-1996. 5-string version.			
1994-1996		$475	$625
Toby Pro 5 Bass			
1994-1996. Solidbody 5-string, Toby Pro logo on truss rod cover, neck-thru body.			
1994-1996		$375	$525
Toby Pro 6 Bass			
1994-1996. Solidbody 6-string, Toby Pro logo on truss rod cover, neck-thru body.			
1994-1996		$450	$650

Tokai

1947-present. Tokai started making guitars and basses around '70 and by the end of that decade they were being imported into the U.S. Today Tokai offers electrics, acoustics, and electric basses made in Japan and Korea.

MODEL YEAR	FEATURES	EXC. COND. LOW	HIGH
Vintage Bass			
1970s-1980s. Tokai offered near copies of classic U.S. basses.			
1970s-80s	Copy models	$400	$825

Tonemaster

1960s. Guitars and basses, imported from Italy, with typical '60s Italian sparkle plastic finish and push-button controls, bolt-on neck.

MODEL YEAR	FEATURES	EXC. COND. LOW	HIGH
Electric Bass			
1960s	Various models	$500	$700

Traben

Intermediate grade, production, solidbody basses imported by Elite Music Brands of Clearwater, Florida, starting in 2004.

Travis Bean

1974-1979, 1999. The unique Travis Bean line included a couple of bass models. Travis Bean announced some new instruments in '99, but general production was not resumed.

MODEL YEAR	FEATURES	EXC. COND. LOW	HIGH
TB-2000 Bass			
1974-1979. Aluminum neck, T-slotted headstock, longer horned, double-cut body, 2 pickups, 4 controls, dot markers, various colors.			
1974-1979		$2,700	$3,500
TB-4000 (Wedge Vee) Bass			
1974-1979. Bass version of Bean's Wedge guitar, few made.			
1974-1979		$3,600	$4,700

True Tone

1960s. Western Auto retailed this line of basses, guitars and amps which were manufactured by Chicago builders like Kay. The brand was most likely gone by '68.

MODEL YEAR	FEATURES	EXC. COND. LOW	HIGH
Electric Bass			
1960s		$225	$350

Univox

1964-1978. Univox started out as an amp line and added guitars and basses around '69. Guitars were imported from Japan by the Merson Musical Supply Company, later Unicord, Westbury, New York. Generally mid-level copies of American designs.

MODEL YEAR	FEATURES	EXC. COND. LOW	HIGH
Badazz Bass			
1971-ca. 1975. Based on the Guild S-100.			
1971-1977		$350	$450
Bicentennial Bass			
1976. Carved eagle in body, matches Bicentennial guitar (see that listing), brown stain, maple 'board.			
1976		$650	$850
Hi Flier Bass			
1969-1977. Mosrite Ventures Bass copy, 2 pickups, rosewood 'board.			
1969-1977		$425	$550
'Lectra (Model 1970F) Bass			
1969-ca. 1973. Violin bass, walnut.			
1969-1973		$525	$675
Model 3340 Semi-Hollow Bass			
1970-1971. Copy of Gibson EB-0 semi-hollow bass.			
1970-1971		$425	$550
Precisely Bass			
1971-ca. 1975. Copy of Fender P-Bass.			
1971-1975		$425	$550
Stereo Bass			
1976-1977. Rickenbacker 4001 Bass copy, model U1975B.			
1976-1977		$425	$550
Thin Line Bass			
1960s. EB-2 style, f-holes, 2 pickups.			
1960s		$425	$550

Ventura

1970s. Import classic bass copies distributed by C. Bruno (Kaman). They also had guitars.

MODEL YEAR	FEATURES	EXC. COND. LOW	HIGH
Vintage Electric Bass			
1970s	Copy models	$425	$550

Vox

1954-present. Guitars and basses bearing the Vox name were offered from 1961-'69 (made in England, Italy), '82-'85 (Japan), '85-'88 (Korea), '98-2001 (U.S.), with a limited edition teardrop bass offered in late '07. Special thanks to Jim Rhoads of Rhoads Music in Elizabethtown, Pennsylvania, for help on production years of these models.

MODEL YEAR	FEATURES	EXC. COND. LOW	HIGH
Apollo IV Bass			
1967-1969. Single-cut hollowbody, bolt maple neck, 1 pickup, on-board fuzz, booster, sunburst.			
1967-1969		$675	$875
Astro IV Bass			
1967-1969. Violin-copy bass, 2 pickups.			
1967-1969		$850	$1,100
Bassmaster Bass			
1961-1965. Offset double-cut, 2 pickups, 2 knobs.			
1961-1965		$625	$800

MODEL YEAR	FEATURES	EXC. COND. LOW	HIGH

Clubman Bass
1961-1966. Double-cut 2-pickup solidbody, red.

1961-1966		$425	$550

Constellation IV Bass
1967-1968. Teardrop-shaped body, 2 pickups, 1 f-hole, 1 set of controls, treble, bass and distortion boosters.

1967-1968		$1,100	$1,450

Cougar Bass
1963-1967. Double-cut semi-hollow body, 2 f-holes, 2 pickups, 2 sets of controls, sunburst.

1963-1967		$850	$1,100

Delta IV Bass
1967-1968. Five-sided body, 2 pickups, 1 volume and 2 tone controls, distortion, treble and bass boosters.

1967-1968		$1,050	$3,050

Guitar-Organ Bass
1966. The 4-string bass version of the Guitar-Organ, Phantom-style body, white.

1966	Excellent cond	$1,950	$2,550
1966	Functional	$600	$1,650

Mark IV Bass
1963-1969. Teardrop-shaped body, 2 pickups, 1 set of controls, sunburst.

1963-1965	England, white	$2,150	$2,850
1965-1969	Italy, sunburst	$1,325	$1,725

Panther Bass
1967-1968. Double-cut solidbody, 1 slanted pickup, rosewood 'board, sunburst.

1967-1968		$475	$625

Phantom IV Bass
1963-1969. Five-sided body, 2 pickups, 1 set of controls.

1963-1964	England	$2,000	$2,600
1965-1969	Italy	$1,450	$1,900

Saturn IV Bass
1967-1968. Single-cut, 2 f-holes, 1 set of controls, 1 pickup.

1967-1968		$550	$725

Sidewinder IV Bass (V272)
1967-1968. Double-cut semi-hollow body, 2 f-holes, 2 pickups, 1 set of controls, treble, bass, and distortion boosters.

1967-1968		$1,000	$1,300

Stinger Bass
1968. Teardrop-shaped, boat oar headstock.

1968		$725	$925

Violin Bass
1966. Electro-acoustic bass with violin shaped body, 2 extended range pickups, sunburst.

1966		$850	$1,100

Wyman Bass
1966. Teardrop-shaped body, 2 pickups, 1 f-hole, 1 set of controls, sunburst.

1966		$1,325	$1,725

Wal

1976-present. Founded in England by luthier Ian Waller and his partner Peter Stevens, forming the company under the name Electric Wood in '78. Waller died in '88, Stevens enlists help of luthier

Paul Herman, and in 2000s Stevens retires and Herman takes over. In the early years, the Mark designation was used generically. Newer contemporary models are named Mk1, Mk2 and Mk3. Prices shown will increase 5% with LED option, or 10% with rare top, but no value difference between fretted and fretless. MIDI electronics does not increase the value.

Custom (IV) Bass
1980s-1990s. 4-string, active, no guard, generally highly figured front and back.

1980	Mark I	$4,500	$5,800
1985	Mark II	$5,200	$6,800
1994	Mark III	$5,200	$6,800

Custom (V) Bass
1980s-1990s. 5-string, active, no guard, generally highly figured front and back.

1985	Mark II	$5,200	$6,800
1994	Mark III	$5,200	$6,800

Custom (VI) Bass
1990s. 6-string, active, no guard, generally highly figured front and back.

1994	Mark III	$5,200	$6,800

JG Bass
1976-1978. 4-string, passive with either tooled leather (34 made), or leather guard.

1976-1978	Non-tooled	$5,200	$6,800
1976-1978	Tooled	$5,800	$7,500

Pro (Mark I) Bass
1978. Passive, black guard.

1978		$2,800	$3,800

Wandre (Davoli)

Ca. 1956/57-1969. Italian-made guitars and basses.

Electric Bass

1956-1969	Common models	$1,000	$3,000
1956-1969	Rare models	$3,000	$8,000

Warwick

1982-present. Professional and premium grade, production/custom, electric and acoustic basses made in Markneukirchen, Germany; founded by Hans Peter Wilfer, whose father started Framus guitars. They also build amps.

Welson

1960s. Italian-made copy model guitars and basses.

Electric Bass

1960s	Copy models	$100	$300

Wurlitzer

Large music retailer Wurlitzer marketed a line of American-made guitars in the 1920s. They also offered American- and foreign-made guitars starting in '65. In '67, Wurlitzer switched to Italian-made Welson guitars.

Hollowbody Electric Bass
1960s. Italian-made.

1967		$475	$625

1967 Vox Apollo IV
Rivington Guitars

Wal Pro (Mark I)

BASSES

Zemaitis GZB-2500

Zon Legacy

MODEL YEAR	FEATURES	EXC. COND. LOW	HIGH

Yamaha

1946-present. Budget, intermediate, professional and premium grade, production, electric basses. They also build guitars. Yamaha began producing solidbody instruments in '66.

Electric Bass

1960-present. Various models.

1960-2019		$100	$1,300

Zemaitis

1960-1999, 2004-present. Tony Zemaitis began selling his guitars in '60 and he retired in '99. He emphasized simple lightweight construction and his instruments are known for hand engraved metal fronts. Each hand-built custom guitar or bass was a unique instrument. Approximately 10 custom guitars were built each year. In '04, Japan's Kanda Shokai, with the endorsement of Tony Zemaitis, Jr., started building the guitars again.

Zen-On

1946-ca.1968. Japanese-made. By '67 using the Morales brandname. Not heavily imported into the U.S., if at all (see Morales).

Electric Solidbody Bass

1950s	Various models	$100	$300

Zim-Gar

1960s. Japanese guitars and basses imported by Gar-Zim Musical Instrument Corporation of Brooklyn, New York.

Electric Solidbody Bass

1960s	Various models	$100	$300

MODEL YEAR	FEATURES	EXC. COND. LOW	HIGH

Zon

1981-present. Luthier Joe Zon builds his professional and premium grade, production/custom, solidbody basses in Redwood City, California. Zon started the brand in Buffalo, New York and relocated to Redwood City in '87. He has also built guitars.

Legacy Elite Bass

1989-present. 34" scale carbon-fiber neck, Bartolini pickups, ZP-2 active electronics.

1989-2019	V, 5-string	$1,300	$1,700
1989-2019	VI, 6-string	$1,350	$1,750

Scepter Bass

1984-1993. Offset body shape, 24 frets, 1 pickup, tremolo.

1984-1993		$1,150	$1,500

Sonus Custom Bass

1990s-present. Offset swamp ash body, 2 pickups.

1990s-2019		$1,800	$2,350

Zorko

Late-1950s-early-1962. Original maker of the Ampeg Baby Bass (see that listing), sold to Ampeg in 1962, Zorko logo on scroll.

Baby Bass

1950s-1962		$1,750	$2,250

AMPS

3 Monkeys Amps
Nashville Howler

65amps Lil' Whiskey

1980 Acoustic 165 JBL
M1 Series 1x12 Combo

3 Monkeys Amps
2007-present. Intermediate and professional grade, production/custom, amps and cabinets built by Greg Howard in Raleigh, North Carolina.

3rd Power
Mid-2009-present. Professional grade, production/custom, guitar amps built in Franklin, Tennessee by Jamie Scott.

65amps
2004-present. Founded by Peter Stroud and Dan Boul, 65amps builds tube guitar head and combo amps and speaker cabs in Valley Village, California.

Ace Tone
Late-1960-1970s. Made by Sakata Shokai Limited of Osaka, Japan, early importer of amps and effects pedals. Later became Roland/Boss.

B-9 Amp
Late-1960s-early-1970s. Solid-state bass amp head.

		LOW	HIGH
1960s-70s		$120	$155

Mighty-5 Amp
Late-1960s-early-1970s. Tubes, 50-watt head.

1960s-70s		$95	$120

Solid A-5 Amp
Late-1960s-early-1970s. Solidstate 2x12 combo with verticle cab, reverb and tremolo, black tolex, silver grille.

1960s-70s		$140	$180

Acoustic
Ca.1965-ca.1987, 2001-2005, 2008-present. The Acoustic Control Corp., of Los Angeles, California, was mostly known for solidstate amplifiers. Heads and cabinets were sold separately with their own model numbers, but were also combined (amp sets) and marketed under a different model number (for example, the 153 amp set was the 150b head with a 2x15" cabinet). The brand was revived by Samick in '01 for a line of amps. In '08 brand back again on line of amps sold through Guitar Center and Musician's Friend.

114 Amp
Ca.1977-mid-1980s. Solidstate, 50 watts, 2x10", reverb, master volume.

1977-1984		$200	$250

115 Amp
1977-1978. Solidstate, 1x12", 50 watts, reverb, master volume.

1977-1978		$200	$250

116 Bass Amp
1978-mid-1980s. Solidstate, 75 watts, 1x15", power boost switch.

1978-1984		$200	$250

120 Amp Head
1977-mid-1980s. Solidstate head, 125 watts.

1977-1984		$150	$200

123 Amp
1977-1984. 1x12" combo.

1977-1984		$150	$200

124 Amp
1977-mid-1980s. Solidstate, 4x10", 5-band EQ, 100 watts, master volume.

1977-1984		$225	$275

125 Amp
1977-mid-1980s. Solidstate, 2x12", 5-band EQ, 100 watts, master volume.

1977-1984		$225	$275

126 Bass Amp
1977-mid-1980s. Solidstate, 100 watts, 1x15", 5-band EQ.

1977-1984		$225	$275

134 Amp
1972-1976. Solidstate, 100-125 watts, 4x10" combo.

1972-1976		$225	$275

135 Amp
1972-1976. Solidstate, 125 watts, 2x12" combo, reverb, tremolo.

1972-1976		$225	$275

136 Amp
1972-1976. Solidstate, 125 watts, 1x15" combo.

1972-1976		$225	$275

140 Bass Amp Head
1972-1976. Solidstate, 125 watts, 2 channels.

1972-1976		$150	$200

150 Amp Head
1960s-1976. Popular selling model, generally many available in the used market. Solidstate, 110 watts until '72, 125 watts after.

1968-1976		$175	$225

150b Bass Amp Head
1960s-1971. Bass amp version of 150 head.

1968-1971		$150	$200

153 Bass Amp Set
1960s-1971. 150b head (bass version of 150) with 2x15" 466 cabinet, 110 watts.

1968-1971		$350	$450

165 Amp
1979-mid-1980s. All tube combo, switchable to 60 or 100 watts, brown tolex.

1979-1984		$275	$350

220 Bass Amp Head
1977-1980s. Solidstate, 5-band EQ, either 125 or 160 watts, later models 170 or 200 watts, black tolex.

1977-1984		$200	$250

230 Amp Head
1977-1980s. Solidstate head, 125/160 watts, 5-band EQ.

1977-1984		$200	$250

260 Amp Head
1960s-1971. Solidstate, 275 watt, stereo/mono.

1968-1971		$325	$400

270 Amp Head
1970s. 400 watts.

1970s		$325	$400

320 Bass Amp Head
1977-1980s. Solidstate, 5-band EQ, 160/300 watts, 2 switchable channels, black tolex.

1977-1984		$325	$400

360 Bass Amp Head
1960s-1971. One of Acoustic's most popular models, 200 watts. By '72, the 360 is listed as a "preamp only."

1968-1971		$550	$700

The *Vintage Guitar Price Guide* shows low to high values for items in all-original excellent condition, and, where applicable, with original case or cover.

MODEL YEAR FEATURES	EXC. COND. LOW	HIGH

370 Bass Amp Head
1972-1977. Solidstate bass head, 365 watts early on, 275 later, Jaco Pastorius associated.

| 1972-1977   275 or 365 watt | $550 | $700 |

402 Cabinet
1977-1980s. 2x15" bass cab, black tolex, black grille.

| 1977-1984 | $175 | $225 |

404 Cabinet
1970s. 6x10", Jaco Pastorius associated.

| 1970s | $350 | $450 |

450 Amp Head
1974-1976. 170 watts, 5-band EQ, normal and bright inputs.

| 1974-1976 | $275 | $350 |

455 Amp Set
1974-1977. 170 watt 450 head with 4x12" cabinet, black.

| 1974-1977 | $550 | $700 |

470 Amp Head
1974-1977. 170 watt, dual channel.

| 1974-1977 | $275 | $350 |

AG15 Amp
2008-2016. Small combo, 15 watts.

| 2008-2016 | $35 | $45 |

B100 Amp (MK II)
2008-2016. Classic style bass combo, 100 watts, 1x15.

| 2008-2016 | $100 | $125 |

B200 Amp (MK II)
2009-2019. Bass combo, 200 watts, 1x15.

| 2009-2019 | $150 | $200 |

G20-110 Amp
1981-mid-1980s. Solidstate, 20 watts, 1x10". The G series was a lower-priced combo line.

| 1981-1985 | $75 | $100 |

G20-120 Amp
1981-mid-1980s. Solidstate, 20 watts, 1x12".

| 1981-1985 | $75 | $100 |

G60-112 Amp
1981-mid-1980s. Solidstate, 60 watts, 1x12".

| 1981-1985 | $100 | $125 |

G60-212 Amp
1981-mid-1980s. Solidstate, 60 watts, 2x12".

| 1981-1985 | $125 | $150 |

G60T-112 Amp
1981-1987. Tube, 60 watts, 1x12".

| 1981-1985 | $200 | $275 |

Tube 60 Amp
1986-1987. Combo, 60 watts, 1x12", spring reverb, bright switch, master volume control, effects loop.

| 1986-1987 | $200 | $275 |

ADA
1977-2002. ADA (Analog/Digital Associates) was located in Berkeley, California, and introduced its Flanger and Final Phase in '77. The company later moved to Oakland and made amplifiers, high-tech signal processors, and a reissue of its original Flanger.

Aguilar
1995-present. U.S.-made tube and solidstate amp heads, cabinets, and pre-amps from New York City, New York. They also made effect pedals.

Aiken Amplification
2000-present. Tube amps, combos, and cabinets built by Randall Aiken originally in Buford, Georgia, and since '05 in Pensacola, Florida.

Airline
Ca.1958-1968, 2004-present. Brand for Montgomery Ward, built by Danelectro, Valco and others. In '04, the brand was revived on a line of reissues from Eastwood guitars.

Tube Amp 1x6" Speaker
| 1958-1960s | $175 | $250 |

Tube Amp 1x8" Speaker
| 1958-1960s | $225 | $325 |

Tube Amp 1x10" Speaker
| 1958-1960s | $325 | $475 |

Tube Amp 1x12" Speaker
| 1958-1960s | $475 | $650 |

Tube Amp Higher-End
| 1958-1960s | $550 | $725 |

Tube Amp Highest-End
| 1958-1960s | $650 | $950 |

Alamo
1947-1982. Founded by Charles Eilenberg, Milton Fink, and Southern Music, San Antonio, Texas, and distributed by Bruno and Sons. Alamo started producing amps in '49 and the amps were all-tube until '73; solidstate preamp and tube output from '73 to ca. '80; all solidstate for ca. '80 to '82.

Bass Solidstate Preamp-Tube Output Amp
1973-ca.1979. Solidstate preamp section with tube output section, 35 or 40 watts, 15" speakers, combo or piggyback. Models include the Paragon Bass, Paragon Bass Piggyback, Paragon Country Western Bass, Paragon Super Bass, and the Fury Bass.

| 1973-1979 | $125 | $175 |

Bass Tube Amp
1960-1972. Leatherette covered, all tube, 20 to 35 watts, 15" speakers, combo or piggyback, some with Lansing speaker option. Models include the Paragon Special, Paragon Bass, Piggyback Band, Piggyback Bass, Fury Bass, and Paragon Bass (piggyback).

| 1960-1972 | $325 | $450 |

Birch "A" Combo Amp
1949-1962. Birch wood cabinets with A-shaped grill cutout, 2 to 5 tubes. Models include the Embassy Amp 3, Jet Amp 4, Challenger Amp 2, Amp 5, and the Montclair.

| 1949-1962 | $275 | $375 |

Mid-Power Solidstate Preamp-Tube Output Amp
1973-ca.1979. Solidstate preamp section with tube output section, 25 watts, 12" speaker, with reverb and tremolo. Models include the Montclair.

| 1973-1979 | $125 | $175 |

Acoustic Model 135

1964 Airline Tremolo Reverb
Tom Pfeifer

1974 Alamo Montclair Reverb 2565
Tom Pfeifer

AMPS

1960s Alamo Embassy
Imaged by Heritage Auctions, HA.com

Alessandro 1/2AZZ

Allen Hot Blond

MODEL YEAR	FEATURES	EXC. COND. LOW	HIGH

Mid-Power Tube Amp
1960-1970. Leatherette covered, all tube, 15 to 30 watts, 12" or 15" speakers, some with tremolo and reverb, some with Lansing speaker option. Models include Montclair, Paragon, Paragon Band, Titan, and Futura.

1960-1970		$350	$500

Small Solidstate Preamp-Tube Output Amp
1973-ca.1979. Solidstate preamp section with tube output section, 3 to 12 watts, 5" to 12" speaker, some with reverb. Models include the Challenger, Capri, Special, Embassy, Dart, and Jet.

1973-1979		$125	$175

Small Tube Amp
1960-1972. Leatherette covered, all tube, 3 to 10 watts, 6" to 10" speakers, some with tremolo. Models include the Jet, Embassy, Challenger, Capri, Fiesta, Dart, and Special.

1960-1972		$225	$300

Solidstate Amp
Ca.1980-1982. All solidstate.

1980-1982		$30	$40

Twin Speaker Combo (Tube/Hybrid) Amp
1973-ca.1979. Solidstate preamp section with tube output section, 20 or 70 watts, 10", 12" and 15" speaker configurations, some with reverb and tremolo. Models include the 70-watt Paragon Super Reverb Piggybacks, the 45-watt Futura 2x12, and the 20-watt Twin-Ten.

1973-1979		$225	$300

Twin Speaker Tube Amp
1962-1972. Leatherette covered, all tube, up to 45 watts, 8", 10", 12" or 15" speaker configurations, some with tremolo and reverb, some with Lansing speaker option. Models include the Electra Twin Ten, Century Twin Ten, Futuramic Twin Eight, Galaxie Twin Twelve, Galaxie Twin Twelve Piggyback, Piggyback Super Band, Alamo Pro Reverb Piggyback, Futura, Galaxie Twin Ten, Twin-Ten, and Band Piggyback.

1962-1972		$400	$550

Alden
Small budget grade solidstate guitar and bass amps from Muse, Inc. of China.

Aletsis
1992-present. Alesis has a wide range of products for the music industry, including digital modeling guitar amps. They also offer guitar effects.

Alessandro
1998-present. Tube amps built by George Alessandro in Huntingdon Valley, Pennsylvania. Founded in '94 as the Hound Dog Corporation, in '98 the company name was changed to Alessandro. The Redbone ('94) and the Bloodhound ('96) were the only models bearing the Hound Dog mark. Serial numbers are consecutive regardless of model (the earliest 20-30 did not have serial numbers). In '98 the company converted to exotic/high-end components and the name changed to Alessandro High-End Products. In '01, he added the Working Dog brand line of amps.

Allen Amplification
1998-present. Tube combo amps, heads and cabinets built by David Allen in Walton, Kentucky. He also offers the amps in kit form and produces replacement and upgrade transformers and a tube overdrive pedal.

Allston Amplifiers
2005-present. Professional and premium grade, custom, amps and cabinets built by Rob Lohr in Allston, Massachusetts.

Aloha
Late-1940s. Electric lap steel and amp Hawaiian outfits made for the Dallas-based Aloha.

Ampeg
1949-present. Ampeg was originally primarily known for their bass amps. In the eastern U.S., Ampeg was Fender's greatest challenger in the '60s and '70s bass amplifier market. Currently offering tube and solidstate heads, combos and speaker cabinets. They have also built guitars.

Amp Covering Dates: Wood veneer 1946-1949, Smooth brown 1949-1952, Dot tweed 1952-1954, Tweed 1954-1955, Rough gray 1957-1958, Rough tan 1957-1958, Cream 1957-1958, Light blue 1958, Navy blue 1958-1962, Blue check 1962-1967, Black pebble 1967, Smooth black 1967-1980, Rough black 1967-1985.

AC-12 Amp
1970. 20 watts, 1x12", accordion amp that was a market failure and dropped after 1 year.

1970		$275	$375

AX-44 C Amp
1990-1992. AX hybrid amp with solidstate power section and 1 preamp tube, 22 watts, 2x8 combo.

1990-1992		$175	$225

B-2 Bass Amp
1994-2000. Solidstate, 200 watts, 1x15" combo or 4x8" combo, black vinyl, black grille, large A logo.

1994-2000 1x15"		$375	$500

B-2 R Bass Amp Head
1994-2005. 200 watts, rackmount, replaced by 450 watt B2RE.

1994-2005		$250	$325

B-3 Amp
1995-2001. Solidstate head, 150 watts, 1x15".

1995-2001		$375	$500

B-4 Bass Amp Head
1998-2008. Solidstate 1000-watt head, early models made in USA, then outsourced.

1998-2008		$300	$400

B-5 R Bass Amp Head
2000-2005. 500 watts, 2-channel.

2000s		$300	$400

B-12 N Portaflex Amp
1961-1965. 25 watts, 2x12", 2 6L6 power tubes.

1961-1965		$1,400	$1,850

MODEL YEAR	FEATURES	EXC. COND. LOW	HIGH

B-12 X/B-12 XT Portaflex Amp
1961-1969. Tube, 50 watts, 2x12", reverb, vibrato, 2x7027A power tubes.

1961-1969		$1,400	$1,850

B-15 N (NB, NC, NF) Portaflex Amp
1960-1970. Introduced as B-15 using 2 6L6 power tubes, B-15 N in '61, B-15 NB in '62, B-15 NC with rectifier tube in '64, B-15 NF with fixed-bias 2 6L6 power tubes and 30 watts in '67, 1x15".

1960-1965		$1,400	$1,850
1966-1970	1x15"	$1,400	$1,850
1967-1968	2x15"	$1,400	$1,850

B-15 R Portaflex Amp (Reissue)
1997-2007. Reissue of '65 Portaflex 1x15", blue check, 60/100 watts.

1997-2007		$1,100	$1,425

B-15 S Portaflex Amp
1971-1977. 60 watts, 2x7027A power tubes, 1x12".

1971-1977		$900	$1,175

B-18 N Portaflex Amp
1964-1969. Bass, 50 watts, 1x18".

1964-1969		$1,400	$1,850

B-25 Amp
1969 only. 55 watts, 2 7027A power tubes, 2x15", no reverb, guitar amp.

1969		$1,000	$1,300

B-25 B Bass Amp
1969-1980. Bass amp, 55 watts, 2 7027A power tubes, 2x15".

1969-1980		$1,000	$1,300

B-50 R Rocket Bass Amp (Reissue)
1996-2005. 50 watts, 1x12" combo, vintage-style blue check cover.

1996-2005		$250	$325

B-100 R Rocket Bass Amp (Reissue)
1996-2005. Solidstate, 100 watts, 1x15" combo bass amp, vintage-style blue check cover.

1996-2005		$250	$325

B-115 Amp
1973-1980. 120 watts, solidstate, 1x15" combo.

1973-1980		$250	$325

B-115 E Amp Cabinet
2006-2017. Bass cab, 1x15".

2006-2017	1x15	$200	$260

B-410 Bass Amp
1973-1980. Solidstate, 120 watts, 4x10", black vinyl, black grille.

1973-1980		$300	$400

BA Series Amp
1999-present. Solidstate bass combo amps, model number is speaker configuration.

1999-2019	BA-112, 50w, 1x12	$100	$130
1999-2019	BA-115, 100w, 1x15	$100	$130
2008-2016	BA-210, 300w, 2x10	$175	$225
2008-2016	BA-210, 600w, 2x10	$215	$275
2011-2019	BA-108, 25w, 1x8	$20	$30

BT-15 Amp
1966-1968. Ampeg introduced solidstate amps in '66, the same year as Fender. Solidstate, 50 watts, 1x15", generally used as a bass amp. The BT-15D has 2 1x15" cabinets. The BT-15C is a 2x15" column portaflex cabinet.

1966-1968		$325	$425

BT-18 Amp
1966-1968. Solidstate, 50 watts, 1x18", generally used as a bass amp. The BT-18D has dual 1x18" cabinets. The BT-18C is a 2x18" column portaflex cabinet.

1966-1968		$325	$425

Continental I Amp
1956-1959. Single-channel version of Duette, 30 watts, 1x15".

1956-1959		$550	$725

Dolphin Amp
1956-1960. Smallest combo offered during this era, 15 watts, 1x12", single-channel (I) and dual-channel (II) options.

1956-1959	Dolphin I	$425	$550
1956-1960	Dolphin II	$525	$675

Duette Amp
1956-1958. Dual-channel, 3 combo models offered; Zephyr (20w, 1x15"), Continental (30w, 1x15") and Duette 50 D-50 (50w, 2x12", tremolo).

1956-1958	Continental Duette	$550	$725
1956-1958	Zephyr Duette	$550	$725
1957-1958	Duette 50 D-50	$800	$1,050

ET-1 Echo Twin Amp
1961-1964. Tube, 30 watts, 1x12", stereo reverb.

1961-1964		$850	$1,100

ET-2 Super Echo Twin Amp
1962-1964. Tube, 2x12", 30 watts, stereo reverb.

1962-1964		$950	$1,250

G-12 Gemini I Amp
1964-1971. Tube, 1x12", 22 watts, reverb.

1964-1971		$600	$800

G-15 Gemini II Amp
1965-1968. Tube, 30 watts, 1x15", reverb.

1965-1968		$600	$800

G-18 Amp
1977-1980. Solidstate, 1 channel, 10 watts, 1x8", volume, treble, and bass controls.

1977-1980		$65	$85

G-20 Gemini 20
1969-1970. Tubes, 35 watts, 2x10".

1968-1969		$600	$800

G-110 Amp
1978-1980. Solidstate, 20 watts, 1x10", reverb, tremolo.

1978-1980		$105	$135

G-115 Amp
1979-1980. Solidstate, 175 watts, 1x15" JBL, reverb and tremolo, designed for steel guitar.

1979-1980		$125	$165

G-212 Amp
1973-1980. Solidstate, 120 watts, 2x12".

1973-1980		$150	$200

GS-12 Rocket 2 Amp
1965-1968. This name replaced the Reverberocket 2 (II), 15 watts, 1x12".

1965-1968		$600	$775

GS-12-R Reverberocket 2 Amp
1965-1969. Tube, 1x12", 18 watts, reverb. Called the Reverberocket II in '68 and '69, then Rocket II in '69.

1965-1969		$600	$775

1965 Ampeg B-12 X Portaflex
Tom Pfeifer

1969 Ampeg B-15 N
Imaged by Heritage Auctions, HA.com

2005 Ampeg B-50 R Rocket Bass

AMPS

AMPS

1968 Ampeg GV-15 Gemini V
Ted Wulfers

Early-1960s Ampeg J-12 Jet

1968 Ampeg SB-12 Portaflex
Tom Pfeifer

MODEL YEAR	FEATURES	EXC. COND. LOW	HIGH
GS-15-R Gemini VI Amp			
1966-1967. 30 watts, 1x15", single channel, considered to be "the accordion version" of the Gemini II.			
1966-1967		$600	$775
GT-10 Amp			
1971-1980. Solidstate, 15 watts, 1x10", basic practice amp with reverb.			
1971-1980		$115	$150
GV-15 Gemini V			
1968-1971. Unimusic-era tube amp, 30 watts, 1x15" combo, reverb and tremolo.			
1968-1971		$575	$750
GV-22 Gemini 22 Amp			
1969-1972. Tube, 30 watts, 2x12".			
1969-1972		$625	$800
J-12 A Jet Amp			
1964. Jet Amp with 7591A power tubes.			
1964		$375	$500
J-12 D Jet Amp			
1966. Jet Amp with new solidstate rectifier.			
1966		$350	$450
J-12 Jet Amp			
1958-1964, 1967-1972. 20 watts, 1x12", 6V6GT power tubes. Second addition, also known as the Jet II, was like the J-12 D Jet but with 12AX7s.			
1958	Rough tan	$525	$675
1959	Blue	$500	$650
1960-1964	Blue	$375	$500
1967-1972	Model reappears	$275	$350
J-12 R Reverbojet Amp			
1967-1970. Part of Golden Glo Series, nicknamed 'copper front', 18 watts, 1x12" combo, single channel, tremolo and reverb, printed circuit replaces point-to-point wiring.			
1967-1970		$375	$500
J-12 T Jet Amp			
1965, 2006-2008. J-12 A with revised preamp.			
1965		$375	$500
J-20 Jet Amp			
2007-2008. Tubes, 20 watts, 1x12.			
2007-2008		$350	$450
Jet II/J-12 T			
2007-2008. 15 watts, 1x12".			
2007-2008		$225	$300
Jupiter Amp			
1956-1958. Part of Accordiamp Series, similar to Dolphin except preamp voiced for accordion, 15 watts, 1x12".			
1956-1958		$400	$500
M-12 Mercury Amp			
1957-1965. 15 watts, 2 channels, Rocket 1x12".			
1957-1965		$500	$650
M-15 Big M Amp			
1959-1965. 20 watts, 2x6L6 power, 1x15".			
1959-1965		$575	$750
Model 815 Bassamp Amp			
1955. 15 watt combo, 1 channel. Ampeg Bassamp logo on control panel.			
1955		$575	$750
Model 820 Bassamp Amp			
1956-1958. 20 watt combo, 1 channel.			
1956-1958		$625	$800

MODEL YEAR	FEATURES	EXC. COND. LOW	HIGH
Model 822 Bassamp Amp			
1957-1958. 2 channel 820.			
1957-1958		$650	$825
Model 830 Bassamp Amp			
1956-1958. 30 watt combo.			
1956-1958		$700	$900
Model 835 Bassamp Amp			
1959-1961. 35 watt 1x15" combo, 2 channels.			
1959-1961		$700	$900
New Yorker Amp			
1956-1958. Part of Accordiamp Series, similar to Continental except preamp voiced for accordion, 30 watts, 1x15".			
1956-1958		$475	$625
PB Series Amp			
2002-2008. Portabass Series amps and speaker cabs.			
2002-2004	PB-122H Cab	$225	$300
2002-2008	PB-250 Head	$225	$300
Portaflex (PF) Series Amp			
2011-present. Portaflex (PF) ultra-compact amp heads offered with flip-top cabs, 350 watt or 500 watt head and 115, 210 or 410 cab options.			
2011-2019	PF350	$200	$260
2011-2019	PF500	$200	$260
R-12 Rocket Amp			
1957-1963. 12 watts, 1x12", 1 channel.			
1957-1963		$500	$650
R-12 B Rocket Amp			
1964. 12 watts, 1x12", follow-up to the R-12 Rocket.			
1964		$500	$650
R-12 R Reverberocket Amp			
1961-1963. Rocket with added on-board reverb.			
1961-1963		$600	$800
R-12 R Reverberocket Amp (Reissue)			
1996-2007. 50 watts, 2xEL34 power tubes, 1x12" (R-212R is 2x12").			
1996-2007		$375	$450
R-12 R-B Reverberocket Amp			
1964. 7591A power tubes replace R-12-R 6V6 power tubes.			
1964		$525	$700
R-12 R-T Reverberocket Amp			
1965. 7591A or 7868 power tubes, revised preamp.			
1965		$525	$700
R-15 R Superbreverb (Supereverb) Amp			
1963-1964. 1x15 combo, originally called Supereverb, but Fender had a problem with that name.			
1963-1964		$700	$900
R-50H Reverberocket Amp			
1997-2003. 50 watt head usually sold with a 4x12" bottom, blue check covering.			
1997-2003	Head and cab	$500	$650
R-212 R Reverberocket Combo 50 Amp (Reissue)			
1996-2007. 50 watts, 2x12", all tube reissue, vintage-style blue check cover, vintage-style grille.			
1996-2007		$450	$550

The *Vintage Guitar Price Guide* shows low to high values for items in all-original excellent condition, and, where applicable, with original case or cover.

MODEL YEAR	FEATURES	EXC. COND. LOW	HIGH

Rhapsody Amp
1956-1958. Part of Accordiamp Series, similar to Zephyr except preamp voiced for accordion, 20 watts, 1x15".

1956-1958		$500	$650

SB-12 Portaflex Amp
1965-1971. 22 watts, 1x12", designed for use with Ampeg's Baby Bass, black.

1965-1971		$675	$875

SBT Amp
1969-1971. 120 watts, 1x15", bass version of SST Amp.

1969-1971		$625	$750

SE-412 Cabinet
1996-1999. 4x12" speakers.

1996-1999		$275	$340

SJ-12 R/RT Super Jet Amp
1996-2007. 50 watts, tube, 1x12", SJ-12 RT has tremolo added.

1996-2007		$350	$425

SS-35 Amp
1987-1992. Solidstate, 35 watts, 1x12", black vinyl, black grille, large A logo.

1987-1992		$150	$185

SS-70 Amp
1987-1990. Solidstate, 70 watts, 1x12".

1987-1990		$175	$225

SS-70 C Amp
1987-1992. Solidstate, 70 watts, 2x10", chorus, black vinyl.

1987-1992		$200	$250

SS-140 C Amp
1987-1992. Solidstate, 2x12 combo, chorus and reverb.

1987-1992		$225	$275

SS-150 Amp Head
1987-1992. Solidstate, 150 watts.

1987-1992		$275	$335

SS-412 Cabinet
1987-1992. Matching 4x12 cab for SS series heads.

1987-1992		$275	$335

Super Comboamp/Model 833 Comboamp/Model 950C Super
1956-1960. 30 watts, 3 channels. 950C is 50 watts with 2 15" speakers (very few made).

1956-1957	Super Comboamp	$650	$825
1958	Model 833	$650	$825
1959-1960	Model 950C	$650	$825

SVT Bass Amp Head
1969-1985. 300 watt head only.

1969	Stones World-Tour Assoc	$1,625	$2,150
1970-1979		$1,325	$1,750
1980-1985		$1,175	$1,550

SVT Bass Cabinets
1969-1985. Two 8x10" cabs only.

1969		$1,150	$1,500
1970-1985		$1,050	$1,400

SVT-II Bass Amp Head
1989-1994. Rackmount, 300 watts, tube.

1989-1994		$900	$1,150

SVT-2 Pro Bass Amp Head
1993-2014. 300 watts, rackmount, tube preamp and power section, black metal.

1993-2014		$925	$1,200

SVT-III Bass Amp Head
1991-1994. Mosfet, 275/450 watts.

1991-1994		$500	$650

SVT-3 Pro Bass Amp Head
1993-present. Tube preamp and MOS-FET power section, 450 watts, rackmount, black metal.

1993-2019		$450	$575

SVT-4 Pro Bass Amp Head
1997-present. Rackmount, all tube preamp, MOS-FET power section yielding 1600 watts.

1997-2019		$575	$750

SVT-5 Pro Bass Amp Head
2002-2005. Rackmount, all tube preamp, MOS-FET power section yielding 1350 watts.

2002-2005		$575	$750

SVT-6 Pro Bass Amp Head
2005-2009. Rackmount, all tube preamp, MOS-FET power section yielding 1100 watts.

2005-2009		$375	$500

SVT-15 E Bass Cabinet
1994-2017. Compact 1x15.

1994-2017		$325	$425

SVT-100 T Bass Combo Amp
1990-1992. Solidstate, ultra-compact bass combo, 100 watts, 2x8".

1990-1992		$350	$450

SVT-200 T Amp Head
1987 only. Solidstate, 200 watts to 8 ohms or 320 watts to 4 ohms.

1987		$325	$425

SVT-350 Amp Head
1995-2005. Solidstate head, 350 watts, graphic EQ.

1995-2005		$425	$550

SVT-400 Amp Head
1987-1997. Solidstate, 2 200 watt stereo amps, rack-mountable head with advanced (in '87) technology.

1987-1997		$425	$550

SVT-410 HE Bass Cabinet
1994-present. 4x10, horn/driver.

1994-2019		$425	$550

SVT-450 H Amp Head
2007-2017. Solidstate head, 275/450 watts.

2007-2017		$425	$550

SVT-610 HLF Cabinet
2003-present. 6x10, horn/driver.

2003-2019		$425	$550

SVT-810 E Cabinet
1994-present. 8x10.

1994-2019		$425	$550

SVT-AV Anniversary Edition Amp
300 watt head.

2001		$700	$900

SVT-CL Classic Bass Amp Head
1994-present. Tube, 300 watts.

1994-2019		$850	$1,100

1996 Ampeg R-12 R Reverberocket
Denny Harmison

Ampeg SVT-4 Pro

2008 Ampeg SVT Micro 210AV Cab

AMPS

Anderson 45 RT

Andrews Spectraverb 22

Aria Pro II Revolution II

MODEL YEAR	FEATURES	EXC. COND. LOW	HIGH
V-2 Amp Cabinet	*1971-1980. 4x12" cab, black tolex.*		
1971-1980		$400	$515
V-2 Amp Head	*1971-1980. 60 watt tube head.*		
1971-1980	Head only	$450	$600
V-4 B Bass Amp Head	*1972-1980. Bass version of V-4 without reverb.*		
1972-1980	Head only	$700	$900
V-4 Cabinet	*1970s. Single 4x12" cabinet only.*		
1970-1980		$400	$515
V-7 SC Amp	*1981-1985. Tube, 100 watts, 1x12", master volume, channel switching, reverb.*		
1981-1985		$500	$650
VH-70 Amp	*1991-1992. 70 watts, 1x12" combo with channel switching.*		
1991-1992		$300	$400
VH-140 C Amp	*1992-1995. Varying Harmonics (VH) with Chorus (C), two 70-watt channel stereo, 2x12".*		
1992-1995		$375	$500
VH-150 Amp Head	*1991-1992. 150 watts, channel-switchable, reverb.*		
1991-1992		$275	$350
VL-502 Amp	*1991-1995. 50 watts, channel-switchable, all tube.*		
1991-1995		$350	$450
VL-1001 Amp Head	*1991-1993. 100 watts, non-switchable channels, all tube.*		
1991-1993		$325	$425
VL-1002 Amp Head	*1991-1995. 100 watts, channel-switchable, all tube.*		
1991-1995		$350	$450
VT-22 Amp	*1970-1980. 100 watt combo version of V-4, 2x12".*		
1970-1980		$450	$600
VT-40 Amp	*1971-1980. 60 watt combo, 4x10".*		
1971-1980		$450	$600
VT-60 Amp Head	*1989-1991. Tube head only, 6L6 power, 60 watts.*		
1989-1991		$350	$450
VT-60 Combo Amp	*1989-1991. Tube, 6L6 power, 60 watts, 1x12".*		
1989-1991		$325	$425
VT-120 Amp Head	*1989-1992. 120 watts, 6L6 tube head.*		
1989-1992		$350	$450
VT-120 Combo Amp	*1989-1992. Tube, 6L6 power, 120 watts, 1x12", also offered as head only.*		
1989-1992		$350	$450
Zephyr I Amp	*1956-1959. Single-channel, 20 watts, 1x15".*		
1956-1959		$450	$600

MODEL YEAR	FEATURES	EXC. COND. LOW	HIGH

Anderson Amplifiers

1993-present. Tube amps and combos built by Jack Anderson in Gig Harbor, Washington.

Andrews

2006-present. Professional grade, production/ custom, amps and cabinets built by Jeff Andrews in Dunwoody, Georgia.

ARACOM Amplifiers

1997-present. Jeff Aragaki builds his tube amp heads, combos, and cabinets in Morgan Hill, California.

Area 51

2003-present. Guitar amps made in Newaygo, Michigan (made in Texas until early '06), by Dan Albrecht. They also build effects.

Aria/Aria Pro II

1956-present. The Japanese instrument builder offered a range of amps from around '79 to '89.

Ariatone

1962. Another private brand made by Magnatone, sold by private music and accordion studios.

Model 810

1962. 12 watts, 1x8, tremolo, brown cover.

1962		$500	$650

Ark

Owners Matt Schellenberg and Bill Compeau build professional and premium grade, production/custom amps in Farmington Hills, Michigan (cabinet shop), with all wiring done in Windsor, Ontario. They started in 2005.

Ashdown Amplification

1999-present. Founded in England by Mark Gooday after he spent several years with Trace Elliot, Ashdown offers amps, combos, and cabinets.

Audio Guild

1960s-1974. Audio Guild was already making amps under such brands as Universal and Versatone and others when they launched their own brand in the '60s.

Grand Prix Amp

1969-1974. Tube combo 1x12, reverb and tremolo, dual channel.

1969-1974		$550	$725

Ultraflex Amp

1969-1974. All-tube, higher power combo, 2 speakers, reverb and tremolo.

1969-1974		$800	$1,025

Universal Amp

1960s-1974. Universal was a brand of Audio Guild. Tube combo amp, reverb, tremolo.

1960s-1974		$550	$725

MODEL		EXC. COND.	
YEAR	FEATURES	LOW	HIGH

Versatone Pan-O-Flex Amp

1960s-1974. Versatone was a brand of Audio Guild. Mid-power tube amp, 1x12" and 1x8" combo, high and low gain input, volume, bass, treble and pan-o-flex balance control knobs, black cover.

1960s-1974		$800	$1,025

Audiovox

Ca.1935-ca.1950. Paul Tutmarc's Audiovox Manufacturing, of Seattle, Washington, was a pioneer in electric lap steels, basses, guitars and amps.

Auralux

2000-2011. Founded by Mitchell Omori and David Salzmann, Auralux built effects and tube amps in Highland Park, Illinois.

Austin

1999-present. Budget and intermediate grade, production, guitar and bass amps imported by St. Louis Music. They also offer guitars, basses, mandolins, ukes and banjos.

Bacino

Tube combo amps, heads and cabinets built by Mike Bacino in Arlington Heights, Illinois starting in 2002.

Backline Engineering

2004-present. Gary Lee builds his tube amp heads in Camarillo, California. He also builds guitar effects.

Bad Cat Amplifier Company

1999-present. Originally located in Corona, California, and now in Santa Ana, Bad Cat offers class A combo amps, heads, cabinets and effects.

Baer Amplification

2009-present. Professional grade, production, bass amps built in Palmdale, California by Roger Baer.

Baldwin

Piano maker Baldwin offered amplifiers from 1965 to '70. The amps were solidstate with organ-like pastel-colored pushbutton switches.

Exterminator Amp

1965-1970. Solidstate, 100 watts, 2x15"/2x12"/2x7", 4' vertical combo cabinet, reverb and tremolo, Supersound switch and slide controls.

1965-1970		$450	$625

Model B1 Bass Amp

1965-1970. Solidstate, 45 watts, 1x15"/1x12", 2 channels.

1965-1970		$225	$325

Model B2 Bass Amp

1965-1970. Solidstate, 35 watts, 1x15", 2 channels.

1965-1970		$200	$300

Model C1 Custom (Professional) Amp

1965-1970. Solidstate, 45 watts, 2x12", reverb and tremolo, Supersound switch and slide controls.

1965-1970		$350	$450

Model C2 Custom Amp

1965-1970. Solidstate, 40 watts, 2x12", reverb and tremolo.

1965-1970		$350	$450

Model D1 Deluxe (Professional) Amp

1965-1970. Solidstate, 30 watts, 1x12", reverb and tremolo, Supersound switch and slide controls.

1965-1970		$350	$450

Barcus-Berry

1964-present. Pickup maker Barcus-Berry offered a line of amps from '75 to '79.

Barth

1950s-1960s. Products of Paul Barth's Barth Musical Instrument Company. Barth was also a co-founder of Rickenbacker. He also produced guitars and lap steels.

Studio Deluxe 958 Amp

1950s-1960s. Small practice combo amp.

1950s-60s		$300	$450

Basson

Speaker cabinets for guitar, bass and PA made by Victor Basson in Carlsbad, California, starting in 2001.

BC Audio

2009-present. Bruce Clement builds his production/custom, professional grade, tube amps in San Francisco, California.

Bedrock

1984-1997. Tube amp company founded by Brad Jeter and Ron Pinto in Nashua, New Hampshire. They produced 50 amps carrying the brand name Fred before changing the company name to Bedrock in '86. Around '88, Jay Abend joined the company. In '90, Jeter left and, shortly after, Pinto and Abend moved the company to Framingham, Massachusetts. The company closed in '97.

Behringer

1989-present. Founded in Germany by Uli Behringer, offering a full line of professional audio products. In '98 they added tube, solidstate, and modeling amps. They also offer effects and guitars.

Beltone

1950s-1960s. Japan's Teisco made a variety of brands for others, including the Beltone line of amps. There were also guitars sold under this name made from a variety of builders.

Benson

1967-1974. Ron Benson designed and built amps in conjunction with jazz ace Howard Roberts who needed a more versatile amp for recording sessions. Some featured built-in fuzz and plug-in equalizer modules. Originally built in California, later in Seattle. Some 2,000 amps total production.

Ashdown RM-C210T-500 EVO II Combo

Backline Engineering Zentone 7

Bad Cat Mini Cat

AMPS

Black Wing Black Hawk 15

Blackstar Artist Series

Bogner Mephisto

Big M

1966-1967, 1975-1976. The Marshall name in Germany was owned by a trumpet maker, so Jim Marshall marketed his amps and cabs there under the Big M Made In England brand name until the issue was resolved. A decade later, in a failed attempt to lower speaker cabinets prices in the U.S., Marshall's American distributor built cabs, with Marshall's permission, on Long Island, mainly for sales with Marshall solidstate lead and bass heads of the time, and labeled them Big M. They were loaded with cheaper Eminence speakers, instead of the usual Celestions.

Big M Cabinets

1975-1976. The M2412 with 4x12 for lead and the M2212F 2x12 bass cabs.

Model Year	Features	Exc. Cond. Low	Exc. Cond. High
1975-1976	2x12	$315	$410
1975-1976	4x12	$600	$800

JTM-45 Amp Head

1966-1967. Branded Big M.

Model Year	Features	Exc. Cond. Low	Exc. Cond. High
1966-1967		$5,000	$6,450

BigDog Amps

2005-2007. Tube head and combo guitar and bass amps and speaker cabinets built in Galveston, Texas, by Steve Gaines.

Bird

Ca. 1959-1965. Bird built electronic organs in the U.K. and also offered tubes amps from around '59 to '65.

Blackstar Amplification

2007-present. Intermediate and professional grade guitar amps and cabinets from Joel Richardson of Northampton, U.K. He also offers effects pedals.

Blackwing

2016-present. Professional and premium grade head and combo amps, and cabinets built in Corona, California by James Heidrich.

Blankenship Amplification

2005-present. Roy Blankenship builds his tube head and combo amps and cabinets in Northridge, California. He also built amps under the Point Blank brand.

Bluetone Amplifiers

2002-present. Founded by Alex Cooper in Worcestershire, England, Bluetone offers professional grade, production amps employing their virtual valve technology.

Bogen

1932-present. Founded in New York City by David Bogen, this company has made a wide range of electronic products for consumers and industry including a few small guitar combo tube amps such as the GA-5 and GA-20 and tube PA equipment. The company name (David Bogen, New York) and model number are on the lower back panel. The '50s Bogen tube amps are well respected as tone-generating workhorses. In '56 he sold the company and it was moved to New Jersey, and they continue to offer pro audio PA gear.

Bogner

1988-present. Tube combos, amp heads, and speaker cabinets from builder Reinhold Bogner of North Hollywood, California.

Bolt

Professional grade, production, tube amps and cabinets built in Salt Lake City, Utah starting in 2009. They also built the Morpheus brand effects.

Brand X

2004-2007. Small solidstate combo amps from Fender Musical Instruments Corporation.

Bronson

1930s-1950s. Private brand utilized by Detroit lap steel instruction George Bronson. These amps often sold with a matching lap steel and were made by other companies.

Lap Steel Amp

Model Year	Features	Exc. Cond. Low	Exc. Cond. High
1930s-50s	Melody King 1x10	$350	$475
1930s-50s	Pearloid	$200	$300
1947	Supreme 1x10, 12w	$400	$550

Bruno (Tony)

1995-present. Tube combos, amp heads, and speaker cabinets from builder Tony Bruno of Cairo, New York.

Budda

1995-present. Amps, combos, and cabinets originally built by Jeff Bober and Scott Sier in San Francisco, California. In '09, Budda was acquired by Peavey and they started building Budda products in their Meridian, Mississippi Custom Shop. They also produce effects pedals.

Bugera

2008-present. Uli Behringer builds his budget and intermediate grade, production, tube amps in China. He also offers the Behringer brand.

Burriss

2001-present. Bob Burriss builds custom and production guitar and bass tube amps, bass preamps and speaker cabinets in Lexington, Kentucky. He also builds effects.

Byers

2001-2010. Tube combo amps built by Trevor Byers, in Corona, California. His initial focus was on small early-Fender era and K & F era models.

Cage

1998-present. Production/custom, professional grade, amp heads and cabinets built in Damascus, Maryland by Pete Cage.

MODEL YEAR	FEATURES	EXC. COND. LOW	HIGH

California
2004-present. Student/budget level amps and guitar/amp packs, imported by Eleca International.

Callaham
1989-present. Custom tube amp heads built by Bill Callaham in Winchester, Virginia. He also builds solidbody electric guitars.

Campbell Sound
Intermediate and professional grade, production/custom, guitar amps built by Walt Campbell in Roseville, California, starting in 1999.

Carl Martin
1993-present. In '05, the Denmark-based guitar effects company added tube combo amps.

Carlsbro
1959-present. Guitar, bass, and keyboard combo amps, heads and cabinets from Carlsbro Electronics Limited of Nottingham, U.K. They also offer PA amps and speaker cabinets.

Carol-Ann Custom Amplifiers
2003-present. Premium grade, production/custom, tube guitar amps built by Alan Phillips in North Andover, Massachusetts.

Carr Amplifiers
1998-present. Steve Carr started producing amps in his Chapel Hill, North Carolina amp repair business in '98. The company is now located in Pittsboro, North Carolina, and makes tube combo amps, heads, and cabinets.

Artemus Amp
2010-2015. Combo 1x12", 15/30 watts.

2010-2015		$1,300	$1,750

Bloke Amp
2012-2015. 48 watts, 1x12".

2012-2015		$1,150	$1,500

Hammerhead MK 1/MK 2 Amp
2000-2004 (MK 1), 2004-2008 (MK 2). 25 watts (28 for MK 2), head or combo, 1x12", 2x10" or 2x12".

2000-2004 2x12 combo		$900	$1,200

Impala Amp
2013-present. Combo 1x12", 44 watts - max 55 watts, reverb.

2013-2019		$1,400	$1,850

Imperial Combo Amp
2000-2004. 60 watts, with 1x15", 2x12" or 4x10".

2000-2004 4x10"		$2,300	$3,000

Mercury Combo Amp
2002-2014. 1x12", tube, 8 watts, reverb, built-in attenuator.

2002-2014		$1,500	$1,950

Raleigh Amp
2008-present. Practice/studio amp, 1x10", 3 watts.

2008-2019		$950	$1,250

Rambler Amp
1999-present. Class A, tubes, 28 watts pentode/14 watts triode, with 1x12", 2x10", 2x12" or 1x15" speakers.

1999-2019	1x12"	$1,500	$1,950
1999-2019	2x12"	$1,700	$2,200

Slant 6V (Dual 6V6) Amp
1998-present. 40 watts, 2 channel, combo amp, 2x12" or 1x15", also available as a head.

1998-2019		$1,600	$2,100

Sportsman Amp
2011-present. Available in 1x12 and 1x10 combos and head, 16-19 watts.

2011-2019	1x10"	$1,300	$1,750

Viceroy Amp
2006-2018. Class A, tubes, 33 or 7 watts, 1x12" or 1x15".

2006-2018		$1,400	$1,850

Carvin
1946-present. Founded in Los Angeles by Lowell C. Kiesel who sold guitars and amps under the Kiesel name until late-'49, when the Carvin brand was introduced. They added small tube amps to their product line in '47 and today offer a variety of models. They also build guitars, basses and mandolins.

Caswell Amplification
2006-present. Programmable tube amp heads built by Tim Caswell in California.

Chicago Blues Box/Butler Custom Sound
Tube combo amps built by Dan Butler of Butler Custom Sound originally in Elmhurst, then Lombard, Illinois. He began in 2001.

Clark Amplification
1995-present. Tweed-era replica tube amplifiers from builder Mike Clark, of Cayce, South Carolina. He also makes effects.

Club Amplifiers
2005-present. Don Anderson builds intermediate to premium grade, custom, vacuum tube guitar amps and cabinets in Felton, California.

CMI
1976-1977. Amps made by Marshall for Cleartone Musical Instruments of Birmingham, U.K. Mainly PA amps, but two tube heads and one combo amp were offered.

CMI Electronics
Late-1960s-1970s. CMI branded amplifiers designed to replace the Gibson Kalamazoo-made amps that ceased production in '67 when Gibson moved the electronics lab to Chicago, Illinois.

Carlsbro 60TC
Alex Drinkall

Carr Rambler

Carvin V3MC

AMPS

CMW Amps Plexi Junior

Cruzer CR-15RG

Mid-1950s Danelectro 68
Erick Warner

MODEL YEAR	FEATURES	EXC. COND. LOW	HIGH

Sabre Reverb 1 Amp
Late-1960s-early-1970s. Keyboard amp, 1x15" and side-mounted horn, utilized mid- to late-'60s cabinets and grilles, look similar to mid-late '60s Gibson black tolex and Epiphone gray amp series, black or gray tolex and silver grille.

1960s-70s		$300	$400

CMW Amps
2002-present. Chris Winsemius builds his premium grade, production/custom, guitar amps in The Netherlands.

Colby
2012-present. Professional and premium grade, production/custom, tube amp heads, combos and cabinets built by Mitch Colby in City Island, New York. He also builds Park amps.

Comins
1992-present. Archtop luthier Bill Comins, of Willow Grove, Pennsylvania, introduced a Comins combo amp, built in collaboration with George Alessandro, in '03.

Coral
1967-1969. In '66 MCA bought Danelectro and in '67 introduced the Coral brand of guitars, basses and amps. The amp line included tube, solidstate, and hybrid models ranging from small combo amps to the Kilowatt (1000 Watts of Peak Power!), a hybrid head available with two 8x12" cabinets.

Cornell/Plexi
Amps based on the '67 Marshall plexi chassis built by Denis Cornell in the U.K. Large Plexi logo on front.

Cosmosound
Italy's Cosmosound made small amps with Leslie rotating drums in the late '60s and '70s. They also made effects pedals.

Crafter USA
1986-present. Giant Korean guitar and bass manufacturer Crafter also builds an acoustic guitar amp.

Crate
1979-present. Solidstate and tube amplifiers originally distributed by St. Louis Music. In '05 LOUD Technologies acquired SLM and the Crate brand.
CA Series Amps
1995-2019. Crate Acoustic series.

1990s		$150	$200

Solidstate Amp
1979-1990s. Various student to mid-level amps, up to 150 watts.

1979-90s		$50	$75

Vintage Club Series Amps
1994-2001. Various tube amps.

MODEL YEAR	FEATURES	EXC. COND. LOW	HIGH
1994-1997	5310/VC-5310	$225	$300
1994-1999	20	$175	$250
1994-1999	30/VC-2110	$250	$325
1994-1999	30/VC-3112	$275	$350
1994-1999	50/VC-50	$250	$325
1994-1999	60/VC-60	$250	$325
1994-2001	5212/VC-5212	$225	$300

Cruise Audio Systems
1999-2003. Founded by Mark Altekruse, Cruise offered amps, combos, and cabinets built in Cuyahoga Falls, Ohio. It appears the company was out of business by '03.

Cruzer
Solidstate guitar amps built by Korea's Crafter Guitars. They also build guitars, basses and effects under that brand.

Custom Kraft
Late-1950s-1968. A house brand of St. Louis Music Supply, instruments built by others. They also offered basses and guitars.
Import Student Amp

1960s	1x6 or 1x8	$50	$75

Valco-Made Amp

1960s	1x12 or 1x15	$350	$450

Da Vinci
Late-1950s-early-1960s. Another one of several private brands (for example, Unique, Twilighter, Titano, etc.) that Magnatone made for teaching studios and accordion companies.
D60 Custom
1965. 2x12", reverb, vibrato.

1965		$1,125	$1,450

Model 250 Amp
1958-1962. Similar to Magnatone Model 250 with about 20 watts and 1x12".

1958-1962		$925	$1,250

Model 440A/D40 Custom Amp
1964-1966. 1x12", reverb, vibrato.

1964-1966		$1,000	$1,350

Danelectro
1946-1969, 1997-present. Founded in Red Bank, New Jersey, by Nathan I. "Nate" or "Nat" Daniel. His first amps were made for Montgomery Ward in '47, and in '48 he began supplying Silvertone Amps for Sears. His own amps were distributed by Targ and Dinner as Danelectro and S.S. Maxwell brands. In '96, the Evets Corporation, of San Clemente, California, reintroduced the Danelectro brand on effects, amps, basses and guitars. In early '03, Evets discontinued the amp line, but still offers guitars, basses, and effects.
Cadet Amp
1955-1969. A longstanding model name, offered in different era cabinets and coverings but all using the standard 3-tube 1x6" format. Models 122 and 123 had 6 watts. 1x6", 3 tubes, 1 volume, 1 control, 2 inputs,

MODEL YEAR	FEATURES	EXC. COND. LOW	HIGH

16x15x6" 'picture frame' cabinet with light-colored cover, dark grille.

1955-1969 Various models	$150	$225

Challenger Amp

1950s. Compact combo amp, 5 tubes including 2x6L6, 2 channels, bass and treble control, 2 vibrato controls, golden-brown cover, tan woven cloverleaf-shaped grille.

1950s	$350	$450

DM-10 Amp

1965-1967. Combo 'large knobs' cabinet, 10 watts, 1x8", 2 control vibrato, 2 inputs, 1 volume, 1 tone, dark vinyl with light grille, DM-10 logo next to script Danelectro logo right upper front.

1965-1967	$260	$350

DM-25 Amp

1965-1967. Stow-away piggyback, 25 watts, 1x12", reverb, vibrato, 4 inputs, 9 control knobs, dark vinyl cabinet with light grille, DM-25 logo next to script Danelectro logo below control knobs.

1965-1967	$600	$775

DS-50 Amp

1965-1969. 75 watts, 3x10" stow-away piggyback cabinet, reverb and tremolo, suitable for bass accordion.

1965-1969	$700	$925

DS-100 Amp

1967-1969. 150 watts, stow-away piggyback cabinet, 6x10" Jensens, reverb, tremolo, suitable for bass accordion, 36x22x12" cabinet weighs 79 lbs.

1965-1969	$1,300	$1,725

DTR-40 Amp

1965. Solidstate combo, 40 watts, 2x10", vibrato, DTR-40 logo under control knobs.

1965	$350	$450

Model 68 Special Amp

1954-1957. 20 watts, 1x12", light tweed-fabric cover, light grille, leather handle, script Danelectro plexi-plate logo.

1954-1957	$475	$625

Model 72 Centurion Amp

1954-1957. Series D 1x12" combo, blond tweed, rounded front D cabinet.

1954-1957	$475	$625

Model 78A Amp

1954-1957. Artist Series D, 115 watts,

1954-1957	$475	$625

Model 88 Commando Amp

1954-1957. Series D, 25 watts with 4x6V6 power, suitcase-style amp with 8x8" speaker, light beige cover.

1954-1957	$800	$1,050

Model 89 Amp

1954-1957. Series D 1x15" combo, blond tweed, rounded front D cabinet.

1954-1957	$550	$725

Model 98 Twin 12 Amp

1954-ca.1957. Rounded front Series D 2x12", blond tweed-style cover, brown control panel, vibrato speed and strength.

1954-1957	$800	$1,050

Model 132 Corporal Amp

1962-1964. 2x8", 4 tubes, 3 inputs, 4 control knobs, 19x15x7" picture frame cabinet in light-colored material with dark grille.

1962-1964	$400	$550

Model 142 Viscount Amp

Late-1950s. Combo amp, lower watts, 1x12", light cover, brown grille, vibrato.

1959	$500	$650

Model 143 Viscount Amp

1962-1964. 12 watts, 1x12", 6 tubes, 2 control vibrato, 1 volume, 1 tone, 'picture frame' narrow panel cabinet, light-colored cover with dark grille.

1962-1964	$400	$550

Model 217 Twin-Fifteen Amp

1962-1964. Combo amp, 60 watts, 2x15" Jensen C15P speakers, black cover, white-silver grille, 2 channels with tremolo.

1962-1964	$700	$900

Model 274 Centurion Amp

1961-1962. 15 watts, 1x12", 6 tubes, 2 channels with separate volume, treble, bass controls, Vibravox electronic vibrato, 4 inputs, 20x20x9 weighing 25 lbs., 'picture frame' cabinet with black cover and light grille.

1961-1962	$400	$525

Model 275 Centurion Amp

1963-1964. Reverb added in '63, 15 watts, 1x12", 7 tubes, Vibravox vibrato, 2 channels with separate volume, bass, treble, picture frame cabinet with black cover and light grille.

1963-1964	$500	$675

Model 291 Explorer Amp

1961-1964. 30 watts, 1x15", 7 tubes, 2 channels each with volume, bass, and treble controls, Vibravox vibrato, square picture frame cabinet, black cover and light grille.

1961-1964	$500	$650

Model 300 Twin-Twelve Amp

1962-1964. 30 watts, 2x12", reverb, 8 tubes, 2 channels with separate volume, bass, and treble, Vibravox vibrato, picture frame cabinet with black cover and light grille.

1962-1964	$800	$1,050

Model 354 Twin-Twelve Amp

Early 1950s. Series C twin 12" combo with diagonal speaker baffle holes, brown cover with light gold grille, Twin Twelve script logo on front as well as script Danelectro logo, diagonally mounted amp chassis, leather handle.

1950s	$800	$1,050

Dean

1976-present. Acoustic, electric, and bass amps made overseas. They also offer guitars, banjos, mandolins, and basses.

Dean Markley

The string and pickup manufacturer added a line of amps in 1983. Distributed by Kaman, they now offer combo guitar and bass amps and PA systems.

1961 Danelectro Model 142 Viscount

Rivington Guitars

Early-1960s Danelectro Model 275 Centurion Series F

Erick Warner

Dean DA25C

AMPS

Demeter TGA-2.1

Divided By Thirteen RSA 23

Dr. Z Amps Z-Lux

MODEL YEAR	FEATURES	EXC. COND. LOW	HIGH

K Series Amps
1980s. All solidstate, various models include K-15 (10 watts, 1x6"), K-20/K-20X (10 to 20 watts, 1x8", master volume, overdrive switch), K-50 (25 watts, 1x10", master volume, reverb), K-75 (35 watts, 1x12", master volume, reverb), K-200B (compact 1x12 combo).

1980s	K-15, 20, 20X	$32	$40
1980s	K-200B	$110	$135
1980s	K-50	$36	$45
1980s	K-75	$56	$70

DeArmond
Pickup manufacturer DeArmond starting building tube guitar amps in 1950s. By '63, they were out of the amp business. They also made effects. Fender revived the name for a line of guitars in the late '90s.

R-5T Studio Amp
1959-1960. 1x10", low power, 1-channel, brown.

1959-1960		$2,300	$3,000

R-15 Amp
1959-1961. 1x12", 15 watts, 2 channels, no tremolo, tan.

1959-1961		$2,700	$3,500

R-15T/Model 112 Amp
1959-1961. 1x12", 15 watts, 2 channels, tremolo, tan.

1959-1961		$2,800	$3,600

Decca
Mid-1960s. Small student-level amps made in Japan by Teisco and imported by Decca Records. They also offered guitars and a bass.

Demeter
1980-present. James Demeter founded the company as Innovative Audio and renamed it Demeter Amplification in '90. Originally located in Van Nuys, in '08 they moved to Templeton, California. First products were direct boxes and by '85, amps were added. Currently they build amp heads, combos, and cabinets. They also have pro audio gear and guitar effects.

Devilcat
2012-present. Professional grade, production/custom, tube amps built in Statesboro, Georgia by Chris Mitchell.

Diaz
Cesar Diaz restored amps for many of rock's biggest names, often working with them to develop desired tones. By the early '80s he was producing his own line of professional and premium grade, high-end custom amps and effects. Diaz died in '02; his widow Maggie and longtime friend Peter McMahon resumed production in '04 under Diaz Musical Products.

Dickerson
1937-1947. Dickerson was founded by the Dickerson brothers in 1937, primarily for electric lap steels and small amps. Instruments were also private

branded for Cleveland's Oahu company, and for the Gourley brand. By '47, the company changed ownership and was renamed Magna Electronics (Magnatone). Amps were usually sold with a matching lap steel.

Oasis Amp
1940s. Blue pearloid cover, 1x10", low wattage, Dickerson silk-screen logo on grille with Hawaiian background.

1940s		$225	$300

Dime Amplification
2011-ca. 2014. Solidstate combo and head amps and cabinets from Dean Guitars, designed by Gary Sunda and Grady Champion.

Dinosaur
2004-2015. Student/budget level amps and guitar/amp packs, imported by Eleca International. They also offered effects.

Divided By Thirteen
Mid-1990s-present. Fred Taccone builds his tube amp heads and cabinets in the Los Angeles, California area. He also builds effects.

Dr. Z
1988-present. Mike Zaite started producing his Dr. Z line of amps in the basement of the Music Manor in Maple Heights, Ohio. The company is now located in its own larger facility in the same city. Dr. Z offers combo amps, heads and cabinets.

Drive
Ca. 2001-ca. 2011. Budget grade, production, import solidstate amps. They also offered guitars.

DST Engineering
2002-2014. Jeff Swanson and Bob Dettorre built their tube amp combos, heads and cabinets in Beverly, Massachusetts. They also built reverb units.

Duca Tone
The Duca Tone brand was distributed by Lo Duca Brothers, Milwaukee, Wisconsin, which also distributed EKO guitars in the U.S.

Tube Amp
1950s. 12 watts, 1x12".

1950s		$425	$575

Dumble
1963-present. Made by Howard Alexander Dumble, an early custom-order amp maker from California. Initial efforts were a few Mosrite amps for Semie Moseley. First shop was in '68 in Santa Cruz, California. Early on, Dumble also modified other brands such as Fender and those Dumble-modified amps are also valuable, based on authenticated provenance. Top dollar goes for combos or heads with the cab. A head alone would be 10-20% lower. Higher values are considered for an amp that has not been

AMPS

MODEL YEAR	FEATURES	EXC. COND. LOW	HIGH

modified in any way, unless the mod is certified as being done by Dumble. The used/vintage Dumble market is a sophisticated luxury-market for those musicians and collectors that are wealthy enough to afford these amps. Each amplifier's value should be considered on a case-by-case basis. Dealers have reported that some Dumbles can sell for $90,000 to $100,000 or more.

Dynamic Amps
2008-present. David Carambula builds production/custom, professional grade, combo amps, heads and cabinets in Kalamazoo, Michigan.

Dynamo
2010-present. Professional and premium grade, production/custom, amps and cabinets built by Ervin Williams in Lake Dallas, Texas.

Earth Sound Research
1970s. Earth Sound was a product of ISC Audio of Farmingdale, New York, and offered a range of amps, cabinets and PA gear starting in the '70s. They also made Plush amps.

2000 G Half-Stack Amp
1970s. 100 watts plus cab.

1970s		$375	$500

Model G-1000 Amp Head

1970s	Reverb	$190	$250

Original 2000 Model 340 Amp
1970s. Black Tolex, 400-watt head and matching 2x15" cab.

1970s		$375	$475

Producer Model 440 Amp
1970s. 700-watt head and matching 2x15" cab.

1970s		$375	$475

Revival Amp
1970s. 2x12" tweed twin copy, with similar back mounted control panel, tweed covering, but with solid-state preamp section and 4x6L6 power.

1970		$350	$470

Super Bass/B-2000 Amp
1970s. Tuck & roll black cover, 2 channels - super and normal, volume, bass, mid range, and treble tone controls, no reverb or tremolo.

1970s	Cabinet	$190	$250
1970s	Head only	$190	$250

Traveler Amp
1970s. Vertical cab solidstate combo amp, 50 watts, 2x12 offset, black tolex.

1977		$275	$350

EBS
1988-present. The EBS Sweden AB company builds professional grade, production bass amps and cabinets in Stockholm, Sweden. They also build effects.

EchoSonic
1950s. Tube combo amps with built-in tape echo built by Ray Butts in Cairo, Illinois, with the first

in '53. Used by greats such as Chet Atkins, Scotty Moore and Carl Perkins, probably less than 70 were made. Butts also developed the hum bucking Filter'Tron pickup for Gretsch.

Eden
1976-present. Founded by David Nordschow in Minnesota as a custom builder, Eden now offers a full line of amps, combos, and cabinets for the bassist, built in Mundelein, Illinois. In '02, the brand became a division of U.S. Music Corp (Washburn, Randall). They also produce the Nemesis brand of amps.

Egnater
1980-present. Production/custom, intermediate and professional grade, tube amps, combos, preamps and cabinets built in Berkley, Michigan by Bruce Egnater. He also imports some models.

Rebel Amp
2008-present. 20-watt head, 1x12" cabinet.

2008-2019		$390	$500

Renegade Amp Head
2009-present. 65 watts, 2 channel head.

2009-2019		$390	$500

Tourmaster Series Amp
2009-present. 100-watt, all-tube amp and combo.

2009-2019	Various models	$390	$800

Tweaker Amp
2013-present. 15 to 88-watt, tube heads and cabinets.

2013-2019	1x12 combo	$290	$375
2013-2019	40 watt head/1x12 cab	$390	$500

EKO
1959-1985, 2000-present. In '67 EKO added amps to their product line, offering three piggyback and four combo amps, all with dark covering, dark grille, and the EKO logo. The amp line may have lasted into the early '70s. Since about 2000, EKO Asian-made, solidstate guitar and bass amps are again available. They also make basses and guitars.

El Grande
1951-1953. Tube combo amps built by Chicago's Valco Manufacturing Co., most likely for a retailer, and sold together with lap steels.

Valco Spectator
1952. Same as Supro Spectator, 1x8, 5 watts, volume and tone, red and white two-tone.

1952		$290	$375

Eleca
2004-present. Student level imported combo amps, Eleca logo on bottom of grille. They also offer guitars, effects and mandolins.

Electar
1996-2008. The Gibson owned Electar brand offered tube and solidstate amps, PA gear and wireless systems. Though branded separately, Electar amps

Ca. 1977 Overdrive Special Dumble OD-50WC
Imaged by Heritage Auctions, HA.com

AMPS

Eden ENC112

Egnater Rebel 30 MK2

Emery Sound Combo

Emery Sound Superbaby

1965 Epiphone EA-12 RVT Futura
George Healey

AMPS

were often marketed with other Epiphone products, so see them listed there. Epiphone also had amp models named Electar in the 1930s.

Electro-Harmonix
1968-1981, 1996-present. Electro-Harmonix has offered a few amps to go with its line of effects.
Freedom Brothers Amp
Introduced in 1977. Small AC/DC amp with 2x5 1/2" speakers. E-H has reissued the similar Freedom amp.
1977 — $190 — $250
Mike Matthews Dirt Road Special Amp
1970s. 25 watts, 1x12" Celestion, built-in Small Stone phase shifter. A 40 watt version was released in 2019.
1977 — $190 — $250

Electromuse
1940s-1950s. Tube amps made by others, like Valco, and usually sold as a package with a lap steel. They also offered guitars.
Amps
Late-1940s. Vertical cabinet with metal handle, Electromuse stencil logo on front of cab.
1948-1949 — Lower power — $175 — $225

Electrosonic Amplifiers
2002-2009. Intermediate and professional grade, production/custom, tube amps built by Josh Corn in Boonville, Indiana. He also builds effects.

Elk
Late-1960s. Japanese-made by Elk Gakki Co., Ltd. Many were copies of American designs. They also offered guitars and effects.
Custom EL 150L Amp
Late-1960s. Piggyback set, all-tube with head styled after very early Marshall and cab styled after large vertical Fender cab.
1968 — $300 — $375
Guitar Man EB 105 (Super Reverb) Amp
Late-1960s. All-tube, reverb, copy of blackface Super Reverb.
1968 — $250 — $325
Twin Amp 60/Twin Amp 50 EB202 Amps
Late-1960s. All-tube, reverb, copy of blackface Dual Showman set (head plus horizontal cab).
1968 — $300 — $375
Viking 100 VK 100 Amp
Late-1960s. Piggyback set, head styled after very early Marshall and cab styled after very large vertical Fender cab.
1968 — $300 — $375

Elmwood Amps
1998-present. Jan Alm builds his production/custom, professional and premium grade, guitar tube amps and cabinets in Tanumshede, Sweden.

Elpico
1960s. Made in Europe, PA tube amp heads sometimes used for guitar.

PA Power Tube Amp
1960s. Tubes, 20-watt, metal case, 3 channels, treble and bass control, 2 speaker outs on front panel, Elpico logo on front, small Mexican characterization logo on front.
1960s — $300 — $400

Emery Sound
1997-present. Founded by Curt Emery in El Cerrito, California, Emery Sound specializes in custom-made low wattage tube amps.

Emmons
1970s-present. Owned by Lashley, Inc. of Burlington, North Carolina. Amps sold in conjunction with their steel guitars.

Epiphone
1928-present. Epiphone offered amps into the mid-'70s and reintroduced them in '91 with the EP series. Currently they offer tube and solidstate amps.
Century Amp
1939. Lap steel companion amp, 1x12" combo, lattice wood front with Electar insignia "E" logo.
1939 — $375 — $475
Cornet Amp
1939. Lap steel companion amp, square shaped wood box, Electar insignia "E" logo.
1939 — $310 — $400
E-30 B Amp
1972-1975. Solidstate model offered similarly to Gibson G-Series (not GA-Series), 30 watts, 2x10", 4 knobs.
1972-1975 — $140 — $180
E-60 Amp
1972-1975. Solidstate, 30 watts, 1x10", volume and tone knobs.
1972-1975 — $105 — $135
E-60 T Amp
1972-1975. E-60 with tremolo, volume, tone, and tremolo knobs.
1972-1975 — $105 — $135
E-70 T Amp
1971-1975. Solidstate, tremolo, 1x10", 3 knobs.
1971-1975 — $105 — $135
E-1051 Amp
Ca. 1971-1974. Tube practice amp, 1x10".
1971-1974 — $140 — $180
EA-12 RVT Futura Amp
1962-1967. 50 watts, originally 4x8" but 4x10" by at least '65, '60s gray tolex, light grille.
1962-1967 — $450 — $575
EA-14 RVT Ensign Amp
1965-1969. Gray tolex, silver-gray grille, 50 watts, 2x10", split C logo.
1965-1969 — $400 — $525
EA-15 RVT Zephyr Amp
1961-1965. 14 or 20 watts, 1x15", gray tolex, light grille, split C logo on panel, tremolo and reverb, script Epiphone logo lower right grille.
1961-1965 — $400 — $525

MODEL YEAR	FEATURES	EXC. COND. LOW	HIGH

EA-16 RVT Regent Amp
1965-1969. 25 watts, 1x12", gray vinyl, gray grille, tremolo, reverb. Called the Lancer in first year.

1965-1969		$325	$425

EA-22 RVT Mighty Mite Amp
1964-1967. 1x12", mid-level power, stereo, reverb, vibrato, old style rear mounted control panel.

1964-1967		$725	$950

EA-26 RVT Electra Amp
1965-1969. Gray tolex, reverb, tremolo, footswitch, 1x12".

1965-1969		$325	$428

EA-28 RVT Pathfinder Amp
Mid-1960s. Similar to Gibson's GA-19 RVT, medium power, 1x12, reverb and tremolo.

1964-1966		$425	$550

EA-30 Triumph Amp
1959-1961. Low-power, limited production, 1x12, light colored cover, 3 knobs.

1959-1961		$625	$800

EA-32 RVT Comet Amp
1965-1967. 1x10", tremolo, reverb.

1965-1967		$300	$400

EA-33 RVT Galaxie Amp
1963-1964. Gray tolex, gray grille, 1x10".

1963-1964		$325	$425

EA-35 Devon Amp
1961-1963. 1x10" until '62, 1x12" with tremolo in '63.

1961-1963		$325	$425

EA-35 T Devon Amp
1963. Tremolo, 6 knobs.

1963		$325	$425

EA-50 Pacemaker Amp
1961-1969. 1x8" until '62, 1x10" after. EA-50T with tremolo added in '63. Non-tremolo version dropped around '67.

1961-1965	1x8"	$300	$400
1966-1969	1x10"	$325	$425

EA-300 RVT Embassy Amp
1965-1969. 90 watts, 2x12", gray vinyl, gray grille, tremolo, reverb.

1965-1969		$450	$600

EA-500T Panorama Amp
1963-1967. 65 watts, head and large cabinet, tremolo, 1x15" and 1x10" until '64, 1x15" and 2x10" after.

1964-1967		$385	$500

EA-600 RVT Maxima Amp
1966-1969. Solidstate Epiphone version of Gibson GSS-100, gray vinyl, gray grille, two 2x10" cabs and hi-fi stereo-style amp head.

1966-1969		$275	$355

Electar Amp
1935-1939. All models have large "E" insignia logo on front, first model Electar in rectangular box with 1x8" speaker, 3 models introduced in '36 (Model C, Model M, and Super AC-DC), the Special AC-DC was introduced in '37, later models were 1x12" combos. Old Electar amps are rarely found in excellent working condition and prices shown are for those rare examples.

1935	Electar	$385	$500
1936-1939	Model C	$550	$725
1936-1939	Model M	$550	$725
1936-1939	Super AC-DC	$625	$825
1937-1939	Special AC-DC	$600	$775

Electar Tube 10 Amp
1997-2004. These modern Electar amps were branded as Electar, not Epiphone, but since they were often marketed with other Epi products, they are included here. 10 watt combo, all tube, 8" speaker.

1997-2004		$100	$130

Electar Tube 30 Amp
1997-2004. 30 watt combo, all tube, 10" speaker, reverb added in 2002.

1997-2004		$100	$130

Model 100 Amp
1960s. Made in Kalamazoo, label with serial number, Model 100 logo on small 10" speaker, blue cover, 3 tubes, 3 knobs.

1960s		$320	$415

Zephyr Amp
1939-1957. Maple veneer cabinet, 30 watts with 2x6L6 power, 1x12" until '54, 1x15" after, made by Danelectro using their typical designs, Dano D-style blond covering, large split "E" logo on front, brown grille cloth, large block Zephyr logo on back panel.

1939-1953	1x12"	$600	$775
1953-1957	1x15"	$625	$800

Zephyr Dreadnaught Amp
1939. Similar to Zephyr amp but higher power and added microphone input.

1939		$600	$775

Esteban
2005-2007. Imported brand from China, student budget level compact amps.

Compact Amp

2005-2007		$20	$45

Estey
Late-1960s. In 1959, Magnatone merged with the Estey Organ Company and in late '66/early '67 they introduced models branded Estey and based on their budget Magnatone Starlite series.

Model T12 Amp
Late-1960s. Based on Magnatone Starlite model 412.

1967		$325	$425

Model T22 Amp
Late-1960s. Based on Magnatone Starlite model 422 but with larger 12" speaker.

1967		$400	$525

Model T32 Amp
Late-1960s. Based on Magnatone Starlite model 432 with reverb and vibrato.

1967		$450	$600

Model T42 Amp
Late-1960s. Based on Magnatone Starlite model 442 bass amp.

1967		$450	$600

Ca. 1961 Epiphone Zephyr Gray Amplifier
Imaged by Heritage Auctions, HA.com

1960s Epiphone EA-30 Triumph
Imaged by Heritage Auctions, HA.com

1960s Epiphone EA-50 Pacemaker
Imaged by Heritage Auctions, HA.com

EVH 5150III

Evil Robot Custom 214

Fargen Mini Plex MK III

MODEL YEAR	FEATURES	EXC. COND. LOW	HIGH

Evans Custom Amplifiers

1994-present. Professional grade, production, solidstate head and combo amps built by Scot Buffington in Burlington, North Carolina.

EVH

2007-present. Eddie Van Halen's line of professional and premium grade, production, tube amp heads and cabinets built by Fender. They also build guitars.

5150 III 50-watt Amp

2011-present. 50 watt head with 2x12 cab.

2011-2019		$850	$1,150

Evil Robot

2010-2014. Produced by David Brass and Fretted Americana, made in the U.S.A., initial product produced in limited quantities is based on the '59 Tonemaster (Magnatone) Troubadour amp. Production ceased in '14.

Excelsior

The Excelsior Company started offering accordions in 1924 and had a large factory in Italy by the late '40s. They started offering guitars and amps, uaually built by others including Valco and possibly Sano, around '62. By the early '70s they were out of the guitar business.

Americana Stereophonic High Fidelity Amp

Late 1960s. 50 watts, 1x15", 2x8", 2x3x9" ovals, 2xEL34 power, tube rectifier, large Excelsior logo and small Excelsior The House of Music logo, guitar and accordion inputs, stereo reverb and vibrato.

1968-1969		$925	$1,250

Citation C-15 Amp

1962. Made by Sano, mid power with 2x6V6 power tubes, single speaker combo amp, large Citation by Excelsior logo on front panel.

1962		$600	$800

Fargen

1999-present. Benjamin Fargen builds his professional and premium grade, production/custom, guitar and bass tube amps in Sacramento, California. He also builds guitar effects.

Fender

1946-present. Leo Fender developed many ground-breaking instruments, but Leo's primary passion was amplifiers, and of all his important contributions to musicians, none exceed those he made to the electric tube amplifier.

Tweed Fender amp circuits are highly valued because they defined the tones of rock and roll. Blackface models remained basically the same until mid-'67. Some silverface circuits remained the same as the blackface circuits, while others were changed in the name of reliability. Price Guide values are for all original, excellent condition amps. Small differences in an amp's condition can generate larger differences in selling prices. Non-original speakers will significantly reduce a pre-'68 amp's value. Reconed speakers will reduce the value, but a reconed speaker is preferable to a replacement speaker. Multi-speaker amps generally have matching speaker codes. Different speaker codes require explanation. Fender leather handles are often broken and replaced. A replacement handle drops the value of an amp. Grille cloths should have no tears and a single tear can drop the value of an amp. Each Tweed amp should be evaluated on a case-by-case basis, and it is not unusual for a Tweed amp to have a wide range of values. Alnico speaker replacement is more significant than ceramic speaker replacement. Fender converted to ceramic about '62. Speaker replacement is of less concern in post-'70 Fender amps.

From 1953 to '67, Fender stamped a two-letter date code on the paper tube chart glued inside the cabinet. The first letter was the year (C='53, D='54, etc.) with the second the month (A=January, etc.).

The speaker code found on the frame of an original speaker will identify the manufacturer, and the week and year that the speaker was assembled. The speaker code is typically six (sometimes seven) digits. The first three digits represent the Electronics Industries Association (E.I.A.) source code which identifies the manufacturer. For example, a speaker code 220402 indicates a Jensen speaker (220), made in '54 (4) during the second week (02) of that year. This sample speaker also has another code stamped on the frame. ST654 P15N C4964 indicates the model of the speaker, in this case it is a P15N 15" speaker. The sample speaker also had a code stamped on the speaker cone, 4965 1, which indicates the cone number. All of these codes help identify the originality of the speaker. The value ranges provided in the Guide are for amps with the original speaker and original speaker cone.

Most Fender speakers from the '50s will be Jensens (code 220). By the late-'50s other suppliers were used. The supplier codes are: Oxford (465), C.T.S. (137), Utah (328). JBL speakers were first used in the late-'50s Vibrasonic, and then in the Showman series, but JBL did not normally have a E.I.A. source code. An amp's speaker code should be reconciled with other dating info when the amp's original status is being verified.

Piggyback amps from '68-'79 utilize rather heavy, bulky cabinets, which can be difficult and expensive to ship. Therefore a standalone amp head from this period is worth significantly more than a standalone cabinet.

General Production Eras: Diagonal tweed era, Brown tolex era, Blackface era, Silverface era with raised Fender logo with underlining tail, Silverface era with raised Fender logo without underlining tail, Silverface era with raised Fender logo with small MADE IN USA designation.

Nameplate and Logo Attribution: Fender nameplate with city but without model name (tweed era), Fender nameplate without city

MODEL YEAR	FEATURES	EXC. COND. LOW	EXC. COND. HIGH

or model name (tweed era), Fender nameplate with model name noted (tweed era), Fender flat logo (brown era), Fender script raised logo (blackface era).

30 Amp
1980-1981. Tube combo amp, 30 watts, 2x10" or 1x12".

1980-1981	1x12"	$425	$550
1980-1981	2x10"	$450	$600

75 Amp
1980-1982. Tube, 75 watts, offered as a 1x15" or 1x12" combo, or as head and 4x10" or 2x12" cab.

1980-1982	1x15"	$450	$600
1980-1982	2x12"	$475	$625
1980-1982	4x10"	$525	$675

85 Amp
1988-1992. Solidstate, 85 watt 1x12" combo, black cover, silver grille.

1988-1992	$225	$295

800 Pro Bass Amp Head
2004-2008. Rack-mount, 800 watts, 5-band EQ.

2004-2008	$365	$475

Acoustasonic 15 Amp
2013-present. Student 1x6" amp, 15 watts.

2013-2019	$50	$75

Acoustasonic 30/30 DSP Amp
2000-2011. Small combo, brown tolex, wheat grille. Upgrade model includes DSP (Digital Signal Processor) effects.

2000-2005	30	$200	$260
2000-2011	30 DSP	$225	$290

Acoustasonic 100 Combo Amp
2012-2013. 100 watts, 1x8", horn.

2012-2013	$275	$375

Acoustasonic 150 Combo Amp
2012-2017. 150 (2x75 stereo) watts, 2x8", piezo horn.

2012-2017	$275	$375

Acoustasonic Junior/Junior DSP Amp
1998-2011. 2x40 watts, 2x8", Piezo horn.

1998-2011	$225	$290

Acoustasonic SFX/SFX II Amp
1998-2011. SFX technology, 32 stereo digital presents, 2x80 watts, SFX is taller combo with one 10", a sideways mounted 8", and a horn. SFX II is shorter cab with 8", sideways 6".

1998-2003	SFX, tall cab	$290	$375
2003-2011	SFX II, short cab	$300	$385

Acoustasonic Ultralight Amp
2006-2009. Small 2x125-watt 2 channel head with 2x8 w/tweeters stereo cab.

2006-2009	$475	$625

Acoustic Pro Amp
2016-2019. 200-watt digital combo, 12" & tweeter, natural blonde cab.

2016-2019	$500	$650

Acoustic SFX Amp
2016-2019. 160-watt digital combo, 8" & 6.5" & tweeter, natural blonde cab.

2016-2019	$500	$650

AmpCan Amp
1997-2008. Cylindrical can-shaped battery powered portable amp.

1997-2008	$145	$190

Automatic SE Amp
1998-2000. Solidstate 25-watt, 1x10" (12" in 2000) combo, blackface cosmetics.

1998-2000	$90	$120

Bandmaster Amp
1953-1974. Wide-panel 1x15" combo '53-'54, narrow-panel 3x10" combo '55-'60, tolex '60, brownface with 1x12" piggyback speaker cabinet '61, 2x12" '62, blackface '62-'67, silverface '68-'74.

The Fender tweed 4x10" Bassman and tweed 3x10" Bandmaster amps are highly sensitive to condition. Because there are so few that are truly excellent, the price ranges listed may be misleading. Most Bassman amps are at best very good minus (VG-) because their tweed is so damaged and stained. It is also rare to find the original speakers, and if the frames are original, they have often been reconed. 4x10" Bassman and 3x10" Bandmasters that are excellent plus plus (Exc++) may have price ranges that are much higher than the values listed. It is estimated that 90% of the vintage 4x10" Bassman are really only VG or less. Because of the extreme condition factor for these tweed amps, the prices below include amps in very good (VG) condition. Therefore the condition for these listed amps is VG to Exc. Exc+ will be more than the values listed here. As per other high-end collectible, each amp should be taken on a case by case basis.

Fender piggyback amps include a head and separate cabinet. The prices shown are for a factory-original matching set. A factory-original set is worth 25% more than the combined value of a head and cabinet that were not originally sold together when new. Heads are worth more than cabinets. The value of a separate head is 40% of the value shown here, and the value of a separate cabinet is 35% of the value shown. In summary, the math is as follows: 40% head + 35% cabinet + 25% premium = 100% value of factory-original set.

1953-1954	Tweed, 1x15"	$2,900	$3,800
1955-1958	Tweed, 3x10"	$6,600	$8,500
1959-1960	Old style cab, pink-brown tolex	$6,700	$8,700
1959-1960	Tweed, 3x10"	$6,700	$8,700
1960	Brown tolex, 3x10"	$3,400	$4,400
1960	Brown tolex, 3x10", reverse controls	$6,200	$7,900
1961	Rough white/ oxblood, 1x12"	$2,200	$2,900
1961-1962	Rough white/ oxblood, 2x12"	$1,800	$2,350
1963-1964	Smooth white/ gold, 2x12"	$1,800	$2,350
1964-1967	Black tolex, 2x12"	$1,050	$1,400
1967-1968	Black, 2x12"	$750	$1,000
1967-1969	Silverface, 2x12"	$600	$800
1970-1974	Silverface, 2x12"	$525	$675

Fender Acoustasonic 15

AMPS

1962 Fender Bandmaster
Ted Wulfers

1964 Fender Bandmaster
Tom Pfeifer

1963 Fender Bassman
Peter Guild

AMPS

1964 Fender Bassman
Michael Butler

1960 Fender Bassman
Dennis Delzer

MODEL YEAR	FEATURES	EXC. COND. LOW	HIGH
Bandmaster Reverb Amp			
1968-1980. 45 watt silverface head with 2x12" cabinet.			
1968-1972		$725	$975
1973-1980		$675	$900
Band-Master VM Amp Set			
2009-2012. Vintage Modified, 40 watts, piggyback, DSP reverb and effects.			
2009-2012		$450	$600
Bantam Bass Amp			
1969-1971. 50 watts, large unusual 1x10" Yamaha speaker.			
1969-1971	Original speaker	$525	$675
Bassbreaker 15 Amp			
2015-present. Tube, 15 watts, 1x12" combo, master volume, gray tweed standard. Also offered in FSR limited editions.			
2015-2019	Combo, gray tweed	$350	$450
2015-2019	Head only, gray tweed	$300	$400
2017	Combo, LE		
	Blonde Nubtex	$375	$475
2017	Combo, LE		
	British Green	$375	$475
Bassbreaker 45 Amp			
2015-present. Head (until '18) or 2x12" combo, 45 watts, gray tweed.			
2016-2019	Combo	$650	$850
2015-2018	Head	$575	$750
Bassman Amp			
1952-1971. Tweed TV front combo, 1x15" in '52, wide-panel '53-'54, narrow-panel and 4x10" '54-'60, tolex brownface with 1x12" in piggyback cabinet '61, 2x12" cabinet '61-'62, blackface '63-'67, silverface '67-'71, 2x15" cabinet '68-'71. Renamed the Bassman 50 in '72.			

The Fender tweed 4x10" Bassman and tweed 3x10" Bandmaster amps are highly sensitive to condition. Because there are so few that are truly excellent, the price ranges listed may be misleading. Most Bassman amps are at best very good minus (VG-) because their tweed is so damaged and stained. It is also rare to find the original speakers, and if the frames are original, they have often been reconed. 4x10" Bassmans and 3x10" Bandmasters that are excellent plus plus (Exc++) may have price ranges that are much higher than the values listed. It is estimated that 90% of the vintage 4x10" Bassman are really only VG or less. Because of the extreme condition factor for these tweed amps, the prices below include amps in very good (VG) condition. Therefore the condition for these listed amps is VG to Exc. Exc+ will be more than the values listed here. As per other high-end collectibles, each amp should be taken on a case by case basis.

Fender piggyback amps include a head and separate cabinet. The prices shown are for a factory-original matching set. A factory-original set is worth 25% more than the combined value of a head and cabinet that were not originally sold together when new. Heads are worth more than cabinets. The value of a separate head is 40% of the value shown here, and the value of a separate cabinet is 35% of the value shown. In summary, the math is as follows: 40%

MODEL YEAR	FEATURES	EXC. COND. LOW	HIGH
head + 35% cabinet + 25% premium = 100% value of factory-original set.			
1952	TV front, 1x15"	$2,150	$2,800
1953-1954	Wide panel, 1x15"	$2,000	$2,600
1955-1957	Tweed, 4x10",		
	2 inputs	$5,300	$6,900
1957-1958	Tweed, 4x10"		
	4 inputs	$6,700	$8,700
1959-1960	Old style cab,		
	pink-brown tolex	$6,800	$8,800
1959-1960	Tweed, 4x10",		
	4 inputs	$6,800	$8,800
1961	White 1x12", 6G6,		
	tube rectifier	$2,500	$3,300
1962	Late '62, white 2x12	$1,850	$2,400
1962	White 1x12",		
	6G6A, ss rectifier	$2,300	$3,000
1963-1964	Smooth white		
	2x12", 6G6A/B	$1,850	$2,400
1964	Transition, black,		
	white knobs	$1,350	$1,750
1965-1966	AA165/AB165,		
	black knobs	$1,100	$1,450
1967-1969	Silverface,		
	vertical 2x15"	$650	$850
1970-1971	Silverface, 2x15"	$550	$700
'59 Bassman Amp			
1990-2003. Tube, 45 watts, 4x10", birch ply cab, solidstate rectifier.			
1990-2003		$675	$875
'59 Bassman LTD Amp			
2004-present. Lacquered Tweed (LTD), tube, 45 watts, 4x10", solid pine cab, tube rectifier.			
2004-2019		$850	$1,100
Bassman 10 Amp			
1972-1982. 4x10" combo, silverface and 50 watts for '72-'80, blackface and 70 watts after.			
1972-1980	50w	$475	$625
1981-1982	70w	$475	$625
Bassman 20 Amp			
1982-1985. Tubes, 20 watts, 1x15".			
1982-1985		$375	$500
Bassman 25 Amp			
2000-2005. Wedge shape, 1x10", 25 watts, 3-band EQ.			
2000-2005		$75	$95
Bassman 50 Amp			
1972-1977. 50 watts, with 2x12" cab.			
1972-1977		$475	$625
Bassman 60 Amp			
1972-1976. 60 watts, 1x12".			
1972-1976		$475	$625
Bassman 60 Amp (later version)			
2000-2005. Solidstate, 60 watts, 1x12".			
2000-2005	Combo	$90	$120
Bassman 70 Amp			
1977-1979. 70 watts, 2x15" cab.			
1977-1979		$475	$625

MODEL YEAR	FEATURES	EXC. COND. LOW	HIGH

Bassman 100 Amp
1972-1977, 2000-2009. Tube, 100 watts, 4x12", name reused on solidstate combo amp.

| 1972-1977 | 4x12" | $475 | $625 |
| 2000-2009 | 1x15" combo | $195 | $255 |

Bassman 100 T Amp
2012-present. 100-watt head, master volume, '65 blackface cosmetics. Usually paired with Bassman NEO cabs.

| 2012-2019 | Head only | $825 | $1,100 |

Bassman 135 Amp
1978-1983. Tube, 135 watts, 4x10".

| 1978-1983 | | $475 | $625 |

Bassman 150 Combo Amp
2005-2009. Solidstate 1x12" combo, 150 watts.

| 2005-2009 | | $195 | $260 |

Bassman 250 Combo Amp
2006. Import from Indonesia, 250 watts, 2x10".

| 2006 | | $200 | $260 |

Bassman 300 Pro Amp Head
2002-2012. All tube, 300 watts, 6x6550, black cover, black metal grille.

| 2002-2012 | | $750 | $975 |

Bassman 400 Amp
2000-2004. Solidstate, 350 watts with 2x10" plus horn, combo, black cover, black metal grille.

| 2000-2004 | Combo | $250 | $325 |
| 2000-2004 | Head | $225 | $285 |

Bassman Bassbreaker (Custom Shop) Amp
1998-2003. Classic Bassman 4x10" configuration. Not offered by 2004 when the '59 Bassman LTD was introduced.

| 1998-2003 | 2x12" | $675 | $900 |
| 1998-2003 | 4x10" | $700 | $925 |

Bassman NEO Cabinet
2012-present. Cabinets used with Bassman 100 T head and Super Bassman head, standard '65 blackface cosmetics.

2012-2019	115	$360	$470
2012-2019	410	$450	$590
2012-2019	610	$490	$640
2012-2019	810	$575	$750

Bassman Solidstate Amp
1968-1971. Small head, piggyback cab. The whole late 1960s Solidstate series were unreliable and prone to overheating, more of a historical novelty than a musical instrument.

| 1968-1971 | | $370 | $485 |

B-Dec 30 Amp
2006-2009. Bass version of the G-Dec, 30 watts, 1x10.

| 2006-2009 | | $100 | $130 |

Blues Deluxe Amp
1993-2005. All tube, 40 watts, reverb, 1x12", tweed covering (blond tolex optional '95 only).

| 1993-2005 | Tweed | $375 | $485 |
| 1995 | Blond | $375 | $485 |

Blues Deluxe Reissue Amp
2006-present. All tube, tweed, 40 watts, reverb, 1x12".

| 2006-2019 | | $375 | $485 |

Blues DeVille Amp
1993-1996. All tube Tweed Series, 60 watts, 4x10" (optional 2x12" in '94), reverb, high-gain channel, tweed cover (blond tolex optional '95 only).

| 1993-1996 | | $475 | $625 |

Blues DeVille Reissue Amp
2006-2015. 60 watts, 4x10, tweed.

| 2006-2015 | | $475 | $625 |

Blues Junior Amp (III) (IV)/LE
1995-present. Tube, 15 watts, 1x12", spring reverb, tweed in '95-'96, '04-'05, '08-'10, black tolex with silver grille standard '96 on, blond '00-'09, brown '08, surf green '09. Woody Custom Shop (hardwood) in '02-'03. III update in '10, IV in '18. Limited Edition After the Gold Rush, Surf-Tone Green, Red Nova Two-Tone, Creamy Wine Two-Tone, Navy Blues, Silver Noir Two-Tone, and Chocolate Tweed offered in '12.

1995-2019	Black	$275	$375
2002-2003	Woody Custom Shop	$525	$675
2015-2019	Lacquer tweed	$350	$450

Bronco 40 Bass Amp
2012-2018. 40 watts, 1x10", 12 effects.

| 2012-2019 | | $135 | $175 |

Bronco Amp
1968-1974, 1993-2001. 1x 8" speaker, all tube, 5 watts until '72, 6 watts for '72-'74, ('90s issue is 15 watts), solidstate, tweed covering (blond tolex was optional for '95 only).

| 1968-1974 | Tubes | $450 | $575 |
| 1993-2001 | 15w, no reverb | $85 | $115 |

Bullet/Bullet Reverb Amp
1994-2005. Solidstate, 15 watts, 1x8", with or without reverb.

| 1994-2005 | | $30 | $65 |

BXR Series Bass Amp
1987-2000. Various models.

| 1987-2000 | | $65 | $185 |

Capricorn Amp
1970-1972. Solidstate, 105 watts, 3x12".

| 1970-1972 | | $500 | $640 |

Champ Amp
1953-1982. Renamed from the Champion 600. Tweed until '64, black tolex after, 3 watts in '53, 4 watts '54-'64, 5 watts '65-'71, 6 watts '72-'82, 1x6" until '57, 1x8" after.

1953-1954	Wide panel, 1x6"	$1,325	$1,725
1955-1956	Narrow panel, 1x6"	$1,325	$1,725
1956-1964	Narrow panel, 1x8"	$1,700	$2,300
1964	New cab, black tolex, 1x8", AA764	$675	$900
1964	Old cab, black, 1x8", last F51	$1,350	$1,800
1965-1967	New cab, black tolex, 1x8", AA764	$600	$800
1968-1972	Silverface, 1x8"	$450	$600
1973-1980	Silverface, 1x8"	$400	$525
1981-1982	Blackface	$400	$525

Champ II Amp
1982-1985. 18 watts, 1x10".

| 1982-1985 | | $420 | $545 |

Fender Blues Deville Reissue

AMPS

1995 Fender Blues Junior
Denny Harmison

1964 Fender Champ
Ken Ypparila

1948 Fender Champion 800

1962 Fender Concert
KC Cormack

1955 Fender Deluxe
Jerome Pinkham

MODEL YEAR	FEATURES	EXC. COND. LOW	HIGH

'57 Champ/'57 Custom Champ Amp
2009-2011, 2016-present. Custom Series reissue, tweed, leather handle, 5 watts, 1x8". Custom added to model name in '16.

| 2009-2019 | | $625 | $825 |

Champ 12 Amp
1986-1992. Tube, 12 watts, overdrive, reverb, 1x12".

| 1986-1992 | Black | $250 | $320 |
| 1986-1992 | Other colors | $325 | $420 |

Champ 25 SE Amp
1992-1993. Hybrid solidstate and tube combo, 25 watts, 1x12".

| 1992-1993 | | $175 | $225 |

Champion 20 Amp
2014-present. Solidstate, 20 watts, 1x8", black and silver.

| 2014-2019 | | $55 | $75 |

Champion 30/30 DSP Amp
1999-2003. Small solidstate combo, 30 watts, 1x8", reverb.

| 1999-2003 | | $65 | $85 |

Champion 40 Amp
2014-present. Solidstate, 40 watts, 1x12".

| 2014-2019 | | $90 | $120 |

Champion 100 Amp
2014-present. Solidstate, 100 watts, 2x12", 2 channels.

| 2014-2019 | | $150 | $200 |

Champion 100XL Amp
2019-present. 100 watts, 2x12", 16 on-board effects, black.

| 2019 | | $260 | $340 |

Champion 110 Amp
1993-2000. Solidstate, 25 watts, 1x10", 2 channels.

| 1993-2000 | | $90 | $115 |

Champion 300 Amp
2004-2007. 30 watt solidstate combo, Dyna-Touch Series, DSP effects.

| 2004-2007 | | $140 | $180 |

Champion 600 Amp
1949-1953. Replaced the Champion 800, 3 watts, 1x6", 2-tone tolex, TV front. Replaced by the Champ.

| 1949-1953 | | $1,100 | $1,450 |

Champion 600 Amp (later version)
2007-2012. Small 5 watt combo.

| 2007-2012 | | $125 | $165 |

Champion 800 Amp
1948. About 100 made, TV front, luggage tweed cover, 1x8, 3 tubes, becomes Champion 600 in '49.

| 1948 | | $1,175 | $1,525 |

Concert Amp
1960-1965. Introduced with 40 watts and 4x10", brown tolex until '63, blackface '63-'65. In '62 white tolex was ordered by Webbs Music (CA) instead of the standard brown tolex. A wide range is noted for the rare white tolex, and each amp should be valued on a case-by-case basis. In '60, the very first brown tolex had a pink tint but only on the first year amps.

| 1960 | Brown (pink) tolex | $2,100 | $2,700 |
| 1960 | Brown (pink), tweed grille | $2,000 | $2,600 |

MODEL YEAR	FEATURES	EXC. COND. LOW	HIGH

1961-1963	Brown tolex	$1,800	$2,400
1962	White tolex (Webb Music)	$1,900	$2,500
1963-1965	Blackface	$1,800	$2,400

Concert (Pro Tube Series) Amp
1993-1995. Tube combo, 60 watts, 1x12, blackface.

| 1993-1995 | | $525 | $675 |

Concert Reverb (Pro Tube Series) Amp
2002-2005. 4x10" combo, reverb, tremolo, overdrive.

| 2002-2005 | | $525 | $700 |

Concert 112 Amp
1982-1985. Tube, 60 watts, 1x12", smaller Concert logo (not similar to '60s style logo).

| 1982-1985 | | $600 | $800 |

Concert 210 Amp
1982-1985. Tube, 60 watts, 2x10".

| 1982-1985 | | $625 | $825 |

Concert 410 Amp
1982-1985. Tube, 60 watts, 4x10".

| 1982-1985 | | $675 | $875 |

Concert II Amp Head
1982-1987. 60 watts, 2 channels.

| 1982-1987 | | $550 | $725 |

Cyber Champ Amp
2004-2005. 65 watts, 1x12", Cyber features, 21 presets.

| 2004-2005 | | $175 | $225 |

Cyber Deluxe Amp
2002-2005. 65 watts, 1x12", Cyber features, 64 presets.

| 2002-2005 | | $190 | $250 |

Cyber-Twin (SE) Amp
2001-2011. Hybrid tube/solidstate modeling amp, 2x65 watts, head or 2x12" combo, becomes the SE in '05.

2001-2003	Head only	$275	$375
2001-2004	Combo	$325	$425
2005-2011	2nd Edition SE	$325	$425

Deco-Tone (Custom Shop) Amp
2000. Art-deco styling, 165 made, all tube, 15 watts, 1x12", round speaker baffle opening, uses 6BQ5/ES84 power tubes.

| 2000 | | $700 | $900 |

Deluxe Amp
1948-1966. Name changed from Model 26 ('46-'48). 10 watts (15 by '54 and 20 by '63), 1x12", TV front with tweed '48-'53, wide-panel '53-'55, narrow-panel '55-'60, brown tolex with brownface '61-'63, black tolex with blackface '63-'66.

1948-1952	Tweed, TV front	$2,700	$3,500
1953-1954	Wide panel	$2,700	$3,500
1955	Narrow panel, small cab	$4,100	$5,400
1956-1960	Narrow panel, large cab	$4,000	$5,300
1961-1963	Brown tolex	$2,000	$2,600
1964-1966	Black tolex	$1,800	$2,400

Deluxe Reverb Amp
1963-1981. 1x12", 20 watts, blackface '63-'67, silverface '68-'80, blackface with silver grille option introduced in mid-'80. Replaced by Deluxe Reverb II.

MODEL YEAR	FEATURES	EXC. COND. LOW	HIGH

Reissued as Deluxe Reverb '65 Reissue.

1963-1967	Blackface	$2,300	$3,000
1967-1968	Silverface	$1,700	$2,200
1969-1970	Silverface	$1,400	$1,800
1971-1980	Silverface	$1,000	$1,300
1980-1981	Blackface	$1,000	$1,300

Deluxe Reverb Solidstate Amp
1966-1969. Part of Fender's early solidstate series.

1966-1969		$400	$510

'57 Deluxe/'57 Custom Deluxe Amp
2007-2011, 2014-present. Custom Series reissue, hand-wired, 12 watts, 1x12" combo, tweed. Custom added to model name in '17. A '57 Deluxe head version was offered '14-'16 and Limited Editions in '18-'19.

2007-2011		$1,150	$1,500
2014-2016	Head only	$1,025	$1,350
2017-2019		$1,150	$1,500
2018	LE Blond	$1,200	$1,550
2019	LE Exotic Wood, 5 offered	$5,000	$6,500

'65 Deluxe Reverb Reissue Amp
1993-present. Blackface reissue, 22 watts, 1x12".

1993-2019		$625	$825

'68 Custom Deluxe Reverb Amp
2014-present. Vintage Modified silverface reissue with modified circuit, 1x12".

2014-2019		$625	$825

Deluxe Reverb II Amp
1982-1986. Updated Deluxe Reverb with 2 6V6 power tubes, all tube preamp section, black tolex, blackface, 20 watts, 1x12".

1982-1986		$775	$1,025

Deluxe 85 Amp
1988-1993. Solidstate, 65 watts, 1x12", black tolex, silver grille, Red Knob Series.

1988-1993		$225	$300

Deluxe 90 Amp
1999-2003. Solidstate, 90 watts, 1x12" combo, DSP added in '02.

1999-2002		$150	$200
2002-2003	DSP option	$175	$225

Deluxe 112 Amp
1992-1995. Solidstate, 65 watts, 1x12", black tolex with silver grille.

1992-1995		$150	$200

Deluxe 112 Plus Amp
1995-2000. 90 watts, 1x12", channel switching.

1995-2000		$175	$225

Deluxe 900 Amp
2004-2006. Solidstate, 90 watts, 1x12" combo, DSP effects.

2004-2006		$200	$275

Deluxe VM Amp
2009-2013. Vintage Modified Series, 40 watts, 1x12", black.

2009-2013		$450	$600

MD20 Mini Deluxe Amp
2007-present. One-watt, dual 2" speakers, headphone jack, 9V adapter jack.

2007-2019		$15	$20

The Edge Deluxe Amp
2016-2019. 12-watts, 1x12" combo, tube, tweed. The Edge front panel badge.

2016-2019		$1,250	$1,600

Dual Professional Amp
1994-2002. Custom Shop amp, all tube, point-to-point wiring, 100 watts, 2x12" Celestion Vintage 30s, fat switch, reverb, tremolo, white tolex, oxblood grille.

1994-2002		$1,100	$1,400

Dual Professional/Super Amp
1947. V-front, early-'47 small metal name tag "Fender/Dual Professional/Fullerton California" tacked on front of cab, 2x10 Jensen PM10-C each with transformer attached to speaker frame, tube chart on inside of cab, late-'47 renamed Super and new metal badge "Fender/Fullerton California".

1947		$4,500	$5,800

Dual Showman Amp
1962-1969. Called the Double Showman for the first year. White tolex (black available from '64), 2x15", 85 watts. Reintroduced '87-'94 as solidstate, 100 watts, optional speaker cabs.

Fender piggyback amps include a head and separate cabinet. The prices shown are for a factory-original matching set. A factory-original set is worth 25% more than the combined value of a head and cabinet that were not originally sold together when new. Heads are worth more than cabinets. The value of a separate head is 40% of the value shown here, and the value of a separate cabinet is 35% of the value shown. In summary, the math is as follows: 40% head + 35% cabinet + 25% premium = 100% value of factory-original set.

1962	Rough blond/ oxblood	$2,900	$3,700
1963	Smooth blond/ wheat	$2,400	$3,100
1964-1967	Black tolex, horizontal cab	$1,600	$2,100
1968	Blackface, large vertical cab	$850	$1,100
1968-1969	Silverface	$700	$900

Dual Showman Reverb Amp
1968-1981. Black tolex with silver grille, silverface, 100 watts, 2x15".

1968-1972		$750	$1,000
1973-1981		$700	$900

Fender '57 Amp
2007. Only 300 made, limited edition combo, hand-wired, 1x12", retro styling.

2007		$1,150	$1,500

FM Series Amp
2003-2010. Lower-priced solidstate amps, heads and combos.

2003-2006	FM-212R, 2x12	$195	$250
2003-2010	FM-100 Head/Cab	$205	$270

Frontman Series Amp
1997-present. Student combo amps, models include 10G (10 watts, 1x6"), 15/15B/15G/15R (15 watts, 1x8"), 25R (25 watts, 1x10", reverb), 212R (100 watts, 2x12", reverb).

1997-2004	15DSP w/15 FX selections	$40	$60

Fender '65 Deluxe Reverb Reissue

1967 Fender Dual Showman
Imaged by Heritage Auctions, HA.com

Fender Frontman 25R

AMPS

2004 Fender Hot Rod Deluxe Limited
Carter Vintage Guitars

1977 Fender Musicmaster Bass
Tom Pfeifer

Fender Pawn Shop Special Excelsior

MODEL YEAR	FEATURES	EXC. COND. LOW	HIGH
1997-2004	25DSP	$55	$75
1997-2006	65DSP	$115	$150
1997-2011	15/15B/15G/15R	$30	$50
1997-2011	65R	$75	$100
1997-2013	25R	$40	$60
2007-2013	212R	$150	$200

G-Dec Amp
2005-2012. Digital, amp and effects presets.

2005-2009	G-Dec (small cab)	$70	$90
2006-2009	G-Dec 30 (large cab)	$100	$130
2007-2008	G-Dec Exec, maple cab	$165	$215
2011-2012	G-Dec Jr, Champ cab	$50	$65

H.O.T. Amp
1990-1996. Solidstate, 25 watts, 1x10", gray carpet cover (black by '92), black grille.

1990-1996		$70	$95

Harvard Solidstate Amp
1980-1983. Reintroduced from tube model, black tolex with blackface, 20 watts, 1x10".

1980-1983		$120	$155

Harvard Tube Amp
1956-1961. Tweed, 10 watts, 1x10", 2 knobs volume and roll-off tone, some were issued with 1x8". Reintroduced as a solidstate model in '80.

1956-1961		$1,950	$2,550

Harvard Reverb Amp
1981-1982. Solidstate, 20 watts, 1x10", reverb, replaced by Harvard Reverb II in '83.

1981-1982		$120	$155

Harvard Reverb II Amp
1983-1985. Solidstate, black tolex with blackface, 20 watts, 1x10", reverb.

1983-1985		$120	$155

Hot Rod Blues Junior Limited Amp
2000s. Compact tube combo, rough blond tolex, dark tolex sides, wheat grille.

2000s		$300	$400

Hot Rod Deluxe/Deluxe III Amp
1996-present. Updated Blues Deluxe, tube, 40 watts, 1x12", black tolex. Various covering optional by '98, also a wood cab in 2003. III added to name in '11 with various limited edition colors.

1996-2019	Various colors	$375	$485

Hot Rod DeVille 212 Amp
1996-2011. Updated Blues DeVille, tube, 60 watts, black tolex, 2x12".

1996-2011	Various colors	$475	$625

Hot Rod DeVille 410/DeVille 410 III Amp
1996-2018. Tube, 60 watts, black tolex, 4x10". III added to name in '11.

1996-2018	Various colors	$475	$625

Hot Rod Pro Junior III Amp
2010-2018. 15 watts, 1x10", black textured vinyl covering with blackface-style black/silver grille cloth.

2010-2018		$275	$375

Hot Rod Pro Junior IV Amp
2018-present. 15 watts, 1x10", modified volume circuit, tweed with vintage-style '50s grille cloth.

2018-2019		$275	$375

J.A.M. Amp
1990-1996. Solidstate, 25 watts, 1x12", 4 preprogrammed sounds, gray carpet cover (black by '92).

1990-1996		$60	$75

Jazz King Amp
2005-2008. 140 watt solidstate 1x15" combo.

2005-2008		$450	$600

KXR Series Amp
1995-2002. Keyboard combo amps, 50 to 200 watts, solidstate, 1x12" or 15".

1995-2002	Various models	$75	$200

Libra Amp
1970-1972. Solidstate, 105 watts, 4x12" JBL speakers, black tolex.

1970-1972		$475	$625

London 185 Amp
1988-1992. Solidstate, 160 watts, black tolex.

1988-1992	Head only	$210	$275

London Reverb 112 Amp
1983-1985. Solidstate, 100 watts, black tolex, 1x12".

1983-1985		$290	$375

London Reverb 210 Amp
1983-1985. Solidstate, 100 watts, black tolex, 2x10".

1983-1985		$310	$400

London Reverb Amp Head
1983-1985. Solidstate head, 100 watts.

1983-1985		$210	$275

M-80 Series Amp
1989-1994. Solidstate, 90 watts, 1x12", also offered as head only, Bass (160w, 1x15"), Chorus (90w, 2x12") and Pro (90w, rackmount).

1989-1994	M-80	$140	$185
1990-1994	M-80 Chorus	$140	$185
1990-1994	M-80 Bass	$140	$185
1989-1993	M-80 Pro	$140	$185

Machette Amp
2012-2013. 50 watts, 1x12" tube combo, casters, inlaid white piping and gray vinyl accents on black tolex.

2012-2013		$1,700	$2,200

Model 26 Amp
1946-1947. Tube, 10 watts, 1x10", hardwood cabinet. Sometimes called Deluxe Model 26, renamed Deluxe in '48.

1946-1947		$1,750	$2,300

Montreux Amp
1983-1985. Solidstate, 100 watts, 1x12", black tolex with silver grille.

1983-1985		$290	$375

Musicmaster Bass Amp
1970-1983. Tube, 12 watts, 1x12", black tolex.

1970-1980	Silverface	$375	$500
1981-1983	Blackface	$375	$500

Mustang Series Amp
2010-present. Mustang I thru V, modeling amp effects, small combo up to a half-stack.

2010-2016	II, 40w, 1x12	$100	$130
2010-2019	I, 20w, 1x8	$50	$70
2011-2016	III, 100w, 1x12	$150	$195
2011-2016	IV, 150w, 2x12	$225	$325
2011-2016	V, 150w, 4x12	$285	$375

The *Vintage Guitar Price Guide* shows low to high values for items in all-original excellent condition, and, where applicable, with original case or cover.

MODEL YEAR	FEATURES	EXC. COND. LOW	HIGH
PA-100 Amp Head			
Early to mid-1970s. All tube head, 100 watts, 4 channels with standard guitar inputs, master volume.			
1970s		$400	$525
PA-135 Amp Head			
Later 1970s. All tube head, 135 watts, 4 channels, master volume.			
1970s		$400	$525
Pawn Shop Special Excelsior/Excelsior Pro Amp			
2012-2013. Retro late-'40s vertical combo slate-grille cab, 13-watt 1x15" combo tube amp, tremolo, brown textured vinyl covering.			
2012-2013		$225	$300
Pawn Shop Special Greta Amp			
2012. Mini tube tabletop amp, 2 watts, 1x4" vintage radio-style cab, red.			
2012		$125	$175
Pawn Shop Special Ramparte Amp			
2014. Tube amp, 9 watts, 1x12", 2-tone chocolate and copper grille cloth with wheat.			
2014		$225	$300
Pawn Shop Special Vaporizer Amp			
2014. Tube amp, 12 watts, 2x10", Rocket Red, Slate Blue or Surf Green dimpled vinyl covering with silver grille cloth.			
2014		$250	$325
Performer 650 Amp			
1993-1995. Solidstate hybrid amp with single tube, 70 watts, 1x12".			
1993-1995		$180	$230
Performer 1000 Amp			
1993-1995. Solidstate hybrid amp with a single tube, 100 watts, 1x12".			
1993-1995		$180	$230
Princeton Amp			
1948-1979. Tube, 4.5 watts (12 watts by '61), 1x8" (1x10" by '61), tweed '48-'61, brown '61-'63, black with blackface '63-'69, silverface '69-'79.			
1948-1953	Tweed, TV front	$1,350	$1,800
1953-1954	Wide panel	$1,350	$1,800
1955-1956	Narrow panel, small cab	$1,800	$2,400
1956-1961	Narrow panel, large cab	$1,800	$2,400
1961-1963	Brown, 6G2	$1,700	$2,225
1963-1964	Black, 6G2	$1,600	$2,100
1964-1966	Black, AA964, no grille logo	$1,375	$1,800
1966-1967	Black, AA964, raised grille logo	$1,200	$1,600
1968-1969	Silverface, alum grille trim	$750	$1,000
1969-1970	Silverface, no grille trim	$675	$900
1971-1979	Silverface, AB1270	$675	$900
1973-1975	Fender logo-tail	$675	$900
1975-1978	No Fender logo-tail	$675	$900
1978-1979	With boost pull-knob	$675	$900

MODEL YEAR	FEATURES	EXC. COND. LOW	HIGH
Princeton Reverb Amp			
1964-1981. Tube, black tolex, blackface until '67, silverface after until blackface again in '80.			
1964-1967	Blackface	$2,100	$2,750
1968-1972	Silverface, Fender logo-tail	$875	$1,150
1973-1979	Silverface, no Fender logo-tail	$875	$1,150
1980-1981	Blackface	$875	$1,150
Princeton Reverb II Amp			
1982-1985. Tube amp, 20 watts, 1x12", black tolex, silver grille, distortion feature.			
1982-1985		$750	$975
'65 Princeton Reverb Reissue Amp			
2009-present. Vintage Reissue series, includes various Limited Edition colors.			
2009-2019	Various colors	$550	$725
Princeton Chorus Amp			
1988-1996. Solidstate, 2x10", 2 channels at 25 watts each, black tolex. Replaced by Princeton Stereo Chorus in '96.			
1988-1996		$150	$200
Princeton 65 Amp			
1999-2003. Combo 1x2", reverb, blackface, DSP added in '02.			
1999-2001		$130	$170
Princeton 112/112 Plus Amp			
1993-1997. Solidstate, 40 watts (112) or 60 watts (112 Plus), 1x12", black tolex.			
1993-1994	40 watts	$130	$170
1995-1997	60 watts	$130	$170
Princeton 650 Amp			
2004-2006. Solidstate 65 watt 1x12" combo, DSP effects, black tolex.			
2004-2006		$130	$170
Princeton Recording Amp			
2007-2009. Based on classic '65 Princeton Reverb, 15 watts, 1x10" combo, 2 on-board effects (overdrive/compression), 4-button footswitch, blackface cosmetics.			
2007-2009		$500	$650
Pro Amp			
1946-1965. Called Professional '46-'48. 15 watts (26 by '54 and 25 by '60), 1x15", tweed TV front '48-'53, wide-panel '53-'54, narrow-panel '55-'60, brown tolex and brownface '60-'63, black and blackface '63-'65.			
1946-1953	Tweed, TV front	$2,900	$3,800
1953-1954	Wide panel	$3,100	$4,100
1955	Narrow panel (old chassis)	$3,500	$4,500
1955-1959	Narrow panel (new chassis)	$3,600	$4,600
1960	Pink/brown, tweed-era cover	$2,000	$2,600
1961-1962	Brown tolex	$1,800	$2,400
1963-1965	Black tolex	$1,800	$2,400
'57 Custom Pro Amp			
2016-2019. Hand-wired, 26 watts, 1x15", lacquered tweed.			
2016-2019		$1,300	$1,700

Fender Pawn Shop Special Vaporizer

1963 Fender Princeton
Roger Myers

1959 Fender Pro
Ted Wulfers

AMPS

1967 Fender Pro Reverb
Michael Butler

AMPS

2015 Fender Pro Junior III
Rivington Guitars

Fender Rumble 100

MODEL YEAR	FEATURES	EXC. COND. LOW	HIGH
Pro Reverb Amp			
1965-1982. Tube, black tolex, 40 watts (45 watts by '72, 70 watts by '81), 2x12", blackface '65-'69 and '81-'83, silverface '69-'81.			
1965-1967	Blackface	$1,600	$2,100
1968	Silverface	$1,100	$1,450
1969-1970		$1,050	$1,350
1971-1980	Silverface	$700	$900
1981-1982	Blackface	$700	$900
Pro Reverb Solidstate Amp			
1967-1969. Fender's first attempt at solidstate design, the attempt was unsuccessful and many of these models will overheat and are known to be unreliable. 50 watts, 2x12", upright vertical combo cabinet.			
1967-1969		$400	$515
Pro Reverb Reissue (Pro Series) Amp			
2002-2005. 50 watts, 1x12", 2 modern designed channels - clean and high gain.			
2002-2005		$650	$850
Pro 185 Amp			
1989-1991. Solidstate, 160 watts, 2x12", black tolex.			
1989-1991		$200	$275
Pro Junior Amp (III) (IV)			
1994-present. All tube, 2xEL84 tubes, 15 watts, 1x10" Alnico Blue speaker, tweed '94-'96, blond in '95, black tolex '96-'17. Lacquered Tweed '18-present. III update in '10, IV in '18.			
1995	Blond	$275	$375
1994-1995	Tweed	$375	$500
1996-2017	Black tolex	$225	$300
Pro Junior 60th Anniversary Woody Amp			
2006. Recreation of original Fender model (1946-2006), 15 watts, 1x10, lacquered wood cab.			
2006		$550	$700
Pro Junior Masterbuilt Custom Shop Amp			
Late 1990s. Transparent white-blond wood finish.			
1990s		$550	$700
Prosonic Amp			
1996-2001. Custom Shop 2x10" combo or head/4x12" cab, 60 watts, 2 channels, 3-way rectifier switch, tube reverb, black, red or green.			
1996-2001	Cab	$300	$400
1996-2001	Combo	$650	$850
1996-2001	Head	$525	$700
Quad Reverb Amp			
1971-1978. Black tolex, silverface, 4x12", tube, 100 watts. Large Fender combo amps built in the '70s are not often in excellent condition. Any grille stain or tear to the grille can mean an amp is not in excellent condition and can significantly reduce the values shown.			
1971-1978		$750	$975
R.A.D. Amp			
1990-1996. Solidstate, 20 watts, 1x8", gray carpet cover until '92, black after.			
1990-1996		$55	$75
R.A.D. Bass Amp			
1992-1994. Solidstate, 25 watts, 1x10", renamed BXR 25.			
1992-1994		$55	$75

MODEL YEAR	FEATURES	EXC. COND. LOW	HIGH
Roc-Pro 1000 Amp			
1997-2001. Hybrid tube combo or head, 100 watts, 1x12", spring reverb, 1000 logo on front panel.			
1997-2001	Combo	$175	$25
1997-2001	Half stack, head & cab	$225	$325
Rumble Bass Amp			
1994-1998. Custom Shop tube amp, 300 watts, 4x10" cabs, blond tolex, oxblood grille. Not to be confused with later budget Rumble series.			
1994-1998	Cab	$525	$700
1994-1998	Head	$975	$1,250
1994-1998	Head & 2 cabs	$2,100	$2,800
Rumble Series Amp			
2003-present. Solidstate bass amps, model number indicates watts (i.e. Rumble 15 = 15 watts), models include Rumble 15 (1x8"), 25 (1x10"), 30 (1x10"), 40 (1x10"), 60 (1x12"), 75 (1x12"), 100 (1x15" or 2x10"), 150 (1x15") and 350 (2x10"). Some models discontinued '09 then restarted in '14.			
2003-2009	Rumble 60	$115	$150
2003-2013	Rumble 150	$135	$175
2003-2013	Rumble 150 Head	$105	$135
2003-2013	Rumble 30	$95	$125
2003-2013	Rumble 350	$195	$250
2003-2013	Rumble 350 Head	$135	$175
2003-2013	Rumble 75	$120	$155
2003-2019	Rumble 100	$135	$175
2003-2019	Rumble 15	$45	$60
2003-2019	Rumble 25	$55	$75
2003-2019	Rumble 40	$105	$135
Scorpio Amp			
1970-1972. Solidstate, 56 watts, 2x12", black tolex.			
1970-1972		$475	$625
Showman 12 Amp			
1960-1966. Piggyback cabinet with 1x12", 85 watts, blond tolex (changed to black in '64), maroon grille '61-'63, gold grille '63-'64, silver grille '64-'67.			
1960-1962	Rough blond/ oxblood	$2,775	$3,600
1963-1964	Smooth blond/gold	$2,375	$3,100
1964-1966	Black	$1,550	$2,000
Showman 15 Amp			
1960-1968. Piggyback cabinet with 1x15", 85 watts, blond tolex (changed to black in '64), maroon grille '61-'63, gold grille '63-'64, silver grille '64-'67.			
1960-1962	Rough blond oxblood	$2,600	$3,400
1963-1964	Smooth blond/gold	$2,300	$3,000
1964-1967	Blackface	$1,450	$1,900
1967-1968	Silverface	$625	$825
Showman 112 Amp			
1983-1987. Solidstate, 1x12", 200 watts, 2 channels, reverb, 4-button footswitch, 5-band EQ, effects loop.			
1983-1987		$300	$400
Showman 115 Amp			
1983-1987. Solidstate, 1x15", 200 watts, 2 channels, reverb, EQ, effects loop, black tolex.			
1983-1987		$300	$400

MODEL YEAR	FEATURES	EXC. COND. LOW	HIGH

Showman 210 Amp
1983-1987. Solidstate, 2x10", 200 watts, 2 channels, reverb, EQ, effects loop, black tolex.

1983-1987		$300	$400

Showman 212 Amp
1983-1987. Solidstate, 2x12", 200 watts, 2 channels, reverb, EQ, effects loop, black tolex.

1983-1987		$300	$400

Sidekick 10 Amp
1983-1985. Small solidstate Japanese or Mexican import, 10 watts, 1x8".

1983-1985		$50	$60

Sidekick Bass 30 Amp
1983-1985. Combo, 30 watts, 1x12".

1983-1985		$60	$75

Sidekick Reverb 15 Amp
1983-1985. Small solidstate import, reverb, 15 watts.

1983-1985		$70	$85

Sidekick Reverb 20 Amp
1983-1985. Small solidstate Japanese or Mexican import, 20 watts, reverb, 1x10".

1983-1985		$75	$95

Sidekick Reverb 30 Amp
1983-1985. Small solidstate Japanese or Mexican import, 30 watts, 1x12", reverb.

1983-1985		$80	$100

Sidekick Reverb 65 Amp
1986-1988. Small solidstate Japanese or Mexican import, 65 watts, 1x12".

1986-1988		$100	$125

Sidekick 100 Bass Amp Head
1986-1993. 100 watt bass head.

1986-1993		$75	$90

Squier Champ 15 Amp
1990s-2000s. 1x8, 15 watts, solidstate.

1990s-00s		$45	$55

Squier SKX Series Amp
1990-1992. Solidstate, 15 watts, 1x8", model 15R with reverb. Model 25R is 25 watts, 1x10, reverb.

1990-1992	15, non-reverb	$30	$40
1990-1992	15R, reverb	$35	$45
1990-1992	25R, reverb	$45	$55

Squier SP10 Amp
2003-2012. 10 watt solidstate, usually sold as part of a Guitar Pack.

2003-2012		$30	$40

Stage 100/Stage 1000 Amp
1999-2006. Solidstate, 1x12", combo or head only options, 100 watts, blackface. Head available until 2004.

1999-2004	Head only	$200	$250
1999-2006	Combo	$250	$325
1999-2006	Combo stack, 2 cabs	$325	$425

Stage 1600 DSP Amp
2004-2006. Solidstate, 160 watts, 2x12" combo, 16 digital effects (DSP).

2004-2006		$300	$400

Stage Lead/Lead II Amp
1983-1985. Solidstate, 100 watts, 1x12", reverb, channel switching, black tolex. Stage Lead II has 2x12".

1983-1985	1x12"	$175	$225
1983-1985	2x12"	$175	$225

Starcaster by Fender 15G Amp
2000s. Student economy pac amp, sold with a guitar, strap and stand, Starcaster by Fender logo. Sold in Costco and other discounters.

2000s		$20	$30

Steel-King Amp
2004-2009. Designed for pedal steel, 200 watts, solidstate, 1x15".

2004-2009		$475	$625

Studio 85 Amp
1988. Studio 85 logo on upper right front of grille, solidstate, 1x12" combo, 65 watts, red knobs.

1988		$175	$225

Studio Bass Amp
1977-1980. Uses Super Twin design, tube, 200 watt combo, 5-band eq, 1x15".

1977-1980		$500	$650

Studio Lead Amp
1983-1986. Solidstate, 50 watts, 1x12", black tolex.

1983-1986		$200	$260

Super Amp
1947-1963, 1992-1997. Introduced as Dual Professional in 1946, renamed Super '47, 2x10" speakers, 20 watts (30 watts by '60 with 45 watts in '62), tweed TV front '47-'53, wide-panel '53-'54, narrow-panel '55-'60, brown tolex '60-'64. Reintroduced '92-'97 with 4x10", 60 watts, black tolex.

1947-1952	V-front	$4,500	$6,000
1953-1954	Tweed, wide panel	$3,400	$4,400
1955	Tweed, narrow panel, 6L6	$4,500	$6,000
1956-1957	Tweed, narrow panel, 5E4, 6V6	$3,800	$5,000
1957-1960	Tweed, narrow panel, 6L6	$5,700	$7,400
1960	Pink, tweed-era grille	$2,100	$2,700
1960	Pink/brown metal knobs	$2,200	$2,850
1960	Pink/brown reverse knobs	$2,200	$2,850
1960-1962	Brown, oxblood grille, 6G4	$1,900	$2,500
1962-1963	Brown, tan/wheat grille, 6G4	$1,900	$2,500

Super 60 Amp
1989-1993. Red Knob series, 1x12", 60 watts, earlier versions with red knobs, later models with black knobs, offered in optional covers such as red, white, gray or snakeskin.

1989-1993	Combo	$250	$350
1989-1993	Head	$250	$350

Super 112 Amp
1990-1993. Red Knob series, 1x12", 60 watts, earlier versions with red knobs, later models with black knobs, originally designed to replace the Super60 but the Super60 remained until '93.

1990-1993		$325	$425

Super 210 Amp
1990-1993. Red Knob series, 2x10", 60 watts, earlier versions with red knobs, later models with black knobs.

1990-1993		$325	$425

1963 Fender Showman
Imaged by Heritage Auctions, HA.com

Fender Showman head and cab
Carter Vintage Guitars

1956 Fender Super
Rivington Guitars

AMPS

Fender Super Bassman Head

1967 Fender Super Reverb

1968 Fender Super Reverb
Michael Campbell

MODEL YEAR	FEATURES	EXC. COND. LOW	HIGH

Super 410 Amp
1992-1997. 60 watts, 4x10", black tolex, silver grille, blackface control panel.
| 1992-1997 | | $525 | $700 |

Super Bassman Amp Head
2012-present. 300-watt head, 6x6550 power tubes, master volume, standard '65 blackface cosmetics.
| 2012-2019 | | $975 | $1,250 |

Super Champ Amp
1982-1986. Black tolex, 18 watts, blackface, 1x10".
| 1982-1986 | | $725 | $925 |

Super Champ Deluxe Amp
1982-1986. Solid oak cabinet, 18 watts, upgrade 10" Electro-Voice speaker, see-thru brown grille cloth.
| 1982-1986 | | $925 | $1,200 |

Super Champ XD Amp
2008-2011. Tube amp with extra preamp voicing, 1x10" combo, blackface cosmetics. Replaced by X2 version.
| 2008-2011 | | $195 | $250 |

Super Reverb Amp
1963-1982. 4x10" speakers, blackface until '67 and '80-'82, silverface '68-'80. Large Fender combo amps built in the '70s are not often in excellent condition. Any grille stain or tear to the grille can mean an amp is not in excellent condition and can significantly reduce the values shown.
1963-1964	Blackface, Fender Elec	$1,900	$2,450
1965-1967	Blackface, FMI	$1,800	$2,300
1968	Silverface, AB763	$1,100	$1,450
1969-1970	Silverface	$1,050	$1,350
1970-1972	Silverface, AA270	$900	$1,200
1972-1975	Int Master	$850	$1,100
1975-1980	MV with pull	$750	$1,000
1981-1982	Blackface	$750	$1,000

Super Reverb Solidstate Amp
1967-1970. 50 watts, 4x10".
| 1967-1970 | | $400 | $525 |

'65 Super Reverb Reissue Amp
2001-present. 45 watts, all tube, 4x10", blackface cosmetics.
| 2001-2019 | | $700 | $900 |

Super Showman XFL-1000/XFL-2000 Amp
1969-1971. Solidstate Super Showman head controlled 1 or more powered speaker cabs. The XFL-1000 was a 4x12" cab with 2 70-watt power amps, the 8x10" XFL-2000 had same power amps.
| 1969-1971 | | $450 | $590 |

Super Six Reverb Amp
1970-1979. Large combo amp based on the Twin Reverb chassis, 100 watts, 6x10", black tolex. Large Fender combo amps built in the '70s are not often in excellent condition. Any grille stain or tear to the grille can mean an amp is not in excellent condition and can significantly reduce the values shown.
| 1970-1979 | | $850 | $1,200 |

Super Twin Amp
1975-1980. 180 watts (6 6L6 power tubes), 2x12", distinctive dark grille.
| 1975-1976 | Non-reverb | $700 | $900 |
| 1976-1980 | Reverb | $750 | $950 |

Super-Sonic/60 Amp
2006-present. All tube, 60 watts, various options, 1x12" combo or 2x12" piggyback, blonde/oxblood or blackface. Straight and slant 4x12" cab added '11.
2006-2013	1x12", blonde/oxblood	$575	$775
2006-2014	1x12", blackface	$525	$700
2006-2015	2x12" piggyback, blonde	$775	$1,000

Super-Sonic 22 Combo Limited Edition "Black Gold" FSR Amp
2012. 150 made, 1x12, 2-tone gold and black vinyl with white piping, black grille.
| 2012 | | $575 | $775 |

Taurus Amp
1970-1972. Solidstate, 42 watts, 2x10" JBL, black tolex, silver grille, JBL badge.
| 1970-1972 | | $400 | $515 |

Tonemaster Amp Set
1993-2002. Custom Shop, hand-wired head with Tonemaster 2x12" or 4x12" cabinet, blond or oxblood.
| 1993-2002 | | $1,200 | $1,550 |

Tremolux Amp
1955-1966. Tube, tweed, 1x12" '55-'60, white tolex with piggyback 1x10" cabinet '61-'62, 2x10" '62-'64, black tolex '64-'66.
1955-1960	Tweed, 1x12", narrow panel	$3,300	$4,300
1961	Rough white/oxblood, 1x10"	$2,200	$2,900
1961-1962	Rough white/oxblood, 2x10"	$2,100	$2,700
1962-1963	Rough white/wheat, 2x10"	$1,800	$2,400
1963-1964	Smooth white/gold, 2x10"	$1,800	$2,400
1964-1966	Black tolex, 2x10"	$1,500	$2,000

EC Tremolux Amp
2011-2016. Eric Clapton's variation on a '57, hand-wired, 12 watts, 1x12".
| 2011-2016 | | $1,150 | $1,500 |

Twin Amp
1952-1963, 1996-2010. Tube, 2x12"; 15 watts, tweed wide-panel '52-'55; narrow-panel '55-'60; 50 watts '55-'57; 80 watts '58; brown tolex '60; white tolex '61-'63. Reintroduced in '96 with black tolex, spring reverb and output control for 100 watts or 25 watts.
1952-1954	Tweed, wide panel	$6,500	$8,500
1955-1957	Tweed, 50 watts	$9,500	$12,500
1958-1959	Tweed, 80 watts	$13,500	$18,000
1960	Brown tolex, 80 watts	$10,000	$13,000
1960-1962	Rough white/oxblood	$6,000	$8,000
1963	Smooth white/gold	$5,300	$7,000

'57 Twin-Amp/'57 Custom Twin-Amp
2004-2011, 2016-present. Custom Series reissue, tweed, 40 watts, 2x12". Custom added to model name in '16.
| 2004-2011 | | $1,200 | $1,575 |
| 2016-2019 | | $1,350 | $1,750 |

MODEL YEAR	FEATURES	EXC. COND. LOW	HIGH

Twin Reverb Amp
1963-1982. Black tolex, 85 watts (changed to 135 watts in '81), 2x12", blackface '63-'67 and '81-'82, silverface '68-'81, blackface optional in '80-'81 and standard in '82. Large Fender combo amps built in the '70s are not often in excellent condition. Any grille stain or tear to the grille can mean an amp is not in excellent condition and can significantly reduce the values shown.

1963-1967	Blackface	$2,000	$2,600
1968	Silverface, no master vol	$1,100	$1,450
1969-1970	Silverface, no master vol	$1,050	$1,350
1971-1972	Silverface, no master vol	$700	$900
1973-1975	Silverface, master vol	$700	$900
1976-1980	Silverface, push/pull	$700	$900
1980-1982	Blackface	$700	$900

Twin Reverb Solidstate Amp
1966-1969. 100 watts, 2x12", black tolex.

1966-1969		$400	$515

'65 Twin Reverb Amp
1991-present. Black tolex, 2x12", 85 watts.

1991-2019		$700	$900

'65 Twin Custom 15 Amp
2009-2017. 85 watt Twin Reverb with 1x15".

2009-2017		$725	$925

'68 Custom Twin Reverb Amp
2014-present. Vintage Modified silverface reissue, 1x12", 85 watts, modified all-tube circuitry.

2014-2019		$700	$900

Twin Reverb II Amp
1983-1985. Black tolex, 2x12", 105 watts, channel switching, effects loop, blackface panel, silver grille.

1983-1985		$775	$1,025

Twin "The Twin"/"Evil Twin" Amp
1987-1992. 100 watts, 2x12", red knobs, most black tolex, but white, red and snakeskin covers offered.

1987-1992		$600	$800

EC Twinolux Amp
2011-2016. Eric Clapton's variation on a '57, hand-wired, 40 watts, 2x12".

2011-2016		$2,100	$2,700

Two-Tone (Custom Shop) Amp
2001-2003. Limited production, modern styling, slanted grille, 15 watts, 1x10" and 1x12", 2-tone blond cab, based on modified Blues Deluxe circuit, Two Tone on name plate.

2001-2003		$825	$1,075

Ultimate Chorus DSP Amp
1995-2001. Solidstate, 2x65 watts, 2x12", 32 built-in effect variations, blackface cosmetics.

1995-2001		$205	$265

Ultra Chorus Amp
1992-1994. Solidstate, 2x65 watts, 2x12", standard control panel with chorus.

1992-1994		$195	$250

Vibrasonic Amp
1959-1963. First amp to receive the new brown tolex and JBL, 1x15", 25 watts.

1959-1963		$1,900	$2,500

Vibrasonic Custom Amp
1995-1997. Custom Shop designed for steel guitar and guitar, blackface, 1x15", 100 watts.

1995-1997		$650	$850

Vibrasonic Reverb Amp
1972-1981. Black tolex, 100 watts, 1x15", silverface.

1972-1981		$650	$850

Vibro-Champ Amp
1964-1982. Black tolex, 4 watts, (5 watts '69-'71, 6 watts '72-'80), 1x8", blackface '64-'68 and '82, silverface '69-'81.

1964-1967	Blackface, AA764	$800	$1,050
1968-1972	Silverface	$500	$650
1973-1981	Silverface	$480	$625
1982	Blackface	$480	$625

EC Vibro Champ Amp
2011-2016. Eric Clapton's variation on a '57 Champ, hand-wired, 5 watts, 1x8".

2011-2016		$675	$875

Vibro-Champ XD Amp
2008-2011. Made in China, 5 watts, 1x8.

2008-2011		$140	$180

Vibro-King Custom Amp
1993-2012. Custom Shop combo, 60 watts, 3x10", vintage reverb, tremolo, single channel, all tube, blond or black.

1993-2012		$1,325	$1,725

Vibro-King 212 Amp Cabinet
1993-2012. Custom Shop extension cab, blond tolex, 2x12" Celestion GK80.

1993-2012		$400	$525

Vibro-King Custom Limited Edition Amp
2012-2013. Limited Edition production of unique colors, Chocolate Crème Two-Tone, wheat grille (25 made) and Tequila Sunrise, 3-color sunburst on figured birdseye maple cab, oxblood grille.

2012	Chocolate Crème	$1,650	$2,150
2013	Tequila Sunrise	$2,100	$2,700

Vibrolux Amp
1956-1964. Narrow-panel, 10 watts, tweed with 1x10" '56-'61, brown tolex and brownface with 1x12" and 30 watts '61-'62, black tolex and blackface '63-'64.

1956-1961	Tweed, 1x10"	$2,700	$3,500
1961-1962	Brown tolex, 1x12"	$2,500	$3,300
1963-1964	Black tolex, 1x12"	$2,300	$3,000

Vibrolux Reverb Amp
1964-1982. Black tolex, 2x10", blackface '64-'67 and '81-'82, silverface '70-'80. Reissued in '96 with blackface and 40 watts.

1964-1967	Blackface	$2,400	$3,150
1968	Silverface	$1,625	$2,100
1969-1970	Silverface	$1,225	$1,600
1971-1980	Silverface	$925	$1,200
1981-1982	Blackface	$925	$1,200

Fender Super-Sonic

AMPS

1962 Fender Twin
Jim Sheehan

1959 Fender Vibrolux
Ted Wulfers

To get the most from this book, be sure to read "Using *The Guide*" in the introduction.

1966 Fender Vibrolux Reverb
Steve Brandt

1963 Fender Vibroverb

Fryette Aether

MODEL YEAR	FEATURES	EXC. COND. LOW	HIGH
Vibrolux Reverb Solidstate Amp			
1967-1969. Fender CBS solidstate, 35 watts, 2x10", black tolex.			
1967-1969		$400	$515
Vibrolux Custom Reverb Amp			
1995-2013. Part of Professional Series, Custom Shop designed, standard factory built, 40 watts, 2x10", tube, white knobs, blond tolex and tan grill for '95 only, black tolex, silver grille after. Does not say Custom on face plate.			
1995-2013	Various colors	$700	$900
'68 Custom Vibrolux Reverb Amp			
2014-present. Silverface-style, 35 watts, 2x10", black vinyl with silver-turquoise grille.			
2014-2019		$700	$900
Vibroverb Amp			
1963-1964. Brown tolex with 35 watts, 2x10" and brownface '63, black tolex with 1x15" and blackface late '63-'64.			
1963	Brown tolex, 2x10"	$5,500	$7,200
1963-1964	Black tolex, 1x15"	$4,000	$5,100
'63 Vibroverb Reissue Amp			
1990-1995. Reissue of 1963 Vibroverb, 40 watts, 2x10", reverb, vibrato, brown tolex.			
1990-1995		$875	$1,125
'64 Vibroverb Custom Shop Amp			
2003-2008. Reissue of 1964 Vibroverb with 1x15" blackface specs.			
2003-2008		$1,100	$1,425
Yale Reverb Amp			
1983-1985. Solidstate, black tolex, 50 watts, 1x12", silverface.			
1983-1985		$285	$370

FireBelly Amps

2008-present. Production/custom, professional and premium grade, vintage tube amps built by Steven Cohen in Santa Monica, California.

Fishman

2003-present. Larry Fishman offers professional grade, production, amps that are designed and engineered in Andover, Massachusetts and assembled in China. They also build effects.

MODEL YEAR	FEATURES	EXC. COND. LOW	HIGH
Loudbox 100 Amp			
2006-2013. 100 watts, 1x8" with dome.			
2006-2013		$235	$305
Loudbox Artist Pro-LBX-600 Amp			
2006-present. 120 watts,			
2006-2019		$250	$325
Loudbox Mini Pro-LBX-500 Amp			
2006-present. 60 watts.			
2006-2019		$160	$210
Loudbox Performer Pro-LBX-700 Amp			
2006-present. 180 watts.			
2006-2019		$325	$425

Flot-A-Tone

Ca.1946-early 1960s. Flot-A-Tone was located in Milwaukee, Wisconsin, and made a variety of tube guitar and accordion amps. Most were distrubuted by the Lo Duca Brothers.

MODEL YEAR	FEATURES	EXC. COND. LOW	HIGH
Large Amp			
1960s. Four speakers.			
1960s		$525	$675
Small Amp			
1960s. 1x8" speaker.			
1960s		$275	$375

Fortune

1978-1979. Created by Jim Kelley just prior to branding Jim Kelley Amplifiers in 1980, Fortune Amplifiers logo on front panel, specifications and performance similar to early Jim Kelley amplifiers, difficult to find in original condition, professional grade, designed and manufactured by Active Guitar Electronics company.

Fox Amps

Marc Vos builds professional grade, production/custom, guitar amps and cabinets, starting 2007, in Budel, Netherlands.

Framus

1946-1977, 1996-present. Tube guitar amp heads, combos and cabinets made in Markneukirchen, Germany. They also build guitars, basses, mandolins and banjos. Begun as an acoustic instrument manufacturer, Framus added electrics in the mid-'50s. In the '60s, Framus instruments were imported into the U.S. by Philadelphia Music Company. The brand was revived in '96 by Hans Peter Wilfer, the president of Warwick, with production in Warwick's factory in Germany. Distributed in the U.S. by Dana B. Goods.

Fred

1984-1986. Before settling on the name Bedrock, company founders Brad Jeter and Ron Pinto produced 50 amps carrying the brand name Fred in Nashua, New Hampshire.

Frenzel

1952-present. Jim Frenzel built his first amp in '52 and began using his brand in '01. He offers intermediate and professional grade, production/custom, hand-wired, vintage tube, guitar and bass amps built in Mabank, Texas.

Frudua Guitar Works

1988-present. Intermediate grade, production, guitar and bass amps built by guitar luthier Galeazzo Frudua in Calusco d'Adda, Italy. He also builds guitars and basses.

Fryette

2009-present. Professional and premium grade amps, combos, and cabinets built by Steven M. Fryette, who also founded VHT amps. At the beginning of '09 AXL guitars acquired the VHT name to build their own product. Fryette continues to manufacture the VHT amp models under the Fryette brand in Burbank, California.

MODEL		EXC. COND.	
YEAR	FEATURES	LOW	HIGH

Fuchs Audio Technology

2000-present. Andy Fuchs started the company in '99 to rebuild and modify tube amps. In 2000 he started production of his own brand of amps, offering combos and heads from 10 to 150 watts. They also custom build audiophile and studio tube electronics. Originally located in Bloomfield, New Jersey, since '07 in Clifton, New Jersey.

Fulton-Webb

Steve Fulton and Bill Webb build their tube amp heads, combos and cabinets in Austin, Texas, beginning 1997.

Gabriel Sound Garage

2004-2014. Gabriel Bucataru built his tube amp heads and combos in Arlington Heights, Illinois.

Gallien-Krueger

1969-present. Gallien-Krueger has offered a variety of bass and guitar amps, combos and cabinets and is located in San Jose, California.

Garcia

Tube amp heads and speaker cabinets built by Matthew Garcia in Myrtle Beach, South Carolina, starting in 2004. He also built effects.

Garnet

Mid 1960s-1989. In the mid '60s, "Gar" Gillies started the Garnet Amplifier Company with his two sons, Russell and Garnet, after he started making PA systems in his Canadian radio and TV repair shop. The first PA from the new company was for Chad Allen & the Expressions (later known as The Guess Who). A wide variety of tube amps were offered and all were designed by Gar, Sr. The company also produced the all-tube effects The Herzog, H-zog, and two stand-alone reverb units designed by Gar in the late '60s and early '70s. The company closed in '89, due to financial reasons caused largely by a too rapid expansion. Gar repaired and designed custom amps up to his death in early 2007.

GDS Amplification

1998-present. Tube amps, combos and speaker cabinets from builder Graydon D. Stuckey of Fenton, Michigan. GDS also offers amp kits. In January, '09, GDS bought the assets of Guytron Amplification.

Genesis

Genesis was a 1980s line of student amps from Gibson.

B40 Amp
1984-late-1980s. Bass combo with 40 watts.

1984-1989		$100	$130

G Series Amps
1984-late-1980s. Small combo amps.

1984-1989	G10, 10w	$55	$75
1984-1989	G25, 25w	$75	$100
1984-1989	G40R, 40w, reverb	$125	$150

MODEL		EXC. COND.	
YEAR	FEATURES	LOW	HIGH

Genz Benz

Founded by Jeff and Cathy Genzler in 1984 and located in Scottsdale, Arizona, the company offers guitar, bass, and PA amps and speaker cabinets. In late 2003, Genz Benz was acquired by Kaman (Ovation, Hamer, Takamine). On January 1, '08, Fender acquired Kaman Music Corporation and the Genz Benz brand.

George Dennis

1991-present. Founded by George Burgerstein, original products were a line of effects pedals. In '96 they added a line of tube amps. The company is located in Prague, Czech Republic.

Gerhart

2000-present. Production/custom, intermediate and professional grade, amps and cabinets from builder Gary Gerhart of West Hills, California. He also offers an amp in kit form.

Germino

2002-present. Intermediate to professional grade tube amps, combos and cabinets built by Greg Germino in Graham, North Carolina.

Gibson

1890s (1902)-present. Gibson has offered a variety of amps since the mid-'30s to the present under the Gibson brandname and others. The price ranges listed are for excellent condition, all original amps though tubes may be replaced without affecting value. Many Gibson amps have missing or broken logos. The prices listed are for amps with fully intact logos. A broken or missing logo can diminish the value of the amp. Amps with a changed handle, power cord, and especially a broken logo should be taken on a case-by-case basis.

Vintage amplifiers are rarely found in original, excellent condition. Many vintage amps have notable wear and have a non-original speaker. The prices shown are for fully original (except tubes and caps) amplifiers that are pleasing clean, and contain no significant wear, blemishes, grille stains, or damage.

Atlas IV Amp
1963-1967. Piggyback head and cab, introduced with trapezoid shape, changed to rectangular cabs in '65-'66 with black cover, simple circuit with 4 knobs, no reverb or tremolo, mid-power with 2 6L6, 1x15".

1963-1965	Brown	$475	$600
1966-1967	Black	$475	$600

Atlas Medalist Amp
1964-1967. Combo version with 1x15".

1964-1967		$450	$585

B-40 Amp
1972-1975. Solidstate, 40 watts, 1x12".

1972-1975		$210	$270

BR-1 Amp
1946-1948. 15 watts, 1x12" field-coil speaker, brown leatherette cover, rectangular metal grille with large G.

1946-1948		$585	$765

Fuchs ODS-II

Garnet Gnome Reverb
John Maysenhoelder

Germino Club 40

Gibson EH-150
Rich E. Hall

1959 Gibson GA-5
David Stuckey

Gibson GA-5 Les Paul Junior

MODEL YEAR	FEATURES	EXC. COND. LOW	HIGH
BR-3 Amp			
1946. 12 watts, 1x12" Utah field-coil speaker (most BR models used Jensen speakers).			
1946		$585	$765
BR-4 Amp			
1946-1948. 14 watts, 1x12" Utah field-coil speaker (most BR models used Jensen speakers).			
1946-1948		$500	$650
BR-6 Amp			
1946-1954. 10 to 12 watts, 1x10", brown leatherette, speaker opening split by cross panel with G logo, bottom mounted chassis with single on-off volume pointer knob.			
1946-1947	Verticle cab	$500	$650
1948-1954	Horizontal cab	$500	$650
BR-9 Amp			
1948-1954. Cream leatherette, 10 watts, 1x8". Originally sold with the BR-9 lap steel. Renamed GA-9 in '54.			
1948-1954		$385	$500
Duo Metalist Amp			
1968-early 1970s. Upright vertical combo cab, tubes, faux wood grain panel, mid-power, 1x12".			
1968-1970s		$400	$525
EH-100 Amp			
1936-1942. Electric-Hawaiian companion amp, 1x10". AC/DC version called EH-110.			
1936-1942		$550	$725
EH-125 Amp			
1941-1942. 1x12", rounded shoulder cab, brown cover in '41 and dark green in '42, leather handle.			
1941-1942		$600	$800
EH-126 Amp			
1941. Experimental model, 6-volt variant of EH-125, about 5 made.			
1941		$975	$1,250
EH-135 Amp			
1941. Experimental model, alternating and direct current switchable, about 7 made.			
1941		$1,050	$1,350
EH-150 Amp			
1935-1942. Electric-Hawaiian companion amp, 1x12" ('35-'37) or 1x10" ('38-'42). AC/DC version called EH-160.			
1935	13 3/4" square cab	$1,050	$1,350
1936-1937	14 3/4" square cab	$1,050	$1,350
1937-1942	15 3/8" round cab	$1,050	$1,350
EH-185 Amp			
1939-1942. 1x12", tweed cover, black and orange vertical stripes, marketed as companion amp to the EH-185 Lap Steel. AC/DC version called EH-195.			
1939-1942		$1,300	$1,700
EH-195 Amp			
1939-1942. EH-185 variant with vibrato.			
1939-1942		$1,300	$1,700
EH-250 Amp			
1940. Upgraded natural maple cabinet using EH-185 chassis, only 2 made, evolved into EH-275.			
1940		$1,650	$2,150
EH-275 Amp			
1940-1942. Similar to EH-185 but with maple cab and celluloid binding, about 30 made.			
1940-1942		$1,600	$2,075
Epoch Series			
2000s. Solidstate student practice amps.			
2000s	G-10	$20	$30
Falcon III F-3 Amp			
Early 1970s. Solidstate, 1x12" combo, 65 watts, made in Chicago by CMI after Gibson ceased amp production in Kalamazoo ('67), black tolex, dark grille.			
1970		$225	$300
Falcon Medalist (Hybrid) Amp			
1967. Transitional tube 1x12" combo amp from GA-19 tube Falcon to the solidstate Falcon, Falcon logo and Gibson logo on front panel, brown control panel, dark cover and dark grille, vertical combo cabinet.			
1967		$260	$340
Falcon Medalist (Solidstate) Amp			
1968-1969. Solidstate combo, 15 watts, 1x12".			
1968-1969		$260	$340
G-10 Amp			
1972-1975. Solidstate, 10 watts, 1x10", no tremolo or reverb.			
1972-1975		$90	$115
G-20 Amp			
1972-1975. Solidstate with tremolo, 1x10", 10 watts.			
1972-1975		$105	$135
G-25 Amp			
1972-1975. 25 watts, 1x10".			
1972-1975		$140	$180
G-35 Amp			
1975. Solidstate, 30 watts, 1x12".			
1975		$155	$200
G-40/G-40 R Amp			
1972-1974. Solidstate with tremolo and reverb, 40 watts, 1x12" (G-40) and 2x10" (G-40 R).			
1972-1974		$210	$275
G-50/G-50 A/G-50 B Amp			
1972, 1975. Solidstate with tremolo and reverb, models G-50 and 50 A are 1x12", 40 watts, model 50 B is a bass 1x15", 50 watts.			
1972-1975		$225	$295
G-55 Amp			
1975. 50 watts, 1x12".			
1975		$225	$295
G-60 Amp			
1972-1973. Solidstate with tremolo and reverb, 1x15", 60 watts.			
1972-1973		$245	$315
G-70 Amp			
1972-1973. Solidstate with tremolo and reverb, 2x12", 60 watts.			
1972-1973		$270	$350
G-80 Amp			
1972-1973. Solidstate with tremolo and reverb, 4x10", 60 watts.			
1972-1973		$310	$400
G-100 A/G-100 B Amp			
1975. 100 watts, model 100 A is 2x12" and 100 B is 2x15".			
1975		$310	$400

MODEL YEAR	FEATURES	EXC. COND. LOW	HIGH

G-105 Amp
1974-1975. Solidstate, 100 watts, 2x12", reverb.

1974-1975		$310	$400

G-115 Amp
1975. 100 watts, 4x10".

1974-1975		$340	$440

GA-5 Les Paul Jr. Amp
1954-1957. Tan fabric cover (Mottled Brown by '57), 7" oval speaker, 4 watts. Renamed Skylark in '58.

1954-1957		$400	$525

GA-5 Les Paul Jr. Amp (Reissue)
2004-2008. Goldtone Series, class A, 5 watts, 1x8".

2004-2008		$260	$340

GA-5 Skylark Amp
1958-1968. Gold cover (brown by '63 and black by '66), 1x8" (1x10" from '64 on), 4.5 watts (10 watts from '64 on), tremolo. Often sold with the Skylark Lap Steel.

1958-1959	Gold, 45w, 1x8"	$365	$475
1960-1962	Gold, 45w, 1x8"	$350	$450
1963	Brown, 45w, 1x8"	$325	$425
1964	Brown, 10w, 1x10"	$300	$385
1965-1967	Black, 10w, 1x10"	$270	$350
1968	Skylark, last version	$195	$250

GA-5 T Skylark Amp
1960-1968. Tremolo, 4.5 watts early, 10 later, gold covering and 1x8" until '63, brown '63-'64, black and 1x10" after.

1960-1962	Gold, 45w, 1x8"	$350	$450
1963	Brown, 45w, 1x8"	$325	$425
1964	Brown, 10w, 1x10"	$325	$425
1965-1967	Kalamazoo, black, 10w, 1x10"	$270	$350
1968	Norlin, vertical cab, 10w, 1x10, tubes	$195	$250

GA-5 W Amp
Late-1960s. Norlin-era, post-Kalamazoo production, 15 watts, small speaker, volume and tone controls.

1969		$70	$90

GA-6 Amp
1956-1959. Replaced the BR-6, 8 to 12 watts, 1x12", has Gibson 6 above the grille. Renamed GA-6 Lancer in '60.

1956-1959		$560	$725

GA-6 Lancer Amp
1960-1961. Renamed from GA-6, 1x12", tweed cover, 3 knobs, 14 watts.

1960-1961		$650	$850

GA-7 Les Paul TV Model Amp
1954-1956. Basic old style GA-5 with different graphics, 4 watts, small speaker.

1954-1956		$385	$500

GA-8 Discoverer Amp
1962-1964. Renamed from GA-8 Gibsonette, gold fabric cover, 1x12", 10 watts.

1962-1964		$385	$500

GA-8 Gibsonette Amp
1955-1962. Tan fabric cover (gold by '58), 1x10", 8 watts (9 watts by '58). See Gibsonette for 1952-'54. Name changed to GA-8 Discoverer in '62.

1955-1957	Gibsonette logo, square hole	$425	$550

1958-1959	Gibson logo	$375	$500
1960-1962	Gibson logo, tweed	$375	$500

GA-8 T Discoverer Amp
1960-1966. Gold fabric cover, 1x10", 9 watts (tan cover, 1x12" and 15 watts by '63), tremolo.

1960-1962	Tweed, 9w, 1x10"	$400	$525
1963-1964	Brown, 15w, 1x12"	$350	$450
1965-1966	Black, 15w, 1x12"	$325	$425

GA-9 Amp
1954-1959. Renamed from BR-9, tan fabric cover, 8 watts, 1x10". Often sold with the BR-9 Lap Steel.

1954-1957	Gibson 9 logo	$500	$650
1958-1959	Tweed, 6V6s	$500	$650

GA-14 Titan Amp
1959-1961. About 15 watts using 2x6V6 power tubes, 1x10", tweed cover.

1959-1961		$500	$700

GA-15 RV Goldtone Amp
1999-2004. 15 watts, Class A, 1x12", spring reverb.

1999-2004		$425	$550

GA-15 RVT Explorer Amp
1965-1967. Tube, 1x10", tremolo, reverb, black vinyl.

1965-1967		$325	$425

GA-17 RVT Scout Amp
1963-1967. Low power, 1x10", reverb and tremolo.

1963	Smooth brown	$425	$550
1964-1965	Textured brown	$425	$550
1966-1967	Black	$325	$425

GA-18 Explorer Amp
1959. Tweed, tube, 14 watts, 1x10". Replaced in '60 by the GA-18 T Explorer.

1959		$700	$900

GA-18 T Explorer Amp
1960-1963. Tweed, 14 watts, 1x10", tremolo.

1960-1962	Tweed	$725	$950
1963	Brown	$500	$650

GA-19 RVT Falcon Amp
1961-1967. One of Gibson's best selling amps. Initially tweed covered, followed by smooth brown, textured brown, and black. Each amp has a different tone. One 12" Jensen with deep-sounding reverb and tremolo.

1961-1962	Tweed, 6V6	$975	$1,250
1962-1963	Smooth brown	$550	$725
1964	Textured brown	$500	$650
1965-1967	Black	$375	$500

GA-20 Amp
1950-1962. Brown leatherette (2-tone by '55 and tweed by '60), tube, 12 watts early, 14 watts later, 1x12". Renamed Crest in '60.

1950-1954	Brown, single G logo on front	$575	$750
1955-1958	2-tone salt/maroon	$775	$1,000
1959	2-tone blue/blond	$775	$1,000

GA-20 Crest Amp
1960-1961. Tweed, tube, 14 watts, 1x12".

1960-1961		$800	$1,050

GA-20 RVT Amp
2004-2007. 15 watts, 1x12", reverb, tremolo.

2004-2007		$560	$725

1964 Gibeon GA-5 T Skylark
Tom Pfeifer

AMPS

1960 Gibson GA-8 T Discoverer
David Stuckey

Gibson GA-20 RVT

1952 Gibson GA-40 Les Paul
Ted Wulfers

2008 Gibson GA-42 RVT

1955 Gibson GA-55 V
Joey Abella

MODEL YEAR	FEATURES	EXC. COND. LOW	HIGH
GA-20 RVT Minuteman Amp			
1965-1967. Black, 14 watts, 1x12", tube, reverb, tremolo.			
1965-1967		$375	$475
GA-20 T Amp			
1956-1959. Tube, 16 watts, tremolo, 1x12", 2-tone. Renamed Ranger in '60.			
1956-1958	2-tone	$775	$1,000
1959	New 2-tone	$775	$1,000
GA-20 T Ranger Amp			
1960-1961. Tube, 16 watts, tremolo, 1x12", tweed.			
1960-1962	Tweed	$850	$1,100
GA-25 Amp			
1947-1948. Brown, 1x12" and 1x8", 15 watts. Replaced by GA-30 in '48.			
1947-1948		$900	$1,175
GA-25 RVT Hawk Amp			
1963-1968. Reverb, tremolo, 1x15".			
1963	Smooth brown	$575	$750
1964	Rough brown	$425	$550
1965-1967	Black	$400	$525
1968	Last version	$345	$445
GA-30 Amp (Invader)			
1948-1961. Brown until '54, 2-tone after, tweed in '60, 1x12" and 1x8", 14 watts. Renamed GA-30 Invader in '60.			
1948-1954	Brown	$750	$1,000
1955-1959	2-tone salt/maroon	$750	$1,000
1960-1961	Invader, tweed	$750	$1,000
GA-30 RV Invader Amp			
1961. Tweed, 1x12" and 1x8", 14-16 watts, reverb but no tremolo.			
1961		$750	$1,000
GA-30 RVH Goldtone Amp Head			
1999-2004. 30 watts, Class A head, reverb.			
1999-2004		$700	$925
GA-30 RVS (Stereo) Goldtone Amp			
1999-2004. 15 watts per channel, Class A stereo, 2x12", reverb.			
1999-2004		$850	$1,100
GA-30 RVT Invader Amp			
1962-1967. Updated model with reverb and tremolo, 25 watts, 1x12" and 1x10" speakers, first issue in tweed.			
1962	Tweed	$1,125	$1,450
1963	Smooth brown	$650	$850
1964	Rough brown	$500	$650
1965-1967	Black	$425	$550
GA-35 RVT Lancer Amp			
1966-1967. Black, 1x12", tremolo, reverb.			
1966-1967		$425	$575
GA-40 Les Paul Amp			
1952-1960. Introduced with the Les Paul Model guitar, 1x12" Jensen speaker, 14 watts early and 16 later, recessed leather handle using spring mounting (the handle is easily broken and replacement handle is more common than not). Two-tone leatherette covering, '50s checkerboard grille ('52-early-'55), Les Paul script logo on front of the amp ('52-'55), plastic grille insert with LP monogram, gold Gibson logo above grille. Cosmetics changed dramatically in early/mid-'55. Renamed GA-40 T Les Paul in '60.			
1952-1955	Brown 2-tone, LP grille	$1,200	$1,600

MODEL YEAR	FEATURES	EXC. COND. LOW	HIGH
1955-1957	2-tone salt/maroon	$1,175	$1,525
1958-1959	2-tone blue/blond	$1,175	$1,525
GA-40 RVT Limited Edition Amp			
2008-2011. GA-40RVT Limited Edition logo, 200 made, 2-tone brown/tan, front control panel, 30/15 switchable watts.			
2008-2011		$475	$625
GA-40 T Les Paul Amp			
1960-1962. Renamed from GA-40 Les Paul, 1x12", 16 watts, tremolo. Renamed Mariner in '62-'67.			
1960-1961	Tweed	$1,775	$2,300
1962	Smooth brown	$475	$625
GA-40 T Mariner Amp			
1962-1967. 1x12" combo, 25 watts, tremolo.			
1962-1963	Smooth brown	$475	$625
1964	Rough brown	$365	$475
1965-1967	Black	$350	$450
GA-45 RVT Saturn Amp			
1965-1967. 2x10", mid power, tremolo, reverb.			
1965-1967		$425	$550
GA-50/GA-50 T Amp			
1948-1955. Brown leatherette, 25 watts, 1x12" and 1x8", T had tremolo.			
1948-1955	GA-50	$1,450	$1,900
1948-1955	GA-50 T	$1,550	$2,000
GA-55 RVT Ranger Amp			
1965-1967. Black cover, 4x10", tremolo, reverb.			
1965-1967		$450	$585
GA-55/GA-55 V Amp			
1954-1958. 2x12", 20 watts, GA-55 V with vibrato.			
1954-1958	GA-55	$2,000	$2,600
1954-1958	GA-55 V	$2,000	$2,600
GA-60 Hercules Amp			
1962-1963. 25 watts, 1x15, no-frills 1-channel amp, no reverb, no tremolo.			
1962-1963		$500	$650
GA-60 RV Goldtone Amp			
1999-2004. 60 watts, A/B circuit, 2x12", spring reverb, earliest production in England.			
1999-2004		$850	$1,100
GA-70 Country and Western Amp			
1955-1958. 25 watts, 1x15", 2-tone, longhorn cattle western logo on front, advertised to have extra bright sound.			
1955-1958		$2,000	$2,600
GA-75 Amp			
1950-1955. Mottled Brown leatherette, 1x15", 25 watts.			
1950-1955		$1,250	$1,625
GA-75 L Recording Amp			
1964-1967. 1x15" Lansing speaker, no reverb or tremolo, 2 channels, dark cover, gray grille.			
1964-1967		$460	$600
GA-75 Recording Amp			
1964-1967. 2x10" speakers, no reverb or tremolo, 2 channels, dark cover, gray grille.			
1964-1967		$480	$625
GA-77 Amp			
1954-1959. 1x15" JBL, 25-30 watts, 2x6L6 power tubes, 2-tone covering, near top-of-the-line for the mid-'50s.			
1954-1958	2-tone salt/maroon, leather handle	$1,225	$1,600

AMPS

MODEL YEAR	FEATURES	EXC. COND. LOW	HIGH
1958-1959	2-tone blue/blond, metal handle	$1,225	$1,600

GA-77 RET Vanguard Amp
1964-1967. Mid-power, 2x10", tremolo, reverb, echo.

1964	Rough brown	$610	$790
1965-1967	Black	$450	$575

GA-77 RETL Vanguard Amp
1964-1967. GA-77 RET with 1x15" Lansing speaker option (L).

1964-1967		$560	$725

GA-77 RVTL Vanguard Amp
1962-1967. 50 watts, 1x15", Lansing speaker option (L), tremolo, reverb, smooth brown.

1962-1967		$560	$725

GA-77 Vanguard Amp
1960-1961. 1x15" JBL, 25-30 watts, 2 6L6 power tubes, tweed cover, first use of Vanguard model name.

1960-1961		$1,200	$1,575

GA-78 Bell Stereo Amp
1960. Gibson-branded amp made by Bell, same as GA-79 series, Bell 30 logo on front, 30 watts, 2x10" wedge cab.

1960		$1,600	$2,100

GA-79 RV Amp
1960-1962. Stereo-reverb, 2x10", 30 watts.

1960-1961	Tweed	$1,900	$2,500
1962	Textured brown	$1,700	$2,250

GA-79 RVT Multi-Stereo Amp
1961-1967. Introduced as GA-79 RVT, Multi-Stereo was added to name in '61. Stereo-reverb and tremolo, 2x10", tweed (black and brown also available), 30 watts.

1961	Tweed	$1,900	$2,500
1961-1962	Gray sparkle	$1,700	$2,250
1963-1965	Textured brown	$1,700	$2,250
1965-1967	Black	$1,600	$2,100

GA-80/GA-80 T/Vari-Tone Amp
1959-1961. 25 watts, 1x15", 2 channels, described as "6-in-1 amplifier with improved tremolo," 6 Vari-Tone pushbottons which give "six distinctively separate sounds," 7 tubes, tweed cover.

1959-1961		$1,325	$1,725

GA-83 S Stereo-Vibe Amp
1959-1961. Interesting stereo amp with front baffle mounted 1x12" and 4x8" side-mounted speakers (2 on each side), 35 watts, Gibson logo on upper right corner of the grille, tweed cover, brown grille (late '50s Fender-style), 3 pointer knobs and 3 round knobs, 4 inputs.

1959-1961		$1,975	$2,550

GA-85 Bass Reflex Amp
1957-1958. Removable head, 25 watts, 1x12", very limited production.

1957-1958		$980	$1,275

GA-86 Ensemble Amp
1960. 25 watt head plus 1x12" cab, tweed.

1960		$1,325	$1,725

GA-88S Stereo Twin Amp
1960. Control panel and 2 separate 1x12" speaker cabs, 35 watts, 8 tubes, tweed.

1960		$2,900	$3,800

GA-90 High Fidelity Amp
1953-1960. 25 watts, 6x8", 2 channels, advertised for guitar, bass, accordion, or hi-fi.

1953-1960		$1,125	$1,450

GA-95 RVT Apollo Amp
1965-1967. 90 watts, 2x12", black vinyl, black grille, tremolo, reverb.

1965-1967		$500	$650

GA-100 Bass Amp
1960-1963. 35 watts, 1x12" cabinet, for '60-'61 tweed and tripod included for separate head, for '62-'63 brown covering and Crestline Tuck-A-Way head.

1960-1961	Tweed	$1,000	$1,300
1962-1963	Smooth brown	$575	$750

GA-200 Rhythm King Amp
1957-1961. Introduced as GA-200, renamed Rhythm King in '60, 2-channel version of GA-400. Bass amp, 60 watts, 2x12".

1957-1959	2-tone	$1,600	$2,100
1959-1961	Tweed	$1,600	$2,100
1961	Smooth brown	$1,500	$2,000

GA-300 RVT Super 300 Amp
1962-1963. 60 watts, 2x12" combo, reverb, tremolo, smooth brown.

1962-1963		$1,475	$1,900

GA-400 Super 400 Amp
1956-1961. 60 watts, 2x12", 3 channels, same size as GA-200 cab, 1 more tube than GA-200.

1956-1959	2-tone	$1,800	$2,300
1959-1961	Tweed	$1,800	$2,300
1961	Smooth brown	$1,700	$2,200

GA-CB Custom-Built Amp
1949-1953. 25-30 watts, 1x15", the top model in Gibson's '51 line of amps, described as having sound quality found only in the finest public address broadcasting systems, about 47 made, this high-end amp was replaced by the GA-77 and a completely different GA-90.

1949-1953		$1,500	$2,000

Gibsonette Amp
1952-1954. Gibsonette logo on front, round hole. See GA-8 Gibsonette for later models.

1952-1954		$425	$550

GM05 Amp
2009-2012. Small 5 watt solidstate amp usually sold with Maestro guitar pack.

2009-2012		$20	$35

GSS-50 Amp
1966-1967. Solidstate, 50 watts, 2x10" combo, reverb and tremolo, black vinyl cover, silver grille, no grille logo.

1966-1967		$310	$400

GSS-100 Amp
1966-1967, 1970. Solidstate, 100 watts, two 24"x12" 2x10" sealed cabs, black vinyl cover, silver grille, 8 black knobs and 3 red knobs, slanted raised Gibson logo. Speakers prone to distortion. Reissued in '70 in 3 variations.

1966-1967		$310	$400

Early-1960s Gibson Vanguard 15
Rick Buckendahl

AMPS

1961 Gibson GA-79 RV

Gibson GA-200 Rhythm King

Ca. Late-1960's Gibson Plus 50 Power Amp
Imaged by Heritage Auctions, HA.com

Gibson Thor Bass

Green Electric

MODEL YEAR	FEATURES	EXC. COND. LOW	HIGH
Lancer Amp			
1968-1969. CMI-Chicago produced, small combo, black upright cab, dark grille, post-McCarty era Gibson logo.			
1968-1969		$60	$80
LP-1/LP-2 Amp Set			
1970. Les Paul model, piggyback amp and cab set, LP-1 head and LP-2 4x12" plus 2 horns cab, large vertical speaker cabinet, rather small compact 190 watt solidstate amp head.			
1970		$310	$400
Medalist 2/12 Amp			
1968-1970. Vertical cabinet, 2x12", reverb and temolo.			
1968-1970		$365	$475
Medalist 4/10 Amp			
1968-1970. Vertical cabinet, 4x10", reverb and tremolo.			
1968-1970		$365	$475
Mercury I Amp			
1963-1965. Piggyback trapezoid-shaped head with 2x12" trapezoid cabinet, tremolo, brown.			
1963-1965		$430	$560
Mercury II Amp			
1963-1967. Mercury I with 1x15" and 1x10", initially trapezoid cabinets then changed to rectangular.			
1963-1964	Brown trapezoid cabs	$500	$650
1965-1967	Black rectangular cabs	$430	$560
Plus-50 Amp			
1966-1967. 50 watts, powered extension amplifier. Similar to GSS-100 cabinet of the same era, 2x10" cab, black vinyl cover, silver grille, slant Gibson logo.			
1966-1967		$400	$520
Super Thor Bass Amp			
1970-1974. Solidstate, part of the new G-Series (not GA-Series), 65 watts, 2x15", black tolex, black grille, upright vertical cab with front control, single channel.			
1970-1974		$330	$430
Thor Bass Amp			
1970-1974. Solidstate, smaller 2x10" 50 watt version of Super Thor.			
1970-1974		$295	$385
Titan I Amp			
1963-1965. Piggyback trapezoid-shaped head and 2x12" trapezoid-shaped cabinet, tremolo.			
1963-1965		$430	$560
Titan III Amp			
1963-1967. Piggyback trapezoid-shaped head and 1x15" + 2x10" trapezoid-shaped cabinet, tremolo.			
1963-1964	Brown	$470	$610
1965-1967	Black	$470	$610
Titan Medalist Amp			
1964-1967. Combo version of Titan Series with 1x15" and 1x10", tremolo only, no reverb, black.			
1964-1967		$485	$630
Titan V Amp			
1963-1967. Piggyback trapezoid-shaped tube head and 2x15" trapezoid-shaped cabinet, tremolo.			
1963-1964	Brown	$485	$630
1965-1967	Black	$485	$630

MODEL YEAR	FEATURES	EXC. COND. LOW	HIGH
TR-1000 T/TR-1000 RVT Starfire Amp			
1962-1967. Solidstate, 1x12" combo, 40 watts, tremolo, RVT with reverb.			
1962-1967		$260	$340

Ginelle
Rick Emery builds his tube combo amps in Ardmore, Pennsylvania starting in 1996.

Giulietti
1962-1965. The Giulietti Accordion Company, New York, offered guitars and amps in the '60s. The amps were made by Magnatone and the models and model numbers are often similar to the Magnatone model.

MODEL YEAR	FEATURES	EXC. COND. LOW	HIGH
Pearloid Lap Steel Amp			
1962. Small student level, 1x12", 2-channel, tremolo.			
1962		$175	$225
S 1x12" Combo Amp			
1962. Tremolo, 2-channel.			
1962		$800	$1,050
S-9 Amp (Magnatone 460)			
1962. 35 watts, 2x12 plus 2 tweeters, true vibrato combo, black sparkle.			
1962		$1,150	$1,500

Gjika Amplification
1980-present. Premium and presentation grade tube amp heads and cabinets built by Robert Gjika in Escondido, California.

Gnome Amplifiers
2008-present. Dan Munro builds professional grade, production, guitar amps and cabinets in Olympia, Washington. He also builds effects.

Gomez Amplification
2005-2015. Tube combo amps built by Dario G. Gomez in Rancho Santa Margarita, California.

Goodsell
2004-present. Tube head and combo amps built by Richard Goodsell in Atlanta, Georgia.

Gorilla
1980s-2009. Small solidstate entry-level amps, distributed by Pignose, Las Vegas, Nevada.

MODEL YEAR	FEATURES	EXC. COND. LOW	HIGH
Compact Practice Student Amp			
1980s-2009. Solidstate, 10 to 30 watts, compact design.			
1980s-2009		$20	$50

Goya
1955-1996. Goya was mainly known for acoustics, but offered a few amps in the '60s. The brand was purchased by Avnet/Guild in '66 and by Martin in the late '70s.

Grammatico Amps
2009-present. Production/custom, professional and premium grade, hand-wired, guitar and bass amps built by John Grammatico in Austin, Texas.

MODEL YEAR	FEATURES	EXC. COND. LOW	HIGH

Green

1993-present. Amp model line made in England by Matamp (see that brand for listing), bright green covering, large Green logo on the front.

Greer Amplification

1999-present. Tube guitar amps and speaker cabinets built by Nick Greer in Athens, Georgia. He also builds effects.

Gregory

1950s-1960s. Private branded amps sold via music wholesalers, by late '60s solidstate models made by Harmony including the 007, C.I.A., Mark Six, Mark Eight, Saturn 80, most models were combo amps with Gregory logo.

Solidstate Amp

1960s	Various models	$125	$300

Gretsch

1883-present. In '05, Gretsch again starting offering amps after previously selling them from the 1950s to '73. Initially private branded for them by Valco (look for the Valco oval or rectangular serialized label on the back). Early-'50s amps were covered in the requisite tweed, but evolved into the Gretsch charcoal gray covering. The mid-'50s to early-'60s amps were part of the Electromatic group of amps. The mid-'50s to '62 amps often sported wrap-around and slanted grilles. In '62, the more traditional box style was introduced. In '66, the large amps went piggyback. Baldwin-Gretsch began to phase out amps effective '65, but solidstate amps continued being offered for a period of time. The '73 Gretsch product line only offered Sonax amps, made in Canada and Sho-Bud amps made in the U.S. In '05, they introduced a line of tube combo amps made in U.S. by Victoria Amp Company.

Artist Amp

1946. Early post-war Gretsch amp made before Valco began to make their amps. Appears to be made by Operadio Mfg. Co., St. Charles, Illinois. Low power small combo amp, Gretsch Artist script logo on grille, round speaker baffle hole.

1946		$250	$325

Broadkaster Mini Lead 50 Amp

Late 1960s. Solidstate compact verticle combo amp.

1969		$200	$275

Carousel Amp

1960s. Solidstate, 1x10" and 1x3" speakers, tremolo speed and depth knobs, brown cover.

1960s		$550	$725

Electromatic Amp

1947-1949. Valco-made with era-typical styling, 3 slat speaker baffle openings, leather handle, two-tone leatherette, 3 tubes with small speaker, single volume knob.

1947-1949		$600	$800

Electromatic Artist Amp (6155)

1950s. Small amp, 2x6V6 power, 1x10", volume and tone knobs.

1950s		$525	$675

Electromatic Deluxe Amp (6163)

1950s. 1x12", 2x6L6, brown tweed grille. Also offered in Western Finish.

1950s		$775	$1,025

Model 6150 Compact Amp

Late-1950s-1960s. Early amps in tweed, '60s amps in gray covering, no tremolo, single volume knob, no treble or bass knob, 1x8".

1950s	Brown tweed	$425	$550
1960s	Gray	$425	$550

Model 6151 Electromatic Standard/ Compact Tremolo Amp

Late-1940s-late-1960s. 1x8", various covers.

1940s-60s		$425	$550

Model 6152 Compact Tremolo Reverb Amp

Ca.1964-late-1960s. Five watts, 11"x6" elliptical speaker early on, 1x12" later.

1964-1966		$575	$800

Model 6153T White Princess Amp

1962. Compact combo, 6x9" oval speaker, higher priced than the typical small amp because it is relatively rare and associated with the White Princess guitar - making it valuable in a set, condition is very important, an amp with any issues will be worth much less.

1962		$825	$1,075

Model 6154 Super-Bass Amp

Early-1960s-mid-1960s. Gray covering, 2x12", 70 watts, tube.

1960s		$675	$875

Model 6156 Playboy Amp

Early-1950s-1966. Tube amp, 17 watts, 1x10" until '61 when converted to 1x12", tweed, then gray, then finally black covered.

1950s-1960	Tweed, 1x10"	$600	$775
1961-1962	Tweed, 1x12"	$600	$775
1963-1966	Black or gray, 1x12"	$600	$775

Model 6157 Super Bass (Piggyback) Amp

Mid-late-1960s. 35 watts, 2x15" cabinet, single channel.

1960s		$500	$650

Model 6159 Dual Bass Amp

Mid-late-1960s. 35 watts, tube, 2x12" cabinet, dual channel, black covering. Replaced by 6163 Chet Atkins Piggyback Amp.

1965		$650	$850

Model 6160 Chet Atkins Country Gentleman Amp

Early-late-1960s. Combo tube amp, 35 watts, 2x12" cabinet, 2 channels. Replaced by 6163 Chet Atkins Piggyback amp with tremolo but no reverb.

1960s		$675	$875

Model 6161 Dual Twin Tremolo Amp

Ca.1962-late-1960s. 19 watts (later 17 watts), 2x10" with 5" tweeter, tremolo.

1962-1967		$700	$900

Model 6161 Electromatic Twin Amp

Ca.1953-ca.1960. Gray Silverflake covering, two 11x6" speakers, 14 watts, tremolo, wraparound grille '55 and after.

1953-1960		$775	$1,025

1947 Gretsch Electromatic
Imaged by Heritage Auctions, HA.com

Gretsch Model 6156 Playboy

Late-1950s Gretsch 6161
Imaged by Heritage Auctions, HA.com

AMPS

AMPS

*1969 Gretsch Model 6162
Dual Twin Tremolo/Reverb*
Rivington Guitars

*1964 Gretsch Model
6164 Variety*

Gries 5

MODEL YEAR	FEATURES	EXC. COND. LOW	HIGH
Model 6162 Dual Twin Tremolo/Reverb Amp			
Ca.1964-late-1960s. 17 watts, 2x10", reverb, tremolo. Vertical combo amp style introduced in '68.			
1964-1967	Horizontal	$700	$900
1968-1969	Vertical	$600	$800
Model 6163 Chet Atkins (Piggyback) Amp			
Mid-late-1960s. 70 watts, 1x12" and 1x15", black covering, tremolo, reverb.			
1960s		$600	$775
Model 6163 Executive Amp			
1959. 1x15, gray cover.			
1959		$1,250	$1,625
Model 6164 Variety Amp			
Early-mid-1960s. 35 watts, tube, 2x12".			
1960s		$700	$900
Model 6165 Variety Plus Amp			
Early-mid-1960s. Tube amp, 35 watts, 2x12", reverb and tremolo, separate controls for both channels.			
1960s		$725	$950
Model 6166 Fury (Combo) Amp			
Mid-1960s. Tube combo stereo amp, 70 watts, 2x12", separate controls for both channels, large metal handle, reverb.			
1960s		$725	$950
Model 6169 Electromatic Twin Western Finish Amp			
Ca.1953-ca.1960. Western finish, 14 watts, 2-11x6" speakers, tremolo, wraparound grill '55 and after.			
1953-1960		$4,900	$6,300
Model 6169 Fury (Piggyback) Amp			
Late-1960s. Tube amp, 70 watts, 2x12", separate controls for both channels.			
1960s		$725	$950
Model 6170 Pro Bass Amp			
1966-late-1960s. 25 or 35 watts, depending on model, 1x15", vertical cabinet style (vs. box cabinet).			
1966-1969		$600	$775
Model 7154 Nashville Amp			
Introduced in 1969. Solidstate combo amp, 4' tall, 75 watts, 2x15", reverb, tremolo, magic echo.			
1969-1970s		$425	$550
Model 7155 Tornado PA System Amp			
Introduced in 1969. Solidstate piggyback head and cab, 150 watts, 2 column speaker cabs, reverb, tremolo, magic echo.			
1969-1970s	2x2x15"	$375	$500
1969-1970s	2x4x15"	$450	$575
Model 7517 Rogue Amp			
1970s. Solidstate, 40 watts, 2x12", tall vertical cabinet, front control panel.			
1970s		$175	$250
Model G6156 Playboy Amp			
2005-2007. 15 watts, 1x12" combo amp with retro Gretsch styling, made by Victoria.			
2005-2007		$1,000	$1,275
Model G6163 Executive Amp			
2005-2007. Boutique quality made by Victoria for FMIC Gretsch, 20 watts, 1x15", cabinet Uses to the modern retro early '60s Supro Supreme modified-			

MODEL YEAR	FEATURES	EXC. COND. LOW	HIGH
triangle front grille pattern, maroon baffle with white grille, tremolo and reverb.			
2005-2007		$1,000	$1,275
Rex Royal Amp Model M-197-3V			
1950s. Small student compact amp, low power, 1x8", Rex Royal logo on grille, Fred Gretsch logo on back panel, single on-off volume knob.			
1951		$350	$450

Gries

2004-present. Dave Gries builds his intermediate and professional grade, production/custom, amps and cabinets in Mattapoisett, Massachusetts.

Groove Tubes

1979-present. Started by Aspen Pittman in his garage in Sylmar, California, Groove Tubes is now located in San Fernando. GT manufactures and distributes a full line of tubes. In '86 they added amp production and in '91 tube microphones. Aspen is also the author of the Tube Amp Book. The Groove Tubes brand was purchased by Fender in June, '08.

Guild

1952-present. Guild offered amps from the '60s into the '80s. Some of the early models were built by Hagstrom.

MODEL YEAR	FEATURES	EXC. COND. LOW	HIGH
Double Twin Amp			
1953-1955. 35 watts, 2x12" plus 2 tweeters, 2-tone leatherette covered cab.			
1953-1955		$800	$1,050
G-1000 Stereo Amp			
1992-1994. Stereo acoustic combo amp with cushioned seat on top, 4x6 and 1x10 speakers.			
1992-1994		$525	$700
Master Amp			
Ca. 1957- Ca. 1959. Combo 2x6L6 power, tremolo, 2-tone tweed and leatherette.			
1957-1959		$450	$575
Maverick Amp			
Late-1960s-early-1970s. Dual speaker combo, 6 tubes, verticle cab, tremolo, reverb, red/pink control panel, 2-tone black and silver grille.			
1960s-70s		$375	$500
Model One Amp			
Mid-1970s-1977. Solidstate 1x12" vertical cab combo, 30 watts, reverb and tremolo.			
1970s		$150	$200
Model Two Amp			
Mid-1970s-1977. Solidstate 2x10" vertical cab combo, 50 watts, reverb and tremolo.			
1977-1978		$200	$275
Model Three Amp			
Mid-1970s-1977. Solidstate 1x15" vertical cab bass combo, 60 watts, organ and guitar.			
1977-1978		$175	$225
Model Four Amp			
Early-1980s. Solidstate, 6 watts.			
1980s		$75	$125

MODEL YEAR	FEATURES	EXC. COND. LOW	HIGH

Model Five Amp
Early-1980s. Solidstate, 10 watts, 6.25" speaker.
1980s — $100 — $150

Model Six Amp
Early-1980s. Same as Model Five but with reverb.
1980s — $175 — $225

Model Seven Amp
Early-1980s. Solidstate, 12 watts, small amp for guitar, bass and keyboard.
1980s — $175 — $225

Model 50-J Amp
Early-1960s. 14 watts, 1x12", tremolo, blue/gray vinyl.
1962-1963 — $525 — $700

Model 66 Amp
1953-1955. 15 watts, 1x12", tremolo, 2-tone leatherette.
1953-1955 — $525 — $700

Model 66-J Amp
1962-1963. 20 watts, 1x12", tremolo, blue/gray vinyl.
1962-1963 — $525 — $700

Model 98-RT Amp
1962-1963. The only stand-alone reverb amp from Guild in the early '60s, 30 watts, 1x12", blue/gray vinyl.
1962-1963 — $650 — $850

Model 99 Amp
1953-1955. 30 watts, 1x12", tremolo, 2-tone leatherette.
1953-1955 — $500 — $675

Model 99-J Amp
Early-1960s. 30 watts, 1x12", tremolo, blue/gray vinyl.
1962-1963 — $500 — $675

Model 99-U Ultra Amp
Early-1960s. Piggyback 30-watt head with optional 1x12" or 1x15" cab, cab and head lock together, tremolo, blue/gray vinyl.
1962-1963 — $525 — $700

Model 100-J Amp
Early-1960s. 35 watts, 1x15", blue/gray vinyl.
1962-1963 — $525 — $700

Model 200-S Stereo Combo Amp
Early-1960s. 25 watts per channel, total 50 watts stereo, 2x12", tremolo, blue/gray vinyl, wheat grille.
1962-1963 — $725 — $975

Model RC-30 Reverb Converter Amp
Early-1960s. Similar to Gibson GA-1 converter, attaches with 2 wires clipped to originating amp's speaker, 8 watts, 1x10", blue/gray vinyl.
1962-1963 — $525 — $700

Superbird Amp
1968. Piggyback tube amp with 2x12 cab.
1968 — $600 — $800

SuperStar Amp
Ca.1972-ca.1974. 50 watts, all tubes, 1x15" Jensen speakers, vertical combo, reverb, tremolo, black vinyl cover, 2-tone black/silver grille.
1972-1974 — $425 — $575

Thunder 1 Amp
1965-1972. Combo with single speaker, no reverb, light tan cover, 2-tone tan grille.
1965-1972 1x10" — $300 — $400
1965-1972 1x12" — $325 — $425

Thunder 1 (Model T1-RVT)/T1 Amp
1965-1972. Combo with dual speakers and reverb, light tan cover, 2-tone tan grille.
1965-1972 — $525 — $700

ThunderBass Amp
1965-1972. Piggyback combo, 2x15".
1965-1972 100 watt — $525 — $700
1965-1972 200 watt — $550 — $725

ThunderBird Amp
1965-1972. 50 watts, tube, 2x12", reverb, tremolo, with or without TD-1 dolly, black vinyl, black/silver grille.
1965-1972 — $525 — $700

ThunderStar Bass Amp
1965-1972. Piggyback bass tube head or combo, 50 watts.
1965-1972 Full stack, 2x1x15" — $600 — $800
1965-1972 Half stack, 1x1x15" — $525 — $700

ThunderStar Guitar Amp
1965-1972. Combo, 50 watts, 1x12".
1965-1972 — $525 — $700

Guyatone
1933-present. Started offering amps by at least the late '40s with their Guya lap steels. In '51 the Guyatone brand is first used on guitars and most likely amps. Guyatone also made the Marco Polo, Winston, Kingston, Kent, LaFayette and Bradford brands.

Guytron
1995-present. Tube amp heads and speaker cabinets built by Guy Hedrick in Columbiaville, Michigan. In January, '09, GDS Amplification bought the assets of Guytron Amplification.

Hagstrom
1921-1983, 2004-present. The Swedish guitar maker built a variety of tube and solidstate amps from ca. 1961 into the '70s. They also supplied amps to Guild.

Hanburt
1940-ca. 1950. Harvey M. Hansen built electric Hawaiian guitars in Seattle, Washington, some sold as a set with a small amp. The wooden amps have a large HB in the speaker cutout. He also built at least one mandolin.

Harmony
1892-1976, late-1970s-present. Harmony was one of the biggest producers of guitars, and offered amps as well. MBT International offered Harmony amps for 2000-'02.

H Series Amps
1940s-1960s. Harmony model numbers begin with H, such as H-304, all H series models shown are tube amps unless otherwise noted as solidstate.
1940-1950s H-190/H-191 — $375 — $475
1940-1950s H-200 — $375 — $475
1950s   H-204, 18w, 1x12" — $375 — $475

Ca. 1958 Guild Masteramp Two-Tone
Imaged by Heritage Auctions, HA.com

AMPS

Guild Thunder 1 (T1-RVT)
Greg Gagliono

Guytron GT100 F/V

AMPS

Ca. 1963 Harmony H-303A
Rivington Guitars

Headstrong Lil' King

Headstrong Santa Cruz 20

MODEL YEAR	FEATURES	EXC. COND. LOW	HIGH
1960s	H-303A, 8w, 1x8"	$200	$250
1960s	H-304, low pwr, small spkr	$200	$250
1960s	H-305A, low pwr, small spkr	$200	$250
1960s	H-306A, combo 1x12"	$300	$375
1960s	H306C, piggyback 2x12"	$350	$450
1960s	H-400, 8w, 1x8", vol	$175	$225
1960s	H-400A, 8w, 1x8", vol/tone	$200	$255
1960s	H-410A, 10w, 1x10"	$350	$450
1960s	H-415, 18w, 2x12"	$450	$600
1960s	H-420, 20w, 1x15	$375	$500
1960s	H-430, 30w, 2x10"	$450	$600
1960s	H-440, 2x12", trem/verb	$500	$650
1960s	H-512, solidstate, large	$525	$675

Solidstate Amps
1970s. Dark covering, dark grille.

MODEL YEAR	FEATURES	EXC. COND. LOW	HIGH
1970s	Large amp	$175	$650
1970s	Small amp	$25	$50

Harry Joyce
1993-2011, 2015-present. Hand-wired British tube amps, combos, and cabinets from builder/designer Harry Joyce. Joyce was contracted to build Hiwatt amps in England during the '70s. Joyce died in 2002, and the brand was carried on by Charles Bertonazzi and George Scholz until 2011. Brand brought back by Kevin Wood and Scholz through Harry Joyce USA with new versions of the classic models.

Hartke
1984-present. Guitar and bass amps, combos and cabinets made in the U.S. Founded by Larry Hartke, since the mid-'80s, Hartke has been distributed by Samson Technologies. Hartke also offered basses in the past.

Haynes
Haynes guitar amps were built by the Amplifier Corporation of America (ACA) of Westbury, New York. ACA also made an early distortion device powered by batteries. Unicord purchased the company in around 1964, and used the factory to produce its Univox line of amps, most likely discontinuing the Haynes brand at the same time.
Jazz King II Amp
1960s. Solidstate, stereo console-style, 2x12", Haynes logo upper left side.

1960s		$300	$400

Headstrong
2003-present. Tube combo amps and cabinets built by Wayne Jones in Asheville, North Carolina.

Henriksen JazzAmp
2006-present. Professional grade, production, solidstate amps voiced for jazz guitar built by Peter Henriksen in Golden, Colorado.

Heritage
Founded in 2004 by Malcolm MacDonald and Lane Zastrow who was formerly involved with Holland amps. Located in the former Holland facility in Brentwood, Tennessee, they built tube combo and piggyback amps.

Hilgen
1960s. Mid-level amplifiers from Hilgen Manufacturing, Hillside, New Jersey. Dark tolex covering and swiggle-lined light color grille cloth. Examples have been found with original Jensen speakers.
Basso B-2501 Amp
1960s. 25 watts, 1x15" combo, swirl grille, Hilgen crest logo, compact size.

1965		$350	$450

Basso B-2502 Amp
1960s. 25 watts, 1x15" combo, swirl grille, Hilgen crest logo, large cab.

1965		$375	$500

Basso Grande B-2503 Amp
1960s. Brown sparkle cover, piggyback, 2x12".

1965		$500	$650

Basso Profondo B-2502 Amp
1965. Combo 1x15".

1965		$375	$500

Champion R-2523 Amp
Mid-1960s. Highest offering in their amp line, piggyback with 2x12" cab, tremolo, reverb, swirl grille cloth.

1965		$500	$650

Galaxie T-2513 Amp
1960s. 25 watts, 2x12" piggyback cab, tremolo.

1965		$500	$650

Metero T-2511 Amp
Mid-1960s. Compact 1x12" combo, tremolo.

1965		$375	$500

Pacesetter R-2521 Amp
Mid-1960s. 1x12" combo, tremolo, reverb, swirl grille cloth.

1965		$375	$500

Star T-2512 Amp
1960s. 25 watts, 1x12" combo, tremolo.

1965		$375	$500

Troubadour T-1506 Amp
Mid-1960s. Small practice amp.

1965		$275	$350

Victor R-2522 Amp
Mid-1960s. 1x12" combo, larger cab, reverb, tremolo.

1965		$500	$650

HiWatt
1963-1984, ca.1990-present. Amp builder Dave Reeves started his Hylight Electronics in a garage in England in the early 1960s, doing amp and other electronic repairs. By 1964 he had produced the first amps bearing the Hiwatt brand. By the early '70s,

MODEL YEAR	FEATURES	EXC. COND. LOW	HIGH

Hiwatt's reputation was growing and production was moved to a factory in Kingston-upon-Thames, expanding the amp line and adding PA gear. In '81, Reeves suffered a fatal fall, and ownership of Hiwatt was taken over by Biacrown Ltd, a company made up of Hiwatt employees. Biacrown struggled and closed up in '84. From ca.1990 to ca.1994, a line of American-made Hiwatts, designed by Frank Levi, were available. By the mid-'90s, amps with the Hiwatt brand were again being built in England and, separately, imported from Asia by Fernandes.

Bass 100 Amp Head

1980s	100w, England	$1,300	$1,700

Bulldog SA112 Amp
1980s, 1994-2019. 50 watts, combo, 1x12".

1980s		$1,200	$1,575
1994-2019		$1,100	$1,475

Bulldog SA112FL Amp
1980s-1990s. 100 watts, combo, 1x12".

1980s		$1,200	$1,575
1990s		$1,100	$1,475

Custom 100 Amp Head

2007	100w	$1,300	$1,700

DR-103 Custom 100 Amp Head
1970-late-1980s, 2005-present. Tube head, 100 watts, custom Hiwatt 100 logo on front.

1970-1980s		$2,100	$2,700

DR-201 Hiwatt 200 Amp Head
1970s. 200-watt amp head, Hiwatt 200 logo on front.

1970s		$2,100	$2,700

DR-405 Hiwatt 400 Amp Head
1970s. 400-watt amp head.

1970s		$2,100	$2,700

DR-504 Custom 50 Amp Head
1970-late-1980s, 1995-1999. Tube head, 50 watts.

1970-1980s		$2,100	$2,700

Lead 20 (SG-20) Amp Head
1980s. Tube amp head, 30 watts, black cover, rectangular HiWatt plate logo.

1980s		$575	$750

Lead 50R Combo Amp
1980s. Combo tube amp, 50 watts, 1x12", reverb, dark cover, dark grille, HiWatt rectangular plate logo.

1980s		$825	$1,100

OL-103 Lead 100 Amp Head

1982	100w, England	$1,200	$1,575

PW-50 Tube Amp
1989-1993. Stereo tube amp, 50 watts per channel.

1989-1993		$825	$1,075

S50L Amp Head
1989-1993. Lead guitar head, 50 watts, gain, master volume, EQ.

1989-1993		$725	$950

SA 112 Combo Amp

1970s	50w, 1x12"	$2,500	$3,250

SA 212 Combo Amp

1970s	50w, 2x12"	$2,700	$3,500

SA 412 Combo Amp

1970s	50w, 4x12"	$3,300	$4,350

SE 2150 Speaker Cabinet

1970s	2x15" vertical	$1,750	$2,300

SE 4121 Speaker Cabinet

1970s	4x12", half stack	$1,825	$2,425

SE 4122 (Lead) Speaker Cabinet
1971- mid-1980s. 4x12", Fane speakers, 300 watts.

1971-1980s	4x12", half stack	$1,825	$2,425

SE 4123 (Bass) Speaker Cabinet
1970s. Bass version of SE, often used with DR103 head, straight-front cab and stackable, black tolex with gray grille, Hiwatt logo plate in center of grille.

1970s		$1,825	$2,425

SE 4129 (Bass) Speaker Cabinet
1970s. SE series for bass, 4x12", often used with DR 201 head.

1970s		$1,825	$2,425

SE 4151 Speaker Cabinet
1970s. SE series with 4x15".

1970s		$1,825	$2,425

Hoagland

Professional grade, production, guitar amps built by Dan Hoagland in Land O Lakes, Florida starting in 2008.

Hoffman

1993-present. Tube amps, combos, reverb units, and cabinets built by Doug Hoffman from 1993 to '99, in Sarasota, Florida. Hoffman no longer builds amps, concentrating on selling tube amp building supplies, and since 2001 has been located in Pisgah Forest, North Carolina.

Hoffmann

1983-present. Tube amp heads for guitar and other musical instruments built by Kim Hoffmann in Hawthorne, California.

Hohner

1857-present. Matthias Hohner, a clockmaker in Trossingen, Germany, founded Hohner in 1857, making harmonicas. Hohner has been offering guitars and amps at least since the early '70s.

Panther Series Amps
1980s. Smaller combo amps, master volume, gain, EQ.

1980s	P-12, 12w	$65	$90
1980s	P-20, 20w	$70	$95
1980s	P-25R, 25w	$70	$95
1980s	PBK-20, 25w	$75	$100

Sound Producer Series Amps
1980s. Master volume, normal and overdrive, reverb, headphone jack.

1980s	BA 130 bass	$75	$100
1980s	SP 35	$75	$100
1980s	SP 55	$75	$100
1980s	SP 75	$95	$125

Holland

1992-2004. Tube combo amps from builder Mike Holland, originally in Virginia Beach, Virginia, and since 2000 in Brentwood, Tennessee. In 2000, Holland took Lane Zastrow as a partner, forming L&M Amplifiers to build the Holland line. The company closed in '04.

Henriksen JazzAmp

AMPS

HiWatt Bulldog SA112

1977 HiWatt DR-505 Head
Imaged by Heritage Auctions, HA.com

MODEL YEAR	FEATURES	EXC. COND. LOW	HIGH

Holmes Pro 112

Holmes

1970-late 1980s. Founded by Harrison Holmes. Holmes amplifiers were manufactured in Mississippi and their product line included guitar and bass amps, PA systems, and mixing boards. In the early '80s, Harrsion Holmes sold the company to On-Site Music which called the firm The Holmes Corp. Products manufactured by Harrison have an all-caps HOLMES logo and the serial number plate says The Holmes Company.

Performer PB-115 Bass Amp
60 watts, 1x15", black tolex.

1982		$100	$140

Pro Compact 210S Amp
60 watts, 2x10", 2 channels, active EQ, black tolex.

1982		$100	$140

Pro Compact 212S Amp
2x12" version of Pro.

1982		$130	$170

Rebel RB-112 Bass Amp
35 watts, 1x12", black tolex.

1982		$80	$105

Hondo

1969-1987, 1991-2005. Hondo has offered imported amps over the years. 1990s models ranged from the H20 Practice Amp to the H160SRC with 160 watts (peak) and 2x10" speakers.

Amps
1970s-1990s. Various models.

1970s-90s	Mid-size	$40	$70
1970s-90s	Small	$20	$30

Hottie Super Chef

Hottie

Jean-Claude Escudie and Mike Bernards build their budget and intermediate grade, production/custom, solid state "toaster" amps in Portland, Oregon, starting in 2005. They also offered guitars in '09.

Hound Dog

1994-1998. Founded by George Alessandro as the Hound Dog Corporation. Name was changed to Alessandro in 1998 (see that brand for more information).

Hughes & Kettner

1985-present. Hughes & Kettner offers a line of solidstate and tube guitar and bass amps, combos, cabinets and effects, all made in Germany.

Humphrey

2010-present. Custom, professional and premium grade, tube amps built in Chanhassen, Minnesota by Gerry Humphrey. He also builds preamps and reverb units.

Hurricane

Tube guitar and harmonica combo amps built by Gary Drouin in Sarasota, Florida. Drouin started the company in 1998 with harp master Rock Bottom, who died in September, 2001.

Hughes & Kettner Duotone

MODEL YEAR	FEATURES	EXC. COND. LOW	HIGH

Hy Lo

1960s-1970s. Budget grade, small compact amps made in Japan, Hy Lo logo on grille.

Ibanez

1932-present. Ibanez added solidstate amps to their product line in '98. They also build guitars, basses and effects.

Idol

Late-1960s. Made in Japan. Dark tolex cover, dark grille, Hobby Series with large Idol logo on front.

Hobby Series Amps

1968	Hobby 10	$80	$110
1968	Hobby 100	$165	$225
1968	Hobby 20	$95	$124
1968	Hobby 45	$150	$200

Impact

1963-early 1970s. Based in London, England, tube amps made by Don Mackrill and Laurie Naiff for Pan Musical Instrument Company and their music stores. About a dozen different models of combos, piggyback half-stacks and PAs were offered.

Imperial

Ca.1963-ca.1970. The Imperial Accordion Company of Chicago, Illinois offered one or two imported small amps in the '60s.

Jack Daniel's

2004-2017. Tube guitar amp built by Peavey for the Jack Daniel Distillery, offered until about '10. They offered guitars until '17.

Jackson

1980-present. The Jackson-Charvel Company offered budget to intermediate grade amps and cabinets in the late '80s and the '90s.

Jackson Ampworks

2001-present. Brad Jackson builds his tube amp heads and speaker cabinets in Bedford, Texas.

Jackson-Guldan

1920s-1960s. The Jackson-Guldan Violin Company, of Columbus, Ohio, offered lap steels and small tube amps early on. They also built acoustic guitars.

Jay Turser

1997-present. Smaller, inexpensive imported solidstate guitar and bass amps. They also offer basses and guitars.

JCA Circuits

Tube guitar combo amps built by Jason C. Arthur in Pottstown, Pennsylvania, starting in 1995.

MODEL		EXC. COND.	
YEAR	FEATURES	LOW	HIGH

Jennings

Late 1960s. Tom Jennings formed another company after resigning from Vox. Large block letter Jennings logo on front panel, Jennings Amplifier logo on back control plate with model number and serial number.

Jet City Amplification

2009-present. Budget to professional grade, production/custom, guitar amps and cabinets designed in Seattle, Washington by Doug White, Dan Gallagher, Michael Soldano and built in Asia.

Jim Kelley

1979-1985. Channel-switching tube amps, compact combos and heads, hardwood cabinets available, made by Jim Kelley at his Active Guitar Electronics in Tustin, California. He produced about 100 amps a year. In 1978 and early '79 he produced a few amps under the Fortune brand name for Fortune Guitars.

JMI (Jennings Musical Industries)

2004-present. Jennings built the Vox amps of the 1960s. They are back with tube amp heads and cabinets based on some of their classic models.

Johnson

Mid-1990s-present. Line of solidstate amps imported by Music Link, Brisbane, California. Johnson also offers guitars, basses, mandolins and effects.

Johnson Amplification

Starting in 1997, intermediate and professional grade, production, modeling amps and effects designed by John Johnson, of Sandy, Utah. The company is part of Harman International. In 2002, they quit building amps, but continue the effects line.

JoMama

1994-present. Tube amps and combos under the JoMama and Kelemen brands built by Joe Kelemen in Santa Fe, New Mexico.

Jordan

1966-early 1970s. Jordan Electronics, of Alhambra, California, built a range of electronics, including, starting around 1966, solid state guitar amps and effects.

Juke

1989-present. Tube guitar and harmonica amps built by G.R. Croteau in Troy, New Hampshire. He also built the Warbler line of amps.

Kafel

Jack Kafel built his tube amp heads in Chicago, Illinois, starting in 2004.

MODEL		EXC. COND.	
YEAR	FEATURES	LOW	HIGH

Kalamazoo

1933-1942, 1965-1970. Kalamazoo was a brand Gibson used on one of their budget lines. They used the name on amps from '65 to '67.

Bass Amp
1965-1967. Enclosed back, 2x10", flip-out control panel, not a commonly found model as compared to numerous Model 1 and 2 student amps.

1965-1967		$500	$650

Bass 30 Amp
Late 1960s-early 1970s. Tube combo, verticle cabinet, 2x10".

1970		$375	$500

KEA Amp
1948-1952. Small compact amp, round speaker baffle grille, slant Kalamazoo logo on front, oxblood leatherette.

1948-1952		$400	$525

Lap Steel Amp
1940s. Kalamazoo logo on front lower right, low power with 1-6V6, round speaker grille opening, red/brown leatherette.

1940s		$350	$450

Model 1 Amp
1965-1967. No tremolo, 1x10", front control panel, black.

1965-1967		$250	$325

Model 2 Amp
1965-1967. Same as Model 1 with tremolo, black.

1965-1967	Black panel	$325	$425
1967	Silver panel	$200	$250

Model 3 Amp
Late 1960s-early 1970s. Made by CMI Electronics in Chicago, post Gibson Kalamazoo era, student compact solidstate combo, Kalamazoo 3 logo on front panel, Kalamazoo Model 3 logo on label on speaker magnet.

1960s-70s		$90	$115

Model 4 Amp
Late 1960s-early 1970s. Made by CMI Electronics in Chicago, post Gibson Kalamazoo era, student compact solidstate combo, 3 control knobs, tone, tremolo, volume, Kalamazoo 4 logo on front panel, Kalamazoo Model 4 logo on label on speaker magnet.

1960s-70s		$90	$115

Reverb 12 Amp
1965-1967. Black vinyl cover, 1x12", reverb, tremolo.

1965-1967		$500	$650

Kay

Ca.1931-present. Kay originally offered amps up to around '68 when the brand changed hands. Currently they offer a couple small solidstate imported amps. They also make basses, guitars, banjos, mandolins, ukes, and violins.

K506 Vibrato 12" Amp
1960s. 12 watts, 1x12", swirl grille, metal handle.

1960s		$375	$500

K507 Twin Ten Special Amp
1960s. 20 watts, 2x10", swirl grille, metal handle.

1960s		$425	$550

Jackson Ampworks The McFly

Kafel S150 Head

1963 Kalamazoo Bass 30
Rivington Guitars

AMPS

Kelemen JoMama OverDrive

2019 Kendrick Double Trouble 2x10" Combo Amp

Kingsley ToneBaron

K700 Series Amp
Introduced in 1965. Value Leader/Vanguard/Galazie models, transistorized amps promoted as eliminates tube-changing annoyance and reliable performance, combo amps with tapered cabinets, rear slant control panel, rich brown and tan vinyl cover, brown grille cloth.

Year	Features	Low	High
1965	700, 1x8"	$100	$150
1965	703, 1x8"	$100	$150
1965	704, 1x8"	$100	$150
1965	705, 1x10"	$125	$175
1965	706, 1x15"	$125	$175
1965	707, 1x12"	$125	$175
1965	708, 1x12"	$125	$175
1965	720 bass, 1x15"	$125	$175
1966	760, 1x12"	$125	$175

Model 703 Amp
1962-1964. Tube student amp, small speaker, 3 tubes, 1 volume, 1 tone, 2-tone white front with brown back cabinet, metal handle, model number noted on back panel, Kay logo and model number badge lower front right.

Year		Low	High
1962-1964		$200	$275

Model 803 Amp
1962-1964. Student amp, 1x8", 3 tubes, 1 volume, 1 tone, metal handle, 14.75x11.75x6.75" cabinet with dark gray cover.

1962-1964		$200	$275

Model 805 Amp
1965. Solidstate, 35 watts, 1x10", 4 control knobs, 2-tone cabinet.

1965		$115	$155

Small Tube Amp
Year	Features	Low	High
1940s	Wood cabinet	$275	$375
1950s	Various models	$275	$375
1960s	Models K503, K504, K505	$325	$425

Kelemen
1994-present. Tube amps and combos under the JoMama and Kelemen brands built by Joe Kelemen in Santa Fe, New Mexico.

Kendrick
1989-present. Founded by Gerald Weber in Austin, Texas and currently located in Kempner, Texas. Mainly known for their intermediate to professional grade, tube amps, Kendrick also offers guitars, speakers, and effects.

Kent
Ca.1962-1969. Imported budget line of guitars and amps.
Guitar and Bass Amps
1960s. Various models.

Year	Features	Low	High
1966	1475, 3 tubes, brown	$55	$80
1966	2198, 3 tubes, brown	$55	$80
1966	5999, 3 tubes, brown	$75	$110
1966	6104, piggyback, 12w	$115	$155
1969	6610, solidstate, small	$35	$50

Kiesel
See Guitar section.

King Amplification
Tube combo amps, head and cabinets built by Val King in San Jose, California startin in 2005.

Kingsley
1998-present. Production/custom, professional grade, tube amps and cabinets built by Simon Jarrett in Vancouver, British Columbia.

Kingston
1958-1967. Economy solidstate amps imported by Westheimer Importing, Chicago, Illinois.
Cat Series Amp
Mid-1960s. Solidstate Cat Series amps have dark vinyl, dark grilles.

Year	Features	Low	High
1960s	P-1 3w, P-2 5w	$50	$75
1960s	P-3 8w, P-8T 20w	$55	$80

Cougar BA-21 Bass Piggyback Amp
Mid-1960s. Solidstate, 60 watts, 2x12" cab, dark vinyl, light silver grille.

1960s		$110	$160

Cougar PB-5 Bass Combo Amp
Mid-1960s. Solidstate, 15 watts, 1x8".

1960s		$55	$90

Lion 2000 Piggyback Amp
Mid-1960s. Solidstate, 90 watts, 2x12" cab.

1960s		$140	$190

Lion 3000 Piggyback Amp
Mid-1960s. Solidstate, 250 watts, 4x12" cab.

1960s		$175	$225

Lion AP-281 R Piggyback Amp
Mid-1960s. Solidstate, 30 watts, 2x8" cab, dark vinyl cover, light silver grille.

1960s		$100	$150

Lion AP-281 R10 Piggyback Amp
Mid-1960s. Solidstate, 30 watts, 2x10" cab.

1960s		$125	$175

Kinsman
2012-present. Budget and intermediate grade, production, guitar amps and cabinets built in China and distributed worldwide by John Hornby Skewes & Co. Ltd. in England. They also use the brand on a line of guitar effects.

Kitchen-Marshall
1965-1966. Private branded for Kitchen Music by Marshall, primarily PA units with block logos. Limited production.
JTM 45 MKII 45-Watt Amp Head
1965-1966. Private branded for Kitchen Music, JTM 45 Marshall with Kitchen logo plate, 45 watts.

1965-1966		$5,500	$7,200

Slant 4x12 1960 Cabinet
1965-1966. Slant front 4x12" 1960-style cab with gray bluesbreaker grille, very limited production.

1965-1966	Black on green vinyl	$3,300	$4,400

MODEL		EXC. COND.	
YEAR	FEATURES	LOW	HIGH

KJL

1995-present. Founded by Kenny Lannes, MSEE, a professor of Electrical Engineering at the University of New Orleans. KJL makes budget to intermediate grade, tube combo amps, heads and an ABY box.

KMD (Kaman)

1986-ca.1990. Distributed by Kaman (Ovation, Hamer, etc.) in the late '80s, KMD offered a variety of amps and effects.

Koch

All-tube combo amps, heads, effects and cabinets built in The Netherlands.

Komet

1999-present. Intermediate to professional grade, tube amp heads built in Baton Rouge, Louisanna, by Holger Notzel and Michael Kennedy with circuits designed by Ken Fischer of Trainwreck fame. They also build a power attenuator.

Kona Guitar Company

2001-present. Budget solidstate amps made in Asia. They also offer guitars, basses, mandolins, ukes and banjos.

Krank

1996-2013, 2015-present. Founded by Tony Krank and offering tube amp heads, combos and speaker cabinets built in Tempe, Arizona. They also build effects.

Kustom

1965-present. Kustom, a division of Hanser Holdings, offers guitar and bass combo amps and PA equipment. Founded by Bud Ross in Chanute, Kansas, who offered tuck-and-roll amps as early as '58, but began using the Kustom brand name in '65. From '69 to '75 Ross gradually sold interest in the company (in the late '70s, Ross introduced the line of Ross effects stomp boxes). The brand changed hands a few times, and by the mid-'80s it was no longer in use. In '89 Kustom was in bankruptcy court and was purchased by Hanser Holdings Incorporated of Cincinnati, Ohio (Davitt & Hanser) and by '94, they had a new line of amps available.

Prices are for excellent condition amps with no tears in the tuck-and-roll cover and no grille tears. A tear in the tuck-and-roll will reduce the value, sometimes significantly.

Kustom model identification can be frustrating as they used series numbers, catalog numbers (the numbers in the catalogs and price lists), and model numbers (the number often found next to the serial number on the amp's back panel). Most of the discussion that follows is by series number (100, 200, 300, etc.) and catalog number. Unfortunately, vintage amp dealers use the serial number and model number, so the best way is to cross-check

speaker and amplifier attributes. Model numbers were used primarily for repair purposes and were found in the repair manuals. In many, but not all cases, the model number is the last digit of the catalog number; for example the catalog lists a 100 series Model 1-15J-1, where the last digit 1 signifies a Model 1 amplifier chassis which is a basic amp without reverb or tremolo. A Model 1-15J-2 signifies a Model 2 amp chassis that has reverb and tremolo. In this example, Kustom uses a different model number on the back of the amp head. For the 1-15J-2, the model number on the back panel of the amp head would be K100-2, indicating a series 100 (50 watts) amp with reverb and tremolo (amp chassis Model 2).

Model numbers relate to the amplifier's schematic and electronics, while catalog numbers describe the amp's relative power rating and speaker configuration.

Amp Chasis Model Numbers ('68-'72)
Model 1 Amp (basic)
Model 2 Amp with reverb
Model 3 Amp with Harmonic Clip and Boost
Model 4 Amp with reverb, tremolo, vibrato, Harmonic Clip and Selective Boost
Model 5 PA with reverb
Model 6 Amp (basic) with Selectone
Model 7 Amp with reverb, tremolo, vibrato, boost (different parts)
Model 8 Amp with reverb, tremolo, vibrato, boost (different parts)

Naugahyde Tuck-&-Roll 200 ('65-'67)
The very first Kustoms did not have the model series on the front control panel. The early logo stipulated Kustom by Ross, Inc. The name was then updated to Kustom Electronics, Inc. 1965-'67 amp heads have a high profile/tall "forehead" area (the area on top of the controls) and these have been nicknamed "Frankenstein models." The '65-'67 catalog numbers were often 4 or 5 digits, for example J695. The first digit represents the speaker type (J = Jensen, etc.), other examples are L995, L1195, L795RV, etc. Some '67 catalog numbers changed to 2 digits followed by 3 digits, like 4-D 140f, or 3-15C (3 CTS speakers), etc. Others sported 5 characters like 4-15J-1, where 4 = 4 speakers, 15 = 15" speakers, J = Jensen, and 1 = basic amp chassis with no effects. The fifth digit indicated amp chassis model number as described above.

Naugahyde Tuck-&-Roll 100/200/400 ('68-'71)
Starting in '68, the Kustom logo also included the model series. A K100, for example, would have 100 displayed below the Kustom name. The model series generally is twice the relative output wattage, for example, the 100 Series is a 50-watt amp. Keep in mind, solidstate ratings are often higher than tube-amp ratings, so use the ratings as relative measurements. Most '68-'70 Kustom catalog numbers are x-xxx-x, for example 1-15L-1.

KJL Companion

Krank 10 Watt Combo

1971 Kustom K150-8
Tom Pfeifer

AMPS

1970s Kustom Hustler
Imaged by Heritage Auctions, HA.com

1972 Kustom K50-2 SC
Randy Bacus

*1971 Kustom K100 Head
and Matching Cabinet*
Bob Calla

First digit represents the number of speakers, the 2nd and 3rd represent the speaker size, the fourth represents the speaker type (A = Altec Lansing, L = J.B.L., J = Jensen, C = C.T.S. Bass), the fifth digit represents the amp chassis number. The power units were interchangeable in production, so amps could have similar front-ends but different power units (more power and different effect options) and visa versa. Some '68 bass amp catalog numbers were 4 digits, for example 2-12C, meaning two 12" CTS speakers. Again, there were several different numbers used. Kustom also introduced the 200 and 400 amp series and the logo included the series number. The catalog numbers were similar to the 100 series, but they had a higher power rating of 100 equivalent watts (200 series), or 200 equivalent watts (400 series). Kustom U.S. Naugahyde (tuck-&-roll) covers came in 7 colors: black (the most common), Cascade (blue/green), silver (white-silver), gold (light gold), red, blue, and Charcoal (gray). The market historically shows color options fetching more. The market has not noticeably distinguished power and features options. Condition and color seem to be the most important. Gold and Cascade may be the rarest seen colors.

Naugahyde Tuck-&-Roll 150/250/300/500/600 (c.'71-c.'75)
The amp heads changed with a slightly slanted control panel and the Kustom logo moved to the right/upper-right portion of the front panel. They continued to be tuck-&-roll offered in the same variety of colors. The sales literature indicated a 150 series had 150 watts, 250 had 250 watts, etc.

Naugahyde Tuck-&-Roll SC (Self Contained) Series
Most SC combo amps were rated at 150 watts, with the 1-12SC listed at 50 watts. They were offered in 7 colors of tuck-and-roll. Again the model numbers indicate the features as follows: 4-10 SC is a 4 x 10", 2-10 SC is a 2x10", etc.

Super Sound Tuck-and-Roll Combo Series
The last tuck-and-roll combo amps with slightly smaller tucks. Amp control panel is noticeably smaller and the Kustom logo is in the right side of the control panel.

Black Vinyl ('75-c.'78)
By '75 ownership changes were complete and the colorful tuck-and-roll was dropped in favor of more traditional black vinyl. The products had a slant Kustom logo spelled-out and placed in a position on the grille similar to a Fender blackface baffle. Models included the I, II, III, and IV Lead amps. Heads with half- and full-stacks were available. Bass amps included the Kustom 1, Bass I, II, III, IV, and IV SRO.
Black Vinyl K logo ('78-'83)

MODEL YEAR	FEATURES	EXC. COND. LOW	HIGH
This era is easily recognized by the prominent capital K logo.			
Bass V Amp			
1990s. Large Kustom Bass V logo upper right side of amp, 35 watts, 1x12", black vinyl.			
1990s		$60	$85
Challenger Combo Amp			
1973-1975. 1x12" speaker.			
1973-1975	Black	$200	$275
1973-1975	Color option	$275	$375
Hustler Combo Amp			
1973-1975. Solidstate, 4x10", tremolo, tuck-and-roll.			
1973-1975	Black	$225	$300
1973-1975	Color option	$300	$400
K25/K25 C-2 SC Amp			
1960s. SC (self-contained) Series, small combo tuck-and-roll, 1x12", solidstate, reverb, black control panel.			
1971-1973	Black	$200	$275
1971-1973	Color option	$300	$400
K50-2 SC Amp			
1971-1973. Self-contained (SC) small combo tuck-and-roll, 1x12", reverb and tremolo.			
1971-1973	Black	$200	$275
1971-1973	Color option	$300	$400
K100-1 1-15C Bass Amp Set			
1968-1972. The K100-1 with 1-15C speaker option with matching 1x15" cab, black tuck-and-roll standard, but several sparkle colors offered, C.T.S. bass reflex speaker.			
1968-1972	Black	$200	$275
1968-1972	Color option	$300	$400
K100-1 1-15L-1/1-15A-1/1-15J-1 Amp Set			
1968-1972. K100-1 with matching 1x15" cab, black tuck-and-roll standard, but several colors offered, speaker options are JBL, Altec Lansing or Jensen.			
1968-1972	Black	$200	$275
1968-1972	Color option	$300	$400
K100-1 1-D140F Bass Amp			
1968-1972. K100-1 with matching 1x15" JBL D-140F cab, black tuck-and-roll standard, but several sparkle colors offered.			
1968-1972	Black	$200	$275
1968-1972	Color option	$300	$400
K100-1 2-12C Bass Amp Set			
1968-1972. K100-1 with matching 2x12" cab, black tuck-and-roll standard, but several sparkle colors offered, C.T.S. bass reflex speakers.			
1968-1972	Black	$250	$325
1968-1972	Color option	$500	$700
K100-2 1-15L-2/1-15A-2/1-15J-2 Amp Set			
1968-1972. K100-2 head and matching 1x15" cab, black tuck-and-roll standard, but several sparkle colors offered.			
1968-1972	Black	$200	$275
1968-1972	Color option	$300	$400
K100-2 2-12A-2/2-12J-2 Amp Set			
1968-1972. K100-2 head with matching 2x12" cab, black tuck-and-roll standard, but several sparkle colors offered.			
1968-1972	Black	$250	$325
1968-1972	Color option	$500	$700

MODEL YEAR	FEATURES	EXC. COND. LOW	HIGH

K100-5 PA Amp Head
1968-1972. 50 watts, 2 channels with 8 control knobs per channel, reverb.

| 1968-1972 | Black | $275 | $375 |

K100-6 SC Amp
1970-1972. Basic combo amp with selectone, no reverb.

| 1970-1972 | Black | $175 | $230 |

K100-7 SC Amp
1970-1972. Combo amp with reverb, tremolo, vibrato and boost.

| 1970-1972 | Black | $200 | $275 |
| 1970-1972 | Color option | $300 | $400 |

K100-8 SC Amp
1970-1972. Combo amp with reverb, tremolo, vibrato and boost.

| 1970-1972 | Black | $200 | $275 |
| 1970-1972 | Color option | $300 | $400 |

K100C-6 Combo Amp
1968-1970. Kustom 100 logo middle of the front control panel, 1x15" combo, selectone option.

| 1968-1970 | Black | $200 | $275 |
| 1968-1970 | Color option | $300 | $400 |

K100C-8 Combo Amp
1968-1970. Kustom 100 logo middle of the front control panel, 4x10" combo, reverb, tremolo, vibrato.

| 1968-1970 | Black | $275 | $375 |

K150-1 Amp Set
1972-1975. Piggyback, 150 watts, 2x12", no reverb, logo in upper right corner of amp head, tuck-and-roll, black or color option.

| 1972-1975 | Color option | $300 | $400 |

K150-2 Amp Set
1972-1975. K150 with added reverb and tremolo, piggyback, 2x12", tuck-and-roll, black or color option.

| 1972-1975 | Color option | $300 | $400 |

K150-5 PA Amp Set
1972-1975. PA head plus 2 PA cabs.

| 1972-1975 | | $250 | $335 |

K150/150C Combo Amp
1972-1975. Combo, 2x10".

| 1972-1975 | Black | $200 | $260 |

K200-1/K200B Bass Amp Set
1966-1972. K200 head with 2x15" cab.

| 1966-1972 | Black | $300 | $400 |
| 1966-1972 | Color option | $450 | $600 |

K200-2 Reverb/Tremolo Amp Set
1966-1972. K200-2 head with 2x15" or 3x12" cab, available with JBL D-140F speakers, Altec Lansing (A) speakers, C.T.S. (C), or Jensen (J).

| 1966-1972 | Black | $300 | $400 |
| 1966-1972 | Color option | $450 | $600 |

K250 Amp Set
1971-1975. K250 head with 2x15" cab, tuck-and-roll cover.

| 1971-1975 | Black | $265 | $350 |
| 1971-1975 | Color option | $475 | $625 |

K300 PA Amp and Speaker Set
1971-1975. Includes 302 PA, 303 PA, 304 PA, 305 PA, head and 2 cabs.

| 1971-1975 | Color option | $450 | $600 |

K400-2 Reverb/Tremolo Amp Set
1968-1972. 200 relative watts, reverb, tremolo, with 6x12" or 8x12" cab, available with JBL D-140F speakers, Altec Lansing (A), C.T.S. (C), or Jensen (J). The K400 was offered with no effects (suffix 1), with reverb and tremolo (suffix 2), with Harmonic Clipper & Boost (suffix 3), and Reverb/Trem/Clipper/Boost (suffix 4). The 400 heads came with a separate chrome amp head stand.

| 1968-1972 | Black | $250 | $325 |
| 1968-1972 | Color option | $475 | $625 |

KBA-10 Combo Amp
Late-1980s-1990s. Compact solidstate bass amp, 10 watts, 1x8".

| 1990s | | $30 | $40 |

KBA-20 Combo Amp
Late-1980s-early-1990s. KBA series were compact solidstate bass amps with built-in limiter, 20 watts, 1x8".

| 1989-1990 | | $30 | $40 |

KBA-30 Combo Amp
Late-1980s-early-1990s. 30 watts, 1x10".

| 1989-1990 | | $30 | $40 |

KBA-40 Combo Amp
Late-1980s-early-1990s. 40 watts, 1x12".

| 1989-1990 | | $55 | $75 |

KBA-80 Combo Amp
Late-1980s-early-1990s. 80 watts, 1x15".

| 1989-1990 | | $80 | $105 |

KBA-160 Combo Amp
Late-1980s-early-1990s. Solidstate bass amp with built-in limiter, 160 watts, 1x15".

| 1989-1990 | | $110 | $150 |

KGA-10 VC Amp
1999-2006. 10 watts, 1x6.5" speaker, switchable overdrive.

| 1999-2006 | | $30 | $40 |

KLA-15 Combo Amp
Late-1980s-early-1990s. Solidstate, overdrive, 15 watts, 1x8".

| 1989-1990 | | $55 | $75 |

KLA-20 Amp
Mid-1980s-late-1980s. 1x10", MOS-FET, gain, EQ, reverb, headphone jack.

| 1986 | | $55 | $75 |

KLA-25 Combo Amp
Late-1980s-early-1990s. Solidstate, overdrive, reverb, 25 watts, 1x10".

| 1989-1990 | | $55 | $75 |

KLA-50 Combo Amp
Late-1980s-early-1990s. Solidstate, overdrive, reverb, 50 watts, 1x12".

| 1989-1990 | | $80 | $105 |

KLA-75 Amp
Mid-1980s-late-1980s. 75 watts, reverb, footswitching.

| 1987 | | $110 | $145 |

KLA-100 Combo Amp
Late-1980s-early-1990s. Solidstate, reverb, 100-watt dual channel, 1x12".

| 1989-1990 | | $110 | $145 |

Kustom K150C
Randy Bacus

1970s Kustom K250
Tom Pfeifer

1965 Kustom K400
Craig Brody

AMPS

Laboga AD5200 SA
Carter Vintage Guitars

Lace 20 Watt

Landry LS100

MODEL YEAR	FEATURES	EXC. COND. LOW	HIGH

KLA-185 Combo Amp
Late-1980s-early-1990s. Solidstate, reverb, 185-watt dual channel, 1x12".

1989-1990		$130	$170

KPB-200 Bass Combo Amp
1994-1997. 200 watts, 1x15".

1994-1997		$210	$275

SC 1-12 SC Amp
1971-1973. 50 watts, 1x12" Jensen speaker.

1971-1973	Black	$200	$275
1971-1973	Color option	$300	$400

SC 1-15 SC Amp
1971-1973. 150 watts, 1x15" C.T.S. speaker.

1971-1973	Black	$200	$275
1971-1973	Color option	$300	$400

SC 1-15AB SC Amp
1971-1973. 150 watts, 1x15" Altec Lansing speaker.

1971-1973	Black	$200	$275
1971-1973	Color option	$300	$400

SC 2-12A SC Amp
1971-1973. 150 watts, 2x12" Altec Lansing speakers.

1971-1973	Black	$225	$300
1971-1973	Color option	$300	$400

SC 2-12J SC Amp
1971-1973. 150 watts, 2x12" Jensen speakers.

1971-1973	Black	$225	$300
1971-1973	Color option	$300	$400

SC 4-10 SC Amp
1971-1973. 150 watts, 4x10" Jensen speakers.

1971-1973	Black	$225	$300
1971-1973	Color option	$300	$400

Lab Series

1977-1980s. Five models of Lab Series amps, ranging in price from $600 to $3,700, were introduced at the '77 NAMM show by Norlin (then owner of Gibson). Two more were added later. The '80s models were Lab Series 2 amps and had a Gibson logo on the upper-left front.

B120 Bass Amp Combo
Ca.1984. 120 watts, 2 channels, 1x15".

1984		$250	$325

G120 R-10 Amp Combo
Ca.1984. 120 watts, 3-band EQ, channel switching, reverb, 4x10".

1984		$275	$375

G120 R-12 Amp Combo
Ca.1984. 120 watts, 3-band EQ, channel switching, reverb, 2x12".

1984		$275	$375

L2 Amp Head
1977-ca.1983. 100 watts, black covering.

1977-1983		$190	$250

L3 Amp Combo
1977-ca.1983. 60-watt 1x12".

1977-1983		$250	$325

L4 Amp Head
1977-ca.1983. Solidstate, 200 watts, black cover, dark grille, large L4 logo on front panel.

1977-1983		$190	$250

L5 Amp Combo
1977-ca.1983. Solidstate, 100 watts, 2x12" combo.

1977-1983		$275	$375

L5 Amp Set
1977-ca.1983. Solidstate, 100 watts, 2x12" piggyback.

1977-1983		$275	$375

L7 Amp Set
1977-ca.1983. Solidstate, 100 watts, 4x10" piggyback.

1977-1983		$325	$425

L9 Amp Combo
1977-ca.1983. Solidstate, 100 watts, 1x15".

1977-1983		$250	$325

L11 Amp Set
1977-ca.1983. 200 watts, 8x12" piggyback.

1977-1983		$350	$475

Laboga

1973-present. Adam Laboga builds intermediate and professional grade, production, tube guitar amps and cabinets in Wroclaw, Poland.

Lace Music Products

1979-present. Lace Music Products, founded by pickup innovator Don Lace Sr., offered amplifiers for a while starting in '96. They also offered amps under the Rat Fink and Mooneyes brands.

Lafayette

Ca.1963-1967. Japanese-made guitars and amps sold through the Lafayette Electronics catalogs.

Tube Amp
1960s. Japanese-made tube, gray speckle 1x12" with art deco design or black 2x12".

1960s	Larger, 2 speakers	$175	$225
1960s	Small, 1 speaker	$125	$175

Landry

2008-present. Production, professional grade, amps and cabinets built by Bill Landry in St. Louis, Missouri.

Laney

1968-present. Founded by Lyndon Laney and Bob Thomas in Birmingham, U.K. Laney offered tube amps exclusively into the '80s. Currently they offer intermediate and professional grade, tube and solidstate amp heads and combos and cabinets.

L60 60-Watt Amp Head
1968-1969. 60 watts

1968-1969		$1,100	$1,400

L100 100-Watt Amp Head
1968-1969. Similar to short head Plexi Marshall amp cab, 100 watts, large Laney with underlined "y" logo plate on front upper left corner, black vinyl cover, grayish grille.

1968-1969		$1,100	$1,400

Lectrolab

1950s-1960s. Budget house brand for music stores, made by Sound Projects Company of Cicero,

MODEL YEAR	FEATURES	EXC. COND. LOW	HIGH

Illinois. Similar to Valco, Oahu, and Danelectro student amps of the '50s, cabinets were generally made from inexpensive material. The Lectrolab logo can generally be found somewhere on the amp.

Tube Amp

| 1950s-60s | Larger | $300 | $400 |
| 1950s-60s | Small | $225 | $300 |

Legend
1978-1984. From Legend Musical Instruments of East Syracuse, New York, these amps featured cool wood cabinets. They offered heads, combos with a 1x12" or 2x12" configuration, and cabinets with 1x12", 1x15", 2x12" or 4x12".

A-30 Amp
1978-1984. Natural wood cabinet, 30 watts, 1x12".

| 1978-1984 | | $300 | $400 |

A-60 Amp
1978-1984. Natural wood cabinet, transtube design dual tube preamp with solidstate power section.

| 1978-1984 | | $375 | $500 |

Rock & Roll 50 Amp
1978-1983. Mesa-Boogie-style wood compact amp, head/half stack or 1x12", 1x15" or 2x12" combo, tube preamp section and solidstate power supply.

1978-1983	1x12" combo	$300	$400
1978-1983	1x15" combo	$300	$400
1978-1983	2x12" combo	$375	$500
1978-1983	Half Stack Set	$575	$750

Super Lead 50 Amp
1978-1983. Rock & Roll 50-watt model with added bass boost and reverb, 1x12", hybrid tube and solidstate.

| 1978-1983 | | $300 | $400 |

Super Lead 100 Amp
1978-1983. 100-watt version, 2x12".

| 1978-1983 | | $375 | $500 |

Lenahan
Professional grade, production/custom, vintage-style amps and cabinets built by James T. Lenahan – presently in Fort Smith, Arkansas and prior to '91 in Hollywood, California – starting in 1983. He also built guitar effects.

Leslie
Most often seen with Hammond organs, the cool Leslie rotating speakers have been adopted by many guitarists. Many guitar effects have tried to duplicate their sound. And they are still making them.

122 Amp/122RV Amp
A Hammond-only model, considered the official Hammond B-3 Leslie. RV indicates reverb.

| 1960s | | $700 | $950 |

125 Amp
Late-1960s. All tube amp with 2-speed rotating 1x12" speaker, bottom rotor only, less features.

| 1960s | | $475 | $625 |

142 Amp
A Hammond-only model, smaller cabinet than 122 Amp.

| 1960s | | $600 | $800 |

145 Amp
Similar to 147 Amp, but smaller and easier to move.

| 1960s | | $625 | $825 |

147 Amp/147RV Amp
A universal-use model, "7" denotes "universal" useage. RV has added reverb.

| 1960s | | $625 | $825 |

Lickliter Amplification
In 2009, Michael Lickliter began building professional and premium grade, custom, guitar amps in Punta Gorda, Florida.

Line 6
1996-present. Founded by Marcus Ryle and Michel Doidic and specializing in digital signal processing in both effects and amps. They also produce tube amps. Purchased by Yamaha in 2014.

Little Lanilei
1997-present. Small hand-made, intermediate grade, production/custom, amps made by Mahaffay Amplifiers (formerly Songworks Systems & Products) of Aliso Viejo, California. They also build a reverb unit and a rotary effect.

Little Walter
2008-present. Phil Bradbury builds his professional grade, production, amp heads and cabinets in West End, North Carolina.

London City
Late 1960s-early 1970s. Intermediate to professional grade amps and cabinets made in Netherlands, London City logo.

Louis Electric Amplifier Co.
1993-present. Founded by Louis Rosano in Bergenfield, New Jersey. Louis produces custom-built tweeds and various combo amps from 35 to 80 watts.

Luker
Professional grade, production/custom, guitar and bass amps and cabinets built in Eugene, Oregon by Ken Luker, starting in 2006.

Luna Guitars
2005-present. Located in Tampa, Florida, Yvonne de Villiers imports her budget to professional grade, production, acoustic and electric guitars from Japan, Korea and China. She also imports guitars, basses and ukes.

Lyric
Late 1950s-ca. 1965. One of several private brands that Magnatone made for others, these were built for Lyric Electronics, located in Lomita, California.

Model 660 Custom
Ca. 1959-ca. 1965. 2x12" combo amp, 35 watts.

| 1959-1965 | | $1,150 | $1,500 |

Laney L5T-1

Little Walter 9H10 Hipster
Shawn Penney

Louis Electric Columbia Reverb

AMPS

AMPS

Mack Atomsmasher DB-40

Mad Professor OS 21RT

1958 Maestro GA-45 Maestro
Rivington Guitars

Mack

2005-present. Made in Toronto, Ontario by builder Don Mackrill, the company offers intermediate and professional grade, production, tube amps.

Mad Professor

2002-present. Bjorn Juhl and Jukka Monkkonen build their premium grade, production/custom, tube amps in Tampere, Finland. They also offer effects pedals.

Maestro

Maestro amps are associated with Gibson and were included in the Gibson catalogs. For example, in the '62-'63 orange cover Gibson catalog, tweed Maestro amps were displayed in their own section. Tweed Maestro amps are very similar to Gibson tweed amps. Maestro amps were often associated with accordions in the early-'60s but the amps featured standard guitar inputs. Gibson also used the Maestro name on effects in the '60s and '70s and in 01, Gibson revived the name for a line of effects, banjos, and mandolins and added guitars and amps in '09.

The price ranges listed are for excellent condition, all original amps though tubes may be replaced without affecting value. The prices listed are for amps with fully intact logos. A broken or missing logo may diminish the value of the amp. Amps with a changed handle, power cord, and especially a broken logo, should be taken on a case-by-case basis.

Amp models in '58 include the Super Maestro and Maestro, in '60 the Stereo Maestro Accordion GA-87, Super Maestro Accordion GA-46 T, Standard Accordion GA-45 T, Viscount Accordion GA-16 T, in '62 the Reverb-Echo GA-1 RT, Reverb-Echo GA-2 RT, 30 Stereo Accordion Amp, Stereo Accordion GA-78 RV.

GA-1 RT Reverb-Echo Amp
1961. Tweed, 1x8".
1961	$450	$575

GA-2 RT Deluxe Reverb-Echo Amp
1961. Deluxe more powerful version of GA-1 RT, 1x12", tweed.
1961	$725	$950

GA-15 RV/Bell 15 RV Amp
1961. 15 watts, 1x12", gray sparkle.
1961	$525	$675

GA-16 T Viscount Amp
1959-1961. 14 watts, 1x10", white cab with brown grille.
1959-1961	$425	$550

GA-45 Maestro Amp
1955-1961. 14-16 watts, 4x8", 2-tone.
1955-1961	$900	$1,175

GA-45 RV Standard Amp
1961. 16 watts, 4x8", reverb.
1961	$1,000	$1,300

GA-45 T Standard Accordion Amp
1961. 16 watts, 4x8", tremolo.
1961	$900	$1,175

GA-46 T Super Maestro Accordion and Bass Amp
1957-1961. Based on the Gibson GA-200 and advertised to be designed especially for amplified accordions, 60 watts, 2x12", vibrato, 2-tone cover, large Maestro Super logo on top center of grille.
1957-1961	$1,450	$1,900

GA-78 Maestro Series Amps
1960-1961. Wedge stereo cab, 2x10", reverb and tremolo.
1960-1961	GA-78 RV		
	Maestro 30	$1,800	$2,350
1960-1961	GA-78 RVS	$1,600	$2,100
1960-1961	GA-78 RVT	$1,600	$2,100

Magnatone

Ca.1937-1971, 2013-present. Magnatone made a huge variety of amps sold under their own name and under brands like Dickerson, Oahu, Bronson, and Estey (see separate listings). They also private branded amps for several accordion companies or accordion teaching studios like Ariatone, Audio Guild, Da Vinci, Excelsior, Giulietti, Lyric, Noble, PAC-AMP, PANaramic, Titano, Tonemaster, Twilighter, and Unique (see separate listings). In 2013, Ted Kornblum revived the Magnatone name on a line of tube amps based on the earlier models and built in St. Louis, Missouri.

Model 108 Varsity Amp
1948-1954. Gray pearloid cover, small student amp or lap steel companion amp.
1948-1954	$300	$400

Model 109 Melodier Amp
1950s. 10 watts, 2 speakers.
1950s	$600	$775

Model 110 Melodier Amp
1953-1954. 12 watts, 1x10", brown leatherette cover, light grille.
1953-1954	$550	$725

Model 111 Student Amp
1955-1959. 1x8", 2-3 watts, brown leatherette, brown grille.
1955-1959	$500	$650

Model 112/113 Troubadour Amp
1955-1959. 18 watts, 1x12", brown leatherette, brown grille, slant back rear control panel.
1955-1959	$775	$1,000

Model 118 Amp
1960. Compact, tubes, low power, volume and tone knobs, brown tolex era, Model 118 logo on rear-mounted control panel.
1960	$400	$525

Model 120B Cougar Bass Amp
1967-1968. Initial Magnatone entry into the solidstate market, superseded by Brute Series in '68, 120 watts, 2x12" solidstate bass piggyback amp, naugahyde vinyl cover with polyester rosewood side panels.
1967-1968	$325	$425

Model 120R Sting Ray Reverb Bass Amp
1967-1968. Initial Magnatone entry into the solidstate market, superseded by Brute Series in '68, 150

MODEL YEAR FEATURES	EXC. COND. LOW	HIGH

watts, 4x10" solidstate combo amp, naugahyde vinyl cover with polyester rosewood side panels.

| 1967-1968 | $375 | $500 |

Model 130V Custom Amp
1969-1971. Solidstate 1x12" combo amp.

| 1969-1971 | $225 | $300 |

Model 150R Firestar Reverb Amp
1967-1968. Initial Magnatone entry into the solid-state market, superseded by Brute Series in '68, 120 watts, 2x12" solidstate combo amp, naugahyde vinyl cover with polyester rosewood side panels.

| 1967-1968 | $250 | $350 |

Model 180 Triplex Amp
Mid-to-late-1950s. Mid-level power using 2 6L6 power tubes, 1x15" and 1x8" speakers.

| 1950s | $800 | $1,050 |

Model 192-5-S Troubadour Amp
Early-1950s. 18 watts, 1x12" Jensen Concert speaker, brown alligator covering, lower back control panel, 3 chicken-head knobs, Magnatone script logo on front, Troubadour script logo on back control panel.

| 1950s | $575 | $750 |

Model 194 Lyric Amp
1947-mid-1950s. 1x12" speaker, old-style tweed vertical cab typical of '40s.

| 1940s | $500 | $650 |

Model 195 Melodier Amp
1951-1954. Vertical cab with 1x10" speaker, pearloid with flowing grille slats.

| 1951-1954 | $525 | $700 |

Model 196 Amp
1947-mid-1950s. 1x12", 5-10 watts, scroll grille design, snakeskin leatherette cover.

| 1940s | $500 | $650 |

Model 197-V Varsity Amp
1948-1952. Small compact student amp, 1x8", tubes, Varsity model logo and model number on back panel, old style layout with back bottom-mounted chasis, curved cross-bars on front baffle, brown lizard leatherette, leather handle.

| 1948-1952 | $450 | $600 |

Model 198 Varsity Amp
1948-1954. 1x8", tubes.

| 1948-1954 | $500 | $650 |

Model 199 Student Amp
1950s. About 6 to 10 watts, 1x8", snakeskin leatherette cover, metal handle, slant grille design.

| 1950s | $500 | $650 |

Model 210 Deluxe Student Amp
1958-1960. 5 watts, 1x8", vibrato, brown leatherette, V logo lower right front on grille.

| 1958-1960 | $500 | $650 |

Model 213 Troubadour Amp
1957-1958. 10 watts, 1x12", vibrato, brown leatherette cover, V logo lower right of grille.

| 1957-1958 | $950 | $1,250 |

Model 240 SV Magna-Chordion Amp
1967-1968. Initial Magnatone entry into the solid-state market, superseded by Brute Series in '68, 240 watts, 2x12" solidstate stereo accordion or organ amp,

naugahyde vinyl cover, polyester rosewood side panels, input jacks suitable for guitar, reverb and vibrato, lateral combo cab, rear mounted controls.

| 1967-1968 | $325 | $425 |

Model 250 Professional Amp
1958-1960. 20 watts, 1x12", vibrato, brown leatherette with V logo lower right front of grille.

| 1958-1960 | $975 | $1,300 |

Model 260 Amp
1957-1958. 35 watts, 2x12", brown leatherette, vibrato, V logo lower right front corner of grille.

| 1957-1958 | $1,400 | $1,800 |

Model 262 Jupiter/Custom Pro Amp
1961-1963. 35 watts, 2x12", vibrato, brown leatherette.

| 1961-1963 | $1,025 | $1,350 |

Model 280/Custom 280 Amp
1957-1958. 50 watts, brown leatherette covering, brown-yellow tweed grille, 2x12" plus 2x5" speakers, double V logo.

| 1957-1958 | $1,400 | $1,800 |

Model 280A Amp
1958-1960. 50 watts, brown leatherette covering, brown-yellow tweed grille, 2x12" plus 2x5" speakers, V logo lower right front.

| 1958-1960 | $1,400 | $1,800 |
| 1958-1960 With matching cab | $1,800 | $2,400 |

Model 410 Diana Amp
1961-1963. Five watts, 1x12", advertised as a 'studio' low power professional amp, brown leatherette cover, vibrato.

| 1961-1963 | $575 | $775 |

Model 412 Amp
1960s. Estey era compact student amp, low power, 1x8", tubes.

| 1960s | $250 | $325 |

Model 413 Centaur Amp
1961-1963. 18 watts, 1x12", brown leatherette cover, vibrato.

| 1961-1963 | $875 | $1,150 |

Model 415 Clio Bass Amp
1961-1963. 25 watts, 4x8", bass or accordion amp, brown leatherette cover.

| 1961-1963 | $925 | $1,200 |

Model 422 Amp
1966-1967. Low power 1x12", 3 inputs, black vinyl, light swirl grille.

| 1966-1967 | $500 | $650 |

Model 425 Amp
1961. Tube, 55 watts, 4x12".

| 1961 | $1,150 | $1,450 |

Model 432 Amp
Mid-1960s. Compact student model, wavey-squiggle art deco-style grille, black cover, vibrato and reverb.

| 1960s | $575 | $750 |

Model 435 Athene Bass Amp
1961-1963. 55 watts, 4x10", piggyback head and cab, brown leatherette.

| 1961-1963 | $1,150 | $1,500 |

Model 440 Mercury Amp
1961-1963. 18 watts, 1x12", vibrato, brown leatherette.

| 1961-1963 | $1,000 | $1,300 |

Magnatone Model 108 Varsity

AMPS

Late-1950s Magnatone Model 213 Troubadour

Imaged by Heritage Auctions, HA.com

1960 Magnatone Model 280 Custom

Imaged by Heritage Auctions, HA.com

Magnatone Model 480 Venus

Ca. 1969 Magnatone Model M15

Imaged by Heritage Auctions, HA.com

1950s Magnatone Starlet Model 107

Imaged by Heritage Auctions, HA.com

MODEL YEAR	FEATURES	EXC. COND. LOW	HIGH

Model 450 Juno/Twin Hi-Fi Amp
1961-1963. 25 watts, 1x12" and 1 oval 5"x7" speakers, reverb, vibrato, brown leatherette.

1961-1963		$1,150	$1,500
1961-1963	Extension cab only	$575	$750

Model 460 Victory Amp
1961-1963. 35 watts, 2x12" and 2 oval 5"x7" speakers, early-'60s next to the top-of-the-line, reverb and vibrato, brown leatherette.

1961-1963		$1,150	$1,500

Model 480 Venus Amp
1961-1963. 50 watts, 2x12" and 2 oval 5"x7" speakers, early-'60s top-of-the-line, reverb and stereo vibrato, brown leatherette.

1961-1963		$1,150	$1,500

Model M2 Amp
1963-1964. 1x8", 12-15 watts, 1 channel.

1963-1964		$350	$450

Model M6 Amp
1964 (not seen in '65 catalog). 25 watts, 1x12", black molded plastic suitcase amp.

1964		$475	$625

Model M7 Bass Amp
1964-1966. 38 watts, 1x15" bass amp, black molded plastic suitcase amp.

1964-1966		$475	$625

Model M8 Amp
1964-1966. 27 watts, 1x12", reverb and tremolo, black molded plastic suitcase amp.

1964-1966		$550	$725

Model M9 Amp
1964-1966. 38 watts, 1x15", tremolo, no reverb, black molded plastic suitcase amp.

1964-1966		$550	$725

Model M10/M10A Amp
1964-1966. 38 watts, 1x15", tone boost, tremolo, transistorized reverb section, black molded plastic suitcase amp.

1964-1966		$500	$650

Model M12 Bass Amp
1964-1966. 80 watts, 1x15" or 2x12", mid-'60s top-of-the-line bass amp, black molded plastic suitcase amp.

1964-1966		$650	$725

Model M13 Imperial Amp
Mid-1963-1964. 1x15", 45 watts, 3 channels.

1963-1964		$550	$725

Model M14 Amp
1964-1966. Stereo, 75 watts, 2x12" plus 2 tweeters, stereo vibrato, no reverb, black molded plastic suitcase amp.

1964-1966		$675	$900

Model M15 Amp
1964-1966. Stereo 75 watts, 2x12" plus 2 tweeters, stereo vibrato, transistorized reverb, black molded plastic suitcase amp.

1964-1966		$725	$925

Model M27 Bad Boy Bass Amp
1968-1971. 150 watts, 2x15" (1 passive), reverb, vibrato, solidstate, vertical profile bass amp, part of Brute Series.

1968-1971		$275	$350

Model M30 Fang Amp
1968-1971. 150 watts, 2x15" (1 passive), 1 exponential horn, solidstate, vibrato, reverb, vertical profile amp.

1968-1971		$275	$350

Model M32 Big Henry Bass Amp
1968-1971. 300 watts, 2x15" solidstate vertical profile bass amp.

1968-1971		$275	$350

Model M35 The Killer Amp
1968-1971. 300 watts, 2x15" and 2 horns, solidstate, vibrato, vertical profile amp.

1968-1971		$275	$350

Model MP-1 (Magna Power I) Amp
1966-1967. 30 watts, 1x12", dark vinyl, light grille, Magnatone-Estey logo on upper right of grille.

1966-1967		$525	$700

Model MP-3 (Magna Power 3) Amp
1966-1967. Mid-power, 2x12", reverb, dark vinyl, light grille, Magnatone-Estey logo on upper right of grille.

1966-1967		$600	$775

Model MP-5 (Magna Power) Amp
1966-1967. Mid-power, piggyback 2x12", Magnatone-Estey logo on upper right of grille.

1966-1967		$675	$875

Model PS150 Amp
1968-1971. Powered slave speaker cabinets, 150 watts, 2x15" linkable cabinets.

1968-1971		$175	$225

Model PS300 Amp
1968-1971. Powered slave speaker cabinets, 300 watts, 2x15" (1 passive) linkable cabinets.

1968-1971		$175	$225

Small Pearloid Amp
1947-1955. Pearloid (MOTS) covered low- and mid-power amps generally associated with pearloid lap steel sets.

1947-1955	Fancy grille	$325	$425
1947-1955	Plain grille	$225	$300

Starlet Model 107 Amp
1951-1952. Student model, 1x8", pearloid cover early, leatherette later, low power, single on-off volume control, Starlet logo on back panel, Magnatone logo plate upper left front of grille.

1951-1954	Pearloid	$275	$365
1955-1959	Leatherette	$275	$365

Starlite Model 401 Amp
1964-1966. Magnatone produced the mid-'60s Starlite amplifier line for the budget minded musician. Each Starlite model prominently notes the Magnatone name. The grilles show art deco wavy circles. Magnatone 1960-'63 standard amps offer models starting with 12" speakers. Starlite models offer 10" and below. Model 401 has 15 watts, 1x8" and 3 tubes.

1964-1966		$300	$400

Starlite Model 411 Amp
1964-1966. 15 watts, 1x8", 5 tubes, tremolo (not advertised as vibrato), art deco wavy grille.

1964-1966		$325	$425

MODEL YEAR	FEATURES	EXC. COND. LOW	HIGH

Starlite Model 441A Bass Amp
1964-1966. Lower power with less than 25 watts, 1x15", tube amp.

1964-1966		$450	$600

Starlite Model Custom 421 Amp
1964-1966. Tube amp, 25 watts, 1x10".

1964-1966		$450	$600

Starlite Model Custom 431 Amp
1964-1966. Tube amp, 30 watts, 1x10", vibrato and reverb.

1964-1966		$500	$650

Mahaffay Amplifiers
2009-present. See Little Lanilei.

Mako
1985-1989. Line of solidstate amps from Kaman (Ovation, Hamer). They also offered guitars and basses.

Marlboro Sound Works
1970-1980s. Economy solidstate amps imported by Musical Instruments Corp., Syosset, New York. Initially, Marlboro targeted the economy compact amp market, but quickly added larger amps and PAs.

GA-2 Amp
1970-1980s. 3 watts, 1x8".

1970s-80s		$15	$20

GA-3 Amp
1970-1980s. 3 watts, 1x8", tremolo.

1970s-80s		$20	$30

GA-20B Amp
1970-1980s. Bass/keyboard amp, 25 watts, 1x12".

1970s-80s		$30	$70

GA-20R Amp
1970-1980s. 25 watts, 1x12", tremolo, reverb.

1970s-80s		$30	$70

GA-40R Amp
1970-1980s. 30 watts, 1x12", tremolo, reverb.

1970s-80s		$75	$125

Model 520B Amp
1970-1980s. 25 watts, 1x15", bass/keyboard amp.

1970s-80s		$75	$125

Model 560A Amp
1970-1980s. 45 watts, 2x10".

1970s-80s		$75	$125

Model 760A Amp
1970-1980s. Guitar/bass/keyboard, 60 watts, 1x15".

1970s-80s		$75	$125

Model 1200R Amp Head
1970-1980s. 60 watts, reverb.

1970s-80s		$75	$125

Model 1500B Bass Amp Head
1970-1980s. 60 watts.

1970s-80s		$75	$125

Model 2000 Bass Amp Set
1970-1980s. 1500B head and 1x12" cab.

1970s-80s		$75	$125

Marshall
1962-present. Drummer Jim Marshall (1923-2012) started building bass speaker and PA cabinets in his garage in 1960. He opened a retail drum shop for his students and others and soon added guitars and amps. When Ken Bran joined the business as service manager in '62, the two decided to build their own amps. By '63 they had expanded the shop to house a small manufacturing space and by late that year they were offering the amps to other retailers. Marshall also made amps under the Park, CMI, Narb, Big M, and Kitchen-Marshall brands.

Mark I, II, III and IVs are generally '60s and '70s and also are generally part of a larger series (for example JTM), or have a model number that is a more specific identifier. Describing an amp only as Mark II can be misleading. The most important identifier is the Model Number, which Marshall often called the Stock Number. To help avoid confusion we have added the Model number as often as possible. In addition, when appropriate, we have included the wattage, number of channels, master or no-master info in the title. This should help the reader more quickly find a specific amp. Check the model's description for such things as two inputs or four inputs, because this will help with identification. Vintage Marshall amps do not always have the Model/Stock number on the front or back panel, so the additional identifiers should help. The JMP logo on the front is common and really does not help with specific identification. For example, a JMP Mark II Super Lead 100 Watt description is less helpful than the actual model/stock number. Unfortunately, many people are not familiar with specific model/stock numbers. VG has tried to include as much information in the title as space will allow.

Marshall amps are sorted as follows:
AVT Series - Advanced Valvestate Technology
Club and Country Series (Rose-Morris)-introduced in '78
JCM 800 Series - basically the '80s
JCM 900 Series - basically the '90s
JCM 2000 Series - basically the '00s
JTM Series
Micro Stack Group
Model Number/Stock Number (no specific series, basically the '60s, '70s) - including Artist and Valvestate models (Valvestate refers to specific Model numbers in 8000 Series)
Silver Jubilee Series

Acoustic Soloist (AS) Series Amps
1994-present. Acoustic guitar amps, models include AS50R and D (50 watts, 2 channels, 2x8"), AS80R (40-watt x2 stereo, 3 channels, 2x8"), AS100D (50-watt x2 stereo, 4 channels, 2x8").

1994-2019	Various models	$200	$400

AVT 20 Series Amp
2001-2011. Solidstate, 20 watts, 12AX7 preamp tube, 1x10", Advanced Valvestate Technology (AVT) models have black covering and grille, and gold panel.

2001-2011	Combo	$175	$225

Mahaffay The Little Lanilei 3350LT

Mako MAK2

Marshall AS100D

AMPS

Marshall AVT-50

1984 Marshall JCM 800 2203
Craig Brody

1986 Marshall JCM 800 Model 2204
Scott Davis

MODEL YEAR	FEATURES	EXC. COND. LOW	HIGH
AVT 50 Series Amp			
2001-2011. Solidstate, 50 watts, 4x12".			
2001-2011	Combo	$245	$315
2001-2011	Head & cab	$390	$510
AVT 100 Series Amp			
2001-2011. Solidstate, 100 watts, tube preamp, 1x12".			
2001-2011		$270	$360
AVT 150 Series Amp			
2001-2011. Solidstate, additional features over AVT 100. Combo (100 watts, 1x12"), Half-Stack (150 watts, 4x12") and Head only (150 watts).			
2001-2011	Combo	$295	$385
2001-2011	Half-stack	$375	$500
AVT 275 Series Amp			
2001-2007. Solidstate DFX stereo, 75 watts per side, 2x12".			
2001-2007	Combo	$360	$475
Class 5 Amp			
2009-2014. 5 watts, 1x10" tube combo.			
2009-2014	Head	$290	$385
2009-2014	Head/cab set	$315	$415
Club and Country Model 4140 Amp			
1978-1982. Tubes, 100 watts, 2x12" combo, Rose-Morris era, designed for the country music market, hence the name, brown vinyl cover, straw grille.			
1978-1982		$725	$950
Club and Country Model 4145 Amp			
1978-1982. Tubes, 100 watts, 4x10" combo, Rose-Morris era, designed for the country music market, hence the name, brown vinyl, straw grille.			
1978-1982		$725	$950
Club and Country Model 4150 Bass Amp			
1978-1982. Tubes, 100 watts, 4x10" bass combo, Rose-Morris era, designed for the country music market, hence the name, brown vinyl cover, straw grille.			
1978-1982		$725	$950
Code Series Amp			
2016-present. Marshall-Softube (MST) modelling, digital capabilities, series includes; CODE25, 50, 100 and 100H. Number indicates watts.			
2016-2019		$120	$195
Haze (MHZ) Series Amp			
2009-2014. All tube, multi-functional amp, 15-watt head, 40-watt combo.			
2009-2014	MHZ15	$590	$775
2009-2014	MHZ40C	$340	$440
JCM 600 Series			
1997-2000. All tube, 60 watt models with modern features, includes the JCM600 head, JCM601 1x12" combo and JCM602 2x12" combo.			
1997-2000	JCM600	$355	$470
1997-2000	JCM601	$378	$495
1997-2000	JCM602	$450	$590
JCM 800 Model 1959 Amp Head			
1981-1991. 100 watts.			
1981-1991		$1,190	$1,525
JCM 800 Model 1987 Amp Head			
1981-1991. 50 watts.			
1981-1991		$1,190	$1,525

MODEL YEAR	FEATURES	EXC. COND. LOW	HIGH
JCM 800 Model 1992 Bass Amp Head			
1981-1986. Active tone circuit.			
1981-1986		$1,190	$1,525
JCM 800 Model 2000 Amp Head			
1981-1982. 200 watts.			
1981-1982		$1,190	$1,525
JCM 800 Model 2001 Amp Head			
1981-1982. Bass head, 300 watts.			
1981-1982		$1,190	$1,525
JCM 800 Model 2004 Amp Head			
1981-1990. 50 watts, master.			
1981-1990		$1,190	$1,525
JCM 800 Model 2004S Amp Head			
1986-1987. 50 watts, short head.			
1986-1987		$1,190	$1,525
JCM 800 Model 2005 Amp Head			
1983-1990. 50 watts, split channel.			
1983-1990		$1,190	$1,525
JCM 800 Model 2005 Full Stack Amp			
1983-1990. Limited Edition, 2005 head with 2 2x12 cabs.			
1983-1990		$1,750	$2,275
JCM 800 Model 2203 20th Anniversary Half Stack Amp			
1982. 20th Anniversary plate in lower right corner of matching 1960A cab, matching white tolex cover.			
1982		$2,080	$2,675
JCM 800 Model 2203 Amp Head			
1981-1990, 2002-present. 100 watts, master volume, reissued '02 in Vintage Series.			
1981-1990		$1,350	$1,800
2002-2019	Reissue	$850	$1,100
JCM 800 Model 2203KK Kerry King Signature Amp			
2008-2012. King Signature logo, 100 watts, 3-band EQ.			
2008-2012		$825	$1,100
JCM 800 Model 2203ZW Zack Wylde Signature Amp			
2002. About 600 amp heads and 60 half-stacks made.			
2002	Half-stack	$2,625	$3,400
2002	Head only	$1,450	$1,900
JCM 800 Model 2204 Amp Head			
1981-1990. 50 watts, 1 channel, 2 inputs, master volume, front panel says JCM 800 Lead Series, back panel says Master Model 50w Mk 2.			
1981-1990		$875	$1,175
JCM 800 Model 2204S Amp Head			
1986-1987. Short head, 50 watts.			
1986-1987		$875	$1,175
JCM 800 Model 2205 Amp			
1983-1990. 50 watts, split channel (1 clean and 1 distortion), switchable, both channels with reverb, 4x12" cabinet, front panel reads JCM 800 Lead Series.			
1983-1990	4x12 cab	$500	$675
1983-1990	Head only	$875	$1,175
JCM 800 Model 2210 Amp Head			
1983-1990. 100 watts.			
1983-1990		$875	$1,175

MODEL YEAR	FEATURES	EXC. COND. LOW	HIGH

JCM 800 Model 4010 Combo Amp
1980-1990. 50 watts, 1x12", non-reverb ('80), reverb begins '81, single channel master volume.

1980-1990		$1,025	$1,350

JCM 800 Model 4103 Combo Amp
1981-1990. Lead combo amp, 100 watts, 2x12".

1981-1990		$1,175	$1,550

JCM 800 Model 4104 Combo Amp
1980-1990. Tube lead amp, 50 watts, 2x12".

1980-1990	Black	$1,025	$1,350
1980-1990	Head only	$850	$1,125
1980-1990	White option	$1,025	$1,350

JCM 800 Model 4210 Combo Amp
1982-1990. 50 watts, 1x12" tube combo, split-channel, single input, master volume.

1982-1990		$1,115	$1,450

JCM 800 Model 4211 Combo Amp
1983-1990. Lead combo amp, 100 watts, 2x12".

1983-1990		$1,115	$1,450

JCM 800 Model 4212 Combo Amp
1983-1990. 2x12" 50-watt combo.

1983-1990		$1,115	$1,450

JCM 800 Model 5010 Combo Amp
1983-1991. Solidstate, 30 watts, master volume, 1x12".

1983-1991		$290	$375

JCM 800 Model 5150 Combo Amp
1987-1991. Solidstate, 150 watts, 12" Celestion, 2 channels, presence and effects-mix master controls.

1987-1991		$350	$450

JCM 800 Model 5210 Combo Amp
1986-1991. Solidstate, 50 watts, channel switching, 1x12".

1983		$290	$375

JCM 800 Model 5212 Combo Amp
1986-1991. Solidstate, 50 watts, 2x12" split channel reverb combo.

1986-1991		$360	$475

JCM 800 Model 5213 Combo Amp
1986-1991. Solidstate, 2x12", channel-switching, effects loop.

1986-1991		$290	$375

JCM 800 Model 5215 Combo Amp
1986-1991. Solidstate, 1x15", Accutronics reverb, effects loop.

1986-1991		$290	$375

JCM 900 Model 2100 Mark III Amp Head
1990-1993. FX loop, 100/50-watt selectable lead head.

1990-1993		$725	$950

JCM 900 Model 2100 SL-X Amp Head
1992-1998. Hi-gain 100 watt head amp, additional 12AX7 preamp tube.

1992-1998		$725	$950

JCM 900 Model 2500 SL-X Amp Head
1990-2000. 50 watt version of SL-X.

1992-1998		$725	$950

JCM 900 Model 4100 Dual Reverb Amp
1990-2017. Vintage Series, 100/50 switchable head, JCM 900 on front panel, 4x10 or 2x12 matching cab, black with black front.

1990-2017	4x10 or 2x12	$450	$600
1990-2017	Head only	$650	$850

JCM 900 Model 4101 Combo Amp
1990-2000. All tube, 100 watts, 1x12" combo.

1990-2000		$675	$900

JCM 900 Model 4102 Combo Amp
1990-2000. Combo amp, 100/50 watts switchable, 2x12".

1990-2000		$700	$925

JCM 900 Model 4500 Amp Head
1990-2000. All tube, 2 channels, 50/25 watts, EL34 powered, reverb, effects loop, compensated recording out, master volume, black.

1990-2000		$600	$800

JCM 900 Model 4501 Dual Reverb Combo Amp
1990-2000. 50/25 switchable, 1x12".

1990-2000		$675	$875

JCM 900 Model 4502 Combo Amp
1990-2000. 50/25 switchable, 2x12".

1990-2000		$700	$900

JCM 2000 DSL Series Amp
1998-2015. DSL is Dual Super Lead, 2 independent channels labelled classic and ultra, JCM 2000 and DSL logos both on front panel.

1998-2015	Half-stacks/combos	$240	$825

JCM 2000 TSL Series Amp
1998-2013. TSL is Triple Super Lead, 3 independent channels labelled clean, crunch and lead, 8 tubes, JCM 2000 and TSL logos both on front panel.

1998-2013	Full stacks	$1,200	$1,825
1998-2013	Half-stacks/combos	$630	$1,225

JCM Slash Signature Model 2555SL Amp Set
1996. Based on JCM 800 with higher gain, matching amp and cab set, JCM Slash Signature logo on front panel, single channel, Slash Signature 1960AV 4x12" slant cab, black.

1996	4x12 cab	$700	$900
1996	Head only	$1,550	$2,000

JMD Series
2010-2013. JMD is Jim Marshall Digital. Models include JMD50 & 100 heads and JMD 102 (100w, 2x12) & 501 (50w, 1x12) combos.

2010-2013	501	$490	$650

JTM 30 Series Amp
1995-1997. Tube combo, reverb, 30 watts, effects loops, 5881 output sections, footswitchable high-gain modes. Available as 1x15", 1x12", 2x12" or 3x10" combo or as 4x10" half-stack.

1995-1997	Combo 1x12	$435	$560
1995-1997	Combo 2x10	$460	$600
1995-1997	Combo 2x12	$485	$630
1995-1997	Combo 3x10	$485	$630

JTM 45 Amp Head
1962-1964. Amp head, 45 watts. The original Marshall amp. Became the Model 1987 45-watt for '65-'66.

1962		$8,300	$10,800
1963-1964		$7,300	$9,500

JTM 45 Model 1961 MK IV 4x10 Combo Amp
1965-1966. 45 watts, 4x10", tremolo, JTM 45 MK IV on panel, Bluesbreaker association.

1965-1966		$7,000	$9,100

Mid-1980s Marshall JCM 800 Model 2204
Tony Romagna

Marshall JCM 800 Model 4010
Stephan Brown

Marshall JCM 2000 TSL 100

To get the most from this book, be sure to read "Using **The Guide**" in the introduction.

1964 Marshall JTM 45
Eddie Daurelle

Marshall JTM 45
Model 1961 MK IV
Pang Leo

Marshall Model 1922

JTM 45 Model 1962 MK IV 2x12 Combo Amp
1965-1966. 45 watts, 2x12", tremolo, JTM 45 MK IV on panel, Bluesbreaker association.

MODEL YEAR	FEATURES	EXC. COND. LOW	HIGH
1965-1966		$7,200	$9,400

JTM 45 Model 1987 Amp Head Reissue
1988-1999. Black/green tolex.

1988-1999		$1,025	$1,350

JTM 45 Model 1987 Mark II Lead Amp Head
1965-1966. Replaced JTM 45 Amp ('62-'64), but was subsequently replaced by the Model 1987 50-watt Head during '66.

1965-1966		$4,900	$6,500

JTM 45 Offset Limited Edition Amp Set Reissue
Introduced in 2000. Limited run of 300 units, old style cosmetics, 45-watt head and offset 2x12" cab, dark vinyl cover, light gray grille, rectangular logo plate on front of amp and cab, Limited Edition plate on rear of cab, serial number xxx of 300.

2000		$2,450	$3,250

JTM 50 Amp Head
1966-1967. JTM 50 panel logo, EL34 power tubes.

1966-1967		$5,000	$6,550

JTM 50 Model 1961 MK IV 4x10 Amp
1965-1972. 50 watts, 4x10", Bluesbreaker association, tremolo, JTM 50 MK IV on front panel to '68, plain front panel without model description '68-'72.

1966-1967		$6,300	$8,200
1968		$5,900	$7,700
1969		$5,300	$7,000
1970		$4,500	$6,000
1971-1972		$3,800	$5,000

JTM 50 Model 1962 Bluesbreaker Amp Reissue
1989-1999. 50 watts, 2x12", Model 1962 reissue Bluesbreaker.

1989-1999		$1,200	$1,600

JTM 50 Model 1962 MK IV 2x12 Amp
1966-1972. 50 watts, 2x12", tremolo, Bluesbreaker association, JTM 50 MK IV on front panel to '68, plain front panel without model description '68-'72.

1966-1967		$7,700	$10,000
1968		$7,100	$9,300
1969		$5,900	$7,700
1970		$5,400	$7,100
1971-1972		$4,600	$6,000

JTM 50 Model 1963 PA Amp Head
1965-1966. MK II PA head, block logo.

1965-1966		$2,000	$2,600

JTM 60 Series Amp
1995-1997. Tube, 60 watts, 1x12", 1x15", 2x12" or 3x10" combo or as 4x10" half-stack.

1995-1997	1x12 Combo	$475	$615
1995-1997	2x12 Combo	$500	$650
1995-1997	3x10 Combo	$525	$675
1995-1997	4x10 Mini half-stack	$525	$675

JTM 310 Amp
1995-1997. JTM 30 with 2x10".

1995-1997		$500	$650

JTM 612 Combo Amp
1995-1997. Tube combo amp, 60 watts, 1x12", EQ, reverb, effects loop.

MODEL YEAR	FEATURES	EXC. COND. LOW	HIGH
1995-1997		$475	$615

JVM Series
2007-present. Models (H for Head, C Combo) include 205H/205C (50-watt head/combo 2x12), 210H/210C (100-watt head/combo 2x12), 215C (50-watt 1x12 combo), 410H/410C (100-watt head/combo 2x12, 4-channel).

2007-2017	JVM410C	$975	$1,300
2008-2019	JVM205H	$775	$1,025
2008-2019	JVM210C	$1,075	$1,400
2008-2019	JVM210H	$825	$1,075

MA Series Amp
2009-2013. Models include 50C (50 watts, 1x12"), 50H (50-watt head), 100C (100 watts, 2x12"), 100H (100-watt head) and 412 (4x12" slant cabinet).

2009-2013	Half-stacks/combos	$315	$485

MB Series Amp
2006-2012. Bass Combo Series, models include 30C (30watts, 1x10").

2006-2012	MB30C	$110	$145

MG Series Amp
1999-present. Models include 10KK (10 watts, 1x6"), 15CD, 15RCD or CDR (15 watts, 1x8"), 15MS (15 watts, micro stack, 1x8" slant and straight cabs), 15MSII, (in '02, 10" speakers), 15MSZW (15 watts, 2x1x10"), 50DFX (50 watts, 1x12"), 100DFX (100 watts, combo), 100HDFX (100-watt head), 100RCD (Valvestate Series, 100-watt), 102FX (100 watts, 2x12"), 250DFX (250 watts, combo), 412A (4x12" cabinet).

1999-2019	Various models	$25	$240

Micro Stack 3005 Amp
1986-1991. Solidstate head, 12 watts, 2 1x10" stackable cabs (one slant, one straight). Standard model is black, but was also offered in white, green, red, or the silver Silver Jubilee version with Jubilee 25/50 logo.

1986-1991	Black	$270	$360
1986-1991	Green or red	$360	$485
1986-1991	White	$340	$460
1987-1989	Silver Jubilee/silver	$460	$605

Mini-Stack 3210 MOS-FET Amp Head with 2x4x10"
1984-1991. Model 3210 MOS-FET head with 2 4x10" cabs, designed as affordable stack.

1984-1991		$320	$430

Model 1710 Bass Cabinet
1990s. 1x15" speaker.

1990s		$270	$360

Model 1912 Cabinet
1989-1998, 2013-2017. 1x12", 150 watts.

2013-2017		$270	$360

Model 1917 PA-20 Amp Head
1967-1973. PA head with 20 watts, but often used for guitar, matching cabinet.

1967-1968	Matching cab	$1,000	$1,300
1967-1968	Plexi head	$2,300	$3,000
1969-1973	Aluminum head	$1,800	$2,300
1969-1973	Matching cab	$825	$1,100

AMPS

MODEL YEAR	FEATURES	EXC. COND. LOW	HIGH
Model 1922 Amp Cabinet			
1989-2018. 2x12" extension cab for JCM 800 Series amps.			
1989-2019		$215	$280
Model 1930 Popular Combo Amp			
1969-1973. 10 watts, 1x12", tremolo.			
1969-1972		$1,875	$2,450
1973		$2,000	$2,600
Model 1933 Amp Cabinet			
1981-1991. 1x12" extension cab for JCM 800 Series amps.			
1981-1991		$270	$345
Model 1935/1935A/1935B Bass Cabinet			
1967-1990s. Models 1935, 4x12", black, A slant front, B straight front.			
1967-1970	75w	$1,875	$2,450
1971-1972	Black, weave	$975	$1,275
1973-1975	Black, checkerboard	$925	$1,200
1976-1979	Black	$825	$1,100
1979-1983	260w	$490	$650
1983-1986	280w	$435	$580
1990s		$340	$435
Model 1936 Amp Cabinet			
1981-2011. Extension straight-front cab for JCM 800/900 Series amps, 2x12" speakers, black.			
1981-2011		$340	$435
Model 1937 Bass Cabinet			
1981-1986. 4x12", 140 watts.			
1981-1986		$435	$580
Model 1958 18-Watt Lead Amp			
1965-1968. 18 watts, 2x10" combo, Bluesbreaker cosmetics.			
1965-1968		$4,700	$6,100
Model 1958 20-Watt Lead Amp			
1968-1972. 20 watts, 2x10" combo, tremolo.			
1968		$4,200	$5,500
1969		$3,700	$4,900
1970		$3,600	$4,700
1971-1972		$3,200	$4,200
Model 1959 Super Lead Amp			
1966-1981. Two channels, 100 watts, 4 inputs, no master volume. Plexiglas control panels until mid-'69, aluminum after. See Model T1959 for tremolo version. Early custom color versions are rare and more valuable.			
1966-1969	Black, plexi	$3,700	$4,900
1966-1969	Custom color, plexi	$5,300	$7,000
1969-1970	Black, aluminum	$2,200	$2,900
1969-1970	Custom color, aluminum	$4,400	$5,700
1971-1972	Black, hand-wired, small box	$2,200	$2,900
1971-1972	Custom color, hand-wired	$2,600	$3,400
1973-1975	Black, printed CB, large box	$1,450	$1,925
1973-1975	Custom color, printed CB	$1,950	$2,600
1976-1979	Black	$1,250	$1,650
1976-1979	Custom color	$1,450	$1,925

MODEL YEAR	FEATURES	EXC. COND. LOW	HIGH
1980-1981	Black	$1,175	$1,550
1980-1981	Custom color	$1,350	$1,750
Model T1959 Super Lead (Tremolo) Amp Head			
1966-1973. Head amp, 100 watts, plexi until mid-'69, aluminum after. Tremolo version of the Model 1959 Amp.			
1966-1969	Black, plexi	$3,900	$5,100
1966-1969	Custom color, plexi	$5,700	$7,400
1969-1970	Black, aluminum	$1,875	$2,450
1969-1970	Custom color, aluminum	$1,425	$5,800
1971-1973	Black, hand-wired, small box	$1,700	$2,200
1971-1973	Custom color, hand-wired	$2,450	$3,200
35th Anniversary Marshall Limited Edition Set			
1997. Limited Edition 1997 logo, includes matching Super Lead MKII 100-watt head, PB100 power brake and MKII 1960A slant cab, all in white covering.			
1997		$2,100	$2,800
Model 1959 SLP Reissue Amp Head			
1992-2017. Vintage Series, Super Lead Plexi (SLP).			
1992-1999	Black vinyl	$1,000	$1,300
1992-1999	Purple vinyl or white	$1,200	$1,550
2000-2017	Black vinyl	$1,200	$1,550
Model 1959 SLP Reissue Amp Set			
1992-2013. Vintage Series, 100 watt Super Lead head and matching 4x12" slant cab.			
1992-2013	4x12 Cab	$475	$625
Model 1959HW Amp			
2005-present. Hand-wired, 100 watts, 4x12" slant front cab.			
2005-2014	Cab	$475	$625
2005-2019	Head only	$1,000	$1,300
Model 1959RR Ltd. Ed. Randy Rhoads Amp			
2008-2013. Randy Rhoads Tribute, full stack, 100 watts.			
2008-2013		$2,100	$2,800
Model 1960 4x12 Speaker Cabinet			
1964-1979. Both straight and slant front. The original Marshall 4x12" cab designed for compact size with 4x12" speakers. First issue in '64/'65 is 60-watt cab, from '65-'70 75 watts, from '70-'79 100 watts. After '79, model numbers contained an alpha suffix: A for slant front, B straight.			
1966-1970	Black, weave	$2,000	$2,600
1966-1970	Custom color, weave	$2,800	$3,700
1971-1972	Black, weave	$1,100	$1,450
1971-1972	Custom color, weave	$1,525	$2,000
1973-1975	Black, checkerboard	$800	$1,050
1973-1975	Custom color, checkerboard	$1,200	$1,600
1976-1979	Black	$750	$1,000
1976-1979	Custom color	$1,200	$1,600

1967 Marshall Model 1958 18-Watt Lead
Kris Blakely

1971 Marshall Model 1959 Super Lead
William Bethurem

Marshall Model 1959HW

1960 Marshall Slant Cab

*Marshall Model 1962
Bluesbreaker Combo*

Marshall Model 1974X

Model 1960A/1960B 4x12 Speaker Cabinet

1980-1983 (260 watts), '84-'86 (280 watts, JCM 800 era), '86-'90 (300 watts, JCM 800 era), '90-present (300 watts, JCM 900 era, stereo-mono switching). A slant or B straight front.

YEAR	FEATURES	LOW	HIGH
1980-1983	Black	$435	$575
1980-1983	Custom color	$625	$825
1984-1986	Black	$375	$500
1984-1986	Custom color	$575	$750
1984-1986	Rare color	$775	$1,000
1987-1990	Black	$350	$450
1987-1990	Custom color	$475	$625
1987-1990	Rare color	$675	$900
2000-2007	Black	$315	$415

Model 1960AC/1960BC Classic Speaker Cabinet

2005-2013. 100 watts, 4x12" Celestion G-12M-25 greenback speakers, black, AC slant front, BC straight front.

2005-2013	AC	$575	$750
2005-2013	BC	$525	$700

Model 1960AHW/1960BHW 4x12 Cabinet

2005-present. Half stack cab for HW series, AHW slant or BHW straight front.

2005-2019		$575	$750

Model 1960AV/1960BV 4x12 Cabinet

1990-present. JCM 900 updated, stereo/mono switching, AV slant, BV straight front.

1990-1999	Red vinyl, tan grille	$450	$600
1990-2012	Black vinyl, black grille	$435	$575

Model 1960AX/1960BX 4x12 Cabinet

1990-present. Cab for Model 1987X and 1959X reissue heads, AX slant, BX straight.

1990-2019	AX	$435	$575
1990-2019	BX	$435	$575

Model 1960TV 4x12 Slant Cabinet

1990-2012. Extra tall for JTM 45, mono, 100 watts.

1990-2012	Various colors	$350	$450

Model 1962 Bluesbreaker Combo Amp

1999-2017. Vintage Series, similar to JTM 45 but with 2 reissue 'Greenback' 25-watt 2x12" speakers and addition of footswitchable tremolo effect.

1999-2017		$975	$1,300

Model 1964 Lead/Bass 50-Watt Amp Head

1973-1976. Head with 50 watts, designed for lead or bass.

1973-1976		$875	$1,150

Model 1965A/1965B Cabinet

1984-1991. 140 watt 4x10" slant front (A) or straight front (B) cab.

1984-1991		$315	$415

Model 1966 Cabinet

1985-1991. 150 watt 2x12" cab.

1985-1991		$315	$415

Model 1967 Major 200-Watt Amp Head

1968-1974. 200 watts, the original Marshall 200 Pig was not popular and revised into the 200 'Major'. The new Major 200 was similar to the other large amps and included 2 channels, 4 inputs, but a larger amp cab.

1968	Plexi	$2,200	$2,900
1969-1970	Aluminum	$2,000	$2,600
1971-1972	Small box	$1,050	$1,400
1973-1974	Large box	$1,025	$1,350

Model 1967 Pig 200-Watt Amp Head

1967-early-1968 only. Head with 200 watts. The control panel was short and stubby and nicknamed the Pig, the 200-watt circuit was dissimilar (and unpopular) to the 50-watt and 100-watt circuits.

1967-1968		$2,300	$3,000

Model 1968 100-Watt Super PA Amp Head

1966-1975. PA head with 100 watts, 2 sets of 4 inputs (identifies PA configuration), often used for guitar, matching cabinet.

1966-1969	Matching cab	$1,200	$1,600
1966-1969	Plexi	$2,725	$3,575
1969-1972	Aluminum	$2,050	$2,700
1969-1975	Matching cab	$850	$1,100

Model 1973 Amp

1965-1968. Tube combo, 18 watts, 2x12".

1965		$6,500	$8,500
1966		$6,200	$8,100
1967		$5,100	$6,600
1968		$4,500	$5,900

Model 1973 JMP Lead/Bass 20 Amp

1973 only. Front panel: JMP, back panel: Lead & Bass 20, 20 watts, 1x12" straight front checkered grille cab, head and cab black vinyl.

1973		$1,875	$2,425

Model 1974 Amp

1965-1968. Tube combo, 18 watts, 1x12".

1965		$4,000	$5,300
1966		$3,800	$5,000
1967		$3,500	$4,600
1968		$3,200	$4,250

Model 1974X Amp

2004-present. Handwired Series, reissue of 18-watt, 1x12" combo, extension cabinet available.

2004-2019	Combo	$1,175	$1,550

Model 1974X/1974CX Amp

2004-present. Handwired Series, reissue of 18-watt, 1x12" combo, extension cabinet available (CX).

2004-2019	1974CX cab	$475	$625

Model 1982/1982A/1982B Cabinet

1967-1987. Bass and lead 4x12", 100 watt 1982/1982B, upped to 120 watts in '70. Becomes higher powered 320 and 400 watts Model 1982A/B in '81 and '82.

1967-1970		$2,000	$2,600
1971-1980		$750	$1,450
1981-1982		$435	$575
1983-1987		$350	$575

Model 1986 50-Watt Bass Amp Head

1966-1981. Bass version of 1987, 50-watt.

1966-1969	Black, plexi	$3,100	$4,100
1969-1970	Black, aluminum	$2,100	$2,800
1971-1972	Black, hand-wired, small box	$1,700	$2,300

MODEL YEAR	FEATURES	EXC. COND. LOW	HIGH
1973-1975	Black, printed CB, large box	$1,450	$1,925
1976-1979	Black	$1,250	$1,650
1980-1981	Black	$1,175	$1,550

Model 1987 50-Watt Amp Head
1966-1981. Head amp, 50 watts, plexiglas panel until mid-'69, aluminum panel after.

1966-1969	Black, plexi	$3,100	$4,100
1966-1969	Custom color, plexi	$4,800	$6,200
1969-1970	Black, aluminum	$2,100	$2,800
1969-1970	Custom color, aluminum	$3,900	$5,200
1971-1972	Black, hand-wired, small box	$1,700	$2,300
1971-1972	Custom color, hand-wired	$2,600	$3,400
1973-1975	Black, printed CB, large box	$1,450	$1,925
1973-1975	Custom color, printed CB	$1,950	$2,600
1976-1979	Black	$1,250	$1,650
1976-1979	Custom color	$1,450	$1,925
1980-1981	Black	$1,175	$1,550
1980-1981	Custom color	$1,350	$1,750

Model 1987X Amp Head
1992-present. Vintage Series amp, all tube, 50 watts, 4 inputs, plexi.

1992-2019		$975	$1,300

Model 1992 Super Bass Amp Head
1966-1981. 100 watts, plexi panel until mid-'69 when replaced by aluminum front panel, 2 channels, 4 inputs.

1966-1969	Black, plexi	$3,700	$4,900
1966-1969	Custom color, plexi	$5,300	$7,000
1969-1970	Black, aluminum	$2,200	$2,900
1969-1970	Custom color, aluminum	$4,400	$5,700
1971-1972	Black, hand-wired, small box	$2,200	$2,900
1971-1972	Custom color, hand-wired	$2,600	$3,400
1973-1975	Black, printed CB, large box	$1,450	$1,925
1973-1975	Custom color, printed CB	$1,950	$2,600
1976-1979	Black	$1,250	$1,650
1976-1979	Custom color	$1,450	$1,925
1980-1981	Black	$1,175	$1,550
1980-1981	Custom color	$1,350	$1,750

Model 1992LEM Lemmy Signature Super Bass Amp
2008-2013. Lemmy Kilmister specs, matching 100-watt head with 4x12" and 4x15" stacked cabinets.

2008-2013	Full-stack	$3,200	$4,200

Model 2040 Artist 50-Watt Combo Amp
1971-1978. 50 watts, 2x12" Artist/Artiste combo model with a different (less popular?) circuit.

1971-1978		$1,550	$2,000

Model 2041 Artist Head/Cabinet Set
1971-1978. 50 watts, 2x12" half stack Artist/Artiste cab with a different (less popular?) circuit.

1971-1978		$1,800	$2,300

Model 2046 Specialist 25-Watt Combo Amp
1972-1973. 25 watts, 1x15" speaker, limited production due to design flaw (amp overheats).

1972-1973		$525	$700

Model 2060 Mercury Combo Amp
1972-1973. Combo amp, 5 watts, 1x12", available in red or orange covering.

1972-1973		$550	$725

Model 2061 20-Watt Lead/Bass Amp Head
1968-1973. Lead/bass head, 20 watts, plexi until '69, aluminum after. Reissued in '04 as the Model 2061X.

1968-1969	Black, plexi	$3,000	$4,000
1969-1970	Black, aluminum	$2,100	$2,700
X1971-1972	Black, aluminum	$1,600	$2,100
1973	Black, aluminum	$1,450	$1,900

Model 2061X 20-Watt Lead/Bass Amp Head Reissue
2004-2017. Handwired Series, reissue of 2061 amp head, 20 watts.

2004-2014	1x12 cab	$359	$475
2004-2015	2x12 cab	$375	$500
2004-2017	Head only	$875	$1,125

Model 2068 Artist (JMP) Amp Set
1971-1978. 100-watt head with matching Artist cab, reverb, small logo.

1971-1978		$1,550	$2,000

Model 2078 Combo Amp
1973-1978. Solidstate, 100 watts, 4x12" combo, gold front panel, dark cover, gray grille.

1973-1978		$700	$925

Model 2103 100-Watt 1-Channel Master Combo Amp
1975-1981. One channel, 2 inputs, 100 watts, 2x12", first master volume design, combo version of 2203 head.

1975-1981		$1,100	$1,450

Model 2104 50-Watt 1-Channel Master Combo Amp
1975-1981. One channel, 2 inputs, 50 watts, 2x12", first master volume design, combo version of 2204 head.

1975-1981		$1,100	$1,450

Model 2144 Master Reverb Combo Amp
1978 only. Master volume similar to 2104 but with reverb and boost, 50 watts, 2x12".

1978		$1,200	$1,600

Model 2150 100-Watt 1x12 Combo Amp
1978. Tubes.

1978		$700	$925

Model 2159 100-Watt 2-Channel Combo Amp
1977-1981. 100 watts, 2 channels, 4 inputs, 2x12" combo version of Model 1959 Super Lead head.

1977-1981		$1,025	$1,350

Model 2199 Amp
1979. Solidstate 2x12" combo.

1979		$460	$600

Marshall Model 1987X

1972 Marshall Model 2040 Artist
Mark K

1971 Marshall Model 2060 Mercury
Steve Lee

AMPS

AMPS

Late-1980s Marshall Model 4001 Studio 15 Black
Imaged by Heritage Auctions, HA.com

1981 Marshall Model 2203
Stephan Brown

2007 Marshall Model 2466 Vintage/Modern
Joseph Bradshaw Jr.

MODEL YEAR	FEATURES	EXC. COND. LOW	HIGH
Model 2200 100-Watt Lead Combo Amp			
1977-1981. 100 watts, 2x12" combo, early solidstate, includes boost section, no reverb.			
1977-1981		$525	$675
Model 2203 Lead Amp Head			
1975-1981. Head amp, 100 watts, 2 inputs, first master volume model design, often seen with Mark II logo.			
1975-1981	Black	$1,175	$1,550
1975-1981	Fawn Beige	$1,250	$1,650
Model 2203X JCM800 Reissue Amp Head			
2002-2010. 100 watts.			
2002-2010		$1,175	$1,550
Model 2204 50-Watt Amp Head			
1975-1981. Head only, 50 watts with master volume.			
1975-1981		$1,175	$1,550
Model 2266 50-Watt Combo Amp			
2007-2013. Vintage Modern series, 2x12".			
2007-2013		$650	$850
Model 2466 100-Watt Amp Head			
2007-2013. Vintage Modern series.			
2007-2013		$650	$850
Model 3203 Artist Amp Head			
1986-1991. Tube head version of earlier '84 Model 3210 MOS-FET, designed as affordable alternative, 30 watts, standard short cab, 2 inputs separated by 3 control knobs, Artist 3203 logo on front panel, black.			
1986-1991		$390	$520
Model 3210 MOS-FET Amp Head			
1984-1991. MOS-FET solidstate head, refer Mini-Stack listing for 3210 with 4x10" stacked cabinets. Early-'80s front panel: Lead 100 MOS-FET.			
1984-1991		$270	$355
Model 3310 100-Watt Lead Amp			
1988-1991. Solidstate, 100 watts, lead head with channel switching and reverb.			
1988-1991		$420	$555
Model 4001 Studio 15 Amp			
1985-1992. 15 watts using 6V6 (only model to do this up to this time), 1x12" Celestion Vintage 30 speakers.			
1985-1992		$675	$875
Model 4104 50-Watt Combo Amp			
1981-1990. Combo version of 2204 head, 50 watts, 2x12", master volume.			
1981-1990		$1,300	$1,675
Model 4203 Artist 30 Combo Amp			
1986-1991. 30-watt tube hybrid combo, 1x12", channel switching.			
1986-1991		$390	$510
Model 5002 Combo Amp			
1984-1991. Solidstate combo amp, 20 watts, 1x10", master volume.			
1984-1991		$170	$225
Model 5005 Lead 12 Amp			
1983-1991. Solidstate student amp, 12 watts, master volume, 1x10".			
1983-1991		$195	$245
Model 5205 Reverb 12 Amp			
1986. Solidstate, 12 watts, 1x10", Reverb 12 logo on front panel.			
1986		$195	$245

MODEL YEAR	FEATURES	EXC. COND. LOW	HIGH
Model 5302 Keyboard Amp			
1984-1988. Solidstate, 20 watts, 1x10", marketed for keyboard application.			
1984-1988		$170	$230
Model 5502 Bass Amp			
1984-ca.1992. Solidstate bass combo amp, 20 watts, 1x10" Celestion.			
1984-1992		$170	$230
Model 6100 30th Anniversary Amp			
1992-1998. Head with 100/50/25 switchable watts and 4x12" cabinet (matching colors), first year and into early '93 was blue tolex, black afterwards.			
1992-1998	4x12 cab	$365	$480
1992-1998	Head only	$725	$975
Model 6101 30th Anniversary Combo Amp			
1992-1998. 1x12" combo version of 6100 amp, first year and into early '93 was blue tolex, black afterwards.			
1992-1998		$1,050	$1,350
Model 8008 Valvestate Rackmount Amp			
1991-2001. Valvestate solidstate rack mount power amp with dual 40-watt channels.			
1991-2001		$145	$195
Model 8010 Valvestate VS15 Combo Amp			
1991-1997. Valvestate solidstate, 10 watts, 1x8", compact size, black vinyl, black grille.			
1991-1997		$125	$170
Model 8040 Valvestate 40V Combo Amp			
1991-1997. Valvestate solidstate with tube preamp, 40 watts, 1x12", compact size, black vinyl, black grille.			
1991-1997		$145	$195
Model 8080 Valvestate 80V Combo Amp			
1991-1997. Valvestate solidstate with tube 12AX7 preamp, 80 watts, 1x12", compact size, black vinyl, black grille.			
1991-1997		$145	$195
Model 8100 100-Watt Valvestate VS100H Amp Head			
1991-2001. Valvestate solidstate head, 100 watts.			
1991-2001		$170	$220
Model 8200 200-Watt Valvestate Amp Head			
1993-1998. Valvestate solidstate reverb head, 2x100-watt channels.			
1993-1998		$195	$255
Model 8222 Valvestate Cabinet			
1993-1998. 200 watts, 2x12 extention cab, designed for 8200 head.			
1993-1998		$145	$195
Model 8240 Valvestate Stereo Chorus Amp			
1992-1996. Valvestate, 80 watts (2x40 watts stereo), 2x12" combo, reverb, chorus.			
1992-1996		$220	$290
Model 8280 2x80-Watt Valvestate Combo Amp			
1993-1996. Valvestate solidstate, 2x80 watts, 2x12".			
1993-1996		$245	$315
Model 8412 Valvestate Cabinet			
1991-2001. 140 watts, 4x12 extention cab, designed for 8100 head.			
1991-2001		$195	$255

MODEL YEAR	FEATURES	EXC. COND. LOW	HIGH

MS-2/R/C Amp
1990-present. Microamp series, 1 watt, battery operated, miniature black half-stack amp and cab. Red MS-2R and checkered speaker grille and gold logo MS-2C added in '93.

1990-2019		$25	$40

MS-4 Amp
1998-present. Full-stack version of MS-2, black.

1998-2019		$35	$50

Origin (OR) Series
2018-present. Various tube models include; ORIGIN5, 20C, 20H and 50C. Number indicates watts, C is combo, H is head only.

2018-2019		$220	$290

Silver Jubilee Model 2550 50/25 (Tall) Amp Head
1987-1989. 50/25 switchable tall box head for full Jubilee stack, silver vinyl and chrome control panel.

1987-1989		$1,700	$2,275

Silver Jubilee Model 2551 4x12 Cabinet
1987-1989. Matching silver 4x12" cabs for Jubilee 2550 head, various models, silver vinyl.

1987-1989	2551A, slant	$725	$950
1987-1989	2551AV, Vintage 30	$725	$950
1987-1989	2551B, straight	$725	$950
1987-1989	2551BV, Vintage 30	$725	$950

Silver Jubilee Model 2553 50/25 (Short) Amp Head
1987-1988. 50/25 switchable small box head for mini-short stack, silver vinyl and chrome control panel.

1987-1988		$1,550	$2,050

Silver Jubilee Model 2554 1x12 Combo Amp
1987-1989. 50/25 watts, 1x12" combo using 2550 chassis, silver vinyl and chrome control panel.

1987-1989		$1,400	$1,850

Silver Jubilee Model 2555 Amp Head
1987-1989. 100/50 version of 2550 head, silver vinyl and chrome control panel.

1987-1989		$1,450	$1,950

Silver Jubilee Model 2556 2x12 Cabinet
1987-1989. Matching silver 2x12" cabs for Jubilee heads, various models, silver vinyl.

1987-1989	2556A, slant	$725	$975
1987-1989	2556AV, Vintage 30	$725	$975
1987-1989	2556B, straight	$725	$975
1987-1989	2556BV, Vintage 30	$725	$975

Silver Jubilee Model 2558 2x12 Combo Amp
1987-1989. 50/25 watts, 2x12" combo using 2550 chassis, silver vinyl and chrome control panel.

1987-1989		$1,550	$2,050

Silver Jubilee Model 3560 600 Amp Head
1987. Rackmount 2x300 watts.

1987		$390	$510

SL-5 Amp
2013-2015. Tube combo, 5 watts, 1x12", script logo signature on front panel.

2013-2015		$545	$725

Super 100 40th Anniversary JTM45 MK II Full Stack
2005. 100 watts, 2 4x12 cabs, 250 made.

2005		$3,775	$4,950

Martin
Martin has dabbled in amps a few times, under both the Martin and Stinger brand names. The first batch were amps made by other introduced with their electric acoustics in 1959.

Model 112 Amp
1959-1961. Branded C.F. Martin inside label, made by Rowe-DeArmond, 1x12 combo, limited production, 2x6V6 power tubes, 2x12AX7 preamp tubes, with tube rectifier, 4 inputs, 3 control knobs.

1959-1961		$2,800	$3,600

SS140 Amp

1965-1966		$675	$875

Stinger FX-1 Amp
1988-1990. 10 watts, EQ, switchable solidstate tube-synth circuit, line out and footswitch jacks.

1988		$120	$155

Stinger FX-1R Amp
1988-1990. Mini-stack amp, 2x10", 15 watts, dual-stage circuitry.

1989		$150	$200

Stinger FX-6B Amp
1989-1990. Combo bass amp, 60 watts, 1x15".

1989		$150	$200

Masco
1940s-1950s. The Mark Alan Sampson Company, Long Island, New York, produced a variety of electronic products including tube PA amps and small combo instrument amps. The PA heads are also popular with harp players.

Massie
1940s. Ray Massie worked in Leo Fender's repair shop in the 1940s and also built tube amps. He later worked at the Fender company.

Matamp
1966-present. Tube amps, combos and cabinets built in Huddersfield, England, bearing names like Red, Green, White, Black, and Blue. German-born Mat Mathias started building amps in England in '58 and designed his first Matamp in '66. From '69 to '73, Mathias also made Orange amps. In '89, Mathias died at age 66 and his family later sold the factory to Jeff Lewis.

1x15" Cabinet

1970s		$650	$850

GT-120 Amp Head

1971		$1,800	$2,300

GT-120 Green Stack Amp
1990s. 120 watt GT head with 4x12" straight front cab.

1993-1999		$1,350	$1,750

Marshall MS-4

Ca. 1950s Masco MU-5
Imaged by Heritage Auctions, HA.com

Matamp GT2 MK II

AMPS

2011 Matchless DC-30
Jacques Menache Masri

Matchless HC-30

Matchless Independence 35

Matchless

1989-1999, 2001-present. Founded by Mark Sampson and Rick Perrotta in California. Circuits based on Vox AC-30 with special attention to transformers. A new Matchless company was reorganized in 2001 by Phil Jamison, former head of production for the original company.

Avalon 35 Amp Head
2009-2010. 35 watts head, reverb.

2009-2010	$1,250	$1,625

Brave 40 112 Amp
1997-1999. 40 watts class A, 1x12", footswitchable between high and low inputs.

1997-1999	$1,200	$1,575

Brave 40 212 Amp
1997-1999. 2x12" version of Brave.

1997-1999	$1,300	$1,675

Chief Amp Head
1995-1999. 100 watts class A, head.

1995-1999	$2,050	$2,650

Chief 212 Amp
1995-1999. 100 watts class A, 2x12", reverb.

1995-1999	$2,150	$2,800

Chief 410 Amp
1995-1999. 100 watts class A, 4x10", reverb.

1995-1999	$2,225	$2,900

Chieftan Amp Head
1995-1999. 40 watts class A head, reverb, chickenhead knobs.

1995-1999	$1,350	$1,750

Chieftan 112 Amp
1995-1999, 2001. 40 watts class A, 1x12", reverb.

1995-1999		$1,775	$2,300
2001	Jamison era	$1,775	$2,300

Chieftan 210 Amp
1995-1999. 40 watts class A, 2x10", reverb.

1995-1999	$1,950	$2,500

Chieftan 212 Amp
1995-1999, 2001-present. 40 watts class A, 2x12", reverb.

1995-1999		$1,950	$2,500
2001-2019	Jamison era	$1,950	$2,500

Chieftan 410 Amp
1995-1999. 40 watts class A, 4x10", reverb.

1995-1999	$2,050	$2,650

Clipper 15 112 Amp
1998-1999. 15 watts, single channel, 1x12".

1998-1999	$850	$1,100

Clipper 15 210 Amp
1998-1999. 15 watts, single channel, 2x10".

1998-1999	$900	$1,200

Clubman 35 Amp Head
1993-1999. 35 watts class A head.

1993-1999	$1,500	$1,950

DC-30 Standard Cabinet
1991-1999. 30 watts, 2x12", with or without reverb.

1991-1999	$2,200	$2,900

DC-30 Exotic Wood Cabinet Option
1995-1999. 30 watts, 2x12", gold plating, limited production.

1995-1999	$3,700	$4,800

ES/EB Cabinet
ES = speaker cabinets and EB = bass speaker cabinets.

1991-1999	1x12	$350	$450
1993-1999	2x10	$425	$560
1993-1999	2x10+2x12	$525	$700
1993-1999	2x12	$450	$575
1993-1999	4x12	$575	$750
1997-1999	1x15	$360	$465
1997-1999	4x10	$500	$650

HC-30 Amp Head
1991-1999, 2003. The first model offered by Matchless, 30 watts class A head.

1991-1999		$1,675	$2,150
2003	Jamison era	$1,675	$2,150

HC-85 Amp Head
1992. Only 25 made, similar to HC-30 but more flexible using various tube substitutions.

1992	$1,775	$2,275

Hurricane Amp Head
1997. 15 watts class A head.

1997	$1,000	$1,300

Hurricane 112 Amp
1994-1997. 15 watts class A, 1x12".

1994-1997	$1,000	$1,300

Hurricane 210 Amp
1996-1997. 15 watts class A, 2x10".

1996-1997	$1,200	$1,575

Independence 35 Amp Head
2005-2017. 35 watts, with or without reverb.

2005-2017	$1,500	$1,950

JJ-30 112 John Jorgensen Amp
1997-1999. 30 watts, DC-30 chasis with reverb and tremolo, 1x12" Celestion 30, offered in white, blue, gray sparkle tolex or black.

1997-1999	$2,975	$3,800

Lightning 15 Amp Head
1994-1997, 2005-present. 15 watts class A head.

1994-1997	$1,075	$1,400

Lightning 15 112 Amp
1994-1999, 2001-present. 15 watts class A, 1x12".

1994-1999		$1,525	$2,000
2001-2019	Jamison era	$1,525	$2,000

Lightning 15 210 Amp
1996-1997, 2001-2006. 15 watts class A, 2x10".

1996-1997		$1,625	$2,100
2001-2006	Jamison era	$1,625	$2,100

Lightning 15 212 Amp
1998, 2001-present. 15 watts class A, 2x12".

1998-2019	$1,650	$2,150

Little Monster Amp
2007-2009. 9 watts, offered as head, and 1x12" or 2x12" combo.

2007-2009	$1,050	$1,400

Nighthawk Amp
2003-present. 15 watts, offered as head, and 1x12", 2x10" or 2x12" combo.

2003-2014	2x10	$1,000	$1,300
2003-2019	1x12	$925	$1,200
2003-2019	2x12	$1,050	$1,350

MODEL YEAR FEATURES	EXC. COND. LOW	HIGH
Phoenix 35 (PH-35) Amp Head		
2003-present. 35-watt head, red.		
2003-2019	$1,500	$1,950
SC-30 Standard Cabinet Amp		
1991-1999. 30 watts class A, 1x12".		
1991-1999	$2,200	$2,875
2001-2006 Jamison era	$2,050	$2,700
SC-30 Exotic Wood Cabinet Amp		
1995-1999. 30 watts class A, 1x12", gold plating, limited production.		
1995-1999	$3,550	$4,550
Skyliner Reverb 15 112 Amp		
1998-1999. 15 watts, 2 channels, 1x12".		
1998-1999	$750	$975
Skyliner Reverb 15 210 Amp		
1998-1999. 15 watts, 2 channels, 2x10".		
1998-1999	$825	$1,075
Spitfire 15 Amp Head		
1997. 15 watts, head.		
1997	$975	$1,300
Spitfire 15 112 Amp		
1994-1997. 15 watts, 1x12".		
1994-1997	$1,100	$1,450
Spitfire 15 210 Amp		
1996-1997. 15 watts, 2x10".		
1996-1997	$1,200	$1,575
Starliner 40 212 Amp		
1999. 40 watts, 2x12".		
1999	$1,250	$1,625
Superchief 120 Amp Head		
1994-1999. 120 watts, class A head.		
1994-1999	$1,950	$2,500
TC-30 Standard Cabinet Amp		
1991-1999. 30 watts, 2x10" class A, low production numbers makes value approximate with DC-30.		
1991-1999	$2,150	$2,750
TC-30 Exotic Wood Cabinet Amp		
1991-1999. 30 watts, 2x10" class A, limited production.		
1991-1999	$2,750	$3,525
Thunderchief Bass Amp Head		
1994-1999. 200 watts, class A bass head.		
1994-1999	$1,525	$2,000
Thunderman 100 Bass Combo Amp		
1997-1998. 100 watts, 1x15" in portaflex-style flip-top cab.		
1997-1998	$2,125	$2,750
Tornado 15 112 Amp		
1994-1995. Compact, 15 watts, 1x12", 2-tone covering, simple controls – volume, tone, tremolo speed, tremolo depth.		
1994-1995	$725	$925

Maven Peal

Amps, combos and cabinets built by David Zimmerman in Plainfield, Vermont, beginning in 1999. Serial number format is by amp wattage and sequential build; for example, 15-watt amp 15-001.

Mega Amplifiers

Budget and intermediate grade, production, solidstate and tube amps from Guitar Jones, Inc. of Pomona, California.

Merlin

Rack mount bass heads built in Germany by Musician Sound Design. They also offer the MSD guitar effects.

Mesa-Boogie

1971-present. Founded by Randall Smith in San Francisco, California. Circuits styled on high-gain Fender-based chassis designs, ushering in the compact high-gain amp market. The following serial number information and specs courtesy of Mesa Engineering.

MODEL YEAR FEATURES	EXC. COND. LOW	HIGH
.50 Caliber/.50 Caliber+ Amp Head		
Jan. 1987-Dec. 1988, 1992-1993. Serial numbers: SS3100 - SS11,499. Mesa Engineering calls it Caliber .50. Tube head amp, 50 watts, 5-band EQ, effects loop. Called the .50 Caliber Plus in '92 and '93.		
1987-1988 Caliber	$500	$650
1992-1993 Caliber+	$500	$650
.50 Caliber+ Combo Amp		
Dec. 1988-Oct. 1993. Serial numbers FP11,550 - FP29,080. 50 watts, 1x12" combo amp.		
1988-1993	$550	$725
20/20 Amp		
Jun. 1995-2010. Serial numbers: TT-01. 20-22 watts per channel.		
1995-2010	$550	$725
50/50 (Fifty/Fifty) Amp		
May 1989-2001. Serial numbers: FF001-. 100 watts total power, 50 watts per channel, front panel reads Fifty/Fifty, contains 4 6L6 power tubes.		
1989-2001	$525	$700
395 Amp		
Feb. 1991-Apr. 1992. Serial numbers: S2572 - S3237.		
1991-1992	$725	$950
Bass 400/Bass 400+ Amp Head		
Aug. 1989-Aug. 1990. Serial numbers: B001-B1200. About 500 watts using 12 5881 power tubes. Replaced by 400+ Aug.1990-present, serial numbers: B1200- . Update change to 7-band EQ at serial number B1677.		
1989-1990 Bass 400	$925	$1,225
1990-1999 Bass 400+	$975	$1,300
Big Block Series Amp		
2004-2014. Rackmount bass amps, models 750 and Titan V-12.		
2004-2014 750 Bass Head, 750w	$925	$1,225
2006-2010 Titan V-12, 650-1200w	$925	$1,225
Blue Angel Series Amp		
Jun. 1994-2004. Serial numbers BA01-. Switchable between 15, 33 or 38 watts, offered as head, 1x12" combo or 4x10" combo, blue cover.		
1994-2004 Combo 1x12"	$700	$925
1994-2004 Combo 4x10"	$800	$1,050

1994 Mesa-Boogie .50 Caliber
Imaged by Heritage Auctions, HA.com

Mesa-Boogie Big Block 750

Mesa Boogie Blue Angel

AMPS

Mesa Boogie Express 5:50

Mesa Boogie Lone Star 1x12 Combo

1977 Mesa-Boogie Mark I

MODEL YEAR	FEATURES	EXC. COND. LOW	HIGH

Buster Bass Amp Head
Dec. 1997-Jan. 2001. Serial numbers: BS-1-999. 200 watts via 6 6L6 power tubes.

1997-2001		$525	$700

Buster Bass Combo Amp
1999-2001. 200 watts, 2x10", wedge cabinet, black vinyl, metal grille.

1999-2001		$525	$700

Coliseum 300 Amp
Oct. 1997-2000. Serial numbers: COL-01 - COL-132. 200 watts/channel, 12 6L6 power tubes, rack mount.

1997-2000		$1,000	$1,350

D-180 Amp Head
Jul. 1982-Dec. 1985. Serial numbers: D001-D681. All tube head amp, 200 watts, preamp, switchable.

1982-1985		$775	$1,025

DC-3 Amp
Sep. 1994-Jan. 1999. Serial numbers: DC3-001 - DC3-4523. 35 watts, 1x12".

1994-1999	Combo 1x12"	$500	$650
1994-1999	Head only	$425	$550

DC-5 Amp
Oct. 1993-Jan. 1999. Serial numbers: DC1024 - DC31,941. 50-watt head, 1x12" combo.

1993-1999	Combo 1x12"	$500	$650
1993-1999	Head only	$425	$550

DC-10 Amp
May 1996-Jan. 1999. Serial numbers: DCX-001 - DCX-999. Dirty/Clean (DC), 100 watts (6L6s), 2x12".

1993-1996	Combo 2x12"	$575	$750
1996-1999	Head only	$525	$700

Electra Dyne Amp Head
2009-2013. 45/90 watts, Black Taurus/black grille or British Tan Bronco/tan grille.

2009-2013		$850	$1,100

Express Series Amp
2007-2017. Compact combo tube amps with power switching.

2007-2016	5:50, 2x12", 5-50w	$775	$1,025
2007-2017	5:25, 1x10", 5-25w	$675	$875
2007-2017	5:50, 1x12", 5-50w	$725	$950
2008	5:25, short head, 25w	$600	$800

Extension Cabinet
1980s-present. Mesa-Boogie offered 'extension cabinets' which could be mixed and matched with amp heads, using different configurations with correct impedance. Other manufacturers often consider an extension cab as an extra cab, but Mesa Engineering considers it to be the main cab (not an extra). The company has generic cabs as well as cabs associated with specific models, but both generic and model-specific fall into similar price ranges. Some other variances include; vertical or horizontal, open back or closed, slant or straight front, grille could be metal or cloth, and some cabs are designated for bass guitar. Specialized cabinets may be more than values shown.

1980-2019	Various sizes	$225	$900

F-30 Amp
2002-Feb. 2007. Combo, 30 watts, 1x12".

2002-2007		$400	$525

F-50 Amp
2002-Feb. 2007. Combo, 50 watts, 1x12", AB 2 6L6 power.

2002-2007		$575	$750
2002-2007	Head only	$525	$700

F-100 Amp
2002-Feb. 2007. Combo, 100 watts, 2x12".

2002-2007	Combo 2x12"	$725	$925
2002-2007	Head only	$625	$800

Formula Preamp
Jul. 1998-2002. Serial numbers: F-01. Used 5 12AX7 tubes, 3 channels.

1998-2002		$350	$450

Heartbreaker Amp Head
1996-2001. Head only, 100 watts.

1996-2001		$800	$1,025

Heartbreaker Combo Amp
Jun. 1996-2001. Serial numbers: HRT-01. 60 to 100 watts switchable, 2x12" combo, designed to switch-out 6L6s, EL34s or the lower powered 6V6s in the power section, switchable solidstate or tube rectifier.

1996-2001		$875	$1,125

Lone Star Series Amp
2004-present. Designed by founder Randall Smith and Doug West with focus on boutique-type amp. Class A (EL84) or AB (4 6L6) circuits, long or short head, 1x12" combo, 2x12" combo, and short head 4x10" cab, and long head 4x12" cab.

2004-2016	Combo 1x12", hardwood	$1,525	$2,000
2004-2016	Combo 4x10", blue	$1,150	$1,500
2004-2019	Combo 1x12"	$1,025	$1,350
2004-2019	Combo 2x12"	$1,150	$1,500
2004-2019	Head, class A or AB	$950	$1,250

Lone Star Special Amp
2005-present. Smaller lighter version using EL84 power tubes, 5/15/30 watts, long or short head amp or 1x12", 2x12" or 4x10" combo.

2005-2019	Combo 1x12"	$1,125	$1,475

M-180 Amp
Apr. 1982-Jan. 1986. Serial numbers: M001-M275. Rack mount tube power amp.

1982-1986		$575	$750

M-190 Amp
1980s. Rack mount tube power amp.

1980s		$425	$550

M-2000 Amp
Jun. 1995-2003. Serial numbers: B2K-01.

1995-2003		$625	$800

M6 Carbine Bass Amp Head
2011-2017. 600-watt head, also offered in 2x12 combo.

2011-2017		$500	$650

Mark I Amp Head
1990. 60/100 watts, tweed cover.

1990		$1,300	$1,675

Mark I Combo (Model A) Amp
1971-1978. The original Boogie amp, not called the Mark I until the Mark II was issued, 60 or 100 watts, 1x12", Model A serial numbers: 1-2999, very early se-

MODEL YEAR	FEATURES	EXC. COND. LOW	HIGH
rial numbers 1-299 had 1x15".			
1971-1978	1x12" or 1x15"	$1,300	$1,675

Mark I Reissue Amp

Nov. 1989-Sept. 2007. Serial numbers: H001-. 100 watts, 1x12", reissue features include figured maple cab and wicker grille.

2000-2007	Hardwood cab	$1,250	$1,600
2000-2007	Standard cab	$925	$1,225

Mark II B Amp Head

1981-1983. Head only.

1981-1983		$575	$750

Mark II B Combo Amp

1980-1983. Effective Aug. '80 1x12" models, serial numbers 5575-110000. May '83 1x15" models, serial numbers 560-11000. The 300 series serial numbers K1-K336.

1981-1983	1x12" or 1x15", tolex	$800	$1,050
1981-1983	Hardwood cab	$1,100	$1,450

Mark II C/Mark II C+ Amp

May 1983-Mar. 1985. Serial numbers 11001-14999 for 60 watts, 1x15", offered with optional white tolex cover. 300 series serial numbers after C+ are in the series K337-K422.

1983-1985		$2,150	$2,850
1985	Hardwood cab	$2,600	$3,450

Mark II C+ Amp Head

1983-1985. 60-watt head.

1983-1985	Hardwood cab	$2,500	$3,350
1983-1985	Standard cab	$2,050	$2,750

Mark II Combo Amp

1978-1980. Late-'78 1x12", serial numbers: 3000-5574. Effective Aug.'80 1x15", serial numbers: 300-559 until Mark II B replaced.

1978-1980	1x12" or 1x15"	$725	$950

Mark III Amp Head

1985-1999. 100 watts, black vinyl.

1985-1990		$800	$1,050
1985-1990	Custom hardwood	$1,250	$1,625
1990-1999	Graphic EQ model	$900	$1,175

Mark III Combo Amp

Mar. 1985-Feb. 1999. Serial numbers: 15000-28384. 300 series serialization K500-. Graphic equalizer only Mark III since Aug.'90, 100 watts, 1x12" combo. Custom cover or exotic hardwood cab will bring more than standard vinyl cover cab. There is also a Simul-Class Mark III which can run in 25, 60 or 85 watts.

1985-1990	Black	$900	$1,175
1985-1990	Custom color	$1,050	$1,400
1985-1999	Custom hardwood	$1,450	$1,900
1990-1999	Graphic EQ, standard cab	$1,050	$1,375

Mark IV (Rack Mount) Amp Head

1990-May 2008. Rack mount version.

1990-2008		$850	$1,100

Mark IV Amp Head

1990-May 2008. Clean rhythm, crunch rhythm and lead modes, 85 watts, EQ, 3-spring reverb, dual effects loops, digital footswitching. Also available in custom hardwood cab with wicker grille.

1990-2008	Custom hardwood	$1,300	$1,700
1990-2008	Short head, tolex	$850	$1,100

Mark IV/Mark IV B Combo Amp

May 1990-May 2008. Changed to Model IV B Feb.'95, serial numbers: IV001. Clean rhythm, crunch rhythm and lead modes, 40 watts, EQ, 3-spring reverb, dual effects loops, digital footswitching.

1991-1999		$1,000	$1,275
1991-1999	Custom hardwood	$1,550	$2,050
2000-2008		$1,000	$1,275
2000-2008	Custom hardwood	$1,625	$2,100

Mark V Private Reserve 40th Anniversary Amp

2009-2010. Limited production, 1x12 combo, 40th Anniversary logo.

2009-2010		$3,350	$4,400

Mark V Private Reserve Amp

2011-2016. Special order, 1x12" combo.

2011-2016		$3,175	$4,200

Mark V/Mark Five Amp

2010-present. 3 channels, 10/45/90 watts, also in 1x12" combo.

2010-2019	Combo 1x12"	$1,400	$1,800
2010-2019	Head	$1,250	$1,650

Mark V:35/Mark Five:35 Amp

2015-present. 35/25/10 watts, also 1x12" combo, black.

2015-2019	Combo 1x12"	$1,050	$1,400
2015-2019	Head	$1,300	$1,700

Maverick Dual Rectifier Amp Head

1994-Feb. 2005. 35 watts, Dual Rectifier head, white/blond vinyl cover.

1994-2005		$700	$900

Maverick Dual Rectifier Combo Amp

1997-Feb. 2005. Dual channels, 4 EL84s, 35 watts, 1x12", 2x12" or 4x10" combo amp, 5AR4 tube rectifier, cream vinyl covering. Serial number: MAV. Also available as head.

1997-2005	1x12"	$750	$975
1997-2005	2x12"	$850	$1,100
2005	4x10"	$900	$1,150

Mini Rectifier Twenty-Five Amp Head

2012-present. Ultra compact design, 10/25 watts, 2 channels.

2012-2019		$625	$800

M-Pulse 360 Amp

Jul. 2001-2005. Serial numbers: MP3-01-. Rack mount, silver panel.

2001-2003		$600	$775

M-Pulse 600 Amp

Apr. 2001-2011. Serial numbers: MP6-01- . Rack mount bass with 600 watts, tube preamp.

2001-2011		$650	$850

Nomad 45 Amp Head

1999-Feb. 2005. 45 watts, dark vinyl cover, dark grille.

1999-2005		$400	$525

Nomad 45 Combo Amp

Jul. 1999-Feb. 2005. Serial numbers: NM45-01. 45 watts, 1x12, 2x12" or 4x10" combo, dark vinyl cover, dark grille.

1999-2005	1x12"	$450	$600
1999-2005	2x12"	$500	$650
1999-2005	4x10"	$575	$750

Mesa-Boogie Mark II

AMPS

1980s Mesa-Boogie Mark III Combo

Imaged by Heritage Auctions, HA.com

Mesa-Boogie Mini Rectifier Twenty-Five

Mesa-Boogie Road King II Dual Rectifier Combo

1984 Mesa-Boogie Son Of Boogie

Tom Pfeifer

Mesa Boogie Stiletto Black

Imaged by Heritage Auctions, HA.com

MODEL YEAR	FEATURES	EXC. COND. LOW	HIGH
Nomad 55 Amp Head			
1999-2004. 55 watt head only.			
1999-2004		$400	$525
Nomad 55 Combo Amp			
Jul. 1999-2004. Serial numbers: NM55-01. 55 watts, 1x12", 2x12" or 4x10" combo.			
1999-2004	1x12"	$450	$600
1999-2004	2x12"	$500	$650
Nomad 100 Amp Head			
Jul. 1999-Feb. 2005. 100 watts, black cover, black grille.			
1999-2005		$450	$600
Nomad 100 Combo Amp			
Jul. 1999-Feb. 2005. 100 watts, 1x12" or 2x12" combo, black cover, black grille.			
1999-2005	1x12"	$500	$650
1999-2005	2x12"	$525	$675
Princeton Boost Fender Conversion Amp			
1970. Fender Princeton modified by Randall Smith, Boogie badge logo instead of the Fender blackface logo on upper left corner of the grille. About 300 amps were modified and were one of the early mods that became Mesa-Boogie.			
1970		$2,000	$2,600
Quad Preamp			
Sep. 1987-1992. Serial numbers: Q001-Q2857. Optional Quad with FU2-A footswitch Aug.'90-Jan.'92, serial numbers: Q2022-Q2857.			
1990-1992	With footswitch	$550	$725
Recto Recording Preamp			
2004-2018. Rack mount preamp.			
2004-2018		$750	$975
Rect-O-Verb Combo Amp			
Dec. 1998-2001. Serial numbers R50-. 50 watts, 1x12", black vinyl cover, black grille.			
1998-2001		$775	$1,000
Rect-O-Verb I Amp Head			
Dec. 1998-2001. Serial numbers: R50-. 50 watts, head with 2 6L6 power tubes, upgraded Apr.'01 to II Series.			
1998-2001		$725	$950
Rect-O-Verb II Amp Head			
Apr. 2001-2010. Upgrade, serial number R5H-750.			
2001-2010		$725	$950
Rect-O-Verb II Combo Amp			
April 2001-2010. Upgrade R5H-750, 50 watts, AB, 2 6L6, spring reverb.			
2001-2010		$800	$1,025
Road King Dual Rectifier Amp Head			
2002-May 2017. Tube head, various power tube selections based upon a chasis which uses 2 EL34s and 4 6L6, 2 5U4 dual rectifier tubes or silicon diode rectifiers, 50, 100 or 120 watts. Series II upgrades start in '06.			
2002-2011		$1,725	$2,200
2006-2017	Series II	$1,725	$2,200
Road King Dual Rectifier Combo Amp			
2002-2015. 2x12" combo version, Series II upgrades start in '06.			
2002-2005	Select watts	$1,800	$2,325
2006-2015	Series II	$1,800	$2,325

MODEL YEAR	FEATURES	EXC. COND. LOW	HIGH
Roadster Dual Rectifier Amp			
2006-May 2017. 50/100 watts, head only, 1x12" or 2x12" combo.			
2006-2014	Combo 1x12	$1,525	$1,950
2006-2017	Combo 2x12	$1,575	$2,025
2006-2017	Head	$1,450	$1,850
Rocket 44 Amp			
2011. 45 watts, 1x12" combo, spring reverb, FX loop.			
2011		$425	$550
Rocket 440 Amp			
Mar. 1999-Aug. 2000. Serial numbers: R440-R44-1159. 45 watts, 4x10".			
1999-2000		$550	$725
Satellite/Satellite 60 Amp			
Aug. 1990-1999. Serial numbers: ST001-ST841. Uses either 6L6s for 100 watts or EL34s for 60 watts, dark vinyl, dark grille.			
1990-1999		$500	$675
Solo 50 Rectifier Series I Amp Head			
Nov. 1998-Apr. 2001. Serial numbers: R50. 50-watt head.			
1998-2001		$600	$775
Solo 50 Rectifier Series II Amp Head			
Apr. 2001-2011. Upgrade, serial numbers: S50-S1709. Upgrades preamp section, head with 50 watts.			
2001-2011		$600	$775
Solo Dual Rectifier Amp			
1997-2011. Dual Rectifier Solo logo on front panel, 3x5U4, 150 watts.			
1997-2011		$1,100	$1,425
Solo Triple Rectifier Amp			
1997-2011. Triple Rectifier Solo logo on front panel, 3x5U4, 150 watts.			
1997-2011		$1,100	$1,425
Son Of Boogie Amp			
May 1982-Dec. 1985. Serial numbers: S100-S2390. 60 watts, 1x12", considered the first reissue of the original Mark I.			
1982-1985		$500	$650
Stereo 290 (Simul 2-Ninety) Amp			
Jun. 1992-present. Serial numbers: R0001-. Dual 90-watt stereo channels, rack mount.			
1992-2019		$700	$900
Stereo 295 Amp			
Mar. 1987-May 1991. Serial numbers: S001-S2673. Dual 95-watt class A/B stereo channels, rack mount. Selectable 30 watts Class A (EL34 power tubes) power.			
1987-1991		$450	$600
Stiletto Ace Amp			
2007-2011. 50 watts, 2 channels, head or combo.			
2007-2011	Combo 1x12"	$800	$1,050
2007-2011	Combo 2x12"	$875	$1,125
2007-2011	Head only	$775	$1,000
Stiletto Series Amp Head			
2004-2011. Series includes the Deuce (50 or 100 watts, 4 EL-34s) and Trident (50 or 150 watts, 6 EL-34s).			
2004-2011	Deuce	$950	$1,225
2004-2011	Trident	$1,000	$1,300

The *Vintage Guitar Price Guide* shows low to high values for items in all-original excellent condition, and, where applicable, with original case or cover.

MODEL YEAR	FEATURES	EXC. COND. LOW	HIGH

Strategy 400 Amp
Mar. 1987-May 1991. Serial numbers: S001-S2627. 400 to 500 watts, power amplifier with 12 6L6 power tubes.

1987-1991		$700	$925

Strategy 500 Amp
Jun. 1991-Apr. 1992. S2,552- . Rack mount, 500 watts, 4 6550 power tubes.

1991-1992		$875	$1,150

Studio .22/Studio .22+ Amp
Nov. 1985-1988. Serial numbers: SS000-SS11499, black vinyl, black grille, 22 watts, 1x12". Replaced by .22+ Dec. '88-Aug. '93. Serial numbers: FP11,500-FP28,582. 22 watts.

1985-1988	22	$500	$650
1988-1993	22+	$500	$650

Studio Caliber DC-2 Amp
Apr. 1994-Jan. 1999. Serial numbers: DC2-01 - DC2-4247 (formerly called DC-2). 20 watts, 1x12" combo, dark vinyl, dark grille.

1994-1999		$400	$525

Studio Preamp
Aug. 1988-Dec. 1993. Serial numbers: SP000-SP7890. Tube preamp, EQ, reverb, effects loop.

1988-1993		$400	$525

Subway Reverb Rocket Amp
Jun. 1998-Aug. 2001. Serial numbers: RR1000-RR2461. 20 watts, 1x10".

1998-2001		$500	$675

Subway Rocket (Non-Reverb) Amp
Jan. 1996-Jul. 1998. Serial numbers: SR001-SR2825. No reverb, 20 watts, 1x10".

1996-1998		$500	$675

Subway/Subway Blues Amp
Sep. 1994-Aug. 2000. Serial numbers: SB001-SB2515. 20 watts, 1x10".

1994-2000		$475	$625

TA-15 Amp Head
2010-2015. TransAtlantic series, lunchbox-sized tube head, 2 channels, 5/15/25 watts.

2010-2015		$500	$650

TA-30 Combo Amp
2012-2015. TransAtlantic series, 15/30/40 watts, 1x12" or 2x12" combo, 2 channels.

2012-2015		$850	$1,125

Trem-O-Verb Dual Rectifier Amp Head
Jun. 1993-Jan. 2001. 100-watt head version.

1993-2001		$925	$1,200
1993-2001	Rackmount version	$925	$1,200

Trem-O-Verb Dual Rectifier Combo Amp
Jun.1993-Jan.2001. Serial numbers: R- to about R-21210. 100 watts, 2x12" Celestion Vintage 30.

1993-2001		$925	$1,200

Triaxis Programmable Preamp
Oct. 1991-2016. Serial numbers:T0001-. 5 12AX7 tube preamp, rack mount.

1991-2016		$925	$1,200

Venture Bass (M-Pulse) Amp

2007-2009		$750	$1,000

V-Twin Rackmount Amp
May 1995-Jun. 1998. Serial numbers: V2R-001 to V2R-2258.

1995-1998		$425	$550

WalkAbout M-Pulse Bass Amp Head
Sep. 2001-May 2017. Serial numbers: WK-01-. Lightweight 13 pounds, 2 12AX7s + 300 MOS-FET.

2001-2017		$550	$725

WalkAbout Scout Convertible Combo Amp
2001-May 2017. Head and 1x12 combo.

2001-2017		$800	$1,025

Meteoro
1986-present. Guitar, bass, harp and keyboard combo amps, heads, and cabinets built in Brazil. They also build effects.

Metropoulos Amplification
2004-present. George Metropoulos builds his professional and premium grade amps in Flint, Michigan.

MG
2004-present. Tube combo guitar amps built by Marcelo Giangrande in São Paulo, Brazil. He also builds effects.

Mighty Moe Ampstraps
Peter Bellak built his guitar amp straps in Sacramento, California, starting in 2007. He also offered an amp strap for ukulele.

Milbert Amplifiers
2009-present. Professional and premium grade, production/custom, amps for guitars and cars, built in Gaithersburg, Maryland by Michael Milbert.

Mission Amps
1996-present. Bruce Collins' Mission Amps, located in Arvada, Colorado, produces a line of custom-made combo amps, heads, and cabinets.

Mojave Amp Works
2002-present. Tube amp heads and speaker cabinets by Victor Mason in Apple Valley, California.

Montgomery Ward
Amps for this large retailer were sometimes branded as Montgomery Ward, but usually as Airline (see that listing).

1x12" Combo Amp
1950s. 1x12", about 2 6L6 power tubes, includes Model 8439 and brown covered Maestro C Series with cloverleaf grille.

1950s		$400	$600

Model 55 JDR 8437 Amp
1950s. 4x8" speakers in 'suitcase' amp cabinet, brown control panel.

1950s		$500	$700

1999 Mesa Boogie Subway Blues
Mark Aftab Sackoor

AMPS

MG Raven

Milbert GAGA D-90

Mosrite 400 Fuzzrite
Dennis Carden

1979 Music Man Seventy Five
Rivington Guitars

Music Man 112 HD130
Terry Loose

Mooneyes

Budget solid state amp line from Lace Music Products. They also offered amps under the Rat Fink and Lace brands. Lace had a Mooneyes guitar model line.

Morley

Late-1960s-present. The effects company offered an amp in the late '70s. See Effects section for more company information.

Bigfoot Amp

1979-ca.1981. Looks like Morley's '70s effects pedals, produced 25 watts and pedal controlled volume. Amp only, speakers were sold separately.

Model Year	Features	Low	High
1979-1981		$175	$225

Mosrite

1968-1969. Mosrite jumped into the amp business during the last stages of the company history, the company was founded as a guitar company in 1954 and attained national fame in the '60s but by the time the company entered the amp business, the guitar boom began to fade, forcing the original Mosrite out of business in '69.

Model 400 Fuzzrite Amp

1968-1969. Solidstate, 1x15 combo, black tolex with silver grille, reverb and tremolo.

Model Year	Features	Low	High
1968-1969		$625	$825

Model SS-550 The Gospel Amp

1968. Solidstate, 1 speaker combo, 2 channels normal and tremolo, reverb, black tolex.

Model Year	Features	Low	High
1968		$575	$750

Mountain

Mountain builds a 9-volt amp in a wood cabinet. Originally built in California, then Nevada; currently being made in Vancouver, British Columbia.

Multivox

Ca.1946-ca.1984. Multivox was started as a subsidiary of Premier to manufacture amps, and later, effects. Generally student grade to low intermediate grade amps.

Murph

1965-1967. Amps marketed by Murph Guitars of San Fernado, California. At first they were custom-made tube amps, but most were later solidstate production models made by another manufacturer.

Music Man

1972-present. Music Man made amps from '73 to '83. The number preceding the amp model indicates the speaker configuration. The last number in model name usually referred to the watts. RD indicated Reverb Distortion. RP indicated Reverb Phase. Many models were available in head-only versions and as combos with various speaker combinations.

Sixty Five Amp Head

1973-1981. 65 watts, reverb, tremolo.

Model Year	Features	Low	High
1973-1981		$350	$450

Seventy Five Reverb/75 Reverb Amp

1973-1981. Head amp, 75 watts, reverb.

Model Year	Features	Low	High
1973-1981		$375	$475

110 RD Fifty Amp

1980-1983. 50 watts, 1x10", reverb, distortion.

Model Year	Features	Low	High
1980-1983		$400	$525

112 B Bass Amp

1983. 50 watts, 1x12".

Model Year	Features	Low	High
1983		$400	$525

112 RD Fifty Amp

1980-1983. 50 watts, 1x12", reverb, distortion.

Model Year	Features	Low	High
1980-1983		$400	$525

112 RD Sixty Five Amp

1978-1983. 65 watts, 1x12", reverb, distortion.

Model Year	Features	Low	High
1978-1983		$400	$525

112 RD One Hundred Amp

1978-1983. 100 watts, 1x12", reverb, distortion, EVM option for heavy duty 12" Electro-Voice speakers.

Model Year	Features	Low	High
1978-1983		$475	$625
1978-1983	EVM option	$475	$625

112 RP Sixty Five Amp

1978-1983. 65 watts, 1x12", reverb, built-in phaser.

Model Year	Features	Low	High
1978-1983		$475	$625

112 RP One Hundred Amp

1978-1983. Combo amp, 100 watts, 1x12", reverb, built-in phaser.

Model Year	Features	Low	High
1978-1983		$475	$625

112 Sixty Five Amp

1973-1981. Combo amp, 65 watts, 1x12", reverb, tremolo.

Model Year	Features	Low	High
1973-1981		$475	$625

115 Sixty Five Amp

1973-1981. Combo amp, 65 watts, 1x15", reverb, tremolo.

Model Year	Features	Low	High
1973-1981		$475	$625

210 HD130 Amp

1973-1981. 130 watts, 2x10", reverb, tremolo.

Model Year	Features	Low	High
1973-1981		$525	$700

210 Sixty Five Amp

1973-1981. 65 watts, 2x10", reverb, tremolo.

Model Year	Features	Low	High
1973-1981		$525	$700

212 HD130 Amp

1973-1981. 130 watts, 2x12", reverb, tremolo.

Model Year	Features	Low	High
1973-1981		$525	$700

212 Sixty Five Amp

1973-1981. 65 watts, 2x12", reverb, tremolo.

Model Year	Features	Low	High
1973-1981		$525	$700

410 Sixty Five Amp

1973-1981. 65 watts, 4x10", reverb, tremolo.

Model Year	Features	Low	High
1973-1981		$525	$700

410 Seventy Five Amp

1982-1983. 75 watts, 4x10", reverb, tremolo.

Model Year	Features	Low	High
1982-1983		$525	$700

HD-130 Amp

1973-1981. Head amp, 130 watts, reverb, tremolo.

Model Year	Features	Low	High
1973-1981	Head only	$375	$475

HD-150 Amp

1973-1981. Head amp, 75/100 watts.

Model Year	Features	Low	High
1973-1981	Head only	$375	$475

AMPS

MODEL YEAR	FEATURES	EXC. COND. LOW	HIGH

RD Fifty Amp
1980-1983. Head amp, 50 watts, reverb, distortion.

| 1980-1983 | Head only | $375 | $475 |

Nady
1976-present. Wireless sound company Nady Systems started offering tube combo and amp heads in '06.

NARB
1973. Briefly made by Ken Bran and Jim Marshall, about 24 made, all were Marshall 100-watt tremolo half-stack, NARB logo on amp and cabinet.

100 Watt Half-Stack
1973. 100 watts, 4x12".

| 1973 | | $2,800 | $3,700 |

National
Ca.1927-present. National/Valco amps date back to the late-'30s. National introduced a modern group of amps about the same time they introduced their new Res-O-Glas space-age guitar models in '62. In '64, the amp line was partially redesigned and renamed. By '68, the Res-O-Glas models were gone and National introduced many large vertical and horizontal piggyback models which lasted until National's assets were assigned during bankruptcy in '69. The National name went to Chicago importer Strum N' Drum. Initially, Strum N' Drum had one amp, the National GA 950 P Tremolo/Reverb piggyback.

Aztec Amp
1950s. Combo, early '50s version with 3 Rola 7x11" speakers using 3 speaker baffle openings, about 20 watts using 2x6L6 power tubes, 2-tone brown leatherette and tweed cover. By '56, amp has one 15" speaker and does not have segmented grill.

| 1950s | 3 Rola 7x11 | $775 | $1,025 |
| 1956 | 1x15 | $725 | $950 |

Bass 70/Bass 75 Amp
1962-1967. 35 watts (per channel), 2x12" (often Jensen) speakers, large knobs, Raven Black tolex with silver and white grille, designed for bass. New model name in '64 with nearly identical features but listed as total of 70 watts, in '62 called Bass 70 but renamed Bass 75 in '64.

| 1962-1963 | Bass 70 | $700 | $900 |
| 1964-1967 | Bass 75 N6475B | $700 | $900 |

Chicagoan Model 1220 Amp
1950s. 17 watts, 1x10", tube, says "Valco Chicago 51" on control panel.

| 1950s | | $650 | $850 |

Dynamic 20 Amp
1962-1963. 17 watts, 2x8" (often Jensen) speakers, 2 large knobs, Raven Black tolex with silver and white grille, compact student-intermediate amp.

| 1962-1963 | | $675 | $900 |

Glenwood 90 Amp
1962-1967. 35 watts, 2x12" (often Jensen) speakers, large knobs, reverb, tremolo, Raven Black tolex with silver and white grille, top of the line, becomes the

nearly identical N6490TR in '64.

| 1962-1963 | | $1,025 | $1,375 |
| 1964-1967 | Model N6490TR | $950 | $1,250 |

Glenwood Vibrato Amp
Two 12" speakers, reverb, tremolo.

| 1964-1967 | Model N6499VR | $1,025 | $1,375 |

Model 75 Amp
1940s. Vertical tweed combo cabinet, volume and tone knobs, 3 inputs.

| 1940s | | $450 | $600 |

Model 100 Amp
1940. Tube amp, 40 watts, 1x12".

| 1940 | | $525 | $675 |

Model 1202 Twin Amp
1954. 18 watts, 2x8" Jensen speaker, 2 channels (Instrument and microphone), horizontal flying bird logo on grille.

| 1954 | | $700 | $900 |

Model 1210 High Fidelity Amp
1954. 20 watts, 1x15" Jensen speaker, 4 input jacks, 2 channels (instrument and microphone), 20x24x10" combo, metal handle.

| 1954 | | $700 | $900 |

Model 1212 Amp
1954. 12 watts, 1x12", 5 tubes, 3 inputs, 15x18x8" combo, diving flying bird logo on grille, plastic handle.

| 1954 | | $650 | $850 |

Model 1215 Amp
1952. 1x12", 2 channels.

| 1952 | | $650 | $850 |

Model 1275 Amp
1953. Combo 1x10", 12 watts, 5 tubes, light tan weave cover, deep brown grille cloth.

| 1953 | | $625 | $825 |

Model GA 950-P Tremolo/Reverb Piggyback Amp
1970s. Strum N' Drum/National model, solidstate, 50 watts, 2-channel 2x12" and 1x7" in 32" tall vertical cabinet, black.

| 1970s | | $260 | $335 |

Model N6800 - N6899 Piggyback Amps
1968-1969. National introduced a new line of tube amps in '68 and most of them were piggybacks. The N6895 was sized like a Fender piggyback Tremolux, the N6875 and N6878 bass amps were sized like a '68 Fender large cab piggyback with a 26" tall vertical cab, the N6898 and N6899 were the large piggyback guitar amps. These amps feature the standard Jensen speakers or the upgrade JBL speakers, the largest model was the N6800 for PA or guitar, which sported 3x70-watt channels and 2 column speakers using a bass 2x12" + 1x3" horn cab and a voice-guitar 4x10" + 1x3" horn cab.

| 1968-1969 | | $500 | $650 |

Model N6816 (Model 16) Amp
1968-1969. Valco-made tube amp, 6 watts, 1x10" Jensen speaker, 17" vertical cab, tremolo, no reverb, black vinyl cover and Coppertone grille.

| 1968-1969 | | $350 | $450 |

1978 Music Man 212 HD130
Federico Garibotti

1938 National Model C

National Model 100
Imaged by Heritage Auctions, HA.com

AMPS

National Stagestar

Naylor Electra-Verb 60 Head

Nobels Streetman 15

AMPS

MODEL YEAR	FEATURES	EXC. COND. LOW	HIGH
Model N6820 Thunderball Bass Amp			
1968-1969. Valco-made tube amp, about 35 watts, 1x15" Jensen speaker, 19" vertical cab, black vinyl cover and Coppertone grille.			
1968-1969		$425	$550
Model N6822 (Model 22) Amp			
1968-1969. Valco-made, 6 watts tube (4 tubes) amp, 1x12" Jensen speaker, 19" vertical cab, tremolo and reverb, black vinyl cover and Coppertone grille.			
1968-1969		$375	$500
National Dobro Amp			
1930s. Sold by the National Dobro Corp. when the company was still in Los Angeles (they later moved to Chicago). National Dobro plate on rear back panel, suitcase style case that flips open to reveal the speaker and amp, National logo on outside of suitcase. The noted price is for an all-original amp in excellent condition (this would be a rare find), there are other 1930s models included in the price range below.			
1930s	Early metal baffle	$525	$700
1930s	Later standard baffle	$400	$525
1930s	Suitcase style	$500	$650
Newport 40 Amp			
1964-1967. 17 watts, 2x10", tremolo only.			
1964-1967	Model N6440T	$650	$850
Newport 50 Amp			
1964-1967. 17 watts, 2x10", tremolo and reverb.			
1964-1967	Model N6450TR	$650	$850
Newport 97 Amp			
1964-1967. 35 watts, 1x15", rear mounted chasis, tremolo.			
1964-1967	Model N6497T	$650	$850
Sportsman Amp			
1950s. Tweed combo with brown leatherette speaker surround, 1x10".			
1950s		$625	$825
Student Practice Amp			
1970s. Strum N' Drum era, small solidstate, single control.			
1970s		$35	$45
Studio 10 Amp			
1962-1967. Five watts, 1x8", 3 tubes, 1 channel, 1 volume control, no tone control, no reverb or tremolo.			
1962-1963		$425	$550
1964-1967	Model N6410	$425	$550
Tremo-Tone Model 1224 Amp			
1956-1959. Small combo, tremolo, dual Rola oval 6x11" speakers, tweed, by Valco, flying bird pattern on lower front grille.			
1956-1959		$925	$1,225
Val-Pro 80 Amp			
1962-1963. 35 watts, 2x12" (often Jensen) speakers, 8 tubes, large control knobs, tremolo, black cover with white and silver trim, replaced by Glenwood 90 in '64 with added reverb.			
1962-1963		$1,000	$1,300
Val-Trem 40 Amp			
1962-1963. 17 watts, 2x10" (often Jensen) speakers, large knobs, Val-Trem logo on back panel, Clear-Wave tremolo, Raven Black tolex with silver and white grille, open back combo amp, becomes Newport 40 in '64.			
1962-1963		$800	$1,050

MODEL YEAR	FEATURES	EXC. COND. LOW	HIGH
Val-Verb 60 Amp			
1962-1963. 17 watts, 2x10" (often Jensen) speakers, large knobs, Val-Verb logo on back panel, reverb, no tremolo, Raven Black tolex with silver and white grille, open back combo amp.			
1962-1963		$950	$1,250
Westwood 16 Amp			
1964-1967. Five watts using 1 6V6 power, 2 12AX7 preamp, 1 5Y3GT rectifier, tremolo, 2x8", dark vinyl cover, silver grille.			
1964-1967	Model N6416T	$650	$850
Westwood 22 Amp			
1964-1967. 5 watts, 2x8", reverb and tremolo, 1 channel, 6 tubes.			
1964-1967	Model N6422TR	$700	$925

Naylor Engineering

1994-present. Joe Naylor and Kyle Kurtz founded the company in East Pointe, Michigan, in the early '90s, selling J.F. Naylor speakers. In '94 they started producing amps. In '96, Naylor sold his interest in the business to Kurtz and left to form Reverend Guitars. In '99 David King bought the company and moved it to Los Angeles, California, then to Dallas, Texas. Currently Naylor builds tube amps, combos, speakers, and cabinets.

Nemesis

From the makers of Eden amps, Nemesis is a line of made-in-the-U.S., FET powered bass combos and extension cabinets. The brand is a division of U.S. Music Corp.

Newcomb

1950s. Newcomb Audio Products, Hollywood, California, Newcomb script logo on back panel along with model number, they offered instrument amplifiers that could also be used as small PA.

MODEL YEAR	FEATURES	EXC. COND. LOW	HIGH
Model G 12			
1953. 1x12" (Rolla) combo amp, 2 controls (volume and tone), large metal handle, oxblood-brown leatherette.			
1953		$325	$425

Nobels

1997-present. Effects manufacturer Nobels Electronics of Hamburg, Germany also offers a line of small practice and portable amps.

Noble

Ca. 1950-ca. 1969. From Don Noble and Company, of Chicago, Illinois, owned by Strum N' Drum by mid-'60s. They also offered guitars and amps.

MODEL YEAR	FEATURES	EXC. COND. LOW	HIGH
Model 381/Custom 381 Amp			
1950s. 2x12" and 2x5".			
1958-1960		$1,025	$1,350

Norma

1965-1970. Economy line imported and distributed by Strum N' Drum, Wheeling (Chicago), Illinois. As noted in the National section, Strum

MODEL YEAR	FEATURES	EXC. COND. LOW	HIGH

N' Drum acquired the National brand in the '70s. Some early amps were tube, but the majority were solidstate.

GA-93 Amp
1969-1970. 6 watts, 1x6".

1969-1970		$55	$75

GA-97 T Amp
1969-1970. 13 watts, 1x8", tremolo.

1969-1970		$60	$80

GA-725 B Amp
1969-1970. Bass amp, 38 watts, 1x10".

1969-1970		$60	$80

GA-918 T Amp
1969-1970. 24 watts, 1x12", tremolo and reverb.

1969-1970		$70	$95

GA-930 P (Piggyback) Amp
1969-1970. 40 watts, 2x12", piggyback.

1969-1970		$80	$105

GA-6240 Amp
1969-1970. 50 watts.

1969-1970		$80	$105

GAP-2 Amp
1969-1970. 3 watts, 1x4".

1969-1970		$55	$75

Oahu

The Oahu Publishing Company and Honolulu Conservatory, based in Cleveland, Ohio, started with acoustic Hawaiian and Spanish guitars, selling large quantities in the 1930s. As electric models became popular, Oahu responded with guitar/amp sets. The brand has been revived on a line of U.S.-made tube amps.

Combo Amp
1965. Small 1x10" combo, 1 6V6, 4 12AX7, 15Y3GT, white cover, light grille, Oahu script logo upper left grille.

1965		$625	$825

Mid-Size Amp
1940s-1950s. 1x10".

1940s-50s		$450	$600

Small Guitar/Lap Steel Amps
1940s-1950s. 1x8", various colors.

1940s-50s		$325	$425

Thunderbolt
1965. 1x12", 6 tubes.

1965		$1,300	$1,700

Oliver

Ca.1966-ca. 1978. The Oliver Sound Company, Westbury, New York, was founded by former Ampeg engineer, Jess Oliver, after he left Ampeg in '65. Tube amp designs were based upon Oliver's work at Ampeg. The Oliver Powerflex Amp is the best-known design, and featured an elevator platform that would lift the amp head out of the speaker cabinet.

Model B-120 Amp Head
1970s. B-120 logo on front panel, 35 watts, all tube head.

1970s		$425	$550

Model G-150R Combo Amp
1970s. Reverb, tremolo, 2 6L6 power tubes, 40 watts, 1x15", black tolex with black grille, silver control panel.

1970s		$500	$650

Model P-500 Combo Amp
1960s. All tube combo with 15" motorized amp chassis that rises out of tall lateral speaker cabinet as amp warms up.

1960s		$675	$875

Orbital Power Projector Amp
Late-1960s-early-1970s. Rotating speaker cabinet with horn, Leslie-like voice.

1960s-70s		$675	$875

Sam Ash Oliver Amp Head
Late-1960s-early-1970s. Private branded for Sam Ash Music, about 30 watts using the extinct 7027A power tubes, Sam Ash script logo on front grille.

1960s-70s		$325	$425

Omega

2009-present. James Price builds his premium grade, production/custom, amps in Moravian Falls, North Carolina.

Orange

1968-1981, 1995-present. Orange amps and PAs were made in the U.K. by Cliff Cooper and Matthew Mathias. The Orange-colored amps were well-built and were used by many notable guitarists. Since '95, Cliff Cooper is once again making Orange amplifiers in the U.K., with the exception of the small Crush Practice Combo amps, which are made in Korea. '68-'70 amps made by Matamp in Huddersfield, classic designs started in '71 at Bexleyheath/London plant.

Model GRO-100 Graphic Overdrive Amp Head
1969-1971. Four EL34 power, only 2 pre-amp tubes, short-style head, model number on back panel.

1969-1971		$2,500	$3,200

Model OR-80 Amp
1971-1981. Half-stack head and cab, 80 watts, 4x12" straight-front cab with Orange crest on grille, orange vinyl and light orange grille.

1971-1975		$2,300	$3,100
1976-1981		$2,000	$2,700

Model OR-80 Combo Amp
1971-1981. About 80 watts, 2x12" combo.

1971-1975		$2,000	$2,600
1976-1981		$1,700	$2,200

Model OR-120 Graphic Amp
1972-1981. Half-stack head and cab, 120 watts, 4x12" straight front cab with Orange crest on grille, orange vinyl and light orange grille.

1972-1975		$2,400	$3,200
1976-1981		$2,200	$2,900

Model OR-200 212 Twin Amp
1970s. 120 watts, 2x12" combo, orange vinyl, dark grille, Orange crest on grille, reverb and vibrato, master volume.

1971-1975		$2,300	$3,000
1976-1981		$1,800	$2,400

1950 Oahu
Bill Parsons

Oliver Powerflex 500
Don Oflinden

1977 Orange Model OR-120
Eric Van Gansen

AMPS

1970s The Kat (Model 6012) Amp
Imaged by Heritage Auctions, HA.com

Park Little Head 18

PRS Archon 50

MODEL YEAR	FEATURES	EXC. COND. LOW	HIGH

Orepheus

Early 1960s. Private branded for Coast Wholesale Music Co., Orepheus logo on control panel along with model number.

Small Tube Amp
1960s. Student compact tube amps, some with 2 knobs, volume and tone.

1960s	Model 708	$325	$425

Orpheum

Late-1950s-1960s. Student to medium level amps from New York's Maurice Lipsky Music.

Small/Mid-Size Amp
Late-1950s-1960s. U.S.-made, 2 6V6 power tubes, Jensen P12R 12" speaker, light cover with gray swirl grille.

1950s-60s	Mid-Size	$425	$550
1950s-60s	Small	$325	$425

Osborne Sound Laboratories

Late 1970s. Guitar amps built by Ralph Scaffidi and wife guitarist Mary Osborne in Bakersfield, California. They also offered guitars.

Ovation

1966-present. Kaman made few amps under the Ovation name. They offered a variety of amps under the KMD brand from '85 to around '94.

Little Dude Amp
1969-ca.1971. Solidstate combo, 100 watts, 1x15" and horn, matching slave unit also available.

1970s		$160	$210

The Kat (Model 6012) Amp
1970s. Solidstate, 2x12" combo.

1970s		$160	$210

Overbuilt Amps

1999-2007. Tube amps and combos built by Richard Seccombe in West Hills, California. He nows works at Fender R&D.

PAC-AMP (Magnatone)

Late-1950s-early-1960s. Private branded by Magnatone, often for accordion studios.

Model 213 Troubadour Amp
1957-1958. 10 watts, 1x12".

1957-1958		$950	$1,250

Model 280-A Amp
1961-1963. About 50 watts, 2x12" + 2x5", brown leatherette, light brown grille, stereo vibrato, PAC-AMP nameplate logo.

1961-1963		$1,400	$1,800

Palette Amps

Robert Wakeling began building his tube amp heads and combos and speaker cabinets in Stillwater, Oklahoma in 2003.

MODEL YEAR	FEATURES	EXC. COND. LOW	HIGH

PANaramic (Magnatone)

1961-1963. Private branded equivalent of '61-'63 Magnatone brown leatherette series, large PANaramic logo. Many Magnatone private brands were associated with accordion companies or accordian teaching studios. PANaramic was a brand name of PANaramic accordion. They also made guitars.

Model 260/262-style Amp
1961-1963. 35 watts, 2x12", gray vinyl and light grille, vibrato, large PANaramic logo.

1961-1963		$1,400	$1,800

Model 413-style Amp
1961-1963. 18 watts, 1x12", black leatherette cover, light silver grille, vibrato, large PANaramic logo.

1961-1963		$875	$1,150

Model 450-style Amp
1961-1963. 20 watts, 1x12", reverb and vibrato, reverb not generally included in an early-'60s 1x12" Magnatone amp, dark vinyl, dark cross-threaded grille, large PANaramic logo.

1961-1963		$1,150	$1,500

Model 1210 (250-style) Amp
1961-1963. 1x12" combo, 20 watts, 2.5 channels, true vibrato.

1961-1963		$975	$1,300

Paris

1960s. Brand name used on a line of solidstate amps distributed by a music wholesaler. Possibly built by Kay.

Master Series Amp
1960s. Compact combo, 1x12", black tolex-style cover, silver grille, rear mounted slanted control panel.

1960s		$70	$95

Park

1965-1982, 1993-1998, 2013-present. Park amps were made by Marshall from '65 to '82. Park logo on front with elongated P. In the '90s, Marshall revived the name for use on small solidstate amps imported from Asia. Brand name acquired by Mitch Colby (Colby Amps) in '13 and used on tube head amps and cabs built in New York City.

G Series Amp
1992-2000. Student compact amps, models include G-10 (10 watts, 1x8"), G-25R (25w, reverb), G-215R (15w, 2x8") and GB-25 (25w, 1x12" bass).

1990s	G-10	$50	$90
1990s	G-15R	$55	$100
1990s	G-215R	$65	$105
1990s	G-25R	$60	$100
1990s	GB-25	$55	$100

Model 50 Amp Head
1967-1969. Plexi, 50 watts.

1967-1969		$2,500	$3,300

Model 1001L 75W Lead Amp Head
1967-1971. Plexi (later aluminum), 75 watts, black tolex.

1967-1969	Plexi	$3,600	$4,700
1969-1971	Aluminum	$2,100	$2,700

MODEL YEAR	FEATURES	EXC. COND. LOW	HIGH
Model 1008A 4x12 Slant Cabinet			
Late-1960s-early-1970s. Similar to Marshall 1960 4x12" cab.			
1960s-70s		$1,600	$2,100
Model 1206 50W Master Volume Amp Head			
Late-1970s-1982. 50 watts, similar to JCM 800 50-watt made during same era.			
1970s-82		$1,600	$2,100
Model 1212 50W Reverb Combo Amp			
Late-1960s-early-1970s. 50 watts, 2x12", reverb, tube.			
1960s-70s		$2,100	$2,700
Model 1213 100W Reverb Combo Amp			
Late-1960s-early-1970s. 100 watts, 2x12", reverb, tube.			
1960s-70s		$2,100	$2,700
Model 1228 50W Lead Amp Head			
Late-1970s-1982. 50 watts, based upon Marshall 50-watt made during same era.			
1970s-82		$1,600	$2,100
Model 1229 100W Lead Amp Head			
Late-1970s-1982. 100 watts, tube.			
1970s-82		$1,600	$2,100
Model 1231 Vintage 20 LE Combo Amp			
Late-1970s-1982. 20 watts, 1x12".			
1970s-82		$1,700	$2,300
Model 1239 50W Master Volume Reverb Combo Amp			
Late-1970s-1982. 50 watts, 1x12".			
1970s-82		$1,700	$2,300

Paul Reed Smith

1985-present. In the late '80s, PRS offered two amp models. Only 350 amp units shipped. Includes HG-70 Head and HG-212 Combo. HG stands for Harmonic Generator, effectively a non-tube, solid-state amp. In '09, PRS introduced tube combo and head amps and cabinets designed by Doug Sewell.

Paul Ruby Amplifiers

2000-present. Professional grade, custom, tube amps built by Paul Ruby in Folsom, California.

Peavey

1965-present. Hartley Peavey's first products were guitar amps. He added guitars to the mix in '78. Headquartered in Meridan, Mississippi, Peavey continues to offer a huge variety of guitars, amps, and PAs. TransTube redesign of amps occurs in '95.

3120 Amp Head
2009-2016. Tubes, 120 watts, 3 foot-switchable channels.

2009-2016		$350	$450

5150 212 Combo Amp
1995-2004. Combo version of 5150 head, 60 watts, 2x12", large 5150 logo on front panel, small Peavey logo on lower right of grille.

1995-2004		$450	$600

MODEL YEAR	FEATURES	EXC. COND. LOW	HIGH
5150 EVH Head/Cabinet Amp Set			
1995-2008. Half stack 5150 head and 4x12" cab, large 5150 logo on front of amp.			
1995-2008	Half-stack	$900	$1,200
5150 II Amp			
2004. Has 5051 II logo on front, look for 'II' designation.			
2004	Half-stack	$825	$1,100
6505 Series Amp			
2008-present. Promoted for modern "heavy" metal sound.			
2008-2019	2x12 combo, 60w	$475	$625
2008-2019	6505+ head, 120w	$450	$600
2008-2019	6505+, 1x12 combo	$450	$600
Alphabass Amp			
1988-1990. Rack mount all tube, 160 watts, EQ, includes 2x15" Black Widow or 2x12" Scorpion cabinet.			
1988-1990		$225	$300
Artist Amp			
Introduced in 1975 as 120 watts, 1x12", bright and normal channels, EQ, reverb, master volume.			
1970s		$225	$300
Artist 110 Amp			
1990s. TransTubes, 10 watts.			
1990s		$110	$140
Artist 240 Amp			
1975-1980s. 120 watt combo, 1x12".			
1975-80s		$175	$225
Artist 250 Amp			
1990s. 100 watts, 1x12", solidstate preamp, 4 6L6 power tubes.			
1990s		$190	$235
Artist VT Amp			
1990s. Combo amp, 120 watts, 1x12".			
1990s		$250	$310
Audition 20 Amp			
1980s-1990s. 20 watts, single speaker combo.			
1980-1990s		$40	$50
Audition 30 Amp			
1980s-1990s. 30 watts, 1x12" combo amp, channel switching.			
1980-1990s		$45	$55
Audition 110 Amp			
1990s. 25 watts, 1x10" combo, 2 channels.			
1990s		$50	$70
Audition Chorus Amp			
1980s. 2x10-watt channels, 2x6", channel switching, post gain and normal gain controls.			
1980s		$80	$100
Audition Plus Amp			
1980s. Solidstate, 20 watts, 1x10".			
1980s		$50	$65
Backstage 30/Plus/50/110 Amp			
1977-1991. 1x10 combo, Backstage 30 (15 then 18 watts) '77-'83, Backstage Plus (35w) '84-'87, Backstage 50 (50w) '88-'89, Backstage 110 (65w) '89-'91. Name reused in 2000s on small 10-watt amp.			
1977-1991		$55	$75
Backstage Chorus 208 Amp			
1990-1996. 150 watts, 2x8", reverb, channel switching.			
1990-1996		$95	$125

Paul Ruby AX84 High Octane

AMPS

2007 Peavey 5150 EVH Head/Cabinet
Imaged by Heritage Auctions, HA.com

Peavey 6505+

AMPS

Peavey Bandit 65

Peavey Classic 30

1980s Peavey KB-100
Imaged by Heritage Auctions, HA.com

MODEL YEAR	FEATURES	EXC. COND. LOW	HIGH

Bandit/65/75 Amp
1981-1989. 1x12" combo, originally 50 watts, upped to 65 watts in '85 and 75 in '87, renamed Bandit 112 in '90.

1981-1984	Bandit	$105	$135
1985-1986	Bandit 65	$105	$135
1987-1989	Bandit 75	$105	$135

Bandit 112/Bandit II 112 Amp
1990-present. 80 watts (II is 100), 1x12", active EQ circuit for lead channel, active controls. TransTube in '95.

1990-1994		$130	$160
1994-2019	TransTube	$180	$225

Basic 40 Amp
1980s. 40 watts, 1x12".

1980s		$85	$105

Basic 60 Amp
1988-1995. Solidstate combo amp, 50-60 watts, 1x12", 4-band EQ, gain controls, black.

1988-1995		$130	$160

Basic 112 Bass Amp
1996-2006. 75 watts, 1x12" bass combo, 2000-era red border control panel.

1996-2006		$130	$160

Blazer 158 Amp
1995-2005. 15 watts, 1x8", clean and distortion, later called the TransTube Blazer III.

1995-2005		$70	$90

Bluesman Amp
1992. Tweed, 1x12" or 1x15".

1992		$235	$300

Bravo 112 Amp
1988-1994. All tube reverb, 25 watts, 1x12", 3-band EQ, 2 independent input channels.

1988-1994		$200	$275

Butcher Amp Head
1985-1987, 2010-2017. All tube head, 120 watts. Current version is all tube, 100 watts with half power switch

1985-1987		$275	$375

Classic 20 Amp
1990s. Small tube amp with 2xEL84 power tubes, 1x10" narrow panel combo, tweed cover.

1990s		$275	$375

Classic 30/112 Amp
1994-present. Tweed combo, 30 watts, 1x12", EL84 tubes.

1994-2019	Narrow panel combo	$315	$415
2008-2014	Badge front	$315	$415
2008-2014	Head	$275	$375

Classic 50/212 Amp
1990-present. Combo, 50 watt, 2x12", 4 EL84s, 3 12AX7s, reverb, high-gain section.

1990-2019		$350	$450

Classic 50/410 Amp
1990-present. Combo amp, 4x10", EL84 power, reverb, footswitchable high-gain mode.

1990-2019		$350	$450

Classic 120 Amp
1988-ca.1990. Tube, 120 watts.

1988-1990		$300	$375

Combo 300 Amp
1982-1993. 1x15" bass combo, 300 watts.

11982-1993		$155	$195

DECA/750 Amp
1989-ca.1990. Digital, 2 channels, 350 watts per channel, distortion, reverb, exciter, pitch shift, multi-EQ.

1989-1990		$205	$255

Decade Amp
1970s. Practice amp, 10 watts, 1x8", runs on 12 volt or AC.

1970s		$75	$95

Delta Blues Amp
1995-2014. 30 watts, tube combo, 4 EL84 tubes, 1x15" or 2x10", tremolo, large-panel-style cab, blond tweed.

1995-2014		$350	$450

Deuce Amp
1972-1980s. 120 watts, tube amp, 2x12" or 4x10".

1972-1980s		$175	$215

Deuce Amp Head
1972-1980s. Tube head, 120 watts.

1972-1980s		$130	$165

Ecoustic Series Amp
1996-present. Acoustic combo amps, 110 (1x10) and 112 (1x12, offered until '10) at 100 watts, digital effects (EFX, later E) added in '03. E20 and E208 added in '11.

1996-2010	112	$125	$155
2003-2019	E110	$125	$155

Encore 65 Amp
1983. Tube combo, 65 watts.

1983		$230	$290

Envoy 110 Amp
1988-present. Solidstate, 40 watts, 1x10", Trans-Tubes.

1988-2019		$100	$130

Heritage VTX Amp
1980s. 130 watts, 4 6L6s, solidstate preamp, 2x12" combo.

1980s		$155	$195

Jazz Classic Amp
1980s. Solidstate, 210 watts, 1x15", electronic channel switching, 6-spring reverb.

1980s		$155	$195

JSX (Joe Satriani) Amp
2004-2010. Joe Satriani signature, 120 watt tube head. Also offered were JSX 50 (50 watts, '09-'10), JSX 212 Combo ('05-'10) and 5-watt JSX Mini Colossal ('07-'10).

2004-2010	120w head	$515	$650

KB Series Amp
1980s. Keyboard amp, models include KB-60 (60 watts, 1x12", reverb), KB-100 (100w, 1x15"), and KB-300 (300w, 1x15" with horn).

1980s	KB-100	$145	$190
1980s	KB-300	$200	$260
1980s	KB-60	$125	$160

LTD Amp
1975-1980s. Solidstate, 200 watts, 1x12" Altec or 1x15" JBL.

1975-1982		$155	$195

MODEL YEAR	FEATURES	EXC. COND. LOW	HIGH

Mace Amp Head
1976-1980s. Tube, 180 watts.
1976-1980s — $235 — $295

Mark III Bass Amp Head
1978-1983. 300 watts, 2 channels, graphic EQ.
1978-1983 — $165 — $205

MegaBass Amp
1986-ca. 1992. Rack mount preamp/power amp, 200 watts per 2 channels, solidstate, EQ, effects loop, chorus.
1986-1992 — $185 — $230

Microbass Amp
1988-2005. 20 watts, 1x8" practice amp, made in China.
1988-2005 — $40 — $50

Minx 110 Bass Amp
1987-2005. Solidstate, 35 watts RMS, 1x10" heavy-duty speaker.
1987-2005 — $90 — $110

Musician Amp Head
Introduced in 1965 as 120 watt head, upped to 210 watts in '72.
1965-1970s — $125 — $155

Nashville 112 Steel Guitar Amp
2008-present. Compact size, 1x12", 80 watts.
2008-2019 — $375 — $500

Nashville 400 Steel Guitar Amp
1982-2000. 210 watts, 1x15" solidstate steel guitar combo amp.
1982-2000 — $400 — $525

Nashville 1000 Steel Guitar Amp
1998-2008. 1x15" speaker, solidstate steel guitar combo amp.
1998-2008 — $400 — $525

Pacer Amp
1974-1985. Master volume, 45 watts, 1x12", 3-band EQ.
1974-1985 — $70 — $90

Penta Amp Head/Gary Rossington Signature Penta
2005-2015. Tubes, 140 watts, 4x12", 5 selectable preamp settings. Becomes the Gary Rossington Signature Penta in 2009.
2005-2015 Cab — $240 — $300
2005-2015 Head — $290 — $350

ProBass 1000 Amp
1980s. Rack mount, effects loops, preamp, EQ, crossover, headphone output.
1980s — $130 — $165

Rage/Rage 158 Amp
1988-2008. Compact practice amp, 15 watts, 1x8". 158 starts '95. Replaced by 25 watt Rage 258.
1988-2008 — $35 — $45

Reno 400 Amp
1984-late 1980s. Solidstate, 200 watts, 1x15" with horn, 4-band EQ.
1980s — $130 — $165

Renown 112 Amp
1989-1994. Crunch and lead SuperSat, 160 watts, 1x12", master volume, digital reverb, EQ.
1989-1994 — $130 — $165

Renown 212 Amp
1989-1994. Crunch and lead SuperSat, 160 watts, 2x12", master volume, digital reverb, EQ.
1989-1994 — $155 — $195

Renown 400 Amp
1981-late 1980s. Combo, 200 watts, 2x12", channel switching, Hammond reverb, pre- and post-gain controls.
1980s — $205 — $255

Revolution 112 Amp
1992-2002. 100 watts, 1x12" combo, black vinyl, black grille.
1992-2002 — $175 — $220

Session 400 Amp
1974-ca. 1999. 200 watts, 1x15 or early on as 2x12, steel amp, available in the smaller box LTD, offered as a head in '76, available in wedge-shaped enclosure in '88.
1974-1999 — $400 — $500

Session 500 Amp
1979-1980s. 250 watts, 1x15", steel amp.
1979-1985 — $400 — $500

Special 112 Amp
1981-1994. 160 watts, 1x12". In 1988, available in wedge-shaped enclosure.
1981-1994 — $150 — $185

Special 130 Amp
1980s. 1x12", 130 watts.
1980s — $150 — $185

Special 212 Amp
1995-2005. 160 watts, 2x12", transtube, solidstate series.
1995-2005 — $175 — $220

Stereo Chorus 212 Amp
1990s. 2x12" combo.
1990s — $235 — $315

Studio Pro 50 Amp
1986-late 1980s. 50 watts, 1x12".
1980s — $105 — $130

Studio Pro 112 Amp
1980s. Repackaged and revoiced in 1988. Solidstate, 65 watts, 1x12", Peavey SuperSat preamp circuitry, new power sections.
1980s — $115 — $145

TKO Series Bass Amp
1978-2011. Solidstate, 1x15, original TKO was 40 watts, followed by TKO 65 (65 watts) for '82-'87, TKO 75 for '88-'90, and TKO 80 for '91-'92. Renamed TKO 115 in '93 with 75, 80 or 100 watts until '09 when jumping to 400 watts.
1982-1987 TKO 65 — $105 — $130
1988-1990 TKO 75 — $140 — $175
1991-1992 TKO 80 — $175 — $225

TNT Series Bass Amp
1974-2009. Solidstate, 1x15, original TNT was 45 watts, upped to 50 for '79-'81, followed by TNT 130 (130 watts) for '82-'87, TNT 150 for '88-'90, and TNT 160 for '91-'92. Renamed TNT 115 in '93 with 150, 160 or 200 watts until '09 when jumping to 600 watts (Tour TNT 115 - see Tour Series).
1982-1987 TNT 130 — $250 — $350
1988-1990 TNT 150 — $250 — $350
1991-1992 TNT 160 — $250 — $350

1990 Peavey Nashville 400
Imaged by Heritage Auctions, HA.com

Peavey Penta Head/ Gary Rossington Sig.

2000s Peavey Rage 258
Imaged by Heritage Auctions, HA.com

AMPS

Pignose Hog

1970s Plush PRB 1000S
Imaged by Heritage Auctions, HA.com

Ca. 1990s Polytone Taurus
Imaged by Heritage Auctions, HA.com

MODEL YEAR	FEATURES	EXC. COND. LOW	HIGH

Tour Series
2004-2019. Imported bass heads and cabinets, various models.

| 2004-2019 | Various models | $265 | $350 |

Transchorus 210 Amp
1999-2000. 50 watts, 2x10 combo, stereo chorus, channel switching, reverb.

| 1999-2000 | | $230 | $290 |

Triple XXX Series Amp
2001-2009. Made in USA.

| 2001-2009 | Head, 120w | $490 | $615 |
| 2001-2009 | Super 40, 40w, 1x12 | $440 | $550 |

Triumph 60 Combo Amp
1980s. Tube head, effects loop, reverb, 60 watts, 1x12", multi-stage gain.

| 1980s | | $150 | $190 |

Triumph 120 Amp
1989-1990. Tube, 120 watts, 1x12", 3 gain blocks in preamp, low-level post-effects loop, built-in reverb.

| 1989-1990 | | $180 | $225 |

Ultra 60 Amp Head
1991-1994. 60 watts, all tube, 2 6L6 power, black, black grille.

| 1991-1994 | | $230 | $290 |

Ultra Series Amp
1998-2002. All tube combos and cabs.

1998-2002	Ulta 112, 60w	$225	$280
1998-2002	Ulta 212, 60w	$275	$350
1998-2002	Ulta 410, 60w	$275	$350
1998-2002	Ulta Plus 120 Head	$325	$400

ValveKing Series Amp
2005-2018. Tube head, combos and cabs.

2005-2016	VK212, 100w, 2x12	$250	$325
2005-2018	VK100, 100w head	$200	$275
2005-2018	VK112, 50w, 1x12	$225	$300

Vegas 400 Amp
1984-late 1980s. 210 watts, 1x15, some prefer as a steel guitar amp.

| 1980s | | $335 | $425 |

VTM Series Amp
1987-1993. Vintage Tube Modified series, tube heads, 60 or 120 watts.

| 1987-1993 | VTM120, 120w | $275 | $375 |
| 1987-1993 | VTM60, 60w | $275 | $375 |

Vypyr Series Amp
2008-2014. Modeling amp heads and combos, 60 and 120-watt tube and 15, 30, 75 and 100-watt solidstate models. Changes to Vypyr VIP in late '14.

2008-2014	15w, combo	$60	$75
2008-2014	30w, 1x12 combo	$130	$165
2010	75w, combo	$175	$225

Wiggy 212 Amp
2001-2008. 100-watt head in mono (2x75-watt in stereo) with matching 2x12" cab, 2 EQ, 5-band sliders, rounded amp head.

| 2001-2008 | | $400 | $500 |

Penn
Tube amps, combos, and cabinets built by Billy Penn, starting in 1994, originally in Colts Neck, then in Long Branch, New Jersey.

MODEL YEAR	FEATURES	EXC. COND. LOW	HIGH

Pignose
1972-present. Pignose was started by people associated with the band Chicago, including guitarist Terry Kath, with help from designers Wayne Kimball and Richard Erlund. In '74, it was sold to Chicago's band accountant, who ran it until '82, when ownership passed to the company that made its sturdy, wood cabinets. They also offer guitars and effects.

7-100 Practice Amp
1972-present. The original Pignose, 7"x5"x3" battery-powered portable amplifier, 1x5".

| 1972-2019 | | $50 | $75 |

30/60 Amp
1978-ca.1987. Solidstate, 30 watts, 1x10", master volume.

| 1978-1987 | | $75 | $100 |

60R Studio Reverb Amp
Solidstate, 30 watts.

| 1980 | | $95 | $125 |

G40V Amp
1997-2009. Tubes, 1x10", 40 watts.

| 1997-2009 | | $200 | $275 |

G60VR Amp
1998-2009. Tubes, 1x12", 60 watts.

| 1998-2009 | | $225 | $300 |

Hog 20/Hog 30 Amp
1995-present. Rechargeable solidstate models.

| 1995-2020 | | $100 | $150 |

Plush
Late 1960s-early 1970s. Tuck and roll covered tube amps made by the same company that made Earth Sound Research amps in Farmingdale, New York.

Tube Amplifiers
Early 1970s. All tube heads and combos including the 450 Super 2x12" combo, 1000/P1000S head, and 1060S Royal Bass combo.

| 1971-1972 | | $500 | $1,200 |

Point Blank
2002-2004. Tube amps built by Roy Blankenship in Orlando, Florida before he started his Blankenship brand.

Polytone
Beginning in the 1960s and made in North Hollywood, California, Polytone offers compact combo amps, heads, and cabinets and a pickup system for acoustic bass.

Guitar or Bass Amps
1980s-2000s. Various models.

| 1980-2000s | | $250 | $450 |

Port City
2005-present. Daniel Klein builds his amp heads, combos, and cabinets in Rocky Point, North Carolina.

MODEL YEAR	FEATURES	EXC. COND. LOW	HIGH

Premier

Ca.1938-ca.1975, 1990s-2010. Produced by Peter Sorkin Music Company in Manhattan. First radio-sized amplifiers introduced by '38. After World War II, established Multivox subsidiary to manufacture amplifiers ca.'46. By mid-'50s at least, the amps featured lyre grilles. Dark brown/light tan amp covering by '60. By '64 amps covered in brown woodgrain and light tan. Multivox amps were made until around '84.

B-160 Club Bass Amp
1963-1968. 15 to 20 watts, 1x12" Jensen speaker, '60s 2-tone brown styling, 6V6 tubes.

1963-1968		$600	$775

Model 50 Amp
1940s-1960s. In '62 this was their entry-level amp, 4 to 5 watts, 1x8" similar to Fender Champ circuit with more of a vertical suitcase-style cab.

1940s-60s		$375	$475

Model 71 Amp
1961-1962. Combo with 1x12" (woofer) and 2 small tweeters, 24 watts. '61 styling with circular speaker baffle protected with metal X frame, 2 tweeter ports on upper baffle, 2-tone light tan and brown, 8 tubes, tremolo. The '62 styling changed to baffle with a slight V at the top, and 2-tone cover.

1961	Round baffle	$825	$1,075
1962	V-baffle	$825	$1,075

Model 76 Amp
1950s-1960s. Suitcase latchable cabinet that opens out into 2 wedges, 2-tone brown, lyre grille, 1x12".

1950s-60s		$675	$900

Model 88 Multivox Amp
1962. Multi-purpose combo amp, organ-stop control panel, 1x15" woofer with 2 tweeters, vertical suitcase cab, 2-tone cover, classic circular speaker baffle with X brace, 10 tubes, top-of-the-line in '62 catalog.

1962		$825	$1,075

Model 88N Amp
1950s-1961. Rectangular suitcase cabinet, 2-tone tan and brown, Premier and lyre logo, 25 watts, 1x12".

1950s-1961		$825	$1,075

Model 100R Amp
1960s. Combo amp, 1x12", reverb and tremolo.

1960s		$825	$1,075

Model 110 Amp
1962. 12-watt 1x10 student combo, lyre grille logo, 2-tone cab.

1962		$525	$675

Model 120/120R Amp
1958-1963. 12-watt 1x12" combo, tremolo, reverb ('62), 2-tone brown cab.

1958-1963		$600	$775
1962	With reverb	$650	$850

Model 200 Rhythm Bass Amp
1962. 1x15" combo bass amp.

1962		$625	$800

T-8 Twin-8 Amp
1950s, 1964-1966. 20 watts, 2x8", tremolo, reverb.

1950s		$1,200	$1,550
1964-1966		$1,100	$1,450

T-12 Twin-12 Amp
1958-1962. Early reverb amp with tremolo, 2x12", rectangular cabinet typical of twin 12 amps (Dano and Fender), brown cover.

1958-1959		$1,300	$1,650
1960-1962		$1,200	$1,550

Pritchard Amps

2004-present. Professional grade, production/custom, single and two-channel amps and cabinets built by Eric Pritchard in Berkeley Springs, West Virginia.

Pyramid Car Audio

Inexpensive student models, imported.

Quantum

1980s. Economy amps distributed by DME, Indianapolis, Indiana.

Q Terminator Economy Amp
1980s. Economy solidstate amps ranging from 12 to 25 watts and 1x6" to 1x12".

1980s	Various models	$25	$35

Quidley Guitar Amplifiers

Intermediate and professional grade, production/custom, tube guitar amp heads, combos and cabinets built by Ed Quidley in Wilmington, North Carolina, starting in 2006.

Quilter

2011-present. Patrick Quilter builds his intermediate and professional grade, production, guitar amps in Costa Mesa, California.

Quinn

Professional and premium grade, production/custom, amps and cabinets built by Shadwell J. Damron III, starting 2005, in Vancouver, Washington.

Randall

1960s-present. Randall Instruments was originally out of California and is now a division of U.S. Music Corp. They have offered a range of tube and solid-state combo amps, heads and cabinets over the years.

Rastop Designs

2002-present. Professional grade, custom amps built by Alexander Rastopchin in Long Island City, New York. He also builds effects.

Rat Fink

Early 2000s. Solidstate amp line from Lace Music Products. They also sold guitars and basses under this brand and offered amps under the Mooneyes and Lace brands.

Realistic

Radio Shack offered a couple made-in-the-U.S. combo tube amps in the '60s, including the Entertainer 34 with a flip down record turntable in the back! Their radio and stereo gear were also branded Realistic.

1964 Premier B-160 Club Bass
Imaged by Heritage Auctions, HA.com

AMPS

Premier Twin-8
Ängkvist

Realistic MPA-20
Bernunzio Uptown Music

Red Iron Mil Spec

Reeves Custom 12

1950s Rickenbacker M-8

Imaged by Heritage Auctions, HA.com

MODEL YEAR	FEATURES	EXC. COND. LOW	HIGH

Reason

2007-2016. Professional grade, production/custom, amps and cabinets built by Obeid Khan and Anthony Bonadio in St. Louis, Missouri.

Red Bear

1994-1997. Tube amps designed by Sergei Novikov and built in St. Petersburg, Russia. Red Bear amps were distributed in the U.S. under a joint project between Gibson and Novik, Ltd. Novik stills builds amps under other brands.

MK 60 Lead Tube Amp

1994-1997. Head with 4x12" half stack, Red Bear logo on amp and cab.

1994-1997		$650	$850

MK 100 Full Stack

1994-1997. 100 watts, 2x4x12".

1994-1997		$1,000	$1,300

Red Iron Amps

2001-present. Paul Sanchez builds his tube amp heads in Lockhart, Texas.

RedPlate Amps

2006-present. Professional and premium grade, production/custom, guitar amplifiers built in Phoenix, Arizona by Henry Heistand.

Reeves Amplification

2002-present. Started by Bill Jansen, Reeves builds tube amps, combos, and cabinets in Cincinnati, Ohio, based on the classic British designs of Dan Reeves.

Regal

Ca.1895-1966, 1987-present. The original Regal company distributed instruments built by them and others.

Gibson EH Amp

1936. Rare private-branded Gibson EH amp, 1x10", single control, alligator tweed.

1936		$550	$725

Reinhardt

2004-2012. Bob Reinhardt builds his professional grade, production/custom, guitar and bass amps and cabinets in Lynchburg, Virginia. He also builds effects pedals.

Resonant Amplifiers

2007-present. Owners Wes Kuhnley and Peter Bregman build their professional grade, vacuum tube guitar and hi-fi amps in Minneapolis, Minnesota. They also build the Field Effects.

Retro-King Amplifier Company

2004-present. Tube combo and head amps built by Chuck Dean in Marcellus, New York.

Revenge Amps

Greg Perrine began building in 1996, intermediate grade, production/custom, guitar amplifiers and attenuators in Conway, Arkansas. He also imports a line of amps.

Reverend

1996-present. Joe Naylor started building amps under the Naylor brand in '94. In '96 he left Naylor to build guitars under the Reverend brand. From '01 to '05, Reverend offered tube amps, combos, and cabinets built in Warren, Michigan, that Naylor co-designed with Dennis Kager.

Rex

1950s-1960s. Tube amps built by the Lamberti Bros. Co. in Melbourne, Australia. They also built guitars. In the 1920s-1940s, Gretsch has an unrelated line of guitars with that brand.

Reynolds Valveart

1997-present. Professional and premium grade, production/custom, amps and cabinets built by Peter Reynolds in Windsor, Australia.

Rickenbacker

1931-present. Rickenbacker made amps from the beginning of the company up to the late '80s. Rickenbacker had many different models, from the small early models that were usually sold as a guitar/amp set, to the large, very cool, Transonic.

E-12 Amp

1963. 1x12" combo with tremolo depth and speed, volume, and on-off tone knobs.

1963		$500	$650

Electro-Student Amp

Late-1940s. Typical late-'40s vertical combo cabinet, 1x12" speaker, lower power using 5 tubes, bottom mounted chassis, dark gray leatherette cover.

1948-1949		$475	$625

Hi Fi Model 98

1956. Tube amp, long horizontal cab with 3 speakers, Rickenbacker Hi Fi and Model 98 logo on back panel, blond cover, wheat grille cloth.

1956		$1,075	$1,400

Model B-9E Amp

1960s. 1x12" combo, 4 knobs, gray.

1960s		$600	$800

Model M-8 Amp

1950s-1960s. Gray, 1x8".

1950s-60s		$425	$550

Model M-9 Amp

1960s. Green, 1x12".

1960s		$550	$700

Model M-10 Amp

1930s. Silver metal, 1x10".

1935		$450	$575

Model M-11 Amp

1950s. 12-15 watts, 1x12", 2x6V6 power. There was a different M-11 offered in the 1930s.

1950s		$650	$850

AMPS

MODEL YEAR	FEATURES	EXC. COND. LOW	HIGH

Model M-12 Amp
1950s. 12-15 watts, 1x12", M-12 logo on back panel, brown leatherette. There was a different M-12 offered in the 1930s.

1950s		$650	$850

Model M-14A Amp
Late 1950s-early 1960s. 1x12 combo, mid-power 2x6V6, dual channel with vibrato, rough-brown tolex cover.

1950s-60s		$650	$850

Model M-15 Amp
1950s-Early 1960s. 1x15" combo, 35 watts, 2 x 6L6 power tubes, model name on top panel.

1950s-60s		$675	$875

Model M-16 Amp
1950s-Early 1960s. 1x15", 35 watts, model name on top panel.

1950s-60s		$675	$875

Model M-30 EK-O-Sound Amp
1961. Recording echo chamber and amp in 1x12 combo format, 11 tubes, gray grille and cover, very limited production.

1961		$3,200	$4,200

Model M-59 Amp
1930s. Small lap steel amp.

1935		$375	$500

Professional Model 200-A Amp
1938. 15 watts, was sold with the Vibrola Spanish guitar.

1938		$475	$625

RB and RG Series Amp
1987-1989. Various bass (RB) and guitar (RG) amp models.

1987-1989		$125	$275

Supersonic Model B-16 Amp
1960s. 4x10" speakers, gray cover.

1960s		$700	$925

Supersonic Model B-22 Amp Head
1960s. Tube head, gray cover.

1960s		$575	$725

TR7 Amp
1978-1982. Solidstate, 7 watts, 1x10", tremolo.

1978-1982		$100	$150

TR14 Amp
1978-ca.1982. Solidstate, 1x10", reverb, distortion.

1978-1982		$100	$150

TR25 Amp
1979-1982. Solidstate, 1x12" combo, reverb, tremolo, distortion.

1979-1982		$150	$200

TR35B Bass Amp
1978-ca.1982. Solidstate, mid-power, 1x15".

1978-1982		$150	$200

TR50 Amp
1977-ca. 1982. Solid state with Rick-o-Sound stereo inputs.

1977-1982		$200	$250

TR75G Amp
1978-ca.1982. 75 watts, 2x12", 2 channels.

1978-1982		$200	$250

TR75SG Amp
1978-ca.1983. 1x10" and 1x15" speakers.

1978-1982		$200	$250

TR100G Amp
1978-ca.1982. Solidstate, 100 watts with 4x12", 2 channels.

1978-1982		$250	$350

Transonic TS100/TS200 Amp
1967-1973. Trapezoid shaped combo, solidstate, 100 (2x12") or 200 (2x15") watts, Rick-O-Select.

1967-1973	100w	$2,400	$3,100
1967-1973	200w	$2,800	$3,600

Risson
1970-1984, 2012-present. Bob Rissi builds his intermediate, professional and premium grade, production/custom, guitar and bass amplifiers in Placentia, California. From 1970-84 they were built in Santa Ana.

Rivera
1985-present. Amp designer and builder Paul Rivera modded and designed amps for other companies before starting his own line in California. He offers heads, combos, and cabinets. He also builds guitar pedals.

Chubster 40 Amp
2000-present. 40 watts, 1x12" combo, burgundy tolex, light grille.

2000-2019		$625	$825

Clubster 25 Amp
2005-2016. 25 watts, 1x10", 6V6.

2005-2016		$525	$700

Clubster 45 Amp
2005-2015. 45 watts, 1x12" combo.

2005-2015		$625	$825

Fandango 112 Combo Amp
2001-present. 55 watts, 2xEL34, 1x12".

2001-2019		$850	$1,100

Fandango 212 Combo Amp
2001-2015. 55 or 100 watts, 2x12" tube amp.

2001-2015		$900	$1,200

Jake Studio Combo Amp
1997. 55 watts, 1x12", reverb and effects loop.

1997		$650	$850

Knucklehead 55 Amp
1994-2002. 55-watt amp head, replaced by reverb model.

1994-2002		$525	$700

Knucklehead 100 Amp
1994-2002. 100-watt amp head, replaced by reverb model.

1994-2002		$575	$750

Knucklehead Reverb 112 Amp
2003-2007. 55 watts, 1x12" amp combo, reverb.

2003-2007		$800	$1,050

Los Lobottom/Sub 1 Amp
1999-2004. 1x12" cabinet with 300-watt powered 12" subwoofer.

1999-2004		$375	$500

Ca. 1980 Rickenbacker TR-100 GT
Imaged by Heritage Auctions, HA.com

AMPS

Rivera Clubster 45

Rivera Fandango

Rivera Venus

Roland Blues Cube Artist

1979 Roland Cube 60B

Imaged by Heritage Auctions, HA.com

MODEL YEAR	FEATURES	EXC. COND. LOW	HIGH
M-60 Amp Head			
1990-2009. 60 watts.			
1990-2009		$475	$625
M-60 112 Combo Amp			
1989-2009. 60 watts, 1x12".			
1989-2009		$550	$725
M-100 Amp Head			
1990-2009. 100 watts.			
1990-2009		$525	$675
M-100 212 Combo Amp			
1990-2009. 100 watts, 2x12" combo.			
1990-2009		$625	$800
Pubster 25 Amp			
2005-2017. 25 watts, 1x10".			
2015-2017		$375	$475
Pubster 45 Amp			
2005-2014. 45 watts, 1x12".			
2005-2014		$400	$525
Quiana Combo Amp			
2000-present. Combo, 55 watts.			
2000-2014	2x12	$750	$850
2000-2014	4x10	$850	$1,100
2000-2019	1x12	$650	$850
R-30 112 Combo Amp			
1993-2007. 30 watts, 1x12", compact cab, black tolex cover, gray-black grille.			
1993-2007		$625	$825
R-100 212 Combo Amp			
1993-2007. 100 watts, 2x12".			
1993-2007		$700	$925
Sedona 112 Amp			
2011-present. 55 watts, 1x12".			
2011		$850	$1,125
Sedona Lite 55 Combo Amp			
2005-present. For electric and acoustic guitars, 55 watts, 1x12".			
2005-2019		$775	$1,025
Suprema R-55 112/115 Combo Amp			
2000-present. Tube amp, 55 watts, 1x12" (still available) or 1x15" ('00-'01).			
2000-2019	1x12 or 1x15	$750	$975
TBR-1 Amp			
1985-1999. First Rivera production model, rack mount, 60 watts.			
1985-1999		$600	$775
Venus Series			
2007-present. Series includes the 7/15-watt 3 combo (1x10 or 1x12), and the 15-watt 5 and 35-watt 6, both as combos (1x12, 2x12) and heads with cabs (1x12, 2x12).			
2007-2019	Venus 6, 17/35w head	$750	$975
2007-2019	Venus 6, 1x12	$775	$1,000
2007-2019	Venus 6, 2x12	$875	$1,125
2009-2017	Venus 3, 1x10	$675	$875
2009-2019	Venus 5, 1x12	$700	$925

Roccaforte Amps

1993-present. Tube amps, combos, and cabinets built by Doug Roccaforte in San Clemente, California.

MODEL YEAR	FEATURES	EXC. COND. LOW	HIGH
Rocktron			

1980s-present. Tube and solidstate amp heads, combos and cabinets. Rocktron is a division of GHS Strings and also offers stomp boxes and preamps.

Rogue

2001-present. They offered student-level solidstate import (Korea) compact amps up to around '06. They also offer guitars, basses, lap steels, mandolins, banjos, ukuleles and effects.

Small Solidstate Amps			
2001-2006. Various models.			
2001-2006		$35	$90

Roland

Japan's Roland Corporation's products include amplifiers and keyboards and, under the Boss brand, effects.

Acoustic Chorus (AC) Series Amp			
1995-present. Number in model indicates wattage (i.e. AC-60 = 60 watts).			
1995-2009	AC-100, 1x12", 2x5"	$350	$450
1995-2019	AC-60, 2x6"	$275	$375
1995-2019	AC-90, 2x8"	$350	$450
Blues Cube			
1996	BC60, 1x12	$190	$250
1996	BC60, 3x10	$225	$300
2000s	BC30	$175	$225
Bolt 60 Amp			
Early 1980s. Solidstate/tube, 1x12".			
1980s		$175	$225
Cube Series Amp			
1978-present. Number in model indicates wattage (i.e. Cube-15X = 15 watts).			
1978-1982	100, 1x12"	$175	$225
1978-1982	20, 1x8"	$95	$125
1978-1983	40, 1x10"	$175	$225
1978-1983	60, 1x12"	$175	$225
1978-1983	60B, 1x12"	$175	$225
2000-2009	30 Bass, 1x10"	$115	$150
2000s	80GX, 1x12	$175	$225
2000s	80XL, 1x12	$175	$225
2006-2010	30X, 1x10"	$115	$150
2006-2013	15X, 1x8"	$95	$125
2006-2013	20X, 1x8"	$95	$125
2008-2013	80X, 1x12"	$175	$225
Jazz Chorus (JC) Series Amp			
1975-present. Includes the JC-50 (50 watts, 1x12"), JC-55 (50 watts, 2x8"), JC-77 (80 watts, 2x10"), JC-90 (90 watts, 2x10") and JC-120 (120 watts, 2x12" and 4x12").			
1975-2014	JC-120, 2x12"	$400	$500
1980s	JC-50, 1x12"	$300	$400
1987-1994	JC-55, 2x8"	$300	$400
1987-1994	JC-77, 2x10"	$350	$450
1990s	JC-120, 4x12"	$425	$550
1990s	JC-90, 2x10"	$350	$450
Micro Cube Amp			
2000-present. Compact AC power or battery, 2 watts, 1x5".			
2000-2019		$75	$100

MODEL YEAR	FEATURES	EXC. COND. LOW	HIGH

Spirit Series Amp
1982-1989. Compact, model number indicates wattage.

MODEL YEAR	FEATURES	EXC. COND. LOW	HIGH
1982-1989	Spirit 30, 1x12	$75	$100
1982-1989	Spirit 40A, combo	$75	$100
1982-1989	Spirit 50, combo	$75	$100

Studio Bass Amp

1979		$175	$225

VGA3 V-Guitar Amp
2003-2009. GK digital modeling amp, 50 watts, 1x12" combo.

2003-2009		$175	$225

VGA5 V-Guitar Amp
2001-2004. GK digital modeling amp, 65 watts, 1x12".

2001-2004		$175	$225

VGA7 V-Guitar Amp
2000-2009. 65 + 65 watts, 2x12", digital modeling with analog-style controls.

2000-2009		$200	$250

S.S. Maxwell
See info under Danelectro.

Sadowsky
1980-present. From '05 to '07, luthier Roger Sadowsky built a bass tube amp head in Brooklyn, New York. He also builds basses and guitars.

Sam Ash
1960s-1970s. Sam Ash Music was founded by Sam Ash (formerly Ashkynase) in Brooklyn, New York, in 1924, and by '66 there were about four Ash stores. During the '60s they private branded their own amp line, was built by Jess Oliver of Oliver Amps and based upon Oliver's Ampeg designs.

Sam Ash Mark II Pro Combo Amp
1960s. 2x12" with reverb combo amp.

1960s		$525	$700

SamAmp
2004-present. Intermediate and professional grade, boutique amps built by Sam Timberlake in Vestavia Hills, Alabama.

Sano
1951-ca. 1980. Combos, heads and cabinets made in three factories around New Jersey. Founded by Joseph Zonfrilli, Louis Iorio, and Nick Sano, initially offering accordion pickups, amplifiers, and all-electric accordions. Sano patented his accordion pickup in '44 and also developed a highly acclaimed stereophonic pickup accordion and matching amp. By '66 the Sano Corporation augmented their all-tube accordion amps with new solidstate circuitry models. In the mid-'60s they offered a new line of amps specifically designed for the guitar and bass market. Sano amps are generally low-gain, low power amplifiers. They also marketed reverb units and guitars.

Compact Combo Amp

MODEL YEAR	FEATURES	EXC. COND. LOW	HIGH
1960s	160R, 15w, 1x12"	$400	$525
1960s	Sano-ette	$325	$425

Satellite Amplifiers
2004-present. Professional and premium grade, production/custom, tube amps, preamps and cabinets built by Adam Grimm in San Diego, California. He also builds effects.

Savage
1994-present. Tube combos, amp heads and cabinets built by Jeff Krumm at Savage Audio, in Savage, Minnesota.

Sceptre
1960s. Canadian-made. Sceptre script logo on upper left side of grille ('60s Fender-style and placement).

Signet Amp
1960s. Low power, 1x10", Class-A 6V6 power.

1960s		$250	$325

Schaller
The German guitar accessory company began in 1945, main products in the late '50s were tube amps and they had solid-state amps in the '60s.

Schertler
Made in Switzerland, model logo (e.g. David model) on front, intermediate to professional grade, modern designs for modern applications.

SDG Vintage
2003-present. Intermediate and professional grade, production/custom, tube amps, combos and heads built by Steven Gupta in Bristow, Virginia.

Selmer
1930s-late 1970s. The Selmer UK distributor offered mid- to high-level amps starting as early as 1935 and by the '50s was one of the strongest European brands of amps.

Bassmaster 50 Amp
1960s. Amp and cabinet set.

1964		$2,000	$2,600

Constellation 14 Amp
1962-1965. Single speaker combo, 14 watts, gray snakeskin tolex-type cover.

1962-1965		$1,950	$2,500

Futurama Caravelle Amp
1960s. Mid-size 1x12" combo.

1964		$900	$1,200

Futurama Corvette Amp
1960s. Class A low power 1x8", 4 tubes, volume and tone controls, plus amplitude and speed tremolo controls, large script Futurama logo on front of amp, Futurama Corvette and Selmer logo on top panel.

1960s		$750	$1,000

Little Giant Amp
1960s. Small combo, red.

1963		$1,075	$1,400

1978 Roland Jazz Chorus-160
Alf Tengs-Pedersen

AMPS

Roland Micro Cube

1975 Sano Supernova
Tom Pfeifer

AMPS

1964 Selmer Zodiac Twin 30
Imaged by Heritage Auctions, HA.com

Shaw Retro-Mod 15

Sherlock Angry Ant

Mark 2 Treble and Bass Amp Head
1960s. About 30 watts (2xEL34s), requires power line transformer for U.S. use, large Selmer logo on grille.

1960s	$1,075	$1,400

Thunderbird Twin 30 Amp
1960s. 30 watts, 2x12".

1962-1965	$4,000	$5,200

Thunderbird Twin 50 Amp
1960s. 50 watts, 2x12".

1964	$4,000	$5,200
1968	$2,450	$3,200

Truvoice Amp
1960s. Truvoice and Selectortone logo on top-mounted chasis, 30-watt combo, 1x15 or 2x12 Goodmans speaker, 2xEL34 power tubes, tremolo, 6 push button Selectortone Automatic.

1961	1x15 combo	$2,000	$2,600
1965	2x12 combo	$2,600	$3,400

Zodiac Twin 30 Amp
1964-1971. Combo amp, gray snakeskin tolex cover.

1964-1971	$2,900	$3,800

Sewell
1998-2008. Doug Sewell built his tube combo and head amps in Texas. He currently is the senior amp designer for Paul Reed Smith.

Seymour Duncan
Pickup maker Seymour Duncan, located in Santa Barbara, California, offered a line of amps from around 1984 to '95.

84-40/84-50 Amp
1989-1995. Tube combo, 2 switchable channels, 1x12", includes the 84-40 ('89-'91, 40 watts) and the 84-50 ('91-'95, 50 watts).

1989-1995	84-40 or 84-50	$225	$300

Bass 300 x 2 Amp
1986-1987. Solidstate, 2 channels (300 or 600 watts), EQ, contour boost switches, effects loop.

1986-1987	$225	$300

Bass 400 Amp
1986-1987. Solidstate, 400 watts, EQ, contour boost, balanced line output, effects loop.

1986-1987	$225	$300

Convertible Amp
1986-1995. 60-watt; dual-channel; effects loop; Accutronics spring reverb; 3-band EQ.

1986-1987	Head only	$300	$400
1988-1995	Combo	$300	$400

KTG-2075 Stereo Amp
1989-1993. Part of the King Tone Generator Series, 2 channels with 75 watts per channel.

1989-1993	$225	$300

SG Systems
1970s. A Division of the Chicago Musical Instrument Company (CMI), who also owned Gibson Guitars. Gibson outsourced amplifier production from Kalamazoo to CMI in '67 and CMI (Chicago) continued for a year or two with Gibson-branded amplifiers. In the early '70s CMI introduced the SG Systems brand of hybrid amplifiers, which had a tube power section and a solidstate preamp section. CMI was trying to stay modern with SG Systems by introducing futuristic features like the Notch Shift which would quickly switch between popular rock sounds and mellow jazz delivery. SG amps have a large SG logo on the front baffle and were built with metal corners. Amplifiers have similar power specs; for example, the models issued in '73 all were rated with 100-watt RMS with 200-watts peak music power, so models were based on different speaker configurations.

SG Series Amp

1970s	SG-115, 1x15	$310	$400
1970s	SG-212, 2x12	$330	$430
1970s	SG-215 Bass, 2x15	$330	$430
1970s	SG-410, 4x10	$330	$430
1970s	SG-610, 6x10	$350	$450
1970s	SG-812 PA	$210	$275

Shaw
2008-present. Custom/production, intermediate and professional grade, guitar amp heads and cabinets built by Kevin Shaw in Lebanon, Tennessee.

Sherlock Amplifiers
1990-present. Dale Sherlock builds his intermediate to premium grade, production/custom, tube guitar amps and cabinets in Melbourne Victoria, Australia.

Sherwood
Late 1940s-early 1950s. Amps made by Danelectro for Montgomery Ward. There are also Sherwood guitars and lap steels made by Kay.

Sho-Bud
Introduced and manufactured by the Baldwin/Gretsch factory in 1970. Distributed by Kustom/Gretsch in the '80s. Models include D-15 Model 7838, S-15 Model 7836, Twin Tube Model 7834, and Twin Trans Model 7832.

Compactra 100 Amp
1960s. Hybrid tube, 45 watts, 1x12".

1960s	$450	$600

D15 Double Amp
Introduced in 1970. Solidstate, 100 watts. 2 channels 1x15" JBL speaker.

1970s	$450	$575

S15 Single Amp
Introduced in 1972. Like D15, but with single channel.

1970s	$300	$400

Sho-Bass Amp
Introduced in 1972. 100 watts, 1x15", solidstate combo, black grille, black vinyl cover.

1970s	$300	$400

Twin Trans Amp
Introduced in 1972. 100 watts, solidstate combo, 2x12", reverb, black vinyl cover, dark grille, Sho-Bud script logo front upper right.

1970s	$425	$550

MODEL		EXC. COND.	
YEAR	FEATURES	LOW	HIGH

Twin Tube Amp
Introduced in 1972. 100 watt tube combo, 4 6L6s, 2x12", reverb, black vinyl cover, dark grille.
1970s $525 $700

Siegmund Guitars & Amplifiers
1993-present. Chris Siegmund builds his tube amp heads, combos and cabinets in Los Angeles, California. He founded the company in Seattle, moving it to Austin, Texas for '95-'97. He also builds effects pedals and guitars.

Silvertone
1941-ca.1970, present. Brand used by Sears. All Silvertone amps were supplied by American companies up to around '66.

Model 1300 Amp
1948. Vertical combo cab, treble-clef logo on grille, 2-tone, 3 inputs, 2 controls.
1948 $375 $500

Model 1304 Amp
1949-1951. 18 watts, 1x12, 2x6L6 power tubes, 2-tone leatherette cover, round speaker baffle hole, volume, treble, bass and tremolo control knobs, becomes Model 1344.
1949-1951 $375 $500

Model 1330 Amp
1954-1957. Introduced in Sears Fall '54 catalog, 3 tubes (with rectifier), 1x6", wide-panel 13x13.75x7.5" cab in tan artificial leather, 9 lbs., replaced Model 1339 at the same price but with new wide-panel style, small Silvertone logo above the grille, replaced in '58 by Model 1390 Silvertone Meteor.
1954-1957 $195 $250

Model 1331 Amp
1954-1957. Made by Danelectro, 14 lbs., 1x8" student combo, 3 tubes (with rectifier), 1 volume, 1 tone, 2 inputs, tan tweed-effect cover with brown alligator trim, large-thread wheat-gold grille, brown metal control panel.
1954-1957 $225 $300

Model 1333 Amp
1954-1957. Made by Danelectro, 23 lbs., 1x12" combo, 2x6V6 power, 5 tubes (with rectifier), 2 volumes, 1 tone, 3 inputs, 2-control vibrato, tan tweed-effect cover with brown alligator trim, large-thread wheat-gold grille, brown metal control panel.
1954-1957 $400 $525

Model 1334 Amp
1954-1957. Made by Danelectro, 29 lbs., heavy-duty 1x12" combo, 6 tubes (with rectifier), 2 volumes, 2 tones, 3 inputs, 2-control vibrato, tan tweed-effect cover with brown alligator trim, large-thread wheat-gold grille, brown metal control panel.
1954-1957 $425 $575

Model 1335 Amp
1954-1957. Made by Danelectro, 99 lbs., heavy-duty 1x15" combo, 6 tubes (with rectifier), 2 volumes, 2 tones, 4 inputs, 2-control vibrato, tan tweed-effect cover with brown alligator trim, large-thread wheat-gold grille, brown metal control panel.
1954-1957 $450 $600

Model 1336 (Twin Twelve) Amp
1954-1957. Made by Danelectro, 26.75x17.5x9.25" cab, 45 lbs., 2x12" combo, 4x6L6 powe tubes, 3 volumes, 2 tones, 4 inputs, 2-control vibrato, tan tweed-effect cover with brown alligator trim, large-thread wheat-gold grille, brown metal control panel.
1954-1957 $675 $900

Model 1337 "Wide Range Eight Speaker" Amp
1956. Odd-looking suitcase cab that opens into 2 separate speaker baffles each containing 4x8" speakers, 2 preamps, 2 channels with separate controls for volume, bass and treble, 2-control vibrato, 42 lbs.
1956 $675 $900

Model 1339 Amp
Ca.1952-1954. Sears lowest-priced amp, 3 tubes (with rectifier), 1x6", 1 input, 1 knob, maroon artificial leather cover over 10.5x8x5" verticle cab, script Silvertone logo on low right grille, 7 lbs.
1952-1954 $225 $300

Model 1340 Amp
Ca.1952-1954. Sears second lowest-priced amp, 3 tubes (with rectifier), 1x6", 2 inputs, 1 knob, brown and white imitation leather cover over 15x12x8.5" verticle cab, script Silvertone logo on low right grille, 14 lbs.
1952-1954 $225 $300

Model 1342 Streamlined Amp
Ca.1952-1954. Sears third lowest-priced amp, 4 tubes (with rectifier), 1x12", 3 inputs, 2 knobs, green and beige imitation leather cover over 16x19x7.25" slanted-side cab, script Silvertone logo on low right grille, 23 lbs.
1952-1954 $400 $525

Model 1344 Amp
1950-1954. Retro-styled vertical 22.5x15.5x9.5" cab with round speaker baffle hole, 1x12" combo, first Silvertone built-in vibrato, 6 tubes (with rectifier), 3 inputs, 3 controls (treble, bass, volume) plus vibrato control, maroon imitation leather cover with sports-stripe around the bottom, 33 lbs., script Silvertone logo low right side of cab.
1952-1954 $400 $525

Model 1346 (Twin Twelve) Amp
Ca.1952-1954. Danelectro-made, brown control panel, 2x12", 4 6L6s, vibrato, leather handle, tan smooth leatherette cover, 2 speaker baffle openings.
1952-1954 $675 $900

Model 1390 Meteor Amp
1958-1959. Renamed from Model 1330, Meteor logo on front panel, 1x6" practice amp, 3 tubes (with rectifier), tan simulated leather cover, in '60 renamed Model 1430 (but no longer a Meteor).
1958-1959 $225 $300

Model 1391 Amp
1958-1959. Modern-style cab, 3 tubes (with rectifier), 5 watts, 1x8".
1958-1959 $225 $300

Model 1392 Amp
1958-1959. Modern-style cab, 6 tubes (with rectifier), 10 watts, 1x12", vibrato.
1958-1959 $400 $525

Siegmund Sound King

Silvertone Model 1333
Imaged by Heritage Auctions, HA.com

Silvertone Model 1336
Imaged by Heritage Auctions, HA.com

AMPS

1961 Silvertone Model 1472
Kevin Lozinski

*Ca. 1961 Silvertone
Model 1474 Twin 12*
Imaged by Heritage Auctions, HA.com

1963 Silvertone Model 1482
Kevin Lozinski

AMPS

MODEL YEAR	FEATURES	EXC. COND. LOW	HIGH

Model 1393 Amp
1958-1959. Modern-style cab, 7 tubes (with rectifier), 15 watts, heavy-duty 1x12", vibrato.

| 1958-1959 | | $400 | $525 |

Model 1396 Two-Twelve Amp
1958-1959. Script Two-Twelve logo on lower left front and Silvertone logo on lower right front, 50 watts, 2x12", 4x6L6 power tubes, 9 tubes (with rectifier), vibrato, 26.75x17.5x9.25" with gray and metallic fleck cover, white grille, 45 lbs.

| 1958-1959 | | $675 | $900 |

Model 1420 Amp
1968. Tube-powered, 5 watts, 1x8" student combo.

| 1968 | | $275 | $350 |

Model 1421 Amp
1968. Tube-powered, 10 watts, 1x8" combo, covered in dark olive vinyl.

| 1968 | | $275 | $350 |

Model 1422 Amp
1968. Tube-powered, 40 watts, 1x12" combo, covered in dark olive vinyl.

| 1968 | | $400 | $525 |

Model 1423 Amp
1968. Solidstate, 125 watts, 2x12" cab, 55 lbs., dark olive.

| 1968 | | $325 | $425 |

Model 1425 Amp
1968. Solidstate, 200 watts, 6x10" cab, 86 lbs., dark olive.

| 1968 | | $675 | $900 |

Model 1426 Amp
1968. Solidstate, 250 watts, 6x15" cab, slide switches instead of control knobs, automatic E-tone for tuning, casters for 149 lb. head and cab.

| 1968 | | $675 | $900 |

Model 1428 Amp
1968. Solidstate, 60 watts, 1x15" cab, 36 lbs., dark olive.

| 1968 | | $325 | $425 |

Model 1430 Amp
1959-1966. Silvertone's lowest-price model, 3 tubes, 1x6", previously called Model 1390 Meteor, and prior to that named Model 1330, retro cab basically unchanged since first introduced in '54.

| 1959-1966 | | $225 | $300 |

Model 1431 Amp
1959-1961. 5 watts, 1x8", overhanging-top wrap-around grille cab, 3 tubes (with rectifier), light gray cover with white grille.

| 1959-1961 | | $225 | $300 |

Model 1431 Bass Amp
1968. Solidstate, 200 watts, 6x12" cab, 91 lbs., dark olive.

| 1968 | | $675 | $900 |

Model 1432 Amp
1959-1961. 10 watts, 1x12", vibrato, overhanging-top wrap-around grille cab, 6 tubes (with rectifier), dark gray tweed-effect cover with white grille.

| 1959-1961 | | $400 | $525 |

Model 1433 Amp
1959-1961. 15 watts, 1x15", vibrato, overhanging-top wrap-around grille cab, 7 tubes (with rectifier), gray with metallic fleck cover with white grille.

| 1959-1961 | | $525 | $700 |

Model 1434 Twin Twelve Amp
1959-1961. 50 watts using 4x6L6 power, 2x12" combo, vibrato, 2 channels each with volume, bass and treble controls, black cover with gold-colored trim.

| 1959-1961 | | $675 | $900 |

Model 1459 Amp
1960s. Student tube amp, 3 watts, 1x8", black vinyl, square cab, 1 tone, 1 volume, 1 channel, 2 inputs.

| 1967-1968 | | $275 | $350 |

Model 1463 Bass Amp
1967-1968. Solidstate, 1x15", piggyback, 60 lbs., reverb, tremolo.

| 1967-1968 | | $325 | $425 |

Model 1464 Amp
1967-1968. Solidstate, 100 watts, 2x12", piggyback, 60 lbs., reverb, tremolo, gray vinyl cover.

| 1967-1968 | | $375 | $500 |

Model 1465 Amp
1966-1968. Solidstate, piggyback, 150 watts, 6x10", reverb, tremolo, gray vinyl cover, replaces Model 1485.

| 1966-1968 | | $675 | $900 |

Model 1466 Bass Amp
1966-1968. Solidstate, 150 watts, 6x10", gray vinyl cover.

| 1966-1968 | | $550 | $725 |

Model 1471 Amp
1961-1963. 5 watts, 1x8", 3 tubes, 1 volume, 1 tone, 2 inputs, black leathette cover with white grille.

| 1961-1963 | | $275 | $350 |

Model 1472 Amp
1960s. 10 watts, 2 6V6s provide mid-level power, 1x12", front controls mounted vertically on front right side, black cover with silver grille, large stationary handle, tremolo.

| 1961-1963 | | $400 | $525 |

Model 1473 Bass Amp
1961-1963. Designed for bass or accordion, 25 watts, 1x15" combo, 6 tubes (with rectifier), 2 channels, 4 inputs, 19x29x9" cab, 43 lbs., black leatherette with white grille.

| 1961-1963 | | $525 | $700 |

Model 1474 Twin Twelve Amp
1961-1963. Silvertone's first reverb amp, 50 watts, 4x6L6 power, 10 tubes (with rectifier), 2x12" combo, 2 control vibrato with dual remote footswitch, 2 channels each with bass, treble, and volume, 4 inputs, ground switch, standby switch, 19x29x9" combo cab, 54 lbs., black leatherette with silver grille.

| 1961-1963 | | $675 | $900 |

Model 1481 Amp
1963-1968. Compact student amp, 5 watts, 1x8", 3 tubes (with rectifier), volume and tone controls, gray leatherette cover with white grille, replaces Model 1471.

| 1963-1968 | | $275 | $350 |

Model 1482 Amp
1960s. 15 watts, 1x12", 6 tubes, control panel mounted on right side vertically, tremolo, gray leatherette.

| 1963-1968 | | $400 | $525 |

MODEL		EXC. COND.	
YEAR	FEATURES	LOW	HIGH

Model 1483 Bass Amp
1963-1966. 23 watts, 1x15" piggyback tube amp, gray tolex and gray grille.

1963-1966		$525	$700

Model 1484 Twin Twelve Amp
1963-1966. 60 watts, 2x12" piggyback tube amp, tremolo and reverb, gray cover with light grille.

1963-1966		$675	$900

Model 1485 Amp
1963-1965. 120 watts, 6x10" (Jensen C-10Q) piggyback, 10 tubes with 5 silicon rectifiers, 2 channels, reverb, tremolo, charcoal-gray tolex-style cover, white grille, replaced in '66 by solidstate Model 1465.

1963-1965		$900	$1,150

Model 4707 Organ Amp
1960s. Interesting '60s family room style cabinet with legs, 45-watt tube amp with vibrato, 1x12", front controls, could be used for organ, stereo, or record player turntable.

1960s		$350	$450

Simms-Watts
Late 1960s-1970s. Tube amp heads, combos, PA heads and cabinets made in London, England. Similar to Marshall and HiWatt offerings of the era.

Skip Simmons
1990-present. Custom and production tube combo amps built by Skip Simmons in Loma Rica, California.

Skrydstrup R&D
1997-present. Production/custom, premium grade, amps and cabinets built by Steen Skrydstrup in Denmark. He also builds effects.

Sligo Amps
2004-present. Intermediate and professional grade, production/custom, amps built by Steven Clark in Leesburg, Virginia.

SMF
Mid-1970s. Amp head and cabinets from Dallas Music Industries, Ltd., of Mahwah, New Jersey. Offered the Tour Series which featured a 150 watt head and 4x12" bottoms with metal speaker grilles and metal corners.

Tour MK 2 Amp Head
1970s. 150-watt head, high- and low-gain inputs, master volume, 8xEL34 power tubes, black.

1970s		$850	$1,100

SMF (Sonic Machine Factory)
2002-2009. Tube amps and cabinets designed by Mark Sampson (Matchless, Bad Cat, Star) and Rick Hamel (SIB effects) and built in California.

Smicz Amplification
Tube combos and extension cabinets built by Bob Smicz in Bristol, Connecticut.

Smith Custom Amplifiers
All tube combo amps, heads and speaker cabinets built by Sam Smith in Montgomery, Alabama starting in 2002.

Smokey
1997-present. Mini amps often packaged in cigarette packs made by Bruce Zinky in Flagstaff, Arizona. He also builds Zinky amps and effects and has revived the Supro brand on a guitar and amp.

Snider
Jeff Snider has been building various combo tube amps in San Diego, California, since '95. In 1999 he started branding them with his last name.

Soldano
1987-present. Made in Seattle, Washington by amp builder Mike Soldano, the company offers a range of all-tube combo amps, heads and cabinets. They also offer a reverb unit.

Astroverb 16 Combo Amp
1997-present. Atomic with added reverb.

1997-2019		$675	$875

Atomic 16 Combo Amp
1996-2001. Combo, 20 watts, 1x12".

1996-2001		$575	$750

Avenger Amp Head
2004-present. Single channel, 4 preamp tubes, 100-watt with 4 power tubes, or 50-watt with 2.

2004-2019		$1,075	$1,400

Decatone Combo Amp
1998-present. 2x12" 100-watt combo, rear mounted controls, still available as a head.

1998-2008	2x12 combo	$1,600	$2,100
2009-2019	Head only	$1,250	$1,650

HR 50/Hot Rod 50 Amp Head
1992-2012. 50-watt single channel head.

1992-2012		$875	$1,125

HR 100/Hot Rod 100 Amp Head
1994-2001. 100-watt single channel head.

1994-2001		$875	$1,125

Lucky 13 Combo Amp
2000-present. 100 watts (50 also available), 2x12" combo.

2000-2019		$1,200	$1,575

Reverb-O-Sonic Combo Amp
1990s-present. 50 watts, 2 channels, 2x12" combo, reverb.

1990s-2019		$1,050	$1,375

SLO-100 Super Cabinet
1988-2019. 4x12" slant-front or straight-front cabinet, prices shown are for slant, deduct $100 for straight.

1988-1989		$650	$850
1990-2019		$575	$750

SLO-100 Super Lead Overdrive 100-Watt Amp
1988-present. First production model, 100-watt amp head, snakeskin cover, 4x12" cabinet.

1988-1989		$2,550	$3,300
1990-2009		$2,450	$3,200
2010-2019		$2,400	$3,100

1964 Silvertone Model 1483
Imaged by Heritage Auctions, HA.com

AMPS

Smokey

Soldano Decatone
Eric Van Gansen

Sommatone Roaring 40 2008

*1970s Sound City 120
Head and L-412 Cabinet*

Imaged by Heritage Auctions, HA.com

Sound Electronics Model X-101

Tom Novak

MODEL YEAR	FEATURES	EXC. COND. LOW	HIGH

Sommatone

1998-present. Jim Somma builds his tube combo and head amps and cabinets in Somerville, New Jersey.

Sonax

Introduced in 1972. Budget line of solidstate amps offered by Gretsch/Baldwin, made by Yorkville Sound (Traynor) in Toronto. Introduced with dark grille and dark cover.

530-B Bass Amp
1970s. Solidstate, 30 watts, 1x12".

1970s		$115	$150

550-B Bass Amp
1970s. Solidstate, 50 watts, 1x15".

1970s		$135	$175

720-G Amp
1970s. Solidstate student amp, 20 watts, 2x8", reverb.

1970s		$135	$175

730-G Amp
1970s. Solidstate, 30 watts, 2x10", reverb and tremolo.

1970s		$195	$250

750-G Amp
1970s. Solidstate, 50 watts, 2x12", reverb and tremolo.

1970s		$210	$275

770-G Amp
1970s. Solidstate, 75 watts, 4x10", reverb and tremolo.

1970s		$225	$300

Songworks Systems

See listing under Little Lanilei.

Sonny Jr.

1996-present. Harmonica amplifiers built by harmonica player Sonny Jr. in conjunction with Cotton Amps in Tolland, Connecticut.

Sonola

Tube combo amps made for the Sonola Accordian company of Chicago in the 1950s and '60s, possibly built by Guild or Ampeg. There are also Sonola tube amp heads from the '70s made by MHB Amplifiers in Adelaide, South Australia.

Sound City

Made in England from 1966-'67 to the late-'70s, the tube Sound City amps were Marshall-looking heads and separate cabinets. They were imported, for a time, into the U.S. by Gretsch.

50 PA Plus Amp
Late-1960s-late-1970s. Similar to 50 Plus but with 4 channels.

1970s		$575	$750

50 Plus/50R Amp Head
Late-1960s-late-1970s. Amp head, labeled 50 Plus or 50 R.

1960s-70s		$750	$1,000

120 Energizer Slave Unit Amp
1970s. 120-watt power amp only, no preamp, Energizer Slave Unit logo on front panel.

1970s		$475	$625

120/120R Amp Head
Early-late-1970s. The 120-watt head replaced the late-1960s 100-watt model.

1970s	120 no reverb	$775	$1,050
1970s	120R reverb	$850	$1,150

200 Plus Amp Head

1970s		$900	$1,175

Concord Combo Amp
80 watts, 2x12" Fane speakers, cream, basketweave grille.

1968		$800	$1,050

L-80 Cabinet
1970s. 4x10" speaker cabinet.

1970s		$425	$550

L-412 Cabinet
1970s. 4x12" speaker cabinet.

1970s		$475	$625

X-60 Cabinet
1970s. 2x12" speaker cabinet.

1970s		$450	$600

Sound Electronics

Sound Electronics Corporation introduced a line of amplifiers in 1965 that were manufactured in Long Island. Six models were initially offered, with solidstate rectifiers and tube preamp and power sections. Their catalog did not list power wattages but did list features and speaker configurations. The initial models had dark vinyl-style covers and sparkling silver grille cloth. The amps were combos with the large models having vertical cabinets, silver script Sound logo on upper left of grille. The larger models used JBL D120F and D130F speakers. Stand alone extension speakers were also available.

Various Model Amps
Mid-1960s. Includes X-101, X-101R, X-202 Bass/Organ, X-404 Bass and Organ, X-505R amps, hi-fi chassis often using 7868 power tubes.

1960s		$400	$600

Southbay Ampworks/ Scumback Amps

2002-present. Tube combo amps and speaker cabinets built by Jim Seavall in Whittier, California. He also builds Scumback Speakers. In '14, name changed to Scumback Amps.

Sovtek

1992-1996. Sovtek amps were products of Mike Matthews of Electro-Harmonix fame and his New Sensor Corporation. The guitar and bass amps and cabinets were made in Russia.

Mig Cabinet

1992-1996	2x12"	$300	$400

MODEL YEAR	FEATURES	EXC. COND. LOW	HIGH

Mig Series Amp Head

1992-1996. Tube amp heads, model number indicates watts, point-to-point wiring, models include; Mig 30, 50, 60, 100, 100B (bass).

1992-1996	Various models	$450	$600

Space Tone

See Swart Amplifiers.

Specimen Products

1984-present. Luthier Ian Schneller added tube amps and speaker cabinets in '93. He also builds guitars, basses and ukes in Chicago, Illinois.

Speedster

1995-2000, 2003-2007. Founded by Lynn Ellsworth, offering tube amps and combos designed by Bishop Cochran with looks inspired by dashboards of classic autos. In '03, Joe Valosay and Jevco International purchased the company and revived the brand with help from former owner Cory Wilds. Amps were originally built by Soldono, but later ones built by Speedster in Gig Harbor, Washington. They also built effects pedals.

Splawn

2004-present. Production, professional grade, tube amps and cabinets built by Scott Splawn in Dallas, North Carolina.

St. George

1960s. There were Japanese guitars bearing this brand, but these amps may have been built in California.

Mid-Size Tube Amp

1965. Low power, 1x10" Jensen, 2 5065 and 2 12AX7 tubes.

1960s		$175	$225

Standel

1952-1974, 1997-present. Bob Crooks started custom building amps part time in '52, going into full time standard model production in '58 in Temple City, California. In '61 Standel started distributing guitars under their own brand and others. By late '63 or '64, Standel had introduced solidstate amps, two years before Fender and Ampeg introduced their solidstate models. In '67 Standel moved to a new, larger facility in El Monte, California. In '73 Chicago Musical Instruments (CMI), which owned Gibson at the time, bought the company and built amps in El Monte until '74. In '97 the Standel name was revived by Danny McKinney who, with the help of original Standel founder Bob Crooks and Frank Garlock (PR man for first Standel), set about building reissues of some of the early models in Ventura, California.

A-30 B Artist 30 Bass Amp

1964-early-1970s. Artist Series, the original Standel solidstate series, 80 watts, 2x15".

1964-1969		$300	$400

A-30 G Artist 30 Guitar Amp

1964-early-1970s. Solidstate, 80 watts, 2x15".

1964-1974		$325	$425

A-48 G Artist 48 Guitar Amp

1964-early-1970s. Solidstate, 80 watts, 4x12".

1964-1974		$375	$500

A-60 B Artist 60 Bass Amp

1964-early-1970s. Solidstate, 160 watts, 4x15".

1964-1974		$375	$500

A-60 G Artist 60 Guitar Amp

1964-early-1970s. Solidstate, 160 watts, 4x15".

1964-1974		$375	$500

A-96 G Artist 96 Guitar Amp

1964-early-1970s. Solidstate, 160 watts, 8x12".

1964-1974		$425	$550

Artist XV Amp

1960s. Piggyback, hybrid solidstate preamp with power tubes.

1962		$300	$400

C-24 Custom 24 Amp

Late-1960s-1970s. Custom Slim Line Series, solidstate, 100 watts, 2x12", dark vinyl, dark grille.

1960s-70s		$325	$450

I-30 B Imperial 30 Bass Amp

1964-early-1970s. Imperial Series, the original Standel solidstate series, 100 watts, 2x15".

1964-1974		$350	$475

I-30 G Imperial 30 Guitar Amp

1964-early-1970s. Imperial Series, the original Standel solidstate series, 100 watts, 2x15".

1964-1974		$375	$500

S-10 Studio 10 Amp

Late-1960s-1970s. Studio Slim Line Series, solidstate, 30 watts, 1x10", dark vinyl, dark grille.

1960s-70s		$275	$350

S-24 G Amp

1970s. Solidstate, 2x12".

1970s		$325	$450

S-50 Studio 50 Amp

Late-1963 or early-1964-late-1960s. Not listed in '69 Standel catalog, 60 watts, gray tolex, gray grille, piggyback.

1960s		$325	$450

SM-60 Power Magnifier Amp

1970s. Tall, verticle combo solidstate amp, 100 watts, 6x10".

1970		$325	$425

Tube Amp

1953-1958. Early custom made tube amps made by Bob Crooks in his garage, padded naugahyde cabinet with varying options and colors. There are a limited number of these amps, and brand knowledge is also limited, therefore there is a wide value range. Legend has it that the early Standel amps made Leo Fender re-think and introduce even more powerful amps.

1953-1958	Various models	$2,000	$4,500

Specimen Horn

Standel Model 25L15
Imaged by Heritage Auctions, HA.com

Star Gain Star

AMPS

Suhr Badger
Rob Bernstein

Sundown

1975 Sunn Model T
Stephan Brown

MODEL YEAR	FEATURES	EXC. COND. LOW	HIGH

Star
Tube amps, combos and speaker cabinets built by Mark Sampson in the Los Angeles, California area, starting 2004. Sampson has also been involved with Matchless, Bad Cat, and SMF amps.

Starcaster
See listing under Fender.

Starlite
Starlite was a budget brand made and sold by Magnatone. See Magnatone for listings.

Stella Vee
1999-2005. Jason Lockwood built his combo amps, heads, and cabinets in Lexington, Kentucky.

Stephenson
1997-present. Mark Stephenson builds his intermediate to premium grade, production/custom, tube amps and cabinets in Regina, Saskatchewan 1997-'99, in Hope, British Columbia 2000-'06, and since in Parksville, British Columbia. He also offers effects.

Stevenson
1999-present. Luthier Ted Stevenson, of Lachine, Quebec, added amps to his product line in '05. He also builds basses and guitars.

Stimer
Brothers Yves and Jean Guen started building guitar pickups in France in 1946. By the late '40s they had added their Stimer line of amps to sell with the pickups. Early amp models were the M.6, M.10 and M.12 (6, 10 and 12 watts, respectively). An early user of Guen products was Django Reinhardt.

Stinger
1980s-1990s. Stinger was a budget line of guitars and solidstate amps imported by Martin.

Strad-O-Lin/Stradolin
Ca.1920s-ca.1960s. The Strad-O-Lin company primarily made mandolins for wholesalers but around '57 Multivox/Premier bought the company and used the name on guitars and amps.
Compact Solidstate Amp
1960s. Made in U.S.A., logo on control panel and grille, black grille and cover.

| 1960s | | $95 | $125 |

Stramp
1970s. Stramp, of Hamburg, Germany, offered audio mixers, amps and compact powered speaker units, all in aluminum flight cases.
Solidstate Amp
1970s. Solidstate amp head in metal suitcase with separate Stramp logo cabinet.

| 1970s | | $300 | $400 |

Straub Amps
2003-present. Harry Straub builds his professional grade, production/custom, amps in St. Paul, Minnesota.

Suhr
1997-present. John Suhr builds his production/custom amps in Lake Elsinore, California. He also builds guitars and basses.

Sundown
1983-1988. Combo amps, heads and cabinets designed and built by Dennis Kager. By '88, he had sold his interest in the company.

Sunn
1965-2002. Started in Oregon by brothers Conrad and Norm Sundhold (Norm was the bass player for the Kingsman). Sunn introduced powerful amps and extra heavy duty bottoms and was soon popular with many major rock acts. Norm sold his interest to Conrad in '69. Conrad sold the company to the Hartzell Corporation of Minnesota around '72. Fender Musical Instruments acquired the brand in '85 shortly after parting ways with CBS and used the brand until '89. They resurrected the brand again in '98, but quit offering the name in '02.
100S Amp and Cabinet Set
1965-1970s. 60 watts, 1x15" JBL D130F and 1 LE 100S JBL Driver and Horn, piggyback, 5 tubes (with rectifier).

| 1965-1969 | | $1,125 | $1,500 |

190L Amp and Cabinet Set
1970s. Solidstate, 80 watts, 2 speakers.

| 1970s | | $575 | $750 |

200S/215B Amp and Cabinet Set
1966-1970s. 60 watts, 2x6550s, large vertical cab with 1x15" or 2x15" speakers.

| 1966-1969 | 1x15" | $1,125 | $1,500 |
| 1966-1969 | 2x15" | $1,125 | $1,500 |

601-L Cabinet
1980s. 6x10" plus 2 tweeters cab.

| 1980s | | $350 | $450 |

2000S Amp
1968-1970s. 4x6550 power tubes, 120 watts.

| 1968-1970s | Head & cab | $1,300 | $1,700 |

Alpha 112 Amp
1980s. Solidstate, MOS-FET preamp section, 1x12" combo, reverb, overdrive, black.

| 1980s | | $150 | $200 |

Alpha 115 Amp
1980s. Solidstate, MOS-FET preamp section, 1x15", clean and overdrive.

| 1980s | | $175 | $225 |

Alpha 212 R Amp
1980s. Solidstate, MOS-FET preamp section, 2x12", reverb.

| 1980s | | $225 | $300 |

MODEL YEAR	FEATURES	EXC. COND. LOW	HIGH

Beta Bass Amp
1978-1980s. Solidstate 100-watt head and combos, large Beta Bass logo on front panel.

1978-1980s	4x12"	$525	$700
1978-1980s	6x10"	$525	$700
1978-1980s	Combo 1x15"	$525	$700
1978-1980s	Combo 2x12"	$525	$700
1978-1980s	Combo 4x10"	$525	$700

Coliseum 300 Bass Amp
1970s. Solidstate, Coliseum-300 logo on front.

1970s	Head & cab	$675	$900

Coliseum Lead Amp
1970s. Solidstate, Coliseum Lead logo on front.

1970s	Head & cab	$675	$900

Coliseum Lead Full Stack Amp
1970s. Coliseum Lead logo on amp head, two 4x12" cabs.

1970s		$1,025	$1,350

Concert 215S Bass Amp Set
1970s. Solidstate head, 200 watts, Model 215S tall vertical cabinet with 2x12" Sunn label speakers, dark vinyl cover, silver sparkle grille.

1970s		$625	$825

Concert Lead 610S Amp Set
1970s. Solidstate, 200 watts, 6x10" piggyback, reverb and built-in distortion.

1970s		$775	$1,025

Enforcer Amp
1980s. Tube, 60/100 watt 2x12" or 100 watt head.

1980s	Combo	$750	$975
1980s	Head & cab	$800	$1,050

Fuse 200S Amp
1970s. Sunn Fuse logo and model number on front panel, 140 watts.

1970s		$850	$1,125

Model T Amp Head
Early-1970s. 100 watts.

1970s		$2,150	$2,825

Model T Amp Reissue
1998-2002. Reissue of '70s Model T, 100 watts, with 4x12" cab.

1998-2002	Head & cab	$1,250	$1,625

SB-160 Bass Amp
1985. Combo, 60 watts.

1985		$325	$425

SB-200 Amp
1985. 200 watts, 1x15", 4-band EQ, master volume, compressor.

1985		$350	$475

Sceptre Amp
1968-1972. 60 watts, 6550 power tubes, tremolo, reverb.

1968-1972	Head & cab	$1,050	$1,375

Sentura Amp
1967-1970s. Rectifier and power tubes, I and II versions.

1967-1969	I, 1x15" set	$950	$1,250
1967-1969	II, 2x15" set	$1,000	$1,300

SL 250 Amp
1980s. 60 watts, 2x12" combo, SL 250 logo.

1980s		$450	$600

SL 260 Amp
1982-ca.1985. 60 watts, 2x12" combo with reverb, SL 260 logo.

1982-1985		$525	$675

Solarus Amp
1967-1970s. Tube amp (EL34s), reverb, tremolo, 2x12" 40 watt combo to '68; 60 watt head with 2x12" cab for '69 on.

1967-1968	Combo	$525	$700
1969-1970s	Head & cab	$650	$850

Solo II Amp
Early-1970s. Solo II logo on front panel, 120 watts, 2x12" combo, black tolex.

1970s		$525	$700

Sonaro Amp
Early-1970s. Head and 1x15" cab, 60 watts.

1970s		$575	$750

Sonic 1-40 Amp
1967-1969. Tube head, 1x15" bass amp, 40 watts.

1967-1969	Head & cab	$900	$1,200

Sonic I Amp
1967-1969. 125 watts, 1x15" JBL D130F in short cabinet, 5 tubes (with rectifier), piggyback, dark tolex.

1967-1969	Head & cab	$900	$1,200

Sonic II Amp
1967-1969. 250 watts, 2x15" JBL D130F in folding horn large cabinet, 5 tubes (with rectifier), piggyback, dark tolex.

1967-1969	Head & cab	$950	$1,250

Sorado Amp
1970s. 50 watts, tubes, 2x15" matching cab.

1970s	Head & cab	$825	$1,100

Spectrum I Amp
1967-1969. 125 watts, 1x15" JBL D130F large cabinet, 5 tubes (with rectifier), piggyback, dark tolex cover.

1967-1969	Head & cab	$875	$1,150

Spectrum II Amp
1967-1969. 250 watts, 2x12", piggyback, 5 tubes (with rectifier), Spectrum II logo on front panel.

1967-1969	Head & cab	$925	$1,225

SPL 7250 Amp
Dual channels, 250 watts per channel, forced air cooling, switch-selectable peak compressor with LEDs.

1989	Head & cab	$475	$625

Stagemaster
1980s. 120 watts, 2x12".

1980s	Combo	$400	$525
1980s	Head & cab	$475	$625

T50C
1998-2002. Combo 1x12", 50 watts.

1998-2002		$525	$700

Supersound
1952-1974. Founded in the U.K. by Alan Wootton, building custom amps and radios, the firm continued to build amps and effects into the early '60s. They also built guitars and basses.

1970s Sunn Solos
Imaged by Heritage Auctions, HA.com

Ca. 1970 Sunn Sceptre
Imaged by Heritage Auctions, HA.com

Sunn Stagemaster 2×12
Robert Curd

AMPS

Supro 1688T
Carter Vintage Guitars

Supro 1695T Black Magick

Mid-1960s Supro Corsica
Imaged by Heritage Auctions, HA.com

MODEL YEAR	FEATURES	EXC. COND. LOW	HIGH

Supertone

1914-1941. Supertone was a brand used by Sears for their musical instruments. In the '40s Sears started using the Silvertone name on those products. Amps were made by other companies.

Amp

1930s		$200	$350

Supro

1935-1968, 2004-present. Supro was a budget brand of the National Dobro Company, made by Valco in Chicago, Illinois. Amp builder Bruce Zinky revived the Supro name in '04 for a line of guitars and amps. In '13, Absara Audio, LLC acquired the Supro trademark and started releasing amps in July '14. In 2020 D'Angelico Guitars acquired the brand.

Accordion 1615T Amp

1957-1959. Compact combo, 1x15", 24 watts, 2x6L6 power, 5V4, 3x12AX7, 2 channels, tremolo, 3 control knobs, Accordion (model) logo upper left corner of grille, Supro logo lower right, Rhino-Hide gray with white sides.

1957-1959		$725	$950

Bantam Amp

1961-1966. Petite, 4 watts, 3 tubes, 1x 8" Jensen, gold weave Saran Wrap grille, Spanish Ivory fabric cover, red in '64, gray in '66. Also sold as matching set, for example in '64 with student-level red and white lap steel, add 65% to price for matching guitar and amp set.

1961-1963	1611S, Spanish ivory	$325	$425
1964-1965	S6411, red cover	$325	$425
1966	Gray cover	$325	$425

Bass Combo Amp

Early 1960s. 35 watts, 2x12", 2 channels (bass and standard), 7 tubes, tremolo, woven embossed black and white tolex that appears grey. The '61 model 1688T has a narrow panel body style somewhat similar to the Fender narrow panel cab style of the late '50s, in '62 the cab panel was removed and the 'no panel' style became the 1688TA model, the new cab was less expensive to build and Supro offered a price reduction on applicable models in '62.

1961	1688T, narrow panel	$700	$900
1962-1963	1688TA, no panel	$700	$900

Big Star Reverb S6451TR Amp

1964. 35 watts, 2x12", reverb and tremolo, 'no panel' cab.

1964		$900	$1,200

Brentwood 1650T Amp

Mid-1950s. Advertised as Supro's "finest amplifier", model 1650T described as the "professional twin speaker luxury amplifier", 2 channels including high-gain, tremolo with speed control.

1956		$900	$1,200

Combo Amp

1961-1964. 24 watts, 6 tubes, 1x15" Jensen, Rhino-Hide covering in black and white, light grille, tremolo.

1961	1696T, narrow panel	$650	$850
1962-1963	1696TA, no panel	$650	$850

Combo Tremolo S6497T Amp

1964. 35 watts, 1x15", standard 'no panel' cab, tremolo.

1964		$675	$900

Comet 1610B Amp

1957-1959. Gray Rhino-Hide, 1x10".

1957-1959		$600	$800

Comet 1610E Amp

Mid-1950s. Supro's only 1x10" amp from the mid-'50s, 3 input jacks, 2 control knobs, woven tweed and leatherette 2-tone covering.

1956		$600	$800

Coronado Amp

1960-1963. 24 watts, 2x10", tremolo, 2 channels, 6 tubes, Supro logo upper right above grille, black and white mixed tolex appears gray, described as tremolo twin-speaker pro amp, '61 has 'narrow panel' body style, new body style in '62 becomes 1690TA model with grille only and no panel.

1960-1961	1690T, narrow panel	$725	$975
1962-1963	1690TA, no panel	$725	$975

Corsica Amp

Mid-1960s. Redesigned vertical combo amp, reverb, tremolo, blue control panel, black tolex, silver grille.

1965-1967		$500	$650

Dual-Tone Amp

1961-1965. 17 watts, 6 tubes, 1x12" Jensen, organ tone tremolo, restyled in '64, Trinidad Blue vinyl fabric cover, light color grille.

1961	1624T, narrow panel	$700	$925
1962-1963	1624TA, no panel	$700	$925
1964-1965	S6424T, no panel	$700	$925

Galaxy Tremolo S6488 Amp

1965. 35 watts, 2x12" (often Jensen), 7 tubes, tremolo, multi-purpose for guitar, bass and accordion.

1965		$725	$950

Galaxy Tremolo S6688 Amp

1966-1967. 35 watts, 2x12" (often Jensen), turquoise front control panel with Supro logo (not on grille), model name/number also on front control panel.

1966-1967		$725	$950

Golden Holiday 1665T Amp

Mid-1950s. Supro's model for the 'semi-professional', 2 oval 11x6" speakers, 14 watts, 6 tubes, tremolo, 2 control knobs, black and tweed cover.

1956		$750	$975

Model 24 Amp

1965. 18 watts, 1x12 combo, 2 channels each with bass and treble inputs, tremolo, Model 24 logo on top panel, Calypso Blue vinyl cover.

1965		$650	$850

Reverb 1650R Amp

1963. 17 watts, 1x10", 'no panel' grille front style cab, reverb.

1963		$650	$850

Royal Reverb 1650TR Amp

1963-1965. 17 watts, 15 tubes, 2x10" Jensens, catalog says "authentic tremolo and magic-reverberation."

1963-1965		$825	$1,100

MODEL		EXC. COND.	
YEAR	FEATURES	LOW	HIGH

YGA1 Amp Head
1966-1967. 45 watts guitar amp, tremolo.

| 1966-1967 | | $475 | $625 |

YGL3 Mark III Amp
1971-1979. All tube, 80 watts, 2x12" combo, reverb, tremolo.

| 1971-1979 | | $625 | $800 |

YGM3 Guitar Mate Reverb Amp
1969-1979. Tubes, 25 watts, 1x12", black tolex, gray grille until '74, black after.

| 1969-1979 | | $625 | $800 |

YGM3 Guitar Mate Reverb Reissue Amp
2011-2013. 1x12" combo, 'flying wing' Traynor badge.

| 2011-2013 | | $440 | $575 |

YRM1 Reverb Master Amp Head
1973-1979. 45 watt tube amp, reverb, tremolo.

| 1973-1979 | | $450 | $575 |

YRM1SC Reverb Master Amp
1973-1979. YRM1 as a 4x10" combo.

| 1973-1979 | | $625 | $800 |

YSR1 Custom Reverb Amp Head
1968-1973. 45 watt tube amp, reverb, tremolo.

| 1968-1973 | | $450 | $575 |

YVM Series PA Amp Head
1967-1980. Public address heads, models include tube YVM-1 Voice Master, and solidstate YVM-2 and 3 Voice Mate and YVM-4, all with 4 inputs.

1967-1972	1, tubes	$375	$500
1969-1975	2, solidstate	$155	$200
1970-1980	3, solidstate, reverb	$215	$275
1972-1977	4, solidstate, reverb	$215	$275

Trillium Amplifier Company
2007-present. Brothers Stephen and Scott Campbell build their professional and premium grade, production/custom tube amps in Indianapolis, Indiana.

Trinity Amps
2003-present. Stephen Cohrs builds his production/custom, professional grade, tube amps and cabinets in Toronto, Ontario.

True Tone
1960s. Guitars and amps retailed by Western Auto, manufactured by Chicago guitar makers like Kay.

Hi-Fi 4 (K503 Hot-Line Special) Amp
1960s. Similar to K503, 4 watts from 3 tubes, gray cabinet, gray grille, metal handle.

| 1960s | | $225 | $300 |

Model 5 (K503A) Amp
1960s. 4 tubes, 1x8".

| 1960s | | $225 | $300 |

Vibrato 704 Amp
1960s. Solidstate, 10 watts, 1x8", white sides and gray back, gray grille.

| 1960s | | $105 | $140 |

Vibrato 706 Amp
1960s. Solidstate, 15 watts, 1x15", white sides and gray back, brown grille.

| 1960s | | $120 | $155 |

MODEL		EXC. COND.	
YEAR	FEATURES	LOW	HIGH

Tube Works
1987-2004. Founded by B.K. Butler in Denver, Tube Works became a division of Genz Benz Enclosures of Scottsdale, Arizona in 1997. Tube Works' first products were tube guitar effects and in '91 they added tube/solidstate amps, cabinets, and DI boxes to the product mix. In '04, Genz Benz dropped the brand.

Twilighter (Magnatone)
Late-1950s-early-1960s. Magnatone amps private branded for LoDuca Brothers. Prominent block-style capital TWILIGHTER logo on front panel, generally something nearly equal to Magnatone equivalent. This is just one of many private branded Magnatones. Covers range from brown to black leatherette, and brown to light silver grilles.

Model 213 Amp
1961-1963. About 20 watts, 1x12", vibrato, brown leatherette and brown grille.

| 1961-1963 | | $950 | $1,250 |

Model 260R Amp
1961-1963. About 18 to 25 watts, 1x12", vibrato, brown leatherette cover.

| 1961-1963 | | $1,100 | $1,500 |

Model 280A Amp
Late-1950s-early-1960s. About 35 watts, 2x12", vibrato, brown leatherette cover.

| 1961-1963 | | $1,200 | $1,500 |

Two-Rock
1999-present. Tube guitar amp heads, combos and cabinets built by Joe Mloganoski and Bill Krinard (K&M Analog Designs) originally in Cotati, California, currently in Rohnert Park. They also build speakers.

Ugly Amps
2003-present. Steve O'Boyle builds his tube head and combo amps and cabinets in Burbank, California and Reading, Pennsylvania.

UltraSound
A division of UJC Electronics, UltraSound builds acoustically transparent amps, designed by Greg Farres for the acoustic guitarist, in Adel, Iowa.

Unique (Magnatone)
1961-1963. Private branded, typically for an accordion company or accordion studio, uses standard guitar input jacks.

Model 260R Amp
1961-1963. Based on Magnatone 260 Series amp, 35 watts, 2x12" but with reverb, black vinyl-style cover with distinctive black diamond-check pattern running through the top and sides.

| 1961-1963 | | $1,400 | $1,800 |

Model 460 Amp
1961-1963. 35 watts, 2x12" and oval 5"x7" speakers, reverb and vibrato make it one of the top models, black vinyl, black grille.

| 1961-1963 | | $1,150 | $1,500 |

1970s Traynor YGM3 Guitar Mate Reverb

AMPS

Two-Rock Coral

Ugly Lil' Ugly 20W Head

1971 Univox U-1226
Carter Vintage Guitars

AMPS

Valvetech Suplex

Valvetrain Bennington Reverb

MODEL YEAR	FEATURES	EXC. COND. LOW	HIGH

Universal (Audio Guild)

See Audio Guild amps.

Univox

1964-ca.1978. From '64 to early-'68, these were American-made tube amps with Jensen speakers. By '68, they were using Japanese components in American cabinets, still with Jensen speakers. Electronics were a combination of tube and transistors during this time; this type lasted until the mid-'70s. Around '71, Univox introduced a line of all solidstate amps, as well.

Lead Model Tube Amp
1960s. Tube amp, 2x10" or 2x12".

1965-1969		$525	$700

Model U45B Bass Amp
1965-1968. 1x12" combo tube bass amp, 10 watts.

1965-1968		$275	$350

Model U60A Amp
1965-1968. 1x12" tube combo.

1965-1968		$300	$390

Model U65R Amp
1965-1968. 20 watts, 1x12" tube combo.

1965-1968		$345	$450

Model U65RD Lead 65 Amp
1976-1978. Solidstate, 65 watts, reverb, 1x12" or 2x12" in a vertical cab.

1976-1978		$45	$60

Model U102 Amp
1965-1968. 1x12" tube combo.

1965-1968		$345	$450

Model U130B Bass Amp
1976-1978. Solidstate, 130 watts, 1x15".

1976-1978		$125	$165

Model U130L Lead Amp
1976-1978. Solidstate, 130 watts.

1976-1978		$125	$165

Model U155R Amp
1965-1968. 20 watts, 1x12" tube combo.

1965-1968		$450	$575

Model U202R Amp
1965-1968. 1x12" tube combo.

1965-1968		$450	$575

Model U305R Amp
1965-1968. 30 watts, 1x15" tube combo.

1965-1968		$525	$675

Model U1011 Lead Amp Head
1976-1978. Solidstate, 100 watts, reverb, tremolo. Name also used on earlier tube head.

1976-1978		$190	$250

Model U1061 Bass Amp Head
1976-1978. Solidstate.

1976-1978		$190	$250

Model U1220 Amp
1968-1971. Tubes or tube-hybrid, piggyback, 2x12".

1968-1971		$300	$400

Model U1226 Amp Head
1971-1972. 60-watt tube amp head.

1971-1972		$450	$575

Model U1246B Bass Amp Head
1976-1978. Solidstate, 60 watts.

1976-1978		$190	$245

Model U1246L Lead Amp Head
1976-1978. Solidstate.

1976-1978		$190	$245

Valco

Valco, from Chicago, Illinois, was a big player in the guitar and amplifier business. Their products were private branded for other companies like National, Supro, Airline, Oahu, El Grande and Gretsch.

Valvetech

Production/custom, professional grade, amps built by Rob Pierce, starting in 1997, in Ossian, Indiana.

Valvetrain Amplification

2005-present. Tube combos, amp heads, and speaker cabinets built by Rick Gessner in Sorrento, Florida. He also builds reverb units.

Vamp

1970s. Tube and solidstate amps and speaker cabinets built at Triumph Electronics in England.

Bass Master Amp Head

1970s	100 watts	$1,000	$1,300

VanAmps

Tim Van Tassel, started in 1999, builds professional, production/custom, amps and cabinets in Golden Valley, Minnesota. He also builds effects.

Vega

The original Boston-based company (1903) was purchased by C.F. Martin in '70. In '80, the Vega trademark was sold to a Korean company.

A-49 Amp
1960s. Tubes, 6 watts, 1x8", tan cover.

1960s		$250	$325

Director Combo Amp
1950s. Small to mid-size tube amp, 2-tone cover, 2 volume and 1 tone controls, rear mounted control chassis similar to Fender or Gibson from the '50s.

1950s		$375	$500

Lap Steel Amp
1930s-1940s. Various models.

1936	1x12, dark cover	$375	$500
1940s	1x10, tweed	$375	$500

Super Amp
Early 1950s. 1 6L6, 1x10", vertical combo amp typical of the era.

1950s		$375	$500

Triumphal Amp
Late-1940s. Vega Triumphal logo on back control pane, 6L6 power, 1x12".

1940s		$375	$500

Versatone (Audio Guild)

See Audio Guild amps.

MODEL YEAR	FEATURES	EXC. COND. LOW	HIGH

Vesta Fire
1980s. Japanese imports by Shiino Musical Instruments Corp.; later by Midco International. Mainly known for effects pedals.

VHT
1989-present. Founded by Steven M. Fryette, VHT built amps, combos, and cabinets in Burbank, California. At the beginning of '09 AXL guitars acquired the VHT name and manufactures their own product under that brand. Fryette continues to build the VHT amp models under Fryette Amplification.

Vibe Amplification
2008-2013. Intermediate grade, production, tube amps, imported from Asia by Lorenzo Brogi in Bologna, Italy.

Victor
Late-1960s. Made in Japan.

Victoria
1994-present. Tube amps, combos, and reverb units built by Mark Baier in Naperville, Illinois. In '08, they changed the logo from the original script Victoria Amp Co. to the current stylized lightning bolt Victoria logo.

Cherry Bomb Amp
2011-present. Tube tremolo, 40 watts, 1x15", alligator/cream tolex.

2011-2019		$1,400	$1,850

Double Deluxe Amp
1994-present. 35 watts, 2x12".

1994-2019		$1,400	$1,850

Electro King Amp
2008-present. 1957 GA-40 type circuit, tubes, 15 watts, 1x12".

2008-2019		$1,275	$1,675

Golden Melody Amp
2008-present. Tubes, reverb, 50 watts, 2x12", alligator/brown tolex.

2008-2019		$1,400	$1,850

Ivy League Amp
2010-present. Tweed Harvard specs, 14 watts, 1x10".

2011-2019		$800	$1,050

Model 518 Amp
1994-present. Tweed, 1x8".

1994-2019		$750	$1,000

Model 5112-T Amp
2001-present. Tweed, 5 watts, 5F1 circuit, 1x12".

2001-2019		$800	$1,050

Model 20112 Amp
1994-present. Tweed, 20 watts, 1x12", tweed.

1994-2019		$1,050	$1,350

Model 35115 Amp
1994-present. Tweed combo, 28 watts, 1x15".

1994-2019		$1,350	$1,750

Model 35210 Amp
1994-present. Tweed, 28 watts, 2x10", tweed.

1994-2019		$1,450	$1,850

Model 35212-T Amp
1990s. Tweed, 35 watts, 2x12".

1990s		$1,400	$1,800

Model 35310-T Amp
1994-present. Tweed, 28 watts, 3x10".

1994-2019		$1,475	$1,900

Model 45115-T Amp
2008-2009. Tweed, 45 watts, 1x15".

2008-2009		$1,350	$1,750

Model 45410-T Amp
1994-present. Tweed, 45 watts, 4x10" combo, tweed.

1994-2019		$1,400	$1,800

Model 50212-T Amp
2002-present. Tweed, 50 watts, 2x12" combo.

2002-2019		$1,400	$1,800

Model 80212 Amp
1994-present. Tweed, 80 watts, 2x12", tweed.

1994-2019		$1,450	$1,900

Regal Amp
2004-2006. Class A with 1 x 6L6, 15 watts, 1x15", brown tolex cover, rear mount controls.

2004-2006		$1,325	$1,725

Regal II/Regal Amp
2006-present. Class A, 35 watts, 1x15", tweed or vanilla tolex, rear mount controls. The II removed from name about '13.

2006-2019		$1,375	$1,775

Reverberato Amp
1996-2016. Tube reverb unit with vibrato, tweed or color options.

1996-2016		$1,000	$1,300

Silver Sonic Amp
2011-present. Tube reverb, 20 watts, 1x12", 2-tone black/cream cab with Sonic Blue or black tolex.

2011-2019		$1,400	$1,800

Trem D'La Trem Amp
2007-present. Tweed design, 14 watts, 1x15".

2007-2019		$1,350	$1,750

Victoriette Amp
2001-present. 20 watts, 1x12" or 2x10", reverb, tremolo in '01.

2001-2019	2x10	$1,450	$1,850

Victorilux Amp
2001-present. 45 watts, 2x12", 3x10" or 1x15", EL84s, reverb, tremolo.

2001-2019	3x10	$1,525	$1,950

Vintage47
2010-present. Founder/builder David Barnes, of California, builds retro-inspired compact amps that reflect old-school Valco values, handwired, intermediate and professional grade.

Vivi-Tone
1933-1938. Founded in Kalamazoo, Michigan, by former Gibson designer Lloyd Loar and others, Vivi-Tone sold small amps built by Webster Electric to accompany their early electric solidbody guitars.

1950s Vega Commander
Imaged by Heritage Auctions, HA.com

AMPS

Victoria 35115
Carter Vintage Guitars

Victoria Silver Sonic

Voodoo Hex

2006 Vox AC15CC
Ted Wulfers

*1966 Vox AC50 Head
and 2X12" Cabinet*
Tom Scarcella

MODEL YEAR	FEATURES	EXC. COND. LOW	HIGH

V-M (Voice of Music) Corp.

1944-1977. Started out building record changers in Benton Harbor, Michigan. By the early '50s had added amplified phonographs, consoles, and tape recorders as well as OEM products for others. Their portable PA systems can be used for musical instruments. Products sport the VM logo.

Small Portable Amp

1950s. Standard phono input for instrument, phono and microphone controls, wood combo cabinet, 1x10" or 1x12" Jensen.

1950s		$250	$350

Voltmaster

Trapezoid-shaped combo amps and reverb units made in Plano, Texas, in the late 1990s.

Voodoo

1998-present. Tube amp heads and speaker cabinets built in Lansing, New York by Trace Davis, Anthony Cacciotti, and Mike Foster.

Vox

1954-present. Tom Jennings and Dick Denney combined forces in '57 to produce the first Vox amp, the 15-watt AC-15. The period between '57-'68 is considered to be the Vox heyday. Vox produced tube amps in England and also the U.S. from '64 to '65. English-made tube amps were standardized between '60 and '65. U.S.-made Vox amps in '66 were solidstate. In the mid-'60s, similar model names were sometimes used for tube and solidstate amps. In '93 Korg bought the Vox name and current products are built by Marshall. Those amps that originally came with a trolley or stand are priced including the original trolley or stand, and an amp without one will be worth less than the amount shown. Smaller amps were not originally equipped with a trolley or stand (if a speaker cabinet mounts to it and it tilts, it is called a trolley; otherwise referred to as a stand).

4120 Bass Amp
1966-1967. Hybrid solidstate and tube bass amp.

1966-1967		$365	$475

7120 Guitar Amp
1966-1967. Hybrid solidstate and tube amp, 120 watts.

1966-1967		$365	$475

AC-4 Amp
1961-1965. Made in England, early Vox tube design, 3.5 watts, 1x8", tremolo.

1961-1965		$1,000	$1,300

AC-4TV Amp
2009-2019. Tube, 4 watts, in 1x10 (AC-4TV8 is 1x8) combo or amp head with 1x12 cab, EL84 power tube, 12AX7 powered preamp. AC-4TVmini combo has 6.5 inch speaker.

2009-2013	1x12	$105	$140
2009-2013	1x8	$110	$145
2009-2013	Head only	$125	$165
2009-2019	1x10	$125	$165

MODEL YEAR	FEATURES	EXC. COND. LOW	HIGH

AC-10 Amp
1958-1965. Made in England, 12 watts, 1x10", tremolo, this tube version not made in U.S. ('64-'65).

1958-1965		$1,800	$2,400

AC-10 Twin Amp
1962-1965. Made in England, also made in U.S. '64-'65, 12 watts (2xEL84s), 2x10".

1962-1965		$2,100	$2,800

AC-15 Amp
1958-1965. 15 watts, 1x12", TV front changed to split front in fall '60.

1958	TV front	$2,950	$3,900
1958-1965	Split front	$2,500	$3,200

AC-15 Twin Amp
1961-1965. Tube, 2x12", 18 watts.

1961-1965	Standard colors	$2,750	$3,600
1962-1965	Custom colors	$2,950	$3,850

AC-15 50th Anniversary Amp
2007. 50th Anniversary 1957-2007 plaque on lower left front of grille, hand wired, white tolex.

2007		$700	$900

AC-15H1TV Amp
2008-2009. Part of Heritage Collection, limited edition, 200 made, hand wired, oiled mahogany cabinet.

2008-2009		$1,000	$1,300

AC-15HW1 Amp
2015-present. Hand-wired, 15 watts, 1x12".

2015		$800	$1,050

AC-15TB/TBX
1996-2004. 15 watts, top boost, 1x12" Celestion (lower cost Eminence available).

1996-2004	TB	$725	$975
1996-2004	TBX	$850	$1,150

AC-15C1 Amp
2010-present. China, 15 watts, 1x12", tube, reverb and tremolo.

2010-2019		$365	$475

AC-15CC Custom Classic Amp
2006-2012. Made in China, 15 watts, 1x12" tube combo, master volume, reverb, tremolo, 2-button footswitch.

2006-2012		$365	$475

AC-30 Reissue Model Amp
1980s-1990s-2000s. Standard reissue and limited edition models with identification plate on back of amp. Models include the AC-30 Reissue and Reissue custom color (1980s-1990s), AC-30 25th Anniv. (1985-1986), AC-30 30th Anniv. (1991), AC-30 Collector Model (1990s, mahogany cabinet) and the AC-30HW Hand Wired (1990s).

1980s	Rose Morris era	$1,250	$1,650
1985-1986	25th Anniv	$1,250	$1,650
1990s	Collector Model	$1,750	$2,300
1990s	Custom colors	$1,325	$1,750
1990s	Hand wired	$1,850	$2,500
1990s	Reissue	$1,050	$1,400
1991	30th Anniv	$1,500	$1,950
1995	TBT, LE, tan	$1,325	$1,750
2000s	Reissue	$1,100	$1,450

AC-30 Super Twin Amp Set
1960-1965. Piggyback head and 2x12" pressure cabinet with amp trolley.

1960-1965		$3,400	$4,475

MODEL YEAR	FEATURES	EXC. COND. LOW	HIGH

AC-30 Twin/AC-30 Twin Top Boost Amp
1960-1973. Made in England, tube, 30-watt head, 36 watts 2x12", Top Boost includes additional treble and bass, custom colors available in '60-'63.

1960-1963	Custom colors	$2,725	$3,600
1960-1965		$2,400	$3,200
1966		$2,100	$2,800
1967-1973		$1,750	$2,300

AC-30BM Brian May Limited Edition Amp
2007. 30 watts, 2x12" combo.

2007		$1,100	$1,450

AC-30C2X Custom Amp
2004-2018. 30 watts, 2x12" Celestion Alnico Blue speakers.

2004-2018		$550	$725

AC-30CC Custom Classic Amp
2004-2012. 30 watts, 2x12", tubes, 2-button footswitch.

2004-2012		$550	$725

AC-30VR Valve Reactor Amp
2010-2019. 2x12" combo, digital reverb, 30 watts.

2010-2019		$300	$400

AC-50 Amp Head
1963-1975. Made in England, 50-watt head, U.S. production '64-'65 tube version is Westminster Bass, U.S. post-'66 is solidstate.

1963-1975		$2,000	$2,600

AC-50 Cabinet

1963-1975	Black	$600	$800

AC-100 MK I Amp
1963-1965. All tube 100-watt with 4x12 cab, due to reliability concerns it was transitioned to AC-100 Super De Luxe MK II in '65.

1963-1965		$3,000	$4,000

AC-100 Super De Luxe MK II Amp
1965. Solidstate 100-watt head with 4x12 cab on speaker trolley.

1965		$1,850	$2,400

AD Series Amp
2004-2008. Import small to large modeling amps with single 12AXT preamp tube, chrome grills, includes applicable footswitch, some available with amp trolley (i.e. AD-60VT).

2004-2006	AD120VT	$365	$475
2004-2006	AD-60VT	$215	$275
2004-2008	AD100VTH	$175	$225
2004-2008	AD-15VT	$95	$125
2004-2008	AD-30VT	$100	$130
2004-2008	AD-50VT	$145	$190
2006-2008	AD-100VT	$250	$345

Berkeley II V108 (Tube) Amp
1964-1966. U.S.-made tube amp, revised '66-'69 to U.S.-made solidstate model V1081, 18 watts, 2x10" piggyback.

1964-1966		$900	$1,175

Berkeley II V1081 (Solidstate) Amp
1966-1967. U.S.-made solidstate model V1081, 35 watts, 2x10" piggyback, includes trolley stand.

1966-1967		$600	$775

Berkeley III (Solidstate) Amp
1968. Berkeley III logo on top panel of amp.

1968		$750	$1,000

Buckingham Amp
1966-1968. Solidstate, 35 watts, 2x12" piggyback, includes trolley stand.

1966-1968		$825	$1,075

Cambridge 15 Amp
1999-2001. 15 watts, 1x8", tremolo.

1999-2001		$130	$175

Cambridge 30 Reverb Amp
1999-2002. 30 watts, 1x10", tremolo and reverb.

1999-2002		$150	$200

Cambridge 30 Reverb Twin 210 Amp
1999-2002. 30 watts hybrid circuit, 2x10", reverb.

1999-2002		$190	$250

Cambridge Reverb V1031/V1032 (Solidstate) Amp
1966-1968. Solidstate, 35 watts, 1x10", model V1031 replaced tube version V103.

1966-1968		$600	$775

Cambridge Reverb V3/V103 (Tube) Amp
1965-1966. U.S-made tube version, 18 watts, 1x10", a Pacemaker with reverb, superceded by solidstate Model V1031 by '67.

1965-1966		$850	$1,100

Churchill PA V119 Amp Head and V1091 Cabinet Set
Late-1960s. PA head with multiple inputs and 2 column speakers.

1960s	Head & cabs	$625	$825
1960s	PA head only	$350	$450

Climax V-125/V-125 Lead Combo Amp
1970-1991. Solidstate, 125 watts, 2x12" combo, 5-band EQ, master volume.

1970-1991		$500	$650

DA Series Amp
2006-2013. Small digital modeling amps, AC/DC power, solidstate.

2006-2013	DA5, 5w, 1x65	$80	$105
2007-2009	DA10, 10w, 2x6	$100	$130
2007-2009	DA20, 20w, 2x8	$105	$140
2010	DA15, 15w, 1x8	$90	$120

Defiant Amp
1966-1970. Made in England, 50 watts, 2x12" + Midax horn cabinet.

1966-1970		$1,225	$1,600

Escort Amp
Late 1960s-1983. 2.5 watt battery-powered portable amp.

1968-1986		$290	$375

Essex V1042 Bass Amp
1966-1968. U.S.-made solidstate, 35 watts, 2x12". Also called Essex Bass Deluxe.

1966-1968		$400	$525

Foundation Bass Amp
1966-1970. Tube in '66, solidstate after, 50 watts, 1x18", made in England only.

1966	Tubes	$1,200	$1,550
1967-1970	Solidstate	$525	$675

Kensington V1241 Bass Amp
1966-1968. U.S.-made solidstate bass amp, 22 watts, 1x15", G-tuner, called Kensington Bass Deluxe in '67.

1966-1968		$525	$675

Vox AC-30C2RD
Andrew McIntosh

1967 Vox Berkeley II V1081 (Solidstate)
Rivington Guitars

1970 Vox Escort
Steve Lee

AMPS

1967 Vox Royal Guardsman
Imaged by Heritage Auctions, HA.com

1967 Vox Super Beatle V1141
Imaged by Heritage Auctions, HA.com

Wallace Amplification Sophia

MODEL YEAR	FEATURES	EXC. COND. LOW	HIGH
Night Train Series Amp			
2009-2016. Small tube head and combo, 2 channels, Celestion speaker, models available; NT15C1 (15w, 1x12 combo), NT15H-G2 (15w, 1x12 head/cab), NT50H-G2 (50w, 2x12 head/cab).			
2009-2016	NT 2x12 cab	$200	$265
2009-2016	NT15H-G2 cab	$175	$225
2009-2016	NT15H-G2 head	$285	$375
2015-2016	NT15C1 combo	$425	$550
Pacemaker V1021 (Solidstate) Amp			
1966-1968. U.S.-made solidstate amp, 35 watts, 1x10", replaced Pacemaker model V102.			
1966-1968		$350	$450
Pacemaker V2/V102 (Tube) Amp			
1965-1966. U.S.-made tube amp, 18 watts, 1x10", replaced by solidstate Pacemaker model V1021.			
1965-1966		$675	$875
Pathfinder (Import) Amp			
1998-present. Compact amps with 1960s cosmetics.			
1998-2013	15, 15w, 1x8"	$65	$90
2002-2019	10, 10w, 65"	$55	$75
Pathfinder V1/V101 (Tube) Amp			
1965-1966. U.S.-made tube amp, 4 watts, 1x8", '66-'69 became U.S.-made solidstate V1011.			
1965-1966		$675	$900
Pathfinder V1011 (Solidstate) Amp			
1966-1968. U.S.-made solidstate, 25 watts peak power, 1x8".			
1966-1968		$325	$425
Royal Guardsman V1131/V1132 Amp			
1966-1968. U.S.-made solidstate, 50 watts piggyback, 2x12" + 1 horn, the model below the Super Beatle V1141/V1142.			
1966-1968		$1,025	$1,325
Scorpion (Solidstate) Amp			
1968. Solidstate, 120 watts, 4x10" Vox Oxford speaker.			
1968		$425	$550
Super Beatle Reissue Amp Cabinet			
2011-2012. 2x15" cab only.			
2011-2012		$325	$425
Super Beatle V1141/V1142 Amp			
1965-1966. U.S.-made 120 watt solidstate, 4x12" + 2 horns, with distortion pedal (V1141), or without (V1142).			
1965-1966		$2,400	$3,200
T-60 Amp			
1962-1966. Solidstate bass head, around 40 watts, sold with 2x15" or 1x12" and 1x15" cabinet.			
1962-1966		$550	$725
VBM1 Brian May Special Amp			
2010. Compact 10-watt, 1x6" speaker, also called VBM1 Brian May Recording Amp, white cover, includes headphone/recording line out, Brian May logo on lower right grille.			
2010		$125	$160
Viscount V1151/V1152 Amp			
1966-1968. U.S.-made solidstate, 70 watts, 2x12" combo, 1151, 1153, and 1154 with distortion.			
1966-1968		$675	$900

MODEL YEAR	FEATURES	EXC. COND. LOW	HIGH
VT Valvetronix/Valvetronix + Series Amps			
2008-present. Line of digital modeling combo amps, ranging from the 15-watt, 1x8" VT15 ('08-'11) to the 120-watt, 2x12" VT120+.			
2008-2011	VT15	$95	$125
2012-2019	VT20+	$95	$125
2015-2016	VT80	$155	$200
2015-2019	VT40+	$145	$190
Westminster V118 Bass Amp			
1966. Solidstate, 120 watts, 1x18".			
1966		$475	$625

V-Series
See Crate.

Wabash
1950s. Private branded amps, made by others, distributed by the David Wexler company. They also offered lap steels and guitars.

Model 1158 Amp
1955. Danelectro-made, 1x15", 2x6L6 power tubes, tweed.

1955		$450	$600

Small Amp

1940s	3 tubes	$175	$225

Wallace Amplification
2000-present. Production/custom, professional grade, amps built by Brian Wallace in Livonia, Michigan. (Not affiliated with a 1970's amp company from the United Kingdom also called Wallace that has since gone out of business.)

Warbler
See listing under Juke amps.

Warwick
1982-present. Combos, amp heads and cabinets from Warwick Basses of Markneukirchen, Germany.

Washburn
1962-present. Imported guitar and bass amps. Washburn also offers guitars, banjos, mandolins, and basses.

Watkins
1957-present. England's Watkins Electric Music (WEM) was founded by Charlie Watkins. Their first commercial product was the Watkins Dominator (wedge Gibson stereo amp shape) in '57, followed by the Copicat Echo in '58. They currently build accordion amps.

Clubman Amp
1960s. Small combo amp with typical Watkins styling, blue cover, white grille.

1960s		$800	$1,050

---

*The **Vintage Guitar Price Guide** shows low to high values for items in all-original excellent condition, and, where applicable, with original case or cover.*

MODEL YEAR	FEATURES	EXC. COND. LOW	HIGH

Dominator MK Series Amp
1970s. Similar circuit to '50s tube amps except solidstate rectifier, 25 watts, different speaker used for different applications.

1970s	MK I, bass, 1x15	$475	$625
1970s	MK II, organ, 1x12	$475	$625
1970s	MK III, guitar, 1x12	$475	$625

Dominator V-Front Amp
Late-1950s-1960s, 2004. 18 watts, 2x10", wedge cabinet similar to Gibson GA-79 stereo amp, tortoise and light beige cab, light grille, requires 220V step-up transformer. Was again offered in '04.

1959-1962	$2,000	$2,600

Scout Amp
1960s. 17 watts, 1x10 combo, 6 tubes.

1960	$800	$1,050

Westminster Tremolo Amp
1959-1962. 10-watt 1x10" combo, Westminster Tremolo logo on top panel, 3 control knobs, blue and white cover.

1959-1962	$800	$1,050

Webcor
1940s-1950s. The Webster-Chicago Company built recording and audio equipment including portable amplifiers suitable for record turntables, PAs, or general utility. Low power with one or two small speakers.

Small Amp

1950s	1 or 2 speakers	$200	$265

West Laboratories
1965-1970s, 2005-2015. Founded by David W. West in Flint, Michigan, moved to Lansing in '68. The '71 catalog included three tube and two solidstate amps, speaker cabinets, as well as Vocal Units and Mini Series combo amps. Amps were available as heads, piggyback half-stacks and full-stacks, with the exception of the combo Mini Series. The Fillmore tube amp head was the most popular model. West equipment has a West logo on the front and the cabinets also have a model number logo on the grille. David West reestablished his company in 2005, located in Okemos, Michigan, with models offered on a custom order basis, concentrating on lower power EL84 designs. West died November, '15.

Avalon Amp Head
1970s. 50 watts, 2 6CA7 output tubes.

1970s	$525	$700

Fillmore Amp Head
1970s. 200 watts, 4 KT88 output tubes.

1970s	$2,000	$2,600

Grande Amp Head
1970s. 100 watts, 2 KT88 output tubes.

1970s	$650	$850

Mini IR Amp
1970s. 50 watts, 1x12 tube combo with reverb, black tolex, large West logo and model name Mini IR on front panel.

1970s	$725	$950

White
1955-1960. The White brand, named after plant manager Forrest White, was established by Fender to provide steel and small amp sets to teaching studios that were not Fender-authorized dealers. The amps were sold with the matching steel guitar. See Steel section for pricing.

White (Matamp)
See Matamp listing.

Winfield Amplification
2001-present. Intermediate and professional grade, production, vacuum tube amps built by Winfield N. Thomas first in Greensboro, Vermont and presently in Cochise, Arizona.

Wizard
1988-present. Professional and premium grade, production/custom, guitar and bass, amps and cabinets built by Rick St Pierre in Cornwall, Ontario.

Woodson
Early 1970s. Obscure builder from Bolivar, Missouri. Woodson logo on front panel and Woodson Model and Serial Number plate on back panel, solidstate circuit, student level pricing.

Working Dog
2001-2014. Lower cost tube amps and combos built by Alessandro High-End Products (Alessandro, Hound Dog) in Huntingdon Valley, Pennsylvania.

Wright Amplification
Aaron C. Wright builds his professional grade, production/custom, amps and cabinets in Lincoln, Nebraska starting in 2004.

Yamaha
1946-present. Yamaha started building amps in the '60s and offered a variety of guitar and bass amps over the years. The current models are solidstate bass amps. They also build guitars, basses, effects, sound gear and other instruments.

Budokan HY-10G II Amp
1987-1992. Portable, 10 watts, distortion control, EQ.

1987-1992	$45	$60

G30-112 Amp
1983-1992. Solidstate combo, 30 watts, 1x12".

1983-1992	$115	$150

G50-112 Amp
1983-1992. 50 watts, 1x12".

1983-1992	$135	$175

G100-112 Amp
1983-1992. 100 watts, 1x12" combo, black cover, striped grille.

1983-1992	$140	$185

1963 Watkins Control ER15
Nicholas Kennett

AMPS

Winfield

Wizard Modern Classic Combo

AMPS

1968 Yamaha TA-60
Tom Pfeifer

Zeppelin Design Labs Percolator

Zinky Blue Velvet

MODEL YEAR	FEATURES	EXC. COND. LOW	HIGH
G100-212 Amp			
1983-1992. 100, 2x12" combo, black cover, striped grille.			
1983-1992		$160	$210
JX30B Amp			
1983-1992. Bass amp, 30 watts.			
1983-1992		$95	$125
TA-20 Amp			
1968-1972. Upright wedge shape with controls facing upwards, solidstate.			
1968-1972		$85	$115
TA-25 Amp			
1968-1972. Upright wedge shape with controls facing upwards, 40 watts, 1x12", solidstate, black or red cover.			
1968-1972		$100	$135
TA-30 Amp			
1968-1972. Upright wedge shape, solidstate.			
1968-1972		$115	$150
TA-50 Amp			
1971-1972. Solidstate combo, 80 watts, 2x12", includes built-in cart with wheels, black cover.			
1971-1972		$130	$175
TA-60 Amp			
1968-1972. Upright wedge shape, solidstate, most expensive of wedge-shape amps.			
1968-1972		$170	$225
VR3000 Amp			
1988-1992. Combo 1x12", 2 channels, identical control sections for each channel, settings are completely independent.			
1988-1992		$105	$135
VR4000 Amp			
1988-1992. 50-watt stereo, 2 channels, EQ, stereo chorus, reverb and dual effects loops.			
1988-1992		$160	$210
VR6000 Amp			
1988-1992. 100-watt stereo, 2 channels which can also be combined, EQ, chorus, reverb and dual effects loops.			
1988-1992		$210	$280
VX-15 Amp			
1988-1992. 15 watts.			
1988-1992		$75	$100
VX-65D Bass Amp			
1984-1992. 80 watts, 2 speakers.			
1984-1992		$100	$135
YBA-65 Bass Amp			
1972-1976. Solidstate combo, 60 watts, 1x15".			
1972-1976		$100	$135
YTA-25 Amp			
1972-1976. Solidstate combo, 25 watts, 1x12".			
1972-1976		$100	$135
YTA-45 Amp			
1972-1976. Solidstate combo, 45 watts, 1x12".			
1972-1976		$100	$135
YTA-95 Amp			
1972-1976. Solidstate combo, 90 watts, 2x12".			
1972-1976		$100	$135
YTA-100 Amp			
1972-1976. Solidstate piggyback, 100 watts, 2x12".			
1972-1976		$130	$175

MODEL YEAR	FEATURES	EXC. COND. LOW	HIGH
YTA-110 Amp			
1972-1976. Solidstate piggyback, 100 watts, 2x12" in extra large cab.			
1972-1976		$130	$175
YTA-200 Amp			
1972-1976. Solidstate piggyback, 200 watts, 4x12".			
1972-1976		$150	$200
YTA-300 Amp			
1972-1976. Solidstate piggyback, 200 watts, dual cabs with 2x12" and 4x12".			
1972-1976		$225	$300
YTA-400 Amp			
1972-1976. Solidstate piggyback, 200 watts, dual 4x12".			
1972-1976		$225	$300

Z.Vex Amps

2002-present. Intermediate grade, production amps built by Zachary Vex in Minneapolis, Minnesota with some subassembly work done in Michigan. He also builds effects.

Zapp

Ca.1978-early-1980s. Zapp amps were distributed by Red Tree Music, Inc., of Mamaroneck, New York.

Z-10 Amp
1978-1980s. Small student amp, 8 watts.

1979-1982		$25	$30

Z-50 Amp
1978-1980s. Small student amp, 10 watts, reverb, tremelo.

1978-1982		$30	$35

Zeppelin Design Labs

2014-present. Brach Siemens and Glen van Alkemade build budget and intermediate grade amps and cabinets in Chicago, Illinois. They also offer their products as DIY kits.

Zeta

1982-2010. Solid state amps with MIDI options, made in Oakland, California. They also made upright basses and violins.

Zinky

1999-present. Tube head and combo amps and cabinets built by Bruce Zinky in Flagstaff, Arizona. He also builds the mini Smokey amps (since '97), effects, and has revived the Supro brand on a guitar and amp.

ZT Amplifiers

2009-present. Ken Kantor of Berkeley, California imports intermediate grade, production, solid state compact amps from China. He also offers effects.

EFFECTS

Aguilar Filter Twin

Ampeg Scrambler Fuzz

Amptweaker TightDrive

EFFECTS

MODEL YEAR FEATURES	EXC. COND. LOW	HIGH

Ace Tone

1968-1972. Effects from Ace Electronic Industry, which was a part of Sakata Shokai Limited of Osaka, Japan, which also made organs, amps, pioneering Rhythm Ace FR-1 and FR-2 drum machines, etc. Their Ace Tone effects line was the predecessor to Roland and Boss.

Echo Chamber EC-10
1968-1972. Solidstate tape echo.

1968-1972	$300	$580

Expander EXP-4
1968-1972. "Expander" effect.

1968-1972	$175	$200

Fuzz Master FM-1
1968-1972. Distortion and overdrive.

1968-1972	$300	$450

Fuzz Master FM-2
1968-1972. Fuzz. Black housing. 2 Control knobs.

1968-1972	$175	$400

Fuzz Master FM-3
1968-1972. Distortion and clean boost.

1968-1972	$450	$650

Stereo Phasor LH-100
1968-1972. Phaser.

1968-1972	$275	$340

Wah Master WM-1
1968-1972. Filter wah.

1968-1972	$75	$150

Acoustyx

1977-1982. Made by the Highland Corporation of North Springfield, Vermont.

Image Synthesizer IS-1
1977-ca.1982. Synthesizer effects.

1977-1982	$50	$60

Phase Five
1977-ca.1982. Used 6 C cell batteries!

1977-1982	$50	$60

ADA

1975-2002. Analog/Digital Associates was located in Berkeley, California, and introduced its Flanger and Final Phase in '77. The company later moved to Oakland and made amplifiers, high-tech signal processors, and a reissue of its original Flanger.

Final Phase
1977-1979. Reissued in '97.

1977-1979	$375	$450

Flanger
1977-1983, 1996-2002. Reissued in '96.

1977-1979	No control pedal	$325	$400
1977-1979	With control pedal	$375	$475
1980-1983		$225	$300
1996-2002		$75	$100

MP-1
1987-1995. Tube preamp with chorus and effects loop, MIDI.

1987-1995	No foot controller	$150	$200
1987-1995	With optional foot controller	$200	$260

MP-2
Ca.1988-1995. Tube preamp with chorus, 9-band EQ and effects loop, MIDI.

1988-1995	$225	$275

Pit chtraq
1987. Programmable pitch transposer including octave shifts.

1987	$150	$200

Stereo Tapped Delay STD-1
Introduced in 1981.

1980s	$150	$200

TFX4 Time Effects
Introduced in 1982, includes flanger, chorus, doubler, echo.

1980s	$150	$200

Aguilar

1995-present. The New York, New York amp builder also offers a line of tube and solidstate pre-amps.

Akai

1984-present. In '99, Akai added guitar effects to their line of electronic samplers and sequencers for musicians.

Alamo

1947-1982. Founded by Charles Eilenberg, Milton Fink, and Southern Music, San Antonio, Texas. Distributed by Bruno & Sons. Mainly known for guitars and amps, Alamo did offer a reverb unit.

Reverb Unit
1965-ca.1979. Has a Hammond reverb system, balance and intensity controls. By '73 the unit had 3 controls - mixer, contour, and intensity.

1965-1970	$300	$400

Alesis

1992-present. Alesis has a wide range of products for the music industry, including digital processors and amps for guitars.

Allen Amplification

1998-present. David Allen's company, located in Richwood, Kentucky, mainly produces amps, but they also offer a tube overdrive pedal.

Altair Corp.

1977-1980s. Company was located in Ann Arbor, Michigan.

Power Attenuator PW-5
1977-1980. Goes between amp and speaker to dampen volume.

1977-1980	$90	$120

Amdek

Mid-1980s. Amdek offered many electronic products over the years, including drum machines and guitar effects. Most of these were sold in kit form so quality of construction can vary.

MODEL YEAR	FEATURES	EXC. COND. LOW	HIGH

Delay Machine DMK-200
1983. Variable delay times.

1983		$85	$115

Octaver OCK-100
1983. Produces tone 1 or 2 octaves below the note played.

1983		$75	$100

Phaser PHK-100

1983		$65	$100

Phlanger

1983		$50	$60

Ampeg

Ampeg entered the effects market in the late-1960s. Their offerings in the early-'60s were really amplifier-outboard reverb units similar to the ones offered by Gibson (GA-1). Ampeg offered a line of imported effects in '82-'83, known as the A-series (A-1 through A-9), and reintroduced effects to their product line in '05.

Analog Delay A-8
1982-1983. Made in Japan.

1982-1983		$75	$125

Chorus A-6
1982-1983. Made in Japan.

1982-1983		$50	$75

Compressor A-2
1982-1983. Made in Japan.

1982-1983		$50	$75

Distortion A-1
1982-1983. Made in Japan.

1982-1983		$50	$75

Echo Jet Reverb EJ-12
1963-1965. Outboard, alligator clip reverb unit with 12" speaker, 12 watts, technically a reverb unit. When used as a stand-alone amp, the reverb is off. Named EJ-12A in '65.

1963-1965		$550	$700

Echo Satellite ES-1
1961-1963. Outboard reverb unit with amplifier and speaker alligator clip.

1961-1963		$550	$675

Flanger A-5
1982-1983. Made in Japan.

1982-1983		$50	$75

Multi-Octaver A-7
1982-1983. Made in Japan.

1982-1983		$50	$100

Over Drive A-3
1982-1983. Made in Japan.

1982-1983		$50	$75

Parametric Equalizer A-9
1982-1983. Made in Japan.

1982-1983		$45	$70

Phaser A-4
1982-1983. Made in Japan.

1982-1983		$50	$75

Phazzer
1975-1979. Phase shifter, single speed knob.

1975-1979		$50	$125

Scrambler Fuzz
1969-1970. Distortion pedal, black housing. 2 Control knobs. Reissued in '05.

1969-1970		$200	$450

Sub Blaster SCP-OCT
2005-2007. Bass octave pedal.

2005-2007		$225	$380

Amplifier Corporation of America

Late '60s company that made amps for Univox and also marketed effects under their own name.

Amptweaker

2010-present. James Brown, an amp design engineer previously employed by Peavey, then for Kustom amps, now designs and builds effects in Batavia, Ohio.

amukaT Gadgets

2006-present. Guitar effects built by Takuma Kanaiwa in New York, New York.

Analog.Man

1994-present. Founded by Mike Piera in '94 with full-time production by 2000. Located in Danbury, Connecticut (until '07 in Bethel), producing chorus, compressor, fuzz, and boost pedals by '03.

Astro Tone
2000s-present. Fuzz.

2000s-2019		$120	$160

Bad Bob
2000s-present. Boost.

2000s-2019		$90	$150

Beano Boost
2000s-present. Boost.

2000s-2019		$100	$160

Dual Analog Delay
2000s-present. Delay.

2000s-2019		$200	$250

Envelope Filter
2000s-present. Envelope 'auto-wah'.

2000s-2019		$140	$200

Juicer
2000s-present. Compressor.

2000s-2019		$120	$160

King of Tone
2000s-present. Overdrive pedal, 4 generations, numerous options available.

2000s-2019		$350	$700

Peppermint Fuzz
2000s-present. Fuzz.

2000s-2019		$120	$230

Prince of Tone
2000s-present. Overdrive.

2000s-2019		$120	$150

Sun Bender
2000s-present. Fuzz.

2000s-2019		$200	$240

Sun Face
2000s-present. Fuzz.

2000s-2019		$200	$300

amukaT Gadgets Tweaker

Analog.Man Sun Bender

EFFECTS

Analog.Man King of Tone

Area 51 The Alienist

Arion Delay SAD-1
Keith Myers

Bad Cat Siamese Drive

EFFECTS

MODEL YEAR	FEATURES	EXC. COND. LOW	HIGH

Aphex Systems

1975-present. Founded in Massachusetts by Marvin Caesar and Curt Knoppel, to build their Aural Exciter and other pro sound gear. Currently located in Sun Valley, California, and building a variety of gear for the pro audio broadcast, pro music and home-recording markets.

Apollo

Ca.1967-1972. Imported from Japan by St. Louis Music, includes Fuzz Treble Boost Box, Crier Wa-Wa, Deluxe Fuzz. They also offered basses and guitars.

Crier Wa-Wa
Ca.1967-1972.

1967-1972		$125	$200

Fuzz/Deluxe Fuzz
Ca.1967-1972. Includes the Fuzz Treble Boost Box and the Deluxe Fuzz.

1967-1972		$125	$240

Surf Tornado Wah Wah
Ca.1967-1972.

1967-1972		$180	$300

Arbiter

Ivor Arbiter and Arbiter Music, London, began making the circular Fuzz Face stompbox in 1966. Other products included the Fuzz Wah and Fuzz Wah Face. In '68 the company went public as Arbiter and Western, later transitioning to Dallas-Arbiter. Refer to Dallas-Arbiter for listings.

Area 51

2003-present. Guitar effects made in Newaygo, Michigan (made in Texas until early '06), by Dan Albrecht. They also build amps.

Aria/Aria Pro II

1956-present. Aria provided a line of effects, made by Maxon, in the mid-'80s.

Analog Delay AD-10
1983-1985. Dual-stage stereo.

1983-1985		$65	$75

Chorus ACH-1
1986-1987. Stereo.

1986-1987		$40	$50

Chorus CH-10
1983-1985. Dual-stage stereo.

1983-1985		$40	$50

Chorus CH-5

1985-1987		$40	$50

Compressor CO-10

1983-1985		$40	$50

Digital Delay ADD-100
1984-1986. Delay, flanging, chorus, doubling, hold.

1984-1986		$65	$75

Digital Delay DD-X10

1985-1987		$65	$75

Distortion DT-10
1983-1985. Dual-stage.

1983-1985		$40	$50

Distortion DT-5

1985-1987		$40	$50

Flanger AFL-1
1986. Stereo.

1986		$50	$60

Flanger FL-10
1983-1985. Dual-stage stereo.

1983-1985		$50	$60

Flanger FL-5

1985-1987		$50	$60

Metal Pedal MP-5

1985-1987		$40	$50

Noise Gate NG-10

1983-1985		$30	$40

Over Drive OD-10
1983-1985. Dual-stage.

1983-1985		$40	$50

Parametric Equalizer EQ-10

1983-1985		$40	$50

Phase Shifter PS-10
1983-1984. Dual-stage.

1983-1984		$50	$70

Programmable Effects Pedal APE-1
1984-1986. Compression, distortion, delay, chorus.

1984-1986		$50	$60

Arion

1984-2014. Arion offers a wide variety of budget imported effects.

Guitar and Bass Effects

1984-2014		$15	$75

Arteffect

Tom Kochawi and Dan Orr started building analog effects in 2006, in Haifa and Natanya, Israel.

Asama

1970s-1980s. This Japanese company offered solidbody guitars with built-in effects as well as stand-alone units. They also offered basses, drum machines and other music products.

Astrotone

Late 1960s. By Universal Amp, which also made the Sam Ash Fuzzz Boxx.

Fuzz
1966. Introduced in '66, same as Sam Ash Fuzzz Boxx.

1966		$175	$275

ATD

Mid-1960s-early 1980s. Made by the All-Test Devices corporation of Long Beach, New York. In the mid-'60s, Richard Minz and an associate started making effects part-time, selling them through Manny's Music in New York. They formed All-Test and started making Maestro effects and transducer pickups for CMI, which owned Gibson at the time. By '75, All-Test was marketing effects under their own brand. All-Test is still making products for other industries, but by the early to mid-'80s they were no longer making products for the guitar.

MODEL YEAR	FEATURES	EXC. COND. LOW	HIGH

PB-1 Power Booster
1976-ca.1980.

1979-1980		$50	$60

Volume Pedal EV-1
1979-ca.1980.

1979-1980		$30	$40

Wah-Wah/Volume Pedal WV-1
1979-ca.1981.

1979-1981		$50	$60

Audio Matrix

1979-1984. Effects built by B.K Butler in Escondido, California. He later designed the Tube Driver and founded Tube Works in 1987. He nows operates Butler Audio, making home and auto hybrid tube stereo amps.

Mini Boogee B81
1981. Four-stage, all-tube preamp, overdrive, distortion.

1981		$100	$135

Audioworks

1980s. Company was located in Niles, Illinois.

F.E.T. Distortion

1980s		$40	$55

Auralux

2000-2011. Founded by Mitchell Omori and David Salzmann, Auralux built effects and tube amps in Highland Park, Illinois.

Austone Electronics

1997-2009. Founded by Jon Bessent and Randy Larkin, Austone offered a range of stomp boxes, all made in Austin, Texas. Bessent passed away in '09.

Overdrive and Fuzz Pedals
1997-2009. Various overdrive and fuzz boxes.

1997-2009		$125	$245

Automagic

Wah pedals and distortion boxes made in Germany by Musician Sound Design, starting in 1998.

Avalanche

Late 1980s. Effects built by Brian Langer in Toronto, Ontario.

Brianizer
Late-1980s. Leslie effect, dual rotor, adjustable speed and rates.

1980s		$75	$90

Axe

1980s. Early '80s line of Japanese effects, possibly made by Maxon.

B & M

1970s. A private brand made by Sola/Colorsound for Barns and Mullens, a U.K. distributor.

Fuzz Unit
1970s. Long thin orange case, volume, sustain, tone knobs, on-off stomp switch.

1970s		$275	$325

MODEL YEAR	FEATURES	EXC. COND. LOW	HIGH

Backline Engineering

2004-present. Guitar multi-effects built by Gary Lee in Camarillo, California. In '07, they added tube amps.

Bad Cat Amplifier Company

2000-present. Amp company Bad Cat, originally of Corona, California, also offers guitar effects. In '09 the company was moved to Anaheim.

Baldwin

1965-1970. The piano maker got into the guitar market when it acquired Burns of London in '65, and sold the guitars in the U.S. under the Baldwin name. They also marketed a couple of effects at the same time.

Banzai

2000-present. Effects built by Olaf Nobis in Berlin, Germany.

Bartolini

The pickup manufacturer offered a few effects from around 1982 to '87.

Tube-It
1982-ca.1987. Marshall tube amplification simulator with bass, treble, sustain controls.

1982-1987	Red case	$80	$90

Basic Systems' Side Effects

1980s. This company was located in Tulsa, Oklahoma.

Audio Delay
1986-ca.1987. Variable delay speeds.

1986-1987		$75	$100

Triple Fuzz
1986-ca.1987. Selectable distortion types.

1986-1987		$50	$60

BBE

1985-present. BBE, owner of G & L Guitars and located in California, manufactures rack-mount effects and added a new line of stomp boxes in '05.

Behringer

1989-present. The German professional audio products company added modeling effects in '01 and guitar stomp boxes in '05. They also offer guitars and amps.

Beigel Sound Lab

1980, 2013-present. Music product designer Mike Beigel helped form Musitronics Corp, where he made the Mu-Tron III. In 1978 he started Beigel Sound Lab to provide product design in Warwick, New York, where in '80 he made 50 rack-mount Enveloped Controlled Filters under this brand name. As of 2013, Mike Beigel's Beigel Sound Lab has started making a Mu-FX Tru-Tron 3X and Octave Divider.

Banzai Cold Fusion Overdrive

BBE Sonic Stomp

Beigel Sound Lab Tru-Tron 3X

EFFECTS

Beigel Sound Lab Boostron 3

Bigsby Foot Volume and Tone Control
Monte Klein

Boss Rocker Distortion PD-1
Garrett Tung.

MODEL YEAR	FEATURES	EXC. COND. LOW	HIGH

Boostron 3
2016-2017. Combines preamp boost, compression and distortion in one pedal.

2016-2017		$225	$325

Octave Divider
2015. Updated and expanded version of original Musitronics Mu-Tron Octave Divider.

2015		$325	$400

Tru-Tron 3X
2015-2019. Updated and expanded version of original Musitronics Mu-Tron III envelope filter.

2015-2019		$325	$500

Bell Electrolabs
1970s. This English company offered a line of effects in the '70s.

Vibrato

1970s		$150	$200

Bennett Music Labs
Effects built in Chatanooga, Tennessee by Bruce Bennett.

Bigsby
1948-1966. Paul Bigsby made steel guitars, pedal steels, and electric guitars and mandolins, as well as developing the Bigsby vibrato tailpiece and other components.

Foot Volume and Tone Control
1950s-1960s. Beautifully crafted pedal in a cast-aluminum housing featuring a side-to-side tone sweep.

1950s-60s		$400	$625

Binson
Late 1950s-1982. Binson, of Milan, Italy, made several models of the Echorec, using tubes or transistors. They also made units for Guild, Sound City and EKO.

Echorec
Ca.1960-1979. Four knob models with 12 echo selections, 1 head, complex multitap effects, settings for record level, playback and regeneration. Includes B1, B2, Echomaster1, T5 (has 6 knobs), T5E, and Baby. Used a magnetic disk instead of tape. Guild later offered the Guild Echorec by Binson which is a different stripped-down version.

1960s	Tube	$2,500	$3,350
1970s	Solidstate	$700	$800

Bixonic
1995-2007. The round silver distortion pedals were originally distributed by SoundBarrier Music, later by Godlyke, Inc.

Expandora EXP-2000
1995-2000. Analog distortion, round silver case, internal DIP switches.

1995-2000		$170	$210

Black Cat Pedals
1993-2007, 2009-present. Founded by Fred Bonte and located in Texas until late 2007 when produc-

tion was discontinued. In '09, using Bonte's same designs, new owner Tom Hughes restarted production in Foxon, Connecticut.

Black Cat OD-1
2010-present. Overdrive.

2010-2019		$70	$120

Blackbox Music Electronics
2000-2009. Founded by Loren Stafford and located in Minneapolis, Minnesota, Blackbox offered a line of effects for guitar and bass. The Blackbox models are now made under the Ooh La La brand.

Blackout Effectors
Kyle Tompkins began building effects pedals in 2007, in Vancouver, British Columbia and now builds them in Asheville, North Carolina.

Blackstar Amplification
2007-present. Guitar effects pedals built by Joel Richardson in Northampton, U.K. He also builds amps.

Blackstone Appliances
1999-present. Distortion effects crafted by Jon Blackstone in New York City.

Mosfet Overdrive
1999-present. Though the designation doesn't appear on the housing, the original was subsequently called 2Sv1 after later versions were issued.

1999	2Sv1, no controls on top	$125	$240
2000	2Sv2	$100	$200
2006-2019	2Sv3, 2Sv31, 2Sv32, 2Sv33	$95	$200
2012	Billybox Limited Edition	$150	$250

Bon, Mfg
Bon was located in Escondido, California.

Tube Driver 204
1979-ca.1981.

1979-1981		$100	$150

Boomerang
1995-present. Effects pedals built in Grapevine, Texas by Boomerang Musical Products, Ltd.

Boss
1976-present. Japan's Roland Corporation first launched effect pedals in '74. A year or two later the subsidiary company, Boss, debuted its own line. They were marketed concurrently at first but gradually Boss became reserved for effects and drum machines while the Roland name was used on amplifiers and keyboards. Boss still offers a wide line of pedals.

Acoustic Simulator AC-2
1997-2007. Four modes that emulate various acoustic tones.

1997-2007		$50	$65

MODEL YEAR	FEATURES	EXC. COND. LOW	HIGH
Acoustic Simulator AC-3			
2007s-present. Four modes that emulate various acoustic tones.			
2007-2019		$50	$85
Auto Wah AW-2 and AW-3			
1991-1999 (AW-2), 2000-present (AW-3).			
1991-2019		$40	$70
Bass Chorus CE-2B			
1987-1995		$40	$50
Bass Equalizer GE-7B			
1987-1995. Seven-band, name changed to GEB-7 in '95.			
1987-1995		$40	$50
Bass Flanger BF-2B			
1987-1994		$40	$50
Bass Limiter LM-2B			
1990-1994		$35	$40
Bass Overdrive ODB-3			
1994-present. Yellow case.			
1994-2019		$40	$50
Blues Driver BD-2			
1995-present. Blue case.			
1995-2019		$40	$75
Chorus Ensemble CE-1			
1976-1978. Vibrato and chorus.			
1976-1978		$275	$500
Chorus Ensemble CE-2			
1979-1982		$100	$250
Chorus Ensemble CE-3			
1982-1992		$30	$75
Chorus Ensemble CE-5			
1991-present. Pale blue case.			
1991-2019		$45	$95
Compressor Sustainer CS-1			
1978-1982		$70	$95
Compressor Sustainer CS-2			
1981-1986		$70	$110
Compressor Sustainer CS-3			
1986-present. Blue case.			
1986-2019		$50	$75
Delay DM-2			
1981-1984. Analog, hot pink case.			
1981-1984		$100	$245
Delay DM-3			
1984-1988		$145	$195
Digital Delay DD-2			
1983-1986		$60	$150
Digital Delay DD-3			
1986-present. Up to 800 ms of delay, white case.			
1986-1989		$120	$170
1990-2019		$95	$145
Digital Delay DD-5			
1995-2005. Up to 2 seconds of delay.			
1995-2005		$100	$145
Digital Delay DD-6			
2003-2007. Up to 5 seconds of delay.			
2003-2007		$55	$100
Digital Delay DD-7			
2008-present. Up to 6.4 seconds of delay, crème case.			
2008-2019		$80	$105

MODEL YEAR	FEATURES	EXC. COND. LOW	HIGH
Digital Dimension C DC-2			
1985-1989. Two chorus effects and tremolo.			
1985-1989		$135	$245
Digital Metalizer MZ-2			
1987-1992		$80	$95
Digital Reverb RV-2			
1987-1990		$95	$145
Digital Reverb RV-5			
2003-2019. Dual imput and dual output, four control knobs, silver case.			
2003-2019		$60	$95
Digital Reverb/Delay RV-3			
1994-2004		$95	$120
Digital Sampler/Delay DSD-2			
1985-1986		$100	$150
Digital Space-D DC-3/Digital Dimension DC-3			
1988-1993. Originally called the Digital Space-D, later changed to Digital Dimension. Chorus with EQ.			
1988-1993		$130	$180
Digital Stereo Reverb RV-70			
1994-1995. Rack mount, MIDI control, reverb/delay, 199 presets.			
1994-1995		$130	$180
Distortion DS-1			
1978-1989, 1990s-present. Orange case.			
1978-1989		$75	$150
1990-1999		$30	$50
2000-2019		$20	$25
Dr. Rhythm DR-55			
1979-1989. Drum machine.			
1979-1989		$145	$195
Dual Over Drive SD-2			
1993-1998		$45	$55
Dynamic Filter FT-2			
1986-1988. Auto wah.			
1986-1988		$70	$95
Dynamic Wah AW-3			
2000-present. Auto wah with humanizer, for guitar or bass.			
2000-2019		$50	$60
Enhancer EH-2			
1990-1998		$35	$45
Flanger BF-1			
1977-1980		$55	$70
Flanger BF-2			
1980-1989		$60	$100
1990-2005		$40	$55
Foot Wah FW-3			
1992-1996		$45	$55
Graphic Equalizer GE-6			
1978-1981. Six bands.			
1978-1981		$60	$75
Graphic Equalizer GE-7			
1981-present. Seven bands, white case.			
1982-1989		$50	$90
1990-2019		$45	$70
Graphic Equalizer GE-10			
1976-1985. 10-band EQ for guitar or bass.			
1976-1985		$75	$150

Boss Chorus Ensemble CE-3

1989 Boss Delay DM-3
Rivington Guitars

EFFECTS

1984 Boss Distortion DS-1
Rivington Guitars

To get the most from this book, be sure to read "Using *The Guide*" in the introduction.

Boss Super Over Drive SD-1
Rivington Guitars

Boss Super Shifter PS-5
Keith Myers

Boss Touch T Wah TW-1
Scott Mills

MODEL YEAR / FEATURES	EXC. COND. LOW	HIGH
Harmonist HR-2		
1994-1999. Pitch shifter.		
1994-1999	$80	$105
Heavy Metal HM-2		
1983-1991. Distortion.		
1983-1991	$60	$140
Hyper Fuzz FZ-2		
1993-1997	$45	$150
Hyper Metal HM-3		
1993-1998	$35	$45
Limiter LM-2		
1987-1992	$25	$65
Line Selector LS-2		
1991-present. Select between 2 effects loops, white case.		
1991-2019 With adapter	$45	$85
Mega Distortion MD-2		
2003-present. Red case.		
2003-2019	$45	$55
Metal Zone MT-2		
1991-present. Distortion and 3-band EQ, grey case.		
1991-2019	$30	$50
Multi Effects ME-5		
1988-1991. Floor unit.		
1988-1991	$70	$140
Multi Effects ME-6		
1992-1997	$50	$100
Multi Effects ME-8		
1996-1997	$70	$120
Multi Effects ME-20		
1990s	$60	$90
Multi Effects ME-25		
1990s	$70	$120
Multi Effects ME-30		
1998-2002	$70	$120
Multi Effects ME-50		
2003-2009. Floor unit.		
2003-2009	$100	$160
Multi Effects ME-70		
2000s	$70	$170
Multi Effects ME-80		
2000s-present.		
2000s-2019	$100	$195
Noise Gate NF-1		
1979-1988	$40	$75
Noise Suppressor NS-2		
1987-present. White case.		
1987-2019	$40	$65
Octaver OC-2/Octave OC-2		
1982-2003. Originally called the Octaver.		
1982-2003	$75	$130
Overdrive OD-1		
1977-1979	$95	$185
1980-1985	$70	$145
Overdrive OD-3		
1997-present. Yellow case.		
1997-2019	$45	$60
Parametric Equalizer PQ-4		
1991-1997	$45	$70
Phaser PH-1		
1977-1981. Green box, 2 knobs.		
1977-1981	$70	$95

MODEL YEAR / FEATURES	EXC. COND. LOW	HIGH
Phaser PH-1R		
1982-1985. Resonance control added to PH-1.		
1982-1985	$70	$120
Phaser PH-2		
1984-2001. 12 levels of phase shift, 4 knobs.		
1984-2001	$40	$65
Phaser PH-3		
2000-present. Added effects.		
2000-2019	$40	$70
Pitch Sifter/Delay PS-2		
1987-1993	$95	$150
Reverb Box RX-100		
1981-mid-1980s.		
1981-1985	$70	$95
Rocker Distortion PD-1		
1980-mid-1980s. Variable pedal using magnetic field.		
1980-1985	$45	$70
Rocker Volume PV-1		
1981-mid-1980s.		
1980-1985	$45	$55
Rocker Wah PW-1		
1980-mid-1980s. Magnetic field variable pedal.		
1980-1985	$55	$65
Slow Gear SG-1		
1979-1982. Violin swell effect, automatically adjusts volume.		
1979-1982	$300	$440
Spectrum SP-1		
1977-1981. Single-band parametric EQ.		
1977-1981	$325	$375
Super Chorus CH-1		
1989-present. Blue case.		
1989-2019	$45	$70
Super Distortion & Feedbacker DF-2		
1984-1994. Also labeled as the Super Feedbacker & Distortion.		
1984-1994	$95	$120
Super Octave OC-3		
2004-present. Super Octave.		
2004-2019	$60	$90
Super Over Drive SD-1		
1981-present. Yellow case.		
1981-1989	$50	$105
1990-2019	$30	$50
Super Phaser PH-2		
1984-1989	$45	$85
1990-2001	$30	$50
Super Shifter PS-5		
1999-2013. Pitch shifter/harmonizer, aqua case.		
1999-2013	$95	$120
Touch Wah TW-1/T Wah TW-1		
1978-1987. Auto wah, early models were labeled as Touch Wah.		
1978-1987	$95	$120
Tremolo TR-2		
1997-present. Aqua case.		
1997-2019	$65	$75
Tremolo/Pan PN-2		
1990-1995	$120	$145

MODEL YEAR	FEATURES	EXC. COND. LOW	HIGH

Turbo Distortion DS-2
1987-present. Orange case.

1987-2019		$70	$120

Turbo Over Drive OD-2
1985-1994. Called OD-2R after '94, due to added remote on/off jack.

1985-1994		$40	$90

Vibrato VB-2
1982-1986. True pitch-changing vibrato, warm analog tone, 'rise time' control allows for slow attach, 4 knobs, aqua-blue case.

1982-1986		$325	$460

Volume FV-50H
1987-1997. High impedance, stereo volume pedal with inputs and outputs.

1987-1997		$45	$55

Volume FV-50L
1987-1997. Low impedance version of FV-50.

1987-1997		$35	$45

Volume Pedal FV-100
Late-1980s-1991. Guitar volume pedal.

1987-1991		$35	$45

Brimstone Audio
2011-present. Shad Sundberg builds his guitar effects in California.

Browntone Electronics
2006-2012. Guitar effects built in Lincolnton, North Carolina by Tim Brown.

Bruno
Music distributor Bruno and Sons had a line of Japanese-made effects in the early '70s.

Budda
1995-present. Wahs and distortion pedals originally built by Jeff Bober and Scott Sier in San Francisco, California. In '09, Budda was acquired by Peavey Electronics. They also build amps.

Bud Wah
1997-2018. Wah pedal.

1990s-2018		$100	$145

Build Your Own Clone
2005-present. Build it yourself kits based on vintage effects produced by Keith Vonderhulls in Othello, Washington. Assembled kits are offered by their Canadian distributor.

Burriss
2001-present. Guitar effects from Bob Burriss of Lexington, Kentucky. He also builds amps.

Carl Martin
1993-present. Line of effects from Søren Jongberg and East Sound Research of Denmark. In '06 they added their Chinese-made Vintage Series. They also build amps.

Carlsbro
1959-present. English amp company Carlsbro Electronics Limited offered a line of effects from '77 to '81.

Carrotron
Late-1970s-mid-1980s. Carrotron was out of California and offered a line of effects.

Noise Fader C900B1
1981-ca.1982.

1981-1982		$50	$60

Preamp C821B
1981-ca.1982.

1981-1982		$55	$65

Carvin
1946-present. Carvin introduced its line of Ground Effects in '02 and discontinued them in '03.

Castle Instruments
Early 1980s. Castle was located in Madison, New Jersey, and made rack-mount and floor phaser units.

Phaser III
1980-1982. Offered mode switching for various levels of phase.

1980-1982		$100	$175

Catalinbread
2003-present. Nicholas Harris founded Catalinbread Specialized Mechanisms of Music in Seattle, Washington, in '02 to do mods and in '03 added his own line of guitar effects.

Cat's Eye
Dean Solorzano and Lisa Kroeker began building their analog guitar effects in Oceanside, California in 2001.

Cause & Effect Pedals
2009-present. Guitar effects pedals built in Ontario by Mark Roberts and Brian Alexson.

Celmo
2008-present. The Celmo Sardine Can Compressor is made by Kezako Productions in Montcaret, France.

Chandler
Located in California, Chandler Musical Instruments offers instruments, pickups, and pickguards, as well as effects.

Digital Echo
1992-2000. Rackmount, 1 second delay, stereo.

1992-2000		$275	$425

Tube Driver
1986-1991. Uses a 12AX7 tube. Not to be confused with the Tube Works Tube Driver.

1980s	Large Box	$175	$330
1980s	Rackmount	$100	$215
1990s	Rackmount	$90	$150

Boss Tremolo TR-2

Carl Martin Dual Injection

Catalinbread Antichthon

EFFECTS

Chunk Systems Agent 00Funk

Crazy Tube Circuits Starlight

Creation Audio Labs Holy Fire 9

EFFECTS

MODEL YEAR	FEATURES	EXC. COND. LOW	HIGH

Chapman
1970-present. From Emmett Chapman, maker of the Stick.
Patch of Shades
1981, 1989. Wah, with pressure sensitive pad instead of pedal. 2 production runs.

1980s		$50	$75

Chicago Iron
1998-present. Faithful reproductions of classic effects built by Kurt Steir in Chicago, Illinois.

Chunk Systems
1996-present. Guitar and bass effects pedals built by Richard Cartwright in Sydney, Australia.

Clark
1960s. Built in Clark, New Jersey, same unit as the Orpheum Fuzz and the Mannys Music Fuzz.
SS-600 Fuzz
1960s. Chrome-plated, volume and tone knobs, toggle switch.

1960s		$150	$200

Clark Amplification
1995-present. Amplifier builder Mike Clark, of Cayce, South Carolina, offers a reverb unit and started building guitar effects as well, in '98.

ClinchFX
2006-present. Hand made pedals by Peter Clinch in Brisbane, Queensland, Australia.

Coffin
Case manufacturer Coffin Case added U.S.-made guitar effects pedals to their product line in 2006.

Colorsound
1967-2010. Colorsound effects were produced by England's Sola Sound, beginning with fuzz pedals. In the late-'60s, wah and fuzz-wah pedals were added, and by the end of the '70s, Colorsound offered 18 different effects, an amp, and accessories. Few early Colorsound products were imported into the U.S., so today they're scarce. Except for the Wah-Wah pedal, Colorsound's production stopped by the early '80s, but in '96 most of their early line was reissued by Dick Denny of Vox fame. Denny died in 2001. Since then, Anthony and Steve Macari build Colorsound effects in London.

Mutronics offered a licensed rack mount combination of 4 classic Colorsound effects for a short time in the early 2000s.
Flanger

1970s		$110	$210

Fuzz Phazer
Introduced in 1973.

1970s		$160	$235

Jumbo Tone-Bender
1974-early 1980s. Replaced the Tone-Bender fuzz, with wider case and light blue lettering.

1974-1980s		$275	$335

MODEL YEAR	FEATURES	EXC. COND. LOW	HIGH

Octivider
Introduced in 1973.

1970s		$160	$235

Overdriver
Introduced in 1972. Controls for drive, treble and bass.

1970s		$160	$235

Phazer
Introduced in 1973. Magenta/purple-pink case, slanted block Phazer logo on front.

1970s		$160	$235

Power Booster

1970s		$750	$900

Ring Modulator
Introduced in 1973. Purple case, Ring Modulator name with atom orbit slanted block logo on case.

1970s		$260	$285

Supa Tone-Bender Fuzz
1977-early 1980s. Sustain and volume knobs, tone control and toggle. Same white case as Jumbo Tone-Bender, but with new circuit.

1970s		$275	$350

Supa Wah-Swell
1970s. Supa Wah-Swell in slanted block letters on the end of the pedal, silver case.

1970s		$160	$195

Supaphase

1970s		$160	$235

Supasustain

1960s		$135	$210

Swell

1970s		$80	$90

Tremolo

1970s		$160	$210

Tremolo Reissue
1996-2009. Purple case.

1996-2009		$110	$135

Wah Fuzz Straight
Introduced in 1973. Aqua-blue case, Wah-Fuzz-Straight in capital block letters on end of wah pedal.

1970s		$185	$300

Wah Fuzz Swell
Introduced in 1973. Yellow case, block letter Wah Fuzz Swell logo on front, three control knobs and toggle.

1970s		$260	$360

Wah Swell
1970s. Light purple case, block letter Wah-Swell logo on front.

1970s		$235	$285

Wah Wah
1970s. Dark gray case, Wah-Wah in capital block letters on end of wah pedal.

1975		$310	$350

Wah Wah Reissue
1996-2005. Red case, large Colorsound letter logo and small Wah Wah lettering on end of pedal.

1996-2005		$85	$150

Wah Wah Supremo
1970s. Silver/chrome metal case, Wah-Wah Supremo in block letters on end of wah pedal.

1975		$435	$485

MODEL YEAR	FEATURES	EXC. COND. LOW	HIGH

Companion
1970s. Private branded by Shinei of Japan, which made effects for others as well.
Tape Echo

1960-1970		$400	$650

Wah Pedal

1970s		$150	$240

Conn
Ca.1968-ca.1978. Band instrument manufacturer and distributor Conn/Continental Music Company, of Elkhart, Indiana, imported guitars and effects from Japan.
Strobe Tuner
Brown or later, grey, case.

1960s	ST-4	$50	$100
1960s	ST-6	$75	$100
1960s	ST-8	$75	$125
1968	ST-2	$50	$100
1970s	Strobotuner ST-11	$75	$100
1970s	Strobotuner ST-12	$75	$100

Coopersonic
2006-present. Martin Cooper builds his guitar effects in Nottingham, UK.

Coron
1970s-1980s. Japanese-made effects, early ones close copies of MXR pedals.

Cosmosound
Italy's Cosmosound made small amps with Leslie drums and effects pedals in the late '60s and '70s. Cosmosound logo is on top of pedals.
Wah Fuzz CSE-3
1970s. Volume and distortion knobs, wah and distortion on-off buttons, silver case.

1970s		$275	$350

Wild Sound

1970s		$175	$195

Crazy Tube Circuits
2004-present. Guitar effects designed and built by Chris Ntaifotis in Athens, Greece.

Creation Audio Labs
2005-present. Guitar and bass boost pedal and re-amplifying gear built in Nashville, Tennessee.

Crowther Audio
1976-present. Guitar effects built by Paul Crowther, who was the original drummer of the band Split Enz, in Auckland, New Zealand. His first effect was the Hot Cake.

Crucial Audio
2005-present. Effects by Steve Kollander engineered and assembled in Sussex County, Delaware, with chassis manufactured by machine shops within the U.S. They also provide OEM products and design engineering services to companies in-

cluding Matchless, Requisite Audio & West Coast Pedal Boards.
Apollo-18 Vacuum Tube Leslie Interface Module
2015-present. High-voltage vacuum tube interface module for Leslie 122 or 147 type rotary speaker systems; can be used with a tube preamp and/or two channel vacuum tube direct box.

2015-2019		$960	$1,200

Die Götterdämmerung Ring Modulator/ Germanium Fuzz Pedal
2017-present. Provides full function controls combined with germanium fuzz generated from matched NOS 2N404.

2017-2019		$280	$360

DUB-1 Wideband Vacuum Tube Direct Box/Tube Buffer
2016-present. Interface for recording studios or live sound to sweeten the tone of instruments.

2016-2019		$370	$460

Echo-Nugget Vacuum Tube Analog Delay
2008-present. Tube-driven analog delay with selectable boost/tone preamp.

2008-2019		$450	$550

Time Warp Vacuum Tube Analog Delay Pitch Modulator
2008-present. Tube-driven analog delay with selectable modulation/warp function.

2008-2019		$450	$550

Cruzer
Effects made by Korea's Crafter Guitars. They also build guitars, basses and amps under that brand.

Crybaby
See listing under Vox for early models, and Dunlop for recent versions.

CSL
Sola Sound made a line of effects for C. Summerfield Ltd., an English music company.

Cusack Music
2003-present. Effects built in Holland, Michigan by Jon Cusack.

Dallas/Dallas Arbiter
Dallas Arbiter, Ltd. was based in London and it appeared in the late-1960s as a division of a Dallas group of companies headed by Ivor Arbiter. Early products identified with Dallas logo with the company noted as John E. Dallas & Sons Ltd., Dallas Building, Clifton Street, London, E.C.2. They also manufactured Sound City amplifiers and made Vox amps from '72 to '78. The Fuzz Face is still available from Jim Dunlop.
Fuzz Face
1966-1975, 1977-1981, 1986-1987, 1993-present. Late '70s and '80s version was built for Dallas Arbiter by Crest Audio of New Jersey. The current reissue is built by Jim Dunlop USA (see that listing).

1968-1969	Red	$1,000	$2,100

Crowther Audio Hotcake

Crucial Audio Apollo-18 Vacuum Tube Leslie Interface Module

1981 Dallas Fuzz Face
Keith Myers

EFFECTS

Damage Control Solid Metal

Danelectro Daddy-O
Jim Schreck

*DeArmond Square Wave
Distortion Generator*
Jim Schreck

MODEL YEAR	FEATURES	EXC. COND. LOW	EXC. COND. HIGH
1970	Red	$950	$1,600
1970-1975	Blue	$800	$1,600
1977-1980	Blue	$650	$850
1981	Grey, reissue	$450	$550

Fuzz Wah Face

1970s	Black	$550	$650
1990s	Reissue copy	$65	$80

Rangemaster Treble Booster

1966. 2000s. Grey housing. 1 Control knob. On-off slider switch. Old-style round-barrel 9-volt battery powered; many converted to later rectangular battery. Various current reissues built by JMI and other firms.

1966		$1,675	$2,850
2000s	JMI reissue	$175	$225

Sustain

1970s		$400	$500

Treble and Bass Face

1960s		$500	$600

Trem Face

Ca.1970-ca.1975. Reissued in '80s, round red case, depth and speed control knobs, Dallas-Arbiter England logo plate.

1970-1975		$500	$600

Wah Baby

1970s. Gray speckle case, Wah Baby logo caps and small letters on end of pedal.

1970s		$500	$600

Damage Control

2004-2009. Guitar effects pedals and digital multi-effects built in Moorpark, California. The company was founded with the release of a line of tube-driven effects pedals. In '09, it began developing products under the Strymon brand name.

Demonizer

2004-2009. Class A distortion preamp pedal powered by dual vacuum tubes.

2004-2009		$180	$255

Liquid Blues

2004-2009. Class A overdrive pedal powered by dual vacuum tubes.

2004-2009		$180	$245

Solid Metal

2004-2009. Class A distortion pedal powered by dual vacuum tubes.

2004-2009		$180	$260

TimeLine

2004-2009. Delay pedal powered by dual vacuum tubes.

2004-2009		$240	$300

Womanizer

2004-2009. Class A overdrive preamp pedal powered by dual vacuum tubes.

2004-2009		$170	$220

Dan Armstrong

1976-1981. In '76, Musitronics, based in Rosemont, New Jersey, introduced 6 inexpensive plug-in effects designed by Dan Armstrong. Perhaps under the influence of John D. MacDonald's Travis McGee novels, each effect name incorporated a

color, like Purple Peaker. Shipping box labeled Dan Armstrong by Musitronics. They disappeared a few years later but were reissued by WD Products from '91 to '02 (See WD for those models). From '03 to '06, Vintage Tone Project offered the Dan Armstrong Orange Crusher. Since '06, a licensed line of Dan Armstrong effects that plug directly into the output of a guitar or bass (since '07 some also as stomp boxes) has been offered by Grafton Electronics of Grafton, Vermont. Dan Armstrong died in '04.

Blue Clipper

1976-1981. Fuzz, blue-green case.

1976-1981		$100	$200

Green Ringer

1976-1981. Ring Modulator/Fuzz, green case.

1976-1981		$100	$280

Orange Squeezer

1976-1981. Compressor, orange case.

1976-1981		$125	$300

Purple Peaker

1976-1981. Frequency Booster, light purple case.

1976-1981		$100	$170

Red Ranger

1976-1981. Bass/Treble Booster, light red case.

1976-1981		$85	$100

Yellow Humper

1976-1981. Yellow case.

1976-1981		$85	$100

Danelectro

1946-1969, 1996-present. The Danelectro brand was revived in '96 with a line of effects pedals. They have also offered the Wasabi line of effects. Prices do not include AC adapter, add $10 for the Zero-Hum adapter.

Chicken Salad Vibrato

2000-2009. Orange case.

2000-2009		$20	$50

Cool Cat

1996-2018		$30	$35

Cool Cat Chorus

1996-2018. Blue case.

1996-2018		$20	$40

Corned Beef Reverb

2000-2009. Blue-black case.

2000-2009		$15	$40

Daddy-O Overdrive

1996-2009. White case.

1996-2009		$35	$40

Dan Echo

1998-2009. Lavender case.

1998-2009		$40	$45

Echo Box

1953-ca. 1958. Reverb unit, metal housing with black endplates.

1953-1958		$200	$450

Fab Tone Distortion

1996-2014. Red case.

1996-2014		$30	$40

MODEL YEAR	FEATURES	EXC. COND. LOW	HIGH

Dredge-Tone
Located in Berkeley, California, Dredge-Tone offers effects and electronic kits.

DST Engineering
2001-2014. Jeff Swanson and Bob Dettorre built reverb units in Beverly, Massachusetts. They also built amps.

Dunlop
Jim Dunlop, USA offers the Crybaby, MXR (see MXR), Rockman, High Gain, Heil Sound (see Heil), Tremolo, Jimi Hendrix, Rotovibe, Uni-Vibe and Way Huge brand effects.

Crybaby Bass
1985-present. Bass wah.

1985-2019		$75	$100

Crybaby Multi-Wah 535/535Q
1995-present. Multi-range pedal with an external boost control.

1995-2019		$70	$90

Crybaby Wah-Wah GCB-95
1982-present. Dunlop began manufacturing the Crybaby in '82.

1982-1989		$45	$75
1990-1999		$40	$70
2000-2019		$35	$50

Fuzz Face
1993-present. Reissue of the classic Dallas Arbiter effect (see that listing for earlier versions).

1993-2019	Red, reissue	$100	$165

High Gain Volume + Boost Pedal

1983-1996		$35	$45

High Gain Volume Pedal GCB-80

1983-2010		$40	$50

Jimi Hendrix Fuzz JH-2 (Round)
1987-1993. Round face fuzz, JH-2S is the square box version.

1987-1993		$50	$75

Rotovibe JH-4S Standard
1989-1998. Standard is finished in bright red enamel with chrome top.

1989-1998		$100	$160

Tremolo Volume Plus TVP-1
1995-1998. Pedal.

1995-1998		$125	$140

Uni-Vibe UV-1
1995-2012. Rotating speaker effect.

1995-1999		$225	$350
2000-2012		$200	$225

Durham Electronics
2001-present. Alan Durham builds his line of guitar effects in Austin, Texas.

Dutch Kazoo
2013-present. Guitar effects pedals built in Parker Ford, Pennsylvania by Corinne Mandell.

Dynacord
1950-present. Dynacord is a German company that makes audio and pro sound amps, as well as other electronic equipment and is now owned by TELEX/EVI Audio (an U.S. company), which also owns the Electro-Voice brand. In the '60s they offered tape echo machines and guitars. In '94 a line of multi-effects processors were introduced under the Electro-Voice/Dynacord name, but by the following year they were just listed as Electro-Voice.

EchoCord
Introduced in 1959. Tape echo unit.

1959-1960s		$275	$400

Dyno
See Dytronics.

Dytronics
Mid-1970s-early 1980s. The Japanese Dytronics company made a chorus rackmount unit for electric piano called the Dyno My Piano with flying piano keys or a lightning bolt on the front. Another version was called the Tri-Stereo Chorus and a third, called the Songbird, had a bird's head on the front.

E Bow
See Heet Sound Products.

E.W.S. (Engineering Work Store)
2007-present. Guitar effects pedals built in Tokyo, Japan for Prosound Communications in Van Nuys, California.

EarthQuaker Devices
2005-present. Jamie Stillman started building Fuzz Face and Rangemaster clones for friends and in '07, he built a modified Big Muff for Dan Auerbach of the Black Keys, who he tour-managed at the time. After extensive revisions, this became the Hoof Fuzz and he began retailing his pedals.

Acapulco Gold
2015-present. Power amp distortion. Grandma Cyclops limited-edition version was made '16 in collaboration with visual artist and Devo co-founder Mark Mothersbaugh and the Akron Art Museum.

2015-2019		$60	$90
2016	Grandma Cyclops	$75	$120

Afterneath
2014-present. Ambient reverb.

2014-2019		$100	$190

Amp Hammer II

2009		$50	$100

Arpanoid
2013-present. Polyphonic arpeggiator.

2013-2019		$140	$190

Arrows
2014-present. Preamp boost.

2014-2019		$45	$80

Avalanche Run
2016-present. Stereo reverb and delay.

2016-2019		$180	$225

1979 DOD Phasor 201
Rivington Guitars

Dunlop Crybaby Multi-Wah 535Q

Durham Crazy Horse

EFFECTS

EarthQuaker Devices Bellows

EarthQuaker Devices Fuzz Master General

EarthQuaker Devices Interstellar Orbiter

MODEL YEAR	FEATURES	EXC. COND. LOW	HIGH
Bellows			
	2016-2019. Fuzz driver.		
2016-2019		$75	$100
Bit Commander			
	2011-present. Guitar synthesizer.		
2011-2019		$75	$145
Black Eye			
2007		$50	$100
Bows			
	2016-2019. Germanium preamp.		
2016-2019		$75	$100
Chrysalis			
2010		$50	$100
Cloven Hoof			
	2014-present. Fuzz grinder.		
2014-2019		$75	$115
Cloven Hoof Reaper			
	2015-2017. Fuzz.		
2015-2017		$90	$140
Crimson Drive			
2007		$50	$100
Dirt Transmitter			
	2008-2019. Fuzz driver.		
2008-2019		$80	$100
Disaster Transport			
	2007. Delay pedal.		
2007		$50	$150
Disaster Transport Jr.			
2010		$50	$100
Disaster Transport SR			
	2013-present. Advanced modulation delay and reverb.		
2013-2019		$225	$275
Dispatch Master			
	2011-present. Hi-fi digital delay and reverb.		
2011-2019		$80	$130
Dream Crusher			
2009		$50	$100
Dunes			
	2015-present. Mini mega overdrive.		
2015-2019		$80	$120
Erupter			
	2017-present. Fuzz.		
2017-2019		$75	$100
Fuzz Master General			
	2015-2019. Octave fuzz pedal.		
2015-2019		$80	$130
Ghost Disaster			
2010		$50	$100
Ghost Echo			
	2009-present. Vintage-voiced reverb.		
2009-2019		$75	$140
Grand Orbiter			
	2009-present. Phaser/vibrato.		
2009-2019		$90	$130
Gray Channel			
	2016-present. Dynamic dirt doubler.		
2016-2019		$90	$130
Hoof			
	2007-present. Germanium/silicon hybrid fuzz.		
2007-2019		$90	$125

MODEL YEAR	FEATURES	EXC. COND. LOW	HIGH
Hoof Reaper			
	2012-present. Dual fuzz octave.		
2012-2019		$150	$200
Hummingbird			
	2007-present. Repeat percussion/tremolo.		
2007-2019		$75	$110
Interstellar Orbiter			
	2015-present. Dual resonant filter built in collaboration with turntablist Kid Koala for his "Turntable Orchestra" tour. Features original artwork by Koala.		
2015-2019		$120	$180
Levitation			
	2008-present. Psychedlic reverb.		
2008-2019		$80	$125
Monarch			
2010		$50	$120
Night Wire			
	2016-present. Harmonic tremolo.		
2016-2019		$90	$130
Organizer			
	2012-present. Polyphonic organ emulator.		
2012-2019		$90	$135
Palisades			
	2014-present. Mega ultimate overdrive.		
2014-2019		$120	$190
Park Fuzz Sound			
	2015-present. Reissue of the Park Amplification fuzz pedal built in cooperation with Park.		
2015-2019		$75	$120
Pitch Bay			
	2014-2017. Dirty polyphonic harmonizer.		
2014-2017		$100	$180
Pulse Machine Tremolo			
2007		$50	$100
Rainbow Machine			
	2011-present. Polyphonic pitch-shifting modulator.		
2011-2019		$120	$175
Royal Drive			
2007		$50	$100
Sea Machine			
	2010-present. Chorus.		
2010-2019		$75	$120
Sound Shank			
2009		$50	$100
Space Spiral			
	2017-present. Modulation delay.		
2017-2019		$75	$140
Spatial Delivery			
	2016-present. Envelope filter with sample and hold functions.		
2016-2019		$75	$130
Spires			
	2016-2019. Nü-Face double fuzz.		
2016-2019		$75	$130
Stealth Fuzz			
2007		$50	$100
Talons			
	2012-2017. Hi-gain overdrive.		
2012-2017		$75	$100
Tentacle			
	2015-present. Analog octave up. Grandpa Cyclops		

*The **Vintage Guitar Price Guide** shows low to high values for items in all-original excellent condition, and, where applicable, with original case or cover.*

MODEL YEAR	FEATURES	EXC. COND. LOW	HIGH

limited-edition version was made '16 in collaboration with visual artist and Devo co-founder Mark Mothersbaugh and the Akron Art Museum.

| 2015-2019 | | $75 | $100 |
| 2016 | Grandpa Cyclops | $75 | $120 |

Terminal
2014-2019. Fuzz.

| 2014-2019 | | $75 | $110 |

The Depths
2013-2017. Optical vibrato.

| 2013-2017 | | $90 | $140 |

The Grim Reefer
2014-2017. Fuzz pedal.

| 2014-2017 | | $75 | $100 |

The Warden
2013-present. Optical compression.

| 2013-2019 | | $90 | $140 |

Tone Job
2012-present. EQ and boost.

| 2012-2019 | | $75 | $100 |

Tone Reaper

| 2009 | | $50 | $100 |

Transmisser
2016-2019. Reverb.

| 2016-2019 | | $125 | $190 |

White Light

| 2008 | | $50 | $100 |

Zap Machine

| 2010 | | $50 | $100 |

Z-Drive
2015-2017. Overdrive built in collaboration with Dr. Z Amplification.

| 2015-2017 | | $175 | $220 |

EBS
1992-present. Bass and guitar effects built in Stockholm, Sweden by the EBS Sweden AB company. They also build bass amps.

Ecco-Fonic
1959-1968. The Ecco-Fonic was designed by Ray Stolle and sold from his radio and TV repair shop in Los Angeles. Theis first Ecco Ecco-Fonic was distributed by Fender in 1958-'59. Stolle sold the company to E.S. "Eddie" Tubin in late 1959-'60, who sold the company in 1961 to Milton Brucker. Starting in 1963, Fender offered a solidstate Ecco-Fonic designed by new-owner Bob Marks and Russ Allee and labeled as the Fender Echo.

Model 109
1959-1960. Tube-driven tape-echo unit, 2 control knobs, revised to 3 knobs, 1-piece top, gold housing.

| 1959 | Brown case | $900 | $1,500 |

Model 109-B
1960-1962. Tube-driven tape echo unit, 4 Control knobs, 2-piece top, gold housing.

| 1960-1962 | Brown or black case | $400 | $1,250 |

Model 109-C
1961-1962. Tube-driven tape echo unit, multiple playback heads, black housing.

| 1961-1962 | Black case | $400 | $1,000 |

Echoplex
The Echoplex tape echo unit was invented around 1959 in Akron, Ohio, by Don Dixon and Mike Battle, who originally produced it in small numbers. Production was soon moved to Market Electronics in Cleveland, and those units were sold under the Maestro brand (see listings under Maestro). After Maestro dropped the Echoplex, it was marketed under the Market Electronics name from the late-'70s to the late-'80s (see listing under Market Electronics for '80s models). In '94, Gibson's Oberheim division introduced a rackmount unit called the Echoplex. In '01, it was relabeled as Gibson.

Echoplex
1959. Dixon- and Battle-built pre-Maestro production tube-driven tape echo. Black case.

| 1959 | | $900 | $1,200 |

Eden Analog
Guitar effects pedals built by Chris Sheppard and Robert Hafley in Pelham, Alabama, starting in 2004.

Effector 13
2002-2008. Guitar effects built by Devi Ever in Minneapolis, Minnesota. Located in Austin, Texas until mid-'04. Name changed to Devi Ever : Fx in '09.

Effectrode
1996-present. Effects pedals built in Corvallis, Oregon by Phil Taylor.

EFX
1980s. Brand name of the Los Angeles-based EFX Center; they also offered a direct box and a powered pedal box/board.

Switch Box B287
1984. Dual effects loop selector.

| 1984 | | $25 | $35 |

EKO
1959-1985, 2000-present. In the '60s and '70s EKO offered effects made by EME and JEN Elettronica, which also made Vox effects.

Eleca
2004-present. Guitar effects pedals imported by Eleca International. They also offer guitars, mandolins and amps.

Electra
1970-1984, 2013-present. Guitar importer St. Louis Music offered Electra effects in the late '70s.

Chorus 504CH
Ca.1975-ca.1980.

| 1975-1980 | | $55 | $75 |

Compressor 502C/602C
Ca.1975-ca.1980.

| 1975-1980 | | $45 | $55 |

EarthQuaker Devices Pitch Bay

EBS ValveDrive DI

Electra Phase 501
Christopher Wright

EFFECTS

E-H Attack/Decay
Jim Schreck

E-H Bad Stone Phase Shifter
Keith Myers

1970s E-H Big Muff Pi
Keith Myers

MODEL YEAR	FEATURES	EXC. COND. LOW	HIGH
Distortion 500D			
Ca.1976-ca.1980.			
1976-1980		$55	$75
Flanger (stereo) 605F			
Ca.1975-ca.1980.			
1975-1980		$55	$75
Fuzz Wah			
Ca.1975-ca.1980.			
1975-1980		$75	$150
Pedal Drive 515AC			
Ca.1976-ca.1980. Overdrive.			
1976-1980		$40	$50
Phaser Model 501P			
Ca.1976-ca.1980.			
1976-1980		$50	$60
Phaser Model 875			
Ca.1975-ca.1980.			
1975-1980		$50	$60
Roto Phase I			
1975-ca.1980. Small pocket phaser.			
1975-1980		$70	$85
Roto Phase II			
1975-ca.1980. Pedal phasor.			
1975-1980		$80	$95

Electro-Harmonix

1968-1984, 1996-present. Founded by Mike Matthews in New York City, the company initially produced small plug-in boosters such as the LPB-1. In '71, they unveiled the awe-inspiring Big Muff Pi fuzz and dozens of innovative pedals followed. After closing in '84, Matthews again began producing reissues of many of his classic effects as well as new designs in '96.

MODEL YEAR	FEATURES	EXC. COND. LOW	HIGH
10 Band Graphic Equalizer			
1977-1981. Includes footswitch.			
1977-1981		$60	$70
16-Second Digital Delay			
Early-1980s, 2004-2008. An updated version was reissued in '04.			
1980s	No foot controller	$500	$625
1980s	With foot controller	$675	$850
1990s		$325	$500
2004-2008		$275	$375
3 Phase Liner			
1981		$50	$60
5X Junction Mixer			
1977-1981		$30	$40
Attack Equalizer			
1975-1981. Active EQ, a.k.a. "Knock Out."			
1975-1981		$150	$200
Attack/Decay			
1980-1981. Tape reverse simulator.			
1980-1981		$200	$225
Bad Stone Phase Shifter			
1975-1981.			
1975-1981	Three knobs	$200	$250
1975-1981	Two knobs, color switch	$175	$225
Bass Micro-Synthesizer			
1981-1984, 1999-present. Analog synthesizer sounds.			

MODEL YEAR	FEATURES	EXC. COND. LOW	HIGH
1981-1984		$225	$300
1999-2019		$150	$175
Bassballs			
1978-1984, 1998-present. Bass envelope filter/ distortion.			
1978-1984		$200	$225
Big Muff Pi			
1971-1984. Sustain, floor unit, issued in 3 different looks, as described below.			
1970s	Black graphics, knobs in triangle pattern	$300	$475
1970s	Red/black graphics, 1/2" letters	$200	$425
1980s	Red/black graphics, 1" letters	$125	$275
Big Muff Pi (Reissue)			
1996-present. Originally made in Russia, but currently both Russian- and U.S.-made versions are available.			
1996-2019	Russian-made	$40	$65
Big Muff Sovtek			
2000s. Big Muff Pi, Electro Harmonix, and Sovtek logos on an olive green case. Sold in a wooden box.			
2000s	With wooden box	$150	$300
Black Finger Compressor Sustainer			
1977, 2003-2019. Original has 3 knobs in triangle pattern.			
1977		$125	$400
2003-2019		$75	$150
Clap Track			
1980-1984. Drum effect.			
1980-1984		$40	$60
Clone Theory			
1977-1981. Chorus effect, The Clone Theory logo.			
1977-1981		$150	$175
Crash Pad			
1980-1984. Percussion synth.			
1980-1984		$40	$60
Crying Tone Pedal			
1976-1978. Wah-wah.			
1976-1978		$175	$225
Deluxe Big Muff Pi			
1978-1981. Sustain, AC version of Big Muff Pi, includes a complete Soul Preacher unit.			
1978-1981	Red graphics	$125	$200
Deluxe Electric Mistress Flanger			
1977-1983, 1996-present. AC.			
1977-1979		$150	$250
1980-1983		$125	$175
Deluxe Memory Man			
1977-1983, 1996-present. Echo and delay, featured 4 knobs '77-'78, from '79-'83 it has 5 knobs and added vibrato and chorus.			
1977-1978	4 knobs	$250	$520
1979-1983	5 knobs	$200	$350
1996-2019		$150	$165
Deluxe Octave Multiplexer			
1977-1981		$200	$250
Digital Delay/Chorus			
1981-1984. With digital chorus.			
1981-1984		$250	$300

MODEL YEAR	FEATURES	EXC. COND. LOW	HIGH
Digital Rhythm Matrix DRM-15			
1981-1984		$225	$250
Digital Rhythm Matrix DRM-16			
1979-1983		$225	$250
Digital Rhythm Matrix DRM-32			
1981-1984		$225	$250
Doctor Q Envelope Follower			
1976-1983, 2001-present. For bass or guitar.			
1976-1983		$80	$200
2001-2019		$30	$60
Domino Theory			
1981. Sound sensitive light tube.			
1981		$50	$100
Echo 600			
1981		$175	$225
Echoflanger			
1977-1982. Flange, slapback, chorus, filter.			
1977-1982		$200	$250
Electric Mistress Flanger			
1976-1979		$250	$460
1980-1984		$175	$240
Electronic Metronome			
1978-1980		$25	$30
Frequency Analyzer			
1977-1984, 2001-present. Ring modulator.			
1977-1984		$200	$250
Full Double Tracking Effect			
1978-1981. Doubling, slapback.			
1978-1981		$100	$150
Fuzz Wah			
Introduced around 1974.			
1970s		$175	$225
Golden Throat			
1977-1984		$500	$800
Golden Throat Deluxe			
1977-1979. Deluxe has a built-in monitor amp.			
1977-1979		$600	$800
Golden Throat II			
1978-1981		$150	$300
Guitar Synthesizer			
1981. Sold for $1,495 in May '81.			
1981		$225	$300
Hog's Foot Bass Booster			
1977-1980		$70	$90
Holy Grail			
2002-present. Digital reverb.			
2002-2019		$75	$90
Hot Foot			
1977-1978. Rocker pedal turns knob of other E-H effects, gold case, red graphics.			
1977-1978		$75	$100
Hot Tubes			
1978-1984, 2001-2007. Tube distortion.			
1978-1984		$125	$200
Linear Power Booster LPB-1			
1968-1983.			
1976-1979		$55	$80
1980-1983		$45	$75
Linear Power Booster LPB-2			
Ca.1968-1983.			
1968-1983		$90	$100

MODEL YEAR	FEATURES	EXC. COND. LOW	HIGH
Little Big Muff Pi			
1976-1980, 2006-present. Sustain, 1-knob floor unit.			
1976-1980		$140	$175
2006-2019		$90	$125
Little Muff Pi			
1971-1975. Sustain, 1-knob floor unit, issued in 2 styles; blue or red graphics.			
1971-1975		$250	$360
Memory Man/Stereo Memory Man			
1976-1984, 1999-present. Analog delay, newer version in stereo.			
1976-1979		$200	$250
1980-1984		$125	$155
Micro Synthesizer			
1978-1984, 1998-present. Mini keyboard phaser.			
1978-1979		$225	$250
1978-1984		$225	$250
1998-2019		$150	$170
Mini Q-Tron/Micro Q-Tron			
2002-present. Battery-operated smaller version of Q-Tron envelope follower, changed to identical effect in smaller box Micro in '06.			
2002-2019		$40	$45
Mini-Mixer			
1978-1981. Mini mic mixer, reissued in '01.			
1978-1981		$30	$40
MiniSynthesizer			
1981-1983. Mini keyboard with phaser.			
1981-1983		$300	$400
MiniSynthesizer With Echo			
1981		$375	$500
Mole Bass Booster			
1968-1978.			
1968-1969		$60	$80
1970-1978		$40	$60
Muff Fuzz			
1976-1983. Fuzz and line boost, silver case with orange lettering.			
1976-1983		$85	$100
Muff Fuzz Crying Tone			
1977-1978. Fuzz, wah.			
1977-1978		$150	$250
Octave Multiplexer Floor Unit			
1976-1980		$175	$275
Octave Multiplexer Pedal			
1976-1977, 2001-present.			
1976-1977		$150	$250
2001-2019		$40	$45
Panic Button			
1981. Siren sounds for drum.			
1981		$30	$40
Poly Chorus/Stereo Polychorus			
1981, 1999-present. Same as Echoflanger.			
1981		$175	$300
1999-2019		$125	$150
Polyphase			
1979-1981. With envelope.			
1979-1981		$175	$225
Pulsar/Stereo Pulsar			
2004-present. Variable wave form tremolo.			
2004-2019		$45	$55

E-H Crying Tone Pedal
Jim Schreck

E-H Digital Rhythm Matrix DRM-15
Jim Schreck

EFFECTS

E-H Muff Fuzz
Keith Myers

To get the most from this book, be sure to read "Using *The Guide*" in the introduction.

E-H Soul Preacher
Jim Schreck

1977 E-H Zipper Envelope Follower
Rivington Guitars

E-H Volume Pedal
Jim Schreck

MODEL YEAR	FEATURES	EXC. COND. LOW	HIGH
Pulse Modulator	*Ca.1968 -ca.1972. Triple tremolo.*		
1968-1969		$250	$325
1970-1972		$200	$250
Q-Tron	*1997-2017. Envelope controlled filter.*		
1997-2017		$125	$175
Q-Tron +	*1999-present. With added effects loop and Attack Response switch.*		
1999-2019		$70	$80
Queen Triggered Wah	*1976-1978. Wah/Envelope Filter.*		
1976-1978		$125	$150
Random Tone Generator RTG			
1981		$40	$60
Rhythm 12 (Rhythm Machine)			
1978		$75	$125
Rolling Thunder	*1980-1981. Percussion synth.*		
1980-1981		$40	$50
Screaming Bird Treble Booster	*Ca.1968-1980. In-line unit.*		
1968-1980		$75	$100
Screaming Tree Treble Booster	*1977-1981. Floor unit.*		
1977-1981		$100	$150
Sequencer Drum	*1981. Drum effect.*		
1981		$40	$50
Slapback Echo	*1977-1978. Stereo.*		
1977-1978		$150	$200
Small Clone	*1983-1984, 1999-present. Analog chorus, depth and rate controls, purple face plate, white logo.*		
1983-1984		$150	$200
1999-2019		$35	$40
Small Stone Phase Shifter	*1975-1984, 1996-present. Both Russian and U.S. reissues were made.*		
1975-1979		$150	$225
1980-1984		$100	$175
Soul Preacher	*1977-1983, 2007-present. Compressor sustainer. Nano version for present.*		
1977-1983		$100	$150
Space Drum/Super Space Drum	*1980-1981. Percussion synthesizer.*		
1980-1981		$125	$175
Switch Blade	*1977-1983. A-B Box.*		
1977-1983		$45	$55
Talking Pedal	*1977-1978. Creates vowel sounds.*		
1977-1978		$350	$550
The Silencer	*1976-1981. Noise elimination.*		
1976-1981		$60	$80

MODEL YEAR	FEATURES	EXC. COND. LOW	HIGH
Tube Zipper	*2001-2018. Tube (2x12AX7) envelope follower.*		
2001-2018		$100	$120
Vocoder	*1978-1981. Modulates voice with instrument.*		
1978-1981	Rackmount	$425	$525
Volume Pedal			
1978-1981		$45	$65
Wiggler	*2002-2019. All-tube modulator including pitch vibrato and volume tremolo.*		
2002-2019		$100	$110
Worm	*2002-present. Wah/Phaser.*		
2002-2019		$55	$65
Y-Triggered Filter			
1976-1977		$140	$160
Zipper Envelope Follower	*1976-1978. The Tube Zipper was introduced in '01.*		
1976-1978		$200	$300

Electrosonic Amplifiers
2002-2010. Amp builder Josh Corn also offers a preamp pedal, built in Boonville, Indiana.

Elk
Late-1960s. Japanese company Elk Gakki Co., Ltd. mainly made guitars and amps, but did offer effects as well.

Elka
In the late '60s or early '70s, Italian organ and synthesizer company Elka-Orla (later just Elka) offered a few effects, likely made by JEN Elettronica (Vox, others).

EMMA Electronic
Line of guitar effects built in Denmark and distributed by Godlyke.

ReezaFRATzitz RF-1/ReezaFRATzitz II
2004-present. Overdrive and distortion, red case.

2004-2019		$80	$95

Empress Effects
2005-present. Guitar effects pedals built by Steve Bragg and Jason Fee in Ottawa, Ontario.

EMS
1969-1979. Peter Zinnovieff's English synth company (Electronic Music Studios) also offered a guitar synthesizer. The company has reopened to work on original EMS gear.

eowave
2002-present. Effects built first in Paris and now in Burgundy, France by Marc Sirguy.

Epiphone
Epiphone pedals are labeled G.A.S Guitar Audio System and were offered from around 1988 to '91.

MODEL YEAR	FEATURES	EXC. COND. LOW	HIGH

Pedals
Various models with years available.

1988-1989	Chorus EP-CH-70	$35	$45
1988-1989	Delay EP-DE-80	$45	$60
1988-1991	Compressor EP-CO-20	$35	$40
1988-1991	Distortion EP-DI-10	$35	$45
1988-1991	Flanger EP-FL-60	$40	$55
1988-1991	Overdrive EP-OD-30	$35	$45

Ernie Ball
1972-present. The Ernie Ball company also builds Music Man instruments.

Volume Pedals
1977-present. Aluminum housing.

| 1977-2019 | | $35 | $75 |

Euthymia Electronics
Line of guitar effects built by Erik Miller in Alameda, California.

Eventide
1971-present. This New Jersey electronics manufacturer has offered studio and rackmount effects since the late '70s. In '08 they added guitar effects pedals.

EXR
The EXR Corporation was located in Brighton, Michigan.

Projector
1983-ca.1984. Psychoacoustic enhancer pedal.

| 1983-1984 | | $65 | $75 |

Projector SP III
1983-ca.1984. Psychoacoustic enhancer pedal, volume pedal/sound boost.

| 1983-1984 | | $65 | $70 |

Farfisa
The organ company offered effects pedals in the 1960s. Their products were manufactured in Italy by the Italian Accordion Company and distributed by Chicago Musical Instruments.

Model VIP 345 Organ
Mid-1960s. Portable organ with Syntheslalom used in the rock and roll venue.

| 1960s | | $500 | $600 |

Repeater

| 1969 | | $100 | $150 |

Sferasound
1960s. Vibrato pedal for a Farfisa Organ but it works well with the guitar, gray case.

| 1960s | | $275 | $375 |

Wah/Volume

| 1969 | | $100 | $150 |

Fargen
1999-present. Guitar effects built in Sacramento, California by Benjamin Fargen. He also builds amps.

Fender
1946-present. Although Fender has flirted with effects since the 1950s (the volume/volume-tone pedal and the Ecco-Fonic), the company concentrated mainly on guitars and amps. Fender effects ranged from the sublime to the ridiculous, from the tube Reverb to the Dimension IV. In 2013 Fender added a line of pedals.

'63 Tube Reverb
1994-2017. Reissue spring/tube Reverb Units with various era cosmetics as listed below. Currently offered in brown or, since '09, in lacquered tweed.

1994	White (limited run)	$375	$450
1994-1997	Black	$350	$400
1994-1997	Blond	$375	$450
1994-1997	Tweed	$375	$450
1994-2008	Brown	$350	$425
2009-2017	Lacquered Tweed	$300	$375

Blender
1968-1977, 2005-2010. Battery-operated unit with fuzz, sustain, and octave controls.

1968-1969		$290	$410
1970-1977		$275	$350
2005-2010	Reissue	$125	$175

Contempo Organ
1967-1968. Portable organ, all solidstate, 61 keys including a 17-key bass section, catalog shows with red cover material.

| 1967-1968 | | $525 | $550 |

Dimension IV
1968-1970. Multi-effects unit using an oil-filled drum.

| 1968-1970 | | $195 | $300 |

Echo and Electronic Echo Chamber
1963-1968. Solidstate tape echo built by Ecco-Fonic, up to 400 ms of delay, rectangle box with 2 controls '63-'67, slanted front '67-'68.

| 1963-1967 | | $300 | $500 |
| 1967-1968 | | $225 | $350 |

Echo-Reverb
1966-1970. Solidstate, echo-reverb effect produced by rotating metal disk, black tolex, silver grille.

| 1966-1970 | | $300 | $350 |

Fuzz-Wah
1968-1984, 2007-2011. Has Fuzz and Wah switches on sides of pedal '68-'73, has 3 switches above the pedal '74-'84. Newer version ('07-'11) has switches on sides.

1968-1973	Switches on side	$150	$225
1974-1984	Switches above	$100	$200
2007-2011	Switches on side	$80	$90

Phaser
1975-1977, 2007-2011. AC powered, reissued in '07.

| 1975-1977 | | $95 | $175 |
| 2007-2011 | | $50 | $80 |

Reverb Unit
1961-1966, 1975-1978. Fender used a wide variety of tolex coverings in the early-'60s as the coverings matched those on the amps. Initially, Fender used rough blond tolex, then rough brown tolex, followed by smooth white or black tolex.

| 1961 | Blond tolex, Oxblood grille | $1,000 | $1,400 |

Ernie Ball 500K Stereo Volume/Pan

Fender Blender
Wade Jones

Fender Electronic Echo Chamber

EFFECTS

*Field Effects by Resonant
Electronic Design
Acceleron Fuzz*

*Fishman Fission Bass
Powerchord*

Foxx Wa and Volume
Keith Myers

MODEL YEAR	FEATURES	EXC. COND. LOW	HIGH
1961	Brown tolex	$1,000	$1,200
1962	Blond tolex, Oxblood grille	$1,000	$1,250
1962	Brown tolex, Wheat grille	$800	$1,100
1963	Brown tolex	$800	$1,100
1963	Rough blond tolex	$800	$1,200
1963	Smooth white tolex	$800	$1,200
1964	Black tolex	$800	$1,200
1964	Brown tolex, gold grille	$800	$1,100
1964	Smooth white tolex	$800	$1,100
1965-1966	Black tolex	$775	$1,000
1966	Solidstate, flat cabinet	$150	$225
1975-1978	Tube reverb reinstated	$500	$600

Vibratone

1967-1972. Fender's parent company at the time, CBS, bought Leslie in 1965, and Fender began offering a Leslie-type rotating-speaker-emulator as the Vibratone in 1967. Based on the Leslie Model 16 cabinet and made specifically for the guitar, it featured a single fixed 4-ohm 10-inch speaker fronted by a rotating drum. Designed to be powered by an external amp. 2-speed motor. Black tolex.

1967-1968	Fender cast logo in upper left corner	$600	$850
1968-1972	Fender logo plate through center	$500	$850

Volume-Tone Pedal

1954-1984, 2007-2018. Swivel foot controller.

1954-1984		$90	$100
2007-2018		$35	$40

Field Effects by Resonant Electronic Design

2010-present. Guitar effects pedals built in Minneapolis, Minnesota by Wes Kuhnley and Peter Bregman. They also build the Resonant brand amps.

Fishman

2003-present. Larry Fishman of Andover, Massachusetts offers a line of acoustic guitar effects pedals. He also builds amps.

FJA Mods

In 2002, Jerry Pinnelli began building guitar effects in Central Square, New York. He added professional grade, production, guitar amps in '07, then relocates to Charlotte, North Carolina in '18 and takes a hiatus from building.

FlexiSound

FlexiSound products were made in Lancaster, Pennsylvania.

F. S. Clipper

1975-ca.1976. Distortion, plugged directly into guitar jack.

1975-1976		$55	$65

The Beefer

1975. Power booster, plugged directly into guitar jack.

1975		$40	$50

Flip

Line of tube effects by Guyatone and distributed in the U.S. by Godlyke Distributing.

Tube Echo (TD-X)

2004-2017. Hybrid tube power delay pedal.

2004-2017		$90	$100

FM Acoustics

FM Acoustics pedals were made in Switzerland.

E-1 Pedal

1975. Volume, distortion, filter pedal.

1975		$70	$80

Foxx

Foxx pedals are readily identifiable by their fur-like covering. They slunk onto the scene in 1971 and were extinct by '78. Made by Hollywood's Ridinger Associates, their most notable product was the Tone Machine fuzz. Foxx-made pedals also have appeared under various brands such as G & G, Guild, Yamaha and Sears Roebuck, generally without fur. Since 2005, reissues of some of the classic Foxx pedals are being built in Provo, Utah.

Clean Machine

1974-1978		$250	$275

Down Machine

1971-1977. Bass wah.

1971-1977	Blue case	$225	$275

Foot Phaser

1975-1977, 2006-present.

1975-1977		$450	$675

Fuzz and Wa and Volume

1974-1978, 2006-present. Currently called Fuzz Wah Volume.

1974-1978		$225	$400

Guitar Synthesizer I

1975		$300	$350

Loud Machine

1970s. Volume pedal.

1970s		$30	$45

O.D. Machine

1972-ca.1975.

1972-1975		$150	$250

Phase III

1975-1978		$100	$150

Tone Machine

1971-1978, 2005-present. Fuzz with Octave, blue or black housing.

1971-1978		$250	$540

Wa and Volume

1971-1978		$200	$225

Wa Machine

1971-ca.1978.

1971-1978		$150	$200

MODEL YEAR	FEATURES	EXC. COND. LOW	HIGH

Framptone
2000-present. Founded by Peter Frampton, Framptone offers hand-made guitar effects.

3 Banger
2000-present. Three-way amp switch box, white housing.

| 2000-2019 | | $200 | $240 |

Amp Switcher
2000-present. A-B switch box, white housing.

| 2000-2019 | | $80 | $100 |

Talk Box
2000-present. Talk box, white housing, no control knobs, on-off footswitch.

| 2000-2019 | | $160 | $250 |

Frantone
1994-present. Effects and accessories hand built in New York City.

Fulltone
1991-present. Effects based on some of the classics of the past and built in Los Angeles, California, by Michael Fuller.

DejàVibe
1991-2004. Uni-Vibe-type pedal, later models have a Vintage/Modern switch. Stereo version also available.

| 1991-1993 | Mono, gold housing | $175 | $225 |
| 1993-2004 | Mono, black housing | $150 | $175 |

DejàVibe 2
1997-2018. Like DejàVibe but with built-in speed control. Stereo version also available.

| 1997-2018 | Mono | $200 | $225 |

Distortion Pro
2002-2008. Red case, volume and distortion knobs with four voicing controls.

| 2002-2008 | | $125 | $150 |

Fat Boost
2001-2007. Clean boost, silver-sparkle case, volume and drive knobs.

| 2001-2007 | | $125 | $135 |

Full-Drive 2
1995-present. Blue case, four control knobs.

| 1995-2019 | | $120 | $145 |

Mini-DejàVibe
2004-2018. Uni-Vibe-type pedal, white housing, 3 Control knobs, stereo version also available.

| 2004-2018 | Mono | $125 | $150 |

Octafuzz
1996-2019. Copy of the Tycobrahe Octavia.

| 1996-2019 | | $100 | $135 |

Soul Bender
1994-present. Volume, tone and dirt knobs.

| 1994-2019 | | $100 | $125 |

Supa-Trem
1996-2019. Black case, white Supa-Trem logo, rate and mix controls.

| 1996-2019 | | $100 | $150 |

Supa-Trem2
2000s. Yellow housing, 3 control knobs.

| 2000s | | $150 | $200 |

Tube Tape Echo
2000s. Echo-Plex-style echo unit, white case.

| 2000s | | $675 | $800 |

Tube Tape Echo TTE
2004-present. Echoplex-style tube-powered tape unit, different colored housings.

| 2004-2019 | | $725 | $1,000 |

Furman Sound
1993-present. Located in Petaluma, California, Furman makes audio and video signal processors and AC power conditioning products for music and other markets.

LC-2 Limiter Compressor
1990s. Rackmount unit with a black suitcase and red knobs.

| 1990s | | $40 | $50 |

PQ3 Parametric EQ
1990s. Rackmount preamp and equalizer.

| 1998-1999 | | $110 | $150 |

PQ6 Parametric Stereo
| 1990s | | $135 | $175 |

RV1 Reverb Rackmount
| 1990s | | $110 | $150 |

Fxdoctor
2003-present. Joshua Zalegowski originally built his effects in Amherst, Massachusetts, and in 2005 moved to Boston.

Fxengineering
2002-present. Production and custom guitar effects built by Montez Aldridge in Raleigh, North Carolina.

G2D
1999-present. David Manning and Grant Wills build their guitar effects pedals in Auckland, New Zealand.

Garcia
Guitar effects built by Matthew Garcia in Myrtle Beach, South Carolina, starting in 2004. He also built amps.

Geek MacDaddy
See listing under The Original Geek.

George Dennis
1991-present. Founded by George Burgerstein, original products were a line of effects pedals. In '96 they added a line of tube amps. The company is located in Prague, Czech Republic.

Gibson
Gibson did offer a few effects bearing their own name, but most were sold under the Maestro name (see that listing).

Foxx O.D. Machine
Rich Kislia

Fulltone Supa-Trem ST-1

Fxdoctor Ray Gun Phaser

EFFECTS

Gig-FX VOD

Gizmoaudio Sawmill

Guild Foxey Lady
Jim Schreck

EFFECTS

Echoplex Digital Pro Plus
1994-2010. Rackmount unit with digital recording, sampling and digital delay. Labeled as just Echoplex until '01 when Gibson name added.

Model Year	Features	Low	High
1994-2010		$425	$650

GA-3RV Reverb Unit
1964-1967. Small, compact, spring reverb unit, black tolex, gray grille.

1964-1967		$325	$400

GA-4RE Reverb-Echo Unit
1964-1967. Small, compact, lightweight accessory reverb-echo unit that produces complete reverberation and authentic echo, utilizes Gibson's "electronic memory" system for both reverb and echo, black tolex, gray grille.

1964-1967		$375	$550

Gig-FX
2004-present. Founder Jeff Purchon of Waltham, Massachusetts, imports guitar effects pedals built at his company-owned factory in Shenzhen, China.

Gizmo, Inc.
Ca.1980. Short-lived company that grew out of the ashes of Musitronics' attempt to make the Gizomotron. See Mu-Tron.

Gizmoaudio
2009-present. Guitar effects built by Charles Luke in Cumming, Georgia.

Gnome Amplifiers
2008-present. Guitar effects pedals built by Dan Munro in Olympia, Washington. He also builds amps.

Godbout
Godbout sold a variety of effects do-it-yourself kits in the 1970s, which are difficult to value because quality depends on skills of builder.

Effects Kits
1970s		$20	$30

Godley Crème
1978-1980. Kevin Godley and Lol Crème, members of the band 10cc, developed the Gizmotron, which mounted on the face of a bass or guitar and continously strummed the strings to give a bowed-string effect. The device was built by Musitronics of New Jersey, which built the MuTron III and other effects.

Gizmotron
1978-1980. A "ultimate sustain" mechanical add-on to guitar or bass bridges with rotating plectrums.

1978-1980		$300	$500

Goodrich Sound
1970s-present. Originally located in Michigan, and currently in Dublin, Georgia, Goodrich currently offers volume pedals and a line boost.

Match Box Line Boost
Early-1980s-2011. Small rectangular line buffer/driver.

1980s-2011		$45	$55

Volume Pedal 6122
Late-1970s-1980s. Uses a potentiometer.

1970s		$45	$55

Volume Pedal 6400ST
Late-1970s-1980s. Stereo pedal, using photocells.

1970s		$45	$55

Volume Pedal 6402
Late-1970s-1980s. Uses photocell.

1970s		$45	$55

Goran Custom Guitars
1998-present. Luthier Goran Djuric from Belgrade, Serbia also offers guitar pedals.

Greer Amplification
1999-present. Guitar stomp box effects built by Nick Greer in Athens, Georgia. He also builds amps.

Gretsch
Gretsch has offered a limited line of effects from time to time.

Controfuzz
Mid-1970s. Distortion.

1970s		$150	$225

Deluxe Reverb Unit Model 6149
1963-1969. Similar to Gibson's GA-1 introduced around the same time.

1963-1969		$475	$700

Expandafuzz
Mid-1970s. Distortion.

1970s		$200	$375

Reverb Unit Model 6144 Preamp Reverb
1963-1967. Approximately 17 watts, preamp functionality, no speaker.

1963-1967		$450	$600

Tremofect
Mid-1970s. Tremolo effect, 3-band EQ, speed, effect, bass, total, and treble knobs.

1970s		$225	$300

Guild
Guild marketed effects made by Binson, Electro-Harmonix, Foxx, WEM and Applied in the 1960s and '70s.

Copicat
1960s-1979. Echo.

1970s		$300	$450

DE-20 Auto-Rhythm Unit
1971-1974. 50 watt rhythm accompaniment unit. Included 20 rhythms and a separate instrument channel with its own volume control. 1x12" plus tweeter.

1971-1974		$200	$300

Echorec (by Binson)
Ca.1960-1979. Stripped-down version of the Binson Echorec.

1960s		$675	$875

Foxey Lady Fuzz
1968-1977. Distortion, sustain.

Model Year	Features	Low	High
1968-1975	2 knobs, made by E-H	$200	$540
1976-1977	3 knobs in row, same as Big Muff	$250	$550

MODEL YEAR FEATURES	EXC. COND. LOW	HIGH

Fuzz Wah FW-3
1975-ca.1979. Distortion, volume, wah, made by Foxx.
| 1970s | $80 | $150 |

HH Echo Unit
1976-ca.1979.
| 1970s | $200 | $300 |

VW-1
1975-ca.1979. Volume, wah, made by Foxx.
| 1970s | $200 | $250 |

Guyatone
1998-present. Imported stomp boxes, tape echo units and outboard reverb units distributed by Godlyke Distributing.

HAO
Line of guitar effects built in Japan by J.E.S. International, distributed in the U.S. by Godlyke.

Harden Engineering
2006-present. Distortion/boost guitar effects pedals built by William Harden in Chicago, Illinois. He also builds guitars.

Heathkit
1960s. These were sold as do-it-yourself kits and are difficult to value because quality depends on skills of builder.

TA-28 Distortion Booster
1960s. Fuzz assembly kit, heavy '60s super fuzz, case-by-case quality depending on the builder.
| 1960s | $140 | $150 |

Heavy Metal Products
Mid-1970s. From Alto Loma, California, products for the heavy metal guitarist.

Raunchbox Fuzz
| 1975-1976 | $75 | $100 |

Switchbox
1975-1976. A/B box.
| 1975-1976 | $25 | $35 |

Heet Sound Products
1974-present. The E Bow concept goes back to '67, but a hand-held model wasn't available until '74. Made in Los Angeles, California.

E Bow
1974-1979, 1985-1987, 1994-present. The Energy Bow, hand-held electro-magnetic string driver.
| 1974-1979 | $50 | $60 |

E Bow for Pedal Steels
1979. Hand-held electro-magnetic string driver.
| 1979 | $35 | $55 |

Heil Sound
1960-present. Founded by Bob Heil, Marissa, Illinois. Created the talk box technology as popularized by Joe Walsh and Peter Frampton. In the '60s and '70s Heil was dedicated to innovative products for the music industry. In the late-'70s, innovative creations were more in the amateur radio market, and by the '90s Heil's focus was on the home theater market. The Heil Sound Talkbox was reissued by Jim Dunlop USA in '89.

Talk Box
1976-ca.1980, 1989-present. Reissued by Dunlop.
1976-1980	$100	$150
1989-1999	$60	$85
2000-2019	$60	$80

Henretta Engineering
2009-present. Analog guitar effects built by Kevin Henretta first in Chicago, Illinois and presently Saint Paul, Minnesota.

Hermida Audio
2003-present. Alfonso Hermida builds his guitar effects in Miramar, Florida.

High Gain
See listing under Dunlop.

Hohner
Hohner offered effects in the late-1970s.

Dirty Booster
1977-ca.1978. Distortion.
| 1977-1978 | $55 | $65 |

Dirty Wah Wah'er
1977-ca.1978. Adds distortion.
| 1977-1978 | $65 | $75 |

Fuzz Wah
1970s. Morley-like volume pedal with volume knob and fuzz knob, switch for soft or hard fuzz, gray box with black foot pedal.
| 1970s | $65 | $75 |

Multi-Exciter
1977-ca.1978. Volume, wah, surf, tornado, siren.
| 1977-1978 | $60 | $70 |

Tape Echo/Echo Plus
1970s. Black alligator suitcase.
| 1970s | $200 | $275 |

Tri-Booster
1977-ca.1978. Distortion, sustain.
| 1977-1978 | $55 | $65 |

Vari-Phaser
1977-ca.1978.
| 1977-1978 | $55 | $65 |

Vol-Kicker Volume Pedal
1977-ca.1978.
| 1977-1978 | $30 | $40 |

Wah-Wah'er
1977-ca.1978. Wah, volume.
| 1977-1978 | $55 | $65 |

HomeBrew Electronics
2001-present. Stomp box effects hand made by Joel and Andrea Weaver in Glendale, Arizona.

Honey
1967-1969. Formed by ex-Teisco workers after that firm was acquired by Kawai. Honey launched

Guild Tri-Oct
Mary-Anne Hammer

1970s Guyatone PS-104 Crossover Auto Wah
Rivington Guitars

EFFECTS

HomeBrew Electronics Psilocybe
Keith Myers

EFFECTS

Hughes & Kettner Tube Rotosphere MKII

1980 Ibanez Analog Delay AD80
Bernunzio Uptown Music

Ibanez Auto Wah AW7 (Tone-Lok)

MODEL YEAR	FEATURES	EXC. COND. LOW	HIGH

several effects designed by engineer Fumio Mieda, before going bankrupt in March, '69. The company was reborn as Shin-ei and many of its designs continued production in various forms; see Shin-ei for more.

Psychedelic Machine
1967-1969. Amp head-sized effect with numerous controls.

1967-1969		$750	$1,100

Hughes & Kettner
1985-present. Hughes & Kettner builds a line of tube-driven guitar effects made in Germany. They also build amps and cabinets.

Ibanez
1932-present. Ibanez effects were introduced ca. 1974, and were manufactured by Japan's Maxon Electronics. Although results were mixed at first, a more uniform and modern product line, including the now legendary Tube Screamer, built Ibanez's reputation for quality. They continue to produce a wide range of effects.

60s Fuzz FZ5 (SoundTank)
1991-1992, 1996-1998. Fuzz with level, tone and distortion controls, black plastic case, green label.

1990s		$25	$30

7th Heaven SH7 (Tone-Lok)
2000-2004. Lo, high, drive and level controls, gray-silver case, blue-green label.

2000-2004		$20	$30

Acoustic Effects PT4
1993-1998. Acoustic guitar multi-effect with compressor/limiter, tone shaper, stereo chorus, digital reverb, with power supply.

1993-1998		$75	$100

Analog Delay AD9
1982-1984. 3 control analog delay, Hot Pink metal case.

1982-1984		$200	$275

Analog Delay AD80
1980-1981. Pink case.

1980-1981		$200	$275

Analog Delay AD99
1996-1998. Reissue, 3 control knobs and on/off switch, winged-hand logo, black case.

1996-1998		$125	$150

Analog Delay AD100 (Table Unit)
1981-1983. Stand-alone table/studio unit (not rack mount) with power cord.

1981-1983		$200	$250

Analog Delay 202 (Rack Mount)
1981-1983. Rack mount with delay, doubling, flanger, stereo chorus, dual inputs with tone and level.

1981-1983		$200	$300

Auto Filter AF9
1982-1984. Replaces AF201 model.

1982-1984		$150	$200

MODEL YEAR	FEATURES	EXC. COND. LOW	HIGH

Auto Filter AF201
1981. Two min-max sliders, 3 mode toggle switches, orange metal case.

1981		$175	$200

Auto Wah AW5 (SoundTank)
1994-1999. Plastic case SoundTank series.

1994-1999		$30	$40

Auto Wah AW7 (Tone-Lok)
2000-2010. Silver case.

2000-2010		$20	$30

Bass Compressor BP10
1986-1991		$70	$80

Bi-Mode Chorus BC9
1984. Dual channel for 2 independent speed and width settings.

1984		$75	$100

Chorus CS-505
1980-1981. Speed and depth controls, gray-blue case, stereo or mono input, battery or external power option.

1980-1981		$200	$250

Chorus Flanger CF7 (Tone-Lok)
1999-2010. Speed, depth, delay, regeneration controls, mode and crazy switches.

1999-2010		$35	$55

Classic Flange FL99
1997-1999. Analog reissue, silver metal case, winged-hand artwork, 4 controls, 2 footswitch buttons.

1997-1999		$90	$110

Classic Phase PH99
1995-1999. Analog reissue, silver metal case, winged-hand artwork, speed, depth, feedback, effect level controls, intense and bypass footswitches.

1995-1999		$90	$110

Compressor CP5 (SoundTank)
1991-1998		$20	$30

Compressor CP10
1986-1992		$75	$80

Compressor CP830
1975-1979		$100	$125

Compressor II CP835
1980-1981		$100	$125

Compressor Limiter CP9
1982-1984		$100	$125

Delay Champ CD10
1986-1989. Red case, 3 knobs.

1986-1989		$125	$150

Delay Echo DE7 (Tone-Lok)
1999-2010. Stereo delay/echo.

1999-2010		$40	$80

Delay Harmonizer DM1000
1983-1984. Rack mount, with chorus, 9 control knobs.

1983-1984		$175	$225

Delay III DDL20 Digital Delay
1988-1989. Filtering, doubling, slap back, echo S, echo M, echo L, Seafoam Green coloring on pedal.

1988-1989		$100	$125

Delay PDD1 (DPC Series)
1988-1989. Programmable Digital Delay (PDD) with display screen.

1988-1989		$125	$150

MODEL YEAR FEATURES	EXC. COND. LOW	HIGH

Digital Chorus DSC10
1990-1992. 3 control knobs and slider selection toggle.

| 1990-1992 | $75 | $100 |

Digital Delay DL5 (SoundTank)

| 1991-1998 | $35 | $45 |

Digital Delay DL10
1989-1992. Digital Delay made in Japan, blue case, 3 green control knobs, stompbox.

| 1989-1992 | $100 | $125 |

Distortion Charger DS10

| 1986-1989 | $70 | $90 |

Distortion DS7 (Tone-Lok)
2000-2010. Drive, tone, and level controls.

| 2000-2010 | $40 | $45 |

Dual Chorus CCL

| 1990s | $60 | $100 |

Echo Machine EM5 (SoundTank)
1996-1998. Simulates tape echo.

| 1996-1998 | $45 | $95 |

Fat Cat Distortion FC10
1987-1989. 3-knob pedal with distortion, tone, and level controls.

| 1987-1989 | $50 | $105 |

Flanger FFL5 (Master Series)
1984-1985. Speed, regeneration, width, D-time controls, battery or adapter option.

| 1984-1985 | $70 | $90 |

Flanger FL5 (SoundTank)

| 1991-1998 | $25 | $35 |

Flanger FL9
1982-1984. Yellow case.

| 1982-1984 | $100 | $150 |

Flanger FL301
1979-1982. Mini flanger, 3 knobs, called the FL-301 DX in late '81-'82.

| 1979-1982 | $100 | $125 |

Flanger FL305
1976-1979. Five knobs.

| 1976-1979 | $100 | $125 |

Flying Pan FP777
1976-1979. Auto pan/phase shifter, 4 control knobs, phase on/off button, pan on/off button, silver metal case with blue trim and Flying Pan winged-hand logo.

| 1976-1979 | $575 | $725 |

Flying Pan FP777 Reissue

| 2007 | 777 made | $275 | $350 |

Fuzz FZ7 (Tone-Lok)
2000-2010. Drive, tone and level controls, gray-silver case, blue-green FZ7 label.

| 2000-2010 | $45 | $50 |

Graphic Bass EQ BE10
1986-1992. Later labeled as the BEQ10.

| 1986-1992 | $60 | $80 |

Graphic EQ GE9
1982-1984. Six EQ sliders, 1 overall volume slider, turquoise blue case.

| 1982-1984 | $60 | $80 |

Graphic EQ GE10
1986-1992. Eight sliders.

| 1986-1992 | $60 | $80 |

Graphic Equalizer GE601 (808 Series)
1980-1981. 7-slider EQ, aqua blue metal case.

| 1980-1981 | $75 | $100 |

Guitar Multi-Processor PT5
1993-1997. Floor unit, programmable with 25 presets and 25 user presets, effects include distortion, chorus, flanger, etc, green case.

| 1993-1997 | $100 | $125 |

LA Metal LM7
1988-1989. Silver case.

| 1988-1989 | $55 | $65 |

LoFi LF7 (Tone-Lok)
2000-2010. Filter, 4 knobs.

| 2000-2010 | $20 | $30 |

Metal Charger MS10
1986-1992. Distortion, level, attack, punch and edge control knobs, green case.

| 1986-1992 | $45 | $55 |

Metal Screamer MSL
1985. 3 control knobs.

| 1985 | $55 | $65 |

Modern Fusion MF5 (SoundTank)
1990-1991. Level, tone and distortion controls.

| 1990-1991 | $45 | $50 |

Modulation Delay DM500
1983-1984. Rack mount.

| 1983-1984 | $75 | $100 |

Modulation Delay DM1000
1983-1984. Rack mount with delay, reverb, modulation.

| 1983-1984 | $100 | $125 |

Modulation Delay PDM1
1988-1989. Programmable Digital Modulation pedal.

| 1988-1989 | $100 | $125 |

Mostortion MT10
1990-1992. Mos-FET circuit distortion pedal, 5 control knobs, green case.

| 1990-1992 | $50 | $60 |

Multi-Effect PUE5/PUE5 Tube (Floor Unit)
1990-1993. Yellow version has tube, blue one does not. Also available in PUE5B bass version.

| 1990-1993 | Tube | $350 | $450 |

Multi-Effect UE300 (Floor Unit)
1983-1984. Floor unit, 4 footswitches for super metal, digital delay, digital stereo chorus, and master power, 3 delay modes.

| 1983-1984 | $275 | $350 |

Multi-Effect UE300B (Floor Unit)
1983-1984. Floor unit for bass.

| 1983-1984 | $275 | $350 |

Multi-Effect UE400 (Rackmount)
1980-1984. Rack mount with foot switch.

| 1980-1984 | $300 | $375 |

Multi-Effect UE405 (Rackmount)
1981-1984. Rack mount with analog delay, parametric EQ, compressor/limiter, stereo chorus and loop.

| 1981-1984 | $300 | $375 |

Noise Buster NB10
1988-1989. Eliminates 60-cycle hum and other outside signals, metal case.

| 1988-1989 | $70 | $75 |

Ibanez Compressor Limiter CP9

1980s Ibanez Flanger FL301-DX
Bernunzio Uptown Music

Ibanez Metal Charger MS10
Keith Myers

EFFECTS

1984 Ibanez Phaser PT9
Rivington Guitars

Ibanez Stereo Chorus CS9
Keith Myers

Ibanez Tube King TK999US
Keith Myers

MODEL YEAR	FEATURES	EXC. COND. LOW	HIGH
Overdrive OD850			
1975-1979		$275	$400
Overdrive II OD855			
1977-1979. Distortion, tone, and level controls, yellow/green case, large Overdrive II logo.			
1977-1979		$300	$400
Pan Delay DPL10			
1990-1992. Royal Blue case, 3 green control knobs.			
1990-1992		$95	$125
Parametric EQ PQ9			
1982-1984		$125	$175
Parametric EQ PQ401			
1981. 3 sliders, dial-in knob, light aqua blue case.			
1981		$125	$175
Phase Tone PT909			
1979-1982. Blue box, 3 knobs, early models with flat case (logo at bottom or later in the middle) or later wedge case.			
1979-1982		$140	$150
Phase Tone PT999			
1975-1979. Script logo, 1 knob, round footswitch, becomes PT-909.			
1975-1979		$125	$150
Phase Tone PT1000			
1974-1975. Morley-style pedal phase, light blue case, early model of Phase Tone.			
1974-1975		$200	$300
Phase Tone II PT707			
1976-1979. Blue box, script logo for first 2 years.			
1976-1979		$100	$130
Phaser PH5 (SoundTank)			
1991-1998		$20	$30
Phaser PH7 (Tone-Lok)			
1999-2010. Speed, depth, feedback and level controls.			
1999-2010		$35	$40
Phaser PT9			
1982-1984. Three control knobs, red case.			
1982-1984		$75	$100
Powerlead PL5 (SoundTank)			
1991-1998. Metal case '91, plastic case '91-'98.			
1991	Metal	$25	$40
1991-1998	Plastic	$15	$20
Renometer			
1976-1979. 5-band equalizer with preamp.			
1976-1979		$75	$100
Rotary Chorus RC99			
1996-1999. Black or silver cases available, requires power pack and does not use a battery.			
1996-1999	Black case	$100	$125
Session Man SS10			
1988-1989. Distortion, chorus.			
1988-1989		$70	$80
Session Man II SS20			
1988-1989. 4 controls plus toggle, light pink-purple case.			
1988-1989		$70	$80
Slam Punk SP5 (SoundTank)			
1996-1999		$35	$40
Smash Box SM7 (Tone-Lok)			
2000-2010		$30	$35

MODEL YEAR	FEATURES	EXC. COND. LOW	HIGH
Sonic Distortion SD9			
1982-1984		$75	$100
Standard Fuzz (No. 59)			
1974-1979. Two buttons (fuzz on/off and tone change).			
1974-1979		$175	$200
Stereo Box ST800			
1975-1979. One input, 2 outputs for panning, small yellow case.			
1975-1979		$175	$225
Stereo Chorus CS9			
1982-1984		$75	$100
Stereo Chorus CSL (Master Series)			
1985-1986		$70	$90
Super Chorus CS5 (SoundTank)			
1991-1998		$20	$30
Super Metal SM9			
1984. Distortion.			
1984		$75	$95
Super Stereo Chorus SC10			
1986-1992		$75	$100
Super Tube Screamer ST9			
1984-1985. 4 knobs, light green metal case.			
1984-1985		$225	$300
Super Tube STL			
1985		$75	$95
Swell Flanger SF10			
1986-1992. Speed, regeneration, width and time controls, yellow case.			
1986-1992		$55	$100
Trashmetal TM5 (SoundTank)			
1990-1998. Tone and distortion pedal, 3 editions (1st edition, 2nd edition metal case, 2nd edition plastic case).			
1990-1998		$15	$20
Tremolo Pedal TL5 (SoundTank)			
1995-1998		$45	$95
Tube King TK999			
1994-1995. Has a 12AX7 tube and 3-band equalizer.			
1994-1995	Includes power pack	$125	$200
Tube King TK999US			
1996-1998. Has a 12AX7 tube and 3-band equalizer, does not have the noise switch of original TK999. Made in the U.S.			
1996-1998	Includes power pack	$125	$200
Tube Screamer TS5 (SoundTank)			
1991-1998		$20	$25
Tube Screamer TS7 (Tone-Lok)			
1999-2010. 3 control knobs.			
1999-2010		$30	$35
Tube Screamer TS9			
1982-1984, 1993-present. Reissued in '93.			
1982-1984		$300	$700
1993-2019		$75	$125
Tube Screamer Classic TS10			
1986-1993		$175	$225
Tube Screamer TS808			
1980-1982, 2004-present. Reissued in '04.			
1980-1982	Original	$600	$1,300
2004-2019	Reissue	$75	$120

The ***Vintage Guitar Price Guide*** shows low to high values for items in all-original excellent condition, and, where applicable, with original case or cover.

MODEL YEAR / FEATURES	EXC. COND. LOW	HIGH

Turbo Tube Screamer TS9DX
1998-present. Tube Screamer circuit with added 3 settings for low-end.
1998-2019 $70 $85

Twin Cam Chorus TC10
1986-1989. Four control knobs, light blue case.
1986-1989 $75 $100

Virtual Amp VA3 (floor unit)
1995-1998. Digital effects processor.
1995-1998 $55 $75

VL10
1987-1997. Stereo volume pedal.
1987-1997 $50 $75

Wah Fuzz Standard (Model 58)
1974-1981. Fuzz tone change toggle, fuzz on toggle, fuzz depth control, balance control, wah volume pedal with circular friction pads on footpedal.
1974-1981 $225 $300

Wah WH10
1988-1997 $50 $75

Ilitch Electronics
2003-present. Ilitch Chiliachki builds his effects in Camarillo, California.

Indy Guitarist
See listing under Wampler Pedals.

Intersound
1970s-1980s. Intersound, Inc. was located in Boulder, Colorado and was a division of Electro-Voice.

Reverb-Equalizer R100F
1977-1979. Reverb and 4-band EQ, fader.
1977-1979 $75 $100

J. Everman
Analog guitar effects built by Justin J. Everman in Richardson, Texas, starting in 2000.

Jack Deville Electronics
2008-present. Production/custom, guitar effects built in Portland, Oregon by Jack Deville.

Jacques
One-of-a-kind handmade stomp boxes and production models made in France.

JAM Pedals
2007-present. Pedals built by Jannis Anastasakis Marinos of Athens, Greece.

Black Muck
2017-2018. Fuzz distortion.
2017-2018 $190 $240

Boomster
2007-2019. Silicon clean boost.
2007-2019 $75 $100

Boomster Mini
2017-present. Silicon clean boost.
2017-2019 $50 $100

DanComp
2007-2015. Compressor based on the Dan Armstrong Orange Squeezer compressor circuit.
2007-2015 $200 $220

Delay Llama
2007-present. Analog delay.
2007-2019 $150 $200

Delay Llama Supreme
2014-2019. Analog delay with tap tempo modulation.
2014-2019 $275 $325

Delay Llama+
2009-2019. Analog delay with hold function.
2009-2019 $150 $200

Dyna-ssoR
2007-present. Compression/sustainer.
2007-2019 $140 $175

Fuzz Phase
2007-2018. Germanium fuzz.
2007-2018 $200 $240

LucyDreamer Supreme
2017-present. Overdrive/boost.
2017-2019 $180 $210

Rattler
2008-present. Distortion.
2008-2019 $140 $175

Rattler+
2008-2018. Distortion with low-gain stage.
2008-2018 $175 $200

Red Muck
2008-2018. Fuzz distortion.
2008-2018 $140 $175

Retro Vibe
2007-present. Vibe/vibrato.
2007-2019 $230 $275

Ripple
2007-present. Two-stage phaser.
2007-2019 $120 $160

Ripply Fall
2017-present. Chorus/vibrato/phaser.
2017-2019 $220 $280

Rooster
2007-2018. Frequency booster.
2007-2018 $160 $200

The Big Chill
2011-present. Super tremolo with 2 speeds and chop effect.
2011-2019 $175 $200

The Chill
2007-present. Sine-wave tremolo.
2007-2019 $120 $160

Tube Dreamer 58
2007-present. Overdrive with selectable high-gain stage.
2007-2019 $120 $150

Tube Dreamer 72
2007-2018. Overdrive.
2007-2018 $130 $160

Tube Dreamer 88
2007-2018. Double overdrive.
2007-2018 $160 $200

Ibanez Tube Screamer TS9

Jack Deville Deuce Coupe Overdrive

JAM Pedals LucyDreamer Supreme

EFFECTS

Jen Variophaser
Niclas Löfgren

JHS Pedals Sweet Tea

Jordan Boss Tone Fuzz

MODEL YEAR	FEATURES	EXC. COND. LOW	HIGH
Tube Dreamer+			
2007-2017. Overdrive with footswitchable high-gain stage.			
2007-2017		$140	$180
Wahcko+			
2007-present. Wah-wah.			
2007-2019		$180	$220
WaterFall			
2007-present. Chorus/vibrato.			
2007-2019		$150	$200

JangleBox

2004-present. Stephen Lasko and Elizabeth Lasko build their guitar effects in Springfield, Virginia and Dracut, Massachusetts.

Jan-Mar Industries

Jan-Mar was located in Hillsdale, New Jersey.

MODEL YEAR	FEATURES	EXC. COND. LOW	HIGH
The Talker			
1976. 30 watts.			
1976		$75	$125
The Talker Pro			
1976. 75 watts.			
1976		$100	$150

Jax

1960s-1970. Japanese imports made by Shin-ei.

MODEL YEAR	FEATURES	EXC. COND. LOW	HIGH
Fuzz Master			
1960s		$350	$425
Fuzz Wah			
1960s		$125	$300
Vibrachorus			
1969. Rotating-speaker simulator, with control pedal. Variant of Uni-Vibe.			
1969		$575	$775
Wah-Wah			
1960s		$400	$500

Jen

Italy's Jen Elettronica company made a variety of guitar effects pedals in the 1960s and '70s for other brands such as Vox and Gretsch name. They also offered many of them, including the Cry Baby, under their own name.

Jersey Girl

1991-present. Line of guitar effects pedals made in Japan. They also build guitars.

Jet Sounds LTD

1977. Jet was located in Jackson, Mississippi.

MODEL YEAR	FEATURES	EXC. COND. LOW	HIGH
Hoze Talk Box			
1977. Large wood box, 30 watts.			
1977		$90	$125

Jetter Gear

2005-present. Brad Jeter builds his effects pedals in Marietta, Georgia.

JHD Audio

1974-1990. Hunt Dabney founded JHD in Costa

Mesa, California, to provide effects that the user installed in their amp. Dabney is still involved in electronics and builds the BiasProbe tool for tubes.

MODEL YEAR	FEATURES	EXC. COND. LOW	HIGH
SuperCube/SuperCube II			
1974-late 1980s. Plug-in sustain mod for Fender amps with reverb, second version for amps after '78.			
1974-1980s		$50	$75

JHS Pedals

2007-present. Located in Mississippi 2007-08, Josh Scott presently builds his guitar and bass effects in Kansas City, Missouri.

Jimi Hendrix

See listing under Dunlop.

John Hornby Skewes & Co.

Mid-1960s-present. Large English distributor of musical products, which has also self-branded products from others, over the years. The early Zonk Machines, Shatterbox and pre-amp boosts were designed and built by engineer Charlie Ramskirr of Wilsic Electronics, until his death in '68. Later effects were brought in from manufacturers in Italy and the Far East.

MODEL YEAR	FEATURES	EXC. COND. LOW	HIGH
Bass Boost BB1			
1966-1968. Pre-amp.			
1966-1968		$250	$400
Fuzz FZIII			
1970s. Fuzz pedal, 2 control knobs, 1 footswitch.			
1970s		$150	$200
Phaser PZ111			
1970s. Phaser pedal made in Italy, 2 control knobs, 1 footswitch.			
1970s		$80	$200
Selectatone TB2			
1966-1968. Pre-amp combining treble and bass boost.			
1966-1968		$250	$650
Treble Boost TB1			
1966-1968. Pre-amp.			
1966-1968		$250	$750
Zonk Machine I			
1965-1968. Fuzz pedal, gray-blue housing, 2 control knobs, 1 footswitch, 3 germanium transistors.			
1965-1968		$1,500	$2,000
Zonk Machine II			
1966-1968. Fuzz pedal, gray-blue housing, 2 control knobs, 1 footswitch, 3 silicon transistors.			
1966-1968		$1,000	$1,500
Zonk Machine Reissue			
2000s. Reissued by JMI starting in 2013, reissues also made by the British Pedal Company, 2 control knobs, 1 footswitch.			
2000s		$150	$200
Zonk Shatterbox			
1966-1968. Combined the Zonk Machine II fuzz circuit with the Treble Boost, 2 control knobs, gold housing, 2 foot switches.			
1966-1968		$1,500	$2,000

MODEL YEAR	FEATURES	EXC. COND. LOW	HIGH

Zonk Shatterbox Reissue
2000s. Reissues made by the British Pedal Company, gold housing, 2 foot switches.

2000s		$150	$200

Zoom Spring Reverb Unit

1967-1968		$500	$700

Johnson
Mid-1990s-present. Budget line of effects imported by Music Link, Brisbane, California. Johnson also offers guitars, amps, mandolins and basses.

Johnson Amplification
Modeling amps and effects designed by John Johnson, of Sandy, Utah, starting in 1997. The company is part of Harman International. In '02, they quit building amps, but continue the effects line.

Jordan
1966-early 1970s. Jordan Electronics - originally of Alhambra, California, later in Pasadena - built a range of electronics, including, starting around 1966, solid state guitar amps and effects. Sho-Bud of Nashville, Tennessee, licensed the Boss Tone and sold it as the Sho-Sound Boss Tone. Mahoney later reissued the Boss Tone as the Buzz Tone.

Boss Tone Fuzz
1967-1970s. Tiny effect plugged into guitar's output jack, 2 control knobs, black plastic housing, extremely delicate wiring.

1967-70s		$100	$225

Compressor J-700
1967-1970s. Sustain and Level control knobs.

1967-70s		$75	$100

Creator Volume Sustainer Model 600
1967-1970s. Volume pedal and sustainer, side controls for Sustain and Tone.

1967-70s		$400	$540

Gig Wa-Wa Volume Pedal
1967-1970s.

1967-70s		$125	$145

Phaser
1967-1970s. Black case, yellow knobs.

1967-70s	Black case	$125	$150

Vibrasonic

1967-70s		$145	$195

Kay
1931-present. Kay was once one of the largest instrument producers in the world, offering just about everything for the guitarist, including effects.

Effects Pedals
1970s. Includes the Graphic Equalizer GE-5000, Rhythmer, and Tremolo.

1970s		$50	$75

Fuzz Tone

1970s		$175	$350

Wah

1970s		$90	$120

Keeley
2001-present. Line of guitar effects designed and built by Robert Keeley in Edmond, Oklahoma. Keeley Electronics also offers a range of custom modifications for other effects.

Kendrick
1989-present. Texas' Kendrick offers guitars, amps, and effects.

ABC Amp Switcher

1990s		$100	$140

Buffalo Pfuz

1990s		$70	$100

Model 1000 Reverb
1991-2003. Vintage style, 3 knobs: dwell, tone, and mix, brown cover, wheat grille with art deco shape.

1991-2003		$400	$450

Powerglide Attenuator
1998-present. Allows you to cut the output before it hits the amp's speakers, rack mount, metal cab.

1998-2019		$180	$200

Kent
1961-1969. This import guitar brand also offered a few effects.

Kern Engineering
Located in Kenosha, Wisconsin, Kern offers pre-amps and wah pedals.

Kinsman
2012-present. Guitar effects pedals built in China and distributed by John Hornby Skewes & Co. Ltd.

Klon
1994-present. Originally located in Brookline, Massachusetts, and now located in Cambridge, Massachusetts, Klon was started by Bill Finnegan after working with two circuit design partners on the Centaur Professional Overdrive.

Centaur
2010. Smaller overdrive unit with burnished silver case.

2010		$700	$950

Centaur Professional Overdrive
1994-2009. Standard size with gold case. A smaller unit was introduced in '10.

1994-2009	Gold, horse logo	$2,000	$3,000
1994-2009	Silver, no horse logo	$1,500	$2,100

KMD (Kaman)
1986-ca. 1990. Distributed by Kaman (Ovation, Hamer, etc.) in the late '80s.

Effects Pedals

1986-1990	Analog Delay	$45	$60
1986-1990	Overdrive	$30	$45
1987-1990	Distortion	$30	$45
1987-1990	Flanger	$30	$50
1987-1990	Phaser	$30	$50
1987-1990	Stereo Chorus	$30	$50

Kay Rhythmer R-12
Keith Myers

Keeley Electronics Dual Fixed Filter
Keith Myers

Keeley Hooke Reverb

EFFECTS

Kustom The Bag
The Bag Man

Line 6 DL-4 Delay Modeler

Line 6 POD X3

Korg

Most of the Korg effects listed below are modular effects. The PME-40X Professional Modular Effects System holds four of them and allows the user to select several variations of effects. The modular effects cannot be used alone. This system was sold for a few years starting in 1983. Korg currently offers the Toneworks line of effects.

PEQ-1 Parametric EQ
1980s. Dial-in equalizer with gain knob, band-width knob, and frequency knob, black case.

MODEL YEAR	FEATURES	EXC. COND. LOW	HIGH
1980s		$40	$50

PME-40X Modular Effects

MODEL YEAR	FEATURES	LOW	HIGH
1983-1986	KAD-301 Delay	$60	$70
1983-1986	KCH-301 Chorus	$25	$35
1983-1986	KCO-101 Compressor	$45	$55
1983-1986	KDI-101 Distortion	$45	$55
1983-1986	KDL-301 Echo	$90	$110
1983-1986	KFL-401 Flanger	$40	$50
1983-1986	KGE-201 Graphic EQ	$25	$35
1983-1986	KNG-101 Noise Gate	$25	$35
1983-1986	KOD-101 Over Drive	$45	$55
1983-1986	KPH-401 Phaser	$45	$55
1983-1986	OCT-1 Octaver	$70	$80

PME-40X Professional Modular Effects System
1983-ca.1986. Board holds up to 4 of the modular effects listed below.

		LOW	HIGH
1983-1986		$125	$150

SSD 3000 Digital Delay
1980s. Rack mount, SDD-3000 logo on top of unit.

		LOW	HIGH
1980s		$775	$925

KR Musical Products

2003-present. Kevin Randall presently builds his vintage style, guitar effects in White Marsh, Virginia.

Krank

1996-2013, 2015-present. Tempe, Arizona, amp builder Tony Krank also builds effects pedals.

Kustom

1965-present. Founded in '64 by Charles "Bud" Ross in his Chanute, Kansas, garage to build amps for his band. While Fender, Rickenbacker, and others tried and failed with solid-state amps, Ross' Kustom creations were a big hit. Kustom likely only ever made one foray into effects, producing The Bag, designed by Doug Forbes.

The Bag
1969-1971. Pioneering "talk box" effect housed in a "bota" wineskin-type bag worn over the player's shoulder. Covered in multiple styles of mod fabrics.

		LOW	HIGH
1969-1971		$900	$1,500

Lafayette Radio Electronics
1960s-1970s. Effects that claimed to be made in the U.S., but were most likely built by Shin-ei of Japan.

Deluxe AC Super Fuzz
1969-1970s. Made by Shin-ei, AC power.

		LOW	HIGH
1969-70s		$300	$500

Echo Verb/Echo Verb II
1970s. Solid-state echo/reverb. Likely made by Shin-ei.

MODEL YEAR	FEATURES	LOW	HIGH
1970s	2 instrument inputs	$175	$300
1970s	Instrument & mic inputs	$75	$250

Fuzz Sound
1970s. Likely made by Shin-ei.

		LOW	HIGH
1970s		$150	$250

Roto-Vibe
1969-1970s. Rotating-speaker simulator, with control pedal. Variant of Uni-Vibe made by Shin-ei.

		LOW	HIGH
1969-70s		$575	$850

Super Fuzz
1969-1970s. Made by Shin-ei.

		LOW	HIGH
1969-70s		$300	$500
1969-70s	Battery power	$300	$500

Laney

1968-present. Founded by Lyndon Laney and Bob Thomas in Birmingham, U.K., this amp builder also offered a reverb unit.

Reverberation Unit
1968-1969. Sleek reverb unit, plexi-style front panel, black vinyl cover.

		LOW	HIGH
1968-1969		$300	$400

Larry Alan Guitars

2003-present. Luthier Larry Alan Daft offers effects pedals built in Lansing, Michigan. He also builds guitars and basses.

Lehle

2001-present. Loop switches from Burkhard Georg Lehle of Lehle Gitarrentechnik in Voerde, Germany.

D.Loop Signal Router

		LOW	HIGH
2004		$150	$175

Lenahan

Amp builder James Lenahan also offered a line of guitar pedals, built in Fort Smith, Arkansas.

Leslie

1966-1970s. In 1941, Donald Leslie began building speakers for Hammond organs to emulate pipe-organ sounds. Using a rotating baffle in front of a stationary speaker, he replicated the tremolo sound. He sold his company to CBS in 1965, and Fender launched its Vibratone based on Leslie technology in 1967. Leslie also offered its Model 16 and 18 speakers for guitarists. The Leslie 16/18 were also sold by Selmer as the Selmer-Leslie.

Model 16
1966-1970s. Rotating-speaker emulator, single fixed 4-ohm 10-inch speaker fronted by a rotating drum. Designed to be powered by an external amp. Black covering, cast Leslie badge in upper left corner.

		LOW	HIGH
1966-70s		$600	$750

EFFECTS

MODEL YEAR	FEATURES	EXC. COND. LOW	HIGH

Model 18

1966-1970s. Rotating-speaker emulator, single fixed 4-ohm 12-inch speaker fronted by a rotating drum. Designed to be powered by an external amp. Black covering, cast Leslie badge in upper left corner.

1966-70s		$500	$700

Line 6

1996-present. Founded by Marcus Ryle and Michel Doidic. Purchased by Yamaha in 2014. They also produce amps and guitars. All prices include Line 6 power pack if applicable.

DL-4 Delay Modeler
1999-present. Green case.

1999-2019		$145	$175

DM-4 Distortion Modeler
1999-2018. Yellow case.

1999-2018		$100	$125

FM-4 Filter Modeler
2001-2018. Purple case.

2001-2018		$175	$225

MM-4 Modulation Modeler
1999-2018. Aqua blue case.

1999-2018		$100	$150

POD 2.0
2001-2014. Updated version of the original Amp Modeler.

2001-2014		$150	$200

Little Lanilei

1997-present. Effects made by Mahaffay Amplifiers (formerly Songworks Systems & Products) of Aliso Viejo, California. They also build amps.

Lizard Leg Effects

2007-2016. Steve Miller built a line of effects pedals in Gonzales, Louisiana.

Lock & Rock

Line of floor pedal guitar and microphone effects produced by Brannon Electronics, Inc. of Houston, Texas starting in 2003.

Loco Box

1982-1983. Loco Box was a brand of effects distributed by Aria Pro II for a short period starting in '82. It appears that Aria switched the effects to their own brand in '83.

Effects

1982-1983	Analog Delay AD-01	$35	$45
1982-1983	Chorus CH-01	$55	$65
1982-1983	Compressor CM-01	$35	$45
1982-1983	Distortion DS-01	$40	$55
1982-1983	Flanger FL-01	$35	$45
1982-1983	Graphic Equalizer GE-06	$25	$35
1982-1983	Overdrive OD-01	$40	$50
1982-1983	Phaser PH-01	$45	$55

Lotus Pedal Designs

2009-present. Guitar effects pedals built in Duluth, Minnesota by Sean Erspamer.

Lovepedal

2000-present. Sean Michael builds his preamps and guitar stomp boxes in Detroit, Michigan.

Lovetone

Hand-made analog effects from Oxfordshire, U.K. starting in 1995.

Ludwig

For some reason, drum builder Ludwig offered a guitar synth in the 1970s.

Phase II Guitar Synth
1970-1971. Oversized synth, mushroom-shaped footswitches, vertical silver case.

1970-1971		$650	$800

M.B. Electronics

Made in San Francisco, California.

Ultra-Metal UM-10
1985. Distortion.

1985		$35	$40

Mad Professor

2002-present. Guitar effects pedals built by Bjorn Juhl and Jukka Monkkonen in Tampere, Finland. They also build amps.

Maestro

1950s-1970s, 2001-2012. Maestro was a Gibson subsidiary; the name appeared on 1950s accordian amplifiers. The first Maestro effects were the Echoplex tape echo and the FZ-1 Fuzz-Tone, introduced in the early-'60s. Maestro products were manufactured by various entities such as Market Electronics, All-Test Devices, Lowrey and Moog Electronics. In the late-'60s and early-'70s, they unleashed a plethora of pedals; some were beautiful, others had great personality. The last Maestro effects were the Silver and Black MFZ series of the late-'70s. In 2001, Gibson revived the name for a line of effects, banjos and mandolins, adding guitars and amps in '09. By '12 the brand is no longer listed with Gibson.

Bass Brassmaster BB-1
1971-ca.1974. Added brass to your bass.

1971-1974		$775	$1,100

Boomerang
Ca.1969-ca.1972. Wah pedal made by All-Test Devices.

1969-1972		$175	$200

Boomerang BG-2
1972-ca.1976. Wah pedal made by All-Test Devices.

1972-1976		$200	$225

Echoplex EM-1 Groupmaster
Ca.1970-ca.1977. Two input Echoplex, solidstate.

1970-1977	Without stand	$900	$1,400

Echoplex EP-1
1959-mid-1960s. Original model, smaller green box, tube-driven tape echo, separate controls for echo volume and instrument volume, made by Market Electronics. Though not labeled as such, it is often referred to as the EP-1 by collectors.

1959-60s	Earlier small box	$800	$1,200

Lizard Leg Effects Draconis Dual Boost

Lovetone Meatball

Mad Professor Fire Red Fuzz

EFFECTS

Maestro Fuzz-Tone FZ-1B
Bob Cain

Maestro Rover RO-1
Kyle Stevens.

1968 Maestro Sound System for Woodwinds W-1
Rivington Guitars

MODEL YEAR	FEATURES	EXC. COND. LOW	HIGH
Echoplex EP-2			
Mid-1960s-ca.1970. Larger gray or green box than original, tube-driven tape echo, single echo/instrument volume control, made by Market Electronics. Around '70, the EP-2 added a Sound-On-Sound feature. Limited-edition EP6T reissue made by Market in 1980s (see Market Electronics listing).			
1960s	Larger box	$550	$1,200
Echoplex EP-3			
Ca.1970-1977. Solidstate, made by Market Electronics, black box.			
1970-1977		$400	$1,000
Echoplex EP-4 (IV)			
1977-1978. Solidstate, last version introduced by Maestro. See Market Electronics and Echoplex brands for later models.			
1977-1978		$350	$750
Echoplex Groupmaster EM-1			
1970s. Large, multi-channel echo unit.			
1970s		$1,400	$2,000
Echoplex Sireko ES-1			
Ca.1971-mid-1970s. A budget solidstate version of the Echoplex, made by Market.			
1971-1975		$250	$350
Envelope Modifier ME-1			
1971-ca.1976. Tape reverse/string simulator, made by All-Test.			
1971-1976		$150	$225
Filter Sample and Hold FSH-1			
1975-ca.1976.			
1975-1976		$475	$700
Full Range Boost FRB-1			
1971-ca.1975. Frequency boost with fuzz, made by All-Test.			
1971-1975		$150	$200
Fuzz MFZ-1			
1976-1979. Made by Moog.			
1976-1979		$150	$200
Fuzz Phazzer FP-1			
1971-1974		$200	$300
Fuzztain MFZT-1			
1976-1978. Fuzz, sustain, made by Moog.			
1976-1978		$200	$250
Fuzz-Tone FZ-1			
1962-1963. Brown housing, uses 2 AA batteries.			
1962-1963		$300	$460
Fuzz-Tone FZ-1A			
1965-1967, 2001-2009. Brown housing, uses 1 AA battery. Early model "Kalamazoo, Michigan" on front, later "Nashville, Tennessee".			
1965-1967	Kalamazoo	$275	$470
2001-2009	Nashville	$75	$280
Fuzz-Tone FZ-1B			
Late-1960s- early-1970s. Black housing, uses 9-volt battery.			
1970s		$275	$325
Mini-Phase Shifter MPS-2			
1976. Volume, speed, slow and fast controls.			
1976		$110	$125

MODEL YEAR	FEATURES	EXC. COND. LOW	HIGH
Octave Box OB-1			
1971-ca.1975. Made by All-Test Devices.			
1971-1975		$225	$300
Parametric Filter MPF-1			
1976-1978. Made by Moog.			
1976-1978		$350	$450
Phase Shifter PS-1			
1971-1975. With or without 3-button footswitch, made by Oberheim.			
1971-1975	With footswitch	$275	$325
1971-1975	Without footswitch	$175	$225
Phase Shifter PS-1A			
1976		$150	$250
Phase Shifter PS-1B			
1970s		$150	$250
Phaser MP-1			
1976-1978. Made by Moog.			
1976-1978		$250	$325
Repeat Pedal RP-1			
1970s		$200	$300
Rhythm King MRK-2			
1971-ca.1974. Early drum machine.			
1971-1974		$400	$500
Rhythm Queen MRQ-1			
Early 1970s. Early rhythm machine.			
1970s		$125	$150
Rhythm'n Sound G-2			
Ca.1969-1970s. Multi-effect unit.			
1969-1975		$600	$750
Ring Modulator RM-1			
1971-1975	No control pedal	$550	$600
1971-1975	With MP-1 control pedal	$650	$700
Rover Rotating Speaker			
1971-ca.1973. Rotating Leslie effect that mounted on a large tripod.			
1971-1973	RO-1 model	$1,200	$1,500
Sound System for Woodwinds W-1			
1960s-1970s. Designed for clarinet or saxaphone input, gives a variety of synthesizer-type sounds with voices for various woodwinds, uses Barrel Joint and integrated microphone.			
1960-1970s		$350	$400
Stage Phaser MPP-1			
1976-1978. Has slow, fast and variable settings, made by Moog.			
1976-1978		$175	$275
Super Fuzz-Tone FZ-1S			
1971-1975		$200	$300
Sustainer SS-2			
1971-ca.1975. Made by All-Test Devices.			
1971-1975		$100	$150
Theramin TH-1			
1971-mid-1970s. Device with 2 antennae, made horror film sound effects. A reissue Theremin is available from Theremaniacs in Milwaukee, Wisconsin.			
1971-1975		$775	$975
Wah-Wah/Volume WW-1			
1970s. Wah-Wah Volume logo on end of pedal, green foot pad.			
1971-1975		$150	$250

MODEL YEAR	FEATURES	EXC. COND. LOW	HIGH

Magnatone

Ca.1937-1971, 2013-present. Magnatone built very competitive amps from '57 to '66. In the early-'60s, they offered the RVB-1 Reverb Unit. The majority of Magnatone amps pre-'66 did not have on-board reverb.

Model RVB-1 Reverb Unit
1961-1966. Typical brown leatherette cover, square box-type cabinet. From '64-'66, battery operated, solidstate version of RVB-1, low flat cabinet.

1961-1963		$275	$400
1964-1966	Battery & solidstate	$200	$300

Mahoney
2000s. Reissues of the Jordan Boss Tone.

Buzz Tone
2000s. Similar black-plastic housing to the original Boss Tone. 2 Control knobs.

2000s		$40	$75

Manny's Music
Issued by the New York-based retailer.

Fuzz
1960s. Same unit as the Orpheum Fuzz and Clark Fuzz.

1960s		$275	$490

Market Electronics
Market, from Ohio, made the famous Echoplex line. See Echoplex and Maestro sections for earlier models.

Echoplex EP-6T
1980-ca.1988. Limited-edition all-tube reissue of the Echoplex EP-2.

1980-1988		$400	$500

Marshall
1962-present. The fuzz and wah boom of the '60s led many established manufacturers, like Marshall, to introduce variations on the theme. They got back into stomp boxes in '89 with the Gov'nor distortion, and currently produce several distortion/overdrive units.

Blues Breaker
1992-1999. Replaced by Blues Breaker II in 2000.

1992-1999		$130	$260

Blues Breaker II BB-2
2000-present. Overdrive pedal, 4 knobs.

2000-2019		$50	$65

Drive Master
1992-1999		$70	$140

Guv'nor
1989-1991. Distortion, Guv'nor Plus introduced in '99.

1989-1991		$125	$160

Jackhammer JH-1
1999-present. Distortion pedal.

1999-2019		$55	$60

Power Brake PB-100
1993-1995. Speaker attenuator for tube amps.

1993-1995		$190	$230

Shred Master
1992-1999		$75	$100

Supa Fuzz
Late-1960s. Made by Sola Sound (Colorsound).

1967		$550	$850

Supa Wah
Late-1960s. Made by Sola Sound (Colorsound).

1969		$300	$425

Vibratrem VT-1
1999-present. Vibrato and tremolo.

1999-2019		$50	$75

Matchless
1989-1999, 2001-present. Matchless amplifiers offered effects in the '90s.

AB Box
1990s. Split box for C-30 series amps (DC 30, SC 30, etc.).

1990s		$175	$300

Coolbox
1997-1999. Tube preamp pedal.

1997-1999		$275	$350

Dirtbox
1997-1999. Tube-driven overdrive pedal.

1997-1999		$300	$500

Echo Box
1997-1999. Limited production because of malfunctioning design which included cassette tape. Black case, 8 white chickenhead control knobs.

1990s	Original unreliable	$300	$400
1990s	Updated reliable	$700	$900

Hotbox/Hotbox II
1995-1999. Higher-end tube-driven preamp pedal.

1995-1999		$395	$565

Mix Box
1997-1999. 4-input tube mixer pedal.

1997-1999		$375	$425

Reverb RV-1
1993-1999. 5 controls, tube-driven spring-reverb tank, various colors.

1993-1999		$1,400	$1,675

Reverb RV-2
2000s. 5 controls, tube-driven spring-reverb tank, various colors.

2000s		$900	$1,000

Split Box
1990s. Tube AB box.

1997	Standard AB	$275	$325

Tremolo/Vibrato TV-1
1993-1995. Tube unit.

1993-1995		$350	$480

Maxon
1970s-present. Maxon was the original manufacturer of the Ibanez line of effects. Currently offering retro '70s era stomp boxes distributed in the U.S. by Godlyke.

AD-9/AD-9 Pro Analog Delay
2001-present. Purple case.

2001-2019		$175	$275

Maestro Wha-Wha/Volume
Robbie Keene

Magnatone RVB-1 Reverb Unit

Marshall Guv'nor
Keith Myers

EFFECTS

Maxon OD-820 Over Drive Pro

Meteoro Doctor Metal

Mica Wau-Wau SG-150
Jim Schreck

MODEL YEAR FEATURES	EXC. COND. LOW	HIGH
CS-550 Stereo Chorus		
2001-2017. Light blue case.		
2001-2017	$100	$130
DS-830 Distortion Master		
2001-present. Light blue-green case.		
2001-2019	$100	$125
OD-820 Over Drive Pro		
2001-present. Green case.		
2001-2019	$140	$175

McQuackin FX Co.

Rich McCracken II began building his analog guitar effects in 1997, first in Nashville, Tennessee, then Augusta, Georgia.

Mesa-Boogie

1971-present. Mesa added pre-amps in the mid '90s, then pedals in 2013.

MODEL YEAR FEATURES	EXC. COND. LOW	HIGH
V-Twin Bottle Rocket		
2000-2004	$100	$180
V-Twin Preamp Pedal		
Dec. 1993-2004. Serial number series: V011-. 100 watts, all tube preamp, floor unit, silver case.		
1993-1999	$225	$275
2000-2004 Updated tone adj	$275	$325

Metal Pedals

2006-present. Brothers Dave and Mike Pantaleone build their guitar effects in New Jersey.

Meteoro

1986-present. Guitar effects built in Brazil. They also build guitar and bass amps.

MG

2004-present. Guitar effects built by Marcelo Giangrande in São Paulo, Brazil. He also builds amps.

Mica

Early 1970s. These Japanese-made effects were also sold under the Bruno and Marlboro brand names.

MODEL YEAR FEATURES	EXC. COND. LOW	HIGH
Tone Fuzz		
1970s. Silver case, black knobs.		
1970s	$200	$250
Tone Surf Wah Siren		
1970s. Wah pedal.		
1970s	$150	$195
Wailer Fuzz		
1970	$75	$100
Wau Wau Fuzz		
1970s. Wau Wau Fuzz logo on end of pedal, black.		
1970s	$150	$175

Mooer

2012-present. A line of guitar pedals built by Mooer Audio in China.

Moog/Moogerfooger

1964-present. Robert Moog, of synth fame, introduced his line of Moogerfooger analog effects in 1998. They also offer guitars.

MODEL YEAR FEATURES	EXC. COND. LOW	HIGH
Misc. Effects		
2004-present.		
2004-2010 MF-105 MuRF	$250	$400
2004-2010 Theremin	$250	$400

Moonrock

Fuzz/distortion unit built by Glenn Wylie and distributed by Tonefrenzy starting in 2002.

Morley

Late-1960s-present. Founded by brothers Raymond and Marvin Lubow, Morley has produced a wide variety of pedals and effects over the years, changing with the trends. In '89, the brothers sold the company to Accutronics (later changed to Sound Enhancements, Inc.) of Cary, Illinois.

MODEL YEAR FEATURES	EXC. COND. LOW	HIGH
ABY Switch Box		
1981-ca.1985. Box no pedal.		
1981-1985	$25	$35
Auto Wah PWA		
1976-ca.1985.		
1976-1985	$25	$35
Bad Horsie Steve Vai Signature Wah		
1997-present.		
1997-2019	$65	$80
Black Gold Stereo Volume BSV		
1985-1991	$25	$35
Black Gold Stereo Volume Pan BSP		
1985-1989	$30	$40
Black Gold Volume BVO		
1985-1991	$25	$35
Black Gold Wah BWA		
1985-1991	$30	$40
Black Gold Wah Volume BWV		
1985-1989	$30	$40
Chrystal Chorus CCB		
1996-1999. Stereo output.		
1996-1999	$25	$30
Deluxe Distortion DDB		
1981-1991. Box, no pedal.		
1981-1991	$40	$60
Deluxe Flanger FLB		
1981-1991. Box, no pedal.		
1981-1991	$55	$65
Deluxe Phaser DFB		
1981-1991. Box, no pedal.		
1981-1991	$40	$60
Distortion One DIB		
1981-1991. Box, no pedal.		
1981-1991	$35	$45
Echo Chorus Vibrato ECV		
1982-ca.1985.		
1982-1985	$150	$225
Echo/Volume EVO-1		
1974-ca.1982.		
1974-1982	$150	$225
Electro-Pik-a-Wah PKW		
1979-ca.1982.		
1979-1982	$55	$65

MODEL YEAR	FEATURES	EXC. COND. LOW	HIGH
Emerald Echo EEB			
1996-1999. 300 ms delay.			
1996-1999	Green case	$40	$50
Jerry Donahue JD-10			
1995-1997. Multi-effect, distortion, overdrive.			
1995-1997		$80	$90
Power Wah PWA/PWA II			
1992-2006. Wah with boost. Changed to II in '98.			
1992-2006		$40	$50
Power Wah PWO			
Ca.1969-1984, 2006-present. Reissued in '06.			
1969-1984		$60	$160
Power Wah/Boost PWB			
Introduced in 1973, doubles as a volume pedal.			
1970s		$80	$150
Power Wah/Fuzz PWF			
Ca.1969-ca.1984.			
1969-1984		$125	$250
Pro Compressor PCB			
1978-1984. Stomp box without pedal, compress-sustain knob and output knob.			
1978-1984		$45	$55
Pro Flanger PFL			
1978-1984		$100	$125
Pro Phaser PFA			
1975-1984		$100	$125
Rotating Sound Power Wah Model RWV			
1971-1982		$325	$425
Select-Effect Pedal SEL			
1980s. Lets you control up to 5 other pedals.			
1980s		$20	$30
Slimline Echo Volume 600			
1983-1985. 20 to 600 ms delay.			
1983-1985		$45	$55
Slimline Echo Volume SLEV			
1983-1985. 20 to 300 ms delay.			
1983-1985		$50	$60
Slimline Variable Taper Stereo Volume SLSV			
1982-1986		$70	$100
Slimline Variable Taper Volume SLVO			
1982-1986		$35	$50
Slimline Wah SLWA			
1982-1986. Battery operated electro-optical.			
1982-1986		$55	$75
Slimline Wah Volume SLWV			
1982-ca.1986. Battery operated electro-optical.			
1982-1986		$55	$75
Stereo Chorus Flanger CFL			
1980-ca. 1986. Box, no pedal.			
1980-1986		$60	$70
Stereo Chorus Vibrato SCV			
1980-1991. Box, no pedal.			
1980-1991		$80	$100
Stereo Volume CSV			
1980-ca. 1986. Box, no pedal.			
1980-1986		$30	$45
Volume Compressor VCO			
1979-1984		$30	$45

MODEL YEAR	FEATURES	EXC. COND. LOW	HIGH
Volume Phaser PFV			
1977-1984. With volume pedal.			
1977-1984		$125	$180
Volume VOL			
1975-ca.1984.			
1975-1979		$30	$45
1980-1984		$25	$40
Volume XVO			
1985-1988		$25	$40
Volume/Boost VBO			
1974-1984		$50	$60
Wah Volume CWV			
1987-1991. Box, no pedal.			
1987-1991		$65	$80
Wah Volume XWV			
1985-ca.1989.			
1985-1989		$65	$90
Wah/Volume WVO			
1977-ca.1984.			
1977-1984		$80	$100

Morpheus

Guitar effects pedals manufactured in Salt Lake City, Utah by the same builders of the Bolt brand amps.

Mosferatu

Line of guitar effects pedals built by Hermida Audio Technology.

Mosrite

Semie Moseley's Mosrite company dipped into effects in the 1960s.

Fuzzrite

1960s-1970s, 1999. Silver housing as well as some painted housings, 2 front-mounted control knobs. Sanner reissued in '99.

1960s-70s	Mosrite logo	$250	$550
1999	Reissue, Sanner logo	$100	$225

Mu-FX

See Beigel Sound Lab.

Multivox

New York-based Multivox offered a variety of effects in the 1970s and '80s.

Big Jam Effects

Multivox offered the Big Jam line of effects from 1980 to ca. '83.

1980-1983	Analog Echo/Reverb	$100	$125
1980-1983	Bi-Phase 2, Flanger, Jazz Flanger	$50	$60
1980-1983	Chorus	$45	$55
1980-1983	Compressor, Phaser, 6-Band EQ, Spit-Wah	$40	$80
1980-1983	Distortion	$70	$80
1980-1983	Octave Box	$40	$55
1981-1983	Noise Gate, Parametric EQ	$35	$45
1981-1983	Space Driver, Delay	$60	$70
1982-1983	Volume Pedal	$30	$35

Morley Bad Horsie Steve Vai Signature Wah

Morley Rotating Wah RWV
Nate Westgor

Mosrite Fuzzrite

EFFECTS

1970s Multivox Full Rotor MX-2
Keith Myers

Mu-Tron Bi-Phase

MXR Six Band EQ
Keith Myers

MODEL YEAR	FEATURES	EXC. COND. LOW	HIGH
Full Rotor MX-2			
1978-ca.1982. Leslie effect.			
1978-1982		$300	$350
Little David LD-2			
1970s. Rotary sound effector in mini Leslie-type case.			
1970s	With pedal	$325	$500
1970s	Without pedal	$325	$375
Multi Echo MX-201			
1970s. Tape echo unit, reverb.			
1970s		$200	$250
Multi Echo MX-312			
1970s. Tape echo unit, reverb.			
1970s		$225	$300
Rhythm Ace FR6M			
1970s. 27 basic rhythms.			
1970s		$60	$80

Mu-Tron

1972-ca.1980. Made by Musitronics, founded by Mike Beigel and Aaron Newman in Rosemont, New Jersey, these rugged and unique-sounding effects were a high point of the '70s. The Mu-Tron III appeared in '72 and more products followed, about 10 in all. Musitronics also made the U.S. models of the Dan Armstrong effects. In '78 ARP synthesizers bought Musitronics and sold Mutron products to around '80. In '78, Musitronics also joined with Lol Creme and Kevin Godley of 10cc to attempt production of the Gizmotron, which quickly failed (see listing under Godley Crème). A reissue of the Mu-Tron III was made available in '95 by NYC Music Products and distributed by Matthews and Ryan Musical Products. As of 2013, Mike Beigel's Beigel Sound Lab has started making a hot-rodded Tru-Tron III.

MODEL YEAR	FEATURES	LOW	HIGH
Bi-Phase			
1975-ca.1980. Add $50-$75 for Opti-Pot pedal.			
1971-1980	Optical pedal option	$900	$1,500
1975-1980	2-button footswitch	$900	$1,250
C-100 OptiPot Control Pedal			
1975-1980	Blue case	$550	$700
C-200 Volume-Wah			
1970s		$300	$350
Flanger			
1977-ca.1980.			
1977-1980		$800	$1,700
III Envelope Filter			
1972-ca.1980. Envelope Filter.			
1972-1980		$450	$790
Micro V			
Ca.1975-ca.1977. Envelope Filter.			
1970s		$200	$250
Octave Divider			
1977-ca.1980.			
1977-1980		$540	$780
Phasor			
Ca.1974-ca.1976. Two knobs.			
1974-1976		$275	$480
Phasor II			
1976-ca.1980. Three knobs.			
1976-1980		$200	$395

MODEL YEAR	FEATURES	EXC. COND. LOW	HIGH
Muza			

2006-present. Digital guitar effects made in China by Hong Kong's Medeli Electronics Co., Ltd. They also build digital drums.

MXR

1972-present. MXR Innovations launched its line of pedals in '72. Around '77, the Rochester, New York, company changed lettering on the effects from script to block, and added new models. MXR survived into the mid-'80s. In '87, production was picked up by Jim Dunlop. Reissues of block logo boxes can be differentiated from originals as they have an LED above the switch and the finish is slightly rough; the originals are smooth.

MODEL YEAR	FEATURES	LOW	HIGH
Six Band EQ			
1975-1982. Equalizer.			
1975-1979		$70	$85
1980-1982		$60	$70
Six Band EQ M109 (Reissue)			
1987-present. Reissued by Jim Dunlop.			
1987-2019		$30	$40
Ten Band EQ M108			
1975-1981, 2004-present. Graphic equalizer.			
1975-1981	With AC power cord	$80	$100
Analog Delay			
1975-1981. Green case, power cord.			
1975-1979	Earlier 2-jack model	$300	$325
1980-1981	Later 3-jack model	$150	$200
Blue Box			
1972-ca.1978. Octave pedal, M-103.			
1970s	Earlier script logo	$290	$400
1970s	Later block logo	$225	$250
Blue Box M103 (Reissue)			
1995-present. Reissued by Jim Dunlop, blue case. Produces 1 octave above or 2 octaves below.			
1995-2019		$40	$45
Carbon Copy M169			
1987-present. Analog delay. 3 Control knobs. I Toggle switch. Green housing.			
1987-2019		$90	$110
Commande Effects			
1981-1983. The Commande series featured plastic housings and electronic switching.			
1981-1983	Overdrive	$40	$50
1981-1983	Phaser	$100	$110
1981-1983	Preamp	$40	$50
1981-1983	Stereo Chorus	$60	$70
1981-1983	Sustain	$60	$70
1981-1983	Time Delay	$70	$80
1982-1983	Stereo Flanger	$70	$80
Distortion +			
1972-1982.			
1970s	Earlier script logo	$185	$225
1970s	Later block logo	$85	$110
1980s	Block logo	$80	$95
Distortion + (Series 2000)			
1983-1985		$60	$70
Distortion + M104 (Reissue)			
1987-present. Reissued by Jim Dunlop, yellow case.			
1987-1990		$55	$65
1991-2019		$45	$55

MODEL YEAR	FEATURES	EXC. COND. LOW	HIGH
Distortion II			
1981-1983	With AC power cord	$140	$180
Distortion III M115			
1987-present. 3 Control knobs. Red housing.			
1987-2019		$25	$60
Double Shot Distortion M151			
2003-2005. 2 channels.			
2003-2005		$65	$75
Dyna Comp			
1972-1982. Compressor.			
1970s	Block logo, battery	$90	$120
1970s	Script logo, battery	$175	$200
1980s	Block logo, battery	$65	$80
Dyna Comp (Series 2000)			
1982-1985		$65	$75
Dyna Comp M102 (Reissue)			
1987-present. Reissued by Jim Dunlop, red case.			
1987-2019		$35	$40
Envelope Filter			
1976-1983		$125	$225
Flanger			
1976-1983, 1997-present. Analog, reissued by Dunlop in '97.			
1976-1979	AC power cord, 2 inputs	$175	$225
1980-1983	AC power cord	$100	$150
1997-2019	M-117R reissue	$60	$70
Flanger/Doubler			
1979	Rack mount	$150	$175
Fullbore Metal M116			
1987-present. 6 Control knobs. Bare metal housing.			
1987-2019		$35	$100
Limiter			
1980-1982. AC, 4 knobs.			
1980-1982	AC power cord	$125	$200
Loop Selector			
1980-1982. A/B switch for 2 effects loops.			
1980-1982		$50	$60
Micro Amp			
1978-1983, 1995-present. Variable booster, creme case, reissued in '95.			
1978-1983		$75	$100
1995-2019	M-133 reissue	$40	$45
Micro Chorus			
1980-1983. Yellow case.			
1980-1983		$125	$175
Micro Flanger			
1981-1982		$100	$150
Noise Gate Line Driver			
1974-1983.			
1970s	Script logo	$75	$125
1980s	Block logo	$75	$100
Omni			
1980s. Rack unit with floor controller, compressor, 3-band EQ, distortion, delay, chorus/flanger.			
1980s		$425	$475
Phase 45			
Ca.1976-1982. Battery, earlier script logo, later block.			
1970s	Script logo	$125	$200
1980s	Block logo	$100	$125

MODEL YEAR	FEATURES	EXC. COND. LOW	HIGH
Phase 90			
1972-1982.			
1970s	Earlier script logo	$325	$425
1970s	Later block logo	$200	$275
1980s	Block logo	$150	$200
Phase 90 M101 (Reissue)			
1987-present. Reissued by Jim Dunlop, orange case.			
1987-1989	Block logo	$60	$85
1990-2019	Block or script logo	$50	$75
Phase 100			
1974-1982.			
1970s	Earlier script logo	$250	$325
1970s	Later block logo, battery	$175	$275
Phaser (Series 2000)			
1982-1985. Series 2000 introduced cost cutting die-cast cases.			
1982-1985		$60	$85
Pitch Transposer			
1980s		$400	$475
Power Converter			
1980s		$45	$60
Smart Gate M135			
2002-present. Noise-gate, single control, battery powered, gray case.			
2002-2019		$60	$80
Stereo Chorus			
1978-1985. With AC power cord.			
1978-1979		$175	$275
1980-1985		$150	$220
Stereo Chorus (Series 2000)			
1983-1985. Series 2000 introduced cost cutting die-cast cases.			
1983-1985		$55	$75
Stereo Flanger (Series 2000)			
1983-1985. Series 2000 introduced cost cutting die-cast cases, black with blue lettering.			
1983-1985		$60	$80
Super Comp M132			
2002-present. 3 knobs, black case.			
2002-2019		$40	$55

Nobels

1997-present. Effects pedals from Nobels Electronics of Hamburg, Germany. They also make amps.

ODR-1 Natural Overdrive

1997-present. Classic overdrive, green case.

1997-2019		$30	$40

TR-X Vintage Tremolo

1997-2017. Tremolo effect using modern technology, purple case.

1997-2017		$30	$40

Nomad

1960s. Effects that claimed to be made in the U.S., but most likely built by Shinei of Japan. Models include the Verberola and the Fuzz wah, both of which were sold under other brands such as Applied, Jax USA, and Companion.

MXR Carbon Copy M169

MXR Dyna Comp M102
Keith Myers

MXR Phase 90
Keith Myers

EFFECTS

Origin Effects SlideRig

Peavey Companded Chorus CMC-1

Pigtronix FAT Drive

EFFECTS

Fuzz Wah
1960s. Fuzz wah pedal similar to Morley pedals of the era with depth and volume controls and fuzz switch, silver and black.

1960s	$75	$125

Oddfellow Effects
Jon Meleika, began in 2013, builds guitar effects pedals in Riverside, California.

Olson
Olson Electronics was based in Akron, Ohio.
Reverberation Amplifier RA-844
1967. Solidstate, battery-operated, reverb unit, depth and volume controls, made in Japan.

1967	$100	$150

Ooh La La Manufacturing
2007-2014. Hand-made guitar effects built in St. Louis Park, Minnesota, including the models formerly offered under the Blackbox brand.

Option 5
2002-present. Jay Woods builds his guitar effects pedals in Mishwaka, Indiana.

Origin Effects
2012-present. Custom-built and production guitar effects made in Oxfordshire, U.K. by Simon Keats.

Ovation
Ovation ventured into the solidstate amp and effects market in the early '70s.
K-6001 Guitar Preamp
1970s. Preamp with reverb, boost, tremolo, fuzz, and a tuner, looks something like a Maestro effect from the '70s, reliability may be an issue.

1970s	$100	$125

PAIA
1967-present. Founded by John Paia Simonton in Edmond, Oklahoma, specializing in synthesizer and effects kits. PAIA did make a few complete products but they are better known for the various electronic kit projects they sold. Values on kit projects are difficult as it depends on the skills of the person who built it.
Roctave Divider 5760
1970s. Kit to build analog octave divider.

1970s	$70	$85

Pan*Damn*ic
2007-2012. Guitar effects pedals made by PLH Professional Audio in West Chester, Pennsylvania.

Park
1965-1982, 1992-2000. Sola/Colorsound made a couple of effects for Marshall and their sister brand, Park. In the '90s, Marshall revived the name for use on small solidstate amps.

Pax
1970s. Imported Maestro copies.
Fuzz Tone Copy

1970s	$125	$150

Octave Box Copy
1970s. Dual push-buttons (normal and octave), 2 knobs (octave volume and sensitivity), green and black case.

1970s	$125	$150

Pearl
Pearl, located in Nashville, Tennessee, and better known for drums, offered a line of guitar effects in the 1980s.
Analog Delay AD-08
1983-1985. Four knobs.

1983-1985	$100	$150

Analog Delay AD-33
1982-1984. Six knobs.

1982-1984	$175	$225

Chorus CH-02
1981-1984. Four knobs.

1981-1984	$75	$100

Chorus Ensemble CE-22
1982-1984. Stereo chorus with toggling between chorus and vibrato, 6 knobs.

1982-1984	$125	$175

Compressor CO-04

1981-1984	$50	$75

Distortion DS-06

1982-1986	$40	$60

Flanger FG-01
1981-1986. Clock pulse generator, ultra-low frequency oscillator.

1981-1986	$75	$100

Graphic EQ GE-09

1983-1985	$40	$55

Octaver OC-07

1982-1986	$100	$225

Overdrive OD-05

1981-1986	$75	$145

Parametric EQ PE-10

1983-1984	$45	$60

Phaser PH-03
1981-1984. Four knobs.

1981-1984	$75	$95

Phaser PH-44
1982-1984. Six knobs.

1982-1984	$150	$175

Stereo Chorus CH-22
1982-1984. Blue case.

1982-1984	$75	$125

Thriller TH-20
1984-1986. Exciter, 4 knobs, black case.

1984-1986	$175	$225

Peavey
1965-present. Peavey made stomp boxes from '87 to around '90. They offered rack mount gear after that.

MODEL YEAR	FEATURES	EXC. COND. LOW	HIGH
Accelerator Overdrive AOD-2			
1980s		$30	$35
Biampable Bass Chorus BAC-2			
1980s		$30	$35
Companded Chorus CMC-1			
1980s		$25	$30
Compressor/Sustainer CSR-2			
1980s		$35	$40
Digital Delay DDL-3			
1980s		$30	$35
Digital Stereo Reverb SRP-16			
1980s		$50	$55
Dual Clock Stereo Chorus DSC-4			
1980s		$30	$35
Hotfoot Distortion HFD-2			
1980s		$25	$30

PedalDoctor FX

1996-present. Tim Creek builds his production and custom guitar effects in Nashville, Tennessee.

Pedalworx

In 2001, Bob McBroom and George Blekas began building guitar effects in Manorville, New York and Huntsville, Alabama. They also do modifications to wahs.

Pharaoh Amplifiers

1998-2010. Builder Matt Farrow builds his effects in Raleigh, North Carolina.

Pignose

1972-present. Guitar stomp boxes offered by the amp builder in Las Vegas, Nevada. They also offer guitars.

Pigtronix

2003-present. Originally in Brooklyn, and currently in Yonkers, New York offering, offering a range of guitar effects. In 2020 D'Angelico Guitars acquired the brand.

Plum Crazy FX

Guitar effects built by Kaare Festovog in Apple Valley, Minnesota starting in 2005.

Premier

Ca.1938-ca.1975, 1990-2010. Premier offered a reverb unit in the '60s.
Reverb Unit
1961-late-1960s. Tube, footswitch, 2-tone brown.

1960s		$250	$350

Prescription Electronics

Located in Portland, Oregon, Jack Brossart began offering a variety of hand-made effects in 1994.
Dual-Tone
1998-2009. Overdrive and distortion.

1998-2009		$165	$175

Throb
1996-2014. Tremolo.

1996-2014		$165	$175

MODEL YEAR	FEATURES	EXC. COND. LOW	HIGH
Yardbox			
1994-2014. Patterned after the original Sola Sound Tonebender.			
1994-2014		$90	$125

Pro Tone Pedals

2004-present. Guitar effects pedals built by Dennis Mollan in Dallas, Texas until early-2011, and presently in Summerville, South Carolina.

ProCo

1974-present. Located in Kalamazoo, Michigan and founded by Charlie Wicks, ProCo produces effects, cables and audio products.
Rat
1979-1987. Fuzztone, large box until '84. The second version was 1/3 smaller than original box. The small box version became the Rat 2. The current Vintage Rat is a reissue of the original large box.

1979-1984	Large box	$250	$400
1984-1987	Compact box	$95	$170

Rat 2
1987-present. Classic distortion.

1987-1999		$75	$150
2000-2019		$40	$55

Turbo Rat
1989-present. Fuzztone with higher output gain, slope-front case.

1989-2019		$40	$50

Vintage Rat
1992-2005. Reissue of early-'80s Rat.

1992-2005		$40	$50

Pro-Sound

The effects listed here date from 1987, and were, most likely, around for a short time.
Chorus CR-1

1980s		$25	$40

Delay DL-1
1980s. Analog.

1980s		$35	$55

Distortion DS-1

1980s		$20	$35

Octaver OT-1

1980s		$25	$40

Power and Master Switch PMS-1

1980s		$15	$25

Super Overdrive SD-1

1980s		$20	$35

Providence

1996-present. Guitar effects pedals built in Japan for Pacifix Ltd. and distributed in the U.S. by Godlyke Distributing, Inc.

Radial Engineering

1994-present. Radial makes a variety of products in Port Coquitlam, British Columbia, including direct boxes, snakes, cables, splitters, and, since '99, the Tonebone line of guitar effects.

Premier Reverb Unit

Prescription Electronics Yardbox
Rivington Guitars

Radial Tonebone Texas Dual Overdrive

EFFECTS

Red Witch Eve Tremolo

Rocktron Banshee Talk Box
Rivington Guitars

Rocktron Rampage Distortion

MODEL YEAR	FEATURES	EXC. COND. LOW	HIGH

Rapco

The Jackson, Missouri based cable company offers a line of switch, connection and D.I. Boxes.

The Connection AB-100

1988-2017. A/B box.

1988-2017		$25	$35

Rastop Designs

2002-present. Alexander Rastopchin builds his effects in Long Island City, New York. He also builds amps.

Ray Butts Music Co.

1950s. Ray Butts ran a music store in Cairo, Illinois, where he built his famous EchoSonic amp. He experimented with building a pioneering fuzz box that never went into production and offered his NovaMatch buffer in very limited production.

NovaMatch

Late-1950s. Buffer with 1Db of gain in a lipstick-tube-like unit that plugged into guitar jacks.

1950s		$200	$300

Real McCoy Custom

1993-present. Wahs and effects by Geoffrey Teese. His first wah was advertised as the Real McCoy, by Teese. He now offers his custom wah pedals under the Real McCoy Custom brand. He also used the Teese brand on a line of stomp boxes, starting in '96. The Teese stomp boxes are no longer being made. In '08 he moved to Coos Bay, Oregon.

Recycled Sound

2009-present. Greg Perrine designs attenuators in Conway, Arkansas, which are then built in China.

Red Witch

2003-present. Analog guitar effects, designed by Ben Fulton, and made in Paekakariki, New Zealand.

Reinhardt

2004-2012. Amp builder Bob Reinhardt of Lynchburg, Virginia also offers a line of effects pedals.

Retro FX Pedals

2006-ca. 2010. Guitar effects pedals built by John Jones in St. Louis, Missouri.

Retroman

2002-present. Joe Wolf builds his retro effects pedals in Janesville, Wisconsin.

Retro-Sonic

2002-present. Tim Larwill builds effects in Ottawa, Ontario.

Reverend

1996-present. Reverend offered its Drivetrain effects from '00 to '04. They also build guitars.

MODEL YEAR	FEATURES	EXC. COND. LOW	HIGH

RGW Electronics

2003-present. Guitar effects built by Robbie Wallace in Lubbock, Texas.

Rivera

1985-present. Amp builder Paul Rivera also offers a line of guitar pedals built in California.

Rocco

Introduced in 1937, the Rocco Tonexpressor was a volume pedal designed by New York City steel-guitarist Anthony Rocco and built and distributed by Epiphone. Generally credited with being the first guitar effect pedal.

Rockman

See listings under Scholz Research and Dunlop.

Rocktek

1986-2009. Imports formerly distributed by Matthews and Ryan of Brooklyn, New York; and later by D'Andrea USA.

Effects

1986-2009	Delay, Super Delay	$30	$40
1986-2009	Distortion, 6 BandEQ, Bass EQ, Chorus, Compressor	$15	$25
1986-2009	Overdrive, Flanger, Metal Worker, Phaser, Vibrator Tremolo	$15	$20

Rocktron

1980s-present. Rocktron is a division of GHS Strings and offers a line of amps, controllers, stomp boxes, and preamps.

Austin Gold Overdrive

1997-2011. Light overdrive.

1997-2011		$25	$35

Banshee Talk Box

1997-present. Includes power supply.

1997-2019		$65	$120

Hush Rack Mount

1980s-present.

2000-2019		$50	$100

Hush The Pedal

1996-present. Pedal version of rackmount Hush.

1996-2019		$25	$50

Rampage Distortion

1996-2013. Sustain, high-gain and distortion.

1996-2013		$25	$35

Surf Tremolo

1997-2000		$60	$80

Tsunami Chorus

1996-2009. Battery or optional AC adapter.

1996-2009	Battery power	$40	$50
1996-2009	With power supply	$50	$60

Vertigo Vibe

2003-2006. Rotating Leslie speaker effect.

2003-2006	Battery power	$50	$60
2003-2006	With power supply	$60	$70

MODEL YEAR	FEATURES	EXC. COND. LOW	HIGH

XDC
1980s. Rack mount stereo preamp, distortion.

1980s		$100	$150

Roger Linn Design
2001-present. Effects built in Berkeley, California by Roger Linn.

Roger Mayer Electronics
1964-present. Roger Mayer started making guitar effects in the U.K. in '64 for guitarists like Jimmy Page and Jeff Beck. He moved to the U.S. in '69 to start a company making studio gear and effects. Until about 1980, the effects were built one at a time in small numbers and not available to the general public. In the '80s he started producing larger quantities of pedals, introducing his rocket-shaped enclosure. He returned to the U.K. in '89.

Axis Fuzz
1987-present.

1987-2019		$125	$150

Classic Fuzz
1987-present. The Fuzz Face.

1987-2019		$175	$200

Metal Fuzz
Early 1980s-1994.

1987-1994		$125	$150

Mongoose Fuzz
1987-2017.

1987-2017		$125	$250

Octavia
1981-present. Famous rocket-shaped box.

1981-2019		$180	$400

Voodoo-1
Ca.1990-present.

1990-2019		$100	$300

Rogue
2001-present. Budget imported guitar effects. They also offer guitars, basses, lap steels, mandolins, banjos, ukuleles and amps.

Roland
Japan's Roland Corporation first launched effect pedals in 1974; a year or two later the subsidiary company, Boss, debuted its own line. They were marketed concurrently at first, but gradually Boss became reserved for compact effects while the Roland name was used on amplifiers, keyboards, synths and larger processors.

Analog Synth SPV
1970s. Multi-effect synth, rack mount.

1970s		$750	$900

Bee Baa AF-100
1975-ca.1980. Fuzz and treble boost.

1975-1980		$300	$550

Bee Gee AF-60
1975-ca.1980. Sustain, distortion.

1975-1980		$75	$125

Double Beat AD-50
1975-ca.1980. Fuzz wah.

1975-1980		$175	$200

Expression Pedal EV-5

1970s		$50	$75

Expression Pedal EV-5 Reissue
2000. Black pedal, blue foot pad.

2000		$25	$30

Guitar Synth Pedal GR-33 and Pickup GK-2A
2000-2005. Requires optional GK-2A pickup, blue case.

2000-2005		$300	$550

Human Rhythm Composer R-8
1980s. Drum machine, key pad entry.

1980s		$175	$250

Human Rhythm Composer R-8 MK II
2000s. Black case.

2000s		$300	$400

Jet Phaser AP-7
1975-ca.1978. Phase and distortion.

1975-1978		$525	$650

Phase Five AP-5
1975-ca.1978.

1975-1978		$200	$225

Phase II AP-2
1975-ca.1980. Brown case.

1975-1980		$125	$175

Space Echo Unit
1974-ca. 1980. Tape echo and reverb, various models.

1970s	RE-101	$350	$500
1970s	RE-150	$350	$550
1970s	RE-200	$500	$750
1970s	RE-201	$750	$1,250
1970s	RE-301	$700	$950
1970s	RE-501	$700	$1,000
1970s	SRE-555 Chorus		
	Echo	$950	$1,100

Vocoder SVC-350
Late-1970s-1980s. Vocal synthesis (vocoder) for voice or guitar, rack mount version of VP-330.

1980		$550	$700

Vocoder VP-330 Plus
Late-1970s-1980s. Analog vocal synthesis (vocoder) for voice or guitar, includes 2 1/2 octaves keyboard.

1978-1982		$750	$900

Wah Beat AW-10
1975-ca.1980.

1975-1980		$70	$100

Rosac Electronics
1969-1970s. Founded by Ralph Scaffidi and former Mosrite engineer Ed Sanner with backing from Morris Rosenberg and Ben Sacco in Bakersfield, California. Made the Nu-Fuzz which was a clone of Mosrite's Fuzzrite and the Nu-Wah. Closed in mid- to late- '70s and Scaffidi went on to co-found Osborne Sound Laboratories.

Roger Mayer Voodoo Axe

Roland Bee Baa AF-100
Niclas Löfgren

Roland Space Echo

EFFECTS

1978 Ross Distortion
Rivington Guitars

Sam Ash Fuzzz Boxx

Satellite Eradicator

Ross

Founded by Bud Ross, who also established Kustom, in Chanute, Kansas, in the 1970s. Ross produced primarily amplifiers. In about '78, they introduced a line of U.S.-made effects. Later production switched to Asia.

10 Band Graphic Equalizer

MODEL YEAR / FEATURES	EXC. COND. LOW	HIGH
1970s	$80	$100

Compressor
1970s. Gray or black case.

1970s	$325	$475

Distortion
1978-ca.1980. Brown.

1979-1980	$50	$70

Flanger
1977-ca.1980. Red.

1977-1980	$100	$125

Phase Distortion R1
1979. Purple.

1979	$100	$125

Phaser
1978-ca.1980. Orange.

1978-1980	$65	$90

Stereo Delay
1978-ca.1980.

1978-1980	$125	$175

Rotovibe

See listing under Dunlop.

S. Hawk Ltd.

1970s. Various effect pedals, no model names on case, only company name and logo.

Hawk I Fuzz
1970s. Linear pre-amp, fuzz, headphone amp, 1 slider.

1970s	$300	$400

Sam Ash

1960s-1970s, 2013-present. Sam Ash Music was founded by Sam Ash (nee Askynase), in '24, in Brooklyn, and by '66, there were about four Ash stores. During this time, Ash Music private branded their own amps and effects. In 2013, Sam Ash reissued the Fuzzz Boxx.

Fuzzz Boxx
1966-1967, 2013-2019. Red, made by Universal Amplifier Company, same as Astrotone Fuzz. There is also a Fuzzola II. Fuzzz reissued in '13.

1967	$200	$325

Volume Wah
1970s. Italian-made.

1970s	$175	$200

Sanner

1999. Reissue from Eddie Sanner, who was the engineer behind the 1960s Mosrite Fuzzrite, using the identical circuitry as the original. Issued as a limited edition.

Sano

1944-ca. 1970. Sano was a New Jersey-based accordion company that built their own amps and a reverb unit. They also imported guitars for a few years, starting in '66.

Satellite Amplifiers

2004-present. Analog effects pedals made in San Diego, California by amp builder Adam Grimm.

Schaffer-Vega

1975-1982, 2015-present. After Mick Jagger's wireless system for the 1975 Rolling Stones Tour of the Americas began broadcasting police calls and lottery numbers, New York recording engineer Ken Schaffer invented his Schaffter-Vega Diversity System (SVDS) as a better wireless system – although it also could be used to affect guitar tones, offering overdrive as used by AC/DC's Angus Young.

Diversity System
1975-1982. Wireless mic and guitar transmitter and receiver.

1975-1982	$1,000	$1,500

Replica Pedal
2015-present. Stompbox replicating the SVDS guitar effects made by SoloDallas.

2015-2019	$300	$350

Replica Tower
2015-present. Replica of the original SVDS made by SoloDallas.

2015-2019	$1,000	$1,300

Schaller

The German guitar accessories company, which began in 1945, offered guitar effects off and on since the '60s and currently has reissue versions of its volume pedal and tremolo.

Scholz Research

1982-1995. Started by Tom Scholz of the band Boston. In '95, Jim Dunlop picked up the Rockman line (see Dunlop).

Power Soak

1980s	$100	$160

Rockman

1980s	$70	$130

Rockman X100
1980s. Professional studio processor.

1980s	$100	$150

Soloist
1980s. Personal guitar processor.

1980s	$50	$80

Seamoon

1973-1977, 1997-2002. Seamoon made effects until '77, when Dave Tarnowski bought up the remaining inventory and started Analog Digital Associates (ADA). He reissued the brand in '97.

Fresh Fuzz
1975-1977. Recently reissued by ADA.

1975-1977	$150	$200

MODEL YEAR	FEATURES	EXC. COND. LOW	HIGH

Funk Machine
1974-1977. Envelope filter. Recently reissued by ADA.

1974-1977		$200	$345

Studio Phase
1975-1977. Phase shifter.

1975-1977		$75	$125

Sekova
Mid-1960s-mid-1970s. Entry level instruments imported by the U.S. Musical Merchandise Corporation of New York.

Seymour Duncan
In late 2003, pickup maker Seymour Duncan, located in Santa Barbara, California, added a line of stomp box guitar effects.

Shin-ei
1969-1970s. When the Honey company went bankrupt in March, '69, it was reborn as Shin-ei and many Honey designs continued in production in various forms. Their chief engineer was Fumio Mieda who later did design work for Korg. Shin-ei also made effects for Univox (including the Uni-Fuzz, Super-Fuzz and Uni-Vibe), Companion, Applied, Apollo, Jax, Nomad, Shaftsbury, Pax, Crown, Royal, Mica, Kent, Marlboro, Memphis, Bruno, Boomer, Alex, Ace Tone, Aria, Goya, Kimbara, Lord, National, Northland, Tele Star, Tempo, and probably others.

Fuzz Wah

1970s		$250	$400

FY-2 Fuzz Box
1969-1970s. 2 transistors.

1969-1970s		$250	$450

FY-6 Super Fuzz
1969-1970s. Built from fuzz circuitry of Psychedelic Machine, 6 transistors.

1969-1970s		$750	$1,100

Psychedelic Machine
1969. Amp head-sized effect with numerous controls.

1969		$750	$1,100

Resly (Repeat Time) Machine
1970s. Black case, 3 speeds.

1970s		$400	$500

Sho-Bud
1956-1980. This pedal steel company offered volume pedals as well.

Sho-Sound Boss Tone
1970s-1980. Licensed version of the Jordan Boss Tone, 2 control knobs, similar black plastic housing.

1970s-80		$65	$150

Volume Pedal

1965		$90	$170

SIB
Effects pedals from Rick Hamel, who helped design SMF amps.

Siegmund Guitars & Amplifiers
1993-present. Los Angeles, California amp and guitar builder Chris Siegmund added effects to his product line in '99.

Sitori Sonics
Emanual Ellinas began building his guitar effects in Birmingham, Alabama, in 2006.

Skrydstrup R&D
1997-present. Effects pedals built by Steen Skrydstrup in Denmark. He also builds amps.

Skull Crusher
2009-2015. Partners John Kasha and Shawn Crosby of Tone Box Effects, built their guitar effects in Simi Valley, California.

Snarling Dogs
Started by Charlie Stringer of Stringer Industries, Warren, New Jersey in 1997. Stringer died in May '99. The brand is now carried by D'Andrea USA.

Sobbat
1995-present. Line of effects from Kinko Music Company of Kyoto, Japan.

Sola/Colorsound
1962-2010. Sola was founded by London's Macari's Musical Exchange in '62, which was launched by former Vox associate Larry Macari and his brother Joe. The first product was the Tone-Bender fuzz box, designed by Gary Stewart Hurst and modeled in part on the Maestro Fuzz-Tone FZ-1. The first readily available fuzz in Britain, it was an instant success. Sola soon began making effects for Vox, Marshall, Park, and B & M and later under their own Colorsound brand. Refer to Colorsound for further listings and more company info.

Tone Bender Mk 1.5
1966-late 1960s.

1966-1969		$1,000	$2,100

Tone Bender Mk I

1965-1966		$1,500	$2,450

Tone Bender Professional Mk II
Late 1960s.

1960s		$900	$2,100

Soldano
1987-present. Seattle, Washington amp builder Soldano also built a reverb unit.

Sho-Space Box
1987-2018. Tube-driven spring reverb.

1987-2018		$800	$900

Songbird
See Dytronics.

1970s Shin-ei Fuzz Wah
Keith Myers

Skull Crusher Chrome

Sola/Colorsound Fuzz/Wah/Swell
Shane Richardson

EFFECTS

Strymon Deco

Strymon TimeLine

Swart FuzzyBoost

Sonic Edge

Guitar and bass effects pedals built by Ben Fargen in Sacramento, California starting in 2010. He also builds the Fargen amps.

Sonuus

2009-present. Guitar effects built in China and imported by owners James Clark and John McAuliffe in the U.K.

Speedster

1995-2000, 2003-2007. Amp builder Speedster added guitar effects pedals to their product line in '04, built in Gig Harbor, Washington.

StarTouch

2001-present. Tony Chostner builds production/custom, effects pedals in Salem, Oregon.

Stephenson

1997-present. Amp builder Mark Stephenson in Parksville, British Columbia also offers a line of guitar pedals.

Stinger

Stinger effects were distributed by the Martin Guitar Company from 1989 to '90.

Effects

MODEL YEAR	FEATURES	EXC. COND. LOW	HIGH
1989-1990	CH-70 Stereo Chorus	$25	$55
1989-1990	CO-20 Compressor	$35	$55
1989-1990	DD-90 Digital Delay	$45	$65
1989-1990	DE-80 Analog Delay	$50	$70
1989-1990	DI-10 Distortion	$40	$65
1989-1990	FL-60 Flanger	$40	$65
1989-1990	OD-30 Overdrive	$40	$65
1989-1990	TS-5 Tube Stack	$45	$65

Strymon

2009-present. Founded in 2004 as Damage Control, the company began offering effects pedals under the Strymon name in 2009. Owners Gregg Stock, Pete Celi, and Dave Fruehling build their line of guitar pedals in Chatsworth, California.

Big Sky
2013-present. Reverberator pedal.

		EXC. COND. LOW	HIGH
2013-2019		$390	$490

BlueSky
2010-present. Digital reverb pedal.

2010-2019		$230	$280

Brigadier
2010-present. dBucket delay.

2010-2019		$175	$200

Deco
2014-present. Tape saturation and doubletracker pedal.

2014-2019		$245	$270

DIG
2015-present. Dual digital delay.

2015-2019		$220	$250

El Capistan
2010-present. Tape echo.

MODEL YEAR	FEATURES	EXC. COND. LOW	HIGH
2010-2019		$210	$280

Flint
2012-present. Tremolo and reverb.

2012-2019		$175	$290

Lex
2011-present. Rotary effects pedal.

2011-2019		$230	$300

Mobius
2012-present. Modulation pedal.

2012-2019		$335	$405

OB.1
2009-present. Optical compressor and clean boost.

2009-2019		$125	$150

Ojai
2016-present. High current DC power supply.

2016-2019		$125	$175

Ola
2010-present. dBucket chorus and vibrato.

2010-2019		$180	$235

Orbit
2010-present. dBucket flanger.

2010-2019		$170	$190

Riverside
2016-present. Multistage drive.

2016-2019		$200	$230

Sunset
2017-present. Dual overdrive pedal.

2017-2019		$230	$275

TimeLine
2011-present. Delay pedal.

2011-2019		$315	$380

Zuma
2016-present. High current DC power supply.

2016-2019		$160	$220

Studio Electronics

1989-present. Synth and midi developer Greg St. Regis' Studio Electronics added guitar pedal effects to their line in '03.

Subdecay Studios

2003-present. Brian Marshall builds his guitar effects in Woodinville, Washington.

Supersound

1952-1974. Founded by England's Alan Wootton, this firm built echo units in the 1960s. They also built amps, guitars and basses.

Supro

1935-1968, 2004-present. Supro offered a few reverb units in the '60s. Brand name was revived in '04.

500 R Standard Reverb Unit
1962-1963. Outboard reverb unit.

1962-1963		$250	$500

600 Reverb Power Unit
1961. Independent reverb unit amp combination to be used with Supro Model 1600R amp or other amps, 3 tubes, 1x8" speaker.

1961		$300	$700

EFFECTS

MODEL YEAR	FEATURES	EXC. COND. LOW	HIGH

Swart Amplifier

2003-present. Effects pedals built by Michael J. Swart in Wilmington, North Carolina. He also builds amps.

Sweet Sound

1994-present. Line of effects from Bob Sweet, originally made in Trenton, Michigan, and then in Coral Springs, Florida. Bob died in 2008. Currently built by his brother Gerald.

Swell Pedal Company

1997-2012. Mike Olienechak builds his line of tube pedals for guitar and bass in Nashville, Tennessee.

SynapticGroove

Benjamin Harrison and Chrystal Gilles build their guitar effects in Edmond, Oklahoma, starting in 2013.

Systech (Systems & Technology in Music, Inc)

1975-late-1970s. Systech was located in Kalamazoo, Michigan.

Effects

MODEL YEAR	FEATURES	LOW	HIGH
1975-1979	Envelope & Repeater	$75	$125
1975-1979	Envelope Follower	$75	$125
1975-1979	Flanger	$75	$125
1975-1979	Harmonic Energizer	$150	$225
1975-1979	Overdrive Model 1300	$75	$125
1975-1979	Phase Shifter Model 1200	$75	$125

T.C. Jauernig Electronics

2004-present. Tim Jauernig, of Rothschild, Wisconsin, built effects for several years before launching his T.C. Jauernig brand in '04.

TC Electronic

1976-present. Brothers Kim and John Rishøj founded TC Electronic in Risskov, Denmark, and made guitar effects pedals for several years before moving into rack-mounted gear. Currently they offer a wide range of pro audio gear and rack and floor guitar effects.

Booster + Distortion

1980s		$325	$400

Dual Parametric Equalizer

1980s		$275	$350

Stereo Chorus/Flanger SCF

Introduced in 1982, and reissued in '91.

1980s		$175	$275

Sustain + Equalizer

1980s		$225	$300

Tech 21

1989-present. Tech 21 builds their SansAmp and other effects in New York City. They also build amps.

Sansamp

1989-present. Offers a variety of tube amp tones.

1989	1st year	$125	$175
1990-2019		$100	$125

XXL Pedal

1995-2000, 2005-2012. Distortion, fuzz.

1995-2012		$50	$75

Teese

Geoffrey Teese's first wah was advertised as the Real McCoy, by Teese. He now offers his custom wah pedals under the Real McCoy Custom brand. The Teese brand was used on his line of stomp boxes, starting in '96. The Teese stomp boxes are no longer being made.

TEN

2013-present. Guitar effects built in Spokane, Washington by Ryan Dunn and Doug Harrison. From 2001-'13 they used the ToadWorks brand.

The Original Geek

Jeff Rubin began building guitar effects pedals in Los Angeles, California under the Geek MacDaddy brand in 2004. After a breakup with his business partner in '09 he began using The Original Geek brand.

Thomas Organ

The Thomas Organ Company was heavily involved with Vox from 1964 to '72, importing their instruments into the U.S. and designing and assembling products, including the wah-wah pedal. Both Thomas Organ and JMI, Vox's European distributor, wanted to offer the new effect. The problem was solved by labeling the Thomas Organ wah the Crybaby. The Crybaby is now offered by Dunlop. Refer to Vox listing for Crybaby Stereo Fuzz Wah, Crybaby Wah, and Wah Wah.

ThroBak Electronics

2004-present. Jonathan Gundry builds his guitar effects in Grand Rapids, Michigan. He also builds guitar amps and pickups.

ToadWorks

See listing for TEN.

TomasZewicZ or TZZ

2008-present. Guitar effects pedals built by John Tomaszewicz in Coral Springs, Florida, which he labels TZZ. He also builds amps.

Tone Box Effects

See listing for Skull Crusher.

Tonebone

See Radial Engineering listing.

ToneCandy

2007-present. Mike Marino builds his guitar effects pedals in Santa Rosa, California.

Top Gear

1960s-1970s. Top Gear was a London music store. Their effects were made by other manufacturers.

TC Electronics HOF Mini
Keith Myers

TEN Bananas At Large Stereo Buffer

ThroBak Electronics Strange Master

EFFECTS

T-Rex Diva Drive

Tube Works Real Tube
Keith Myers

Univox Micro Fazer

EFFECTS

MODEL YEAR	FEATURES	EXC. COND. LOW	HIGH
Rotator			
1970s. Leslie effect.			
1970s		$100	$175

Top Hat Amplification

1994-present. Brian Gerhard builds his amps and effects in Fuquay-Varina, North Carolina. He previously built them in La Habra, California and Apex, North Carolina.

Traynor

1963-present. Amp and PA builder Traynor also built two spring reverb units, one tube and one solidstate, in Canada from 1966-'72 and a 7-band EQ from '73-'78.

Tremolo

See listing under Dunlop.

T-Rex

2003-present. Made in Denmark and imported by European Musical Imports.

TSVG

Mike Klein started building his guitar effects in his shop located in Philadelphia, Pennsylvania in 2011.

Tube Works

1987-2004. Founded by B.K. Butler (see Audio Matrix) in Denver, Colorado, Tube Works became a division of Genz Benz Enclosures of Scottsdale, Arizona in 1997 which dropped the brand in 2004. They also offered tube/solidstate amps, cabinets, and DI boxes.

MODEL YEAR	FEATURES	EXC. COND. LOW	HIGH
Blue Tube			
1989-2004. Overdrive bass driver with 12AX7A tube.			
1989-2004		$100	$150
Real Tube			
Ca.1987-2004. Overdrive with 12AX7A tube.			
1987-1999		$100	$150
Tube Driver			
1987-2004. With tube.			
1987-2004		$100	$150

TWA (Totally Wycked Audio)

2009-present. Boutique analog effect pedals made in the U.S. and offered by Godlyke, Inc.

Tycobrahe

The Tycobrahe story was over almost before it began. Doing business in 1976-1977, they produced only three pedals and a direct box, one the fabled Octavia. The company, located in Hermosa Beach, California, made high-quality, original devices, but they didn't catch on. Now, they are very collectible. Reissues were made by Chicago Iron.

MODEL YEAR	FEATURES	EXC. COND. LOW	HIGH
Octavia			
1976-1977, 2000s. Octave doubler.			
1976-1977		$1,100	$1,900
2000s	Octavia & Octavian reissue	$260	$300

MODEL YEAR	FEATURES	EXC. COND. LOW	HIGH
Parapedal			
1976-1977, 2000s. Wah.			
1976-1977		$700	$1,350
2000s	Reissue, light blue	$200	$300
Pedalflanger			
1976-1977. Blue pedal-controlled flanger.			
1976-1977		$1,100	$1,350

Uni-Vibe

See listings under Univox and Dunlop.

Univox

Univox was a brand owned by Merson (later Unicord), of Westbury, New York. It marketed guitars and amps, and added effects in the late-'60s. Most Univox effects were made by Shin-ei, of Japan. They vanished in about '81.

MODEL YEAR	FEATURES	EXC. COND. LOW	HIGH
Drum Machine SR-55			
1970s		$175	$200
EC-80 A Echo			
Early-1970s-ca.1977. Tape echo, sometimes shown as The Brat Echo Chamber.			
1970s		$75	$100
EC-100 Echo			
1970s. Tape, sound-on-sound.			
1970s		$75	$160
Echo-Tech EM-200			
1970s. Disc recording echo unit.			
1970s		$130	$170
Fuzz FY-2			
1970s		$185	$350
Micro 41 FCM41 4 channel mixer			
1970s		$35	$50
Micro Fazer			
1970s. Phase shifter.			
1970s		$75	$115
Noise-Clamp EX110			
1970s		$45	$55
Phaser PHZ1			
1970s. AC powered.			
1970s		$50	$75
Pro-Verb UR-3			
1970s. Reverb (spring) unit, black tolex, slider controls for 2 inputs, 1 output plus remote output.			
1970s		$85	$100
Square Wave SQ150			
Introduced in 1976. Distortion, orange case.			
1970s		$75	$125
Super-Fuzz			
1968-1973. Made by Shin-ei and similar to the FY-6 Super Fuzz, built from fuzz circuitry of Honey/Shin-ei Psychedelic Machine, 6 transistors, battery powered.			
1968-1973	Gray box, normal bypass switch	$400	$925
1968-1973	Unicord, various colors, blue bypass pedal	$350	$500
Surf Siren			
1970s. Wah pedal.			
1970s		$90	$150

MODEL YEAR	FEATURES	EXC. COND. LOW	HIGH
Uni-Comp			
1970s. Compression limiter.			
1970s		$50	$100
Uni-Drive			
1970s		$150	$200
Uni-Fuzz			
1969-1973. Fuzz tone in blue case, 2 black knobs and slider switch. Made by Shin-ei, AC-powered version of Super-Fuzz, built from fuzz circuitry of Honey/Shin-ei Psychedelic Machine.			
1969-1973		$300	$590
Uni-Tron 5			
1975. A.k.a. Funky Filter, envelope filter.			
1975		$200	$525
Uni-Vibe			
Introduced ca. 1969-1970s. Rotating-speaker simulator, with control pedal. Made by Shin-ei, built from circuitry of Honey/Shin-ei Psychedelic Machine.			
1960s		$1,200	$2,500
1970s		$800	$1,600
Uni-Wah Wah/Volume			
1970s		$800	$125

VanAmps

Amp builder Tim Van Tassel of Golden Valley, Minnesota, also offers a line of reverb effects pedals.

Vesta Fire

Ca.1981-ca.1988. Brand of Japan's Shiino Musical Instrument Corp.

Effects			
1981-1988	Chorus/Flange FLCH	$35	$50
1981-1988	Distortion DST	$35	$50
1981-1988	Flanger	$35	$50
1981-1988	Noise Gate	$25	$40
1981-1988	Stereo Chorus SCH	$35	$50

Vintage Tone Project

Line of guitar effects made by Robert Rush and company in Delmar, New York, starting in 2003. They also built reissues of Dan Armstong's '70s effects from '03 to '06.

VintageFX

2003-present. Effects based on vintage pedals from the '60s and '70s built by Dave Archer in Grand Island, New York.

Visual Sound

1995-2015. Effects pedals designed by Bob Weil and R.G. Keen in Spring Hill, Tennessee and built in China. They changed name to Truetone in '15.

VooDoo Lab

1994-present. Line of effects made by Digital Music Corp. in California.

Analog Chorus			
1997-2012. Based on '76 CE-1.			
1997-2012		$100	$120

MODEL YEAR	FEATURES	EXC. COND. LOW	HIGH
Bosstone			
1994-1999. Based on '60s Jordan Electronics Fuzz.			
1994-1999		$70	$110
Microvibe			
1996-present. Uni-Vibe rotating-speaker simulator.			
1996-2019		$65	$100
Overdrive			
1994-2002. Based on '70s overdrive.			
1994-2002		$55	$65
Superfuzz			
1999-present.			
1999-2019		$75	$90
Tremolo			
1995-present.			
1995-2019		$55	$75

Vox

1954-present. The first Vox product was a volume pedal. Ca. '66, they released the Tone Bender, one of the classic fuzzboxes of all time. A year or so later, they delivered their greatest contribution to the effects world, the first wah-wah pedal. The American arm of Vox (then under Thomas Organ) succumbed in '72. In the U.K., the company was on-again/off-again.

Clyde McCoy Wah-Wah Pedal
Introduced in 1967, reissued in 2001-2008. Clyde's picture on bottom cover.

1967	Clyde's picture	$800	$1,050
1968	No picture	$600	$800
2001-2008	Model V-848	$150	$175

Crybaby Wah
Introduced in 1968. The Thomas Organ Company was heavily involved with Vox from '64 to '72, importing their instruments into the U.S. and designing and assembling products. One product developed in conjunction with Vox was the wah-wah pedal. Both Thomas Organ and JMI, Vox's European distributor, wanted to offer the new effect. The problem was solved by labeling the Thomas Organ wah the Crybaby. The original wahs were built by Jen in Italy, but Thomas later made them in their Chicago, Illinois and Sepulveda, California plants. Thomas Organ retained the marketing rights to Vox until '79, but was not very active with the brand after '72. The Crybaby brand is now offered by Dunlop.

1960s	Jen-made	$200	$250
1970	Sepulveda-made	$125	$175

Double Sound
1970s. Jen-made, Double Sound model name on bottom of pedal, double sound derived from fuzz and wah ability.

1970s		$200	$250

Flanger

1970s		$200	$250

King Wah
1970s. Chrome top, Italian-made.

1970s		$200	$250

Repeat Percussion
Late-1960s. Plug-in module with on-off switch and rate adjustment.

1968		$100	$125

Univox Super-Fuzz U-1095
Kai Hawkins

Voodoo Lab Tremolo

Vox Clyde McCoy Wah
Garrett Tung

EFFECTS

Vox Tone Bender MKIII
Shane Richardson

Whirlwind OC-Bass
Optical Compressor

Xotic Effects Bass RC Booster

MODEL YEAR	FEATURES	EXC. COND. LOW	HIGH
Stereo Fuzz Wah			
1970s		$150	$200
Tone Bender V-828			
1966-1970s. Fuzz box, reissued as the V-829 in '93.			
1966-1968	Mark I, gray case	$550	$750
1969	Mark II, black case	$475	$625
1970s	Mark III	$475	$600
ToneLab Valvetronix			
2003-2019. Multi-effect modeling processor (ToneLab EX or ToneLab ST), 12AX7 tube preamp.			
2003-2019		$400	$425
V-807 Echo-Reverb Unit			
1967. Solidstate, disc echo.			
1967		$275	$375
V-837 Echo Deluxe Tape Echo			
1967. Solidstate, multiple heads.			
1967		$350	$450
V-846 Wah			
1969-1970s. Chrome top, Italian-made.			
1969	Clyde McCoy	$450	$600
1970s		$300	$425
V-847 Wah-Wah			
1992-present. Reissue of the original V-846 Wah.			
1992-2019		$55	$80
Volume Pedal			
1954-late 1960s. Reissued as the V850.			
1960s		$50	$270

Wampler Pedals
2004-present. Brian Wampler began building effects under the brand Indy Guitarist in 2004, and changed the name to Wampler Pedals in 2007. They are built in Greenwood, Indiana.

Warmenfat
2004-present. Pre-amps and guitar effects built in Sacramento, California, by Rainbow Electronics.

Wasabi
2003-2008. Line of guitar effect pedals from Danelectro.

Washburn
Washburn offered a line of effects from around 1983 to ca. '89.

Effects			
1980s	Analog Delay AX:9	$30	$35
1980s	Flanger FX:4	$35	$40
1980s	Phaser PX:8	$40	$45
1980s	Stack in a Box SX:3	$30	$35

Watkins/WEM
1957-present. Watkins Electric Music (WEM) was founded by Charlie Watkins. Their first commercial product was the Watkins Dominator amp in '57, followed by the Copicat Echo in '58.

Copicat Tape Echo
1958-1970s, 1985-present. The Copicat went through several detail changes, subsequently known as the Marks I, II, III, and IV versions. It has been reissued in various forms by Watkins.

MODEL YEAR	FEATURES	EXC. COND. LOW	HIGH
1958-1970s	Solidstate	$525	$1,000
1958-1970s	Tube	$850	$1,100

Way Huge Electronics
1995-1998, 2008-present Way Huge offered a variety of stomp boxes, made in Sherman Oaks, California. Jim Dunlop revived the brand in '08.

WD Music
Since 1978, WD Music has offered a wide line of aftermarket products for guitar players. From '91 to '02, they offered a line of effects that were copies of the original Dan Armstrong color series (refer to Dan Armstrong listing).

Blue Clipper
1991-2002. Fuzz.

1991-2002		$30	$45

Orange Squeezer
1991-2002. Signal compressor.

1991-2002	Light Orange case	$40	$50

Purple Peaker
1991-2002. Mini EQ.

1991-2002		$40	$50

Westbury
1978-ca.1983. Brand imported by Unicord.

Tube Overdrive
1978-1983. 12AX7.

1978-1983		$150	$200

Whirlwind
1976-present. Effects from Michael Laiacona, who helped found MXR, originally made in Rochester, New York. Currently the company offers guitar effects, DI boxes and other music devices built in Greece, New York.

Commander
1980s. Boost and effects loop selector.

1980s		$75	$100

Wilson Effects
2007-present. Guitar effects built by Kevin Wilson in Guilford, Indiana.

WMD (William Mathewson Devices)
2008-present. William Mathewson builds his instrument effects in Denver, Colorado.

Wurlitzer
Wurlitzer offered the Fuzzer Buzzer in the 1960s, which was the same as the Clark Fuzz.

Xotic Effects
2001-present. The roots of Xotic go back to a small garage in the San Fernando Valley of Southern California in 1996, producing and designing bass guitars and bass preamps, soon expanding to build boutique pedals.

MODEL YEAR	FEATURES	EXC. COND. LOW	HIGH

AC Booster
2002-present. Light overdrive with 20db+ of boost and 2-band EQ.
| 2002-2019 | | $75 | $100 |

AC Plus
2007-2018. Stackable 2-channel light overdrive with 3-band EQ and compression.
| 2007-2018 | | $100 | $130 |

AC-COMP
2010-2018. Custom Shop light overdrive with 3 compression modes. Internal DIP switches control level of compression, tonal character, and treble/presence levels.
| 2010-2018 | | $120 | $130 |

Bass BB Preamp
2006-present. Bass overdrive with 2 overlapping EQs and ±15dB boost/cut.
| 2006-2019 | | $130 | $160 |

Bass RC Booster
2006-present. Bass boost with 2-band active EQ and ±15dB boost/cut.
| 2006-2019 | | $50 | $80 |

BB Plus
2008-present. Stackable 2-channel overdrive with 3-band EQ and compression.
| 2008-2019 | | $115 | $130 |

BB Preamp
2005-present. Overdrive with 30dB+ boost and 2-band EQ.
| 2005-2019 | | $80 | $100 |

BBP-COMP
2011-2018. Custom Shop overdrive with 3 compression modes and 2-band EQ.
| 2011-2018 | | $140 | $160 |

BBP-MB
2009-2018. Custom Shop overdrive with 12dB+ mid-treble boost and 2-band EQ.
| 2009-2018 | | $125 | $140 |

EP Booster
2009-present. Mini boost pedal with 20db+ of boost. Internal DIP switches control boost frequencies and EQ.
| 2009-2019 | | $75 | $90 |

RC Booster
2002-2017. Clean boost with 20dB+ of transparent boost and 2-band EQ.
| 2002-2017 | | $50 | $60 |

RC Booster V2
2016-present. Clean boost with 20dB+ transparent boost and 2-band EQ. Added gain channel with gain 2 control knob.
| 2016-2019 | | $75 | $90 |

Robotalk
1998-2009. Envelope filter, random arpeggiator and low-pass filter. Ultra-boutique pedal, made from scratch, in limited quantities.
| 1998-2009 | | $200 | $300 |

Robotalk 2
2009-present. Envelope filter with 2 separate envelope filter channels that can be combined or used individually. Internal input pad controls passive/active signals. Internal DIP switches control frequency settings.
| 2009-2019 | | $125 | $180 |

Robotalk-RI
2011-2018. Custom Shop envelope filter with an enhanced arpeggiator for more wonderfully strange and mesmerizing sounds.
| 2011-2018 | | $150 | $200 |

SL Drive
2013-present. Mini overdrive pedal produces tones from legendary amplifiers, the Super Lead and Super Bass. Internal DIP switches control boost frequencies and EQ settings.
| 2013-2019 | | $65 | $90 |

Soul Driven
2017-present. Boost/overdrive with mid-boost and tone knobs. Internal bass boost DIP switches control up to 6dB+ of boost.
| 2017-2019 | | $130 | $140 |

SP Compressor
2012-present. Mini compressor featuring a wide variety of compressor tones from vintage to subtle to modern, and more. Internal DIP switches control attack.
| 2012-2019 | | $85 | $95 |

Stereo X-Blender
2011-2017. Custom Shop effects looper with 3 parallel effects loops equipped with a transparent buffer amplifier allowing feeding and mixing of effects without signal deterioration.
| 2011-2017 | | $130 | $160 |

X-Blender
2006-present. Series and parallel effects looper with boost switch for 6dB+ volume boost, treble and bass EQ and phase inverter switch. Dry/Wet knob in parallel mode.
| 2006-2019 | | $85 | $140 |

Xotic Wah
2014-present. Wah pedal that features a 20% smaller size, bias, wah-Q, treble, and bass controls, plus internal DIP switches for even more tonal possibilities.
| 2014-2019 | | $175 | $200 |

Yamaha
1946-present. Yamaha has offered effects since at least the early '80s. They also build guitars, basses, amps, and other musical instruments.

Analog Delay E1005
1980s. Free-standing, double-space rack mount-sized, short to long range delays, gray case.
| 1980s | | $160 | $180 |

Yubro
Yubro, of Bellaire, Texas, offered a line of nine effects in the mid- to late-'80s.

Analog Delay AD-800
| 1980s | 300 ms | $75 | $125 |

Stereo Chorus CH-600
| 1980s | | $50 | $75 |

Xotic Effects Robotalk 2

Xotic Effects Soul Driven

Xotic Effects X-Blender

EFFECTS

Z.Vex Effects Box of Rock

Z.Vex Fuzz Factory 7

Z.Vex Super Seek Wah

MODEL YEAR	FEATURES	EXC. COND. LOW	HIGH

Z.Vex Effects

1995-present. Zachary Vex builds his effects in Minneapolis, Minnesota, with some subassembly work done in Michigan. Painters on staff create stock and custom versions of many pedals, which often bring higher prices. Vexter pedals are silkscreened pedals made in Taiwan. U.S. Vexters are manufactured in Taiwan, but engraved in Minnesota. California Mini models are manufactured in California. In 2000-2002, Vex built the solidbody Drip Guitar with an onboard Wah. In 2002, Vex also began building amps.

Basstortion

2011-present. Bass distortion, bright/dark switch.

2011-2019		$95	$130

Box of Metal

2007-present. High-gain distortion, switchable noise gate.

2007-2019		$120	$150

Box of Rock

2005-present. 2-in-1 pedal. Tube amp-type distortion pedal and clean post-gain boost.

2005-2019		$100	$150

Channel 2

2014-present. Mini boost pedal, master volume.

2014-2019		$70	$90

Distortion

2009-present. Tube amp-style distortion, sub contour and gain switches.

2009-2019		$60	$75

Double Rock

2012-present. Dual switchable distortion/boost pedal.

2012-2019		$175	$200

Fat Fuzz Factory

2011-present. Fuzz Factory with additional 3-position mini toggle to select frequency range.

2011-2019		$175	$200

Fuzz Factory

1995-present. Powerful, tweaky, and unique germanium fuzz pedal, with idiosyncratic hand-painted housings. Also available as Vexter and US Vexter models.

1995-2014		$120	$145
1995-2019	Hand-painted	$140	$200

Fuzz Factory 7

2013-2018. Limited edition Fuzz Factory with footswitchable EQ and 9-position rotary frequency selector.

2013-2018		$300	$375

Fuzz Probe

2000-present. Theremin-controlled Fuzz Factory.

2000-2019		$100	$175

Fuzzolo

2014-present. Mini footprint 2-knob silicon fuzz for guitar and bass.

2014-2019		$80	$100

Instant Lo-Fi Junky

2011-present. Filter, compression, and wave shapeable vibrato and blend for chorus effect.

2011-2019		$150	$175

Inventobox

2010-present. Dual pedal chassis for DIY builders or for use with Z.Vex modules.

2010-2019		$150	$200

Jonny Octave

2005-present. Octave pedal.

2005-2019		$140	$185

Lo-Fi Loop Junky

2002-present. Sampler, single 20-second sample with vibrato.

2002-2019		$150	$200

Loop Gate

2012-present. Audio looping mixer with foot switchable noise gate.

2012-2019		$100	$130

Machine

1996-present. Crossover distortion generator.

1996-2019		$150	$200

Mastrotron

2009-present. Silicon fuzz with mini toggle sub contour.

2009-2019		$70	$95

Octane I, II, and III

1995-present. Ring modulator fuzz.

1995-2019		$85	$125

Ooh Wah I and II

2003-2013. 8-step sequencer using wah filters with random sequencing.

2003-2013		$90	$115

MODEL YEAR	FEATURES	EXC. COND. LOW	HIGH
Ringtone and Ringtone TT			
2006-2013. 8-step sequencer using ring modulator.			
2006-2013		$175	$190
Seek Trem I and II			
2006-2013. 8-step sequencer using volume.			
1999-2013		$135	$175
Seek Wah I and II			
2006-2013. 8-step sequencer using wah filters.			
2006-2013		$140	$180
Sonar Tremolo and Stutter			
2012-present. Tremolo with wave shaping, distortion circuit, tap tempo, and auto tempo ramping.			
2012-2019		$175	$190
Super Duper 2-in-1			
2001-present. Dual boost with master volume on 2nd channel.			
2001-2019		$120	$170
Super Hard On			
1996-present. Sparkly clean boost.			
1996-2019		$110	$170
Super Ringtone			
2013-present. 16-step sequencer using ring modulator with MIDI sync, tap tempo, tap tempo sync, and glissando.			
2013-2019		$150	$225
Super Seek Trem			
2013-present. 16-step sequencer using volume with MIDI sync, tap tempo, tap tempo sync, and glissando.			
2013-2019		$150	$195
Super Seek Wah			
2013-present. 16-step sequencer using wah filters with MIDI sync, tap tempo, tap tempo sync, and glissando.			
2013-2019		$150	$195
Tremolo Probe			
2000-present. Theremin-controlled volume.			
2000-2019		$100	$175
Tremorama			
2004-2013. 8-step sequencer using volume with random sequencing.			
2004-2013		$195	$230
Volume Probe			
2000-2002. Theremin-controlled volume using coiled cable for antenna.			
2000-2002		$100	$175

MODEL YEAR	FEATURES	EXC. COND. LOW	HIGH
Wah Probe			
2000-present. Theremin-controlled wah.			
2000-2019		$100	$175
Woolly Mammoth			
1999-present. Silicon fuzz for guitar and bass.			
1999-2019		$200	$290

Zinky

1999-present. Guitar effects built by Bruce Zinky in Flagstaff, Arizona. He also builds amps and has revived the Supro brand on a guitar and amp.

Zoom

Effects line from Samson Technologies Corp. of Syosset, New York.

MODEL YEAR	FEATURES	EXC. COND. LOW	HIGH
503 Amp Simulator			
1998-2000		$25	$40
504 Acoustic Pedal			
1997-2000. Compact multi-effects pedal, 24 effects, tuner, replaced by II version.			
1997-2000		$25	$40
505 Guitar Pedal			
1996-2000. Compact multi-effects pedal, 24 effects, tuner, replaced by II version.			
1996-2000		$30	$40
506 Bass Pedal			
1997-2000. Compact multi-effects bass pedal, 24 effects, tuner, black box, orange panel. Replaced by II version.			
1997-2000		$35	$45
507 Reverb			
1997-2000		$25	$40
1010 Player			
1996-1999. Compact multi-effects pedal board, 16 distortions, 25 effects.			
1996-1999		$40	$75

ZT Amplifiers

2009-present. Effects pedals built in China and offered by Ken Kantor in Berkeley, California. He also imports amps.

Z.Vex Tremolo Probe

Zoom Choir
Jim Schreck

EFFECTS

ZT Amplifiers Extortion

MANDOLINS

MANDOLINS

*1900s American
Conservatory Bowlback*
Imaged by Heritage Auctions, HA.com

Apitius Grand Classic

MODEL YEAR	FEATURES	EXC. COND. LOW	HIGH

Airline

Ca. 1958-1968. Brand for Montgomery Ward. Instruments were built by Kay, Harmony and Valco.

Electric Mandolin (Kay K390)

Early-1960s. In '62 the K390 was advertised as the Kay Professional Electric Mandolin. Venetian shape with sunburst spruce top, curly maple back and sides, tube-style pickup, white 'guard, rope-style celluloid binding.

1962		$375	$500

Mandolin (Lower-End)

1960s. Acoustic, plain features.

1960s		$200	$275

Alvarez

1965-present. An import brand for St. Louis Music, Alvarez currently offers intermediate grade, production, mandolins. They also offer guitars, lap steels and banjos.

Mandolins

1970s-2000s. Classic style mandolin features, round soundhole or f-holes.

1970s	A style	$400	$525
1970s	F style	$450	$575

American Conservatory (Lyon & Healy)

Late-1800s-early-1900s. Mainly catalog sales of guitars and mandolins from the Chicago maker. Marketed as a less expensive alternative to the Lyon & Healy Washburn product line.

Arched Back Mandolin

1910s. Flat back with a mild arch, standard appointments, nothing fancy.

1910s		$200	$400

Bowl Back Mandolin

1917. Bowl back style, 14 ribs, Brazilian.

1917		$100	$350

Bowl Back Mandolin Style G2603

Early-1900s. Bowl back-style, 28 rosewood ribs (generally more ribs and use of rosewood ribs versus mahogany indicates higher quality), color corded soundhole and edge inlay, inlaid tortoise shell celluloid guard plate underneath strings and below the soundhole, bent top, butterfly headstock inlay.

1917		$200	$550

Bowl Back Mandolin Style G2604

Early-1900s. Bowl back-style, 42 rosewood ribs (generally more ribs indicated higher quality), extra fancy color corded soundhole and edge inlay around, extra fancy inlaid tortoise shell celluloid guard plate underneath strings and below the soundhole, bent top, butterfly headstock inlay.

1917		$350	$650

Apitius

1976-present. Luthier Oliver Apitius builds his premium and presentation grade, production/custom, mandolins in Shelburne, Ontario.

Applause

1994-present. Applause offered intermediate grade, production, Ovation-styled, imported mandolins. They also offer ukes.

Mandolin

1990s		$100	$200

Aria/Aria Pro II

1956-present. Intermediate grade, production, acoustic and electric mandolins from Aria/Aria Pro II, which added Japanese and Korean mandolins to their line in '76.

AM200 Mandolin

1994-2012. Pear-shaped A body, plywood.

1994-2012		$175	$250

AM400 Mandolin

1994-2012. F-style, plywood.

1994-2012		$275	$375

AM600 Mandolin

1994-2008. F-style, solid wood.

1994-2008		$325	$425

PM750 Mandolin

1976-ca. 1982. F-style Loar copy, maple plywood body, sunburst.

1976-1982		$425	$550

Bacon & Day

Established in 1921 by David Day and Paul Bacon, primarily known for fine quality tenor and plectrum banjos in the '20s and '30s.

Mandolin Banjo Orchestra

1920s. Mandolin neck and banjo body with open back, headstock with Bacon logo.

1920s		$300	$400

Professional Mandolin

1920s. Figured birch back and sides, spruce top, oval sound hole, 2-point flat back.

1920s		$1,300	$1,700

Senorita Banjo Mandolin

1930s		$700	$900

Silverbell #1 Banjo Mandolin

1920s. Fancy appointments, closed-back resonator.

1920s		$750	$1,000

Bauer (George)

1894-1911. Luthier George Bauer built guitars and mandolins in Philadelphia, Pennsylvania. He also built instruments with Samuel S. Stewart (S.S. Stewart).

Acme Professional Bowl Mandolin

1894-1911. Bowl back, 29 ribs, Brazilian.

1894-1911	Fancy	$400	$600
1894-1911	Mid-level	$300	$400
1894-1911	Plain	$100	$300

Beltone

1920s-1930s. Acoustic and resonator mandolins and banjo-mandolins made by others for New York City distributor Perlberg & Halpin. Martin did make a small number of instruments for Beltone, but most were student-grade models most likely made by one of the big Chicago builders. They also made guitars.

MODEL YEAR	FEATURES	EXC. COND. LOW	HIGH

Resonator Mandolin
1930s. F-hole top, banjo-style resonator back.

1930s		$350	$500

Bohmann
1878-ca.1926. Established by Czechoslavakian-born Joseph Bohmann in Chicago, Illinois.

Bowl Mandolin
1890-1900. Spruce top, marquetry trimmed, inlay, pearl.

1890-1900	Fancy	$600	$1,200
1890-1900	Mid-level	$400	$600
1890-1900	Plain	$100	$400

Brandt
Early 1900s. John Brandt started making mandolin-family instruments in Chicago, Illinois around 1898.

Mandola
1900s. Spruce top, rosewood body, scroll headstock, pearl and abalone fretboard binding.

1900s		$600	$1,200

Presentation Mandolin
1900s. Spruce top, tortoise shell-bound.

1900s		$400	$1,000

Breedlove
1990-present. Breedlove started building professional and premium grade, mandolins in Bend, Oregon in 1997. In '15, they ceased U.S. mando production, but continued with their import line. They also produce guitars, basses, laps and ukes.

Alpine Mandolin
2000s-2013. Master Class series, O-style body, spruce/maple.

2000s-2013		$1,750	$2,250

K-5 Mandolin
1990s. Asymmetric carved top, maple body.

1990s		$1,450	$1,900

Olympic Mandolin
1990s. Solid spruce top, teardrop-shaped, oval soundhole, highly flamed maple back, sunburst.

1990s		$1,100	$1,450

Quartz OF/OO Mandolin
2000s. Basic A-style body with f-holes.

2000s		$825	$1,075

Bruno and Sons
Established in 1834 by Charles Bruno, primarily as a distributor, Bruno and Sons marketed a variety of brands, including their own. In the '60s or '70s, a Japanese-made solidbody electric mandolin was sold under the Bruno name.

Banjo Mandolin
1920s. Open back, 10" model.

1920s		$100	$300

Bowl Back Mandolin
1890s-1920s. Brazilian rosewood, spruce, rosewood ribs.

1920s	Less fancy	$100	$400
1920s	More fancy	$350	$600

MODEL YEAR	FEATURES	EXC. COND. LOW	HIGH

Calace
1825-present. Nicola Calace started The Calace Liuteria lute-making workshop in 1825 on the island of Procida, which is near Naples. The business is now in Naples and still in the family.

Lyre/Harp-Style Mandolin
Late-1800s-early-1900s. Lyre/harp-style, 8 strings, round soundhole, slightly bent top. Condition is important for these older instruments and the price noted is for a fully functional, original or pro-restored example.

1900		$600	$1,200

Carvin
1946-present. Carvin offered solidbody electric mandolins from around '56 to the late '60s, when they switched to a traditional pear-shaped electric/acoustic. They also offer guitars, basses and amps.

MB Mandolin
1956-1968. Solidbody, 1 pickup, single-cut Les Paul shape until '64, double-cut Jazzmaster/Strat shape after. Models include the #1-MB and the #2-MB, with different pickups.

1950s		$1,200	$1,700

Cole
1890-1919. After leaving Fairbanks & Cole in 1890, W.A. Cole started his own line. He also made guitars and banjos.

Imperial G Bowl Back Mandolin
1905-1910. 27 ribs.

1905-1910		$700	$1,000

Collings
1986-present. Professional and premium grade, production/custom, mandolins built in Austin, Texas. Collings added mandolins to their line in '99. They also build guitars and ukuleles.

MF Mandolin
1999-present. F-style, carved top and back.

1999-2019		$3,000	$4,000

MF-5 Deluxe Mandolin
2005. Limited production, varnish finish, hand engraved nickel tailpiece unique to each instrument.

2005		$7,700	$10,000

MF-5V Mandolin
2007. Carved Adirondack spruce top, highly flamed maple body.

2007		$6,000	$8,000

MT Mandolin
1999-present. A-style, 2 f-holes, carved top and back, matte finish, tortoise-bound top.

1999-2019		$2,025	$2,650

MT-2 Mandolin
1999-present. MT with high gloss finish, ivoroid body, neck and headstock binding.

1999-2019		$2,900	$3,800

MT-2V Mandolin
2009-present. Like MT-2, but with oil-based varnish finish and ivoroid-bound ebony 'guard.

2009-2019		$3,200	$4,200

Breedlove KO

Collings MT

MANDOLINS

MANDOLINS

1966 Epiphone Venetian
Kerry Brown

Epiphone MM-50

MODEL		EXC. COND.	
YEAR	FEATURES	LOW	HIGH

Crestwood
1970s. Copy models imported by La Playa Distributing Company of Detroit.
Mandolin
1970s. Includes models 3039 (electric A-style), 3041 (bowl back-style, flower 'guard), 3043 (bowl back-style, plain 'guard), 71820 (A-style), and 71821 (F-style).

1970s		$150	$200

Cromwell
1935-1939. Private branded instruments made by Gibson at their Parsons Street factory in Kalamazoo, Michigan. Distributed by a variety of mail order companies such as Continental, Grossman, and Richter & Phillips.
GM-2 Mandolin
1935-1939. Spruce top, mahogany back and sides, similar to KM-11.

1935-1939		$425	$550

GM-4 Mandolin
1935-1939. Style A, f-holes, solid wood arched top, mahogany back and sides, block capital letter Cromwell headstock logo, dot markers, elevated 'guard, sunburst.

1935-1939		$500	$650

Dayton
1910-late 1930s. Mandolins built by luthier Charles B. Rauch in Dayton, Ohio. He also built banjos, violins, guitars and banjo-ukuleles.
Style B Mandolin

1911		$1,400	$1,800

DeLucia, Vincenzo
1910s-1920s. Luthier Vincenzo DeLucia built mandolins in Philadelphia, Pennsylvania.
Mandolin
Early-1900s. High quality material, rosewood body, fine ornamentation.

1910s		$950	$1,250

Ditson
Mandolins made for the Oliver Ditson Company of Boston, an instrument dealer and music publisher. Turn of the century and early-1900s models were bowl back-style with the Ditson label. The '20s Ditson Style A flat back mandolins were made by Martin. Models were also made by Lyon & Healy of Boston, often with a Ditson Empire label.
Mandola
1920. Bowl back.

1920		$900	$1,200

Style A Mandolin
1920s. Style A flat back made by Martin, mahogany sides and back, plain ornamentation.

1920s		$900	$1,200

Style B Mandolin
Style B flat back made by Martin, Adirondack top, Brazilian rosewood sides and back, herringbone soundhole trim.

1918		$1,700	$2,200

MODEL		EXC. COND.	
YEAR	FEATURES	LOW	HIGH

Victory Mandolin
1890s. Brazilian rib bowl back with fancy inlays.

1890s		$500	$800

Dobro
1929-1942, 1954-2019. Dobro offered mandolins throughout their early era and from the '60s to the mid-'90s.
Mandolin
1930s-1960s. Resonator on wood body.

1930s-60s		$825	$1,100

Dudenbostel
1989-present. Luthier Lynn Dudenbostel builds his limited production, premium and presentation grade, custom, mandolins in Knoxville, Tennessee. He started with guitars and added mandolins in '96.
F-5 Mandolin
1996-2012. Loar-style, about 30 made.

1996-2012		$18,000	$24,000

Duff Mandolins
1982-present. Premium and presentation grade, custom/production, mandolin family instruments built by luthier Paul Duff in Palmyra, Western Australia.
F-5 (Loar) Mandolin

1990-2000s Adirondack		$5,500	$7,100

H-5 Mandola

2000-2010s Adirondack		$6,100	$7,900

EKO
1961-1985, 2000-present. The Italian-made EKOs were imported by LoDuca Brothers of Milwaukee. The brand was revived around 2000, but does not currently include mandolins.
Baritone Mandolin
1960s. Baritone mandolin with ornate inlays.

1960s		$375	$500

Octave Mandolin
1960s. Octave mandolin with ornate inlays.

1960s		$375	$500

Epiphone
1928-present. Intermediate grade, production, acoustic mandolins. Epiphone has offered several mandolin-family models over the years. Those from the '30s to the '60s were U.S.-made, the later models imported.
Adelphi Mandolin
1932-1948. A-style body, maple back and sides, f-holes, single-bound top and back.

1932-1948		$800	$1,050

Mandobird VIII Mandolin
2004-2012. Reverse Firebird-style body with mandolin neck, electric, various colors.

2004-2012		$165	$210

MM Series Mandolin
1979-present. Imported A and F styles.

1979-1985	MM70, F-style		$400	$550
1979-2013	MM50, F-style		$300	$400

MODEL YEAR	FEATURES	EXC. COND. LOW	HIGH
1980-2019	MM30, A-style	$120	$150
1998-2013	MM20, A-style	$90	$125

Strand Mandolin
1932-1958. Walnut back and sides, f-holes, multi-bound, sunburst.

1944-1947		$875	$1,150

Venetian Electric Mandolin
1961-1970. Gibson-made, pear-shaped body, 4 pole P-90 'dog-ear' mounted pickup, volume and tone knobs, dot markers, sunburst finish.

1961-1970		$1,300	$1,675

Windsor Special Mandolin
1936-1949. Scroll body, f-holes, slot-block inlays.

1940s	Rare, high-end	$9,800	$12,700

Zephyr Mandolin
1939-1958. A-style, electric, f-holes, maple body, 1 pickup, slotted block inlay.

1950s		$575	$750

Esquire
1930s. Student level instruments with painted Esquire logo and painted wood grain.

Mandolin
1930s. Laminate A-style wood body, sunburst.

1930s		$200	$300

Fairbanks
1875-1922. Primarily known for banjos, Fairbanks also offered banjo mandolins when owned by Vega.

Little Wonder Banjo Mandolin
1920s. Banjo body, mando neck, dot inlays.

1921		$425	$550

Style K Banjo Mandolin
1920s. Banjo body, mando neck, dot inlays.

1920		$375	$500

Fender
1946-present. Intermediate grade, production, acoustic and acoustic/electric mandolins. Fender also offered an electric mandolin for 20 years.

FM Series Mandolin
2001-2017. Made in Korea, acoustic and acoustic-electric, models include 52E (acou-elec, A-style), 53S (acoustic, A-style), 60E (5 string, 2 pu) and 61SE (8-string, 1 pu) (both acou-elec, double-cut, block-end 'board), 62SE (acou-elec, double-cut, extended 'board), 63S (acoustic, F-style), 63SE (acou-elec, F-style), 100 (acoustic, A-style).

2001-2002	FM-60E/61SE	$335	$435
2001-2007	FM-62SE/62SCE	$335	$435
2001-2014	FM-52E	$120	$155
2001-2017	FM-53S	$145	$190
2001-2017	FM-63S	$275	$360
2011-2017	FM-63SE/63SCE	$335	$435
2013-2017	FM-100	$75	$100

Mandolin
1956-1976. Electric solidbody, often referred to as the Mandocaster by collectors.

1956-1957	Blond	$2,475	$3,200
1958-1959	Sunburst	$2,100	$2,750

MODEL YEAR	FEATURES	EXC. COND. LOW	HIGH
1960-1965	Sunburst	$1,825	$2,375
1966-1976	Sunburst	$1,650	$2,175

Flatiron
1977-2003, 2006-2009. Gibson purchased Flatiron in 1987. Production was in Bozeman, Montana until the end of '96, when Gibson closed the Flatiron mandolin workshop and moved mandolin assembly to Nashville, Tennessee. General production tapered off after the move and Flatirons were available on a special order basis for a time. The brand was revived in '06 on an import model sold through Epiphone.

A Style Mandolins
Includes A style Performer series (1990-'95, maple back & sides, mahogany neck, ebony board, top binding, sunburst) and Festival series (1988-'95, same, in cherry finish and with no binding).

1988-1995	Festival	$1,000	$1,350
1990-1995	Performer	$1,100	$1,450

A-2 Mandolin

1977-1987	Early, no truss rod	$2,500	$3,300

A-5 Mandolin
Teardrop shape, f-holes, figured maple body and neck, carved spruce top, X-bracing, unbound ebony 'board, nickel hardware, fleur-de-lis headstock inlay.

1987-1994	Gibson Montana	$1,275	$1,625
1996-2003		$1,275	$1,625

A-5 1 Mandolin
Carved top and back, bound body, dot inlays, The Flatiron headstock inlay.

1983-1985	Pre-Gibson	$2,600	$3,400

A-5 2 Mandolin
Carved top and back, bound body, neck, headstock and pickguard, dot inlays, modified fern headstock inlay.

1983-1985	Pre-Gibson	$3,150	$4,000

A-5 Artist Mandolin
A-5 with highly figured maple body and neck, bound ebony headstock, gold hardware, fern headstock inlay.

1987-1990	Gibson Montana	$2,200	$2,900
1996-2003		$1,700	$2,300

A-5 Junior Mandolin
As A-5 but with tone bar bracing, mahogany neck, The Flatiron headstock inlay.

1987-1990	Gibson Montana	$900	$1,150
1996-2003		$900	$1,150

Cadet Mandolin
Flat-top, teardrop body, spruce top, maple body, rosewood 'board, nickel hardware.

1990-1996		$450	$600

F Style Mandolin
Includes F style Performer series (1990-'95, maple back & sides and neck, ebony board, fern/banner headstock inlay, top and back of body and headstock bound, sunburst top) and Festival series (1988-'95, same, but without headstock or back binding).

1988-1995	Festival	$2,400	$3,100
1990-1995	Performer	$2,500	$3,200
2001	Festival, Gibson Montana	$2,400	$3,100

F-2 Mandolin

1977-1987	Early, no truss rod	$5,000	$6,500

1964 Fender Mandocaster
Reess Sutherland

1993 Flatiron A-5
Steven Squire

MANDOLINS

Ca. 1900 A. Galiano Bowl Back
William Ritter, courtesy of George Gruhn.

MANDOLINS

1924 Gibson A
David Stone

MODEL YEAR	FEATURES	EXC. COND. LOW	HIGH
F-5 Mandolin			
F-style body, f-holes, flamed maple body and neck, carved spruce top, tone bar bracing, bound ebony 'board and headstock, nickel hardware, flower pot headstock inlay, cherry finish.			
1987-1990	Gibson Montana	$3,100	$4,100
F-5 Artist Mandolin			
F-5 but with X-braces, bound ebony 'board, gold hardware, fern headstock inlay, and sunburst.			
1984-1985	Pre-Gibson	$3,700	$4,900
1987-1995	Gibson Montana	$3,500	$4,500
1996-2003	Modified fern	$3,500	$4,500
Model 1 Mandola			
Model 1 features.			
1977-1987	Pre-Gibson	$725	$950
1983-1995	Gibson Montana	$575	$750
Model 1 Mandolin			
Oval shape, spruce top, maple body, rosewood 'board, walnut headstock veneer.			
1977-1987	Pre-Gibson	$725	$950
1988-1995	Gibson Montana	$575	$750
Model 2 Mandola			
Model 2 features, birdseye maple (MB) or curly maple (MC) body.			
1977-1987	Pre-Gibson	$800	$1,050
1988-1995	Gibson Montana	$700	$950
Model 2 Mandolin			
Like Model 1, but with curly maple (MC) or birdseye maple (MB) back and sides, ebony 'board, rosewood headstock veneer.			
1977-1987	Pre-Gibson	$700	$900
1977-1995	Flamed koa back/sides	$750	$950
1988-1995	Gibson Montana	$650	$825
Model 3 Octave Mandolin			
Model 2 features, birdseye maple (MB) or curly maple (MC) body.			
1977-1987	Pre-Gibson	$800	$1,050
1988-1995	Gibson Montana	$700	$950

Framus

1946-1977, 1996-present. Founded in Erlangen, Germany by Fred Wilfer. In the '60s, Framus instruments were imported into the U.S. by Philadelphia Music Company. They offered acoustic and electric mandolins. The brand was revived in '96.

12-String Mandolin

1960s		$400	$525

Freshwater

1992-2011. Luthier Dave Freshwater and family built mandolin family instruments in Beauly, Inverness, Scotland. They also built bouzoukis, dulcimers and harps.

Galiano/A. Galiano

New Yorkers Antonio Cerrito and Raphael Ciani offered instruments built by them and others under the Galiano brand during the early 1900s.

MODEL YEAR	FEATURES	EXC. COND. LOW	HIGH
Mandolin			
Bowl back, some fancy appointments.			
1920s		$300	$400

Gaylord

1940s. Private brand made by Harmony, painted Gaylord logo on headstock.

Artistic A Mandolin

1940s	Painted logo	$170	$225

Gibson

1890s (1902)-present. Orville Gibson created the violin-based mandolin body-style that replaced the bowl back-type. Currently Gibson offers professional, premium and presentation grade, production/custom, mandolins.

Special Designations:

Snakehead headstock: 1922-1927 with production possible for a few months plus or minus.

Lloyd Loar era: Mid-1922-late 1924 with production possible for a few months plus or minus.

Mandolin (Orville Gibson)

1890s-1902. Mandolin models built during Orville Gibson era, before he sold out to others in 1902, covering a range of features and levels of appointments.

1890s-1902	Less rare, plain	$2,500	$6,100
1980s-1902	Rare, fancy	$20,000	$27,000

A Mandolin

1902-1933. Oval soundhole, snakehead headstock '22-27, Loar era mid-'22-late-'24.

1902-1918	Orange	$1,050	$1,400
1918-1921	Brown	$1,050	$1,400
1922-1924	Loar era	$2,100	$2,700
1925-1933		$1,900	$2,500

A-0 Mandolin

1927-1933. Replaces A Jr., oval soundhole, dot inlay, brown finish.

1927-1933		$1,200	$1,600

A-00 Mandolin

1933-1943. F-hole, dot inlay, carved bound top.

1933-1943	Sunburst	$1,200	$1,600

A-1 Mandolin

1902-1918, 1922-1927, 1933-1943. Snakehead headstock '23-'27.

1902-1918	Orange	$1,250	$1,600
1922-1924	Loar era	$2,300	$3,000
1925-1927	Black	$1,800	$2,300
1927	Not snaked	$1,800	$2,300
1927	Snaked	$1,800	$2,300
1929		$1,800	$2,300
1932	Re-intro, oval	$1,800	$2,300
1933-1943	Sunburst, f-holes	$1,200	$1,600

A-2/A-2Z Mandolin

1902-1908, 1918-1928. A-2Z '22-'27. Renamed A-2 '27-'28. Snakehead headstock '23-'27. Lloyd Loar era mid-'22-late-'24.

1902-1908	Orange	$1,200	$1,600
1918-1921	Brown	$1,200	$1,600
1922-1924	Loar Era	$3,700	$4,800

MODEL YEAR	FEATURES	EXC. COND. LOW	HIGH
1923-1924	Loar era, extra binding	$3,700	$4,800
1925-1928		$1,600	$2,100

A-3 Mandolin

1902-1922. Oval soundhole, single-bound body, dot inlay.

1902-1917	Orange	$1,700	$2,200
1918-1922	Ivory	$1,700	$2,200

A-4 Mandolin

1902-1935. Oval soundhole, single-bound body, dot inlay, snakehead '23-'27.

1902-1917	Various colors	$1,800	$2,400
1918-1921	Dark mahogany	$1,800	$2,400
1922-1924	Loar era	$4,600	$6,000
1925-1935	Various colors	$2,100	$2,800

A-5 Mandolin

1957-1979. Oval soundhole, maple back and sides, dot inlay, scroll headstock, sunburst. Name now used on extended neck version.

1957-1964		$900	$1,200
1965-1969		$900	$1,200
1970-1979		$825	$1,100

A-5G Mandolin

1988-1996. Less ornate version of the A-5 L, abalone fleur-de-lis headstock inlay.

1988-1996		$825	$1,100

A-5L/A-5 Mandolin

1988-2013. Extended neck, raised 'board, flowerpot headstock inlay, curly maple and spruce, sunburst, based on custom-made 1923 Loar A-5. L has been dropped from name.

1988-2013		$1,800	$2,400

A-9 Mandolin

2002-2013. Spruce top, maple back and sides, black bound top, satin brown finish.

2002-2013		$900	$1,200

A-12 Mandolin

1970-1979. F-holes, long neck, dot inlay, fleur-de-lis inlay, sunburst.

1970-1979		$825	$1,100

A-40 Mandolin

1948-1970. F-holes, bound top, dot inlay, natural or sunburst.

1948-1949		$1,050	$1,375
1950-1959		$1,000	$1,300
1960-1964		$850	$1,125
1965-1970		$800	$1,050

A-50 Mandolin

1933-1971. A-style oval bound body, f-holes, sunburst.

1933	Oval soundhole	$1,150	$1,500
1934-1941	Larger 1125" body	$1,150	$1,500
1942-1949	Smaller 10" body	$1,000	$1,300
1950-1959		$950	$1,250
1960-1964		$850	$1,150
1965-1971		$825	$1,075

A-75 Mandolin

1934-1936. F-holes, raised fingerboard, bound top and back.

1934-1936		$1,600	$2,100

A-C Century Mandolin

1933-1934, 1936-1937. A body, built to commemorate the 1933-1934 Century of Progress Exhibition in Chicago, pearloid 'board.

1933-1937		$2,700	$3,500

A-Junior Mandolin

1920-1927. The Junior was the entry level mandolin for Gibson, but like most entry level Gibsons (re: Les Paul Junior), they were an excellent product. Oval soundhole, dot markers, plain tuner buttons. Becomes A-0 in '27.

1920-1927	Sheraton Brown	$1,200	$1,600

AN-Custom (Army-Navy) Mandolin

Mid-1990s. Made in Bozeman, Montana, round teardrop shape, flat spruce top, flat maple back, maple rims, Gibson script logo on headstock.

1995		$850	$1,150

Army and Navy Special Style DY/Army-Navy Mandolin

1918-1922. Lower-end, flat top and back, round soundhole, no logo, round label with model name, brown stain. Reintroduced as Army-Navy (AN Custom) '88-'96.

1918-1922		$525	$700

C-1 Mandolin

1932. Flat top, mahogany back and sides, oval soundhole, natural, painted on 'guard, a '32 version of the Army and Navy Special. This model was private branded for Kel Kroydon in the early-'30s.

1932		$525	$700

CB-3 Mando-Cello (Cello Banjo)

1930s. TB-3 Mastertone rim, 4 strings.

1930s		$2,800	$3,700

D "The Alrite" Mandolin

1917. Round body style, round soundhole, The Alrite on inside label, colored wood on top binding and around center hole.

1917		$625	$825

EM-100/EM-125 Mandolin

1938-1943. Initially called EM-100, renamed EM-125 in '41-'43. Style A (pear-shape) archtop body, 1 blade pickup, 2 knobs on either side of bridge, dot markers, tortoise 'guard, sunburst.

1938-1940	EM-100	$975	$1,275
1941-1943	EM-125	$975	$1,275

EM-150 Mandolin

1936-1971. Electric, A-00 body, 1 Charlie Christian pickup early on, 1 P-90 later, bound body, sunburst.

1936-1940	Charlie Christian pickup	$2,050	$2,650
1941-1949	Rectangular pickup	$1,100	$1,400
1949-1964	P-90 pickup	$1,100	$1,400
1965-1971	P-90 pickup	$900	$1,200

EM-200/Florentine Mandolin

1954-1971. Electric solidbody, 1 pickup, gold-plated hardware, 2 control knobs, dot markers, sunburst. Called the EM-200 in '60 and '61.

1954-1960	Florentine	$2,000	$2,600
1960-1961	Renamed EM-200	$2,000	$2,600
1962-1965	Renamed Florentine	$2,000	$2,600
1966-1971	Florentine	$1,700	$2,200

1920 Gibson A-4
Craig Brody

1935 Gibson A-C Century
John C. Ellig

MANDOLINS

1924 Gibson F-4

Bob Moreland

1924 Gibson F-5

Laurence Wexer

MANDOLINS

F Mandolin

1900-1903. 1900 model has O.H. Gibson Kalamazoo label, 3-point unbound body, early Gibson F-style, historically important design, inlaid star and crescent headstock. 1903 model is 3-point F-style, bound top rope-style, fancy inlay below-the-string guard, inlaid star and crescent headstock, large dot markers, black finish. Early F-style mandolin ornamentation can vary and values will vary accordingly.

1900	1900, signed by Orville	$4,000	$25,000
1900	1900, unsigned	$3,000	$20,000
1901-1902		$2,000	$13,000
1903		$1,800	$12,000

Bill Monroe Model F Mandolin

1991-1995. Limited run of 200, sunburst.

1991-1995	Lacquer	$7,800	$10,200
1991-1995	Varnish	$7,800	$10,200

Doyle Lawson Signature F Mandolin

2003-2018. Artist Series, F-5 style, carved spruce top, figured maple sides and back, sunburst finish.

2003-2018		$5,000	$6,600

F-2 Mandolin

1902-1934. Oval soundhole, pearl inlay, star and crescent inlay on peghead.

1902-1909	3-point	$2,700	$3,500
1910-1917	2-point	$2,700	$3,500
1918-1921	2-point	$2,500	$3,300
1922-1924	Loar era	$3,800	$4,900
1925-1934		$3,100	$4,000

F-3 Mandolin

1902-1908. Three-point body, oval soundhole, scroll peghead, pearl inlayed 'guard, limited production model, black top with red back and sides.

1902-1908		$3,100	$4,000

F-4 Mandolin

1902-1943. Oval soundhole, rope pattern binding, various colors.

1902-1909	3-point	$4,600	$6,100
1910-1921	2-point	$4,600	$6,100
1922-1924	Loar era	$5,300	$6,950
1925-1943		$3,500	$4,500

F-5 Mandolin

1922-1943; 1949-1980. F-holes, triple-bound body and 'guard. The '20s Lloyd Loar era F-5s are extremely valuable. Reintroduced in '49 with single-bound body, redesigned in '70. The Loar era F-5 market is very specialized to the point that individual instrument valuations can vary based upon the actual sound of the particular instrument. Valuations should be considered on a case-by-case basis.

1922	Loar no virzi	$82,000	$114,000
1923	Loar Apr 12, 1923	$86,000	$120,000
1923	Loar Feb 8, 1923	$86,000	$120,000
1923	Loar Jul 9, 1923, side bound	$94,000	$130,000
1923	Loar non-side bound	$82,000	$114,000
1924	Late-1924, unsigned	$58,000	$81,000
1924	Loar Feb 18, 1924	$86,000	$120,000
1924	Loar Mar 31, 1924	$86,000	$120,000

1924	Loar no virzi	$83,000	$115,000
1924	Loar with virzi	$73,000	$102,000
1925-1929	Fern, Master Model	$40,000	$56,000
1928-1929	Fern, not Master Model	$32,000	$45,000
1930-1931	Fern peghead inlay	$28,000	$39,000
1932-1935	Fern peghead inlay	$25,000	$35,000
1936-1937	Fern peghead inlay	$18,000	$25,000
1938-1940		$18,000	$25,000
1940-1943	Fleur-de-lis peghead inlay	$16,000	$22,000
1949	Flower pot, mahogany neck	$7,000	$9,300
1950-1953	Flower pot, maple neck	$5,400	$7,200
1954	Flower pot peghead inlay	$5,400	$7,200
1955-1956	Flower pot peghead inlay	$5,300	$7,000
1957-1959	Flower pot peghead inlay	$4,300	$5,700
1960-1965		$3,900	$5,200
1966-1969	Sunburst	$3,200	$4,200
1970-1980	Sunburst	$2,900	$3,800

F-5 CMS Mandolin

2016. Flamed maple back and sides, aged hand-carved spruce top.

2016		$4,900	$6,500

F-5 Distressed Master Model Mandolin

2004-2009. Aged finish and hardware.

2004-2009		$12,000	$15,500

F-5 Fern Mandolin

2003-2010. Custom Shop model.

2003-2010		$5,000	$6,600

F-5 Master Model Mandolin

2002-2018. F-holes, triple-bound body and guard, red spruce top, maple back and sides, flowerpot inlay.

2002-2018		$10,100	$13,500

F-5G/F-5G Deluxe Mandolin

1997-2018. Two-point style F, Deluxe has a slightly wider neck profile.

1997-2018		$3,000	$4,000

F-5L/F-5L "The Fern" Mandolin

1978-2018. Reissue of Loar F-5, gold hardware, fern headstock inlay (flowerpot inlay with silver hardware also offered for '88-'91), sunburst.

1978-1984	Kalamazoo-made	$4,800	$6,200
1984-1999		$4,800	$6,200
2000-2018		$3,900	$5,100

F-5V Mandolin

1990s-2000s. Based on Lloyd Loar's original F-5s of 1922-24, varnish Cremona Brown sunburst finish.

1990-2000s		$5,675	$7,375

F-5X Mandolin

1996. F-5 Fern model, X-braced.

1996		$4,150	$5,400

MODEL YEAR	FEATURES	EXC. COND. LOW	HIGH

Adam Steffey F-5 Mandolin
2002-2003. Only 50 offered, signature logo on truss rod cover.

2002-2003		$4,600	$6,100

Bella Voce F-5 Mandolin
1989. Custom Shop master-built model, high-end materials and construction, engraved tailpiece with Bella Voce F-5, sunburst.

1989		$5,700	$7,400

Ricky Skaggs Distressed F-5 Master Model Mandolin
2007-2008. Distressed Master Model (DMM), limited to 30, hand-carved red spruce top, hand-carved Eastern flamed maple back, sides and neck.

2007-2008		$14,000	$18,600

Sam Bush Signature F-5 Mandolin
2000-2018. Artist Series model, carved spruce top, gold hardware, built at Opry Mill plant in Nashville.

2000-2018		$4,325	$5,700

Wayne Benson Signature F-5 Mandolin
2003-2006. Limited edition of 50, solid spruce top, figured maple back, sides and neck, gold hardware, vintage red satin.

2003-2006		$4,500	$5,850

F-7 Mandolin
1934-1940. F-holes, single-bound body, neck and 'guard, short neck, fleur-de-lis peghead inlay, sunburst.

1934-1937		$6,200	$8,000

F-9 Mandolin
2002-2018. F-5 style, carved spruce top, no inlays, black bound body.

2002-2018		$1,700	$2,200

F-10 Mandolin
1934-1936. Slight upgrade of the '34 F-7 with extended 'board and upgraded inlay, black finish.

1934-1936		$9,900	$12,900

F-12 Mandolin
1934-1937, 1948-1980. F-holes, bound body and neck, scroll inlay, raised 'board until '37, 'board flush with top '48-on, sunburst.

1934-1937		$7,575	$9,850
1948-1959		$2,900	$3,900
1960-1964		$2,800	$3,700
1965-1969		$2,250	$3,000
1970-1980		$2,150	$2,800

H-1 Mandola
1902-1936. Has same features as A-1 mandolin, but without snakehead headstock.

1902-1908	Orange	$1,350	$1,800
1918-1921	Brown	$1,700	$2,350
1922-1924	Loar era	$2,600	$3,400
1925-1928		$2,350	$3,050

H-1E Mandola
Late-1930s. Limited number built, electric with built-in adjustable bar pickup, sunburst.

1938		$2,900	$3,900

H-2 Mandola
1902-1922. Has same features as A-4 mandolin.

1902-1917	Various colors	$2,400	$3,200
1918-1922	Dark Mahogany	$2,900	$3,800

H-4 Mandola
1910-1940. Same features as F-4 mandolin.

1910-1921		$6,000	$7,800
1922-1924	Loar era	$6,900	$9,000
1925-1940		$5,900	$7,700

H-5 Mandola
1923-1929 (available by special order 1929-1936), 1990-1991. Same features as the high-end F-5 Mandolin. This is a very specialized market and instruments should be evaluated on a case-by-case basis.

1923-1924	Loar era	$54,000	$72,000
1990-1991	Limited production	$4,000	$5,300

J Mando Bass
1912-1931. Large 24" wide A-style body, 4 strings, extension endpin for upright bass-style playing, optional colors available.

1912-1917	Sunburst	$4,200	$5,500
1918-1922	Brown	$4,200	$5,500
1923-1931	Black	$4,200	$5,500

K-1 Mandocello
1902-1943. Same features as H-1 mandola, off & on production, special order available.

1902-1908	Orange	$2,800	$3,700
1918-1921	Brown	$2,800	$3,700
1922-1924	Loar era	$3,400	$4,500
1925-1943		$3,400	$4,500

K-2 Mandocello
1902-1922. Same features as A-4, black or red mahogany..

1902-1917		$4,000	$5,300

K-4 Mandocello
1912-1929 (offered as special order post-1929). Same features as F-4 mandolin, sunburst.

1912-1921		$7,200	$9,500
1922-1924	Loar era	$12,500	$16,500
1925-1929		$7,500	$9,800

M-6 (Octave Guitar)
2002-2006. A-style mandolin body, short-scale 6-string guitar neck.

2002-2006		$1,075	$1,400

MB-00 Mandolin Banjo
1932-1942.

1939		$750	$975

MB-1 Mandolin Banjo
1922-1923, 1925-1937.

1922-1923	Trap door	$500	$650
1925-1937		$675	$875

MB-2 Mandolin Banjo
1920-1923, 1926-1937.

1920-1923	Trap-door	$525	$700
1926-1937		$750	$975

MB-3 Mandolin Banjo
1923-1939.

1923-1924	Trap-door	$750	$975
1925-1939		$1,625	$2,100

MB-4 Mandolin Banjo
1923-1932. Fleur-de-lis inlay.

1923-1924	Trap-door	$800	$1,050
1925-1932		$1,775	$2,350

1920s Gibson K-2
Bernunzio Uptown Music

1926 Gibson MB-3
Bernunzio Uptown Music

MANDOLINS

MANDOLINS

Gilchrist Model 5

Godin A-8

MODEL YEAR	FEATURES	EXC. COND. LOW	HIGH
MB-11 Mandolin Banjo			
1931-1942.			
1941	Pearloid headstock	$2,700	$3,525
MB-Junior Mandolin Banjo			
1924-1925. Open back, budget level.			
1924-1925		$375	$500
SPF-5 Mandolin			
1938. F-style, single bar pickup with volume and tone controls, very limited production, natural.			
1938		$18,000	$24,00

Gilchrist

1977-present. Premium and presentation grade, custom, mandolins made by luthier Steve Gilchrist of Camperdown, Australia. Custom ordered but were also initially distributed through Gruhn Guitars, Nashville, Tennessee and then exclusively by Carmel Music Company. Designs are based upon Gibson mandolins built between 1910 and '25.

Mandola			
1999. Classical styling.			
1999		$18,500	$24,000
Model 1 Mandolin			
A style, maple back and sides, black binding.			
2000		$6,100	$8,000
Model 3 Mandolin			
A style, sugar maple back and sides, ivoroid binding, black/shite purfling.			
2011-2019		$12,500	$16,500
Model 4 Junior Mandolin			
F style, sugar maple back and sides, ivoroid binding.			
2012		$9,500	$12,500
Model 4 Mandolin			
F style, sugar maple back and sides, ivoroid binding.			
1978-2006		$12,500	$16,500
Model 5 Mandolin			
1978-present. Based on the Gibson '22-'24 Loar-era F-5 mandolin, Gilchrist slant logo, spruce top, flamed maple back, sides, and neck, ebony 'board, multiple binding, sunburst.			
1978-2019		$18,000	$23,000
Model 5C Classical Mandolin			
Part of "Classical" quartet commissioned by the Nashville Mandolin Ensemble.			
1993	Blond	$18,500	$24,000

Givens

1962-1992. Luthier R. L. (Bob) Givens handcrafted about 800 mandolins and another 700 in a production shop.

A Mandolin			
1962-1975. Early production A-style.			
1962-1975		$2,600	$3,400
A-3 Mandolin			
1975-1988. Distinguished by use of decal (the only model with Givens decal).			
1975-1988		$2,600	$3,400
A-4 Mandolin			
1988-1993. No 'board binding, simple block-like multiple-line RL Givens inlay, nicer maple.			
1988-1993		$2,600	$3,400

MODEL YEAR	FEATURES	EXC. COND. LOW	HIGH
A-5 Mandolin			
1988-1993. Bound 'board, pearl headstock inlay.			
1988-1993		$2,600	$3,400
A-6 (Torch) Mandolin			
1988-1992. Narrow neck, torch inlay (the only A model with this), gold hardware, snowflake markers.			
1988-1992		$3,000	$3,900
A-6 Custom Mandolin			
1991-1992. Elaborate customized A-6 model.			
1991-1992		$3,400	$4,400
A-6 Legacy Mandolin			
2007. Givens brand made by long time associate Steven Weill, Engelmann spruce top, Mother-of-Pearl and abalone R.L. Givens flowerpot inlay, 3-tone sunburst.			
2007		$1,600	$2,100
F-5 (Fern) Mandolin			
1973-1985. Givens' own version with fern ornamentation.			
1973-1985		$6,500	$8,500
F-5 (Loar) Mandolin			
1962-1972. Givens' own version based upon the Loar model F-5.			
1962-1972		$6,500	$8,500
F-5 (Torch) Mandolin			
1988-1992. Givens F-5 with torch inlay (the only F model with this).			
1988-1992		$7,500	$9,500
F-5 (Wheat Straw) Mandolin			
1986-1988. Givens F-5-style with wheat straw ornamentation.			
1986-1988		$7,000	$9,000

Godin

1987-present. Intermediate grade, production, acoustic/electric mandolins from luthier Robert Godin. They also build basses and guitars.

A-8 Mandolin			
2000-present. Single-cut chambered body, acoustic/electric.			
2000-2019		$375	$500

Goya

1955-1996. Originally made in Sweden, by the late '70s from Japan, then from Korea.

Mandolin			
1960s	Japan/Korea	$200	$300
1960s-70s	Sweden built	$325	$500

Gretsch

1883-present. Gretsch started offering mandolins by the early 1900s, then stopped after the late '50s. In 2012 they again offered mandolins.

New Yorker Mandolin			
Late 1940s-late 1950s. Teardrop shape, f-holes, arched top and back, spruce top, maple back, sides, and neck, rosewood 'board.			
1940s-50s		$425	$575

MODEL YEAR	FEATURES	EXC. COND. LOW	HIGH

G Series Mandolins
2012-2017. Part of the Roots Collection, spruce top, mahogany body, rosewood 'board, includes G9300 New Yorker Standard and acoustic/electric G9320 New Yorker Deluxe.

| 2012-2017 | New Yorker Deluxe | $105 | $135 |
| 2012-2017 | New Yorker Standard | $85 | $110 |

GTR
1974-1978. GTR (for George Gruhn, Tut Taylor, Randy Wood) was the original name for Gruhn Guitars in Nashville, Tennessee (it was changed in '76). GTR imported mandolins and banjos from Japan. An A-style (similar to a current Gibson A-5 L) and an F-style (similar to mid- to late-'20s F-5 with fern pattern) were offered. The instruments were made at the Moridaira factory in Matsumoto, Japan by factory foreman Sadamasa Tokaida. Quality was relatively high but quantities were limited.

A-Style Mandolin
1974-1978. A5-L copy with GTR logo on headstock.

| 1974-1978 | | $1,000 | $1,300 |

F-Style Mandolin
1974-1978. F-5 Fern copy with slant GTR logo on headstock, sunburst, handmade in Japan.

| 1974-1978 | | $1,850 | $2,400 |

Harmony
1892-1976, late 1970s-present. Founded by Wilhelm Schultz in 1892, and purchased by Sears in 1916. The company evolved into one of the largest producers of stringed instruments in the U.S. in the '30s.

Baroque H35/H835 Electric Mandolin
Late 1960s-early 1970s. Electric version of Baroque H425 with single pickup and two controls.

| 1969-1970 | H35 | $325 | $425 |
| 1971-1976 | H835 | $325 | $425 |

Baroque H425/H8025 Mandolin
F-style arched body, extreme bass bout pointy horn, close grained spruce top, sunburst.

| 1969-1970 | H425 | $300 | $400 |
| 1971-1976 | H8025 | $300 | $400 |

Lute H331/H8031 Mandolin
1960s-1970s. A-style, flat top and back, student level.

| 1960s | H331 | $300 | $400 |
| 1970s | H8031 | $300 | $400 |

M-100 Mandolin
1980s. A-style, sunburst.

| 1980s | | $120 | $195 |

Monterey H410/H417/H8017 Mandolin
1950s-1970s. A-style arched body with f-holes, sunburst.

| 1950s-70s | All models | $125 | $210 |

Heritage
1985-present. Heritage offered mandolins for a number of years.

H-5 Mandolin
1986-1990s. F-style scroll body, f-holes.

| 1986-1990s | | $2,100 | $2,800 |

Höfner
1887-present. Höfner has offered a wide variety of instruments, including mandolins, over the years. They currently again offer mandolins.

Model 545/E545 Mandolin
1960s. Pear-shaped A-style with catseye f-holes, 545 (acoustic), E545 (acoustic-electric), block-style markers, engraved headstock, Genuine Höfner Original and Made in Germany on back of headstock, transparent brown.

| 1968-1969 | 545 | $350 | $450 |
| 1968-1969 | E545 | $425 | $550 |

Hondo
1969-1987, 1991-2005. Budget grade, production, imported mandolins. They also offered banjos, basses and guitars. Hondo also offered mandolins from around '74 to '87.

Mandolin
1974-1987. Hondo offered F-style, A-style, and bowl back mandolin models.

1974-1987	Acoustic	$95	$125
1974-1987	Acoustic-electric	$140	$185
1974-1987	Style F	$215	$275

Howe-Orme
1897-ca. 1910. Elias Howe patented a guitar-shaped mandolin on November 14, 1893 and later partnered with George Orme to build a variety of mandolin family instruments and guitars in Boston.

Mandola
1897-early-1900s. Guitar body-style with narrow waist, not the common mandolin F- or S-style body, pressed (not carved) spruce top, mahogany back and sides, flat-top guitar-type trapeze bridge, decalomania near bridge.

| 1890s | | $1,450 | $1,875 |

Style 3 Mandolin
Brazilian rosewood, plain style.

| 1900 | | $1,600 | $2,100 |

Style 4 Mandolin
Guitar-shaped, Brazilian rosewood, fancy style.

| 1900 | | $1,800 | $2,400 |

Style 6 Mandolin
Brazilian rosewood, top-of-the-line.

| 1900 | | $3,800 | $5,000 |

Ianuario Mandolins
1990-2009. Professional and premium grade, custom, mandolins built by luthier R. Anthony Ianuario in Jefferson, Georgia. He also built banjos and violins. Tony and his wife Ann died in an auto accident in '09.

Ibanez
1932-present. Ibanez offered mandolins from '65 to '83. In '04 they again added mandolins to the product line.

Model 511 Mandolin
1974-1980. A-style, f-holes, dot markers, sunburst.

| 1974-1980 | | $210 | $275 |

1970s Harmony Model H8025
Bernunzio Uptown Music

1960s Höfner Model 545
Imaged by Heritage Auctions, HA.com

MANDOLINS

Ibanez M522S

J.L. Smith Deluxe 5-String

MANDOLINS

MODEL YEAR / FEATURES	EXC. COND. LOW	HIGH
Model 513 Mandolin		
1974-1979. A-5 copy with double cutaways, oval sound hole, dot markers, sunburst.		
1974-1979	$230	$300
Model 514 Mandolin		
1974-1979. Arched back, spruce, rosewood, dot inlays, sunburst.		
1974-1979	$230	$300
Model 522 Mandolin		
1974-1978. Symmetrical double point.		
1974-1978	$275	$350
Model 524 Artist Mandolin		
1974-1978. F-5 Loar copy, solid wood carved top and solid wood carved top and solid wood back, sunburst.		
1974-1978	$600	$775
Model 526 (Electric) Mandolin		
1974-1978. A-style body, single pickup, two control knobs, sunburst.		
1974-1978	$290	$375
Model 529 Artist Mandolin		
1982-1983. F-5 Loar era copy, solid wood carved top and solid wood spruce top and solid maple sides and back, sunburst.		
1982-1983	$750	$975
Model M500 Series Mandolins		
2004-present. F-Style and A-Style bodies, acoustic and acoustic-electric option, various finishes.		
2004-2019	$35	$150

Imperial
1890-1922. Imperial mandolins were made by the William A. Cole Company of Boston, Massachusetts.

Bowl Back Mandolin		
1890s	$210	$275

J.L. Smith
2008-present. Custom, intermediate and professional grade, mandolins built by luthier John L. Smith first in Myrtle Beach, South Carolina, and presently in Sebastian, Florida.

Johnson
Mid-1990s-present. Budget and intermediate grade, production, mandolins imported by Music Link, Brisbane, California. Johnson also offers guitars, amps, basses and effects.

MA Series A-Style Mandolins		
Mid-1990s-2013. Import, A-style copy. Several levels offered; the range shown is for all value levels.		
1990s-2013	$100	$145
MF Series F-Style Mandolins		
Mid-1990s-2006. Import, F-style copy. Several levels offered; the range shown is for all value levels.		
1990s-2006	$100	$220

Kalamazoo
1933-1942, 1946-1947, 1965-1970. Budget brand produced by Gibson in Kalamazoo, Michigan. They offered mandolins until '42.

Kalamazoo/Oriole A-Style Mandolin		
1930s. Kalamazoo and Oriole on the headstock, KM/A-style.		
1930s	$575	$750
KK-31 Mandocello		
1935-1938. Archtop, f-hole body, sunburst.		
1935	$2,500	$3,300
KM-11 Mandolin		
1935-1941. Gibson-made, A-style, flat top and back, round soundhole, dot inlay, sunburst.		
1935-1941	$425	$550
KM-12N Mandolin		
1935-1941. A-style with f-holes, spruce top, flamed maple sides and back, bound top and bottom, natural finish.		
1935-1941	$500	$650
KM-21 Mandolin		
1936-1940. Gibson-made, A-style, f-holes, arched bound spruce top and mahogany back, sunburst.		
1936-1940	$600	$800
KM-22 Mandolin		
1939-1942. Same as KM-21 with bound top and back.		
1939-1942	$675	$900
KMB Mandolin/Banjo		
1930s. Banjo-mandolin with resonator.		
1930s	$300	$400

Kay
1931-present. Located in Chicago, Illinois, the Kay company made an incredible amount of instruments under a variety of brands, including the Kay name. From the beginning, Kay offered several types of electric and acoustic mandolins. In '69, the factory closed, marking the end of American-made Kays. The brand survives today on imported instruments.

K68/K465 Concert Mandolin		
1952-1968. Pear-shape, spruce top, mahogany back and sides, natural. Renamed the K465 in '66. Kay also offered a Venetian-style mandolin called the K68 in '37-'42.		
1952-1968	$300	$390
K70 Mandolin		
1939-1966. Venetian-style, bound top and back, f-holes.		
1939-1940s	$525	$700
K73 Mandolin		
1939-1952. Solid spruce top, maple back and sides, A-style body, f-holes, cherry sunburst.		
1939-1952	$300	$390
K390/K395 Professional Electric Mandolin		
1960-1968. Modified Venetian-style archtop, 1 pickup, f-hole, spruce top, curly maple back and sides, sunburst finish. Renamed K395 in '66.		
1960-1968	$350	$450
K494/K495 Electric Mandolin		
1960-1968. A-style archtop, single metal-covered (no poles) pickup, volume and tone control knobs, sunburst. The K494 was originally about 60% of the price of the K390 model (see above) in '65. Renamed K495 in '66.		
1960-1968	$250	$375

MODEL YEAR	FEATURES	EXC. COND. LOW	HIGH

Kay Kraft

1931-1937. First brand name of the newly formed Kay Company. Brand replaced by Kay in '37.

Mandocello

1928-1935. Venetian octave mandolin.

1935		$700	$1,100

Mandola

1937		$400	$700

Mandolin

1931-1937. Kay Kraft offered Venetian- and tear-drop-shaped mandolins.

1931-1937		$200	$400

Style C Mandolin

1928-1935. Deluxe Venetian, rosewood back and sides.

1935		$1,100	$1,500

Kel Kroydon (by Gibson)

1930-1933. Private branded budget level instruments made by Gibson. They also had guitars and banjos.

KK-20 (Style C-1) Mandolin

1930-1933. Flat top, near oval-shaped body, oval soundhole, natural finish, dark finish mahogany back and sides.

1930-1933		$775	$1,025

Kent

1961-1969. Japanese-made instruments. Kent offered teardrop, A style, and bowlback acoustic mandolins up to '68.

Acoustic Mandolin

1961-1968. Kent offered teardrop, A-style, and bowlback acoustic mandolins up to '68.

1961-1968		$130	$190

Electric Mandolin

1964-1969. Available '64-'66 as a solidbody electric and '67-'69 as hollowbody Venetian-style.

1964-1969		$175	$230

Kentucky (Saga M.I.)

1977-present. Brand name of Saga Musical Instruments currently offering budget, intermediate, and professional grade, production, A- and F-style mandolins. Early models made in Japan, then Korea (roughly the '90s), currently made in China.

KM Series Mandolin

1980s-present. Originally made in Japan, then Korea and now China.

1980s	KM-1000 F-style	$875	$1,150
1980s	KM-180 A-style	$225	$300
1980s	KM-650 F-style	$450	$600
1980s	KM-700 F-style	$450	$600
1980s	KM-800 F-style	$650	$850
1988-2009	KM-850 F-style	$1,025	$1,350
1990-2000s	KM-250S A-style	$250	$325
1990s	KM-200S A-style	$250	$325
1990s	KM-500S A-style	$475	$625
1990s	KM-620 F-style	$450	$600
1990s	KM-675	$415	$550
2000-2017	KM-675	$475	$625
2000-2017	KM-700 F-style	$300	$400
2000-2019	KM-1000 F-style	$875	$1,150
2000-2019	KM-140 A-style	$95	$125
2000-2019	KM-150/160 A-style	$150	$200
2000s	KM-380S	$210	$275
2000s	KM-620 F-style	$275	$375
2000s	KM-630 F-style	$325	$425
2000s	KM-750 F-style	$650	$850
2000s	KM-800 F-style	$300	$400
2010-2019	KM-1500 F-5 style	$1,450	$1,900
2010s	KM-615 F-style	$340	$450
2011	KM-171 A-style	$175	$230
2011-2017	KM-900 A-style	$600	$800
2019	KM-606	$500	$650
2020	KM-855 F-style	$825	$1,075

Kimble

2000-present. Luthier Will Kimble builds his premium grade, custom/production, mandolins, mandocellos, and mandolas in Cincinnati, Ohio.

Kingston

Ca. 1958-1967. Mandolins imported from Japan by Jack Westheimer and Westheimer Importing Corporation of Chicago, Illinois. They also offered guitars, basses and banjos.

Acoustic Mandolin

1960s		$135	$190

EM1 Electric Mandolin

1964-1967. Double-cut solidbody electric, 15.75" scale, 1 pickup.

1960s		$175	$240

Knutsen

1890s-1920s. Luthier Chris J. Knutsen of Tacoma and Seattle, Washington. He moved to Los Angeles, California around 1916. He also made guitars, steels, and ukes.

Harp Mandolin

1910s. Harp mandolin with tunable upper bass bout with 4 drone strings, and standard mandolin neck. The mandolin version of a harp guitar.

1910s-20s		$1,400	$1,800

Lakeside (Lyon & Healy)

1890-early-1900s. Mainly catalog sales of guitars and mandolins from the Chicago maker. Marketed as a less expensive alternative to the Lyon & Healy Washburn product line.

Style G2016 12-String Mandolin

1890-early-1900s. 12-string, 18 mahogany ribs with white inlay between, celluloid guard plate.

1890-1900s		$320	$425

Lyle

Ca. 1969-1980. Instruments imported by distributor L.D. Heater of Portland, Oregon. Generally Japanese-made copies of American designs. They also had basses and guitars.

TM-200 Mandolin

1970s	A-style	$150	$200

1930's Kalamazoo KM-21
Imaged by Heritage Auctions, HA.com

Kentucky KM-1000 Master F-Style

MANDOLINS

1953 Martin Style 2-15
Greg Perrine

1916 Martin Style B
Larry Briggs

MODEL YEAR	FEATURES	EXC. COND. LOW	HIGH

Lyon & Healy

1864-present. Lyon & Healy was an early large musical instrument builder and marketer, and produced instruments under many different brands.

Style A Mandocello
1910s-1920s. Scroll peghead, symmetrical 2-point body, natural.

1910s-20s		$4,900	$6,400

Style A Professional Mandolin
1918-1920s. Violin scroll peghead, natural.

1918-1920s	Basic options	$4,900	$6,400
1918-1920s	Fancy options	$6,200	$8,100

Style B Mandolin
1920s. Maple back and sides, 2-point body, natural.

1920s		$1,775	$2,350

Style C Mandolin
1920s. Like Style A teardrop Gibson body style, oval soundhole, carved spruce top, carved maple back, natural.

1920s		$1,950	$2,550

Lyra

1920s-1930s. Private brand made by Regal, Lyra name plate on headstock.

Style A (Scroll) Mandolin
1920s-1930s. Scroll on upper bass bout.

1925-1935		$425	$550

Mann Mandolins

2002-present. Luthier Jonathan Mann builds his professional grade, production/custom, acoustic and electric mandolins in Joelton, Tennessee.

Martin

1833-present. Martin got into the mandolin market in 1895 starting with the typical bowl back designs. By 1914, Gibson's hot selling, innovative, violin-based mandolin pushed Martin into a flat back, bent top hybrid design. By '29, Martin offered a carved top and carved back mandolin. Most models were discontinued in '41, partially because of World War II. Production resumed and standard models are offered up to 1993. From '94 to '02 mandolins are available on a custom order basis only. Martin offered a Backpacker mandolin up to '06.

Backpacker Mandolin
1998-2006. Bell-shaped body.

1998-2006		$120	$155

Style 0 Mandolin
1905-1925. Bowl back-style, 18 rosewood ribs, solid peghead.

1905-1925		$725	$925

Style 00 Mandolin
1908-1925. Bowl back-style, 9 rosewood ribs (14 ribs by '24), solid peghead.

1908-1925		$650	$850

Style 000 Mandolin
1914 only. Bowl back, solid peghead, dot inlay, 9 mahogany ribs.

1914		$650	$850

MODEL YEAR	FEATURES	EXC. COND. LOW	HIGH

Style 1 Mandolin
1898-1924. Bowl back, German silver tuners, 18 ribs.

1898-1924		$775	$1,025

Style 2 Mandolin
1898-1924. Bowl back, 26 rosewood ribs, higher appointments than Style 1.

1898-1924		$925	$1,200

Style 2-15 Mandolin
1936-1964. Carved spruce top, maple back and sides, f-hole, single-bound back, solid headstock.

1936-1964		$925	$1,200

Style 2-20 Mandolin
1936-1941. Carved spruce triple-bound top and bound maple back and sides, f-hole, dot inlay.

1936-1942		$1,700	$2,200

Style 2-30 Mandolin
1937-1941. Carved spruce top and maple back and sides, multi-bound, f-holes, diamond and square inlays.

1937-1941		$1,900	$2,500

Style 3 Mandolin
1898-1922. Bowl back, 26 rosewood ribs, abalone and ivory-bound soundhole.

1898-1922		$1,300	$1,700

Style 4 Mandolin
1898-1921. Bowl back, 30 rosewood ribs.

1898-1921		$1,450	$1,875

Style 5 Mandolin
1898-1920. Bowl back, vine inlay, abalone top trim.

1898-1920		$1,500	$1,950

Style 6 Mandolin
1898-1921. Bowl back, top bound with ivory and abalone, vine or snowflake inlay.

1898-1921		$1,550	$2,000

Style 20 Mandolin
1929-1942. Symmetrical 2-point body, carved top and back with oval soundhole, dot markers.

1929-1942		$1,700	$2,200

Style A Mandolin
1914-1995. Flat back, oval soundhole, dot inlay, solid headstock.

1914-1949		$725	$950
1950-1995		$625	$825

Style AA Mandola
1915-1931, 1935, 1941. Mandola version of Style A mandolin.

1915-1941		$1,550	$2,000

Style AK Mandolin
1920-1937. Koa wood version of Style A, flat back.

1920-1937		$1,250	$1,625

Style A Bitting Special Mandolin
1917. Private branded, small number produced, Martin and model impressed on back of headstock.

1917		$850	$1,125

Style B Mandolin
1914-1946, 1981-1987. Flat back with bent top, spruce top and rosewood back and sides, herringbone back stripe, multi-bound.

1914-1939		$1,200	$1,550
1940-1946		$1,100	$1,400
1981-1987		$825	$1,050

MODEL YEAR	FEATURES	EXC. COND. LOW	HIGH

Style BB Mandola
1917-1921, 1932-1939. Brazilian rosewood, herringbone trim, features like Style B mandolin. This is the only Mandola offered.

1917-1939		$2,000	$2,600

Style C Mandolin
1914-1934. Flat back.

1914-1916		$1,700	$2,200
1917-1934		$2,100	$2,700

Style D Mandolin
1914-1916. Flat back.

1914-1916		$2,600	$3,400

Style E Mandolin
1915-1937. Flat back, rosewood back and sides, bent spruce top, Style 45 snowflake fretboard inlay and other high-end appointments. Highest model cataloged.

1915-1919		$4,500	$6,000
1920-1937		$5,700	$7,400

May Flower
Ca. 1901-1910. H. J. Flower's Chicago-based May Flower Music Company offered bowl back mandolins that he may or may not have built. There were also May Flower harp guitars built by others.

Bowl Back Mandolin
1901-1910. Mid-level bowl back-style with 19 rosewood ribs and mid-level appointments.

1901-1910	Fancy	$725	$950
1901-1910	Plain	$600	$800

Menzenhauer & Schmidt
1894-1904. Founded by Frederick Menzenhauer and Oscar Schmidt International. Menzenhauer created the guitar-zither in the U.S. He had several patents including one issued in September 1899 for a mandolin-guitar-zither. Control of operations quickly went to Oscar Schmidt.

12-String Mandolin
1890s. Bowl back mandolin with 3 strings per course that were tuned in octaves, designed during an experimental era for mandolin-related instruments, 13 rosewood ribs, spruce top, inlays.

1890s		$200	$290

Mid-Missouri/The Big Muddy Mandolin Company
1995-present. Intermediate grade, production, acoustic and electric mandolins and mandolas built by luthier Michael Dulak in Columbia, Missouri. In late '06, they changed their name to The Big Muddy Mandolin Company.

M Series Mandolin
1995-present. Teardrop A-style body, solid spruce top, solid maple, mahogany or rosewood back and sides.

1995-1999	M-0	$300	$400
1995-1999	M-1	$300	$400
1995-2016	M-3	$350	$450
1995-2019	M-15 Mandola	$450	$600
1995-2019	M-2	$325	$425
1995-2019	M-4	$400	$525

Mix
Carbon fiber mandolins built by Peter Mix, Will Kimball, and Matt Durham of New Millennium Acoustic Design (NewMAD) in Waterville, Vermont. They started in 2007.

Monteleone
1971-present. Primarily a guitar maker, luthier John Monteleone also builds presentation grade, custom, mandolins in West Islip, New York.

Morales
Ca.1967-1968. Japanese-made, not heavily imported into the U.S.

Electric Mandolin

1967-1968		$250	$450

Mozzani
Late-1800s-early-1900s. Founder Luigi Mozzani was an Italian (Bologna) master luthier and renowned composer and musician. There are original Mozzani-built mandolins and also factory-built instruments made later at various workshops.

Mandolin
1920s. Factory-built bowl back model.

1920s		$325	$450

Original Bowl Back Mandolin
Late-1800s-early-1900s. Handcrafted by Luigi Mozzani, about 24 ribs, soundhole ornamentation, snowflake-like markers.

1800-1900s		$950	$1,250

National
Ca.1927-present. The National brand has gone through many ownership changes and offered resonator mandolins from around 1927 to '41.

Style 0 Mandolin
1931-early-1940s. Metal body with Hawaiian scenes, single-cone resonator.

1930s		$1,900	$2,500

Style 1 Mandolin
1928-1936. Plain metal body, tri-cone resonator.

1928-1936	Single cone	$1,600	$2,150
1928-1936	Tricone version	$2,200	$2,900

Style 2 Mandolin
1928-1936. Metal body with rose engraving, tri-cone resonator.

1928-1936	Single cone	$2,500	$3,500
1928-1936	Tricone version	$4,500	$7,500

Style 3 Mandolin

1930s	Single cone	$3,500	$4,500
1930s	Tricone version	$5,000	$8,500

Style 97 Mandolin
1936-1940. Metal body, tri-cone resonator.

1936-1940		$4,200	$5,500

Triolian Mandolin
1928-1940. Metal body with palm trees, single-cone resonator.

1928-1940	Single cone	$2,050	$2,700

Monteleone Grand Artist
Laurence Wexer

1935 National Style 1
Bernunzio Uptown Music

MANDOLINS

Nugget Deluxe F

Ovation MSC148 (Celebrity)

MANDOLINS

MODEL YEAR	FEATURES	EXC. COND. LOW	HIGH

Nouveau (Gibson)

1986-1989. Mandolin bodies and necks made in Japan, assembled and finished in U.S. Became Nouveau (by Epiphone) in '88 and the brand was discontinued in '89. They also made guitars.

C7 Mandolin

1986-1987. F-style, white wood body and neck.

1986-1987		$1,400	$1,900

Nugget

1970s-present. Luthier Mike Kemnitzer builds his premium grade mandolins in Central Lake, Michigan.

O'Dell, Doug

See listing under Old Town.

Old Hickory

2005-2010. Budget grade, production, imported F- and A-style acoustic mandolins from Musician's Wholesale America, Nashville, Tennessee. They also offer banjos.

Style A Mandolin

2005-2010	AC-100 mid-level	$50	$125
2005-2010	FC-100 highest level	$85	$165
2005-2010	M-1 lowest level	$45	$60

Style F Mandolin

2005-2010	Various models	$175	$250

Old Kraftsman

1930s-1960s. Brand name used by the Siegel Company on instruments made by Kay and others (even Gibson). Quality was mixed, but some better-grade instruments were offered.

Mandolin

1950s		$245	$320

Old Town

1974-2007. Luthier Doug O'Dell built his professional and premium grade, production/custom acoustic and electric mandolins in Ohio.

EM Series Electric Mandolin

1980s-2007	Various models	$1,700	$2,200

Old Wave

1990-present. Luthier Bill Bussmann builds his professional and premium grade, production/custom, mandolins and mandolas in Caballo, New Mexico. He has also built guitars and basses.

Orpheum

1897-1942, 1944-early 1970s, 2001-2006. Intermediate grade, production, mandolins. They also offered guitars. An old brand often associated with banjos, 1930s branded guitars sold by Bruno and Sons. 1950s branded guitars and mandolins sold by Maurice Lipsky Music, New York, New York. The brand was revived for '01 to '06 by Tacoma Guitars.

Electric Mandolin Model 730 E

1950s. Private branded for Maurice Lipsky as a student model, A-style body, 1 bar pickup, 2 side-mounted knobs, maple back and sides, dots, sunburst.

1950s		$500	$650

Mandolin-Banjo

1910-1930. Mandolin neck on small banjo body, fancy headstock and fretboard inlay, carved heel.

1910-1930	Model No 1	$300	$450
1910-1930	Model No 2	$400	$550
1910-1930	Model No 3	$500	$650

Style A Mandolin

1950s		$250	$425

Oscar Schmidt

1879-ca. 1939, 1979-present. Currently offering budget and intermediate grade, production, mandolins. They also offer guitars, basses, banjos, ukuleles and the famous Oscar Schmidt autoharp. The original Schmidt company offered innovative mandolin designs during the 1900-'30 mandolin boom.

Mandolin Harp Style B

1890s. More zither-autoharp than mandolin, flat autoharp body with soundhole.

1890s		$175	$225

Sovereign Mandolin

1920s. Bowl back, bent top, rope-style binding, mahogany ribs, dot inlay, plain headstock, natural.

1920s	Basic	$250	$350
1920s	Fancy	$500	$900

Ovation

1966-present. Ovation added mandolins in '94 and currently offers intermediate and professional grade, production, mandolins. They also offer guitars and basses.

MCS148 (Celebrity) Mandolin

1994-2017. Single-cut, small Ovation body, Ovation headstock, red sunburst.

1994-2017		$275	$400

Paris Swing

2005-2008. Intermediate grade, production, imported acoustic mandolins from The Music Link, which also offers instruments under Johnson and other brands.

Phoenix

1990-present. Premium grade, production/custom, mandolins built by luthier Rolfe Gerhardt (formerly builder of Unicorn Mandolins in the '70s) in South Thomaston, Maine. Gerhardt's Phoenix company specializes in a 2-point Style A (double-cut) body style.

Ramsey

1990s. Built by luthier John Ramsey of Colorado Springs, Colorado.

Ratliff

1982-present. Professional and premium grade, production/custom, mandolin family instruments built by luthier Audey Ratliff in Church Hill, Tennessee.

MODEL YEAR	FEATURES	EXC. COND. LOW	HIGH

R Series Mandolin
1990s-present. R-5 is an F-style mando, R-4 is round-hole version of 5.

1995-2016	R-4	$1,400	$1,800
1995-2019	R-5	$2,100	$2,700

Silver Eagle Mandolin

1998	A-style	$1,200	$1,550

Recording King
1929-1943. Montgomery Ward house brand. Suppliers include Gibson, Kay, Regal, and Gretsch. Brand name revived by The Music Link in '05.

Style A Mandolin
1929-1943. Gibson-made, plain appointments, sunburst.

1929-1943		$300	$525

Red Diamond
Early 1980s-present. Luthier Don MacRostie builds his premium grade, production/custom, mandolins in Athens, Ohio.

Regal
Ca. 1895-1966, 1987-present. Large Chicago-based manufacturer which made their own brand name and others for distributors and mass merchandisers. Absorbed by the Harmony Company in 1954.

Bicentennial 76 Mandolin
1976. A-style body, flat back, oval soundhole, '76 logo on 'guard, white body, red peghead, blue stars on front and back.

1976		$325	$425

Mandolin

1920s	A-style	$325	$425
1930s	Standard	$425	$550
1930s	Ultra Grand Deluxe	$550	$750

Octofone Mandolin

1920s-30s		$400	$525

Resonator Mandolin

1937	Model 250	$950	$1,250
1950s		$550	$725

Rickenbacker
1931-present. Rickenbacker had the Electro Mandolin in the late '30s and introduced 4-, 5- and 8-string electric models in 1958 and currently offers one model.

Model 5002V58 Mandolin
1997-present. 8 strings, maple front, walnut back, rosewood 'board.

1997-2019		$1,225	$1,600

Rigel
1990-2006. Professional and premium grade, production/custom mandolins and mandolas built by luthier Pete Langdell in Hyde Park, Vermont.

Roberts
1980s. Built by luthier Jay Roberts of California.

MODEL YEAR	FEATURES	EXC. COND. LOW	HIGH

Tiny Moore Jazz 5 Mandolin
1980s. Based on Bigsby design of the early-1950s as used by Tiny Moore, five-string electric, sunburst.

1985		$1,450	$1,850

Ryder
1992-present. Luthier Steve Ryder builds his professional and premium grade, production/custom solid and semi-hollowbody electric mandolins, mandola and octave mandolins in South Portland, Maine.

S. S. Stewart
1878-1904. S.S. Stewart of Philadelphia was primarily known for banjos. Legend has it that Stewart was one of the first to demonstrate the mass production assembly of stringed instruments.

Mandolin Banjo
Early-1900s. Mandolin neck and a very small open back banjo body, star inlay in headstock.

1900s		$125	$300

Sekova
Mid-1960s-mid-1970s. Entry level, imported by the U.S. Musical Merchandise.

Electric Mandolin
Mid-1960s-mid-1970s. Kay-Kraft-style hollowbody with f-holes, 1 pickup and Sekova logo on the headstock.

1960s-70s		$325	$425

Sigma
1970-2007. Budget and intermediate grade, production, import mandolins distributed by C.F. Martin Company. They also offered guitars, basses and banjos.

SM6 Mandolin
1970-2007. Made in Korea.

1970-2007		$150	$275

Silvertone
1941-ca.1970, present. Brand name used by Sears on their musical instruments.

Mandolin
1941-ca.1970. Arched top and back, sunburst.

1940s-50s		$200	$300

Sovereign
Ca. 1899-ca. 1938. Sovereign was originally a brand of the Oscar Schmidt company of New Jersey. In the late '30s, Harmony purchased several trade names from the Schmidt Company, including Sovereign. Sovereign then ceased as a brand, but Harmony continued using it on a model line of Harmony guitars.

Mandolin
1920s-1930s. Old-style bent top.

1920s-30s		$225	$325

Stanley Mandolins
2003-present. Luthier Chris Stanley builds his premium grade, production/custom, A-style and F-style mandolins in Rhinelander, Wisconsin.

1930s Regal Flat Back Teardrop
Bernunzio Uptown Music

Roberts Tiny Moore J5

MANDOLINS

MANDOLINS

Stelling S-5

1930s Strad-O-Lin Style A
Bernunzio Uptown Music

MODEL YEAR	FEATURES	EXC. COND. LOW	HIGH

Stathopoulo

1903-1916. Original design instruments, some patented, by Epiphone company founder A. Stathopoulo.

A-Style Mandolin

1903-1916. A-style with higher-end appointments, bent-style spruce top, figured maple back and sides.

1912		$700	$900

Stella

Ca. 1899-1974, 2000s. Stella was a brand of the Oscar Schmidt Company which was an early contributor to innovative mandolin designs and participated in the 1900-'30 mandolin boom. Pre-World War II Stella instruments were low-mid to mid-level instruments. In '39, Harmony purchased the Stella name and '50s and '60s Stella instruments were student grade, low-end instruments. The Stella brand was reintroduced in the 2000s by MBT International.

Banjo-Mandolin

1920s. One of several innovative designs that attempted to create a new market, 8-string mandolin neck with a banjo body, Stella logo normally impressed on the banjo rim or the side of the neck.

1920s		$100	$175

Bowl Back Mandolin

1920s. Typical bowl back, bent top-style mandolin with models decalomania, about 10 (wide) maple ribs, dot markers.

1920s		$100	$175

Pear-Shape Mandolin

1940s-1960s. Harmony-made lower-end mandolins, pear-shaped (Style A) flat back, oval soundhole.

1940s-60s		$175	$250

Stelling

1974-present. Mainly known for banjos, Stelling also builds premium grade, production/custom mandolins in Afton, Virginia.

Sterling

Early-1900s. Distributed by wholesalers The Davitt & Hanser Music Co.

Stiver

1971-present. Premium grade, custom/production, mandolins built by luthier Louis Stiver in Polk, Pennsylvania.

A Model Mandolin

1982-2019		$2,400	$3,100

F-5 Mandolin

1982-2019		$3,100	$4,000

Strad-O-Lin/Stradolin

Ca.1920s-ca.1960s. The Strad-O-Lin company was operated by the Hominic brothers in New York, primarily making mandolins for wholesalers. In the late '50s, Multivox/Premier bought the company and used the name on mandolins, guitars and amps.

MODEL YEAR	FEATURES	EXC. COND. LOW	HIGH

Baldwin Electric Mandolin

1950s-1960s. A-Style, single pickup, tone and volume knobs, spruce top, maple back and sides, Baldwin logo on headstock, natural.

1950s-60s	Various models	$200	$300

Junior A Mandolin

1950s-1960s. A-Style, Stradolin Jr. logo on headstock, dot markers, sunburst.

1950s-60s		$145	$190

Style A Mandolin

1920s-1950s. A-style body with f-holes, dot markers.

1920s-30s		$400	$525
1940s-50s		$400	$525

Summit

1990-present. Professional and premium grade, production/custom mandolins built by luthier Paul Schneider in Hartsville, Tennessee. He was originally located in Mulvane, Kansas.

Supertone

1914-1941. Brand used by Sears before they switched to Silvertone. Instruments made by other companies.

Mandolin

Spruce top, mahogany back and sides, some with decalomania vine pattern on top.

1920s-30s	Fancy	$400	$525
1920s-30s	Standard	$225	$325

Supro

1935-1968, 2004-present. Budget line from the National Dobro Company. Brand name was revived in '04.

T30 Electric Mandolin

1950s		$525	$700

Tacoma

1995-2009. Tacoma offered intermediate, professional and premium grade, production, electric and acoustic mandolins up to '06. They also built guitars and basses.

M Series Mandolin

1999-2006. Solid spruce top, typical Tacoma bodystyle with upper bass bout soundhole, E (i.e. M-1E) indicates acoustic/electric.

1999-2004	M2/M2E, rosewood	$350	$475
1999-2006	M1/M1E, mahogany	$350	$475
1999-2006	M3/M3E, maple	$425	$575

Unicorn

1970s-late 1980s. Luthier Rolfe Gerhardt (currently luthier for Phoenix Mandolins) founded Unicorn in the mid-'70s. Gerhardt built 149 mandolins before selling Unicorn to Dave Sinko in '80. Sinko closed Unicorn in the late-'80s.

Vega

1889-present. The original Boston-based company was purchased by C.F. Martin in '70.

MODEL YEAR	FEATURES	EXC. COND. LOW	HIGH

10-String Lute Mandola
1915. 15" scale, few made.

1915		$1,900	$2,500

Lansing Special Bowl Mandolin
1890s. Spruce top, abalone, vine inlay.

1890s		$350	$450

Little Wonder Mandolin Banjo
1920s. Maple neck, resonator.

1920s		$425	$550

Mando Bass Mandolin
1910s-1920s. Large upright bass-sized instrument with bass tuners, body-style similar to dual-point A-style, scroll headstock.

1910s-20s		$3,000	$4,000

Mandolin Cittern
1910s. 10-string (five double strings tuned in 5ths), vague A-style with oval soundhole and cylinder back, natural.

1910s		$1,700	$2,200

Style 202 Lute Mandolin
Early-1900s. Basic A-style with small horns, natural spruce top, mahogany sides and cylinder back, dot markers.

1910s		$1,700	$2,200

Style 205 Cylinder Back Mandolin
1910s-1920s. Rounded tube cylinder shape runs the length of the back.

1910s		$1,150	$1,500
1920s		$1,000	$1,300

Style A Mandolin

1910s		$450	$600

Style D 100 Electric Hollowbody Mandolin

1940		$500	$650

Style F Mandolin
1910s. Scroll upper bass bout, oval soundhole, Vega and torch inlay in headstock.

1910s		$700	$900

Style K Mandolin Banjo

1910s-30s		$200	$300

Style L Banjo Mandolin/Whyte Laydie
1910s-1920s. Open back banjo body and mandolin 8-string neck.

1910s-20s		$600	$825

Style S Mandolin Banjo

1915		$500	$700

Super Deluxe Mandolin

1910s	Sunburst	$675	$900

Tubaphone Style X Mandolin Banjo

1922-1923		$675	$900

Vinaccia
Italian-made by Pasquale Vinaccia, luthier.

Bowl Back Mandolin
1900-1920s. High-end appointments and 'guard, 30 rosewood ribs.

1900-1920s		$1,550	$2,050

Vivi-Tone
1933-ca. 1936. Lloyd Loar's pioneering guitar company also built early electric mandolins and mandocellos in Kalamazoo, Michigan.

Acoustic Mandolin
1933-1935. Spruce top, back and sides.

1933-1935		$4,100	$5,300

Electric Mandocello
1933-1935. Traditonal guitar-arch body, Vivi-Tone silkscreen logo on headstock.

1933-1935		$4,800	$6,300

Electric Mandola
1933-1935. Traditonal European teardrop/pear-shaped top, Vivi-Tone silkscreen logo on headstock.

1933-1935		$4,500	$5,800

Electric Mandolin
1933-1935. Vivi-Tone silkscreen logo on headstock.

1933-1935		$4,100	$5,300

Waldo
1891-early 1900s. Mandolin family instruments built in Saginaw, Michigan.

Bowl Back Mandolin
1890s. Alternating rosewood and maple ribs, some with script Waldo logo on pickguard.

1890s		$180	$230

Washburn
1962-present. Currently offering imported intermediate and professional grade, production, mandolins.

Mandolin/Mandolin Family
1974-present. Various models plywood to carved.

1974-2019		$75	$300

Washburn (Lyon & Healy)
1880s-ca.1949. Washburn was founded in Chicago as one of the lines for Lyon & Healy to promote high quality stringed instruments, ca. 1880s. The rights to Washburn were sold to Regal which built Washburns by the mid-'30s until ca. '49. In '74 the brand resurfaced.

Bowl Back Mandolin
1890s-1900s. Lyon and Healy sold a wide variety of bowl back mandolins, Brazilian ribs with fancy inlays and bindings.

1890-1900s	Fancy	$550	$1,000
1890-1900s	Plain	$200	$300
1900s	Standard appointments	$300	$400

Style A Mandolin
1920s. Professional quality.

1920s		$2,400	$3,200

Style E Mandolin
1915-1923. Brazilian rosewood.

1915-1923		$525	$675

Weber
1996-present. Intermediate, professional, and premium grade, production/custom, mandolins, mandolas, and mandocellos. Many former Flatiron employees, including Bruce Weber, formed Sound To Earth, Ltd., to build Weber instruments when Gibson moved Flatiron from Montana, to Nashville. Originally in Belgrade, Montana, and after

Ca. 1898 Washburn Model 118
Izzy Miller

1920 Washburn #1648 Bowl Back
Bernunzio Uptown Music

MANDOLINS

Weber Bitterroot A14-O
Bernunzio Uptown Music

Wurlitzer
Imaged by Heritage Auctions, HA.com

MANDOLINS

'04, in Logan, Montana. They also build guitars. In '12, Two Old Hippies (Breedlove, Bedell) acquired the brand, moving production in '13 to Oregon where Bruce Weber oversees development.

Absaroka Mandolin
2000s. A style body, white binding, diamond inlays.

MODEL YEAR	FEATURES	EXC. COND. LOW	HIGH
2002		$1,650	$2,150

Alder #1 Mandola
Celtic A style body, black binding, diamond inlays.

| 1997 | | $975 | $1,300 |

Alder #2 Mandola
2000-2012. Teardrop body, X-braced, spruce top, maple back and sides.

| 2000-2012 | | $1,000 | $1,325 |

Aspen #1 Mandolin
1997-2011. Teardrop A-style, solid spruce top, maple sides and back, mahogany neck.

| 1997-2011 | | $825 | $1,100 |

Aspen #2 Mandolin
1997-2011. Like #1, but with maple neck.

| 1997-2011 | | $875 | $1,150 |

Beartooth Mandolin
1997-2009. Teardrop A-style, solid spruce top, curly maple sides, back, and neck.

| 1997-2009 | | $1,550 | $2,000 |

Big Sky Mandolin
1999. F-style.

| 1999 | | $2,700 | $3,500 |

Bighorn Mandolin
2006-2008. A-style, oval, double Venetian.

| 2006-2008 | | $2,100 | $2,700 |

Bitterroot Mandolin
2002-present. Style A or F.

| 2002-2019 | A-style | $1,600 | $2,100 |
| 2002-2019 | F-style | $1,900 | $2,450 |

Bridger Mandolin
2000-2015. A-style, long neck.

| 2003 | A-Celtic style | $1,600 | $2,100 |

Custom Vintage Mandolin
2007-present.

| 2007-2019 | A-style | $2,400 | $3,100 |
| 2007-2019 | F-style | $3,300 | $4,300 |

Fern Mandolin
1997-present. Top of the product line.

| 1997-2019 | A-style | $3,600 | $4,700 |
| 1997-2019 | F-style | $4,400 | $5,700 |

Gallatin Mandolin
1999-present.

| 1999-2019 | A-style | $700 | $1,000 |

| 1999-2019 | F-style | $1,400 | $1,800 |

Octar Mandolin
2008. Octave mando, 15" archtop body.

| 2008 | | $1,800 | $2,300 |

Sage #1 Octave Mandolin
2000s. Octave mando, diamond inlays.

| 2006 | | $825 | $1,100 |

Sweet Pea Mandolin
2009-2012. Travel mando.

| 2009-2012 | | $275 | $350 |

Y2K Mandolin
2000. Celtic-style teardrop body, satin natural finish.

| 2000 | | $575 | $750 |

Yellowstone Mandolin
1997-present. A-style and F-style available, solid spruce top, curly maple sides, back, and neck, sunburst.

1997-2019	A-style	$2,100	$2,700
1997-2019	F-style	$2,900	$3,800
2003-2019	Mandola	$2,700	$3,500
2010	Octave	$2,200	$2,900

Weymann
1864-1940s. H.A. Weymann & Sons was a musical instrument distributor located in Philadelphia. They also built their own instruments.

Keystone State Banjo Mandolin
1910s. Maple rim and back, ebony fretboard.

| 1910s | | $200 | $375 |

Mandolin Banjo
1920s. Mandolin neck on an open banjo body.

| 1920s | Various models | $200 | $375 |

Mando-Lute
1920s. Lute-style body, spruce top, flamed maple sides and back, rope binding, deluxe rosette, natural.

| 1920s | Various models | $450 | $700 |

Wurlitzer
The old Wurlitzer company would have been considered a mega-store by today's standards. They sold a wide variety of instruments, gave music lessons, and operated manufacturing facilities.

Banjolin
1920s. Mandolin neck on banjo body.

| 1920s | | $400 | $550 |

Mandolin
1920s. Various woods and appointments.

| 1920s | | $325 | $500 |

Mandolin Banjo
1900-1910. Mandolin neck on open back banjo body, plain-style.

| 1900-1910 | | $175 | $250 |

BANJOS

Bacon Blue Ribbon
Intermountain Guitar and Banjo

1924 Bacon & Day

Banjo collectors, hobbyists, and dealers often think nothing of changing the neck on a banjo; a banjo may have a true vintage neck or a new replacement neck. So, our all original parts concept that applies to the rest of this Price Guide doesn't always apply to vintage banjos.

The banjo market operates somewhat differently than many of the other markets that are covered in the Guide. The prices shown are guidance prices only and each instrument should be evaluated on a case-by-case basis.

Acme

1893-early 1900s. Banjos made for Sears by S.S. Stewart, and later George Bauer, both of Philadelphia.

The Pearl
Open back, 5-string, pearl fretboard.

MODEL YEAR	FEATURES	EXC. COND. LOW	HIGH
1908		$775	$1,000

The Professor
Tree-of-Life board, 5-string.

1900		$775	$1,000

Aria/Aria Pro II

1956-present. Aria offered banjos from time to time under both the Aria and Aria Pro II brand names. They also make guitars, basses, and mandolins.

Resonator 5-String
1976-1978. 5-string resonator back, Aria Pro II brand, models PB450, PB550 and PB650.

1975		$425	$550

Bacon

1906-1967. Frederick Bacon was a well-known banjo player when he started selling banjos under his own name. The earliest Bacon banjos were built by other companies. By 1920, they were building their own models including the B&D (Bacon & Day) models. In 1940 Gretsch purchased the company and took over production.

FF Professional No. 3
1906-1907	5-string	$10,000	$13,000

Special
1914	5-string	$2,150	$2,800

Style C/Super Tenor
1920-1926	Tenor	$400	$525

Bacon & Day (B&D)

1921-1967. B&D was not a separate company, but a line of banjos from the Bacon Banjo Company. David Day left Vega to join up with Fred Bacon in '21. Gretsch purchased Bacon in '40, and offered Bacon and B&D banjos until '67.

Blue Bell
1922-1939	Tenor	$675	$875

Blue Ribbon 17
1933-1939	Tenor	$550	$700

Blue Ribbon Deluxe
1933-1939	Tenor	$1,300	$1,700

Blue Ribbon Orchestra
1933-1939	Tenor	$800	$1,050

FF Professional No. 1
1921	5-string	$1,275	$1,650

MODEL YEAR	FEATURES	EXC. COND. LOW	HIGH
FF Professional No. 2			
1921	5-string	$1,275	$1,650
FF Professional No. 3			
1920-1922	Tenor	$600	$775
Ne Plus Ultra			
1920s	#5, plectrum	$5,400	$7,000
1920s	#5, tenor	$5,400	$7,000
1920s	#6, plectrum	$6,400	$8,300
1920s	#6, tenor	$6,200	$8,000
1920s	#7, plectrum	$9,600	$12,500
1920s	#7, tenor	$9,300	$12,000
1920s	#8, plectrum	$15,500	$20,000
1920s	#8, tenor	$14,700	$19,000
1920s	#9, plectrum	$15,500	$20,000
1920s	#9, tenor	$14,600	$19,000
1930s	Tenor	$6,150	$8,000
1948	Plectrum	$2,300	$3,000
1950s-60s	Tenor	$1,550	$2,000
Roy Smeck			
1930s. Silver Bell #1, tenor.			
1930s		$1,475	$1,900
Senorita			
1930s	Plectrum	$600	$775
1950s	4-string	$450	$575
Silver Bell Series			
1920-1933	#1, tenor/plectrum	$1,050	$1,350
1920-1933	#2, tenor	$1,250	$1,600
1920-1933	#3 Montana, tenor	$1,850	$2,400
1920-1933	#3, tenor	$1,550	$2,000
1920-1939	#1, 5-string	$1,875	$2,450
1920s	#5, 5-string	$3,450	$4,500
1927	#6 Montana, tenor	$3,850	$5,000
1928	#4 Montana, tenor	$2,700	$3,500
1928	#4, tenor	$2,700	$3,500
1931	#3 Sultana, tenor	$1,850	$2,400
1933-1939	#1 Montana, tenor/plectrum	$1,050	$1,350
1933-1939	#1 Serenader, tenor	$1,050	$1,350
1933-1939	#1 Symphonie, tenor	$1,600	$2,100
1933-1939	#3 Montana, plectrum	$2,400	$3,100
Super			
1920-1925	Tenor, non-carved neck	$700	$900
1926-1927	5-string, carved neck	$2,150	$2,775
1926-1927	5-string, non-carved neck	$1,900	$2,475
1926-1927	Tenor, non-carved neck	$850	$1,125
Symphonie Silver Bell			

1960. By Gretsch, script Symphonie logo on headstock, fancy ornamentation, gold-plated hardware.

1960	5-string	$1,700	$2,200

Baldwin

1966-1976. Baldwin was one of the largest piano retailers in the Midwest and in 1965, they got into the guitar market. In '66 they bought the ODE Banjo company. From '66 to '71 the banjos were labeled as Baldwin; after that ODE was added below the Baldwin banner. In '76 Gretsch took over ODE production.

BANJOS

MODEL YEAR	FEATURES	EXC. COND. LOW	HIGH
Ode 2R			
1968	Plectrum, 4-string	$800	$1,050
Ode Style C			
1968	Bluegrass, 5-string	$1,125	$1,475
Style D			
1968-1969	5-string	$2,075	$2,700

Barratt

1890s. Made by George Barratt in Brooklyn, New York.

Style D 5-String

1890s	Victorian era	$290	$375

Benary and Sons

1890-1899. Manufactured by the James H. Buckbee Co. for music instrument wholesaler Robert Benary.

Celebrated Benary

1890-1899. 5-string, open back, plain appointments.

1890-1899		$600	$775

Bishline

1985-present. Professional and premium grade, production/custom, banjos built by luthier Robert Bishline in Tulsa, Oklahoma.

Boucher

1830s-1850s. William Boucher's operation in Baltimore is considered to be one of the very first banjo-shops. Boucher and the Civil War era banjos are rare. The price range listed is informational guidance pricing only. The wide range reflects conservative opinions. 150 year old banjos should be evaluated per their own merits.

Double Tack

1840s		$7,700	$10,000

Single Tack

1840s		$6,900	$9,000

Bruno and Sons

Established in 1834 by Charles Bruno, primarily as a distributor, Bruno and Sons marketed a variety of brands, including their own.

Royal Artist Tenor

1920s	Figured resonator	$500	$650

Buckbee

1863-1897. James H. Buckbee Co. of New York was the city's largest builder. The company did considerable private branding for companies such as Benery, Dobson, and Farland.

5-String

1890-1897. 5-string, open back, plain appointments.

1890-1897	High-level models	$1,150	$1,500
1890-1897	Low-level models	$375	$500
1890-1897	Mid-level models	$600	$800

Christy

1960s. Banjos built by luthier Art Christianson in Colorado.

5-String Long Neck Folk Banjo

1965	Rare models	$500	$675
1965	Standard models	$375	$500

Cole

1890-1919. W.A. Cole, after leaving Fairbanks & Cole, started his own line in 1890. He died in 1909 but the company continued until 1919. He also made guitars and mandolins.

Eclipse

1890-1919	Dot diamond inlays	$1,450	$1,900
1890-1919	Flower inlays	$1,700	$2,200
1890-1919	Man-in-the-moon inlays	$1,925	$2,500

Deering

1975-present. Greg and Janet Deering build their banjos in Spring Valley, California. In 1978 they introduced their basic and intermediate banjos. They also offer banjos under the Goodtime and Vega brands.

40th Anniversary

2015	5-string	$2,050	$2,650

B-6

1986-2002. Mahogany neck and resonator, ebony 'board, 6 strings, satin finish.

1986-2002		$750	$1,000

Basic

1979-1982. Resonator back, 5 strings.

1979-1982		$725	$925

Black Diamond

1998-present. Black head, mahogany neck, 5 strings, ebony 'board, diamond inlays, resonator back.

2001		$1,050	$1,400

Boston

1982-present. Mahogany resonator and neck, 5 or 6 strings, ebony 'board, seed and vine inlays.

1982	5-string	$700	$900
2012	6-string	$950	$1,250

Calico

1998-present. Curly maple resonator and neck, 5 strings, ebony 'board, plectrum and tenor available.

2007-2010		$2,400	$3,200

Calico Custom

1997-2007.

2007	5-string	$2,850	$3,700

Crossfire

1998-2016. Alder body, maple neck, 5 strings, ebony 'board, diamond inlays. Available in tenor.

2005-2016		$1,800	$2,300

D-6 Banjo Guitar

1995	Resonator, 6-string	$1,400	$1,825

Deluxe

1995-present. Mahogany resonator, mahogany or maple neck, ebony 'board, white and gold inlays on 6-string. Available 5-, 6- or 12-string, plectrum 4-string, 17- or 19-fret tenor 4-string.

1995-2003	5- or 6-string	$1,500	$1,950
1995-2003	Plectrum 4-string	$1,150	$1,500

Ca. 1890 Benary and Sons Celebrated Benary
Elderly Instruments

ca.1890s Buckbee
Kenneth Parr

BANJOS

Deering Maple Blossom

1993 Deering Golden Era
Imaged by Heritage Auctions, HA.com

MODEL YEAR	FEATURES	EXC. COND. LOW	HIGH

Eagle II
2010-present. Resonator back, available as 5-string, 6-string, openback 5-string and 19-fret tenor.

| 2010-2016 | Resonator | $1,200 | $1,600 |

G.D.L. Greg Deering Limited Edition
2001-2010. Figured walnut neck, burl walnut resonator, abalone and mother-of-pearl inlays, ebony 'board, 5 strings.

| 2001 | | $3,000 | $3,900 |

Golden Era
1995-present. Deeper resonator sound chamber, curly maple, 5 strings, ebony 'board, Cremona Sunburst stain finish.

| 1995-2016 | | $1,975 | $2,600 |

Golden Wreath
2006-present. Deep resonator, 5 strings, mahogany neck, ebony 'board, mother of pearl wreath inlay.

| 2006 | | $1,950 | $2,550 |

Goodtime 5-String
| 2010-2013 | | $300 | $400 |

Goodtime Special
2001-present. Maple neck, rim and resonator, black inlays and binding. Available 4-string plectrum and 19-fret tenor, or 5-string openback.

| 2010-2013 | 5-string | $500 | $675 |

Grand Ole Opry
2005. Limited Edition for Opry's 80th anniversary, hand signed by Greg and Janet Deering, only 80 produced.

| 2005 | 5-string | $3,300 | $4,400 |

Ivanhoe
High-end appointments, 5-string.

| 1986 | | $7,000 | $9,000 |

John Hartford
Resonator back, curly maple, 5-string, offered in 22 or 24 frets.

| 2007-2015 | | $2,100 | $2,800 |

Maple Blossom
1983-present. Dark walnut stained maple neck, 4, 5, or 6 strings, fancy inlays, high gloss finish. Originally called the Advanced ('78-'82).

| 1983-2016 | 5-string | $1,400 | $1,850 |
| 1983-2016 | Tenor | $1,200 | $1,550 |

Saratoga Star
| 2004 | 5-string | $3,300 | $4,200 |

Sierra
1998-present. Mahogany or maple neck and resonator, maple rim, ebony 'board, 4- or 5-string, electric/acoustic or openback.

| 1996-2014 | | $1,100 | $1,450 |

Standard
| 1992 | 5-string | $1,100 | $1,450 |

Tenbrooks Saratoga Star
Curly maple neck and deep resonator, 5-string, ebony 'board.

| 2010 | | $2,850 | $3,700 |

Texas Calico
1986. Limited run of 150, Texas and 1836-1986 logo on fretboard, engraved gold-plated metal hardware, 5 strings.

| 1986 | | $7,200 | $9,300 |

Ditson
1916-1930. The Oliver Ditson Company of Boston offered a variety of musical instruments.
Tenor
Resonator with typical appointments, 4 strings.

| 1920 | | $425 | $550 |

Dobro
1929-1942, ca. 1954-2019. Guitars and mandolins were also made under the Dobro name. In '93 Gibson purchased the brand and built Dobros in Nashville, Tennessee. For more info refer to the guitar section.
Dojo Banjo
Resonator guitar body with 5-string banjo neck.

| 1988-1994 | | $1,250 | $1,650 |

Dobson, C. Edgar
1880s. The Dobson brothers – Henry Clay, Charles Edgar, George Clifton, Frank Prescott, and Edward Clarendon – were banjo teachers and performers who marketed banjos in various ways over the years.
Great Echo
| 1888 | 5-string | $850 | $1,100 |

Dobson, George
1870-1890. Marketed by renown banjo instructor George C. Dobson of Boston, Massachusetts.
Matchless
| 1880s | 5-string | $600 | $800 |

Dobson, H.C.
1860s-early 1900s. The oldest of the Dobson brothers, Henry C. was a successful musical instrument distributor out of New York. They were designed by Henry, but most, if not all, were made by others.
Silver Chime 5-String
| 1890 | Fancy | $1,050 | $1,375 |
| 1890 | Plain | $500 | $650 |

Epiphone
1873-present. Epiphone introduced banjos in the early 1920s, if not sooner, offering them up to WW II. After Gibson bought the company in '57, they reintroduced banjos to the line, which they still offer.
Black Beauty Tenor
| 1920 | | $375 | $500 |

EB-44 Campus
1962-1970. Long neck, open back, folk-era 5-string.
| 1962-1970 | | $800 | $1,050 |

EB-88 Minstrel
1961-1969. Flat head, standard neck, 5 strings.
| 1961-1969 | | $1,400 | $1,800 |

EB-99
1970s. Import, higher-end, 5-string.
| 1970s | | $525 | $700 |

EB-188 Plantation
1962-1968. Long neck, open back, 5 strings.
| 1962-1968 | | $1,150 | $1,500 |

BANJOS

MODEL YEAR	FEATURES	EXC. COND. LOW	HIGH
Electar (Electric)			
1930s	Tenor	$725	$950
MB-200			
1998-2015. Mahogany neck and body, rosewood 'board, 5 strings.			
2009		$225	$300
MB-250			
1998-2013. Mahogany resonator body and neck, rosewood 'board, 5 strings.			
2012		$385	$500
Peerless Plectrum			
1920-1925. Fancy headstock.			
1920-1925		$400	$525
Recording A			
Ca. 1925-ca. 1935. Epiphone Recording logo on headstock, flamed maple neck and resonator, fancy pearl inlay markers.			
1920s	Tenor	$1,700	$2,200
Recording B			
Ca. 1925-ca. 1935.			
1930s	Tenor	$2,000	$2,600
Recording Concert C Special			
1930s. Tenor, maple body, fancy appointments, resonator.			
1932		$2,600	$3,400
TB-100			
Mid 1960s.			
1960s	Tenor	$625	$825
White Beauty Tenor			
1920. Closed-back resonator, large dot markers, White Beauty headstock logo.			
1920		$375	$500

Excelsior

Ca.1885-ca. 1990. Brand name of guitars and banjos marketed by Boston's John C. Haynes & Company. Instruments were more basic without tone rings. Brand most likely faded out in very early 1890s when Haynes started their more refined line of Bay State instruments.

MODEL YEAR	FEATURES	EXC. COND. LOW	HIGH
Model 218			
1889	Open back, 5-string	$1,225	$1,600

Fairbanks/Vega Fairbanks/ A.C. Fairbanks

1875-1922. From 1875 to 1880, A. C. Fairbanks built his own designs in Boston. In 1880, W. A. Cole joined the company, starting Fairbanks & Cole, but left in 1890 to start his own line. The company went by Fairbanks Co. until it was purchased by Vega in 1904. The banjos were then branded Vega Fairbanks (see Vega listings) until 1922.

MODEL YEAR	FEATURES	EXC. COND. LOW	HIGH
Acme (F & C)			
1880-1890. 5-string, open back, fancy markers.			
1880-1890		$650	$850
Electric 5-String Series			
1890s	Electric	$3,200	$4,300
1890s	Imperial	$1,900	$2,500
1890s	No. 3	$3,400	$4,400
1890s	No. 5	$4,700	$6,000
1890s	No. 6	$5,200	$6,700
1901	Special	$2,200	$2,900
Electric Banjeaurine			
1890s	5-string	$2,000	$2,600
Imperial Open Back			
1888	5-string	$2,600	$3,400
Regent			
1900-1904	5-string	$2,000	$2,600
Senator No. 1			
1900-1909	5-string	$900	$1,150
Special #0			
1890-1904		$600	$800
Special #2			
1890-1904	5-string	$725	$950
Special #4			
1900-1904	5-string	$900	$1,200
Tubaphone #3			
1908	5-string	$2,500	$3,200
Whyte Laydie #2			
1901-1904	5-string	$3,000	$4,000
Whyte Laydie #7			
1901	1st year	$7,000	$9,000
1902-1908		$6,100	$7,900

Farland

Ca. 1890-1920s. Buckbee and others made instruments for New York banjo teacher and performer A. A. Farland.

MODEL YEAR	FEATURES	EXC. COND. LOW	HIGH
Concert Grand			
1900-1920	5-string	$825	$1,100
Grand Artist No. 2			
1890s-1910. Ornate floral markers, open back, 5-string.			
1890s-1910		$1,600	$2,000

Fender

1946-present. Fender added banjos to their product mix in the late 1960s, and continues to offer them.

MODEL YEAR	FEATURES	EXC. COND. LOW	HIGH
Allegro			
Late 1960s-1970s. Tenor or 5-string.			
1960s		$725	$925
Artist			
1960s-70s	5-string	$1,100	$1,425
FB Series			
1998-2017. Various imported 5-string models.			
2007-2012	FB-54	$200	$250
2007-2012	FB-55	$275	$375
2007-2012	FB-58	$350	$450
2007-2012	FB-59	$450	$600
Leo Deluxe			
1980-1988. Fancy inlay, Japanese-made.			
1970s		$626	$800

Framus

1946-1977, 1996-present. The new Framus company, located in Markneukirchen, Germany, continues to offer banjos.

MODEL YEAR	FEATURES	EXC. COND. LOW	HIGH
Various Models			
1960s		$150	$350
1970s		$125	$250

Fairbanks Electric
Intermountain Guitar and Banjo

Early-1970s Fender Artist Tenor
William Ritter / Gruhn Guitars

BANJOS

1927 Gibson Bella Voce

William Ritter/Gruhn Guitars

1924 Gibson GB-5

Intermountain Guitar and Banjo

BANJOS

MODEL YEAR	FEATURES	EXC. COND. LOW	HIGH

Gibson

1890s (1902)-present. Gibson started making banjos in 1918. Vega and Gibson were the only major manufacturing companies that offered banjos in their product catalog in the '50s.

RB prefix = regular banjo (5-string)

TB prefix = tenor banjo (4-string, tenor tuning)

PB prefix = plectrum banjo (4-string, plectrum tuning)

The prices shown are guidance prices only and each instrument should be evaluated on a case-by-case basis.

All American

1930-1937, 1970-1986. Tenor banjo, fancy appointments, historic art, gold hardware. Reissue offered in RB, TB, or PB.

1930-1937	Arch top, 2-pc Flange	$8,600	$11,400
1930-1937	Flat head, 1-pc Flange, rare	$37,000	$49,000
1975-1980	5-string	$5,600	$7,000

Bella Voce

1927-1931. Tenor or plectrum, fancy appointments, flower-pattern art, gold hardware.

1927-1931	Plectrum	$18,000	$23,000
1927-1931	Tenor	$18,000	$23,000

Christmas Banjo Limited Edition

2008-2009. Christmas theme, 5-string, flame maple, gold parts, 12 offered.

2008-2009	$5,800	$7,500

Earl Scruggs '49 Classic

1992-2008. Figured maple resonator and neck, rosewood 'board, multiple bindings.

2001-2002	$3,000	$3,800

Earl Scruggs Flint Hill Special

2005. Commemorative Limited Edition, 20 made with first 5 signed by Earl, Flint Hill Special on headstock, figured maple resonator and neck, classic Amber Brown finish.

2005	$3,700	$4,900

Earl Scruggs Golden Deluxe

1991-2010. Satin gold hardware, hearts and flowers inlay.

1997	$3,600	$4,800

Earl Scruggs Standard

1984-2010. 5-string, high-end appointments, Standard added to model name in '92.

1984-2010	$2,900	$3,700

ETB Electric Tenor

1938-1941. Electric Tenor Banjo, Charlie Christian pickup.

1934-1941	$2,600	$3,400

Flint Hill Special

2005-2006. Earl Scruggs style, 5-string.

2005-2006	$3,600	$4,500

Florentine Plectrum

1927-1937. High-end appointments, gold hardware.

1925-1930	2-pc Flange	$14,000	$18,000

Florentine Tenor

1927-1937. High-end appointments, gold hardware.

1927-1935	40-hole	$13,000	$17,000

MODEL YEAR	FEATURES	EXC. COND. LOW	HIGH

GB-1

1922-1940. Guitar-banjo, style 1 appointments, 6-string neck, walnut. Trap door '22-'24, resonator diamond-flange '25-'30, 1-piece flange '31-'40.

1922-1924	Trap door	$1,150	$1,450
1925-1930		$1,600	$2,000
1931-1940		$2,300	$2,900

GB-3

1918-1937. Guitar-banjo, style 3 appointments, mahogany. Trap door '18-'24. Mastertone, 2-piece flange, ball-bearing arch-top tone ring for '25-'26 and cast arch-top tone ring for '26-'29. Mastertone, 40-hole tone ring '28-'37. Flat head option '31-'37.

1918-1924	Trap-door	$1,000	$1,300
1925-1926		$2,600	$3,500
1926-1929		$2,600	$3,500
1928-1937		$2,600	$3,500

GB-4

1918-1931. Guitar-banjo, style 4 appointments, maple. Very early models were called GB without -4 suffix. Trap door '18-'24. Mastertone, 2-piece flange, ball-bearing arch-top tone ring for '25-'26 and cast arch-top tone ring for '26-'29. Mastertone, 40-hole tone ring '28-'31. Flat head option '31.

1918-1924	GB/GB-4	$2,200	$2,900
1925-1926		$3,200	$4,100
1926-1929		$3,200	$4,100
1928-1931		$3,200	$4,100

GB-5

1924. Rare, gold plated, trap-door.

1924	$5,200	$6,700

GB-6/GB-6 Custom

1922-1934. Guitar-banjo, style 6 appointments, special order availability. Trap door '22-'24. Mastertone, 2-piece flange, ball-bearing arch-top tone ring for '25-'26 and cast arch-top tone ring for '26-'29. Mastertone, 40-hole tone ring '28-'34. Flat head option '31-'34.

1922-1924	Trap door	$3,000	$3,900
1925-1926		$4,500	$5,900
1926-1929		$4,500	$5,900
1928-1934		$4,500	$5,800

Granada PB

1929-1939. Plectrum, flat head tone ring.

1929-1939	$80,000	$105,000

Granada RB

1925-1939. 5-string banjo with either a 2-piece flange ('25-'30), or a 1-piece flange ('33-'39).

1925-1926	Ball bearing	$17,800	$22,200
1927-1930	40-hole arched	$27,500	$35,100
1929-1939	Flat head	$143,000	$186,000

Granada RB (Reissue)

1986-2010. Resonator back, hearts & flowers or flying eagle inlay, 5-string.

1986-2006	Flying eagle	$3,400	$4,400
1986-2010	Hearts & flowers	$3,400	$4,400

Granada RB Pot and Reneck

1933-1939. Original pot and replacement neck, flat head tone ring.

1933-1939	$42,000	$53,000

MODEL YEAR	FEATURES	EXC. COND. LOW	HIGH
Granada TB			
1925-1930. Tenor banjo with a 2-piece flange.			
1925-1926	Ball bearing	$4,500	$6,000
1927-1930	40-hole arched	$6,000	$8,000
PB-1			
1926-1930s. Plectrum Banjo (PB), bracket-shoe.			
1920s		$750	$1,000
PB-2			
1920s-1930s. Plectrum, bracket-shoe for '20s and 1-piece flange for '30s..			
1920s		$750	$1,000
1930s		$2,900	$3,900
PB-3			
1925-1927, 1929-1939. Laminated maple resonator Mastertone model, plectrum neck and tuning. Tube and plate, 2-piece flange for '25-'27. Flat head tone ring '29-'39.			
1925-1927	Tube & plate	$1,900	$2,500
1929-1939	Flat head	$57,000	$75,000
PB-4			
1925-1940. Plectrum with either a 2-piece flange ('25-'32), or 1-piece ('33-'40).			
1925-1927	Ball bearing	$2,300	$3,000
1928-1932	Archtop	$3,000	$3,900
1933-1940	Archtop	$7,700	$10,000
1933-1940	Flat head	$47,000	$61,000
PB-7			
1937-1943. Plectrum, 40-hole flat tone ring.			
1940		$47,000	$61,000
PB-11			
1931-1942. Plectrum, 1-piece flange, pearloid 'board, headstock and resonator cover.			
1931-1942		$3,000	$3,900
PB-100			
1948-1979. Plectrum with either a 1-piece flange ('48-'68), or 2-piece ('69-'79).			
1969-1979		$750	$1,000
RB Jr.			
1924-1925. Budget line, 5-string, open back.			
1924-1925		$1,100	$1,425
RB-00			
1932-1942. Maple resonator, 1-piece flange.			
1933-1939		$3,200	$4,300
RB-1			
1922-1940. Resonator Banjo (RB), 1-piece or diamond flange.			
1922-1930	Early specs	$3,400	$4,500
1930-1932	1-pc Flange	$3,400	$4,500
1933-1940	Diamond flange	$3,400	$4,500
RB-1 Reissue			
1990-1993. Fleur-de-lis, brass tone ring.			
1990-1993		$1,500	$2,000
RB-2			
1933-1939		$6,000	$7,800
RB-3			
1923-1937. Resonator, dot inlay, 5 strings.			
1922-1924	Trap or non-trap	$2,150	$2,800
1925-1926	Ball bearing, Mastertone	$6,000	$8,000
1927-1929	Archtop, 40-hole or no hole, MT	$8,000	$14,000

MODEL YEAR	FEATURES	EXC. COND. LOW	HIGH
RB-3 Reissue			
1988-2010. Called the RB-3 Wreath at end of production.			
1988-2010		$2,400	$3,200
RB-4			
1922-1937. Resonator 5-string with either a 2-piece flange ('25-'31), or 1-piece ('33-'37). Trap or non-trap door on earlier models ('22-'24).			
1922-1924	Trap or non-trap	$2,700	$3,300
1925-1931	Archtop	$13,000	$16,000
1929-1937	Flat head	$74,000	$96,000
1933-1937	Archtop	$28,000	$35,000
RB-4/R-4/Retro 4			
1991-2006. Resonator, flying eagle inlay, multi-bound.			
1998-2006		$3,350	$4,350
RB-5			
1995-2008. Resonator.			
1996		$5,000	$6,500
RB-6 New Century Style 6 Gold Sparkle			
1995-2008. Figured-maple, gold sparkle binding.			
2005	5-string	$5,300	$7,000
RB-7 Top Tension			
1994-2008. Maple, bow-tie inlay.			
2003		$3,400	$4,400
RB-11			
1931-1942. Pearloid covered 'board, headstock and resonator.			
1933-1939		$4,400	$6,000
RB-12			
1995-2008. Carved walnut resonator, rosewood 'board, art deco inlay.			
1996-2003		$3,500	$4,500
RB-75 J.D. Crowe			
1997-2006. Based on Crowe's instrument.			
1997-2006		$3,000	$3,900
RB-100			
1948-1979. Maple resonator.			
1948-1965		$1,400	$1,825
1966-1979		$1,150	$1,500
RB-150			
1948-1959. Laminated mahogany resonator, bow tie inlay.			
1948-1959		$1,900	$2,500
RB-170			
1960-1973. No resonator, 5-string, dot markers, decal logo, multi-ply maple rim.			
1960-1973		$900	$1,200
RB-175			
1962-1973. 2000s. Open back, long neck typical of banjos of the '60s. Models include the RB-175, RB-175 Long Neck, RB-175 Folk.			
1962	RB-175	$1,100	$1,450
1962-1964	Long Neck	$1,100	$1,450
1965-1969	Folk	$1,100	$1,450
1970-1973	RB-175	$1,100	$1,450
RB-180			
1961-1967. Longneck.			
1961-1967		$1,550	$2,000

1930 Gibson Granada

2000 Gibson RB-4 Mastertone
Imaged by Heritage Auctions, HA.com

BANJOS

1959 Gibson RB-250
Jay Hunt

Gold Star G-11HF
Elderly Instruments

BANJOS

MODEL YEAR	FEATURES	EXC. COND. LOW	HIGH
RB-250			
1954-2010. Mahogany, 2-piece flange until '88, 1 after.			
1954-1959		$2,700	$3,500
1960-1965		$2,500	$3,300
1966-1969	Flat head	$1,900	$2,500
1970-1989	Mastertone	$1,800	$2,400
1990-1999		$1,800	$2,400
2002-2004	Reissue	$1,800	$2,400
RB-500			
1964-1969. Maple, 1-piece flange, gold hardware.			
1967		$2,700	$3,500
RB-800			
1964-1971, 1979-1986. Maple resonator, 1-piece flange until '69, 2 after.			
1964-1986		$2,500	$3,300
TB			
1918-1923. Renamed TB-4.			
1919		$1,100	$1,400
TB-00			
1939-1944. Maple resonator, 1-piece flange.			
1939-1944		$1,600	$2,000
TB-1			
1922-1939. Tenor banjo with a 1-piece flange.			
1922-1925		$575	$750
1926		$625	$825
1933-1939		$2,600	$3,350
TB-2			
1922-1928	Wavy flange	$750	$950
1933-1937	Pearloid board	$2,750	$3,550
TB-3			
1925-1937. Tenor banjo with either a 2-piece flange, or a 1-piece flange.			
1925-1926		$2,000	$2,600
1927-1929		$2,500	$3,300
1930-1937		$6,000	$8,000
TB-4			
1922-1937. Dot inlay.			
1922-1924	Trap door	$700	$925
1925-1926	Ball bearing	$2,500	$3,300
1927-1931	40 or no hole ring	$2,700	$3,600
1933-1937	40 or no hole ring	$4,300	$5,700
TB-5			
1922-1924	Trap door	$900	$1,200
1925-1926	Ball bearing	$6,000	$8,000
1927-1931	40 or no hole ring	$7,500	$10,000
TB-6			
1927-1939	Tube plate flange	$10,000	$13,000
TB-11			
1931-1942. Pearloid covered 'board, headstock and resonator.			
1931-1942		$2,200	$3,000
TB-12			
1937-1939. Produced in limited quantities, 1-piece flange, flat head tone ring, double bound walnut resonator, price levels include both original and conversion instruments, conversions with original flat head tone rings are somewhat common in the vintage banjo market.			
1937	Top tension pot assembly	$43,000	$57,000

MODEL YEAR	FEATURES	EXC. COND. LOW	HIGH
TB-18			
1937. Rare model.			
1937	Flat head top tension	$62,000	$80,000
TB-100			
1949-1959		$1,250	$1,600
1960-1969		$1,100	$1,400
TB-250			
1954-1996.			
1954-1959		$1,450	$1,850
1960-1969	Mastertone	$1,250	$1,650
1970-1996	Mastertone	$1,150	$1,500
TB-800			
1964	2 made	$2,900	$3,800
1975	Flying eagle markers	$2,400	$3,200
Trujo Plectrum			
1928-1934		$2,200	$2,900

Gold Star

1970s-present. A brand name of Saga Musical Instruments offering professional and premium grade, production banjos.

5-String

1970s-present. Various 5-string models.

YEAR	MODEL	LOW	HIGH
1970s	G-11HF	$1,150	$1,475
1980s-2017	GF-85	$1,150	$1,475
1984	JD Crowe	$3,700	$4,750
2000-2017	GF-200	$1,150	$1,475
2006	GF-100FE	$1,150	$1,475

Gold Tone

1993-present. Professional and premium grade, production/custom banjos and banjitars built by Wayne and Robyn Rogers in Titusville, Florida. They also offer guitars, basses, lap steels, mandolins and ukuleles.

5-String

Various 5-string models.

YEAR	MODEL	LOW	HIGH
2009	Banjola Deluxe Mandola	$525	$675
2011	BG-250F BG Special	$450	$575
2011	CC-100 Cripple Creek	$375	$500
2011	OB-250AT	$650	$850
2011	OT-800	$525	$675
2014	TB-250 Travel	$525	$675
2014	WL-250 Open Back	$525	$675

Tenor

Various tenor models.

YEAR	MODEL	LOW	HIGH
2011	IT250R Irish (China)	$425	$550

Goya

1952-1996. Martin offered Goya banjos while they owned the brand name in the '70s.

Student 5-String

1976-1996. Goya-Martin era.

YEAR		LOW	HIGH
1976-1996		$200	$300

Gretsch

1883-present. Gretsch offered banjos in the '20s and again in the '50s and '60s. In 2012 they again started building them.

MODEL YEAR	FEATURES	EXC. COND. LOW	HIGH

5-String
| 1977 | | $310 | $410 |

Broadkaster
1920s-1939. Tenor or 5-string banjo with pearloid head and board.
1920s	Tenor	$375	$500
1932-1939	5-string	$800	$1,050
1932-1939	Tenor	$275	$375

Model 6536 Folk
1960s. Open-back, 5-string, long-neck style.
| 1964 | | $450 | $600 |

New Yorker
1930s-1960s. New Yorker logo on headstock, 5-string or tenor.
| 1930s-60s | | $225 | $300 |

Orchestella
1925-1929. Tenor or 5-string banjo with gold engravings.
| 1925-1929 | 5-string | $1,250 | $1,650 |
| 1925-1929 | Tenor | $475 | $625 |

Tenor Short-Scale
| 1925-1929 | Plain styling | $225 | $300 |
| 1950s | Plain styling | $225 | $300 |

GTR
1974-1978. GTR (for George Gruhn, Tut Taylor, Randy Wood) was the original name for Gruhn Guitars in Nashville, and they imported mandolins and banjos from Japan.
5-String Copy
| 1974-1978 | | $625 | $825 |

Harmony
1892-1976, late 1970s-present. Huge, Chicago-based manufacturer of fretted instruments, mainly budget models under the Harmony name or for many other American brands and mass marketers.
Bicentennial
1976. Red, white and blue, '76 logo, 5-string.
| 1976 | | $525 | $675 |

Electro
1950s. Electric banjo, 5-string, wood body, 1 pickup.
| 1950s | | $525 | $675 |

Holiday Folk
1960s. Long neck, 5-string.
| 1960s | | $150 | $250 |

Reso-Tone Tenor
| 1960s | | $150 | $250 |

Roy Smeck Student Tenor
| 1963 | | $150 | $250 |

Sovereign Tenor
| 1960s | | $150 | $250 |

Howard
Howard is a brand name of Cincinnati's Wurlitzer Co. used in the 1920s on banjos built by The Fred Gretsch Manufacturing Co. The brand name was also appeared on guitars in the mid-'30s by Epiphone.
Tenor
| 1930s | Open back | $150 | $200 |
| 1930s | Resonator | $365 | $475 |

Huber
1999-present. Premium grade, production, 5-string banjos built by luthier Steve Huber in Hendersonville, Tennessee.

Ibanez
1932-present. Ibanez introduced their Artist line of banjos in 1978 in a deal with Earl Scruggs, but they were dropped by '84.
Model 591
1978-1984. Flat head, 5-string.
| 1978-1984 | | $825 | $1,100 |
Model 593
1977. Vine inlay, 5-string.
| 1977 | | $1,100 | $1,400 |

John Wesley
Introduced in 1895 by Kansas City, Missouri instrument wholesalers J.W. Jenkins & Sons, founded by cello builder John Wesley Jenkins. May have been built by Jenkins until circa 1905, but work was later contracted out to others.

Kalamazoo
1933-1942, 1965-1970. Budget brand built by Gibson. Made flat-tops, solidbodies, mandolins, lap steels, banjos and amps.
Banjo
| 1935-1940 | KPB, plectrum | $350 | $450 |
| 1935-1941 | KRB, 5-string | $600 | $800 |

Kay
Ca. 1931 (1890)-present. Kay was a huge manufacturer and built instruments under their name and for a large number of other retailers, jobbers, and brand names.
Silva
1950s. Top of the line 5-string, Silva verticle logo along with Kay logo on headstock, block markers.
| 1950s | | $375 | $500 |
Student Tenor
| 1950s | | $135 | $175 |

Kel Kroydon
1930-1933. Private branded budget level instruments made by Gibson. They also had guitars and banjos. The name has been revived on a line of banjos by Tom Mirisola and made in Nashville.
KK-11 Tenor
| 1933-1937 | | $1,850 | $2,400 |

Kingston
Ca. 1958-1967. Imported from Japan by Westheimer Importing Corp. of Chicago. They also offered guitars, basses and mandolins.
Student Tenor
| 1965 | | $50 | $75 |

Gretsch Broadkaster
Bernunzio Uptown Music

Huber VRB-G

BANJOS

Luscomb Lion Heel
Bernunzio Uptown Music

2003 OME Mockingbird
Grand Artist SB Plectrum
William Ritter/Gruhn Guitars

BANJOS

MODEL YEAR	FEATURES	EXC. COND. LOW	HIGH

Lange

1920s-1942, Late 1940s. The William L. Lange Company began selling Paramount banjos, guitar banjos and mandolin banjos in the early 1920s. Gretsch picked up the Paramount name and used it on acoustics and electrics for a time in the late '40s. See Paramount for more listings.

Tourraine Deluxe

1920s	Tenor	$525	$675

Leedy

1889-1930. Founded in Indianapolis by U. G. Leedy, the company started making banjos in 1924. Leedy was bought out by C. G. Conn in '30.

Arcadian

1925	Plectrum	$400	$525

Olympian

1930	Tenor	$425	$550

Solotone

1924-1930	A Tenor	$750	$1,000
1924-1930	B Tenor	$950	$1,250
1924-1930	C Tenor	$1,050	$1,400
1924-1930	D Tenor	$1,200	$1,600

Libby Bros.

1890s. Made in Gorham, Maine, rarity suggests limited production.

Open Back

1890-1895. Fancy position markers, 5-string.

1890-1895		$1,000	$1,325

Ludwig

The Ludwig Drum Company was founded in 1909. They saw a good business opportunity and entered the banjo market in '21. When demand for banjos tanked in the '30s, Ludwig dropped the line and concentrated on its core business.

Ambassador

1920s-1932	Tenor	$750	$1,000

Bellevue

1920s. Tenor, closed-back banjo with fancy appointments.

1920s		$575	$750

Big Chief

1930. Carved and engraved plectrum banjo.

1930		$5,000	$6,500

Capitol

1920s		$450	$600

Columbia

1920s	Tenor, student-level	$300	$400

Commodore

1930s. Tenor or plectrum, with gold hardware and fancy appointments.

1930s	Tenor, Ambassador	$950	$1,250
1932	Plectrum	$1,150	$1,500

Deluxe

1930s. Engraved tenor, with gold hardware.

1930s		$1,500	$2,000

Dixie

1930s	Tenor	$285	$375

Kenmore Plectrum

1920s	Open back	$450	$600

Kingston

1924-1930	Tenor	$400	$525

Standard Art Tenor

1924-1930. Tenor banjo with fancy appointments.

1924-1930		$2,300	$3,000

The Ace

1920s. Tenor banjo, resonator and nickel appointments.

1920s		$850	$1,100

Luscomb

1888-1898. John F. Luscomb was a well-known banjo player who designed a line of instruments for Thompson & Odell of Boston.

Open Back 5-String

1890s		$525	$700

Matao

1967-1983. Japanese copies of American brands, offered guitars, basses, banjos and ukes.

Bluegrass

1970s	5-string	$225	$300

Mitchell (P.J.)

1850s. Early gut 5-string banjo maker from New York City.

Gut 5-String

1850s		$2,300	$3,000

Morrison

Ca. 1870-ca. 1915. Marketed by New Yorker James Morrison, made by Morrison or possibly others like Buckbee. After 1875, his instruments sported the patented Morrison tone ring.

5-String

1885-1890		$500	$650

ODE/Muse

1961-1980. Founded by Charles Ogsbury in Boulder, Colorado, purchased by Baldwin in '66 and moved to Nashville. Until '71 the banjos were branded as Baldwin; afterwards as Baldwin ODE. Gretsch took over production in '76. Muse was a retail store brand of banjos produced by ODE from '61 to '66. In '71, Ogsbury started the OME Banjo Company in Colorado.

Model C

1976-1980. 5-string banjo, resonator and fancy markers.

1976-1980		$1,150	$1,500

Model D

1976-1980. 5-string banjo, resonator and gold engravings.

1976-1980		$1,500	$2,000

OME

1971-present. Charles Ogsbury started OME outside Boulder, Colorado after he sold his first banjo company, ODE, to Baldwin.

MODEL YEAR	FEATURES	EXC. COND. LOW	HIGH
Bright Angel			
2012-2019	5-string	$2,100	$2,800
Columbine			
2012-2015	Tenor	$2,800	$3,600
Grubstake			
1972-1980	5-string	$750	$1,000
Juggernaut			
1973-1979	5-string	$1,750	$2,250
Juggernaut II			
1974	5-string	$2,100	$2,800
Juniper Megatone			
2016	5-string	$2,100	$2,800
Magician			
1997	5-string, gold	$2,800	$3,700
Mogul			
1973	5-string, silver	$2,300	$3,000
1973	Plectrum, black	$2,100	$2,800
1973	Plectrum, silver	$2,000	$2,600
1974	5-string, gold	$3,000	$3,900
Monarch			
1986	Plectrum	$1,800	$2,400
Primrose			
2013-2019	5-string	$2,400	$3,100
X 5-String			
1971		$950	$1,250
XX 5-String			
1971		$1,050	$1,350
1972	Extra Long Neck	$950	$1,250
1975		$950	$1,250
XX Tenor			
1973		$950	$1,250
XXX 5-String			
1971		$1,350	$1,750

Orpheum

1897-1922. Lange and Rettberg purchased the J.H. Buckbee banjo factory in 1897 and started making banjos under the Orpheum label. William Lange took control in 1922 and changed the name to Paramount.

MODEL YEAR	FEATURES	EXC. COND. LOW	HIGH
Model #1			
1910s-20s	Tenor	$500	$650
1914-1916	5-string, open back	$1,800	$2,400
1920-1922	Plectrum	$575	$750
Model #2			
1920-1922	5-string	$1,300	$1,700
1920-1922	Tenor	$600	$775
Model #3			
1900-1910s	5-string	$2,600	$3,400
1910s	Plectrum, fancy	$1,500	$1,900
1910s	Tenor, fancy	$825	$1,100

Paramount

1921-1935. William Lange and his Paramount company are generally accredited with commercializing the first modern flange and resonator in 1921.

MODEL YEAR	FEATURES	EXC. COND. LOW	HIGH
Aristocrat			
1921-1935	Plectrum	$1,275	$1,650
1921-1935	Tenor	$1,050	$1,350

MODEL YEAR	FEATURES	EXC. COND. LOW	HIGH
Aristocrat Special			
1921-1935. Plectrum or tenor with fancy appointments.			
1921-1935	Plectrum	$1,925	$2,500
1921-1935	Tenor	$1,550	$2,000
Artists Supreme			
1930s. High-end appointments, 19-fret tenor, engraved gold-plated hardware.			
1930s	Tenor	$3,300	$4,300
Junior			
1921-1935	Plectrum	$600	$800
1921-1935	Tenor	$525	$725
Leader			
1921-1935	Plectrum	$725	$950
1921-1935	Tenor	$650	$850
Style 1			
1921-1935	Plectrum	$600	$800
1921-1935	Tenor	$500	$650
Style 2			
1921-1935. Tenor banjo, resonator and plain appointments.			
1921-1935		$500	$650
Style A			
1921-1935. Models include the Style A Tenor, Plectrum, and the 5-string (with resonator and fancy appointments).			
1921-1935	5-string	$1,050	$1,350
1921-1935	Plectrum	$600	$800
1921-1935	Tenor	$575	$750
Style B			
1921-1935. Models include the Style B Tenor, and the Plectrum (with resonator and fancy appointments).			
1921-1935	Plectrum	$1,000	$1,300
1921-1935	Tenor	$850	$1,100
Style C			
1921-1935. Models include the Style C Tenor, Plectrum, and the 5-string (with resonator and fancy appointments).			
1921-1935	5-string	$2,925	$3,800
1921-1935	Plectrum	$1,000	$1,300
1921-1935	Tenor	$925	$1,200
Style D			
1921-1935	Plectrum	$1,450	$1,900
1921-1935	Tenor	$1,300	$1,700
Style E			
1921-1935	Plectrum	$1,850	$2,400
1921-1935	Tenor	$1,700	$2,200
Style F			
1921-1935	Plectrum	$2,550	$3,300
1921-1935	Tenor	$2,375	$3,100
Super/Super Paramount			
1929-1935	Plectrum	$2,800	$3,600
1929-1935	Tenor	$2,550	$3,300
Tenor Harp II			
1924	Fancy, 4-string	$775	$1,000
Trooper			
1921-1935	Plectrum	$500	$650
1921-1935	Tenor	$425	$550

Penco

Ca. 1974-1978. Japanese-made banjos imported into Philadelphia. They also offered guitars, basses and mandolins.

1920s Orpheum Model #1
Imaged by Heritage Auctions, HA.com

1925 Paramount Style E Tenor
William Ritter/Gruhn Guitars

BANJOS

1895 S.S. Stewart Banjeaurine
William Ritter/Gruhn Guitars

Slingerland May Bell

MODEL YEAR	FEATURES	EXC. COND. LOW	HIGH
Deluxe Tenor			
1970s	Japan	$190	$250

Recording King

1929-1932, 1936-1941. Brand name used by Montgomery Ward for instruments made by various American manufacturers, including Kay, Gibson and Gretsch.

Studio King Tenor
1929-1932. Gibson-made, 40 hole archtop.

1929-1932		$2,700	$3,600

Regal

Ca. 1895-1966, 1987-present. Mass manufacturer Regal made brands for others as well as marketing its own brand. In '87 the Regal name was revived by Saga.

Bicentennial '76
1976. Part of a series of Regal instruments with Bicentennial themed appointments.

1976	5-string	$325	$425

S.S. Stewart

1878-1904. S.S. Stewart of Philadelphia is considered to be one of the most important and prolific banjo manufacturers of the late 19th century. It's estimated that approximately 25,000 banjos were made by this company. The brand name was used on guitars into the 1960s.

MODEL YEAR	FEATURES	LOW	HIGH
20th Century			
1890s		$800	$1,050
American Princess			
1890s. 5-string, 10" rim.			
1890s		$725	$925
Banjeaurine			
1890s. 5-string banjo, 10" head with an open back.			
1890	Plain appointments	$800	$1,050
1890	Style 3, fancy	$1,500	$2,000
Champion			
1895. Open back, 5-string.			
1895	Plain appointments	$800	$1,050
Concert No. 1 Pony			
Open back 5-string, short scale.			
1891		$800	$1,050
Orchestra			
1890s. 5-string, various styles.			
1893-1894	#1, with frets	$1,050	$1,350
1893-1894	#2, fretless	$2,200	$2,900
1893-1894	#2, with frets	$1,700	$2,250
Piccolo			
1880s. 5-string, 7" rim.			
1880s	Plain appointments	$800	$1,050
Special Thoroughbred			
1890s-1900s. Open back, 5-string, carved heel.			
1890-1900s	Plain appointments	$800	$1,050
Universal Favorite			
1892. 11" head.			
1892	Plain appointments	$725	$950

Silvertone

1941-ca. 1970, present. Brand of Sears instruments which replaced their Supertone brand in '41. Currently, Samick offers a line of amps under the Silvertone name.

MODEL YEAR	FEATURES	LOW	HIGH
4-String			
1960s		$70	$125
5-String			
1960s		$175	$300

Slingerland

Ca. 1914-present. The parent company was Slingerland Banjo and Drums, Chicago, Illinois. The company offered other stringed instruments into the '40s. Slingerland Drums is now owned by Gibson.

Deluxe			
1920s	Tenor, high-end	$1,150	$1,500
May Bell			
1920s-30s	Various styles	$250	$950
Student/Economy			
1930s	Tenor	$200	$275

Stathopoulo

1917-1928. House of Stathopoulo evolved from the A. Stathopoulo brand in 1917, and in 1929 became the Epiphone Banjo Corporation which later became Epiphone, the well known guitar brand.

Super Wonder XX Tenor			
1920s		$675	$875

Stelling

1974-present. Founded by Geoff Stelling, building premium and presentation grade, production/custom banjos in Afton, Virginia. They also build mandolins.

5-String
1974-present. Various 5-string models.

1976-1984	Staghorn	$3,700	$4,800
1977-1978	Bell Flower	$2,250	$3,000
1978-1981	Whitestar	$1,950	$2,600
1983	Hartford	$2,250	$3,000
1985	Golden Cross	$3,050	$4,100
1985	Master Flower	$3,050	$4,100
1990	Masterpiece	$4,450	$5,800
2001	Red Fox	$2,400	$3,100
2003	Sunflower	$2,700	$3,500
2004	Crusader Deluxe	$3,950	$5,200
2006	Crusader	$3,000	$3,900
2012	Swallowtail	$3,050	$4,100

Stetson, J.F.

1880s-1900s. J. F. Stetson branded banjos were distributed by W.J. Dyer & Bros. of St. Paul, Minnesota and others.

Presentation
1890s. Highest-end style, by Fairbanks, open back, 5-string.

1890s		$9,000	$11,700

Studio King

1930s. Banjos made by Gibson, most likely for a mail-order house or a jobber.

MODEL YEAR	FEATURES	EXC. COND. LOW	HIGH
Studio King			
1933-1934	Tenor TB-3, 2-pc Flange	$3,500	$4,500
1935-1937	Tenor TB-3, 1-pc Flange	$5,500	$7,300

Superb

1920s. Private brand made by House of Stathopoulo, Inc., the company name of Epiphone from 1917 to 1928. The brand was also used on banjo ukuleles.

Tenor			
1920s		$365	$475

Supertone

1914-1941. Brand used by Sears, Roebuck and Company for instruments made by various American manufacturers, including its own Harmony subsidiary Harmony. In '40, Sears began making a transition to the Silvertone brand.

Prairie Wonder
1925. 5-string, open back banjo.

1925		$365	$475

Thompson & Odell

1875-1898. Boston instrument importers Thompson & Odell started building banjos in the 1880s. They sold the company to Vega in 1898.

Artist			
1880s	Various models	$575	$775

Tilton

1850s-late 1800s. Built by William B. Tilton, of New York City. He was quite an innovator and held several instrument-related patents. He also built guitars.

Toneking

1927. Private brand of the NY Band Instruments Company, Toneking logo on headstock.

Tenor			
1927		$290	$375

Univox

1964-1978. Instruments imported from Japan by the Merson Musical Supply Company, later Unicord, Westbury, New York.

Tenor			
1970s	Import	$250	$325

Van Eps

1920s. Designed by virtuoso banjo artist Fred Van Eps and sold through Lyon & Healy.

Recording			
1920s	5-string	$1,000	$1,300
1920s	Tenor	$850	$1,100

Vega

1889-1980s, 1989-present. Vega of Boston got into the banjo business in 1904 when it purchased Fairbanks. Vega and Gibson were the only major manufacturing companies that offered banjos in their product catalog in the 1950s. The Deering

Banjo Company acquired the brand in '89 and uses it on a line of banjos.

MODEL YEAR	FEATURES	EXC. COND. LOW	HIGH
Artist			
1927-1929	Tenor	$1,100	$1,400
1929	Plectrum, open back	$1,100	$1,400
Artist Deluxe			
1931	Tenor	$1,450	$1,900
Artist Professional #9			
1923-1929	Tenor	$1,900	$2,400
Earl Scruggs STII			
1969	5-string, resonator	$1,450	$1,900
Folk Ranger FR-5			
1960s	5-string, open back	$525	$700
Folk Wonder			
1960s	5-string	$625	$825
Folklore SS-5			
1966. Open back, long neck folk banjo.			
1963-1966	5-string	$1,000	$1,300
FP-5 Folk Professional			
1961	Rare, 5-string	$1,425	$1,850
Imperial Electric			
1918-1921	5-string	$1,900	$2,500
Little Wonder			
1910s-1950s.			
1910s-20s	Guitar banjo	$900	$1,125
1920s	Plectrum	$525	$700
1920s-30s	Tenor	$450	$600
1950s	5-string	$900	$1,100
Moderne Tenor			
1931		$1,600	$2,000
Pete Seeger			
1958-1970. 5-string, long neck banjo.			
1958-1961	Dowel-stick	$2,300	$3,000
1962-1970	Folk era	$2,300	$3,000
Professional			
1960. 5-string banjo with a Tubaphone tone ring.			
1960	Pro II, slits	$1,200	$1,600
1960	Professional, holes	$1,350	$1,750
Ranger			
1960s. Standard appointments, dot markers.			
1966	5-string	$500	$625
Regent			
1920s. Open back and dot markers.			
1920s	5-string	$1,475	$1,925
Soloist			
1920s. Oettinger tailpiece.			
1920s	5-string	$4,500	$6,000
Style M			
1920-1929. Tenor, with Tubaphone TR.			
1920-1929		$800	$1,050
Style N			
1910s-20s	Tenor	$400	$500
Style X No. 1			
1922-1930	Tenor	$1,500	$1,950
Style X No. 9			
1922-1930. Tenor with fancy appointments.			
1922-1930	Tenor	$2,000	$2,600
Tubaphone #3			
1908-1930	5-string	$1,850	$2,450

Stelling Master Flower
Elderly Instruments

1927 Vega Artist
Imaged by Heritage Auctions, HA.com

BANJOS

Vega Vegaphone De-Luxe

1923 Vega Whyte Laydie #7

Imaged by Heritage Auctions, HA.com

MODEL YEAR	FEATURES	EXC. COND. LOW	HIGH
Tubaphone #9			
1921-1929	5-string	$5,700	$7,500
Tubaphone Deluxe			
1920s. Higher-end appointments, carved heel, Deluxe logo on tailpiece.			
1923	5-string	$8,000	$10,000
V.I.P. Tenor			
1970s. 4-string, open back, fancy engraved pearl markers, on-board electronics.			
1970		$1,225	$1,525
V-45			
1970. Plectrum banjo, flat head tone ring, fancy appointments.			
1970s		$2,700	$3,300
Vega Lady's Banjo			
1913		$800	$1,000
Vegaphone De-Luxe			
1929	Plectrum	$3,000	$3,700
Vegaphone Professional			
1920s	Plectrum	$950	$1,250
1920s-30s	Tenor	$875	$1,150
1960s	5-string	$850	$1,050
Vegavox I 5-String			
1964		$1,500	$1,900
Vegavox I Plectrum			
1956-1959		$1,500	$1,850
Vegavox I Tenor			
1930s-1969. Vox-style deep resonator, alternating block/dot markers.			
1930s		$1,900	$2,400
1956-1959		$1,500	$1,850
1960-1969		$1,400	$1,750
Vegavox IV			
1956-1975. IV logo on truss rod cover, high-end appointments, 4-string plectrum neck.			
1956-1975	Plectrum or tenor	$2,500	$3,300

MODEL YEAR	FEATURES	EXC. COND. LOW	HIGH
Vegavox IV Deluxe			
1970-1973	Tenor	$3,300	$4,300
Whyte Laydie			
1975	5-string	$1,650	$2,150
Whyte Laydie #2			
1919	Vega Fairbanks	$2,600	$3,300
1923-1928	5-string	$2,600	$3,300
1923-1928	Plectrum	$1,075	$1,400
Whyte Laydie #7			
1905	5-string	$6,300	$8,200
1909	5-string	$5,900	$7,700
1920s	Tenor	$2,000	$2,600
1921-1928	5-string	$5,900	$7,700
Whyte Laydie Style L			
1922		$850	$1,100
Whyte Laydie Style R			
1920s-1930s. Tenor banjo with closed back.			
1920s-30s		$850	$1,100
Wonder			
Made by C.F. Martin (brand owner in the '70s), closed back resonator style, tenor or plectrum.			
1967	Plectrum	$600	$800
1973	Tenor	$600	$800

Vega/Deering

1989-present. Deering purchased the Vega brand in '89. They also make banjos under the Deering brand.

Kingston Trio

1990s-present. Folk-style banjo similar to '50s and '60s Vega Long Neck, 5-string.

1990s-2006		$2,400	$3,100

Little Wonder

Maple neck, ebony 'board, 5-string.

1999		$500	$675

MODEL YEAR	FEATURES	EXC. COND. LOW	HIGH
Long Neck			
2006	5-string	$2,400	$3,100
Old Tyme Wonder			
2012-2018. Maple neck, ebony 'board, 5 strings, brown stained satin finish.			
2012		$925	$1,150
Senator			
2009-present. Open back, 5-string.			
2009-2011		$1,000	$1,300
Tubaphone #2			
2005. Open back, 5-string.			
2005-2011		$2,100	$2,700

Washburn (Lyon & Healy)

1880s-ca.1949. Washburn was the brand name of Lyon & Healy of Chicago. They made banjos from 1880-1929.

MODEL YEAR	FEATURES	EXC. COND. LOW	HIGH
5-String			
1896	Old 1890s style	$800	$1,000
Irene			
1920s	5-string	$700	$875
Model 1535			
1917	5-string, open back	$1,475	$1,850

Weymann

1864-1940s. The Weymann company was founded in 1864 and got seriously into the banjo manufacturing business in 1917. They manufactured banjos until around 1930.

MODEL YEAR	FEATURES	EXC. COND. LOW	HIGH
Keystone State Style 2			
1920s		$800	$1,000
Plectrum			
1924-1928	Style A	$675	$875
1927	Style #1	$1,150	$1,550
1927	Style #2	$1,250	$1,650

MODEL YEAR	FEATURES	EXC. COND. LOW	HIGH
Tenor			
1924-1928	Style #1	$1,000	$1,300
1924-1928	Style #2	$1,100	$1,450
1924-1928	Style #4	$2,100	$2,800
1924-1928	Style #50	$450	$575
1924-1928	Style #6	$3,400	$4,500
1924-1928	Style A, low pro model	$675	$900

Wildwood Banjos

1973-2018. Traditional and bluegrass banjos made originally in Arcata, California, and after '07, in Bend, Oregon.

MODEL YEAR	FEATURES	EXC. COND. LOW	HIGH
Minstrel			
1990s-2018. Maple neck, ebony 'board, tubaphone-style tone ring, 5 strings.			
2013		$975	$1,275
Paragon			
1990s-2018. Curly maple or Claro black walnut neck, ebony 'board, mother-of-pearl inlay, 5 strings.			
1990s		$1,425	$1,850
Troubador			
1973-2018. Curly maple neck, ebony 'board, tubaphone-style tone ring, 5 strings.			
1970s-2010		$1,125	$1,475

Wilson Brothers

1915-1928. Brand name, possibly made by Lyon & Healy, for the Wilson Brothers Manufacturing Company, of Chicago, which was better known as a builder of drums.

MODEL YEAR	FEATURES	EXC. COND. LOW	HIGH
Tenor			
1920s-30s	Resonator	$350	$450

Yosco

1900-1930s. Lawrence L. Yosco was a New York City luthier building guitars, round back mandolins and banjos under his own brand and for others.

MODEL YEAR	FEATURES	EXC. COND. LOW	HIGH
Style 3			
1920s	Tenor	$950	$1,200

Wildwood Troubador
Elderly Instruments

1924 Weymann #4 Tenor
William Ritter/Gruhn Guitars

BANJOS

BIBLIOGRAPHY

By Ken Achard: *The Peavey Revolution*, 2005, Backbeat.

By Tony Bacon: *60 Years of Fender*, 2010; *50 Years of Gretsch Electrics*, 2005; *Six Decades of the Fender Telecaster*, 2005; *Squier Electrics*, 2012, all Backbeat Books.

By Tony Bacon & Paul Day: *The Bass Book*, 1994; *The Gretsch Book*, 1996; *The Rickenbacker Book*, 1994, all Balafon Books/GPI Books; *The Ultimate Guitar Book*, 1991, Alfred A. Knopf.

By Paul Bechtoldt: *G&L: Leo's Legacy*, 1994, Woof Associates.

By J.W. Black and Albert Molinaro: *The Fender Bass, An Illustrated History*, 2001, Hal Leonard.

By Klaus Blasquiz: *The Fender Bass*, 1990, Mediapresse.

By Bob Brozman: *The History and Artistry of National Resonator Instruments*, 1993, Centerstream.

By Dave Burrluck: *The PRS Guitar Book*, 1999, Outline Press.

By Bob Carlin: *Regal Musical Instruments 1895-1955*, 2011, Centerstream.

By Walter Carter: *Epiphone: The Complete History*, 1995, *The History of the Ovation Guitar*, 1996, both Hal Leonard; *Gibson Guitars: 100 Years of An American Icon*, 1994, W. Quay Hays.

By Paul Day: *The Burns Book*, 1990, PP Publishing/Bold Strummer; *The Classical Guitar Book*, 2002, Balafon.

By Michael Doyle: *The History of Marshall*, 1993, Hal Leonard.

By Andre Duchossoir: *The Fender Telecaster*, 1991; *Gibson Electrics, The Classic Years*, 1994; *Guitar Identification: Fender-Gibson-Gretsch-Martin*, 1983, all Hal Leonard; *The Fender Stratocaster*, 1988, Mediapresse.

By Jim Elyea: *Vox Amplifiers, The JMI Years*, 2009, The History For Hire Press.

By Steve Evans and Ron Middlebrook: *Cowboy Guitars, 2002*, Centerstream.

By Jim Fisch & L.B. Fred: *Epiphone: The House of Stathopoulo*, 1996, Amsco.

By Paul Fox: *The Other Brands of Gibson*, 2011, Centerstream.

By Frank W/m Green: *The Custom Guitar Shop and Wayne Richard Charvel*, 1999, Working Musician Publications.

By George Gruhn and Walter Carter: *Acoustic Guitars and Other Fretted Instruments*, 1993; *Electric Guitars and Basses*, 1994, both GPI Books; *Gruhn's Guide to Vintage Guitars*, 3rd Ed., 2010, Backbeat.

By Philip F. Gura and James F. Bollman: *American's Instrument, The Banjo in the 19th Century*, 1999, University of North Carolina.

By Hal Leonard Publishing: *The Boss Book*, 2001.

By Robert Carl Hartman: *The Larson's Creations, Guitars & Mandolins*, 2007, Centerstream.

By Gil Hembree: *Gibson Guitars: Ted McCarty's Golden Era: 1948-1966*, 2007, Hal Leonard.

By Gregg Hopkins and Bill Moore: *Ampeg - The Story Behind The Sound*, 1999, Hal Leonard Publishing.

By Tom Hughes: *Analog Man's Guide to Vintage Effects*, 2004, Musicians Only Publishing.

By Dave Hunter and Walter Carter: *Gibson Bible*, 2008, Jawbone.

By Dave Hunter and Paul Day: *Fender Bible*, 2007, Jawbone.

By J.T.G.: *Gibson Shipping Totals 1948-1979*, 1992.

By Richard Johnston and Dick Boak: *Martin Guitars, A Technical Reference*, 2009, Hal Leonard.

By Mark Kasulen & Matt Blackett: *The History of Yamaha Guitars*, 2006, Hal Leonard.

By Robb Lawerence: *The Les Paul Legacy 1968-2009*, 2009, Hal Leonard.

By Mike Longworth: *Martin Guitars, A History*, 1988, 4 Maples Press.

By Wallace Marx Jr.: *Gibson Amplifiers, 1933-2008*, 2009, Blue Book.

By John Morrish: *The Fender Amp Book*, 1995, Balafon/GPI.

By Hans Moust: *The Guild Guitar Book: The Company and the Instruments 1952-1977*, 1995, GuitArchives.

By David Peterson and Dick Denney: *The Vox Story, A Complete History of the Legend*, 1993, Bold Strummer.

By Jim Roberts: *American Basses*, 2003, Backbeat.

By Paul William Schmidt: *Acquired of the Angels*, 1998, Scarecrow Press.

By Norbert Schnepel and Helmuth Lemme: *Elektro-Gitarren Made in Germany*, 1987, Musik-Verlag Schnepel-Lemme oHG.

By Jay Scott: *The Guitars of the Fred Gretsch Company*, 1992, Centerstream.

By Michael John Simmons: *Taylor Guitars, 30 Years of a New American Classic*, 2003, PPVMedien.

By Richard R. Smith: *The Complete History of Rickenbacker Guitars*, 1987, Centerstream; *Fender: The Sound Heard 'Round the World*, 1995, Garfish.

By Joesph E. Spann: *Spann's Guide to Gibson 1902-1941*, 2011, Centerstream.

By Paul Specht, Michael Wright, and Jim Donahue: *Ibanez, the Untold Story*, 2005, Hoshino (U.S.A.) Inc.

By John Teagle: *Washburn: Over 100 Years of Fine Stringed Instruments*, 1996, Amsco.

By John Teagle and John Sprung: *Fender Amps: The First 50 Years*, 1995, Hal Leonard.

By Art Thompson: *Stompbox*, 1997, Miller Freeman.

By Doug Tulloch: *Neptune Bound, The Ultimate Danelectro Guitar Guide*, 2008, Centerstream.

By Thomas A. Van Hoose: *The Gibson Super 400, Art of the Fine Guitar*, 1991, GPI.

By Jim Washburn & Richard Johnston: *Martin Guitars: An Illustrated Celebration of America's Premier Guitarmaker*, 1997, Rodale.

By Tom Wheeler: *American Guitars, An Illustrated History*, 1992, Harper Collins; *The Dream Factory*, 2011, Hal Leonard.

By Eldon Whitford, David Vinopal, and Dan Erlewine: *Gibson's Fabulous Flat-Top Guitars*, 1994, GPI.

By Hans-Peter Wilfer: *Framus Vintage*, 2009, Framus.

By Michael Wright: *Guitar Stories, Vol. I*, 1994; *Guitar Stories, Vol. II*, 2000, both Vintage Guitar Books.

Magazines (various issues): *Acoustic Guitar, Guitar Player, Guitar World, Musicial Merchandise Review, The Music Trades, Vintage Guitar.*

Various manufacturer catalogs, literature, and web sites.

DEALER DIRECTORY
A GEOGRAPHICAL GUIDE

Australia
Guitar Emporium
Darren Garth
20 Lalor St
Port Melbourne, Victoria 3207
61.3.9696.8032
emporium@ozemail.com.au
www.guitaremporium.com.au

Canada
Folkway
22 Dupont Street East
Waterloo, Ontario N2J-2G9
(855) 772-0424 (toll free)
info@folkwaymusic.com
www.folkwaymusic.com

Twelfth Fret
Grant MacNeill/Chris Bennett
2132 Danforth Avenue
Toronto, Ontario
M4C 1J9
416-423-2132
416-423-1554 (Repairs)
sales@12fret.com
www.12fret.com

England
Denmark Street Guitars
27 Denmark Street
London, WChH 8HJ
011-44-207-379-1139
www.londonvintageguitars.com

Japan
H I Guitars
7-59-103 Higashi OmiyaSaitama-Shi,
SAITAMA 330-0021 Japan
011-81-3-3257-7117
higuitars@aol.com
www.hi-guitars.com

United States of America
Arizona
CE Distribution
6221 S Maple Ave
Tempe, AZ 85283
480-755-4712
www.cedist.com

California
California Vintage Guitar and Amp
Dave Swartz
5244 Van Nuys
Sherman Oaks, CA
91401
818-789-8884
sales@californiavintageguitarandamp.com
www.californiavintageguitarandamp.com

California World Guitar Shows
Larry Briggs
918-288-2222
www.CalShows.TV

Drew Berlin's Vintage Guitars
Drew Berlin
213-400-4244
Drew@DrewBerlin.com
www.DrewBerlin.com

Gryphon Strings
Richard Johnston
211 Lambert Ave
Palo Alto, CA 94306
650-493-2131
info@gryphonstrings.com
www.gryphonstrings.com

Neal's Music
Neal Shelton
Huntington Beach , CA
714-330-9428
nealmuzic@aol.com
www.nealsmusic.com

Players Vintage Instruments
Lowell Levinger
Inverness, CA
415-669-1107
info@vintageinstruments.com
www.vintageinstruments.com

Schoenberg Guitars
Eric Schoenberg
106 Main Street
Tiburon, CA 94920
415-789-0846
eric@om28.com
www.om28.com

Union Grove Music
Richard Gellis
PO Box 2635
Aptos, CA, 95001
(831) 427-0670
www.uniongrovemusic.com/

Florida
Guitar Broker
Craig & Dustin Brody
816 NW 6th Ave
Ft. Lauderdale, FL 33311
954-646-8819
vintage@guitarbroker.com
www.guitarbroker.com

Kummer's Vintage
Timm Kummer
12231 NW 49th Dr
Coral Springs, FL 33076
954-752-6063
prewar99@aol.com
www.kummersvintage.com

Replay Guitar Exchange
Jim Brady
3944 Britton Plaza
Tampa, FL 33611
813-254-8880
info@replayguitar.com
www.replayguitar.com

Georgia
Atlanta Vintage Guitars
Greg Henderson
3778 Canton Road, Ste. 400
Marietta, GA 30066
770-433-1891
atlantavintageguitars@gmail.com
www.atlantavintageguitars.com

Illinois
Chicago Guitar Show
Ruth Brinkmann
817.312.7659
ruthmbrinkmann@gmail.com
www.wacovintageinstruments.com

Chicago Music Exchange
Daniel Escauriza
3316 N Lincoln Ave
Chicago, IL 60657
773-525-7775
info@chicagomusicexchange.com
www.CME6.com

SS Vintage
George Coutretsis
4422 N Clark St
Chicago, IL 60640
773-472-3333
george@ssvintage.com
www.ssvintage.com

Kansas
Mass Street Music
Jim Baggett
1347 Massachusetts St
Lawrence, KS 66044
785-843-3535
sales@massstreetmusic.com
www.massstreetmusic.com

Maryland
Garrett Park Guitars
Rick Hogue
7 Old Solomans Island Rd

Annapolis, MD 21401
410-571-9660
info@gpguitars.com
www.gpguitars.com

Nationwide Guitars, Inc.
Bruce or Brad Rickard
P.O. Box 2334
Columbia, MD 21045
410-489-4074
nationwideguitar@gmail.com
www.nationwideguitars.com

Southworth Guitars
Gil Southworth
southworthguitar@aol.com
www.southworthguitars.com

Massachusetts
Bay State Vintage Guitars
A.J. Jones
481 Washington St
Norwood, MA 022062
617-267-6077
info@baystatevintageguitars.com
www.baystatevintageguitars.com

Michigan
Elderly Instruments
Stan Werbin
100 North Washington
Lansing, MI 48906
888-473-5810
elderly@elderly.com
www.elderly.com

Minnesota
Vintage Guitars & Parts Guitarville' by Eddie Vegas
Ed Matthews
Duluth, MN 55720
218-879-3796
e.matthews@mchsi.com
www.eddievegas.com

Willies American Guitars
254 Cleveland Avenue South
St. Paul, MN 55105
651-699-1913
info@williesguitars.com
williesguitars.com

Missouri
Fly by Night Music
Dave Crocker
103 S Washington
Neosho, MO 64850-1816
417-451-5110
crocker@joplin.com
www.amigoguitarshows.com

Killer Vintage
Dave Hinson
PO Box 190561
St. Louis, MO 63119
314-647-7795
info@killervintage.com
www.killervintagespecialtyguitars.com/

Nevada
A.J.'s Music
Peter Trauth
1203 Santa Ynez
Henderson, NV 89002
702-436-9300
ajsmusic@earthlink.net
www.ajsmusic.com

New Hampshire
Retromusic
Jeff Firestone
38 Washington Street
Kenne, NH 03431
603-357-9732
retromusicnh@gmail.com
www.retroguitar.com

New Jersey
Lark Street Music
Buzz Levine
479 Cedar Ln
Teaneck, NJ 07666
(201) 287-1959
larkstreet@gmail.com
www.larkstreetmusic.com

New Jersey Guitar and Bass Center
Jay Jacus
995 Amboy Ave
Edison, NJ 08837
732-225-4444
njgtrbass@aol.com
www.newjerseyguitarandbasscenter.com

New Mexico
GuitarVista
Stanley Burg
3117 Silver Ave SE
Albuquerque, NM 87106
505-268-1133
gitmaven@yahoo.com
www.guitarvistanm.com

New York
Bernunzio Uptown Music
122 East Ave
Rochester, NY 14604
585-473-6140
info@bernunzio.com
www.bernunzio.com

Imperial Guitars
Bill Imperial
2A Cherry Hill Rd
New Paltz, NY 12561
845-255-2555
IGS55@aol.com
www.imperialguitar.com

Laurence Wexer, LTD
Larry Wexer
By appointment only
New York, NY 10036
212-532-2994
lwexer@gmail.com
www.wexerguitars.com

Mountain Cat
Doug Myer
471 Haverstraw Rd
Suffern, NY 10901-3135
845-918-1607
mountaincatguitars@gmail.com
www.mountaincatguitars.com

Rivington Guitars
Howie Statland
73 E 4th St
New York, NY 10003
212-505-5313
rivingtoninfo@gmail.com
www.rivingtonguitars.com

Sam Ash
Sammy Ash
516-686-4104
sam.ash@samashmusic.com

We Buy Guitars
Richie Friedman
PO Box 60736
Staten Island, NY 10306
516-221-0563
Webuyguitars@aol.com

Well Strung Guitars
David Davidson
439 Main St
Farmigndale, NY 11735
516-221-0563
info@wellstrungguitars.com
www.wellstrungguitars.com

North Carolina
Coleman Music
Chip Coleman
1021 S Main St
China Grove, NC 28023-2335
704-857-5705
OR120@aol.com
www.colemanmusic.com

Midwood Guitar Studio
Douglas Armstrong
1517 Central Ave
Charlotte, NC 28205-5013
980-265-1976
sales@midwoodguitarstudio.com
www.midwoodguitarstudio.com

Ohio
DHR Guitar Experience
Dale Rabiner
577 Delta Ave Unit C
Cincinnati, OH 45226
513-260-8260
dale@dhrguitarexperience.com
www.dhrguitarexperience.com

Gary's Classic Guitars
Gary Dick
Cincinnati, OH
513-891-0555
garysclssc@aol.com
www.garysguitars.com

The Loft at Lay's
Dan Shinn
74 Kenmore Blvd
Akron, OH 44314
330-848-1392
info@laysguitar.com
www.theloftatlays.com

Mike's Music
Mike Reeder
2615 Vine St
Cincinnati, OH 45219
513-281-4900
www.mikesmusicohio.com

Oklahoma
Strings West
Larry Briggs
PO Box 999 - 109 N Cincinnati Ave
Sperry, OK 74073
918-288-2222
larryb@stringswest.com
www.stringswest.com

Oregon
McKenzie River Music
Artie Leider
455 West 11th
Eugene, OR 97401
541-343-9482
artie@mrmgtr.com
www.mckenzierivermusic.com

Pennsylvania
Jim's Guitars
Jim Singleton
651 Lombard Rd #119
Red Lion, PA 17356
717-417-5655
info@jimsguitars.com
www.jimsguitars.com

Vintage Instruments
Fred Oster
507 South Broad Street
Philadelphia, PA 19147
215-545-1000
vintagephiladelphia@gmail.com
www.vintage-instruments.com

Tennessee
Blues Vintage
Gabriel Hernandez
212-A McGavock Pike
Nashville, TN 37214
888-407-2717
info@bluesvintageguitars.com
www.bluesvintageguitars.com

Carter's Vintage Guitars
Christie and Walter Carter
625 8th Ave S
Nashville, TN 37203
615-915-1851
walter@cartervintage.com
www.cartervintage.com

Gruhn Guitars
George Gruhn
2120 8th Ave S
Nashville, TN 37204
615-256-2033
gruhn@gruhn.com
www.gruhn.com

Rumble Seat Music
Eliot Michael
1805 8th Ave S
Nashville, TN 37203
615-915-2510
sales@rumbleseatmusic.com
www.rumbleseatmusic.com

Texas
Boingosaurus Music LLC
Garrett Tung
Austin, TX
boingosaurusmusic@gmail.com
www.boingosaurus.com

Dallas International Guitar Festival
Jimmy Wallace
PO Box 4997186
Garland, TX 75049
972-240-2206
info@guitarshow.com
www.guitarshow.com

Ellis Music & Accessories
John Ellis
11008 Salado Springs Cir
Salado, TX 79571-5298
951-347-5197
jolinmusic@earthlink.net
www.ellisvintage.com

Heritage Auctions
Aaron Piscopo
2801 W. Airport Frwy.
Dallas, TX 75261
214-409-1183
AaronP@HA.com
www.HA.com

Jimmy Wallace Guitars
Jimmy Wallace
514 Main St
Garland, TX 75040
469-562-8545
info@JimmyWallaceGuitars.com
www.JimmyWallaceGuitars.com

Kebo's Bassworks
Kevin 'KeBo" Borden and Dr. Ben Sopran-
zetti
info@kebosbassworks.com
www.kebosbassworks.com

Killer Vintage Specialty Guitars of Texas
Dave Hinson
3738 Haggar Way Ste 108
Dallas, TX 75209
972-707-0409
killervintagedallas@gmail.com
www.killervintagespecialtyguitars.com/

Southpaw Guitars
Jim
5813 Bellaire Blvd
Houston, TX 77081
713-667-5791
info@southpawguitars.com
www.southpawguitars.com

Texas Amigos Guitar Shows
Ruth Brinkmann
800-473-6059
www.amigoguitarshows.com

Van Hoose Vintage Instruments
Thomas VanHoose
2722 Raintree Drive
Carrollton, TX 75006
972-998-8176
tv0109@yahoo.com
www.vanhoosevintage.com

Utah
Intermountain Guitar and Banjo
Leonard or Kennard
712 East 100 South
Salt Lake City, UT 84102
801-322-4682
guitarandbanjo@earthlink.net
www.guitarandbanjo.com

Virginia
Action Music
Matt Baker
111 Park Ave
Falls Church, VA 22046
703-534-4801
actionmusiconpark@gmail.com
www.actionguitar.com

Vintage Sound
Bill Holter
PO Box 11711
Alexandria, VA 22312
703-300-2529
bhvsound@vintagesound.com
www.vintagesound.com

West Virginia
King's Row LTD
John Carlin
Williamson, WV
615-864-5667
JRCarlin54@gmail.com

Wisconson
Brian Goff's Bizarre Guitars
Brain Goff
Madison, WI
608-235-3561
Bdgoff@sbcglobal.net
www.bizarreguitars.net

Cream City Music
John Majdalani
12505 W Bluemound Rd
Brookfield, WI 53005-8026
262-860-1800
johnm@creamcitymusic.com
www.creamcitymusic.com

Dave's Guitar Shop
Dave Rogers
1227 South 3rd St

LaCrosse, WI 54601
608-785-7704
info@davesguitar.com
www.davesguitar.com

Dave's Guitar Shop
Dave Rogers
914 S 5th St
Milwaukee, WI 53204
608-790-9816
info@davesguitar.com
www.davesguitar.com

Dave's Guitar Shop
Dave Rogers
2990 Cahill Main #200
Madison, WI 53711
608-405-8770
info@davesguitar.com
www.davesguitar.com

MANUFACTURER DIRECTORY

Arizona
CE Distribution
6221 S Maple Ave
Tempe, AZ 85283
480-755-4712
www.cedist.com

California
Alleva Coppolo
Jimmy Coppolo
1245 W 9th St
Upland, CA 91786-5706
909-981-9019
jimmy@allevacoppolo.com
www.allevacoppolo.com

NEW York
Mirabella
Cris Mirabella
PO Box 483
St. James, NY 11780
631-842-3819
mirguitars@aol.com
www.mirabellaguitars.com

Other
EMG Pickups
www.emgpickups.com

Gibson
www.gibson.com

Godlyke Distributing / Maxon
www.maxonFX.com

Lindy Fralin Pickups
www.fralinpickups.com

Mesa Boogie
www.mesaboogie.com

RWK Guitars
www.rwkguitars.com

Slidewinder Ring
www.slidewinderring.com

TECH/REPAIR

Canada
Burlesk Custom Guitars & Repair
James Burley
Calgary, Alberta T3K-2G6
jmwburley@shaw.ca
www.burleskguitars.com

United States of America
California
National Guitar Repair
Marc Schoenberger
805-481-8532 805-471-5905
Luthier17@aol.com
www.nationalguitarrepair.com

Delaware
Dana Sound Research
Dana Sutcliffe, Master Luthier
Wilmington DE, 19810

302-439-3677
danasoundresearchinc@gmail.com
www.danamusic.com

New York
The Guitar Specialist, Inc
Doug Proper
380 Adams Street
Bedford Hills, NY 10507
914-401-9052
info@guitarspecialist.com
www.guitarspecialist.com

Ohio
Lays Guitar Restoration
Dan Shinn
974 Kenmore Blvd
Akron, OH 44314
330-848-1392

info@laysguitar.com
www.laysguitar.com

Wyoming
Anton's Musical Instrument Repair
Anton
1841 Lane 12
Powell, WY 82435
307-754-5341
luthier82435@yahoo.com
www.antonsinstrumentrepair.com